MARLBOROUGH'S AMERICA

THE LEWIS WALPOLE SERIES IN
EIGHTEENTH-CENTURY CULTURE AND HISTORY

The Lewis Walpole Series, published by Yale University Press with the aid of the Annie Burr Lewis Fund, is dedicated to the culture and history of the long eighteenth century (from the Glorious Revolution to the accession of Queen Victoria). It welcomes work in a variety of fields, including literature and history, the visual arts, political philosophy, music, legal history, and the history of science. In addition to original scholarly work, the series publishes new editions and translations of writing from the period, as well as reprints of major books that are currently unavailable. Though the majority of books in the series will probably concentrate on Great Britain and the Continent, the range of our geographical interests is as wide as Horace Walpole's.

Marlborough's America

Stephen Saunders Webb

Yale UNIVERSITY PRESS

NEW HAVEN & LONDON

Published with assistance from the Annie Burr Lewis Fund.

Yale University Press books may be purchased in quantity for educational, business, or promotional use. For information, please e-mail sales.press@yale.edu (U.S. office) or sales@yaleup.co.uk (U.K. office).

Set in Janson type by Newgen North America.

Printed in the United States of America.

Library of Congress Cataloging-in-Publication Data

Webb, Stephen Saunders, 1937–
  Marlborough's America / Stephen Saunders Webb.
    p. cm. — (The Lewis Walpole series in eighteenth-century culture and history)
  Includes bibliographical references and index.
  ISBN 978-0-300-17859-3 (cloth : alk. paper)
  1. Marlborough, John Churchill, Duke of, 1650–1722—Military leadership.   2. Great Britain—Colonies—America—Administration.   3. Great Britain—Colonies—America—History—18th century.   4. Great Britain—Politics and government—1660–1714.   5. Imperialism—History—18th century.   6. Military government of dependencies.
  I. Title.
  DA462.M3W53 2013
  941.06'9092—dc23

                                                                              2012018059

A catalogue record for this book is available from the British Library.
This paper meets the requirements of ANSI/NISO Z39.48–1992 (Permanence of Paper).

10 9 8 7 6 5 4 3 2 1

For Margaret

August 13, *1704*
Dr B
I have not time to say more,
but to beg You will give my Duty to the Queen,
and lett her know Her Army has had a Glorious Victory
Monsr. Tallard and two other Generals are in my Coach
and I am following the rest:
the bearer my Aid de Camp Coll Parkes
will give Her an account of what has pass'd.
I shal doe it in a day or two by a nother more att large

—MARLBOROUGH

Contents

Illustrations

THE HANOVERIANS: MONARCHS, MINISTERS, AND MILITARY MEN

MARLBOROUGH'S AMERICA

MAPS

Preface: Army and Empire

The military revolution created an imperial state in Britain and in the British empire in America. Each stage in the conquest of the British Isles was followed by a plan to dominate America. In 1569, the arquebusiers of Queen Elizabeth destroyed the feudal levies of the northern earls. In 1584, the queen received from Raleigh and Hakluyt the "Discourse of Western Planting." Cromwell's New Model Army annihilated the cavaliers at Naseby in 1645. In 1651, the "Declaration of the Commonwealth" declared that the English in America should answer to an imperial authority in London. In 1689, the declaration of war against France listed as a casus belli the violated frontiers of English colonies in America. In 1713, the treaty of Utrecht ended that war by conceding British imperial advances in America. In 1721, to consolidate these gains, officer administrators on both sides of the Atlantic produced a comprehensive plan of garrison government in their report "On the Government of the American Plantations." In 1746, the Scots clansmen were eviscerated by the regiments of king George at Culloden. In 1748, the president of the lords commissioners of trade and plantations produced the plans exemplified by the creation of the military colony at Halifax in a new Scotland, Nova Scotia. In 1763, the Peace of Paris, which ejected France from North America, was accompanied by the Knox memorandum and the expansion of garrison government in North America. The dynamic of domestic security followed by imperial advance goes far to contradict the clever, but false, dictum that the British empire "was founded in a fit of absence of mind," and it rebuts the received wisdom that England stumbled into a "commercial and colonial" connection with America "without any fixed policy, in fact without any clear idea of what she and her people were doing," and with no thought of the military means to imperial advantage. The leaders of "Greater Britain" could and did quarrel about imperial strategy— whether to invest more in the navy and treaty ports or in the army and conquered colonies—but they were agreed that imperial accumulation could break the zero-sum game of European war.

The identity of the imperial state with the military revolution was manifested by the army service of 90 percent of the royal governors of overseas provinces between the restoration of the monarchy (by elements of the army) in 1660 and the accession of the last soldier-prince, George II, in 1727. These army officers applied to America the forms of garrison government they had developed in the British Isles between the battles of Naworth and Naseby. In 1654, the Cromwellian conquest of Jamaica transferred militarized administration from the British Isles across the Atlantic. It was modified by American experience. To survive, the conquerors of Jamaica created regimental plantations. The exchange of their crops, and their comrades' privateering plunder, for capital equipment involved the conquerors in commerce. The need to draw experienced planters from older possessions produced a civilian population. So military law was leavened with property protection and civil liberty. Courts-martial became courts of law. So much was confirmed when the restored monarchy continued in Jamaica the policies of the protectorate.

Royal government involved the colony in restoration politics. Anglo-Jamaican military administration shifted with every ministry. So the character of the governors general alternated between militaristic and legalistic. At last, in 1681, the Exclusion Crisis produced an imperial constitutional settlement. It preserved Cromwellian military command, introduced royal legislative initiative, and secured a permanent revenue for the imperial executive, all in return for the enfranchisement of a bicameral colonial legislature and the everyday operations of local law.

The imperial constitutional compromise of 1681—between a militarized and royalized imperial executive and a more or less civilian legislature—was also influenced by the outcomes of Bacon's revolution in Virginia, repressed by royal commissioners, a regiment of the royal Guards, royal naval reserves, and a squadron of the royal navy. As the garrison of Virginia for five years, the Guards steeled the transformation of Virginia from an autonomous and abusive autocracy of a pre–Civil War sort to an imperial possession, commanded by soldiers of the crown. They cramped, but they did not break, the Berkelean baronage of the Old Dominion. So the Exclusion Crisis moderated executive authority in Virginia as it had in Jamaica. The dominion's executives and representatives, with the help of English "moderates"—all of whom wanted a degree of provincial autonomy—secured provincial political privileges within an imperial constitution. Nonetheless, the armed authority of the imperial state remained preeminent.

1676 marked the end of American independence. Hitherto, the mainland colonies had rendered only a symbolic subordination to the English executive, save for a brief, Cromwellian military imposition in the Chesapeake. Now North American autonomy was shattered. The Susquehanna revenge and the English military repression of Nathaniel Bacon's attempt at independence eliminated Virginia's autonomy. King Philip's War decimated and demoralized the puritan republics of New England. The condominium of the English crown and the Iroquois league, with its headquarters in a more-than-royal New York, both rescued and confined New England. The covenant chain alliance also shaped the new "middle" colonies. Protected by the Iroquois and given

English institutions, five new colonies were hived off of the vast proprietary province of James, duke of York, afterward king James II. At its maximum, "New York" had extended, with puritan interruptions, from the St. Croix to the Delaware. It was administered by the duke's lieutenants, among them John Churchill, members of the duke's household, the shadow cabinet of a king-in-waiting, an imperial nexus.

The new king's military favorite had been raised in a royalist household broken by the civil wars. After the restoration of the monarchy, Churchill became a page in the household of the duke of York. He came of age as an officer in the royal Guards (combining two militant models, Churchill learned the manual of arms, the pattern of discipline, from an ex-Cromwellian sergeant). As a captain of marines, Churchill fought at sea under James's command in the second Dutch War. Promoted to an English regiment in the French service, Churchill forwarded his military education in combat under Marshal Turenne's command before coming home to serve once again in James's household. There he helped launch the punitive expedition to Virginia, administer New York, and direct the Hudson's Bay Company (HBC). Churchill became governor of the HBC when James succeeded to the imperial crown, but king James was a public, devout, Catholic in a kingdom Protestant by law.

By now it was clear that Churchill was not a mere military automaton. In 1678 he had been the English liaison-officer with William of Orange, the Protestant champion, helping to effect the Triple Alliance against French, Catholic, aggression. Churchill resisted James's pressure to convert to Catholicism. He was associated with the earl of Halifax when that personification of "moderation" brokered the imperial settlement of 1681. Still, Churchill was, first and foremost, a soldier of the king. Ennobled at king James's coronation in 1685, lord Churchill led the royal army in the repression of the duke of Monmouth's Protestant revolt. Churchill's troops guarded the torturous executions of hundreds of rebels. Now lord Churchill, baron of Aymouth in the peerage of Scotland (where he had served under James's ruthless command), the king's most able commander would repress rebels but he would not betray the interests of England's empire or its constitution, in church and state.

In 1686, lord Churchill persistently and presciently protested King James's Treaty of American Neutrality with Louis XIV. Churchill joined the imperial secretariat, headed by William Blathwayt, secretary at war and of plantations, in impassioned objections to the concessions King James made to France on every American frontier, from Hudson's Bay and Acadia in the north, along the boundaries of the Anglo-Iroquois condominium, all the way to the Carolinas, and in the Leeward Islands. Even more menacing to the anglican imperialists than the treaty's American concessions was its embodiment of King James's entente with Louis XIV. If the two Catholic kings had their way, French bayonets would coerce anglicans as they had huguenots. The Protestant Reformation would be destroyed in the British kingdoms and in English America as well.

King James was not unmindful of anglican opposition. He redoubled the size of his army. He dispensed with the law in order to commission Catholic officers in both the English army and navy. The king catholicized the army of occupation in Ireland. Refugee officers from Ireland warned their English counterparts that they, too, would be cashiered if they did not convert to Catholicism. Torn between his conscience and his king, Churchill consulted with his confessor. Assured that religious faith superseded military duty, lord Churchill began to conspire with colleagues in the most disaffected regiments: the former garrison of Tangier, Christian crusaders brought home in the Exclusion Crisis. Churchill contacted notably Protestant and/or professional officers in the garrisons. The officers of the Guards regiments in the capital's barracks were canvassed. So were Churchill's brother George's naval colleagues. Churchill himself met with agents of Prince William to pledge English military support for a Dutch invasion. Churchill believed that desertion, subversion, and invasion would defang the King. James would be forced to abandon his unconstitutional coercion of the church, the armed forces, and the universities (where James was ardently supported by William Penn). The king would have to submit to a Protestant regency. To these ends, Churchill was able to promise the support of James's younger daughter, the Princess Anne (who was deeply dependent on Churchill's wife, Sarah) and her husband, Prince George of Denmark (who was almost as reliant on lord Churchill).

Paradoxically, lord Churchill's coup promised to be so effective because the royal restoration of the Cromwellian garrisons, the creation of a royal army, and the expansion of the navy, had confirmed military power as the indispensable instrument of monarchy. If the garrisons could be subverted and the citadels seized, the battleships kept to their anchors, and the king's field army divided by desertion and disaffection, King James could neither govern the country nor resist even the small invasion force—perhaps 12,000 men—which Prince William could spare from the defense of the Netherlands against France. Even these soldiers could not be embarked for England unless Louis XIV diverted his army to the Rhine. Reassured by the scale of King James's military preparations—the king had doubled the English army to 40,000 men and was importing additional regiments from Ireland and Scotland—the French monarch made a fatal miscalculation.

So, on November 5, 1688, a Dutch fleet, commanded by an English admiral, put Prince William's army ashore at Torbay. The English fleet, paralyzed by dissention, lay to its moorings. Even so, the prince's army was outnumbered two to one by the king's field force, but as it marched west to meet the invaders, the King was demoralized by desertions led by Princess Anne's relations and dependents, "the Denmark connection," and by the most professional, imperialist, and Protestant officers. On November 23, Churchill himself decamped, with hundreds of other officers. He left behind a declaration that he would not help King James conquer the constitution established by law in church and state. In less than two weeks, Prince William and his Blue Guards were in command of the capital. Threatened (it was said by lord Churchill) with imprisonment in the Tower (from which, King James said, no monarch had ever escaped with his life), the king fled to France, following his stalwart Catholic queen and their son, "the warming-pan baby," afterward the soi-disant James III.

The events of 1688 were not a revolution, "glorious" or otherwise. They were a Protestant putsch. The coup was effected, as King James himself said, by lord Churchill's disruption of the royal field army. The irregular forces raised around the person of Princess Anne (who had fled from London in the company of lady Churchill) manifested aristocratic dissension but it hardly affected the outcome. So too the copycat coups in the colonies, where provincial Protestant militias displaced the king's commissioners. In America, King James had eliminated the imperial settlement of 1681 in favor of armed autocracy, first in New York, then in Jamaica, and finally, fatally, in the Dominion of New England. It was in Boston, the capital of the dominion, that the first of the colonial coups took place. On April 19, 1689, the Massachusetts provincial army overwhelmed the scanty garrison (the bulk of the regular troops were fighting the French-backed Abenaki on the Maine frontier). Officers of the Massachusetts provincial army arrested the governor general, Sir Edmund Andros. His deputy in New York, Captain Francis Nicholson, lost control of the citadel to the city militia regiment. His subordinates abandoned Albany to republican rebels from Connecticut. The Protestant militia of Maryland rose against the royalist deputy of the Catholic proprietor. Forming an "Association in Arms" on the English model, the Maryland military took over the government. Like their colonial counterparts everywhere, the Maryland associators justified their aggression by denouncing Catholics, the French, King James, and all Indians whatsoever (the bogeymen equivalent to the Irish in England), and declared for Prince William.

The new regime had more than enough to do in fighting for control of the British Isles and defending the Netherlands against France. The few regiments which could be spared, or had to be exiled as loyalists, went to the English West Indies. To its adherents in North America, the new regime sent munitions, admonitions, and executives for King William, who was determined to preserve the royal prerogative in the colonies. A larger view of English America was retained by lord Churchill. The English declaration of war with France on May 7, 1689, made French aggression on American frontiers the casus belli. The language was the same as that of lord Churchill's protest against the Treaty of American Neutrality three years earlier.

Churchill was created earl of Marlborough when William was crowned king. Now a lieutenant general, Marlborough purged the English army in William's name and for his own aggrandizement. Leading reorganized and increasingly professional troops to tactical successes in the Netherlands, to the capture of Cork and Kinsale in Ireland, and in the defense of England itself,

Marlborough made the English army so much his own that he was a menace to the new regime. Cashiered, disgraced, imprisoned, Marlborough was released only when his peers refused to do business without him. In parliament, Marlborough championed the English princess, Anne, as heiress apparent to Dutch William, and the earl excited the English army against the Dutch occupiers. Marlborough took advantage of the truce of 1697 and the so-called standing army crisis to force the Dutch army out of England. So Marlborough ensured Anne's accession and his own ascendancy. King William acquiesced in the inevitable. He commissioned Marlborough to negotiate a Grand Alliance to resist Louis XIV's determination to make Spain, and Spanish America, a Bourbon fiefdom. On the eve of Anne's accession, King William recommended Marlborough as "the coolest head and the warmest heart" to head her ministry and command her army in what became the war of the English as well as the Spanish succession.

Louis XIV had been forced to recognize William III's right to the English throne but, on the death of James II at Saint-Germain, on August 27, 1701, the French monarch declared that James's son, raised a Catholic in France, was the rightful king of England, not James's surviving daughter, the Protestant princess Anne who was, as she said, "intirely English." As the effective commander of the English army, Marlborough threatened to "walk over the bellies" of any armed opponents of Anne's accession. He more than repaid Dutch support for the Protestant succession by securing parliamentary legislation committing 40,000 men to fight France in the Netherlands. At the head of an expanded English army and its European auxiliaries, Marlborough was the obvious candidate to command the armies of the Grand Alliance.

In 1702 and in the ten campaigns that followed, the allied armies under Marlborough's command defeated the French for the first time in living memory. In a string of unbroken victories—five pitched battles and thirteen sieges—the captain general and his men rescued the Hapsburg empire, secured the British union, and reconquered Flanders and Brabant. So they forced Louis XIV to accept a peace that made the British empire preeminent in the Atlantic world. By exhausting the greatest power in Europe, by forcing France (and its Spanish allies) to concede to Britain the Mediterranean bases, the Newfoundland fisheries, and the vast western empire claimed by England's Iroquois allies, Marlborough proved the truth of his dictum that "if we can be so fortunate as to force them [the French] here [in Europe], we may have by one dash of a pen, much more than any expeditions [to America] can gaine in many yeares." Each of Marlborough's battlefield victories and successful sieges did indeed secure more territory and greater security for British America than the fatally flawed and invariably failed attempts to attack France in America directly.

After the battle of Blenheim on August 13, 1704, so the historian commissioned by Napoleon to write Marlborough's biography wrote, the duke's preeminence in the west was indisputable: "Dès-lors le nom de Marlborough fut, pour ainsi dire, un puissance qui entra dans la conféderation, et qui la soutint par un terreur le cours d'un siècle n'a pu effacer les traces profondes." ("Thenceforward the name of Marlborough became as it were a new power which entered into the confederacy [against France] and upheld it by a terror, the profound marks of which the passage of a century has not effaced.") Therefore, *Marlborough's America* is, first, the story of a man whom his most unprincipled English enemy called "the greatest statesman and the greatest general that this country or any other country has produced." Yet these, "the prejudices of a partisan," the historian of the British army writes, "are but a sorry standard for the measure of one whose transcendent ability as a general, a statesman, a diplomatist, and an administrator, guided not only England but Europe through the War of the Spanish Succession, and delivered them safe for a whole generation from the craft and ambition of France." So much and more can be said for Marlborough's legates in America. They not only defended England's imperial possessions and populations from France, they also built into the structures and ideals of American governance the principles they derived from lord Churchill's coup, from its consequences, "the Glorious Revolution," and from their long service and, in the case of his staff, close association, with the captain general.

In Britain, in Europe, and often, even, in America, Marlborough exercised command through the agency of his staff officers. They executed the captain general's commands. They prepared the estimates that led to legislation, the appropriation, tax, and recruiting acts, each a victory in "the winter campaign" in parliament. Marlborough's victories depended more largely on the statutes previously enacted to pay for the military defense of the Glorious Revolution, the Protestant Netherlands, and English America. That legislation had created a national bank, which administered a national debt, expressed in treasury and bank bills, the new instruments of finance capital, obligations to be retired by long-term taxes. As executors of the ensuing "military-fiscal revolution," Marlborough's staff officers made the logistical arrangements for tens of thousands of men. These were not trivial achievements. A single convoy numbered 16,000 horses, 150 pieces of artillery, and thousands of carts with munitions and supplies, extended over fifteen miles of road, escorted by 50,000 men, which traveled for 75 miles in the face of two enemy armies.

To reward his accomplished staff, and so to exercise his overweening influence everywhere in the empire, the captain general formalized the customary military monopoly of royal governments. On Marlborough's nomination, the queen commissioned his senior officers to command the political centers and the seaports of the British Isles. There they commanded the garrison governments that, ever since the crisis of the Elizabethan regime, had secured the supremacy of the state, "the court," over the counties, "the country." And Marlborough's general officers commanded the enormous garrisons of the new conquests, Gibraltar and Minorca, the keys to the Mediterranean, from which the outposts of empire in America and the West Indies were frequently reinforced.

To impose the authority of the empire over its provinces, Marlborough rewarded his junior staff officers with governments in America and the West Indies. They were veterans not just of the captain general's campaigns, European and parliamentary, but of the garrison governments of Marlborough's European conquests, and they had served in the garrisons of Britain and Ireland as well. Ireland supported the royal army's largest reserves, paid for by taxes on this, the greatest of England's colonies. The Irish garrison employed and educated officers who deployed to American government. So did Scotland, the unwilling partner in a shotgun marriage with England. British union was the price Scots paid for access to empire and for imperial commands for Scots officers, especially from Marlborough's staff. Extensive influence must also be attributed to the dozens of Marlborough's junior officers and the scores of his sergeants who came out to drill and discipline American regiments, regular and provincial, and who remained to found American families and extend imperial frontiers.

Repressive though they might be, and authoritarian as they all were, Marlborough's American legates, like their general, were self-conscious defenders of "Revolution Principles," which they applied in the context of the imperial settlement of 1681. These principles and that settlement enshrined the primacy of protestantism, in the forms of the church of England but with toleration for dissenters, and recognized constitutional government, in which bicameral legislatures proposed binding statutes, subject to royal approval. The royal sanction was pro forma in Britain but, in the provinces, laws were subject to not just the sovereign's approval but that of the governors general. They retained in the eighteenth century a more-than-royal prerogative of veto and a high degree of executive discretion. Underlying every principle and practice was the unvarying hostility of Marlborough's men to the empires of France and Spain as tyrannical, Catholic aggressors. For all of the duke's delegates, protestantism and patriotism were one, an inextricable knot of religiously ordered liberty and politically fervent nationality. These anglican officers' political principles were deeply dyed with military morality, the trinity of "Duty, Honor, Country." As professional soldiers, they had dutiful obligations to the responsibilities of rank. As commanding officers, they partook of aristocratic self-regard. As patriots, their ultimate loyalty lay with the nation. Responsible, proud, patriotic, these officers saw civilians, particularly their political opponents, as selfish, sniveling, and subversive. Opposition was "mutiny."

Marlborough's legates brought with them across the Atlantic administrative ability, exemplified in the march to the Danube; valor, proven in pitched battles, obscure skirmishes, and arduous sieges; political acumen, honed in garrison government; and diplomatic skill, required to combine selfish civilians, contentious allies, and disparate nationalities in the work of self-defense and imperial expansion. These officers were also economically adept. Staff officers, such as Hunter and Spotswood, calculated all the requisites of an army: pay, rations, and transport; appropriations, requisitions, and routes. Parke, a combat aide, not a planner, nonetheless had been a most successful planter, shipbuilder, and marketeer before being commissioned. He, like all of Marlborough's legates, had been well educated academically. They served for decades in the era's most modern institution, the army, the largest consumer of goods and services, commodities and cash. Such officers were materialists—applied scientists, if you will—creative in cartography and optics, ballistics, fortification, and architecture.

Commissioned imperial executives, these officers took command of garrison governments that had always been unavoidably economic in their operations. Not only was physical protection the prerequisite of prosperity, but crown contributions of men and munitions, pay and plunder, governmental purchases of soldier's rations and ship's repairs, had long underwritten colonial economies. In Marlborough's America, all of these contributions continued, but they were consolidated and multiplied manifold by his officers' imposition of the military-fiscal revolution.

Colonel Parke's privateers and flags of truce, his fostering of farmer-militiamen, and his proposals for forcible conquest and colonization by Scots clansmen, were traditional elements of garrison government. General Hunter hatched sophisticated statutes which finally repaid the debts of revolution and the consequent wars with France. Creating a paper currency in government bills, Hunter underwrote a new capitalist class devoted to government. Spotswood created a crown corporation, the Virginia Indian Company (so like Marlborough's Hudson's Bay Company in its combination of private profit with imperial expansion at the expense of France), passed a tobacco act that combined quality control with taxation, and produced a paper currency. Spotswood recruited a syndicate of speculators in frontier lands that pushed settlement west to the Blue Ridge. He even mapped the armed advance of Anglo-American empire all the way to the Ohio River and Lake Erie. It was the extensive military service of Marlborough's officers which equipped and inspired them to mobilize, even revolutionize, the economies of the American polities most deeply engaged in the contest with France for America. Of course, the duke's legates had to enlist local elites to do the work of royal government. So they created a new class of officials and entrepreneurs tied to government, war, and empire.

All of Marlborough's officers were gentlemen. Their model of gentle behavior was their commander, the duke of Marlborough. The arbiter of the Augustan age wrote that "of all the men I ever knew in my life (and I knew him extremely well), the late duke of Marlborough possessed the Graces in the highest degree, not to say engrossed them. . . . With all his gentleness and gracefulness, no man living was more conscious of his situation, nor maintained his dignity better." He was, in a word, charming. It was said, and his officers knew this all too well, that he could refuse a favor more gracefully than other men could grant one. Grace has also been said to be "beauty in action." Marlborough had been the very model both of masculine good looks and battlefield bravery. Even as the wars wore him down, age thickened him, and he fought from calculation rather than inclination, he retained a predilection for the handsome, rakish, foolhardy aides who recalled his salad days. The Virginian Colonel Daniel Parke was an outstanding example. Many of Marlborough's most responsible staff officers were less than beautiful—Cadogan, the chief of staff, was fat; Spotswood, his deputy, was plain—but all of them sought to emulate the captain general's coolness under fire, his politeness even in crisis, his famous sangfroid. The duke's staff knew that Marlborough's unfailing politesse and apparent calm masked an iron will, an unrelenting purpose, and an acquisitive temper. He and they sought wealth, power, fame, victory.

The captain general and all of his staff were combat veterans. They led from in front. When civilian associates chided Marlborough for risking his life in the melee, he replied that, even as his lust for personal combat waned with age, he had to show his men that he exposed himself to the same risks that he imposed on them. Hardship was not confined to the day of battle. Like his men, Marlborough suffered from the spring rains, the summer heat, and the mud of autumn, wet through woolen clothing and leather footgear. In the rapid movements by which the captain general "stole a march" from the enemy, he and his men advanced by day and by night. They did not halt to cook a meal or change their clothes, much less to camp and sleep. At the end of the march they went right into combat. There they fought hand to hand in the choking, blinding, fog of hundreds of thousands of black powder explosions, an awful atmosphere of deafening noise and incessant danger. If they survived—every battle, every siege, culled candidate viceroys—these officers emerged hard men, and proud.

They kept always before them remembrances of the war that had made them what they were. Marlborough commissioned the tapestries that still hang in that monument to military merit and royal favor, Blenheim Palace. Military tapestries also graced Cliveden, the palatial home of Marlborough's senior general of infantry, the earl of Orkney, titular governor general of Virginia. Lesser officers had simpler, if not more modest, mementoes. The duke's major of brigade for the dragoons, Robert Hunter, hung his portrait, showing the half-armor, leopard skin, and sash of his staff rank and mounted service, in his official residence, the city citadel, as governor general of New York. Parke wore to his death in command of the Leeward Islands the decoration (her portrait miniature, set in jewels) given him by queen Anne when he brought home Marlborough's Blenheim dispatch. A fortification, perhaps one of the dozens which he helped the captain general capture, is said to have formed the background of Alexander Spotswood's portrait, which he hung in the governor's mansion in Williamsburg. In the intervals of marching and fighting, Marlborough and his staff had spent happy hours planning the gardens they would plant when peace came. The same gardener planned the landscapes of Marlborough's Blenheim Palace at Woodstock and "the Palace" that Spotswood built in Williamsburg. There, his councilors complained, Colonel Spotswood never ceased speaking of the service with Marlborough that had won him the command of Virginia.

The military indoctrination of Marlborough's officers—the governors general in training—emerges here from an analysis of the captain general's ten triumphant campaigns, punctuated by four unprecedented victories. At Blenheim, on the banks of the Danube, Marlborough and Eugene destroyed the French and Bavarian armies invading the Hapsburg empire, turned back the aggression of Louis XIV after forty triumphant years, and recast the balance of power in the Atlantic world. At Ramillies, for the first time, Marlborough's tactical genius had full play. Flanders was recovered from France. Oudenarde was won after a forced march and against long odds. It was followed by a relentless pursuit of the beaten French and the reconquest of Brabant. At Malplaquet, in France itself, suicidal charges apparently opened the road to Paris, a reformation of the ancien regime, and a drumhead peace that would win America for Britain.

Key staff officers demanded American rewards for their shares in these "European" victories: Colonel Parke's fatal frontier administration in Antigua; Colonel Hunter's transformation of New York in arts and empire; Colonel Spotswood's conversion of Virginia's parochial grandees into pioneers of continental conquest. The liberty of the American provinces depended upon the independence of England from France, that is, on the Protestant succession to the imperial throne. In 1714, for the third time in his long career in command, Marlborough directed the military determinants of the Anglo-American succession. Again, Marlborough had won America in Europe. His former subordinates secured America for Britain.

Even after his death in 1722, Marlborough's veterans extended his legacy in America. The generation that separated England's wars with France for America, so it is usually said, was one of "salutary neglect," but the duke's delegates in American commands used continuous contention with Bourbon Spain to promulgate plans for another imperial war. Marlborough's veteran legates based their plans of hemispheric conquest on the armies they intended to recruit from the burgeoning populations of the American provinces. In 1739, their repeated proposals were realized in the "American Regiment": four battalions; more than 4,000 men; officered by the sons of the provincial elite, scores of whom were anxious to enter the royal army, the ruling class of the empire. Marlborough's veterans then led the American Regiment to the Caribbean.

The Cartagena campaign was an unmitigated disaster. It exposed the military imbecility and anti-American prejudice of a new peacetime generation of English (not Scottish) army officers. Conversely, the expedition excited an "American" identity. Even the American Regiment's failures educated its officers in the identity of arms and empire. This was nowhere more apparent than in the achievements and the aspirations of the American Regiment's senior captain, Lawrence Washington. The most distinguished of the American officers, Captain Washington came home to Virginia, collected the half pay of his royal army rank, and was commissioned adjutant general of Virginia by his regimental colonel, the Marlborough veteran, general Sir William Gooch, commander in chief of Virginia. Obedient to the king's commands, Sir William granted Lawrence Washington's Ohio Company 200,000 acres on the new western frontier with France in America. Major Washington was succeeded as an adjutant and major by the Ohio Company's surveyor of western lands, his devoted younger brother George. With astonishing rapidity, having in hand Marlborough's commission as captain general and trying to instill in his reluctant recruits the drill and discipline of Marlborough's army, George Washington rose to be Virginia's general in the British empire's decisive war with France for dominion of the Atlantic world. So were linked Marlborough's America and Washington's Empire.

"The Sunshine Day"

O N SUNDAY, MARCH 8, 1702, King William III died and princess Anne of Denmark, younger daughter of the exiled King James II, was proclaimed queen. She immediately met her privy council and declared herself determined to protect the Protestant succession to the imperial throne and to resist the aggression of France everywhere in the Atlantic world. For nineteen years, "The Sunshine day" of Anne's accession had been the boundary of expectation for the Denmark-Churchill connection. Now, suddenly, all their dreams of power and favor came true. On the Monday, Queen Anne commissioned John Churchill, earl of Marlborough, as general and commander in chief of her forces in the Netherlands. On Tuesday, she commissioned him captain general of England, with the fullest military powers possessed by any subject since the death, in 1670, of the previous military kingmaker, George Monck, the duke of Albemarle. On Wednesday, the queen named Marlborough a knight of the garter. On Friday, she commissioned him master general of the ordnance. This was a great office of state as well as of war. The cannon was *ultima regio regis*. The ordnance office was exceeded in bureaucratic range, monetary influence, and political patronage only by the treasury (that, Marlborough insisted, should be returned to the hands of his friend Sidney Godolphin).[1]

Every ordnance appointment—from the administrative board at the Tower of London down to gunners in every garrison in the empire—was at the disposal of the master general. So were the supplies of munitions that defended every imperial frontier. The munitions that the ordnance sent to the American provinces were the most expensive contributions of English government to its empire. Among Marlborough's first acts as master general was to order a new train of artillery for the West Indies, a colonel's command, with thirty-nine officers and 144 skilled artificers. Before the end of the year, Bermuda, New York, Jamaica, Massachusetts, and Nevis had received additional grants of ordnance, despite the navy's impressment of the crews of eight storeships loading munitions for America. This impressment was protested by James Lowther, principal storekeeper in the ordnance (and afterwards governor general of Barbados), so that Marlborough could put a stop to the navy's exactions. The master general was the more apt to be listened to because his longtime coadjutor, Prince George of Denmark, the queen's consort, was now lord high admiral. The actual work of naval administration lay in a commission dominated by Marlborough's brother, Admiral George Churchill.[2]

Having obeyed the master general's orders to supply munitions to the American provinces, the board asked him to obtain a supplementary grant from parliament "that we may be enabled forthwith to replenish the Stores, which by reason of the many Issues made to the Plantations (the charge whereof amounts to £19021/10/10 1/4 as apears by the annexed Abstract for which no allowance has been made by parliament or otherwise) our Stores are so much exhausted." Arms for empire were the master general's first concern.[3]

Just six days after King William's death, Queen Anne appointed Marlborough her ambassador extraordinary to the states general of the Netherlands. Already England's preeminent politician, obviously in control of England's foreign policy, effectively in command of the army and the ordnance, influential at the admiralty, Marlborough could effectively assure the Dutch of England's fidelity to every existing engagement. More, as Marlborough had written to Anton Heinsius, the pensioner of Holland, on the day of Anne's accession, and as he told the assembled Dutch delegates on March 28, England under Anne was prepared to enter into "such other stricter Alliances and Engagements, which shall conduce to the Interests of both Nations, the preservation of the Liberty of *Europe* and Reducing, within just Bounds, the Exorbitant Power of *France*."[4]

Marlborough declared to the Dutch that he had the queen's authority to concert immediate military action against France. The regiments that had been held in the three British kingdoms to ensure Anne's succession would now complete their recruiting to a war establishment and sail for the Netherlands. Marlborough explained that these British troops, together with those already in the Netherlands garrisons, would make up about half of the 40,000 troops to be paid for by England in the Low Countries. In return for this English investment in the defense of the Protestant Netherlands (a commitment unprecedented since the reign of Elizabeth), Marlborough asked the Dutch deputies for a substantial contribution to a "blue water" operation. The high tory imperialists—Henry Hyde, earl of Rochester, restored as lord lieutenant of Ireland, and Daniel French, earl of Nottingham, an imperial secretary of state (supported by William Blathwayt, secretary at war and auditor of the plantations)—had vastly expanded the scope of the assault on Spanish commerce and colonies which Marlborough had previously proposed. The tories called for a great Anglo-Dutch expedition to assault Cadiz. The allied troops would be com-

manded by the tory champion James Butler, duke of Ormonde. The allied fleet
would be directed by the tory admiral Sir George Rooke. Success at Cadiz was
expected to provide a base from which a part of the expedition would sail up
the Mediterranean to persuade Andalucia to declare for the Hapsburg candidate, "Charles III." The rest of the force would cross the Atlantic from Cadiz
to reinforce John Benbow's fleet in the West Indies for a sweep of the Franco-
American coasts all the way from the Antilles to Newfoundland. Perhaps even
Quebec could be attacked. France might be driven from America altogether.
The endgame of the war with France for America was already in tory minds.[5]

As soon as he had won Dutch consent to three imperial campaigns—in
Flanders, Iberia, and America—Marlborough went home to face a new government divided over contradictory imperial strategies. The continental conception (essentially whig) held that America, and every other war objective, could
be best won by helping the Dutch fight France in Europe. The maritime view
(essentially tory) saw England's advantage in giving the Dutch no more than
the 10,000 men the 1678 treaty required. Already defeated in that desire, the
tories not only resisted every subsequent increase in Marlborough's field force,
they also tried to draw off his regiments to make amphibious "descents" on
coastal France, embark on Iberian adventures, or man American expeditions.
For the high tories deplored the cost of a growing English army in Europe as
the impetus of a financial revolution. That revolution, begun to finance king
William's war, was creating a new capitalist elite. It, together with military patronage, were the underpinnings of a novel state power wielded by the new class
of which Marlborough was the exemplar. Fearful and jealous, xenophobic and
reactionary, the tory right wing's American policy was to conquer commercial
bases at the termini of the transatlantic trade routes and to expand England's
territorial dominion in both the West Indies and North America. Commerce
and colonies would strengthen England's traditional economic elites: landlords
and merchants. Politically, the tories believed that if they could keep the army
small and stationed overseas, they would check both the growth of the state
and the autonomy of the American colonies. The secretary of state, the earl of
Nottingham, put the maritime and colonial concept bluntly to Marlborough:
"I am byast by an opinion that we shall never have any decisive success nor be
able to hold out a war agt France but by making a Sea-War & such a Sea-War
as accompanies & supports attempts on land." These "attempts" were to be
raids against French ports, occupation of Iberian port cities, whether in the
Old World or the New, and assaults on the American littoral, from the Lesser
Antilles to the St. Lawrence.[6]

In his previous period of power, which had ended ten years earlier, Marlborough had been identified with this tory maritime strategy. Now, Marlborough's own hopes of inheriting the late king's command of the allied army, even
of taking King William's place at the head of the Grand Alliance, had begun

to convince the captain general that America was best won in Europe. The terrible military cost of West Indian campaigns (which had at last horrified even a king so prodigal of English lives as Dutch William) was quickly brought home to Marlborough by the death of his longtime colleague Governor General Selwyn and by the destruction of the 12th Regiment in Jamaica by provincial neglect and epidemic disease. Marlborough considered Nottingham's (and Blathwayt's) newest proposal for a grand American operation, extending from Guadeloupe to Canada, as the last trial of tory imperial strategy.[7]

Marlborough's movement away from tory commercialism and colonialism and toward whig capitalism and imperialism was accelerated by his wife's deepening partisanship. The countess's whig politics had been masked by her hatred for King William and by her resentment of his whig ministers. With William's death and his ministers' replacement by tories, however, lady Marlborough's fear of the tory right became an undisguised obsession. "The Church Party" seemed to Sarah to be the champions of the exiled Stuarts, collaborators with those exiles' French master, Louis XIV, and, like him, religious persecutors. Lady Marlborough relentlessly pressed her phobia on her husband and on their queen. Anne was a churchwoman of deepest dye, however, and a tory down to her gouty toes. Now that Anne was queen, lady Marlborough's habitual forwardness and growing censoriousness seemed to the monarch disrespectful and distrustful, even impudent and insulting to her majesty. But old love died hard. So, for several years, Sarah retained an access to Anne and an influence over the queen that, in a monarchical age of personalized politics, expressed itself in the facilitation of innumerable appointments, military, civil, and religious. In the first two classes lady Marlborough almost invariably acted at the instance of her husband, the captain general, or their closest friend, the lord treasurer. In church patronage, Queen Anne always interposed her own deep convictions. Nevertheless, the countess of Marlborough's unique intimacy with a sick, shy queen was an indispensable conduit of patronage and power for Marlborough and Godolphin.[8]

It was to the lord treasurer that Sarah addressed a complaint, typical of many others both in its partisanship and in its concern for imperial administration. From Margate (where, on May 19, 1702, she was seeing her husband off to his command), she wrote to Godolphin that "though I know my opinion is very insignifycant upon most occasions," she had to complain that only "faction and nonsense" would have placed high tory puppets, the lords Dartmouth and Weymouth, on the commission for trade and plantations. She would do things differently, said lady Marlborough: "if I had any power to dispose of places, the first rule should bee to have those that were proper for the business; the next those that had deserved on any occation; and whenever there was room without hurting the publick, I think that one would with pleasure give employments to those that were in soe unhappy a condition as to want it."[9]

Whatever her importance as a channel to the queen, particularly on matters of patronage, the countess understood that the moderate tory triumvirs—her husband, their friend the treasurer, and their junior partner, the speaker, Robert Harley—did not agree with her about policy or accept her politics. What compelled their cooperation, personal relations apart, and what split them all from the high tories, "the Church Party," was religion. The triumvirs, like lady Marlborough, admitted dissent and rejected coercion in matters spiritual. All four accepted what latitudinarianism implied: freedom of thought and of debate and an acceptance of that cultural sea change which marked the transition from traditional to modern society. Thus it was that Speaker Harley kept up a connection with dissenters, famous in the case of his intelligencer Daniel Defoe, but effective as well with the Quaker patriarch and American proprietor William Penn (who also offered Harley a clandestine connection with the party of the exiled Stuarts, the jacobites).[10]

Penn's nemesis was William Blathwayt, the secretary at war and of plantations. He reminded Godolphin that the duke of York had given Delaware to Penn for the yearly fee of a rose, never paid. Anxious for Marlborough's "protection," "sensible" that, as a Nottingham tory, he had "wanted the opportunity of shewing my real devotion to your Service," Blathwayt suggested to Marlborough that the queen resume her father's gift to Penn. Then Delaware, the "tract of land between Maryland and Pennsylvania," could become the captain general's own province, alienating "the Greatest Part of Mr Penn's best County, called Chester County." Blathwayt suggested that as an American proprietor, Marlborough could reconcile personal profit with imperial strength, in good seventeenth-century fashion, developing Delaware as the basis of a trade in naval stores, reducing the English navy's dependency on the caprice of Swedes. It was a measure of Blathwayt's political desperation that so determined a royal centralizer should have offered to expand the number of private proprietors in America. Blathwayt recognized that the deal was so shady that Marlborough might "scruple" to appear. So Blathwayt proposed that the conscienceless lord Cornbury, misgovernor of New York, should front for Marlborough.[11]

The captain general passed all this on to Godolphin with the remark that the secretary at war and plantations had obviously outlived his usefulness. Marlborough quickly transferred most of Blathwayt's responsibilities as secretary at war to his own secretary, Adam de Cardonnel. Godolphin drastically reduced Blathwayt's authority as auditor general of the American revenues. Blathwayt was blamed not for his appeal to Marlborough's cupidity, but rather for failing to recognize that the earl was now so elevated that petty pelf was insulting to his greatness and the offer of a private propriety was inimical to his imperial duty. The captain general's sense of the public interest had grown with his elevation. Born to a modest family impoverished by civil war, "fiel pero desdichado," Marlborough had risen by professional merit and princely favor to the operational command of England's army. Now he aspired to the confederate command that had been king William's.[12]

There were princes aplenty who claimed command of the allied armies, the elector of Brandenburg first among them. The house of Hanover offered several princely generals (including its elector, the future king of Great Britain). The queen ordered Marlborough to seek the command for her beloved husband, Prince George. Marlborough dutifully told the allied envoys that no English officer would submit to any authority but the queen's, exercised by a general she commissioned. Of course, everyone knew that it was Marlborough who had anglicized the English army and he who had made it both the prop of Anne's accession and the arbiter of her authority. The earl's argument for Prince George (backed as it was by England's status as the paymaster of the alliance) worked even more effectively for Marlborough himself.[13]

While the contest over the allied command dragged on, France advanced on every front. Not until the campaign of 1702 was into mid-June did the heer van Dykevelt's decisive declaration that Marlborough had been King William's own choice for the command at last persuade the states general to resolve that the general of the English expeditionary forces would command the field army of which his troops were a part. Marlborough's authority, however, was to be restricted by a council of war dominated by the Dutch generals and the political commissars, or "field deputies," of the states. So restricted, this was a command only vaulting ambition could covet and military genius effect. Marlborough had never held an independent command in Europe. He was hamstrung by his allies, jealous and insubordinate Dutch generals and captious Dutch deputies, most of whom hated Englishmen. His avowed enemies were the marshals of France. The French were undefeated in living memory. They now possessed the strongest positions they had enjoyed since William of Orange led the Dutch back from the brink of disaster in 1672. The French now held every one of the Dutch barrier fortresses in the Spanish Netherlands. The subsequent defection from the empire to France of the governor general of the Spanish Netherlands, the elector of Bavaria, and of his brother, the elector of Cologne, meant that the armies of Louis XIV also controlled every one of the indispensable riverain routes from the Danube to the Scheldt.

Under existing conceptions of warfare, the allied position was irrecoverable and the balance of power in the west was irredeemable. In the nine years of war that had ended in 1697, the allies had regained but one major city from the French, Namur. In the Spanish Netherlands alone, there were now nine barrier fortresses, Namur included, in French hands. Each fortress city commanded a vital water route. These routes were indispensable to eighteenth-century armies which, fed on fresh bread and paid in specie, seldom moved more than a day's march—say, fifteen miles—from their magazines of supplies. Even in summer, the roads were often impassable and the fortress cities also controlled the major bridges. The land communications between the river routes or around their headwaters were covered by defensible camp sites, each a day's march apart. The whole of Flanders and much of western Europe, save for heavily forested or very rough terrain, was a chessboard. Divided by rivers and marches, dominated by fortresses, small and discrete territories were the squares of a war game, played by rigid rules. France held all the major pieces.

In this chess game, a coup was a day's march stolen from enemy observation; a victory was the enemy's grass forage interrupted or its bread convoy cut off; a triumph was to check the movement of a hostile force. This war of feints and countermarches occasionally produced an endgame: the siege of a fortress. It, too, had rules for those pieces in the great game of war: the besiegers and besieged; the covering and relieving armies; the convoy escorts and attackers; the foragers and raiders; the outpost guards and infiltrators. In these war games sizable actions were few and actual encounters between armies were usually accidents. King William had stumbled into Steinkirk and been surprised at Landen. His only triumph, Namur, was a siege. Orthodox generals avoided battle as an incalculable expense of men and material, a cast of the dice, "a game at hazard," rather than a chess match. To the conventional military mind, battle was a disaster. Primarily concerned to keep the game in play and avoid fatal conclusions until October—the end of the grass-growing season and the onset of autumnal rains—closed the campaign, no conventional general would ever willingly fight. The Dutch generals, by whom Marlborough and his staff were surrounded, outnumbered, and obstructed, were intensely conventional.

In June 1702, Marlborough took command (if that is the word to describe his limited authority) of a losing position. From the west and south, along the Meuse and the Rhine, the armies of France were advancing on the Netherlands, under the (relatively) creative command of Louis-François, duc de Boufflers, marshal of France. During Marlborough's visit to The Hague in March, he had agreed to an allied attack on the enemy outpost, the town of Kaiserwerth, a small place on the north bank of the Rhine, downstream from Cologne. On April 18, even before Marlborough's return from England, his accession to the allied command, and the declaration of war (which was delayed in England until May 2 and in France until June 18), "the trenches were opened" against the fortifications of Kaiserwerth. In the words of that poetic private, John Scot, "We keeped the trenches and held in the Frenches." After two tedious months, the allied mortars and siege guns had "reduced Keyfwerfwert to a Heap of Rubbish." On June 9, its counterscarp and ravelin were taken by storm. On June 15, the garrison capitulated. The next day they marched away with the honors of war, drums beating, flags flying, bullet in mouth, cannon and wagons in train, to rejoin Boufflers' army. The allies had taken 2,500 casualties to seize a ruin whose garrison they released and whose fortifications they demolished to prevent its reoccupation.[14]

At the penultimate moment of the siege, the day after the storm of the Kaiserwerth counterscarp, Marshal Boufflers executed his plan to destroy the allies' covering army, which included all the English infantry. Boufflers' French outnumbered the allies two to one. His army marched without word reaching the allies' inept commander, Godert, baron van Reede-Ginkel, earl of Athlone. The French were already closing the pinchers that would surround the allies and cut them off from their base at Nimwegen when Athlone accidentally learned of the French approach. The allied army escaped only by a prodigious cross-county march. All through the night of June 18, the allied retreat was covered by the disciplined rearguard action of Richard Ingoldsby's brigade of English infantry (under John, baron Cutts's command). The retreating troops were rescued by the citizens of Nimwegen. Without a garrison, abandoned by the gunners, and betrayed by the municipal authorities (all of whom had sold out to the French), the people of Nimwegen broke into the arsenal, pulled the artillery up the ramps to the bastions, and opened fire on the advancing French. Boufflers was just minutes away from snapping up the only allied field army and winning the war at a stroke. "Half an hour more," wrote an English officer, "would have cut us to pieces."[15]

Marlborough landed at The Hague to be greeted with the news of Athlone's narrow escape and his troops' bitter censure of the Dutch general "for not having better intelligence." In the crisis, other of the allies' generals, even the royal Dane, Charles Rudolph, duke of Württemberg-Neustadt, who had contested Marlborough's command in Ireland, were now prepared to give way to his rank as captain general of the English and to recognize the earl as the army's senior officer. Godert de Ginkel, earl of Athlone, whose title memorialized his displacement of Marlborough from the Irish command in 1691, refused to step down, but the states general were profoundly alarmed by their field army's narrow escape, by the danger to Nimwegen, and by the French occupation of the strategic triangle between the Meuse and the Rhine. That spear point pressed against the allied army sheltering under the guns of Nimwegen. So it threatened the heart of Holland. At last, on June 2/13, the states displaced Athlone and conceded the command of the field army to Marlborough.[16]

Marlborough immediately rewarded Ingoldsby for his brigade's bravery and discipline by authorizing the addition of a grenadier company to the general's regiment and by promoting Ingoldsby's son to be its captain. In the brigade's rearguard action, the 16th Regiment had been especially distinguished, inflicting losses of five to one on the French household troops who attacked them. This was the baptism of fire for four of the regiment's new crop of ensigns. In the retreat to Nimwegen, Hugh Drysdale, John Fermor, William Gooch, and John Montgomery advanced toward the command of Virginia, Minorca, and New York, for the grateful captain general took a personal interest in their subsequent promotions.[17]

The other English regiment that saw especially hard fighting in the retreat to Nimwegen was Sir Bevil Granville's (the 10th), commanded by its recently promoted executive officer, Lieutenant Colonel Roger Elliot. The bravery of

Elliot's half brother, Lieutenant Alexander Spotswood, was marked in the action. Marlborough brevetted him captain. Replacing an officer casualty of the 10th, Spotswood took another step up the military ladder toward the government of Virginia. Even as Granville's regiment was in action near Nimwegen, its colonel's commission as governor general of Barbados was being written in London. Sir Bevil offered substantial military assets both in Flanders and in England in exchange for an independent and lucrative command in America. At first it seemed that Granville would be "obliged to quit the Government of Pendennis, the Command of a Regiment of Foot, and of his Rank in the Army which gave him a pretence to the Post of Brigadier General (Being the oldest Colonel of Foot) which he did upon the assurance that He should Enjoy the said Government of Barbados with all the Advantages that his predecessors had done . . . without parting with anything they had in England." When the lord treasurer, and so the commissioners of trade and plantations, refused to let any of the governors general accept gratuities from their provincial assemblies without the prior permission of the crown, Granville demanded compensation. He insisted that Marlborough pass the command of the 10th Regiment to the tory lord North and Grey (presumably his lordship paid Sir Bevil a handsome price for such a senior corps). Marlborough agreed. He also gave the government of Pendennis to another Granville (but he was expected to vote the fortress borough's parliamentary seat for the Marlborough-Godolphin moderates, not the Granville ultras). Finally, Marlborough approved Sir Bevil's promotion to brigadier general. Such were the military counters of imperial politics.[18]

The general and the treasurer had planned to give Granville's regiment to Colonel George Villiers. Then Villiers's garrison regiment in England could go to Colonel Rupert Billingsly, the lieutenant governor of Berwick, an original member of the Denmark-Churchill connection and the leader of the 15th during lord Churchill's coup. Billingsly's lieutenant governorship was then to pass to Major Edward Nott, another of the Denmark-Churchill connection and field officer of the 15th during the coup at Berwick. Subsequently, Nott had raised a North Country regiment to go out to the West Indies. He had come home to serve with Marlborough at Cork and Kinsale, but his largest claim to Marlborough's present favor was a decade of West Indian service. By making Nott lieutenant governor of Berwick, Marlborough not only served present partisan interests and rewarded Nott's long loyalty, he also secured the key to the Scots border. To make assurance doubly sure, Marlborough intended to promote Colonel Edmund Maine, "who was formerly Lieut to my Lords [Marlborough's, 3d] Troop of Guards," as the titular governor of Berwick. This post, with its salary of £1,000 per annum, was Marlborough's recompense to an old comrade who, as a Marlborough man, had passed the entirety of king William's reign without a single promotion. Although the regimental succession was diverted from Villiers (who did not wish to go on campaign) to lord North and Grey (who did), the gubernatorial changes went forward as planned.

Marlborough was now sure of Berwick and Major Nott took a long step up the ladder of imperial command toward the government of Virginia.[19]

Marlborough now turned from the Scots border to London's river. He was determined that the command of the Thames garrisons should continue in trustworthy hands. General William Selwyn, the governor of Tilbury, had died in command of Jamaica. Marlborough nominated a soldier connection of Godolphin's for transfer from the Scilly Isles to command the fort, town, and dockyard at Tilbury (the lord treasurer saw to it that Scilly stayed in the family). General Selwyn, much lamented by Marlborough, had also to be replaced in Jamaica. That island dominion, with its garrison and naval base, was to be the headquarters of the tory ministry's American expedition. Marlborough, while he was still at The Hague trying to secure the command of the allied army in Flanders, had responded to Godolphin's three suggestions for a new Jamaican governor general of high enough military rank to command in chief the army intended for America. Marlborough pointed out that two of Godolphin's nominees (Thomas Livingstone, viscount Teviot, and Major General William Stewart) were Scots. As such, they were barred by act of parliament from administering the trade and navigation statutes. So the Scots were incapable of the civil side of the Jamaica command. Godolphin's third candidate was lord Cutts. Given his strong American interests and his outstanding combat record (not to mention his relative poverty), Cutts would do, Marlborough agreed, but Cutts declined the commission.[20]

"The General," although he was tiring of officers "who refus'd the West India Service, & made terms with the Queen," next pursued lord Nottingham's suggestion of Major General Ingoldsby as "generall in the Indies." Ingoldsby said "he will goe any where her Maty thinks him capable of Serving her, but should take it as a great favor if he might have time to know if his wife wou'd give her consent." The champion of Anne and the husband of Sarah assured Ingoldsby that "I thought the Service might allow soe much time, and that the Queen would not like him the worse for being soe good a husband; I shall want him here, but doe for the good of her Maty, and England wish that his wife may let him goe."[21]

Pending Mrs. Ingoldsby's decision, Marlborough assumed that Ingoldsby would be the next governor general of Jamaica and commander in chief in America. He had Ingoldsby meet at The Hague both with Pensioner Heinsius and the English admiral Sir David Michell, sent over by Nottingham to concert "the great force both English and Dutch" to be sent on from Cadiz "into the West Indies to receive those under their protection who would submit to the House of Austria" in the monarchy of Spain, "and to conquer those who were obstinate." Presumably at Nottingham's instance (and probably on Blathwayt's information), Havana and Cartagena were now added to an already overlong list of targets. Each addition required an increased investment of men, munitions, and ships. The American expedition, atop that to Cadiz, would drain the garrisons in Ireland and England, weaken the navy in home waters, and tax Marlborough's ordnance establishment. As Nottingham called for more and more troops to be taken from Marlborough's army and sent to the West Indies, it seemed to both England's captain general and Holland's pensioner that this latest tory imperial effort put at risk the Grand Alliance's central purposes: the protection of the Netherlands from French aggression and so the maintenance of English independence. Nonetheless, the parliamentary strength of the tory right compelled both Heinsius and Marlborough to appear to support this ulti-mate expression of "blue water" imperialism. On October 6, 1702, Nottingham concluded a long dispatch to Marlborough by declaring flatly that Europe was to be won in America: "It was more practicable to make Spain, & the other Dominions in Europe follow the fate of the West Indies, than to make the West Indies (if once in the Power of France) follow the fate of Spain." Nottingham insisted that "the Indies . . . are certainly the principall Batteries from whence our Potent Enemys may be Soonest Disabled & Distressed," since "by seizure of a few Ports & Places there, her Majesty may become Sovereign of the prin-cipall Sources or Springs of the Trade & Treasure of the World."[22]

The Dutch were asked to provide three regiments for the force concen-trating at Jamaica to seize all America (Marlborough suggested the Scots Dutch brigade, another instance of his determination to make the American empire as "British" as the army already was). The troops were to sail under convoy of a squadron of warships at the end of the 1702 campaign in Flanders. As negotia-tions went forward at The Hague during July 1702, Marlborough suggested a change of commander. Although General Ingoldsby, "a very brave and a very honest man," in Marlborough's view, continued to gratify his chief by saying "he would goe when ever I pleased," he had not yet heard from his wife (she not only said no, she also produced a wealthy relative who swore he would disinherit Ingoldsby if he went to the Indies). Besides, Marlborough valued In-goldsby as the drillmaster of the uniform discipline Marlborough now imposed on every British regiment. Ingoldsby himself wanted an English government. It had three admitted advantages over the American command: he could hold an English governorship in absentia during the war; the command would give him a parliamentary interest in the borough; his salary and perquisites as governor would pay for his campaigning costs in Flanders. The inadmissible advantage was that it was much less risky to take the field in Flanders than it was to face yellow fever in the West Indies.[23]

So, even as Marlborough maneuvered the allied army, in the presence of the French, on the Heaths of Peer, he wrote Godolphin to ask, inter alia, "(Is [it] impossible to make use of Lord Peterborough)"? In this extraordinary pa-renthesis, Marlborough suggested that the peer who had tried to destroy him as recently as the Fenwick episode should become the prospective viceroy of all America. "Ld. Peterborough has long had it in his head," Marlborough ex-plained in his next letter to Godolphin. Now that the American prospect was so vast and so political, "I suppose there are an hundred pretenders" to be viceroy. Of them, Charles Mordaunt, earl of Peterborough, was not the worst, Marlborough wrote. At least he would be better than the likes of William O'Brien, the new earl of Inchiquin, who had inherited Marlborough's contempt for his father, dating back to Inchiquin's misgovernment of Tangier. The young peer's appointment "wou'd be a libel upon the Queen's government," the captain general exclaimed.[24]

Peterborough seemed to Marlborough someone best out of England. First, Marlborough resented the fascination the seductively feminist Peterborough had for Sarah. "What Histories ever gave us leave to think your Sex insignificant, rather what age of the world does not prove the contrary?" Peterborough wrote lady Marlborough. He added that she was proof enough of woman's equality, even superiority. Besides Peterborough's attentions to Sarah, Marlborough disapproved of the relentless campaign Peterborough was waging to obtain the hand of Marlborough's exquisite daughter, Mary, for Peterborough's heir, John, viscount Mordaunt. Admittedly, Mordaunt had military (and political) virtues. He was an especially brave aide de camp to the captain general. Mordaunt aspired both to be an efficient noble commander of the sort personified by North and Grey of the 10th, "and with fewer words be as serviceable in the winter wars" in parliament. Both in the field and in the commons, Mordaunt pledged his obedience to Marlborough, but, as Marlborough wrote to his wife, Mordaunt was a rakehell, "which can never make a good husband." Lady Marlborough could not be charmed into allowing an unsuitable alliance if Peterborough was overseas. Better yet, the American appointment might well end in Peterborough's disgrace (Marlborough's faith in the plan had diminished in direct proportion to its escalating ends) or even death.[25]

Peterborough needed an experienced second in command. Marlborough agreed with Godolphin that the Scots veteran Sir David Colyear, lord Portmore, was qualified, the more so because of his long service with the Scots-Dutch brigade. Portmore's brother had just been killed leading the Scots-Dutch at Kaiserwerth, adding to his claims to an independent command. Marlborough admitted to some doubts about Portmore's capacity: he was one "of a great many [who] are good officers whilst they receive orders, that are not capable of commanding in chief." Portmore (like Peterborough) had long since discussed possible imperial assignments with the captain general. "I know he has his heart sett on being left Governor of Cadiz," Marlborough wrote. Despite his reservations, Marlborough secured Portmore's commission to command the prospective conquest in Spain with an option to take command of the detachment from the Cadiz expedition, which was supposed to rendezvous with Peterborough to conquer the Spanish West Indies and French America.[26]

In the meantime, at Nimwegen, on June 21, 1702, the captain general of England took command of the allied army, now numbering 60,000. The conventional Dutch generals saw only danger and counseled the defensive, fearing that the French army would bombard their cities and levy "contributions" from their countryside, but Marlborough, concluding that the French had over-stretched their communications, saw an opportunity to attack. The Dutch generals thought that the enemy was a threat to the heart of Holland, but Marlborough declared that the French were trapped between Nimwegen, at the apex of the Meuse-Rhine triangle, and the Dutch frontier fortress at Maestricht, eighty miles up the line of the Meuse. He argued that the allied army had only to advance and the French would retreat to secure their supply routes. As soon as the French withdrew, Marlborough predicted, the enemy would be forced to choose whether to defend Brabant to the west or to cover the easternmost Flanders fortresses (on the Meuse between Nimwegen and Maestricht). That is, the French would be forced to choose whether to lose a great province or a line of riverine fortresses. As one of Marlborough's officers explained, the captain general intended, simply by advancing, to force the French "to quit their camp and dance after him." After two weeks of argument with Athlone and the desperately defensive Dutch generals, Marlborough appealed over their heads to the states general. He won their permission to advance, but only if he divided his army, leaving eighteen battalions of infantry and twenty squadrons of cavalry to garrison Nimwegen.[27]

At last, on July 16/27, the allies crossed the Meuse and put themselves astride the French communications westward with Brabant. The enemy immediately abandoned their strong camp at Genape and retreated up the east bank of the Meuse. The allies followed, march for march, along the west bank, for forty miles. Cutts and the English infantry then captured the castle of Graven-broeck. There Marlborough encamped his army. While his patrols dismantled the French supply stations at Peer and Bree, Marlborough waited for the French "either to quite the Meuse, or abandon Brabant." Marlborough anticipated that if the French chose to leave the line of the Meuse and march west for Brabant, they must cross the allied front. There he intended to bring the enemy to bay, on the move (at a terrible disadvantage, given the linear tactics of the time), on a battlefield of Marlborough's choosing. As one of his captains put it, the French saw "we were just between them and home, and they had no way homeward but by marching over a heath within half a league of our camp."[28]

That night, August 1/12, Marlborough met a council of war. He persuaded the reluctant Dutch generals (the generals commanding the troops of all the other nations in the allied army readily supported Marlborough) to advance to take the French in flank as they crossed the Heath of Peer the next morning. At first light, Marlborough convened the generals to distribute their orders. The Dutch, dominated by Athlone's appeals to their defensiveness, refused to march. Marlborough could only ride out with the generals and the political commissars of the states general to show them the French retreating "in the greatest confusion and disorder imaginable; upon this they all acknowledged that they had lost a fair opportunity of giving the enemy a fatal blow." When the French encamped, they were still vulnerable, at least in Marlborough's view. Again the Dutch refused to attack. Two chances for a decisive battle had been lost to the Williamite generals. Just as Marlborough had predicted, however, the French had been maneuvered out of the province of the Spanish Guelderland. In fact, the French retreat looked very like flight, Orkney wrote, "for from the time that we crossed the Meuse they have marched night and day and have been five days sometime without having off their cloths or putting up their tents." Forced across the Meuse, lying behind the River Demer, the French had to eat up Brabant.[29]

Conventional opinion considered this outcome little short of miraculous, given the sorry state of the allies less than a month before, but Marlborough's devastating headaches testified to his fury at missing two decisive battles no Dutch general wanted to fight. "He realy was sike with vexation it was not done," Orkney declared. Still, the French had not only been forced from their gains in Guelderland but also, as the captain general had anticipated, the allied advance had compelled the French to uncover the fortress cities of the Meuse between Nimwegen and Maestricht. Now the allies tried to establish a supply line to fuel the forthcoming sieges. The French advanced to threaten the allied communications.[30]

On August 16, the allied convoy, the 6,000 Dutch soldiers whom Marlborough had sent out to meet it, and the French advance guard under Marlborough's nephew James Fitzjames, duke of Berwick, all were within a mile of each other. The French main body was coming up hotfoot, but it was still separated from Berwick by a river when Marlborough and the allies suddenly appeared on the French army's southern flank. The French flinched and the whole solar system, still in orbit around that magnetic convoy, moved south. On August 23, Marlborough deployed the allied army in line of battle across the Heath of Helchteren just as the French, exhausted and hungry, emerged onto the plain. The allied artillery opened the engagement in midafternoon but, to spring Marlborough's trap, the Dutch general of the left wing, Opdam, had to obey Marlborough's orders to attack. These orders were at last supported by the Dutch political commissars. Still, Opdam refused to march, claiming that difficult terrain prevented his troops from getting at the disordered enemy. Night fell, the French withdrew, and the allied cavalry pursuit at dawn was inconclusive, only the English cavalry making contact.[31]

The English officer corps, furious at the Dutch generals' obstruction, could not be muzzled. So the English public, accustomed by a decade of Williamite military mismanagement to expect the worst of "the boors," expressed its outrage at Dutch timidity and perversity, but Marlborough's critics now began to say that he was avoiding action in order to prolong the war and so increase the profits of command. Marlborough's correspondence to his intimates reveals that the captain general was literally prostrate with repressed fury and frustration. Still, as Cardonnel's bulletin declared, the hasty retreat of the outmaneuvered French back across the Demer to shelter once again in Brabant left "the Spanish Guelder open to us so that we are at liberty to besiege any place on the Meuse between the Grave [the crossings of the Meuse at Nimwegen] and Maestricht," the frontier of the Dutch republic.[32]

With his supplies in hand and the enemy at a distance, Marlborough moved against the strongest of these petty places, Venloo. He had it invested, from both banks of the Meuse, on September 5. The trenches were opened on the 7th, but there were weeks of delay before the Dutch siege train could be gotten the few miles upriver from Nimwegen. Then the Dutch engineers insisted on treating this little fortification as if it were a vast urban masterpiece by Vauban, but they could neither agree among themselves nor with any of their allies about a single step of the classic siege ritual. Cautious with the enemy and quarrelsome with everyone else, the Dutch besiegers drove Marlborough to distraction as he watched from the headquarters of the covering army. If "England that is famous for negligence," Marlborough wrote to Godolphin, found anyone in its service "guilty of half what I see here, it would be impossible for them to avoid being justly torn to peces by the parliament."[33]

The Dutch acted at last only because Marlborough threatened "that if they would not besiege Venloo he would quit the Army and I really believe," Orkney concluded, "that if he was not here that nothing would be done at all." Not until September 18 were the outworks of Venloo attacked. Fort St. Michael was the key to the position and the objective of the English infantry detached to the siege. Just before the attack began, lord Cutts called together the officers of the Royal Irish (18th) and three companies of grenadiers. As Captain Richard Kane (that governor general in the making) recalled, Cutts gave them unprecedented orders. They were to follow up their storm of the counterscarp by a headlong assault on the walls beyond it. At 4:00 p.m. the English attacked. The enemy ran. The English grenadiers and fusiliers pursued the fleeing French along the covered way into a ravelin. They killed most of its garrison. Then they chased the survivors across a deep moat on a narrow, 100-foot-long wooden catwalk. The English pursued the French so closely that they could not throw down the loose planks. Friend and foe reached the foot of the curtain wall almost together. They found the sally port closed in their faces. The French engineers had not reveted the great earthwork with stone, however, and the French governor had not had the grass cropped. So the fleeing Frenchmen pulled themselves overhand up the embankment, grasping the long grass. The English infantry followed, despite the musketry from above, "for we had no Choice, but to carry the Fort or all perish." When the first wave of attackers reached the ramparts, the garrison tumbled down into the fort, "where they threw down their Arms and called for Quarter, which we gave them, and the Plunder of the Fort to the Soldiers. Thus were lord Cutts' unaccountable Orders as madly executed . . . which got Lord Cutts great applause, of which he boasted all his life after, tho' neither he nor any of the Noblemen stirred one foot out of the

Trenches till we were master of it, except the young Earl of Huntington, who [still hobbled by a wound received at Kaiserwerth] stole out of the Trenches from them, and kept up with the foremost." Marlborough immediately authorized a regiment to be raised for this noble volunteer. It was actions, not titles, that impressed the army, another alarming indication of its professional, not patrician, values. The defenders of Venloo were also impressed. A week after the mad English attack, the French mistook a salute as the signal of another assault. They immediately surrendered.[34]

In the meantime, Marlborough detached the earl of Orkney with his Royal Scots and eight other British battalions, together with the English artillery, to take the island fortress of Stevensweart in the Meuse. This they did with dash and éclat in just five days. Orkney, an orthodox general, brave but unadventuresome, was learning initiative from Marlborough. "I always thought to play a sure Gaime," Orkney wrote, "but now it is easy to be seen a head is wanted." The day after Venloo surrendered, the allies moved up the Meuse to Ruremond, the last barrier to the allied river communications with Maestricht. Ruremond's 2,000-man garrison made but the weakest resistance. After just nine days, they surrendered themselves and a huge magazine of munitions. Two days later, on October 6, Marlborough had the pleasure of announcing to the states general that the River Meuse had been opened to allied navigation all the way to the Dutch frontier at Maestricht. By conventional standards, Marlborough's campaign had come to a triumphant conclusion. In June, the allies had their backs to the walls of Nimwegen and feared for the heart of Holland. In October, they were conquerors of a province and three riverine fortresses, the Dutch frontier was regained, and the French were exhausted and embarrassed.[35]

Although his wool-clad troops were soaked through by autumn rains and his horses were starving as the forage failed, Marlborough was determined, against the unanimous advice of the Dutch generals, to keep the allied army in the field. He had the engineers build bridges across the Meuse so that the allies could forage in the Guelderland. The British dragoons under their brigade major, Robert Hunter, scoured the captured town of Waert and its dependencies "to the last extremity." Hunter was responsible for securing, by force if necessary, tens of thousands of horse rations—oats, hay, and straw—from the farmers of the conquered countryside, from the magistrates of its towns, and from commercial commissaries. At the same time Marlborough ordered Hunter both to repress the notorious plundering by British dragoons and to see to their medical treatment (the troopers were suffering from dysentery caused, Marlborough thought, from gorging on captured honey).[36]

Hunter's exactions fed the siege of Liège, "one of the Great Cities of Europe," the seat of an ancient diocese, the home of 100 churches, and the last crossing of the Meuse this side of Namur itself. When the Dutch generals clamored to go into winter quarters after Venloo fell, Marlborough insisted that, having opened the river route to Maestricht and having reunited the several siege detachments, the allies should advance once again. Marlborough told the generals that Boufflers was so badly beaten that an advance on Liège would force him back beyond the French fortified lines, deep into Brabant, and so make the enemy "content themselves with winter quarters in their own country." That, under the rules of eighteenth-century warfare, was a check. What Marlborough did not tell the Dutch generals and commissars was that he had checkmate in mind.[37]

Using a double agent to set up Boufflers, Marlborough made a night march as if to attack the French in their camp at Tongres, midway between Liège and the French lines covering Brabant. Boufflers was so alarmed that he escaped, as he thought, from a trap at Tongres (so quickly that he left his engineering equipment behind) to take the usual camp for covering Liège. Arriving at the campsite early on the morning of October 12, Boufflers found to his horror that Marlborough had anticipated him. The allies were already in battle line across the plain. For the fourth time, the Dutch generals refused to attack the disordered French army. For the fourth time, the French retreated, crossing their lines and encamping in Brabant. Marlborough was so chagrined at losing another opportunity to bring the French to battle that he actually wrote the enemy commander to explain that he had not taken the opportunity Boufflers had so kindly offered him because, "as you know, I am the head of a confederate army, of whose acts I am not absolutely the master."[38]

The next day, the allies invested Liège. To escape bombardment, the city itself capitulated as soon as the allied batteries were in place. The city fathers surrendered to Marlborough personally. He refused to let Athlone or the other Dutch generals share in the conquest or command of a city outside the Dutch frontier, a city whose capture they had done all they could to impede. Instead, Marlborough encouraged jacobite English exiles such as the earl of Ailesbury to set up their households in Liège. They could anglicize a jurisdiction where "the Dutch locusts and plunderers" did not command. Indeed, it was only Marlborough's "natural good temper" and his ability to look forward to "the common cause" of victory that had kept the mutual hatreds of the English and the Dutch under any control. "If we had a General of another disposition," Ailesbury wrote, "the two Nations might have come to hostilities." When Athlone's Dutch cavalry seized the forage collected for the English horse, Hunter and the British staff barely averted bloodshed. They took their grievance to the captain general. Marlborough simply said, "advise my Lord Athlone's men to be aware of doing that twice."[39]

Before the city surrendered, its French garrison withdrew into the citadel and the Chartreuse fortress. Trenches were opened against the citadel on October 19. The usual sally, led by the French governor in person, was beaten back. Three days of terrific bombardment exploded most of the French magazines. Then "eight battalions and a thousand commanded grenadiers of the allies" stormed the counterscarp. As they moved forward, the enemy called for terms but they were overrun by two English units under Cutts's command. Cutts's vanguard was led by Lieutenant Colonel Elliot at the head of the grenadier company of the 10th. The capture of the counterscarp, at a cost of 590 English casualties, opened the citadel itself to assault. As soon as the siege batteries, firing at point-blank range from the lip of the counterscarp, had battered a breach in the curtain wall, the English again moved to the attack. As Marlborough wrote to Nottingham (in the same letter in which he deplored the utter failure of Nottingham's pet plan for the capture of Cadiz), "for the honor of her Majesty's subjects, the English were the first that got upon the breach, and the Governor was taken by a Lieutenant of Stewart's."[40]

Marlborough was proud of his compatriots and their first foreign conquest. "This has been an action of so great vigor," he wrote to Godolphin, "that it is impossible to say to much of the bravery that was shown by all the officers and soldiers." He commissioned Cutts governor of Liège and made his first duty the custody of 2,263 French prisoners, all elite troops. The allied batteries moved to bombard the Chartreuse from a height so commanding "that we could see the very bottom of their works." A mortar barrage enveloped the Chartreuse "in fire and flame." Before the cannon could open up, the fortress garrison surrendered as prisoners of war, closing the campaign of 1702. Orkney summed up the views that Marlborough's staff reported to correspondents around the empire: "we have had a long Campagne, a great deale of fatigue, and I hope glorious to England, tho' I must doe justice to say that it is all owing to Ld Marlborrow for he has had a constant struggle with the Dutch, and theres not one place taken that he has not in a manner forced them to undertake, and this last place was down right against all their Consents . . . tell the truth Ld. Marlb. has soe much a superiority of understanding to all the rest of our Generalls that I can assure you it suppplys double the want of Equall Service with them." Genius had outdone experience.[41]

Liège was refortified in five days by the allied armies. Then Marlborough named the winter quarters for the 40,000 troops in English pay. These he had chosen a month earlier, on the assumption that Boufflers would be baffled and that Liège would fall. So Marlborough could place his winter quarters advantageously for an early spring campaign to clear the Rhine, just as this one had opened the Meuse. Even a baffled Boufflers was not to be ignored, however, and Marlborough kept the allies together until the army reached Maestricht. Then he boarded a canal barge and set off down the river to visit each of the fortresses he had captured in his first campaign as commander in chief.[42]

On the second night of his voyage, halfway between Venloo and Grave, opposite the isolated French outpost at Guelder, Marlborough's yacht was separated from both its larger companion and their cavalry escort riding along the bank. French raiders from Guelder were waiting in ambush. They killed the mule drivers on the towpath, pulled the barge in to the shore, threw a shower of grenades onto the deck, boarded in the smoke, overwhelmed the twenty-five guards, and captured the yacht. The lieutenant in command of the French raiders examined the passports which every officer, except Marlborough, had obtained from Boufflers. Too proud to take a pass from his enemy to travel through country he had conquered, Marlborough was subject to seizure. The allied cause was exposed to disaster. As the French officer reached Marlborough, one of his servants slipped the captain general a pass dating from the last war, made out to Marlborough's brother, General Charles Churchill. It was accepted by the French officer. (The officer was an Irish deserter from the English army. He soon afterward deserted the French as well. Appearing at The Hague, he received a full pardon from Queen Anne and a command in the Dutch army.) The raiders then plundered the barge, taking a rich haul of gold and silver plate. The French retired. They took with them the captain general's cook, but not the captain general.[43]

The tardy cavalry escort had fled from the firing. They spread the word that Marlborough had been taken to Guelder. Before dawn, the allied garrisons of Ruremond and Venloo surrounded the fort. The states general dispatched a courier to Germany to order a captured French marshal held for exchange. As the bad news spread during the day, the streets of The Hague filled with despairing crowds. At last, toward evening, Marlborough's yacht arrived. Astonishment gave way to celebration as the captain general landed. "I was not ashore one minet," Marlborough wrote to Godolphin, "before I had great crowds of common pepell, some endeavouring to take mee by the hands, all cryeing out welcome. But that which moved the most was to see a great many of both sexes crye for joye. I have been extreamly obliged by the kind reception I have meet with, for from five in the afternoon till after ten at night, there was a perpetuall fyering in the streets, which is their way of rejoycing. I pray God bless the Queen and her undertakings, for the liberty of Christendom depends upon itt."[44]

Like the citizens crying and firing in the streets, like the English soldiers who surged out of their quarters to celebrate Marlborough's escape, so the allied leaders who crowded into Marlborough's rooms declared that the queen's general had become the champion of freedom in the west. Speaking for the states general, the pensioner of Holland said that Marlborough's capture would have "put it in the power of *France* to have extended her uncontroulable Dominion over all *Europe*, by detaining that Person . . . whom we cannot but look upon as destin'd by Providence to be its Instrument in ascertaining the Liberties of the better part of the Christian World." Apparently embarrassed, Marlborough replied that it was queen Anne who was the instrument of the divine will. It was glory enough to be her agent. It was Marlborough's rival for command, however, who best, and most generously, credited Marlborough for rescuing the Netherlands in 1702. "The success of this campaign," wrote the earl of Athlone, "is solely due to this incomparable chief, since I confess that I, serving as second in command, opposed in all circumstances his opinion and proposals."[45]

It was too much to say, as the English did, that Marlborough's successes in the Flanders campaign of 1702 exceeded those of king William's seven campaigns combined, but all the allies agreed that the captain general's achievements were unprecedented and unrepeatable. Marlborough himself remarked privately to Sarah that "it was not reasonable to expect ever to have so much success in any other campaigne as in this." That being so, pensioner Heinsius wrote to Marlborough, this was the time to accept the dukedom that queen Anne had offered him when the house of lords addressed her in praise of her general's victories. The title would enhance his standing in Europe, Marlborough was told. It would strengthen his command of the allied army. It could not be thought the effect of royal favor, for "it is visable to the whole world that it is not done upon your own account," but was the recognition due military achievement. Sarah, as always, was bitterly opposed to her husband's elevation. He agreed with her "that we ought not to wish for a greater title, till we have a better estate," but he pointed out that the queen had anticipated this objection by a grant of £5,000 per annum from the post office revenues during her lifetime. She was even prepared to ask parliament to make the grant for Marlborough's life. Whatever the springs of his wife's objection—social caution or economic circumstance, principled opposition or personal jealousy—Marlborough was not about to reject the one reward still outstanding for his leadership of the coup of 1688 and for his militant support for the accession of Queen Anne. A ducal title was an English subject's ultimate ambition.[46]

On December 14, 1702, queen Anne created the earl of Marlborough marquess of Blandford and duke of Marlborough. She asked parliament to continue for Marlborough's life the £5,000 per annum she had given him for hers. Small men defeat large projects. The high tory Sir Christopher Musgrave resented the refusal of Marlborough's ordnance office to remove the gunner (a former page of the earl of Carlisle) from Carlisle castle and replace him with Musgrave's election agent. Musgrave led the tory majority in the house of commons against what they now declared to be mere monarchical munificence to an unworthy favorite. To justify their position and to testify to their support for tory imperial strategy, the tory majority declared that Marlborough's victories in Flanders were no more meritorious than the services of Ormonde and Rooke in the failed Cadiz expedition. Marlborough had taught the tories too well how to oppose royal largess and how to politicize the military. Soon after he arrived from The Hague, he asked the queen to withdraw her request. This unpleasant episode was but one shot in the tory campaign to discredit Marlborough and the war in Europe, and to exalt Ormonde, Rooke, and a war naval and colonial. Such a war presented far fewer dangers, so the tories thought, than Marlborough's continental victories, with all the power they were giving to the army, the state, and "King John."[47]

PART I

WINNING AMERICA IN EUROPE

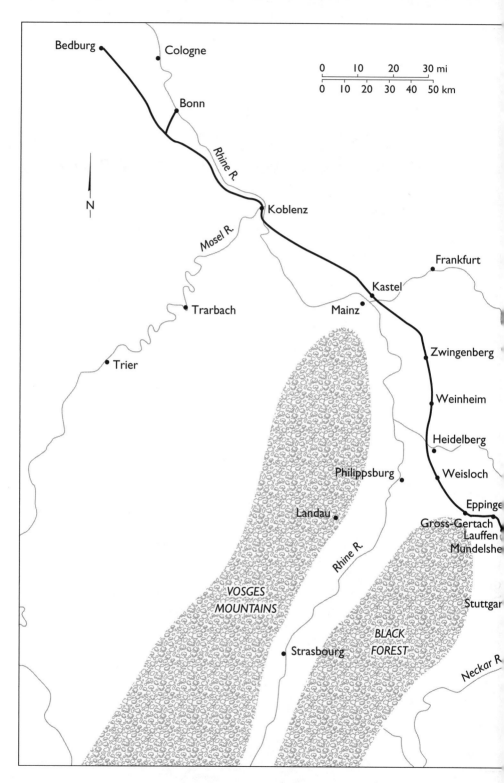

The March to Danube

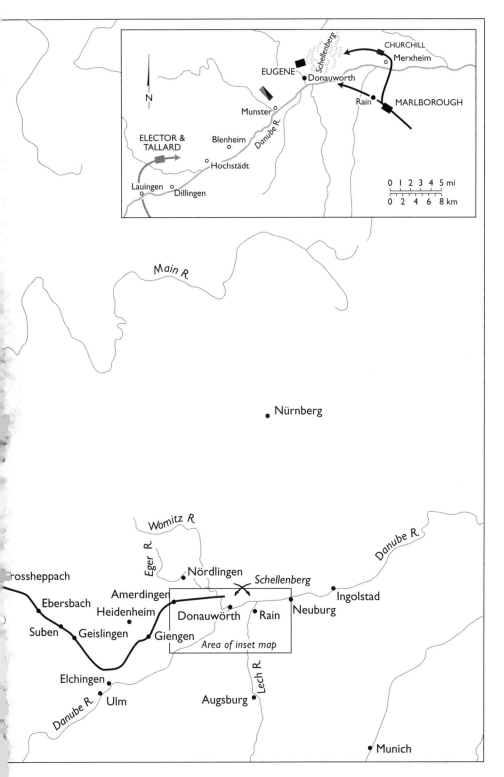

and the concentration on Blenheim

THE COCKPIT CIRCLE

Serenissima et Potentissima Anna D.G. Anglia Scotia Francia et Hibernia Regina &c. Inaugurata XXIII.ᵈ die Aprilis Anno 1702.

Queen Anne, mezzotinto engraving by Smith after a portrait by Kneller, 1702. Unless otherwise indicated, the mezzotinto portrait engravings reproduced here are by Smith after Kneller, date from the period, and are taken from the collection of the author.

When, in the summer of 1683, Princess Anne of England married Prince George of Denmark, King Charles gave the newlyweds a residence, the Cockpit, in Whitehall Palace. Resident with them were their principal advisors, the most beautiful couple in England, John, lord Churchill, and his lady, Sarah. The following year, their intimate the widower Sidney Godolphin was named first lord of the treasury and created baron Godolphin. This, "the Cockpit circle," remained intact through rebellion and revolution to "the sunshine day" of Anne's accession in 1702 and beyond, until the death of the prince in 1708. Prince George is usually remembered for King Charles's dismissive remark about the portly prince that "he had tried him drunk and sober, but 'God's fish,' there was nothing in him." Yet the prince had been a serving soldier, he was a devoted husband and, as lord admiral in his wife's reign, he was an aegis for Admiral George Churchill, Marlborough's younger brother, and one of the captain general's conduits to the queen.

By the time of the prince's death, the strains of world war, compounded by the personal tragedy most poignant in an aristocratic age, the death of heirs, had strained the Cockpit

George, prince of Denmark

John, duke of Marlborough

Sarah, duchess of Marlborough

Sidney, earl of Godolphin

Præstantissimus, Nobilissimusq, Johannes Churchill Marchio de Blandford
Illustrissimorum Johannis et Saræ et Ducis et Ducissæ de Marlborough Filius.
Summa Parentum Nobilitate inter primos Clarus Virtutibus suæ tam minus celebris, Corporisq, ac animi dotibus
paucos habuit pares, priorem neminem. Natus 9° Jan. Ær. Christi. MDCLXXXVI. Obijt X Kal. Mart: MDCCII.

John, marquess of Blandford

connection. In July 1700, eleven-year-old William, duke of Gloucester, the only surviving child of Anne's seventeen pregnancies, died. On February 20, 1703, another death from smallpox, that of the Marlboroughs' son and heir, the marquess of Blandford, aged seventeen, "the finest young man that could be seen," shattered Sarah. When lady Marlborough reluctantly returned to court, her behavior to the queen, always familiar, became abusive. The buffer of intimacy lost, the duchess' lifelong whiggery clashed with the queen's innate toryism. They finally parted in April 1710.

In August 1710, the queen, in the hands of a new female favorite, her dresser Abigail Hill Masham, a vehicle for the tory chief Robert Harley, dismissed lord treasurer Godolphin. In January 1711, the queen deprived the duchess of all her munificent court appointments. Anne cashiered the captain general in December. Dying, Godolphin took refuge in the Marlboroughs' modest house at St. Albans. Sarah nursed him through his last days. Following Godolphin's death on September 15, 1712, the Marlboroughs went into exile. They did not return to England until the day Queen Anne died, August 1, 1714.

The accession of the Protestant heir, the elector of Hanover, as king dictated the restoration of his champion, the duke of Marlborough, to all his British commands, but the strain of the '15, the death of the duke's favorite daughter, Anne, countess of Sunderland, and her father's subsequent strokes, led to the military ascendancy of Marlborough's officers Stanhope and Cadogan and the political preeminence of the duke's son-in-law, Sunderland. The duke was left in the hands of the duchess who, like a savage dog with a bone, cut Marlborough off from his family, friends, and colleagues until at last the duke died on June 16, 1722.

His bequest and her own investments made the dowager duchess of Marlborough the wealthiest woman in Britain, well able to support the "patriots" who championed the late duke's program of European alliance and Atlantic aggression against France and Spain. To the patriots' most promising leader, William Pitt, the dowager duchess bequeathed £10,000 on her death, at Marlborough House on October 18, 1744. The last survivor of the Cockpit circle, Sarah, duchess of Marlborough, was the most notable link between the age of Anne and the renewed war for Atlantic American empire.

PRÉCIS

IN TEN VICTORIOUS campaigns, from 1702 to 1711, captain general the duke of Marlborough educated and promoted the officers who, as governors general, transformed England's autonomous American colonies into provinces of a British empire. Indeed, the duke's disciples dominated the imperial army throughout the six decades in which Britain achieved dominion in the Atlantic world and imposed an Augustan aegis on the entirety of "Greater Britain." Their accomplishments, extended for nearly forty years after the death of the duke in 1722, make a mockery of the idea of "salutary neglect."

They passed the test of battle in the storm of the Schellenberg and at the battle of Blenheim, August 13, 1704. The Blenheim bounty rolls include at least fourteen future American governors general, but the influence of Blenheim on America was immediate. His army's catastrophic losses prevented Louis XIV from dispatching to French Canada the reinforcements required to conquer Boston, New York, their hinterlands, and the empire of the Iroquois. Blenheim amplified English ambition to deprive France of "Spain and the Indies" by placing an Austrian instead of a Bourbon prince on the Spanish throne. The three wars with Spain conducted by Marlborough's veterans between 1719 and 1748, and their persistent portrayal of France as the ultimate imperial enemy, manifested their intention to deprive both Bourbon monarchies of their American possessions.

Essential to England's own empire was union with Scotland. It would solve England's greatest security problem. An independent Scotland might choose its own monarch, distinct from that of England, to succeed queen Anne. A Scots king would perforce embrace the "auld alliance" with France even as the English army lost 10,000 Scots troops and England's influence over the Scots brigades in the Dutch service as well. On the other hand, union would harness Scots imperial energies. They had been deeply damaged by William III at Darien but were still manifest in Scots interlopers in American trades, especially Virginia tobacco. Scots should be subjected to the acts of trade, and so help support English armed forces. Marlborough's appointment of Scots officers to his own staff attested to his appreciation of their superior education, cultivation, and the imperial ambition of gentlemen who knew that "the only good road in Scotland was the road out."

The Scots project, so portentous for British security, American cultivation, and the empire militant, depended utterly on the outcome of Marlborough's European enterprise. It was so direfully affected by Dutch defensiveness in the campaigns of 1702 and 1703 that the duke determined to lead all of the troops in English pay out of the Netherlands in the spring of 1704, march them hundreds of miles up the Rhine and down the Danube to "save the Empire." The captain general intended to check the Franco-Bavarian invasion of Austria, an invasion supposed to conquer Vienna and take the Empire out of the Grand Alliance against France.

The New Year's honors list in 1704 was headed by the earl of Orkney's promotion to lieutenant general (at the same time, Marlborough promised Orkney the government of Virginia, once the serving tory officer was removed, but that commission could only be made official and effective if and when the union made Scots capable of American commands). Orkney's was but the first of dozens of Marlborough's nominations to the queen of serving officers in 1704. Once abroad, the captain general added 150 brevet promotions to officers serving under his command. Marlborough also dictated 495 new regimental appointments. Multiplied yearly, these officers recruited the military-administrative class so vastly enlarged by a decade of war, a new class which strengthened and stabilized government everywhere in Greater Britain by 1720.

Each officer candidate had a promotion précis, prepared for the captain general by his military secretary, Adam de Cardonnel. The précis' priorities were Marlborough's. The first qualification for any promotion was prior service in America, the most dangerous and demanding duty in England's army. Second, subalterns were preferred from the cadet companies of noble households (or, in time, from the cadets trained by governors general in, say, New York, or the Leeward Islands). Third, Marlborough favored for promotion, to every rank, those officers who had "come off" with him when he deserted king James at the revolution, the crucial moment of the then lord Churchill's coup. Lastly, every officer candidate who could do so produced recommendations from parliamentarians, preferably lords but also commoners, the more the better. The outcome of this, and half a dozen more annual promotions on the like lines, was an officer corps every year more professional and more hardened, more imperial and more gentlemanly, more political and more authoritarian.

The reconstituted staff led the captain general's march to the Danube. This was to be Marlborough's demonstration that America was to be won, the political and religious liberty of Protestant Europe (and so of America) preserved, and the English as well as the Spanish successions secured from Catholic and absolutist France by defeating Louis XIV in Europe. If, however, the captain general failed to defeat the French (and Bavarians) in Germany, he would be impeached and executed. "We will break him as hounds upon a hare," declared the tory leader in the commons. Alternatively, as William Penn wrote from Philadelphia, Marlborough "will be Xenophon and Cyrus too if he beats the great D[uke] of Bavaria, so great a Captain and a Sovereign Prince, now the French [have] joined him."

Joined himself by the greatest of the Imperial generals, Prince Eugene of Savoy, Marlborough destroyed the French army at Blenheim. He led the decisive cavalry charge in person. Eugene bloodied the Bavarians. Louis XIV had committed 70,000 men to the Danube campaign. Fewer than 13,000 returned to France. The elector of Bavaria had 20,000 men in the field before Blenheim. He took fewer than 3,000 with him into exile in Belgium. Marlborough sent Marshal Tallard, formerly the ambassador of Louis XIV to his English client state, with eighteen other French generals as prisoners to London. Each prisoner was an unimpeachable evidence of the victory which had changed the balance of power in the Western world.

Marlborough instantly saw that the victory at Blenheim was the "firm foundation of future Power and Greatness." Much of that power and greatness was to be achieved in America. The captain general's laconic victory dispatch was borne from the Blenheim battlefield to the queen at Windsor by Marlborough's aide, the Virginian Daniel Parke. In the Old Dominion, the serving governor general, Francis Nicholson, had the news that "Coll. Parke, a Gent. & Native of this Country," had carried Marlborough's dispatch proclaimed in every church and courthouse in the colony. Parke was but one, and the least successful, of the duke's fourteen officers whom, blooded at Blenheim, Marlborough promoted to command Virginia, the Leeward Islands, Jamaica, Newfoundland, Massachusetts, and New York. The acknowledgments his legates made to the captain general prefaced what were, for the most part, long, moderate, and constructive regimes. During the decades in American commands, the duke's delegates cemented the culture of an Augustan age, and the institutions of the military-fiscal revolution, on Britain's American provinces.

In the spring of 1705, the captain general's military and political patronage was multiplied by his disposal of more than 200 new regimental commissions. He filled the field-grade posts of an entire regiment with officers who had survived the West Indian expedition of the previous reign. Marlborough named their sons the regiment's subaltern officers. His brevets elevated field-grade veterans of American service and his promotions of general officers rewarded former commanders of West Indian garrisons. He secured the seniority of every officer serving in America and he preserved the rank of garrison regiments, a morale-sustaining regulation for the units which spent a generation in, say, the Leeward Islands or Nova Scotia before being repatriated.

The captain general himself was downcast, however, and his reputation dimmed, by the disasters that opened the next campaign. Late in the spring of 1705, Marlborough invaded Lorraine along the line of the Moselle, but his advance was bogged down by bad weather, a shortage of provisions, and the absence of German support. In the Netherlands, absent the captain general, the French recaptured Huy and besieged Liège. The Dutch begged Marlborough to come to the rescue. He was hard pressed to extricate his army at night, in heavy rain, through a narrow pass, but, on the mere rumor of his approach, the French abandoned their siege and retreated behind the supposedly impregnable lines of Brabant. Marlborough "bubbled" the Dutch generals into following his night march. His troops overran the lines at daybreak. Again, the duke in person led the cavalry charge which consolidated the breakthrough but, once the Dutch columns caught up, their humiliated generals refused to join the pursuit. Then they declined to develop a bridgehead over the Dyle. When, by miracles of maneuver, the captain general caught the French army in the open, a Dutch general ran his baggage train right across the advance of the allied artillery. Apoplectic, Marlborough was reduced to leveling the lines of Brabant in hopes that, in the next campaign, he could somehow escape Dutch obstruction, and that the French would be foolish enough to give him another chance to attack them.

Fortunately, Marlborough's failures in 1705 convinced Louis XIV that Blenheim had been a fluke. Instead of deploying behind the Dyle, while the Dutch demoralized the English and their alliance decayed, the French army crossed the Dyle and advanced to the famous camp at Ramillies. It was, in the Dutch view, impregnable, but Marlborough did not ask the Dutch generals' opinion. Instead, the allies advanced toward Ramillies. There, on July 23, 1706, 55,000 allied troops attacked 63,000 French, Swiss, and Bavarians. For a third time, Marlborough himself led the decisive cavalry charge. Broken, the French army fled west for 100 miles, not stopping until they reached their own frontier. The allies had achieved their original, seemingly chimerical, war aim. They had driven the French out of the Low Countries.

The queen's troops seized, garrisoned, and governed one famous city after another. Recognizing that they could spare few men from the ongoing pursuit of the French to control the Belgian cities, the duke's officers perforce honored Marlborough's promise to respect provincial civil and religious liberties and observed his admonition to limit their requisitions: "a little money, more or less, ought not in my opinion to come in competition" with civic peace and popular support. Would that a later generation of British leaders who, "to gain a peppercorn, have lost an empire," had been so forbearing. Admittedly, there were exceptions to this benign behavior in Belgium. Ordered by Marlborough to prevent an untoward election, Colonel Hunter had his garrison regiment assemble silently under the windows of the town hall. Then he ordered the drums beaten and the cadence called. Terrified, the burghers burst from the building, even as Hunter's troops marched on to the parade ground. The election was cancelled (and Governor General Hunter's New York political practices anticipated).

Belgium lost to the allies, their own frontier attacked, the French offered to make peace. The duke demanded, inter alia, that the French withdraw from Maine and from the empire of Iroquois; cede Acadia and Nova Scotia; and return to England the Hudson's Bay posts in the north and Nevis and St. Kitts in the Caribbean. All these American cessions were more than Louis XIV would concede, short of Marlborough's march on Paris. Confined by his allies' timidity, Marlborough had to begin the invasion of France with the siege of Menin. The citadel's garrison capitulated on August 22, 1706.

The victory at Ramillies, the conquest of Belgium, and the assault on France itself, made the union of the British kingdoms inevitable. The union, by making the Scots natural-born subjects of the imperial crown, would legalize their entry into what would become the "British" empire. But Scots "patriots" were determined to defeat the union. To them it entailed parliamentary taxation, the loss of civil liberty, and the imposition of an anglican episcopacy. The patriots would defend their independence by mob demonstrations and popular petitions to their legislature but, civil protest failing, by force. So Marlborough stripped the English guards and garrisons and sent every possible man to the Border fortresses. He ordered the Irish garrison's dragoons concentrated in Belfast, ready to repress Scots rebellion, but before they were called up or Marlborough's English regiments shipped from Flanders, at the height of the crisis in Edinburgh in December 1706, the recruiting parties of Marlborough's Scots regiments arrived from Flanders. They tipped the balance of power in Edinburgh to the unionists, for the French, after Ramillies, had no troops with which to sustain Scots independence. The auld alliance was toothless. The attractions of a British empire were obvious. The union treaty passed the Scots parliament on January 16, 1707. Marlborough welcomed "great Britain" by raising new Scots regiments with which to reward the unionists, and he nominated his Scots veterans for further promotion in the British army and to the governments of British America.

CHAPTER ONE

Grand Designs

ARLBOROUGH'S ANNUAL PARLIAMENTARY campaign had closed and his annual military campaign was about to begin when, on February 20, 1703, his hopes and his wife's happiness were destroyed. The marquess of Blandford, the Marlboroughs' sole surviving son and heir, was amiable and able. He possessed his father's masculine beauty and his military ambition. "The finest young man that could be seen," Blandford had begged to join his father's staff, but lady Marlborough had held her son out of danger, as she thought, in university. At Cambridge, Blandford suddenly sickened and died of smallpox, aged seventeen. His parents were at his bedside. Devastated, the duke and duchess retired to St. Albans. There, for months to come, lady Marlborough remained in seclusion, the balance of her mind in question. Fatally for her family's fortunes, the duchess was never willing to return to regular attendance on Queen Anne. After just five days at St. Albans, however, Marlborough was called to his command overseas. He sailed in mourning, deprived of that familial future, the continuance of his name and blood, the end-all of ambition in that dynastic age. "I have lost what is so dear to me," Marlborough said to an old friend, "it is fit for me to retire and not to toil and labour for I know not who." All the world knew and said that the duke of Marlborough had suffered "la plus grande affliction du monde."[1]

Marlborough reached the Dutch coast on March 6/17, 1703. From his headquarters, the elegant Mauritshuis at The Hague, he tried to lose his grief in work. He worked to get a Dutch fleet out of port to reinforce the English in the Mediterranean. He worked to persuade the Dutch to let him bypass the siege of Bonn and either resume his proposed campaign on the Moselle or advance into Brabant. His loss was inescapable. Mourning their son and hoping for another heir, he wrote to Sarah that "you are dearer to mee ten thousand times then ever you were, I am soe entirely yours, that if I might have all the world given mee, I could not be happy but in your love." He hoped that political hatred might distract Sarah from her grief and send her back to court. The malignity of all of the high tories was profound, Marlborough reminded her, but Rochester's hatred was limitless, "for he is not capable of having anything but revenge in his heart." Certainly Rochester's "Church Party" ought not keep the government of Virginia in the person of Colonel Francis Nicholson, but the tory candidate to replace Nicholson, General Arthur Forbes, the jacobite earl of Grenard, would do dreadful damage to the Marlboroughs' determination to make moderation prevail in America. The duke told his duchess that when Grenard "desired I would speak to the Queen that he might have the government of Virginia . . . I excused myself upon my being to goe away the next day. He then desired I would lett Lord Treasurer know his desires, which I did." Now Grenard had contacted lady Marlborough. Warned by the duke, she would not assist a tory extremist to extend his party's influence in America. Nicholson could hold onto the Virginia command until Marlborough identified a suitable replacement, perhaps from the imperial general staff he built during the campaign of 1703 in Flanders.[2]

As soon as he closed his letter to his lady on Anglo-American politics, Marlborough turned to the coming campaign. He reviewed his options with the allied generals, he arranged payments to the English auxiliary troops and, for ten days, the captain general toured the garrisons on the allied army's three fronts: the Rhine, the Meuse, and the frontier of Brabant. By the time Marlborough returned to The Hague, he had acquiesced in the Dutch determination that he begin the campaign by besieging Bonn. As usual, however, the Dutch siege train was slow to assemble. April 9 found a fretful duke watching from his window the great Good Friday procession in Cologne: "thoughts how pleased poor Lord Churchill would have been with such a sight has added much to my uneasyness. Since it has pleased God to take him, I doe wish from my soull I could think less of him."[3]

After the procession passed, Marlborough sat down with his secretariat to dictate the appointment of some of the staff officers who would make his army the most efficient in Europe and who, carrying the duke's command ethos to America, would open there the Augustan age he personified. Marlborough's men were fed, paid, and equipped on a scale unparalleled and with a regularity unequalled elsewhere in Europe. They moved with a speed, directness, and decision that was the military marvel of the age. The bureaucratic efficiency and personal dexterity that Marlborough's staff officers acquired in ten victorious campaigns educated the greatest generation of governors general ever to serve in America. For it was the ambition of every staff officer to merit from Marlborough the military promotions which led to independent imperial commands: garrison governments.[4]

A staff career that eventuated in the transformation of Virginia from a tobacco colony to a frontier of empire began on that Good Friday in Cologne. Marlborough promoted a brevet captain, Lieutenant Alexander Spotswood, to succeed his elder half brother, Roger Elliot, as a captain in the 10th Regiment. The duke made Elliot colonel of a new regiment. Obviously, the general had been impressed with both of these army brats. Elliot and Spotswood were children of the Tangier Regiment. They had spent their youths in the Tangier garrison, educated in the regiment's schools, quarters, and camps. They had risen through the officer ranks of the Tangier Regiment's daughter corps, the 10th Regiment, during king William's wars in Flanders, without either a noble family or a parliamentary interest to recommend them. Roger Elliot was the lieutenant colonel of the 10th at the Peace of Ryswick. As the regiment's executive officer during its peacetime posting in Ireland, Elliot had seen to recruiting, clothing, and equipment, the elements of the regimental economy. On the outbreak of war, the 10th sailed for Flanders but its colonel, Sir Bevil Granville, was going out to command Barbados—or, rather, as the establishment had it, Granville was "in England." For purposes of military accounting, all America was part of England.[5]

Marlborough now named Granville's second in command, Lieutenant Colonel Elliot, to raise a second regiment in the Granville family's interest. From Elliot's own family, Marlborough promoted Alexander Spotswood. The duke had already brevetted Spotswood captain over the heads of all of the lieutenants of the 10th. They included John Ligonier (whom Marlborough subsequently promoted captain and brevetted major of the 10th, the foundation of Ligonier fame and so of his role as chief of staff during Britain's imperial triumph in America) and George Wade (who would command American troops in the repression of the last tribal uprising in the British Isles). When Marlborough also declared that Captain Lieutenant Spotswood would succeed his brother in command of the senior company of the 10th, the regiment's new colonel, William North, lord North and Grey, protested that "yr Grace was pleas'd to promise me yt you would not alter anything in my Regiment without my knowledge." He suggested that, instead, "Capt Spotsworth" should succeed to James Granville's company, he being promoted major of Elliot's new regiment. North and Grey pointed out that Elliot's company should, by seniority, go to George Wade, the brevet major of the 10th. Besides, Granville's company in the 10th was weakly manned. North pointed out that Colonel Elliot could order his major, James Granville, to recruit his former company in the 10th from the Granville country in Cornwall and Dorset when they raised the new regiment there. Nevertheless, Spotswood kept Elliot's company. Elliot took his new regiment out to Spain. With it he would garrison his government, again acquired by Marlborough's favor, the English conquest Gibraltar.[6]

That Elliot had by no means exhausted the family favor with the captain general was further confirmed when Captain Spotswood received an additional, decisive, promotion. He was named Marlborough's lieutenant quartermaster general, that is, deputy chief of staff. Captain Spotswood was to second Marlborough's quartermaster general, that big, rough Irish cavalryman, Major William Cadogan. As Spotswood explained, his staff appointment "is an Employ, that in all other Services of the World, is possest by Men of an high[er] degree than that of a Captain." In Marlborough's new staff, however, junior officers could rise. They would be more bureaucratic and functional, less dignified and honorific, than were their equivalents, the camp marshals of European armies.[7]

Camp marshals designed army encampments (on the model of the Roman *castra*). They determined the rank and duties of units both in camp and on service. Marlborough's quartermasters general combined these, the European camp marshal's duties, with those of the Cromwellian and restoration scout-masters general, the chiefs of reconnaissance and intelligence. Marlborough's quartermasters took over the functions of the old army's provost marshal general (the police chief) and supervised its wagon master general (the coordinator of transport services). Marlborough's quartermasters general worked with the paymaster general and with a multitudinous corps of commissaries for hospitals, bread rations, and for the custody and exchange of prisoners. Finally, Marlborough's quartermasters general exercised some control over the field artillery and the engineering staff, subsections of "the train of artillery." As the earl of Orkney had suggested, the artillery train now had regimental status and was commanded by a colonel aptly named Blood. Cadogan's and Spotswood's liaison with the artillery train was Captain Richard King until he was promoted quartermaster general in America.[8]

Marlborough's quartermasters general literally led his army. They staked out the line of march for each column, assisted by the regimental quartermasters (Lieutenant Charles Gookin, afterward deputy governor of Pennsylvania, was quartermaster of Major General Erle's regiment) and by the quartermasters of each line of horse or foot. The quartermasters general not only directed their color men to flag a route for each column on the march, they then had that column's position flagged in line, either in the campsite or on the battlefield. Into these premarked positions the regimental and line quartermasters led their particular regiment or, subsequently, a brigade of three or more regiments. While the army encamped, the quartermasters general posted the camp guards. Then, working with the majors of brigade (Robert Hunter, afterward governor general of New York, New Jersey, and Jamaica, became major of brigade for the dragoons), the quartermasters established a rotation for the camp guard and the guards of the market and the artillery park. The quartermasters general also detailed a subaltern and thirty dragoons to protect each general's quarters. At the head of other mounted detachments, the quartermasters general checked straggling and plundering.[9]

Toward the close of the 1703 campaign, the chaplain of Orkney's regiment (the Royal Scots) wrote that, as the allied army was marching for Limbourg, "some of Our Danes, 2 officers being with them, barbarously plundering a very pretty church and the Priest's House, spoyling everything they could not carry off even to the knocking the heads of Barrels and such like; Capt. Spotswood,

Quarter Master General under Cadoughan, saw them all the while but did not dare speak, for he had like to have been killed once before this year for endeavoring to hinder their plundering, but his party [escort] presently coming up he took them all prisoners and particularly seized the 2 Officers coming out of the church with plunder on their backs. He delivered them to the [Danish general] Duke Wirtemburgh, who immediately handcufft them with Irons at the head of the Regiment and declared the Way of their country was to shoot them without any further tryal or enquiry."[10]

The quartermasters general were active, and exposed, in every army movement. Besides enforcing, as best they could, Marlborough's stringent orders against plundering, they arranged and protected the grazing of horses, and they directed the army's vast operations to harvest forage and crops, cut fascines, collect wood, and draw water. The quartermasters led the army's scouting and reported field intelligence. All these motions provoked constant cavalry skirmishes with the enemy. Both Cadogan and Spotswood were captured. Hunter and Parke won single combats in these encounters. To execute their innumerable duties, quartermasters general kept in hand the army's most ready troops, not only their own mounted escorts (typically a troop of dragoons or cavalry apiece) but also the camp pickets, the grand guard of the camp, the provost marshal's police, and the "market guard" or sutlers' police. During the 1703 campaign, as the quartermasters' responsibilities multiplied, Marlborough began to assign the entire picket of the old camp as the quartermasters general's escort whenever the army marched. Their multitudinous mounted escorts and colorful flag bearers made the quartermasters general the obvious indication to every enemy observer of Marlborough's immediate line of march. By their selection of campsite or battlefield, the quartermasters signaled the captain general's apparent intent. So Marlborough frequently used his staff to mislead the enemy and to bait traps. The quartermasters general's most famous exploit was the race for the Scheldt crossings, the organization of the encounter battle beyond that river, and the first fighting at Oudenarde in 1708, but every motion of Marlborough's army put them to the fore.[11]

It was, as Spotswood wrote at the end of his first campaign as lieutenant quartermaster general, a post whose pay was far less than its responsibility, "but there are accidents in it that may content a man in another manner; & if the War lasts, & I live some lucky Hits may happen towards the making of one's Fortune." Spotswood's promotions, the command of Virginia among them, were "hits" more deserved than lucky. Certainly, the officer who had laid out the camps of an army of 50,000 men or more would find the planning of a colonial capital, Williamsburg, Virginia, a mere bagatelle. As deputy chief of staff, Spotswood helped organize Marlborough's army and lead it into the most famous European battles of a century. Consequently, Spotswood found reshaping the Virginia provincial army, resisting a Tuscarora uprising, or even helping to recruit or supply Anglo-American armies little more than enlivening incidents in the quiet world beyond the Atlantic. Colonel Spotswood would be succeeded in Virginia, and in command of the American Regiment, more than 4,000 strong, by William Gooch. Marlborough named Gooch an ensign in Flanders in this spring of 1703.[12]

Another familyless, unconnected, entirely professional Scots staff officer, Major Robert Hunter, was promoted to Marlborough's staff in 1703. Already distinguished as a regimental major—"and the Life of a Regiment turns upon that Post"—Hunter was brevetted lieutenant colonel by Marlborough in recognition of his services as major of brigade to the British dragoons. The logistical and organizational duties of the brigade major had been expanded to include the communication and implementation of Marlborough's action orders. As a link between the general staff and the fighting brigades, the majors of brigade, Lieutenant Colonel Hunter prominent among them, increased their authority and responsibility in every one of Marlborough's campaigns.[13]

Every forenoon, the general officers met at the duke's headquarters or command post to receive his orders. They always stood, for, to the astonishment of contemporaries, the captain general took only two, folding, chairs on campaign. No one sat around at Marlborough's headquarters. After the captain general issued his orders to the senior officers, the brigadier generals met in the orderly room with their majors of brigade to detail each unit's particular duty. Detailing called for an intimate and current knowledge of the capacity and readiness of each element of the army of 50,000 men in English pay in 1703. Detailing also required a good deal of diplomacy. In this multinational army of proudly distinctive units, difficult, distasteful, or dangerous duties were supposedly taken in turn. Officers were selected for details by lot "and the men by equal Dividend of each Nation or Battalion." This accounting led to constant disputes. It was the duty of the brigade major to settle them "according to the Rules of War, and the Custom of the Army, and for the Good of the Service." As a training in multinational arbitration, adjudication, and the installation of corporate purpose, Hunter's experience as brigade major would stand in him in good stead as he directed the war against the French and defined the public good in contention with the quarrelsome, multiethnic elites of New York, New Jersey, and Jamaica.[14]

When Hunter converted royal commands into provincial practice, he drew upon stressful experience in the chain of command. It was the brigade major who met the general's aides-de-camp when they brought Marlborough's action orders from headquarters to the brigade, on the march or in battle. The major broke down the brigade's task into regimental or company assignments. Sergeant orderlies both made copies of the general's orders and took the brigade major's dictation. The resulting orderly books detail the history of every regiment fortunate enough to retain them. The orderly sergeants also helped the regimental adjutants keep up the records of each unit's postings, rotations, duty tours, and strength. Educated in the army, the greatest school of the age, at least sixty of Marlborough's sergeants became instructors in American provincial armies. They were commissioned as company grade officers, unusual promotions in Europe. These officers founded military dynasties on American frontiers.[15]

Each Friday morning, the orderly sergeants brought the rosters to the brigade major. He reviewed them and took them to Marlborough's headquarters, together with a summary of the reports about stragglers from the sweepers behind the line of march, patrols' accounts of their reconnaissances and losses, and captains' lists of their company's casualties. It was from the brigade majors' reports that the captain general calculated his army's strength (or dealt knowledgeably with captious colonels). The brigade majors were essential links in the command chains of the army, itself the greatest bureaucracy, the central support, and the forcible instrument of the new state. So, on parade, at reviews, and in battle, the majors of brigade took the post of honor at the right of the brigade line. When it was Colonel Hunter's turn to serve as major of brigade of the day at Marlborough's headquarters, he (and his orderlies, a sergeant from each squadron in the British dragoon brigade) attended the captain general. At the battle of Ramillies, Colonel Hunter, as major of brigade, would advance his military career toward its apex: imperial administration in America.[16]

The captain general and his new staff got the army into the field in the spring of 1703 a month earlier than had been the allied wont, but the Dutch delays in bringing their siege guns held up the attack on Bonn until April 14/25. Meanwhile, the duke agonized about the liability to surprise of "the great army" that covered the siege. Under Hendrick van Nassau, Heer van Overkirk, the covering army was encamped along the Meuse, sixty miles from Bonn. Marlborough's fears were well founded. Just as in the previous year, a sudden advance by the French, unanticipated and undetected by the Dutch generals, nearly trapped the allies' field army. Only the heroic resistance, for twenty-nine hours, against the entire French army, by two regiments, Dutch and Scots-Dutch, quartered at Tongres (the Dutch general commanding them fled at the sight of the enemy) gave the allied main body just enough time to flee to the ramparts of Maestricht. So they had fled the year previous to the works of Nimwegen. "We picht our tents in a confused manner, near the very walls of Maestricht as if we were afraid of them," Orkney's chaplain grumbled. Orkney himself sent a courier to Marlborough calling for him to ride to the rescue of the outclassed Dutch generals.[17]

Marlborough joined the covering army at Maestricht on May 7/18, just three days after he had personally accepted the surrender of Bonn. The Dutch generals were almost as angry at Marlborough's presumption in taking Bonn while they fled from the French as the tory right wing was at his success in again defeating troops of the sun king. These jealousies, military and political, and the prospect of another campaign spent alternatively rescuing Dutch generals from their blunders and being accused in England of prolonging the war for his own profit, deeply depressed Marlborough. As soon as his migraine relented enough so that he could write to Sarah, Marlborough denounced partisanship and predicted his own downfall: "As for myself I doe assure you, I shall meadle with nether partys, having noe privat ends of my own, but whilest I am in the world endeavour to serve her Majesty the best I can. I know by this methode whichever party is uppermost will be angry with mee, soe that at last the Queen will be obliged by them to let me retir." Marlborough begged Sarah to adopt his moderation, "for my dearest soull, when wee come to live together, my happyness will depend upon our having but one thought, in order to which we must renounce all partys, and content ourselves in praying for the Queen's long life, and that France may never have it in their power to impose laws upon England."[18]

The duchess, still deep in her own depression, passed this despairing letter on to Queen Anne. Lady Marlborough intimated that she would join her husband in retiring from the royal service. The queen's reply bespoke the force of the cockpit connection. It had survived coup and disgrace, spent years in opposition, and managed two succession crises, to arrive at the rim of world power. If "my dear Mrs. Freeman and Mr. Freeman" retired, Queen Anne wrote, she would abdicate, "for what is a Crown, when ye support of it is gon, I will never forsake your dear self, Mr. Freeman nor Mr. Montgomery [Godolphin], but always be your constant faithful servant, & we four must never part, till death mows us down with his impartiall hand." But Marlborough was right. His wife was a whig. The queen was a tory. The two parties were implacable. Eventually the queen would be driven to cashier her captain general. The prospect was ever present in Marlborough's mind. It was the background of his every military decision and it was the calculus that drove his staff to seek refuge and reward in America while their general still had the power to place them in colonial commands.[19]

Marlborough's prospects, and those of his staff officers, were further diminished by the expansion of the second front in the War of the Spanish Succession. It was on the day that Bonn surrendered to Marlborough that the allies signed the treaties with Portugal which committed them to place Charles of Austria on the imperial throne of Spain. This campaign to reverse the Bourbon seizure of the Spanish empire was a vast extension of the allied war aim to exclude the French from Spanish American ports and trade, but Marlborough anticipated that assaults on the Spanish empire's frontiers in Portugal, Catalonia, and Savoy would divert French resources from Flanders and Germany. Given their naval superiority, it would be easier for the allies to sustain Iberian and Savoyard diversions than it would be for the French to resist them. Marlborough thought that the opening of the port of Lisbon to the allied fleets would be the greatest English imperial benefit of Portuguese alliance, for he saw Lisbon as the base from which England could conquer ports and create colonies in the western Mediterranean.[20]

Yet the price of Mediterranean conquest was the detachment of troops from Flanders. As captain general of England, Marlborough acquiesced in the reduction of his personal command. He gave professional spine to the allied command in Iberia. He transferred lord Portmore from the failed Peterborough expedition to America. Marlborough promoted Portmore colonel of the 2d Queen's royal regiment and added it to the Spanish expeditionary force. (Portmore immediately asked Marlborough to promote his captain lieutenant, Richard Phillips, to command a company of the 2d. Phillips was afterward governor general of Nova Scotia and the officers of his regiment, the 40th, shaped that infant society.) Marlborough sent a favorite officer, Colonel James Stanhope, as his liaison with the soi-disant Charles III of Spain. He added Stanhope's own regiment to the force designed to invade Spain from Portugal. In Iberia, Stanhope built up the military connection from whom he secured American and Minorcan commands for his staff officers in Marlborough's last years.[21]

What made the Iberian effort finally fatal to the war in Flanders, crippled Marlborough's command, and drove his officers to transfer to America was that the high tories saw Spain not as a second and subsidiary front but as the primary means of achieving their linked imperial ends: winning oceanic trade and American territory from Spain and France and draining military resources and political power from the Marlborough moderates and the whig continentalists. As secretary of state and the senior surviving minister of the tory right, Nottingham spent 1703 trying to transfer more of Marlborough's best and most devoted units to Portugal. Nottingham wrote "royal" orders to take Marlborough's own former regiment (the 24th) from his army. Nottingham even tried to detach Charles Churchill's 3d Regiment from his brother's command. Then Nottingham called for the withdrawal of 2,000 additional English troops from the allied army in Flanders. As he had in the American expedition, the secretary of state added one objective to another, each requiring an additional force. Nottingham's tory bias had concluded that only an amphibious, primarily naval, war—"a fleet and army accompanying it"—could make any impression on French power. Marlborough's army must be drawn down, first for Cadiz, Martinique, Guadeloupe, Cartagena, and Newfoundland, then for Canada, Portugal, the Cevannes, a "Descent." When, in August 1703, Nottingham announced the raising of several new regiments in England without consulting Marlborough, the captain general's enormous professional and political embarrassment drove him to begin the political campaign that, building on the failure of the Graydon expedition to America, ousted Nottingham from the ministry and with him most of the tory right wing. So the government of queen Anne would be opened to the whigs.[22]

Still and all, Marlborough was committed to the Spanish second front. Although he hung on to the "near four thousand men" of the picked English regiments designated for Iberia until the last stages of the 1703 campaign in Flanders, he had then to detach his own former command, the Royal Dragoons, and "four old regiments, and I think very good ones"—Stanhope's, Stewart's, Bridges's and Barrymore's. This last was not, as Marlborough wrote, "Baltimore's," for the Maryland proprietor had held no English command since his arrest by Churchill's troopers in 1688. The slip was a natural one, however, for Marlborough was thinking about the Chesapeake. He intended the government of Maryland for a colonel of the Guards. He had his eye on a change in the Virginia command. The duke also planned to utilize the Chesapeake tobacco convoy. He ordered horse and foot shipped from Flanders to English ports to rendezvous with the great tobacco ships. Outbound and lightly laden, they were to serve as troop transports to Portugal en route to Virginia.[23]

The Hapsburg candidate for the Spanish imperial throne must be proclaimed in Madrid. So 12,000 allied troops invaded Spain, but the Castilian people were already embittered by the English outrages at Cadiz. The Spanish grandees resented the Grand Alliance's proposed partition of their empire. Noblemen were reluctant to desert the Bourbon prince in possession, Philip of France. Portmore immediately wrote to Marlborough that the hoped-for "general tendency to a revolution" in Spain was a myth, that the Portuguese were all talk, and that Marlborough must be prepared for continued bad news from Iberia. Such intimations of Spanish reality had no effect in England. Nottingham's popular slogan "No Peace Without Spain" had replaced the goal of partition of the Spanish empire with a fatal determination to seize everything Spanish from Italy to the Philippines. This unwinnable war eviscerated the allied efforts in America, to the disappointment of the tories, but it achieved their objective of weakening Marlborough's army in the one theater where the genius of the captain general and the ferocity of his island troops made possible a victory previously unimaginable (and profoundly unwelcome to insular conservatives): the capture of Paris, the fall of France, the eclipse of the sun king.[24]

From the moment he arrived in the Maestricht camp, Marlborough, daily more audacious in the face of all his enemies, foreign and domestic, had rallied the allied armies to take the offensive. On May 7/18, 1703, the grand parade when Marlborough took command was followed by a *feu de joi* for the capture of Bonn and by the duke's personal and particular review of the troops in English pay. Then, in a duplication of the previous year's advance, Marlborough pushed the French back from their positions menacing Maestricht. As the allies advanced, the French retreated behind their lines in Brabant. Marlborough ordered the allied cavalry to press forward and "to Scour al the little villages upon the Jarr or Jecker, from each of which the Enemy retreated as soon as our men appeared." Behind dozens of these outpost skirmishes and cavalry encounters, always seeking battle, Marlborough led his army forward through the mud of Flanders. Orkney's veteran chaplain wrote of "the worst dayes march that I ever saw: T'was very cold, winds very high and in our faces, wayes very deep, and it rain'd very hard al day." By the end of May, the rain-soaked rival armies were in presence. For three weeks, they faced each other while Marlborough attempted to persuade the states general of the Netherlands to override their generals and authorize him to attack.[25]

In the interim, the captain general had time to attend to the imperial politics of the English army. Guards captain (and so lieutenant colonel) John Seymour of the First Guards wrote to Marlborough, "my only patron," to ask his favor, first with the lord treasurer and then with the secretary at war and of plantations. Seymour was preparing to "perform my duty in ye Station your Grace has bin pleased to place me," the government of Maryland. It was the captain general's assurance that the lord treasurer would allocate funds for Lieutenant Colonel Seymour's passage to Maryland and his equipage as governor that had persuaded Seymour to sell (to Marlborough's nominee) for £500 the Guards' commission that had cost him £1,100. Writing to the duke to promise his care and fidelity to the queen and his faith and duty to the captain general, Lieutenant Colonel Seymour asked for "two lines to the lord treasurer." Marlborough did write something a bit stronger than was his wont to Godolphin in such cases: "I have had a very pressing letter from Seamor that is to goe to Meryland, to recomend him to your favour." The captain general also had his secretary write to the secretary at war and of plantations that "Lt Col John Seymour . . . may depend upon his Grace's favour and Protection on all occasions." Seymour already looked forward to a specific occasion for Marlborough's further favor: "if any accident should happen to remove Coll. Nickholson, I may hope to Succeede, wthout any prejudice to him." Seymour said to Marlborough that it would reflect poorly on them both if he, "constituted by your Graces [liking] & favor" as governor of Maryland, was passed over for command of the Old Dominion.[26]

Instead of advancing Colonel Seymour, the government of Virginia contributed to Marlborough's campaign to build a British imperial army, Scots as much as English. Marlborough had preserved the officer corps of the six Scots regiments in the service of the states "entire in the Scots nation." He increasingly preferred Scots officers to his own staff, as in the cases of Hunter and Spotswood, and Marlborough gave the command of the British infantry to George Hamilton, earl of Orkney. Each of them would be commissioned to command Virginia. Marlborough also preserved the naval rank of Orkney's younger brother, lord Archibald Hamilton, "for the officers speakes very well of him." Subsequently, lord Archibald became governor general of Jamaica. These appointments would be legalized by the union of Scotland with England. So was satisfied the Scots imperial impulse so marked at Darien. Anne, duchess of Hamilton, had subscribed heavily in Darien in the names of her sons, George and Archibald, because, she said, as military men, they should be invested in empire. Marlborough moved to propitiate Scots imperialism in naming officers for the imperial expedition of 1703. He was increasingly determined to win by military promotion and officer influence the union he would otherwise have to impose by force, for Scotland was essential to England's security.[27]

British union had been the aim of every English sovereign since Elizabeth. It was King William's deathbed counsel to Princess Anne. As William lay dying, the earl of Orkney discussed the central question of the misnamed war, the British (not the Spanish) succession. Anne's succession was contested by the French. It was not immediately agreed to by the Scots. And Anne had no heirs. Would the Scots accept Anne's Hanoverian successor, as laid down by the English parliament's act of settlement? Orkney agreed with his brother, the duke of Hamilton, that no such succession would occur unless the union of England and Scotland was first completed. The Hamilton brothers domiciled in England—George, earl of Orkney, in the army; lord Archibald Hamilton in the navy; and Charles, earl of Selkirk, at court—urged their brother the duke to come up to London (from his wife's estates in Lancaster) to meet with Marlborough and affirm the family's loyalty both to Anne and to her successor. Instead, Hamilton went to Scotland to prevent Anne's succession or British union by any act of the Scots parliament that did not serve his own interests. Hamilton had his own claim to the throne of Scotland to consider. The duke sent his excuses to Anne's champion. He was, Hamilton wrote to Marlborough, entirely loyal to Anne, but the illness of one of his children, combined with a need to sound popular sentiment on a proposed union of the British kingdoms, compelled him up to Edinburgh rather than down to London. The existing Scots parliament must meet by law within twenty days of King William's death, Hamilton wrote. Otherwise, any legislative recognition of Anne's succession and all support for the war with France would be invalid. Those measures would be best taken, the duke declared, if King William's leftover Scots ministers were dismissed and a new management (headed, it is fair to presume, by Scotland's premier nobleman) was named by Queen Anne. She should demonstrate that she "will be Queen of her People and not of a party."[28]

Even in the field, the duke of Marlborough kept in the closest touch with the politics of the northern kingdom. Orkney complained that the duke was better informed than he was about Scots affairs. That was especially dangerous to the Hamiltons, Orkney told his brothers in England and Scotland, because Marlborough was building an alternative Scots interest. During the rain delay in the spring of 1703, Marlborough intervened both with the Scots ministers and with Queen Anne on behalf of John Campbell, the young duke of Argyll. He was Ian Roy Cean, "Red John the Warrior"; MacCullummore, the chief of clan Campbell; colonel and brigadier of the Scots-Dutch. Marlborough found this arrogant and ambitious, spoiled and ill-mannered young man almost insufferable. "Very hote headed," was the restrained duke's cry of protest, but he considered Argyll to be politically reliable: he "seems to be very honest as to the Revolution." Few Scots nobles were free of the taint of jacobitism. None, given

Arygll's ambition for an English peerage, were more in favor of union. So Marlborough had secured Argyll's commission as colonel of the Scots Life Guards. Despite his promises of duty and faithfulness to Marlborough, however, Argyll quickly began to set himself up as Marlborough's rival for command of the army, and so of the imperial executive.[29]

Scots resentment of English imperial dominion deepened during 1703. It was expressed by resistance to the Hanoverian succession. Andrew Fletcher of Saltoun was the intellectual spokesman of the Scots opposition (his notorious republicanism was the brush Nicholson used to tar the Scots-led opposition to his government in Virginia). Fletcher now helped to inspire the 1703 act of the Scottish parliament anent peace and war, conferring on the Scots parliament the power to declare war or make peace independent of the English monarch. An "act of security" declared that, at the next succession, the crowns of Scotland and England should be separated, unless in the meantime Scotland was granted full access to the English empire. Never again, wrote Fletcher, should the Scots be so poorly repaid for their investment of lives in the royal military as they had been by the English discountenance of Darien.[30]

The immediate English response was the house of lords' declaration that Scots rebellion was imminent. Godolphin warned his Scots correspondents that the modern, armed English state would respond to Scots contumacy with a power unimagined in 1639–41, when a Scots invasion had determined English politics. The government's Scots ministers reported that the duke of Hamilton, leader of the opposition, was taking French money (which he probably was) and planning to enthrone the pretender in Scotland (which he certainly was not). Orkney wrote to his brother the duke that he had "allways told Ld Marlb. that I believed you wish the present government as well as he did tho you might not approve the Management." Nonetheless, Marlborough ordered Anglo-Irish troops redeployed to Belfast, ready for embarkation to Scotland. Although he took care to see to it that Berwick and Carlisle were in safe hands, Marlborough did not yet send additional English forces up to the Scots Borders. Hamilton warned that any such troop movement would indicate that England was prepared to impose union by force. An English invasion would be repelled. The crisis passed for the moment. Union negotiations were indecisive. The occasional conformity crisis in England boded ill for a union with Presbyterian Scotland. The captain general had no troops to spare from Flanders for the Borders of Scotland because he could neither reduce the garrisons of the south and east of England nor take the political risk of increasing the army in England beyond the limit of 7,000 men that the parliament had imposed in 1698.[31]

In the Netherlands as well as in England, political restrictions limited Marlborough's military deployments. The captain general was unable to persuade the states to overrule the Dutch generals and authorize him to attack the French lines in Brabant. "You cant belive how disirous the Duke of Marlb. is that something of consequence should be done," Orkney wrote. So Marlborough proposed "The Great Design." This, the centerpiece of the 1703 campaign, was premised on the captain general's hope that the riches of the great ports of Ostend and Antwerp would tempt the covetous Dutch into an offensive. Material results would be welcome in mercantile England as well. Marlborough always understood that the maritime powers were motivated *spe praemii vel lucri*. In mid-May 1703, he proposed feints that would force the French to uncover either Ostend or Antwerp. The capture of either port would unhinge the French lines at the coast. Then, Marlborough explained, he would either lead the allies south into Flanders from Antwerp along the line of the River Scheldt, or advance west from Ostend along the coast into France itself, supplied and supported by allied seapower.[32]

"The Great Design" and its author were frustrated, first by "Cohorn" (Menno, baron van Coehoorn), who took a Dutch division on a plundering raid into the Paes de Waes (the sixty miles of countryside between Antwerp and Ostend). The raid, "undertaken not only against the Duke's opinion but almost without his consent," enriched Cohorn, alerted the French to Marlborough's plan, and alienated the peasants of the paes. Meanwhile, the Dutch deputies began to worry out loud that, if Marlborough did capture one of the great channel ports, he might keep it for England. Dutch political support for the Great Design began to evaporate. Then, despite Marlborough's explicit and repeated warnings, a Dutch detachment under Opdam was entrapped at Eckern, near Antwerp. On the night of July 1/12, Opdam fled to Breda. He reported to Marlborough and to the states that his command had been annihilated. "I pray God it be not soe," wrote Marlborough, "for he is very capable of having itt happen to him," but the treasurer of Holland took Opdam's place in command and the Dutch infantry fought their way out of the trap. One of Marlborough's aides, the Virginian Daniel Parke, remarked that although "there is no persuading the Dutch to Attack they are like Ratts if you Surround them & leave them no way to Escape (as the French did at Eckern) then they will fight like Divels." Still, the Dutch retreat compelled Marlborough to find another avenue to attack Antwerp.[33]

In frightful weather, Marlborough marched his men fifty miles from Maestricht to the very suburbs of Antwerp. "It is not to be imagin'd what our poor foot has suffered in this last march by the excessive rain we have had," the captain general wrote, but he had brought the main army close to the objective. Now Marlborough explained to the states that an assault on the French lines near their conclusion at Antwerp was a risk worth taking, "for if you have a mind to Antwerp, and a speedy end of the war, you must venture something for it." The states agreed. Despite every delay and obstruction that the Dutch generals could conceive, at 3:00 a.m. on July 24/August 4, the allied army advanced in two divisions. One was commanded by Marlborough, the other by Frederick van Baer van Slangenburg, "the Dutch beast," the English soldiers called him. Marlborough fully expected to drive the French army into the Scheldt.

The French burned their camp and retreated behind their entrenchments as Marlborough advanced, but Slangenburg and his Dutch colleagues refused to obey Marlborough's orders to attack. Then the disobedient Dutch generals demanded a council of war. After two days of bickering, they would agree to only one course of action: a return to the Meuse and the siege of Huy, a little town on the river between the allies' frontier at Maestricht and the French-held fortress city of Namur.[34]

When he reported the depressing demise of the Grand Design, Daniel Parke added that he himself had a delightful morning during the allied advance on Antwerp. Colonel Parke and count Maurice of Nassau had led the first of the allies, a troop of the Royal Dragoons. When they saw their opposite numbers "making their escape to their Camp," Nassau and Parke pursued. "I was upon the fleetest horse," Parke recalled, "therefore came up with them first I Got before them presented my pistoll at which they put up their Armes." Parke left the prisoners with Nassau and rode on to capture a splendid loose steed, only to find himself almost in the grasp of two French dragoons, but one of the Royals "came to my Assistance for wch I gave him two Guineas."[35]

The dashing Daniel Parke had enjoyed his day, but the Dutch generals had sabotaged Marlborough's march on Antwerp. They were, as Cadogan put it, "equally incapable of shame as reason." Marlborough was left to undertake the siege of Huy, which was, "as the French expression is a pis aller." Its capture would do nothing but add to the security of Liège and make it possible to attack Namur, "if it shall ever be thought reasonable." Marlborough only hoped that, rather than concede Huy, the French would offer battle "by which God may give us more success in three or four hours time than we dare promise ourselves" from thirty years of sieges. Nine days of muddy marching up from Antwerp put the allies over the Meuse on both sides of Huy. The town was invested on August 4/15. It instantly surrendered and was garrisoned by the 10th Regiment. As the siege of the citadel began, Marlborough entrenched the approaches to his camp at Val Notre Dame. He longed for a "viset" from Marshal Villeroy but, as Orkney's chaplain wrote, "we don't suspect he will be so foolhardy as to give us opportunity of a Battell." Eight days later, the garrison of the citadel surrendered ("the Commander was a merchants Son who had bought his commission to a Company, and not being used to those things was frightened out of his wits by cannon and Bombes"). From this vantage point, the castle of Huy and its two other forts were bombarded and their garrisons were forced to surrender unconditionally. This Marlborough insisted on with uncharacteristic vehemence—"he used the little Dutch Generall like any dog," Orkney said—rejecting the Dutch desire to get the French out as cheaply as possible by giving the garrison the honors of war and letting them march away. Marlborough wanted French prisoners whom he could exchange for the gallant defenders of Tongres, the saviors of the allied army from Overkirk's error.[36]

Marlborough also hoped that the calculated insult of making Huy's garrison prisoners of war under the very eyes of the French army would provoke Villeroy to attack. Failing this, Marlborough determined to advance, despite what the Dutch generals said was the impenetrability of the French lines. On August 24, Marlborough demanded that the council of war approve the attack. All the allied generals, except the Dutch, agreed. "The Enemy being superior in *Italy* and the *Empire*, and being out-number'd no where but here, the Eyes of all the *Allies* are fixed upon us," expecting that relief which an advance in Flanders alone could afford them. So Marlborough and the un-Dutch generals wrote to the states. A victory here, Marlborough added, would not only force the French to withdraw resources from their campaign in the Tyrol and from their advance along the Danube toward Vienna but also enable the allies to seize all of Flanders in a fortnight. Again, the defensive Dutch generals opposed Marlborough's aggression. They wrote to their employers that, even if the enemy were weaker than the allies, and even if their entrenchments could be taken, both of which the Dutch generals doubted, the French had only to retreat to the impregnable position at Ramillies. (Three years later, Marlborough would demonstrate how pregnable Ramillies was.) Again, all that the Dutch generals would agree to was a minor, safe, predictable siege of another small town, Limbourg. This, they explained, "is not a place of so little consequence as men imagine." As usual, the states agreed with their generals and restrained Marlborough. Reduced to the siege of Limbourg, Marlborough commanded it in person. He left the Dutch generals with the covering army, "in hopes to recover my health . . . for I have been these last six days in a perpetual dispute, and there I shall have nobody but such as will willingly obey me."37

Even before this, the sixth Dutch veto of the 1703 campaign, Marlborough had matured his plan to escape the cautious counsels of his confederates. If the disappointments of 1703 did not enable his enemies to bring him down during the "winter campaign" in parliament, the captain general would advance in 1704, in person, at the head of the troops in English pay. He would march hundreds of miles from the Netherlands to the Danube valley and rescue the Austrian empire from the French and Bavarian attack. As early as February 1703, Marlborough had predicted to Heinsius that the crux of the 1704 campaign would be in Germany. In April of 1703, he had his staff plan cantonments of supplies up the Rhine as far as Coblenz. In May, Marlborough had observed that the French advance into Bavaria would elicit calls for an allied diversion on the Moselle, but he declined to send detachments that the imperial generals would fritter away. He replied to imperial promises of cooperation that "we have seen by long experience that we can by no means rely upon any promises from Germany." Nevertheless, by June of 1703, Marlborough had concluded that the fate of the alliance depended upon the outcome of the war in Germany. He resolved to take the queen's army into that distant theater in 1704. He would leave the Dutch generals to enjoy their paralyzing quarrels and to exercise their instinct for the defensive on their own frontier. To save the empire, the captain general would himself lead into Germany every man whom he could recruit and England could pay. In late July, Marlborough told his intimates that after he had satisfied the Dutch generals by taking Limbourg, he would organize the winter quarters of the queen's troops in such a way that in the following spring he could escape up the Rhine.[38]

Marlborough's avowed objective was an attack from the Rhine at Coblenz up the Moselle into France, but the logic of his scattered letters demonstrates that he already looked further down the Rhine and beyond the Black Forest to the Danube and an assault on Bavaria. He could hardly say as much. In an age when his advance of 80 miles up the Meuse was accounted a miracle, a march of 350 miles to the upper Danube and perhaps much further, down and across that great river, deep into Bavaria, was almost unthinkable. Marlborough's strategic imagination was driven to bold conclusions no one else, friend or foe, could anticipate by his desperation to escape the Dutch generals: "if I might have *millions* given mee to serve another yeare, and be obliged to doe notheing but by the *unanimous consent* of the Generals, I would much sooner dye." To Godolphin he confided that he was near death already, "for the unreasonable opposition I have meet with has heated my blood soe that I am almost madd with the head ecke." Neither secrecy in planning nor discipline in execution were possible as things were. "Soe for the future," Marlborough proposed, "the onely expedient I can think of" to make decisive "use of the braverie of the troupes," was to make "the troupes paid by England" his independent command.[39]

On September 27, the 1,400-man garrison of Limbourg surrendered as prisoners of war. Marlborough hurried to The Hague. There he was again greeted as a hero. His own opinion was that not having brought the French to battle, he had done nothing "worth the being commended," but his successful sieges, first on the Rhine and then along the Meuse, had pushed the enemy back and relieved the Dutch from their abiding fear that the French invasion of 1672 would be repeated. Moreover, by completing the conquest of three provinces—Cologne, Liège, and Guelderland—and by occupying the French field army while the Dutch raided the Paes de Waes, Marlborough had greatly expanded Dutch territory and resources. He was, the Dutch crowds rejoiced, "Victorious without Slaughter."[40]

Yet the capture of Limbourg, like the disposition of Liège, intimated that division of interests between Dutch and English which would grow with every victory in the Netherlands. Limbourg was the first allied conquest in the Spanish Netherlands. Marlborough had arranged to take it himself, with his own troops. So he had been able to install a "Spanish" (that is, Austrian) governor of his own choosing. Out of pique with the Dutch, as a diplomatic gesture to the Austrian prince whom the allies had acclaimed as Charles III of Spain, and perhaps with a view to claiming for himself the quasi-royal command of Flanders,

Marlborough took both personal and public pleasure in presenting the keys of the conquest to Charles III when they met at Düsseldorf on October 16. The English officers in Marlborough's suite at Düsseldorf had chafed at his public acquiescence in Dutch disobedience and defensiveness. They had, like Daniel Parke, written to their friends that "had my Ld. Marlborough had an absolute command wee had made a Glorious Campaigne." Now, in the presence of the king of Spain, they rejoiced to hear Marlborough's "Invectives against the Dutch for holding his Hands from reaping that glorious Harvest of Honour which he, and the Troops under him, must have unavoidably reaped had he not been obstructed in his Measures." The English officers shared in the prestige of their commander's embassy to king Charles. Royalist that he was, the duke exulted in the "very great compliment and a [diamond-hilted] sword from the Emperor, which the King of Spain gave mee," taking it from his own side.[41]

The king and the duke journeyed in company to The Hague but the luster of their state entry was dimmed for Marlborough when he discovered that the states general had reappointed the generals whom he hated most to commands in the coming campaign. Then Nottingham further embarrassed Marlborough by suddenly demanding that another 2,000 troops be transferred to Portugal. The captain general was gratified, however, to receive a long letter from the duke of Savoy announcing that he had turned against the French. So the master of the Italian passes had temporarily diverted the Franco-Bavarian advance away from Vienna. In return, Savoy asked Marlborough to come to his rescue or send English aid by sea. Marlborough's ability to assist Savoy, indeed, his own future, was uncertain. The captain general repeated his intention to retire rather than serve again with the Dutch generals. He did not have the approval of the queen or her cabinet for his adventure up the Rhine. He had yet to face the hostility of the high tories in parliament.[42]

The captain general reached England on the last day of October 1703 to meet the parliament, whose opening had been delayed until he could get home. This year there were no parliamentary addresses congratulating the duke on his campaign, however, and private praises rang rather hollow. From Jamaica, for instance, Colonel Handasyde (who "next to the obedience Due to her mast Sacred Majesties Commands am proud of being under Yor Graces") wrote in hopes that his dispatch would find Marlborough returned to England and "Crowned with Laurells after having made a Glorious Campagne, and brought Success and Victory along with you for the Service of her Maties and your Country, and An Augmentation of your lops particular honour." Instead, Marlborough's hopes of honor were focused on the coming campaign. When he escorted Charles III to meet queen Anne at Windsor, Marlborough presented to the two sovereigns his purported plan for an assault along the Moselle, designed to divert the French both from Germany and Italy. The queen not only personally approved the plan, she also publicly expressed her continued favor to her captain general by commissioning him as governor of Greenwich

Hospital. This was an appropriate honor for a commander whose provision for the health of his troops and his concern for his wounded soldiers was unique in the age.[43]

War and sacrifice, the queen's plea for national unity and political moderation, and the crisis of the west, epitomized by the Franco-Bavarian advance on Vienna—none of these diverted the tory majority in the commons, agitated by Rochester and Nottingham, from their obsession with the passage of the second bill against occasional conformity. The obvious intention of the bill's tory authors was to destroy England's civil peace, and so to undercut the war effort, by legislating a religious and political monopoly for the church of England. So the duumvirs arranged the bill's defeat in the lords on December 14, 1703. Religious toleration was the measure of Marlborough's political moderation. Although he would not yet break entirely with his lifelong tory constituency by voting against the bill, Marlborough correctly assured his wife that "the bill will certainly be thrown out, unless my Lord Treasurer and I will both speake to pepell and speak in the House, which I doe assure you for myself I will not doe."[44]

The defeat of the high tories' religious offensive at home ensured parliamentary support for the war in Europe. Marlborough reported to the allies' ambassadors that parliament would finance an additional fifteen regiments, 10,000 more troops, for the army under his command in Flanders; that it would extend the controversial recruiting act; that it would expand English subsidies to the allies and for auxiliary troops; and, finally, that the parliament would finance another expedition to Portugal, where England already had 8,000 troops. Marlborough also persuaded parliament to meet the ordnance debt of £150,324/19/4, largely owing, as the principal officers wrote, "to the great Squadrons which have been sent to the West Indies" and to the "very Extraordinary" cost of munitions sent to the American colonies, from Newfoundland to Jamaica. Finally, Marlborough reported that the commons would agree to rebuild the English navy, decimated by the great storm of November 26, 1703, "which late o'er pale Britannia pass'd." Every one of these measures was pressed by the captain general in the lobbies, in debate, and in late-night meetings with Godolphin and Harley. Marlborough had ceased to talk of retirement. Now he spoke of a campaign on the Moselle, a campaign free from Dutch generals, a campaign managed by an enlarged staff of "the queen's subjects," both Scots and English.[45]

On January 1, 1704, the captain general had the queen commission George Hamilton, earl of Orkney, a lieutenant general. Marlborough also promised Orkney the government of Virginia as soon as the impending ousters of Nottingham and Blathwayt exposed their high tory clients to recall from the colonial commands. In the same general promotion, the precedent by which officers in command of American provinces continued to rise by seniority in military rank was set by Brigadier General Sir Bevil Granville, the governor general of Barbados. He was promoted major general. The captain general's brevet for the Huguenot soldier Charles Sybourg, who was to command in Jamaica, evidenced Marlborough's constant favor to military merit, even in the ranks of naturalized refugees. Mostly Huguenots, they were valued by Marlborough, if not by the immoderate tories, for their professional contributions to the army and the empire. These officers, and the others on the promotions lists which Marlborough forwarded to the queen from January to April 1704, were to command the enlarged army. A new regiment of dragoons, an additional squadron for the quartermaster general's regiment, and two more troops of Scots Greys were the cavalry raised in the late winter of 1703–4. Much ampler fields of military patronage were the fifteen new regiments of infantry. Seven were to be recruited primarily in Ireland, eight in England. In the first week of January 1704, the floodgates of military patronage opened. A wave of commissions buoyed up the military-political ship of state commanded by the captain general of England. It was manned by the new class, the militarized oligarchy of Greater Britain. Just as parliament funded the army, so its members found unprecedented patronage opportunities in the expanded corps. The military-fiscal revolution had found political expression. As Adam de Cardonnel, Marlborough's military secretary, complained to his opposite number in Ireland, "I have Scarce had any rest Night or Day since it [the regimental commissions list for Ireland] has been in Agitation, there is hardly a Member in either House but has been soliciting for his friend."[46]

Cardonnel was tactfully trying to explain to the resentful officers of the lord lieutenant the duke of Ormonde's Irish military establishment why they had so few commissions to assign. The first of these was simply seniority. Within regiments, seniority ruled promotion, but seniority was also the strongest claim to steps between regiments. Next to seniority was service, military and imperial. Then "interest," familial and political, had its place in appointment and promotion, making the army one with the establishment. At the apex of the establishment, only ultimately subject to the queen, Marlborough could express his professional preferences. He favored officers who had survived military service in America, or who were the products of aristocratic military noble households or whose political reliability had been proven when they went "of with my Lord Duke at the Revolution," that is, officers who deserted the army of James II to join in lord Churchill's coup. Marlborough recognized the new political reality, the power of parliament so enhanced by the revolution, so every one of the forty-five men appointed by Marlborough to commands in the regiments raising in Ireland who was able to do so gave references to members of the house of commons or to politically active lords. The political-military connections exposed by Marlborough's military promotions underlay imperial government.[47]

Captain Thomas Foulkes had been promoted captain when king James expanded the army in the Sedgemoor summer of 1685, but the bulk of his career was typical of the army of king William. From service in the reconquest of Ireland, Foulkes went out to the Leeward Islands with the Wheeler-Foulkes expedition in 1693. There, Foulkes parlayed his company command into the lieutenant governorship of Antigua. In the imperial political upheaval of 1697, the so-called "standing army crisis," Foulkes's unit was disbanded and he was replaced in the government. Ranked as a lieutenant colonel of infantry because of his American government, Foulkes asked to be commissioned either as the executive officer of a new marching regiment or as a captain of dragoons. Either Foulkes had aimed a little too high or his patronage from the Howe interest in parliament was a bit insufficient. Only at the last possible moment, when Marlborough was at sea, bound for the campaign of 1704, did he cross off a junior officer's name from the list of the new North Country regiment of Sir Charles Hotham so that Foulkes could take the senior captaincy.[48]

Lieutenant John Farmer (Fermor) had no need of parliamentary recommendations. He had been a lieutenant under Marlborough himself in the Royal Fusiliers. Farmer was further fortunate in that the earl of Orrery, who was raising a regiment from his family's estates in Ireland and so was anxious to recruit experienced officers, asked Marlborough to promote Farmer to a company command in his corps. Farmer also claimed an endorsement from Colonel Richard Brewer, late commander in chief of Jamaica. Commissioned in Orrery's Regiment, Captain Farmer won the favor of the duke of Argyll. He would see to Farmer's promotion as his own lieutenant governor in England's newly conquered Mediterranean base, Minorca.[49]

Lieutenant John Doucet's credentials were those of a vanishing medieval world of martial households. The son of a field officer in the Anglo-Irish garrison, Doucet had been a page to the duke of Ormonde and had marched in the viceroy's cadet company. Ormonde had pulled Doucet out of Fox's marines before they went to the West Indies. So Doucet survived to receive Admiral George Churchill's nomination to a company in the new levies. Given this impeccable tory background, Doucet naturally was a client of the far right, and it is not clear that he was allowed to take command of his company until Marlborough began to build some political backfires in 1709. Doucet did join Marlborough's command in time to win distinction on the dreadful day of Malplaquet. Then he found a peacetime billet as the lieutenant governor of an imperial conquest especially prized by the tories: Annapolis, Nova Scotia.[50]

An American officer who actually wanted a post in the West Indies was a welcome candidate for promotion. Cardonnel told Marlborough that John Syms, "a gentn of ye Leeward Is. where he has a considerable estate, prays one of the two new Companys to be sent to these Islds." Backed by both the feudal authority of the duke of Devonshire and the military testimony of Colonel Henry Cornewall of the Horse Guards, Syms received Marlborough's mandate for a commission to command a company in the Leeward Islands garrison.[51]

Scholarly qualifications to command were especially appropriate on the eve of the Augustan age. Martin Bladen had "dedicated [his newly published translation of] Caesar's Commentary to his Grace," the English Augustus, so

Cardonnel minuted Bladen's résumé. It also included military service "as an Ensign during the last Warr in Colonel Fairfax's Regiment." As a command in that regiment implied, Bladen also had "a good Interest in Yorkshire," an interest headed by lord Fairfax himself. "Several other members" of parliament were willing to speak for Bladen. So he jumped from being that lowest form of officer life, a half-pay ensign, to being a company commander in the new regiment of Sir Charles Hotham. Captain Bladen's company was to be raised in Yorkshire, where his interest would help recruiting and where professional advice was at hand from the new regiment's senior captain, Colonel Foulkes.[52]

Doubtless Foulkes regaled his juniors with tales of his West Indian government. Bladen certainly put that imperial information to administrative use. After staff service with Galway in Portugal and Stanhope in Spain—for which he won a field promotion to colonel's rank—Bladen became a comptroller of the mint and the dominant commissioner of trade and plantations. This last was a doubly appropriate position for a scholar of empire and an officer whose military and political patron, lord Fairfax, was the proprietor of the Northern Neck of Virginia and whose family both patronized and married the Washingtons. During his decades of a service on "the board of trade," Colonel Bladen was the most influential strategic and political planner for America, calling for an enhanced garrison government of strategic provinces and a continental captain general to direct the transmontane conquest of a "Greater Britain in America."[53]

Henry Pulleyne was another of the well-connected North Country men who, like Bladen, Marlborough had commissioned in Hotham's Yorkshire regiment. Pulleyne was recommended by "several Noblemen for a Company in the New Levies." Not only did Pulleyne have the support of three dukes, his father was high sheriff of Yorkshire (an enormous help to forced recruiting under the new act). Most important of all, he "claims his grace's promise." Marlborough was as good as his word. Pulleyne served out the war in Hotham's regiment. Then he took his army half pay out to Bermuda as lieutenant governor.[54]

With only three knights "and several other members" of parliament to recommend him to Marlborough's attention, William (Tailer) Taylor's aspirations were more modest than those of a Yorkshire Pulleyne backed by three dukes. Taylor wanted a step up from ensign to lieutenant in a marching regiment. He did much better than that, however, for Marlborough made Taylor a lieutenant in Major General Erle's dragoons. Taylor's ascent to mounted service was helped by traditional credentials. He had been a page in the duke of Norfolk's household. Then Taylor had served two campaigns in Flanders as a volunteer with General Piercy Kirke (would-be governor general of New England). From the outbreak of the war of the English and Spanish successions, Taylor saw active service as an ensign, perhaps under Codrington in the West Indies, certainly under Stanhope in Spain. Major General Erle helped Taylor to another American command, under General Francis Nicholson (like Taylor a ducal page and Kirke protégé). Taylor became colonel of a provincial regiment, participated in the capture of Port Royal, Nova Scotia, and became lieutenant governor of Massachusetts. Taylor had begun his service, as had Nicholson, Doucet, and many others recorded in Marlborough's promotions file, in an older, aristocratic, army of medieval antecedents. He rose to American command in a more modern military force, the bureaucratic and authoritarian basis of an overseas empire.[55]

The transformation of empire and army—from the colonies and patriarchs of the seventeenth century to the provinces and professionals of the eighteenth—was especially apparent in the cockpit of the imperial struggle, the Leeward Islands. Ever since Marlborough had been commissioned captain general of the queen's army, he had fended off inquiries about the Guards command which had been linked to the Leeward Islands government. The former Guards officer Governor Christopher Codrington, paralyzed by anger, illness, and opium after the failed invasion of Guadeloupe, had asked to be relieved. It was expected by everyone (except Colonel Thomas Whetham, who held the dormant commission for the Leeward Islands command, who was serving there with his regiment, and who had been distinguished at Guadeloupe) that Codrington would be succeeded by another Guards officer, a native of the islands, the lieutenant colonel of the Coldstream Guards, Brigadier General Sir William Mathew. Sir William was a son of Abednego Mathew, the officer of the Barbados Regiment who had become patriarch of the Leeward Islands. Sir William himself was a veteran of the Virginia expedition of 1676, of Tangier, and of Sedgemoor. At the end of December 1703, the Irish secretary at war, Edward Southwell, had written to his principal, the duke of Ormonde, that "Mathews of the Guards has got the governmt of the Leeward Islands. 'I fear he is under contribution.'"[56]

"Under contribution" to whom is not clear. Marlborough wrote to his duchess that "since the Queen came to the crown, I have never taken one farthing from anybody living for any favour or employment what soe ever; and be assured as long as I live I never will." Moreover, Colonel Mathew was so preeminent a product of the Anglo-American military elite that his gubernatorial commission was a matter of course. Marlborough treated it as such. Marlborough also had his eye out for the next member of the Mathew dynasty, the younger William, quartermaster of the Coldstream Guards. Marlborough promoted him a company captain in the Coldstream in succession to his father. The younger Mathew would be distinguished under Marlborough's command, and Stanhope's, before he eventually became the third generation of the Mathew military family to command their home province, the Leeward Islands.[57]

Sir William Mathew's successor as lieutenant colonel of the Coldstream Guards and, by favor of "his Highness, the Prince and Duke of Marlborough," was Mathew's major, Edward Braddock. There was, Braddock wrote to the captain general, "no body in the Regiment [who] will serve you to ye hazard of my Life with more Sincerety." Braddock's son Edward the younger, like the second William Mathew, was also promoted by Marlborough. Likewise, he followed his father through the ranks of the regiment toward service in America. "Braddock of the Coldstream," in command of an army of British regulars and Virginia provincials, fell in the fatal ambush at the Monongahela on July 9, 1755. He was buried by a provincial colonel, George Washington, manifesting the transfer of imperial authority from the British to the American army.[58]

Sir William Mathew had been felled by disease soon after he arrived to take command of the Leeward Islands. The garrison officers succeeded to the government by military seniority and were coached by Colonel Codrington, the former governor general. One of these officers was Major John Johnson of the 27th. He had led the grenadiers of the regiment ashore at the River Baliff, Guadeloupe. Johnson was Sir William Mathew's immediate successor as governor general of the Leeward Islands. Murdered in 1706, Johnson was replaced by Marlborough's own aide-de-camp, a Virginian, Colonel Daniel Parke. Parke, a proud scion of the Evelyns, observed that Johnson had begun life as "a bricklayer, went into ye Army, was first a Serjeant. Tiffeny [Zachariah Tiffin] made him a Captain for bringing him a good store of black cattle in the Irish warr. Codrington made him Major, Lieutenant Colonel and Governor [of Nevis], he could neither write nor read." Be that as it may, Marlborough confirmed Codrington's promotions of Johnson and other officers at the end of December 1703, extraordinary instances of the Anglo-American social mobility that military careers provided.[59]

Provincial officers were frequently promoted into the regular service. Given luck and merit, these Americans could rise to command their native colonies. Both the recruitment of provincial officers by regular regiments on American service and those officers' subsequent return to American commands were impelled by English officers' fears of New World disease. Not one of the colonels of the four regiments that went out with Sir Hovenden Walker to the Caribbean in 1703 made the voyage themselves. Because they were general officers, town governors, or aides-de-camp, the four colonels, and two of their field officers, received six months' leave from Marlborough when their regiments sailed for America. The influence of patrons or family also secured furloughs from American service for eight captains, three subalterns, and two chaplains. The captain general tried to fill all of their places with half-pay officers from Ireland. Many of them refused to serve in the West Indies. Marlborough cashiered the lot. This did nothing to solve the problem of officer shortages, a problem that was greatly magnified by casualties at sea and on Guadeloupe. So provincial officers joined regular regiments. Two of them, Walter Douglas and George Phenney, were recommended for promotion by Codrington after Guadeloupe. The captain general of Jamaica, Thomas Handasyde, duly commissioned the two Leeward Islands' officers into the 12th Regiment as captains.

Douglas went home with the regiment, served under Marlborough, notably in defense of Leffinghe in 1708, and succeeded Parke as governor general of the Leeward Islands in 1711. Phenney took the Bahamas command in 1721.[60]

Marlborough kept the field-grade commands of the regiments in America in his own hands. Handasyde's promotion to colonel of the 22d as well as the lieutenant colonel's and major's promotions were the captain general's exclusive prerogative. When Blathwayt recommended that Lieutenant Colonel John Livesay of Brewer's (12th) regiment in the Jamaica garrison succeed by seniority, Marlborough agreed, but he held back the colonel's commission until he could issue it himself in England (recall that the Jamaica garrison, like all the army units in America, were carried on the English establishment). Blathwayt himself had to submit a full file and formal application to get Marlborough to act on his recommendation of a relation by marriage, Captain Wynter, "an able vigorous officer but uneasy in his fortune at home," to fill a company command in Livesay's regiment in Jamaica. The command of Jamaica itself illustrated the degree to which Marlborough had established military seniority, regulated by his own promotions lists, as the measure of imperial command. In mid-February 1704, Colonel Handasyde was commissioned captain general and governor in chief.[61]

Handasyde was commissioned the moment Marlborough returned to England from a winter journey to The Hague. In November 1703, the crisis in Germany had suddenly deepened. The Imperial forces on the Rhine, under Louis William, margrave of Baden-Baden, allowed a second French army to pass the river and reinforce the Bavarians. Ingolstadt fell to the Franco-Bavarian forces in December. The road to Vienna would be open in the spring. The empire was in danger and with it the Grand Alliance. Alarmed for Germany and suffering from a domestic political and fiscal crisis, the states general called on queen Anne to send Marlborough across the Channel to advise them. The duke embarked late on the afternoon of January 16. By midnight his ship was out of control, driving before a full gale under bare poles. A day passed before she could be gotten under storm canvas, "during which time I was extreamly sick," Marlborough reported. The storm was still raging when the ship struggled into the Goere. Nonetheless, Marlborough risked taking a small boat ashore, leaving his staff behind. He was the first person to land from England in six weeks. He reached The Hague, sick and alone, to find that none of his staff's plans for the Rhine supply depots had been executed, that none of the subsidies for the German circles and princes had been paid, and that the allied troop contracts had not been negotiated.[62]

In a monthlong flurry of orders, admonitions, and pledges of English gold, Marlborough made "my applications for an early campaign," with an army of his own (ostensibly) on the Moselle. In fact, Marlborough was daily more concerned to "retablir les affaires en Allemagne." His public objective, the junction of the Moselle with the Rhine at Coblenz, was more than halfway to his real target, Bavaria. The same arrangements would serve both Marlborough's ostensible plan and his real design. Immense magazines were stocked. Rendezvous between the queen's army and the troops of German princely states in English pay were designated. Marlborough asked that the twelve Dutch battalions serving with the Imperialists be transferred to his command. Marlborough also laid plans with the Dutch to send troops to Portugal to support Charles III. He asked the Dutch for warships to divert the French from Savoy by supporting an allied attack on the great French naval base at Tulon. Marlborough justified these detachments to Iberia and Italy, and his own excursion as well, by assuring the doubtful Dutch that, to draw the French away from the Netherlands, he had only to march up the valley of the Rhine. Yet, the Dutch insisted on keeping their field army and garrisons at full strength. Marlborough could not yet see where he could find troops enough to save Vienna. Nevertheless, he trusted that "wee have a just cause, and that God Almighty will enable us some way or other to secure the libertys of Europe."[63]

"God helps those who help themselves." Marlborough quickly returned to London. He reached the imperial metropolis at 3:00 a.m. on February 13. Later that morning he obtained the queen's permission to compose, with his staff and Godolphin's, the bank orders that Cadogan and Spotswood took to Amsterdam in mid-March. They transferred £100,000 to the Circle of Suabia, the regional government of the empire on the upper Rhine, to purchase supplies for the army's magazines there. To set a good example both to the Dutch deputies and to her own parliament, the queen advanced monies from her own civil list to help the margrave of Baden recruit the imperial regiments on the Rhine. Marlborough arranged an English subsidy for the Danish auxiliary troops and he paid their commander, the duke of Württemberg. Marlborough had English bankers contact the Amsterdam bourse to open a line of credit with the financial houses in Frankfurt for the use of the queen's army in Germany. As soon as Marlborough's expensive, but reliable, intelligence service (he financed English espionage from the enormous kickback he extracted from the army's bread contractors) reported that the French had shelved for the coming year their perennial plan to invade Scotland, Marlborough ordered his staff to move 14,000 British troops from the Channel garrisons to the landward frontiers of the Netherlands. There the British relieved the Dutch garrisons for a month. While the Dutch troops rebuilt their frontier fortifications, the English and the Scots regiments prepared, as they thought, to march up the Rhine valley to a campaign on the Moselle.[64]

On February 21, 1704, Cadogan returned to London with Baden's promises to cooperate. The queen announced to her cabinet that she had empowered the captain general to arrange the operations of the 1704 campaign with the states general but that he might use her troops to divert the Franco-Bavarian armies from their march on Vienna in whatever way he thought best. Marlborough was "to take the necessary measures" to prevent "an entire Revolution and

Desolation of all Germany." Marlborough pocketed the queen's blank check, extracted his newly promoted generals from the comforts of the capital and, despite the dreadful distractions of a bitter quarrel with his wife (lady Marlborough had been misinformed by her son-in-law's malice or self-righteousness—Sunderland could never tell the difference—that her lord was unfaithful, and she had left his bed), Marlborough himself boarded a yacht at Harwich, bound for Holland. His generals did the same. On April 7, 1704, the great annual convoy for Flanders set sail. Besides the generals' yachts, the Channel Fleet escorted horse transports with the remounts for Marlborough's cavalry (the duke declared that English horses, like English men, were braver than any others); troop transports for the new recruits, the annual reclothing of the regiments abroad, and two complete new regiments; munition ships and storeships.[65]

As Marlborough boarded his yacht, he warned Godolphin that Nottingham, embittered by the defeat of the occasional conformity bill, would attack the moderates' hold on the queen's government. Nottingham would demand "such alterations in the Cabinet Councell as he thinkes absolutely necessary for the Safety of the Church." If the queen refused to remodel her cabinet to suit "the Church Party," Nottingham would use the high tory majority in the commons to tack the bill against occasional conformity to the land tax. So the religious right would hold the war effort hostage. "If all this be trew, as I really believe itt is," Marlborough wrote Godolphin, then Nottingham "is in my opinion doing Her Maty all the hurt he is capable of."[66]

Waiting for the tide to turn in the English Channel (and in imperial politics), Marlborough forwarded to Secretary Hedges more of the promotion lists that, when they were confirmed by the queen, would strengthen the captain general politically as much as they did the armies of the empire militarily. When the duke of Ormonde, the high tories' military champion, complained that Marlborough's latest list would leave him without military patronage in his own Irish lieutenancy, the captain general blandly replied that "most of these gentlemen, or at least their [parliamentary] friends for them, have already made their acknowledgements to her majesty for her favour on this occasion, so that her Majesty can't go back from what she had promised." Nevertheless, Marlborough wrote, the queen had graciously allowed Ormonde's nominees to retain their half pay. Half pay would not satisfy high church.[67]

Nottingham was indeed confident that the church party majority in the commons could block war finance and so compel the queen to purge the cabinet of moderates. He was mortified to find that his own partisans were to be ousted instead. Nottingham threatened to resign. His bluff was called. On April 22, 1704, under great pressure from Marlborough, Speaker Harley accepted the northern (European) secretaryship of state, the official conduit from Marlborough's command to the queen. "I am sensible of the advantage I shall reap by it," Marlborough wrote to Harley, "in having so good a friend near her Majesty's person to represent in the truest light my faithful endeavors for her service and the advantage of the public." A functionary, James Hedges, was transferred to the southern (American and Iberian) secretaryship that had been Nottingham's.[68]

The fall of a great oak bore down lesser trees. On April 1, "St. Taffy's Day," Blathwayt was told ("in jest") that Henry St. John, Harley's brilliant and beautiful protégé and an eloquent admirer of Marlborough, would take over the war office. For five days, Blathwayt "saw no man alive . . . but who he entertained with it till it came really to effect, tho' no such thing was intended at first." By April 6, "the prints" had the story. On that day, Blathwayt wrote his last letter to Marlborough, pledging a smooth transition. On April 22, 1704, the day of Nottingham's fall, Blathwayt wrote his final war office letter (to Colonel Gibson at Portsmouth, to take nine companies of Colonel Elliot's new regiment into the garrison). As he obviously anticipated, Blathwayt's removal was inevitable, April Fool's joke or no. He had used his bureaucratic grip on the army and the empire to forward the tory program of maritime commerce, colonial expansion, and anglican administration in America. That program had dominated imperial politics for twenty years, ever since Blathwayt, Nottingham, and Marlborough had come to office together. Now, the tory imperial agenda was increasingly at odds both with Marlborough's deepening concentration on the war against France in Europe and with his growing concern to moderate ideological strife in Greater Britain. With the resignation of Rochester, the ideological leader of "the Church Party"; of Nottingham, high church imperialism's leading statesman; and of Blathwayt, militant anglicanism's chief bureaucrat, the ways were cleared for Marlborough to launch his campaign to win America in Europe.[69]

CHAPTER TWO

The March to the Danube

O N THE NIGHT of April 9, 1704, John Churchill, the duke of Marlborough, crossed the English Channel to open the epic campaign that would preserve English national independence, make England's empire British, secure the Protestant succession to the imperial throne, and rescue both European and American liberty from the aggression of Louis XIV. The campaign would, so its genius hoped, make a deathless reputation for the name "Marlborough" in a world that had forgotten "the detested names of Whigg and Torry." For once, the Channel crossing itself had that Augustan calmness which poets and praetorians alike now ascribed to the captain general. Quiet crossings "I prefer to most things," Marlborough admitted, but he was as anxious as ever to get ashore. He left the becalmed *Peregrine* in a small boat, had himself rowed to the nearest port, and took horse to The Hague, all on April 10. There he found the Dutch generals determined to destroy his campaign.[1]

Since he was taking the queen's troops to assist the Germans by an assault on the Moselle frontier with France, the Dutch generals said, they had recommended that the states general withdraw the twelve Dutch battalions already with the Imperialists, troops whose aid Marlborough had been promised. The duke declined to be daunted. Instead, he told the duchess and the treasurer, the queen and her consort, and no one else that he would order the British battalions to assemble at Maestricht, march thence to Coblenz (at the junction of the Rhine and the Moselle), and rendezvous in route with the Hessians, Hanoverians, and Prussians in English pay. Only when he had assembled his little army in Coblenz would Marlborough inform the states general that he was marching into Germany and ask the Dutch deputies for those twelve battalions (under their courageous commander, that invaluable staff officer Major General Johan van Goor). If Marlborough could also secure the services of the Anglo-Dutch auxiliary troops marching from Denmark, he would concentrate an army of

50,000 men at Coblenz. Then, the duke wrote to his intimates, "I shall make no difficulty of marching directly to the Danub."[2]

A march to the Danube might present no difficulty to the mind of Marlborough, but it was unimaginable to insular Englishmen. Its goal, the rescue of the Hapsburg empire, was repugnant to anglican xenophobes. The high tories were both. Therefore, if Marlborough's march was anything but an unimaginable success, he expected not only to lose parliamentary support for the European alliance but also to be impeached himself for high crimes. "If he fails," wrote Sir Edward Seymour when news of Marborough's march at last became public, "we will break him up as hounds upon a hare." "I am very sensible," Marlborough admitted, "that I take a great deal upon mee. But should I act otherways the Empire would be undone, and consequently the whole confederacy."[3]

Marlborough worked by day and night, despite blinding headaches, to overcome Dutch defensiveness. When, on April 21/May 2, he declared to the states general that, with or without their concurrence, he was ordering the queen's troops and the English auxiliaries to march to the Moselle, the Dutch deputies were doubly generous in reply. They declared that General Goor's battalions could remain on the Rhine and would link up with Marlborough's army when it reached the Moselle junction. They agreed to supply the expeditionary army with artillery, munitions, and river transport. They declared to Marlborough (and so to his Dutch detractors and his English enemies) that "they should be satisfied with whatever I should think was for the publick service." In the event, the Dutch deputies were even better than their promises. When, as Marlborough predicted, the best units of the French field army followed him out of the Netherlands and up the Rhine, the states general also released to Marlborough the elite Danish auxiliary troops: eight regiments and twenty squadrons. But it was a measure of the precariousness of English politics, and Marlborough's constant mindfulness of their military makeweight, that he had to leave six English infantry regiments and four squadrons of cavalry in Dutch seaport garrisons "soe that," as he wrote to Godolphin, "if you should have any alarme they are at hand."[4]

On April 25/May 6, 1704, Marlborough's military career came full circle. Thirty-seven years had passed since John Churchill had received his first commission, a pair of colors in the First Guards. On this day, Queen Anne commissioned her captain general colonel of the royal bodyguard. Henceforward, the serving battalion of the First Guards would be Marlborough's own escort.[5]

Marlborough now dominated the greatest of regimental connections. The First Guards supplied many more imperial administrators and commanders than any line regiment. It had done so ever since its formation at the restoration of the monarchy in 1660. When, in the spring of 1704, Marlborough took command of the Guards, Andrew Wheeler, a veteran of the Guards' first American expedition, to Virginia in 1676, was still among his captains. By virtue of his Guards captaincy, Wheeler told Marlborough, the Virginia veteran was the eldest lieutenant colonel of the English army. Having served the whole war in Flanders under king William, Wheeler sought Marlborough's brevet as colonel "to keep his seniority in the Army." To obtain that brevet, Wheeler volunteered to take command of the winter quarters of the Guards in Ghent in succession to Brigadier Braddock: "I shall Entirely submitt my self to yr Grace's Benign Consideration; And as I am a Souldier of ffortune, and that my Commission is my Bread, for which I have serv'd now above Thirty Years." Like so many Guards officers, Wheeler's every promotion, from captain lieutenant up, had been earned by administrative service abroad. Following three winters at Ghent, Andrew Pitcairn Wheeler was brevetted colonel by Marlborough, the final promotion of an officer whose regimental career had begun in the repression of Bacon's revolution and the royalization of Virginia three decades earlier.[6]

For most of the two decades after 1704, Marlborough's mediation sent Guards officers to imperial posts. Captain (and Lieutenant Colonel) Henry Worsley was a connection of Harley's. Worsley both survived his patron's eclipse and benefited from Marborough's restoration to the Guards command. He became governor general of Barbados in 1722. William Dobbyn had been Sir Edmund Andros's subaltern in the Barbados Regiment and in the garrison of New York. As an officer of the 15th, Dobbyn had joined lord Churchill's coup and become lieutenant governor of Antigua when the regiment sailed out to the Leeward Islands, the cockpit of the West Indies. Dobbyn was a newly promoted captain of the Guards when Marlborough took command of the regiment. He reassigned Dobbyn to the old headquarters of the 15th, the vital frontier fortress at Berwick. There he succeeded as lieutenant governor another veteran of the 15th, Edward Nott, when Marlborough sent Nott out to command Virginia. Dobbyn's promotion to Berwick made room in the Guards for Michael Richards, whom Marlborough rewarded for his defense of Newfoundland from the French. The same intake of Guards officers added to Marlborough's command William Blakeney, who afterward recruited the American Regiment, was distinguished at Cartagena, and became a famous lieutenant governor of Minorca (1748–56). John Selwyn, son of the late governor general of Jamaica, was now commissioned in the Guards. Marlborough's promise to another dying officer brought James Edward Oglethorpe, afterward the founder of Georgia, into the premier officer corps. The last year of Marlborough's first term in command of the Guards saw Philip Anstruther, also a commandant of Minorca (1740–43), added to the roster of the duke's disciples. Indeed, as late as 1756, First Guards officers appointed or promoted by Marlborough were still in command in the empire. When, on the eve of the march to the Danube, Marlborough was commissioned colonel of the First Guards, he became the center of a regimental connection that spanned nearly ninety years of England's first imperial administration.[7]

At least a dozen other future governors general were serving with the line regiments of foot and horse that followed the duke toward the Danube. They were headed by the newly promoted lieutenant general, George Hamilton, earl of Orkney (titular governor general of Virginia, 1705–37). Orkney was colonel of the Royal Scots, the first of foot, "Pontius Pilate's Bodyguard." Both battalions of Orkney's regiment marched with the expeditionary army up the valley of the Rhine in May 1704. Ahead of the infantry, in Wood's cavalry, rode Captain Samuel Shute (governor general of Massachusetts, 1716–23) and Lieutenant John Pitt (now Marlborough's master of horse, afterward governor of Bermuda, 1727–37). Pitt was a son of the famous governor of Fort Madras, "Diamond" Pitt, and brother of another soldier, Thomas, lord Londonderry (governor general of the Leeward Islands, 1727–29). William Cosby (successively governor general of Minorca and of New York, 1732–36) rode as a volunteer in Cadogan's Horse, to which he was commissioned as a cornet in August. The duke of Schomberg's horse were commanded by Lieutenant Colonel Charles de Sybourg, who would hold several West Indian commands in the 1720s. Robert Hunter (who was commissioned lieutenant governor of Virginia in 1706 and who served as governor general of New York and New Jersey, 1709–20, and Jamaica, 1727–34) was the major of Charles Ross's Irish dragoons. As major of the dragoon brigade, Hunter was brevetted lieutenant colonel by Marlborough. Captaincies in the 10th Regiment were held by Alexander Spotswood, Marlborough's deputy quartermaster general (lieutenant governor and commander in chief of Virginia, 1710–22, quartermaster general in Scotland after 1725, and colonel of the American Regiment and major general of the Cartagena expedition in 1739) and John Ligonier, imperial chief of staff in "the Great War for the Empire." William Gooch (lieutenant governor and commander in chief of Virginia, 1727–51) commanded a company in the earl of Derby's regiment. Richard Kane, "Marlborough's drillmaster" (governor of Gibraltar, 1720–27, and of Minorca, 1730–37), commanded as major in the Royal Irish by Marlborough's "act" or brevet. General Ingoldsby's hard-fighting corps was commanded by Lieutenant Colonel Joseph Sabine (governor of Gibraltar, 1730–38). One of his captains, James Jones, as colonel of a garrison regiment would become the nemesis of brevet Colonel Daniel Parke, Marlborough's aide-de-camp, when Parke became governor general of the Leeward Islands. Parke, a wealthy and well-connected Virginian, had just ridden into the camp at Bedburg, either on his 30-guinea pad, "a very pretty young" hunter, or his charger, "a Stone horse that I was offered Sixty Guineas for in London."[8]

All of these officers, as William Penn wrote excitedly from far-off Pennsylvania, were enlisted in "this mighty march, to the Danube, of the D[uke] of M[arlborough]'s with so prodigious an artillery requiring 2000 horse to draw it." The actual number was 5,000 horse, but Penn's perceptive point was that Marlborough's expedition to the Danube "will give a turn to the French affairs, and may England, poor England, ever prevail. He will be Xenophon and Cyrus too if he beats the great D[uke] of Bavaria, so great a Captain and a Sovereign Prince, now the French [have] joined him."9

Even before Marlborough's march began, Marshal Tallard had pushed some 12,000 recruits over the Rhine and through the defiles of the Black Forest to reinforce the Franco-Bavarian army on the Danube. Tallard's success was owing to the supine behavior, if not the outright treason, of the Imperial commander on the Rhine, the margrave of Baden. It was Baden with whom Marlborough would have to cooperate, but both Baden and the French still thought that Marlborough intended to leave the Rhine near Coblenz and invade France along the line of the Moselle. The French had a much shorter march from their field army's quarters behind the lines of Brabant to a point on the Moselle, Trèves, say, at which they could meet Marlborough's invasion. So they let Marlborough start off ahead of them, never dreaming that from Coblenz he would turn east to the Danube rather than west up the Moselle. "If thay should lett mee get ten days before them," the captain general wrote to his wife, the French might be too late to prevent his march to the Danube and his rescue of the empire.10

The officers and men of Marlborough's little army were still just as ignorant of their Danube destination as were the French and the allies when the captain general reached Bedburg on May 14, 1704. There Marlborough's staff not only issued every regiment its full arrears of pay and allowances but, to complete every soldier's astonishment, also advanced a full month's subsistence money, all in gold. For once, an army was not to live off the countryside. Instead, Marlborough's men would pay cash for provisions provided at prearranged campsites. The results of a year's planning and preparation now became apparent to the ranks, even as the quartermasters general turned to their more immediate task of sorting out the expeditionary force's transport: 1,700 carts, 6,000 cart horses, 5,000 artillery horses, and 4,000 cavalry horses. Four thousand peasants were conscripted as "pioneers" to execute the engineers' orders to level the roads, bridge the rivers, and assist the soldiers in building camp defenses and field fortifications. That last task was not necessary for Marlborough's army, uniquely mobile and aggressive among the armies of its age, never entrenched in 1704.11

At first light on May 19, the British drums beat the "General." The army rose, dressed, and packed. At dawn, the drums beat the "Assembly." The army struck tents, loaded baggage, called in pickets, and stood to arms. At 6:00 a.m., the drums beat the "March." The regiments formed up. After a moment of silent anticipation, a single drum to the right of each regiment began to beat the slow British cadence. The regiments faced right, turned from a line of battle into a column of march, and followed the drums toward Germany.12

Fifty-one battalions and ninety-two squadrons filed away from the camp at Bedburg toward Bonn and the Rhine. As they moved out, Marlborough wrote to his duchess, rejoicing that he had at last a prospect of victory, "for the troops

I carry with me are very good, and will do whatever I will have them." As soon as he learned of Marlborough's march toward the Rhine, Marshal Villeroy explained to Versailles that "there was only danger at the point where the Duke in person stood at the head of the allied troops." So Louis XIV ordered his marshal to encamp most of the French field army behind the barriers of Brabant and to set out himself with elite units to cross the Ardennes and head off Marlborough from France. Villeroy took with him "thirty-five battalions and forty-five squadrons of the best troops in the Low Countries, with orders, as I am informed," Marlborough wrote, "to observe me wheresoever I march." Villeroy's detachment fulfilled Marlborough's prediction: with the weakened French on the defensive in Flanders, the Dutch could, if they would, release reinforcements to Marlborough's command. More men were of the essence for, as Marlborough was told when he reached Bonn on May 23, the French had now gotten 26,000 recruits through the imperial defenses to reinforce the Franco-Bavarian army on the Danube. "If the Dutch doe not consent to the strengthening the Troupes I have," Marlborough told Godolphin, "wee shall be overpowered by numbers."[13]

On May 25, Marlborough and his advance guard of cavalry were in Coblenz, at the junction of the Rhine and the Moselle. His infantry crossed the Moselle at Coblenz four days later. Then, to their utter astonishment, instead of turning right, up that river, into France, the British soldiers were ordered to wheel left and cross the Rhine itself over two long pontoon bridges. From the bridgeheads, the British columns turned right and marched south along the bowstring of the great bend in the Rhine between Coblenz and Mainz. As Marlborough's men crossed Hesse, they were joined by Hessian and Prussian contingents, and they learned that the Dutch had released seven or eight battalions and twenty-one squadrons of Danes to follow the captain general up the valley of the Rhine. When the growing army reached Mainz, it was but ten miles from the magazines and credits organized at Frankfurt by Marlborough's staff. The captain general wrote to the lord treasurer that he would draw on the Frankfurt bankers "to take up a months pay for the English. . . . For notwithstanding the continual marching, the men are extremely pleased with this expedition, soe that I am sure you will approve of my taking all the care possible that they may not want."[14]

His quartermasters general executed Marlborough's orders for the care of the men on the march with unprecedented efficiency and effectiveness. Captain Parker of the Royal Irish recalled that "we generally began our march about three in the morning, proceeded about four leagues or four and a half [twelve to fifteen miles] each day, and reached our ground about nine. As we marched through the countries of our Allies, commissaries were appointed to furnish us with all manner of necessaries for man and horse; these were brought to the ground before we arrived, and the soldiers had nothing to do, but pitch their tents, boil their kettles, and lie down to rest. Surely never was such a march carried on with more order and regularity, and with less fatigue both to man and horse."[15]

Despite the exacting care of Colonel Frederick Thomas van Hangest-Genlis d'Ivoy, the Dutch quartermaster general, and of his English colleagues, for the ease of the troops and the provision of supplies and forage, Marlborough had to issue the strictest orders he could devise against foraging and looting. Captain Spotswood and his guards arrested numerous armed English marauders. Another Scot, the pious Major Blackadder of the Cameronians, concluded (perhaps for the edification of his brother in Maryland) that "the English army are sinners exceedingly before the Lord, and I have no hopes of success, or that this expedition shall prove to our honor."[16]

Honorable or not, on June 3, the allied infantry, artillery, and heavy baggage, all under the command of Charles Churchill, crossed the River Main where it joins the Rhine at Mainz. They found themselves in the principality of the elector of Mayence. The elector had made a very good thing out of filling the shopping lists of Marlborough's quartermasters general, for they paid on the spot, in gold. This was "a thing hitherto unknown in Germany" where both the Imperialists and the French lived off the land, the former paying in worthless chits on a bankrupt treasury, the latter paying not at all. So, after the grateful elector invited General Churchill and his officers to dine and dance at his palace, they invited him to review their commands beforehand. "The Regiments were drawn out on purpose, and were so fresh, and so clean" that the elector and his staff "were greatly surprised at their handsome appearance. But when his Highness came to Her Majesties Battalion of Guards, which then consisted of above 700 able men, and was drawn up by itself, on the Right of all, he Seem'd to view each man from Head to Foot and observing not only their order, but the[ir] cleanliness, and their Arms, Accoutrements, Clothes, Shoes and Linnen, he said to the General 'Certainly all these Gentlemen are Dressed for the Ball.'"[17]

After the ball was over, Churchill's command set out again "thro' that mountainous Country, where one Hill took up a whole days march and could hardly have been ascended in that time but for the Indefatigable care and pains of Colonel Blood," commander of the artillery train. Marlborough and the cavalry were far ahead, already at the point of decision for the entire army, the campaign, the course of the war, and the future of three empires. That decisive spot was the crossings of the River Neckar upstream of its junction with the Rhine.[18]

There the duke and his advanced guard were less than a day's ride from Philipsburg. Toward that town Marlborough had ordered the Dutch, Hessian, and Lunenberg troops already cantoned along the upper Rhine to make a feint. At Philipsburg, Marlborough had ordered a bridge of boats built across the Rhine. With troops and bridge, he threatened the fortress city of Landau and the province of Alsace, two great prizes of Louis XIV's aggressions. Toward this threatened point the French armies were moving, having come on from the Moselle once Marlborough was well past it. But now the French armies, under marshals Tallard and Villeroy, were not only divided from Marlborough and the allies by the Rhine, the French were also two full weeks of forced marches from being able to intercept Marlborough at Philipsburg. And they did not know where he was going next. Once Marlborough disclosed his intentions, it would take the French four weeks to agree on a countermove and get orders for it from Versailles. Then the French generals would discover that they needed another detachment from Flanders. They had yet to get across the Rhine. By the time the French began their pursuit, Marlborough had long since left the Rhine behind him. He had stretched his lead over Villeroy and Tallard to six weeks, time enough to invade Bavaria.[19]

By contrast with the uncertainty of the French about his intentions, Marlborough was fully informed of his enemies' difficulties and deliberations. His intelligence system (which seems to have included at least one very highly placed informant at Versailles) had provided the captain general with complete copies of the French war ministry's memoranda and dispatches. In contrast to the enemy's dispersion, Marlborough was within a week of concentrating 51,000 men of his own. He was in touch with an equal number of Imperialists. The two allied armies lay between the French force in Alsace, building toward 60,000 troops, and the Franco-Bavarian army on the Danube, perhaps 50,000 men. When united, the allies would be twice the size of either enemy force. So, on the one hand, the French marshals were frozen in defense of Alsace. On the other hand, the mere threat of Marlborough's march toward the Danube, and his army's union with the Imperialists to invade Bavaria, had halted the Franco-Bavarian movement to attack Vienna and to put the elector of Bavaria on the Imperial throne. The grateful emperor had already offered Marlborough a princely title and estate as an acknowledgement that the captain general's bold movement up the Rhine had preserved both the capital and the throne of Leopold I. Marlborough had "stolen a march" indeed.[20]

"Wee have for a time saved the Empire by this March," Marlborough wrote Godolphin. Anything more than a reprieve, however, depended upon Marlborough's ability to use the time and space he had put between himself and the French marshals in Alsace to "reduce the Elector of Bavaria." During the first week in June 1704, while the allied infantry marched across the Palatinate to reach Marlborough and the vanguard, the duke informed the states general that he was moving "to the Relief of the Empire." He asked their permission to take with him General Goor and his twelve battalions. Before they acceded to the captain general's request, the states debated the question. So all Europe learned that Marlborough would attack Bavaria. The news "was a terrible Surprize to the French." They had at first believed that Marlborough would invade

France up the line of the Moselle. Then they had thought that he would recross the Rhine into Alsace. Now it was clear that he intended to crush the Franco-Bavarian army on the Danube and devastate Bavaria.[21]

The Danube decision was no less a surprise to the duke's own officers. Even "General Churchill (the Duke's brother) knew nothing of the matter before this time." At least one senior officer had been informed a little earlier. On May 22, Orkney had written to Selkirk that "I don't doubt but the March of an English Army into Germany will make a great noise with you, as it does with us." Now that Orkney could see Marlborough's plan, he agreed that an attack on Bavaria was "the greatest Stroak we could do." It had forced the French to strip their army in the Netherlands of its best troops, leaving the Dutch a huge superiority if, Orkney wrote, the Dutch would only use it. Clearly, the French were willing to bet the outcome of the war in the Netherlands on preserving Bavaria and the Franco-Bavarian assault on Vienna. On the allied side, the Imperial field commander, Prince Louis, the margrave of Baden, was so impressed that he had offered to share alternate days of command with Marlborough, "which I believe is more than he would do with any prince in Germany." Now everything depended on the endurance of the troops. "I really never saw such marching," Orkney exclaimed. "We march day and night" toward a denouement on the Danube.[22]

On June 4, the bulletin of Marlborough's army announced that the cavalry had crossed the Neckar and encamped near Philipsburg while the duke concentrated the Dutch, Hessians, and Lunenberg infantry from the Rhine garrisons. "With them and the English horse," so the bulletin declared, "his Grace designs to proceed to the Danube," followed by the foot and artillery under General Churchill and (at a further remove) by the Danish troops coming up from Holland. To Godolphin, Marlborough was more particular: "I shall, in two days after the junction [with the Imperialists under Louis of Baden], march directly to Donauwörth. If I can take that place, I shall there settle a magazine for the army." Then Marlborough could cross the Donauwörth bridges over the Danube into Bavaria. Donauwörth was the essential objective both as the bridgehead to Bavaria and as the terminus of Marlborough's new line of communications from Frankfurt to the Danube, via Nuremberg, Heidenheim, and Nördlingen. Marlborough had magazines and hospitals prepared at Nördlingen. There the Circles of Franconia and Suabia were stockpiling Imperial requisitions and English purchases of grain, wagons, and forage. On June 8, the day he reported his plans to Godolphin, Marlborough ordered the colonel of every foot regiment to have a new pair of shoes for each of their soldiers sent to Nördlingen so that the men would be freshly shod when they crossed the Danube.[23]

The next day, June 9, 1704, prince Eugene of Savoy, the victor of Zenta, the most renowned captain of the age, rode into Marlborough's camp to help him plan both the defense of the Rhine against the advance of the French marshals from Landau and the allied assault on Bavaria. Eugene and Marlborough agreed that if the elector of Bavaria did not abandon the French, they would destroy his country. The strategic agreement of these, the two most aggressive generals in the Western world, one everywhere famous, the other essentially untried, reflected their instant affection, the spiritual kinship of "the Great Twin Brethren." One of Marlborough's sergeants best expressed what the union of the prince and the duke would mean to the war and the West. His comrades smiled, said Sergeant Millner, when they saw "the two greatest Men in the Age, with Friendship and Confidence in each other" at the head of the allied army.[24]

Eugene and Marlborough rode from their review of the British army up the road to Gross Heppech. There, from June 13 to June 15, 1704, they met with the Imperial theater commander, that crafty veteran of wars courtly and military, Louis, margrave of Baden. After much debate and jockeying for command advantage, they agreed that Prince Eugene would command the defense of the Rhine while Marlborough and his army marched through the Swabian Jura to join prince Louis's force entrenched at Ulm. The united armies would then attack the elector of Bavaria. The operation would be directed on alternate days by Baden and Marlborough. Baden declared that his willingness to share command with the duke was a vast condescension. Since his campaigns against the Turks, prince Louis considered himself "the first general in Christendom." He pointed out that he was now at the head of the Imperial army in the heart of the empire itself. It was only the debt that the empire owed the English queen and her captain general for sending her army so far from home that persuaded Baden to yield any command to Marlborough, he said. The margrave added that he had never made such a concession to Eugene, for all his fame. Marlborough was not at all grateful. He would, as he told his intimates, far rather have served with prince Eugene than share command with the devious, even treacherous, old margrave, but at least he thought that he could count on Eugene to delay the French.[25]

Thus far agreed, the generals set their staffs to work writing and distributing the necessary orders for the movements of three allied armies. Marlborough's staff made their headquarters at the Lamb, a famous hostelry, where they discovered that the strength of the local wines more than compensated for the thinness of German lager. The duke's young, privileged aides-de-camp messed with the veteran officers of the First Guards and Prince George of Denmark's regiment, the infantry escorts of the duke and his brother, General Charles Churchill. Over dinner, an affray occurred between a Guards officer and one of the duke's aides, the notoriously hotheaded Virginian Daniel Parke.[26]

An exceedingly handsome young man, the son of a Virginia councilor, treasurer, and secretary of the same name, Daniel Parke had become the protégé of the veteran governor general Sir Edmund Andros and so a provincial councilor and a visitor of the College of William and Mary. Joining the English army, Parke served as an aide to the earl of Arran in king William's last campaign. He joined Marlborough's own staff in 1703. Parke was a scion of the Evelyn clan. Its head, the famous diarist and silviculturist (and more to the point, gunpowder manufacturer) John Evelyn, was both an acquaintance of Marlborough and an intimate of Godolphin. Parke had planned to pyramid his family connections and his military service into the command of Virginia. His confrontation at the Lamb seemed to have ended his ambitions. A court of honor judged Parke to be at fault. He promised to resign his commission at the close of the campaign.[27]

It was slowed by rain and cold. Marlborough's infantry and artillery took ten days to struggle through the muddy defiles of the Jura (Swabian) uplands, "impassable by any but such as were carry'd on by an invincible Resolution." Major Blackadder's despondent diary entries reflected the hardship: "Marching all day. Great fatigue, bad weather, bad roads." By June 22, Marlborough was once again riding over the ground on which he had fought the Imperialists thirty years before, as a colonel of Louis XIV in Marshal Turenne's army. Now captain general of England, Marlborough had his army in touch with its Imperial allies under Louis of Baden, at Elchingen, ten miles north of Ulm and fifteen miles west of the Danube bridges at Donauwörth. Two days later, General Goor led sixteen Dutch battalions into Marlborough's lines. On the 27th, the English infantry and artillery, with the Hessian and Prussian infantry, all commanded by General Churchill, struggled into camp over roads "very heavy, deep and tedious." Every allied battalion was reviewed by Marlborough as it came into camp. He was relieved to find the men "very hearty and in good Order, after all their tedious marches."[28]

The allies had now concentrated some 85,000 men only two leagues from the camp of 50,000 men commanded by the elector of Bavaria, but this Franco-Bavarian army escaped into a fortified position during Louis of Baden's day of command (and because of his warning to his brother elector that Marlborough would attack the next day). Thwarted by Baden at Ulm, Marlborough learned that the enemy had also been warned of his intention to assault Donauwörth. A peasant reported that the elector of Bavaria had suddenly reinforced the garrison on the heights commanding the town, the famous Schellenberg, with 13,000 men, and that they were digging in.[29]

Nonetheless, Marlborough resolved to attack. On July 1, 1704, he "sent out the Quartermasters General with a party of 400 horse to gain more Particular Inteligence." On their return after dark, the duke dispatched the commissary of hospitals and a medical staff to the Norlingen depot to prepare for a large number of casualties. At midnight, Marlborough ordered 6,000 or 7,000 picked troops from his command, plus three regiments of Imperial grenadiers, to be ready to advance at 2:00 a.m. At 3:00 on the morning of July 2, Marlborough and his brother, with their escorts and elements of the 5,850 infantry under the particular command of Lieutenant General Goor, followed the quartermasters general, their escorts, 400 pioneers, and thirty-six pontoons eastward along the north bank of the Danube toward Donauwörth and the Schellenberg.[30]

By 8:00 a.m. on July 2, 1704, the quartermasters general were again in sight of the Schellenberg. They ordered the regimental quartermasters and their color men to mark a camp, hoping to convince the French and Bavarians that they would not be attacked that day. Marlborough and his generals joined the quartermasters general at 9:00 a.m. and advanced with them to inspect the enemy positions. They observed that the enemy, forewarned of the allied advance, had not only reinforced the garrison of the Schellenberg but also that the cavalry of their main army had encamped in two bodies on the other side of the Danube, in order of battle, leaving a space for the Franco-Bavarian infantry to pitch their tents between the wings of horse when they arrived from Ulm. The duke and his staff noticed that the defenders of the Schellenberg had yet to complete two sections of their entrenchments, one between the counterscarp of Donauwörth itself and the old fort on the crest of the Schellenberg, and the other between that fort and the northwest angle of the elevation. Marlborough decided to attack the second gap. It was the smaller of the two and more difficult of access, but it was the natural assignment for his wing, left and junior, of the allied army. More important, an attack upon this gap would concentrate the defenders to their right, further from the city and away from the larger, more level gap between the Donauwörth fortifications and the old earthwork atop the Schellenberg. Into that weakly defended sector, Marlborough would ask Louis of Baden to lead the Imperialists, who had marched from their camp two hours after Marlborough's assault force. If Marlborough could launch the attack during the day, his day of command, he could prevent the enemy from closing the gaps, from further reinforcing the garrison, or from settling the rest of their army in the camp across the Danube, any one of which events would doubtless give Louis of Baden the excuse he would use not to attack Donauwörth when he took back the command on July 3.[31]

In midmorning, Baden and his staff arrived at the front and Marlborough again went forward, with Baden and the commanders of his own attack, Goor and Orkney, to assign each his part in the storm of the Schellenberg. When they retired at noon, the generals found that Marlborough's storm troops, wading through the sodden fields of the Danube valley and across at least three of the Danube's tributaries, had only just reached the banks of the Wernitz, "a deep still River" that intersected the Danube three miles west of Donauwörth. The Wernitz was crossed by but a single bridge. So the allied engineers had launched thirty-six pontoons, linked them with prefabricated girders, and were now laying the bridge decks. The assault troops were still on the wrong side of the river, however, they were visibly tired from their twelve-mile march through the mud, and they were still three miles from their objective.[32]

At this discouraging moment, prince Eugene's adjutant arrived and rode up to Marlborough to tell him that the French army had reached Strasbourg, was about to cross the Rhine, and would push fifty battalions and sixty squadrons, 40,000 men, through the Black Forest. They would not just reinforce, they would virtually double the size of the Franco-Bavarian army on the Danube. Eugene would delay them if he could, but his force was less than half the strength of Marshal Tallard's. If Marlborough were to invade Bavaria and preserve Vienna, it was now or never. If he could not capture Donauwörth today, he would have to retreat north, along his new line of communications, into Franconia. He would leave the Danube Valley, the Austrian Empire, and the Grand Alliance to the mercy of Louis XIV's armies. He would find himself in the hands of the merciless men of the tory right. It was the movement that would "either gain him a great Reputation, and very much shelter him from his Enemies (which are not a few) or be his Ruin." It was, said the laconic duke, "a case of victory or death."[33]

It was 3:00 in the afternoon, twelve hours since their advance had begun, before Marlborough's picked troops got across the Wernitz. He detailed his thirty-five squadrons of cavalry to cut fascines and to carry these bundles of branches forward on their saddlebows to the waiting infantry. Then, under the cover of the smoke from the burning village of Berg, Marlborough moved up his artillery batteries. Meanwhile, Marlborough's infantry battalions were formed up by General Goor along the face of the adjacent wood, the Boschberg. From the woods, the British and the Dutch looked up a quarter mile of steep slope toward the gap, perhaps 300 yards long, between the old Swedish fort on the Schellenberg and the northwestern angle of the enemy works. Here the Franco-Bavarian entrenchments had been left unfinished for, as the French commander recalled, "we did not believe that the enemy would dream of approaching from this direction." The steepness of the slope and the closeness of the woods impeded the linear formation of infantry and, just 30 yards from the defenders' ditch and parapet was a deep ravine. The attackers knew nothing of that natural moat when, shortly after 4:00, their colors first appeared above the crest of the Boschberg valley and alarmed the defenders of the Schellenberg.[34]

At 5:00 the British cavalry brought up the fascines to the leading infantry regiments, then defiled to the rear, forming two lines close behind and "in support" of the four lines of foot. Marlborough himself rode to the front to look up at his enemy. "Giving his Orders with the greatest Presence of Mind imaginable and exposing his Person to the greatest Danger," the duke organized the assault. All the while, the enemy artillery cut swathes in the tightly packed ranks of redcoats and bluecoats, fully exposed and at point-blank range. Drawn up on the slope behind their trenches, the French and Bavarian battalions were almost equally vulnerable. The first shots from Colonel Blood's English batteries tore through the French grenadier regiment ranked behind the northwest angle. A cannonball cut in half the lieutenant with whom the regiment's colonel was speaking. The colonel recalled that the same salvo killed "twelve grenadiers, who fell side by side in the ranks so that my coat was covered with brains and blood. . . . I had five officers and eighty grenadiers killed on the spot before we had fired a single shot."[35]

At 6:00, Marlborough ordered his infantry to charge. The attack was led by two "forlorne hopes," each of 130 volunteers. One was commanded by captain the lord Mordaunt of the First Guards, Peterborough's heir, the suitor of Marlborough's daughter, Mary. Mordaunt was wounded and fifty of his men were killed by the first blast of case shot from the enemy artillery. The other advance party was led by Henry Blount and William West of the Guards together with their friend, Marlborough's aide, Daniel Parke. "After Blunt and West were kill'd, I lead up those two platoons to the French," Parke recalled. Shot in both legs, Parke nonetheless "remain'd the whole day in the Battle." He would bring back from the assault on the Schellenberg only one sergeant and twenty-six men of the forlorn hope. The doomed volunteers were followed forward by the entire first line of Marlborough's infantry, General Ferguson's command: the First Guards battalion; both battalions of Orkney's Royal Scots; Ingoldsby's regiment (the 23d, whose commanding officer, Joseph Sabine, was wounded as he took his first step toward the Schellenberg); and the 37th. To the right of these five redcoated British battalions an equal number of General Goor's bluecoated Dutch advanced.[36]

Galled by the artillery firing down on them from the Schellenberg and the guns of Donauwörth firing up from the city walls, the allies nonetheless advanced until they were eighty paces from the enemy entrenchments. Then the enemy's first volley of musketry shot down General Goor and most of his staff. The allied assault stopped. While Orkney's officers moved up to take command of the attack, his Royal Scots lost 400 men to another blast of case. Finally, the attackers moved forward again, only to encounter the ravine. Amid slaughter and smoke, they mistook it for the enemy ditch, threw down their fascines, and advanced over them only to find themselves at the edge of the actual ditch, under heavy small-arms fire both from the enemy, who were standing to their parapet less than twenty feet away, and from their own army, twenty ranks deep behind them. The allied vanguard broke and ran. The French and the Bavarians swarmed over the parapets and charged, bayoneting the fugitives. The pursuit ran headlong into the First Guards. The Guards companies had already lost every one of their captains and the Guards platoons had lost all their subaltern officers and three-fourths of their sergeants. Nevertheless, they had reformed as volunteer officers, such as Colonel Parke, struggled to the front. Rallying on the steep and slippery slopes of the Schellenberg, the Guards beat the enemy back into their entrenchments. Meanwhile the allied cavalry stopped their retreating infantry and "forced them up again to the charge."[37]

To lead that charge, the surviving generals and colonels of Marlborough's brigades and battalions now dismounted and walked to the front of the ranks. The cavalry closed up from behind. Led by their senior officers and pressed by their own horse, the allied battalions marched slowly forward to a second attack. "The English infantry led this attack with the greatest intrepidity," the French sector commander reported, "right up to our parapet, but there they

were opposed with a courage at least equal to their own. . . . We were all fighting hand to hand, hurling them back as they clutched at the parapet; men were
slaying, or tearing at the muzzles of guns and the bayonets which pierced their
entrails; crushing under their feet their own wounded comrades, even gouging
out their opponents' eyes with their nails, when the grip was so close that neither could make use of their weapons. It would have been quite impossible to
find a more terrible representation of Hell itself than was shown in the savagery
of both sides on this occasion."[38]

At last, just before 7:00, the British troops fell back once again to the shelter of the Boschberg dip. They left the Schellenberg entrenchment full to the
level of the enemy parapet with the corpses of their comrades, but the ferocity
and the duration of their attack had forced the defenders to concentrate on that
dreadful angle. Ten French and Bavarian battalions had been crammed into
the defense of the Boschberg gap. A front just 300 yards long had consumed
five-eighths of the entire defense of the Schellenberg entrenchments, although
they stretched for nearly two miles. In particular, the defensive concentration
against Marlborough's assault had drawn the troops out of the second gap,
the 700 yards between the Donauwörth counterscarp and the old fort on the
hillcrest.[39]

Into this unguarded gap, Louis of Baden led the right wing of the allies.
The margrave changed the minds of Marlborough's officers about his courage
(if not about his loyalty). "He charged very boldly at the head of his men," Daniel Parke noted, "and was the first that broke the Enemy." Baden was followed
by the Imperial infantry. They crossed the unfinished enemy entrenchments
without firing a shot. The governor of Donauwörth had neglected to line the
counterscarp galleries with musketeers to take the attackers in flank. The Imperialists could therefore form up on the hillside, put their backs to the silent
town, and march, slowly and with shouldered arms, northward up the gentle
slope toward the undefended flank of the enemy infantry bunched at the northwest angle of the Schellenberg defenses. All the enemy attention was directed
outward, at Marlborough's colors flying behind the Boschberg ditch. At last,
too late, the Bavarian cavalry awakened to the Imperial advance and charged.
The countercharge of the German cuirassiers beat the Bavarians back.[40]

At that very moment, just after 7:00 on the evening of July 2, 1704, the
surviving Dutch and British infantry, reinforced by the dismounted Scots
dragoons, made a third attack on the northwest angle. As French defenders
flinched from the menacing approach of the Imperialists on their unguarded
flank, Marlborough's men at last drove over that terrible parapet and pushed
the French and Bavarian infantry back up the slope. Marlborough himself
crossed the entrenchment with the first squadron of the English cavalry. As
the Scots dragoons remounted, the captain general gave his final order of the
battle: "Kill, Kill and destroy." The entire British cavalry swept the scattering
defenders across the mile-broad open plateau, "hackt them down at a miser-

able rate," and drove the survivors off the Schellenberg, either into the woods to the north or down the southern slope to the Danube. The pontoon bridges collapsed under the weight of the fugitives. Thousands drowned. The Bavarian commander, count D'Arco, escaped before the bridges broke (leaving his entire camp, gold plate, guns, tents, and all, to the British plunderers). Fewer than 3,000 of the 12,000 or 13,000 French and Bavarian troops who had defended the Schellenberg ever reached the electoral camp across the Danube: "the rest were killed, or downed, or deserted, or were taken prisoners."[41]

In one and one-quarter hours of fighting at the Boschberg angle, Marlborough's infantry had suffered 1,223 casualties. Altogether, his command lost 1,500 of the 4,000 foot actually engaged. Losses among the field officers were disproportionately high: fifty-three were killed on the spot. Together with the First Guards and the Royal Scots, Ingoldsby's (23d) Regiment was especially hard hit. Its veteran commander, Colonel Joseph Sabine, brevet Lieutenant Colonel James Jones, and Major Richard Ingoldsby, all future provincial commanders, were among the regiment's dozen wounded officers. The wounded faced a dreadful night. No sooner had the firing stopped then "it grew dark and rained heavily, a cold rain, al night, and many poor wretches who could not of themselves creep off the place were left till the next morning and then found expiring."[42]

In the night, Marlborough visited those of the wounded who had been gotten into shelter. One of them was his aide-de-camp Lewis Oglethorpe, son of Marlborough's old comrade Sir Theopolis Oglethorpe. Hit twice, Lewis Oglethorpe was mortally wounded. Marlborough promised his expiring aide that he would make a military career for his younger brother, James Edward Oglethorpe. As soon as he was of an age to serve, Oglethorpe received from Marlborough a commission in the First Guards. So the military career of the founder of Georgia had its beginning on the slopes of the Schellenberg.[43]

The storm of the Schellenberg opened a new epoch in the military reputation, and so the imperial effectiveness, of the redcoated troops and their captain general. Marlborough wrote that "the English in particular have gained a great deal of honour in this action, which I believe to be the warmest that has been known for many years." Prince Louis added his tribute to the deathless courage of the islanders: "the English Troops might be kill'd, but they could not be beaten." Still, the immediate effects of the killing on the surviving fighting men were sobering. "We are not yet recovered out of the confusion the death of Our Friends has put us in," the chaplain of Orkney's Royal Scots wrote. Major Blackadder of the Cameronians walked the battlefield the morning after the fighting and "got a preaching from the dead. The carcasses cold very thick strewed upon the ground all corrupted . . . our comrades and friends lying as dung upon the earth." Yet their sacrifice had seized the Schellenberg, a natural fortress taken only once in forty-three previous attacks, in 1632, by Gustavus Adolphus himself, after a short march and at the second attack. With the commanding heights in hand, the allies advanced that night into the suburbs of Donauwörth. They bridged the streams around the city in preparation for a dawn attack on the town. They even began to bridge the Danube itself, preparatory to an assault on the Franco-Bavarian camp. Dawn showed no camp to attack.[44]

The elector of Bavaria had reached camp just in time to see his men driven into the Danube. The shock of the Schellenberg demoralized the prince as well as his army. They instantly broke camp and retreated right across Bavaria to shelter under the guns of Augsburg. As he fled past Donauwörth, the elector ordered his governor to set fire to the town and the magazines, then to evacuate the garrison, break the Danube bridge behind them, and retreat east along the Danube to Ingolstadt, Marlborough's next obvious target. With the allies already in the suburbs of Donauwörth, however, the Bavarians did not wait to see if the fires they set had caught hold before they fled over the Danube bridge, nor did they pause to break it. The townspeople quickly put out the fires and opened the gates to the allies. So they seized intact both the great military magazines and the vital bridge, material rewards for the Dutch and British losses on the Schellenberg.[45]

As Marlborough had so long foreseen, his capture of Donauwörth both anchored his communications with Frankfurt to the north and opened Bavaria to the south. His enemies, whether the men of the left in Holland or the men of the right in England, gave all the credit to Prince Louis. That prince's own commander, the emperor, nonetheless told Marlborough that the victory which, he reiterated, had saved his empire and the grand alliance, "was chiefly owing to your counsel prudence and conduct, as well as to the bravery of the troops who fought under your command." As Marlborough wrote to his duchess, "in truth it is very plain, that if her Majesty's troupes had not been here, the Elector of Bavaria had now been in Vienna," borne in by French bayonets. The Schellenberg, with all its momentous consequences, was Marlborough's first European triumph. He wrote to his wife that "my name here will not dye for some time, which is a pleasure to mee, though I should be ill used by my own country."[46]

On July 5, 1704, Marlborough's command crossed the Danube on the Donauwörth span and five pontoon bridges. The elector of Bavaria was out of reach, but Marlborough anticipated that the allied advance would force him "to eat up his own country," the endgame of early eighteenth-century warfare. On July 6, the quartermasters general, escorted by 4,000 men and twelve guns, prepared to bridge the River Lech and cross into Bavaria itself. Marlborough hoped that the allied advance into "the heart of the Elector's country" would persuade that recalcitrant prince to leave the French and rejoin the Empire, but Marshal Tallard was advancing to the elector's relief. Once they were joined, the Franco-Bavarian forces would be much stronger than the allies, even if Prince Eugene reached Marlborough and Baden with his force more or less intact after fighting a delaying action. Marlborough had to coerce the elector quickly, but logistical problems peculiar to the well-fed English gave the elector time both to recover from the shock of the Schellenberg and to learn that his French allies were on the march. "Our greatest difficulty," Marlborough explained to Godolphin, "is that of making our bread follow us, for the troups that I have the honour to command can't subsist without it, and the Germains that are used to starve, can't advance without us."[47]

By July 7, 200 additional wagons had been hired to carry the English bread ration. Major Cadogan was taking on the late General Goor's tactical and organizational tasks. Likewise, Captain Spotswood and the staff began to assume the management of the allied armies that king William had preserved as the prerogative of Dutch professionals. So it was an anglicized general staff that got 10,000 men across the Lech. The captain general rejoiced in his deepening authority over march-trained and battle-hardened troops and their even more disciplined officers. "I have great reason to hope that every thing will goe well," Marlborough wrote, "for I have the pleasure to find all the officers willing to obaye, without knowing any other reason than that it is my desire." Menaced by that rarest of eighteenth-century military phenomena, an absolute command of aggressive troops, the Bavarians abandoned Neuburg, "a place of the greatest consequence to us," Marlborough explained, "since it will make it easy for us to have all our provisions for the subsistence of the army, from the Circle of Franconia" transported directly into Bavaria across the Danube. Neuburg was occupied by the British dragoons. Colonel Hunter oversaw the bridging of the Danube to the city. The army was resupplied. Bavaria lay undefended before the allies. They raped it.[48]

"As we advance we burn and destroy," Marlborough declared. The allies torched ancient towns and prosperous villages, cut crops and killed livestock, all the way to the gates of Munich. On July 25, 1704, the day that the elector of Bavaria issued his final refusal to resume his allegiance to the emperor—he would, Max Emmanuel said, rather "serve as a dragoon under the French King than as General in the Emperor's Service"—the allied cavalry fired "372 towns, villages and farmhouses and it was a shocking sight to see the fine country of Bavaria all in a flame." After five dreadful days, Marlborough declared himself sick of burning Bavaria to no purpose: "these poor people suffer onely for their master's ambition" to be emperor himself. Henceforward, Marlborough confined his men to camp, but they had already so pillaged the Bavarian countryside that there was "nothing to be seen for a great way round but an universal Desolation of Sixty Villages in Flames, burning to Ashes, and nothing omitted that the Law of War would allow." The 600-mile journey of the British from Bedburg to Bavaria, the famous march to the Danube, ended at Heidenheim in twelve days of destruction.[49]

CHAPTER THREE

Blenheim

A s THE BRITISH burned Bavaria, the French army under Tallard had marched down the Danube from its headwaters in the Black Forest. They reached the vicinity of Ulm by July 29, 1704. There the French could be joined by the elector of Bavaria and all the troops he dared withdraw from his garrisons. Marlborough admitted that his eastward advance (across the Lech into Bavaria and down the right bank of the Danube through Neuburg and Rain onto the plain of Ingolstadt) had left the roads to the west open, enabling Max Emmanuel to unite his forces with the French. Marlborough had miscalculated. The devastation of the Bavarian countryside had not forced the elector to terms. True, the Franco-Bavarian army could not now winter on the doorstep to Vienna, but neither could the allies easily subsist themselves in the ruined countryside. Nor, without heavy artillery, could the allies take the great cities. "The German gunners are good for little," the British complained. German ammunition was scanty. The Imperial siege train was always and invariably delayed. A shortage of siege guns and shot, Colonel Parke complained, had held up the allied advance for days at that "little foolish Dyrt Pyle called Rain." While the allies burned Bavaria, the elector's army had time to recover from the shock of the Schellenberg and to entrench at Augsburg. They could not be driven further. Parke wrote, "My Lord Duke fretts butt there is no help for it." Now that the French relieving force was at hand, the allied campaign was without any good prospects. The allies could not even retreat the way they had come, for the French lay along the Danube route to the Rhine. Worse yet, if the enemy advanced to Donauwörth, they could cut Marlborough's communications with Frankfurt and sever his line of retreat to Franconia. Indeed, the allied army might not be able to retreat at all. Eugene, observing Tallard's advance, was separated from Marlborough and Baden by forty miles and the Danube River. If the allies could not concentrate their forces quickly, they would be destroyed in detail.[1]

Then Marlborough's ministry would fall, he would be impeached, and Louis XIV would triumph throughout the Atlantic world. Suddenly, the march to the Danube seemed to be the harebrained scheme that the tories had always thought it. Marlborough's own officers agreed "that unless something more material was done, before the duke left the empire, his great undertaking would avail nothing, and the Elector would carry all before him in the next campaign." Then the Empire would become a French fiefdom and the Grand Alliance would collapse. "If things should take this turn, the Duke well knew what must be his fate on his return to England, where he had many powerful enemies," men anxious to execute him and put a client of France on the English imperial throne.[2]

Where others saw disaster, Marlborough saw opportunity. The allied position was desperate enough to tempt the French to advance, the captain general wrote, and "if thay give us any opportunity, we shal be glad to come to a battalie, for that would decide the whole, which would be very much our business, for our troupes are very good." So Marlborough wrote on the last day of July 1704. Within the week the French and Bavarian forces were united at Ulm. On that very day, August 6, one of Marlborough's officers looked out from his tent to see Prince Eugene, unheralded and with just two attendants, ride up the regimental street of the Royal Irish toward Marlborough's marquee at the apex of the British camp.[3]

The next day "the Great Twin Brethren" called on Louis of Baden. They flattered him. As the senior commander, they said, Baden should have the unique honor of besieging Ingolstadt. It had never been taken. Once it was in allied hands, they could bid defiance to the French and retain Bavaria for the Empire. Marlborough would content himself with covering the siege from his position on the south bank of the Danube. Eugene would do the same on the north bank. "In case the enemy should attack either" of the covering armies, they could use the new pontoon bridges that Marlborough's engineers had thrown over both the Lech and the Danube as "bridges of communication to succor each other." Baden accepted their submission as his due and agreed to set off immediately to the post of honor. Of course, Marlborough and Eugene knew that the siege of Ingolstadt was but a by-blow. Marlborough privately observed that Prince Louis could never collect a siege train sufficient to batter down the walls of Ingolstadt. If the Germans had been able to bring up any heavy artillery, he said, the allies would have taken every city in Bavaria weeks earlier. As one of the duke's officers remarked, by sending Baden off to besiege Ingolstadt, Marlborough and Eugene had parked "that cautious old general" out of their way while they sought to strike "a bold and decisive blow."[4]

On August 8, 1704, Marlborough led his army a day's march to the west toward the Lech and Danube bridges. Prince Louis marched for Ingolstadt with the 15,000 men (twenty-three or twenty-four battalions and thirty-one squadrons) that Marlborough and Eugene had given him as the price of their freedom of action. Eugene rode off to rejoin his army of observation, encamped on the north bank of the Danube near a small village—Blenheim, the English called it—an easy day's march west of Donauwörth. At 11:00 a.m., however, the prince rejoined the duke to report that the French and the Bavarians were on the march to cross the Danube at Lauingen and Billigen, near Ulm. The enemy intended to cut off the force that Eugene had left at Blenheim. He had already sent his generals orders to retreat, Eugene said. His dragoons were to hold the line of the River Kessel; his infantry were to take the strong camp at Münster, where the Kessel met the Danube. When Eugene reached Münster, he discovered that "the enemy were marching directly towards him."[5]

His courier reached Marlborough with the news of the French advance at 11:00 p.m. on the night of August 10. Marlborough had already detached 27 squadrons of cavalry to reinforce Eugene and he had ordered General Churchill to take 20 battalions of British infantry and all the English field artillery across the Danube, over a pontoon bridge near the Lech junction, en route to Donauwörth. At midnight, Marlborough's remaining cavalry rode north. At 1:00 a.m. on the morning of August 11, General Churchill and the British infantry marched west. They advanced over the Schellenberg and passed Donauwörth to join prince Eugene. At 2:00 a.m., Marlborough rallied the allied main body. They crossed the Lech at Rain and marched toward the Danube bridges at Donauwörth. During the day, every element of Marlborough's army was moving west and north and west again at its top speed. By 4:00 p.m., the leading elements of the captain general's cavalry had reached the crossings of the Wörnitz. By 6:00, they were in contact with Eugene at Münster. By nightfall, Marlborough himself had come up. Before midnight, he and Eugene had concentrated 65 battalions and 160 squadrons in a strong defensive position behind the Kessel. Their left flank rested on the bank of the Danube and their right flank reached the hills. The First Guards and Rowe's Brigade, the first English infantry on the scene, had crossed the Kessel to hold Münster. At dawn on August 12, the artillery and the wagon train of Marlborough's main body reached the Kessel, having traveled twenty-four miles along rain-soaked roads in as many hours. The allied concentration was complete.[6]

As soon as Colonel Blood led the artillery into camp, the two commanders took their quartermasters general and the grand guard, thirty squadrons of cavalry, and rode west. Two miles before they reached the Nebel stream, Marlborough and Eugene topped a rise and looked down into the broad valley. The famous Blenheim camps lay on either side of the stream. From the point where the Nebel intersected the Danube at Blenheim, the campgrounds ran up three miles of gently rolling fields to the northern escarpment of the Danube valley. The allied generals planned to bring their army forward to the eastern camp. There the Nebel stream would offer them a strong defensive line and the breadth of the Danube plain would permit a nearly full deployment of the allied army. To view the camp, Marlborough and Eugene climbed the steeple of the Tapsheim village church and looked west through their telescopes. They saw that they had been forestalled. The French quartermaster general had already raised his standard on the western slope of the Nebel valley. His deputies were marking out the Franco-Bavarian camp along the three miles of the stream between the village of Blenheim, which stood on the lip of the bank above the Danube's flood plain, and the village of Lutzingen on the edge of the hills to the north. These stone-built villages would anchor the flanks of the Franco-Bavarian armies. They were already somewhat superior to the allies in numbers and very much stronger in artillery. When the Franco-Bavarian forces were deployed atop the long slope which ran up from the natural moat of the Nebel, the Blenheim position would be impregnable. So, according to the earl of Orkney, said every one of Marlborough's staff.[7]

Nonetheless, Marlborough was determined to attack. The French had only to hold the Blenheim camp to sustain their communications with the Rhine and cut off Marlborough's. The Blenheim position also threatened the flank of Marlborough's communications via Nördlingen with Frankfurt. The enemy would grow stronger every day as the elector's scattered battalions marched from their garrisons to the Blenheim rendezvous. Besides, Marlborough saw before him the opportunity that he and his men had long hoped for, "of finishing this business in one day's action." Marlborough recalled the maxim he had learned from Turenne in this very countryside: "that the Conqueror has as much reason to seek for an occasion of fighting as he that is upon the defensive has to avoid it." Marlborough's men were still flushed with victory and pillage whereas some of the enemy had their defeat at the Schellenberg and their retreat across Bavaria freshly in mind. Many more were tired by their long march from France. Marlborough and Eugene therefore concluded that "it was surely the best way to be the aggressors, which would embolden their own men and strike terror into the Enemy." Before they climbed down from the church tower, they had mapped out the avenues of their attack on the Blenheim position. Then they ordered their engineers and pioneers to lay the bridges and level the routes for the advance of their army westward from the Kessel.[8]

By midday the allied generals were themselves back in the Kessel camp. No sooner had they sat down to their meal than couriers galloped up to report that the pickets guarding the pioneers were engaged with a powerful force of French cavalry, surely the vanguard of the French army. Nothing seemed less likely to Marlborough than that the French would have advanced beyond all the advantages of Blenheim to attack the allies. Nevertheless, he and Eugene remounted and led out the camp guard of seven squadrons of dragoons. They were joined by the grand guard of cavalry. The allied horsemen were closely followed by lord Cutts in command of the first infantry line of Marlborough's army wing: the Guards, two British brigades, and a brigade each of Hessians and Prussians. Behind them, the entire allied army cleaned their weapons for instant action.[9]

In fact, the French cavalry were just a patrol. They had withdrawn as soon as they captured a few prisoners to interrogate. Remarkably, every single one of these prisoners told the same two lies. The allied army was united, the prisoners said, for Baden had given up the siege of Ingolstadt and rejoined Marlborough and Eugene. The allies were preparing to retreat to Nördlingen. With these planted messages the allied commanders doubly discouraged an enemy attack. They confirmed Marshal Tallard's assumption that the allies, although they had concentrated their strength, were demoralized by his arrival and would retreat without fighting. This was an ideal result, to the marshal's conventional military mind: mere maneuver had won again. Eugene and Marlborough had set a double psychic trap for Tallard. The supposedly shirking allies were actually going to attack, but the road to Nördlingen left the Danube valley not far east of Blenheim so, when the enemy discovered the allied movement westward, Tallard would read it as the retreat he expected. That "retreat" would be the allied deployment for a surprise attack. The allies' pioneers resumed their road and bridge work, under the added protection of the British and Hessian infantry, while Marlborough and Eugene rode back to Münster. "As soon as they came to camp," they "gave orders for striking our tents, packing up our baggage, and sending all away to the Schellenberg; and that every man should prepare for battle."[10]

At 1:00 in the morning of August 13, 1704, allied drums beat the "General." The soldiers, who had "lain on their arms," were quickly on their feet. At 1:30, "Assembly" was sounded and, at 2:00, "March!" Forty squadrons of cavalry led the way. By 3:00 a.m. the infantry were crossing the Kessel on the bridges built during the previous afternoon and evening. Once across the bridges, the allied army formed eight columns, four of troops in English pay, four of Imperialists, and began to march west toward Blenheim. At Thifflengen, the army picked up its advance guard, the English Guards and Rowe's brigade, who formed a ninth column together with eleven battalions of Hessians and Hanoverians and fifteen squadrons of Ross's Dragoons (with whom Colonel Hunter rode) and of Wood's Horse (whose captains included Shute and Pitts). Commanded by lord Cutts, the ninth column marched westward alongside the Danube.[11]

At first light the allies, 57,000 strong, halted the heads of their columns on the brink of the Nebel valley. The general officers joined Marlborough and Eugene on the height of Schwenningen, about half a mile from the Nebel, to receive their final orders. At 6:00 a.m., the anglicans among them took the Sacrament from Francis Hare, Marlborough's chaplain general. As Marlborough remounted, in elevated spirits and a state of grace, he is even said to have stepped quite out of character and declared that "this day I conquer or die." Afterward, all he would allow was that "he believed he had pray'd more that Day, than all the Chaplains of the Army."[12]

"A little after seven," the nine allied columns advanced over the crest of the Nebel valley and fanned out. The five columns of Marlborough's wing (the allied left) marched down the broad slope toward the stream while Eugene's four columns (the allied right) debouched from the edge of the plain into the foothills. Now the allies could see the camp of their enemies, 63,000 strong, ranged along the opposite slope of the valley. The lines of enemy tents extended from Blenheim village two miles north to the village of Oberglau, which lay "about musket shot" west of the Nebel stream and then ran on for a third mile to Lutzingen, a village situated among the ravines in the edge of the foothills. The denizens of this vast encampment were fast asleep.[13]

Marlborough explained this amazing stupor in the courteous metaphor of a polite society. The French, he said, "did not expect so early a visit." Indeed, they did not. The cavalry commander of Marshal Tallard's right wing, the count of Mérode-Westerloo, had set up his field bed in the lobby of a barn near Blenheim. After a fine dinner in the village with his officers, Mérode-Westerloo was still slumbering soundly when his head groom threw open the bed curtains, shook the count awake, and shouted that the enemy was at hand. The count, an old campaigner, was not easily alarmed: "Thinking to mock him, I asked 'where? there?' and he at once replied 'Yes—there—there!' flinging wide as he spoke the door of the barn. . . . The door opened straight onto the fine sunlit plain beyond and the whole area appeared to be covered by enemy squadrons."[14]

The allies had achieved an astounding tactical surprise, assisted by the French assumption that, inferior in numbers and with their communications in danger, the allies were in retreat. Even after the enemy cavalry were seen to be present in force, the French high command assumed that the allied squadrons were merely masking the retreat of their main body northward to Nördlingen. At first, the mist of a summer dawn in the Danube valley concealed the full scale of the allied attack. When the mist burned off, the rising sun was at the allies' backs all during their deployment, dazzling the French. As the day wore on, the wind rose from the east, blowing back in the faces of the French the smoke and effluvia from the villages that the French pickets had fired as they retreated. Finally, as the battle was joined and grew in intensity, the dense and acrid black powder smoke from the repeated firing of more than 100 heavy guns, scores of field pieces, and almost 100,000 muskets eddied around the French position, blinding and choking. Mist, sun, and smoke all concealed allied deployments from the French commander, and Marshal Tallard was a short-sighted man.[15]

Awakened at last to the arrival of the allies in force, if not to their intention to attack, Marshal Tallard ordered his battery of huge twenty-four-pounders to fire the three salvos that recalled the French foragers and pickets. "Following their usual deplorable custom," Mérode-Westerloo recalled, the retreating French parties "set fire to all the villages, mills and hamlets to our front, and flames and smoke billowed up to the clouds." Escorted by forty squadrons, Marlborough, Eugene, and their staff followed up the retreating French outliers. Led by Alexander Spotswood, Cadogan's deputy, and accompanied by

Daniel Parke, Marlborough's aide, the English quartermasters general actually rode right down to the Nebel stream, dismounted, sounded the depths, measured the morass, and were shocked to discover the obstacle to be "much worse than we expected." So Orkney recalled. The Nebel's banks were higher, its water was both wider and deeper, and its swamps more extensive than the German officers (who had fought, and lost, a great battle on the same site a year earlier) had told their allies. But the English quartermasters general also observed the French to be "in confusion and fear."[16]

Deprived of time to plan or to reorganize, the French and the Bavarians would have to fight as they had camped, in two armies, weakly linked where they met at Oberglau. Tallard's wing, the Franco-Bavarian right, suffered from three maldistributions. All of his infantry had encamped along the riverbank. Most of his cavalry were picketed across the plain, on Tallard's left. The bulk of the marshal's heavy artillery was parked well to the rear. Every minute of delay in getting those guns to the front would save dozens of allied lives. The uneven disposition of both Tallard's horse and his foot forced an unorthodox formation on the marshal. Its fatal biases were reinforced by the order of encampment. Commanded by the elector of Bavaria and by Marshal Marsin, the left wing of Louis XIV's army had camped with their cavalry on the right, almost but (owing to an epidemic among Tallard's horses) not quite in touch with Tallard's cavalry near Oberglau. The moment the allies began to deploy, the elector and the marshal threw fourteen battalions into Oberglau to barricade and garrison the hinge of the French army. Then they began to station their remaining infantry in two lines close to the Nebel, between Oberglau and Lutzingen.[17]

The disposition in which the armies of Louis XIV now found themselves, with most of their cavalry in the center and most of their infantry on the flanks, was the reverse of contemporary practice. It was forced on the French and Bavarians by their order of encampment and by their enemies' surprise attack, but it was also apparently favored by the lay of the land. The vast plain of the center was ideal ground for the French cavalry, even as allied access to it was impeded by the water hazards of the Nebel between Blenheim and Oberglau. These villages, with Lutzingen, provided three strong points for the French infantry. In hurried and testy consultations with his two colleagues, Tallard argued for a plan that would let the allied left wing, Marlborough's, cross the Nebel. Then the allied flanks could be pinned down by infantry attacks from Blenheim and Oberglau. Immobilized, the allied center could be pushed back into the swamp by French cavalry charges downhill. At last, Tallard said, his command would kill Marlborough's survivors as they stood, too crowded to maneuver or to defend themselves, facing uphill into the afternoon sun. The elector and Marsin afterward claimed to have suggested that Tallard's plan might not work as he intended. Certainly, they resolved not to give the allied right wing, Eugene's command, a single inch on the west bank of the Nebel that it did not fight for.

All three of Louis XIV's commanders agreed that victory demanded that they hold the anchors of their line, the villages of Lutzingen and Blenheim.[18]

As 7:00 gave way to 8:00, the French decision to commit most of their infantry to the defense of the villages seemed the sounder as the allies deployed masses of infantry against the French flanks. In particular, the redcoated storm troops, whose aggressive reputation had so recently been reconfirmed at the Schellenberg, were concentrating just across the Nebel from the village of Blenheim. So Marshal Tallard posted all his best infantry, no fewer than twenty-seven battalions, at Blenheim. He ordered nine battalions into the barricaded, loopholed, heavily built village itself. He placed eighteen battalions in two reserves, one behind Blenheim and the other just to the north of the village. Between Blenheim and the river, Tallard stationed twelve squadrons of dismounted dragoons. They also guarded an avenue of wagons, parked parallel to the bank of the Danube, to cover Blenheim's communications westward. Then Tallard backed the Blenheim defenses with his great battery of twenty-four-pounders. He ordered the village defended against the redcoats to the last man and gun.[19]

At 8:30, the French twenty-four-pounders "began to play" (the phrase is Marlborough's) on the English infantry drawn up on the opposite side of the Nebel, at exactly the level of the French battery. Their shot "galled us very much," Orkney said. As Marlborough himself rode along the foremost line of his infantry, followed by a mass of mounted staff officers (always a tempting target for enemy gunners), "one of the first cannon shot came between his horses legs and beat up all the dirt into his face." For a moment man and mount disappeared. The British held their breath. Then the duke emerged from the eruption of earth, apparently unshaken. Without allowing his mount to alter its pace, the captain general rode on to arrange the center of his wing in four lines. Infantry, commanded by General Churchill, made up the first and fourth lines. The first was to seize the crossings of the Nebel. The fourth was to support the cavalry once they had followed the first infantry line across the stream. The two lines of cavalry, commanded by the prince of Hesse, were stationed between the two infantry lines. The first line of cavalry was to expand the bridgeheads seized by the infantry. Then the second line of cavalry was to cross the bridges, and both cavalry lines were to form a front along the foot of the slope, backed by the fourth line of foot, facing up toward the French camp. As this novel deployment went forward, Marlborough himself sited the English artillery in its support. He revisited each battery as soon as it opened up "to observe the range of the guns, and the effect of their fire."[20]

The first effect of the English guns was felt by Tallard's cavalry, drawn up in two lines on the far slope of the Nebel valley. The English "cannonballs inflicted grave disorder on my squadrons," one of their commanders recalled, "I was riding past Forsac's regiment when a shot carried away the head of my horse and killed two troopers." Yet this same officer looked out over the valley of the Nebel with delight: "it would be impossible to imagine a more magnificent spectacle. The two armies in full battle array were so close to each other that they exchanged fanfares of trumpet-calls and rolls of kettle-drums. . . . The brightest sun imaginable shone down on the two armies drawn up in the plain. You could even distinguish the uniforms of each successive unit, a number of generals and aides-de-camp galloped here and there: all in all it was an almost indescribably stirring sight."[21]

As the French looked on, Marlborough's quartermasters general rode back down to the Nebel. There they directed the engineers and pioneers who, "with extreme dilligence," as the French remarked, began to build five causeways and bridges across the morass and stream "with pontoons, beams, planks and trestles." One causeway was aimed at the flank of Oberglau, the hinge not only of the French army but, as the allied deployment developed, of Marlborough's and Eugene's armies as well. Between Oberglau and the two water mills just upstream from Blenheim, four bridges spanned the split streams of the Nebel and their morasses. As he directed the bridging work, the lieutenant quartermaster general, Captain Alexander Spotswood, was crushed when the French artillery brought a bridge down on top of him. Spotswood "broke my uppermost Ribb with the Colar-bone & Shoulderbone" on the left side. Badly injured though he was, Spotswood pushed his working parties to repair the stone bridge, which had carried the main road over the stream. Then the pioneers began to fill in the approaches to the new bridges with the fascines brought down to them by the cavalry of Marlborough's second line.[22]

The bridging units all came under intense artillery fire from the French field batteries on the slope beyond the stream. Their fire also cut swathes through Marlborough's four lines, standing on the opposite slope. The separate force of twenty battalions under lord Cutts, ranked opposite to Blenheim village in four lines and backed by the British dragoons, continued to be especially hard hit by the great French battery behind the village. The bombardment was effective largely because both the divisions of Marlborough's wing had to wait in the open, in line, under fire, for four hours, while Eugene's columns struggled to get into position in the rough terrain to the allied right. As they deployed, the Imperialists, too, were cut up by French artillery. The French gunners claimed that they inflicted more than 2,000 casualties on the allies before the armies ever got to blows. As Marlborough's men grew restive under the pounding, he ordered religious services performed at the head of every regiment. From his place with the Cameronians, whose every private had a Bible in his hand, Major Blackadder looked out at the enemy and had a premonition: "how easy it would be for the Lord to slay or take captive all those thousands before nightfall."[23]

It was "almost half an hour past twelve" before Marlborough, who had at last ordered his infantry to lie down and his cavalry to dismount to reduce the toll that they were paying to the French artillery, and who had sent one aide after another galloping off to ask Eugene if his wing was at last in position, finally was informed that the prince's men were prepared to attack. Marlborough mounted his white horse and sent the young Prince of Hesse racing to lord Cutts with the duke's order that the British brigades were to attack Blenheim village. Cutts ordered Brigadier Rowe and his leading brigade to break into Blenheim "sword in hand."[24]

At 12:45 p.m. on August 13, 1704, Rowe's men fired the first musket shots of the battle as they stormed the mill works above Blenheim. Then they used the milldams as causeways across the Nebel. Those of Rowe's men who survived the blasts of grapeshot fired from the big battery behind Blenheim formed up in the hollow of the Nebel bank. Then Rowe's brigade—the 10th, 15th, 21st, and 24th regiments—marched in the slow British cadence up the riverbank and toward the Blenheim barricades. When the redcoats were within thirty paces, the French fired their first volley. Before they could reload, Rowe struck his sword against the palisade. His men "gave their first volley in the teeth of the enemy." The French replied. Rowe fell. As the Scots Fusiliers' field officers struggled to carry off their fallen colonel, they exchanged thrusts across the barrier with its French defenders. Both the lieutenant colonel and the major of the Scots Fusiliers were killed. Of the Scots' thirty-four officers, twenty-four were disabled. Almost leaderless, the British brigade fell back, a third of their rank and file casualties.[25]

As the British retreated, thirteen squadrons of the elite Gens d'Armes charged in from their right, seized the Scots Fusiliers' colors, and crumpled two regiments. "They would have cut 'em in pieces" had not the Hessians who were marching up in support faced right and "by a great Fire put a sudden Stop to their Career." Then the Hessians charged and recaptured the Scots' colors from the French horsemen. Lord Cutts ordered up the English cavalry. Colonels Palmes and Sybourg took five squadrons into the Nebel swamp. Each trooper led his horse through the morass. These who did not bog down remounted on the far bank only to see eight squadrons of the Gendarmerie bearing down on them. As was the French practice, however, the Gens d'Armes halted to fire their pistols. The English, as Marlborough insisted (he issued no pistol ammunition for field action), "charged up to them sword in hand, and broke and put them to flight."[26]

These five English squadrons charged "with such superior force and superabundant energy," as a French general put it, that they not only broke eight squadrons of their elite opponents, they also killed the French sector commander and rode on, scattering all opposition, until they were taken in flank by musketry from Blenheim village. Captains John Pitts and Samuel Shute of Wood's Horse were wounded, though they kept their saddles, and the English cavalry fell back. They were charged in their retreat by fresh French horse and driven into the Nebel swamp. Once again, the victorious French cavalry were stopped by the musket volleys fired by the solid Hessian formation and fell back.[27]

Into the space that the Hessians had won from the French marched Ferguson's brigade. The senior regiment of Ferguson's brigade was the earl of Derby's (16th). Raised by officers of the Royal Scots at the Revolution, the 16th had fought in every major action of king William's wars, from Walcourt to Namur. When the regiment was recruited to a war footing in 1702, four future governors general had joined the veterans of the 16th as ensigns: Hugh Drysdale, afterward Orkney's lieutenant and commander in chief of Virginia; John Fermor, Argyll's lieutenant governor of Minorca; John Montgomery, governor general of New York; and William Gooch. The 16th had been heavily hit at the Schellenberg. Only Gooch of the four new ensigns was able to fight at Blenheim. There he extended the combat record and deepened the association with Scots general officers that underlay Gooch's long and successful command of Virginia. His gubernatorial term was punctuated by the Cartagena expedition where, as a brigadier general, Gooch again led the 16th. Thirty-six years earlier, he and they, and the survivors of Rowe's brigade, had renewed the assault on Blenheim village.[28]

In three desperate charges the two British brigades cleared the French from the village gardens and outbuildings, but they could not break into the village itself. At last the British took cover on the slope of the Nebel bank, 80 or 100 paces from the village. Each time the French garrison sallied out to drive them into the Nebel, the redcoats advanced to the crest of the bank. Firing by platoons, they overwhelmed the line volleys of the French and forced them back into Blenheim, but Cutts's command could not renew the suicidal assault. "For what with the Barricades they had made in the lanes, the Pales of Orchardes and gardens thro which they had made holes to fire out at, a very strong church yard, they were almost as hard to be beaten as out of a fortifyed Town," one of Orkney's officers observed. Richard Kane, the captain of the Royal Irish, tactician, historian, and a future governor general, who was wounded in the attack on the village, criticized the infantry commanders—Churchill, Cutts, "and some of our warm Genls"—for uselessly sacrificing "my brave Officers and soldiers" in what was now, and in Marlborough's mind perhaps always had been, merely a masking operation, designed to hold Tallard's infantry in play and away from his center.[29]

If this was Marlborough's intention, it was a complete success, for, stalled though they were, the determined and repeated English attacks had two decisive results. First the village commander drew one of Tallard's two infantry reserves into his defenses. Then the incredible success by just five squadrons of the hitherto unheralded English cavalry against eight squadrons of the finest and most famous French horsemen appeared to Tallard to be an omen of defeat in the most vital section of his line. He rode down the hillside himself to put most of his second infantry reserve, and some artillery as well, into Blenheim village to cover the flank of his cavalry. Tallard had overstocked the village with defenders. Some of them could not even shoulder their weapons, much less get into the front line. He had fatally reduced the infantry firepower available to his center. Worst of all, Tallard was so busy in Blenheim that he missed Marlborough's next maneuver altogether.[30]

At about 2:30, Marlborough's aides reached Cutts with orders not to attack again but to hold the French attention, for the crisis of the battle had been reached on the plain between the villages of Blenheim and Oberglau. At the moment Rowe's brigade had attacked Blenheim, Marlborough ordered his first line of infantry to advance across the bridges before them and he ordered the prince of Holstein-Beck to take ten battalions across the causeway near Oberglau. General Churchill got the first allied infantry across the Nebel under cover of the smoke from Unterglau, a village burning on the allied bank. Churchill's crossing point was halfway between the areas swept by the musketry from Oberglau and Blenheim and it was exactly opposite Tallard's center. This, by some accounts, had not yet fully deployed. Perhaps the marshal's cavalry were delayed by his detour to Blenheim village (Marlborough seemed to be sure that the marshal would be drawn into Blenheim by the failure of the French cavalry on the north flank of the village). Even when Tallard returned to the center of his line, he may have been too blinded by smoke to accurately assess the scale and danger of Marlborough's advance across the Nebel. Perhaps Tallard, adhering to his original plan, really did say, "let them pass, the more there comes over, the more we shall have to kill and take Prisoners." Perhaps, as he himself afterward claimed, the marshal's order to his cavalry to attack the allies as they emerged from the morass was disobeyed. Whatever the reason, the first line of Marlborough's infantry crossed the Nebel, hindered only by the stream itself and by French artillery fire, and formed line on the western slope, parallel to the bank. Then the first line of allied cavalry got across the stream and the swamp, passed though the intervals between the infantry units, and deployed, Lumley and the English cavalry on the left, Hompesch and the Dutch cavalry in the center, Württemberg and the Danish cavalry on the right.[31]

At last, the French attacked. Belated though that attack was, it was pushed home. Only the platoon volleys of Orkney's infantry saved the fleeing allied cavalry from being forced back down the bank and into the Nebel swamp. Orkney's nine battalions "marched to sustain the horse, whom I found repulsed, calling out for foot, being pushed by the gendemarie." Orkney's horse was shot under him, but he stepped clear, unscathed, and rallied the squadrons of cavalry that his infantry had rescued. Orkney formed the horse up on the flank of his infantry. He placed in front of his line the four field pieces that his artillerymen had somehow gotten across the Nebel. The English guns fired. Orkney led both horse and foot to the attack. The Gendarmerie fled, but three French infantry units held their ground in battalion squares. They were cut down as they stood. Then dragoons from Lunenberg and Zell "charged the Enemy with such Vigour, that they broke them and drove them beyond the second Rivulet called Meulwagen," the small stream that ran parallel to and west of the lower Nebel.[32]

Marlborough ordered Ross's Dragoons and Wood's Horse to reinforce the troopers from Lunenberg and Zell. In the space covered by these allied horsemen, and by Orkney's foot and guns, Marlborough ordered a new line of cavalry formed by the squadrons Orkney had rallied and by elements of the second line of cavalry. Its squadrons had been led by the Hanoverian general, von Bülow, both in column across the Nebel bridges and "pell-mell" through the swamps, despite the growing volume of enemy fire, from the French infantry at Blenheim and Oberglau and from Tallard's artillery on the Nebel slope. In half an hour, a mile-long front of cavalry—English and Hanoverians, Dutch and Danes, horsemen from Hesse, Lunenberg, Zell, and Switzerland—extended from the edge of the area enfiladed by the musketry from Blenheim to that commanded by the fire of the Oberglau garrison. Under the cover of musketry from Oberglau, the left wing of Tallard's cavalry now charged the allied horsemen. Twice the French drove the Hanoverian and Danish squadrons of Marlborough's right flank back across the Nebel.[33]

It was 3:00 on the afternoon of August 13, 1704. Suddenly it seemed that Tallard's tactics would win. The fire from the garrisons of Blenheim and Oberglau had apparently pinched Marlborough's main body into a killing ground. Backed up against the Nebel, without room to maneuver, the allies would be ridden down and cut to pieces by the famous French cavalry. Blenheim had proven impregnable. Oberglau's garrison and cavalry outguards had beaten off Holstein-Beck's assault. As the first two battalions of the prince's ten (some accounts say eleven) battalions crossed the Nebel causeway in column, they had been met and smashed by a line of nine French battalions, including the Irish exile brigade. Holstein-Beck was wounded and captured. Even as his attack floundered, the Imperial cavalry that formed Prince Eugene's left flank refused to support the attack on Oberglau without orders from the prince. These orders were unlikely to be given because Eugene himself had been thrice beaten back over the Nebel by the army of the elector of Bavaria and Marshal Marsin.[34]

Marlborough saw the crisis of the day before him. "Giving his Orders with all imaginable Calmness," the duke sent a dozen aides racing to find Prince Eugene and ask him to release the Imperial heavy cavalry. Then Marlborough "galloped up" to the causeway and personally led a Hessian brigade over the Nebel to occupy the Oberglau defenders from the south. He ordered an artillery battery moved down from the eastern slope and gotten across the Nebel to support the Hessians. By the time these guns opened up, Marlborough had brought over two more battalions. Then he flanked this little force with the repulsed squadrons of Danes and Hanoverians. As Marlborough ordered this combined force to demonstrate against Oberglau, an aide returned with Eugene's generous order to the Imperial cuirassiers to obey Marlborough's commands. The duke directed the Imperialists to cross the Nebel and charge the French cavalry, which had now joined in the attack on Holstein-Beck's column. Coming down from the north, the Imperial heavy cavalry hit the unsuspecting French on the bridle hand and broke them. The village of Oberglau was now attacked on three sides. Its enlarged garrison was as much engaged by the combined arms of the allies as the French in Blenheim village were preoccupied with the British infantry. Marlborough had thus secured both flanks of his advance from further attack. Tallard's killing ground was again Marlborough's bridgehead.[35]

From it, the allies moved up the Nebel slope in waves, advancing and receding. Each cycle of attack and retreat gained ground and wore down the enemy. First, Marlborough's cavalry pushed the French horse to the crest of the slope. Tallard counterattacked with what infantry battalions he could scrape together. The allied cavalry shrank from their volleys. Yet, as a French officer explained, the allied "squadrons being sustained by several Lines of Horse and Foot, our men were forced to shrink back, and throw themselves on our Second Line, which being at some Distance, gave the Enemy Time to gain Ground, which they maintained by their numbers, and their *slow and close March*. We rallied the Squadrons of our first Line, and they charged again with the same Success; but they were still overpower'd, as also the said Brigades, and, at Last, the second Line."[36]

It was now after 4:00. From his post near Oberglau, the hub of the four armies, Marlborough had watched the center of his line slowly advance up the hill. Now it was Tallard's turn to call on Marsin for help, as Marlborough had called on Eugene, but Marlborough's assault on Oberglau had paralyzed the young marshal. Marsin refused Tallard's order to attack so that Tallard could extract some of the infantry crowded into Oberglau and Blenheim and reinforce his center. Marsin exclaimed that he had "to deal with the duke of Marlborough in person." He could not be expected to do more than hold his own and he could not spare a man to support Marshal Tallard. So neither the Blenheim nor the Oberglau garrisons, fully half of all the French and Bavarian battalions, could be withdrawn to meet Marlborough's impending attack on the center of Tallard's lines.[37]

It was now apparent that Marlborough, by masking the French strongpoints at Oberglau and Blenheim with relatively small forces of infantry, and even smaller ones of cavalry, had multiplied his original advantage over Tallard (for Marlborough commanded more than half of the allies while Tallard led less than half of the Franco-Bavarian army). Where the center of Marlborough's line met the center of Tallard's at the western crest of the Nebel valley, the captain general had achieved a superiority of almost eight to five in cavalry and better than two to one in infantry. As the French batteries withdrew before the allied advance or were overrun by it, Marlborough also acquired his first advantage in artillery.

His two lines of cavalry, eighty-six squadrons, were backed by two lines of infantry, twenty-three battalions. They were faced by about sixty squadrons of Tallard's, supported by just ten recruit battalions. Yet their volleys halted the allied advance just as Marlborough arrived from Oberglau. He brought with him Colonel Blood's batteries and their escort, a Hanoverian brigade. The English gunners unlimbered their weapons within half-musket shot of the French battalions and knocked the young soldiers down with grape and partridge shot. As the ranks of the recruits thinned and their files closed up—for their discipline held to the end and their lines were still exact when everyone in them was dead—the cavalry of the two armies stood, just sixty paces apart, glaring at each other.[38]

The tension, it is said, was too much for "a certain English general." He "was a wheeling off with the Horse in Despair" when, almost at 5:00, Marlborough rode up from the guns. With his customary coolness and a courtesy that was, in the circumstances, a bit pointed, the captain general said, "Mr.——, You are under a mistake, the Enemy lies that Way, you have nothing to do but to face him, and the Day is your Own." This "Gentle Reproof" had its effect. Marlborough rode along the length of both his lines of cavalry. He called on his troopers for "a Home Charge." The trumpets sounded. Thirteen thousand allied horsemen moved forward as one, "sword in hand to the attack." The French horsemen fired their fusils and their pistols at the charging allied thousands, then wheeled and broke. Left all alone, the remnants of the ten brave recruit battalions were cut down as they stood, "none escaping, but a few who threw themselves on the Ground as dead." To observers standing across the valley, "immediately the Field of Battle seem'd to be clear." The French camp was overrun but, behind it, Marshal Tallard rallied the French horsemen yet again.[39]

At 5:30, Marlborough's massed cavalry charged for the third time. The force of their assault split the French squadrons in half. Marlborough and the prince of Hesse led the pursuit of the thousands who raced toward the Danube. The fleeing French were so closely packed that horses in the center of the mass could not put hoof to ground. Lemming-like, more than thirty squadrons of French cavalry plunged over the bank of the Danube and down to the flood plain twenty feet below. The survivors staggered on toward the pontoon bridges. Again, as in the flight from the Schellenberg, the bridges collapsed under the weight of the fugitives. Those who fell from the bridges, or who never reached them, tried to swim the Danube. By nightfall, the river was "ful of Jack Boots." Shoals of shoe leather marked the annihilation of the finest French cavalry formations. Between 2,000 and 3,000 horsemen of this division drowned in the Danube. Perhaps 1,000 troopers reached the further bank.

Most of them were either killed by the peasants whose villages they had burned or surrendered to the allies to escape the boors.[40]

Another mob of French fugitives raced west along the bank of the Danube. Some were caught and killed before they reached the town of Höchstädt and the shelter of its walls, castle, garrison, and inundations. The Gendarmerie had held together as they escaped from Tallard's right flank, however, and they rode straight for Höchstädt. Marlborough ordered Hompesch to pursue them with thirty squadrons. As the allies rode west, they drove smaller fragments of Tallard's cavalry into ravines or the Höchstädt morass. Somehow, a substantial number of French horsemen crossed the Schwanbach swamp and escaped, but Marshal Tallard, his staff, and their escort were backed up against the bank of the Danube by the Hessian horse and surrendered. The captives were immediately taken to Marlborough where he sat his horse, in the former French camp, watching the French cavalry drown in the Danube.[41]

At 6:00, Marlborough borrowed a tavern bill from one aide, a pencil from another, and scribbled a note to Sarah:

> August 13, 1704
>
> Dr B
>
> I have not time to say more, but to beg you will give my Duty to the Queen, and Lett her know Her Army has had a Glorious Victory Monsr. Tallard and two other Generals are in my Coach and I am following the rest: the bearer my Aid de Camp Coll Parkes will give Her an account of what has pass'd. I shal doe it in a day or two by a nother more att large
>
> MARLBOROUGH.[42]

To bear a victory dispatch home to the sovereign was every aide's ultimate aspiration. Fame, fortune, an imperial career awaited such a messenger. In a career of victories—for Marlborough never fought a battle he did not win or besiege a fortress he did not take—it became the captain general's custom to award the custody of his dispatches to the bearer of the battle-winning order. Perhaps Parke's distinction at Blenheim had been to bring back prince Eugene's release of the Imperial cuirassiers. Whatever it was that made Marlborough grateful to his aide, the captain general of England now took a moment to promise Parke every American officer's most prized promotion, the command of his native province: "the Duke promised me the Government of Virginia at ye Battle of Blenheim."[43]

Of course Marlborough only meant that Parke, a professional soldier and provincial gentleman, albeit one of proven "Zeal for Your Grace's Honor & Happiness," could have the actual command as lieutenant governor. The duke had previously pledged the title of royal lieutenant and governor general of

Virginia to "a person of quality," the earl of Orkney, his lieutenant general of infantry at Blenheim. Colonel Parke had yet to discover that the politics of the pending union with Scotland and the double directives of social and military rank had made Marlborough prefer the noble Scots general to the titular command of Virginia. Daniel Parke wanted to be promoted a governor general, to command a government in chief, and to collect an unshared salary and perquisites. So he would settle for the more profitable, and more dangerous, government of the Leeward Islands.

Dreaming in vain of Virginia, Colonel Parke raced north from the Danube, killing horses under him, marked at every stage of his progress by diplomats, journalists, and public officials. The English resident in Frankfurt, Charles Davenant, a commissioner of trade and plantations and long a Parke patron, wrote, "Yesterday Colonel Parke came here with the agreeable news of the victory we have gained over the enemies. . . . The Duke of Marlborough has beyond all dispute saved the Empire." At Rotterdam, the rejoicing Dutch government awarded Parke a gold medal and chain. The news of the most decisive and important victory of a century spread in rings of excitement from the thrown stone of Colonel Parke's famous ride.[44]

In Virginia, Colonel Nicholson published a proclamation that "his grace, John, Duke of Marlborough, Capt. Genll. of her Majtes Land fforces," had won "a Signall and Glorious victory over the french and Bavarian fforces at Blenheim." As a good tory, Nicholson gave credit first to God and then to the queen. She had, Nicholson said, earned the victory by her heavenly credit as a benefactor of the poor clergy of Virginia, and because she had protected the duke of Marlborough and his family in the worst of times (king William's, that is). Nicholson, however, could not avoid giving credit to the man who had once challenged and then horsewhipped him, Daniel Parke. As Nicholson proclaimed to the Virginians, the first account of the victory had been "brought to her most Sacred Majesty by Coll. Parke, a Gent. & Native of this Country, who was sent by his grace." Another Virginian, Augustine Washington, an English schoolboy when Parke arrived in London, never forgot the wild and unprecedented rejoicing that swept the kingdom. When he got back to Virginia, Washington built a memorial, a home called Blenheim, the beloved summer residence of his son, George. Augustine named one of Blenheim's slaves Marlborough and another Eugene, an evil tribute to military genius.[45]

As Parke raced to Nördlingen, Frankfurt, Rotterdam, London, Windsor, and fame, the battle of Blenheim raged on behind him. Marlborough's center had broken through Tallard's cavalry, split his command into fragments, captured the marshal and his staff, and driven thousands of the French to their deaths in the Danube, but the hard-charging cavalry and their commander, the captain general of England, had left behind them the three bastions of the French line. Oberglau was untaken. Blenheim was held by the cream of Louis XIV's infantry, "the best and oldest corps of France." Lutzingen anchored a position of great natural strength against which Prince Eugene had three times thrown his outnumbered troops and three times had been beaten back across the Nebel by the superior forces of the elector of Bavaria and Marshal Marsin.[46]

At 5:00, Eugene had abandoned the Imperial cavalry with bitter words for their cowardice. He took command of the Prussian and Danish infantry as they advanced against the flank of the Franco-Bavarian position. Despite extraordinary personal peril (at one point, Eugene was in the grasp of an enemy dragoon who had his pistol poised to shoot the prince when the dragoon was shot instead), Prince Eugene led the Prussians in hand-to-hand combat. At last they turned the French flank and pushed it back more than two miles "over Hills, Dales, Rocks, and Woods," beyond the bastion of Lutzingen. As the Prussian push was exhausted, however, Eugene faced an impending French cavalry counterattack without horse or guns to support his infantry.[47]

It was by now almost 7:00 in the evening. An aide of Marlborough at last caught up with Eugene with a report, three hours old, that the duke was about to attack Tallard's center, but by then the results of Marlborough's attack were apparent even on the far northern boundary of the Blenheim battlefield. The French force that had assembled to attack Eugene's exposed advance suddenly withdrew. As soon as he could ride back, collect his scattered and demoralized cavalry, and persuade them to cross the Nebel, Eugene followed up Marsin's and the elector's well-organized retreat.[48]

At the same time, Marlborough sent aides westward to call off Hompesch's cavalry from their pursuit of the Gendarmerie and to turn them toward the flank of the retreating French left wing. Marlborough supported Hompesch's horsemen with Hessian infantry as soon as they had compelled the surrender of the last three of Tallard's battalions on the Blenheim battlefield. Marlborough was just as concerned to protect his own right flank, disordered as it was by the pursuit, from any attack by the army of the elector and Marsin as he was to take the Franco-Bavarian wing in flank as it retreated. In the gathering darkness, deepened as it was by the smoke that blew across the battlefield, Marlborough's admonition to be cautious encouraged Hompesch's cavalry to mistake Eugene's advance for Marsin's rear guard. Hompesch sent his aides to obtain Marlborough's permission to halt and investigate.[49]

Eugene, having no idea as yet of the dimensions of Marlborough's victory, mistook Hompesch's waiting squadrons for Tallard's army. He also halted. Marlborough's officers subsequently realized that both elements of the allied pursuit had been frozen in place by mistaken identities, "until they were informed of their mistakes by their Aides de Camp; and that it was by this means that the Elector and Marsin had time to get over the Pass of Nordlingen which was just before them." So the French left wing escaped. Ironically, the French and the Bavarians fled along the very route by which they had thought the allies were retreating before the battle began and over which Daniel Parke had already ridden with the news of Tallard's defeat. Harassed by Eugene's dragoons, the elector and Marsin nonetheless led off their survivors (they left 10,000 casualties on the battlefield), undefeated and in good order, into the night of August 13, 1704.[50]

The only prize left for the allies to collect was a huge one, and highly dangerous. Nearly twenty-eight battalions of Tallard's best infantry were still crammed into the Blenheim village. They were "surrounded by little more than half their numbers, almost al English." The Blenheim garrison had lost contact with the main French army "betwixt three and four o'clock" as Marlborough's combined arms slowly compelled Tallard to retreat. As the allied cavalry advanced, Orkney pulled his own infantry battalions out of the first line and marched them to their left, down the west bank of the Nebel toward Blenheim. As Marlborough led the cavalry pursuit westward, his brother, Charles Churchill, also marched his British battalions from the second line of infantry down the valley toward the village. Together, Orkney's and Churchill's commands trapped the Blenheim garrison between themselves, the bank of the Danube, and Cutts's brigades, still in line beneath the Nebel bank. The British screen around Blenheim was very thin, however, and the men who made it up had been marching and fighting for seventeen hours. The village garrison still had an avenue to the west, covered by the barricade of wagons along the bank of the Danube. It was held by twelve squadrons of dismounted dragoons who had seen no action at all.[51]

About 6:00 in the evening, Webb's (the 8th, King's) Regiment, led by that perennial candidate for American command Lieutenant Colonel Richard Sutton, overran this barricade and captured several hundred of its defenders, completing the encirclement of Blenheim. Resisting the enormous temptation to seize twelve squadrons of dragoon horses that now stood, tied up and unguarded, within easy reach, the soldiers of the 8th took positions from the Danube bank right across the floodplain to the edge of the water. Alarmed, elements of the garrison counterattacked along the line of the bank. The 8th stopped them with platoon fire. The bulk of the counterattackers fell back into the village, but the English infantry drove some of the enemy troops right into the Danube. Among the victims was Philippe, marquis de Clérambault, the general commanding the Blenheim garrison.[52]

Leaderless, the troops in Blenheim nonetheless tried again to break out of the village. This time the French took the western road, but their leading elements were checked by lord John Hay's "regiment of grey dragoons." Hay's dragoons fought dismounted from a position at a rise in the road, and they left their color parties behind the crest so that it appeared that they were well supported. In fact, there was no one behind the Scots. Nonetheless, the French fell back into Blenheim. Next, a French brigade from Blenheim attacked north, along the road to Oberglau. They were halted by five squadrons of Ross's Dragoons. These troopers were holding this blocking post alone because their major, Robert Hunter, had executed Marlborough's orders to detach the English cavalry from Cutts's command to join the movement against the left flank of Marshal Marsin's retreat. Nevertheless, and despite odds of two to one against them, the British had contained the Blenheim breakouts.[53]

As night came on, the outnumbered British counterattacked. Now backed by four English regiments commanded by General Ingoldsby, Ross's Dragoons advanced from the north down the Oberglau road toward Blenheim. They captured the entire French brigade that had attacked them. From the east, lord Cutts obeyed General Churchill's orders to call on the battered British infantry for a fifth assault against the village. This time, they actually broke into Blenheim. They fought through the burning buildings and rubble-choked streets until they came up against the high stone walls of the churchyard, the heart of the defense. The churchyard was also Orkney's objective. He advanced toward it slowly from the west, at the head of seven battalions. His force could not make a front equal to that of the French they attacked, however, so the British were flanked and halted short of their objective. Before Orkney's attack stalled, however, two entire French brigades surrendered.[54]

Orkney and his aides used their officer prisoners to open negotiations with the remainder of the Blenheim garrison. The earl was appalled to discover how numerous they were, for "I had not above seven battalions and 4 escuadrons commanded by Brigadier Ross, which were of great use to me. However I made the best countenance I could." Poker faced, Orkney bluffed the senior surviving French commander: "I told him that the Marshall was already our prisoner and that the duke of Marlborough (who had been everywhere from one attack to another, and had ventured his person too much that day) was already above a leg in pursuit of their horse, and that he had sent me word that I should have 20 battalions to sustain me, with all our cannons."[55]

The Blenheim garrison was assaulted on every side. After Orkney's last attack was repelled, "I sett fire to the Village which did incomode them very much." The French were also suffering from English howitzers, "whose shells set all the Barns and Houses on fire." So the French were "grilled amidst the continually collapsing roofs and beams of the blazing houses." As yet the defenders of the village had neither faced numbers equal to their own nor had they suffered from heavy guns. Both and worse were impending, Orkney said to enemy negotiators. That was all bluff, but Orkney had let the French see one truth: they could expect no relief from their main body. One of Orkney's prisoners, a brigadier, the marquis Denonville, son of the infamous Canadian viceroy and colonel of the Royal Regiment, made all these dangers, real and otherwise, clear to his colleagues. Perhaps Denonville was not the most courageous of men. Certainly he wanted company in his disgrace, having surrendered the Royals to Orkney's officers. Denonville's arguments were amplified when General Ingoldsby's aide-de-camp found his brother, the colonel of a French dragoon regiment, and persuaded him that his life and those of his men were about to be lost to a new attack. Then General Churchill rode up to the negotiators. He observed that it was 7:00, that he intended to carry Blenheim before dark, and that the French generals had no time to lose if they wished to live. All "this bore weight" on the besieged. At last, Orkney's repeated threats to launch Marlborough's battalions and batteries against Blenheim "maide us soon finish matters, tho,' truth to tell, it was a little gasconad in me."[56]

At 8:00, Orkney counted "27 battalions and half a battalion of bombadiers and twelve escuadrons of dragoons," officers and all, as they surrendered. As the French soldiers filed out of Blenheim, they cursed their officers as cowards, broke their weapons, and tried to conceal their colors. The attenuated regiments of redcoats formed a long lane in which were penned more than 10,000 French rank and file. To deprive these French soldiers of leadership, and to make sure that their officers did not go back on their word, Orkney took them all back to his quarters in Münster. A French general officer who escaped from the battle wrote that "this capture of so great a number of troops at one stroke was the most brilliant feature of the day's victory." It was Orkney's triumph.[57]

Through the night after the battle of Blenheim, the British infantry and dragoons took turns guarding the prisoners and "sleeping on their arms." Their quartermasters plundered the French camp for food and pots. Being British, they were disgusted to find piles of cabbage cumbering the floors of the French tents and bundles of herbs tied to the tent poles but, being British, they were delighted to discover 200 fat cattle, already skinned and hung. The British "boyled the pot with French beef" and, in the morning, as Orkney's chaplain gratefully reported, they shared "a mess of admirable broth which was very comfortable."[58]

After breakfast on the morning of August 14, 1704, the survivors of the Royal Scots counted coup. Orkney's was an early estimate and, as it happened, rather below the mark. He told his correspondents in England and Scotland that Marlborough's army had captured "above 1200 officers and 12000 soldiers, above 20 pieces of cannon and of colors and standards vast numbers. I hope the effect of this battle will be great; and I confess it is intirely owing to my Lord Duke; for I declare, had I been to give my opinion, I had been against it, considering the ground wher they were encamped, and the strength of the army; but I believe his Grace knew the necessity of a battle." Orkney's chaplain put the army's opinion pithily: "the Victory was gain'd by my Lord Duke and the whole Glory ought to be his." Both Marlborough and his officers gave full credit to "the bravery of the troops, which he led from the Meuse to the Danube." Orkney spoke for all when he wrote that, "without vanity, I think we did our parts." Their triumph was immediately hailed as "perhaps the greatest and completest victory that has been gained this many ages."[59]

After he had caught three hours' sleep (having spent eighteen hours in the saddle) Marlborough met Eugene. Their first order was to have the trophies of their victory—colors, standards, and cannon—collected and conveyed to Colonel Blood's custody. Their second act was to issue battlefield promotions, many of them to imperial executives in the making. For example, lord North and Grey had lost his right hand, but he still managed to recommend John Ligonier for the coveted captaincy of the 10th's grenadiers. Richard Kane succeeded as major of Hamilton's Regiment. "Marlborough's drillmaster," Kane promoted as his own ensign "Mr Thomas Carter," sergeant of grenadiers, "who in ye late Action & at all other times behaved himself with great Courage." Adjutant William Blakeney received a captaincy. Thomas Stanwix was assured of the command of Carlisle, key to the Borders. George Wade was promoted colonel over the heads of eight officers.[60]

Virtue rewarded, Marlborough and Eugene took their leading generals, Orkney much marked among them (although, after twenty hours in the saddle, he could hardly walk, "& I am so hoarse you could not hear me speak"), to pay a morning call on their French guests. With his usual delicacy, Marlborough tried to avoid any discussion of the battle, only expressing his concern for Tallard's own wound and offering condolences to the marshal for the death of his son in the fighting. Tallard insisted on offering his congratulations to the victor. Marlborough, he said, had "beaten the best troops in the World." The duke demurred. "Your lordship, I presume, excepts those who had the Honor to beat them."[61]

Then the French officers crowded around the captain general, "admired his person, as well as his tender and generous behavior toward them. They all had something to say for themselves," but mostly they were concerned for their king: "Oh Que dira le Roy!" The emperor agreed, writing to Marlborough that Blenheim "will instruct France, that her Forces are not always invincible, and will prove such a Blow as her King never felt in the whole Course of his Reign." Fifty years of French victory had come to an end. Almost a century would pass before the armies of France again bestrode Europe. In the interim, a new empire displaced France in America. Indeed, the shape of the West had changed on August 13, 1704.[62]

After he and his officers had paid their digestive call on the French, who, they said, had received their "visit" so warmly at Blenheim, the captain general wrote to his friend the lord treasurer about the military dimensions of the battle and its political uses. "We doe flatter ourselves here, that the victory we obtain'd yesterday is greater than has been known in the memory of man," Marlborough wrote, "for we have taken about 1500 officers, and above 8,000 soldiers, besides a very great slater, soe that Tallard's army is ruined." Marlborough said that he had decided to send Marshal Tallard (who, as the ambassador of the sun king to the court of St. James, had personified French supremacy) as a prisoner of war to England, together with seventeen other French generals. Eighteen captive French generals, Marlborough declared, should convince even Rochester, Nottingham, and the Francophiles of the tory right—the products of two generations of English clientage to France—that Louis XIV had suffered a complete defeat.[63]

The political results of Marlborough's victory over France in Germany reached across the English empire. At Westminster, the fact of Blenheim broadened the moderate party and strengthened their ministry's hold on public opinion: "we may now at last assure our selves the Wisdom of your Grace & my Lord Treasurer will be enabled to keep us quiet at home." The taxpaying electorate of England rejoiced that at last they had "blood for our money." The Scots had much less hope for French aid in their anticolonial struggle against England and the union. Indeed, British union, the dying wish of King William, the first command of Queen Anne, the goal of every English sovereign for a century, was the most dramatic imperial outcome of Marlborough's victory on the Danube. In America, too, the English empire would be protected because Blenheim drew all French resources to rebuilding the army at home. "A firm foundation of future Power and Greatness," Blenheim had secured "the Protestant Succession," the talisman of anglican authority, national independence, English empire, and the new dynasty. Hanoverian troops had fought under Marlborough's command, helping to win a royal future for their elector. Queen Anne had every reason to congratulate her captain general on "soe Glorious a Victory, which will not only humble our enemys abroad but Contribute very much to ye putting a stop to ye ill designs of those at home."[64]

As the queen suggested, the European effects of Blenheim were as immediate as the English ones: "A new scene opens in Europe." The Austrian empire was preserved. Bavaria was conquered. A French army was eliminated. None of Tallard's 20,000 infantry and few of his 8,000 cavalry escaped the debacle of the French left. The Franco-Bavarian troops of the right wing had suffered 10,000 casualties on the battlefield, a third of their strength. Worse came to the fugitives. Deprivation, desertion, and disease dogged the steps of the fleeing French and Bavarians. All told, Louis XIV had sent more than 70,000 men from France into Bavaria in 1704. Fewer than 13,000 of them got back over the Rhine. The elector of Bavaria had entered the campaign with a field force of 20,000 men. He had fewer than 3,000 left after Blenheim. The French had not only to build a new field army, they had also to reconstitute military morale. Until they did so, they would have to fight on the defensive.[65]

That last was true at sea as well. On the very day of Blenheim, the naval battle off Malaga had left the allied battle fleet in command, and the English in possession of Gibraltar. Drawn though Malaga had been, lord Archibald Hamilton, captain R.N., reported to his brother Orkney (and he to Marlborough) that only a shortage of ammunition had prevented "an Intire Victory." Hamilton had to stand a court-martial, with half a dozen other captains, for withdrawing their ships from the line of battle because they were out of ammunition. Hamilton was honorably acquitted. Admiral Rooke not only testified that he had given Hamilton permission to withdraw but also added that the *Eagle* had been so heavily engaged that she had to be towed clear of the battle line. Orkney asked Marlborough to promote lord Archibald from his captaincy in the Royal Scots to one in the First Guards. A Hamilton in the English Guards "would show the World your Grace did not intend to make distinctions of Nations" now that union was impending. The duke of Hamilton, Orkney's and lord Archibald's brother, complained that these victories would make the English too proud to deal with, but their mother the duchess, Scots patriot though she was, was herself proud of the triumph of the unified armed forces of Scotland and England. It would do as much to forward the union as the necessity "I have often told you off, humbling ye ffr. King." It was as military champions of a Greater Britain that Orkney succeeded to the government of Virginia and lord Archibald Hamilton to that of Jamaica. After Malaga, lord Archibald continued to serve with distinction in the Mediterranean. There, the battered French fleet was penned up in the harbor of Tulon, vulnerable whenever Marlborough's pending plan for a combined operation against that port could be executed.[66]

The captain general's victory had come at a high cost. Orkney lamented that "my Regiment is no more a regiment." Forty officers of the Royal Scots had been casualties at Blenheim. The victory had cost the allies 12,484 men killed or wounded, 25 percent of the force engaged, for, as Marlborough explained, "the dispute lasted above five hours, in which time we had neither hedge nor ditch between us." As Orkney observed, "if it has cost us dear the Enemy has payd well for it." The allies had ended Louis XIV's career of aggression. It had extended from the Danube to the Hudson, from Milan to Maine, from Ostend to Onondaga, but Marlborough's range of strategic vision, his battlefield aggressiveness, and his tactical innovations—"the great and dangerous design of changing the manner of making war with France"—meant that two generations of French supremacy had been reversed. In just two months after Blenheim, the allies drove the French out of Germany, over the Rhine, and recaptured Landau. Marlborough pressed on by amazing mountain marches. On October 29 he seized Trèves and on December 20 he took Trabach, the outer defenses of the Moselle valley. Henceforth, it seemed, Louis XIV would have to defend France itself from Marlborough's army. The sun king was eclipsed. He no longer could spare the resources necessary to execute his viceroys' plans to eliminate English America: to capture Boston and New York; to penetrate Virginia and the Carolinas; to raid Jamaica and to conquer the Leeward Islands.[67]

The altered balance of empire in America appeared as Marlborough's veteran officers were commissioned as Queen Anne's governors general. In Virginia and the Leewards, in Jamaica, Newfoundland, and New York, Marlborough's men protected England's frontiers in America from French aggression, they asserted the politics of moderation in what had been ideologically riven societies, they introduced the imperial culture of the Augustan age—with Marlborough as its imperator—into what had been colonies of England and now became provinces of a Greater Britain.

CHAPTER FOUR

Greater Britain

THE NEW STYLE New Year opened auspiciously for the queen's army and the English empire. On January 3, Guards regiments paraded the flags captured at Blenheim from the Tower of London to Westminster Hall through streets lined with cheering crowds. At a window of St. James's Palace, the Denmark-Churchill connection gathered for the last time. Queen Anne and Prince George, the duke and the duchess of Marlborough, lord Godolphin, lord and lady Fitzharding watched the triumphal procession together. The crashing salutes of "forty Guns in the Park being fired at the same time" punctuated the parade. The Household Cavalry's troopers carried thirty-four captured cavalry standards down the Strand. The Blues were followed by a battalion of the Foot Guards. Their tall pikemen bore 128 captured infantry colors through the gates of the City of London and into the royal precincts of Westminster. To conclude the duke of Marlborough's triumph, the tattered colors of Louis XIV's most famous regiments and the battered flags of France herself were hung high up on the walls of the great hall of the ancient royal palace of Westminster, every flag a martial emblem of England's new place in the world.[1]

On January 6, the City feted Marlborough and his officers, Godolphin and the ministers. After dinner, the hosts subscribed £2 million to underwrite the campaign of 1705. Parliamentary repayment of this loan was a foregone conclusion. As the duke of Marlborough resumed his seat in their house, the lords congratulated him for "The Glorious Victories your Grace has obtained at *Schellenberg* and *Hochstadt*." The Austrian empire had been rescued, "the Exorbitant Power of *France*" had been checked, and "a happy Step" had been made toward "securing the Liberties of *Europe*" by "your Grace's Conduct and Valour." Such was "the unanimous Voice of *England*, and all Her Majesty's *Allies*." Immediately afterward, the house of commons addressed the queen, asking her to reward and to memorialize Marlborough's military merit. Queen

Anne granted Marlborough and his heirs the royal manor of Woodstock and ordered Sir John Vanbrugh to build there "the Castle of Blenheim." It became the greatest English residence of the baroque age, a building comparable to Versailles itself, the palace of "the Sun King" whom Marlborough had eclipsed at the battle of Blenheim. By way of quitrent for Woodstock, 15,000 Oxfordshire acres, the dukes of Marlborough were to present the English sovereign annually, on the day of Blenheim, a banner. Its device, three golden lilies on a silver field, was the achievement of France.[2]

During March, Marlborough's army received its royal reward for the Blenheim campaign. The queen's bounty money was distributed by Marlborough's orders, with the advice of his generals, to every officer and soldier who had served at the Schellenberg or at Blenheim. Fourteen future governors general received shares of the £65,000. Among them, Alexander Spotswood received £75/15 as deputy quartermaster general, £30 as a captain of the 10th Foot (he and John Ligonier were the regiment's only surviving captains), and £30 as recompense for his wound. Spotswood went off to soak his shattered shoulder in the spa waters at Aix La Chapelle until the new campaign began. The captain general's favor extended to Spotswood's half brother. Roger Elliot took the regiment, which Marlborough had authorized him to raise from cadres of the 10th, out to garrison England's new conquest, Gibraltar, and to succeed as its governor.[3]

Gibraltar exemplified Marlborough's imperial principles and military administration. His response to news of the conquest was that Gibraltar "may be of vast use to our trade and navigation in the Mediterranean, and therefore that no cost ought to be spared to maintain it." He ordered the ordnance to spend what the governor needed to make Gibraltar impregnable (£164,361/13/6) and to place forward contracts for munitions to be stockpiled at Gibraltar for future Mediterranean conquests. As the master general issued his orders in England, however, Franco-Spanish attackers were lodged within 100 paces of the breach that their siege artillery had beaten in Gibraltar's walls. Only 100 defenders were left on their feet. They were "very ragged with hard duty," so the Guards brigadier wrote to Marlborough, but relief reached Gibraltar at the moment of the final Franco-Spanish assault. Its defeat, Marlborough saw, meant that he could develop Gibraltar as the new Tangier, the fortress-port that would reestablish England in the Mediterranean. Gibraltar's garrison culture would enhance the army's professional and imperial ethos, as Tangier had Marlborough's. "As an encouragement to all the garrison to exert themselves," Marlborough immediately promoted Gibraltar's officers and he promised further "that I shall be always ready to intercede with her Majesty for those whose good conduct may deserve it." Marlborough's constant attention to distant duty both stimulated his imperial subordinates and manifested the captain general's own continual attentions to Greater Britain.[4]

In the spring of 1705, Marlborough's military patronage was multiplied by the raising of six new regiments. Seeking promotion, veteran officers minuted their imperial service to the captain general. Major James Mountjoy reminded the duke of Marlborough that he had given him his first commission twenty years earlier. Mountjoy had served in the reconquest of Ireland. He had been promoted captain in Foulkes's regiment in 1693. Mountjoy had "suffered very great hardships" during the Wheeler-Foulkes expedition, but he had stayed on as a major in the Jamaica garrison for three years until the imperial disbandment of 1697 had put him on half pay. Now Mountjoy asked Marlborough to award him an English commission at the rank he had won fighting the French in America. Marlborough not only had Mountjoy commissioned major of a new regiment of foot, he officered the entire regiment with veterans of Foulkes's American expedition and with their sons. They would carry Stuart traditions of imperial service right through the Augustan age in America.[5]

Major Thomas Jones claimed credit from Marlborough for service in the coup of 1688. Afterward, Jones had been commissioned a captain in the 13th Foot. Marlborough had brevetted Jones as major for services on the Heaths of Peer in 1702, and then nominated him as a lieutenant colonel in the proposed Peterborough expedition to America. Many officers had refused to serve, Major Jones recalled, but he had been prepared to earn his promotion by American service. When the American expedition was downgraded, however, Jones had lost his step. Diverted from America to Iberia, Jones had been the senior English major in Portugal. Now he asked the captain general for a commission as major of a senior English corps or as lieutenant colonel of a new one. Always responsive to claims of imperial service, Marlborough made Jones major of the 13th and, before the end of the 1705 campaign, brevetted him lieutenant colonel commanding the regiment.[6]

Major Thomas Garth had been a captain in Holt's regiment in the 1693 assault on Guadeloupe. Wounded and promoted major, Garth was captured at sea. He had been imprisoned for six painful and expensive months before being exchanged and going out to Barbados as major of Governor General Russell's garrison regiment. After Russell's death, Garth took command of Barbados until the regiment was disbanded in 1697. Impressed by Garth's American service, Marlborough brevetted him lieutenant colonel.[7]

Colonel Garth's commander in the 1693 American expedition, Henry Holt, also petitioned "Marleburrow" in 1705. Holt recalled more than thirty years of military service in Tangier, Flanders, and France prior to his promotion to colonel for services in lord Churchill's coup. "Since the late revolution," Holt had served "Tenn years in ye West Indies, and often Severely Wounded." He had "Commanded as Lt. Genll in the Leeward Islands and on his Departure thence, the Govemt gave him an Ample Certificate under the Great Seal of ye said Island, of their intire Satisfaction of his Conduct & Good Service dureing his long Stay Among them." As recognition of his unsurpassed American service and his spotless service record, General Holt begged Marlborough's "Favour in preserving and preferring him in his rank amoungst the Genll Officers." Marlborough complied. Holt, whose military record was a shorthand summary of English empire, was promoted major general in the 1705 list.[8]

While many officers reminded Marlborough of their imperial service records, others parlayed less orthodox credentials as they advanced toward American commands. In his application to Marlborough for a lieutenant colonel's commission in the new levies, Elizeus Burgess explained that he had come up from Oxford after the Protestant putsch in 1688 to buy a commission in the remodeled second troop of the Life Guards. He resigned that commission after a falling-out with the Guards colonel, the duke of Ormonde. Nonetheless, Burgess accompanied Ormonde to Flanders as a volunteer. After fighting in three campaigns there, at a cost "visable to the whole army," Burgess won king William's attention and a royal promise of the next available commission in the Household Cavalry. In successive months in 1696, however, Burgess killed two dueling opponents. In the first case, Burgess was convicted of manslaughter but pled his clergy. In the second case, Burgess was indicted for murder. Rather than face trial, he bribed a party of Guards sergeants to break him out of prison. After the king cashiered the fugitive he was outlawed. These untoward events, Burgess explained in the terms characteristic of rakehell officers, were but "misfortunes" that "had no relation to the Service." Burgess's subsequent service in Flanders actually won him the king's pardon and assurance of another commission. Then Burgess fell foul of the law a third time and lost his last chance with king William. Now he applied to Marlborough for a commission.[9]

Marlborough was not inclined to commission this foul-mouthed and murderous drunkard, much less to give him field rank, but Burgess claimed the patronage of both the fastidious duke of Somerset and Marlborough's priggish son-in-law the earl of Sunderland (Marlborough refused to take Burgess's word and insisted that Somerset and Sunderland submit written recommendations). Burgess also alleged that the duke of Ormonde had offered him a commission in the Irish Guards at Dublin, but ingratiatingly, Burgess pled his "great Zeale" for active service under Marlborough: "I fagn would serve in yt Field where I may be of most use to my Country and ye Common Cause." The captain general would have none of him. Burgess had to settle for that lowest form of officer's rank, an adjutant's place in Iberia. Yet Burgess's bravery in Spain would win him a battlefield commission in the dragoons from Stanhope. After peace broke out, Stanhope saw to it that Burgess was named governor general of Massachusetts (horrified, the puritan provincials bought out the blasphemer Burgess).[10]

He was succeeded in the Massachusetts command by Samuel Shute. Captain of horse for a decade before he rode in the decisive charge at Blenheim, Shute collected the £129 due to him as a wounded cavalry captain. He used the bounty to reequip himself and find favor on the battlefields of a new campaign.

Shute's successful service in Flanders (and, it may be, in the military maneuvers which helped secure the Union with Scotland) won him Marlborough's brevet as major of horse in 1707 and lieutenant colonel of cavalry in 1709. At last, in 1716, Colonel Shute rode the Marlborough restoration (and Sunderland's particular favor) to eight years in command of Massachusetts.[11]

There was a colonelcy in 1705 for one of the duchess of Marlborough's poor relations, "Jack" Hill. His sister Abigail was now filling the gap in the queen's affections left by the duchess of Marlborough's retirement from the court. To the needy queen, "hill" seemed to be "Soe good a Creature yt I shall be glad at any time to do anything for her that is not unreasonable." Abigail had taken an opportunity, while dressing the invalid queen on May Day morning, to speak "about her brothers business. She tells me Coll: Stanhope says if the Duke of Marl: must be writt to about his parting with ye regiment, wch is a step he concluds must be made, he feares ye answer will not come before he goes, & then he shall not be able to settle his affairs hear, therfore I desire you would consider of this, & if you think the D of Marl can have no objection against it, I must own to you I should be glad the thing weare don, (tho I am against selling) because I find Mr Hill has persuaded his Sister this would be of Soe much advantage to him, yt she seems to be desirous of it, & she is Soe good a Creature." A week later the queen signed Hill's commission to succeed Stanhope as colonel of the 11th Regiment of Foot. Hill left the command of the regiment in the field to its veteran lieutenant colonel, Jasper Clayton. Clayton, with those other viceroys in the making James Mountjoy and Charles Irwin, led the 11th in Marlborough's next three campaigns. Hill only took command when the regiment left Marlborough's army and was shipped out to Spain. There it was destroyed at Almanza. In 1711, Hill sailed for America with the reconstituted corps, in command of the Canadian expedition, only to watch the men of the 11th drown in the St. Lawrence.[12]

Stanhope had sold his regiment to Hill so that he could equip himself as a general in Spain (reinforcing the widening separation between officers of the line and the general staff). Because Stanhope went to Spain at Marlborough's behest, Godolphin approved the sale to Hill. Marlborough was not consulted before the fact, however, and the sale showed that even at the height of his power, Marlborough could be bypassed by royal favor. The queen's inclination to her dresser had overcome the royal regulation, issued at Marlborough's instance, against sales outside regiments. Queen Anne's affection had advanced a markedly tory officer, at Abigail's instance, and she was Secretary Harley's client in the queen's closet. Hill's appointment was another instance of the queen's resistance (encouraged by Prince George and Admiral Churchill) to the clean sweep of tory partisans demanded by her ministers. In the spring of 1705, that combination of tory assertion and royal affection, which would pull down the moderates in Britain, threaten their imperial legates in America, and restore "blue water" imperial strategy, was already at work.

Contumacious creoles in America were as much a danger to Marlborough's legates in America as the high tories in England were to the captain general. From across the Atlantic, on February 27, 1705, that old campaigner Governor General Handasyde of Jamaica wrote to the duke of Marlborough to "congratulate your safe arrival out of all the great Dangers and hazards that your person has been exposed to." With an old soldier's sincerity, Handasyde wished the captain general "all the joy imaginable" for his victories in Germany, "the Greatness of which no tongue can express, having by your Courage and Conduct succored and relieved that Drooping Empire, out of the paws of the Lion, and given a fatall blowe to ye common Disturber of all Europe." Then Handasyde reported to the captain general the condition of an American outpost of that war. A six months' siege by epidemic disease had left the two regiments in Jamaica, "the most dangerous place in the World," 100 men short of the establishment, despite regular recruiting in England. Yet Handasyde assured Marlborough that "the Island is in ye best Posture of Defence I can possibly put it in Considering ye small Number we have to defend it."[13]

That small number was shrinking because the garrison of Port Royal had "no other lodging but under the [gun] platforms and the Heavens for the Canopee." Refusal to quarter the queen's garrison regiments was only part of the creole assembly's offensive against the royal prerogative, so Handasyde wrote Marlborough. The queen's viceroy, her regimental officers, and her patent officials all were under attack by the opposition in the assembly. The opposition had been organized by a commonwealthsman, the lawyer Hugh Totterdale, a "man of '41." Totterdale was aided and abetted by a peripatetic lawyer named Barrow. Barrow's career of "country" politics had already made him persona non grata with the chief executives of New York, the Carolinas, and Bermuda. Now Handasyde found Barrow lending English ideological meaning to Jamaican provincialism. Barrow was the precursor of those eighteenth-century commonwealthsmen whose revolutionary politics of resistance to the imperial crown and the metropolitan state, borrowed from the "country" and "commonwealth" ideologues of the 1640s and 1650s, inspired the rising resistance of American provincials to English empire.[14]

Handasyde was determined not to allow "Her Majestys Royal authority to be lessened" in Jamaica. Neither would he "attempt to encroach upon the Liberty of Her Subjects, but endeavour to keep everything in a just balance." The governor general was politically moderate, but he was confronted by an assembly, inspired by commonwealthsmen such as Barrow, who "cannot endure Kingly Government" or abide its military instruments. While the royal garrison fought in defense of Jamaican plantations against French raiders, the assembly reacted to the governor general's request for troop subsidies "as thou the Queen was going to Dragoon them." The antimilitary, antiexecutive principles of the country party in the Jamaica assembly reflected the English commonwealth doctrine of "'41," but their parliamentary tactics were up-to-date.

In Jamaica as in England, the opposition "tacked" a political program to the fiscal appropriations on which the war with France depended. Officeholders were to be excluded from assembly seats (as in the 1705 act in England that prohibited governors general—among other royal officers—from sitting in the commons). The Jamaica assembly brought "country" measures to America: they denied the right of the upper house to amend money bills; they required an oath of secrecy from representatives; and they denounced the royal executive's traditional right to appoint the clerk of the assembly and to approve, or disapprove, its choice of speaker.[15]

Handasyde deployed the prerogative's classic defenses. He forced the assembly to expel Totterdale for seditious libel. As chancellor, Handasyde disbarred both Totterdale and Barrow. As commander in chief, Handasyde ordered the reinstatement of the Scots, Dutch, and Huguenot officers whom the xenophobic assemblymen had barred from the militia. He purged the opposition leaders from the provincial army. The governor general asked his patrons in the Marlborough-Godolphin ministry to secure the queen's veto of the Jamaican "tack." Then Handasyde exercised the royal prerogative over legislative meetings: he dissolved the Jamaica assembly and called new elections. The restored officers of the reformed militia captured enough seats to put the governor general in command of the assembly. From it, he received long-term financing for the royal government of Jamaica, subsidies for the salaries of his regular officers, and the payment for their men's quarters. So "the General" had fortified "Her Majesty's Royall Authority and the Interest of old England, neither of which will ever be lost . . . without I have a drop of blood in my veins to defend them." The governor general of Jamaica wrote home to England that planter xenophobia, country politics, hatred of the army, and fear of the state were not just reflections of English commonwealth doctrine, or even expressions of traditional elites' fear of the new professional classes. Rather, Handasyde wrote, provincial exclusiveness had seized upon country doctrine to drive Jamaica toward independence. The Jamaica assembly's antipathy to the crown, to the army, and to "foreigners" was the work of "those Creoles, who will not allow themselves to be called Englishmen" and who "would have all the Imployments in their own hands, that an English man may have no Encouragement to come amongst them."[16]

As were all English newcomers to the West Indies, Handasyde was much more endangered by tropical disease than by creole politics. After just four months in Jamaica, he "lost one of the best of Wyfes, who has left a numerous family of little ones Motherless." Handasyde's military family was also ravaged. So rampant was yellow fever that the recruitment methods usual to the English army failed to fill the ravaged ranks. English regiments at home or in Europe mustered complete, then deducted the "dead pays" of the absentees from each company's payroll to meet the costs of annual recruiting. Handasyde informed Marlborough that such a system could never meet the costs of American recruiting or overcome potential soldiers' well-founded fear of West Indian disease. Besides, the governor general wrote, he could not muster complete lest Marlborough think that his subordinate in Jamaica had 800 men with the colors when there were but 500. Unless a way could be found to reinforce his garrison, Handasyde feared that he might lose the queen's island dominion to the French, the creoles, or the slaves, and so sacrifice "my Honour wch I value above all the World."[17]

Handasyde proposed that the seasoned soldiers of Livesay's Regiment in the Jamaica garrison be absorbed into the 22d and that his regiment be further enlarged by additional companies and fresh recruits. There were, Handasyde wrote, obvious advantages to the queen's service from consolidation. The average company in the 22d would then have more than seventy seasoned soldiers. An exchange of officers between the 22d and Livesay's regiments would let all those officers go home who, through lack of capital, enterprise, health, or acculturation, were not prospering in the province. Handasyde would keep the officers committed to America. Livesay could have the residue to raise a new regiment in England or Ireland. As colonel of the 22d, Handasyde admitted that consolidation would enormously benefit himself, his officers, and their regiment. It would virtually eliminate the cost of recruiting. It would establish the 22d as an overstrength corps, paid accordingly, with swollen perquisites for the officers.[18]

These were by no means all the concessions that the governor general sought for himself and his corps from the imperial high command. As a reward "on behalf of my self and Regiment" for their continued administration of Jamaica, the colonel of the 22d sought Marlborough's own promise "that neither I as a Coll. loose my Post in the Army, nor my Regiment its Corps." That is, Handasyde was to preserve his seniority among English officers and the 22d was to retain its rank in the English regiments while they served in Jamaica. Such a concession by the captain general would ensure promotion for the colonel (Handasyde received his step to brigadier general at Christmas 1705) and would preserve the regiment from disbandment "if a sudden peace should happen." The colonel explained that this was but his corps' due, "since we are of eighteen or twenty years standing, there not being many elder Regiments in the Service."[19]

The principles formulated by the governor general of Jamaica formally integrated army seniority with imperial administration. Now, not only general officers, such as Sir Bevil Granville at Barbados, but virtually all officers commanding American governments continued to rise by seniority in the army. In addition, regiments posted to imperial provinces "kept their corps" in the royal army, with all that implied for the long-term employment and military professionalism of their officers and men. These concessions to officer rank and regimental seniority meant that American governors and garrisons were fully integrated into the new British army being built by Marlborough. Marlborough also saw to it that American service conferred on both colonels and corps an unusual access to the professional concessions about pay and equipment, recruits and promotions, required for regimental success.

As Marlborough's promotion files indicate, officers had previously claimed regimental and brevet promotions as rewards for American service. Now that service would promise general's rank to army officers serving as American administrators. Handasyde, Hunter, Spotswood, and Gooch, like Granville before them, exemplified the governors general and lieutenant governors who attained general's rank in the British army while resident in the American provinces. Secure in their service, these officers led the transformation of the governments, cultures, and societies of Barbados, Jamaica, New York, New Jersey, and Virginia during the first half of the eighteenth century. Their military, political, fiscal, architectural, and scientific leadership, the fruit of transatlantic military careers open to merit, were essential elements in the conversion of English colonies into British provinces.

Such transformative duties could be dangerous. So much Handasyde made clear when he reported his regiment's repression of the latest slave revolt. "I am more apprehensive of some Bloody Design from them than from any other Enemy," the governor general explained. Slave "numbers being so very great and the whites so few, makes me wonder that they have not before destroyed us all." Such was the tropical violence of West Indian society that the danger to government from the dissident assemblymen was almost as great as that from the slaves. The governor general announced to the assembly that the 22d was on alert to thwart the opposition's plan to assassinate him and to rebel against England. The country party's declaration of war against royal government, Handasyde said to the provincial legislators, freed him to purge every militia command, every commission of the peace, every public office of profit or power. So the governor general "broke the factious knot of them that has always opposed Government." Then, taking advantage of repeated French raids, Handasyde put the island under martial law. Using Huguenot, Scots, and Dutch militia officers, he rearmed and reformed the island regiments, forced the islanders to put their slaves to building fortifications, and manned them with "trustworthy Negroes" (black enlistment in the provincial military eventually produced the West Indian black regiments). So, the governor general wrote, he had "disciplined the people, and taught them how they should behave themselves in case of an attempt by the French." Handasyde promised the imperial authorities that "Jamaica shall not be lost without the lives of the best part of us."[20]

To protect Jamaica by sea, Handasyde built up a force of privateers to do the fighting that the royal navy shunned. The governor general manned these privateers from his regiment. The men were paid on prize shares. The officers who commanded the little vessels were promised promotion "so that Bravery may meet with a Reward." The governor general's convoy saw sugar shipments worth £600,000 safely off to England. In a suitable symbiosis of war and trade, Handasyde put his French prisoners into the crews of the English merchantmen. These impressed enemies helped the ships get home. Their removal from Jamaica eliminated that local exchange of prisoners which had previously informed the enemy about English West Indian military plans and problems. The Jamaica convoy also carried home to England £200,000 in silver coin, profits of the new trade with Spanish America, trade protected by the 22d regiment's navy, bullion that would help pay Marlborough's men in Europe.[21]

Impressed by Handasyde's politics, preparedness, and profits, and his determination to protect "Her Majesty's Royal Authority and the Interest of Old England" in Jamaica, the imperial authorities concluded that the governor general and the 22d had earned military rewards: "we do not think Her Majesty can dispense with the service of so good a Regiment in Jamaica and so able a Commander in this Juncture of Affairs," the plantations commissioners declared. Marlborough agreed. He ordered the draft of Livesay's regiment into Handasyde's corps. He promised the reversion of the regimental command to Governor General Handasyde's son Roger (then a serving captain in the 22d regiment, Roger Handasyde subsequently governed Minorca and helped command Scotland). Marlborough assured the officers and men of the 22d that their unit would be preserved even in peacetime, a forecast of the enlarged, permanent, peacetime British imperial army.[22]

Marlborough was "the great Patron of all Officers" who did the work of the imperial crown in England's uneasy dependencies. So a candidate for the Guards command in Edinburgh wrote to the captain general. The dangerous disaffection of queen Anne's northern kingdom, the constant temptation it presented to French intervention, and the danger of a Stuart restoration in Scotland all were constant concerns of the captain general. On his return from the Blenheim campaign, Marlborough received a letter from John Hamilton, lord Belhaven, leader of the Hamilton interest in the Scots parliament (Belhaven's heir, after and because of the union, was commissioned governor general of Barbados, the fifth member of the Hamilton connection to receive an American command). As the captain general had saved the tottering Austrian Empire, so Belhaven begged him to reinforce the threadbare fabric of the Scots polity: "it is much the worse of the wearing." In 1705, Marlborough made the army the makeweight in the balance between Scottish independence and an imperial union.[23]

The crucial post in Scotland was that of commander in chief. Marlborough always preferred to appoint officers from his own general staff to imperial commands. He wanted Orkney to take the Scots post. The earl was not averse to government. His Virginia appointment was Hamilton family news even before he returned to England from the 1704 campaign. It was understood, however, that, as a Scot, Orkney could act in an English colony only by delegation. Therefore his returns would be limited to a £1,500 composition with the officer who held the actual Virginia command, Marlborough's veteran subordinate Governor General Edward Nott. Asked to nominate a Scots episcopal minister to the church in Virginia, Orkney explained that, "Nott is realy Governour and I am nothing, but he is to allow me so much a year out of it." Nonetheless, Orkney believed "my recommendation will have some weight." To increase that weight, that is, to win the Virginia commission outright, Orkney would have to support a union of his native Scotland with the England in which he had made his career and his home. Like every aristocratic officer, Orkney's avowed ambition was to live "a retired country life" on an expansive estate centered on a great house. For lord and lady Orkney, that house was Cliveden, overlooking the Thames, close to London, a house to be hung with tapestries of victory, ordered jointly with Marlborough from de Vos in Brussels, a house ennobled by gardens designed, at Marlborough's recommendation, given in the midst of a siege, by the Blenheim landscape architect, "Capability" Brown. Tied to England, to the captain general, and to war, Orkney flatly refused to leave active service for the snake pit of Scots politics.[24]

Marlborough next nominated Major General Robert Murray, the second-ranking Scots officer in his field force, to the northern command. The earl of Leven then wrote from Scotland to Marlborough to remind the captain general that he was militarily senior to Murray. Godolphin added that Leven's social rank and his backing for the proposed union of the kingdoms made him an apt appointee. Marlborough offered Leven the Scots ordnance office but the earl refused to be bought off. So he got the chief military command in Scotland, the government of Edinburgh Castle, and the ordnance as well. These appointments were explicitly linked to Leven's support of the union. Marlborough rewarded lesser unionists with ten or a dozen captaincies in a new Scots regiment. Not wholly trusting Leven's personal political loyalty (he had whig support), Marlborough then secured General Murray's release from the Dutch service so that he could take command of the Scots Guards, now barracked in Edinburgh Castle.[25]

The chief civil officer in Scotland was the queen's commissioner. He would direct the Scots parliament as it considered the union. Obviously, a serving army officer would be a more biddable representative of queen Anne's imperial interest than some civilian magnate. The duke of Argyll held one of the two greatest titles in the Scots peerage (the duke of Hamilton's was the other, but his own claims to the throne of Scotland made him unreliable on the question of the union). Argyll was a fighting commander of the Scots-Dutch. Marlborough considered him too young, too junior, and too hotheaded to command the queen's troops in Scotland, but he could not deny Argyll's political preeminence among the unionists. Argyll claimed to be one of the "revolution men," "well affected" to the outcomes of the 1688 coup and the champion of the Protestant succession in Scotland. So Argyll was elevated to an English peerage as the price of his service in Scotland as the queen's commissioner (as the jealous Orkney remarked, Argyll was "the fittest for a Court in the World for he will have all he askes else he will doe nothing"). Argyll was instructed to obtain from the Scots parliament the nomination of commissioners to negotiate a treaty of union with England.[26]

The Scots balked. The lowland mobs and the highland clans alike demanded a parliamentary "Act of Security." That act separated the succession to the Scots and English thrones (looking to the duke of Hamilton as king of Scotland) unless Scots grievances (primarily the loss of the Scots American investment in American empire, Darien) were redressed and a union approved on Scots (federal) terms. To this assertion of Scots independence, the English parliament replied with an "Alien Act." It threatened the Scots with economic exclusion from the English empire unless and until the Scots parliament repealed the Act of Security and moved either toward union or a shared Protestant succession to the thrones of both kingdoms.[27]

The duke of Hamilton considered the Alien Act the equivalent of an English declaration of war with Scotland, but the duke's defense of Scots independence and his own claim to the Scottish throne were compromised by an English wife, sons, estate, and by his siblings in the English armed services. Orkney reminded his brother that the Alien Act left Scotland with no alternatives to union: "its impossible to think we can subsist of ourselves, and to be a separat Nation . . . you will find noe such thing as mony in that kingdom soe soon as you have noe more commerce with England." Even Hamilton's mother, duchess Anne, advised him that Scots resistance was only useful insofar as it raised the price of union with England. "Our Independency is now a jest soe we had best make a bargain for itt" was the duke's bitter summary of the duchess's counsel, but even an apparent resistance to union would raise Hamilton's price, and Scotland's, for the loss of independence. Resistance would also enhance the power and popularity that a reputation for patriotism gave Hamilton with the mobs of Edinburgh and Glasgow and the militias of Lanarkshire and the southwest. So he threatened war.[28]

In the wake of Blenheim, no realist could doubt that war's outcome. As captain general, Marlborough had readied the senior English regiments to sail from the Dutch ports direct to Scotland. As master general of the ordnance, Marlborough resupplied the Border fortresses and dispatched engineers to modernize them. As the queen's first minister, Marlborough informed the Border governors that the queen was so antagonized by "all ye unjust unreasonable things those strange people desire" in Scotland that, if fighting began, she would order him to reinforce the Border garrisons with every available unit from the army in England. Naturally, Marlborough continued to pay particular attention to the military ability and political reliability of the officers commanding the Border garrisons.[29]

Berwick was the key to the Borders, but the illness of its governor, Marlborough's old comrade Major General Edmund Maine, threatened the duke's control of the Berwick command, weakened as it was by Marlborough's transfer of Colonel Nott from the Berwick lieutenancy to the command of Virginia. Lord North and Grey, the colonel of the 10th, who had lost a hand at Blenheim, was in line to succeed General Maine as Berwick's governor. Marlborough no more wanted to lose North and Grey in the field than he wanted to allow such a determined tory to command at Berwick. Therefore, Marlborough nominated one of his staff at Blenheim, Brigadier General Francis Palmes, to the Berwick government, for "he did in the last campaign distinguish himself very particularly." General Maine recovered completely, however, and he was able to supervise the refortification and rearmament of both Berwick and Tinmouth, represent Berwick in the English parliament of 1705, and supply Marlborough with a penetrating analysis of the Scots parliament's union debates.[30]

Marlborough called Carlisle "our Frontier Garrison" with the "troublesome neighbours to the north." Concerned at his own military inexperience, the young earl of Carlisle, governor of the town, asked Marlborough to appoint a veteran officer as his lieutenant. The captain general selected Colonel Thomas Stanwix (founder of a military family afterward memorialized in the name of a New York frontier fortress). Stanwix held the Carlisle command during the union crisis, represented the borough in parliament, and organized local forces against the French invasion attempt of 1708. Then Stanwix went out to fight in Spain. He succeeded Roger Elliot in the command of Gibraltar but, cashiered by the tories, was available to become one of Marlborough's key commanders in the suppression of the Scots rebellion of 1715.[31]

In the spring of 1705, mobs and militias threatened the Scots parliamentarians who favored the union negotiation. Not until August could Argyll and the court get the Scots parliament to even discuss the matter. Then the country party held out for parliamentary election of commissioners to negotiate a federal union. At last, the opposition was betrayed by its leader. The duke of Hamilton, after he had persuaded most of his parliamentary majority to be absent, moved that the Scots parliament invite the queen to name the Scots commissioners, knowing full well that commissioners named by the queen, on the advice of the Marlborough-Godolphin ministry, would agree to a union incorporating the kingdoms and uniting their parliaments. In February 1706, Anne named the commissioners. They, like most of the Scots elite, agreed with Orkney that "nothing will ever doe with England but an intire union." Scotland "will be an unhappy poore nation till we be joined" with England for, absent a prevalent sense of the public good among Scots leaders, "our divisions will ever keep us miserable." On the positive side, Orkney predicted that the English commissioners would offer the Scots terms "so good that it will be not in our power to refuse them." One of these terms would open English America to the Scots. As Orkney sailed with Marlborough to begin the campaign of 1706, the Scots commissioners accepted the principle that, while there would continue to be two British kingdoms, with profound differences in religion, law, and local government, the united kingdom would have the same sovereign and a single parliament, albeit one with Scots overrepresentation in both houses. In the euphoria that followed Marlborough's incredible victories that spring, the commissioners further agreed to a complete economic union. It not only opened the English empire to the Scots, it also compensated Scotland for her share of England's war debt with an "equivalent" payment of almost £400,000. Its major recipients were to be the stockholders of the Scots' failed enterprise in empire, the Darien Company. The Hamiltons were first among them. It remained to be seen if the duke of Hamilton, the Scots patriots, and the nationalist mobs and militias would permit the treaty of union to pass the parliament of Scotland.[32]

Just as Marlborough, master general of the ordnance, sent engineers to Scotland to repair the seats of royal authority, Edinburgh Castle especially, so he sent to America military engineers who extended the provincial fortifications that both protected American ports and manifested imperial power. In New York and New England during 1704 and 1705, the pioneering work was Michael Richards's. As he reminded Marlborough, Richards had helped fortify the Medway in king James's time. He had served under king William in Ireland (as Piercy Kirke's chief engineer) and in Flanders. At the siege of Namur, Richards "was soe severely wounded as never to have been able to recover himself perfectly since." After the peace of Ryswick, Richards was sent to Newfoundland, "where he very severely suffered in his health." Thence he was recalled by Marlborough to become the chief English engineer on the duke's staff.[33]

Richards's American surveys and sites were substantially extended by Colonel W. W. Römer and Captain John Redknap. They directed the construction of a modern fort on Castle Island, commanding the harbor and waterfront of Boston. It was "well filled with good workes and one hundred great guns mounted," Governor General Dudley reported to Marlborough, "but I want two good Master Gunners" for the castle and for the two batteries that were now built to protect the main ship channel, "our people here being without the skill necessary for that service." Colonel Dudley "humbly laid" plans for all these works "before his Grace the Duke of Marlborough, and hope they will be to his Lordship's satisfaction." Dudley also exacted a provincial tax from New Hampshire and commanded corvée labor from every militiaman in the province so that the English engineers could fortify Newcastle (Fort William and Mary) on Grand Island in the Piscataqua. They also supervised the construction of harbor defenses at Salem, Marblehead, and Casco Bay. To Marlborough, as the master general, the engineers sent plans for each fort and requests for ordnance from England to arm them.[34]

These fortifications were the bases from which Colonel Dudley ordered out all of the twenty sloops and many of the 2,000 men (one in five Massachusetts men served in the 1704–5 campaigns, a mobilization unequalled anywhere in Europe) who defended the frontiers of Massachusetts and New Hampshire. The war cost the Massachusetts ratepayers £30,000 a year "when the ordinary charge of Government in Peace demands not above a thousand," so Dudley reported to Marlborough. Such were the costs of the new tactics that Dudley had adopted to meet the problems of a wilderness war. He dispatched both levies and volunteers to interdict the Native American and provincial Canadian raiders directed and supplied by the French authorities, both military and religious. During the winter of 1704–5, Dudley told Marlborough, "for Twenty Days at a Time carrying their Provisions on their Backs in the Depths of the Snows," the Massachusetts soldiers had "followed the Enemy and Driven them from all their Ancient Seats to their Terror and Starving." When spring came, the governor general's sloop-borne raiders, 700 strong, coasted north from Casco Bay to the St. Croix, carrying the war to the enemy. Meanwhile, 600 men were garrisoned in frontier hamlets from Marlborough to Wells. Four hundred more men guarded the Maine outposts. Neither campaign could prevent the disaster at Deerfield in February 1704, but the town was not abandoned. The subsequent defense of Lancaster marked the first of a long string of successes that stabilized the New England frontier. As Dudley reported to Marlborough, "since the Eruption of the Indians wherein they did great Spoyl in Burning & Destroying the People in the out parts & open frontiers, I have ever since had so good intillegince of the Marches, that I have mett them every where & disapointed them so as I have not lost one village of a large open frontier of two hundred miles long, that has been beaten in and burned three times in our former troubles within fourty years past."[35]

During 1705, Dudley reestablished the Massachusetts frontier at the line it had reached in 1675, on the eve of King Philip's War, and to which it had again extended before the Abenaki raids of the 1690s. The frontier would not be rolled back again, so the governor general's strategic horizons were widening beyond the "continual hurry" of "marching of small parties all along the Frontiers." Colonel Dudley, "the least & meanest of your Grace's Servants," was inspired by Marlborough's "great & unparalleled Services & Success against the Common Enemy of Christendom, to the Establishment of her Majestys Glory, the Honour of the English armes and your Graces ever lasting triumph." So, he believed, was "every English subject in the Plantations." Dudley felt that "the People of this Province, very easy & all ways Satisfied with the Disposall of their men & moneys" in the war, now, in the light of Blenheim, would provide the infantry to attack the French sources of New England's war, Acadia and Canada itself. To convoy the Massachusetts men's assault, Dudley asked the captain general to persuade the admiralty to send out "four or five frigotts & some Mortars to remove Port Royall & Quebeck the only two places of strength belonging to the French king upon the Continent to the Northward of us." The capture of the capitals of Acadia and New France "would for ever put these Northern Provinces into a secure posture with the Indians."[36]

Dudley's proposal was delivered to the duke of Marlborough by "one of your Grace's officers, . . . who has honoured himself here in his faithful service to her Majesty." Dudley's lieutenant governor and military aide, Captain and Colonel Thomas Povey of the First Guards, had at last recovered sufficiently from "Indisposition contracted upon actuall Service in New England agt. the ffrench & Indians" to sail home. So his uncle, William Blathwayt, wrote to Marlborough when he asked the duke, as colonel of the First Guards, to extend for six months the furlough Marlborough had given Povey "for the time of his being Lieut Governr of New England, which Employment he undertook solely for the better fitting himself for the Queen's Service." So Povey had remained on Marlborough's regimental register of the First Guards, under the heading "Indian." Ill though he was, Povey had advanced the imperial war effort in America. He commanded the provincial companies which protected the New Hampshire logging crews who cut the spars for England's battleships. Colonel Povey also raised and drilled the companies of infantry that had sailed from New England to assist the defense of the English West Indies.[37]

Governor General Dudley wrote home in praise of his lieutenant, "who hath shewed himself in all occasions a very good officer," but Dudley had not been able to get the Massachusetts assembly to allocate Colonel Povey an executive salary. The legislators, the governor general noted, even protested the £100 per annum that he paid Povey as captain of the new fort on Castle Island. The majority of the Massachusetts legislators were bitterly hostile to the Guards colonel, as they were to "every loyal and good man that loves the Church of England and dependance upon H. M. Government." Indeed, the governor general himself had to build backfires with Marlborough to check the creole candidacy of Sir Charles Hobby. This merchant was pushed for the government of Massachusetts by the "unwearied applications" of the Ashursts, agents of the puritan party in both province and parliament. Dudley explained to Marlborough that he had tried to draw Hobby's fangs by commissioning him colonel of the Boston regiment, "but I never thought him capable of the Government." "Always Sensible of the deepest obligation to your Grace for my present situation in her Majestys Service," Dudley rehearsed to Marlborough his qualifications to command Massachusetts and New Hampshire: his "life and manners"; his "twenty years in the Service of the Crown" since being commissioned president of the Dominion of New England, including his decade of service in command of the Isle of Wight; his successive terms in parliament (where he had "never once failed of my Duty to that most Excellent Government"); his popularity with the loyal party in Massachusetts. This Dudley authenticated with addresses "for the Continuance of their Governour" from the provincial officers, both military and civil, "the best of all Sorts in every County." "I know this Country perfectly," Dudley told the duke, "and every hole of it, its Inhabitants their hopes & fears & Dangers, my own Estate is to be defended in Common [with theirs], and the People are Sensible and Satisfied in it." So much was demonstrated because, "notwithstanding the very severe & heavy Charge of the Warr, The Assemblys have allways Cheerfully supported the Service with men and money, and thankt my Conduct therein." Legislative support, as Marlborough knew full well, was the sine qua non of an imperial administration at war.[38]

Dudley boasted as much of his enemies as his allies. He had, the governor general wrote to the captain general, obeyed the queen's orders to extend admiralty jurisdiction to Rhode Island. He had headed the first royal court to sit in Connecticut. Dudley's regional assertion of royal government had excited the enmity of these charter governments. If he were recalled, "the noise of this People would be that I was dismissed for my strict obedience to Her Majesty's Comands." Dudley was, he wrote Marlborough, too old and too ill to recross the Atlantic to solicit for himself, "tho no indisposition has at any time hindred my Travel to ye Frontiers or Seeing the Forces at all Times sent abroad." So he had to "humbly and entirely resign my honor & hopes of her Majestys favour to your Grace's Disposall." Dudley was not disappointed. He remained in command of Massachusetts so long as Marlborough was in charge of the empire.[39]

The duke also heard during 1705 from his engineer in charge of rebuilding the defenses of Port Royal, Jamaica, and the island dominion's new provincial capital, Kingston. Lieutenant Colonel Christian Lilly was the third-ranking engineer of England. As he told the master general, "I have followed the Profession of a Souldier these two and twenty years." He was the veteran of "fifteen several sieges & Generall field battles &c," but he was now "employ'd in the most Irksome and fatiguefull as well as most dangerous Service that can be," a fourth American tour of duty. Having laid the foundations of the Jamaican citadel and capital, Colonel Lilly sailed to Barbados to design the island's only major fortification, at Needham's Point. There, Lilly reported, the governor general, Sir Bevil Granville, by modernizing the provincial army of 4,000 men, had collected £3,000 in commission fees and weapons fines. Lilly's report arrived just as Sir Bevil's kinsman John Granville had been displaced from the board of ordnance, another victim of Marlborough and Godolphin's continuing purge of high tories. Then Sir Bevil himself was replaced in Barbados by Marlborough's agent in Spain, the paymaster general Colonel Mitford Crowe. The Granvilles sought to soften the blow to Sir Bevil, because, they said, he had not made nearly as much money as governors general usually did. They proposed his transfer to the government of Guernsey. Godolphin wrote to Harley, however, that "the Duke of Marlborough has long been engaged to his own brother, C. Churchill" to command in chief the Channel island. It was actually administered by the veteran of four American governments, Virginia most recently, Sir Edmund Andros.[40]

Andros's successor in command of Virginia, Colonel Francis Nicholson, was on the outs as a high tory. A potential successor was at hand. Marlborough had previously arranged Colonel John Seymour's transfer from the First

Guards to Maryland. "It was yr Grace's solie generousity to send me abroad," Seymour recalled in March 1705. He relied upon Marlborough's protection "while I doe my duty" in the Chesapeake government. Everyone in Maryland had rejoiced at the news of Blenheim, Seymour reported. The Maryland assembly congratulated the queen on her captain general's acquisition of "Immortal Honour & the lasting Reputation of her Matys Armes and Kingdome" that he had won. In every church, Marylanders were offering "our best thanks to The Almighty in the most publique and Solemne Manner wee are capable of," their governor declared. His people joined in a chorus that rose from "the remotest plantations" in America in praise of Marlborough's "unerring Glorious conduct." Colonel Seymour sought to ride the Marlborough tide across the Chesapeake Bay. As Colonel Nicholson had been promoted from Maryland to succeed Sir Edmund Andros in Virginia, likewise, "if a Removall happen in Virginia," Seymour again asked Marlborough to promote him to the post. So Seymour could escape the Clarke plotters' attempt to overthrow his government. Maryland's jurors, "like true Americans," Seymour said (note the colonel's nationalization of creole sedition), had refused to convict the conspirators. He added that the shortage of public arms in a province still partly proprietary hindered both the repression of domestic dissidence and the defense of the western frontiers. In asking for arms immediately and promotion afterward, Colonel Seymour threw "My Selfe and the future Welfare of my poore Family" on Marlborough's goodwill, "with all dutiful Dependance by which a person of my lowe Ranke can with any sort of Confidence ever hope to obtyne a favourable Glance from one so deservedly Shining with all the Illustrious Characters imaginable."[41]

Unfortunately for Colonel Seymour, not even the most abject flattery could undo Marlborough's complicated arrangements for the command of Virginia. He had promised the chief command to Orkney and the actual administration to Parke. Orkney's appointment was publicly announced on March 29, 1705, the day on which the queen dissolved the parliament and Marlborough, with Orkney and the other generals, took ship from Harwich to Holland to open the campaign. If Parke took actual command of Virginia, however, he would not only have to share his salary with Orkney, he also feared that he would have to accept Orkney's influence in the management of the tobacco trade. Orkney would not concede control of such an essential element in the Anglo-Scots economy and the politics of the union. Parke's own tobacco went to London. Orkney would champion Glasgow. The (illegal) Scots traders in Virginia were Parke's personal and political enemies. They had not forgotten that Parke had dragged Mrs. Commissary Blair by her hair from a Bruton Parish pew, nor that he was an anglican protégé of Sir Edmund Andros. When Parke's enemies in Virginia, Scots and creoles, learned of his appointment, they informed Orkney, and he told Marlborough that Parke was "Generally hated by the people and they are affray'd they would have very little relief by the Exchange" of Parke for

Nicholson. Orkney asked Marlborough to substitute for Parke an officer "that will be agreeable to that Country and act with prudence." He did not presume to name the officer, having not yet kissed the queen's hands for the command. Nonetheless, Marlborough could not lightly oppose Orkney's wishes. Parke had his own reasons not to press Marlborough to fulfill his promise. If he took the Virginia commission, despite Orkney's opposition, Parke would have to sail with the next tobacco fleet. He had other fish to fry.[42]

First Parke exercised his claim on Marlborough's favor to obtain an independent command, one that he did not have to exercise until he saw what his fame as the bearer of the Blenheim dispatch might win him in England. Another American place was open to Parke because of Sir William Mathew's death, shortly after he had transferred from the Coldstream Guards to the Leeward Islands, and because of the capture in Spain of Mathew's son William, captain and colonel in the Coldstream. Colonel Mathew had been distinguished in the defense of Gibraltar and the capture of Barcelona. He was the heir presumptive to his father's government as well as his Leeward Island plantations, but his exchange was uncertain and the Codrington clique, for generations provincial rivals of the Mathews', welcomed the prospective government of Colonel Christopher Codrington's old messmate Daniel Parke. So the privy council passed the order to prepare Parke's commission as governor general of the Leeward Islands, "that post wch I owe singly to your Grace's countinence and favour," as Parke acknowledged to Marlborough.[43]

Parke's first concern as governor general designate of the Leeward Islands was to lobby in London for orders to reinforce or to replace the remnants of the regular regiment that garrisoned the islands. Marlborough's officers who had estates in the Leewards, Captain William West of Stringer's Regiment, for example, reminded Marlborough of their share in his victory. They prayed "that every year may add fresh lawrels to Tryumphant Blenheim." Then they asked the captain general for commissions to command elements of the Leeward Islands reinforcements. Parke proposed placing these islander officers in command of men drafted from depots in England. They, together with Whetham's seasoned soldiers from the Leeward Islands garrison, would form a new regiment. Parke's cadres would sail out to America in vessels detached from the fleet assembling in Portsmouth harbor to assault Iberia.[44]

In the meantime, Parke had to be replaced in the Virginia command. Colonel Nicholson's recall was issued on April 17. On April 20, 1705, Major Edward Nott's instructions for Virginia were approved by the queen in council. On the 25th his promotion from Berwick to Virginia became official. On May 4, Nott was at Deal, where the Virginia convoy had been held at anchor until he could board its naval escort. In his last moment in England, Nott wrote to Marlborough a letter that bears quoting in full. Its almost blasphemous obsequity, its astonishment that the bureaucrats had been compelled to cooperation by mere assumptions about Marlborough's imperial intent, and its flat declaration that the captain general dictated the command of Virginia, England's most important American colony, all made Nott's acknowledgment to Marlborough a classic of its kind. The governor general wrote to the captain general that,

> as I have infinit reason to be sure that this post of so great honor I have received is owing to your great goodness and Patronage, So would I with the greatest Gratitude Acknowledge itt as I ought ware I capable; the great Mercy we receive from ye good and great God is accepting our indeavours And I implore you to take ye will for ye deed, I beseech your Grace to allow me to observe how great an influence your favour to me has had for it made my Commission pass all ye Offices, So yt I was able to be down at this place in 27 dayes after I was declared Governer; and indeed Mr Blathwait laboured to gett me dispatched believing it was agreeable to your Sentement. I will trouble you no further then [to] intreat you to believe That ye only return I can make is to beg yt God will continue his blessings to you and your family, in this world, And to give you all happenesse & Glory in the World to come. Which shall be ye Constant Prayers of
>
> My Lord
>   Your Graces Most Obleged
>   Most Obedient
>   Most Humble
>   And Devoted
>   Servant
>   Edward Nott.[45]

While Major Nott's orders were being hurried through the mazes of Whitehall by "the imperial fixer," William Blathwayt, Daniel Parke was delayed in England. Perhaps Colonel Parke had used up Marlborough's favor in getting a second government. Certainly the spring season of military organization and departures had passed before Parke could sail. Finally, Parke's instructions were long delayed at the commission of trade and plantations. On July 26, Parke wrote to Marlborough that, had he anticipated this hiatus in his command, he "would have done myself the Honor to have waited on your Grace this Campaigne." The Leeward Island instructions were ready the next day, but Parke was already embroiled in elections for the new parliament, standing for Whitchurch. A rotten borough abides no handling. A well-bribed mayor disqualified Parke's paid voters. Parke's election petitions were scheduled to be heard in the commons on December 4, but they were lost in the extraordinary conjunction of the Scots succession crisis, the English naturalization of the Hanoverians, the annual debate about occasional conformity, and the sensational announcement that the duke of Marlborough had been created a prince of the Austro-Hungarian empire. Eight months after he was commissioned captain general and governor in chief of the Leeward Islands, Parke sailed out to his new command in his own ship, the Virginia-built *Indian King*. In parting, Parke was reassured by Godolphin that "the salary would be the same" in the Leeward Islands as in Virginia. Parke was promised by Marlborough that his promotion as an English brigadier general would occur in the course of Parke's provincial command.[46]

Colonel Parke's parliamentary efforts (like the more successful campaigns by the lieutenant governors whom Marlborough had commissioned to such garrison towns as Hull, Carlisle, and Berwick) were the preface to the Marlborough-Godolphin ministry's all-out attack on the high tories. The tories had tacked to the land tax their party's shibboleth, the bill against occasional conformity to the church of England. So the tories declared their preference for religious exclusiveness and partisan political advantage over national union and victory in the war with France. The tory tack was offensive in itself to the politically moderate and war-minded ministry, but Marlborough was especially offended because it endangered the land tax from which he had promised to pay the Prussians for the 8,000 men with whom Marlborough intended to rescue prince Eugene and win the war in Italy.[47]

The tack was defeated in the commons. This "happy turn" Marlborough considered "as great a victory" as Blenheim. Then, a separate occasional conformity bill was defeated in the lords. To declare their division from the right wing of their party, Marlborough and Godolphin voted against the bill for the first time, rather than, as previously, working behind the scenes to defeat it. Then they persuaded the queen to dissolve the parliament. In the ensuing election, Marlborough declared unlimited political war: "as to the tackers, I think the answer and method that should be taken is what is practised in all armies, that is, if the enemy give no quarter, they should have none given to them." The identity of domestic politics and foreign war was neatly put by Godolphin. Writing to Harley about Cadogan's struggle to win the seat at Woodstock, the lord treasurer declared that "this battle at Woodstock vexes me very much, what good will it do us to have Lord Marlborough beat the French abroad if the French at home must beat him." But Marlborough was not yet dug in at Woodstock. Oxfordshire was the very heart of toryism. Cadogan was "an Irishman" as well as a soldier. Only after the duke of Marlborough demanded that a poll be taken (so that, as he said, he would know who his friends were when he came to live at Blenheim) was Cadogan returned for Woodstock.[48]

Lord and lady Marlborough faced opposition even at home in St. Albans, a borough they had controlled ever since Marlborough quartered the troops of his first command there in 1683. Now the tory corporation admitted king James's freemen to vote and rejected queen Anne's, but to no avail. At Rochester, the tory admiral Sir George Rooke appeared against the Churchillian officers Shovell and Fairburne, "but with no better success than he used to do against the French." At Southampton, Mitford Crowe's electoral interest was cast to Adam de Cardonnel, the duke's secretary, and Crowe was recommissioned governor general of Barbados.[49]

"The pulse of a Nation is allways felt best at the Heart." Despite the efforts of Nottingham's magistrates, the great boroughs of London, Westminster, and Southwark all returned Marlborough moderates. The duke made sure that these decisions, replete with barbed remarks about Nottingham, were well publicized: "a little Mony can not be better placed by those who are in Power, then obliging, and engaging, those who have Wit and Satyr, that may be turned on them, nor the Enemy." Fifty-four tackers lost their seats in one of the great electoral reversals of the age. The election of 1705 produced an ideal parliament, to the minds of the Marlborough-Godolphin ministry. Whig and tory partisans were so nearly balanced that 100 government placemen could hold the balance in the house of commons. Marlborough declared that while the whigs, both lords and commons, must be rewarded for their support of the ministry, "all the care imaginable must be taken that the Queen be not in the hands of any Party, for Party is always unreasonable and unjust."[50]

Of course the whigs did not agree. To insert themselves into the ministry they determined "to drive the nail that would go." They sought the secretaryship of state for the south (including Iberia and the Americas) for one of the whig junto, Marlborough's son-in-law, the earl of Sunderland. The queen disliked Sunderland personally as arrogant and despised him politically as a republican. She considered his appointment at the whig's behest as "throwing myself into the hands of a party." With "a party man secretary of state," the queen declared to the duumvirs, she would "look upon myself tho I have the name of queen, to be in reality but their slave." Despite persistent, even impudent, pressure from Sunderland's mother-in-law, the duchess of Marlborough, the queen refused to make the appointment. Undeterred, the whigs set lady Marlborough to demand another office for her son-in-law: special envoy to the emperor. Diplomatic success, it was hoped, would help qualify Sunderland as a secretary of state.[51]

Marlborough was horrified. He shared the queen's antipathy both to party government and to Sunderland. He feared that once Sunderland was in office, his own prestige would be tied to that of his hated son-in-law. Nonetheless, the queen, pressed both by the whigs and by lady Marlborough, agreed to send Sunderland to Vienna. "Employing him on such an Embassy, for three or four Months, might properly introduce him to the Method of the Business [of the secretaryship], the Queen would be better acquainted with him, and she would soften by degrees" to the idea of his accession to the ministry, to the American secretariat and, ultimately, to replace Marlborough himself as the first minister of the crown. Such was the whig intent, milder only by a degree from the tory intent to reduce Marlborough's height by a head. Small wonder the duke was determinedly nonpartisan. He much preferred unprincipled talent. In the ministerial reshuffle of 1705, Marlborough himself nominated the formidable young parliamentarian Robert Walpole to the admiralty commission. Here began the ministerial career that would make the name Walpole the cognomen of the post-Marlborough age of Anglo-American politics.[52]

CHAPTER FIVE

Ramillies and Union

IN THE GENERATION since he had begun his ascent to power as one of James Stuart's new men, Marlborough's own imperial vision had grown to continental size, in Europe as well as in the Americas. In the spring of 1706, the captain general intended to take forty battalions and forty squadrons, all the northern European troops in English pay, and march to save Savoy, and so Italy, from France. As his British battalions and squadrons moved south, they would be joined by the Prussians, the Danes, and the Hanoverians whom he had recruited during the winter. Marlborough's army was to unite with Prince Eugene's Imperialists. Then Marlborough hoped to turn west and attack Toulon. Its capture would win control of the Mediterranean for England. More, Toulon would be the base from which Marlborough and Eugene could strike up into "the soft underbelly" of France, far removed from Vauban's formidable fortresses and obstructive Dutch generals.[1]

On May 7/18, 1706, the army of the allies took the field in Flanders and "the duke of M. ordered six hand-mills for grinding corn to be delivered to every British regiment, horse as well as foot. This occasioned a report, that he designed to march us to Italy, to the relief of the Duke of Savoy, which had been a fine jaunt indeed." The French, however, were beforehand in every theater of the war that spring. They besieged Barcelona in Spain and Turin in Savoy. They attacked and defeated the Imperial armies, both in Italy and on the Rhine, all before the British were fully in the field. Only in Portugal were the allies successful. There Galway's victory at Alcantra had, as Marlborough hoped, opened the road to Madrid. But the road to Italy was closed.[2]

Worse, the Danes, the Prussians, and the Hanoverians all made such difficulties over the terms of their contracts that they had not advanced to the rendezvous for the march to Italy. They would not even join Marlborough in Flanders for some time to come. At the same time that Marlborough heard this bad news, the states general declared that they would not allow him to take any of their native troops into Italy. On the other hand, the Dutch deputies promised Marlborough that if he stayed in the Netherlands, they would strengthen his authority over both the Dutch troops and those in the joint pay of the maritime powers. The Dutch also agreed, in principle at least, that they would strengthen their treaty commitment to support with troops the Protestant succession in both British kingdoms. This was an attractive lure. Marlborough was pressed for evidence with which to assure the electoral court of the queen's commitment, and his own, to the Hanoverian succession. The Dutch, by reemphasizing the Protestant succession to the English imperial throne as a war aim, had reminded Marlborough of the war's political center of gravity. Another imperial succession besides that of Spain was at stake in "the War of the Spanish Succession." Godolphin declared that domestic political dangers were redoubled by the conjoined crises of the succession and the union. So the lord treasurer rejoiced at "the end of the project of Italy," telling Marlborough that, "I could never swallow so well the thoughts of your being so far out of reach, and for long a time."[3]

Once again, Marlborough and his men marched toward Maestricht to open the campaign. "God knows I go with a heavy heart," the captain general wrote the lord treasurer, "for I have no prospect of doing any thing considerable, unless the french would do what I am confident they will not . . . march out of their lines, which if they do, I will most certainly attack them." The French had been fortifying the line of the Dyle for a decade. They had only to hold that line to frustrate Marlborough and wear out the allies. Louis XIV, however, was convinced that Marlborough's victory at Blenheim was a fluke. The French king was also sure that the Dutch generals would never cooperate with the English duke. Finally, Louis knew that it would be weeks if not months before the Prussians, Hanoverians, and Danes joined the allied armies. Therefore the king insisted that French aggression in every other theater, from New England to Nevis and from Italy to Spain, be matched in the Netherlands. On May 9/20, 1706, the duke of Marlborough was delighted by the news that the French had assembled every available man, crossed the Dyle, taken the camp at Tirlemont, and were in the open field at last.[4]

Marlborough instantly abandoned his plan to surprise Namur. He sent money and messengers to Copenhagen to win the release of the Danish troops from their winter quarters in the Netherlands. Simultaneously, Marlborough sent a personal plea to the commander of the Danish mercenaries to ride hard with his cavalry for the allied camp without waiting for the orders of his court. Whether or not he was reinforced, Marlborough resolved to round the headwaters of the two rivers Gheet and attack the French. "Nothing could be more happy for the Allies than a battle," Marlborough wrote to the Dutch leaders, "since I have good reason to hope, with the blessing of God, we may have a complete victory." The captain general called no council of war nor, did the new Dutch deputies demand one. Rather, the lead elements of the allied army marched west at 1:00 in the morning of Whitsunday, May 23, 1706.[5]

Cadogan, Spotswood, their color men, and a cavalry escort of 600 troopers led Marlborough's army westward. They flagged the routes toward Marlborough's objective: the village of Ramillies. Lying on high ground between the headwaters of four rivers—the two rivers Gheet, the Dyle, and the Mehaigne—Ramillies was a famous choke point and strong camp. Indeed, it was the very camp that the Dutch had declared was impregnable and to which they had predicted that the French would retreat if Marlborough passed the lines of Brabant in 1703.[6]

At 3:00 a.m. on Whitsunday, the main body of the allies, more than 55,000 strong, set out along the quartermasters' flagged routes. In eight columns, Marlborough's army struggled through twelve miles of mud. Far ahead of the mired columns, the quartermasters crossed the leveled lines of Brabant, at Merdorp, "a little after eight." Shortly afterward they had the Ramillies plateau in sight. Their mounted escort drove in parties of French light horse. Then the quartermasters, peering through the mists of morning, discovered that once again, as at Blenheim, the French had already occupied the allied objective and were deploying superior numbers of troops—some 63,000 men—in a position that offered great advantages to the defense.[7]

By 10:00 a.m., after a six-hour ride, Marlborough and Overkirk had caught up with the quartermasters. At 11:00, after further cavalry skirmishing cleared a path for them, the allied commanders rode forward to observe the French deployment. The French left lay behind the ravine formed by the springs of the Gheet. Their right was flanked by the marshes of the Mehaigne. The French front was bastioned by four stone-built villages: Taviers abutted the marshes on the French right; Ramillies itself was the center of the French line; Offus and Autréglise strengthened the French left.[8]

Orkney, in command of the allied right wing, observed that the ground was not only extremely advantageous to the French defense but also that the enemy had long planned to fight there. Marshal Villeroy and the elector of Bavaria, "on Pretence of Hunting," had mapped the battlefield during the preceding winter. They had sent their plans to Louis XIV. As an earnest of his approval they had received the Household troops of France. The Household would bear the brunt of the proposed battle and collect the credit for the inevitable victory. So it was that, on the morning of Pentecost, the French army deploying on the field of Ramillies was in all its glory: "weather and fatigue had hardly yet had time to dim its brilliancy, and it was inspired with a courage born of confidence." Outward confidence and apparent courage concealed a fatal fear. The French officers believed "that France had surpassed herself in the quality of these troops . . . that the enemy had no chance whatever of beating them in the coming conflict," but all in the same breath they added that "if defeated now we could never again hope to withstand them."[9]

Arriving early on the strong ground of their carefully calculated choice, the French extended to their left, behind the Gheet ravine, from Autréglise to Offus "a single line of the worse of their infantry, with squadrons after a scattering manner posted in their rear." Into Ramillies, the dyked and ditched village at the center of their line, the French threw twenty battalions of infantry and emplaced ten triple-barreled cannon. Across the plain of Ramillies were ranked "all the best troops of France." In three lines, each over two miles long, the Household Cavalry of Louis XIV was interlaced with choice infantry battalions and supported by artillery. On the far right flank, the village of Taviers and its satellite, Franquenay, both on the edge of the Mehaigne morass, were held by infantry. Dragoon squadrons were stationed in reserve behind the villages.[10]

Between 10:00 and 11:00 on Whitsunday morning, the allies marched onto the plateau facing the French position. The eight columns of the allied army began the complicated maneuvers by which more than 50,000 men shifted from column into line on a plain too constricted for sweeping movements. With his habitual caution, Orkney feared that the French would attack while the allies were fatally disordered. As their staffs fought chaos, Marlborough and Overkirk analyzed the French disposition. By noon, Marlborough's deployment was apparently complete. All eyes were focused on the redcoated shock troops poised against the French left.[11]

Marlborough had ranked the redcoats of his right wing, fifteen squadrons and nineteen battalions commanded by the earl of Orkney, opposite the single line of infantry and its cavalry support on the French left, apparently secure on the high ground behind the Gheet. At the village of Ramillies itself, Marlborough aimed a column of Dutch infantry headed by the Scots-Dutch brigade and commanded by the duke of Argyll. Back in Marlborough's army after a three-year absence advancing the union in Scotland, Argyll came "galloping fast through our host," a Scots private recalled, to lead the assault on Ramillies.[12]

Against the French center and the Household of Louis XIV, on the plain where the battle would be won and lost, Marlborough massed the Dutch Horse Guards and dragoons, indeed, all the allied cavalry save the British (and the still-absent Danes). To the eye of the enemy, the allied cavalry under Overkirk's command seemed to be "four dense lines like solid walls." And now, to their rear, at an angle inclining away from the front, arrived Marlborough's crucial reserve. 3,150 Danish cavalry stood still in the order of march that had brought them onto the plateau opposite Ramillies at the very end of the allied deployment. The Danes' first task was to support the four Dutch Guards battalions who formed the left flank of the allies and who were defiling along the edge of the Mehaigne morass toward Taviers and the French right.[13]

No sooner were the two armies in presence than, at 12:30 on Sunday, May 23, 1706, the allied artillery, each battery positioned by Marlborough in person, opened fire. The second allied discharge "danged doun" the color party of a French cavalry regiment. The fall of the French standard was marked as an auspicious omen by the allied infantry waiting to attack Ramillies. As the destructive barrage went on, Marlborough reemphasized the British threat against the French left flank. He ordered Orkney to march the British to the crest of the ravine which separated him from the French left wing, thinly stretched between Autréglise and Offus. In case the French generals had forgotten what the redcoats had done at the Schellenberg and at Blenheim, Louis XIV himself had warned his commanders to pay "particular attention to that part of the line which will endure the first shock of the English troops." As Clérambault had done at the Schellenberg and as Tallard had done at Blenheim, so Villeroy at Ramillies transferred choice infantry and dragoons from the center of his line to defend the flank threatened by the British battalions. This last-minute maneuver not only weakened the vital center—among the infantry Villeroy ordered to march more than a mile to a new position on his left were the Swiss Guards and two battalions of the Regiment du Roi—but it disordered the French array at the instant of battle. The first French line across the plain of Ramillies, and even the second line, now showed gaps where the withdrawn infantry battalions had been stationed between the squadrons of the Household. The third French line was reduced to scattered squadrons of dragoons and a few battalions of Swiss. Both were soon siphoned off to meet the developing Dutch attack on the French right flank at Taviers. Villeroy had originally deployed three solid lines of mixed arms. Now, in response to Marlborough's dispositions, even before the main bodies were engaged, Villeroy had fatally reduced his center to two lines, mostly horse, with intervals between the squadrons.[14]

As the French redeployed to meet the British threat, Marlborough's staff got the last of his troops into line. At 2:00 in the afternoon, the allies simultaneously attacked both flanks of the French line and the village of Ramillies at its center. On the allied left, the Dutch Guards advanced against the villages of Taviers and Franquenay, the anchors of the French right flank. On the allied right, Orkney led ten or twelve battalions of British infantry down the slopes of the Gheet ravine. The infantry waded through mud and water up to their armpits. Then they struggled up the slippery slope toward the French line. Somehow, the dragoons, Scots Greys and Royal Irish, managed to lead their mounts through the mire and up the slope in support of Orkney's infantry and under a terrific French fire. "I think I never had more shot about my ears," Orkney recalled, but the French infantry retired as the British advanced. At the head of the grenadier company of the First Guards, Orkney broke into the village of Offus.[15]

He was supported by the 16th Foot, commanded at Ramillies by its lieutenant colonel, Jasper Clayton (the governor general of Gibraltar during the siege of 1727; some of Clayton's victorious but battered regiments would be sent on to Jamaica to fight against the Maroons under the command of Governor General Robert Hunter). Clayton's officers included no fewer than four future imperial legates, Captains Hugh Drysdale and William Gooch, successively Orkney's lieutenants in command of Virginia from 1722 to 1751, and Captains John Fermor (afterward commander of Minorca) and John Montgomery (the future governor general of New York). All four of these captains had been commissioned ensigns in the 16th at the outbreak of the war. All of them would serve to the end of Marlborough's campaigns. Orkney's subsequent favor to Gooch and Drysdale, and Argyll's to Fermor and Montgomery, manifested the approval of these fighting generals for the four captains of the 16th. At Ramillies, it is likely that their regiment served successively on the right under Orkney and in the center under Argyll.[16]

The movement of the 16th from right to center was the consequence of the most important and the most controversial order of the day. The order ended the British attack on the French right at the very moment of victory, or so it seemed to Orkney. Marlborough sent ten messengers to call the earl off. Two of them reached Orkney with Marlborough's warning that his command "would be cut to pieces if it did not withdraw." The reinforced French left wing now had fifty squadrons waiting on the plains behind Offus for the British to emerge from the village. Orkney had but two regiments of dragoons in support. The French infantry called up from the center were also en route to counter the British attack. "I confess it vexed me to retire," Orkney wrote, but his Royal Scots and the First Guards covered the British withdrawal back down the slope, through the Gheet stream, and up to their original position on the ridge above. There Orkney found Cadogan waiting to explain the larger tactical issue. "Since My Lord could not attack everywhere," Cadogan said, Marlborough "would make the grand attack in the center and try to pierce there."[17]

Now that he had forced the French to weaken their center to strengthen their right, Marlborough weakened his right to strengthen his center, first with infantry for the assault on Ramillies. Cadogan conveyed the duke's order for the second line of Orkney's infantry to file away toward the allied center. They left their color parties to mark their former positions. Those positions were masked by the first British line, still stationed on the crest of the ravine. The second British line marched toward Ramillies down the swale which Marlborough had marked at the outset of the battle as a covered communication between his center and his right. Even if the enemy had observed the march of Marlborough's men from right to center, the French could not recover the forces sent to their left wing in time to reestablish their own center before Marlborough attacked. This was so because, as Marlborough had observed to his generals before the fighting began, the French lines at Ramillies were drawn on a great arc, extending from one advanced French flank at Autréglise to the other at Taviers, more than four miles away. Marlborough's men maneuvered on the chord of that arc. One of what Marlborough termed "our two great attacks" on the French center, the infantry assault on the village of Ramillies, was being reinforced along the chord by the battalions marching from the British right. The second attack, an enormous cavalry action, was in crisis on the plain of Ramillies.[18]

Between 3:00 and 3:30, as nearly 28,000 mounted men charged, broke, rallied, and charged again across the great plain of Ramillies, the duke of Marlborough gradually achieved an advantage of four to three. That weight finally broke the Maison du Roi. By 4:00, the allied advantage grew to seven to four. Those odds impelled the final, crushing allied cavalry charge. As the cavalry engaged, Marlborough built up an infantry advantage at the crucial point, just south of the Ramillies village. The duke of Marlborough thereby both saved his own life and won a great battle of abiding consequence in England's war with France for Atlantic empire.[19]

At the outset of the cavalry contest, the Dutch twice broke through the widely separated squadrons of the Franco-Bavarian first line and attacked the French Household. Twice the Maison du Roi counterattacked and drove the Dutch back. The second French counterattack nearly severed the allied lines just south of Ramillies village. "The Duke seeing this, and seeing that things went pretty well elsewhere, stuck by the weak part to make it up by his presence, and still led up new squadrons there to the charge." About 3:30, the duke led fresh Dutch dragoons to the attack. They broke. Marlborough was caught up in their rout. He fell from his horse as it leaped a ravine. He was ridden over by the fleeing dragoons. Bruised and shaken, afoot and in high boots, the captain general stumbled toward the safety of the allied lines.[20]

French dragoons saw Marlborough fall. They bore down on the fugitive duke, "hewing down all in their way," but General Murray had also seen the duke dismounted. He ran to the rescue at the head of two battalions of Swiss. Simultaneously, Marlborough's mounted aides reached their general. Captain Molesworth jumped from his horse. Colonel Bringfield, the duke's equerry, held Molesworth's stirrup for Marlborough. The captain general swung up into the saddle. As he raised his right leg, a cannon ball passed beneath it and beheaded Bringfield. "In truth," wrote Orkney, "there was no scarcity of them," but "we got the duke mounted again." Just then, Murray arrived with the Swiss. Some of the French dragoons, unable to check their charge at the duke, rode right onto the allied bayonets, "but the body of them, seeing the two battalions, shore off to the right and retir'd."[21]

While the duke was down, his chief of staff, Cadogan, saw that the moment had arrived to throw in the cavalry reserves from Orkney's right wing. "As from the duke," General Cadogan "ordered Colonel Hunter to go to the General of the horse on the right and order him to carry all the cavalry from the right . . . and immediately attack the French horse." Hunter was astounded at an order that would denude the British battalions of cavalry support. It was obvious that Cadogan was acting on his own. So Hunter repeated Cadogan's command "in the hearing of several officers and asked if this was his Grace's order to which Mr. Cadogan answered yea." Hunter took a fresh horse (he had already exhausted four mounts that day), raced to the right, persuaded a very reluctant British command to release the cavalry, and returned with Wood's and Lumley's troopers in time for the decisive charge.[22]

When his reinforcements arrived, the captain general, just as he had at Blenheim, rode along the ranks of his cavalry, calling on them for "a Home Charge." At 4:00, the "dense walls" of the allied cavalry rode forward, at a walk, knee to knee. As they approached the enemy, "they broke into a trot to gain impetus for their charge." The French Household advanced to meet them. The shock was audible for miles, even above the din of battle. The allies checked the charge of Louis XIV's Household, "surged through the gaps" between the French squadrons, enveloped the French formations and broke them. Isolated, the French infantry of the center were once again, as at Blenheim, cut down as they stood in battalion squares. The last line of French light horse did not await the allied attack. It fled westward. Marshal Villeroy and the elector of Bavaria rallied some of the Household squadrons and the Bavarian Horse Guards. They recalled the fifty squadrons they had sent from the center to their left wing. With these troops, Louis XIV's commanders formed a new line, at an oblique angle to their original position. The new Franco-Bavarian line extended west from the Ramillies village strong point to the great barrow known as "the Tomb of Ottomund," but both ends of the new French line were imperiled. The Danish cavalry had already reached the tomb. The allied infantry was about to take Ramillies village.[23]

The spearhead of the assault on Ramillies village was the Scots brigade in the Dutch service, commanded by Argyll, and Schultz's battalion of the Dutch Blue Guards. Twenty battalions of French infantry held the ditches and hedges around the village, supported by a battery of the new French triple-barreled cannon. The allies advanced under the cover of a bombardment from the batteries placed by Marlborough. Platoon fire and bayonet charges—Private John Scot sadly remembered one attack which trampled a lovely field of rye—slowly cleared the Ramillies defenses. At about 5:00, after three hours of fighting, the allies got into the village. Argyll "was himself the second or third man who with his sword in his hand broke over the enemy's trenches and chased them out of the village of Ramillies." The allies turned the triple-barreled cannon on the retreating French. As the French fell back, the leading regiments of the two British brigades detached from Orkney's right wing reached Ramillies. The Scots Fusiliers pushed the Regiment of Picardy into a swamp. There the French were dispatched by Borthwick's Scots-Dutch and Churchill's English. At 6:00, Argyll and Schultz, steadily reinforced from the right by English regiments, had in hand seven brigades, nearly 14,000 infantry. They smashed into the French foot holding the eastern end of Villeroy's new line.[24]

As the allied infantry opened their attack on Ramillies village, the Danish cavalry had slipped by Taviers, the boundary of the French right flank. The

Dutch Guards under Werdmuller, who had taken the village at the outset of the battle, now masked the twelve squadrons of dismounted dragoons that Villeroy had detached from the French center to retake Taviers. So the Danes were able to ride unopposed past the village and up onto the Ramillies plateau. At 6:00, just as the allied infantry attacked the Ramillies end of the new French line, the Danes reached the Tomb of Ottomund. They charged down on the French and Bavarian right. Assaulted from both flanks, the whole French formation began to withdraw, but "we had not got forty yards in our retreat when the word *(sauve qui peut) fly that can*, . . . put all in confusion. Then might be seen whole brigades running in disorder, the enemy pursuing close at our heels, and with regularity."[25]

The French retreat was fatally obstructed. Lines of supply wagons, abandoned by their civilian drivers, choked the road junctions. These blockages dispersed French infantry formations and exposed the separated soldiers to the swords of the Danish and Dutch cavalry. Drunk with battle and infuriated by a day of French gasconades, the allied horsemen gave no quarter. As the French fled north and west, their retreat was intercepted by the second attack of the British right wing. When the French center collapsed, the infantry remaining under Orkney's command recrossed the Gheet, climbed the slope, and drove forward around the left flank of the French. The British battalions were accompanied by the dragoons. The Scots Greys (their major, Charles Cathcart, would command the Anglo-American expedition against Cartagena in 1739, an expedition organized by two other Ramillies veterans, Spotswood and Gooch) and the Royal Irish "broke in *a la hussarde* sword in hand and at a gallop upon two battalions du Roi and killed or took them all prisoners." Orkney's British command was now astride the French routes west to the Dyle and safety. Cadogan's and Wood's cavalry charged into the village of Offus (in an action in which John Pitt, afterward governor of Bermuda, distinguished himself, as did his fellow officer in Wood's Horse, Samuel Shute, Dudley's successor in command of Massachusetts). These horse regiments, and Wyndham's, were now joined by two regiments of Dutch dragoons. Combined, the allied troopers struck the Spanish and Bavarian Horse Guards. They nearly captured both Villeroy and the elector, but their escorts sacrificed themselves while Louis XIV's marshals fled.[26]

By 7:00 on the Sunday evening, the French army was shattered. An evenly contested battle had been transformed into a rout by seven successive attacks on the French center. Now began the longest and most destructive pursuit of the century. Marlborough pushed his victorious army westward after the fleeing French. Even the Dutch, who had borne the brunt of the battle of Ramillies, followed the aged Marshal Overkirk five leagues and more down the road toward Louvain. At 2:00 a.m. on Monday, the Dutch advance guard reached Meldert. It halted for just over an hour, resting until first light. Less engaged than the Dutch on the battlefield, many of Marlborough's British regiments marched on through darkness to dawn as Whitsunday became Monday, May 24, 1706. "We look like a beaten army," Orkney wrote at 7:00 a.m., when he halted his men for their first meal in forty-eight hours. By then the allies had already counted 6,760 enemy killed, 4,328 wounded. They had taken more than 5,000 prisoners and had overrun the entire French artillery train. The cost to Marlborough's army was 1,066 killed and 2,567 wounded.[27]

So many French units had been shattered that the allies had captured more than 120 colors and standards. "It is most certain," Marlborough wrote his duchess, "that we have destroyed the greatest part of the best troupes of France." Less than half of Villeroy's original command remained under his control. At midnight, by torchlight, the defeated marshal and the weeping elector had met with their surviving staff in the marketplace at Louvain. They ordered the lines of the Dyle abandoned without a fight. By noon on Monday, Orkney and the British dragoons had crossed the Dyle and were threatening the defenses of the Brussels canal to the north. The French field army fled west more than 100 miles. The French crossed the Dender and the Scheldt and "never looked behind them till they got to Lille," the frontier of France itself. All of Brabant and most of Spanish Flanders, that is, Belgium, were open to the allies. If Marlborough could sustain his absolute command for a few months, if he could make the allies move forward without stopping to divide the military spoils of Ramillies and without debating the political future of the Spanish Netherlands, he could seize Belgium before the French recovered. So Marlborough could achieve the original allied war aim: to drive the armies of Louis XIV out of the Low Countries.[28]

At 11:00 a.m. on Monday, Marlborough temporarily halted the pursuit. His secretary reported that "I am almost dead with the fatigues of marching, fighting (or at least the fright & apprehension of it) and writing for three days together without any rest." It can be imagined how exhausted Marlborough was, but he was buoyed up by victory. While his army took a few hours to regroup and resupply, the captain general of England wrote to the lord treasurer that "the consequence of this battaile is likely to be of greater advantage then that of Blenheim, for we have now the whole summer before us, and with the blessing of God, I will make the best use of itt. For as we had no council of war before the battaile, so I hope to have none this whole campagne, and I think we may make such a campagne as may give the Queen the glory of making an honorable and safe peace, for the blessing of God is certainly with us."[29]

Marlborough sent his victory dispatches home with Colonel Michael Richards, the Newfoundland veteran who had commanded the artillery at Ramillies. Richards was honored partly as a tribute to the decisive role the twenty allied heavy guns had played in the battle and partly because he was going home anyway to take command of the artillery for "the descent." Aimed at the Cevannes, this expedition finally wound up in Spain. There Richards's exploits, and those of his soldier brothers, testified to Marlborough's willingness to invest some of his best officers, as well as seven more battalions of foot and sixteen additional squadrons of dragoons, all from his own command, in the unfinished allied agenda of "Spain and the Indies." For Marlborough grew daily more convinced that his defeat of the French and his conquest of Belgium would make it "very reasonable that King Charles should have the intier monarque of Spain."[30]

Colonel Richards reached London Thursday night, just seventy-two hours after the allies had begun their march toward Ramillies. He carried Marlborough's letters to the treasurer, the duchess, the secretaries of state, and the queen. Awakened by the rejoicing bells, Queen Anne was told by Colonel Richards that her captain general had decisively beaten a much larger French army, taken its cannon, baggage, and more than 6,000 prisoners, and that Marlborough had survived being dismounted in the melee. "I am now soe Sleepy I can hardly hold a pen," the queen wrote the duke, but she rejoiced that he had escaped and she instantly seized upon the domestic political implications of Marlborough's military triumph overseas: "I hope in God it will be a means to Confirm all good & honest people in their principalls & frighten others from being troublesom." The secretary at war elegantly epitomized the same conclusions about Ramillies' results, military and political: "France and faction are the only two enemies England has to fear, and your grace will conquer both; at least, while you beat the french you give a strength to the government, which the other dares not contend with."[31]

Godolphin did not go back to bed after Colonel Richards arrived. Rather, the lord treasurer completed his half-finished letter to the duke about the imperial aims of the Spanish succession war. The captain general, so the lord treasurer wrote, must be alert to prevent the Dutch, satisfied with the conquest of Belgium, from listening to French overtures for peace, at least until the allies took Spain, and with it America, from France. Even as these letters were addressed to the duke, the "happy" consequences of Ramillies unfolded with such speed as to confirm the duumvirs' belief that by the conquest of Belgium, the allies could also win Spain, and so access Spanish America for England.[32]

On Monday night, as Marlborough moved his army to assault the crossings of the Dyle, storm the French lines, and besiege the city of Louvain, he learned that the French had abandoned all three of these allied objectives and were in full flight for Brussels. On Tuesday, May 25, 1706, the allies crossed the Dyle, occupied Louvain, and advanced to Bethlehem on the Brussels road. Before dawn on Wednesday, the allies were on the march again and, at 10:00 a.m., a trumpeter from the governor of Brussels was brought to Marlborough to announce that a revolution was under way in the Spanish Netherlands. The governor of the capital asked Marlborough for safe passage to allied headquarters for the city magistrates and for councilors and representatives from the estates of Brabant. They wished to welcome their liberator and to negotiate with him a new government for the whole of the duchy. The captain general afterward explained to the lord treasurer that "there could not be time for orders from

England" about the form of a new government for the ancient province. The duke and the Dutch must act "before the enemy came to make a stand" and the local authorities had time to recover from the shock of the allied victory. So, when the Burgundian dignitaries reached his camp at Beaulieu (at the crossings of the Senne just five miles north of Brussels), at 4:00 on Tuesday afternoon, the captain general, "in conjunction with the [Dutch] deputies of the army," had prepared a constitution which confirmed the provincial privileges of the Joyeuse Entrée, but that also opened the government, economy, and military of Brabant to the maritime powers. The new government would confer on Marlborough and his staff unprecedented political power while giving England full commercial access to the duchy.[33]

The English duke and the Dutch deputies urged the Burgundian delegates to declare Charles III king in the Spanish Netherlands. The allied representatives assured the provincial leader that, if they proclaimed the allied candidate to the Spanish throne to be their sovereign, the allied army would protect the Catholic Church, despite the protestantism of the Dutch and English. The maritime powers' spokesmen also promised to restore to the duchy of Brabant and to its cities their traditional rights of self-government, for England and the Netherlands were the avowed champions of civil liberty. Finally, Marlborough pledged his word to the Burgundians, and he proclaimed to his army, that offenders against civilian persons or property in the domains of "his most Catholic Majesty, Charles the 3rd" would be instantly executed and their regiments collectively fined. Marlborough wrote that the proposed charter of provincial liberty (and his own promise of physical protection) "had all the good effect we could wish for." Within twenty-four hours, the delegates of city, council, and estates caught up with Marlborough—he had crossed the Senne by then and advanced to Grimsby on the road to Ghent—proclaimed their allegiance to Charles III, and admitted their subordination to the allied armies.[34]

Marlborough immediately made his new authority manifest. He commissioned General Charles Churchill governor of Brussels. Marlborough ordered his brother to occupy the capital of the Low Countries with four battalions and two squadrons. Churchill was to cooperate in the government with Jacob, baron Hop, the treasurer general of the states. Churchill was to act against both the enemies of King Charles and the partisans of the French, hopefully with the cooperation of the local magistrates. After Churchill's troops escorted Marlborough to his triumphal welcome in the provincial capital, they ousted from Brussels every prominent person who would not swear allegiance to Charles III, pay taxes to the Dutch, and trade with the English. More humble men were ordered to enlist in the allied army. Empire, on the Anglo-Dutch military and mercantile model, had occupied Brabant. There Marlborough's staff officers, the executors of an expanding empire, learned lessons they would apply in America.[35]

In Brussels, Governor General Churchill received his brother's orders to supervise the opening of trade with England (facilitated by an act of parliament, forwarded by Marlborough). The governor general's economic and political agency was the new council of state. Churchill was ordered to visit each councilor at home, sound out his political sympathies, and report them to the captain general. Marlborough then sent a full analysis of the new province's material resources and political predilections to the queen and council at Whitehall. In the meantime, Marlborough gave his exhausted men a day of rest. The Sunday, one week after Ramillies, was the first day taken from the pursuit. "Nothing could excuse the giving them so great a fatigue, especially after a battle," Marlborough wrote of his men, "but the necessity of pursuing the enemy and getting thither," to Brussels.[36]

And still the French fled. Having abandoned their wounded in Brussels, they had gotten a garrison and supplies into Antwerp, but Marlborough's march to Grimsby had threatened the French main body's communications with their own frontier. The French field force hastened to be out of Brabant altogether. Writing to Harley from the camp at Grimsby, Marlborough rejoiced in his achievement: "I think a Victory was never more compleat, nor greater Advantages made of the Success in so short a Time." Such splendid results—"more than we read of in modern history in so short a time," the duke reminded Secretary Hedges—deserved a second set of dispatches. Another of Marlborough's aides, his master of horse, Captain and Colonel John Pitt (son of the famous governor of Madras, brother of the future governor general of the Leeward Islands, himself afterward governor of Bermuda) was sent to the imperial capital. Pitt reported that the city of Antwerp had opened its gates to General Cadogan (this was premature: the city fathers had made overtures of surrender, but Cadogan had yet to reach Antwerp and the citadel would hold out for some time), that General Churchill was in full command of Brussels, that a provisional government for the duchy was in place, and that the advance would continue. The Dutch had agreed to strip the garrisons of the Netherlands of men to reinforce Marlborough's determination "to press the Enemy while the Consternation continues amongst them." The allied army was marching on Ghent, the episcopal seat of Flanders.[37]

Early on the morning of Tuesday, June 1, 1706, Pitt reached London with the news that Marlborough had conquered all Brabant and was advancing into Flanders. The guns of the Tower fired salutes all day. Every street crossing was ablaze that night. The next morning the talk of the town was that the privy council would proclaim a free trade between England and Belgium. Captain Pitt was received and rewarded by the delighted and grateful queen. "The account you send by Mr. Pitt of ye great progress you have made since ye Battle is Astonishing," Anne wrote to the duke, and she promised "by all the actions of my Life" to show Marlborough "how truly sensible I am . . . of your great & Faithfull Services to me." Pitt took the queen's letter back to the captain general, but he also bore warnings of the political pressures which would make Anne belie her promises, and he carried the advice that would fissure the Anglo-Dutch alliance in its moment of triumph. Lady Marlborough and the lord treasurer both urged the captain general to take this propitious moment to press queen Anne to permit Sunderland to enter her cabinet as secretary of state for the southern department, that is, Spain, the Mediterranean, and the Americas. This concession to the whigs, essential supporters of the war, so said Marlborough's intimates, would be eased in execution and multiplied in effect if the captain general could add to his conquests one with particular economic and political impact in England: the great port of Ostend, the obvious entrepôt for English trade with the Low Countries and a logistical link to London, independent of the Dutch.[38]

Captain Pitt found the allied army advancing toward the crossings of the River Scheldt at Gavre. If Marlborough's army could anticipate the French at the Scheldt, they could force a final battle on the frontier of France. Another victory, if his allies would let Marlborough bypass the French frontier fortresses rather than besiege them, would open the road to Paris and end the war. On May 31, however, the moment they heard of Marlborough's march from Grimsby, the French decamped. They all but abandoned Ghent in their haste to get into France ahead of the duke. Marlborough thereupon turned away from Gavre, swung north along the Scheldt, encamped at Merelbeck, and sent Cadogan to summon Ghent to surrender. The quartermaster general arrived at the eastern gate of the city just as the last French battalion cleared the western gate. Cadogan was hailed from the city walls by the citizens of Ghent. They insisted that what was true almost everywhere else in the cities of Brabant and Flanders also applied in Ghent: the Spanish and Walloon troops who held the citadel only awaited an invitation to abandon the abusive French and join the victorious allies. Marlborough's chief of staff was not about to take such a triumph on himself. Cadogan carried back to Marlborough the welcome news that Ghent would surrender without a fight. At high noon on June 3, an advance guard having occupied the city and the citadel of Ghent, the commander in chief of the allies made another triumphal entry.[39]

The duke of Marlborough now owed Cadogan a double debt: the quartermaster general had never taken any credit for issuing the decisive order at Ramillies. Now he had given his chief Ghent, the greatest of trophies from that victory. The duke decided that his loyal subordinate should have the honor of taking the surrender of Antwerp, "the most considerable city in Flanders" and seat of its parliament. The capture of Antwerp "alone in former years would have been thought good success for a whole campagne." Surely the ten or eleven battalions in the Antwerp garrison would stand a siege just sufficient to signalize not only Cadogan but also other key British commanders at Ramillies. So Marlborough ordered Orkney, as general of the British division, to send

1,000 horsemen under the command of Colonel Hunter, the executor of Cadogan's crucial order at Ramillies, to invest the city. Orkney was to follow Hunter
with sixteen battalions of infantry. Cadogan was to command the siege artillery
necessary to take the citadel. He would then accept Antwerp's surrender.[40]

When Hunter's horsemen reached the walls of Antwerp, the French commandant of the citadel came out under a flag of truce "to parly." In his train was
a local merchant. He got Hunter aside and arranged for him to communicate
with the secretary of Antwerp's Spanish governor general. The secretary asked
for terms. Hunter offered those typical of the Belgian revolution: if the Spanish
governor general could isolate the French regiments in the garrison and then
persuade his own troops to seize the citadel and surrender it to king Charles III
(that is, to his English allies), the prince and duke of Marlborough would see
to it that the governor general retained his command and that his secretary was
promoted colonel of a garrison regiment. Hunter's courier rushed these terms
to Marlborough. He agreed. The Spanish then announced that they would
"admit the English troops into the citadel at Antwerp." So the French declared
that they would negotiate as well, all before Cadogan, bringing up the artillery,
and Orkney, at the head of the infantry, arrived on the scene.[41]

Marlborough made sure that Cadogan had the honor of negotiating the
final terms of the surrender. These negotiations were protracted and delicate,
depending as they did on the vagaries of the noble governor, "a man of very
great Quality, very little Fortune, and less Understanding," as Cadogan told
Marlborough. The "Spaniards" of the garrison had also to convince (by courier to Courtrai, the rendezvous of the refugees from Ramillies) their governor
general, the elector of Bavaria, of "the impossibility of holding the Town and
keeping the People in order in case of a siege." So the elector would release
them from their promises to hold out against all odds. Then the Spanish garrison had to agree to accept the Hapsburg king, Charles, rather than the Bourbon king, Philip, as their sovereign. Having done so, they had to maneuver
the French out of the citadel, which they had been ordered to hold "to the
last extremity." To preserve appearances, the French garrison in Antwerp required that the English go through all the motions of a siege: invest the city
with Hunter's horse; emplace Cadogan's artillery to bombard it; rank Orkney's
infantry for a storm; and promise to repatriate the French garrison. Overcom-
ing all these obstacles to the surrender of Antwerp meant that there was plenty
of credit to share: Orkney told his correspondents of another of his famous
"gasconades." Marlborough's journalists saw to it that Cadogan received all the
play in the *London Gazette*. Many officers knew how much credit belonged to
Colonel Hunter, however, and Hunter's coup at Antwerp became a coffeehouse
commonplace in London.[42]

The duke of Marlborough was furious that his elaborate plan to honor his
chief of staff had been undercut. The captain general had been shaken by his
close call at Ramillies. He had been criticized by his nearest and dearest for

exposing himself: "where so much consequence turns upon one single life, you must allow your friends the liberty to think and say, that it ought not to have been done without an absolute necessity." By acting as if he were still a colonel of dragoons, the captain general had lost command of the contest. Victory had depended on Cadogan's unorthodox, independent, and timely order to Hunter. The British officers had violently criticized Cadogan, first for withdrawing their second line of infantry, then for calling away the English cavalry, and in both cases for depriving the British forces of a chance to decide the battle. One officer who had written home denouncing Cadogan was already under constant supervision, by Marlborough's orders, lest he further damage the facade of the captain general's sole command and provide more ammunition for Marlborough's political enemies. When Colonel Hunter, full of his triumph at Antwerp and expecting praise, waited on the captain general, he found Marlborough at his most chilling: "Sir, said the Duke, I think you might have trusted me to publish the service you have done." Colonel Hunter protested that he had said nothing of his actions at Antwerp to any outsider. His protests went for naught. In that moment, Robert Hunter knew that he had lost not just credit for his crowning military achievement, the capitulation of Antwerp, but the captain general's future favor, at least in Flanders. If Hunter wanted to advance his military career, he would have to look elsewhere in the empire of England.[43]

On the afternoon of June 12, 1706, the prince and duke of Marlborough was met six miles from the gates of Antwerp by the city's bishop and all his clergy. They hailed the captain general as their liberator "from the Tyrany of *France*." Three miles from the gates, the mayor and magistrates of Antwerp presented Marlborough with a great golden basin containing the keys to the city. At the city gates, the principal inhabitants of Antwerp met their deliverer with lighted torches, although it was broad daylight, and led him through cheering crowds to the episcopal palace. There it was declared that the ancient city had never before been surrendered "*to any Person, since the Great Duke of Parma, and that after a siege of twelve Months.*" The duke of Marlborough was waited on by the Spanish governor general with the honors due to royalty. For the Spanish and the Walloons knew that only the captain general could protect them from a fate worse than French tyranny, Dutch exploitation.[44]

The Dutch deputies wanted all the major fortress cities in Brabant and Flanders included in the barrier against French aggression promised them by the Grand Alliance. From those cities the Dutch government intended to extract the entire cost of the ongoing war by taxes, requisitions, and drafts. The Dutch merchants were determined to exclude even their English allies from trade with the conquered Low Countries. The first consequence of this policy of exploitation and greed was that Dutch generals refused to cooperate in the smallest advance until the necessary ammunition had been paid for by the people of Brabant and Flanders. They immediately intimated that if Marlborough and his officers in the new garrison commands abandoned them to the Dutch, the heirs of Burgundy would stage a counterrevolution in favor of the French. Regardless of who paid for the supplies, the allied armies had outdistanced their ammunition, artillery, and bread wagons. So, in the gap between the surrender of Ghent and that of Antwerp, while his army's logistical tail caught up to its main body, Marlborough took a trip to The Hague to ask the Dutch to lower their demands in Flanders and raise their support for the army there. If the Dutch would keep their promises to strip their own garrisons of troops to reinforce their army in Flanders, help England pay the Prussian and Hanoverian mercenaries, and send up siege guns and ammunition to underwrite the allied advance, and do these things quickly, while the enemy "is still in terror and consternation" and before the French could be reinforced from their army on the Rhine, Marlborough promised to capture Ostend, clear the enemy from the rest of Flanders, and attack the French frontier fortresses of Menin and Mons, all before the end of the campaign. The Dutch agreed "to make as they call it *a vigorous effort against the enemy.*" The lord treasurer concluded that the Dutch merely intended "to gather a *vigorous contribution* from French Flanders, whenever they can come at itt." He asked Marlborough to garner "some share of it for the Queen."[45]

On June 15, determined "to give the enemy no breathing time," Marlborough ordered Marshal Overkirk to besiege Ostend. The duke covered the siege by taking post with fifty battalions and ninety squadrons at Rousselaer, between Ostend and the French rendezvous at Courtrai. It had cost the duke of Parma's Spanish army 80,000 men to take Ostend the last time it fell. Nonetheless, the duke of Marlborough expected that dissension in the garrison, disaffection in the citizens, and bombardment by the English fleet under his old collaborator the Newfoundland veteran Sir Stafford Fairborne would compel Ostend's immediate surrender. Marlborough already had planned to use the port of Ostend to ship out English and Dutch regiments to raid western France and to bring in the supplies he required to invade France from the east. Marlborough had to come up in person, however, the British grenadiers had to storm the seaside fortifications, and allied siege guns had to be dug in on the captured counterscarp before the city capitulated on July 7, 1706. The magistrates of Ostend told Marlborough that it had taken Parma three years to compel their only previous surrender. Marlborough's army had taken Ostend in three weeks.[46]

With the fall of Ostend, Flanders followed Brabant into the lists of Marlborough's conquests. "So many towns have submitted since the battaile," the captain general marveled, "that it really looks more like a dream than truth." On the very day that Ostend surrendered, however, the jealousy of the Dutch forced Marlborough to decline the highest honor, the most lucrative office, and the greatest authority he had ever been offered: the quasi-regal commission as governor general of the entire Spanish Netherlands. The government of Brabant and Flanders was worth £60,000 annually to its captain general. He commanded much of the richest countryside, several of the most cultivated capitals, and a number of the chief ports of Europe. The command had been held by the elector of Bavaria. Its prestige was such that, forced to choose between holding Bavaria as a fief of the empire or retaining the Spanish Netherlands at the behest of France, the elector had chosen the latter. Marlborough was the great elector's nemesis: Blenheim had driven him from Bavaria and destroyed his bid for the Imperial throne; Ramillies had forced the elector from the Low Countries. After Blenheim, the emperor had awarded Marlborough princely rank in the empire. After Ramillies, he offered the substance of sovereignty, the governor generalship of the Spanish Netherlands.[47]

The Dutch were appalled by an appointment which might reverse Marlborough's avowed intent to take England out of Flanders after the war. Certainly the captain general was determined to share in the new government, if only for fear that the Dutch would "cook up such a one as may spoyl all." His brother already commanded in Brussels. Now Ostend gave the captain general of England direct communications across the Channel. The duke had previously promised the councils and estates of Flanders and Brabant that, acting for the queen of England, he would assure them of a moderate government, limited in its taxes and restrained in its military requisitions, respectful of their religious and civil liberties. The queen and the lord treasurer were delighted at this prospect of power for the captain general and for England (the duchess opposed it, as she had every elevation of Marlborough's dignity since the revolution). The queen assured the duke that she would be delighted, "both for your particular, & ye good of ye Common Cause, yt yu had ye Government of Flanders in your hands." English approval only intensified Dutch anger. So angry were the states general, so profound was the alarm of the Dutch financiers, so obvious was the jealousy of the Dutch field deputies, and so deep was the hostility of the Dutch military to Marlborough's command of the Spanish Netherlands that, to preserve the Grand Alliance, Marlborough declined the emperor's commission.[48]

"Jealousy itself could not regard such a refusal but as the mark of a magnanimity, of which History furnishes no example." So the secretary of the Dutch council of state wrote to Marlborough. The duke indeed had put the lie to all charges, contemporary or modern, that he allowed his avarice or his ambition to overcome his sense of public duty. The man who had begun public life as a page had now renounced a principality. Having done so, as he replied to the Dutch secretary, the duke felt himself able to act the honest broker in reconciling allied conflicts about the government of the southern Netherlands. He convinced the Dutch that it was worth their while to stay in the war. He assured the Imperialists that he would protect their prerogatives in the province until peace returned them the government. He promised the people of the conquered countries that the queen of England would secure their privileges, religious and political. The captain general told them all that "the Queen never had, nor will have, the least thought of appropriating any thing of these countries to herself." Acting as the arbitrator of the allies, Marlborough rejected the Dutch declaration that they alone would govern the conquests. He insisted instead upon the reerection of the Burgundian council of state. He recalled George Stepney from Vienna. The veteran diplomat, member of the board of trade and longtime imperial colleague of Blathwayt and Marlborough, would act for England, and for her captain general, in the Anglo-Dutch condominium now established at Brussels. On Stepney's death in 1707, he was replaced by Cadogan as England's envoy extraordinary. The commission to the quartermaster general reiterated Marlborough's reliance on his general staff for the administration of conquered provinces everywhere in England's expanding imperial ambit.[49]

Marlborough made it clear to his deputies in the provincial administration that "our chief aim ought to be to satisfy the people and make them easy under the present administration." Respect for provincial law, custom, and religion was essential, Marlborough told his military administrators, if only because the allies could detach but small garrisons and "must depend in some measure upon the faithfulness of the inhabitants." Taxes ought to take second place to tranquility: "the collecting at present a little money more or less ought not, in my opinion, to come in competition in a matter of this moment." Marlborough was determined to conduct an accommodating, legitimate, and moderate administration of the occupied provinces, "quieting the minds of the people and putting them in a good humour." Such were the lessons the captain general taught his staff of future American administrators. On both continents, however, the self-interest of local elites, the tensions of transoceanic politics, and the abiding enmity of France all were the enemies of Marlborough's moderation. Its success in Flanders depended on the like moderation by the restored Burgundian council of state, the Dutch and Imperialists, and the English political parties. None was forthcoming. French diplomacy successfully roused burgher resentment at allied exactions, reminded the Dutch that their republic was being exhausted to build English empire, told the Imperialists that English whigs would support Dutch republicans, and stirred up tory resentment at Dutch ingratitude and greed.[50]

Allied arguments about the government of the southern Netherlands also envenomed their negotiations about the demands they would make on France as the price of peace. Immediately after Ramillies, Louis XIV approached the pensioner of Holland to negotiate a peace. Heinsius informed Marlborough. The captain general composed the preliminary terms that the allies should offer France. These terms were essentially those that Marlborough had put forward in 1701 as the basis of the Grand Alliance against France, but they were amplified by the victories of 1704 to include the conquest of Gibraltar and of 1706, which had added Minorca, Flanders, and Brabant. In Marlborough's preliminaries, the English made up for their "not pretending to any conquest or increase of dominion" in the Netherlands by demanding Gibraltar and

Minorca and by "leaving room" to demand the recovery of French conquests in America. Moreover, England would retain any American conquests. As they had informed the captain general, the governors general from Virginia to Massachusetts already had in view extraordinary expansions of "her Matys American Dominions." The northern frontiers of New England were to be restored to the Kennebec and extended to Acadia and Nova Scotia. West and northwest from New York, English empire should include the territories claimed or controlled by England's Iroquoian allies. Since 1684, Marlborough had demanded the withdrawal of the French not only from the conquests made by the Five Nations but also from what Marlborough called "encroachments and usurpations on the dominions of England in Newfoundland and Hudson's Bay, and elsewhere in the Indies." Now, as the directors of the Hudson's Bay Company wrote to their former governor, "the same Spirit that lead your Grace to conquer for Great Brittaine in Europe will guide Your Heroick mind, never to consent to an Article by which the Queen shall Relinquish So considerable a part of her Matys American Dominions" to the French. In the autumn of 1706, however, the peace negotiations by which France would make these extensive concessions to English empire were suspended. Marlborough would not concede Italian kingdoms to Philip of France (as a consolation for losing Spain and Spanish America to Charles of Austria). Louis XIV was no more willing to admit English pretensions to trade and territory in America than he ever had been.[51]

The allied contest for power and profit in Flanders and Brabant was related to America in other ways than the suspended peace negotiations. For example, it crippled the allied response to the French devastation of Nevis. Under some pressure from London, Marlborough had outlined an English relief expedition to the Leewards, but the Dutch resented being left out of a force that might go on to make a larger assault on French interests in America. Again, the Dutch apprehended that England alone would win the war in America. So the Dutch pledged ships (which, in the end, they could not supply) to the expedition. Characteristically, they also proposed to add immediate profit to the strategic plan by having the squadron go on from the relief of the Leewards to intercept the Spanish American treasure fleet before it could reach French-controlled ports. This hoary scheme, the dream of Dutch and English sea rovers for two centuries, together with expanded American objectives for the Leeward Island relief fleet, seemed doubly dubious to Marlborough, given a decade of disastrous American expeditions: "I always see soe many accedents happen to almost every thing that is projected for the Sea, that I have little hopes for Success, but what is right ought to be attempted."[52]

His attention drawn anew to the West Indies, Marlborough reviewed Daniel Parke's proposal that the officers of Colonel Whetham's regiment be recalled from the Leeward Islands to reraise their corps, that Whetham's surviving seasoned soldiers remain under Parke's command, and that they be reinforced with a large number of men and a few officers. The arrangement, as Parke wrote to Marlborough, "will save the Queen one halfe the Expense" of a full regiment (Parke knew his chief's inclination to an economical empire) "and be more agreeable to the Planters by Easing them of the Burthen (as they deem it) of Quartering so many officers." In Parke's Leeward Islands, as in Handasyde's Jamaica, the provincial elite valued English soldiers' skills as fighters, overseers, and laborers, but they resented imperial officers as military, economic, and political competitors.[53]

Meanwhile, on July 23, 1706, Marlborough had marched the allied armies south to invest Menin, Vauban's masterpiece of fortification. Marlborough would have preferred to attack Mons. Its capture would both drive the elector of Bavaria from his temporary capital and open the road to Paris for the next campaign. The Dutch generals thought the siege of Mons too hazardous. The Dutch commissars considered that Mons would consume more ammunition than Brabant and Flanders would pay for. The Dutch statesmen had no stomach for the further English aggrandizement that the capture of Mons might entail. Marlborough had to settle for Menin.[54]

On August 16, French raiders beat up Marlborough's foragers. Brigadier General Cadogan was reported missing. The captain general was agonized by the loss of his chief of staff, "for he loved me, and I could rely on him. . . . I shall not be quiet till I know his fate." It took Marlborough just two days to find out that Cadogan was a prisoner at Tournai, to exchange the brigadier for a major general (a marquis, moreover) captured at Ramillies, and to express his relief by promising Cadogan that, at the end of the 1706 campaign, he would succeed Charles Churchill, the new governor of Guernsey, as lieutenant of the Tower of London. From the moment that Churchill's transfer had been rumored, Marlborough had been besieged by "applications" for his command in the Tower. In reply, the captain general wrote to the lord treasurer a letter which illuminates the interaction of the general, the treasurer, and the queen in imperial appointments. "I beg you would not be ingag'd, and that the queen will gratifie me on this occasion" of the Tower lieutenancy, Marlborough wrote. He went on, "I wou'd not have the place disposed as yet, but when I shall think it is a proper time, I wou'd then beg the Queen would be pleased to lett Brigadier Cadogan have itt, since it will be a provision for him in time of Peace." The captain general admitted that he had let lord North and Grey, the colonel of the 10th, know that he might expect the post, but the colonel had voted with the tory right in the previous "winter campaign" in parliament. Then too, nearly losing Cadogan had powerfully reminded Marlborough of the particular value of his chief of staff (a value that Cadogan shared with the other officers of the captain general's staff who earned imperial commands): "as I wou'd put my life in his hands, so I will be answerable for his faithfulness, and Duty to the Queen. I have for the Queen's service oblig'd him in this Warr to expose his life very often, so that in Justice I owe him this good office." Godolphin endorsed

Marlborough's letter "read to Mrs Morley," and he wrote the captain general that "the Queen likes your thought for Cadogan, & will keep that matter as it is till you come" home to make another round of appointments to the officer executive of the empire.[55]

With the help of Cadogan and the general staff, Marlborough conducted against Menin what his officers considered "the best-managed operation of the war." The duke commanded an exiguous covering force, far outnumbered by the new French field army recruited from the Rhine and commanded by the duke of Vendôme, himself recalled from the brink of success at the siege of Turin, the capital of Savoy and the key to Italy. So had Marlborough's success at Ramillies saved Savoy and opened northern Italy to the allies. Outnumbered though he now was before Menin, Marlborough feared no enemy attack, "for our men are in heart and theirs are cowed."[56]

In the key assault on Menin, the British infantry paid for "standing by" at Ramillies. Opening the trenches for the siege, the British took heavy losses from French sorties even before they (together with the newly arrived Prussians) stormed the Menin counterscarp. Commanded by Orkney in person, with Argyll as his brigadier, the allies exploded the mines that their engineers had driven below a salient angle of the Menin defenses. Before the dust settled, the attackers, led by the Royal Irish Regiment, had reached the enemy palisades at the foot of the glacis. The British troops hacked and pushed through the palisades, charged up the glacis, threw in their grenades, and followed them down into the galleries of the covered way. They killed all of the enemy who did not flee. Then the storm troops had to withstand two hours of flanking fire (from the ravelins that projected into the counterscarp) and direct shot (from embrasures in the curtain wall) before support troops could dig artillery emplacements, a parallel, and communications trenches into the slope behind them. When the attackers were relieved, they had sustained 1,400 casualties. Exhausted himself, Orkney nonetheless took care to praise Argyll to Marlborough as "very active" and to report that "our men behaved extremely well."[57]

In just two days, the allied batteries dug in on the Menin glacis beat the inner defenses into rubble. On August 22, 1706, "the enemy at Menin placed a white flag on their breach." "And as I was there," Marlborough wrote, "I imediately ordered an exchange of ostiges. We have this morning posession of on of their gates." Marlborough recognized Argyll's bravery by giving him command of the Bruges Gate at Menin. Through that gate, under Argyll's eye, the 4,500 survivors of the defeated garrison marched out past Marlborough and his staff. From the captured works, Marlborough dismounted artillery embossed with the arms of England, lost by the English under William III at Landen thirteen years earlier. Sent home as trophies, these great guns manifested both Marlborough's vast military superiority to William and the enormous elevation of English arms under Anne.[58]

As he had honored one Scots commander at the surrender of Menin, he gave another its government. The earl of Orkney, governor general of Virginia and now of Menin, relieved the tedium of rebuilding the city walls and leveling the adjacent French frontier fortifications with a round of elegant entertainments. After Orkney attended Marlborough's annual Blenheim Day dinner for "the general officers that were with me at the battaile," Orkney invited his chief to dine and to hear the hautbois of the Guards play the latest Parisian airs. Across the Atlantic, another officer and governor rejoiced that Marlborough's "Calm Conduct" had conquered Flanders and Brabant from France, both "to the everlasting honour of the English Nation," and to the growth of Marlborough's reputation and of English authority "throughout the Amaz'd World."[59]

It was the universal belief of contemporaries that Marlborough's victory at Ramillies impelled the union of the British kingdoms and, as Marlborough was fully aware, it was the union that would bring Scotland fully into the Anglo-American empire. The union of the kingdoms, the opening of the empire to Scotland, and the preeminence of the army in imperial administration meant that Scots generals became the heads of new imperial "interests." One of these new connections in army and empire was the duke of Argyll. Ramillies and Menin capped the military reputation of the young duke. A reluctant Marlborough admitted that Argyll "has really behaved himselfe all this campagne with great willingness and corage." To reward Argyll's military bravery and to encourage his return to Scotland to forward the union, Marlborough had to give way to Argyll's exorbitant demands for promotion. He had the young nobleman successively advanced from colonel and brigadier in the Scots-Dutch service to the command of a senior English regiment and to the rank of major general in the queen's service. To make the point of military merit, Marlborough had both of Argyll's English commissions backdated to the day of Ramillies, but no one missed the political premise of Argyll's promotion. As lord Dalrymple wrote home to Scotland from Marlborough's camp, the promotion of Scots officers after the battle of Ramillies and the conquest of the Low Countries was one way "the Duke of Marlborough's good success will help our part digest the Union, tho' a good part of the members [of the Scots parliament] should swallow it with a little reluctancy." When the military campaign of 1706 in Flanders was over, the union campaign in Scotland would depend upon Argyll's leadership.[60]

"My Lord Mariborrow has now got the Duke of Argyle in a very good humour on making or promising to make him Major-Generall, upon which his Grace has promised to goe to the Parliament and serve the Queen in the affaire of the Union," so wrote a Scots officer. Marlborough asked the queen to approve Argyll's commissions immediately, "so that he may not have an excuse for staying" in London, instead of hurrying north to meet the Scots parliament.

Writing to the lord treasurer, the captain general even put words in her majesty's mouth: "if the Queen will be pleas'd to tel him that she takes it very kindly, his going to Scotland at this time, and that she is very glad of his coming home safe after so much danger, this will please him, and you must not let him stay."[61]

Marlborough also allowed Argyll to "touch the appointments" to the Scots Horse Guards (after the union the 4th Troop of the Royals), the colonelcy of which Marlborough had previously obtained for the Scots grandee. This military-political bargain had imperial consequences outside of Britain and outlasting the age of Marlborough. Argyll immediately nominated lord George Forbes of Holt's Regiment (Forbes's brother, a captain in the Royal Scots and Orkney's friend, had been killed at Blenheim) to a captaincy in the troop. Forbes succeeded Argyll himself in command of Minorca in 1718 and became governor general of the Leeward Islands in 1729. To replace Forbes in the Horse Guards, Argyll would nominate Charles Dilke, who also became a governor general of the Leeward Islands. Between 1706 and 1710, Argyll parlayed military patronage and Scots politics to become Marlborough's most effective imperial rival, the officer to whom such provincial oligarchs as William Byrd II of Virginia applied (in vain) for American governments. Even the careers in the colonies of such Campbells as lord Loudoun were founded in Argyll's achievements at Ramillies, at Menin, and in Edinburgh.[62]

Despite Argyll's ascent, the earl of Orkney remained Marlborough's senior Scots officer and the leading beneficiary of his military patronage, whether to Scottish or American commands. "My Lord Orkney who, both by his quality of oldest [eldest] Lieutenant General of the foot and being at the head of the [10,000] Scots troops here, has a right both to advise and to be bold with the Duke in what relates to Scots regiments," but Orkney's compatriots complained that he was "modest and shy to meddle," unwilling to press Marlborough unless he thought that the captain general was already "inclined" toward a particular officer. In October 1705, however, Orkney's intervention with Marlborough ensured that the command of the Cameronians, a particularly pious, Presbyterian, and parochial unit, raised in Hamilton territory, was determined by regimental seniority, and that every Cameronian officer was promoted in due course, including that dour diarist, Major John Blackadder. He would hold Glasgow and Stirling for Hanover and Britain for, as Blackadder wrote, the Cameronians were firmly founded on "a Revolution foot." Indeed, "most of our army here are Whigs and staunch ones." The Cameronians' marked national, sectarian, and political partisanships, and the regimental officers' astute appeal to the queen's ministers in Scotland, also helped Orkney overcome the united application to Marlborough by the English brigadiers for Colonel George Macartney's appointment to command the Cameronians. Macartney had to seek an American command instead.[63]

The interlocked military and political structures of imperial commands, in England and Scotland, Europe and America, were further exposed when the lord treasurer reported the death of Colonel Edward Nott, governor general of Virginia, a command he had held by an informal compromise with the earl of Orkney. As a Scot, Orkney could not command an English dominion. Godolphin now wrote to Marlborough, "I make no doubt but my Lord Orkney will seize upon that [government], and I don't see why one might not persuade him to go down to Scotland and vote for the Union, without which he can't be capable of it." Orkney was very sick with a fever contracted at the siege of Menin, but he agreed to take leave from his government of that city to organize Scots support for the union. As Godolphin had implied, the union, by making all Scots natural-born subjects of the imperial queen of Great Britain and the British dominions, would enable Orkney both to take title to the Virginia command himself and to claim from Marlborough the nomination of one of Orkney's own Scots military clients as the queen's lieutenant governor. The union would not only open royal governments in America to Scots officers, it would make the American provinces a field for fabled Scots ambition of every kind. The cultural and political, military and economic consequences of the union of England and Scotland for the American future were enormous, but it was the Scots governors general who led the way to America for their compatriots.[64]

Of the Scottish military executives, none would be more influential in America than Colonel Robert Hunter. Smarting from Marlborough's criticism after Antwerp, Hunter was the more inclined to leave the Flanders service after he lost his best friend, lord John Hay, at the siege of Menin. The same epidemic that sickened Orkney had killed Hay, the colonel of the Scots Greys and a son of the marquis of Tweeddale. The marquis's vote, those of his family's interest, and of their political faction, the so-called squadrone volante, might decide the question of union in the parliament of Scotland. Hunter had nursed lord John Hay throughout his final illness. Hunter obtained leave from Marlborough to take Hay's last words to Elizabeth, lady Hay, an heiress in both British kingdoms. She married the messenger. At just this moment, Orkney was urging Marlborough to be "as Civill as you can" to the whole Hay connection. For if the marquis of "Tweedale and that family coud be brought about it might goe a great way to Effectuate the Union." Marlborough ordered Argyll to save a commission in the Scots Horse Guards for lord William Hay "as well as for his own merit as in memory of Lord John Hay; and likewise in consideration of the good services the Marques of Twedale is now doing the Queen in Parliament." Then Marlborough accepted Orkney's nomination of Colonel Robert Hunter as lieutenant governor and commander in chief of Virginia. Besides Orkney's nomination, his Hay family connection, and his distinguished military service, Hunter was the particular friend of lord Dalrymple, heir to the earl of Stair. A leader of the squadrone volante, the earl died while pleading on behalf of the union in the Scots parliament and his son became Hunter's "good lord" and a British field marshal.[65]

The last parliament of an independent Scotland was adjourned until October 3, 1706, so that Argyll, at the head of Marlborough's "reinforcement" for the unionists, could arrive from the Flanders front, and so that the Guards in Edinburgh could be reinforced to resist the city mob. "The mob of this town are mad against us," the union manager wrote. The Edinburgh mob was an estate in itself: "Mr. Fletcher said it was the true spirit of this country, for the Reformation and Revolution were both brought about by them." It was the mob that had so intimidated the Scots privy council that, despite Queen Anne's call for a reprieve, the councilors ordered the judicial murder of officers of an English ship, the *Worcester*, as revenge for the Darien disaster. Now the duke of Hamilton's "patriot" party inflamed the people of the capital city by telling them "they were to loss the Crown and would be taxt excessively." Threatened with an English executive and parliamentary taxation, the Edinburgh street forced the adjournment of the parliament. Then they attacked the house of the leading unionist, "calling out that they would massacre him for being a betrayer and seller of his country."[66]

Newly arrived in Edinburgh, Argyll was at lord Loudoun's for dinner with the unionist lords when the mob rose. The duke led the lords through the howling populace down the Canongate to the palace of Holyrood House. Assembling the available privy councilors, Argyll obtained their order that he, as colonel of the Guards, should call the garrison of Edinburgh Castle down into the city. "The regiment of Foot Guards was got together immediately," ordered to fire on the mob if attacked, and exempted from arraignment for murder if killing proved to be necessary. The Guards quickly seized the city gates and cleared the streets. The next day the opposition "complained of Guards being sent in to town to overawe the Parliament," but the city was cowed. The Scots "patriots" then organized popular petitions against an incorporating union, Scots loss of liberty, and English parliamentary taxation by acts of trade. The patriots roused the Presbyterian clergy to complain of ecclesiastical tyranny (that is, toleration of the few remaining episcopalian clergy). They sent circular letters to their country kinsmen to muster their militias to "give law to the Parliament," if necessary by civil war. The patterns of revolution were laid down, not just for Scotland but also for America.[67]

Marlborough considered the Scots crisis "the most dangerous since Her Majesty's coming to the Crown." In its midst, on November 18, 1706, he arrived in London from The Hague. In every forum, the captain general declared himself for the union and he promised every support to the unionists. He was alerted by Shute, however, that the number of troops now in Edinburgh could do no more than keep down the city mob. The agitation for independence was spreading across the northern kingdom. Outside the capital, garrisons were unreliable because they feared "that after the Union they shall either be disbanded or sent to the plantations" (as regiments opposed to Dutch William had been sent to the West Indies). The queen's commissioner to the Scots parliament wrote to Marlborough, rejoicing in his arrival from Flanders, repeating that popular hostility to the union might affect the Scots troops, and begging Marlborough to hasten English troops to the Borders, for "its easier to discourage the takeing up of armes then to reduce men once in rebellion in a popular cause." The parliament in Edinburgh could not endorse the union "if the country rise and force us from hence."[68]

Marlborough called up the forces of the empire to secure the union. He ordered all available troops to march to the Scots Borders "to be ready in case there was occasion for them" in Scotland. General Carpenter's cavalry, shipped over from Ireland, rode into Leeds. The earl of Essex's dragoons occupied Lancaster, that seat of lost causes. Livesay's new regiment, raised by officers just returned from Jamaica, marched to York. Barrymore's foot, rebuilt by cadres returned from Spain, was headquartered at Hull, with detachments stationed along the Borders. Stripping the army in England, the captain general kept only the Horse Guards and part of the Foot Guards to garrison London. Every other regiment in England was sent north to support the union. Marlborough concentrated three regiments of foot at the fortress town of Berwick, including Orrery's and Erle's foot from the Irish establishment. Four more regiments were concentrated in the northern Irish ports. All the forces had orders to move to repress any rising in Scotland. "You may be sure the forces on the Borders encourage us not a little," the duke of Queensbury wrote Marlborough, "and has quite different effects on the opposers."[69]

On December 7, 1706, Marlborough informed the Scots commander in chief, the earl of Leven, that not only was there a field force of English infantry at Berwick and that Marlborough had added a regiment of Irish dragoons to the troops in Belfast, but also that he had now ordered the entire regiment of the Horse Guards, 800 strong, to ride hard from London for the Borders. The captain general considered cavalry "more usefull than thrice there number of foot" for political police work. He reassured Leven "that all the troops on your borders, as well as those in the North of Ireland are directed to hasten to your assistance" whenever the queen's general in Scotland called. Marlborough hoped, however, that the Scots parliament's suspension of the provision in the Act of Security "that allows the country to arm will entirely dispel the cloud that seems to be hanging over you, and that the Parlament will soon go through this good work so much desired by all who wish well to these nations."[70]

The Scots commander replied to Marlborough that "your Grace's provident care in sending so many horse and foot to our borders has contributed very much to our quiet," but both danger and deliverance were closer at hand. Led by jacobite veterans of George Douglas, the earl of Dumbarton's regiment (Dumbarton was Hamilton's uncle), the Glasgow mob marched toward Edinburgh. Encamped at Hamilton, the mob put "anybody that seems sober or moderate in hazard of his life if he does not speak against the Union." The mob leaders declared that they "would fight while their blood is warm for the independency, religion, etc. of their country against England." They were deflected from Edinburgh by 200 dragoons. The dragoons even arrested the household officers of the duchess of Hamilton in order to make a case against her son, the duke. From London, the earl of Orkney warned his Hamilton kin of the ministerial opinion that "it is nothing but faction that create the confusion that appears amongst the people there and that when once the Union is gained all that ferment will be Allayed." Any armed opposition to the union, sincere or not, Orkney warned, would be crushed by the imperial authorities: "nothing will alter the measure now, let it come to what extremitys they please." The patriots had missed their chance to preserve Scottish independence, Orkney wrote, for the limitations on the power of the next sovereign in Scotland, which would have been accepted by England before Blenheim and Ramillies, were now out of court. An entire union of the two kingdoms would be required. Despite his brother's warning, the duke of Hamilton proposed to substitute an act of succession for the union treaty. He demanded that parliamentary proceedings be adjourned until the queen responded. Hamilton's proposals were voted down in the Scots parliament, but the balance of power in the streets of Edinburgh was still in play: "every day when the D[uke] of H[amilton] comes out of the house, the mob waits of him home with huzzas, and he encourages them not a little."71

In the first week of December, the convoy from the Netherlands made port in Leith. The recruiting parties from Marlborough's Scots regiments marched up to the capital. Added to lord Leven's garrison, these British veterans tipped the balance of force in Edinburgh against Hamilton's patriots. The soldiers also let it be known that Marlborough had left orders with Cadogan to ship entire English regiments to Scotland from their winter quarters in Ghent if there were either serious domestic disturbances or French military intervention. Absent either one, the patriots could only delay, debate, and demand "explanations" to the treaty. They hoped to win time for political opposition to widen in the English parliament, where the church party bridled at protections for presbyterianism, and in Scotland, where addresses against the union now emerged from every shire. The heart of "addressing" was the Hamilton stronghold of Clydesdale. Duchess Anne herself allegedly stirred presbyterian fears that, if the union passed, the kirk was in danger. Her son, the duke, appended to the union treaty a powerfully worded act to protect the kirk, in hopes that it would impede anglican ratification at Westminster.72

Despite recent reinforcements, the queen's ministers in Scotland still so feared a popular revolt that they wrote to the lord treasurer advising adjournment of the union debate. Godolphin reiterated: "orders were given, both in England and Ireland, to have troops ready upon your call; and that if it were necessary, more forces would be ordered from Flanders. The French were in no condition to send any assistance to those who might break out." The union debates should be pushed to a conclusion in Scotland, Godolphin insisted.

The French could only smuggle in ("with the Burgandie wine") rumors that the pretender had converted to protestantism, that he would soon arrive in Scotland, and that the allies had been defeated in Spain. The unionists replied with reports that reemphasized Marlborough's victories over the French. They added that December 19, 1706, had been "a kind of holy day. The Duke of Marlborrow was entertained by the City and the trophies of the last campaign were carry'd befor him, which the Queen came to see." Certainly, the union treaty, which passed the Scots parliament on January 16, 1707, was as much a trophy of Marlborough's victory at Ramillies as were any of the captured French standards, colors, and cannons on display in the imperial metropolis.[73]

From St. James's palace, the duke of Marlborough congratulated the Scots court managers and generals on an event so "very welcome to all good men that wish well to Great Britain." He rewarded an act essential to the Protestant succession and English security with the disproportionate Scots share of military commands, in the army and the empire, that marked the government of Greater Britain in the eighteenth century. Brigadier Hamilton, who had led the recruiting parties up from Leith to protect the parliament from the Edinburgh mob and the country militias, was promoted major general on Marlborough's staff. The duke of Argyll obtained the colonelcy of the Buffs from Charles Churchill (General Churchill got the Coldstream Guards on the death of lord Cutts and was named governor of Guernsey, where the aged Sir Edmund Andros was still lieutenant governor, chief bailiff, and commander in chief). Lord Leven was assured that Marlborough would not draft his exiguous garrisons to form a new regiment for the Hay family. Nonetheless, Leven could nominate as the new unit's officers some of "those who have distinguished themselves by their zeal for the public service."[74]

The Scots had traded political independence for military empire. In executing the bargain, Marlborough was not always magnanimous. By Governor General Orkney's favor and his own interest among the Scots nobility, Colonel Hunter was changing commands. Hunter expected, as did every army officer promoted to an American command, to sell his old commission to finance his voyage and pay for the household appropriate for his viceregal rank. On the eve of Hunter's taking ship for Virginia, Marlborough blocked Hunter's sale of his troop. Orkney reminded Marlborough of every regiment's corporate nature. The officers of Ross's Dragoons, Orkney wrote, would not object if "Hunter, who bought his troop, has the same liberty to sell," but to have a stranger foisted on them for any other reason would "offend the officers of the Regiment that have served long" and who, like Hunter, had risen by seniority. "If a perfect stranger come in they will think it a very great hardship." The morale of an elite regiment, proven at Blenheim and Ramillies, would be destroyed. Besides, if the duke did not let Hunter sell out, he would have to "let him Continue his pay, till he enter on pay in Virginia." Marlborough saw reason. Robert Hunter set sail to help open America to Scotland.[75]

For eighty-five years, from 1603 to 1688, while England founded an empire in America, that is, from the accession of the Stuarts to the English throne until lord Churchill's coup, the Scots parliament had been essentially a colonial assembly, incapable of empire. After 1688, liberation from the lords of the articles had enabled the Scots legislators to sponsor American colonization, but Darien had failed. As the price of their consent to union, the Scots demanded that, as "subjects of the United Kingdom of Great Britain," they should "have full freedom and intercourse of trade and navigation to and from any port or place within the said United Kingdom and the dominions and plantations thereunto belonging." Not just imperial trade but also the imperial legislature and imperial commands were opened to "the North Britons" by the union. For example, the earl of Orkney now sat in the English house of lords as one of the sixteen representative peers from Scotland. Simultaneously, he commanded Virginia (and Menin). While still governor general of Virginia, Orkney would be commissioned governor of Edinburgh Castle, lord lieutenant of Lanarkshire, and the first field marshal of the British army (Argyll succeeded him). Orkney's first Scots deputy in Virginia, Robert Hunter, went on to command New York and Jamaica. His second, Alexander Spotswood, came home from Virginia to serve as Orkney's chief of staff in Scotland. There Spotswood succeeded Charles Dubourgay, who went out to serve in Jamaica in succession to lord Archibald Hamilton, Orkney's brother. For years, Orkney "had tortured lord Marl." for military promotion for "Archy." Once lord Archibald was elected one of the forty-five Scots members of the parliament of Great Britain, the command of Jamaica was added to that of Virginia in the Hamiltons' American "interest." It extended to New England, New York, and New Jersey as well. All were dominions of what was now, more than ever before, "the Imperial Crown of Great Britain."[76]

On March 6, 1706/7, Queen Anne assented to the act that created the United Kingdom. The cannon at the Tower of London and the field artillery in Hyde Park exchanged salutes. With the martial pomp that Marlborough's triumphs had made familiar, the imperial capital celebrated another "glorious victory." To the union the British army and the queen's captain general had manifestly contributed. The Guards on parade and the artillery imparked alike displayed, as they celebrated, the authority of the imperial state. Lord Churchill's coup had secured the independence of England from France. Now, eighteen years afterward, the duke of Marlborough had achieved the imperial goals he had aimed at ever since his formative service under James Stuart. Not only was England independent of France, the British Isles were united under English command, the former English colonies, now British, in America were on the offensive against every rival, the Mediterranean was in the British ambit, national protestantism was safe from Catholic reaction, and the Netherlands were militarily secure. It remained to be seen if Marlborough could achieve total victory in the world war with France.[77]

SOLDIERS, STATESMEN, AND SACHEVERELL

The Right Hon.ᵗᵗᵉ Robert Earl of Oxford & Earl Mortimer, Baron Harley of Wigmore in the County of Hereford, One of the Lords of Her May.ᵗᵗᵉˢ most Hono.ᵗᵗᵉ Privy Council, Knight of y.ᵉ most Noble Order of y.ᵉ Garter & Lord High Treasurer of Great Britain.

Robert, earl of Oxford

In twenty years, 1702–22, England became Britain, Britain surpassed both France and Spain in Atlantic empire, and the united kingdom transformed itself. A century of revolution gave way to the arrogant assurances of an Augustan age. This sea change was managed by an ill-assorted, selfish, but ultimately successful ménage of statesmen, (disproportionately Scots) soldiers, and ecclesiastics. Many of the ministers of Queen Anne were the children of civil strife, veterans of the royal restoration, renewed rebellion, and a "glorious" revolution.

Paradoxically, Robert Harley, the leader of the tories, the party of church and crown, was the son of a parliamentary leader in the civil war. Educated as a Presbyterian, young Harley raised the troops who took Worcester at the revolution. He entered parliament as a "Commonwealthman." Greasing the squeaky wheel, King William summoned this master parliamentarian to legislate the imperial succession. Overnight, Harley became a royalist, a churchman, and a tory. "Robin the Trickster" was elected speaker, and he led the impeachment of the whig ministers for advising the partition of the Spanish empire that he himself subsequently secured. At the accession of Queen Anne, Harley became the junior triumvir, serving with Marlborough and Godolphin, but their growing dependence on the whigs persuaded Harley to play the Sacheverell card, take the treasury from Godolphin, and parlay Marlborough's victories into the South Sea Company. Harley is pictured here in 1714, at the height of his power, his impermeable countenance set off by his robes as earl of Oxford, his garter insignia, and his staff of office.

Among the tories, Oxford's chief rival was Henry St. John, here "late Lord Viscount Bolingbroke." The label of his portrait, reproduced by courtesy of the National Portrait Gallery, London, has been altered to reflect the impeachment and conviction for treason of the most brilliant and most erratic statesman of his generation. The son of an ancient, aristocratic family divided by the civil wars, St. John was educated by dissenting ministers, but the mature man took as his example the Athenian Alcibiades—brilliant orator, political chameleon, and moral delinquent. The tories were in power when St. John entered parliament in 1701, so he joined them. An avowed admirer of Marlborough, St. John became secretary at war in 1704. He was

Henry, late viscount Bolingbroke, by White after Murray, © National Portrait Gallery, London

forced out, with Harley, in 1708. The tory revenge of 1710 found St. John secretary of state for the southern department, America included. He launched the "blue water" alternative to Marlborough's continental focus, the disastrous Quebec expedition of 1711. Two years later, St. John ditched both the duke and the Dutch when he negotiated the separate peace with France. Elevated to the peerage, Bolingbroke panicked at the regime change, fled to France, joined the pretender, and was attainted. After a decade, Bolingbroke returned to England. Public office was closed to him so he became a reformer. Author of "the idea of a patriot king," Bolingbroke proved that "patriotism is the last refuge of scoundrels."

John, lord Somers, was "the conscience of the whigs." His father fought for parliament in the civil war. Called to the bar in 1676, Somers wrote in defense of exclusion and in favor of parliamentary sovereignty. He was counsel for the seven bishops who defied King

John, lord Somers, by Smith after Richardson

Charles, earl of Sunderland, by Simon after Kneller,
© National Portrait Gallery, London

James at the revolution. Elected to the convention parliament, Somers argued for declaring William of Orange king, drafted the bill of rights and, in an effort to reduce royal authority over America, helped shape the commission of trade and plantations. Impeached for his part in Captain Kidd's piracy, Somers was ostracized by Queen Anne but, consulted as to the constitutionality of Marlborough's application to be commissioned captain general for life, Somers destroyed the duke's precedents. So Somers won the queen's affection and gratitude, despite his notorious sensuality, caught by Richardson in this brilliant portrait dated 1713.

Charles Spencer, third earl of Sunderland, was the son of the most notorious politician of the restoration. When, in 1695, Charles reached his majority, he entered parliament as an extreme whig and an ally of Somers. Five years later, in a match arranged by his father and that "true born whig" the duchess of Marlborough, lord Spencer married the duke's favorite daughter, lady Anne Churchill. The earl of Sunderland promised that his son would obey his new father-in-law in politics, a promise long honored only in the breach. Spencer succeeded as earl in 1702, just as the accession of Queen Anne put Marlborough at the apex of imperial authority. Sunderland was seen by the whigs as "the nail that would go" in returning their party to the cabinet, but he embarrassed his father-in-law and offended the queen at every turn.

The queen was compelled to commission Sunderland secretary of state for the southern department at the end of 1706, but he was retained in office only because Marlborough took personally any attempt to remove his son-in-law. Nonetheless, Sunderland tried to undermine Marlborough and Godolphin's choices in the election of Scots representative peers and forwarded plans for a descent on France and for the diversion of forces to Spain and Italy, both in opposition to Marlborough's interests and in defiance of his strategy. Sunderland sought to bypass Marlborough in the abortive peace negotiations of 1709, and he supported the barrier treaty that Marlborough declined to sign. Sunderland insisted on the disastrous prosecution of Sacheverell and yet, when the queen dismissed Sunderland in June 1710, Marlborough took it as a blow to his own interest.

The R.^t Honble James Craggs Esqr
His Majesty's Principal Secretary of State &c

James Craggs (the younger)

After the tory interregnum, Marlborough was once again in the royal confidence, and Sunderland, perhaps more mature and certainly desperate to avoid exile as lord lieutenant of Ireland, began to cooperate with the captain general. Marlborough had arranged for the Stanhope-Sunderland ministry when, in April 1717, his daughter Anne suddenly died, the duke suffered a stroke, and he never resumed authority. Nonetheless, his heirs held power for the next three years until they were brought down by the South Sea stock market crash. Sunderland died on April 19, 1722, in the midst of an ensuing election. A decade later, his second son, Charles Spencer, succeeded as the third earl of Marlborough and, on the strength of his name and fortune, held high military office until his death in 1758.

Sunderland's portrait, dated 1720, engraved by Simon and reproduced courtesy of the National Portrait Gallery, London, shows the earl in his last years, in the plainest of civilian dress, relieved only by the garter star embroidered on his coat.

James Craggs the younger, pictured here at the height of fashion (complete with beauty mark and tricornered hat), and as secretary of state for the southern department in 1718, was the leader in the commons for the Sunderland-Stanhope ministry. Craggs, the son of Marlborough's commons manager, financial agent and, after 1714, the postmaster general, had begun his meteoric career in 1706 as secretary to Marlborough's Mediterranean legate, General James Stanhope. Prominent in the Marlborough restoration, the younger Craggs became secretary at war in 1717. He joined the Sunderland-Stanhope ministry the next year. Like his principals,

James Stanhope

Craggs was a major investor in and manager of South Sea subscriptions. Before this involvement could bring him down, Craggs died of smallpox, followed immediately by his bereaved father, both lifelong props of the Marlborough interest.

Defending his ministry in the midst of the South Sea scandal, James Stanhope, first earl Stanhope, suffered a stroke and died within the day. "Hackum," so named from his violence on the battlefield and in debate, is pictured here as a lieutenant general, his aristocratic mien and fine hand (holding the baton of command) contrasting with the battle raging behind him in Spain. There Stanhope won renown in war and diplomacy, the two faces of power politics. At Almenara, Stanhope killed his opposite number in single combat. He won the day at Saragosa and entered Madrid, but in the allied retreat, he was cut off, with the entire British contingent, at Brihuega. After eighteen months as a prisoner, Stanhope was exchanged and came home to marry Lucy Pitt, daughter of Thomas "Diamond" Pitt, head of the gubernatorial family whose commands ranged from Bombay to the Leeward Islands. Stanhope led the whig opposition to the tory peace with France and its American concessions. Cooperating with Marlborough, Stanhope made military preparations to secure the Protestant succession. In the new regime, Stanhope became secretary of state for the southern department, much to the delight of Marlborough's legates in America. Created earl Stanhope, he led the short war with Spain, 1719–21. Tipped to succeed the ailing duke of Marlborough as captain general, Stanhope had first, fatally, to defend his role in the South Sea bubble.

The death of both Stanhope and Marlborough left the coast clear for William, earl Cadogan, to succeed as master general of the ordnance and colonel of the First Guards. Of an Anglo-Irish military family, Cadogan, aged seventeen, fought for King William at the Boyne. Cadogan began his service under Marlborough's command at Cork and Kinsale. When in 1702 Marlborough took command of the allied armies, he appointed Major Cadogan his quartermaster general. Cadogan's accomplishments in the Blenheim campaign led to his promotion as brigadier general and his election to parliament from Marlborough's new constituency at Woodstock. After Ramillies, Cadogan became a major general and lieutenant of the Tower of London. Following Oudenarde, where the deployment across the Scheldt was his greatest achievement,

Cadogan became a lieutenant general and is here pictured in a rare and remarkable portrait by Louis Laguerre (engraved by Simon). It shows the man as he was, gross of body and manner but a master of war and diplomacy. He wears antique armor to show his rank, and the cartouche shows him engaged in the mandatory victorious single combat. Cadogan combined the essential attributes of a staff officer: ability, reliability, and loyalty. As the captain general put it, "he loved me, and I could rely on him."

Marlborough also relied on John Dalrymple, second earl of Stair, an exemplar of the Scots soldiers who helped secure the union with England. It opened to them a disproportionate share of commands in the royal army and the British empire. Exiled as a child, educated at Lieden, Dalrymple fought at Steinkirk as a teenager. Already a lieutenant colonel in the Scots Guards, viscount Dalrymple joined Daniel Parke as an aide to Marlborough in 1703. By 1706, Dalrymple was colonel of the Cameronians (every man a lay preacher). He commanded

William, earl Cadogan

John, earl of Stair, by Faber after Ramsay

an infantry brigade at Ramillies. Now colonel of the Scots Greys and brigadier of dragoons (Robert Hunter was his brigade major), the earl of Stair brought home Marlborough's dispatches from Oudenarde, was promoted lieutenant general, and commanded the covering force at Bouchain. As a full general, Stair was Marlborough's envoy to the new tory ministry. They forced Stair to sell out.

He led the military preparations at Edinburgh to ensure the Protestant succession, assuring his Scots clients, such as Robert Hunter at New York, that they were safe. Despite his historic ambassadorship at Paris, where he secured the evidence which led to the impeachments of Oxford and Bolingbroke, Stair was at odds with the Walpole ministry. He was denied command of the Cartagena expedition (which went to his Scots clients Cathcart and Spotswood). With the support of the duchess of Marlborough, however, Stair outlasted Walpole and acceded to the high commands listed on the

John Campbell, duke of Argyll and Greenwich

label of the portrait by Stair's compatriot Alan Ramsay. It depicts a figure transitional between the empires of Marlborough and Pitt (that "terrible cornet of horse"). Stair wears an antique breastplate but a modern tricorne is tucked under his arm. An old-style hanger contrasts with a modern telescope. He was both governor general (an ancient rank) of Minorca and field marshal (a new distinction) of Britain.

Because of Stair's devotion to Marlborough, he was always at odds with John Campbell, second duke of Argyll, a good man in a fight and insufferable everywhere else. Colonel of a family regiment at age fifteen, lord Lorne saw no service until, as colonel of Scots-Dutch, he was distinguished in the siege of Kaiserwerth and at the storm of Fort St. Michael. Succeeding as duke, Argyll commanded the Scots brigade at Ramillies. There he personally led the storm of the village strongpoint. To secure his services as the queen's commissioner in the union debates of the Scots parliament, Argyll was commissioned a major general and colonel of the 3d foot. He commanded the British infantry at Oudenarde and was promoted lieutenant general. At Malplaquet, Argyll's heroics were unsurpassed. He set himself up to supplant Marlborough. In the crisis caused by Marlborough's request to be commissioned captain general for life, Argyll offered to bring Marlborough in dead or alive. Now unable to serve under the captain general, Argyll was made governor general of Minorca and sent to retrieve the situation in Spain. He failed. Spain was abandoned to the Bourbons. An organizer of military support for the Protestant succession in Scotland, Argyll checked the rebels at Sheriffmuir in 1715, but, failing to follow up, he was recalled by Marlborough and replaced by Cadogan. Not until Cadogan's death did Argyll retrieve his military commands. He became master general of the ordnance and, at last, in 1736, succeeded Orkney (whom Marlborough had promoted over Argyll's head) as field marshal. In the run-up to Cartagena, Argyll bitterly criticized the selection of Marlborough's

Henricus Sacheverell

Scots loyalists Cathcart and Spotswood. Cashiered, Argyll was restored to rank on the fall of Walpole which, as a Scots parliamentary patron, Argyll did much to effect, but he died within the year, a tenth-generation nobleman at the top of his profession of arms.

Henry Sacheverell was born at Marlborough in 1674. His mother was the daughter of a regicide. His paternal grandfather was a deprived Presbyterian minister. Sacheverell's father was a church of England rector, however, and Henry himself became a bigoted clergyman, loudmouthed and drunken. His now-notorious sermon in November 1709 at St. Paul's to the City corporation denounced the "false brethren" of the Marlborough-Godolphin ministry who tolerated religious dissent, putting "the Church in danger." Sacheverell reiterated the doctrine of nonresistance and denounced the "glorious" revolution, parliamentary sovereignty, and the Protestant succession. The printed sermon ran to 40,000 copies. It is said to have reached every voter in England. Despite Sacheverell's impeachment by the commons and conviction by the lords, his sentiments underlay the tory electoral victory in 1710. Sarah, duchess of Marlborough, wrote of Sacheverell that "he had not one good quality that any man of sense valued him for." This portrait was painted in 1710 by Russell and engraved by Smith at the height of Sacheverell's vogue. It illustrates that, as the duchess observed, Sacheverell's "person was well framed . . . , and he dressed well. A good assurance, clean gloves, white hankerchief well managed . . . moved the hearts of many at his appearance and the solemnity of a trial added much to a pity and concern which had nothing in reason or justice to support him. The weaker part of the ladies [Queen Anne in particular, whose influence reduced the parson's punishment to a pittance] were more like mad or besotted than like persons in their senses." Sacheverell died in obscurity. The church state was buried with him.

PART II

"THE ENDLESS WAR"

Fortified Frontiers

Précis

ARLBOROUGH MIGHT HAVE matched Bonaparte's consolidation of power and extent of victory save that the captain general served the constitutional monarch of a small nation. The febrile politics of Britain and the recuperative power of France both were on display in the spring of 1708. Concluding that the secretary of state, Robert Harley, was an unreconstructed tory, the enemy of moderation at home and conciliatory to France abroad, the duke and duchess of Marlborough and lord treasurer Godolphin demanded that Queen Anne dismiss her secretary. She declined. They threatened to resign. Only the refusal of her ministers to serve, the lords to legislate, and the financiers to support her government without Marlborough forced the queen to acquiesce, but the duke had lost the royal favor.

The first sign of Queen Anne's enmity was American. Despite his dismissal, the queen took Harley's advice to commission Colonel James Jones to command the 38th Regiment, in garrison in the Leeward Islands, without the captain general's imprimatur. Reported to him by his regimental and colonial correspondents, this apparently trivial act indicated to Marlborough that, absent a series of Blenheims and a drumhead peace in Paris, the queen's disfavor would be fatal. The captain general's virtual monopoly of royal military promotions was the font of his power, but if the queen now intervened, Marlborough could not expect political support. His moderation in religion and his nonpartisan politics made the duke suspect to both right and left. Whig hostility appeared when the new secretary of state, Marlborough's own son-in-law, the earl of Sunderland, tried to undercut the duke's influence in the first election of Scots representative peers. The tory right wing still sought to impeach the captain general, end his quixotic war with France, reverse his religious moderation, and reduce the power of "the monied interest," the military nexus of finance capital and armed authority, which Marlborough personified.

In the spring of 1708, the resilience of France after Ramillies appeared in an attempted invasion of Scotland. Foiled though it was, the French sortie delayed the captain general's return to the Flanders front. There he found that, despite his counsels of moderation, the Anglo-Dutch condominium had so exploited the Belgian burghers that they had recalled their viceroy, the elector of Bavaria. That is, they had opened their city gates to the French army, itself at least 10 percent larger than the allied forces. Only their astonishing advance—"such marching is impossible!" Marshal Villars exclaimed—forced on the French the extraordinary encounter at Oudenarde on July 11, 1708. Marlborough admitted that he had fought at a dreadful disadvantage for English political reasons, but the victory saved Brussels from the French and a relentless pursuit again drove the French out of the Low Countries. The troops of Louis XIV were forced, after a half-century career of aggression, to defend the frontiers of France itself.

Marlborough proposed to march on Paris. Fatally, he was checked by his allies. Prince Eugene had a conventional concern for sieges and supply routes. The Dutch, their war aim achieved, sought only to add more fortress cities to their "Barrier" against France. The captain general was reduced to directing the siege of Lille, capital of French Flanders, the second city of France. The siege was apparently doomed by Vauban's formidable fortifications, the approach of winter, and the isolation of the allies in France itself. Marlborough's miraculous victory meant that "King John," as his enemies had called him, was now spoken of as "Caesar." Yet the astonishing campaign of 1708 did not end the war.

Peace negotiations did begin, in February 1709, but the British parliament, with Marlborough prominent in the lords, resolved that the French must acknowledge the legitimacy of the Protestant succession in Britain and the Hapsburg succession in Spain, Spanish America, and Belgium (of which Marlborough had been offered the vice-regency). The duke himself demanded that the French cede all of Newfoundland and return the Hudson's Bay posts (the company directors wrote their former director, now the richest man in England, that this would bring him more power and pelf even than had his interwar combination of the East India companies and his backing of the bank of England). The extent of the imperial ambition excited by the captain general's conquests appeared in William Penn's call on Marlborough to secure for England's American colonies what would be the northern and western boundaries of the United States of America.

Borne by this tide, and weakened politically, the duke failed to oppose in public what he deplored in private: the allies' outrageous demand that Louis XIV surrender the frontier fortresses of France as a pledge that he would force his nephew from the Spanish throne. The failed peace reinforced Marlborough's resolve to march on Paris, reduce the sun king to the status of a constitutional monarch, and secure the peace of western Europe and the Atlantic world from the aggression of France. The European war had produced so few gains in America, however, that both political parties in Britain demanded a resumption of amphibious attacks on Spanish Caribbean ports and on Acadia, Newfoundland, and Quebec. Marlborough deplored all of these proposals as mere buccaneering, doomed by disease, wasteful of resources. Instead, his officers governing in America should use British munitions to arm local levies and attack both the Spanish-American and Franco-American frontiers. Marlborough himself would consolidate his imperial preeminence by obtaining the queen's commission as captain general for life.

Meanwhile, Louis XIV committed the last army of France to prevent the allies from seizing Mons and breaching the French frontier. The two armies met at Malplaquet, 100,000 men to a side, on September 11, 1709. The allies stormed the fortified, forested French positions. In twelve hours of hand-to-hand fighting, the captain general's command drove the enemy from the battlefield, at the cost of 18,500 casualties. Then the allies settled down to a costly but successful siege of Mons. But the French army had survived, the road to Paris was closed, and Marlborough could not win the war. It had, with one interval, gone on for twenty years and exhausted all the combatants. The duke's request for a lifetime command was denied. Henceforward, Marlborough's imperial influence was mostly manifested by his legates in America, sixteen of whom had qualified for governor generalships at Malplaquet. Thirty-two other veterans of that dreadful day subsequently took American military commands. Dozens of other officers survived Malplaquet to form American troops and educate American officers in Marlborough's principles of command, discipline, and drill, as the colonists enlisted, in ever-increasing numbers, in the wars for Atlantic dominion. For five decades after Malplaquet, Marlborough's veterans rose in the British army. They commanded the imperial forces right down to their final circum-Atlantic victory in 1763.

Malplaquet's cost, though the bulk of the casualties were Dutch and those none of Marlborough's doing, deepened war weariness and, as is so often the case in the aftermath of war, amplified political extremes. As moderates, Marlborough and Godolphin were despised by whigs and tories alike while Queen Anne, tottering toward her demise, invited another succession crisis, for she apparently embraced the succession of her half brother, the Catholic French army officer "James III." This, the centerpiece of the jacobite program, was articulated by the popular preacher Henry Sacheverell, that firebrand of high-tory, xenophobic, divine-right, passive-obedience sentiments. He was impeached by the whig commons. Marlborough discountenanced every lord, and even their connections, who voted against impeachment. For example, lord Archibald Hamilton's appointment to command Jamaica was imperiled, despite his gallantry at Malplaquet, because "Archy's" elder brother the duke of Hamilton had voted for acquittal. Marlborough's military authority was the obvious obstacle to divine-right reaction and so, Queen Anne was told, the greatest derogation of her authority. She supported her ministers' every effort to reduce the captain general to a mere theater commander in Flanders.

Marlborough retreated to Flanders early in 1710. He could not risk another Malplaquet. The French would not invite another Ramillies. Yet the captain general thought that he might make an end run around the French defenses and, in another year, march down the Channel coast and up the Seine to Paris. Such a campaign, he wrote, would win "more than ten expeditions can doe" in America. Marlborough masked the lines of La Bassée and seized Douai, but, following the queen's dismissal of Sunderland as secretary of state and his replacement by that articulate but unprincipled tory, Henry St. John, Marlborough concluded that any plan of his for a Channel campaign would be betrayed to the French. Then the queen recast the council of trade and plantations along tory lines, a preface to sacking Godolphin and replacing the lord treasurer with an exchequer headed by Robert Harley, whom the queen created earl of Oxford.

The new tory ministry asked the elector of Hanover, the legal heir apparent to the imperial throne, to supplant Marlborough in command of the allies. His refusal, like the elector's dispatch of his eldest son to serve under Marlborough's command, was a dreadful warning to the high tories of what would happen to them if the Protestant succession took place. Worse, the tories feared that, if the war went on with Marlborough in command, he might become "a second Cromwell," and seize the throne for himself. That the duke, a believer in "the revolution principles" of constitutional monarchy, would never do but, in the lords, Marlborough denounced and defeated the proposed peace with France. The queen then created twelve tory peers who carried the resolution. Still, pressure must be maintained on the French frontier until the peace was signed and the allies deserted. Marlborough was indispensable, but his favorite officers were cashiered and their regiments were detached from the army in Flanders for an attack on Quebec. The tory ministers hoped that, weakened, the captain general could not advance. Better, he might even be defeated by the French.

The Quebec expedition was designed not only to undermine the captain general and capture Quebec, but also to coerce the American colonists. "The whole Empire of North America" should be reduced by force to "One uniform plan of government," with the goal of "riches and power," the one to the sponsoring minister, the other to the entire tory ministry. By "procuring a more solid advantage to England than all those glaring battles and sieges," the conquest of Quebec would put the captain general's victories in the shade. "The whole design was formed by me," wrote St. John. He had Jack Hill, the brother of Mrs. Masham, the queen's dresser and favorite, placed in command of the expedition. On April 24, 1711, queen Anne created St. John viscount Bolingbroke (she refused to advance such a wastrel to an earldom). Three days later, the largest force yet committed to American conquest and coercion sailed for Boston.

The governor general of Massachusetts, Joseph Dudley, a twenty-five-year veteran of imperial administration on both sides of the Atlantic, Marlborough's military correspondent for a decade, took "measures worthy of a military dictatorship" to mobilize Massachusetts, but the professional incompetence of Admiral Walker brought the expedition to grief on the reefs off the Isle of Eggs. The literal "Panic" of Admiral Walker and General Hill in the face of the American environment infected their subordinates. They refused to obey their orders to attack Quebec and declined even to retake Newfoundland, although it lay on their homeward course. Safely back in England, the cowardly commanders blamed their failure on "New England the better to excuse themselves." These tory stalwarts declared that the colonies had sabotaged the expedition so that they could "throw off their Dependence on the Nation, and declare themselves a free State."

Contrast, as contemporaries did, the Canadian fiasco with the captain general's capstone campaign. Marlborough passed the "ne plus ultra lines," the massive French fortifications expressly designed to check his advance into France. On September 14, 1711, Marlborough compelled the unconditional surrender of the fortress town of Bouchain, the anchor of the lines, within cannon shot of the much larger French army, which had failed to relieve the fortress. Marlborough's victory demonstrated to the Atlantic world the captain general's "mastery of the art of war" and, as he proposed, opened the road to Paris in the next campaign. The Oxford-Bolingbroke ministry, however, wished only to keep up the pressure on France until the peace was signed and commercial concessions were wrung from the Bourbon powers. On October 27, 1711, the captain general left his undefeated army. A year later, Marlborough was forced into exile. The grateful Netherlands hailed him as a sovereign prince and he began to organize, for the fourth time, the military forces that would decide Greater Britain's imperial succession.

CHAPTER SIX

Oudenarde

S WORDSMEN KNOW THAT the best defense is a good attack. In 1708, Marlborough exemplified the truth of this axiom, both in politics and in war. He took the offensive against tory critics and jacobite invaders in Britain. He repressed Burgundian revolt and defeated French aggression in Flanders. He authorized amphibious assaults on French empire in the Mediterranean, in the Caribbean, and from New York to Newfoundland along the Atlantic frontier.

At the outset of 1708, the political "winter campaign" was still being fought in parliament. In the lords, Marlborough himself scuttled the "blue water" squadron. He saw to it that the "American bill" for cruisers and convoys spiked the attack in the commons on his brother, Admiral Churchill. By the second week of February, however, Marlborough and Godolphin could no longer ignore Secretary Harley's enmity to themselves and to their rapprochement with the whigs. The disclosure that a French spy had operated unchecked in Harley's office, and the public exposure of Harley's own double agents at Versailles and Saint-Germain, combined to confirm the whig assertion that Harley's faction, the unreformed tories, were Francophiles and jacobites. On February 8, the duchess of Marlborough, the lord treasurer Godolphin, and the captain general severally told the queen that they would leave her service if secretary Harley did not. The queen refused to dismiss her secretary of state. She stunned the duchess and the treasurer by saying that she would accept their resignations. She begged the general to stay on, however, "and if you doe my lord resign your sword, let me tel you, you run it through my head." Then the queen went to the cabinet meeting, imploring Marlborough to follow. He refused. Harley tried to do business without Marlborough, but the duke of Somerset declared that "if her Majesty suffered that fellow to treat of affairs of the war without the advice of the General he could not serve her and so left the council." The threat of Marlborough's resignation convulsed the government. At least four more ministers threatened to step down. The commons refused to take up bills for taxes or make appropriations. The lords voted to investigate the treason in Harley's office with a view to his impeachment. The bank of England suspended loans. Prince George told his wife that civil discontent would follow the destruction of the Marlborough ministry. Shaken but stubborn (like all Stuarts, as Sarah unkindly observed), Anne might have held on to disaster. On February 11, 1708, however, Harley and his followers resigned and were replaced with Marlborough's and Godolphin's nominees.[1]

The reconstituted ministry immediately faced French invasion of a disaffected Scotland. Most Scots hated the union with England. Edinburgh gave a rapturous welcome to a French emissary. Orkney reported the exiled Stuarts at Saint-Germain believed that if the French could put 5,000 troops ashore in Scotland, Orkney's own brother, the duke of Hamilton, would raise 30,000 men in the cause of Scots independence. Like King William before him, Marlborough had drained Scotland of troops, both to strengthen his own army and defang Scots dissidence. Absent troops, Marlborough had provided for Scots security by preoccupying the French armies in the summer. In the winter, he cantoned the queen's regiments in the channel ports of the Netherlands, ready for a rapid redeployment to the British Isles. When Cadogan forwarded a detailed report on the French forces assembling at Dunkirk to invade Scotland, Marlborough ordered deputy quartermaster general Richard King to put ten battalions on board transports at Ostend. "'Tis impossible to express the Goodwill and Heartiness of both officers and Soldiers, on this occasion," Cadogan wrote Marlborough. "They all showed such earnestness for going that to avoid Disputes and Jealousies Mr. Lumley has sent the Ten Eldest Battalions."[2]

As soon as the pretender was reported at Dunkirk, where twelve to fifteen French battalions and 13,000 stand of arms to equip the Scots jacobites awaited his arrival, Marlborough ordered all the available troops in England and Ireland, some 10,000 men, to march either for the Borders or for the northern Irish ports. Lord Leven, the Scots commander in chief, and the other Scots soldiers in the first parliament of Great Britain, hurried north to their commands. Parliament suspended the writ of habeas corpus and proclaimed the pretender and all his supporters traitors. The Marlborough ministry ordered the arrest, "upon suspicion of treason," of every jacobite lord and Scots opposition leader, from the royal duke of Hamilton himself down to the republican commoner Andrew Fletcher of Saltoun. The most prominent Scots opposition figures were escorted up to London and incarcerated in the Tower. In Scotland, "the castles of Stirling and Edinburgh, and all the prisons in Edinburgh, were crammed full of nobility and gentry."[3]

The admiralty, on Marlborough's orders executed by his brother, Admiral Churchill, sent two squadrons, altogether thirty-three British and three Dutch men-of-war, to blockade the French invasion force in Dunkirk (that the allies could simultaneously send off the Virginia and Lisbon convoy, escorted by twelve British and fifteen Dutch warships, suggests something of their enormous superiority at sea). On March 6, bad weather forced Admiral Byng's blockading squadron back across the Channel (Admiral Walker had failed to find Dunkirk!). The wind that was foul for the allies was fair for the French. Their fleet sped north for Scotland, to the dismay of such naval officers as lord Archibald Hamilton, who feared that 30,000 Scotsmen (the Hamiltons seemed fixated on this figure) only awaited the French arrival to proclaim the pretender as King James VIII of Scotland.4

Admiral Byng used his enforced stay in the Downs to resupply and re-inforce the fleet of eighteen battleships and a dozen frigates with which he now pursued the French northwards. The French had a fifteen-hour head start. Better designed and with clean hulls, the French ships were far faster than the cumbersome English vessels, their hulls foul with the marine growth of con-stant service. So Admiral Byng risked the inshore passage, shoal but shorter. The French, well out to sea, overshot the Firth of Forth, beat back, signaled the shore and, while waiting for a reply that did not come, saw the topsails of Byng's squadron on the horizon. The French admiral, Claude de Forbin, bluffed brilliantly. He offered battle. Then, while Byng's more powerful fleet slowly formed its line ahead, Forbin slipped away to the north. His fleet's rear elements exchanged shots with Byng's van, doubled Fife Ness, and disappeared. Outsailing the British pursuit, in two weeks, north about Scotland, the French battle fleet lost only one capital ship, the ex-British *Salisbury*. She had the leading Scots jacobites aboard. Marlborough's calculation and Queen Anne's kindness preserved them from execution. Scotland was saved for the union. Louis XIV's plans to divert Marlborough and his veterans from Flanders were foiled.5

The duke himself sailed from England at the end of March, met Eugene at The Hague, and consulted the Dutch deputies at Amsterdam. The Dutch ordered their commissars, hitherto such a clog to Marlborough, to second his every proposal. Even more astonishing, given Dutch jealousy of the potential for British imperial advantage from the war, was their agreement that James Stanhope, Marlborough's nominee to command the British troops in Spain (an officer, as Cadogan remarked, "entirely in my Lord Duke's hands"), should try to capture a Mediterranean naval base. Once the principal allies agreed on grand strategy, Marlborough and Eugene set off to confer with the elector of Hanover about the levies from the south German states who were to join the allies' widely anticipated campaign on the Rhine and the Meuse.6

In fact, "the Great Twin Brethren" had no intention of fighting along these riverine lines. They intended to draw the French out of their fortified lines to attack Marlborough's outnumbered army in Flanders. Then Eugene was to bring up the Imperial troops from the Meuse to join Marlborough's counter-attack. The elector of Hanover's Germans would be left on the defensive. As they had done to rid themselves of the margrave of Baden, so Marlborough and

Eugene now allocated extra troops to Hanover's command, deceiving both the elector and the French about the focus of the campaign, and risking the enmity of the heir to the British throne when he realized he had been jilted. On the other hand, the electoral heir, the future George II, now joined Marlborough's command "to make the acquaintance of the English officers," a prerequisite to commanding the empire they administered. Marlborough thought that the electoral prince was a dull dog but quite civil, and very anxious to earn the approval of his new comrades, his future subordinates.7

On May 7, 1708, the captain general reviewed the British troops, at once the instrument and the outcome of the union of England and Scotland. In the army, Scots officers were disproportionately represented. So were their compatriots in the parliament of Great Britain. War and politics together meant that Scots would play exaggerated parts in imperial politics. As a class, the Scots officers were now determined to support Marlborough. Formerly highly critical of the captain general, Lieutenant Colonel Cranstoun wrote that "there are no men free of faults, but I do not believe any man living at this time could be put in the Duke of Marlborough's place, but it would prove fatal to Britain and to the interest of the Protestant religion."8

The duke himself despaired of military success, political victory, even his own survival, unless he could quickly win a decisive battle. The struggle to oust Harley had revealed to Marlborough that the favor of the queen, the foundation of his fortune, was lost. The ultra-tories would stop at nothing, even giving victory to France, to bring the captain general down. The junto whigs distrusted Marlborough's monarchism and anglicanism. They would support him only as long as he was victorious. The political nation, now that the invasion crisis was safely past, remembered that it was war weary. The aversion of the landed and commercial elites to military power and executive authority, both personified by "King John," intensified. Much of the increasing political pressure to divert the war to Iberia and America was designed to deprive the duke of the military means to a more-than-Cromwellian command of the British empire. Marlborough, as befit his preeminence, put his problem in public terms. He was, he wrote, "thoroly sensible that the Queen's affairs abroad as well as at home, requires my venturing this campagne, so that no occasion shall be neglected."9

As he opened the campaign of 1708, however, the captain general found the allied position in Flanders was crumbling, both militarily and politically. The French had reinforced their army in Flanders to more than 100,000 men. Marlborough commanded fewer than 90,000. During 1707, the bankrupt Dutch government had mulcted the allied conquests in Flanders, trying to make the conquered principalities pay for their conquest, their occupation, and for the coming campaign. The Dutch had been aided and abetted by the duke's deputy, Cadogan. Abused by both the Dutch and the British, the burghers of every city and town in Flanders believed the emissaries of their former governor general, the elector of Bavaria, when he said that the overbearing allies could be expelled simply by opening the city gates to the waiting French army.[10]

Marlborough was distracted from Belgian disaffection by British politics. He wrote to Stanhope that victory in the ongoing parliamentary elections "will depend in great measure in what we are able to do here this campagne." Marlborough hoped that the foiled invasion of Scotland would win commons seats for the war party in England. In Scotland, Scots peers would elect sixteen of their noble number to sit in the lords. Popular elections would seat forty-five Scots in the commons. Governments expected to control elections in Scotland as they did in England, but the Marlborough ministry was divided. Marlborough himself, a peer of Scotland as baron Aymouth, supported the official unionist slate presented by the Scots commander in chief, the earl of Leven, and by the ministerial spokesman, the duke of Queensbury. Sunderland, although he was Marlborough's son-in-law and now queen Anne's secretary of state as well, connived on behalf of the junto whigs with the Scots opposition, a jumble of jacobites, Scots nationalists, country party adherents, and the mutable "squadrone volante," all under the duke of Hamilton's leadership (if that word can be used of so inconstant a character).[11]

The central figure in the election of Scots peers was the earl of Orkney. The only candidate to appear on both the government's (Marlborough's) and the opposition's (Sunderland's) lists, Orkney himself was divided between his professional duty to the captain general and his connection to the opposition, led by his eldest brother, the duke of Hamilton. Marlborough named only two peers on his proxy, the Scots generals Orkney (whom Marlborough gave leave to attend the elections) and Stair (who remained on duty in Flanders). He left the other fourteen names to be filled in by Queensbury. Marborough's proxy was decisive. It won election for several government candidates (the Scots "have been treated more like a Province than a free People, so they are always carried by the appearances of prevailing power"), but Orkney persuaded a number of Scots officers—"who've risked their bread" thereby—to vote against the "Subaltern Ministry" of unionists.[12]

Orkney was disaffected from the Marlborough ministry because of a failure of imperial income. His share of the royal repayment of Scots investment in the failed Darien colony—the price of union—had gone into the rebuilding of Orkney's great house at Cliveden, "but its gone, besides I am disappointed of a thousand lbs. I was to have from Virginia . . . in the time a new Governour has been a making." Orkney expected to be paid during the interregnum between the death of Colonel Nott and the arrival of Colonel Hunter. Godolphin, as lord treasurer, refused to tap the Virginia quitrent balance. Sunderland, as secretary of state, referred the matter to the lords commissioners for plantations. They did nothing for Orkney, although the board successfully recommended to Godolphin that Hunter, who had been captured en route to Virginia and who was now on parole awaiting a prisoner exchange, be paid for his lost equipage and the half pay of his rank as lieutenant governor, both out of the Virginia quitrents. Orkney was left to depend upon Hunter, from whom he took a bond for repayment once Hunter reached his government, but Marlborough declined to facilitate Hunter's exchange (having promised Virginia to Colonel Spotswood).[13]

Rebuffed by every element of the imperial administration, Orkney complained that "this is using one as ill as can be, and I told my Ld. Marlb. Soe much and that if they were weary of me am sure I was of the war, for att the years end I was not sixpence the better for the service." In his most emollient manner, Marlborough replied that he valued Orkney's service very highly, that he had been responsible for the only creditable actions of the previous campaign—the pursuit of Vendôme and the forage of the Scheldt—and that, unlike the duke of Argyll, Orkney would "do whatever I shall think for the service" without aiming to supplant the captain general himself. It was for those reasons, Marlborough pointed out, that he had put Orkney's name at the head of his proxy for the Scots peers' election, ordered the ministry's united support for Orkney's election to the lords, and given him leave from the army to campaign in Scotland. "They think I can't live without them," Orkney said of the Marlborough ministry and, he admitted, at his present rate of spending, he could not. As the duchess of Marlborough observed, "Lord Orkney is the most covetous wretch in nature." He had proved it by marrying King William's cast-off, Elizabeth Villiers, "that woman, for mere money." Marlborough agreed that Orkney, like his brother the duke of Hamilton, "may be had by those that shall think it worth their while to buy them."[14]

While he prepared to open the campaign of 1708, Marlborough was much more worried by an apparently petty piece of imperial politics than by the Scots elections: the promotion of Lieutenant Colonel James Jones to the colonelcy of the regiment in the Leeward Islands. The governor general, Colonel Daniel Parke, the Virginian who had been given the command as a reward for his service as the captain general's aide-de-camp at Blenheim, had asked Marlborough to prefer him to the colonelcy of the garrison regiment. Parke's security in his turbulent command, Marlborough's control of the imperial officer corps, even the survival of the Marlborough-Godolphin ministry all were put in question by queen Anne's commission to James Jones, because Jones's patron was Robert Harley. Dismissed from office, his party defeated in the recent elections, Harley nonetheless retained the queen's confidence. Moreover, the tories still had champions at court, particularly Prince George and his advisor, Admiral Churchill. *Frater non indignus* was the motto of the envious younger brother of the duke. The admiral clung to the toryism of the Churchills' youth. He deplored his brother's concessions to the regicide, republican, iconoclastic whigs. He promoted tories such as Jones without considering that he thereby imperiled Marlborough's military and imperial hegemony.[15]

The colonel of the Leeward Islands regiment, Luke Lillingston, was an absentee. He had survived two tours in the West Indies. He declared that he would not tempt fate, and yellow fever, in a third. Rather than rejoin his command, Lillingston put the regiment up for sale. A purchaser would pass over the regiment's lieutenant colonel, James Jones, a tory partisan, to whom Harley had promised the regiment. Acting on Admiral Churchill's advice, prince George, as generalissimo of the army, blocked Marlborough's promotion of Lillingston to brigadier, a reward for his previous American service; refused to allow the colonel to sell out, bankrupting him; and then ordered Robert Walpole, now the secretary at war, to send Jones a commission as colonel.[16]

Marlborough wrote to Walpole, "I guess Mr Harley has had a hand in getting Jones Colonel Lillingston's Regt, because I have seen letters upon that Regiment's lmbarkation and since their being in the Leeward Islands, intimating that Jones made his braggs Mr. Harley had promist him, he should have a commission for that Regiment." Marlborough was appalled by Jones's promotion. He "did not think him a fitt person for that Command, while there were so many other officers of the Service better qualified." More important, Marlborough's own authority depended upon his officers' belief that he controlled promotions, both in his own command and in the garrison governments of America (and Great Britain). That Marlborough had not even been consulted, that Harley had made a rabid tory a colonel, and that the ousted minister could act through the agency of the admiral, the prince, and the queen, became the talk of the London coffeehouses. Admiral Churchill, belatedly aware of the damage he had done, tried to blame Walpole. The secretary confronted the admiral with witnesses to the transaction and he reported the proof of Churchill's duplicity to the queen, the prince, and the captain general. To the latter, Walpole protested that he would do nothing of consequence without Marlborough's orders; he had never heard of Jones before this episode; and Admiral Churchill, in saying that Walpole acted independently of the captain general to promote a tory, was saying what he thought would please the queen and her consort. That this last was true confirmed Marlborough's conviction that the court favor that had raised him so high was now gone beyond recall.[17]

It was a shaken captain general who turned from betrayal in Britain to French aggression and Belgian mutiny in Flanders. The French attempt on Scotland had not halted, but it had delayed Marlborough's preparations for the campaign in the Low Countries. Worse, unseasonable rain and stunted grass impeded the allied army's concentration. The Germans and the Imperialists, as usual, were dilatory in bringing up the troops they had promised to help Marlborough meet superior French numbers in Flanders. Nonetheless, the captain general blocked a French thrust at Brussels and, by "marching with a vengance" through the mud, his army caught the French at the River Dender. The allied quartermasters were absent with Prince Eugene. Marlborough's depleted scouts served him badly. He was hoodwinked by the same trick he himself had used at Ramillies. The French "falsified and flourished their Colors apace in the Scrub to our Front" as if offering battle. While Marlborough organized his attack, the French slipped away. Surprised by the speed of the withdrawal, Marlborough was shocked when he discovered that the French feint had covered the betrayal of both Ghent and Bruges to the French.[18]

The subversion of Ghent and Bruges cut Marlborough's army off from Ostend, their most direct link with home, and denied the duke the use of the Scheldt and the Lys, the major river routes to the conquests of 1706. From the safety of the Ghent-Bruges canal line, the French now threatened the Scheldt bridgehead at the fortress town of Oudenarde. Oudenarde was "the chief avenue to their [the allies] other fortresses in Flanders, as well as the only channel for their direct communication with England." Marlborough reinforced the garrison of Oudenarde to prevent its burghers from emulating those of Ghent and Bruges (and he reinforced Antwerp as well, just in the nick of time), but he was prostrated by migraine, by malaria, and by a depression hardly lifted by the arrival of Prince Eugene, since he came without his army.[19]

Superior in numbers, the French invested Oudenarde on July 9 while their main force marched for the strong camp of Lessines, on the banks of the Dender. Thence they could cover the siege of Oudenarde and prevent Marlborough's relief of that fortress. Sick, sleepless for three nights, and too fevered to answer the letters Colonel Sutton, that "safe hand," had brought him from Sarah, Marlborough nevertheless rejoiced that the French had left their impregnable position behind the Ghent-Bruges canal. He posted Orkney, in command of a strong rearguard, to make sure that the French, now that they were on the move, did not double back to take Brussels. Then, "in order to attack the enemy," Marlborough had eight days' bread loaded onto the army's carts, eliminated the officers' baggage, and, now that they had returned with Eugene, launched Cadogan, Spotswood, and their quartermaster corps, together with eight squadrons (commanded by Prince George of Hanover), eight battalions, and the pontoon bridging train, to take the Lessines camp and bridge the Dender. Cadogan's detachment covered twenty-eight miles in twenty-two hours, reached the Dender at Lessines by midnight, and bridged the river in the dark. At daybreak of July 10, the allied advance party saw the heads of the French advance turn back from Lessines and march north, away from the target city. The French would cross the River Scheldt at Gavre and then proceed south along the river's west bank toward Oudenarde.[20]

By midday, the heads of Marlborough's columns reached the Lessines camp. They had marched thirty miles in thirty-six hours. Having forestalled the French at the Dender, Marlborough had now to keep them from using the Scheldt as a shield while they besieged Oudenarde. If Marlborough could intercept the French in the open, he could force them to fight. If the allies won, the battle would reverse the fortunes of the campaign in Flanders, refresh support for the war in England, and so, perhaps, compel Louis XIV to accept a peace treaty which would preserve British independence and empire, European protestantism and liberty. The French feared no such outcome. At Lessines, the allies were fifteen miles from Oudenarde and east of the Scheldt, a river unbridged between Oudenarde and Gavre. At Gavre, the French had an easy crossing of the Scheldt. The river would protect their flank during a short march, just six miles down the road to Oudenarde. Feeling neither danger nor urgency, the French settled into camp at Gavre, expecting to make a leisurely crossing of the Scheldt and an unopposed advance on Oudenarde in the morning.[21]

Marlborough had not allowed the allies to pitch camp at Lessines, or even cook a meal. Instead, at 1:00 in the morning of July 11, the quartermasters, the quarter colors, eight squadrons of Hanoverian cavalry, three infantry brigades (two of them British), thirty-two field guns, the engineers, the bridging train, and a body of pioneers left Lessines with orders to improve the roads for fifteen miles to the Scheldt just north of Oudenarde, throw five pontoon bridges across the river, and attack the French vanguard as it approached. At 8:00 a.m., the main body of the allies followed the vanguard. At 9:00, Cadogan's command had already reached the Scheldt. His scouts reported that the French were still in camp at Gavre. It was 10:00 before the French began to cross the Scheldt. By 10:30, Spotswood's crews had already launched their pontoons, linked them together, anchored them, and were laying the plank roadways. In Oudenarde itself, other allied engineers were augmenting the city's two stone bridges with two pontoon spans. To cross the bridges at Oudenarde, the Dutch division, the allied left wing, had left Marlborough's main body force and marched directly for the city.[22]

By noon, having posted four battalions on the east bank of the Scheldt to guard his bridgehead, Cadogan had led the remainder of the vanguard—twelve battalions and the Hanoverian horse—west over the Scheldt bridges and then north to a position where the Dipenbeck stream met the river. The tributary was interspersed with strongly built villages and it flowed through the midst of a broken landscape, heavily hedged. The eastern anchor of this Dipenbeck line was the village of Eyne, on high ground just north of the point where the Dipenbeck stream entered the marshes of the Scheldt. It was held by elements of the enemy's advance guard, seven battalions of Swiss troops in the French service. Through Eyne ran the high road between Oudenarde, a mile to the south, and Gavre, five miles to the north. Down this road the French main body was advancing. From Eyne, the Dipenbeck ran some two miles west to its source at the castle of Bevere on the high ground of the Boser Couter. South of the Dipenbeck stream lay the plains of Oudenarde. These the French must reach if they were to deploy their superior cavalry and larger numbers of infantry.[23]

At 12:20, Marlborough, Eugene, and the duke's staff crossed Spotswood's pontoon bridges, followed by the Prussian cavalry. By 1:00, the duke had reached Cadogan's position on the south bank of the Dipenbeck and, as was his wont, personally posted his field artillery (on a rise behind the village of Schaerken, where the guns could support the left flank of the British infantry lined up along the stream). Marlborough sent his aides racing back to hurry up the main body of the allies. The marquis de Brion, commanding the French advance party, also called up reinforcements, but the French commander, the royal duke of Burgundy, and his second, the veteran marshal Louis Joseph, duke of Vendôme, simply refused to believe that the allies had reached the Scheldt, much less that they had bridged it and were present in strength between the French and Oudenarde. "If they are there," Vendôme exclaimed, "the Devill must have carried them. Such marching is impossible." In fact, Marlborough had stolen three marches on the French. He had covered fifty miles in sixty hours with 60,000 men, bridged a great river in sight of the enemy, and taken a strong post in the presence of the French advance units. Now, Marlborough offered the French an encounter battle, that rarest of combats in an age of formal fighting. He, or rather Cadogan, had chosen a defensive position that deprived the enemy of their every advantage, in numbers, in cavalry, in artillery. Yet only the divided French command—Vendôme wanted to crush the allied advance units before the main body could come up; Burgundy insisted on a cautious deployment on high ground—gave Marlborough's right wing time to rescue his reckless advance.[24]

At 2:45, at the end of a seven-hour forced march, the duke of Argyll led twenty British battalions onto the Scheldt bridges. With this reinforcement in sight, Marlborough ordered Cadogan's entire force forward. At 3:00 the infantry forded the Dipenbeck stream, led by the 18th Regiment, the Royal Irish, commanded by its major, "Marlborough's drillmaster," Brevet Lieutenant Colonel Richard Kane (Kane would succeed to the colonelcy of the regiment and the governments of Minorca and Gibraltar, and his distillation of Marlborough's drill would educate American soldiers of the next generation). "With their [plug] bayonets in the muzzle of their muskets and not firing a piece," the British infantry stormed into the village of Eyne. They took three of the Swiss battalions prisoner and pushed the other four out onto the plain beyond the village. There "they were cut to pieces" by the Hanoverian cavalry. Eight Hanoverian squadrons, reinforced by Spotswood at the head of the quartermasters and camp color men, now charged onto the plateau north of Eyne. They broke twelve squadrons of French cavalry and pursued them north, right into the main body of the French army. The charge of the allied cavalry cleared the way for Cadogan's infantry to advance from Eyne to occupy another strongpoint, the village of Heurne, but, in the melee, Prince George's horse was shot under him. Fighting on foot, the prince was rescued by his colonel, who sacrificed himself to the future king of Great Britain. Ever afterward, George was "in the habit of calling on all great occasions for his 'Oudenarde sword.'"[25]

The storm of Eyne and Heurne and the Anglo-Hanoverian charge had two tactical results. The annihilation of seven Swiss-French battalions and the flight of the French cavalry, both under the noses of the French commanders, stung them into fighting, but the allied possession of the village strongpoints deflected the advance of the left wing of the French army, under Vendôme, down from the high ground between Eyne and Heurne into the enclosed country along the Dipenbeck stream. The French counterattack, launched at 4:00, despite its superior numbers, was checked on the Dipenbeck line by Collier's and Gronkaus's brigades. That line became the focus of both commanding generals who, "in a manner being taken in their March," abandoned the set-piece tactics of the age. Marlborough, "having no Time to give exact dispositions for attacking the Enemy, order'd what was up, as they were, to begin and attack, and the rest to fall in accordingly." The Prussian cavalry Marlborough had led across the Scheldt bridges he now posted on the plateau west of and between Eyne and Heurne to defend the right flank of the Dipenbeck line and force the French advance down into the valley. Two infantry brigades, one Prussian, the other British, now arrived from the bridges. The duke deployed them on the left flank of the line, westward, toward the next objective, the village of Schaerken.[26]

Vendôme had more men, closer to the front, than Marlborough. So the French infantry began to lap around the allies' left flank. At that moment, Argyll's command, twenty British battalions, arrived from the bridges. Marlborough hurried these, his shock troops, to the left of the allied line. First among them was the 16th regiment, with its four nascent American governors general. The British battalions beat back Vendôme's attack and extended the allied line west toward Schaerken. Now, at the crisis of the battle, thirty-six allied battalions engaged fifty French.[27]

Fighting ferociously, Vendôme's infantry finally outflanked Marlborough's men and pushed them back across the Dipenbeck, but count Lottum's twenty battalions of Prussians and Hanoverians had formed line as they debouched from the Scheldt bridges. At 5:45, Marlborough moved them to the British left flank. Fifteen minutes later, the Prussians and Hanoverians counterattacked. They drove the French back across the Dipenbeck but were themselves instantly imperiled as fresh French battalions sought the allied left. Again, the French flanked the allies and pushed them back across the stream. Again, Marlborough met the French attack with newly arrived units of the allies. All these troops were tired by a forced march of fifteen miles to the Scheldt bridges and a final rush of another mile or more from the bridges to the battle line. They had not had a night's rest or a hot meal for five days. Yet they were possessed by an aggressive spirit which now carried the battle westward toward the headwaters of the Dipenbeck and the high ground of the Boser Couter. Marlborough stationed himself at the center of Lottum's command on the allied left. He asked Prince Eugene to take command of the allied right wing, so long unreinforced and now giving way. At 6:15, the French drove Cadogan's command out of both the villages that anchored the allied right wing. At this moment,

Marlborough advanced on the left with eighteen Hessian and Hanoverian battalions. Through their intervals he withdrew Lottum's twenty battalions. As they marched behind the allied lines to succor Eugene, Cadogan, and the allied right flank, Lottum's men caught their breath, reformed their ranks, and arrived just in time to stabilize the allied right.[28]

Now Marlborough's left flank, weakened by the redeployment of Lottum's battalions, began to crumble. He ordered the Hessians and Hanoverians to counterattack. As the Germans recrossed the stream and fought their way into the village of Dipenbeck, on the edge of the high ground north of the stream, the first units of Dutch infantry reached Marlborough. They had been delayed by the breakdown of two bridges in Oudenarde and by traffic jams crossing the three branches of the Scheldt which ran through the town, but now General Wecke reported to Marlborough with the brigades of the Blue Guards, Nassau-Woudenberg, and the Scots-Dutch. Simultaneously, Lottum's battalions obeyed prince Eugene's orders to support a general advance by the allied right. It retook the villages of Herlegem and Groenwald, reestablished the allied right flank, and began to advance westward against the left flank of the French. "With much to do," Sergeant Millner recalled, "we drove the Enemy from Ditch to Ditch, from hedge to Hedge, and out of one Scrub to another, and Wood, in great Hurry, Disorder, and Confusion." To support Eugene's attack, Marlborough detached all of the British cavalry. They reached the allied right flank at 7:00. His cavalry strength doubled, Prince Eugene ordered twenty squadrons of Prussian cavalry to charge the French Household horse. The Prussians broke the French opposite them. Then, at the cost of three-quarters of their number, the Prussian cavalry smashed through the French left flank, almost reaching French headquarters at the Royegem mill.[29]

Simultaneously, on the allied left flank, Marlborough's Hanoverians fought their way into the Dipenbeck village and Wecke's three brigades of Dutch and Scots cleared out the ravines of the Dipenbeck below the castle of Bevere. As his men pushed north and west, Marlborough now could see that the French had not occupied the high ground to their right, the Boser Couter. Marlborough ordered the aged Dutch marshal count Henry van Nassau, lord of Ouwerkerk—"Overkirk," the British called him—to lead the forces emerging from Oudenarde—sixteen Dutch and four Danish battalions and twelve Danish squadrons—through dead ground up the back of the Boser Couter. At 7:30, Overkirk reported that his men were in position. The duke ordered him to advance downhill, assault the French headquarters, and encircle the French right wing. Just after 8:00, the Dutch and the Danes advanced, led by the young prince of Orange in his first battle. At 8:30, Cadogan led the allied attack from the right. At 9:00, the allied pincers closed in on the French headquarters, but those "court ball champions," as the English labeled the royal duke of Burgundy and the pretended king of England, had already fled with, as Vendôme himself contemptuously observed, "astonishing precipitation."[30]

In the gathering darkness, closing in on the center of the battlefield, the leading allied units fired on each other. "The Night now coming on, and the Fire being directed so many several ways at once, that it was impossible to distinguish Friends from Foes, the Confederate generals gave positive Orders to their Troops to give over Firing, and to let the routed Enemy escape, rather than to venture putting themselves into Disorder. This put an end to the Slaughter, and saved the remainder of the Enemy's Army." As the victors rested on their arms, thousands of the enemy slipped away, but many others were rallied by Huguenot officers such as Captain John Ligonier of the 10th (who would direct "the Great War for the Empire" in America). Their calls—"A moi Touraine. A moi Picardie"—drew the broken regiments into the arms of the allies. And all night long, tens of thousands of allied troops continued to march across the bridges. They took post in the dark and, "in a very soaking rain," awaited renewed fighting at dawn.[31]

At first light on July 12, the French army was gone. Thousands had deserted their colors. Other thousands were dispersed across the countryside. Six thousand were casualties. Eight thousand were prisoners of war. Forty battalions, the entire right wing of the French army, had been destroyed. The remaining French had fled north. At dawn, Marlborough, who had spent the wet night on horseback on the battlefield (although he was so weak with malarial fever that he could hardly keep his saddle), ordered a cavalry pursuit of the beaten enemy. The allied horsemen caught and slaughtered the hindermost French as they piled up at bridges broken to forestall the allied pursuit. The surviving French forces did not stop until they had put the Bruges-Ghent canal between themselves and the victorious allies.[32]

In midmorning, almost blind with migraine, the fevered captain general rode into the market square of Oudenarde. He found it packed with French prisoners. As his officers counted coup—fifty-two standards, fifty-six pairs of colors, ten artillery pieces, 4,500 horses—the duke dictated his victory dispatches. He sent them home with his Scots protégé, the earl of Stair, hoping to fulfill his promise to see Stair elevated to the English peerage (he having lost his election in Scotland "by doing his duty in the Army"). "I believe lord Stair will tell you," Marlborough wrote to Godolphin, that the French "were in as strong a post as is possible to be found; but you know when I left England, I was positively resolved to endeavour by all means a battle, thinking nothing else would make the queen's business go on well. This reason only made me venture yesterday, otherwise I gave them too much advantage." Marlborough had been warned by his electoral agent that the new parliament, for all its whig majority, was as "Tickleish" as any chosen since the Restoration. In it "all depends on the Campaign." Only victory in the field would "put it out of every bodys power to be troublesome." War, politics, and empire were one, especially in a dynastic age when kings were supposed to be commanders and empires were their conquests. Every contemporary commentator contrasted the cowardice of the heir to the throne of France and the panicked flight of the pretender to the throne of England with the courageous charge by the prospective prince of Wales, serving in the army of the victorious allies, under the command of the duke of Marlborough, the champion of Queen Anne and her empire.[33]

> Thus distant Regions echo ANNA'S name,
> Convey'd by the Progressive voice of Fame,
> Whilst ANNA'S Sword is Lodg'd in Marlboro's Hand,
> 'Tis Victory to obey, and Empire to command.

Marlborough gave his vanguard, who had first engaged the enemy and borne the brunt of the battle on the right flank, one day to bury their dead and encamp on the field of their triumph. Then, at midnight of July 13/14, he ordered his leading units—forty squadrons and thirty battalions under Argyll's command—to follow the quartermasters west, past Menin, over the Lys, and on through the following night. Early on the morning of the 15th, the allies reached the French frontier between Warneton and Ypres. The British infantry slung their muskets, grabbed shovels, and charged the French fortifications. "It was like running up the side of a House," Matthew Bishop recalled, but those of the French frontier guards who did not run were captured, the allied infantry threw down the entrenchments, and the province of Flanders, the first conquest of Louis XIV, was open to the allies. Marlborough followed with the allied main body, encamped them on the French frontier, and proposed to march on Paris.[34]

To demonstrate how easy it would be to end the war at a stroke, Marlborough ordered the allied cavalry to raid all across Artois and Picardy. Unopposed, they levied enormous "contributions." The France of Louis XIV, for a generation the aggressor in both Europe and America, lay open to invasion. "Were our Army all composed of English," Marlborough wrote, "the project would certainly be feasible but we have many amongst us who are more afraid of wanting provisions than of the Enemy." Chief among them was Prince Eugene. He insisted that the great fortress city of Lille must be taken as a base for any future "projects in France." When it could come up to the front, Eugene's German army—forty-three squadrons and eighteen battalions—small though it was, would be essential, given the allies' inferiority in numbers, a deficit deepened by the arrival of Berwick's army from the Moselle. Eugene's eminent opinion excused the Dutch deputies (some of whom expected to profit from supplying the siege) from their pledge not to block Marlborough's initiatives. Absent the Dutch, the largest and best-disciplined component of the allied army, Marlborough could not advance into France. The earl of Orkney expressed the British disappointment. He was furious with Marlborough for not somehow having forced the allies to march 150 miles to Paris. It was the only public disagreement the two British generals ever had. It was quickly reported and widely disseminated by a growing number of the political class. They said that Marlborough did not mean to end the war that had made him all-powerful in the British empire.[35]

Lille, the second city of France, was no mean prize. The fortress city was the capital of French Flanders, the masterpiece of Vauban's system of geometric fortification, the nexus of the Lys/Scheldt drainage, even the entrepôt of the Dunkirk privateers. The sun king ordered his marshals to risk everything, even another battle with Marlborough, rather than lose Lille. Marlborough's and Eugene's forces were outnumbered by the French army. It lay across their communications both with England and with Holland. The city and citadel were held by a second French army, under the command of the governor general of French Flanders, the legendary marshal Louis Francois, duke of Boufflers. Against such odds, the siege of Lille was Marlborough's and Eugene's most audacious act of war. "The Eyes of all Europe" were fixed on the frontiers of France.[36]

Vendôme's army at Ghent denied the allies the use of the rivers Scheldt and Lys to bring up their siege artillery. Marlborough ordered it diverted to Brussels, together with hundreds of tons of munitions. An unprecedented convoy was assembled: 16,000 horses were to drag 154 artillery pieces and 3,000 ammunition wagons from Brussels to Lille across seventy-five miles of enemy-occupied territory in a column that itself covered fifteen miles of road escorted by 50,000 men commanded by prince Eugene. While the great convoy gathered, Marlborough, "whose active Genius would never let him spend a Day in vain," had more than three weeks to consider the other fronts of the war with France for Atlantic and Mediterranean empire. Believing that the conquest of Spain required a central Mediterranean base, Marlborough wrote to Stanhope: "I conjure you if possible to take Port Mahon." The deep-water harbor of Minorca, Port Mahon was the safest anchorage in the Mediterranean. Its proximity to the allies' base in Spain, Catalonia, made it an ideal supply depot. A fleet based in Mahon could also cow the contumacious states of Italy and convoy the hugely valuable trade to the Levant.[37]

Stanhope's energy, concentration, and force of will drove reluctant naval officers to escort marines and infantrymen from Barcelona. They took not just Port Mahon but all of Minorca in just two weeks. Sir John Leake, commander in chief of the Mediterranean fleet, sailed for home before the conquest was complete. So it was left to Marlborough, as master general of the ordnance, to equip the naval base that the British held for most of the next century. Although the conquest was made in the name of the soi-disant king of Spain, Charles III, Marlborough ordered Stanhope to garrison the citadel with English troops in support of an English army officer as governor. The garrison government of Minorca would educate officers who would command British provinces in the Caribbean, America, and Scotland.[38]

Recalling the terms of the Grand Alliance, by which the English were to retain whatever they conquered overseas, Marlborough ordered Stanhope to negotiate the cession of the island from Spain. "The resigning of that island to us must be a great advantage to our [trade] in all respects," the duke wrote, "but 'tis a very ticklish point," not just because of the Spanish title but also because of Dutch jealousy. Rather more blunt than Marlborough, "Hackum" Stanhope replied that the Spanish would have no choice in the matter. "Charles III" owed England too much money. The Dutch, Stanhope added, would trade anything for one more city for their "barrier" in Flanders. Stanhope enclosed a promotion list for Marlborough's approval. It included the names of Cope and Wade, who would complete the conquest of Scotland, and William, lord Forbes, afterward governor general of Minorca itself and then commander of the Leeward Islands. Approving military rewards for the conquerors of Minorca, Marlborough also urged the lord treasurer to arrange funding from Genoa for Stanhope so that he could consolidate the conquest. Even as he faced a greatly superior enemy and an apparently impossible siege, Marlborough possessed the self-command and the comprehensive information necessary to direct and consolidate a Mediterranean conquest for the British empire. This despite the distraction of utterly extraneous operations.[39]

One more of the futile expeditions concocted in England to seize a French seaport for "carrying the war into the heart of France" (afterward concisely condemned as "breaking windows with guineas") had been entrusted to Marlborough's lieutenant at the ordnance, General Thomas Erle. Erle was "a man of good sense, a hearty lover of his country and likewise of his bottle." Erle's gout, and a certain disinclination for adventure, had botched the project. The obvious French riposte was an assault on the Channel Islands. Their defense was organized by the lieutenant governor of Guernsey, Sir Edmund Andros, seigneur of Susmarez, bailiff of the island, and hereditary head of its assembly. Sir Edmund had retired to govern Guernsey after a lifetime of soldiering that had culminated in successive American commands: New York, New England, and Virginia. Aged seventy-one, Andros was still so much the soldier that he refused to take his annual leave in London: "being so near the Enemy and in a dangerous time of the year I think it my Duty not to leave the Island."[40]

Marlborough had never had any hope for Erle's operation. Now he refused to take the French threat to the Channel Islands seriously, so he redirected Erle's 6,000 troops to Ostend, thence to reopen a direct communication from England to Lille. Erle's men were feeble from confinement, half rations, and disease on shipboard, but he had them in garrison at Ostend by July 22. Presuming on his achievement, Erle secured the royal consent, and that of Cadogan, acting for Marlborough, for the appointment of Captain Charles Gookin, a seventeen-year veteran of Erle's own (the 19th) regiment, as deputy governor of Pennsylvania for the absentee proprietor, William Penn. During Gookin's service with the 19th it had been distinguished in the reconquest of Ireland, both at Aughrim and the Boyne. Then the 19th had been bloodied at Steinkirk, Landen, and Namur. The regiment lost half its strength at Guadeloupe in 1702 and most of the rest at Newfoundland in 1703. Its historian calls the regiment's record "an epitaph for all the old British regular regiments who . . . have proved over and over again that they were the best empire builders in the world." Gookin was expected to push Pennsylvania toward participation in the widening war on the American continent. If, as Gookin expected, Penn sold the province to the crown, Gookin was in place to become governor general.[41]

On the same day that the crown confirmed Gookin's appointment to Pennsylvania, the duke's designate for New York, lord Lovelace, guidon of the Horse Guards, was ordered to take out with him some of "the poor Palatines." These Protestant refugees from the Rhineland had been driven from their homes by repeated French devastation of the palatinate. With Marlborough's assistance, the Palatines were shipped in military transports to an army tent city on Blackheath. Some of them were to settle plantations in the Irish conquest. Others were to extend the contested frontiers of New York and produce pine products—pitch and tar, turpentine and resin—for the British navy. Lovelace would not live long enough to see the Palatines settled, but his death opened New York to another of Marlborough's staff, Colonel Robert Hunter, to command a vastly increased number of Palatine refugees, to begin a much enlarged naval stores project, and to execute the first stages of a plan to invade Canada.[42]

Hunter, who had been captured en route to Virginia, found his exchange long delayed, in part because Marlborough was indignant at the refusal of the French to admit an equality of English officers with their own, and in part because every exchange at the gubernatorial level involved the complex diplomacy of multistate alliances, supervised by foreign ministers. Ponchartrain, Louis XIV's foreign minister, used Hunter's first prospect for exchange, the marquis de Levy, to trade for an Imperial major general. Instead, Pontchartrain proposed to exchange Hunter for the bishop of Quebec, captured by the British en route to Canada, just as Hunter had been taken on his voyage to Virginia. Ponchartrain argued that, as Hunter was "governor of a province on the same continent where Monsieur de Quebec is a bishop," their exchange had an American logic. Indeed, it was a recognized problem in Euro-American diplomacy and governance that imperial executives en route to or from "America and the West Indies" were very liable to be captured at sea. Stanhope prepared a convention for their speedy exchange. The French endorsed it because the British were dominant at sea, but Hunter's case was not covered. Anyway, Marlborough wanted to exchange the bishop of Quebec for the prince bishop of Méan, an imprisoned ally. At last, the French proposed a general exchange of officers captured at sea. Hunter and two naval captains were exchanged for monsieur de Quebec. Two years had passed since Hunter had been captured. He contrasted his ordeal with the instant exchange Marlborough arranged for his lieutenant quartermaster general, Alexander Spotswood, to whom the golden prospect of replacing Hunter in Virginia had already been offered.[43]

During the raids on Picardy, early in August, Spotswood's horse was shot under him, he was deserted by his escort, a squadron of Wood's cavalry, and taken captive to Lille. Marlborough instantly sent a courier to his nephew, marshal the duke of Berwick, offering to exchange an Irish officer, superior in rank, for Spotswood. Immediately returned, Spotswood brought Wood's officers to court-martial for cowardice. He was supported by Cadogan, for the quartermasters' lives depended on the courage of their escorts, but Marlborough pled political considerations (cavalry officers were notoriously well connected) and arranged an acquittal.[44]

Other, higher political issues may have been at play in Spotswood's speedy exchange. Marlborough appears to have used the process to discuss peace with the French. Spotswood, now trusted by both Berwick and Marlborough, seems to have carried messages between the marshal of France and the captain general of the allies. Marlborough signed himself "oo." His willingness to negotiate, so the French thought, reflected his domestic political weakness and that of the European alliance: "the duke of Marlborough must amidst all his prosperity fear the envy and antagonism of his own class, the general hatred of his countrymen, whose favour is more inconstant than that of any other people, the fickleness of his mistress and the credit of new favourites, perhaps the death of the Princess herself [the French did not yet recognize Anne as queen], and the resentment of the Duke of Hanover . . . and lastly, the breaking up of the Alliance." Only such perilous prospects could make "Marlborough, who rules absolutely the councils of the principal European Powers and who conducts their armies," proffer peace. There was also a potential douceur, which the duke himself proposed, of several million livres. Money was no obstacle. Rather, the French high command argued that, with the French armies astride his communications, Marlborough could neither take Lille nor hold it if he did. Louis XIV personally ordered the peace proposal rebuffed in the most insulting terms. Incensed, Marlborough turned to the siege of Lille.[45]

On August 12, 1708, Marlborough ordered Lille invested. While the city was being surrounded, the captain general read Godolphin's report of rumors that the ships on the Jamaica station had taken seventeen Spanish galleons and millions in treasure. Believing that this stroke would destroy the tottering fortunes of France, that the loyalties of Spain would shift to Charles III, and that the ensuing defection of Peru to the allies would presage the breakup of the Spanish empire in America, Marlborough wrote of his and the army's "great joy." Unfortunately, Governor General Handasyde's dispatches told a different, disgraceful, story. Handasyde had put 170 men of his own regiment, with their officers, on board Sir Charles Wager's flagship. So the admiral could carry out a plan, based on Handasyde's extensive, and expensive, espionage, to attack the Spanish galleons after they sailed from Puerto Bello but before they reached Havana and the French fleet. Wager's three warships duly intercepted the seventeen galleons. Despite the disparity of force, Wager attacked the three

Spanish flagships, destroyed the admiral, took the rear admiral, and only lost the vice admiral because Wager's ship, the aptly named *Resolution*, had been crippled in the unequal combat. The other two English captains repeatedly refused to engage. So the bulk of the Spanish fleet reached Havana. "Escorted" by the French fleet, the Spanish galleons brought Louis XIV enough gold and silver to fund another year of war. Wager court-martialed the guilty captains, Bridges of the *Kingston* and Windsor of the *Portland*. Their dismissal from the service, Handasyde wrote, was "a very favourable sentance" for officers who deserved hanging.[46]

General Handasyde himself was harassed by civilians, both at home and in the Jamaica assembly. The London merchants trading to the West Indies put up Peter Beckford of the plutocratic Jamaica family to replace Handasyde (just as the New England traders touted Sir Charles Hobby and the Virginia merchants advanced William Byrd). The merchants soon realized, however, that not only could no civilian advance to a provincial command in wartime but also that any successful officer candidate must also be a favorite of the captain general. So "the most considerable merchants of the Jamaica trade" put forward General George Macartney, just exchanged after his capture at Almanza. He wrote the captain general to say that, if he could not have the privilege of serving under Marlborough's immediate command, he would advance "the Common Cause" in Jamaica. General Handasyde was anxious to be relieved, provided his regiment was relieved with him, Macartney wrote. General Macartney's case for the Jamaica command was strengthened by the prospect that he could serve as chief of staff to the earl of Peterborough, whose American viceroyalty was being reconsidered by Marlborough even as he organized the siege of Lille. The 1702 plan, coeval with the declaration of war, for an assault on Spanish American ports—Cartagena, the shelter of the galleons, in particular—had been revived both by the news of Wager's action and by the prospect of tapping the growing manpower of the American colonies. Raw provincials, however, required regular stiffening. Peterborough proposed to take 2,500 men from the Irish garrison. The lord lieutenant refused to part with them. Marlborough resisted tapping Erle's garrison at Ostend. Then Peterborough complained that his American commission was not as regal as he had thought it would be. Once again, the plan for an American viceregal command collapsed. It left behind it two poison pills: the prospect of weakening Marlborough by an American diversion of his elite troops and a plan for wasting American lives in ambitious expeditions to forward the original war aim, American conquest. Meanwhile, Handasyde was left to write that "the Good News of the Glorious Success of Her Majesty's fforces under the Command of His Grace the Duke of Marlborough . . . puts me and the Regement under my Comand in hopes of being soon Relieved."[47]

Marlborough's "Glorious Success" was the conquest of Lille and with it all of Flanders. The investment of the city began on August 11. Sergeant Littler of the 16th, the army's champion athlete, swam the River Deule and cut the draw-bridge cables at Marquette Abbey, enabling the allies to take post northwest of Lille (Marlborough immediately commissioned Littler). The next day, the great convoy arrived, unscathed, with the siege artillery and munitions. In its seventy-five-mile passage, the convoy had crossed the front of both Berwick's and Vendôme's armies while their commanders argued about how best to attack it. Now the allies, already much inferior in numbers to the French, divided their forces. Prince Eugene led fifty battalions (five of them British) to the siege of Lille. Marlborough reserved for his covering force the bulk of the British, "as the best troops." The captain general had to fend off a French army that was more than double his numbers. Repeatedly, Marlborough offered battle to the French but, despite their huge numerical advantage, and despite the explicit orders of Louis XIV, they declined to attack the duke's cleverly prepared positions.[48]

Protected by the captain general's covering force, the Dutch gunners sited their pieces too far from the outworks of Lille, the Dutch commissaries embezzled stores and munitions, and the Dutch troops took most of the casualties in repeated, costly assaults of men against masonry. On September 20, Marlborough wrote that the siege guns had "already fired very near as much as was demanded for the taking of the town and citadel and as yet we are not entire masters of the counterscarp." So the success of the siege became a matter of logistics. Argyll led another big convoy of munitions overland from Brussels. Orkney, Stair, and Spotswood scoured Artois and Picardy for grain. Finally, the French armies occupied the line of the River Scheldt, entrenched massively on its eastern bank, placed batteries at every possible crossing, built a fortress opposite Oudenarde, and so cut the allied communications with Brussels. The enemy boasted, Marlborough wrote, that their blockade of the Scheldt would "starve and entirely ruin Our Army" and that the allies would never escape from their foolhardy siege of Lille.[49]

The captain general sent "an intelligent good officer," Spotswood's deputy, Captain John Armstrong, "fully instructed with my thoughts," across enemy territory too dangerous to risk writing, to General Erle in Ostend, ordering him to open the new communication. When the supply convoy left Ostend, Marshal Berwick sent a small army—sixty squadrons and thirty-four battalions—to intercept it. The French caught up with the convoy as it passed through a glade in the woods at Wynendale. As the wagons went forward, General John Richmond Webb (who had begun his military career as a Guards ensign in the Virginia expedition) deployed the escort in the Wynendale opening. The quartermasters, Webb's only mounted men, screened the placement of his twelve battalions across the gap. Then the quartermasters joined the grenadier and flank companies of the infantry, hidden in the woods on either side of the glade. The French advanced in overwhelming numbers: horse, foot, and guns. For three hours the French artillery fired while Webb's infantry lay on their arms. Then the French infantry advanced. Webb's men stood up and, firing by platoons, beat off three French assaults. Finally they fought hand to hand with bayonets and clubbed muskets. At the crisis of the battle, the allied quartermasters, grenadiers, and flank companies fired from the woods. The French flanks collapsed on their center. The attackers fled from the field. They left behind their artillery and 4,000 casualties. Meanwhile, the convoy reached the safety of Cadogan's covering force, the quartermaster general himself, with his cavalry escort, having joined Webb during the fighting. The siege of Lille was resupplied.[50]

The political consequences of Wynendale were less happy. As he had after the surrender of Antwerp to Hunter, Marlborough wanted all the credit to go to Cadogan. So it did in the dispatch printed in the *Gazette*. Unlike Colonel Hunter, however, Webb, a general officer and an outspoken tory, had dozens of parliamentary partisans ready to reflect the widespread resentment of Marlborough's military favoritism to "new men," especially that "bluff blundering booby," the upstart Irishman, William Cadogan. The controversy was the more celebrated because the entire nation was transfixed by the drama of the allied army, isolated in France, attacking the second city of Louis XIV's kingdom. Whigs rejoiced at every success and put money on an early capitulation. Tories toasted every setback and took the whig bets, for "if Duke Marlborough beats the French his enemies must become his footstool . . . Veni, Vidi, Vici."[51]

To cut the allies off from Ostend, Vendôme's troops broke the dikes and drowned the lowlands between the port city and the vital transfer point of Leffinghe. There the allies held a knob of high ground and a bridge across the Ghent canal. To transport munitions across the inundation, the British quartermasters improvised relays of flatboats and high-wheeled wagons from Ostend to Leffinghe. Thence they fought through three more convoys to the allied army attacking Lille. After the heroics of Orkney's Royal Scots at the storm of "the Kattie" eliminated the city's last outwork, the main city wall was exposed to the direct fire of the allied artillery. If the city were to be saved, the French had to take Leffinghe. It had been held for ten days against great odds by Major Walter Douglas commanding Livesay's (12th) Regiment. He was a creole officer, commissioned in the 12th by Handasyde during the regiment's West Indian service (Douglas would go home to the Leeward Islands as governor general). Douglas was seconded at Leffinghe by his creole compatriot George Phenney and by Alexander Cosby and Sir Richard Everard (all of these officers were afterward imperial legates).[52]

The 12th was relieved at Leffinghe by elements of two regiments whose colonels were then in England, having just been exchanged following their capture at Almanza and who were asking Marlborough for American commands, Jack Hill and George Macartney. At the relief of Leffinghe, Macartney's regiment was commanded by Jasper Clayton, afterward colonel of the 12th and governor of Gibraltar. Hill's regiment was led by Samuel Gledhill, who concluded his career with twenty-six years in command of Newfoundland, but the commanding officer was William, viscount Caulfield. His orders were to defend the post to the last man. At 5:00 a.m. on October 24, Leffinghe's defenders were surprised by a French assault, delivered in a rainstorm so severe that most of the garrison were under cover and no one could fire a shot. The French took the entire garrison captive at the point of the bayonet.[53]

The fall of Leffinghe and the blockade of the Scheldt meant that the allies were cut off. At that very moment the city of Lille surrendered. Even as Boufflers evacuated the city and the allies invested the citadel, the elector of Bavaria advanced on Brussels, the lightly garrisoned capital of the Low Countries. Marlborough acted as if he were trapped. He had winter quarters established in and around Lille. "The farce was so well managed that our whole army was imposed on by it," one of the duke's aides recalled. The deception itself was the more effective because Marlborough himself was genuinely sick, exhausted by commanding both the covering force and the siege while Eugene recovered from a head wound. Moreover, Marlborough was deeply depressed by the news of the death of his old comrade and longtime conduit to the queen, her consort, Prince George of Denmark. Suddenly, on the night of December 8, 1708, Marlborough ordered the allies to march. Being too sick to ride, he had himself carried in a litter at the head of the allies as they hastened eastward from Lille toward the line of the Scheldt.[54]

At daybreak, after an eight-hour march, the allied columns attacked four crossing points of the Scheldt. Orkney commanded the vanguard. It took the bridges at Gavre. Cadogan led the main body to a crossing at Kirkhoven. Eugene's column, thwarted in its first attempt, diverted to follow Cadogan across the river, "broad, deep, and rapid." At the fourth attack, the Dutch deputies refused to permit an assault from Oudenarde against the French fortress on the far bank, so Marlborough crossed the river north of Oudenarde and split the French defenders. He drove them north and south from his bridgehead. He crushed the French rearguard. Absent an advance from Oudenarde, however, the captain general could not bring the bulk of the French to bay in a battle that, under the circumstances of French surprise and allied concentration, would have been one of annihilation. Instead, Eugene took the besiegers back to Lille and Marlborough pushed on with his men to relieve Brussels. When they were exhausted, the duke pressed forward with sixty squadrons of cavalry and the two battalions of the Guards, riding double. They had covered another two dozen miles when word came that, on news of the allied breakout, the elector had lifted his siege of Brussels and fled, leaving his wounded men and all of his artillery behind, together with what remained of his military reputation.[55]

Marlborough advanced to a rapturous reception in Brussels, congratulated the men and promoted the officers who had conducted a vigorous defense, and sent 1,000 barrels of gunpowder along the reopened communications with Lille. Sharing in the profound demoralization of the French armies and

facing seven well-supplied batteries, dug in at point-blank range, Boufflers surrendered the citadel of Lille on December 9, 1708. The next day, the 10,000
surviving French defenders marched out, through a gate guarded by Argyll,
between the long lines of the allies. In seventeen weeks of siege, the French had
suffered between 6,000 and 8,000 casualties. The allies had lost double those
numbers. The five British battalions at the siege had lost half of their men. The
16th and its quartet of governors general in training had been especially hard
hit. All the redcoated storm troops had casualties far above the allied average,
but the second city of France had fallen. Louis XIV was again forced to the
peace table.[56]

During the seven months of fighting in 1708, Marlborough had said again
and again that he would not rest until Ghent and Bruges had been recaptured,
the water communications they controlled reopened to the allies, and the winter quarters they had supplied to the British troops reoccupied. On the day that
Boufflers surrendered the citadel of Lille, Marlborough wrote, "we must have
Ghent and Bruges, let it cost what it will." Nine days later, the British invested
Ghent. It was defended by 20,000 French troops. A French sortie decimated
the 10th Regiment, but Marlborough's gunners emplaced 110 artillery pieces to
threaten the city, despite the onset of the worst winter in a century. Unseasonable cold had one advantage for the shivering besiegers. It froze Ghent's water
defenses. Rather than face an assault over the ice, the French capitulated. On
January 2, 1708/9, for ten hours, nineteen French squadrons and thirty-seven
battalions filed out of Ghent. As they passed, they saluted Marlborough. En
route to France, the retreating French evacuated Bruges and Leffinghe. The
allies had recaptured all that they had won in 1706 to add to their astonishing
conquests in 1708. Marlborough declared that his army had "been blessed by
God with more success than ever was known in one campagne."[57]

CHAPTER SEVEN

Malplaquet

MARLBOROUGH DID NOT hurry back to England from the scene of his triumphs in Flanders during the campaign of 1708. Instead, he commuted through the terrible winter from allied headquarters in Brussels to the Mauritshuis in The Hague. In both the Netherlands capitals, the captain general drove forward preparations for the largest army ever fielded by the allies. At the same time, he supervised negotiations for a comprehensive peace with France in Europe and America. Marlborough's preparations for war were supported by the whig-controlled British parliament. It authorized 10,000 additional troops in British pay and made military appropriations of £7 million. As for peace, the duke was directed by repeated parliamentary resolutions that no peace would be safe for Britain or its allies that did not put the whole of the Spanish empire—Flanders, Iberia, Italy, and America—in the hands of the Hapsburg claimant, Charles III. The demand of the Spanish empire for Charles was in effect an expression of English imperialism because Marlborough, through Stanhope, had already imposed on Charles III cessions of Gibraltar and Minorca and a treaty that gave England a monopoly of Spanish American trade.[1]

Peace talks with France had just begun at the end of February 1709 when Marlborough was relieved by Prince Eugene and sailed home. Having received the thanks of parliament for his victories, the duke voted for the addresses that proclaimed England's peace priorities: the security of the Protestant succession; the demolition of Dunkirk; and the cession of the entire Spanish empire to the Hapsburgs. In return for their support of these peace terms, the Dutch were promised British support for a barrier treaty which would put Dutch garrisons in the Flanders fortresses, even when the Low Countries reverted to Spain.[2]

No mention of North America appeared in these votes. Marlborough understood that American cessions were so offensive to France that their discussion would stop preliminary peace negotiations. Neither was it clear how much of French America was to be conquered or claimed. Despite Marlborough's objections to any diversion of force from Flanders, the junto whigs intended to invest heavily in Colonel Samuel Vetch's plan for the conquest of Canada. News had just arrived of the French sack of St. John's, Newfoundland. Merchants from London to Bristol agitated for an American expedition expanded to take all of Newfoundland and Acadia and Quebec as well.3

Still of the opinion that victory in Flanders would do more to win America than any number of expeditions, Marlborough nonetheless secured command of the proposed Canadian expedition for a favorite officer, George Macartney. He had won Marlborough's approval by offering to serve wherever he might be posted. Macartney flattered the captain general by expressing his preference for service under Marlborough's immediate command in Flanders but, Macartney proposed, if Marlborough could expedite his exchange (Macartney had been captured at Almanza), he would take up an American command. A recurrent possibility was the government of Jamaica. Their civilian nominee having been rejected, the London merchant wing of the Jamaica opposition party had approached Godolphin to see if Marlborough would approve of Macartney's relief of Governor General Handasyde. Macartney suggested to Marlborough that if his Almanza regiment were reconstituted, its officers could relieve Handasyde's, "leaving his Seasoned men there for the Service of that Island."4

Marlborough replied that if Macartney took command of the Canadian operation, he could have the Jamaica government as a reward, but Macartney could neither have his own regiment in the island dominion nor could he take over Handasyde's rank and file. Marlborough had promised Handasyde that he would relieve both the governor general and his entire regiment and "it would be for the good of the service that Generall Officers should not have Regiments on Particular Commands." "The good of the service" demanded that generals focus on protecting their commands, not their regiments. Then too, since regiments and governments were equivalents, separating them would help meet the demand for military appointments by the Scots aristocracy, new players in the imperial patronage game. Marlborough would allow the Hamiltons to nominate an officer to the Jamaica viceregency. He knew that Macartney was acceptable to Orkney. Therefore, the first vacant regiment belonged to the rival clan Campbell. It went to Argyll's brother, lord Islay.5

Oddly, Macartney was given the Canadian command without being told that Jamaica was reserved for him. Godolphin thought "it won't be quite right to fill his head with that expectation till his present expedition be over," and it was not clear that Macartney would be free to take any American command. Despite Marlborough's extraordinary efforts—as a purely professional soldier, Macartney's "fortune depends on his liberty," so the captain general wrote to the French minister of war—Macartney's exchange was tied up with that of the Almanza regiments. Macartney had to stretch the terms of his parole to devote his demonic energies to organizing the assault on Canada. He reviewed the composition of the naval squadron. He insisted that its commodore not be selected by seniority but rather be an officer "known to be understanding & acquainted with those parts." Macartney collected arms for the American provincials from Marlborough's ordnance office. He solicited troop transports for the regulars from the transport board.[6]

Colonel Vetch, in London to push his plan to conquer Canada, praised Macartney's "indefatigable zeale for every part of the service." These Scots commanders sought fame, a success that "will transmit your name with lasting honour to posterity." More broadly, the conquest of Canada would "advance the Glory of her Majestys armes, enlarge her Empire and augment the trade and happiness of all her British subjects through her several dominions." Of course, Vetch wrote, the achievement in America would also be a whig coup, exemplifying "the unprecedented zeale, care, prudence and Loyalty of the present matchless ministry."[7]

That ministry was obsessed with America. Marlborough wrote from London to Heinsius that if Heinsius could see "the Zeale everybody here has for carrying on of the Warr . . . you would think me a very moderate man . . . for they would have Newfoundland, and Hudson Bay, as well as our Treaty of Commerce, and some other pretentions to have been in the Preliminaries" of the peace treaty with France, American terms that Louis XIV would not concede in advance of even more allied victories. Before he left London for The Hague and the negotiation of the preliminaries, Marlborough attended to Newfoundland himself. He approved Colonel John Moody's commission to succeed Major Thomas Lloyd in the island command. Lloyd had been captured when the French overran St. John's. He wrote to Marlborough that the French had refused to parole him because, as a prisoner, he had "seen their fortifications in America." So Lloyd could, he said, instruct the expedition against Canada. Reports to the Newfoundland merchants, however, had it that Lloyd had been caught napping at St. John's. Marlborough did nothing to arrange his exchange. Rather, he authorized General Erle at the ordnance to equip Colonel Moody to restore the St. John's garrison and fortifications and to rearm the inhabitants.[8]

The next day Marlborough left London, bound for The Hague to discuss the demands the allies might make on a France defeated on the battlefield in 1708 and debilitated by the arctic winter of 1708–9. The great concern of the Dutch was their fortress barrier against French aggression, but Marlborough wanted to keep the Channel ports, Ostend in particular, free for English trade, and he wished to protect the Hapsburg property in Flanders and Brabant. This would help keep the Imperialists in the war and, despite all his renunciations, Marlborough still hoped to become the Imperial governor general of the Spanish Netherlands. The captain general had made his officers viceroys of the American provinces. He wanted the greatest viceregency in Europe for himself. At this critical juncture, the Imperialists again offered Belgium to Marlborough.[9]

The duke was embarrassed by his own divided desires. He wished to preserve allied unity but he wanted a substantial principality of his own. He disapproved of the inflexibility and scope of the allied demands on France, especially that Louis XIV pledge vital French fortresses and cities as sureties that he
would remove his grandson, Philip of Anjou, from Spain by force if necessary,
but Marlborough also had to cement whig support for a circum-Atlantic settlement. So he returned to England, chose the most agreeable of the whig leaders, Charles, viscount Townshend, as his fellow plenipotentiary, obtained some
modification of the barrier proposal, secured support for a favorable treaty of
commerce with France, and solicited explicit instructions for the restoration
of both Newfoundland and the Hudson's Bay to queen Anne's empire. Fatally,
Marlborough could not modify the demand that the allies be given control of
the frontier of France as an assurance that Louis XIV would expel his grandson
from Spain.[10]

Desperate for peace, Louis XIV had dispatched his foreign minister, Jean-
Baptiste Colbert, marquis de Torcy, to offer Marlborough enormous bribes for
allied concessions about Spain. Marlborough refused the bribes. Instead, he
issued forty-four articles of nonnegotiable demands for the surrender of the
Spanish empire to Charles III, and the withdrawal of French forces and French
merchants from Spanish America. Marlborough intended to win by victory in
Europe the English objectives in the Southern Hemisphere he had laid out in
the imperial plan of 1702. That plan would control English strategy in America
for the rest of the century.[11]

In North America, Marlborough demanded that Newfoundland be restored to the English. Agreeing, Torcy introduced a clause into the Newfoundland article for a mutual restoration of conquests in America. The existence
of this clause stopped preparations for the Canadian expedition for two vital
months while the allies awaited King Louis's ratification of the preliminary
articles of peace. The Canadian expedition was further set back by a change of
commanders. General Macartney was accused of rape by his housekeeper. Advised by the bishop of London, Queen Anne deprived Macartney of command.
The charges were soon dropped (Marlborough and Godolphin considered
them extortionate fabrications), but in the meantime, Macartney's exchange
had come through and he had joined Marlborough's staff. So Marlborough
named Colonel Thomas Whetham, veteran of Guadeloupe and governor general designate of the Leeward Islands, as commander of the Canadian expedition and had him promoted brigadier general. Whetham was already involved
in the expedition as the senior officer of the three regiments from the Irish
garrison assigned to Canada. Just as army officers had long been transferred
from Irish to American commands, now entire regiments were to be detached
from the garrison of England's greatest colony to make American conquests.[12]

It was Newfoundland—"which is in effect all that England asks"—for
which Marlborough negotiated most strenuously with Torcy. Marlborough was

assured by his English correspondents that "Your Grace having gott all New-foundland to be restored to us, gives an unspeakable joy to all the substantial and reputable people of trade and Commerce, from Southampton round the Land's End to Bristoll & . . . will make and keep you more real friends then Bank and both India companies put together." The pressure of the commercial community on the Marlborough-Godolphin ministry for favorable treatment in the peace was relentless. The directors of the Hudson's Bay Company re-called Marlborough's service as the company's governor. Their reaction against Marlborough's proposed Anglo-French commission to determine the bound-aries of Hudson's Bay with Canada and the amount of French reparations due to the company was so hostile that he had to explain that he had conceded the commission—a prescription for inaction—not so much because of the severe French opposition to any concessions in America but rather because of the al-lies' jealousy.[13]

England's allies and her enemy had the same fear: that in the final settle-ment Britain would achieve enormous American advantages. Anglo-American expectations were equally expansive. William Penn wrote to Marlborough that at a general peace conference France would be helpless to resist cessions in America, either because Louis XIV had given up the cautionary French for-tresses or because he had refused the preliminary terms, seen his last army de-feated by Marlborough, and been driven to accept a drumhead peace treaty. In it, Penn expected the captain general to cut the heart of North America out of French Canada. He proposed that Marlborough establish the northern bound-ary of English America at the St. Lawrence River, extend that boundary west-ward through the Great Lakes to the head of the Mississippi River, and project it thence "to the extreme bounds of the continent westward." Penn's prescient prescription of the present Canadian-American border was intended to wipe out the French claim to the Illinois and Louisiana territories, a claim based on LaSalle's exploration which, as Penn doubtless knew, had been challenged by the then lord Churchill in 1686 and 1687. So British America would become a continental empire, invulnerable to the threat of French amphibious attacks which menaced the very existence of the current coastal colonies. Penn sub-mitted this proposal for an Anglo-American continental empire "to the Duke's English head and heart to secure his country so great an one."[14]

The French plenipotentiaries signed the preliminary articles of peace at the end of May 1709. Marlborough was so "sure of a good peace" that he or-dered a canopied chair of state for the diplomatic conference scheduled to be-gin on June 15 (with characteristic frugality, he told Sarah to make sure that the chair could be converted to a bedstead for Blenheim) but, on June 4, Louis XIV refused to accept the preliminaries of peace. The king pointed out that if he surrendered his last frontier fortresses as guarantees that he would force his grandson from Spain in just two months, and failed to do so, the allies would invade an undefended France. From the outset of the negotiations, Marlborough had deplored this unreasonable requirement, the notorious "Article 37." Marlborough's critics, who had demanded that he impose impossible terms, now abused him for doing what they had demanded. They attributed to his warmongering what was due to their greed. As Colonel Cranstoun put it, because France had been willing to concede so much, "people wrought themselves . . . into a persuasion that . . . as they seemed to have given us up their shirt they would give us their skin too." Marlborough's culpability in all this was political cowardice. Because his political position was weak, he had, against "his real judgement," publicly supported what he personally disapproved, the Dutch and whig demand for Article 37. Marlborough feared "what advantage his enemies at home would have made of it" if Spain did not fall to the Hapsburg claimant and so enter the ambit of English empire.[15]

Still, as Cranstoun observed, both the junto whig leaders at home and the whig officers who predominated in the army "seemed pleased at continuing the war." Their views were shared by Godolphin. He wrote Marlborough that the French "had never intended to give up Spain and the Indies" because from Spanish America they drew the income that supported their military. The French negotiation and consideration of the preliminaries had been mere chicane: "this delay & uncertainty has already been of great use to france, it has made us suspend our Expedition to North America." Torcy's restitution clause in the Newfoundland article had made that expedition "pointless," since whatever was taken would have to be returned. Now, said the lord treasurer, there would be no more negotiations: "I see no more room for signing any Treaty, but on a drum head." Marlborough was to impose an unconditional surrender on France. So he was to win both Spain and America for England.[16]

Marlborough agreed. He went further yet. He promised to revolutionize France. The captain general would march "with 150,000 Plenipotentiaries" into France. He would fight a decisive battle. "If God almighty as hitherto bless the Armes of the Allyes," Marlborough would conquer all of France, deflate the French monarchy, and restore the French parliament. Marlborough intended that this French revolution, like his own coup in England twenty years before, would reduce French influence and transform a despotic tyrant into a constitutional monarch. The eclipse of the sun king would cement the European balance of power and secure the peace of the Atlantic world. Marlborough's plan to impose a constitutional monarchy on France, he wrote, "is more likely to give quiet to Christendome then having provinces from them [the French] for the inriching of others," whether Dutch or Austrian.[17]

If Marlborough was to destroy absolutism by force in France, as he had by a coup in England, he must bring the French to battle on the frontier of Flanders. The late start to the campaign—which actually owed more to the ravages of "the great frost" and the wettest of springs and summers than to the chicanes of French diplomacy—limited the allied options to three: a frontal assault on the lines of La Bassée, lines designed to prevent Marlborough's direct advance from Lille to Paris and held by Marshal Villars with 110,000 men; an advance northward to flank the lines by a siege of Ypres, followed by an invasion of France along the Channel coast, supported by the British navy; or a movement southward to take the southern anchors of the La Bassée lines, Tournai and Mons.[18]

Marlborough argued for the assault on Ypres, an advance along the Channel, and a subsequent march on Paris. As always, he was opposed by the Dutch. They already resented England's occupation of Ostend and Marlborough's refusal to give it up to the Dutch barrier. A Channel campaign would take more ports, enhance English commerce, and strengthen Marlborough's claim to command Flanders and Brabant as the imperial viceregent. Because the Dutch supplied most of the allied infantry, they could veto Marlborough's Ypres option. Both the Dutch and prince Eugene, who spoke for the Empire, favored the most conventional course, a set of sieges. The capture of Tournai and Mons would complete the conquest of Flanders for the Empire and add two fortresses to the Netherlands barrier. Once again, the daring dimensions of Marlborough's strategy had been deflated by his allies' political parochialism and by their military conservatism.[19]

Yet, when the allied army marched from Lille on June 26, it seemed that Marlborough had chosen to storm the La Bassée lines. In 1915, "the donkeys" of the British general staff sacrificed the future of England on the same battlefield. As the officers of the Royal Welch recalled, however, "the last time the regiment visited these parts we were under decent leadership. Old Marlborough had more sense than to attack the La Bassee lines; he masked them and went around." Marlborough did march the main body of the allies directly on the lines, capturing Villars' attention, but Marlborough eschewed the attack that Cadogan, speaking for Spotswood and the other quartermasters, had declared to be suicidal. Instead, the duke feinted north, toward Ypres. Villars stripped his southern garrisons to meet this threat, the one he most feared and that Marlborough had openly argued for. As night fell, however, Marlborough doubled back. At daybreak on June 27, 1709, to the surprise of friend and foe alike, the allied army found itself facing the fortifications of Tournai, Vauban's most perfect fortress and the southern anchor of the La Bassée lines.[20]

Drained of defenders by Villars to counter Marlborough's feints, Tournai was nonetheless "one of the best fortify'd Places by Art that is in the World." Even though the most exposed forts had been seized by Orkney's division at the moment of investment, Tournai's garrison of only 5,000 or 6,000 men inflicted 3,200 casualties on the allies before they took the extensive outworks. It took another month of costly fighting before the city surrendered. Then the able-bodied men of the garrison withdrew into the apparently impregnable citadel. It was defended by underground galleries, tunnels, and explosive-packed mines "which the Besiegers could hear [the enemy] working upon under their feet at almost every Step they advanced." An entire battalion of the allies was blown

up in one enormous explosion. So the allies dug countermines. The allied mining parties fought their French counterparts underground with their shovels
and picks. Then men in armor were sent into the mines to engage, sword and
pistol in hand: "every step was taken with Apprehensions of being blown up
with Mines below them, or crushed by the Fall of the Earth above them, and all
this acted in Darkness, has something more terrible than ever is met with in an
other Part of a Soldiers Duty." The citadel of Tournai held out until September 3, 1709. Its capture had cost the allies another month of the already abbrevi-
ated campaigning season and 2,288 additional casualties, each doubly lamented
by his comrades because "every one had been sure of a peace in the spring."[21]

Marlborough was deeply depressed, both by the death of his veterans at
Tournai and by his growing apprehension that he could not end the war. He
knew that he was disappointing both his supporters in the cabinet—who had
assumed that "the best army . . . ever seen" was "ready to march to Paris"
and impose peace on the French—and exciting his parliamentary critics, who
declared that the duke was extending the war to prolong his power. Hearing
the duke's forecast of stalemate, the lord treasurer asked him to approve a plan
that could quiet the leaders of both parties. They believed that American expeditions would "be attended with more advantageous consequences to Great
Britain's Empire then the many millions [that] have been expended in the European wars."[22]

The captain general had laid down a Caribbean strategy at the outset of the
war. It was now refreshed by Governor General Handasyde. He was prepared
to put his entire garrison aboard the Jamaica privateers and attack one or another of the Spanish West Indian ports. The admiralty could supply warships to
escort Handasyde's force. It would be augmented by two additional regiments
from the British Isles and by 1,500 American recruits from New York and New
England. Excited by General Handasyde's plan, the ministers proposed that to
unite these provinces' military resources and employ them in imperial service,
the governments of New York and New England would be recombined in a
new Dominion of New England. It would be commanded by Colonel Hunter.
"If," the lord treasurer wrote to the captain general, "you approve the Scheme
& the person," Colonel Hunter could easily recruit 1,500 provincials "for this
Service to wch the hopes of plunder will naturally incline them." Once again,
the War of the Spanish Succession had produced the plan of Anglo-American
conquest that would be reiterated on ever-larger scales until, after many decades of war, the strategy of 1702 was realized at last, the power of France and
Spain was erased from the American littoral, and the imperial contest of two
centuries was resolved at last in favor of the upstart "English."[23]

Colonel Hunter's friends in Marlborough's army had already asked the
captain general to recommend him to the ministry for another American command. So the duke wrote to the treasurer that Hunter was "a very honest man
and a good officer." When Marlborough received Godolphin's outline of the

plan to unite American and Caribbean forces in an attack on Spanish American ports, he reiterated his belief that "Coll Hunter whome you mention for the West Indies is a very good man, as to the expedition itself it is impossible for me to give any judgement but I know that 4 [Halifax] 17 and 5 [Somers] by the judgement of some marchants, are made very fond of such expeditions, but I do not remember any that has hithertofore ever serv'd for any thing but a pretext to plunder." Godolphin should not be led by the whig junto, especially that "coxcomb" Halifax, to waste money on extravagant expeditions with no aim but the old-fashioned Elizabethan one, plundering the Spanish.[24]

Nonetheless, Marlborough repeated that his veteran subordinate, Colonel Robert Hunter, was "a very good man, and that I am confident he will execute any orders that shall be given him very well." Marlborough also agreed to ask lord Orkney to hold open the lieutenant governorship of Virginia, formerly Hunter's, as an alternative American reward for General Macartney, now serving on Marlborough's staff as a volunteer. What the captain general would not willingly do was nominate anyone but a serving officer under his command to an American government. Godolphin, noticing the clamor against Colonel Mitford Crowe's administration of Barbados, proposed to replace him with Robert Lowther, an ordnance official. Lowther was trying to apply ordnance patronage to his family's parliamentary "interest," much to the master general's annoyance, but he rejected Godolphin's suggestion of an American command for Lowther on the basis of principle, asking, "how will that agree with the Queen's resolution at my desire of giving those governments to the officers of the Army"?[25]

The politicization of the ordnance office manifested the captain general's shrinking authority in all the agencies of the armed state. At the admiralty, Marlborough had lost influence by the death of Prince George and the dismissal of Admiral Churchill. Worse, Marlborough had lost access to Queen Anne, which the prince and the admiral had, however eccentrically, offered. These losses were the more damaging because the queen was now utterly alienated from the duchess of Marlborough. Anne was listening instead to her dresser, Abigail Masham, and through her to Robert Harley. Marlborough's fatal loss of favor at court could not be concealed. Given an opposition to Marlborough led by Argyll and his ilk, even the British army in Flanders was politicized. Desperate to cement his hold on the army, the ultimate source of imperial authority, the duke asked the queen to commission him captain general for life. Marlborough remembered that king Charles II had so commissioned the general who put him on the throne, George Monck, duke of Albemarle. Queen Anne should equally reward the general who had assured her accession. Anne temporized, fearing not only that the commission would make Marlborough effectively "King John" in her own lifetime, but also that it would enable Marlborough, once again, to dictate the imperial succession, this time to the Hanoverians whom Anne feared and hated. In the meantime, lord chancellor Cowper's researches revealed that Monck had commanded only at the royal pleasure. Marlborough's own agent, James Craggs, added that the unprecedented authority Marlborough sought was "lyable to Malicious Constructions." Marlborough shelved his request. To retain even his existing authority, much less to perpetuate his power and secure the peace, the captain general would have to win a decisive battle.[26]

To provoke that battle, even before Tournai fell on September 3, Marlborough ordered a division under lord Orkney to move on Mons. The capital of Hainault, the residence of the elector of Bavaria (as captain general of the Netherlands), the southern anchor of the La Bassée lines, and the last French fortress in Flanders, Mons was a prize for which Louis XIV would risk the last army of France. He had pulled troops from every theater in Europe to protect the frontiers of France. He had canceled the planned dispatch of thousands of troops to Canada. He had called up the last financial reserves of monarchy and aristocracy in France, imperiling both in the event of a defeat. Defeat would entail enormous concessions in North America, put the empire of Spain in the hands of the Hapsburgs, and transfer the trade of Spanish America to British merchants. With the future of France, Spain, and America at stake, the king ordered Marshal Villars to risk everything rather than lose Mons.[27]

On September 2, 1709, lord Orkney led the grenadiers of the allies to the investment of Mons, knowing, as he wrote, that Marshal Boufflers had reached Villars' camp "with orders to risque all and venture a battle." In heavy rain, up to their knees in mud, the elite infantry of the allies began nine days of marching, five of them without bread, to invest Mons and provoke the final battle of the war. On September 6, Orkney's command sundered the French lines between the rivers Haine and Sambre and invested Mons before Villars could reinforce the garrison he had stripped to defend the La Bassée lines.[28]

On September 7, Villars' relieving force reached the long crescent of woodland and broken country which lay between his army and Mons. The allied right wing under Prince Eugene, which had arrived to cover the siege, now moved west to block Villars' passage through the northern gap in the forest line. Sliding south behind the woodland screen, by September 9 Villars reached the southern gap between the Bois de Sart and the Bois de Lanières. In the gap stood a village called Malplaquet. Here Villars' advance encountered Marlborough's.[29]

September 10 was a day of lost opportunities. Villars failed to attack Marlborough before Eugene could come up. Marlborough failed to attack Villars before he could fortify a naturally strong position. Orkney explained that "all the army had orders to advance, which we did, but there came such a prodigious dusty rain that we lost one another, and for some time knew not where we were, and really [were] in a good deal of confusion." The Dutch division found themselves "in woods and a terrible country," isolated far to the left of the allied main body but opposite the French right wing. Marlborough ordered

Orkney to close the gap opposite the Malplaquet opening. This the earl did "after a tedious march." Fortunately, Villars did not attack either the isolated Dutch or the deploying British forces. The French did open up with artillery, "particularly where our English foot were," Orkney recalled, "and killed us a good many men." They could not reply because "wee had no guns come up." The allied cavalry could not attack the French because Villars had infantry deployed in the woods of Taisnières and Lanières on the flanks of the forest opening. So the allies used up the 10th of September forming a line of infantry brigades: the Dutch on the left, the British opposite the Malplaquet gap, the Imperialists and Germans and Danes on the right. The allied cavalry picketed their horses behind the infantry line.[30]

Excuses had to be found for the allies' fatal failure to attack on the 9th or 10th: Eugene's forces had been slow to close up; the same rain that slowed them retarded General Withers, coming up with the last troops from Tournai; and some "people judged twenty battalions, were worth staying another day for." These "people" did not include even the usually cautious Orkney and they certainly did not include Marlborough, but Eugene expected an infantry battle and the Dutch wanted Withers's brigades to reinforce their outnumbered division on the allied left. To bring up Withers's column, the fort guarding the passage across the Haine at St. Ghislain was stormed but, conversely, 100 men were detached from every allied battalion to invest Mons, "a great weakening to us." Meanwhile, "all that day [the 10th] my Lord Duke and Prince Eugene went about reconnoitring and by 2 or 3 in the afternoon could perceive them [the enemy] very well entrenched every where." The French center was apparently impregnable, for the forest gap, two miles wide, now was spanned by five cannon-proof redans, held by three elite infantry brigades, supported by dozens of heavy artillery pieces, well dug in, and backed by the entire French cavalry, 260 squadrons, ready to charge through the intervals of the redans. No one could see into the French infantry dispositions in the forests, but trees felled and chained together, fronted by the abatis of their sharpened tops, produced the impression of a regular fortress. "To tell you freely," Orkney wrote, "I really believ'd since we had not attacked all Tuesday, there would be no battle at all. For indeed . . . I don't believe ever army in the world was attacked in such a post for from their right to the left, I may call it a counterscarp and traverse; in many places 3, 4, and 5 retrenchments one behind another."[31]

An attack seemed the more doubtful because the allied commanders thought themselves opposed by equal numbers, about 100,000 men to a side, but the minimum advantage required for a successful attack on a fortified position was usually reckoned to be at least three to one. To defeat the odds, Marlborough offered his usual plan. Powerful, determined, costly, attacks against the enemy flanks would force him to draw infantry from his center. Then Orkney's fifteen British battalions would storm the enemy earthworks and open the way for Marlborough to lead the allied cavalry onto open ground for a decisive charge.

Only because Withers's command was delayed in its march to the battlefield was there any variation in this, the plan of Blenheim and of Ramillies. Arriving late to the scene of action, Withers's column was ordered to march directly against the French left flank.[32]

During the night of September 10–11, the allies dug in most of their 100 artillery pieces in two great batteries in front of Marlborough's position. One battery would fire over the French redans in the Malplaquet gap. Its cannonballs would ricochet through the ranks of the French Household drawn up on the ridge behind the fortifications. The second allied battery was posted to fire into the French forest line to the right of the Malplaquet gap, in support of an allied infantry attack on a salient of the "Tanniers" forest. As at Blenheim, the allied infantry deployment was covered by a morning mist rising from the sodden fields. Then, at 6:00 a.m., the sun broke through, bedazzling veterans on both sides. Masses of brightly uniformed allied troops were suddenly seen marching toward the forest. From his position in the allied center, Orkney exulted at the "noble sight" of "so many different bodies marching over the plain to attack a thick wood where you could see no men."[33]

Just before 8:00 a.m., "a discharge of all our artillery" announced three allied infantry assaults against the enemy lines in the woods. The allied right wing—thirty-six battalions—was commanded by John Mathias, Reichsgrafen von der Schulenburg. His Prussians and Imperialists were met by "such a fire of musketry and cannon I believe no man alive ever heard." They recoiled from the woods, reformed, and went forward again, and again. Simultaneously, twenty-two battalions of Danes, Hessians, and Saxons, commanded by the Prussian field marshal Philip Carl, count Lottum, with Marlborough in presence, marched up the Malplaquet gap, despite the enfilading fire of fourteen French guns, which "carried off whole ranks at a time." When Lottum's men reached the allied battery that had been pounding the Taisnières salient, they turned a quarter right and charged into the forest. The firestorm drove them back. They were reinforced by a British brigade commanded by Sir Richard Temple and led to the charge by the intrepid duke of Argyll. Argyll tore open his clothes to show the men he wore no body armor. He was seconded by John Richmond Webb who fell, severely wounded, as did most of the other officers. After four hours of fighting, often hand to hand and with no quarter given or taken, "the trees of the wood was guilded with blood." At midday, the allies finally broke through the Taisnières wood only to face a final French entrenchment on the plain, supported by massed cavalry and commanded by Villars in person.[34]

The third attack, by thirty Dutch and Scots-Dutch battalions, the allied left wing, went forward to disaster at 8:30. The divided Dutch command— the aged republican Claude Frederick t'Serclaes, count Tilly, and the youthful prince of Orange-Nassau—ordered five columns to storm the French defenses in the wood of Lanières. The Dutch division carried three lines of French entrenchments, held by forty-six battalions, despite flanking fire from a concealed French battery of twenty guns. By then the Dutch were out of ammunition and most of their officers were killed. They were driven back from a fourth French entrenchment "with such a butchering that the oldest generall alive never saw the like," Orkney wrote. Tilly lacked the force of character to prevent the vainglorious Orange from ordering the ragged battalions back to the charge. The Blue Guards and the Scots-Dutch were annihilated. These, the elite regiments of the Dutch army, lost 5,000 men in the first half hour and more than 8,000 in three hours of action. Officer casualties were appalling. They included the Scots brigade's commander, Orkney's kinsman lord Tullibardine. A French counterattack against the shattered left wing of the allies was checked only by the arrival of the landgrave of Hesse-Cassell with twenty-one squadrons of cavalry and both the allied commanders, Marlborough and Eugene, with a brigade of infantry. They commanded Orange not to attack again without Marlborough's direct order.[35]

The duke's senior subordinates' commanders did not always obey his tactical orders. They were free to respond to the ever-changing circumstances of battle, always providing that, by so doing, they advanced the captain general's larger objectives. Between 10:00 and 11:00 a.m., lord Orkney was "embarrassed" by the retreat of the allied infantry from the Taisnières salient. The French counterattack began to fire into the right flank of Orkney's fifteen battalions. Despite Marlborough's "positive orders to send in none of my foot to the woods, but to keep that line entire" to storm the redans, Orkney "sent in the first battalion of Guards and my own battalion, which very soon redrest matters there again, and, in a little time after that, joyned Count Lottum's and the Duke of Arglie's troops; so we got possession of the corner of the woods which flanked the retrenchments of the enemy" in the Malplaquet gap. Villars was about to counterattack when he saw Marlborough advancing to Orkney's support with thirty Dutch cavalry squadrons. Villars now withdrew the Irish brigade from the defense of the redans and moved it to his left to meet the allies as they emerged from the woods. He then drew two more brigades from his center to attack Lottum and Schulenburg as they cleared the wood of Taisnières. This, the allied center, reinforced by Eugene and, "by a kind of miracle . . . seven big cannon" gotten through the woods by Schulenburg's men, met the French counterattack. As the battle hung in the balance, Withers's column deployed from the north end of the woods. His cavalry were broken by the French horse, but his infantry advanced, took the French counterattack in flank, wounded Villars and his chief subordinate, and killed the third-ranking French general. In the confusion, Prince Eugene led the Dutch cavalry to the charge. At last, the French left wing fell back.[36]

Demoralized by the retreat of the troops on their left flank—or, as a general officer with the French put it, rather than "risk spoiling their beautiful uniforms"—the elite French and Swiss infantry who had manned the redans in the Malplaquet gap moved right to take shelter behind Boufflers' unbroken right wing. It was not so much want of courage that caused these Household regiments to retire, a bitter veteran wrote, but "fear of the embarrassment they might cause the state" if it had to replace such outstanding men as themselves. They left the redans in the Malplaquet glade lightly held. By 1:00, his hussars had assured Orkney that he was not marching into a trap. He led his thirteen remaining battalions up the Malplaquet gap, ably assisted by his brother lord Archibald Hamilton. "Archy," Orkney wrote to one of their brothers, "I believe would have made as good a land officer as a sea one, and I vow very ready to judge well of every thing, and was a great help to me. He only wonders how anybody comes off where bullets fly so thick." Led by the brothers Hamilton, the British battalions took post on the faces of the five redans at the top of the Malplaquet glade and looked out at the double line of French cavalry squadrons on the plain: the French Household and the Gendarmerie under Marshal Boufflers' personal command.[37]

Here was the turning point of the most savage battle of the age. Firing by platoons, Orkney's battalions held off the French cavalry while the allied horse formed up behind the redans. At 1:30, the Dutch squadrons began to debouch onto the plain to face the French Household troops. "Before we got 30 squadrons out," Orkney relates, "they came down and attacked; and there was such pelting at one another that I really never saw the like." The vanguard of some 60,000 horsemen was now engaged. Broken, the Dutch cavalry were seconded by Scots and English mounted regiments, brought up by Marlborough in person. Against the fire of French pistols and carbines, the Scots Greys, under Stair and Campbell, wielded cold steel. Sword in hand, the Scots broke through both French lines. The Greys were followed by Wood's English regiments, but Boufflers' counterattack beat the outnumbered British back through the redan intervals. The Gendarmerie were hard on the heels of the British cavalry when Orkney's battalions "gave them such a fire that it made all that body retreat prodigiously."[38]

For almost two hours, the cavalry battle swayed back and forth across the plain of Malplaquet. Six times the allies advanced. Each time Boufflers' troopers beat the allies' cavalry back to the redans held by Orkney's British infantry. "I really believe," Orkney averred, that "had not ye foot been there, they would have drove our horse out of the field." At last, Prince Eugene came up with the Imperial cavalry, Marlborough committed the last four battalions of his infantry reserve, "and in Person rallied and brought the said disordered squadrons to the charge again." The combined allied assault finally forced Boufflers back. His retreat ended the renewed French infantry assault on the shattered allied left wing, an assault that endangered Orkney's left flank. There Prince Eugene, his head bandaged and his sword in his hand, fought on foot at the head of the shattered Dutch. The landgrave of Hesse-Cassel committed his cavalry to support the final Dutch counterattack. The French right wing withdrew.

Retreating in good order, the French battalions were covered by Boufflers' cavalry as they crossed six miles of watery plain. At last, the French put the Hogneau River between themselves and the allied cavalry pursuit. Unable to extract enough of their exhausted infantry to support their cavalry, break up the French formations, and achieve a bridgehead across the Hogneau, the allies were left masters of the battlefield. They bivouacked there, worn out but sleepless because of "the horrible cries and groans" of thousands of wounded men.[39]

The allies had suffered 18,500 casualties: "in many places they lye as thick as you ever saw a flock of sheep." The French, for the most part entrenched or fighting from cover, had lost perhaps two-thirds as many men. The casualties of Malplaquet had never before been equaled in a single action. They would not be surpassed until the battles of the First World War were fought over the same ground with nearly identical tactics. Hard cases such as Cadogan took the slaughter in stride. "We have lost a good many of our Friends," he wrote, "but victory cannot be bought too dear." Lord Orkney thought otherwise. He recovered the body of his nephew from the human wreckage of the Scots Brigade, men too closely packed together to walk among, men so shattered that most had to be buried on the spot. Orkney got Tullibardine's body as far as Brussels, on its way home to Scotland, before it putrefied and was buried, hastily and amid tears, in the cathedral. "I hope in God it will be the last battle I may ever see," Orkney wrote home of Malplaquet, for "a very few of such would make both parties end the war very soon."[40]

Yet the British had been but lightly hit at Malplaquet. They had casualties of only 1,856 men out of some 13,000 engaged. Nonetheless, these losses, and news of the destruction of the Dutch infantry, suddenly crystallized the war weariness of the queen and her people and reflected terribly on the captain general, the personification of the endless war. Colonel Kane recalled that "Malplaquet was the most desperate and bloody Attack and Battle that had been fought in the Memory of Man; and both our Generals were very much blamed for throwing away so many Men's Lives, when there was no Occasion," for the siege of Mons could have been undertaken without fighting. Malplaquet "was the only rash Thing the duke was ever guilty of, and it was generally believed he was pressed to it by Prince Eugene; And this very Battle gave the Duke's Enemies a Handle to exclaim against him, in saying he delighted in War, and Valued not Men's Lives."[41]

In the wake of the battle, Marlborough comforted himself with the thought that, as he put it to Sarah, it was now "Impossible for the French to continue the warr" and that they would immediately return to the peace table. To Godolphin, Marlborough admitted he had fought "a very murdring battle," but "God had blessed us with a victory, we having first beat their foot, and then their horse. If 110 [Holland] pleases it is now in our power to have what peace we please and . . . this is likely to be the last battel I shall be in." Marlborough was half right. He would never fight another battle, but there would be no quick peace. The last army of France had survived. Emboldened by its effective resistance and unopposed retreat, it manned the lines of La Bassée and blocked the road to Paris. Marlborough was reduced to fighting the sort of indecisive, but costly, siege warfare he despised. Never again would he have the superiority of force, the unquestioning obedience, and the political power necessary to fight a decisive battle. For Marlborough, there would be no peace, no Paris, no restoration of the untrammeled authority over the British army and government that he had enjoyed since Blenheim.[42]

After Malplaquet, the siege of Mons seemed anticlimactic and its surrender inconsequential, even if, by "lyeing very quiet, and not attempting to relieve Mons," the French admitted that they had been defeated. A month after the battle, the allied siege train arrived at Mons and was emplaced in preprepared positions. Cadogan's serious wound put much responsibility for conducting the siege on Spotswood and added to the trials of their aging and exhausted captain general. The rains of the sodden spring and summer continued into the alluvial autumn. In trenches deep in mud and water, the besiegers fell sick. Marlborough was seriously ill himself and he was deeply depressed by the memory of "so many brave men killed with whome I have lived these eight years, when we thought ourselves sure of a peace." When Mons surrendered on October 21, 1709, it had cost the allies another 2,000 casualties. One of them was Marlborough's second application to be captain general for life, denied by the queen on October 25. Four days later, seeking to preserve the prospect of a viceregency in a viable Belgium, Marlborough refused to sign the Barrier Treaty with the Dutch. Townshend signed anyhow and Marlborough sailed for England.[43]

He suffered from another stormy Channel crossing but, once home, appearances altered. It seemed that unending victory had propelled Marlborough to the apex of imperial authority. The duke received the thanks of both houses of parliament for his unprecedented, his eighth, victorious campaign. In the shortest campaign of the long war, the captain general had not only captured the last two French fortress cities in Flanders, he had also won his fourth pitched battle against what had been the dominant army in the Atlantic world. A hitherto critical Scots colonel wrote that Malplaquet "was the most solemn, and well-ordered battle that ever I saw—a noble and fine disposition, and as nobly executed. Every one was at his post, and I never saw troops engage with more cheerfulness, boldness, and resolution. In all the soldiers faces appeared a brisk and cheerful gayness which presaged victory . . . for we never doubted but we would beat them."[44]

Postscript: Malplaquet in America

"War is the school where great men are formed," so contemporaries contended. Malplaquet was especially instructive for the military cadres of the British imperial administration in America. They fought the war for America, which had been declared, in Marlborough's own words, to drive back French aggression along the frontiers of empire from the Hudson's Bay to the Leeward Islands. From that declaration, in May 1689, the war went on for three-quarters of a century. Anticipated in 1709, the Peace of Paris was finally signed in 1763. In remarkable measure, British victory over France in the Atlantic world was the work of Marlborough's officers at Malplaquet. No fewer than sixteen of them became governors general. Sixteen more Malplaquet officer veterans perished in American campaigns. Nine drowned in the St. Lawrence in 1711 (together with 884 rank and file). Seven died in the Cartagena campaign of 1740–41. These thirty-two Malplaquet veterans were joined in American commands by thirty-five senior sergeants, selected for promotion following distinction at Malplaquet. Commissioned as the queen's officers to drill the provincial armies of New York and New England, these Malplaquet veterans led thousands of British and American rank and file in the intersections of army and empire in America. Many of the regiments that fought at Malplaquet already had posted officers to administer the American and Mediterranean campaigns and conquests of the circum-Atlantic war. Now even more followed. That the "regimental connection" was an organ of Anglo-American imperial administration was amply evidenced by the careers of the Malplaquet veterans.[45]

Malplaquet was "the greatest battle I ever saw," said Orkney. No one in the century divided by Malplaquet ever saw a greater. Close to 200,000 men were engaged on a single field of battle. They fought over rough and wooded terrain. They suffered tens of thousands of casualties in a battle punctuated by innumerable crises and improvised responses. The resulting confusion occludes the organization and participation of the British units in the battle. This is especially the case with the British infantry brigade, which formed part of the twenty battalions that advanced from Tournai under the command of Lieutenant General Henry Withers. His British brigade was probably made up of the 16th, 18th, 26th, and Prendergast's regiments. Withers's troops had been the last to leave the siege of Tournai. Thence they had marched sixty miles through the mud, without camping, crossed the Haine at St. Ghislain (stormed to let them through), and strode directly into the battle, which had been delayed until they could arrive. Originally, Withers's column had been intended to reinforce the Dutch on the undermanned left wing of the allies, but to move the Tournai troops all the way across "the terrible country" over which the allies struggled to deploy would have delayed the fighting yet another day. So Marlborough ordered Withers to march directly on the left flank of the French. This improvisation worked to perfection. Unexpected and unchecked, Withers's troops arrived just in time to break the French counterattack on Schulenburg's division. They killed or wounded the three generals in command of the French center and left. In the ensuing confusion, the allied right drove the French left from their last entrenchments and into retreat across the plain of Malplaquet.[46]

The senior regiment of Withers's British brigade was very much a part of the Marlborough connection. Its colonel was the captain general's brother-in-law, Charles Godfrey. Accordingly, the (16th) regiment was a fertile field for governors general. No fewer than seven American executives served with Godfrey's regiment in Marlborough's campaigns. At Tournai, the 16th had seen desperate service in the mines, fighting "in armour and by lanthorn and candle." Four officers of the 16th survived both Tournai and Malplaquet to take up American commands. A captain at Malplaquet, William Gooch, was lieutenant governor and commander in chief of Virginia for twenty-three years (1727–51). As brigadier general, Gooch again commanded the 16th at the siege of Cartagena in 1741, but his own regiment was "Gooch's American Foot," four battalions, thirty-six companies, 4,000 men, from eleven mainland colonies. A lieutenant in the 16th at Malplaquet, Major Benjamin Gregg, died under Gooch's command at Cartagena. John Doucet had been commissioned captain in the 16th at the outset of the 1709 campaign. He made his imperial administrative career in a conquest of this war, Nova Scotia. There he governed Annapolis Royal and helped raise the 40th Regiment, the legionary foundation of Nova Scotia. A noncommissioned officer of the 16th at Malplaquet, Sergeant Abraham Gee, received the queen's commission as a lieutenant when he sailed for America, one of thirty-five veterans who provided essential drill and discipline for American provincial armies in, and after, 1711.[47]

The most famous regiment in Withers's British brigade was the 18th, the "Royal Irish." At Tournai they had stormed the breach of the ravelin, forcing the French to retire to the citadel. During the siege of the citadel, the Royal Irish entered the mines. There they were blown up and suffocated by the dozen. The regimental orderly books of the Royal Irish underwrote three of the (all too rare) participants' histories of Marlborough's campaigns. One was written by the commanding officer of the Royal Irish at Malplaquet, "Marlborough's drill master," Brevet Lieutenant Colonel Richard Kane, afterward commander of Britain's two Mediterranean conquests in this war, Minorca and Gibraltar, and author of the standard history of Marlborough's campaigns (owned by George Washington in the 1757 edition). Like Colonel Kane, Captain Robert Parker was both a historian of Marlborough's wars and one of the drillmasters who taught Marlborough's new fire-discipline to infantry units all across the empire. Parker had spent the 1708 campaign drilling the army in Ireland and writing *The Duke of Marlborough's New Exercise of Firelocks and Bayonets: Appointed by His Grace to Be Used by All the British Forces, and the Militia.* Parker returned to the 18th in time to fight at Malplaquet. There he observed with a proper pride the platoon volleys that, at the moment of allied victory, broke the Royal Regiment of Ireland, the famous "wild geese" in the service of Louis XIV. Marshal Villars had brought up the Irish regiment from the glade of Malplaquet to attack the allies as they emerged from the wood. Withers's battalion took the attackers in flank. Thrice, the Royal Regiment fired its line volleys at the Royal

Irish. Twice, the Royal Irish replied with platoon firings, delivered at a range of 250 feet. Thereupon, the wild geese "retired into the wood in a great disorder. On which we sent our third fire after them, and saw them no more," wrote Captain Parker. In this "fair trial of skill between the two Royal Regiments of Ireland, one in British, the other in the French service," the latter had forty casualties, the former four. The success of Marlborough's drill meant that it was slavishly copied for fifty years, even where, as would be so disastrously the case at Cartagena and the Monongahela, it was utterly unsuitable.[48]

The third regiment in Withers's British brigade were the Cameronians (26th). The lieutenant colonel commanding the Cameronians, James Cranstoun, was perhaps Marlborough's most influential military critic, for his intercepted letters were read by Harley. Cranstoun survived Tournai, wrote home to denounce the lost peace—"we were wrong to push things so far and refuse offers that appeared so reasonable and sincere"—and lost his life at Malplaquet. He was succeeded by another eloquent Scots critic of things English and sinful, Major John Blackadder. He termed Malplaquet the "great Ebenezer" of his life and a "great and glorious victory," but his views may have been colored because, after it, Marlborough's "court" approved his promotion to command the Cameronians, that most pious and puissant of regiments. The Cameronians had been Samuel Vetch's regiment (and his brother's) before the peace of 1697 had sent him out to essay Scots empire, first in Darien, now in "Nova Scotia." Both of Blackadder's successors in command became imperial executives (of a minor sort, the regiment being poorly connected and religiously radical). One of the Cameronians' ensigns at Malplaquet, John Colville, died as lieutenant colonel of General William Gooch's American Regiment at Cartagena in 1741.[49]

The last of Withers's British regiments lost its colonel at Malplaquet. Sir Thomas Prendergast had a premonition of his death but, as General Oglethorpe told his Georgia Rangers, Prendergast survived the attack. He was being twitted by his comrades about false visions when he was killed by the last shot of a French battery which had not received orders to withdraw. Prendergast's death opened a regimental command for General George Macartney, so frequently named to American commands. Macartney succeeded Prendergast only to be dismissed within the year as a whig and a Marlborough loyalist. The regiment was stripped from Marlborough's army in Flanders and shipped to America in 1711. There, after a long summer in Boston, the regiment lost no fewer than five officers and 200 men, shipwrecked in the St. Lawrence. The shattered remnants were disbanded in the tory purge of 1713.[50]

The allied attack on the French salient in the wood of Taisnières was led by the Prussian count Philip Carl Lottum. His command included Sir Richard Temple's British brigade, composed of the duke of Argyll's (3d, the Buffs) regiment; Webb's (8th, the King's); the Royal Scots Fusiliers (21st); and Brigadier Gilbert Primrose's foot (the 24th, formerly Marlborough's). The Buffs were a very senior regiment indeed, having been raised in 1572 by that pioneer of

English empire in America, Sir Humphrey Gilbert. The Buffs had provided at least seven officer governors since 1660, but under Argyll's command, only "red John of the Battles" himself, and his major, received imperial commands during the war. At Minorca, Argyll displaced Marlborough's favored subordinate James Stanhope, the conqueror of the island. The operational command of Minorca was held by Argyll's major at Malplaquet, John Fermor. Years in the future, Argyll would make one of his lieutenants at Malplaquet, Gregory Beale, lieutenant governor of Jersey but, all told, this was a very modest imperial showing for a regiment as senior as the Buffs and for an officer of Argyll's pretensions. Ambitious but ill-informed Americans, William Byrd of Virginia, for example, appealed in vain to Argyll against the dominance of the provinces by Marlborough's men.[51]

Argyll's presumption was unbearable but his bravery was unquestionable. Equally brave, but less lucky, General Webb was seriously wounded seconding Argyll at Malplaquet. Webb was another would-be rival to Marlborough. That, together with his services at Wynendale, had won him the Isle of Wight government, but his regiment sent only a single survivor of Malplaquet to America, Sergeant Philip Buckhurst. One of the nearly three dozen newly commissioned second lieutenants who disciplined companies of the American provincial armies in 1711, Buckhurst stayed on as an officer of the garrison at Placentia, Newfoundland, taken from the French as part of the peace of 1713. The third regiment of this brigade, the Royal Scots Fusiliers—or, in the new union nomenclature, the "British Fusiliers"—lost their colonel, Brigadier General Sampson de Lalo, at the outset of the attack, and recommended none of their survivors to American commands. As for the 24th, another serviceable but not political corps, only Lieutenant Christopher Ganey among the 24th's Malplaquet veterans went on to serve in America. Ganey died a captain of grenadiers at Cartagena in 1741. Of course, the regiment's greatest losses in America were the 302 men drowned in the St. Lawrence in 1711.[52]

The bulk of the British infantry, a double line of fifteen battalions, was under the command of the earl of Orkney. His consistent success as a division commander, especially pronounced at Malplaquet, combined with Orkney's clout as the Hamilton's family's military representative, his importance as the counterpoise to Argyll among Scots soldiers, and, as Marlborough thought, Orkney's service as the captain general's agent in the election of Scots peers to the parliament of Great Britain, gave Orkney a unique capacity to nominate Scots officers for American commands. His aide at Malplaquet, Orkney's younger brother the naval officer lord Archibald Hamilton, was soon Jamaica's viceregent. Orkney also nominated Colonel Alexander Spotswood (who acted as Orkney's chief of staff at Malplaquet) as his lieutenant governor and the royal commander in chief of Virginia. Orkney was prominent among the friends of Colonel Robert Hunter. During the 1709 campaign, Orkney pressed Marlborough to give Hunter command, either of New York and New England or of

Jamaica. Orkney also recommended two sergeants from the first battalion of the Royal Scots as officers in America. One of them, William Moore, went out to serve in the Canadian expedition of 1711.[53]

Orkney ordered his own regiment, the Royal Scots, the 1st of foot, "Pontius Pilate's bodyguard," into the wooded salient, together with a Guards battalion, sixteen companies of the First Guards and six of the Coldstream. Marlborough himself was colonel of the First Guards and General Withers was his lieutenant colonel. Withers nominated three sergeants of the First Guards as lieutenants for American service. Two of them went out in 1711: William Matthews and Thomas Garland. The junior captain of the First Guards at Malplaquet was John Guise. Thirty-one years later, Guise was promoted a brigadier general at Cartagena. He survived yellow jack and Spanish shells to become governor of Berwick.[54]

The Guards' adjutant and drillmaster was Brevet Major and Guards Lieutenant William Blakeney. This Blenheim veteran also survived Malplaquet to serve at Cartagena. Colonel Blakeney had raised the American Regiment, traveling through the mainland provinces of the empire. The regiment established patterns of promotion and recruitment that became the norm for the crown's American regiments: field officers were commissioned directly by the king; company-grade officers were given royal commissions by their respective governors general; lieutenants and sergeants were assigned from regular British regiments to drill each provincial company; the private soldiers were (partially) equipped and (supposedly) paid by the crown. *The New Manual Exercise by General Blakeney* was written for the new American Regiment and printed, in many editions, by Benjamin Franklin. Brigadier General Blakeney came home from the West Indies to be distinguished in the '45. Then his determined defense of Fort St. Philip, Minorca, made Blakeney an Anglo-American hero. Created a knight of the bath and baron Blakeney in 1754, this Malplaquet veteran lived to see the final defeat of France in America.[55]

The lieutenant colonel commanding the Coldstream Guards, Major General Edward Braddock, father of the more famous "Braddock of the Coldstream" who fell at the Monongahela at the outset of "the great war for the empire," was not at Malplaquet, but he did nominate three sergeants to serve in America. Two of them, William Wilkinson and Robert Kitchener, went out. An ensign at Malplaquet, John Huske was captain and lieutenant colonel of the Coldstream and governor of Hurst Castle by 1721, colonel of a regiment (the 32d) at Dettigen, Falkirk, and Culloden, and governor of Jersey. The lieutenant of the Coldstream grenadier company at Malplaquet, William Hanmer, was commissioned colonel of marines for the Cartagena expedition and died of yellow jack. Because the six companies of the Coldstream at Malplaquet took 200 casualties, there were relatively few survivors to make their way in the administration of empire. Besides, the bulk of the regiment was on service elsewhere. Captain and Lieutenant Colonel John Moody was in Boston, reorganizing the

Massachusetts provincial army and arranging to take over his new command at Newfoundland. Lieutenant Thomas Talmarsh was fighting under Stanhope's command in Spain. He would be promoted major and lieutenant governor of Montserrat at the peace. The younger William Mathew, presently lieutenant and quartermaster of the Coldstream (the family regiment of this Leeward Islands clan), would govern Nevis at the peace and served as lieutenant general of the Leeward Islands from 1729 until 1752.[56]

Brigaded with the Guards and the Royal Scots under Orkney's command at Malplaquet was lord North and Grey's (the 10th) regiment. Orkney says nothing of detaching this regiment for the attack on the Taisnières salient, but the regimental historian places the 10th in the forest fighting. Certainly the 10th was up to the task, having perhaps the highest percentage of Blenheim veterans of any regiment at Malplaquet. One of these veterans was the lieutenant quartermaster general, Brevet Lieutenant Colonel Alexander Spotswood. Orkney nominated Spotswood to Marlborough for the Virginia command he held from the year of Malplaquet until 1722. In 1727, Spotswood was tipped for the Jamaica command that finally went to Hunter. On the outbreak of war with Spain in 1739, Spotswood was promoted major general and named quartermaster general and second in command to lord Cathcart for that assault on Spanish American ports that had been pending ever since Marlborough's grand plan of 1702. General Spotswood was also commissioned colonel of the four-battalion American Regiment and raised its Virginia companies. Spotswood died at Annapolis on June 7, 1740, while recruiting Maryland's companies of the American Regiment.[57]

The Huguenot refugee and Blenheim veteran Brevet Major John Ligonier fought within the 10th in the assault on the Taisnières wood. Ligonier's uniform was pierced by twenty-two shots, but he himself was untouched as he led the 10th forward in support of Argyll's attack. The grateful Scots duke brevetted Ligonier lieutenant colonel as his major of brigade in Spain. Colonel Ligonier was Argyll's lieutenant governor of Fort St. Philip, Minorca, and also served as deputy governor of the island conquest under Richard Kane. Forging more links in the chain that bound army to empire, General Ligonier named a young officer, Jeffrey Amherst, as his aide at Dettigen. In 1745, Ligonier was determined to "begin the war where the duke of Marlborough had left it" on the Flanders frontier of France. He was rewarded with the government of Guernsey. Ligonier's career in army and empire ascended until, as general of the horse, he became William Pitt's chief military advisor in the Great War for the Empire. Promoted field marshal, Ligonier, together with lord Anson at the admiralty, was one of "the first two great Chiefs of Staff in our imperial history."[58]

As such, Ligonier supervised the buildup of forces that gave his nominee, John Campbell, earl of Loudoun, more British troops to take Quebec than Marlborough had commanded at Malplaquet. Ligonier hoped to see Loudoun

"return from America with as much honour and applause as the Duke of Marlborough did from Blenheim fields." Ligonier himself became commander in
chief, the title that had replaced Marlborough's rank as captain general. He
succeeded to the master generalship of the ordnance, formerly Marlborough's.
Ligonier was commissioned colonel of the First Guards, as Marlborough had
been. With the duke's military titles, Ligonier inherited Marlborough's responsibility for the ongoing world war with France. In the American theater, Ligonier reiterated, with much great resources and infinitely greater success, the
plan of 1709 for the double assault on Canada: up the St. Lawrence River to
Quebec and down the Lake Champlain corridor to Montreal. Ligonier named
Amherst to command the Champlain attack and Wolfe to lead the riverine
ascent. It was Ligonier who announced to Amherst his reward, the government
of Virginia, the same post lord Orkney had held when he ordered Ligonier
and the 10th to attack the French in the forest at Malplaquet. The name of the
fatal wood, "Taisnières," Ligonier had engraved on his tombstone in Westminster Abbey to commemorate the decisive moment of his career in army and
empire.[59]

The fourth regiment in Orkney's right-hand brigade at Malplaquet was
that of a Marlborough partisan, Lieutenant General Thomas Meredyth. With
Macartney (and Honywood), Meredyth fell victim to the initial tory purge of
the army. Like Macartney's former corps, the 37th Regiment was further vic-
timized by being ordered out to Canada in 1711. Four of its officers who had
survived Malplaquet perished in that expedition. One died of illness at Boston. Three others perished on the reefs of the Isle of Eggs, together with 252
men of the 37th. Laurence Armstrong was more fortunate. Fighting with the
37th, he had survived Oudenarde and Malplaquet. Now Armstrong escaped the
St. Lawrence disaster. He served at Annapolis until, in 1715, after the Marlborough restoration, Armstrong was commissioned as a founding captain of the
40th Regiment, the Nova Scotia legion. Promoted lieutenant colonel of the
40th in 1720, Armstrong took command of the regiment in 1731, in the midst
of his fourteen-year tenure as lieutenant governor and commander in chief of
Nova Scotia.[60]

Orkney's second brigade at Malplaquet was headed by his second battalion.
This unit of the Royal Scots was thick with company-grade officers who had
served throughout Marlborough's campaigns. Hard hit at the Schellenberg and
at Oudenarde, the Royal Scots second battalion had recruited replacements
who sustained its jacobite reputation. None of its Malplaquet veterans became
imperial administrators. The second regiment of Orkney's second brigade was
Sabine's (the 23d) regiment, afterward the Royal Welch Fusiliers. Turnover had
been high since the regiment fought at Blenheim. Only the colonel, Brigadier
General Joseph Sabine, and nine of his officers survived the five intervening
campaigns to fight at Malplaquet. Sabine had joined the 23d as its major in 1691
and commanded as lieutenant colonel at the Schellenberg. Wounded, he was

promoted colonel of the 23d. Greatly distinguished at Ramillies, Sabine was promoted brigadier general and commanded a brigade at Oudenarde and at Malplaquet. As brigadier general, he governed a conquest of this war, Gibraltar, from 1730 until his death in 1739. (In the intervals of service, Sabine built up perhaps the most admired collection in England of the decorative arts.) Sabine nominated Sergeant Walter Harris of the 23d for promotion to lieutenant in America. He brought the discipline of the regiment out to the American provincial forces in 1711.[61]

To the left of Sabine's fusiliers in Orkney's second brigade stood the earl of Orrery's foot, commanded by Lieutenant Colonel John Corbett. Brevet Colonel Corbett had petitioned Marlborough either for a regiment of his own or its equivalent, an American government. Corbett was a veteran officer, having served since he was fourteen. Colonel Corbett's services at Malplaquet won him Marlborough's nomination to the Maryland command in 1710, but he did not go out. Instead, Corbett was promoted brigadier general in 1711 and commissioned colonel of the 23d in 1713. Having been preferred by the tories and tainted with jacobitism, Corbett was not reemployed by Marlborough and died, disappointed, in 1717. Corbett had nominated one of his sergeants at Malplaquet, Christopher Wade, for the American service but, like his colonel, Wade did not go out. Ensign Robert Boyle of the 23d, reduced to half pay in 1713, reappeared on the army list as captain lieutenant in one of the new marine regiments raised for Cartagena. There, in 1741, he died, with so many other Malplaquet veterans, in the renewed Atlantic war.[62]

The third of Orkney's British brigades at Malplaquet probably included Temple's, Evans's, and the 15th and 19th regiments of the line. Major General Richard Temple's regiment had a short life. It was raised for Marlborough's first campaign in 1702 by half-pay officers formerly commissioned in Henry Dutton Colt's regiment during its tour of duty in the West Indies. These officers were very likely creoles. One of them, Brevet Colonel William Newton, commanded the regiment at Malplaquet. Frequently promoted by Marlborough and commissioned colonel of the regiment in 1710, Newton and his regiment were an obvious tory target for disbandment in 1713. At Marlborough's restoration in 1715, Newton, with many of "Temple's" other veteran officers, raised a regiment of dragoons. Captain Edward Richbell, who had served under Newton at Malplaquet, was not among them. He had taken service with Colonel Robert Hunter in the garrison of New York. Richbell's comrade Captain Edward Wolfe had been promoted major by Marlborough. Wolfe, too, was reduced to half pay in 1713, but when Marlborough was restored to command of the First Guards at the accession of George I, the duke had Wolfe commissioned captain and lieutenant colonel. Wolfe commanded a regiment of marines at Cartagena. His martial son was selected by Ligonier to attack Quebec, the apotheosis of the plan for the conquest of Canada that had been laid down in the year of Malplaquet.[63]

The 15th Regiment, so much an imperial legion, also had an American foundation. Boasting the familiar West Indian names of Foulkes and Billingsly among its officers, the 15th had suffered at Tournai, especially by the explosion of a mine beneath the regimental battery. So the regiment was posted in Orkney's second line. Nonetheless, it was damaged in the fighting for the French redans in the Malplaquet gap. Three officers were killed and sixty-four other ranks were casualties. The 15th returned to West Indian service again, and not for the last time, when it suffered enormous losses at Cartagena in 1741. At the moment of Malplaquet, the vacant colonelcy of this senior regiment was being contested at the highest levels of government. Marlborough was finally forced, by queen Anne's order at the instance of the duke of Somerset, to award the command of the 15th to Somerset's heir, Algernon Seymour, earl of Hereford, one of Marlborough's aides at Malplaquet. Conferring the 15th on Hereford thwarted Marlborough's plan to give senior regiments to two serving general officers: "these gentlemen have served all the war, and my Lord Hartford hath both fortun and aige to have a little patience." One of these veterans, Thomas Meredyth, settled for the 37th but, to find a regiment for General Andrew Windsor, the Blenheim and Ramillies veteran who had been wounded at Malplaquet, Marlborough had to look to the British regiments in Iberia where, the captain general claimed, he did not usually meddle in promotions. Aristocratic politics next compelled Marlborough to approve Hereford's commission as governor of Tynemouth Castle, in the heart of his (and the 15th's) home county. The earl went on to govern Minorca during the Spanish War of 1737–42. Thence he transferred to the government of Guernsey, concluding the lifelong career in imperial commands begun at Malplaquet. Such commands were increasingly coveted by aristocratic youth, for Marlborough's victories made the service prestigious. Marlborough's own son-in-law, the duke of Montagu, was with him at Malplaquet. Brevetted colonel of horse in the next promotion list, Montagu left the Horse Guards and became proprietor of St. Lucia and St. Vincent in 1722, the very year when the new Walpole regime decelerated imperial expansion.[64]

Lieutenant General Thomas Erle's regiment (the 19th) was also without its colonel at Malplaquet. Erle was absent administering the ordnance as Marlborough's second in command. Because Erle's regiment had lost half its strength in the Cadiz-Guadeloupe-Newfoundland expedition of 1702–4, it did not again see foreign service until Erle brought it with him to Ostend in 1708 to protect Marlborough's communications for the siege of Lille. In 1709, both the colonel and the regiment still smarted at being implicated in the loss of the vital convoy link between Ostend and Lille at Leffinghe. They were trying to bring the commander at Leffinghe, colonel lord Caulfield, to a court-martial. Cardonnel wrote to Erle on the eve of Marlborough's advance toward the lines of La Bassée that the duke had said, "there is nothing he would not most willingly do to make you easy in the matter of Caulfield," but he had jumped directly from

French custody to an English refuge in order to evade the jurisdiction of Marl-borough's court-martial in Flanders. Nonetheless, Marlborough promised to give Caulfield's conduct "such a turn with the Queen and Lord Treasurer" that he would be cashiered. So he was. Meanwhile, Erle was busy supplying muni-tions and commissions for Boston artillerists to General Vetch. Erle's nominee to Marlborough for the Pennsylvania government, Captain Charles Gookin of the 19th, was pleading, to small avail, with the Quaker legislators for support for the expedition against Canada.[65]

The final regiment in Orkney's third brigade was Brigadier William Ev-ans's. Evans was a Marlborough loyalist and a whig partisan. So the twenty-two-year career of his regiment ended on the tory block in 1713. In 1715, the colonel himself was rewarded for his constancy during Marlborough's exile and the Hanoverian succession crisis by promotion to the colonelcy of a dra-goon regiment. Many of Evans's erstwhile officers—all half-pay veterans of Malplaquet—were recommissioned and, by virtue of acquiring commands in a mounted regiment, promoted. In the meantime, Evans had nominated one of his senior sergeants at Malplaquet, Matthew Low, for promotion to commis-sioned rank in America. Low accepted, as did Sergeant Timothy Bagley, the nominee of the lieutenant colonel commanding the 19th at Malplaquet. Both of these new officers drilled companies in New England.[66]

Ranked in columns behind Orkney's infantry at Malplaquet were the squad-rons of Major General Wood's cavalry brigade, seven regiments strong. Orkney himself, whose infantry brigades sustained the cavalry in combat at Malplaquet, was proudest of his countrymen, the "Grey Dragoons." The colonel of the Scots Greys was major general the earl of Stair (perhaps Marlborough's favorite officer and the patron of another Scot and dragoon officer, Robert Hunter). Stair commanded the British cavalry when it broke the French Household. The major of the Greys was the honorable Charles Cathcart. Major General lord Cathcart died in command of the Cartagena expedition. His regiment at Malplaquet had needed 100 replacements when the day was done. Suffering with them were the Royal Irish dragoons, Colonel Hunter's old outfit (none of them followed him into imperial service). In the British breakout from the redans, "little lord Lumley" was also distinguished. Henry, lord Lumley, heir to the earl of Scarborough who, although he commanded as a lieutenant general, nonetheless charged with his fellow Blenheim veteran brevet colonel Thomas Panton at the head of two squadrons, "one of Lumley's and one of Woods's," af-terward the 1st and 2d Dragoon Guards. None of Lumley's aristocratic officers risked American command, but two officers of Wood's Horse took peacetime assignments in imperial administration.[67]

The major of Wood's regiment at Malplaquet, Samuel Shute, exchanged the lieutenant colonelcy of the regiment for the government of Massachu-setts, where he served from 1716 to 1723. John Pitt, Marlborough's master of the horse, was captain lieutenant of Wood's cavalry at Malplaquet. Promoted captain and lieutenant colonel of the First Guards, Pitt governed Bermuda for a decade after 1727. He had inherited an interest in imperial administration from his father, Thomas ("Diamond") Pitt. The elder Pitt had been governor of Fort St. George, Bombay, for the East India Company. He was commissioned governor general of Jamaica in 1716, but did not go out. "Diamond" Pitt's elder son, the cavalry colonel Thomas Pitt, earl of Londonderry, would serve as governor general of the Leeward Islands, 1727–29.[68]

Lieutenant General Cadogan, the captain general's chief of staff, was the colonel of a veteran cavalry regiment. Its junior cornet, William Cosby, had fought in four of Marlborough's campaigns. One of six sons of that military and imperial clan the Cosbys of Stradbally Hall, Queens County, Ireland, William rose to be the colonel of the Royal Irish Regiment of Foot and governor general of Minorca before he transferred to the command of New York in 1732. There he was promoted brigadier general in 1735 and died in 1737. At Malplaquet, the senior lieutenant of the cavalry regiment nicknamed "Carbineers" was the honorable Richard Ingram. He succeeded as the fifth viscount Irvine in 1714. Obviously well with the Marlborough men of the new ministry, Irvine was successively commissioned colonel of the 16th foot, the 2d horse, and governor of Hull. He died en route to the government of Barbados in 1721.[69]

The brigadier of the British cavalry at Malplaquet was Charles Sybourg, lieutenant colonel of the duke of Schomberg's horse (and perhaps the duke's illegitimate son). Sybourg had held a command in every one of Marlborough's battles. After Malplaquet, Sybourg was promoted major general and he became colonel of his regiment in the tory purge of 1713. This left him out of favor at the Marlborough restoration. Sybourg did not even get the lieutenant governorship of Nevis until after the duke's death in 1722. He did not take up this paltry appointment, of course, but he was commissioned governor of a somewhat less distant post, Fort William, Scotland, in 1725, and died a lieutenant general.[70]

This muster of the Malplaquet regiments' contributions to imperial administration excludes officers who were present at the battle but whose regiments were not. For example, one of Marlborough's aides at Malplaquet, Captain James O'Hara, was on leave from the 7th foot, recovering from a wound incurred in rescuing lord Galway, his commander in Spain and Portugal. O'Hara subsequently became colonel of the 7th, his family's regiment, served as governor general of Minorca and Gibraltar, and rose to become a field marshal and colonel of the Coldstream Guards. He still held both these ranks when he died in 1763, the year of victory over France in America. The links of army and empire reached from Marlborough's last battle to Britain's ultimate imperial triumph in the Atlantic world.[71]

CHAPTER EIGHT

The Duke's Decline

CELEBRATIONS OF THE victory at Malplaquet merely punctuated the collapse of the Marlborough-Godolphin ministry's last, whig, incarnation. The rot had already set in when, on November 10, 1709, Marlborough had returned in triumph to receive the thanks of both houses of parliament and, more tangibly, to secure appropriations totaling £6 million to carry on the war. Yet Marlborough's paymaster wrote that the failure of peace negotiations had so depressed the financial community that "'tis as much as the Bank are able to do to keep their heads above water, that we are brought to our last stroke, and that let our Resolutions be never so Vigorous for Carrying on the Warr our Circumstances are Reduc'd to such a Pass . . . that Peace will be as Welcome to us as I hope 'tis necessary for our Enemies."[1]

War weariness focused on the duumvirs. As tories, Marlborough and Godolphin were viewed with jealousy and suspicion by their whig ministerial colleagues. As moderates in both religion and politics, they were hated by tory "high-flyers," vociferous defenders of the authority of the church and the queen. High-flying hatred was unleashed by Sunderland's ill-advised plan to impeach the tory firebrand, the reverend doctor Henry Sacheverell. Sacheverell had preached to the City corporation, exalting passive obedience to the monarch as God's anointed ruler, denouncing the revolution against James II, denying the sovereignty of William and Mary, and advocating the succession of the soi-disant James III. Sacheverell labeled Marlborough, Godolphin, and the ministry "False Brethren" who had endangered the hegemony of the church and the sovereignty of the queen by religious "Comprehension and Toleration . . . Moderation and Occasional Conformity." Moderation had licensed "the Hellish Principles of fanaticism, regicide, and anarchy." All observers were astonished by the extraordinary popularity of Sacheverell's attack on the "Glorious Revolution" and its principles of parliamentary supremacy (determining by statute, not heredity, the succession to the imperial throne) and religious toleration (a broad and comprehensive state church and the participation in public life of Protestant dissenters from that church). By easy implication, the Sacheverell phenomenon bespoke popular disaffection from the war against France, a war that defended the Protestant succession and fostered a tolerant polity. Sacheverell's xenophobia was as popular as his intolerance. Englishmen apparently despised an alliance with and for the benefit of foreigners, especially their commercial competitors, the politically republican and religiously tolerant Dutch. Xenophobia, intolerance, and loyalism, all were neatly summarized in Sacheverell's slogan. "The Church in Danger" expressed the war-weariness of England and focused it on the ministry of Marlborough and Godolphin at the very moment when Queen Anne decided to attack the essence of their authority, Marlborough's military command.[2]

The earl of Essex's death from debauchery opened two commands, constable of the Tower of London and colonel of dragoons. Urged by Harley, through Mrs. Masham, and without consulting Marlborough, the queen commissioned two tories, earl Rivers as constable and Abigail Masham's brother, "five bottle Jack Hill," as colonel. In the case of the constable, Marlborough was hoist by his own petard for, in his usual devious way, he had intimated that he would not object to Rivers's appointment. Hill's commission, however, was a calculated, unmistakable, and public affront to the captain general. It bypassed officers far better qualified by seniority, combat experience, and by personal and political loyalty to the duke. It favored an officer who was a drunken incompetent, with nothing to recommend him save his relationship to his sister, the queen's dresser, Abigail Hill Masham (who notoriously hated her benefactors, the Marlboroughs). Hill's promotion, by publicly breaking the captain general's monopoly of military patronage, was intended to authorize opposition to the duke among his own officer corps in Flanders, that is, to "set up a standard of disaffection to rally all the malcontent officers in the Army." So much Marlborough declared to his queen. She was warned by her whig ministers that the issue was not just her domestic authority or her personal favor but rather Marlborough's diplomatic and military leadership of the allies: "the duke of Marlborough was not now to be considered as a private Subject that the Eyes of all Europe were upon him. The Princes abroad . . . transacted with him under the notion of one who had her Maty entire trust & favor, and so depended on all he said, wch gave the full force and effect to all he did. That the Army obeyed him unanimously because they depended upon his representations for advancement."[3]

This was precisely the problem, both in Queen Anne's eyes and of "those behind the curtain." Harley and "Hill" prompted Anne to curb her overmighty subject, to escape Marlborough's "tyranny," and to evade the unwelcome counsels of those whom he countenanced: his wife; his son-in-law; the lord treasurer; the hated whigs. Once the captain general's command of military patronage was broken, the ministry it supported would collapse. "The loyal party," which supported the queen, her prerogative, her church, and her family's divine and hereditary right to the throne, would take power. The tories would end this unnatural war against the French king, Louis XIV, who had sheltered and supported the queen's exiled father and brother. The war over, the army purged and reduced, France again preeminent, the Stuart heir might take his natural, divinely sanctified place as Anne's successor. Rather than lose effective command of the army, concede the war to France, and risk the Protestant succession, it is alleged that the captain general threatened to have the whig-controlled house of commons address the queen to remove Mrs. Masham from her presence. Marlborough's partisans proposed that Abigail be exiled "to Ireland (or rather Jamaica, what is vacant)." That is, Colonel Masham was to be given the Jamaica command and ordered to take his wife and her brother, Jack Hill, with him to the fever-ridden West Indies. Certainly, the duke declared that the queen would have to choose between her dresser and himself. He retired to Windsor Lodge without the queen's permission. He refused to attend the cabinet or do any business until the queen canceled her commission to Jack Hill. In the constitutional crisis caused by Marlborough's withdrawal from the government, "the General officers [were] sounded by both sides to discover what they would do if things should come to extremitys." These military consultations cannot have been very reassuring to the court. The queen rescinded Hill's commission, paying him off with a pension from her privy purse. Argyll's offer to "seize the duke at the head of his troops, and bring him away either dead or alive" was not accepted. On the other hand, Marlborough withdrew his latest request for a commission as captain general for life. To avoid further unpleasantness, the captain general arranged for an address from the commons to the queen urging her to dispatch him to the peace conference at Geertruidenberg. He sailed on February 18, 1710, and, after a stormy passage, finally reached The Hague on March 8.[4]

It was, Marlborough wrote, "easier hearing of heats in England than being in the heats themselves." The duke had escaped personal participation in Sacheverell's impeachment before the house of lords. He could not escape the trial's advertisement of the divine right of monarchs and of subjects' religious duty: passive obedience. Those doctrines were as damaging to the captain general's secular military authority as they were to the Protestant and parliamentary "revolution principles" he supported. The whig commoners who managed the impeachment, Robert Walpole outstanding among them, pressed to republican extremes the right of resistance to tyrannical monarchs and the foundations of political authority in popular consent. Party passions were roused to levels not seen since the impeachment of the whig ministers fifteen years earlier. The operations of government were frozen as politicians of all stripes were absorbed in the trial. Colonel Spotswood, trying to prepare for his command of Virginia, could find no one with whom to do business.[5]

The partisan violence excited American assemblies from Antigua to New York. All of them demonstrated their own adherence to whiggish "revolution principles," alarming provincial tories. In Barbados, however, the tories were reinforced as Robert Lowther took command. Lowther did make the usual acknowledgments to Marlborough for the Barbados government. He even added his prayers "that the Almighty will defeat the malicious and base projects of those designing people that are only Enemies to your Grace for those Transcendent virtues which have brought such amazing things to pass." Then John Corbett, an avowed jacobite, was ordered to Maryland. The Corbett case suggests that, although Marlborough thought it now wise to approve tories for American appointments, his official control of the imperial executive was still unimpaired. When he noted that he intended Corbett for South Carolina, the queen and the lord treasurer simply reminded Marlborough that he must mean Maryland as the queen did not commission proprietary executives. Corrected, but not limited, Marlborough refused Colonel Corbett's nomination of Colonel Richard Franks to replace him in Maryland (Corbett wanted a regimental command, not its American equivalent). Instead Marlborough favored the promotion by seniority of the regiment's lieutenant colonel, George Wingfield. He had won Marlborough's favor as lieutenant governor of embattled St. Kitts. The captain general wrote Corbett that if he still wanted the Maryland government, he should hurry to London, take out his patent, and proceed to his command. Hoping for a regiment from a tory ministry, Corbett did not go out.[6]

As Lowther had implied, the captain general could not long escape the rising tory tide. After all, he was still Sarah's devoted husband and it was "the carriage of a certain great lady" that had first affronted the queen's dignity. Tory observers added that Marlborough's opposition to the promotion of Jack Hill had challenged the queen's prerogative and that the Marlboroughs' proposed address for the removal of Abigail Masham had outraged the queen's love. Triply offended, the queen was now prepared to risk all—the war, the state, the succession—to be rid of the duchess of Marlborough and to reduce the duke to a due submission. Once the queen had been persuaded to rid herself of her dependence on the Marlboroughs—for thirty years they had been the primary props of her psyche and her prerogative—it was an easy matter for Robin Harley and his cousin Abigail Hill Masham to undermine the ministry that the duke headed and that the duchess cheered on. One whig minister after another was picked off as an agent of that party which had so profoundly offended the queen, the church, and the country by "the Prosecution of Dr. Sacheverell, with the design of establishing the Doctrine of Resistance by a Law." "The Republican notions that were so openly asserted & maintained" in the impeachment of Sacheverell, tory commentators declared, "have Allarmed to ye greatest degree ye whole Kingdom." The court was inundated with loyal addresses. They supported the royal prerogative and the church's integrity. They opposed

the doctrine of rule by parliamentary majority. They called for the queen's dissolution of the whig parliament because it had asserted the republican doctrine
of an uncontrolled parliamentary sovereignty. Apparently supported by public
opinion, the queen was encouraged to reassert her royal authority over her
army, her church, her parliament, and her empire. So she intended to thwart
the whigs' intended substitution of parliamentary authority for royal sovereignty. The power of parliament was most manifest in the law that mandated
the Protestant succession in the house of Hanover and barred the hereditary
claim of the queen's own brother, the Roman Catholic client of Louis XIV.[7]

With the first principle of the war—the Protestant succession—now in
question, the queen alienated, the ministry—"the whigs in conjunction with
lord treasurer and me," as Marlborough defined that unnatural connection—
divided, and the army factionalized, the captain general could no longer take
the risks required for a decisive victory. Marlborough's political caution decreed
that there would not be another Malplaquet. French military caution ensured
that there would not be another Ramillies. Stalemate in Flanders combined
with reaction in England to give impetus to a peace process whose outcome
would be far more favorable to the Bourbon monarchies than the military situation justified, given Marlborough's astonishing victories and extensive conquests. Marlborough himself withdrew from the peace negotiations before he
was shut out. In any case, he believed that the preliminaries had given too much
to the Dutch and taken too little from the French, in America especially.[8]

Yet Marlborough's military brilliance was neither dimmed by age—he was
now sixty-one—nor by his exhaustion after nine consecutive campaigns in command of the allied armies. He continued to believe that either one more great
battle, if the French could be forced to fight, or the long-awaited conquest of
the Channel ports, which would expose Paris itself in the next campaign, would
make him the arbiter of the Atlantic world. Just as Marlborough still believed
that he might win America in Europe, so he was still sure that no expedition
across the Atlantic could defeat the French there. Probably another victory in
Flanders, certainly a drumhead peace in Paris, would put it "in the power of
those at the head of the army to give what law they please" and win "more at
one stroak than ten expeditions can doe" in America. So believing, the captain
general concentrated the allied armies at Tournai on April 1/12, 1710, a month
before the French could take the field. Two weeks after the allies assembled,
Cadogan and the quartermasters led the army west by night across the French
lines of La Bassée, "which if they had defended must have cost us a great many
thousand lives." Racing westward, Marlborough's men advanced forty miles in
as many hours, overran the French army's base camp, and invested the frontier
fortress of Douai. Douai was the immediate obstacle to an assault on the Channel ports of Boulogne and Calais and so to an attack on Paris supported directly
from England.[9]

A week after the investment of Douai, the city was circumvalled, an operation commanded by major general the earl of Orkney, governor general of Virginia. The earl's brother, lord Archibald Hamilton, was thereupon named governor general of Jamaica. Hamilton owed his American command to political considerations as much as to his brother's military merit or lord Archibald's own service by sea and land. In the lords, Orkney had voted to convict Sacheverell. In the Flanders army, Orkney headed Marlborough's loyal subordinates. "I believe your intention of encouraging 37 [Orkney], is very right and necessary," Godolphin wrote to Marlborough. "But you will have a care how you trust him with your thoughts of any body here [in Britain] for his lady and 28 [Shrewsbury] are all one, and both of them extremely meddling." Elizabeth, lady Orkney, was one of the great politicians of the age (not for nothing had she been king William's mistress, despite her squint). She ate dinner every day with the duchess of Marlborough, and they drank damnation to the tories, but by night she met with Robin Harley, the tory "trickster." She was also close to her brother-in-law, the duke of Hamilton, who had voted to acquit Sacheverell, very much to Marlborough's annoyance.[10]

Marlborough wrote to his duchess, "My Lord Orkney is come and presses me concerning his brother Archebold I have told him what is true, that whatever the Queen would do in itt, I should like it. But the real truth is, that I did promise Duke Hamilton, when I thought that he would have behaved himself better than he has done, that if Meredyth would not accept of the government, I should be for his brother." General Meredyth remained on Marlborough's staff. So lord Archibald Hamilton was commissioned to command Jamaica. Orkney kept Marlborough up to the mark in each stage of the process of lord Archibald's commissioning, instruction, and dispatch. For example, even as he organized the siege of Béthune, Marlborough wrote to Godolphin that "lord Orkney tels me his brother has not gott his commission for the government of Jamaica. It is most certain for the good of the Service that he should go with the next fleet, so that he should be dispatched." The duke of Hamilton, having thanked Marlborough "for your Favour to my brother Ld Archebold for the Government of Jamaica . . . which he owes to your Goodness," assured the captain general that lord Archibald would "doe his diewty soe exactly that your Gr shall have constant reason to be satisfied with the choice you have made." Of course the governor general designate himself pledged that "yr Grace shall allways see my Duty faithfully performed in her Maetys Service & so far [justify] yr recommendation." Personally, lord Archibald promised Marlborough that his "Zeale for your interest and Service" would always demonstrate his "true gratitude and greatest respect."[11]

Duty, service, and zeal were the patriotic and professional characteristics that Marlborough's American legates brought to a generation of imperial governance, but the command of military patronage that had enabled the duke to promote what became the greatest generation of the royal executive in America was now endangered at its source. Once again, the tool with which Robert Harley worked on Queen Anne's emotions was Abigail Masham's brother, Jack Hill. To ensure that the officers "should be in a good humour" after the passage of the La Bassée lines opened the prospect of much hard fighting, the captain general had submitted a promotion list to the queen. Marlborough stopped the promotions to major general one short of Hill (and those to brigadier general three short of Abigail's husband, Colonel Samuel Masham). While she permitted the advancement of officers serving with Marlborough in the field, the queen stopped all other promotions until her favorite's kinsmen were given their steps. Again, Marlborough's efforts to preserve his command authority went unsupported by his whig ministerial colleagues. So Hill became a major general. He devoted the campaign of 1710 to imbibing mineral waters, and other liquids, at the spa. (In his defense, it must be noted that Hill had been jumped over the heads of so many serving officers that he could not command as a general in Flanders.) Marlborough's defeat in the promotions controversy encouraged tory officers in Flanders to voice their discontents with the duke. The result was that "ye Divisions in England have reach'd ye Army & . . . parties are no less active amongst you than they are amongst us."[12]

Even as discipline decayed, the siege of Douai went forward. The allies dug trenches and diverted rivers. They were blown up by mines, thrown against masonry walls, and eviscerated by artillery. They suffered nearly 8,000 casualties before Douai surrendered on June 15/26, 1710. Marlborough then declared that he would have to resign his command immediately because, to spite him, the queen had dismissed his son-in-law, the earl of Sunderland, as her secretary of state for the southern department, America included. Marlborough had begged the queen to retain Sunderland as secretary. He had, he reminded his sovereign, only consented to her promotions of Masham and Hill ("though neither has just pretensions") to retain his command of the allies until the war could be won, but the queen's dismissal of Sunderland was designed to force Marlborough to resign: "his being at this time singled out, has no other reason than his being my son-in-law . . . my enemies have prevailed to have this done in order to make it impossible for me, with honour, to continue at the head of this glorious army, that has, through the whole course of this war, been blessed by God with surprising successes." If this blow to his honor could be put off until the end of the campaign, the captain general informed the queen, he would then resign. The queen rejected both the duke's threats and his pleas in terms of unprecedented acerbity. The fall of Douai, in the sight of the French army, proved that the armies of Louis XIV could not defeat the duke on the battlefield, but the queen's dismissal of Sunderland and her rebuff of Marlborough demonstrated that tory connivance and the queen's concupiscence would combine to bring down the captain general and rescue France. The moment that the news of Sunderland's dismissal reached Versailles, Louis XIV withdrew his ambassador from the peace negotiations.[13]

The whigs, the states general, and the emperor all begged Marlborough not to resign. He agreed to stay on as captain general, but he knew and he said that the loss of royal favor had drained his authority. Now Argyll, at the head of the anti-Marlborough officers, publicly accused the captain general of withholding peace and sacrificing his comrades to keep his military perquisites. Red John was emboldened because Marlborough had been declaring for months that "the queen was weary of my services, which would quickly appear by the removal of Lord Sunderland." The queen herself was unwell, however, and whoever commanded the army would command the succession. Marlborough had made two monarchs already. If he retained the captain generalcy, he could make a third. His enemies even alleged that if Marlborough feared that he was about to lose his command, he might become "a second Cromwell." Dissident officers demanded that "some restraint should be put to that exorbitant power Lord Marlborough has in the army . . . he plainly disposes of preferments here . . . to create a faction sufficient to support him against the Queen and her friends in case every other prop should fail." If Marlborough retained military authority enough to defeat the French, his victory would obliterate the tory reaction: "If Duke Marlborough beats the French his enemies must become his footstool."[14]

Following the fall of Douai, Marlborough marshaled the full allied strength, 120,000 men. On June 27, 1710, he ordered them to cross the Vimy Ridge and deploy opposite Villars' entrenchments behind the River Scarpe. Argyll, having pledged his fidelity to Harley, his "love and honour" to "Brigadier Hill," and having rejoiced in Sunderland's fall, now "made it his business to Shock my Ld Duke in every pointe he could." Red John demanded a full frontal assault, a more than Malplaquet. Colonel Kane observed, however, that "Villars's army much outnumbered ours, and he retired behind the River Sensée, so that there was no coming at him or laying siege to Arras," on the direct road to Paris. Marlborough took the occasion to chagrin Argyll by having Orkney commissioned general of the foot (Sunderland hoped that this would make Argyll shoot himself in the head). The queen, so the captain general wrote, had so favored Argyll as to endanger army discipline and make it "absolutely necessary to countenance 37 [Orkney] in opposition to 221 [Argyll]." "In order to bring the discipline of the army back to that happy posture" of unquestioning obedience, Marlborough declared, the queen must "let me have the power to oblige the officer and not to have anybody encouraged to think that he can meet with preferment by others." Orkney, he said, having been commissioned general of the foot, should be created an English peer. This was a promotion appropriate to an army whose leaders were coming to constitute an imperial aristocracy.[15]

With Orkney in command of the infantry, Marlborough moved the allied army north to the siege of Béthune, a petty place but the first in a sequence of posts which commanded the communications with Boulogne and Calais, the entrepôts of an invasion of northern France supported directly from England. This was Godolphin's dream scheme, the preferred objective of the regiments previously allocated to America. The recapture of Calais, the long-lost but never-forgotten bridgehead to the reconquest of France, was "the particular design that will be of advantage and eclat in England." "No undertaking whatsoever would have been, or yett bee, more popular," Godolphin wrote to Marlborough, "nothing would be more seasonable and necessary to raise the drooping Spirits of 89," the whigs, or prevent the queen from dissolving the parliament. To add Canada to the queen's dominions was far less attractive than the conquest of Calais, the very emblem of England's lost empire in France.[16]

There was a real note of pleasure in Godolphin's report to Marlborough on July 7 that it was now too late to send troops to America. Absent a French invasion of the British Isles, the regiments would be available when Marlborough reached the Channel but, wrote the lord treasurer, then the captain general would have to ask for the regiments withheld from America. This Marlborough never dared to do. The same political dangers that encouraged the lord treasurer to advocate an invasion of northern France prevented the captain general from attempting it. "The little consideration" the queen had for them, Marlborough wrote Godolphin, "makes it not safe for me to make any proposal for employing those regements." "Though if things were as formerly, I could attempt a project on the sea coast . . . but as everything is now, I dare attempt nothing, but what I am almost sure must succeed, nor am I sure that those now in power would keep my secrit" from the French. Indeed, Louis XIV was "so incouraged by what passes in 108 [England] that he has taken a positive resolution for the continuation of 80 [war]." Even if there was some hope that he could break through to Abbeville, Marlborough added, the regiments intended for America should not be "stoped on my account, for that might give a couller to my enemys to lay to my charge the failing of the expedition" against Canada. It was a demoralized captain general who turned his attention to besieging of a series of minor fortresses. Added to Béthune, Aire and St. Venant would clear the River Lys as a logistical line for an invasion of eastern France in 1711.[17]

Whether Marlborough would command the next campaign became daily more problematic. As the siege of Béthune wore on, the direction and strength of the tory wind blowing across the empire became more apparent. Godolphin reported to Marlborough that to replace lord Dartmouth (Sunderland's successor as secretary of state for the south) at the commission for trade and plantations, Matthew Prior had been appointed, without Godolphin's prior knowledge. What neither the lord treasurer or the captain general knew was that Prior was conducting secret negotiations with the French for a peace separate from the rest of the allies. Even so, Marlborough was appalled at Godolphin's loss of power: "Is it possible that you can be so sunke in the Queen's opinion that she should make any Commissioner of Trade, or any other that belongs to your office, without first consulting you?" But the lord treasurer's own place was in peril. On August 8/19, he was summarily dismissed by a messenger from Queen Anne. Godolphin was replaced at the treasury by a commission composed by Robert Harley as chancellor of the exchequer.[18]

The Harley ministry immediately asked the queen to dissolve the whig parliament. This, and the subsequent election of a tory majority were the necessary prerequisites of a peace with France, an exaltation of the church and, so it came to appear, a Stuart succession to the imperial throne. The duumvirate of Marlborough and Godolphin had ended. The two promotion crises and the Sunderland dismissal had already warned Marlborough that he could hope to retain no authority beyond his own field command. During the campaign of 1710, the duke had divested himself of all diplomatic duties, apart from issuing military subsidies to the allies and obtaining recruits from them. He had declared that he could no longer take the great risks for great victories which could compel France to peace and write upon a drumhead a revolution in France and the British character of America. Marlborough's America would now be the work of the captain general's veteran viceroys, whom he had already placed in all the key American commands.[19]

Marlborough himself would be hard pressed to keep the command in Flanders, especially as a series of uninspired sieges dragged on into the rains of autumn and ended in the mud. Ten days after Godolphin's dismissal had left Marlborough "mortified and afflicted," he accepted the capitulation of Béthune and its garrison of 9,000, at a cost of 3,365 allied casualties. Marlborough then moved his main force to block Villars and a French army much superior in numbers to the allies while he took the minor post at St. Venant and besieged the major fortress of Aire. This siege became a terrible struggle against a dogged and resourceful defense. The contest lasted well into November, far beyond the usual close of the campaigning season, because Marlborough simply could not withdraw. The mud was so deep that the duke could not get his artillery pieces out of their batteries. He had no choice but to take Aire as winter quarters for the siege train or abandon his big guns, and with them his record of unbroken military success. So the allies fought on with, as Marlborough wrote, "our poor men up to the knees in mud and water, which is a most grevious sight and will occasion great sickness." So it did. Among the dead were members of Marlborough's "family," his longtime coachman, his favorite cook, and his valet. The invaluable Cardonnel, the secretary at war, lay at death's door. The terrible weather that almost defeated the siege of Aire ended all possibility of an advance to Calais and the Channel. Marlborough's last chance for a decisive military and political stroke was gone. The captain general was sick with disappointment: "I was never more fond of a project since this warr, then this of the sea coast, which the enemy could not have hindered."[20]

After Aire surrendered, it was found that the allies had suffered 7,000 combat casualties and lost twice as many men to disease or desertion. The whole campaign of 1710 had cost the allies 18,901 men, killed or wounded, all to acquire a bridgehead for a potential invasion of northeastern France in another year, presuming that Marlborough retained any authority. No other commander the allies possessed, not even Prince Eugene, could carry them deeper into France. The new ministry in England had already offered the command of the allies to the elector of Hanover, the heir apparent to the British throne. To their amazement, the elector declined this chance to secure the military means of ensuring his succession. Instead, he deferred to Marlborough and declared for continued war against France. The elector's action was a clear indication of his belief in Marlborough's loyalty to his, that is, the Protestant, succession and conveyed an awful warning to the new ministry of the fate that awaited them if the elector came to power as king with Marlborough as his captain general. Sunderland had reminded his father-in-law (who needed no reminder; at last Marlborough had ceased to correspond with the pretender's court) that "that affair of Hanover is, and must be, our sheet anchor, and if it be rightly managed, you will be effectually revenged of all your enemies, and that by securing your Country . . . you will be, if possible, a greater man than you have ever been yet."[21]

If Hanover and Marlborough were one, both might be abandoned by the high tories in favor of the Stuart pretender to the imperial throne. On September 20, 1710, the tory ministerial revolution was completed. The queen dissolved the whig parliament as the preface to an election designed to win control of the commons for the party of church and queen. The tories were certainly determined upon peace with France. Possibly they were prepared to accept the hereditary succession of the Stuart prince presently in French exile. Yet neither of these aims could be publicly admitted. Britain was bound by treaty to the allies and to their war against France. Britain was bound by law to the Protestant, hence Hanoverian, succession. It would take at least a year to work a diplomatic and political counterrevolution. That would give the tories just time enough for one last attempt to realize their blue water strategy of commerce and colonies, of military expeditions and political coercion in America.[22]

So it was that pretenders to office in the new administration revived tory imperial projects. William Patterson, the Scots fixer who wanted to be a commissioner of trade and plantations, declared, in the accents of 1702, that "we ought to insist to have the French possessions not only in Newfoundland but also in Canada, and to have two or three cautionary places in South America from Spain" as a recompense for British campaign costs in Iberia. Harley himself was already evolving the scheme for American trade, based upon the commercial treaties with France and Spain that he anticipated as parts of the peace. His scheme became the stockjobbing, American-focused, South Sea Company. Harley also had in hand Colonel Schuyler's plan for posts among the Five Nations. These would nicely combine anglican evangelism with British trade and even create the nucleus of "English" settlements, all at the cost of French Canada. In his first day in office as secretary of state, Harley's coadjutor (and rival) in the new ministry, Henry St. John, ordered contracts to be let for clothing the expeditionary troops for the next year's campaign against Canada. These contracts potentially advanced the tories' American strategy. They immediately enriched the high-living secretary.[23]

St. John could be sure of the war office's connivance in corruption because George Granville had replaced Walpole (or rather, Cardonnel, for whom Walpole had kept the seat warm) as secretary at war. This without any prior notice to Marlborough, hitherto the secretary's immediate superior. Granville declared that he would not emulate the "servile attendance" of previous secretaries on the captain general. St. John's partner in his American program of personal enrichment and imperial aggrandizement was Arthur Moore, former comptroller of the army accounts and presently m.p. for Grimsby. The paymaster of the forces abroad, James Brydges, was also St. John's close friend and former partner (although Brydges was corrupt on a scale unimaginable by the merely venial St. John). The necessary popular enthusiasm for an American expedition, so profitable personally and politically to the new ministry, had been provided by the visit of the Four Indian Kings. Their return to America was immediately followed by Francis Nicholson's capture of Port Royal and Acadia, news of which reached the imperial metropolis in December 1710. St. John had only to overcome the fiscal reserve, and personal jealousy, of the chancellor of the exchequer, the prime minister, Robert Harley, and to defeat the resistance of the captain general to the loss of five of his best regiments, to launch what Marlborough was sure was a foredoomed attempt to conquer Canada.[24]

Marlborough had to be brought to terms, rather than being dismissed out of hand, because the queen had not yet been convinced to abandon the allies and the war with France, because the elector of Hanover would not take command of the allied armies from Marlborough, and because the new prime minister had both political and military hopes of the advantages to be obtained from a chastened and circumscribed captain general. As the army financier and backstairs operator William Drummond wrote to Harley about Marlborough, "you would strengthen your party more by gaining that one man than by any other thing imaginable." Incredibly, Marlborough had pierced the frontier of France. Louis XIV's only hope of escaping a humiliating peace was if the captain general—"to whom the successes of this war have been so generally ascribed by both friends and foes"—was cashiered. This was inadvisable, Drummond told Harley, because, although Marlborough's "covetousness has gained him much reproach and ill will . . . yet his success in the field, his capacity or rather dexterity in council or in the cabinet, and his personal acquaintance with the heads of the Alliance and the faith they have in him make him still the great man with them and on whom they depend." Harley's response forecast little but personal and professional humiliation for the captain general. He would, the new prime minister wrote, "live and act with the Duke," but Marlborough was vengeful. Besides, his wife and son-in-law would compel Marlborough to contest the new ministry. So his power had to be circumscribed. Marlborough could not be allowed to influence the peace process, nor could he become viceroy of Flanders. He would have to accept the dismissal of his wife from her offices at court and of their friend Godolphin from the treasury, "points hard of digestion for a man of nice honour." Marlborough would be forbidden to direct operations in Iberia or America. Finally, the captain general and his loyal officers were to be shut out of the upcoming elections for the new parliament while their enemies in the army were to be politically supported by the queen herself.[25]

The campaign in Flanders still was in full swing when the October elections came on. To contest seats in parliament, officers had to obtain leave from the captain general to depart the army. Marlborough was generous with political leaves, although it cost him front-line officers, such as Samuel Gledhill. A West Indian veteran, Gledhill was the commander of Sutton's regiment when it took 50 percent casualties at Douai. Severely wounded, stripped, and imprisoned, Gledhill was quickly redeemed by Marlborough, commissioned lieutenant governor of Carlisle, and allowed to go home to seek the parliamentary seat that attended the Carlisle command. Officers more hostile to Marlborough resented the submission implied in having to ask him for leave. Such was the ascendancy of Mrs. Masham, such was Queen Anne's ignorance of the first principles of military discipline, and such was her desire to degrade the captain general (whose military power was daily represented to her as a derogation of her own sovereignty) that she actually sent leaves directly to his enemies. This episode, so subversive of "Keeping Officers to their Duty & to a just subordination," was a mere foretaste of the degradation of the duke that would follow the tory electoral victory of October 1710. That victory crowded the house of commons with backwoodsmen. To them, Marlborough personified the evil alliance of an enlarged army, continental war, religious toleration, finance capitalism, and vaunting plutocracy. In a word, the captain general stood in the Stuart pretender's path to the imperial throne, "the setting up of hereditary right, as they call it." Speaking in Boston, General Nicholson forcefully expressed these high tory sentiments: those who were not for "Indefeasable Hereditary Right were dam'd Whigs and Enemies to the Church and Crown."[26]

For the first time in her reign, the queen's speech at the opening of the parliamentary session made no mention of Marlborough and his victories. In the lords, although the ministry did not command a majority, a motion of thanks to Marlborough was dropped, having been vehemently opposed by Argyll, authorized by the government. Next, the captain general's staff was attacked. Cadogan was removed as envoy to the states general of the Netherlands and to the council of state for Brabant and Flanders. Generals Meredyth, Macartney, and Honywood (to each of whom Marlborough had offered American govern-ments) were cashiered by the queen's order to Secretary Granville. Their of-fense was a report that they had drunk "Damnation and Confusion to the New Ministry, and those who had any Hand in turning out the Old." The queen was told that she was meant. The generals' defense, "that they only drank a health to the Duke of Marlborough and Confusion to all his enemies, a Thing usual in all Armies," was almost equally offensive. It was evidence that the officer corps was "standing by their General," the would-be dictator, so the popular prints had it, who had sought to be commissioned "General for Life." The queen was convinced that the captain general's ambition could only be clipped by leaving him "without Authority in his Army, where it is made Criminal to espouse his Interest, and to fly in his Face is the surest Means to Advancement."[27]

Crippled in the army abroad, Marlborough nonetheless remained hugely popular at home. When he reached London from the battlefront on Decem-ber 28, 1710, his coach was met by crowds cheering, "God Bless the duke of Marlborough!" "No wooden shoes!" "No Popery!" But the duke was not one to exploit popularity. He was "very sensible of the Instability and Emptiness of the Applause of the Vulgar." Besides, the captain general had promised the allies that he would conciliate the new ministry in everything rather than lose his command of the army in Flanders. He was immediately put to the test. The queen bracketed her declaration that she would keep Marlborough in com-mand with an order to him not to permit any parliamentary recognition of his services "because my ministers will certainly oppose it." Secretary St. John then told the duke that he must accept the duchess's dismissal from her of-fices at court, abandon the defense of his subordinates and associates, and ac-cept Argyll's appointment to the command in Spain (displacing Marlborough's protégé Stanhope and rewarding Argyll's opposition to the captain general). If Marlborough balked at any of these conditions, or whatever else the queen's new ministers choose to impose on him, St. John warned, the captain general would be dismissed, disgraced, and impeached. Worst of all, as Marlborough must have known by now, the tory ministry had already begun to negotiate a separate peace with France, a peace that would admit a Bourbon victory in Spain and in Spanish America and that would concede French claims in North America as well.[28]

Yet Marlborough suffered all this to retain the command of the army, the agency of power in the empire. As St. John observed, if the duke remained captain general, he "thinks it possible for him to have the same absolute power which he was once vested with." To prevent this, public opinion had to be convinced that Marlborough's military power menaced civilian authority, that he was vastly overpaid for his military services, and that these services had won no advantages to English empire. To this end, the tory ministry enlisted the services of the reverend Jonathan Swift, dean of St. Patrick's, Dublin, the most brilliant pamphleteer of the age. Swift's fatal assault, first on Marlborough's military power, then on the allies' contribution to the war, and finally on the captain general's honesty and honor, began with publication of the *Examiner* #17, on November 23, 1710.[29]

Swift first dealt with imperialism and ingratitude. Responding to the charge that too little regard had been paid to Marlborough's unprecedented triumphs, Swift contrasted the nominal cost of a tribute for a Roman general to the enormous cost of Blenheim Palace. Swift observed that to obtain a triumph, a Roman general had to have "conquered some great Kingdom, brought the King himself, his Family and Nobles to adorn the Triumph in Chains, and made the Kingdom either a Roman Province, or at best a poor depending State, in humble alliance to that Empire." The contrast with the costly capture of Béthune, Aire, and St. Venant was painfully obvious, and alleged opportunities to expand English empire in America were on every tory tongue. At home, the pretensions of the military to power in the state, epitomized by Marlborough, were as galling as the lack of a triumph over France, or the absence of an addition to empire in America. "In a Kingdom where the People are free," Swift inquired, "how came they to be so fond of having their Councils under the Influence of their Army, or those that lead it? Who in all well-instituted states, had no commerce with the civil Power, further than to receive their Orders, and obey them without Reserve." For half a dozen years, the distinction between civil and military power in the English empire had been essentially meaningless. Marlborough had engrossed both. Now, in the autumn and winter of 1710, the new tory ministry and an embittered, dying queen reduced this former favorite from his imperial preeminence to the role of a theater commander in Flanders.[30]

CHAPTER NINE

Quebec and Bouchain

O N JANUARY 17, 1710/11, the duke of Marlborough paid another install-
ment on the price of retaining his command in Flanders. In return for
a few squadrons of cavalry, he surrendered "five battalions for our attempt upon Quebec. Pray do me the justice," secretary of state St. John wrote
to prime minister Harley, "to believe that I am not light or whimsical in this
project. It will certainly succeed if the secret is preserved, and if it succeeds you
will have done more service to Britain in half a year, then the ministers who
went before you did in all their administration." American conquests would
profit English commerce, so the tories had believed ever since they had become
a political party under James Stuart a half century earlier. They believed it all
the more now that the Protestant crusade, whig continentalism, and Marlborough's ambition all had been stalemated at Malplaquet. The tories' own favorite war, in Spain, had been lost at Brihuega. The new ministry had begun secret
peace talks with France. Now was the tory moment in politics, commerce, and
empire. Militarily, Canadian conquest might bring fame to the least worthy of
the army's senior officers, "five bottle Jack" Hill. Hill's success would tighten
Robert Harley's political liaison with Hill's sister, Abigail Masham. That, because Masham was Queen Anne's present passion, would ensure royal favor
for the tory ministry. Commercially, the ministry's Canada and Newfoundland
project would recapture the trade in furs and fish. Imperially, the conquest of
Canada would provide the military force, the ideological intensity, and the base
of operations required to impose religious conformity and political obedience
on dissenting, republican New England. Successful or not, the expedition would
bolster the bank accounts of the spendthrift secretary of state, Henry St. John.[1]

The American expedition also offered the ministry additional opportuni-
ties to weaken Marlborough's grip on the army and to blunt his offensive against
France. When he proposed the Quebec expedition, St. John also declared that
"I am proposing a state of the General Officers, and if [the queen] pleases will

break Lord Marlborough's faction." So St. John would restore royal, that is, tory, ministerial command of the army now fighting in France. Among the five battalions to be extracted from Marlborough's command for Quebec were the regiments of the three whig generals who had been struck from the staff for drinking damnation to the duke's enemies. The rank and file of these regiments were also devoted to "Corporal John." They would be shipped across the unfriendly Atlantic to a most uncertain fate in North America. Their withdrawal had an additional advantage to a ministry that was engaged in secret peace talks with the French and planning to betray Britain's allies. The loss of five veteran battalions, secretary St. John exulted, would tip the military balance against Marlborough in his death struggle with the French marshal Villars. To do down Marlborough, no act was too petty. Fifty senior sergeants were to be drafted from his battalions, commissioned as lieutenants, and shipped off to Boston, together with Charles Churchill's marines and two dozen officers in second. Seventy-four veterans would suffice to drill and discipline every company of the royal regiments to be raised in New England and New York. These regiments were to be officered, armed, and accoutered by the queen. Their first mission was the conquest of Canada.[2]

Moving the theater of combat from Europe to America would transform the war aim from the preservation of Protestant liberty in Britain and the Netherlands to the subjection of the American colonists and continent. This was the palimpsest of the proposed conquest of Canada. The "Quebec" expedition was intended to discipline not just the New Englanders but, by introducing an army to conquer New France, impose direct and uniform, royal and ecclesiastical government on all the continental colonies. So much secretary St. John made clear to the new governor general of New York, Colonel Robert Hunter. Recognizing Hunter's "extraordinary talents," St. John called on him to "take into your thoughts the whole state of the British Interest in your part of the World." The conquest of Canada would leave on the ground the military instruments with which to realize "the great riches and power which would arise from a good regulation of these colonies." Armed in America, the crown could erase colonial encroachments on its prerogative, buy out the private proprietors, and subject "the whole Empire of North America" to "One uniform plan of government." Even if the expedition failed to conquer Canada, St. John wrote to Hunter, the royal, militant, attention to America that the expedition made manifest would foster "new measures," not just to "render those colonys more useful" to Britain but, by eliminating their indiscipline, make the American colonies better able to resist "that ruin, which the French settlements behind, and their own disorders within, seem to threaten."[3]

Inextricably entwined with the tory ministry's contradictory plan for Canadian conquest (with the assistance of provincial troops) and American discipline (by the royal military) were St. John's personal investments, both in power and in pelf. The Quebec expedition was "my favorite project, which I have been driving on ever since I came last into business," the secretary of state explained. If it failed, it would be "particularly prejudicial to me, who, in carrying it on hitherto have not been back'd by those forms and orders, which are necessary safeguards." The absence of authorization was partly owing to the prime minister's obstruction. Harley did not wish to countenance American conquest and coercion. They contradicted his personal caution, his political moderation, and his sympathy for religious dissent. Neither could Harley endorse an expedition designed to aggrandize St. John, his rival for leadership of the tories. St. John intended to supplant Harley by appealing to the tories' xenophobic desire to "do something in particular for Britain," rather than for ungrateful foreign confederates (that is, the dreadful Dutch). St. John's expedition would indulge tory royalism and imperialism by making "the Queen mistress of the whole continent of North America." He would score personal points with queen Anne by patronizing General Hill, the beloved brother of the Queen's favorite. Finally, as Harley quite correctly suspected, the Canadian expedition was designed to make a solid sordid profit for its projector, St. John.[4]

The most common military corruption involved food contracts, the largest cost of war. Here, as was so often the case, St. John outsmarted himself, lost his profits, and endangered a military objective. To convince the ever-watchful French that the expedition was bound not for Canada but for Spain, St. John ordered it provisioned not for eight months but for three. The balance, he seems to have thought, could be made up in Boston. Having reduced his potential profit from provisions, the secretary of state recurred to shoddy uniforms, weak arms, and inadequate accoutrements. So obvious was the dreadful quality and inflated price of everything from caps to boots and from swords to muskets that St. John had sent to the allied army in Spain that the paymaster general, James Brydges, could only hope that "ye Inspectors are enough in your Interest & power to wink at the Representation" by aggrieved army officers. St. John's own agent admitted that the syndicate sent out "from England ye Cheapest cloathing that we have been able to find there, with directions to put them off here as dear as possible." This agent, who sold the soldiers ill-tempered swords and boys' shoes, was one Theopolis Blyke or Blake. He came home from cheating the soldiers in Spain to act for St. John in supplying the Canadian expedition. On the very day that the fleet made port in Boston, St. John begged the paymaster to intervene, nominally for Blake, actually for himself, with Harley: "Mr. Blake made a very considerable provision of Several Sorts of Stores for ye expedition commanded by Brigadier Hill. As these preparations both for Land & Sea were kept private & went almost Singly thro' my hands, so it fell to my store to contract on this occasion by ye Queen's command." Now Blake had to pay the manufacturers or he would be arrested for debt. "I am sure I had rather be so, than be teas'd at ye rate I have been about this matter," St. John wrote the paymaster, and "I beg yr assistance & shall take it for as great a favor as if I was personally concern'd in it."[5]

Despite the paymaster's intercession, Harley refused to pay £28,036/5 "for clothes sent to Canada," knowing that this was four times their actual cost. Thereupon, St. John burst into Harley's office and "with much passion" protested that allegations of military corruption were only to be made against Marlborough, not against ministers of the new administration. Harley was unrelenting, but Abigail Masham secured the queen's direct order for payment of the full amount. St. John and his associates cleared £21,036/5 in profit, for the first cost of the supplies had been only £7,000. Of course such cheap supplies were shoddy. Francis Nicholson, who had helped placed the clothing contracts, was still trying to force these flimsies on the outraged garrisons of New York and Nova Scotia in 1713. "Extraordinary" costs, that is, sums spent on such things as ship charters and ordnance purchases, came to £79,545/10/9, all of it a fertile field of graft for St. John and his accomplices. As much as 66 percent of the monies billed to the crown for extraordinaries ended up in their accounts. St. John used his illicit gains and his insider's knowledge of the impending peace treaty with France to play the stock market. Unexpected delays in the diplomatic negotiations faced the secretary of state with margin calls. He lost all the gains from his graft. Such was the final fiscal futility of the Canadian expedition.[6]

The lord treasurer's capacity to resist the Canadian expedition collapsed on March 8, 1710/11, when he was stabbed by the marquis de Guiscard during his interrogation for treason. In turn, Guiscard was slightly wounded by St. John. He then "in the utmost confusion ran away to St. James's" Palace and Mrs. Masham. With Harley incapacitated, they could fully exploit the Canada expedition as the mechanism of their assault on Marlborough. Within the week, the queen (by St. John) ordered the captain general to release five specific battalions. Marlborough had thought to thwart Hill's command of the expedition by sending at least two units whose colonels (Hamilton and Sutton, so often before Marlborough's nominees for American posts) were senior to Hill, good tories, and experienced in garrison government. Then, as St. John put it, "either Mr. Hill must not command or a great hardship must be done to officers who have deserved very well; and the reason of that hardship must be her Majesty's partiality to Mr. Hill." St. John had to dig deep to find colonels junior to Hill, so that he could command them, but whose regiments were senior enough so that their loss would damage Marlborough's fighting capacity. To dispose of Generals Sutton and Hamilton, St. John struck their regiments from Marlborough's list. He replaced them with the regiments which had been headed by the cashiered whig generals Meredyth and Macartney but which were now led by tory colonels junior to Jack Hill. Marlborough's submission to Hill's promotion gave Queen Anne enormous satisfaction. Indeed, the whole Canadian expedition seems to have been valued by the queen primarily as an agency by which to anger the captain general, reduce his authority, and produce an American conquest that would put his European victories in the shade.

Without even waiting for Marlborough's acquiescence, the queen (by St. John) ordered Colonel Richard Kane to embark the five battalions at Ostend and ship them to Portsmouth to join the fleet bound to Boston.[7]

The American authorities were to have been warned of the approaching expedition by Francis Nicholson. "Old Nick Nack" had been generously treated by St. John. He promised Nicholson payment of his arrears from the 1710 expedition to Nova Scotia, promotion to lieutenant general in command of the overland assault from Albany against Montreal, a salary of £2 a day, arms for 2,000 provincial troops, and half a battalion of Charles Churchill's marines to enforce his orders. General Nicholson responded with an old-fashioned tory paean of praise for "ye expedition wch Her Most Sacred Majesty hath with so very great equity and wisdom determin'd to be under taken[,] ye success of which will be for God's glory, ye extirpation of ye Roman Catholick religion, the encrease of ye Church of England, the good and welfare of Her Majesty's loyall and dutifull subjects in North America, and others who have ye honor and happiness of being Her Majesty's liege people will reap ye benefitt thereby." But one delay succeeded another. Nicholson's sailing date faded from mid-January to late February. When he finally sailed from Portsmouth with the marines and munitions in two frigates, it was only to put into Plymouth. There the ships were pinned to their moorings by weeks of contrary winter weather.[8]

Meanwhile, the expedition, for whose reception and reinforcement the American colonies were supposedly preparing, was assembled at Portsmouth by that able organizer Colonel Richard King. King had first achieved notice as an engineer at the battle of Blenheim. King was also one of Spotswood's deputies at the siege of Menin. Distinguished at Malplaquet, King was brevetted by Marlborough as lieutenant colonel of foot. On March 1, 1711, King was commissioned quartermaster general of the American expeditionary force and brevetted colonel (his permanent commission was as a captain in that deep-dyed tory corps, the earl of Orrery's foot, commanded by Lieutenant Colonel John Corbett, the governor general designate of Maryland). Colonel King wrote to secretary St. John praising the secretary's patriotism because "this expedition is your own" and because it "must prove in all humane appearance a more solid advantage to England than all those glaring battles, and sieges which have made of late years such a mighty figure in the Gazettes." After this sycophantic slap at Marlborough's accomplishments (and his own service record), the quartermaster general took control of what was now called "Col. King's Expedition." He immediately assembled an artillery train of thirty-eight pieces and 100 gunners. King also did his best elsewhere to fill in for his feckless superiors, General Hill and Admiral Sir Hovenden Walker.[9]

Admiral Walker had disgraced himself in command of the Guadeloupe expedition at the outset of the war. He had lingered for two months at Barbados while Colonel Codrington's force sickened and died on shipboard off the Leeward Islands, waiting for Walker's squadron. When at last he reached

Guadeloupe, Walker had refused to interdict French reinforcements. He declined to take his ships inshore to bombard the French forts. He denied Codrington's forces guns, gunners, and munitions (until Walker was overruled by a council of his own captains). Finally, Walker pled an exaggerated shortage of provisions as an excuse for aborting the invasion. Walker subsequently blamed the fiasco on the Leeward Island troops. His next major command was of a squadron sent to stop the French invasion fleet sailing from Dunkirk to Scotland in 1708. Admiral Walker could not even find Dunkirk. He blamed his pilots. In 1711, Walker was serving ashore in a sinecure at Plymouth when St. John inaugurated the American expedition. The admiralty nominated a seaman, Sir Thomas Hardy, but St. John preferred his friend Sir Hovenden Walker. Although he was an utter incompetent at sea, Walker was, St. John wrote, "a Gentleman of letters, good Understanding, ready Wit, and agreeable Conversation."[10]

St. John also chose the head of the land forces, John Hill. While his main qualification for command was that he was Abigail Masham's brother, Hill's secondary merit was his ability to drink even with St. John. He was one of the dissolute secretary of state's few remaining friends (besides Walker, St. John's other cronies were: the earl of Orrery, who gloried in his insubordination to the captain general; Dean Swift, Marlborough's eloquent enemy; Matthew Prior, the duke's resentful former client, now negotiator of the secret peace with France; and Sir William Wyndham, pack leader of "the October Club" of high tory parliamentarians). St. John had selected two personal friends, officers of marked and public incapacity (Hill himself wrote to St. John that if the expedition failed, "you must blame yourself for pitching upon one So little capable"), over at least five better-qualified nominees. On March 1, 1711, the queen commissioned John Hill as expeditionary general and commander in chief in America. She gave him £1,000 for his personal equipment and £8,000 for "contingencies." Hill immediately nominated a pliable paymaster to manage for his benefit both these monies and the poundage of the expeditionary regiments (allowances taken from Marlborough's depleted accounts for the "particular service" of the American expedition).[11]

Approval for the expedition was carried though Queen Anne's cabinet only over the strongest objections of a wounded prime minister. The absent (Robert Harley, now earl of) Oxford's objections were voiced to the queen and her ministers by no less a tory elder than the earl of Rochester. He said that the expedition was unnecessary, given the prospect of peace, and dangerous, given the uncertainties of the succession, which might demand the service in Great Britain itself of every soldier. As Oxford's and Rochester's objections confirmed, the enterprise was entirely the work of Henry St. John: "the whole design was formed by me, and the management of it solely carried on by me." On April 24, 1711, St. John was created viscount Bolingbroke. The peerage was his reward for forming an expedition designed to serve queen Anne's spite, please her favorite, and advance extreme tory views on both sides of the Atlantic.[12]

On April 27, 1711, the expedition directed by this notorious scoundrel—ten battleships, a cruiser, two bomb ketches, thirty-some transports, seven munitions vessels, and a tender packed with General Hill's provisions, ships manned by about 6,000 sailors and marines, and carrying 5,303 soldiers—the largest force as yet committed to American conquest, cleared Portsmouth, bound for Boston. A quick passage, just eight weeks from land to land, was the expedition's sole stroke of good fortune, but it meant that the fleet reached Boston just two weeks behind Nicholson's long-delayed frigates. The news the frigates brought had astonished "the New-England people," who "were all whigs and supposed the Tory ministry to be determined upon a peace, and rather disposed to suffer France to recover part of what she had lost than to make further acquisition from her." Nonetheless, on June 18, just ten days after Nicholson landed, an intercolonial congress met at New London to prepare for the expedition. Only three days later, a great fleet appeared off Boston. Turned out as if to repel invaders, instead the city regiments lined the streets as the expeditionary commanders processed to the townhouse to meet Boston's civic fathers. Walker and Hill made unwelcome, apparently impossible, demands on the colonists to re-raise provincial regiments and to provision both the provincial and the regular troops and sailors for nine months. These were Herculean labors for a region wrung dry by preparations for four previous expeditions against New France, and by a constant war on the frontiers.[13]

Frontier fighting kept one able-bodied man in five under arms every year in Massachusetts (and an astonishing one in two in New Hampshire): "this would be thought extraordinary in any state in Europe." The overstretched New Englanders did not believe that the tory ministry or its partisans in command of the expedition were in earnest about conquering Canada, but the colonists did believe that the tories intended to reduce provincial liberties. Failure to do everything Hill and Walker asked would provide the tory ministry with an excuse to revoke the New England charters and impose upon the colonists a regular royal government in both state and church. To forestall accusations of disloyalty and dissidence, draconian decrees went forth from the Massachusetts government of Colonel Joseph Dudley to impress provisions, provide credit, recapture deserters, and enlist pilots as well as to requisition transports by the score and draft troops by the thousand.[14]

Credit was the first problem. The tories had antagonized the transatlantic creditor class by dismissing lord treasurer Godolphin and disrupting the Marlborough administration. The merchants who had underwritten the two previous expeditions had yet to be repaid by the English treasury. No one would advance the expedition's purchasing agents a penny. Therefore the Massachusetts legislature immediately authorized an issue of £40,000 in bills of credit to be lent to the supplying merchants, giving them in effect a lien on local tax revenues. The ensuing demand for food, in a season of scarcity, drove up prices. Legislative fiat reduced prices to previous levels. Purveyors refused to sell at the regulated prices. The governor general ordered search and seizure of supplies. That brought hoarded provisions out of hiding, but the question of exchange rates between Massachusetts paper and English bills paralyzed purchasing. At the governor general's request, the legislature doubled the exchange rate from 20 percent to 40 percent in favor of English paper.[15]

Money was one thing, men another. Desertion was the plague of all the armed forces of the age. The British soldiers were encamped on Noodle's Island (where their review by General Hill, in the presence of Governor General Dudley "and a great Concourse of People of all sorts, the Troops making a very fine Appearance, such as had never before been seen in these Parts of the World," introduced the colonists to the drill and discipline of elite troops). Nonetheless, some soldiers got away, "seduced" by high wages and unscrupulous employers. Officers retaliated by enlisting slaves. General Hill ordered them returned to their masters to encourage Massachusetts employers to return British deserters. This failing, recovery of the redcoat runaways (and provincial absconders as well) was executed by force. The governor general ordered the militia companies of nineteen eastern towns to supply twenty-four-hour-a-day patrols of every road and landing place. He commanded the field officers of the provincial regiments, in person or by their captains, to search every district, town, and village "within your Regiment," to arrest all strangers, and to send them under guard to Boston. There they were to face the special court that the legislature authorized to try suspected deserters. The sheriff was to choose the jury, "a thing never before done in that Province."[16]

The next contentious question was pilotage. Admiral Walker had no personal knowledge of the New England coast, of Nova Scotian waters, nor of the St. Lawrence. He had brought no charts. He had accepted the volunteer services of a French prisoner of war who claimed to have the knowledge that the admiral lacked. Everyone who met the French pilot told the admiral that the man was certainly an ignorant rogue and perhaps an enemy agent planted to mislead the expedition. The alternatives were local pilots, who "in general would have preferred a prison on shore to a man of war at sea." So the governor general impressed all the Boston pilots save for the most knowledgeable, Captain Cyprian Southack, the chief provincial naval officer. He had already volunteered to lead the fleet down east. Admiral Walker, however, sent Southack off on a fool's errand to extract unneeded reinforcements from the exiguous garrison of Port Royal. The pilot problem, largely of his own making, inaugurated the admiral's unending complaints that, far from exerting themselves, the colonists had obstructed the queen's service. Admiral Walker warned Governor General Dudley that "Her Majesty will resent such Action in a very signal manner; and when it shall be represented that the people live here as if there were no King in Israel, but every one does what seems right in his own Eyes, measures will be taken to put things on a better foot for the future."[17]

If the queen's resentment were not enough to discipline the colonists, the admiral wrote to St. John that now that there was a high tory majority in parliament and the dissenters' whig friends were out of power, the imperial legislature should act against the colonial charters. For, "instead of assisting, the Government of this Colony have prejudiced the present Expedition, notwithstanding their pretended Declarations to the contrary. . . . they may flatter themselves with a great many Friends in Britain, yet, when the Parliament there shall come to enquire . . . it will produce such a Resentment as perhaps New England may repent."[18]

The doubled discipline of the American colonies, by monarch and parliament, was possible because from the eve of the war, Marlborough had taken pains to consult the parliament (in which he had formerly led the campaign for anglican Atlantic ascendancy). With the accession of Queen Anne, whose personal and political, military and imperial champion he was, Marlborough had ceaselessly striven to unite executive and legislative counsels. The captain general intended both to secure Anne's accession and to advance the conduct of the war with France by amplifying the constitutional authority of the monarch in parliament, thus resolving a century of strife between the Stuart sovereigns and their legislatures. The result had been an unprecedented political stability and governmental authority in England, in Britain, and, as now seemed possible, in America.

No sentient provincial executive could either ignore the need to conciliate the imperial authority born of war or fail to use its methods to consolidate his own colonial command. Joseph Dudley was but one of the queen's viceroys whose provincial mobilization for war utilized military patronage and procurement, and the prerogative power enhanced by the war with France, to win enhanced executive authority and anglicize America. In a month's time, New England, led by Governor General Dudley and with Massachusetts doing the bulk of the work, recruited and regimented 1,160 men (who were armed from royal stores), commissioned sixty officers (each backed by a veteran regular), put the provincial troops under Colonel Samuel Vetch's command, and got them aboard twenty impressed transports, each towing a dozen newly built landing craft. The entire expeditionary force was provisioned for four and a half months. Simultaneously, Dudley ordered out an additional 500 men, plus officers, to defend the frontiers of Massachusetts and New Hampshire.[19]

The English army officers no more appreciated these efforts than the admiral had. Their threats against American autonomy were even more articulate, acrimonious, and anticipatory. Colonel King wrote that "the reluctancy and ill nature that these people shew'd to serve us and forward the expedition" demonstrated "their perverse and wicked intentions . . . to detain us here till the advanc'd season of the year will probably defeat us. . . . its certain that those who rule and profitt by their present disorderly government now see how reasonable it is to change it; that the conquest of Canada will naturally lead the Queen into it, and shew her how absolutely necessary it is to put all this northern continent of America under one form of government, for the real good of the present colonys, for establishing of others, for their mutual support, and the vast advantages that will thereby accrue to Great Britain." Colonel King was prescient indeed. The eventual conquest of Canada did lead the crown in parliament to undertake an imperial reconstruction of American government. By placing an army of occupation in America, the conquest of Canada would work the counterrevolution in government intended in 1711 and provoke the revolt anticipated by the royal military commanders.[20]

Colonel King was quite explicit about the "one form of government" to be imposed on America. If the queen did not herself rescind charters and proprietary rights and impose uniform and direct royal government on the American colonies, so the quartermaster general wrote to the secretary of state, the parliament must, because, "till all their charters are resum'd to the Crown, or taken away by an act of parliament, till they are all settled under one government—with an entire liberty of conscience—and an invitation to all nations to settle here, they will grow every day more stiff and disobedient, more burthensome than advantageous to Great Britain." The objects of the colonel's particular enmity, the New Englanders, could be expected to resent such impositions. "The interestedness, ill nature and sowerness of these people, whose government, doctrine, and manners, whose hypocrisy and canting are insupportable," had already led them not just to impede the expedition but to contemplate treason against the British crown and an alliance with the French.[21]

"There is as much occasion for securing these colonys to Her Majesty as undertaking to reduce the French," so the admiral wrote the secretary of state. Indeed, they were allied! "The mystery of the New Englanders making such delays at Boston" was French instigation. This was discovered when the expedition was at sea and a patrol captured dispatches from the French governor of Newfoundland to Louis XIV's foreign secretary. These revealed that "one Mons. La Ronde Denis (who we found as a pretended prisoner at Boston when we arrived)" had been sent to Massachusetts in response to orders from Paris "to treat with the people of New England as an independent state not to give any assistance to the troops sent from Britain for the reduction of Quebec." It was as obvious to the French ministry as it was to the British government that the conquest of Canada would eliminate American autonomy. Indeed, the French believed that the forces assigned to the "Quebec" expedition were actually intended to destroy the American "republics." The foreign minister, Louis Phélypeaux, comte de Pontchartrain, ordered the governors of Newfoundland and New France to inform "the Council of Boston" "of the designs of the English Court . . . to establish their sovereignty in Boston, and in the Province of New York, the people of these provinces having always maintained themselves in a kind of republic by their Council, without being willing to receive the absolute governors of the Kings of England." In return for New England's and New York's obstruction of the expedition designed to subjugate both them- selves and the Canadians, the king of France would order his Canadian subjects to support the "Bostonnais" in "maintaining their republican state and escaping the yoke sought to be imposed upon them."[22]

The agent chosen to warn the Boston republicans of the imminence of the empire militant was La Ronde Denys, captain of marines. Fluent in English, the French officer was frequently resident in Boston (officially to facilitate pris- oner exchanges, but also, presumably, to forward Boston's illegal trade with Placentia, Quebec, and the eastern Abenaki). Under a flag of truce, Denys had reached Boston before Nicholson. Apparently Denys did not offer the Boston- nais a military alliance with New France. He did promise all New England freedom from French and Indian raids, indeed "de faire cesser toutes sorties d'hostility du cote du Canada," by sea and land, in return for the colonists' obstruction of the Canadian expedition. Denys's message to the colonists was "that the forces which the Queen of England sends to join their own for the conquest of Acadia and Canada have no object whatever but that of ravishing from them the liberties they have kept so firmly and so long, but which would be near ruin if the Queen should become mistress of New France by the for- tune of war; and that either they must have sadly fallen from their ancient spirit, or their chiefs have been corrupted by the Court of London, if they do not see that they are using their own weapons for the destruction of their republic."[23]

Massachusetts's mulishness so exceeded the bounds of war profiteering and puritan perversity as to suggest a real role for political opposition, apart from or in addition to any response to Denys's dubious promises of a truce. A provincial assembly (led by a notorious commonwealthsman, Elisha Cooke) and a con- gregational clergy (whose public authority, if not its very existence, required resistance to the imperial church of England) had ample reason to resent both the militant royalism and anglicanism of the regulars. Ideology apart, there were parents and patriots aplenty to fear the loss of any more of Massachusetts's able-bodied men in badly designed imperial ventures. At the usual odds, the ex- pedition would lose half of the soldiers to disease, even if they captured Quebec without fighting. No wonder that recruitment was difficult or that deserters had "such Encouragement from the Country, that they go armed, and upon their own Defence." Obstruction, desertion, and political hostility there obvi- ously were. Actual resistance, if it was considered, was impossible in the face of an English fleet and army "sufficient to reduce by force all the coloneys." That armada was best gotten away from Boston as soon as possible. Either it would fail and flee or, by conquering Canada, it would give a check to the French and the Abenaki far more effective than any promise by La Ronde Denys.[24]

Allegedly, there were French observers who saw even further than De- nys or his masters. Beyond the British coercion of the American colonists that would inevitably follow the conquest of Canada, the French may have already anticipated the independence movement that conquest and coercion would excite: "Old England will not imagine that these various provinces will then unite, strike off the yoke of the English monarchy, and erect themselves into a democracy." In the summer of 1711, any such speculation was belied not only by the physical incapacity of beleaguered baby societies—"it would not be more absurd to place two of her Majesty's beef-eaters to watch an infant in his cradle, than to guard these weak infant colonies to prevent their shaking off the British yoke"—but also by the belief of Governor General Dudley and the anglicized elites of New England (and New York) that their own tenure in office, the physical security of their provinces, and the diversion of the threatened royal and parliamentary wrath all were best served by bending every effort to conquer Canada. Besides, "Delenda est Canada" had been their slogan for twenty-one years. They were ever more encouraged in pursuing it as the strength of England became the power of Great Britain in successive Atlantic wars. The secretary of the province wrote to Massachusetts's agent in London that "the Expedition (of the last Importance to these Plantations) has been brought forward beyond what could have reasonably been expected, the Supplies demanded being so large. The Government have exerted their utmost Powers to encourage it with all manner of Intention and Application, and I hope the General and Admiral will so represent it in their Favour."[25]

They did not, but on July 30, 1711, "having at last gott our fleet victuall'd for three months and the New England transports mann'd, we all sailed out of Nantasket or Kingroad Harbour with a fair gale at south west to pursue our expedition." Ships' companies of more than 6,000 manned ten battleships, a ship of fifty guns, two frigates, two bomb ketches, Hill's comforts vessel, and sixty or more transports with 7,500 men aboard. The wind was fair, but the mindset of the commanders was not. Additional provisions, requisitioned from as far south as Virginia, had not yet arrived to relieve Admiral Walker's hysterical fears (which he had already spread to his colleague in command) of winter hunger, cannibalism, and a fruitless flight through a frozen wilderness from the ruins of Quebec to the frontiers of New England, in search of sustenance. Even if Quebec could be found (remember, Walker was usually "all at sea") and conquered, the admiral anticipated "how dismal must it have been to have beheld the Seas and Earth lock'd up by Adamantine Frosts, and Swoln with high Mountains of Snow, in a barren and uncultivated Region, and great numbers of brave Men famishing with Hunger, and drawing Lots who should die first to feed the rest, without the least appearance of Relief . . . abandoning all the Ships, naval and military Stores and Ammunition to the Enemy, and desperately attempting to march through uninhabited and wild Woods and Desarts, over deep Snows and Rocks of Ice, to try, if happily we could have reached any part of New England before we had all perished by the way."[26]

The fearful admiral was further convinced, whether by imagination playing on ignorance or by the misinformation of his French pilots, that the St. Lawrence at Quebec froze right to the bottom, 400 feet deep, as he believed, so that he would have to haul out every ship or see them crushed. But he never expected to reach Quebec. Walker thought the river was unnavigable. He believed that powerful tides ran against the wind and that innumerable shoals claimed the lives of almost every ship that entered the St. Lawrence. The admiral accepted no evidence to the contrary. It mattered not to Walker's fears that Sir William Phips had taken every ship of his New England fleet safely up to Quebec in the autumn of 1690 (and Walker had the only copy of Phips's log and sailing directions aboard his flagship). What Walker (not the best name for an admiral) chose to remember, and exaggerate, were Phips's losses on the way home. These "four" ships Walker read as "forty."[27]

Samuel Vetch, the colonel commanding the two New England regiments, had sailed from Boston to Quebec repeatedly under flags of truce, ostensibly (like La Ronde Denys) to arrange prisoner exchanges, probably to facilitate illegal trade, and certainly to prepare for such an invasion as this. So long as Vetch led the fleet, Admiral Walker's panic was bypassed. Sailing in the aptly named *Dispatch*, Vetch knew that he was "myself if not the only, at least the best pilot . . . although none of my province." He confidently led the fleet from Cape Sable to Cape Breton. Vetch sent ahead a flotilla of small craft to sound out and buoy dangers that the fleet might encounter. He sent every ship a list of signals. His coded messages conveyed the sailing directions that kept the unwieldy flotilla clear of danger all the way to the Gulf of St. Lawrence. There, however, off the Isle of St. Paul, Admiral Walker insisted that Vetch come aboard his flagship, the *Edgar*, take the advice of the admiral's two French pilots (the second of whom Walker had just acquired from a French merchant vessel captured outbound from Quebec), and submit to the direction of the admiral and his fleet captain. Vetch thought that the second Frenchman was as much an enemy agent as the first. He had seen enough of the admiral and his captain to know that both were incompetent. So Vetch suggested that it would be best if he continued to lead the fleet from the *Dispatch*. Walker insisted that the flagship should take command. Henceforward, Vetch kept the *Dispatch* at the rear of the fleet to avoid the inevitable disaster.[28]

A fair wind carried the Quebec expedition up the Gulf of St. Lawrence to a position south of Anticosti Island but, at midnight of August 13/14, Admiral Walker, unsure of his position, ordered the fleet to put about until daylight. The fair wind died at dawn. For the next three days, the fleet slatted about in light airs. At dawn on the 18th, the fair wind for Quebec set in again. By now, however, the fleet had drifted so far to the east that the unweatherly transports could not clear Cape Gaspé. To Vetch's disgust, Admiral Walker ordered the fleet to sail back and anchor in Gaspé Bay. It was forty hours before the fleet sailed again. Finally, a steady southwesterly wind let the fleet get its anchors and sail upriver once again. At midday on August 21, the fleet once again reached Anticosti Island. Here the wind backed to the east. Then it dropped. Fog beshrouded the fleet. The consensus of the officers and pilots aboard the flagship was that they were just west of Anticosti Island, and in the center of an estuary seventy miles wide from north to south. So they ordered the fleet to stand southwest under easy sail. In fact, the fleet was nearly forty miles north of the center of the St. Lawrence and almost fifty miles further west than the flagship council had concluded. So the easterly breeze, aided by a northwesterly current, was carrying the fleet into the angle where the north shore of the gulf turned south. An ironbound coast lay right in the fleet's path. Still, a change of course more to the south of west would carry the fleet clear of danger, or so Samuel Vetch thought. He was appalled when, at 10:30 p.m. on the 23d, the flagship signaled the fleet to wear and sail downwind, that is, directly west. Captain Paddon of the *Edgar* had seen land ahead. Admiral Walker, utterly disoriented, thought that it must be the south shore of the estuary. It was the north shore. The admiral was more than 100 miles off course. By ordering the fleet to bear away before the rising easterly wind, Walker put his ships right onto the reefs to the west, the Isle of Eggs.[29]

Having ordered the course change with a nonchalance amazing in an admiral who did not know where he was, who was literally in the dark and in a notoriously treacherous estuary, Walker left the deck of his flagship and went to bed. No sooner was he asleep than Captain George Gauder, quartermaster of Hill's regiment, burst into the admiral's cabin, shouting that there were breakers dead ahead. The admiral had heard nothing of this from the *Edgar*'s captain, the lookouts, or the pilots. He dismissed Gauder as a fearful landsman. Five minutes later, Gauder was back, pleading with Admiral Walker to come and see the danger. Now the admiral heard shouts. He arrived on deck, having taken time to put on his bathrobe and slippers, to see that some of the fleet ahead were already in among the breakers. As the flagship surged downwind toward the reefs, her panicked captain ordered the anchor dropped. Fearing that it would not hold the massive vessel against a rising wind and sea, Admiral Walker took command at last, ordered the anchor rode cut and the ship put about. As the *Edgar* made sail and clawed off the reefs, alarm guns, emergency lights, and the distant shrieks of hundreds of men testified that other vessels of Walker's fleet had not been so fortunate.[30]

At the moment of the alarm, the *Windsor*, with General Hill and Colonel King aboard, was already embayed. As soon as the naval officers' incredulity could be overcome, the *Windsor* tacked and her hands made sail, but the ship was trapped between the north and the northeast reefs off the Isle of Eggs. By great good fortune, there was just room enough between the reefs to bring the battleship head to wind and there was sufficient depth below the ship and scope enough astern for her to anchor. Riding to every anchor she owned, the *Wind-*

sor faced the rising easterly gale. "All the night we heard nothing but ships firing and showing lights in the utmost distress" because, for the ships ahead and to leeward of the *Windsor*, there was no escape. Until the moment of impact, it had "rain'd very hard and blown a perfect storm directly on shore." Now, the onshore wind "and the vast seas that ran" broke the crowded troop transports "in a moment in ten thousand pieces against the rocks; and betwixt them and the shore 'twas at least five miles." In the wreck of seven English transports, 740 officers and men from four royal regiments, the elite of Marlborough's unconquered army were lost, together with thirty-five of their women, some 200 sailors, and all the regimental equipment. Only 200 men survived, "so mangled and bruised on the rocks, and naked withal, that they were not in any condition of service" after they were picked off the isles by boats from the fleet during the next few days.[31]

Few of the fleet could have escaped the fate of the troop transports if the easterly gale had not dropped away at 2:00 a.m. By 4:00, the wind had backed to the southwest. With the wind blowing off the reefs, the anchored ships weighted their sheet anchors, cut their small and bower rodes, and ran away from the north shore. For the next two days, the fleet beat back and forth across the great river, against strong southwesterly winds, unable to find a safe anchorage. On the morning of August 25, Admiral Walker resolved to consult General Hill. Walker found that Hill, overwhelmed by what he believed to be the loss of thousands of his men, had already assembled the colonels aboard the *Windsor* as a council of war. All the landsmen "being dissatisfied with the Difficulties of getting up the River," asked the admiral to add his captains to the council. When they arrived, the naval officers asked why they had not been consulted at Boston. The inadequacy of the pilots (whom Walker now blamed for the disaster) had been known then and the captains had asked for a council to discuss it. Privately, Walker and Hill had agreed with the captains that the expedition was doomed "for, the hazardous Navigation of the River, together with the Unskillfulness of the Pilots . . . were there nothing else was enough to check all Hopes of Success." And not only did both the general and the admiral fear a shortage of provisions and the Canadian winter, they shared, if they did not actually promote, that vague terror of the unknown which pervaded the ranks of all the British officers. Hill and Walker had refused to summon the council of war at Boston only because they knew that the naval captains would vote to abandon the attempt on Quebec and they could offer no arguments to the contrary. They also knew that their untested apprehensions were no grounds for abandoning the attack ordered by the queen. Now the disaster at the Isle of Eggs gave Walker and Hill tangible proof both of pilot error and riverine hazard.[32]

Only Colonel Vetch resisted ignominious retreat. Coming aboard the *Windsor* after a long, wet, cold row to hear, for the first time, exaggerated accounts of the casualties on the reef, Vetch recovered enough to remind the council of war that Phips's fleet had gone up the St. Lawrence in October of 1690 without a single pilot, "upon which the fflag asked me if I would undertake to carry up the fleet I told him I never was bredd to sea nor was it any part of my Province but I would do my best by going ahead and Shewing them where the Difficulty of the River was which I knew pretty well." Instead of accepting Vetch's offer, the council of war, impressed by the French pilots, the incompetent admiral, and the cowardly general, voted to abandon the attempt on Quebec "by reason of the ignorance of the said pilots and as also the uncertainty and rapidity of the currents as by fatal experience we have found."[33]

Back aboard the *Dispatch*, Vetch wrote to Walker, placing the blame where it belonged. "The late fatal Disaster" could not "be in any way Imputed to the Difficulty of the Navigation but to the wrong Course we steered . . . who Directed that Course you best know." The army officers had admitted that there was still ample force to take Quebec, Vetch observed. The navigation up to the city was no more difficult than a return voyage to Cape Breton. Retreat would disgrace the commanders of the expedition, and "it would be of a very fatal Consequence to the Enterest of the Crown and all the British Colonys upon the Continent." Vetch's plan of American continental conquest, adopted by the queen and her ministers, would be abandoned on the doorstep of success: "once we are gott up the town I look upon the greatest part if not all the Difficulty to be over." Again, Colonel Vetch's counsel was ignored. At 7:00 p.m. on August 25, 1711, the expeditionary fleet began to beat back to Gaspé, fighting all the way the easterly winds that would have carried them to Quebec.[34]

By the time, two weeks later, that the fleet anchored in the Spanish River, Cape Breton, Colonel King, at least, had realized the devastating impact on the provinces of the expedition's utter failure: "what a loss it will prove to our poor American coloneys; how much it will contribute to depopulate their frontiers, to diminish their trade, and discourage all people, by the constant wars they must now be oblig'd to maintain, from settling among them or improving their lands. And what is still a more melancholy reflection, they dare hardly expect any relief for the future, when they see this great effort England made to succor them thus ruffled and defeated." Not only would raids from Quebec continue to terrorize the land frontiers of beleaguered New England, but French attacks on New England's fisheries would also go on as before. This because another council of war, also directed by General Hill, concluded that the fleet could not even take its secondary objective, Placentia, Newfoundland, on its way home. Given the expedition's overwhelming force and a navigation so easy that even Admiral Walker could not have missed the most visited and most valuable island in the North Atlantic, an excuse had to be found that would conceal the fact that Hill and Walker were terrified by the (false) news (planted on them in French dispatches carefully put in their way) that the garrison of Placentia had been reinforced to 2,000 men (still less than a third of the expeditionary numbers) and that the harbor was protected by new forts, redoubts, and a boom. Colonel Vetch, a man of more military experience than the court-ier general and the weak-kneed admiral combined, pointed to the expedition's overwhelming numbers and suggested that the heavy battleships could break any boom Placentia could build.[35]

The admiral and the general were proof against any warlike counsels. Hill assured Walker that Mrs. Masham's influence with queen Anne would pro-tect them against all charges of cowardice or incompetence. Besides, Admiral Walker could reuse the excuse St. John's misplaced cleverness had given him at the outset of the expedition: "suppose we had not made ourselves Masters of Placentia before . . . our Provisions have been consumed . . . suppose Winds and Weather had prevented our getting to sea again, had not our Circum-stances been very deplorable? Nay, suppose the best, that we had succeeded in a Month or Six weeks time, where must Provisions have been found to have left with the Garrison, or to bring home all of those Ships and Men." The answer was obvious. Placentia was the greatest fishing port in the Atlantic. No facts could overcome Admiral Walker's fears about food, General Hill's fear of the French, and the vague apprehensions of the council of war. On September 8, the British officers concluded that the shortage of provisions, combined with the lateness of the season, "which makes the navigation of the coast so danger-ous," compelled them to sail directly home.[36]

Samuel Vetch salvaged one crumb from the catastrophe. He pointed out to General Hill that the garrison of Nova Scotia had been dangerously de-pleted by the loss of Major Forbes and seventy men in an Abenaki ambush. Thereupon the general detached a company of New England Indian scouts, a royal engineer, a battery of artillery, and 350 regular troops to Nova Scotia. To command them, he appointed Major Thomas Caulfield, "a gentleman that has serv'd very well." Caulfield displaced that contumacious colonial Sir Thomas Hobby as Samuel Vetch's lieutenant governor. The major and his redcoats be-came cadres of the 40th Regiment, for the next sixty-three years the social backbone as well as the military sinews of Nova Scotia. The reinforcement of Nova Scotia was the sole accomplishment of the expedition of 1711. That expedition had been the largest military mission to North America since 1676. The 1711 attempt would not be equaled again in size or scope for nearly half a century. Nonetheless, it had set the pattern that, as both English and French observers anticipated, would ultimately lead to the conquest of Canada, the coercion of the colonies, and their war for independence.[37]

Admiral Walker, General Hill, and their British officers thought that the military disciplining of America should begin immediately. In their view, it had been the deliberate delaying tactics of the New Englanders, reinforced in their republicanism by La Ronde Denys, that had held the expedition in Boston until it was bound to fail. Colonel Clayton was sent ahead with dispatches. He reached the court at Windsor on October 5, 1711. There he declared that the decisive disaster at the Isle of Eggs was owing to "the several Disappointments which they had met with, and were likely to meet from the Northern Colonies." The first was that the fleet was "detain'd at Boston above a Month" until the season was too advanced for successful navigation. Then, "the Ignorance of the Pilots, which the Governour of New England had furnish'd them with, and answer'd for," had fatal results. Finally, Placentia was not attacked "because the Men of War, which were left to convoy the Stores promis'd by the several Colonies returned without any."[38]

The tory diplomat Matthew Prior informed the speaker of the house of commons that dissenters in religion and politics were to blame for every public difficulty, whether in America or England: "the disappointment we have mett at Canada, . . . is all owing to the avarice or treachery of the godly at New England: the same party are doing all the mischief they can in old England, they are really such a race of men that the Palatines [German refugees] are more our country men than they." It was clear to whig observers, however, that the tory commanders, their patrons, and the ministry "found it necessary to blame New England the better to excuse themselves." So doing, the tories revived the belief, coeval with the foundation of their party, that the colonists' "encreasing Numbers and Wealth, join'd to their great Distance from Britain will give them an Opportunity in the course of some years to throw off their Dependence on the Nation, and declare them selves a free State, if not curb'd in Time by being made entirely subject to the Crown."[39]

The threat of American independence led the tories to demand that every province be royalized and that the queen commission a senior army officer as an American viceroy. As the parliament took its war-driven place alongside the crown in the governance of the empire, its every prescription for the provinces was designed to offset "the Danger of making the Colonies too great," lest they "make Parties, League with Foreigners, and set up for an Independence of Power, separate from England, their Original and Center." In so coercive a context, the tories could construe the failure of the Canadian expedition as a success. It made clear the contumacy of the colonies. So the expedition's commanders were treated as if they had triumphed in America. Hill replaced Marlborough's chief of staff, Cadogan, in the lieutenancy of the Tower of London. Walker was given the West Indian squadron based in Port Royal, Jamaica (where he brutalized the colonists and insulted the new governor general, lord Archibald Hamilton). The senior colonels, Clayton and Kane, were given garrison governments on the continent, governments secured by Marlborough's brilliant campaign of 1711 in Flanders.[40]

On March 4, 1711, seven months before London heard the disastrous news from the St. Lawrence, the duke of Marlborough, "the most necessary man in Europe," arrived at The Hague to take command of the allied armies. "There were those who hoped that he will yet frighten our Enemies into an Honourable Peace" but, as the captain general's spokesman explained, Marlborough was "uneasy in his Thoughts, undermin'd in the Favour of his Sovereign, and vilely represented to the People." Marlborough's bête noire, the duke of Argyll, had been promoted to the command in Spain, replacing Marlborough's favorite, Stanhope. That insolent general the earl of Orrery had displaced Marlborough's chief of staff, Cadogan, as British envoy to The Hague. Marlborough's nominees for command of the Canada expedition had been bypassed in favor of the despised Jack Hill. These rewards to the captain general's most dissident officers could be, and were, represented to Marlborough by St. John as favors, because the malcontents were removed from commands in Marlborough's own army. Moreover, each of them was given an opportunity, which they embraced to the point of disgrace, to show they were better critics than commanders. And St. John's bypassing General Sutton for the Canadian expedition had an unanticipated result: it left Sutton available to win distinction in the key operation of the 1711 campaign, the passage of the French lines.[41]

Despite his loss of power and the war-weariness that had infected the army almost as much as it did English politics, the duke's intentions, as always, were aggressive. So much appeared when, on March 12, he ordered Cadogan to lead 20,000 of the allied troops westward to cover Douai, conquered in the previous campaign, and thence to threaten the French defensive lines. These lines extended more than 150 miles, from the Ardennes to the Channel. Gaps in the water defenses—rivers, canals, and inundations—were filled with fortifications, but the allied advance in the previous campaign had opened the rivers Lys and Scheldt as routes to supply an attack on that sector of the French barrier which extended some twenty-five miles from Bouchain to Aaras. Between these fortresses, the most plausible point of attack was the long causeway which ran from the allied conquest at Douai across the inundations of the Sensée to Arleux, but behind the drowned lands and the fortifications lay Marshal Villars' army, 95,000 men, ready to blunt any allied probe. These impregnable lines, Villars boasted, were "the ne plus ultra of the Duke of Marlborough," the limit of his achievement.[42]

On the last day of April, Marlborough encamped the lead elements of the allies between Bouchain and Douai, at the eastern end of the targeted twenty-five-mile sector of the "ne plus ultra lines." There he concentrated 85,000 men. He was joined by prince Eugene, torn unwillingly from the opera and its women, with 30,000 Imperialists, just in time to celebrate the anniversary of Ramillies on May 23. Eugene's was apt to be but a temporary reinforcement, however, for the Emperor Joseph had died on April 6. Eugene was under orders to withdraw his troops to defend the Rhine crossings the moment that Villars detached forces to fish in the troubled waters of the Imperial election. The successful candidate was apt to be the Austrian prince presently fighting in Spain as Charles III. His accession to the Imperial throne as the Emperor Charles VI would give the new ministry of Queen Anne the excuse it needed to abandon the war for Spain and Spanish America. The tory ministers would argue that a Hapsburg "universal monarchy" would be as dangerous to the balance of power in the Atlantic world as Bourbon hegemony. The ministry of Harley and St. John sought to persuade the French and their candidate for the Spanish throne, Philip of Anjou, to make the same commercial concessions in Spanish America that Marlborough (and Stanhope) had coerced from the Austrian prince, Charles, and from the French negotiators at Geertruidenberg. The prospect of Spanish American trade would underwrite Harley's South Sea Company, the commercial facade of his debt service and stockjobbing scheme. This he introduced in parliament on May 17.[43]

The prime minister's intent was to create a new, tory creditor class to balance "the monied interest" of the whigs, embodied in the Bank of England and the East India Company. Harley also played upon the old tory dream of excluding the Dutch as well as the French from trade with Spanish America. In their place, English merchants would be insinuated into Spanish America under cover of a monopoly of the slave trade, a trade, it was hoped, that would be based on Spanish American treaty ports controlled by English garrisons. At the same time, St. John appealed to another segment of the tories' "blue water" imperialism by forwarding negotiations with the French that would supposedly lead to the cession of the North American fisheries. These enormously valuable and strategic resources were to be secured by the conquest of all Acadia, Newfoundland, and even of Canada, by the Walker expedition.[44]

It was to underwrite a new balance of classes and parties in Britain on the basis of an expanded English empire in the Americas that, early in July 1711, St. John dispatched to Paris his intimate, the poet, diplomat, and veteran imperial administrator Matthew Prior, to renegotiate the preliminary articles of peace. By betraying all of England's allies in return for commercial and colonial concessions from France and Spain, the tories intended to end the war, declaw the duke of Marlborough, and terminate whig predominance in the military-fiscal state created since 1689 to fight the wars with France. Prior's own account of this decisive diplomacy—and we may be sure that his voice was St. John's—passes over without comment the drastic reduction in England's demands upon France since Marlborough's negotiations of 1709. Because the first objective of the ministry was to degrade the captain general "to the rank of an ordinary subject" by making peace on terms agreeable to "the gentlemen of England" on the tory back benches, Harley and St. John were prepared to discount even the enormous, alliance-breaching cession of Spain and Spanish America to the French candidate. Only the Mediterranean conquests of Minorca and Gibraltar and the asiento for the slave trade with New Spain were exceptions to a concentration on the North American objectives. These constituted "the glorious enterprise" of Canadian and maritime conquest now identified with Secretary St. John.[45]

Prior pressed the French for "what we possess or have taken in North America." This was to include Nova Scotia, including all of French Acadia, Cape Breton Island, St. Pierre and Miquelon. If the Canadian expedition succeeded—and the tory ministry was convinced that General Hill "is by this time master of all North America"—Prior was to claim all of Canada and Newfoundland. To this last, Torcy replied that England's real intent was to realize the duke of Marlborough's previous demand for "La Terre Neuve au nom de Dieu, faites la grâce a la reine ma maîtresse," and not otherwise. Prior apologized. The duke's arrogance was characteristic, Prior explained, "of a great general and unacquainted with the particular ways of treaty," but it was Marlborough's defeat of France that alone compelled France to make peace, and it was the captain general's vision of imperial aggrandizement that had inspired demands on France to make unbounded concessions in America. The recovery of the Hudson's Bay posts was also mandated by Prior, the pressure that the company's governors had put on Marlborough being continued on the new ministry. Prior also insisted on British retention of the French quarter of St. Kitts, which Codrington had taken in 1702. Torcy complained that "you ask in America all that which [with] our sweat and our blood we have been endeavouring for a hundred years to acquire."[46]

Prior's demands were those of the tory chiefs, Harley and St. John. Their ministry's very survival required an immediate peace. Moreover, they relied pecuniarily as well as politically on a harvest of its fruits, Harley in South America, St. John in North. Only St. John, of all the cabinet, had sufficient French to negotiate, however, so it was he who separated Cape Breton, Acadia, and the Gulf islands from Nova Scotia, leaving them in French hands, and it was St. John who surrendered "the French shore" of Newfoundland. Whether or not, for so doing, St. John received an enormous bribe, he was responsible for the cessions which, as Torcy acknowledged, recruited the navy of France, fed the French people, and preserved the economy of France's Atlantic provinces. This St. John did over the objection of the lords commissioners of trade and plantations (informed as they were by Francis Nicholson and the Newfoundland and New England merchant lobbies). By St. John's concession, the commissioners pointed out, "the good end of having Newfoundland restor'd to us will be defeated." The cession and fortification of Cape Breton (where the French proceeded to erect the great fortress of Louisburg) would neutralize British Nova Scotia. The failure to make Nova Scotia's western boundary the St. Croix and its northern limit the St. Lawrence would leave most of Acadia to France. So the French menace to the northern frontiers of New England would be sustained. St. John's concessions, made on October 8, 1711, just two days after the news of the Canada expedition's failure reached Windsor, doomed the rival empires in America to three more costly wars, the last of which broke the first British empire and, as had been anticipated in 1711, effected American independence.[47]

Still, it must be said that the agreements of October 1711, although they were achieved at the expense of England's allies and at the price of three generations of war in America, were of inestimable benefit to the new British empire.

Marlborough's defeat of France had secured a peace that achieved the imperial aims with which he had begun the war in 1702: the recovery of Newfoundland, Hudson's Bay, and St. Kitts, and the security of the Jamaica-based trade with New Spain. More important in Marlborough's mind had been the great questions of royal successions. The primary issue was recognition of the legitimacy of Anne's succession and the assurance of a Protestant successor to the imperial throne of what was now a Greater Britain. Anne's sovereignty was assured. The Protestant succession, however, was in doubt, given the possibility of a palace coup by the tory jacobites. The Spanish succession was at least nominally separated from the French monarchy. Both the Mediterranean conquests, Gibraltar and Minorca, together with trade concessions in America, all so much pressed by Marlborough as the roots of maritime empire, were retained. The ambit of the sun king himself had been much reduced. The captain general had achieved unexampled victories against Louis XIV's aggression. He had saved Austria from France at Blenheim and recovered Brabant and Flanders from France at Ramillies and Oudenarde, but every victory had magnified Marlborough's ambition. In a conquered Paris, Marlborough intended to write upon a drumhead peace terms that would revolutionize France itself and cede the New World to a Greater Britain.

Events beyond Marlborough's control now all but erased his hopes of forcing France to an unconditional surrender in Europe and America. On June 13, Prince Eugene withdrew 30,000 troops to the Rhine frontier of the empire to protect the election of Prince Charles as emperor. One after another, the German electoral princes failed to send their promised contingents to join the allied army on the Flanders frontier with France. All these losses made even more bitter the withdrawal of five English battalions for the Quebec expedition and made even more debilitating the divided command that that diversion manifested. Marlborough was left with an army of 85,000 to attack Villars' entrenched 95,000. Nonetheless, on June 14, after long delays owing to a late spring, Marlborough ordered his army to cross the River Scarpe. Early in July, he offered battle to the French on a fair and open field, the plains of Lens. While Marshal Villars' attention was focused on Marlborough's main force, a detachment of the allies advanced along the causeway over the Sensée and, on July 6, took the French position at Arleux. A little allied garrison was left to hold Arleux. It was supposedly covered by a large force encamped on the glacis of Douai. Instead of following up this advantage, however, Marlborough continued to edge his army westward. Villars moved with him, but now he detached a force that beat up the allied camp at Douai and attacked Arleux. The garrison there called for help. Cadogan's relief force was unaccountably slow in coming up. Outnumbered and unsupported, the garrison surrendered as prisoners of war. They were stripped naked, imprisoned, and the fortifications of Arleux were razed by the French.[48]

THE BLENHEIM VICTORIES

Dunawert: The Storm of the Schellenberg

The Blenheim Victories tapestries, designed by the school of Lambert de Hondt and woven at Brussels by Judocus de Vos between 1706 and 1713, memorialize the duke of Marlborough's military accomplishments, save for Ramillies. This omission is the more remarkable because there survives a de Hondt cartoon of the battle. This template of tapestry is centered on the decisive cavalry charge at Ramillies. It shows Marlborough's fight in the midst of the melee. In the background, named village strongpoints are being overrun by the captain general's

Hooghstet: The Battle of Blenheim

infantry. The cartoon is a testimony to the accurate and detailed tactical information shown in the backgrounds of every one of the Blenheim victories, yet a Ramillies tapestry seems never to have been woven. Alan Wace, *The Marlborough Tapestries at Blenheim Palace* (London, 1968), 122, speculates that the duke expected the city of Brussels to commission this particular work, so Marlborough, ever careful with his own money, did not include it in his own set of hangings. Instead of a Ramillies tapestry, Brussels presented Marlborough with a conventional set (if, to

the duke's taste, overrich in gold and silver thread), *The Art of War*. This set was completed in October 1706 and hangs today at Blenheim.

Victorious at Ramillies, the conqueror of Flanders, expecting peace, and with his new home abuilding, the duke began to pester his duchess for the measurements of the Blenheim state rooms in which he intended to hang an individualized tapestry record of his prowess. This was a form of boasting reserved to victorious royalty, but Marlborough now displayed the armorial bearings of a prince of the empire. (It is not beside the point of pride that Marlborough now also commissioned tapestries displaying the achievements of Alexander the Great, to be hung in his bedroom and the duchess's at Blenheim.) The duke kept winning battles and sieges, however, and the duchess was always at odds with the architect of Blenheim, John Vanbrugh, so the tapestry project kept expanding and the measurements were delayed in reaching the duke. Not until February 1713, when the duchess was so good as to leave her friends and her beloved English scenes to join her husband in exile, could Marlborough ask his wife, if it was not too much trouble, to pause in Brussels and approve the finished work: "you may do it in half an hour, whilst they get the dinner ready." Presumably, the Blenheim Victories went home with the triumphant Marlboroughs in August 1714, but the tapestries may not have been hung at Blenheim in the rooms for which they were designed until at last, in 1719, the crippled duke and the protective duchess moved into their palace. Six of the ten "Victories," together with two panels of the earlier *Art of War* set, are reproduced here, all by the kind permission of his grace the duke of Marlborough.

> For Blenheim's lofty rooms in the work design.
> In every piece let Art and Labour shine.
> Let glorious Deeds the Briton's Palace crown,
> Not those of ancient Heroes but his own.

The focal point of the Donauwörth tapestry is the duke of Marlborough, resplendent in a scarlet coat, its color undimmed after the lapse of three centuries, the baton of command in his right hand, his chief of staff, Cadogan, beside him, together with one of the field guides or running footmen who appear with their distinctive caps, tunics, and staffs in so many depictions of Marlborough's triumphs. The command party overlooks columns of cavalry and dragoons, each trooper with a fascine on his saddlebow, riding at full stretch toward the lines of infantry advancing toward the Schellenberg, each fascine destined to fill the ditches defending the heights. Those of the riders whose mounts have not fallen under the strain, having dropped their burdens, return at the gallop over the plain. The walled town of Donauwörth ("Dunawert" on the scroll beneath Marlborough's arms as prince of Mindelheim), the Danube bridgehead, is visible in the center. The great river flows beyond the town. On the right of the tapestry appears a village in flames. Before it (not, as the narrative has it, behind), a battery of English artillery shreds the defenders of the Schellenberg. Their defeat, compared to Marlborough's subsequent successes, was a minor affair. It was the first in an unbroken succession of triumphs, however, and its brutality and completeness made the military reputation of the captain general and his islanders.

The borders of this and every Blenheim tapestry are packed with symbols. Corner medallions associate with the victorious duke the elements of classical *virtù*: wisdom, justice, courage, moderation. The winged horse Pegasus, the mount of the Grecian hero Perseus on the left, is balanced by a Roman legionary shield crossed by the thunderbolt of Jove on the right. The trophy at the foot of the border, spilling over into the battle scene, depicts symbols specific to the action. Here, a bundle of fascines supports a trooper's discarded saddlebag, a dragoon's plug bayonet, and the ax, billhook, and cutlass of the forager. Conventional trophies—weapons and armor, standards, trumpets, and kettledrums—complete the iconography of victory.

Blenheim, the battle that changed the balance of power in the Atlantic world, was fought at the intersection of the River Danube and the Nebel stream on August 13, 1704. It is memorialized in this double tapestry that purports to show the surrender of Camile d'Hostun, comte de Tallard, marshal of France, to the duke of Marlborough, captain general of the allies. The marshal is escorted by two English officers (is the one on the left Daniel Parke?). Cadogan and others of Marlborough's headquarters staff (the hatless officer resembles Cadogan's deputy, Alexander Spotswood) are arrayed behind the triumphant duke. In the left foreground, an English grenadier places the royal standard of Louis XIV, the lilies of France (afterward the Blenheim quitrent banner), atop a most prestigious pile of plunder: French cavalry kettledrums and guidons, regimental colors from the most famous infantry regiments of France. More trophies—armor, weapons, colors—are heaped in the foreground vignette. It is balanced atop the tapestry by the tower of "Hooghstet." The nearest town, Höchstädt, visible here to

"Aldenarda": The Battle of Oudenarde (center panel)
The Art of War: "Pillage" (left to right)
In the Third State Room, Blenheim Palace

the west of Blenheim village, is the name by which the battle is still celebrated in Germany. The arms of the other German cities captured in the campaign of 1704 punctuate the trophy border.

The foreground scene of the Blenheim tapestry is entirely misplaced. For artistic effect, de Hondt has set the surrender on the eastern slope of the Nebel valley, but Tallard was captured on the far western slope during the decisive allied cavalry charge organized by Marlborough in person, which overran French headquarters and drove thousands of Tallard's cavalry to drown in the Danube. What is correctly shown is the sanguinary assault on the French stronghold,

Wynendale:
The Siege of Lille

the Blenheim village, by the English infantry. They had crossed the Nebel on the dams of the mills shown here on the left of the scene, mills broken by artillery and on fire. The action was murderous. The surviving attackers had to be content with penning up the French infantry in Blenheim. The legacy of a bloody stalemate appears in the aid station sheltered at the wheel of one mill and in the naked corpses piled beside the upstream millwheel (all the dead were stripped, either by former comrades or the enemy). Closer at hand, gun crews carry powder

Montes Hannonia:
The Battle of Malplaquet

kegs to supply the artillery Marlborough had placed to fire on the French lines, seen arrayed on the western slope of the Nebel valley.

On the far side of the stream, to the left, Blenheim village is shown surrounded by English infantry and packed with French defenders, lined up behind walls and abatis, so packed that entire battalions could not bring their muskets to bear. Upstream, the allies have crossed the Nebel morass, some wading up to their armpits, others advancing over the bridge (under which

Alexander Spotswood had been crushed as he directed its repair). The allied lines are marked here by clouds of gunpowder smoke. Extending northward up the valley, the smoke defines the conflict of 100,000 men. Forty thousand of the French army perished on the spot, in the river, or at the hands of the peasants whose villages they had pillaged and burned.

Like Blenheim, Oudenarde was fought at the junction of a great river and its tributary, the River Scheldt and the Dipenbeck stream, like the Nebel a minor watercourse with great tactical importance. Once again, stone-built villages and their mills were the key features in the victory that reversed the French counteroffensive of 1708. Oudenarde was the rarest of battles in an age of set pieces, an encounter of armies on the march. The French were advancing to seize the Scheldt bridgehead at Oudenarde. The allies were racing to forestall them. The presence of potential kings also distinguished Oudenarde. The French heir, the duke of Burgundy, and the pretended king of England, James Francis Edward Stuart, complicated the command of the French marshal, Louis-Joseph, duke of Vendôme. Georg Ludwig of Hanover, the future King George II, fought in the melee for the allies, commanded by the prince and duke of Marlborough and by Prince Eugene. It may be that these allied luminaries are featured in the foreground of the Oudenarde tapestry. Perhaps the horseman, hat in hand, being dispatched to the front by the duke of Marlborough, baton in hand, represents Prince Eugene. The splendidly mounted horseman, back to the viewer, consulting the staff might be Prince George. The hint that this is an imagined scene, however, is the hoary figure of the tutelary deity of the River Scheldt, looking up to the horsemen and displaying a plan of Oudenarde.

The reality was otherwise. Far to the right flank and in front of the allied infantry lines, Prince George charged with Rantzau's cavalry. They broke superior numbers of French squadrons. The prince, saved only by the sacrifice of his colonel, fleshed "my Oudenarde sword." Marlborough was posted in the middle of the Dipenbeck line (toward the central windmill in the tapestry) when he asked Prince Eugene to take up command of the allied right flank, endangered by the French riposte to Rantzau's charge. The captain general's own columns are shown here as, at the conclusion of an overnight march, they crossed the Scheldt on the four pontoon bridges with which Cadogan and Spotswood's engineers had spanned the river. In the near foreground, a regiment is seen in the act of changing from a column of march into a line of battle. The grenadier company has already formed line. The flag company is caught in the midst of its evolution, facing left and extending its line behind that of the grenadiers. It is urged on by a gesticulating mounted officer and directed by the beat of the drums grouped on the company's flank. Obscure as this change of front is in this reproduction, its original is still worth many pages in a drill book.

The anchor of the right flank of the allied line was the village of Eyne, on high ground at the junction of the Dipenbeck and the Scheldt. Eyne, its mill, and its people are detailed center right in the Oudenarde tapestry. As the battle is about to envelop them, the villagers are fleeing, driving their livestock before them, carrying valuables from the church or, empty handed, running for their lives. So it is that, obscured in this reproduction by a suite of gilded and lacquered furniture, a pile of commonplace village housewares takes the place of the usual martial trophies at the center of the bottom border. Platters and plates, wine bottles and a cistern, tankards and a sugar caster balance the municipal magnificence of the arms of "Aldenarda," atop the tapestry, the city which gave a name to victory.

The Oudenarde tapestry is flanked by two panels from the conventional *Art of War* hangings presented to Marlborough in October 1706. They are striking reminders of the cost of war to civilians, especially in an age in which armies trekked across the countryside and officers such as Colonel Spotswood tried, often in vain, to enforce Marlborough's stringent orders against plundering. In the foreground of the right panel, a trooper picks a pocket. In the background, horses are laden with the spoils of a village in flames. The left panel shows a hussar beating a young couple, perhaps to make them reveal their "treasure." An old soldier drives off a bound hostage for ransom. Another inhabitant is abused at the door of a house from whose gable window cloth and other valuables are being thrown down to a waiting looter. Piles of mundane spoils—cloth, plates, and pitchers, buckets and fruit baskets—take the place of a military trophy in the foreground. Yet the Churchill arms, supported by Marlborough's imperial eagles, commemorate the captain whose men burned villages and plundered people. These reminders of the cost of war to innocent noncombatants and of the brutality and criminality of the soldiers are the more incongruous in the context of the ormolu objects, the crystal chandelier, and the garish French decorative scheme (installed, to his later regret, by the youthful ninth duke of Marlborough) in Blenheim's third state room.

As usual in the Blenheim Victories, a tactical situation is clearly delineated in *Wynendale*. A convoy of some 700 wagons had been organized by Colonel Armstrong to transport munitions from Ostend across the canal at Leffinghe to the chateau of Wynendale and thence, turning south, reach the allies besieging Lille. Intercepted by forty French battalions, the commander of the convoy's escort, John Richmond Webb, posted his twenty-four battalions across the gap between the chateau (visible at the center right of the tapestry) and the coppice across the glade. Webb stripped his battalions of their grenadiers. He concealed them, together with the quartermasters' escorts, on either side of the opening. Weakened, the allied battalions nonetheless rebuffed charge after charge in the action seen here. With the enemy force fully engaged, the ambush was sprung. The French lost 4,000 men in an hour's fighting. The survivors refused to attack again. At, or just before, the final French assault, Cadogan arrived with the advance elements of twenty-six squadrons of cavalry. Subsequently, there was much controversy over the shares of credit due Webb and Cadogan. Of immediate importance, however, was that two weeks' worth of artillery ammunition that reached the allied besiegers. Marshal Boufflers surrendered Lille to Marlborough on December 9, 1708.

That surrender is also commemorated in tapestry at Blenheim Palace, but the representation of the siege, being veiled in smoke, is of less interest than *Wynendale*, the most informal, the most conventional, and, in composition, the most satisfying of the Blenheim Victories. The central figure is not a famous commander. Rather, an anonymous sergeant threatens a cowardly carter with his halberd, for civilian teamsters always fled the fighting if they could. With shouldered arms, one of the infantry escort looks back to the battle burgeoning behind him. In the foreground, a soldier ties his shoe, hoping, for some reason of his own, to evade the sergeant's attention.

On September 11, 1709, was fought the bloodiest battle of a war-ridden century. Commanded by the duke of Marlborough, the allies had invested the fortress city of Mons ("Montes Hannonia" in the arms atop the tapestry) on the frontier of France. The French, under the duke de Villars, advanced to its relief. The two armies, each 100,000 men, met where a swathe of woodland was divided by the gap of Malplaquet. The tapestry looks over Marlborough's commanding shoulder (Cadogan, severely wounded in the action, is at the duke's left) down into the vital gap. Between the duke and his hatless aide can be seen a British battery. Its six guns are firing into the French abatis in the woods of Taisnières, supporting the assault led by the duke of Argyll, his shirt open to show the men that he wore no armor. Beyond this battery, Orkney's thirteen battalions are divided. Two advance to support Argyll's attack. Eleven battalions back a forty-gun battery. It is firing on the five French redans that block the Trouée d'Aulnois and then, by dreadful ricochet, decimating the four lines of French cavalry ranked on the plain beyond the gap. As the allies broke through the woods to the right of the gap and the Dutch and Scots-Dutch battalions were massacred in the forest to the left, Orkney's battalions stormed the redans in the center and held them in support of the enormous cavalry combat that won the battle for the allies. The French withdrew, having lost 15,000 men. The allies, with losses of 24,000, were too exhausted to follow. By failing to advance to the relief of Mons, the French admitted defeat, but all the commanders—indeed, all Europe— were horrified by the carnage. It was not to be equaled until the twentieth century. Marlborough comforted himself with the thought that he had won peace for the Atlantic world, and he wrote to his duchess "that we have had this day a very bloody Battaile . . . I may be pretty well assur'd of never being in another."

Marlborough was right in one respect: his hopes for peace were dashed, but he did not fight another battle. Political defeat in England meant that the captain general could not risk combat in Europe. He settled instead for the chess game of maneuvers and sieges. His penultimate move was the passage of the La Bassée lines that Villars had boasted were Marlborough's ne plus ultra. Marlborough's final conquest was of the supposedly impregnable fortress anchoring the lines, Bouchain. Marlborough's contemporaries agreed that these actions displayed to the utmost the duke's mastery of the art of war.

So proud was the captain general of this, the triumphant conclusion of his military career, that he commissioned three tapestries to commemorate it. The tapestry here reproduced is said

Bouchain: The Passage of the Lines

to depict the investment of the fortress city. Instead it appears to celebrate the passage of the ne plus ultra lines. The weaver himself is said to have declared that this double tapestry depicted the passage of the lines, was as fine as anything he had ever accomplished, and that it was the best of the *Blenheim Victories*. The scene does not correspond to the investment of Bouchain. There the terrain was flat, not, as here, hilly. The duke famously undertook his reconnaissances at Bouchain alone, not with the large staff and escort pictured here. At Bouchain, the most

visible military features were the thirty miles of fortifications by which Marlborough's 90,000 troops and 6,000 peasant pioneers walled in the besieged city, walled out the French relieving force, and walled off the allied communications. In this image, however, the background is sliced by six columns of allied troops. This disposition corresponds to the formation in which the allied army won its race with the French army to reach the causeway at Arleux, a killing overnight march of thirty-six miles, August 5–6, 1711.

Having won that race and passed the lines without losing a man to combat (although hundreds died of exhaustion), Marlborough's army undertook the siege of a supposedly impregnable fortress, surrounded by a deep morass, within sight of a French army superior in numbers. The French looked on, helpless to intervene, as the entrenched allies strangled the city. Its garrison surrendered unconditionally on September 12, 1711. The road to Paris was open in the next campaign but, advised by a tory ministry already in secret negotiations with Louis XIV, the queen cashiered her captain general. In exile, Marlborough commissioned this tapestry, the lavish memorial of his last campaign.

Marlborough "seemed very much chagrined" at this insult. He vowed that he would avenge himself on a French garrison before the campaign was out. He immediately threatened the French lines at Avesnes-le-Comte, a dozen miles west of Aaras. He pitched camp in sight of "the enemys lines within less than two leagues of us." On July 27, Marlborough personally led a reconnaissance in force, escorted by 2,000 cavalry, Major Samuel Shute prominent among them. Returning to camp, the duke ordered the cavalry to cut and carry forward fascines with which to fill the enemy entrenchments as the infantry stormed the lines. Roads and avenues for the assault were cleared. Marlborough let it be known that he was encouraged in his apparent aggression by French detachments to the Rhine frontier. He drained his garrisons and outposts, echeloning them to the east of his position. There they could cover the heavy baggage withdrawn from the main force as the allies prepared to attack the French lines. Oddly enough, however, on the eve of an assault on a well-entrenched enemy, the train of artillery decamped. Under the cover of darkness and the command of Brigadier Sutton, 100 pieces of field artillery and their ammunition wagons, together with the engineers and pioneers of the army, moved eastward, parallel to the French lines, road building and bridging as they went.[49]

On the eve of a suicidal assault on the colossal lines, the allies were despondent and the French rejoiced, but the duke wrote home that tomorrow "I hope we may find a means of passing some part of the lines." What the captain general meant by this calculated ambiguity appeared the next evening, August 4. The troops struck camp and formed in columns to assault the ne plus ultra lines. Instead, as darkness fell, they were ordered to file off to the left. Without beat of drum, the allies marched eastward over the roads Sutton's engineers had prepared, led "by the duke himself" at the head of the cavalry of the left wing. Meanwhile, the right wing of the allies' horse was making a noisy sweep westward to draw Villars' attention away from the allied main body. At first slowly and in darkness, then more quickly to the light of the rising moon, Marlborough's columns moved east, parallel to the French lines. At 3:00 a.m. on August 5, Cadogan and nearly 12,000 men advanced from Douai, crossed the Sensée causeway, and seized the now unfortified, ungarrisoned Arleux position. At first light, Cadogan's couriers reached Marlborough. They reported that the French lines were breached and that the allies held the Arleux crossing in force. The duke's aides now raced down the long columns of infantry with a courteous but killing request: "the duke desires you will step out." In the next ten hours, the army covered twenty-four miles (having already marched ten miles or more). Half the infantry dropped by the wayside. Thousands are said to have died from exhaustion before, at 10:00 a.m. on August 5, the heads of the allied infantry columns crossed the Sensée at Arleux, followed by Sutton and the artillery. There they joined the left wing of the cavalry (whose troopers, led by Marlborough, had been in the saddle for forty-eight hours, halting only twice to feed their horses before they rode into Arleux) and turned to face the French advancing from Aaras.⁵⁰

By 2:00 a.m., Villars had realized that Marlborough was stealing a march on him. He raced eastward with a small cavalry escort and reached Arleux just as Marlborough did, at 9:00 a.m. The advancing allied horse cut Villars off. He escaped only by sacrificing his escort. So the marshal survived to form up his own army as they arrived, over better roads and along shorter routes than the allies had traveled. With one flank anchored on the fortress of Cambrai and the other at Inchy, a tributary of the Sensée, and with their center behind abbatis in the Bourlon woods, the French faced the allies. They were just half a league apart, but separated by very broken ground. Villars' was a formidable position, but it would not have checked Marlborough in previous years. Without royal favor or political support at home, however, he dared not risk a rebuff. So the captain general called a council of war, a sure sign that he did not intend to attack. For once, it was the Dutch generals who demanded an assault and the British who declined. Marlborough's general of the horse, Lumley, and of the foot, Orkney, pointed out that even the infantry now in line were too exhausted to fight, and that half of the men, even of the elite regiments, had dropped by the wayside, whence the cavalry of the right wing were only now recovering them. Besides, the terrain was too rough to cross under fire and the French flanks were too well supported to turn. Without permitting any further debate, Marlborough declared this to be the opinion of the council.⁵¹

That the duke declined battle clearly announced that his daring had depended upon the assurance of court favor. That lost, any check would expose him to impeachment—"such scenes," said St. John, "as no victories can varnish over"—and the ax. Marlborough was now sixty-one, an advanced age in a short-lived era. He had been bedridden with dizzy spells repeatedly during this campaign, his tenth. "Worn out by continual Fatigues" during a decade at the head of the allied armies, Marlborough was now exhausted by two days in the saddle. He could rest (he went right to bed) assured that history would record that he had succeeded brilliantly in the most decisive move of the military game. He had seized the enemy's "ne plus ultra" lines, defended by an army much superior in numbers to his own, and he had done it without a combat casualty. Still avoiding a battle, he looked for another, less costly, chance to display his unmatched military skill. That would be the siege of Bouchain.⁵²

Bouchain was a fortress town of the third rank but it anchored the east end of the central portion of the ne plus ultra lines. That sector blocked the allies' advance into France. The ne plus ultra lines must be broken, not just pierced, before the allies could advance on Paris in the next campaign (if there were a next campaign). To break the lines, Bouchain must be taken but, in the midst of a morass at the juncture of three rivers, Bouchain was notoriously difficult to besiege. Its capture by Marlborough's 80,000 in the face of the French marshal and his army, now nearly 100,000 men, encamped less than a mile away in plain sight and easy cannon shot of the fortress, would humiliate French arms. It would testify, in the clearest terms, to Marlborough's mastery of the military art.[53]

The capture of Bouchain would be more than a coda to ten successful campaigns, it would open the road to Paris in 1712, provided that the English and the Dutch could be persuaded to bankroll Marlborough's proposal to hold the allies' gains on the French frontier. The captain general planned to take up winter quarters in the most recent conquests and build magazines there for a spring offensive. This the French, even more exhausted by the long war than the allies, could not afford to counter. The campaign of 1712 would be fought entirely in France, with Paris as its objective. England itself, however, its army, and the exchequers and armies of her allies all were enervated by a war that had consumed seventeen of the last twenty-one years. A vindictive queen and an unprincipled ministry would not permit England to make a last sacrifice to defeat France and win America. Peace would let them break Marlborough, dish the whigs, dump the Dutch, and capitalize on the tory chiefs' American investments: the grand fraud of Harley's South Sea Company and the petty peculations of St. John's Canadian expedition military contracts.[54]

If only to confound St. John (who had told the house of commons that "in Flanders we could do nothing"), Marlborough sent home Sutton (to whom St. John had denied command of the Canadian expedition) with dispatches magnifying the capture of the lines. Sutton was rewarded with the government of Hull. St. John had now to admit (privately to Marlborough) that the captain general had "obtained, without losing a man, such an advantage as we should have bought with the expense of several thousand lives, and reckoned ourselves gainers." Sutton announced to the public that Marlborough would now besiege Bouchain. This action mesmerized Europe. So heavy were the odds against the allies and so sustained was the contest between the rival commanders, Marlborough and Villars, that "during the whole course of this long War . . . there was not so critical an instance of this, in which the Reputation of two great Generals was so nearly concern' d, and their Skills in the Art of War so fairly put to the test." The first round in the struggle for Bouchain began on August 6. Marlborough masked Villars' army and the allies crossed the Scheldt. Four days later, Bouchain was invested.[55]

The proximity of the armies made "this undertaking . . . the most hazardous that had happened during the whole Course of the War." The contest was sustained for more than six weeks, with the main forces of the Atlantic world's two greatest armies always in sight of each other. In this test of military skill, "the Duke of Marlborough underwent more Fatigue than he had done in any other," but it was also the captain general's most "favourable Opportunity of exercising his utmost Talent in the Art of War." This was manifest in both the circumvallation and countervallation of Bouchain and in the cavalry raids and repulses that accompanied every convoy from Douai. To protect those convoys,

Marlborough finally bullied the Flanders authorities into the conscription of thousands of peasants. They built twenty miles of walls to cover the allies' supply route from their fortified camp opposite Bouchain to the bridges over the River Scarpe at Marchiennes which connected the besiegers to their depot at Douai. As St. John admitted, Marlborough's achievement was unique in the history of war: "an inferior army posting themselves so as to be able to form a siege and keep communication open with their own country, in sight of an enemy so much superior." Massive amounts of munitions reached the allied batteries along the protected routes. Then the artillery supported infantry assaults. These advanced through morasses so deep in muck that a tall grenadier carried his small officer forward on his shoulders. Both the allied and the French commanders were constantly at the head of their troops. They were in danger day and night for, as Marlborough wrote to Godolphin, "the situation of both arrays are so very extravegant that our army which attacks the town is bombarded by the enemy, and we have several postes so near to each other, that the sentinels have conversations. The whole French army being so camped that they are seen by the garrison of Bouchain, makes the defence more obstenat."[56]

This, Marlborough's thirtieth siege, a success like all the others, was a textbook example of the art military of the age. Under constant fire, the allies excavated approaches to the fortifications of Bouchain, bridged the fosse, seized the counterscarp, and dug in batteries of heavy guns. They punctured Bouchain's outworks. The breaches were then stormed by the infantry and the captured works were reversed to protect breaching batteries. In three days, firing at point-blank range day and night, the heavy guns broke the bastions of Bouchain. The fortress was open to a final assault. To prevent the storm of the city and the slaughter of its inhabitants, the 3,000 survivors of the garrison surrendered, unconditionally, on September 14, 1711. Marlborough modestly remarked that "the Marishall de Villlars has done us the honour of being witness of the garrison being made prisoners at warr." Arleux had been amply avenged at Bouchain. There "the Garrison was numerous, and wanted Nothing; it was supported by the French Army, and yet in the Sight of a Hundred Thousand fighting Men, who endeavour'd to relieve them, they were made prisoners of war."[57]

Marlborough did not want to end the campaign of 1711 at Bouchain, no matter if it, "considered with all its circumstances, must be allow'd to be one of the greatest actions of ye age." He wished to attack the final French defenses at Le Quesnoy and then put the allied army into winter quarters in France, ready to advance on Paris down the line of the River Lys in the spring of 1712. Marlborough had sent his personal representative, that able soldier, brilliant diplomat, and elegant gentleman, the earl of Stair, to present to the ministry the captain general's plan for winning the war. Harley and St. John held Stair in London, fuming and frustrated, until Prior returned from Paris bearing French promises of a separate peace. Then the ministry refused Marlborough the necessary resources for winter quarters in France. So the tories foreclosed a spring advance on Paris. Bouchain, Marlborough now realized, would be his final victory. On October 27, after supervising the refortification of the shattered fortress, the captain general left the allied army for the last time.[58]

A month later, on November 17/28, Marlborough landed at Greenwich together with the Hanoverian envoy, baron Bothmar, with whom the duke was in the closest collaboration. They were determined to resist a peace that would abandon England's allies and that, by making the English ministers the objects of Hanoverian enmity, would cast them into the arms of France and so imperil the Protestant Hanoverian succession. Two days after Marlborough and Bothmar landed, Queen Anne's ministers announced that a congress would meet at Utrecht on January 1 to conclude a peace based on the preliminary articles negotiated by Prior and St. John. Marlborough refused to attend the cabinet council where this decision was made. He would not countenance the proposed peace in public or in private. Instead, "the General putting himself at the head of the whigs" in opposition to the proposed treaty, his incitement and amplification of Hanoverian opposition to the congress, and his reunion with the Hydes, the earl of Nottingham in particular, produced a majority of one vote in the house of lords against the preliminary articles and a majority of eight in favor of Nottingham's motion "that no peace could be safe or honourable to Great Britain, if Spain and the West Indies . . . were allotted to any branch of the house of Bourbon."[59]

To defeat Marlborough and his coalition, Oxford and Bolingbroke persuaded the queen to extreme measures. She created twelve tory peers (including Mrs. Masham's brother) to provide a government majority in the lords. She dismissed the duke of Marlborough from all his offices on the basis of an allegation (put forward by St. John, of all people!) that he had taken a percentage of the army's bread contracts. She commissioned Marlborough's old rival the jacobite duke of Ormonde as captain general (and as recipient of the same traditional percentage on the bread contracts). Marlborough had long anticipated the likelihood of exile if his English enemies triumphed. As soon as Godolphin died, at the Marlboroughs' home at St. Albans, and was buried at Westminster, the duke decamped to the Netherlands. There, at the end of November 1712, Marlborough was received as a sovereign prince. He began to organize the military foundations of yet another royal succession, that of the Hanoverians, but that was a work of years. In the meantime, Marlborough in exile left his officers, the governors general of the American provinces of the British empire, unsupported to face the political and military exigencies of a tory ministry and a failed peace on the unrestricted frontiers of New France.[60]

PART III

MARLBOROUGH'S AMERICA

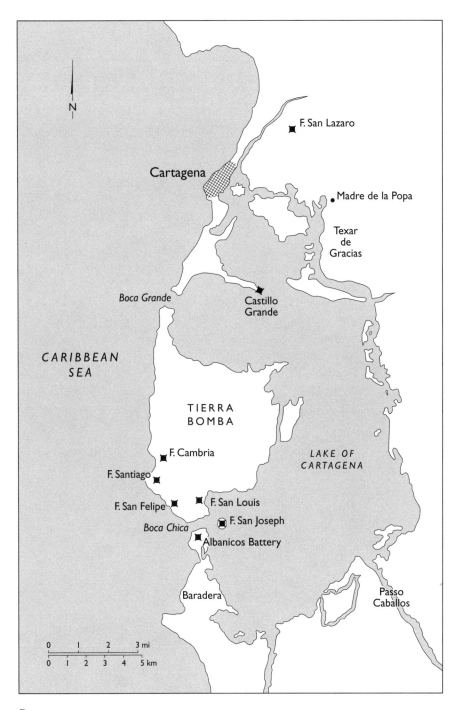

N

F. San Lazaro

Cartagena

Madre de la Popa

Texar
de
Gracias

Boca Grande

Castillo
Grande

CARIBBEAN
SEA

TIERRA
BOMBA

LAKE OF
CARTAGENA

F. Cambria

F. Santiago

F. San Louis

F. San Felipe

F. San Joseph

Boca Chica

Albanicos Battery

Baradera

Passo
Caballos

0		1		2		3 mi
0	1	2	3	4		5 km

Cartagena

Précis

THE MURDER OF Daniel Parke, bearer of the Blenheim dispatch, governor general of the Leeward Islands, was a unique event, unparalleled in the first British empire. His assassination on December 7, 1711, and the killing of most of his bodyguard, the grenadiers of the 38th Regiment, by the militiamen of Antigua, led by their captains, most of them assemblymen, marked the midpoint between republican revolutions, that of 1641 and that of 1776. Ideology excited and excused the fatal quarrel between a soldier of the queen who was a son of the church, a Virginia planter, and a rapacious rake, and his enemies, sugar barons of the Caribbean frontier, republican idealists who were also murderous, miscegenating, drunken deadbeats. The governor general's determination to impose law and order on this Tombstone of a territory, at the same time he was looting the colony and debauching the planters' wives and daughters, excited the fatal enmity of the Antiguan assemblymen. "Patriots" they called themselves. The councilors, and the better sort of planters, were solidly on the side of the royal executive. They called themselves "Loyalists."

The quarrel was overheated by war. Colonel Parke tried to apply "what I have learned from the first Captain of the Age" by regulating the garrison regiment, modernizing the island militia, and fortifying the capital, St. John's. The regiment's new commander, James Jones, commissioned to spite Marlborough and undercut Parke, resisted each of his proposed regimental reforms, for they cut into Jones's looting of the 38th. The island assemblymen, most of whom were militia officers, resisted shrinking the officer corps, opposed the executive's encouragement of small planter-militiamen (whose land the barons wanted to cultivate with slaves), and protested Parke's proposed field fortifications. These would dig up valuable fields for military advantages which the militia-politicians did not comprehend. To justify their opposition to every military reform, the "patriot" assemblymen accused Parke of betraying the island to the French.

It was equally clear to the patriot assemblymen that Parke was a military dictator. When they (for all of them were also magistrates) refused to arrest, indict, or convict the murders, smugglers, and debtors among them, Parke employed his provost marshal as an arresting officer and the grenadiers of the 38th as police. When the offended assemblymen stormed into the council chamber to demand that Parke surrender his commission and leave his command, the grenadiers said they would obey "the general's" orders to shoot those who did not leave. The assemblymen fled, vowing vengeance.

Parke himself was under orders to leave Antigua. Allegedly in response to "5000 good reasons," that ultra whig, secretary of state Sunderland, had rebuffed Parke's pleas to him, as Marlborough's son-in-law, not to condemn one of the duke's appointees without good reason. Ostensibly outraged by Parke's use of the military in civil administration, Sunderland ordered Parke home for a hearing. In the meantime, the secretary of state told Colonel Jones not to allow the 38th to protect the governor general. Understanding that Sunderland was about to be replaced by a tory, Parke hung on, collecting materials for his defense and asserting that the "patriots," Presbyterians, Scots, and republicans as they were, intended nothing less than "an independency from the Crowne of England." Any concession to the rebellious Antiguans would encourage "the fractious Humour" Parke saw prevalent in America.

To quash these would-be king killers, religious dissenters, and independents, Parke proposed that the now-tory parliament and her sacred majesty enact repressive statutes for all America. These would authorize governors general to quarter troops in private buildings; remand to England for trial both royal officers accused of excessive force and republican agitators accused of sedition; strengthen enforcement of the acts of trade, including the use, as Parke had done, of "writs of assistance"; expand the authority of customs collectors; and limit colonial imports of foreign sugar. The funds produced by seizures and duties, Parke suggested, should be appropriated by parliament to the support of imperial executives and royal judges in America, rendering them independent of colonial assemblies. Finally, since political obedience was dependent on religious uniformity, the queen should constitute an anglican episcopate in America. Bishops and clergy would inculcate the doctrine of passive obedience to the lord's anointed sovereign and her representatives, the governors general.

To Parke's prescient anticipation of "the Intolerable Acts," designed to quell the American rebellion he anticipated, the assemblymen-militia captains responded by calling up their companies to the capital, promising them the plunder of the tyrant's palace. Most of the grenadiers and staff officers of the 38th died in defense of the governor general. Parke himself shot the leader of the rebels before being overwhelmed and mutilated. Queen Anne's miniature ripped from his neck, Parke was stripped and left to die in the city square of

St. John's. Fully informed of the murder but facing exile himself, Marlborough could not immediately avenge his aide but, following the captain general's restoration, he saw to it that no implicated officer ever served again.

The "Revolution Principles" that Governor General Robert Hunter, formerly a major of brigade and an aide of the captain general, successfully defended from tory reactionaries in New York were the antithesis of the republican revolutionary ideas that excused the murder of Colonel Parke in Antigua. Hunter was no friend of reaction, however. Like Marlborough, Hunter was a moderate in politics, religion, and race; downright modern in fiscal affairs; and a thoroughgoing authoritarian in matters of public order and military defense. The revolution Hunter defended was that begun by lord Churchill's coup in 1688, as it had developed in the subsequent decade: constitutional monarchy; parliamentary sovereignty; civil liberty; the establishment of the church of England, albeit with religious toleration, publicly for Protestants, practically for all (like London, New York hosted at least seven sorts of sectarians). The ideals of "the Glorious Revolution," that is, preservation of religious and civil liberty, had to be defended from the Catholic and absolutist France of Louis XIV. War compelled fiscal reform: a national currency, bank, and debt, all authorized by statute. This "military-fiscal revolution" became part and parcel of "the Revolution Principles" of Marlborough's generation of imperial executives, for each of them had both to fight and finance his particular province's war with France. Applying "revolution principles" to New York during a decade in command, General Hunter transformed an archaic, even anarchic, colony into a stable Augustan province, well equipped to fight the French in wartime and to prosper in peacetime.

Hunter's commission to command New York (and New Jersey) was produced by Marlborough's manipulation of the military politics of the union with Scotland and impelled by the captain general's extraordinary enthusiasm for his former aide's abilities, whether to settle 3,000 Palatine war refugees or to propel an assault on Quebec. Either would tax the resources and public spirit of a province plundered and demoralized by lord Cornbury and divided by his reactionary politics. Tory reaction also deprived Hunter of the expedition's command, not only by sea against Quebec but also overland, from Hunter's own province, against Montreal. Despite having to defer to a tory political appointee, Francis Nicholson, in six weeks Hunter raised a brigade of more than 2,000 troops, recruited 811 Iroquois warriors, and supplied the army that opened New York's northern frontier. The expedition deepened the war debt the assembly refused to pay, unless they could take control of provincial finance from royal officials, the governor general chief among them.

With the fall of Marlborough, Godolphin, and the whigs, Hunter despaired of success. Whipsawed between a transatlantic tory party and an autonomous assembly, he wrote a Scots comrade, "Only pray take care of my rank in the Army, for there's my refuge at last." Once assured of his promotion to general's rank, despite the change of ministry, and flattered by secretary St. John's admiration of his intellect, Hunter responded to the plan, so much a part of the Quebec expedition's objective, "of putting all North America under one Uniform plan of Government." He deplored the tendency of American assemblies' challenge to the royal fiscal prerogative. Hunter's sacrifice of his salary in defense of the prerogative was mere window dressing. Like all royal executives (and most royal officials), a public salary was the least part of the governor general's income. As could most of Marlborough's legates, Hunter was well able to defy the provincial assembly's pretensions while he evolved methods to co-opt or corrupt them.

The royal prerogative he protected provided the governor general with political ammunition. For example, a polyglot population wanted an act of naturalization so that they could legally hold property in the province, trade within the British empire, vote and hold local office, and so outface New York's overbearing "English" reactionaries. This was especially so because the bulk of the revolutionaries of 1689 in New York were of Dutch descent. All aliens would be grateful to the governor general who naturalized them, and even more grateful if he enfranchised them as well and arranged for the debts due them from defending the revolution and fighting the French to be paid at long last. Forwarding a bill of naturalization, exercising the royal prerogative of re-districting, enfranchising his entire garrison, and conducting an articulate campaign against legislative pretensions, General Hunter won a series of electoral and legislative victories that eventuated in a new system of taxation, a paper currency, and a permanent provincial debt. With the proceeds of this fiscal revolution, Hunter bought the bulk of the provincial legislature. The system he established brought social stability, political peace, and material prosperity to New York for the next half century. Indeed, Hunter's revolution settlement forecast that engineered by another Scots New Yorker in the wake of the next revolution.

Hunter also epitomized the Scots cultural contribution to Augustan empire. Lauded by the London literati, a published Latin poet, a student of government, General Hunter used words as weapons as adeptly as he did his sword. Following Marlborough's own Augustan admonition to recruit "Wit and Satyr" to fight the political wars, Hunter's play, *Androboros, or the Man Eater*, mocked the tory champion General Nicholson, now "governor of governors" and the principal of the church-state party in New York. The general, satirized by Hunter as Androboros, "talks of nothing but battles and Sieges, but he never saw one." "Androboros" arrives on stage supported by two "Men in Black." "Fizle" is that damp squib William Vesey, the high church commissary who aspired to be "the Patriarch of the Western World." "Flip" was Adolph Philipse, so named for the rhyming of his name with his favorite beverage, the leader of the opposition to Hunter. He himself starred as "the Keeper" of that legislative madhouse, the New York "Senate." Hunter pilloried the head of the church-state party, lord Cornbury, as "my lord Oinoborous," "a Devotee of Long Robes of Both Genders," that is, clerics and other whores. That all these denizens of Bedlam were foolish Francophiles, Hunter wrote, was evident from their boasting that the late treaty of commerce with France had divided the trade of the world between France and Britain, generously "yielding to us that of the two Poles." The tories were, quite literally, laughed out of town. Hunter was left to bask in the praise of a transformed legislature. He retired from a modernized and pacified province, as an envious English garrison officer remarked, with enough wealth to buy all of "North Britain."

Life in London bored the veteran officer and governor, so, in 1727, when the accession of that warrior-king, George II, meant fresh commissions to his comrades under Marlborough's command, and the noise of another war with Spain for America offered fresh imperial opportunities, Hunter at last received the post he had asked Marlborough for in 1709. Major General Hunter went out to Jamaica under orders to renew the 1681 constitutional bargain between the crown's military authority and executive power, and the islanders' legislative capacity and civil law. Successful politically, Hunter had also to defend the island dominion in the new war with Spain. More ambitiously, he sought to take command of troops raised in America to seize the Spanish entrepôts. Instead, Hunter died in 1734, at war with the Maroons in the jungles of Jamaica, still as much admired for his cultivation as his courage.

When on June 21, 1710, Colonel Alexander Spotswood, architect of empire, landed in Virginia, he spent his first night at what was still the greatest mansion in America, the rambling jacobean pile named Green Spring. It also was still the headquarters of the Burwell family, determined enemies of every royal executive since 1676. "The Green Spring faction" had resisted every governor general as a military tyrant representing a coercive sovereign. A "country party," that is, American elites allied with London merchants, the Green Spring faction controlled the council, the burgesses, and the church when Colonel Spotswood landed. In time, the lieutenant governor (to the Scots earl of Orkney, Marlborough's senior infantry officer) and commander in chief would declare the Green Spring faction to be "false to the Interest of the Crown, and very much dissatisfied to that of Britain." By the end of his twelve-year tenure, Spotswood had recovered control of the council (a control the royal executive did not lose until the next revolution), achieved equality with the faction in the burgesses, and dominated the church convocation. Such were the monuments to Spotswood's restoration of royal authority and his achievement of political stability.

The inevitable clash of this modern military executive—for nine campaigns Marlborough's deputy chief of staff—with a feudal family faction was delayed. First, the commander in chief of Virginia was preoccupied with the protection of his province. He immediately ordered a reconnaissance beyond the fall line frontier, 100 miles west to the mountains. To secure scouts, Spotswood expanded the ranger service which, like so much of Spotswood's inheritance in Virginia, dated from Colonel Jeffreys's administration. In time, Spotswood himself rode with the rangers the entire length of Virginia's western wilderness boundary, at great personal risk. His abiding objective was the construction of a "Barrier" against the French. That barrier was composed at first of immigrant outposts, red and white, Tuscarora and German, Meherrin and Palatine, workers in iron and naval stores, and cattle ranchers. Next, Spotswood tried to establish a physical frontier, the Virginia Indian Company's Fort Christ-anna, and the fortified trading posts he proposed in the mountain passes, protecting the piedmont, advancing settlement in the Shenandoah valley. From these bases, Spotswood proposed cutting French communications as far west and north as Lake Erie.

So Spotswood fostered Virginia's imperial expansion out of tidewater, beyond tidewater tobacco plantations and slave labor, into a farming piedmont. There smallholder militiamen would settle and defend the 3 million acres Spotswood separated from the Longhouse Extended Lengthwise. The most romantic episode of this often brutal barrier building was Spotswood's real-estate trip with his allies, the Beverley family faction (before Spotswood's time eloquent critics of colonialism and royal governors), with their surveyors and his rangers. "The Knights of the Golden Horseshoe" rode westward right over the Blue Ridge and down to the Shenandoah. There Spotswood buried a bottle (there were lots to choose from) claiming the Great Valley of Virginia for King George.

Spotswood was also distracted from his constant contest with the Green Spring faction by his obsession with architecture. Spotswood's design for an Augustan capital included an executive residence, offices, and armory—popularly "the palace"—a college, church, jail, magazine, even an Indian school. All these "Georgian" structures, the models for subsequent colleges and capitals in America, the ex-quartermaster placed on a Roman camp plan (a grid, overlaying General Nicholson's baroque design). These modern buildings were elegant instruments of imperial government and a monument to neoclassical culture.

Spotswood wanted to modernize Virginia's economy as much as he did its public buildings. Here his corporatism came in constant conflict with the Green Spring faction and their London merchant factors. Spotswood's Virginia Indian company—his HBC—aimed to anchor the barrier, control the arms trade, educate Indian children, and reinforce Colonel Jeffreys's 1677 Indian Treaty. But it ran afoul of the formidable William Byrd II, who had inherited the trade begun with his father's militia's massacre of the Ocanechee middlemen in 1676, and the faction's fur and tobacco factors, Perry of London. The VIC headquarters, Fort Christ-anna, also challenged the faction's monopoly of land development in the upper reaches of the James River valley. The VIC's Indian school exposed the obscene abuse of both native children and the Brafferton endowment for Indian education at the college by the faction's chief priest, commissary James Blair. Next, Spotswood's Tobacco Act created crop inspection, a paper currency, public tobacco agents and agencies. This act threatened big planter monopoly of packing and shipping, and the tax avoidance practices of the London merchants to whom tobacco was consigned. The act favored small planters, English outport merchants, and Scots traders. Worst of all, in the opinion of the faction, the Tobacco Act created patronage enough for Spotswood to buy up the burgesses.

The death of Queen Anne forced Spotswood to dissolve his pet assembly. Elected on a platform of resistance to the Tobacco Act, the newly chosen assembly strung out its session by promising to consider Colonel Spotswood's abiding passion, militia reform. The provincial militia structure exploited the small planter and excused from service every official, and former official, who did not care to acquire the prestige that accompanied rank, collect deficiency fines from the men, or augment slave patrols at public expense. The commander in chief proposed that Marlborough's drill be imposed, by the adjutants Spotswood trained, on a select militia, paid and armed by the province, and mustered in compact districts. (Spotswood acquired from the royal ordnance office fine stands of small arms, built a magazine to store them, and hired artificers to service them.) With such a legion, Spotswood could renew, with effect, his police work in North Carolina, his defense of South Carolina from the Yamasees, and even carry out the assault he proposed against Spanish Florida, and even Cuba.

In "country" accents, the faction protested Spotswood's military initiative, as they had ever since the Guards repressed their fathers in 1676. The governor's "standing army," they declared, "would huff and bully" Virginians and introduce a more than Cromwellian military dictatorship. Not until the administration of yet another Marlborough officer, Major William Gooch (who also revived the Tobacco Act), would the increasing menace of their slaves, and rising tensions with both the Bourbon powers, persuade the planters to admit modernization of the provincial militia by adjutants using Marlborough's manuals. The Washington brothers would be chief among those adjutants.

In 1722, deposed at last by the anti-Marlborough coalition of Argyll and the Walpoles, Spotswood retired to his "enchanted castle" at Germanna, amid the iron mines, naval stores, and farms of his palatine county, "Spotswood." He saw service in Scotland, however, and, in 1727 took the occasion of the accession of George II, Spotswood's comrade in arms at Oudenarde, and the renewal of a conflict with Spain, to produce another report, parallel to General Hunter's, recommending the levying of American troops to oust the Spanish from Florida and Cuba. Disappointed by Walpole's peace with Spain in 1730, Spotswood had to wait until 1739 for promotion to major general and a commission to raise and command a 4,000-man, four-battalion "American" regiment. With it, General Spotswood was ordered to attack the Spanish West Indies, defend

Georgia, and invade Florida. Spotswood died in the midst of raising the American Regiment. His successor in command of the American Regiment, Colonel (afterward General Sir William) Gooch, the lieutenant governor of Virginia, led the regiment to Cartagena at the head of 135 American officers. Their survivors came home to impart Spotswood's and Gooch's—that is, Marlborough's—drill, discipline, and imperial ambition to their comrades in the Great War for the Empire.

CHAPTER TEN

The Dreadful Death of Daniel Parke

T HE CAUSES AND consequences of the Anglo-American counterrevolution appeared early and with unequaled clarity in Antigua. Political passions divided the military. Executive authority encountered legislative pretensions. Corruption of every kind saturated state and society. All this could be said of England, but in the Caribbean colony, the uncertainties and tensions of war on the frontier of empire raised tropical temperatures to the point of military panic, political murder, and provincial insurrection. The Antiguan uprising was also a measure of the duke of Marlborough's changing imperial "interest." Just as the commission to command the Leeward Islands to the Virginian Daniel Parke, one of Marlborough's aides-de-camp, the bearer of the Blenheim dispatches, was an early example of the captain general's control of the imperial executive, so Parke's dreadful death was seen all around the Atlantic ambit of the British empire as an emblem of the duke's decline. Marlborough's failing prestige could not prevent, nor his diminished power avenge, the murder of a favorite officer. Worse, contemporaries in both the kingdom and the colonies believed that the revolution in Antigua reflected widespread American aspirations for independence.[1]

Parke was slaughtered on December 7, 1710. The first report was a letter from an old comrade to Colonel Samuel Gledhill, the West India veteran, dated January 5. It reached him two months later, presumably at Carlisle, where Gledhill was then (by Marlborough's nomination) lieutenant governor. Gledhill immediately forwarded copies to Marlborough at The Hague and to the authorities in London. They read that "the Country all came in well Armed, was divided into two Partys who was commanded by Capts Piggott and Painter in order to kill the Generall provided he would not give up his Commission." Forewarned, Parke "had put all his Affairs in a Posture sent for the Minister & took the Sacrament, and behaved himself with a great deal of Bravery to the last, alleadging that as the Queen had given him a Commission he would not part with it otherwise than with Sword and Pistoll in hand "So the rebels had attacked the governor general and his bodyguard in overwhelming strength. They "forced about 70 of the Queen's Troops and broke open his Chamber Door and Shott him there . . . the Wound of itself was not Mortal, after that they broke his back Bone Dragg'd him by the heels down the Steps, suffering his head to fall from Sep to Step, tore off his Shirt revil'd him and shot him in many Places after dead, Exposing even his privy Parts. . . . The Lieut General [Walter Hamilton] is since gone up [from Nevis to Antigua], and all is hushed up, no enquiry made into anything, but all seems to be easy and quiet, there was about 30 killed and as many wounded in that unheard of Action."[2]

Killing a governor general was indeed "unheard of," but murder, even of imperial officers, was an everyday occurrence in the lawless Leeward Islands. In this "country where murder is never known to be punished," Parke's immediate predecessor, Colonel John Johnson, lieutenant governor of Antigua and acting governor general, had been killed on the eve of Parke's arrival. The murder's agent in London sued for his client's pardon, "saying that killing a man was a misfortune that might happen to anyone." "A Hangman," Parke discovered, "is like to have little business in these Isles." Even the chief justice, Samuel Watkins, had murdered a man in cold blood. The islands' leading businessman, the factor of the Royal African Company, Edward Chester, killed a Virginia visitor shortly after Parke's arrival. A corrupt coroner and a jury packed by a deputy of the provost marshal (himself an absentee in England) found Chester not guilty. The jury foreman himself was a murderer, having just beaten a servant girl to death. Under these lawless and collusive circumstances, Parke wrote, "there was never any inhabitant that I ever heard of brought in guilty of murder."[3]

To arrest and arraign Antiguan killers and to empanel juries to indict and try them, Parke promoted a gentleman ranker of the garrison regiment, Michael Ayon, to be provost marshal. Ayon was "forced to fight severall duels, before he was able to do his duty in quiet." Even then, to arrest the appropriately named Barry Tankard, "son of an Ale-wife" whose "black Banditti" of armed slaves had ambushed Ayon on the highway, the provost marshal had to return by night with six files of soldiers selected from the governor general's guard, break into councilor Tankard's house, and extract him by force from the belligerent company of his drunken companions. In this Tombstone of a territory, the governor general himself was the target of two assassination attempts. The first missed an officer mistaken for Parke. The second, by a Negro sharpshooter "call'd Sandy or Alexander," hired by the reverend James Field, commissary of the bishop of London, cost Parke the use of an arm. The commissary fled from Antigua on the night of the shooting and sailed to London. There parson Field joined other enemies of Parke's administration in complaints to the imperial authorities. "Men who sticke not at Assassinations will Scarce make any Scruple of Perjuries," Parke predicted. Indeed, he wrote, "my first act of tyranny and breaking in upon their constitutions and indeavours to ruin the Countrey" was to try to bring law and order to the Leeward Islands frontier of the British empire.[4]

From that frontier, Parke wrote to Marlborough at the end of November 1709. The governor general recalled to the captain general the worldwide consequences of the victory they had shared: "An Actium, a Pharsala, and a Zama Victories far short of a Blenheim three times decided the fate of a whole World." Now that, at Malplaquet, Marlborough had lopped another limb from Louis XIV, Parke expected "a Glorious Peace." Then he could bask in "the Great honour of having you for my Patron." Now, Parke claimed Marlborough's protection from the "Callumnys a Stobborne Malitious people who can't bear Impartial Justice may have raised and your Grace may have heard. I desire to live no longer than I shall behave my Self Suitable to what I ought to have learned from the first Character of the Age." The captain general would please to consult the lord treasurer on the particulars of Parke's position. It was not the lord treasurer, however, but rather the secretary of state whom Parke had to conciliate. Lord Sunderland, the arch-whig, hated Parke's toryism and militarism. Priggish, censorious, Sunderland deplored Parke's promiscuity. To spite Parke, Sunderland had even, so it was said, helped James Jones to the colonelcy of the Leeward Islands garrison regiment (in the notorious case where Marlborough had been bypassed, supposedly by Admiral Churchill and Prince George). Sunderland was widely believed to have blocked Parke's commission to brigadier general, a promotion promised by Marlborough to Parke when he took the Leeward Islands command. Now the secretary of state pretended concern that Parke had violated the chain of command by taking control of Jones's regiment from its colonel, by issuing brevets to favorite officers, and by giving them leaves. Sunderland professed to believe that Parke had slandered Colonel Jones and ordered him to reside in the unhealthiest of islands, Nevis. The worst of all Parke's military offenses, in Sunderland's whig view, was that Parke had used the soldiers of the garrison regiment to administer the civil affairs of Antigua, the headquarters of the multi-island federation. Incited (perhaps paid) by the agent of the Leeward Islands assembly, Sunderland secured a royal command to Colonel Jones to review and reform the conduct of his regiment and to reprimand those who had served Parke's abusive ends: "H.M. has commanded me to express to you her displeasure that the troops she always desired to be employed for the protection and defence of her subjects should be made use of as instruments of their oppression." Sunderland forbade the governor general to interfere in this regimental inquiry. He also ordered that the troops do nothing to quell complaints against Parke. The regulars were ordered to leave the governor general unprotected.[5]

Simultaneously, two dozen London and Bristol merchants and their clients, the Antiguan sugar barons, complained to Sunderland that Parke, claiming the countenance of the lord treasurer and the duchess of Marlborough (they even implied carnal relations between the colonel and the duchess), had altered the course of justice by seeking to indict Edward Chester for murder and by challenging Antiguan land titles. Parke also sat in chancery, allegedly preferring his own discretion to the common law and ordering judges to sign his illegal decrees. Parke purportedly used the troops to execute writs of assistance to enforce trade regulations. He supposedly compounded with some violators of the acts of trade even as he made "groundless seizures" of other traders' goods, "particularly sixteen Firkins of Butter, belonging to John Barbotaine of the Town of St. John's merchant." Parke was said to have commissioned unsavory characters as privateer captains and taken 10 percent of their prizes to add to the fees he allegedly doubled and the bribes he supposedly took. The merchants and planters reiterated the charges that Parke had "employ'd Parties of arm'd soldiers, not only in the Business properly belonging to Constables, Custom-House Officers, and other Civil Officers, but likewise in the Highest Act of Violence, Force, and Injustice, particularly in ejected Persons out of their Freeholds." (These "Freeholds" turned out to be a single cowshed, requisitioned for soldiers' quarters.) Besides supposed abuse of his military power, Parke had allegedly denigrated the civil authority by: denying the power of the Antigua assembly to redress grievances; dissolving the assembly for resisting his tyranny; meddling with elections for the new assembly by requiring that representatives be freeholders, that is, not merchants; campaigning for particular candidates; and reviewing returns of representatives. Finally, it was said, the governor general had failed in his primary duty, defense of the queen's dominion, by taking measures "contrary to the opinion and Advice of a Council of Officers." He had so alarmed this council of war that they were said to believe that Parke would betray Antigua to the French. After all, Parke communicated with the French by flags of truce, the ships with which, allegedly, he traded with the enemy. All these charges were the more believable, so the merchants and planters insisted, because Parke "frequently and publically declared his implacable Malice against the Island of Antegoa."[6]

In addition to allegations about Parke's abuse of office, he was accused of personal misconduct. By night, it was alleged, the governor general eavesdropped his way around the island capital, St. John's, disguised, armed, and escorted lest his scandalous behavior expose him to harm. On one such "ramble," so it was said, Parke burst into a party at the house of Edward Chester. Backed by ten grenadiers and their company captain, Parke arrested the revelers for riot. Parke supposedly denied Chester and his cronies bail and held them for "thirteen days in a hott loathsome gaol" until they paid him extravagant fines. Finally, Parke was said to be sexually and socially abusive: "said Parke hath threatened to whip the best man's wife in Anteqoa at the cart's arse that should trouble herself with him." Supposedly Parke intended to so provoke the men of substance "that they would rebel and he seize their Estates." Ostensibly outraged, Sunderland had the privy council refer these complaints to the lords commissioners of trade and plantations. In February 1710, the secretary obtained the commissioners' recommendation for an investigation. Following the advice of parson Field, William Nevine, the agent of Parke's enemies, and suggestions by the leading London merchants trading to the islands, Sunderland, in the queen's name, ordered Parke to return to England by the first available warship to face these charges.[7]

Parke replied that his real offense was his effort to substitute the laws of England for "ye Method the fformer Generals used [that is,] to govern as Arbitrarily as Bashaws" but to take bribes to allow Leewards Islands legislatures local autonomy. Parke proposed to reduce the privileges of the island assemblies to those enjoyed by the English house of commons. Parliamentary practice meant that the viceroy would resume the veto power, control the choice of the speaker, name the clerk of the lower house, and himself sit in and dominate the upper house. The Antiguans, said Parke, had confused legality with license. That is, they were "squeeking for their Priviledges, when they would engross the whole Prerogative." The Antiguan lower house "are for the priviledges of the Lords and the Queen's prerogative too." The assembly's nomination of "all Officers from the Judges to the Gunner and paying none but what they recommend, are such essential Parts of the Executive Power, that the Parliament of FORTY-ONE never pretended they had any right to." Like other assertive American assemblies of this decade, the Antiguan lower house had moved beyond the parliamentary claims of right that began the English civil war to the assertions of legislative supremacy that afterward underwrote the American revolution. Parke's position was a moderate one: "few will believe their Liberties to be in Danger, when I deny'd the Assembly nothing claimed by the British Parliament." Moderation, however, was seen as oppressive by aggrandizing American elites. Excited by Irish lawyers, Scots republicans, and English commonwealthsmen, the Antiguan assemblymen rejected royal rule and imperial authority.[8]

He was, Colonel Parke observed, hated as the personification of monarchical empire. He rejected charges of tyranny. He denied the allegations that he profited by flags of truce. He did offer the usual executive defense of these much-abused prisoner exchanges. Cartels, Parke declared, recovered American merchant sailors captured by French privateers. Unredeemed, these sailors would have been shipped to French prisons. Their loss would have curtailed the ever-growing trade with the mainland colonies. Moreover, flags of truce obtained intelligence of the intentions of an ever-aggressive enemy. To protect his province from French raids, Parke went on, he had commissioned privateers "at the request of the Council when there was no Man of War." If the captains he appointed were rather rough-and-ready, this was a requisite for war. If he took 10 percent of their takings, that was both his lawful due as vice admiral and much less than he spent arming the island navy. On the military front, Parke readily admitted that he had pressed the assembly to authorize quarters and appropriate allowances for the garrison regiment. The governor

general added that to increase the islands' military manpower, he tried to preserve the poorer sort of islanders' livelihood in the face of elite engrossment of
land and their slaves' usurpation of trade skills. Parke's "leveling" was resented
by the rich planters. It was his challenge to the depopulation of Barbadua by
the richest planter of all, Christopher Codrington, that was held up as the chief
example of Parke's purported attack on private property. The governor general
observed that "one reason why the Militia is in no better order" was because
"the Poor are so oppress'd by the Rich, who have a Mind to their Land, they
are forced to sell it to them and leave the island."[9]

That these greedy grandees should attack his avarice, especially when
their "law on courts" was designed to prevent the payment of their just debts,
seemed to Parke almost as hypocritical as their implications about his morals.
Apart from being murderers and torturers and extortionists, Parke declared,
the island elite had mulatto bastards by their slaves and they made mistresses
of other men's wives. The planters lived "in professed adultrys and own a mun-
grell race, the living witnesses of their unnatural and monstrous lusts . . . yet
these are the men that charge me of a lewd life and conversation." His much-
maligned "eavesdropping," Parke declared, was simply a plainclothes police
patrol of St. John's. "You may easily imagine," Parke wrote, "that a Seaport
Town in the West Indies, full of Punch-houses and Taverns, cramm'd with
Soldiers and Privateers, to be very licentious; and the greatest care and pains is
wanted to make it habitable and to preserve the Peace, that the Sober Inhabitants may not be insulted or disturbed. And this Fault they accuse me of, has so
reform'd the Town that whereas formerly, almost every Night, some Body was
wounded, or Murder was cry'd out in their Streets, they are now as quiet as
London within her Walls."[10]

Parke declared that he sat in chancery to continue his campaign to bring
law and order to the island capital. He compelled the payments of just debts
(despite the "law on courts" to the contrary). He took "the Part of the Father-
less, and the Widow, to plead for them who have no money to pay others to
plead for them." He acted "to Remember the Interest of the British Crown
and Nation" by trying to preserve the poor whites who could man a militia
to protect the province. He enforced the acts of trade, doubling the customs
revenue. Parke concluded his defense by enclosing to Sunderland addresses
of commendation from the councils of St. Kitts, Nevis, and Antigua. Given
this record of executive accomplishment, Parke declared that as a client of the
captain general, he was owed due process, not arbitrary prosecution by the
secretary of state: "Your Lordship knows very well the Duke of Marlborough
is my Patron and its by his favour that I was sent here. If I have been guilty of
any Mal administration the Duke and your Lordship ought to see that I be not
only removed but Punished but Common Justice requires that I be heard before Condemned." On the other hand, and despite licentious allegations, Parke
expected no support from the duchess of Marlborough. She had cut him dead

when he went to pay his respects on the eve of his departure. If his equipage had not already been on board, Parke told Sunderland that, absent the duchess's favor, he would not have sailed to a post where an indebted elite would "immediately form themselves into cabals, and in proportion to the greatness of their debts" combine to attack the executive whose chancery court forced the planters to pay up. It was their "avow'd Maxim, never to give any Cause, how just so ever on behalf of a Stranger, against an Inhabitant." The planters' war chest for bribery at court was £5,000, Parke reported. Double that amount had been pledged to remove him by those merchants who "are disobliged because I have industriously prevented a Clandestine trade they drove with the French and Dutch Islands." Attacked as a tyrant by planters and merchants for doing his duty to the crown, Parke only asked for "a fair hearing before impartial Judges and not be removed by bribery for pretended Crimes. And if it can be made to appear, that I have acted arbitrarily and Contrary to Law, or that I have neglected my Duty, then lett the Duke and Duchess, your Lordship and Lord Treasurer see that I am punished as I deserve. . . . But till then as I have been placed here by the favour of my Lord Duke, I ought to have the protection of his ffamily."[11]

The frontiersmen's hatred of law and order was the root of the protests against Parke's military administration: "the awe they are in of the Soldiers when they are us'd . . . to reduce them within the limits of the Laws, when the Constables will not assist for Fear . . . is a greater grievance to them than their enemies at a distance," that is, French raiders. Whether to police or to protect the Leeward Islands, Parke explained, he had to take command of Colonel Jones's regiment. He found it unpaid, unclothed, unquartered, unarmed, and unrecruited. When Parke sailed to relieve Montserrat from French assaults, he could not assemble one-third of the regiment. Parke declared that Colonel Jones and his captains returned full, false musters so that their regimental agent could claim full pay and allowances from the queen's paymaster. The governor general ordered the colonel to accompany him to every island, visit every post of the regiment, and muster the men. Of the 834 men on the muster rolls, fewer than 260 were present with the colors. Many soldiers had been sold as servants. Others had deserted rather than starve. The remainder were hungry and ragged, having not been paid or clothed in the two years since Jones took command. Colonel Jones "was not fitt to command a foot Company. Mr. Harley is his relation and got him this post." The same relationship, Parke said, led Jones to believe that if Parke could be cashiered, he would get the government that had previously gone with the command of the regiment. Parke's revelations and Jones's ambitions "made Col. Jones become a bitter Enemy to him, and encouraged his officers in their Slights and Disobedience to the General's Commands, he meriting most of his Colonel who seem'd to be most a Party-Man which did not a little contribute to the Rebellion that follow'd." That is, the incompetent colonel and his corrupt captains allied with the alienated island elite against the governor general. Their opposition to Parke was encouraged because no imperial executive, not the secretaries Sunderland and Walpole, nor John Grubham Howe, paymaster of the English forces, paid the slightest attention to Parke's demonstration that of the more than £14,000 per annum Jones's regiment cost the crown, nothing reached the rank and file or the subaltern officers in the Leeward Islands.[12]

The men of the 38th knew where the fault lay: "All this great Misery has befallen to us since Coll. Jones had the Regiment; for before, we had some Cloathes, and some Money; but since he was our Colonel, which is about two Years, we have had neither Cloathes nor Money. Our Officers tell us, that they receiv'd none from their Colonel." Food was cheap in the islands, and if they had been regularly paid, the men said, they could have bought bread and even saved enough money to buy an occasional bit of beef "to relive us when sick; for the Want of which, a great Number of Us has perish'd and are reduc'd to less than half a Regement." All expected to die soon if General Parke did not report "our sad and deplorable Condition home to the Queen" and obtain her royal orders to their officers for redress. The men of the 38th would have reported their perilous plight previously "but for Fear of our Officers, from whose Fury we now beg Protection."[13]

Parke did shelter the men from the officers, and they protected him, at the cost of their lives. This was especially the case for the grenadiers of the 38th. Their captain, (Brevet) Lieutenant Colonel Thomas Newall, was remarkable not only as "the only Officer that had seen any Service in this Regiment [here Parke was unfair to Colonel Jones, a veteran wounded at Blenheim], but for being more of a Soldier than generally comes into these Parts; having been near Twenty Years in Commission . . . and in most of the Actions, both in this and the last Wars." Certainly Newall's grenadiers were the best paid and best clothed company of the 38th. They were the only unit with a full complement of officers on duty. The grenadiers of the 38th became the governor general's bodyguard and police force in the capital, St. John's. It was grenadiers commanded by Colonel Newall and Provost Marshal Ayon who pursued Parke's would-be assassins and who arrested the Chester rioters. It was on this occasion, as Colonel Newall testified, that Parke justified his use of military force to assist the civilian authorities: "the General said 'what! Have they imprison'd all the Constables, the Marshal and his Men, a Councillor and a Justice of the Peace? Since the Civil Power is imprison'd 'tis time to send for the Military.'" A less friendly witness agreed that it was "the said Company of Grenadiers whom he chiefly employ'd to execute his extraordinary Commands."[14]

Despite its divided loyalties under Daniel Parke, the garrison regiment played a decisive role in provincial life for decades. The 38th Regiment served for fifty-eight years (1707–65) in the Leeward Islands. Like the 40th Regiment in Nova Scotia, the independent companies on the frontiers of New York, and the garrisons of Jamaica and Georgia, the 38th was the foundation of a frontier society. In addition to policing and defending the islands and multiplying the white population, the regiment offered aspirant locals royal commissions in its officer corps. These commissions, by which some Leeward Islanders became field officers in the 38th and held lieutenant governorships in the various islands, were social and professional escalators, carrying young men of the leading island families into the imperial establishment. Their military rank gave these creole officers and those commissioned in other American garrisons or, as will be seen, in the huge American Regiment of colonels Spotswood and Gooch, the wherewithal—half pay and the prestige of a royal commission—with which to build latifundia in the intervals of war. These regiments also constituted bureaucratic, personal, and political links between the provincial administration, the bureaucracy at Whitehall, and the court of St. James.[15]

As "the Generall" of the Leeward Islands, Daniel Parke proposed to the captain general, the duke of Marlborough, a new form of regimental organization, better suited to frontier conditions than the present establishment. With fewer senior officers and more privates, and under the governor general's immediate command, the proposed unit, in the American empire as in its model, Rome, would be called "the legion." As provincial politics heated up, Parke preempted Marlborough's decision. He recruited the best men from the garrison regiment. He armed and quartered them and placed them under the command of junior officers selected and commissioned from among "the young Gentlemen that came over and carried armes in the Regiment." Many governors general brought out such cadets in their military "families." Having given them a military education in American warfare, the executives promoted the cadets to commands in the local forces, either regular or provincial. Parke complained that few of these cadet officers' commissions were confirmed by the crown (that is, Sunderland failed to forward them). Replacements, commissioned in England, left both the serving officers and their men "very hardly used . . . to have strangers put over their heads that never served, and some children." Besides, the governor general complained, most of these officers were political appointees who used their connections to be excused from actual service in the lethal Leewards.[16]

Yet Parke did manage to begin officer careers for his "nephew" Julius Caesar Parke and for his cousin George Sherrard. Both had been commissioned before James Jones took command of the 38th. Both vaulted up to the First Foot Guards (which Parke had led at the Schellenberg). A third Parke protégé, Michael Ayon, had fulfilled the same prerequisites for promotion: "to carry arms as a Cadet and to rise in the service of Her Majesty and their Country by their Courage and Merit." As provost marshal, Ensign Ayon selected juries according to Parke's specifications and he arrested the executive's opponents as rioters or smugglers. He even offered to shoot any man through the head on the general's command. Wounded at Parke's side in the final assault, Ayon was shot again, through the mouth, in cold blood. Miraculously, he survived and reached London to testify against Parke's killers. Another of Parke's ensigns in the 38th, John Lyell, was also left for dead after sharing in the defense of Parke's residence, but he was still in the service three decades later. The general also commissioned officers to higher ranks. For example, he promoted Lieutenant Philip Walsh (his brother Luke, a cadet who became an ensign in the 38th, died in mysterious circumstances). As a captain of the 38th, Walsh was an object of particular animosity from the republican "Faction," both as an enforcer of the acts of trade and as a policeman in St. John's. So he was tried for disobedience by Colonel Jones when Sunderland ordered the regiment returned to the colonel's command. Walsh complained that he and other officers had been "misrepresented to her Majesty, whose Commissions we have the Honour to bear, purely (as I Imagine) for paying the Obedience to Authority, and Respect to the General, which we are directed to do by our Commissions." Nonetheless, Captain Walsh was cashiered. He was replaced by Joseph Rookeby. Rookeby's subsequent refusal to defend the governor general and the queen's government against the insurrection made him notorious, but Rookeby's contumacy was quite in keeping with Colonel Jones's intention to both reclaim control of the 38th and destroy Daniel Parke.[17]

Immediately after Parke's death, Colonel Jones brevetted Captain Rookeby major of the 38th, but he was one of the three regimental officers whose arrest for participating in Parke's murder ended their military careers. Jones himself survived Parke by less than a year. Colonel Jones was a veteran, a captain since 1694, wounded at Blenheim, but he was infamously "factious" and of "an uneasy temper." As lieutenant colonel, Jones had undercut the then colonel of the 38th, General Luke Lillingston, before he took on Parke. Jones was an adept politician but a bad commanding officer. He never paid, clothed, or effectively recruited the regiment. Wanting to get home himself, Jones did not try to keep his officers to service in the islands. Instead, he preferred to recruit provincials opposed to Parke, most despicably Henry Smith, the overseer who spearheaded the final attack on Parke's residence. Ensign Smith was also arrested, shipped home, and indicted for murder in London. The third disgraced officer of the 38th, Lieutenant Thomas Watts, was also promoted captain by Colonel Jones immediately following Parke's murder. Colonel Jones had reclaimed command of his corps, literally, "with a vengeance."[18]

In Antigua, Colonel Jones, and those of the officers and men of the 38th whom he still commanded, had allied themselves with the Antiguan assembly in its protests against the governor general. The most preposterous of these protests was that Parke was "guilty of a most unsoldierly Neglect in time of War, and in the Neighbourhood of a most powerful and watchful Enemy," and that he intended to give up Antigua to the French. The governor general pointed out that apart from the pecuniary fact that he had more of an estate to lose on Antigua than did any of his accusers, his personal honor and professional reputation were at stake in the defense of his government, the queen's dominion.

Parke explained that the root of the problem was that while he had learned his trade from the master soldier of Europe, the provincials were utterly inexperienced in modern warfare, "for all the soldiership any of them can pretend to is what they have seen here." The local elite assumed that their self-promotions gave them military knowledge, "and as every Body almost must be an Officer, there are no soldiers to discipline." Lieutenant Colonel Codrington's company, for example, "consisted of but four Men, vis. Himself, his Lieutenant, and Ensign, and one private man." Parke wanted to consolidate the four Antiguan infantry regiments into one ("which would have been a very small one") and the "Royal Regiment of Caribineers" into a single troop ("which would have been a very weak one"), but this was said "to break into their Constitution . . . worse than delivering them to the French." As it was, each Antiguan unit was at best "a handful of raw indisciplined men, who, as themselves express'd, knew not the exercise or use of their armes." The officers could not teach the men drill they did not know. Neither did they have any knowledge of engineering or artillery. Yet the Antigua assembly would allow nothing to be built "unless a member of their House had the chief management thereof." The result, Parke observed, was that their "forts" were but piles "of loose stone, such as the duke of Beaufort makes around his trees at Badminton." Those of their batteries where the guns were not just lying in the sand lacked the range to hinder the enemy's landing, but the islanders did not propose to contest a French invasion on the beaches. Rather they proposed to retreat to an inland hill fortress, or "deodand." By contrast, General Parke proposed to concentrate men and artillery behind modern earthworks to defend the capital, St. John's. Walls would take the place of drill and discipline for the militia, he observed, and behind the walls of St. John's, 2,000 creole slaves could exercise their vaunted marksmanship.[19]

Parke himself was a competent engineer. Assisted by Colonel Lilly of Marlborough's ordnance office, the governor general proposed to build defenses "as good as the lines in Flanders, which bid defiance to the Confederate armies there for three campaigns." Parke himself, as he reminded everyone, had served in those campaigns "under the duke of Marlborough in which time I was in two battles and was at the taking of 14 strong towns and forts . . . and had the honour of being sent to the Queene by the Duke, with the news of the glorious victory of Blenheim, for which her Majesty gave me her picture and a thousand pounds, and told me she should take care of me. . . . Not withstanding I am charged with unsoldierlike behaviour" by ignorant provincials, wise in their own conceit and antagonized by Parke's publicly expressed contempt for their military ineptitude: "I should have very ill kept up the Dignity of my post, and shew'd I had learned very little of the greatest Captain of this age, had I given up my opinion to Officers much younger [junior], and, I may add, with Modesty, less experienced than my self, because they differ'd with me." No matter that the lines of St. John's would level parson Field's glebe land, or that Parke's plan for more farmer-militiamen meant less land engrossment, and consolidated militia units meant fewer commands for the planter elite, or that the governor general proposed to exact corvée labor from the planters' slaves or, finally, that Parke's modern notions of warfare, learned from Marlborough and applied in Flanders and Germany, contradicted those of Parke's popular predecessor, Colonel Christopher Codrington, learned from William III and practiced in the Lesser Antilles.[20]

The fatal crisis, ostensibly about defense, could have been avoided if Parke had obeyed the order for his recall, dated February 5, 1710. News of that order was received in Antigua to the sound of musketry, toasts to lord Sunderland, and fresh legislative demands for what Parke called "chimerical privileges." The Antiguan assemblymen, Parke declared, were actually republicans, whom every loyal servant of the queen should repress. Those who toasted the secretary "as their chiefest friend," Parke wrote to Sunderland, were rank rebels, antimonarchical, anticlerical. The Scot William Nevine, "who is their agent in England," while in Antigua had lauded the covenanters' murder of the archbishop of St. Andrews. Codrington's Antigua agent, a corrupt collector of customs named Edward Perrie, "justified publicly King Charles's murder, and bid me take warning from him" (presages of Patrick Henry!). Perrie also "professes himself a Presbyterian and an enemy to the Episcopal Church and Monarchy." These men led Calves Head Club celebrations of the execution of King Charles I. If, as the order for Parke's recall suggested, Sunderland had given credit to such traitors, it was no wonder that "it has never been my good fortune to please your Lordship in any one thing I ever proposed." Parke wrote to Sunderland that he could not obey the queen's order (over Sunderland's signature) to return with the first convoy because the machinations of his enemies (using Sunderland's instructions) had prevented him from preparing his defense (as indeed they had).[21]

On the very day that Parke wrote home to excuse his disobedience, he read in the *Gazette* "the agreeable news" of Sunderland's replacement by lord Dartmouth. Sunderland's fall was followed by that of the rest of the whig ministry. This was just what Parke had purportedly boasted: that "he'll get your Lp. [Sunderland], The Presdt. Of her Majesty's Council, and Mr. Walpole Superseded." "Genl. Parke was so puffed up since the Ministry in England was changed" because he was sure that, as a true blue tory, he would now have "the protection at home I ought to have had till it had appeared I did not deserve it." Now it would no longer be true "what his Enemies us'd to report, which was that he had no Friend, except the Duke, and he was out of England." Now Parke could "settle these Islands in an honest method of government." That meant, first of all, taking control of the garrison regiment. "The General" cashiered Colonel Jones. Then Parke "pickt out a sett of men, both officers and soldiers, abandon'd to all his black and gloomy designs." Immediately, the drums of the regiment beat "Round headed cockels Com Dick" at the doors of Parke's enemies.[22]

On September 9, 1710, Parke wrote to lord Dartmouth that the charges against him were the work of their shared ideological enemies: "I am oppress'd only because I am not of the Republican Party." This, Parke wrote, was the key to his bad usage by the whigs Sunderland, Somers, and Walpole. This was the source of the enmity of Nevine, the "Scotch Cameronian," and of Perrie, the "professed Presbyterian." Jones feared a criminal inquiry into his misappropriation of the 38th's pay and allowances. So Jones and his captains supported both "the Court of Inquisition my lord Sunderland erected against me" (to take evidence for Parke's recall) and Sunderland's "other High Commission Court, of which he constituted Col. Jones sole Judge" to condemn Parke's alleged misuse of the regiment. Radical republicanism excused both Jones's corruption and the provincials' resistance to the governor general's authority. The Antiguan republicans, Parke wrote Dartmouth, were enemies not just of the royal prerogative but also of the empire itself. Their opposition was not so much to Parke personally as it was a "bare fac'd . . . attempt on the first branch of her Majesty's sovereignty over them, and of an independency from the Crowne of England."

This was not just an Antiguan crisis, it was also an American one. The queen must quickly "extinguish the factious Humour that reigns not only in this but in most of her Governments," Parke wrote, lest it "oblige her Governours to fall into their own Interest, and rather make their fortunes by humouring the People than mine themselves by endeavouring to maintain her Majesty's honour and the interest of the British Nation." It was not the "interest of her Majesty to have her Governours and her People here hold too near a Correspondenc," Parke observed. Whereas in England, "her Majesty's Happiness is in being a Parent of her People, and having the same Interest with them, here it is very different; the particular Interest of Collonies often clashing with that of the Mother Kingdom." It would take more than royal rescripts and executive discipline to head off American independence. Acts of parliament would be required.[23]

In response to the Antiguan-American crisis, Parke presciently prescribed a set of parliamentary acts. The first act would authorize the quartering of troops in unused colonial buildings. The second would remove to Westminster the trials both of soldiers who were accused of injuring colonists in the course of their duty and of republican agitators who were accused of acting against imperial authority. The third act would regulate customs collection and collectors. The fourth would tighten the regulation of trade, especially the purchase of foreign sugar and molasses by American colonists. Finally, the enhanced royal revenue would be appropriated by an act of the British parliament to the support of the imperial executive and judiciary, thus making them independent of provincial assemblies' allocations. Parke had precisely anticipated "the Intolerable Acts," the parliamentary attentions to imperial administration—military, economic, and judicial—which provoked provincial assemblies to begin an American revolution.

Parke also expected the established church to enhance imperial authority in America, just as its doctrines of passive obedience to royal authority undergirded monarchial government at home. Once he reached London, Parke would "convince all the honest world how villainously I have been persecuted for supporting the Queen's prerogative and the principles of the Episcopal Church." Because "the Episcopall Church is like to be trumps" in the political game, Parke anticipated his own election to parliament and so a leadership in the legislative enactment of a tory program for America. Parke asked Dartmouth to help him to a seat by restoring him to the commission of the peace for Hampshire. There Parke had a parliamentary estate and interest, but the whig lord chancellor had dropped him from the Hampshire magistrates' bench. Parke also claimed interest in the great popular constituency of Middlesex. He asked Dartmouth for a seat on that county commission as well.[24]

This was Daniel Parke's last dispatch. His enemies, both in London and Antigua, feared that the new tory ministry would indeed support their partisan in the Leeward Islands command and advance his parliamentary program for American subordination. Assassination had failed to remove Parke. The Antiguan radicals determined on revolt. A pretext for violence sufficient to excite the island militiamen was at hand in the fact of war, the menace of the French, and the debate over proper defense. The arrival of a French amphibious force at Martinique, its capture of Dutch St. Eustatius, the assumption that the French would attack the always vulnerable St. Kitts, and that, successful there, the French would assault Antigua, was a tissue of possibilities sufficient to panic the planters. So their tactical differences with the governor general became matters of life and death: life for the planter elite, death for the imperial executive.[25]

The council of Antigua asked the governor general to assemble the island legislature to address the emergency. He did so in the first week of December 1710. The opening session broke up over the right of the governor general to name the representatives' speaker. Next the assembly disputed Parke's prerogative to appoint the clerk of the house. Declaring that this constitutional impasse had impeded legislative action against a French invasion, the representatives called on the governor general to withdraw from Antigua and leave them to defend themselves. The representatives carrying this address burst into the chamber where the royal executive sat with the queen's council. Parke silenced the assembly's speaker. He declared that the assembly's address was another attempt to deny the crown's control over legislation. He accused the assemblymen of riot. He ordered the guards to oust them from the council chamber.

The redcoats, nine grenadiers of the 38th, pointed loaded muskets at the legislators and declared that they were prepared to fire on the governor general's command.[26]

The Antiguan assemblymen retreated but, as they went, they shouted that Parke "was no longer Generall and that they would no longer obey him as such." Worse, the representatives threatened that "they would muster up as many forces as should drive him (meaning the Generall) and his Granadiers to the Devil." In reply, the governor general dissolved the assembly to punish "their obstinate resolving to wrest [the prerogative] from HM" and their refusal to make military appropriations for more than one month. The dissolution, so the dismissed assemblymen declared, "set their blood into such a ferment that nothing but the letting out his blood could cure." The Antiguans said that they, "tho dissolv'd, are still accounted the Representatives of the Island, worthy to be entrusted with the Care of the People, whose Destruction, it was now publically said, was intended by the General; the Preservation of their liberty and Property . . . is submitted to those Patriots . . . the Mob . . . were exercised, and taught to form themselves into several military Dispositions. . . . The Common People are told . . . that this rising in arms was but a just reply to the Tyranny of the General, and his Usurpation on their Liberties: That there could be no such Thing as a free Assembly when the Army was made Use of to awe them." The former representatives summoned their constituents to rally, armed, in St. John's, on Thursday, December 7, 1710, alleging that the royal governor general had "betrayed the Island to the French." The "Patriots," as the assemblymen called themselves, called for "an Association in armes" on the usual Anglo-American revolutionary model. Anyone who did not join them was "a traitor to the people." Anyone who would not "be aiding and assisting to them in taking General Parke dead or alive" would have "their estates forefeited and themselves banished off the Island." The Antiguan "Loyalists," as the supporters of the royal prerogative called themselves, were cowed. Some of the loyalists, men "of the best Families and Estates on the Island," lived in outlying areas and were surprised by the speed of events. Others simply refused to believe that the rebels were capable of "that Pitch of Wickedness." Many of the loyalists, together with the neutrals in the struggle, took to small boats and fled downwind to other islands. Others took passage to Virginia, carrying with them news of the Antiguan insurrection.[27]

On December 6, the governor general ordered companies of the garrison regiment to rally at his house. There he supposedly "declared to them that if they would stand by him, they should have all the plunder of the towne and the Plantations of all the islanders that should be killed." Parke placed field artillery on the approaches to his residence. From the island magazine, the governor general also rearmed the grenadier company of the 38th. It now stood by him, but Captain John Marshall of the 38th disobeyed Parke's orders to join him with his company from their post on board the *Larke*, the station ship anchored in St. John's harbor. Her captain, Cunningsby Norbury, also announced that he would not obey the governor general's orders, issued as vice admiral, to defend the queen's government. Instead, Norbury visited the rump meeting of the assembly to announce that the *Larke* would sail immediately for Barbados: "The Assembly or most of them . . . huzzah' d him off." Captain Joseph Rookeby of the 38th then refused the governor general's command to join him. Rookeby declared "that he was not sent to fight against the subject." "General Parke replied, I hope you will support and defend the Queen's Representative when insulted, assuring Rookeby that he would not fire a shott against any person unless they first fired at him." Rookeby responded by ordering his company of the 38th not to defend the governor general. The men defied their captain and manned Parke's artillery. Rookeby then left St. John's. Colonel Jones was at Nevis, on Parke's orders, as he afterward claimed. The remainder of the 38th was either with its colonel on Nevis or at St. Christopher's, the post of danger against the French.[28]

With the grenadiers of the 38th, and six loyal gentlemen by his side, the governor general was outnumbered at least ten to one by the Antiguan militia, or mob. They had come, weapons in one hand and pillowcases for plunder in the other, to storm Parke's residence. He knew that he faced death. The governor general summoned a clergyman to his house. He took Communion at the head of his men, emulating one last time his devout patron, the duke of Marlborough. Parke signed a will leaving his island estates to his mistress (the wife of Edward Chester) and their daughter, Lucy, providing that she took the name of Parke. As the rebel associators and the royal executive faced off, the lieutenant governor, that old soldier John Yeamans, and the council of Antigua, loyalists almost to a man, tried to prevent fighting. They addressed Parke, saying that it was out of their "power to put a stop to the frenzy of an incensed multitude" save by persuading the governor general to sail to another island in his government. Thence they and the representatives would send him laws for the defense of Antigua for his review. Parke rejected the suggestion that he retreat. The speaker of the house then offered final terms: if the governor general disbanded his bodyguard, gave up his commission, and left the island, his life would be spared. Otherwise, "Your Excellency must expect the just resentment of the incensed multitude." The governor general replied that if the assemblymen chose to meet elsewhere in Antigua, "they would not see one Soldier, and they might keep what Party of men they pleased," but the mob at his door had been excited by men who feared that their frauds against the crown and their oppressions of the people would be exposed in the governor general's chancery court. He "expected no quarter from them." He would give them none. He would fire his artillery on any party that attacked him. Then he would set fire to St. John's. He would never give up his commission from the queen or surrender his command.[29]

On the morning of December 7, 1710, the Antigua association in arms, more than 500 strong, fully armed by the queen's military bounty to the province, attacked the governor general's house. They overran the artillery. Captain Rookeby's men fled. Next, the sentries were killed. Then the rebels advanced in rushes under "the Covert of Trees, Stumps, Shrubs, Rocks &c." Parke's regulars stood in their disciplined line, exposed to the fire of hidden rebels until they were driven into the house. It was stormed by parties led by the militia captains (and assemblymen) John Paynter and John Piggott. The governor general, the grenadiers, and a few loyalists put up a desperate defense against overwhelming odds. Fifteen of the redcoats were killed on the spot. Twenty-five were wounded. Some of the surviving soldiers were murdered in cold blood, "poor innocent souls who on their knees begged for quarter in vain, and were murdered for standing guard to their General when they were too few to defend him." Parke and his last defenders retreated, fighting, from room to room of the house. Finally, John Piggott, at the head of forty-five men, cornered Parke and a few followers. Piggott "told the General he was no more such and bid him deliver his Commission, which he refusing they both fired." Parke's shot killed Piggott. Piggott's ball put Parke down with a wound in his thigh. All of Parke's remaining comrades were killed or wounded. George French, afterward the historian of Parke's administration, "lying in his Gore of some Wounds he had before received, was shot in the Mouth." The last of Parke's defenders to go down was Michael Ayon, the provost marshal. He was shot through the body after he surrendered. Then the most brutal members of the mob had their way with the queen's wounded viceroy. The butcher broke Parke's back with a musket butt. The farrier ripped the miniature of queen Anne from the fallen man's neck. The husband of Parke's mistress seized Parke's gold and silver plate. He also found adoring letters to the governor general from many wives of the island elite. Then the disabled governor general was stripped so violently that only the wrists and neckband of his shirt remained on his body. Parke was dragged around the residence by his genitals. Finally he was pulled, by an arm and a leg, down the steps of his house, his head bouncing on every one. He was dragged across the gravel of the market square, "which rak'd the skin from his Bones." He was left to die in the dust, spat upon, reviled, and begging in vain for water.[30]

The lieutenant governor, the veteran John Yeamans, defied threats to his own life to recover the governor general's body. He had it washed and shrouded and given a decent burial in the St. John's parish church. Invited by the rebels, the lieutenant general of the Leeward Islands, Colonel Walter Hamilton, came up from Nevis, together with Colonel Jones. Jones immediately promoted the two officers of the 38th on Antigua who had refused to help Parke. Jones also commissioned the plantation overseer who led the assault, Henry Smith, as an ensign. Jones made the speaker of the assembly, George Lucas, captain lieutenant of the 38th. Lieutenant Colonel Newall, captain of the grenadiers, wounded in Parke's defense, was imprisoned by Hamilton and Jones. He was released so that he could be murdered by two royal navy captains, Cunningsby Norbury and Tobias Lisle, lest Newall go home to testify against Parke's killers. Newall's testimony was expected to have authority "in England especially since he was the Commanding Officer of the Governor's Troops." Colonel Jones imprisoned Sergeant Major Charles Bowes, the senior NCO of the grenadiers, who had also been wounded in Parke's defense. Then Jones falsified an affidavit in Bowes's name to the effect that Parke had declared that "if he had but two companies which he knew in Flanders he would soon drive half the planters of the Island" and that Parke had betrayed the island to the French. When Bowes refused to sign the affidavit or to say "what women came to the General," he was left to rot in the Monkshill dungeon. Lieutenant General Hamilton now had "the Regement entirely of his Side, from the Colonel, to a private Man." Empowered by force, rebel and regular, Hamilton libeled Parke as "the Grand Monster, tyranniseing and tryumphing in Antigua." Hamilton had kept his commission (defying Parke's nominee to replace him) only by the intervention of his kinsman the duke of Hamilton. With Secretary Sunderland, his partner in Scots politics, Hamilton had anticipated, even incited, Parke's assassination. Now "Welcom'd by a large Body of the chiefest Rebels," Walter Hamilton took up residence with "one of the most crucial" patriots. Acting as chief executive, "Lieutenant General" Hamilton legitimized the rebel assembly of Antigua, confirmed Jones's promotions, and rejected the addresses from Nevis and St. Christopher's because they condemned Parke's assassination. Hamilton delayed making any report home. When prodded by the imperial authorities, he declared that the rebels were too numerous, too important, and too provoked by Parke to be punished.[31]

The loyalists were threatened with death for testifying that it was the governor general's "stedfast maintaining H.M. prerogative in all its branches for which he was barbarously murthered, dying a true sone of the Protestant Church as by law established." The loyalists asked that, "if the Pretended Oppression of their Governor appears only to be his maintaining her Dignity and Laws . . . is it not evident, the Affront is to her Majesty, in the person of her Governor; and that they [the rebels] would not, if they could help it, have her reign over them, or to Constitute any Majistrate who would not let them do whatsoever they pleas'd?" Loyalist sentiments infused the first London publication on the rebellion in Antigua, *Forty One in Miniature*. Its title's reference to the puritan and parliamentary revolution against king Charles I and the church of England explicitly linked the Antiguan revolt to the partisanships of other Anglo-American revolutions, past and prospective. "Forty One" also tied the Parke tragedy to immediate imperial politics. It was dedicated to Matthew Prior, the former Marlborough panegyrist, sometime commissioner of trade and plantations, and now the secret envoy of the new tory ministry to France.[32]

Parke, "that brave Hortensio," was martyred, so *Forty-One in Miniature* poetically proclaimed, "Because he did maintain his Sovereign's Cause/ By suffering no Encroachment on the Laws." Parke's murderers called themselves "Patriots," but they were actually the enemies of church and state, law and order. They were commonwealthsmen who, "With Liberty's and Property's loud Cant," had deluded the colonists into thinking that they had been "bought, sold, in short betray'd" by a "popish" (read anglican) Parke, condemned to slavery's "Chains or Wooden Shoes" of poverty, and that each provincial back had been "ready saddled to receive a Pack."

The "patriots" had been told that this royal executive trod in the tyrannical steps of King Charles I. The republican "Brutus" (identified as "S[un]d[e] r[lan]d" in the margin), whom the patriots had bribed to have "Hortensio" removed, could not prevail in the court of good Queen Anne. Frustrated, these believers in "the Good Old Cause" of republican revolution again rose against monarchy:

> At length their Cursed Artifices arm'd
> A Mobb with Rage and Indignation warm'd
> Strain'd their damp Lungs and cryed out One and All,
> We'll this day have the Tyrant, or we'll fall.

To the menaces of the provincial mob, the governor general replied:

> I, by my Gracious Sovereign put in Trust
> Dare strictly be to my Commission just,
> If the Queen's Rights I basely give away,
> And vilely that Depositum betray;
> Curs'd to succeeding Ages may my Name
> Be stigmatiz'd with Infamy and Shame.

So saying, the hero fell:

> For what could such unequal Force repell?
> This is the Effect of all thy Service done,
> Of Zeal approv'd, and signal Valour shewn
> At Schellenbergh, and on the Danube's Banks?

Well advertised and widely condemned, the "rebellious tumult and barbarous murder of Col. Parke, HM late Governor of the Leeward Islands" provoked a series of proposals for a punitive response. Because "the eyes of all the Colonys are on their Mother Kingdom, and how she will punish such an outrage," the lords of trade and plantations proposed that lord Archibald

Hamilton, en route to his command in Jamaica together with the commodore of the convoy, anchor their fleet off Antigua, summon Lieutenant General Walter Hamilton on board, and then send the 250 fleet marines ashore to put down the rebellion, arrest the ringleaders, and ship them to the imperial capital for proceedings under the statute of 35 Henry VIII "for the trial of treasons committed out of the King's dominions." Only by such draconian proceedings could the rebellious example of Antigua be excised and with it be erased the "dangerous consequence such proceedings may be to [the] publick peace of HM subjects in America."[33]

Yet a new governor general had to be commissioned for the Leeward Islands. It soon appeared both obvious and economical that he should be ordered to put down disorder and to send home such miscreants as could not be tried and punished locally. The choice fell on Major Walter Douglas. Douglas was so junior an officer that it was assumed he was the deputy of some Scots military lord, an assumption bolstered by Douglas's recommendation to Oxford by the Scots fixer, George Lockhart, and by Douglas's subsequent care to report to his patron, the leading Scots minister, the duke of Queensbury. But Douglas was also the brother-in-law of Sir John St. Ledger, Antigua's agent. The major was an officer of long but hitherto unrewarded "services in the Army, both in Europe and America, ever since the Revolution, when he came over with the late King William." Douglas had been commissioned lord Cutts's ensign in 1693. He had served in the West Indies. Governor General Handasyde had promoted Douglas captain in Livesay's (the 12th) regiment in Jamaica in 1702. Alex Cosby was Douglas's lieutenant. Samuel Gledhill, the recipient of the dispatch on the Antiguan revolt, was Douglas's fellow captain. Douglas had been distinguished in the defense of Leffinghe, the vital link in the communications to Marlborough's siege of Lille in 1708. When the 12th sailed for Spain in 1710, Douglas was kept in England for a promised promotion.[34]

Douglas's orders for the Leeward Islands government were necessarily tempered by Lieutenant General Hamilton's (tardy) report. He was an enemy of Parke, to be sure, but Hamilton was correct when he wrote that it was manifestly impossible to try the whole assembly of Antigua and hundreds of the island's militiamen for treason. Therefore, in composing Douglas's instructions, the crown adopted the convenient fiction that most of the islanders had been duped by a few malcontents. The queen graciously consented to pardon the misled people, but Douglas was first to arrest at least three and as many as six ringleaders to be tried for treason, in the island if possible, or else in England. In his personal instructions to Douglas, the prime minister made it clear that his concern was to pacify the province and to reassert the royal prerogative, rather than to avenge Marlborough's protégé Daniel Parke.[35]

Major Douglas landed in Antigua on July 10, 1711. He immediately reported that he was going to have difficulties restoring order. Every Antiguan assemblyman save one was implicated in Parke's assassination. Like Nathaniel

Bacon's Virginian revolutionaries before them (and like the American rebels of 1776), the Antiguans were threatening to call in the French to support their subversion of England's empire. If the new governor general tried to act against them, the guilty Antiguans also threatened to arm their Coromantee and creole slaves. Then the island would "see more blood then for a thousand years for the bigness of the place." Douglas lacked the military means to arrest the rebels. The garrison regiment was undisciplined and under strength, ill armed and disaffected. There was "so great an Intimacy and Friendship between the Queen's Troops and the Rebels, that upon the least Motion I should make to apprehend any Planter, the Island would be in an Insurrection, and the Loyalists being the weakest, exposed to certain ruin and destruction." Major Douglas could expect no more help from the royal navy than Colonel Parke had received. Captain Norbury remained an intimate of the rebels and he continued to deny the governor general's vice admiralty authority. Class hatred underlay this interservice hostility. Douglas attributed Norbury's empathy for the rebels and the identification of the other naval captains in the West Indies with the provincial "patriots" to the deficiencies of naval officers' "principles, family, and education." The anarchy and obduracy of the hoi polloi were the order of the day both in Antigua's popular politics and in those of the royal navy. The result, Douglas wrote, was that "The Spirit of Rebellion is so infused into the Majority of the People" that they had reelected to the assembly the murderers of the governor general.[36]

An unrepentant assembly meant that to acquire authority, Douglas had to take control of the 38th from its colonel and the officers implicated in the revolt. As Parke had done, Douglas bypassed Colonel Jones (who sold out to his lieutenant colonel and died within the year, before his conduct in Antigua could be investigated). The governor general arrested the three officers directly implicated in Parke's murder, Captain Joseph Rookeby, Lieutenant Thomas Watts, and Ensign Henry Smith, and sent them home for trial with evidence for the prosecution collected by Sergeant Major Bowes and Provost Marshal Ayon. Douglas then concentrated the 38th on Antigua. He made the able-bodied men—some 200—his personal bodyguard and his government's administrators. In rearming imperial authority in Antigua, Douglas's chief aide was the scion of a Leeward Islands military family, Captain Peter Boar. His people had been officers in Goodwyn's garrison regiment under William III. Douglas now brevetted Boar major of the 38th. For naval force, Douglas detained a Jamaica privateer and her crew of 180, all of them "brave and true hearty men." Douglas quartered soldiers on the plantations of obdurate rebels, purged the militia commands, and suspended the lieutenant general (Hamilton immediately sailed home to denounce Douglas). In physical command of Antigua and the other islands, Douglas reconstituted the judiciary. He voided the Antiguan "act on courts" that protected debtors. To focus political loyalty and authenticate imperial authority, Douglas encouraged the building of episcopal

churches and the recruitment of anglican clergy. He echoed Parke's call for
the resettlement of St. Kitts by the poorer people. Like Parke, Douglas recommended the retention of that disputed island in the upcoming peace with
France, both to provide farms for a free, white, arms-bearing population and to
deny the French a base for the raiding and looting, ransoming and terrorism,
that "most inhumane manner of making war which is still practiced this side of
the Tropick."[37]

Douglas "divided and broke the knot and body of the rebells." Then he
called an assembly and successfully asserted the crown's legislative powers of
appointment, review, and veto. "All thoughts of daring any more to invade the
Prerogative, seem forgot," Douglas reported. It is said that Douglas now took
an extortionate revenge on Parke's killers. To avoid prosecution for treason,
Clem the butcher, having nothing else to give, surrendered his cow. Wealth-
ier, each of the guilty assemblymen was charged £1,600. To fines that totaled
£25,317 in money, bonds, slaves, and sugar, Douglas added all the perquisites
Parke had declined (and some that he had never been offered). So he assembled
"an estate fitter for a nobleman then a breviate major who sells the queen's
mercy by auction." Once most of the rebels were mulcted, Douglas arrested
half a dozen of the leading conspirators, but Thomas Kirby, the former secretary of Antigua who had "fired the first musket against General Parke," had
taken refuge at Codrington's house in Barbados. The new governor general of
Barbados, Robert Lowther, feared that he himself would face an insurrection if
he executed Douglas's warrant to arrest Kirby (another strong suggestion that
the rebellious spirit so violently expressed in Antigua was widespread in British
America). When at last Lowther acted, the naval officer on station refused to
obey the governor general's order to take Kirby prisoner to England, giving
"a great encouragement to all the factious and rebellious people." Lowther
had to hire a ship himself to send Kirby home for trial (he joined the executive chorus demanding that the admiralty order naval officers on colonial stations to subordinate themselves to the governors general). Finally, on February 6, 1712, Queen Anne's birthday, Major Douglas at last published the royal
pardon. Douglas excepted only Kirby, the murderous chief justice (and assembly speaker), the former chief justice, Samuel Watkins, and that meddling
medico, Daniel McKinnon. The latter two fled Antigua. They were sheltered
by the captain of the *Diamond* and taken by him to London, but they were run
down by Daniel Parke's executors, arrested, and indicted for treason by the
crown.[38]

Parke's executors—his sister Evelyn, her husband, Gilbert Pepper, and the
merchant Micaiah Perry, the éminence grise in every province where he did
business—lobbied hard to create a political climate in the imperial metropolis
to help convict the criminals who had killed their kinsman and client the governor general. On March 28, 1713, they submitted to the queen's privy council and

to the lords of trade and plantation a pamphlet entitled *Truth Brought to Light; or, Murder Will Out: Being a Short, but True, Account of the Most Horrid, Barbarous and Bloody* MURTHER *and* REBELLION *Committed at Antego in the West Indies, against Her Majesty and Her Government.* A summary of testimony by "Eye Witnesses" now in London, *Truth Brought to Light* rehearsed the attempts on Parke's life, including the suborning of the 38th. It asserted that these felonies were all independent of and unjustified by any wrongdoing on the governor general's part. Rather, the pamphlet pointed out that the articles against the royal executive were designed to excuse a corrupt courtier's (that is, Sunderland's) intentions to "condemn him first, and try him afterwards." In fact, Parke's administration had been praised by the lieutenant governors and councils of Antigua and St. Christopher's. Their addresses were printed in *Truth Brought to Light.* In short and in sum, Colonel Parke was shown to be a royalist martyr, murdered "as a Faithfull Asserter of the Rights of the British Crown, and a sincere Lover of his Country . . . by Antimonarchial and Disaffected People."[39]

The political wheel turned once again, however, before the accused officers could be brought to trial. The accession of George I and the tory refusal to join his first government produced an essentially whig administration headed by none other than the earl of Sunderland. When Ensign Smith finally went to trial, on June 28, 1715, charged with high treason for "levying war against her Majesty in the Island of Antigua, and murdering Col. Parke, the chief Governor," the defendant pled "a general Pardon granted by General Douglas." The whig attorney general could not find the commitment order to ascertain if Smith had been arrested prior to the pardon being issued. So, although the jury found Smith guilty, the whig chief justice ordered the case dismissed. All the other defendants then successfully pled the queen's pardon for their shares in the dreadful death of Daniel Parke.[40]

On the other hand, Parke's patron, the duke of Marlborough, had been restored as captain general by George I. The duke was treated with the greatest personal consideration by the new regime. When he chose to do so, Marlborough exercised complete military authority. No army officer indicted in the Antigua assassination had his commission confirmed by George I. Officers loyal to Parke were promoted. The full and open file that the captain general collected regarding the murder of his former aide testified to his continuing concern. George French dedicated his *History of Colonel Parke's Administration* to the duke of Marlborough, "the Greatest General in the Field, the Wisest Councellor in the Cabinet, the Best Patriot in the Senate, and the Best Subject in the Commonwealth." French's enormous effusion was designed to demonstrate to Marlborough that his client, Colonel Daniel Parke, "neither abus'd your Favour, nor was unworthy of it," but by then, in 1717, Marlborough had suffered a stroke and was largely retired. The captain general had neither the physical strength nor the political capacity to avenge his former aide. Instead,

Sir Samuel Gerard's selection as lord mayor put the anti-Parke merchants, of whom he was the head, in political power in the imperial capital. They impeded any further prosecution of Parke's murderers.[41]

Legally, the queen's general pardon had muddied the prosecutorial waters. So did Major Douglas's retail of particular pardons, even to ringleaders of the insurrection. Douglas was recalled at the instance of Parke's sister and the Perrys. When the news reached Antigua, the "Patriots" immediately attacked Douglas's residence. They were beaten off by the reformed 38th under its new colonel, Walter Hamilton. He "declared himself now as violently zealous for the Whiggish System as he had been before for the Toryish" and succeeded to the command of the Leeward Islands. With Hamilton's commission, for which, it was said, "there were five thousand good Reasons" given, and with the peace with France and Spain, the Leeward Islands entered into the misnamed era of "salutary neglect." Parke's murderers were preferred, poor planters were expropriated, the royal prerogative was diminished, and the governor general was well paid by an autonomous, elite provincial assembly for his neglect of both sovereign and people, just as Daniel Parke had predicted.[42]

CHAPTER ELEVEN

Defending the Revolution: Robert Hunter in New York

HOME ON PAROLE during 1708, honor bound not to fight against France, Colonel Robert Hunter caroused with England's leading literati: Addison and Steele, Congreve and Swift. Hunter contributed pieces to the *Tatler*, the first fashionable magazine. When Hunter's parole expired and he had to return to Paris, his literary reputation was such, and his identification with "moderation" was so well known, that Jonathan Swift could plausibly attribute to Hunter's pen the famous "Letter on Enthusiasm." Counsels of moderation also infused the "Projects for unity of Partys" and news of the prorogation of convocation that Swift sent Hunter. Swift also regaled the captive with notes on Prior's new poems, the advent of Italian opera in London, and the likelihood that Hunter would become as much "a prisoner to the ladies" of Paris as he was to Louis XIV. In short, Swift so esteemed Hunter that he declared that if the French ministers "exchange you for under six of their Lieutenant Generals, they will be losers by the Bargain." Swift suggested, not wholly in jest, that when he was released, Hunter should take Swift out to Virginia as the first American bishop of the church of England.[1]

Such was Hunter's anxiety to return to duty and cement his commission to command Virginia that the moment his exchange was announced, early in April 1709, he raced from Paris to the Channel, commandeered a row galley for the passage to Dover, and then immediately reembarked to join Marlborough's army in Flanders. There he learned that Virginia was closed to him, even though Hunter had been paid from the colony's quitrents both his half pay as governor general and the entire cost of his captured equipage. While Hunter was a prisoner, the duke of Marlborough had reassigned the Virginia command to two other Scots officers. The first was General George Macartney. The Old Dominion was to recompense Macartney for his loss of the Caribbean command and the government of Jamaica that went with it. Macartney asked to serve with Marlborough instead. The captain general then chose another

Scots officer to command Virginia, his deputy chief of staff, Colonel Alexander
Spotswood. Deprived of Virginia, Hunter concluded that the government of
Jamaica was open. It was a lucrative and responsible command. Besides, his
wife had an estate there which her family wished Hunter to improve. Hunter's
"most intimate and most useful friend," the Scots physician John Arbuthnot,
Queen Anne's favorite doctor, arranged her majesty's approval. In the meantime, however, Marlborough had assigned Jamaica to a third Scots officer,
Orkney's brother, lord Archibald Hamilton. Hunter found himself caught between the queen and the captain general, and at odds with the Hamiltons.[2]

At this embarrassing moment, August 18, 1709, lord treasurer Godolphin
informed the duke of Marlborough of the death of lord Lovelace, viceroy of
New York. Godolphin proposed that Hunter succeed Lovelace and, as commander of a reunited New York and New England, recruit 1,500 provincials
to join the proposed expedition against the Spanish West Indian ports. Marlborough's deteriorating political position left him unable to publicly oppose
this plan, although he wrote Godolphin that tropical disease would kill almost
all the troops involved. If the expedition went forward nonetheless, Marlborough agreed with Godolphin that it would be best if it were well commanded:
"Colonel Hunter, whom you mention for the West Indies is a very good man."
Moreover, Marlborough was relieved to have an American command available that he could press Hunter to accept, thus opening Jamaica for Hamilton.
Hunter duly told Dr. Arbuthnot to tell the queen that he preferred New York
to Jamaica. His appointment was announced on September 9, 1709.[3]

Even as he juggled American commands, Marlborough prepared for a cli-
mactic battle with the army of Louis XIV. Malplaquet was fought on September 11. Hunter may well have seen service there, either on Marlborough's staff
or that of Hunter's "dearest good lord," the Scots earl of Stair, commander of
the dragoon brigade of which Hunter had been major. Even as he fought the
final battle of the War of the Spanish and English Successions—and for Atlantic dominion—Marlborough was bombarded with proposals for American
expeditions. He disapproved of them all, "for they follow no one project, but
they undertake everything and finish nothing, which in the management of a
war is very dangerous." The captain general's criticism crossed in the mail the
lord treasurer's report that the queen "is disposed to give the government of
New York to Collonel Hunter." The captain general replied with what for him
was extraordinary praise: "I have in my former letters assured you of believing
Mr. Hunter to be a very good man, and I am confident he will execute any orders that shall be given him very well."[4]

Hunter was back in England by September 21 to see his commission and
instructions through the seals and to develop the ministerial projects for America and the Caribbean. The first of these plans had been instigated, almost
incidentally, by Marlborough himself. This was the resettlement on the frontiers of New York of thousands of Palatine refugees. The villages of the Ger-

man palatinate had been burned out twice by French armies in the previous twenty-five years. They were destroyed for a third time in 1707 as the homes of Protestants, allied recruits, and Imperial taxpayers. Even as "birds perished on the wing, beasts in their lairs, and mortals fell dead in the way," an escape was offered to "the poor Palatines." "Papers were dispersed among them, and fixed upon the Church Doors, that if they come over into England, the Queen would send them into the Plantations." In April, the vanguard of thousands of Palatine refugees sailed down the Rhine to Rotterdam. They begged the British authorities at The Hague for a passage to England en route to America. Marlborough was present for the peace negotiations by which, among other things, he intended to extend the British empire in America, particularly on the New York frontier with the Iroquois. The captain general saw the Palatines, as he had seen the Huguenot refugees before them, as strengthening Protestant British possessions at the expense of Catholic France. Duly instructed, Marlborough's chaplain publicized the Palatine project, writing that it is "a Fundamental Maxim in Sound Politicks, that the Greatness, Wealth, and Prosperity of a Country consist in the Number of its Inhabitants." In mid-April 1709, the captain general ordered British military transports to carry the refugees to England.[5]

In each crisis of the swelling migration, Marlborough provided additional transports. He added army rations to supplement the Dutch charity (and his own) that sustained the "Poor, Protestant, Palatines." He acknowledged that "the expences may be great but are necessary, if you are in want of these people for the Plantations." On May 17, by "the directions my Lord Duke has thought good to give in relation to the poor Palatines . . . there are almost 1300 embarkt and I believe sail'd by this time." The duke's ordnance office erected entire tent cities to house the Palatines at Greenwich and on Blackheath. As the numbers swelled toward 13,000 in the summer of 1709, Marlborough was warned that many of the refugees were, in fact, Catholics. He replied that "there was no great inconveniency to let them go with the rest." Marlborough's toleration was not reciprocated in England. Three thousand Roman Catholic refugees were returned to the Palatinate. In July, the queen ordered Marlborough not to ship any more refugees until those in England were provided for, something the duke saw easily accomplished by transporting the Palatines to America, as they desired. Despite Anne's order, Palatine passage from the Netherlands to England continued until Christmas 1709.[6]

The Palatine problem was political as much as logistical and parochial as much as imperial. The political issue was epitomized by the naturalization act. Passed on March 29, 1709 (after much lobbying by William Penn, it being "the interest of England to improve and thicken her colonys with people"), the act probably came too late to motivate the migration. Nonetheless, it was blamed for the Palatine influx by the tories. They feared that the whigs intended to drown the church of England with Lutherans and Calvinists. Naturalized, these dissenters would join the whigs to agitate for the repeal of the Test and Corporation acts (which reserved public office to certified communicants of the established church). The tories further declared that this horde of foreigners would drive down the wages of the poor, drive up the taxes of the rich, and that feeding these refugees had already doubled the price of bread. The tories demanded that the Palatines be shipped overseas immediately.[7]

The suggested destinations were an index of British imperial targets. Some of the Palatines, if transported by the navy and supported by regular troops, might "make new Acquisitions for Great Britain" along the Rio de la Plata and in the Canary Islands, even as others reinforced frontier settlements in North America. The tories preferred to place the Palatines in the sugar plantations. Unlike the continental colonists, the Caribbean sugar producers would never compete with English manufacturers. Sugar profits were invested in England. So the sugar islands "will always be restrain'd both by Interest and Affection, from throwing off their Dependency upon us." Whig cynics observed that the Caribbean climate would kill every migrant who survived the voyage, a "most effectual Repeal of the Act of Naturalization." Daniel Parke proposed to re-populate Nevis and St. Kitts with Palatines (a compliment to his tory xenophobic idea that Cuba could be conquered by equally expendable Scots). This idea was squelched by Sunderland. Instead, Thomas, marquess of Wharton, the whig lord lieutenant of Ireland, took 3,000 Palatines to extend the pale of Protestant settlement. Additionally, hundreds of young Palatine men were drafted into the armed forces. Catholic Palatines recruited the British army in Portugal. Protestant Palatines bolstered Marlborough's forces in Flanders. Particularly unfortunate Palatine peasants were impressed into the navy. Saddest of all, families numbering 600 persons were shipped off to North Carolina, where they were decimated by the Tuscaroras.[8]

As the autumn of 1709 came on, 3,000 Palatines were still encamped outside London. On October 19, Colonel Hunter proposed to a lord of the whig junto, John, lord Somers (or was told by his lordship) that the remaining Palatines should sail to New York. On November 4, Sunderland ordered an Atlantic convoy prepared for 3,000 Palatines. A week later, he wrote the president of the New York council about the impending emigration, promising that the crown would recompense the colony for all costs. On November 29, he referred "Colonel Hunter's" plan for Palatine resettlement to the lords commissioners. On December 5, they replied "that the province of New York being the most advanced Frontier of Your Majesty's plantations on the Continent of America, the Defence and Preservation of that Place is of the Utmost Importance to the Security of all the rest." Their lordships concluded that Palatine settlement on the New York frontier would impede French aggression and prevent Indian "Insurrection." The Palatines could also produce naval stores. Pitch and tar, resin and turpentine from New York would help make the royal navy independent of foreign suppliers and redress the British balance of trade. The workers themselves would widen the American market for English manufactures.[9]

This neat summary of "mercantilism" as a plan of imperial power was particularly whig. It embodied the expansion of American frontier settlement by foreign Protestants to resist France in British North America. Every tenet of the whigs' Palatine project was opposed to tory policy: Canadian, commercial, and Caribbean. The church-state tories feared "to Encourage and Encrease our [continental] Colonies for fear of their making themselves Powerful and Independent." To this the whigs replied that Rome had become "mistress of the greatest Part of the then known World" by continental conquest and colonization. It was as necessary "to recruit the Nation with industrious people, as the Army with Soldiers, or the Navy with Sailors." Because "our Colonies are almost become Desart" from losses in two decades of war with France, they had to be repopulated. The whig ministry ordered Colonel Hunter to settle the 3,000 Palatines in New York. They would constitute the largest single European migration to date in any American colony.[10]

Besides the ideological hostility of the tories, Hunter anticipated innumerable pitfalls in the paths to the Palatine project. Was there was land enough in New York for refugee settlement? If not, his Scots patrons, the Hamiltons, had vast claims in Rhode Island and Connecticut. They would gladly sell out to the crown, enriching themselves, settling the Palatines, and royalizing those two troublesome colonial corporations. Hunter was informed that New Hampshire had more suitable forests than New York for naval stores. Should his appointment to command both New York and New England be revived? If he had to produce naval stores with Palatine peasant labor, Hunter said, he would need a staff, supplies, and presents to pacify the Iroquois (their lands might have to be purchased for the Palatine project and the Iroquoian alliance was essential to defend the Palatine frontier). As one of Marlborough's staff, Hunter had ample experience of the capacity of German peasants to resist authority. So, to the lords commissioners' proposal to make the Palatines free farmers, Hunter rejoined that they should be indentured servants until such time as they had paid off their debt to the crown for the cost of their transportation and settlement. Finally, Hunter said, the Palatine project needed cash. He got £8,000 in advance. He had orders placed in the treasury books for an additional £10,000 per year. Hunter had protected himself against every eventuality save one, a political upheaval that would negate every promise made him by the ministry.[11]

On "Gunpowder Day," November 5, 1709, at St. Paul's, at the invitation of the tory lord mayor and before the City corporation, Henry Sacheverell, doctor of divinity, preached his infamous sermon, "In Perils among False Brethren." By "False Brethren," he meant the present ministry. They championed religious toleration, naturalized foreign Protestants, contended for the right of resistance to tyrannical rulers, and decried "the Divine hereditary Right of Kings." So "the divine doctor" damned all moderates and, of course, every whig, as violators of the tory shibboleth: "the subject's obligation to an Absolute and Unconditional Obedience to the Supreme Power in all things lawful." Indeed, it was the subject's duty to passively obey even unlawful acts. Sacheverell proclaimed "the utter illegality of Resistance upon any pretence whatsoever." The tory firebrand specifically condemned the "odious and insufferable" coup of 1688 that had ousted James II. So, in the minds of most of his auditors, Sacheverell sanctified the succession of the French-sponsored Stuart pretender, the Roman Catholic "James III," and this even though the nation was fighting a war to secure the Protestant succession in the house of Hanover. Sacheverell went on to denounce the revolution settlement's toleration of Protestant dissenters from the church of England. "Moderation and Occasional Conformity," by which dissenters were allowed to take part in public life, was, Sacheverell declared, "the crafty insidious work of . . . wily Volpones," lord treasurer Godolphin especially. Even tory moderates, certainly every whig, were to be fought to the death by all good churchmen. Dead moderates and whigs would assuredly be eternally damned by God.[12]

An outraged ministry defended "Revolution Principles." On December 13, a majority of the house of commons voted Sacheverell's sermon a "malicious, scandalous, and seditious libel." The commons announced their intention to impeach the contumacious clergyman. The reaction was instant. Sacheverell was accompanied to his indictment by hundreds of clergymen. Forty thousand copies of "In Perils among False Brethren" were sold before Christmas. On December 29, the newsletters announced both Sacheverell's indictment by the commons and Hunter's departure for New York with the Palatines. Waiting for a fair wind at Plymouth, Hunter, with the rest of the political nation, followed the trial of Dr. Sacheverell. He was impeached by the commons' managers before the lords on February 27, 1709/10. Westminster Hall was surrounded by the London mob, mad for Sacheverell and the church. The lords finally found Sacheverell guilty, but they barely punished him because he had given a voice to the nation's tory majority, supporters of a church-state. With their moderation and toleration under fire and anathema to Anne, Godolphin and the whig ministers were picked off one by one, beginning with Sunderland. He was dismissed by the queen on the day Hunter landed in New York. There, a miniature of Dr. Sacheverell and a corps of the high tory enemies of the revolution were waiting to oppose that "staunch whig," Colonel Robert Hunter. The governor general understood that the tory program, alike in America and England, was "to have Liberty, Claims of Right, Revolution, Succession, Union, Toleration, all trodden under Foot, Parliamentary Limitation and English Constitution overthrown, Hereditary Right Voted Sacred, and then comes the Pretender." Against the tory extremists, Hunter would defend "the Glorious Revolution."[13]

The tory program was counterrevolution, not just in England but in America. Twenty years after the fact, the colonial coup of 1689 still divided New Yorkers. Supporters of the martyred revolutionaries Jacob Leisler and Jacob Milborne, primarily Dutch dissenters of modest means, had been excluded from power by the wealthy, well-connected members of the established churches, both Dutch and English, allied with the tory governors general, most recently lord Cornbury. Having inherited the earldom of Clarendon, his lordship invoked his new parliamentary privilege to defy his creditors, both public (he had so looted the province that the assembly had resolved never to pass another revenue bill) and private (he owed £8,000 to New York merchants). The earl was so impoverished that Hunter paid for his passage home. Clarendon vowed his undying gratitude, but he devoted the next decade to opposing Hunter's every act. The earl acted against Hunter both in person at Westminster and Lambeth and through his tory partisans, "Lord Cornbury's party," still installed in every agency of government in New York. Clarendon's colonial coadjutor was that ultimate tory, General Francis Nicholson. He had just landed in Boston. His orders were to conquer Nova Scotia, but Nicholson also intended to replace the Scots whig Robert Hunter in the command of New York. From New York, Nicholson had been ousted by the coup against King James. This coup Nicholson still, publicly, deplored. So he remained the cynosure of the provincial tory party.[14]

Against these reactionaries, Governor General Hunter promised moderation in all things. Even that crusty old colonel Robert Quary, the chief customs inspector in America and a member, ex officio, of Hunter's council, responded effusively to his desire for "union and reconciliation": "I may truly say that never any Governor was sent into these parts of the world so very well qualified to answer this great end as His Excellency Colonel Hunter is, his Judgement, Prudence and temper is very extraordinary and sufficient to overcome greater difficulties than he will meet with in composing the differences of these Governments." Hunter himself wrote to Sunderland about New York's divided people that he was "not without hopes of striking order out of their confusion and uniting them for her Matys service and their own good." He did say that he would take some time before he convened an assembly so as to let the conviction that a new regime was in power sink in. Unfortunately, time was not on the side of Hunter's moderate whig intentions. Sunderland had just been dismissed as secretary of state for America as the first step in the tory transformation of the imperial ministry.[15]

Ignorant of the ministerial revolution that would leave him at the mercy of the transatlantic tory party, Hunter hastened upriver to Albany. Half of his garrison occupied this, the furthermost inland outpost of British America. There, as the Covenant Chain treaties specified, the representatives of the crown and the colony took counsel with the New York frontier's primary protectors and chief trading partners, the Iroquois. On August 7, 1710, the governor general conferred with "the four Indian Kings . . . lately Come from Great Britain," with other Iroquois sachems, and with the leaders of the Algonquin refugees from New England, "the River Indians." The Five Nations' sachems complained that their warriors had been reduced by half in their war with France and France's aboriginal allies. Moreover, the Iroquois were impoverished by having lost the hunting season of 1709 as their warriors vainly awaited the expedition from England. At the least, the Iroquois asked, the governor general should order their metal goods repaired at the public cost. Hunter agreed. He also distributed the "present" the duke of Marlborough had ordered from the ordnance: 100 light muskets, 500 bars of lead, 1,000 pounds of gunpowder, 2,500 gun flints. To this Hunter added 240 knives, war paint (and 50 mirrors with which to admire its effect), cloth and blankets by the bale, linen shirts and steel hatchets for every sachem, kettles for their wives, tobacco and pipes for all.[16]

The queen who sent them munitions, Colonel Hunter declared, also commanded the armies that had defeated France in Europe. He explained "how vain & groundless the French boasting has been all along, how our Great Queen's armys have year after year, routed all his forces, taken his Townes, and is at this time near his principle town & seat of Government." As a pledge of the queen's protection and an acknowledgement of their alliance, the governor general presented the senior sachem of each nation with a gold medal (twenty war captains received silver medals). The medals bore queen Anne's likeness on one side. On the reverse was a depiction of the battle of Ramillies, in which Hunter himself had played so significant a role. All warriors in their time, the Iroquoian elders rejoiced "that the Queen of Great Britain has been pleased to appoint a person whose character is not only to be a good man [but] a good Soldier to be Govr over ye Christians and Indians in this Country."[17]

The security of New York depended upon the good faith of heathen Indians. This was the message with which, on September 1, 1710, Hunter opened his first assembly. It reissued the provincial mutiny act. In addition to authorizing discipline of the regular troops in the province on the model of the English statute, the New York law provided for regular watches in the colonial incorporations, taxed their inhabitants for the repair of fortifications, and levied provincial excise taxes to help meet other military costs. Local taxes for local uses could be appropriated and controlled by the provincial assembly without controversy. The constitutional conundrum supposedly central to Hunter's administration occurred because the governor general was bound by the queen's instructions not to allow the regular costs of royal government, including his salary, to be received, issued, and accounted for otherwise than by royal officers. So he was forced to veto the (in any case wholly inadequate) bills offered to support his government because the assembly denied the right of the royal council to amend money bills, the royal receiver to collect taxes, the royal auditor to account to the crown, and the viceroy himself, with the assent of the council, to issue warrants for expenditure. The assemblymen's own pay was assessed on their local constituents, so these legislators had no pecuniary need to support the provincial government. Rather, by extending the session by quarreling with the queen's council and her governor general, the assemblymen made politics "a trade" by which the representatives' per diem pay amounted to "more than most of 'em can get by their ordinary Imployments." In vain Hunter pleaded with the assemblymen for "the common interest" and denounced "parties and piques."[18]

At the close of the session, Francis Harrison, St. John's protégé whom Hunter had appointed attorney general, wrote home: "I wish these stupid Americans were competent judges how great a man the Queen has sent 'em, but they have lived so long under the lash of the Tyrant Cornbury that a governor who shall restore 'em to their just rights and privilges sets the prison gates open to a crew of abandoned rascals." The opposition to Hunter was indeed an incongruous lot. Some were Cornbury tories. Hunter, naively believing in his lordship's protestations of eternal gratitude and himself preoccupied with the Palatines and the Five Nations, had neglected to remove them from office. The sheriffs had influenced the elections in favor of the Cornbury party, infusing the voters with his lordship's promise, or threat, to displace Hunter. Others of Hunter's opponents were simply seditious, "uneasy in their Subjection to the Laws, & Crown of this Monarchy." Then there were the city merchants who fenced the loot of the Madagascar pirates and West Indian privateers based in New York. These dealers in stolen merchandise were hardened lawbreakers themselves. They violated the laws of British trade, opposed all local taxes which would reduce their profits, and resisted every effort to strengthen law enforcement. Some provincial lawyers and politicians abetted the pirate party. Even the speaker of the assembly, so Hunter alleged, was one "who from a Sollicitor and Attorney for the Pyrates and other illegal Traders, has set up for their Protector."[19]

Criminality was supported by ideology. A typical opponent of Hunter pictured himself as "an honest South Brittain, and obedient son of the Church, who is no insinuating hypocrite," that is, not a Scot, not religiously tolerant, and not politically moderate. Hunter's enemies declared that they "were more warm than others for the Church and English Interest," even though they were themselves more often than not Dutchmen and congregants of the Dutch Reformed Church. Nonetheless, they pilloried Hunter as "a Dissenter" and contended that he supported "the Dissenting Interest." They "represented" the governor general "as if he were agt the English and Church Interest . . . because he will not be ridden by those who assume that Distinction."[20]

Hunter responded to the provincial assembly's constitutional aggression and its members' partisanship by invoking the taxing authority of the new "British" parliament. While this resort to the supreme legislature was orthodox whig practice, it was especially congenial to a Scots officer whose own command depended upon the act of parliament which created the union of England with Scotland and so constituted a "British" empire. The parliamentary legislation Hunter proposed would have social as well as political consequences. Parliament's imposition of a quitrent on New York landowners would not only make royal government fiscally independent of the assembly, it might also force New York's feudal landlords to sell arable land to ordinary farmers, producers, and fighters, and part with the pine barrens for naval stores. Hunter went further. He proposed that parliament should make all royal governments fiscally independent of the provincial legislatures by imposing an impost on colonial commerce, an excise on retail liquor sales, and by allocating the tax income to the support of royal officials in America.[21]

A British parliamentary tax on New Yorkers would be just, Hunter wrote, because the queen—that is, the British taxpayer—paid £20,000 annually "in maintaining of Forces and Ships of War, for the defence of their Country and Trade." The heart of these forces was the four independent companies of regular troops in the New York garrison. Two companies were stationed in the citadel of New York as the governor general's bodyguard. Two were based in Albany to defend the northern frontier. The independent companies had been very badly treated in the past but, over the course of his administration, Hunter pensioned off fifty invalids and recruited replacements, lowered the exchange rate on the regulars' pay, eliminated the deductions that supposedly paid for staff officers, and put the artillerymen on an independent establishment. Although there were occasional setbacks when well-connected candidates from England obtained commands in New York, Hunter ultimately secured promotions according to seniority and service for the veteran officers of the garrison. Hunter also continued the tradition, begun by Fletcher, of cadet companies to train future officers. Both of Hunter's sons were cadets, as were the sons of the other regular officers, all of them, and their colonial cohorts, educated for careers in the imperial army.[22]

During Hunter's command, the garrison of New York was better paid, clothed, recruited, and armed than at any other period in its history. So the four companies were able to police, protect, and administer the province on the governor general's orders. The regular officers were Hunter's able and obedient lieutenants, whether they were collecting customs in the port of New York or acting as the lords of the Albany frontier. The two companies housed in New York City's citadel protected and dignified the province's commander in chief. The platoon on guard duty turned out, arms presented and drums beating the general officer's salute, whenever the governor general passed through the gates of Fort Anne. The regulars guarded the government's citadel. It sheltered Colonel Hunter's official residence and lovely gardens, the garrison chapel, the city armory, the public records office, and other executive agencies. Red-coated patrols policed the city, held down its servants and slaves, and promised it protection in a world at war. The Albany companies not only were the agents of the governor general on the Mohawk frontier and the masters of the Dutch town but also, as it happened, were able to put down unrest in the Palatine plantations in the Hudson valley.[23]

Hunter had purchased land on the east side of the river from his fellow Scot Robert Livingston. He had long been the chief supplier of the Albany garrison and so was first in line to provision the Palatines. Across the Hudson, Hunter bought the property of Thomas Fullerton, an officer of her majesty's Scottish customs service who had asked Hunter to dispose of his Hudson River holdings. Hunter had settled the Palatines in two "camps" divided into six villages. Named after the queen, Hunter's wife, and their children, the camps were on either bank of the river. The refugees arrived there too late in the year to plant crops or debark pines, much less to leave logs to settle for a season and then refine them into naval stores. Absent any Palatine production, Hunter began to subsist the refugees on his own credit, at a cost of £10,000 per year. He had been assured by the whig ministers that he would be reimbursed, but they had fallen from power. When Hunter's agent, Micaiah Perry, went to the tory-controlled treasury with Hunter's accounts and letters of credit, he was told that there was no parliamentary appropriation to pay for the Palatine project.[24]

There would never be one, given the adamant opposition of the queen's cousin the earl of Clarendon (formerly lord Cornbury) to a whig enterprise directed by a Scot to settle German religious dissenters on the frontier of a province from which Clarendon had been ignominiously recalled. Clarendon's particular hostility was supported by the universal tory opposition to any further "scandalous missapplication of the Publick money" for the support of Palatines. They were alien enemies, so the tories had it, of the English church, the English constitution, even "the English race." The naturalization act, which the tories blamed for drawing these Germans to England in the first place, was repealed. Marlborough and Sunderland were denounced in parliament for their parts in the Palatine migration. Even Hunter's friend Dr. John Arbuthnot, the queen's physician, now declared that the Palatines were the agents of a whig plot against the hegemony of the church of England.[25]

Clarendon's partisans in New York had provoked the Palatines at every turn, saying that Hunter had enslaved them, that they should refuse to manufacture naval stores, and that they should escape to the Schoharie lands (which Hunter had reclaimed from the tory patentees and restored to the Mohawks). There, the Palatines were told, they could rebuild the village communities they had known in Germany. To counter this agitation, Hunter hurried up the Hudson at the beginning of May 1711. He told the Palatine leaders that they were bound by contract to the queen to produce naval stores. Not only were there neither pines nor transportation at Schoharie, Hunter pointed out, but it was also the beleaguered frontier with New France. The governor general did not have troops enough to protect the Palatines there. If they went to Schoharie, "they must lay their account of labouring there as the Israelites did of old, with a sword in one hand and the axe in the other."[26]

To defend themselves against the French, the Palatines had been organized and armed as militia companies by Colonel Hunter. Now the Palatine militia took up arms to win their way to "the Promis'd Land." No sooner had Hunter left the meeting than the Palatine militia "mutinied." Four hundred armed men, led by that former sergeant of Imperial dragoons "Captain Conrad Weiser" forced the governor general "to abscond." He sent orders to Colonel Mathews, in command at Albany, to ship redcoats downriver to Livingston manor. With a platoon of regulars at his back, Hunter confronted the Palatine militia. They retreated, but they fired a salvo in the air as they went and sent back deputies to reiterate their demands. Overnight, Hunter got an additional 130 regulars down from Albany. In the morning he marched against the Palatine militia, dispersed them, disarmed the four Palatine villages on the east bank and, as night fell, embarked troops to sweep the west bank villages. The next day, the Palatines knelt in submission before the governor general. He revoked their leaders' militia commissions. To govern the Palatines as "the Queen's servants," Hunter constituted a special court chaired by Captain Henry Holland. Holland had been a grenadier officer under General Erle. Now an officer in the Albany garrison, Holland was also sheriff of Albany County. He took command of the platoon of regulars Hunter quartered at Livingston manor to police the Palatines. They would "obey no orders without compulsion." So, for the life of the naval stores project, the Palatines were driven to work in the pine barrens in gangs, guarded by regular troops. Those who fled to Albany were arrested by the garrison commander and punished as runaway servants. For the most part, however, the discipline imposed by Hunter and his troops in the spring of 1711 held into the summer. Then more than 300 of the Palatines "volunteered" to serve in the expedition against Canada.[27]

On June 14, as Hunter was sailing back down the Hudson, he was hailed by a messenger from General Francis Nicholson. The messenger conveyed the queen's orders that Hunter was to support, not command, the new expedition against Canada. Hunter was furious. He recalled that Nicholson, "who if I be not mistaken had never seen Troops in the field in his Life, was sent over hither to Command a Land Expedition here with powers Inconsistent . . . with those in my patent" as governor general of New York and "whilst I was actually a Brigdr in ye Army." Nicholson had one essential qualification. He was the most prominent and devoted champion in America of the church of England and of the tory party. So Hunter was denied the command either of the assault on Montreal, his due as governor general of New York, or of the main attack, on Quebec, which Hunter had sought before he took up his American post. Instead, Hunter complained, "all the Drudgery of Commissary of Provisions for the whole [was] Alloted to my share." He had to find three month's provisions for the 5,000 soldiers sent against Quebec (undersupplied by St. John) as well as to raise, outfit, officer, and supply 2,000 men for the diversionary attempt on Montreal.[28]

Hunter sent messengers upriver to Albany to keep the sachems of the Five Nations in town while they called up their warriors to lead the expedition. Hunter sent orders downriver to New York to close the port and to purchase vast quantities of embargoed rum and rice, wine and fish, livestock and wheat. He sent orders to Colonel Spotswood to requisition hundreds of barrels of Virginia pork. One week later, Hunter himself presided over an intercolonial congress of the chief executives of New England and New York and their military staff. To secure supplies for the troops and to restrict information to the enemy, New York's embargo was everywhere applied. To prevent desertion, Massachusetts' stringent measures were adopted by all of New England, New York, and New Jersey. Every chief executive at the New London congress nominated veterans of the previous expedition to execute their orders. General Hunter added thirty of Marlborough's former sergeants, now lieutenants, and two dozen supernumerary officers, all of whom had come out with Nicholson. So every colonial company had a drillmaster adept in Marlborough's fire discipline (save for Rhode Island's companies, for its governor declined to compromise his troops' notorious independence), and every provincial regiment had at least one British field officer from Marlborough's army. The New London congress also directed the chief engineer, Colonel Redknap, and the chief of scouts, Major Livingston, to take their commissions from General Hunter, Marlborough's legate, the senior officer in this massive mobilization against Canada.[29]

The congress assigned a quota of 800 men to New York and New Jersey in addition to the four independent companies and a hoped-for 800 warriors from the Five Nations. To provide for this force, Hunter recalled the New York assembly. In July, the legislators assigned quotas of men to every city and county, asked the governor general to commission the officers "from Europe" to staff the provincial regiment and to drill every company, appointed commissaries to purchase provisions, offered rewards to volunteers, and levied £10,000 to pay the officers and men "in the present Expedition to Canada." Hunter privately corrected the bills before he signed them, lest the assembly take umbrage at council amendments: "this conduct how unparliamentary so ever (for they will be a Parliament) I was obliged to follow or baulk the Expedition."[30]

Although the would-be parliament of New York subjected every able-bodied man, save clergy, to military service, it reduced royal demands on its constituents by insisting that 150 Long Island Indians be made part of New York's contingent (their services as boatmen were highly valued, but they resisted being recruited by men who called themselves "masters" and the Indians "serfs"). The governor general was also asked to make good on the queen's promise that Palatine emigration would strengthen the province. He drafted 200 of them into one of the New York regiments. Hunter enlisted another 100 Palatines to bring the regular companies up to strength. More than 2,000 soldiers were

newly armed. The shortage of weapons, of which Hunter had complained to
Marlborough as late as May 1711, had been erased. Before the end of July, the
governor general "had the troops levy'd, cloathed, accoutred and victualled
and upon their march for Albany, had ready made 330 batteaus, capable of carrying six men each with their provisions, and had sent round to Boston a sufficient quantity of bread and a very considerable stock of other provisions, the
pork from Virginia not being then arrived, and on the 9th of August went in
company with Lieut. Generall Nicholson to Albany." Brigadier Hunter had
mobilized New York and New Jersey, Connecticut and Rhode Island in just six
weeks.[31]

On August 19, the governor general met the sachems of the Five Nations
at Albany. After their emissaries had reviewed the fleet and army at Boston,
the sachems had called up warriors from every nation to the Albany rendezvous, defying French warnings of fire and destruction if they joined the English expedition. On August 24, the warriors arrived, "a jolly crew, about 800
in number, very likely men," in Hunter's estimation (the sachems' tally sticks
recorded 811 warriors). They were feasted and rearmed. On August 30, the
warriors followed the three regiments under Nicholson's command which had
embarked in the 330 bateaus up the Hudson toward the portage to Wood Creek
and Lake Champlain. Colonel Richard Ingoldsby, the independent company
captain who had been New York's lieutenant governor and who was a brevet
lieutenant colonel, commanded a regiment of 600 men: regulars, Palatines,
and New Jersey volunteers. Colonel Peter Schuyler's regiment of 550 men
combined Dutch New Yorkers with Palatines and Long Island Indian draftees.
Colonel William Whiting's 330 Connecticut men completed the brigade. At
the head of 2,310 men, Lieutenant General Nicholson retraced his 1709 route
up the Hudson and overland to Wood Creek, fortifying base camps as he went.
With his bateaus ready to launch on Lake Champlain and the water route to
Montreal open before him, Nicholson was informed of the pusillanimous flight
of Admiral Walker and General Hill. In the face of the entire army, General
Nicholson tore off his wig and stamped on it, shrieking, "Roguery, treachery!"
"The general is drunk," an Iroquoian warrior remarked. A staff officer assured
him that "the general never drinks strong liquor." "I do not mean that he is
drunk with rum," said the Iroquois, "he was born drunk."[32]

Nicholson abandoned the chain of forts leading back to Albany and sailed
home to help "the Cornbury party" displace General Hunter from the command of New York. "I have gott new Enemys as I hear and should I lose my
old friends I am wretched indeed," Hunter wrote at the end of February 1712.
Hunter had but one request for his correspondent, the earl of Stair: "only pray
take care of my rank in the Army for there's my refuge at last." His seniority was
such that Hunter had assumed brigadier's rank and with it the presidency of the
New London congress in 1711, but a year later, he received a new "List of Genll

Officers and my name left out amongst the Brigdrs." Colonel Hunter had been promised promotion when he took the New York command. He was sure that his military service in New York had earned him his step in rank, "for I have had harder military labours than whilst I campaign'd it in Flanders." Hunter's seniority was unquestionable, for "I have serv'd since the Revolution without interruption." Twenty-four years of distinguished service, from his presence in the princess Anne's bodyguard in her escape from St. James's palace at the revolution to his distinguished labors on the duke of Marlborough's staff in Germany and Flanders, Hunter insisted, manifested the seniority and service that justified his promotion to general's rank in his present command, that of New York. Hunter even suggested that Stair should approach Marlborough's replacement as captain general, the jacobite duke of Ormonde. This desperate and degrading step proved to be unnecessary. Hunter had been commissioned brigadier, together with the other serving colonels of his year, on February 12, 1711.[33]

Having learned that Secretary St. John had not blocked his promotion, General Hunter was accommodating in his reply to the secretary's proposal "of putting all North America under one Uniform plan of Government." This was desirable, Hunter agreed, as frequent civil disorder and colonial refusal to raise adequate taxes demonstrated, but it was insufficient. Merely purchasing private governments would not stop the provincial assemblies from attacking the royal prerogative. Every legislature must be told by the queen that representative government existed in the American provinces only by royal grace and favor. Misuse of the legislative privilege would lead to its withdrawal by the crown. Unless assemblies were disciplined, Hunter wrote, their emulation of the house of commons would be copied by provincial councils. They would claim to be the colonial equivalents of the house of lords. The result would be provincial parliaments, each "a body politick co-ordinate with . . . and consequently independent of ye Great Council of ye realm," the British parliament. The provincials sought to create a federal system of imperial government. In it, coordinate legislatures in Britain and in each province would severally acknowledge (and limit) a common sovereign. In each American jurisdiction, federalism "would bring ye Government from Provincial and dependent, to Nationall and independent."[34]

Hunter here quoted the ur-text of English republicanism, James Harrington's *The Commonwealth of Oceana*. Steele had been correct when, praising Hunter's appointment to New York in the *Tatler*, he wrote that "Eboracensis has read all the schemes which writers have formed of government and order, and been long conversant with men who have the reins in their hands; so that he can very well distinguish between Chemerical and practical politics." The learned governor general's pregnant conclusion was "that ye Colonies were infants sucking their mother's breasts, but . . . would weane themselves when they came of age."[35]

The lords commissioners seconded Hunter's recommendation that the queen formally rebuke the assembly of New York. Its pretensions were both of "a very dangerous consequence to that province, and of very ill example to Her Matys other Governments in America, who are already but too much inclined to assume pretended rights tending to an independency on the Crown." The commissioners also resubmitted to parliament their bill for a parliamentary tax on New York to support the royal executive. They denounced the assembly's claim to unique authority as the sole representatives of the people. They endorsed the governor general's attempt to extend his authority and bypass that of the assembly by erecting a court of chancery with himself as chancellor. Before the next session of the assembly adjourned itself, on November 24, 1711, it condemned the chancery court as "dangerous to the Liberty and Property of the Subject," denied the council any share in legislation, refused to recognize the authority of the queen's letters patent, and demanded control of New York's agent at Whitehall. If the assembly had its way, Hunter observed, the queen's viceroy of New York would be "Suffered only to have the name of Govenr, while others, by their influence both at home and abroad, deprive him of that power which is necessary for retaining these Provinces in due Subjection to the Crown of Great Britain; of which that party at New York are so bold as to Complain for its imposing Governors upon them, Declaring they will never be quiet till they have one of their own Chusing." So it was that most of the assemblymen "have but one short step to make towards what I am unwilling to name." The crown had been lavish with privileges to the infant colonies, Hunter concluded, but "if it is expected that . . . now that they are grown up, [they] should be a help . . . to their parent country, there is an evident necessity of an uniformity of their governments. Upon that alone . . . an uniformity of worship intirely depends."[36]

This last was a sop to the tory Cerberus, the reverend William Vesey, the New York friend, associate, and imitator of Dr. Sacheverell. Originally a New England congregationist, Vesey brought a convert's enthusiasm to both religion and politics. The rector of Trinity Church (he styled himself "Rector of the City of New York"), Vesey was, Hunter wrote, "the most impudent and avowed jacobite . . . known in America." Vesey headed the Cornbury party in New York in the absence of his correspondents and patrons, the earl of Clarendon and General Nicholson. The three tory chiefs had prompted the convocation of the anglican clergy to oppose Hunter as "No Churchman" even before he arrived in New York. Now the tory leaders trumped up addresses to the Society for the Propagation of the Gospel against the governor general, caballed with tory officers in the garrison, and encouraged the assembly majority who, Hunter claimed, "have obstructed all settlement [of] the Revenue in order to starve me out."[37]

Vesey was the most outspoken enemy of that revolution in church and state, personified by Marlborough, of which Hunter was the chief champion in New York. The rector was on record as slighting King William, even while "the deliverer" was still alive. Vesey refused to take the oaths abjuring the pretender. He denounced religious toleration. He opposed the immigration of foreigners. He deplored the education of blacks and Indians (the provincial tories lumped them together as "negroes"). Vesey scorned the new class of merchants and officials. As a "high flying" tory politician, Vesey led a jacobite clergy "in the design to distress the Governor in hopes of having the good Churchman Col. Nicholson appointed." Vesey was personally and publicly so abusive during church services that the governor general retired to the chapel he had refurbished in Fort Anne. There the garrison chaplain, the reverend John Sharpe (who, like Hunter, had been born and raised as a Scots Presbyterian) ministered to the governor general, his garrison, the civil officers, and the liberal citizens, all of whom had been driven from Trinity Church by Vesey's partisan, even unpatriotic, invective. Vesey had omitted from public prayers "the Litany for Victory over Her Majesty's enemies and the prayer appointed to be said in the time of war." That is, the jacobite clergyman refused to pray for victory over the Catholic French and the Stuart pretender. He declared that reconsecration of the chapel in Fort Anne was "the Sin of Schism." All who worshiped there were "Schismatics" who put "the Church in Danger." This was the war cry of the tory party on both sides of the Atlantic, and especially of the earl of Clarendon and his faction in the Society for the Propagation of the Gospel (SPG). They endorsed Vesey's denunciation of Hunter to that quasi-governmental body.[38]

Hunter counterattacked on both fronts, metropolitan and provincial. He wrote (by the hand of his garrison chaplain) to his old comrade the commander of Princess Anne's bodyguard, Henry Compton, the bishop of London, the American diocesan and the head of the SPG; to the archbishop of Canterbury; and to Dean Swift. In New York, Hunter's unfailing civility and constant benefactions, his support of public morality, his observance of the Sabbath, and his advocacy of the Christian education of all children, servants, slaves, even Indians, won over a majority of the clerical convocation when it met in February 1712.[39]

That the clerical decision to conciliate the governor general smacked of self-preservation, in a province at war and a city full of slaves, unmistakably appeared at 2:00 on the morning of April 6. Two dozen slaves, "some provided with fire armes, some with swords and others with knives hatchets," set fire to an outbuilding and ambushed the arriving firefighters, killing nine, wounding five. The gunfire alarmed the guard at the citadel. The governor general "order'd a detachment from the fort under a proper officer to march against" the slaves. They fled into the darkness, but Hunter stationed sentries at every Manhattan dock and landing to prevent any escape from the island. At first light, he ordered out the city and the Westchester militia regiments to search every building and "drive the Island." The only fugitive slaves who escaped capture were the six who killed themselves. The survivors were prosecuted by May Bickley, formerly Cornbury's attorney general, before a special slave court of local justices. They condemned twenty-seven slaves to death, all on the coerced testimony of other slaves. "Twenty-one were executed," the horrified governor general reported, "some were burnt, others hanged, one broke on the wheele, and one hung alive in chains in the town, so that there has been the most exemplary punishment inflicted that could possibly be thought of, and which only this act of assembly [punishing slave conspiracy] could justify."[40]

Revolted, Hunter saved those he could from the social wreckage. He reprieved: a pregnant woman; one Mars (prosecuted through three trials before Bickley could satisfy a political grudge against Mars's master); two men against whom even the justices admitted the evidence was insufficient; and two "Spanish Indians." These men had been taken prisoner by a privateer and, "by reason of their colour which is swarthy," were sold as slaves, "among many others of the same colour and country," rather than being exchanged as prisoners of war. Himself an exchanged prisoner of war, the governor general "sincerely pittyed their condition," but he had not been able to relieve any of them until the New York slave court overreached. As Hunter pointed out, the New Yorkers exceeded the West Indian practice of making only a few examples of alleged conspirators. In New York, Hunter wrote, "more have suffered then were active in this bloody affair." So the governor general asked the queen to confirm his reprieves and pardon the surviving slaves. The prosecution, he wrote, "was a party quarrel & the slaves far'd just as the people stood affected to their masters, more have been executed, in a cruel manner too, then were concern'd in the fact, and I'm afraid some who were no way privy to the conspiracy."[41]

Ever alert to ugly opportunity, the earl of Clarendon exerted himself to reverse Hunter's reprieves, both to conceal the tory rancor behind the prosecution and to discredit the whig governor general. Clarendon's clerical toady, Vesey, wrote the SPG. Supported at Lambeth Palace both by the earl and by General Nicholson, Vesey's address denounced the religious instruction of slave children by Elias Neau (he had the additional liability, in tory eyes, of being a Huguenot). Vesey decried the governor general's admission of both the Huguenot catechist and his African pupils to divine service in the Fort Anne chapel (Vesey had refused to admit them to Trinity Church). Vesey also obtained signatures to a petition against any and all concessions to persons of color by telling signers that they were endorsing a new assembly bill authorizing even more summary trials and yet more sanguinary punishments of slaves. Hunter resisted the tory racists. Eventually, his reprieves were confirmed, Elias Neau was reinstated, and Hunter persuaded the assembly to mitigate what he called the "barbarous" terms of the slave act. For the moment, however, the only positive outcome of the conspiracy of 1712 was the realization by the panicked people of the city of New York that it was the quick and forceful response of the governor general and his garrison that had saved them from their slaves.[42]

Provincial insecurity was amplified by the failure of the 1711 expedition against Canada. The very suburbs of Albany were now ravaged by French-directed Algonquin raiders. The Tuscarora war in North Carolina killed many of the Palatines there, involved the neighboring colonies, north and south, in war, and, Hunter wrote, "is like to embroil us all," because "the five nations by the instigation of the French threaten to join" their Iroquoian kinsmen, the Tuscarora. In such circumstances, the worth of so competent a soldier and executive as General Hunter had proved himself to be was apparent to the assembly. When it met in June 1712, the assemblymen were further inclined toward the governor general by his unsparing hospitality, "the prime test of rank," which he sustained in his most impoverished moments.[43]

Hunter faced a huge debt, £22,000, for the subsistence of the Palatines, incurred before he closed the program down in September 1712. Otherwise, the governor general, for all his whining, was doing rather well. As commander in chief, he contracted for the garrison's subsistence. For this, £7,141 were issued annually from the British treasury to Hunter's agent and remitted in merchandise to the governor general. Given the usual markups (200–500 percent) on English goods in New York, Hunter was able to pay the troops in full and still profit handsomely himself. If the governor general skimmed off 40 percent, or £2,856, he was not unusually rapacious. He also clothed the garrison annually. Profits for this varied from £314 to £1,000. Hunter's takings on the rate of exchange between pounds sterling and New York currency netted him between £800 and £1,000 per year. As captain of an independent company, the governor general received £136 annually. He also received the half pay of his rank as brigadier general, £1 per day. Recruiting allowances (the companies were mustered as if they were at full strength and the "dead pays" for missing men constituted a fund for recruiting) brought in anywhere from £280 to £1,300 per year, although, unlike Clarendon, Hunter did recruit. From military sources alone, therefore, the governor general took in close to £5,000 annually. And he had civil income as well: £500 as governor of New Jersey and at least £1,000 per year from fees, fines, and rents in New York. So the governor general earned more than £6,500 each year from the public. If he took nothing under the table, he was unique in his age. Colonel John Riggs estimated Hunter's income as governor general at £9,000 annually. New York was, Riggs wrote, the American equivalent of Ireland in the hierarchy of British commands: the most prestigious and profitable of governments.[44]

The profits of office, mostly military, made New York's commander in chief entirely independent of the salary which, down to the spring of 1712, the assembly had refused to appropriate on any terms that Hunter's royal instructions would permit him to accept. The contest was essentially symbolic. The assembly expressed "the greatest willingness to make me easy (as their phrase is)," Hunter admitted. The legislators levied and appropriated—and their treasurer issued—funds for frontier forts and garrisons, for the provincial bonus paid to the thirty ex-sergeant drillmasters from Marlborough's army, and for arrears owed to the Suffolk County militia companies, on frontier duty since 1709. The assembly even offered to pay the governor general his back salary. Of this appropriation, however, as well as costs for repairs to the Fort Anne complex and fees for the "the British officers" who held the queen's patents, the assembly claimed control. The assembly and its treasurer were determined to exclude the royal governor, council, and receiver general from any share in the fiscal management of provincial tax receipts. Hunter declared that he was bound in principle to reject the assembly's pretensions lest the queen "reserve nothing but the name of a Government."[45]

It was essential that Hunter appear to the tory ministry to be starving himself, in support of the crown, in a contest with an aggressive, even independence-minded assembly. The cessation of hostilities with France, which Hunter proclaimed in New York in the autumn of 1712, removed the most obvious military rationale for the appointment of a combat-hardened officer, especially one of Marlborough's staff. Hunter's aegis, the former captain general, had been disgraced, displaced, and exiled. There had followed a tory purge of whig officers from every command, "down to the meanest." New York was none of those, but its well-advertised contest between a principled and impoverished governor general and a recalcitrant, even aggressive assembly made it an unattractive post, save for the former governors, who knew what a good thing it really was. Given a ministry rapidly moving to the right, however, the earl of Clarendon had other opportunities than the New York command, both as an official in the house of lords and as a (most unlikely) envoy to Hanover. General Francis Nicholson had opposed concessions to France in America. He could not get the attention of the ministry to obtain an appointment to New York. General Hunter himself was not without tory connections. Swift interposed with the ministry on Hunter's behalf, as Hunter was told by "the good old earl of Mar," the secretary of state for Scotland. Moreover, in the time the lords commissioners for trade and plantations could take from writing the commercial treaties with France and Spain, they declared themselves greatly impressed with General Hunter's dramatic defense of the prerogative during the New York assembly election campaign in the spring of 1713.[46]

Announcing that he was disgusted by the assembly's obvious intent of "leaving the Queen a Power and Authority amongst them hardly equal to that of an Indian Sachem," the governor general had dissolved the legislature. He opened the ensuing election campaign with a pamphlet which compared the New York assembly to the Long Parliament. It had plunged the British Isles into civil war and begun a revolution that cut through "all Laws, human and divine, the Constitution, and at last the precious Life of their Sovereign, of ever blessed Memory." New York voters may have cared little about the sacred memory of the martyred Charles I, but Hunter's effusion read well in London.

There the cult of King Charles the Martyr was at the heart of tory ideology. Warming to his royalist theme, Hunter warned New Yorkers that "Republican Visions" might lead them to "withdraw your Allegience." Provoked, the crown would revoke representative government. He warned the electors not to return to office the men who had "Thrown off all Duty and Respect to Her Majesty!" They had "Attack't Her in Her Royal Prerogatives, and made bold steps toward The Subversion of the Constitution of This Government." Assuredly, the queen would no longer "suffer Her Authority to be Trampled under Foot in the Person of Her Governour."[47]

An exciting election was enjoyed by all. The tories raised the specter of the 1689 revolt: "Leysler and Presbyter Rampant." The whigs inflated the bogeymen of royal and ecclesiastical tyranny: "the Gyant Revenue" and "the three Tall Bishops, and an Army of Tythes, Ecclestical Courts, &c." "Religion" and "Liberty" were the rival slogans. The new assembly convened on May 27, 1713, to hear the viceroy's speech from the throne. He admonished the assemblymen that they were "called together to Settle a Revenue," not "to Settle the Government." That was regulated only by "Her Majesty's letters Patent and Instructions." If, however, the assembly submitted to royal authority and supported the queen's government, the governor general said, he was willing to consider popular bills, most important a general naturalization.[48]

By now, the assemblymen were aware of the lords commissioners' support for a parliamentary tax. They had read their lordships' denunciation of the New York assemblymen's governmental pretensions. The commissioners' wholesale removal of the New Jersey councilors opposed to Hunter and the success of Hunter's plea that the crown "pardon the Condemned Negroes here" squelched the Cornbury faction's contention that Hunter "was disregarded at home, and consequently to be recall'd." That "notion" had chilled "the friends of government whilst others triumphed," Hunter complained. Now, however, the lords commissioners publicly praised the governor general's "very commendable" "endeavours and resolutions to support & Maintain Her Majesty's rights and prerogatives."[49]

Supported at Westminster, the governor general threatened to dissolve the New York assembly again. This dissolution would be followed by "a general alteration in the Commissions of peace and militia, that ill men may no longer use her Majesty's authority against her." General Hunter also proposed "an augmentation of the forces here" to strengthen the government. He threatened that he would recommend that the crown veto a pending New York act for the security of titles to land. All this made the assembly majority accommodating. They immediately granted £2,800 directly to the governor general and, led by the governor general's floor manager, Colonel Lewis Morris, began to discuss a long-term revenue. In the fall 1713 session, the assembly agreed in principle to levy an excise for twenty years with which to pay the government's creditors, the governor general chief among them. All claimants were warned to document their demands by June 1, 1714, for the assembly planned to enact a massive measure that would pay every debt incurred by the government since the coup of 1689 in New York.[50]

On the verge of success in New York, Hunter was again in danger at home. The tories purged the imperial army on the eve of the succession crisis. "Reports [were] industriously spread" that Clarendon would return not just to command New York but that the earl would be commissioned "Vice Roy or Generall Governour of all her Maties plantations in America." A jacobite officer, Christopher Fleming, lord Slane, was actually offered New York. Slane had fought for James II at the revolution, followed him to France, and was attained for treason by the convention parliament. Commissioned regimental colonel and lieutenant general in the army of Louis XIV, Slane only returned to his allegiance when Queen Anne came to the throne. Slane then raised a regiment in Ireland for the campaign in Spain. When his regiment was disbanded at the peace, Slane was offered the command of New York as an equivalent. Put off by Hunter's well-advertised financial troubles, however, Slane accepted an Irish peerage as viscount Longford. Hunter's family friend and military patron the earl of Stair seems to have been involved in this transaction. He now broke a long silence to reassure Hunter that, for the moment, his post was secure.[51]

Confirmed in authority, on March 24, 1714, Hunter opened the assembly which brought the fiscal military state to New York, destroyed the tory party in the province, introduced a whig oligarchy, and inaugurated a generation of political stability. This was very much a compromise settlement. The assembly gave up public resistance to royal fiscal and conciliar legislative prerogatives in return for Hunter's assurances that he would honor informal assembly appropriations. Like most gentleman's agreements, this one "combined the useful appearance of virtue with the solid satisfaction of vice." Publicly, it restored the prerogative power over finance to the provincial constitution. Privately, it (apparently) conceded fiscal control to the provincial assembly. The settlement met long-standing public debts, but it was wholly partisan in its choice of beneficiaries. The governor general and the assembly majority agreed to reward the authors and the defenders of the revolution.[52]

In the spring session of 1714, the representatives passed and the governor general and the royal council approved an act that, without any clauses derogative of the royal prerogative, provided £3,222/1/6 for royal officials' salaries. A separate appropriation paid for the annual tribute to the Five Nations. During the summer recess, a committee chaired by Colonel Morris reviewed the claims received during the previous year. In the fall session, Morris introduced a massive revenue bill. It authorized the issue of £27,680 in provincial bills of credit. These bills were to be gradually retired with the income from a twenty-one-year excise on wine, ship tonnage, European goods, and slaves, that is, a tax on the old-order merchants who were among Hunter's chief opponents.

The choice to tax merchants and trade was also a choice to relieve the farmers and landlords of the Hudson valley where Hunter and his aristocratic associates Morris and Livingston were creating the agrarian basis of a new political order.[53]

The political bias of the new order became clear when the governor general immediately passed and published the act. The son of Jacob Leisler, the martyred leader of the revolution, was to receive £2,025. The tory leader, William Smith, got sixpence. The greatest beneficiary was the governor general himself. Hunter was pledged £4,297 in back salary and almost £4,000 as recompense for his support of the garrison. Robert Livingston was promised £4,000, nominally for victualing the Albany garrison during King William's War but actually for canceling Hunter's debt for the Palatines' provisions. Morris was paid for writing the act. Every member of the council and the assembly received a lulu. The governor general had achieved the ambition of every executive of the age: he had bought the legislature.[54]

The flaw in this fiscal and political consolidation of the revolution in New York was that, as Hunter's instructions required, the act had a suspending clause, staying its operation pending the crown's consent. As soon as the New York revenue statute was brought before the plantations commissioners, the earl of Clarendon objected to the bill both in principle and because he did not benefit personally. He promised that he would be more particular in his protest once he had actually read the law. "Of all men, that noble Lord ought to have been most silent in this case," Hunter rejoined, for it was because of "the misapplications during his administration . . . that we owe a great share of these public debts." The rest of the deficit was incurred because, after witnessing Cornbury's corruption, the assembly had refused to authorize any more taxation. Still, Clarendon's caveat, backed by the London correspondents of the established New York merchants, and the gilt brushed by their agents onto the appropriate bureaucratic palms, held up royal approval of the New York revenue act. Hunter's new, whig, court party of officials and landlords, Leislerian farmers and aspirant merchants (both of whom would benefit from the bills of credit, that is, from inflation), had been checked by the tories, cooperating across the Atlantic.[55]

"The Church Party" in New York (indeed, the tories throughout the middle colonies) took on new life with the return of "that eternal teazer Nicholson" to Boston. The tory general had displaced his longtime colleague Colonel Vetch in the government of Nova Scotia, "saying the Ministry had been posses'd with a Character of him as a Partizan of the Whig Ministry, and were resolv'd to keep none in Publick Posts but were intirely in their Interest, And since it was to be given away, he believed he had as good a pretence as any other Person." Nicholson did not reside in Nova Scotia, however, preferring to mulct its garrison from the comfort of Boston. There he repeated his intention "to serve the Pretenders & French Interest." Boston was so much the least likely place to plant royalist, Catholic, and Francophile sentiments that it was reported that the tory ministry intended to use Nicholson's "Madness & Indiscretion" to incite the New Englanders "to committ some Irregularities as might prove a handle to forfeit their Charters."[56]

Nicholson's mischief making was not confined to Nova Scotia and New England. He was commissioned to audit all military expenditure in North America since the queen's accession, to dispose of all military surplus, and to review the accounts of everything he and the tory ministry could imagine might cause trouble to Marlborough's legates in America: the finances and faculty of the College of William and Mary in Virginia; the border disputes between Virginia and North Carolina and between Maryland and Pennsylvania; the Palatine project, customs service, and prize good collections in New York; the Newfoundland fisheries (where Nicholson was authorized to displace the fishing admirals and the convoy commanders in the government). Nicholson was also commissioned to negotiate all questions of trade and settlement.[57]

Arriving in Boston, Nicholson published tory pamphlets (in editions of up to 3,000) to counter what he called the "traiterous, factious" whig alarms about the imperial succession. Yet he told Vetch that the ministry intended to give Nova Scotia and Acadia back to the French as part of the peace settlement. Nicholson told Hunter that he was sending agents to New York to investigate the clothing and deployment of the garrison, the sale of the 1711 expedition's surplus, relations with the Five Nations, and Hunter's alleged disrespect for the tory frontier baron Colonel Schuyler. He demanded that Hunter purchase the Quebec expedition uniforms for which he, Bolingbroke, and Arthur Moore (now on the plantations commission) had so corruptly contracted in 1711. Hunter did so, although he had just reclothed the garrison and knew that if he actually issued Nicholson's unlined, flimsy, and partial outfits, those of the garrison who did not mutiny or desert would freeze. He would put these "scurvy rags" in store for Palatine work clothes, Hunter said, but he did not dare refuse an order to purchase shoddy stuff that had profited Henry St. John, viscount Bolingbroke, and his partners, Nicholson included, more than £20,000. Given Bolingbroke's support and the queen's commission of investigation, Nicholson was "now stiled the Governour of Governours and all obedience and dependence transferr'd to him."[58]

Perhaps even more menacing to Hunter's authority than Nicholson's commissions from the queen was his commission "of spiritual inspection" from the SPG, a charge, endorsed by the tory ministry, that Nicholson invigorate the church of England in America. This authorization was the first fruit of the accession of an old enemy of Hunter, and an old ally of Bolingbroke, Dr. John Robinson, to the see of London and so to the chair of the SPG. Its high tory faction was headed by Clarendon. These churchmen squelched Hunter's chancery case against Trinity Church for the back rents of its landed endowment, "the King's Farm." They allowed New York clergy direct appeals to the crown from the judgments of New York courts without passing their appeals through the highest provincial court, the governor general in council.[59]

Taking advantage of Nicholson's personal proximity and ecclesiastical influence, the rector of Trinity, William Vesey, complained in print, petitions, and finally in person to the SPG that Governor General Hunter was "no Friend of the Church." Hunter's most recent offense, Vesey declared, was his apparent lack of concern about the dreadful defilement of vestments in Trinity Church. Sacrilegious vandals had smeared "odure" on chasubles, stoles, and robes. Vesey insisted that the governor general, although he was absent in Burlington, New Jersey, on the business of his government there, must have been responsible. The reverend Mr. Vesey planned a base revenge. He "proposed to send word to lady Hay [Elizabeth Orby, lady Hay, Hunter's wife] that his Excellency our Governour had to do with Lieut. Rigs wife," and so cause lady Hay to miscarry. In reply, Hunter eschewed scandal but he denounced those who conformed to the church "for filthy lucre" and who, "by their disloyal and seditious conduct showed their aversion to the established constitution in church and state."[60]

To these swipes at Vesey, the convert from congregationalism, rich rector, and jacobite, Hunter added dozens of darts in his *Androboros: A Biographical Farce in Three Acts*, the first stage play written, published, and perhaps performed in British America. Hunter combined his Augustan wit with Colonel Morris's inside information about the opposition assemblymen to produce a play in which Vesey's principal, the high church tory champion General Nicholson, took center stage as "Androboros, or the Man-Eater." He "is now very far gone indeed. He talks of nothing but battles and Sieges, tho' he never saw one, and Conquests over Nations and alliances with Princes who never had a being."

As the play opens, the "Senate" of New York is gathered in their madhouse to honor Androboros. He arrives accompanied by "Two Men in Black," "Fizle" (Vesey), who aspires "to be Patriarch of the Western Empire, of which Androboros is to be Sultan," and "Flip" (Adolph Philipse), the opposition councilor and assembly treasurer who, "for a wonderful Energy in the two most Unruly Members of the Body, has been followed of late by the Women and Boys, but a late sinistrous Accident has Crack't his Voice, and so that now he is but little regarded."

Escorted by the men in black, Androboros boasts to the assembled madmen of his triumphant negotiations with the Four Indian Kings, they of the unintelligible names, demands the senators' support for his pretensions to the sultanate and, as the personification of a less polite age, swears "not to pare these Nails, wash this blew visage, or put off this speckled Shirt" until Louis XIV admits himself "in all his Projects for universal Dominion" Androboros's "Inferior and My Delyma [Belinda Burwell] fairer than the fairest Princess."

Each of the senate's boorish, factious, and captious leaders are pilloried in turn and their republican aspirations and undisciplined proceedings mocked.

Then the mad senators declare their entire support for all of Androboros's claims. They resolve to send "secret Representations and Remonstrances" against the keeper of their lunatic asylum to "my Lord Oinoborous, he being a Devotee of Long Robes of both Genders." That bisexual bashaw lord Clarendon, aka "Oinoborous," will "improve" these slanders to ruin "the Keeper," Governor General Hunter.[61]

Androboros then resumes the stage to report that he has abandoned his expedition against Canada, the French having amiably agreed to unite the Catholic religion with that of England and to divide the commerce of the world between Britain and France, "generously resigning and yielding to us that of the two Poles." The French also promise to give up those forts that they could not hold (in Nova Scotia) as soon as they build replacements (at Cape Breton). Androboros, "(tho it is well known that I hate Boasting)," modestly admits that this "Treaty Litteral and Spiritual" with France was "obtain'd, in a good measure, by the Terror of my Names and Arms."

New York audiences were told that the blowhard Androboros was so unbearable in England that "to get rid of his Noise and Trouble," the ministry "cloth'd him with Sham-Powers" of military and spiritual inspection. Only the death of the Keeper is required for a tory triumph. Androboros, Flip, and Fizle plan to kill him via a secret trap door, but they fall headlong into their own device. A New York grand jury rejoiced that "those who digged the pit . . . are themselves fallen in," evidence that "the general, the clergy and the assembly were so humourously exposed that the laugh was turned upon them in all companies and from this laughing humour, the people began to be in good humour with their Governour and to despise the idol of the Clergy." Vesey fled to Boston to consult with Nicholson. Then he took ship to England to "cry out fire & church" but, as Hunter observed, Vesey had "missed his market."[62]

The libertarian heritage of "the Glorious Revolution," the consequence of the 1688 coup in England, had been in the deepest danger at home. The crisis of the Protestant succession had begun with Queen Anne's near-fatal illness at Christmas 1713. The troops Hunter had asked for in New York were held at home to meet the emergency. Many of the army's remaining whig officers were purged, reducing the military capacity either to resist a jacobite invasion from France or support another coup by Marlborough. The duke, in exile in the Netherlands, was planning to use the army to secure the succession, for the fifth time since 1649. Joined by Cadogan as his chief of staff, Marlborough had tried to persuade the allies to invade England in order to forestall the tory peace with France and to impose the Protestant succession on the British empire. The duke proposed coups in the garrisons and the dissolution of the field army in England, on his model from 1688. General James Stanhope was Marlborough's chief military operative in England. The earl of Sunderland managed the political organization. In Scotland, the earl of Stair was to lead a Hanoverian putsch.[63]

When the allies refused to invade England, Marlborough prepared to obtain the troops necessary to secure the Protestant succession by taking control of the British garrisons at Bruges, Ghent, Nieuport, and Dunkirk. These depots were also targeted by the tory generals. Jack Hill, in command at Dunkirk, offered the port to France for the embarkation of French troops to invade England. These invaders were to support the jacobite field commander, the duke of Ormonde. So the pretender was to be placed on the imperial throne of Great Britain by French force and Stuart soldiers. The results of both the revolution of 1688 and the War of the Spanish and English Successions would be reversed. The Dunkirk garrison thwarted Hill's traitorous intentions, however, and all the British troops in Europe bitterly resented their disgraceful withdrawal from the allied army in the face of the French enemy. The redcoats also hated the peace treaty, which gave up many of their conquests and all of their aspirations for the defeat of France. They were loyal to Marlborough, their "Corporal John." So it was easy for Armstrong and Kane to win over all the British garrisons in the Low Countries. Twelve battalions pledged to accompany Marlborough back to England. To lead the army in the succession crisis, the elector of Hanover, the Protestant and parliamentary heir, commissioned Marlborough as commander in chief of the British army, effective at Queen Anne's death.[64]

The prime minister, the earl of Oxford, was so alarmed by Marlborough's machinations that he advanced £10,000 to the Blenheim building fund, assured the duke that he would not face impeachment if he returned to England, and promised Marlborough that the electoral prince, afterward George II, would be called to take a seat in the lords, helping to ensure the Hanoverian succession. Marlborough published that promise. So he destroyed Oxford's favor with the queen. Anne would tolerate no successor in the kingdom during her lifetime. Bolingbroke came to power. He promised to have Marlborough restored to all his commands, to shunt Ormonde off to command Ireland, and to reassure Hanover about the succession. In midsummer 1714, on the eve of her final illness, Queen Anne herself appears to have asked Marlborough to form a new ministry.[65]

Marlborough landed at Dover on the day of the queen's death, August 1, 1714. He was received rapturously by the London mob. He was briefed by Stanhope on the military preparations in the metropolis to protect the Protestant succession. These included an armed association of half-pay whig officers, clandestine regiments of the rank and file (whose badge was a miniature musket), a Huguenot officer rally, and the subversion of the Guards. Marlborough worked quickly to undo the tory purges which, the duke declared, had "turned officers out of the army after having fought so long in the glorious cause of liberty, some for talking, some for thinking, and wretches put into their place that never serv'd." So Marlborough secured King George's landing at Greenwich on September 18. "My lord duke, I hope your troubles are now all over," said the new monarch. His first private interview was an hour spent with Marlborough. Then the king signed his first royal warrant. It restored the duke as captain general, master general of the ordnance, and colonel of the First Guards.[66]

With Marlborough's restoration, the captain general's American legates were "reprieved." Thanking the earl of Stair for the news that his trial by tories was over, Brigadier Hunter wrote, "I hope the Duke of Marlborough has not forgott me; I have been his faithful servant in all stations of life, and you see I have ye honour to be his fellow sufferer. Pray assure him of my lasting gratitude and devotion, and tell him, if you please, that I am as able to carry a muskett as I was ten years agoe." Yet the security of the imperial capital itself was still uncertain. Every state office was suddenly transformed from tory to whig. Distant commanders were neglected. If Hunter had not accidentally received, via the West Indies, a stray copy of the official *London Gazette* "containing the King's Proclamation for the Continuation of Officers . . . much confusion" might have resulted. As it was, on October 18, 1714, the governor general proclaimed the new monarch to the king's garrison and to his subjects in New York. "Some awkward half huzzas there were," Hunter admitted, and he expected "more trouble" from jacobite diehards once the cheering died away, but not from General Nicholson. He had decamped from Boston and sailed home when his commissions lapsed with the queen's death. "I am pretty easy as to him," Hunter wrote, "for the present folks have no manner of occasion for madmen."[67]

As the spring of 1715 came on, Hunter had yet to receive commission or instructions from the new monarch. Nonetheless, he had "seen so many honest men's names in publish'd lists" that Hunter was sure that his patrons, political and military, would obtain his reappointment. To help his cause along, Hunter sent home one loyal address after another to the new monarch. All reflected "on the fatal consequences which must have attended the success of a Pretender." All deplored the Cornbury-Clarendon regime and the Nicholson misadventures. All praised "the auspicious conduct of Brigadier Hunter . . . who by administration and example has daily inculcated . . . affection to your Majesty's person and Royal progeny. And it was from him we long since learned that the liberties of Great Britain, the Protestant Succession, and the Protestant Religion, howsoever divided or distinguish'd by factious and turbulent spirits must stand or fall together, etc. etc."[68]

On January 25, 1715, despite all that the earl of Clarendon, the merchants' agent Charles Lodwick, the reverend William Vesey, and the bishop of London could do (they especially urged Hunter's pardon of the slaves against him), the secretary of state, General James Stanhope, conveyed the king's commands to the new commissioners of trade and plantations to prepare Brigadier Hunter's commission to command New York and New Jersey. The lords commissioners also dismissed Clarendon and company's objections to the pending New York revenue act and recommended that Hunter be recompensed for his Palatine expenses. So it was that, on May 3, 1715, Brigadier Hunter announced to a new assembly that "notwithstanding the malicious and unjust accusations of some men altogether strangers to me and my conduct" that his administration was "arbitrary, illegal, grievous, oppressive, unjust and destructive," the new king had been pleased to renew Hunter's commission.[69]

Hunter was sure that the assembly would reject criticisms of his government because, following the dissolution of the previous assembly mandated by the death of Queen Anne, he had exercised the royal prerogative of redistricting. Hunter had added three seats in the Hudson and Mohawk regions. The electors in the garrisoned frontier towns of Albany and Schenectady and cooperative manor lords and Leislerian farmers in the valleys voted for Hunter's supporters. These upcountry additions reduced the relative weight of representatives from the New England republican counties of Long Island. "Citizens," they called themselves, not "Subjects." Their tribune was Samuel Mulford. He had published the speech he had made in the previous assembly attacking the governor general's alleged oppression of Long Islanders. The new assembly expelled him for sedition. The tory opposition had its heart in the city. So the governor general copied his predecessors. He enfranchised his garrison. Two hundred soldiers not only voted for Hunter's candidates, they also drove his opponents from the polls.[70]

The capture of all four city seats by the whigs, added to three additional upcountry representatives, gave Hunter's prime minister, Colonel Morris, a solid majority. The new assembly duly passed a five-year grant of support for the royal executive, authorized a "present" for the "wavering" Five Nations and, in a measure they came to regret, shifted payment of their session salaries from county levies to the provincial revenues. In return, the governor general passed a general act of naturalization. At last, fifty-one years after the conquest of New York by the English, and twenty-six years after the revolution for which they were primarily responsible, the Dutch majority (and the refugee Huguenots and Palatines) were made subjects with all "the rights of Englishmen." Concentrated in the city and in the Hudson-Mohawk valley, these newly naturalized subjects, their property rights at last secure, could no longer be intimidated by their and the governor general's "English" opponents.[71]

Both the revenue and the naturalization acts were contentious. Hunter admitted as much to the lords commissioners. The revenue act authorized bills of credit. So it inflated the currency and outraged the established merchants. Their profits were cut and new men now entered the market, financed by paper money. There were constitutional objections as well. The new bills of credit were to be issued by the assembly's treasurer, not by the crown's receiver general. The naturalization act impinged on the royal prerogative of denization and on the parliamentary power of naturalization. Hunter apologized and explained: "If I have done amiss I am sorry for it, but I hope I have now laid a foundation for a lasting settlement in this hitherto unsettled and ungovernable Province." Indeed, the province had been pacified, the revolution defended, and a new class of military clients, economic entrepreneurs, and (mostly Scots) officials had been recruited by the governor general to man the agencies of the fiscal-military state in New York. So the friends of the old order rallied to oppose royal ratification of the acts of revenue and naturalization. In New York, the tories took control of a grand jury which denounced the naturalization act as inimical to the established church. This indictment and mercantile arguments against the New York revenue act as a restraint of English trade were printed in London and placed in every coffeehouse in the City.[72]

The lords commissioners of trade and plantations would have none of this. As whigs, they had long ago dismissed the tory arguments against naturalization as bigoted and xenophobic. The commissioners noted that the naturalization act needed some technical corrections, but they promised to hold it on the table until Hunter could obtain these changes from the assembly. Then they would recommend royal approval. The lords commissioners took the occasion to advise the bishop of London to instruct Vesey (whom Bishop Robinson had just appointed as his commissary in New York) to submit to the governor general. As for the revenue act, the lords commissioners observed that the protesting merchants were as "misinformed on these matters" of economics "as they were on other," that is, political and religious, issues. Their lordships agreed to recommend the revenue act to the crown, again given some explanatory clauses.[73]

Approval of the New York legislation was delayed by "the rebellion & disorders that have been here of late." The earl of Stair, now the British ambassador in Paris, had reported that jacobite risings, with French complicity, were to be expected in Scotland, in the border counties of the north and west of England, and perhaps even in towns and cities of the south and west. The duke of Marlborough accelerated his preparations to defend the new regime. The captain general had already begun to purge recently commissioned tory officers from the Guards. In their places, Marlborough restored officers "who had lost their Commissions for their affection to his Grace, and their Zeal for the Protestant Succession." The Guards were the keys to the kingdom, so it was a most unfortunate moment for a clothing scandal. Marching to change the guard at the Tower, the rank and file of the First Foot Guards threw their shoddy "Hanover shirts" into Marlborough's garden. Everyone involved, from the duke down to the tailor, denied that he was at fault. Nonetheless, as colonel of the First Foot Guards, Marlborough made a personal apology on parade (he lubricated it with a barrel of beer per company), but he took advantage of the outbreak of "the '15" to purge the Guards' ranks of the agitators in the clothing incident. "Irish papists," they were labeled. Three of them were tried for treason and publicly hanged, drawn, and quartered. The centrality of the Guards, "on whom alone his Majesty must depend" for the security of the imperial capital, became apparent to all in July when Marlborough ordered them out of their barracks to encamp in Hyde Park and to patrol the city. The fall in the crime rate was much applauded, and "Hanover rats" were no longer assaulted in the streets.[74]

The tory officers in command of garrison towns and the leading tory regimental colonels were either cashiered or ordered to sell out to politically reliable veterans. Marlborough also had the officer corps of every regiment recruited to full strength from half-pay officers avowedly enthusiastic for the Protestant succession. All leave was canceled as of July 22, 1715. The garrisons of port towns—Southampton, Plymouth, Bristol—were reinforced by the captain general's orders. Both tory Bath and Oxford, the ideological heart of the church party, were occupied by military police. In the northeast, a new post at Newcastle protected London's coal supply. Munitions were stockpiled at the Berwick fortress for the inevitable expedition north into Scotland. At the western terminus of the old Roman wall, Brigadier Stanwix held Carlisle castle for the new king and filled the castle dungeons with the Catholic gentry of Cumberland and Westmoreland.[75]

To hold down England and reduce Scotland, the 8,000 troops actually on foot in Great Britain (about half the establishment) were utterly inadequate. Parliament authorized a fourfold increase in the army. Marlborough used the existing regiments as cadres. He ordered every company of the Guards increased from forty to seventy rank and file, every line regiment's companies expanded from forty to fifty men, and the number of companies in each regiment raised from ten to twelve. Ten veteran battalions were brought back from the Netherlands garrisons. Thirteen came over from the army of occupation in Ireland. Twenty-one new battalions were raised. They were disproportionately dragoons, that is, mounted police. The case of the earl of Stair was typical of Marlborough's avarice being overcome by necessity. The duke offered the earl a regiment of dragoons (to replace the Scots Greys, which Stair had lost to the tories' military purge) for a payment of several thousand pounds. He ended up by seeing that Stair got it gratis. All told, the troops on foot in Great Britain were multiplied from 8,000 to 33,000. Not all these troops were politically reliable, especially where Scotland was concerned (by now, both battalions of Orkney's Royal Scots were notoriously jacobite). Many of the regiments were newly raised. So Marlborough sent Cadogan to the Netherlands to renegotiate the treaty of the (Netherlands fortress) barrier and the (British Protestant) succession, whereby the Dutch were committed to send over 6,000 veterans to support the Protestant succession (shades of 1688!).[76]

In the meantime, Marlborough relied upon Stanhope and his Peninsular War veteran generals—Carpenter, Wills, and Wade—to put down jacobite outbreaks in the north and west of England. Carpenter's dragoons, including Stair's new regiment, pursued the rebels from Northumberland to Lancaster.

Then, just as Marlborough had predicted, the English jacobites were brought to bay at Preston, together with their Scots reinforcements. At the critical moment, General Wills arrived with four English regiments from Ireland. The royal forces invested Preston. On November 14, they forced the unconditional surrender of 1,500 rebels, the only jacobite field force in England.[77]

Like generations of rebels before them, hundreds of the Preston prisoners were transported to servitude in America. The names of 638 survive. The largest numbers were bound for the Chesapeake (they elevated the jacobite temperature in Maryland) and Jamaica. Odd lots were shipped to Barbados, the Leeward Islands, Massachusetts, and New York. Amongst the Scots nobles taken at Preston was James Alexander, whose son was to claim the earldom of Stirling. Secretary Stanhope sent Alexander to New York, where his family's interest was coeval with colonization. Alexander carried a letter of recommendation (probably solicited by the duke of Argyll) from Secretary Stanhope to Governor General Hunter. Alexander hardly needed the secretary of state's chit, for Hunter knew his family personally. The governor general immediately found Alexander a government post in New Jersey, sponsored his legal education in New York, and set the young Scot on the path of preferment that led him to preeminence in the provincial bar (Alexander would be Peter Zenger's counsel), a seat on the council, and a family life which, as was suitable for a rebel against the Hanoverian dynasty, produced a general for George Washington.[78]

Governor General Hunter staffed his cultural and political cadre with Scots who had "left their country for their country's good." "After a liberal education at schools and Colleges in Scotland," Hunter testified, David Jamison had been transported to New York following a hearing before the duke of York (but without trial) as a religious dissident. Defending his nomination of Jamison to the council, Hunter declared him to be "the greatest man I ever knew" in America. The province's leading lawyer, Jamison had written the church of England into the laws of New York (like Hunter, and so many other acculturated Scots, Jamison had not just joined the established church, he had become a lay leader). Hunter observed that if Scots political and religious offenders had been prohibited from public office, especially since the revolution, the empire would have been poorly served. Despite allegations of Cadwallader Colden's complicity in the '15, Hunter brought the young Scots savant to New York and introduced him to the elders of the Five Nations, whose first and greatest historian he would become. As his last act in office, the governor general had Colden promoted surveyor general of the province. So began the career that put Colden in command of New York forty years later. Of course, the xenophobic "English Party," New York's tories, were outraged by Hunter's patronage of "all the North Britons that can be found, though never so scandalous," but these Scots mediated Enlightenment culture to their fellow provincials and the "North Britons" manned a brilliant bureaucracy. It facilitated the imposition of the fiscal-military regime on New York and so transformed a crude and quarrelsome colony into a leading province of the British empire. Shaped by Scots imperialists, New York became "the empire state" of a new nation.[79]

Colonel Alexander Hamilton, writing as "Publius," declared that modern war had origins in female foibles. The "petulance" of the duchess of Marlborough was only matched in importance, Publius wrote, by the "bigotry" of Maintenon and the "cabals" of Pompadour. Larger, "popular," causes of conflict Publius saw in "the antipathies of the English against the French." Such popular hatreds served "the ambition or rather the avarice, of a favorite leader." Publius's example was the duke of Marlborough. Egotism, nationalism, and ambition had recently resulted in unexampled conflict, Publius asserted, because the influx of American specie had multiplied the money supply, "the arts of industry" had advanced apace, and, coordinated by the new "science of finance," cash and manufactures had underpinned "an entire revolution in the system of war," the development of "disciplined armies." Modern finance and force could only be managed in postwar America, Publius concluded, by "the federal authority of a confederate republic," an authority defined by the new constitution whose ratification he advocated, here in *The Federalist* #6–9. Both these essays and that document embodied the lessons which Colonel Hamilton, like other Scots New Yorkers, and the military elite of the new nation, had learned from Marlborough's wars.

On November 13, 1715, one day before the rebels surrendered at Preston, the jacobite cause was defeated in Scotland. There the earl of Mar, whom Marlborough in exile had denounced as the pretender's best friend in the northern kingdom and who had lost his Scots secretaryship when Marlborough was restored, had raised the standard of James III and VII at the Braes of Mar on September 8. With 9,000 swordsmen, Mar advanced on Stirling, the gate of the Highlands. There the duke of Argyll, commanding for King George, had only 3,500 men. On November 13, the two armies fought a drawn battle on the plain of Sheriffmuir. Argyll's cavalry right wing scattered Mar's left. The Highlanders on Mar's right broke the infantry of Argyll's left wing (including the luckless 11th Regiment, recently decimated during the Quebec expedition). Both sides claimed victory, but Argyll's army encamped on the battlefield, held Stirling, and barred the rebels from the lowlands. Further discouraged by the news that Louis XIV had died on September 16 (eliminating any real possibility of formal French involvement), Mar's men took no action until the pretender, James Francis Edward (Stuart), arrived on December 22 and was enthroned at Scone.[80]

Nothing Marlborough could write would persuade Argyll to advance against the Highlanders in winter with regular troops, no matter if they "were used to victory for so many years" under the captain general. So Marlborough sent Cadogan, who had returned with the Dutch battalions from the

Netherlands, to clear the snow-clogged roads from Berwick and bring up the artillery and supplies the master general had stockpiled there. On January 29, 1716, over Argyll's objections, the army advanced through the snow against the rebel headquarters at Perth. On February 4, the pretender, the earl of Mar, and their leading supporters all fled to France. Now that the war was won, Argyll's clansmen turned out and plundered in advance of Cadogan's disciplined and resentful regulars. Argyll was recalled. In April, Cadogan pronounced the rebellion at an end. Marlborough arranged his chief of staff's elevation to the peerage. Argyll was dismissed from all his offices.[81]

In May and November 1716, exhausted by the succession crisis and the rebellion and prostrated by the death of his favorite daughter, Anne, countess of Sunderland, the duke of Marlborough suffered successive strokes. The king retained Marlborough in command for five more years, in part to deny the post to his heir, the prince of Wales, and in part because Cadogan was fully able to administer the army. Marlborough abandoned administrative duties. He appeared in public only in the house of lords. There he pursued the impeachment and ostracism of the tory ministers who had driven him from office and into exile, who had disgraced his army in the face of the allies, who had made a peace that left France powerful in Europe and America, and who had endangered the revolution settlement in church and state.[82]

As Marlborough's vindictiveness demonstrated, the rebellion was over but the repression continued. The whig parliament, elected in the spring of 1715 on an anti-jacobite, anti-French, anti-Catholic platform, had responded to the rebellion by reducing English liberty. Habeas corpus was suspended. Arbitrary arrest and imprisonment were authorized. The English law of treason was applied to Scotland. To prevent electoral reaction—for the Hanoverian regime was desperately unpopular and the whigs still very much a minority party—the triennial act, because it mandated a new election in 1718, was repealed. Instead a seven-year term given to the present, whig, parliament. The defense of revolution principles had produced a whig oligarchy, defensive, oppressive, and convinced that any challenge to parliamentary authority was treason.[83]

In New York, that good whig Brigadier Hunter also used the defense of "Revolution Principles" to impose oligarchy. He excluded from office every public figure who refused to sign an association that denounced the pretender, endorsed the Protestant succession, and pledged allegiance to King George. Hunter then turned to the courts. He had a grand jury indict Thomas Clarke, the "English Party" leader, for declaring that King William had been a mere Dutchman who had no property and hence no rights in England (the parallel with that king's compatriots in New York and tory criticism of their naturalization could not be mistaken). Clarke also had offended Hunter by observing that Scots now monopolized imperial appointments and by demanding that they be replaced by Englishmen.[84]

Directed by the governor general, the grand jury indicted the reverend William Vesey for defaming the Dutch Reformed and French Huguenot congregations in New York, exciting ethnic tensions, and disturbing the public peace. Separate indictments were brought against Vesey for simony and sedition. His salary was stopped by a reformed Trinity vestry. Vesey had returned to New York, "in Triumph like his friend Sacheverell." Vesey had announced that his appointment as commissary of the new bishop of London was evidence that Hunter would be ousted. Vesey's prosecution in New York, however, and the lords commissioners' admonitions to the bishop of London to rein in his seditious subordinate, meant that by the spring of 1716, Hunter could report that "the Commissary here is the humblest Clergyman and warmest whig all of a sudden," a veritable vicar of Bray. The church of England in New York and New Jersey, like its mother church in England, settled into decades of subservience to civil authority. The ideological heart of the old English tory order in church and state had been stilled.[85]

When the governor general reopened the New York assembly on June 5, 1716, political stability and military security were his themes. He rejoiced in the repression of the rebellion in Britain and exalted the loyalty of New York: "his Majesty in the wide extent of his Dominions, has not a Province where fewer took a Squint at his Rightous Title and his Rightous Cause." Now that political danger was past, the governor general declared to the New Yorkers that "Your future Security is all my Aim." The brigadier denounced the recent "Insidious" treaties of peace and commerce at Utrecht. They were, he said, dictated by the French, "whom I can hardly forbear to call still Our Enemies." Bolingbroke's concessions to France in America meant that aggression impended from the new French bases: northeast at Cape Breton; southwest along the Mississippi; northwest at Detroit. Most menacing of all were the old Canadian strongholds due north along the St. Lawrence. To bolster New York's defenses, immediate repairs were required to the city citadel, "which I take to be not only the Security of this Province, but in a great measure that of this Continent," and to the fort at Albany, on which "Depends intirely the Safety of your Frontiers and Remote Settlements." Both repairs could be afforded now that "the Burdensome Expense of the Fruitless Expeditions" was over. Finally, the governor general hinted once again at the final act in his defense of the revolution: the recognition of public debts owed to its most humble champions, a measure that, Hunter said, would call down on the assembly "the Blessing of many Suffering Families."[86]

In two sessions in 1716, the assembly, "the best I have seen here," Hunter wrote, responded to his agenda. They repassed New York's mutiny act. They raised money to repair the fortifications at either end of the Hudson, and to build barracks for the Iroquois at Albany. The legislators agreed to the sachems' request that liquor sales to Indians be outlawed, lest their civil society break down entirely. The legislators raised a new excise on "Negroes and other

Slaves Imported" which, if it did not check the slave trade, did recompense the governor general for lobbying for royal confirmation of the revenue and naturalization bills with the help of a new agent at court. Until news of the royal confirmation of the pending revenue and naturalization statutes arrived, however, the assembly was at something of a stand, and the governor general himself was so crippled by illness and grief that, for a time, he could not act.[87]

Hunter had come down with rheumatism during the winter, the result of a childhood in Scotland and sixteen cold, wet military campaigns. Then, on August 9, 1716, while he was recuperating at his house in Burlington, his wife suddenly died. She left "His Excellency Brigadier Hunter our Governour the most afflicted man alive." After Hunter buried lady Hay in the chapel in Fort George, his thoughts turned to home, his children's inheritance there, and a long soak at Bath. Transportation could not be arranged before the onset of winter in 1716, however, and by February 1717, Hunter believed that the political situation in his provinces was so promising that he postponed his leave for a year. In the interval, the governor general hoped "to have put these governments upon such a foot that anybody may govern them, who has but honesty, though but indifferent capacity." After this anticipation of his own imperial achievement (and an all too accurate estimate of his successors' capacity), Hunter opened the assembly in May.[88]

The brief session was marked only by an act to give manorial status to Robert Livingston's vast landholdings in the Hudson valley. The governor general then conferred an assembly seat on the manor, issued an electoral writ, and welcomed Livingston to a leadership role in the assembly second only to Colonel Morris's. Together, the two manor lords, at the head of the landed interest, saw to it that their champion's political command was complete and his official income assured. As Colonel Riggs put it (when writing to acknowledge his underage son's promotion to lieutenant in the Albany garrison), the governor general "has effectually done his business, and when recalled may, if he pleases, purchase the north of Scotland." The Riggs family, like most of New York's former tories, was now "very easy with H.E.," but, busy as he was purging New Jersey of his remaining opponents, and with major bills in New York still in committee, Hunter postponed most legislation in New York until the fall.[89]

Governor General Hunter opened the fall 1717 session of the New York assembly with the news that, with an explanation in the case of the revenue bill and a minor amendment to the naturalization bill, crown conformation would be forthcoming. Their bargain confirmed, Hunter and the legislators passed the new bills which, by completing Hunter's defense of "the Glorious Revolution," settled a politically stable, whig, Hanoverian, military-fiscal state on the province of New York, a "revolution settlement" that lasted for sixty-nine years until it was overtaken, as Hunter had predicted, by the American Revolution. In 1717 Governor General Hunter first consolidated his legislative majority with an act to pay a new representative from Schenectady and the four new-merchant representatives from New York. At the governor general's request, the assembly explained the previous revenue act and amended the naturalization act (it also altered the act governing slaves to facilitate the manumission of "Negroe, Indian, or Mulatto Slaves"). With the legislative underbrush cut away, the assembly passed an act, prepared by its committees over the summer recess, to authorize the treasurer to issue bills of credit to the amount of 41,517 1/2 ounces of plate (£16,607). These bills were to be redeemed by the extension of the liquor excise until 1739. The bills were to be issued immediately (that is, the act had no suspending clause), in small denominations, to hundreds of the humblest supporters of the revolution of 1689 or their heirs. By instantly rewarding myriads of New Yorkers, Hunter and his legislative managers intended to make it impossible for either the British or the provincial government to undo their fiscal and political settlement. This belated recognition of the revolutionaries of 1689 was now possible because Hunter had shifted the balance of representation from Long Island to the Hudson and Mohawk valleys. This, together with Hunter's electoral coup in the city of New York, had combined to create, for the first time since the revolution, a legislative majority willing to count "our Glorious Deliverer, William the third of Blessed Memory" a blessing indeed.[90]

All "who took up arms in favour of the happy Revolution, and continued in the service in the several Forts, for that very cause, a considerable time at their own Cost without any acknowledgement or satisfaction til now" were to be paid at last. On December 23, 1717, just in time for Christmas, the council approved and the governor general signed an enormous statute, the longest in provincial history. More than 500 named individuals, or their heirs, were recompensed for revolutionary services. Virtually all of them were from New York City, Albany, or the Hudson valley between these urban poles of what had been Leislerian territory. Therefore, the great majority of the grantees were (naturalized) Dutch. Nearly 300 claimants were recompensed for military service in support of the Glorious Revolution in New York, half as Leisler's soldiers and half as suppliers of arms, provisions, or firewood to the revolutionaries. Additionally, eleven English army officers appeared as hitherto unsung heroes of the revolution, having stayed on in the colony after the coup as military advisors to the revolutionary militias.[91]

Other military services both before and after the revolution were also rewarded. One hundred and five additional claimants were paid for enlistment in or supplies for expeditions dating from Governor General Dongan's winter march to Albany in 1687 down to the 1709 expedition against Montreal. The largest single payment in the entire act was 3,710 ounces of plate to Robert Livingston for victualing the garrison in the citadel of New York from 1687 to 1700. The officers currently in command of the four garrison companies were also given bonuses. All told, four-fifths of the persons issued bills of credit under this act were paid for military service or supplies, mostly in support of "the

late happy Revolution." The revenue act of 1717 concluded Governor General
Robert Hunter's defense of the Glorious Revolution. The act recognized that
the dominant public facts of the previous generation had been that revolution
and the cost of the ensuing wars with France. So the act epitomized the conjunction of the military coup with the fiscal state.[92]

There was truth in the objections, both from the right and from the left, to
the 1717 revenue act. On the one hand, it lauded the revolution and rewarded
its soldiers and suppliers. On the other hand, the act corruptly consolidated
a whig oligarchy in New York. Every member of the council and every assemblyman was paid for his vote. Bought and paid for, this assembly was kept
on foot in support of the Hunter settlement for a decade. Only the death of
King George I in 1727 forced its dissolution. Any electoral threat to oligarchical
power and political stability was eliminated in New York for even longer than
in England. The authors of the act were also well paid for their public service,
especially those up-and-coming attorneys and officials Robert Livingston's heir
and George Clarke. The governor general himself collected substantial public
money without any pretense of accounting for it. Hunter received 2,505 ounces
and 7 1/2 pennyweight of plate for "public services." Still, as Colden remarked,
the assembly had "calculated . . . the allowance to the Governor to show how
careful they had been not to allow him half a pennyweight too much."[93]

What the assemblymen had not calculated was that the governor general had inveigled them into enacting the provincial equivalent of a national
debt. The taxes hypothecated to redeem the bills of credit were insufficient,
as Hunter very well knew. So the legislature would have to periodically levy
additional taxes or let what had become the colonial currency fail. Of course,
every executive would make his consent to any new revenue act contingent
on fiscal support for royal government. The legislators were further bound to
pass future revenue acts because Hunter had sequentially shifted the payment
of assemblymen's salaries from their respective constituencies to the provincial
budget. To get paid, the legislators had to obtain the executive's approval of
appropriations. In sum, Hunter's revenue acts, by providing long-term taxes to
redeem bills of credit, had institutionalized a provincial debt and a paper currency, had repaid the revolutionary generation, had honored the unmet costs
of the wars with France, and had made legislators dependent on government.
Only a provincial bank and hard currency were wanted to complete Robert
Hunter's imitation in New York of the British fiscal-military state, and Hunter
had plans for a provincial mint.[94]

Like the English statesmen of the 1690s (and their American imitators in
the 1790s), Robert Hunter sought to defend and to consolidate the libertarian
achievements of the revolution by a fiscal plan which would pay the public debt
incurred by the revolution and the consequent war. So doing, he created the
fiscal instruments that not only strengthened the armed state, and so opened
the road to empire, but that also expanded the commercial, capitalist, and ad-

ministrative class. This "new class" was bound to support the revolutionary state because its fiscal-military institutions enriched, employed, and dignified it. Hunter's provincial settlement, premised on the defense of the Glorious Revolution, lasted until the American Revolution. Then the New York fiscal-military state, and its English parent, was the model on which Hamilton constructed the fiscal-military structure of the United States.[95]

Brigadier Hunter's recurrent illness, the charms of a lovely seamstress, Betty Holland, and of their infant daughter, Elizabeth, together with a pestilence of pirates all held Hunter in New York during 1718. By the spring of 1719, however, encouraged by his hopes for a command in the new war with Spain (for which Hunter, outraged by French-inspired attacks by Spanish "coast guards" on New York vessels in the West Indies, had long been calling), his search for a spa, the need to obtain crown confirmation for his New York acts, and the fortuitous arrival of a warship homeward bound, combined to persuade the governor general to announce his imminent departure. When he closed the spring session of the assembly on June 24, Hunter was at his most ingratiating and statesmanlike. The governor general promised New York's leaders that he would "be watchful and Industrious to promote the Interest and Welfare of this Country, of which I . . . account myself a Countryman." He applauded the achievement of political stability after decades of partisan, ethnic, and social strife: "as the very name of Party or Faction seem to be forgotten, may it lye buried in Oblivion and no Strife ever happen amongst you, but that laudable Emulation, who shall approve himself the most zealous Servant and most dutiful Subject of the best of Princes, and the most useful Member of a well established and flourishing Community."[96]

Chief Justice Morris and Speaker Livingston wrote the reply to the governor general's speech. Every member of the assembly signed it. "You have," the assemblymen told Brigadier Hunter, "governed well and wisely, like a prudent magistrate, like an affectionate Parent. . . . We have seen many Governours, and may see more, but as none of those . . . were ever so justly fixed in the Affections of the Governed, so those to come will acquire no mean Reputation, when it can be said of them, their conduct has been like yours." It was the tragedy of the first British empire that no subsequent governor general of New York "had the honour to carry home with him such a testimonial as this."[97]

CHAPTER TWELVE

Alexander Spotswood: Architect of Empire

THE ROYAL LIEUTENANT governor of Virginia, Colonel Alexander Spotswood was, as he himself wrote, "a Commander in Chief without A Single Centinel to defend me in this Dominion." The leader of the Virginia opposition party declared that although Virginia's military governors were "Tyrants in their nature, yet they are Tyrants without Guards." Nonetheless, Spotswood, like the royal and soldierly legates of the imperial crown generally, and Marlborough's men especially, was obsessed with security, foreign and domestic. Spotswood's particular contribution to imperial security was his determination to marshal the inherent might of an armed provincial populace first to protect and then to extend his sovereign's dominions in America. Colonel Spotswood spent thirteen years in command of the Old Dominion finding ways in which to enlist provincial Virginians in the cause of Augustan empire.[1]

Alexander Spotswood's imperial program was impeded by a contest between the English crown and the colonial elite that dated back to 1676. In that year, the year of Alexander Spotswood's birth in the garrison of Tangier, Nathaniel Bacon's revolution had overwhelmed the baronial regime of Sir William Berkeley in Virginia. The last of the rebels had been repressed, and the vengeful barons had been displaced, by royal legates, backed by a squadron of the navy and a regiment of the Guards. The armed forces of the crown had imposed direct royal government on the formerly autonomous colony. Redcoated rule excited the enmity of the provincial elite: the family, friends, and clients of the ousted Sir William Berkeley. They became known from his mansion, their headquarters, as "the Green Spring Faction." As colonists, they looked to England to find words to express their fear of a royal executive backed by military force. They found those antimilitary slogans in the standing army rhetoric of their English counterparts, the country party. Anglo-American "country" parties paradoxically allied provincial elites with urban oligarchies. Elites and oligarchs shared an antipathy to armed monarchy. Its centralizing authority threatened the self-government of county courts and urban corporations, alike in England and America. In the two decades that followed the "Glorious Revolution," Virginia's country party, the Green Spring faction, became a majority in the colonial council. Their sons and dependents were a plurality in the house of burgesses. Linked to the like-minded merchants of the metropolis who factored their tobacco, Virginia's country party had reached the apogee of its influence during the four-year interregnum caused by the death of Colonel Nott and the capture of Colonel Hunter, Marlborough's legates. Then, on June 21, 1710, Colonel Spotswood, the captain general's deputy chief of staff, landed with his household from the warships of the tobacco convoy. He spent his first night in Virginia at Green Spring.[2]

The most distinguished of the oligarchs who flocked to Green Spring to take the measure of the new executive was William Byrd II. He had himself angled for the Virginia command, but "the duke of Marlborough declared that no one but Soldiers should have the government of a plantation, so I was disappointed." He had even been left off the list of councilors in Colonel Spotswood's royal commission. "The Governor was very courteous to me" nonetheless, Byrd told his diary. Spotswood not only allowed Byrd to take a seat in the council, he even wrote home asking for Byrd's restoration, assuming that, as receiver general of the royal revenues, Byrd would support the interest of the crown in the colony. No wonder that Byrd dreamed "that the lightening almost put out one of my eyes, that I won a tun of money and might win more if I had ventured, that I was great with my Lord Marlborough." As the wielder of the royal thunderbolts, the purveyor of patronage, and the captain general's legate, Colonel Spotswood expected that he would receive the disciplined support of all royal appointees, even Philip Ludwell, the heir to Green Spring, the son of the most inveterate enemy of imperial authority. Ludwell was now both the deputy auditor of the royal revenue and a royal councilor. Spotswood "told the Council that he was come with a full disposition to do the Queen and country service and hoped we would all concur with him in so good a design."[3]

The authority of the royal governor and council depended upon their command of the militia. As soon as the heat of summer had passed and the tobacco harvest was in, Spotswood reviewed Virginia's men in arms. To muster the two militia regiments under Colonel Byrd's command, Virginia's commander in chief met their officers at Byrd's "Westover" mansion. He "was extremely courteous to them" but, much to the surprise of these sunshine soldiers, the veteran commander did not let a driving rain keep him from drilling the men. "The Governor mustered them all the while," Byrd recalled, "and he presented me to the people to be their colonel and commander-in-chief." In a province with few other titles of honor, the rank of Virginians was primarily military. Provincial prestige, patronage, and power depended upon the royal commissions issued by the sovereign's representative to the militia officers. For almost two centuries to come, American elites would equate military rank with social status.[4]

The militia of the older counties, free men of property, could be relied upon to obey orders to suppress domestic unrest, as they did in Spotswood's first summer. To resist the threat of invasions, aboriginal or European, the governor called out the militia. To patrol the fall line frontier, Colonel Spotswood recruited mounted troops of rangers, as had every governor since Colonel Jeffreys in 1677. Beyond the fall line, only a few recent European refugees had settled. The oldest of these colonies was that of the Huguenot pioneers at "Manakin Town" (site of the former Monocan capital). Twenty-five miles further up the James River than any other European settlement, the Manakin Town had been garrisoned and fortified by Colonel Nicholson's command. Now, Colonel Spotswood organized additional French refugees as a troop of dragoons. They reinforced the veteran Huguenot infantry, which "was exercised and performed very well" during Spotswood's review. Beyond Manakin, the interior, westward up the James, southward to the Roanoke, and through the Rock Fish Gap toward Catawba and Cherokee country, insofar as it saw any Europeans at all, was still the domain of the fur traders. This James River frontier region had been the particular preserve of the Byrd family and their partners in the fur trade ever since their Henrico County levies had massacred the native middlemen on Occaneechee Island in 1675.[5]

North of the James, the frontier was defined by the fall line of the Rappahannock and its tributaries. During June of 1710, the Rappahannock rangers reported to Colonel Spotswood that they had obeyed his orders, characteristic of a commander of scouts, to reconnoiter the perimeter of his command. The rangers had followed the rivers west from the fall line, across the Piedmont, to the first ridge of mountains. This distance, they were surprised to discover (so little did official Virginia know of the upcountry), was less than 100 miles. In the autumn, Spotswood ordered "a Company of Adventurers," 100 strong, to follow up the rangers' route. The adventurers' Indian guides led them to a pass through the Blue Ridge. Only the lateness of the season stopped the explorers from descending into the valley beyond. Colonel Spotswood now knew of two potential passes though the Appalachians and he had an idea, also gleaned from the Indians, that the Great Lakes lay not far beyond "the great Mountains." If settlement could be pushed west, up from the falls of one of the rivers, a pass could be seized. Three imperial advantages, Colonel Spotswood declared, were "Manifest." A mountain pass could be held "so strongly that it would not be in the power of the French to dislodge" the Virginians from their new natural frontier, Virginia's "Barrier," the Blue Ridge. A post in the pass would also be a base from which military expeditions could "cut off" communications between Canada and the new French settlements on the Mississippi. The passage fort would also shelter a trading post. British trade goods would win the allegiance of the natives in the disputed lands between the new mountain frontier of Virginia and the new French frontier of lakes and rivers. Marlborough's legate had outlined the Anglo-French struggle for the Ohio country. It would consume imperial energies for a century to come. It would impel the Old Dominion to preeminence in what a subsequent Virginian surveyor, land speculator, and frontier general would call "the Rising Empire" of America.[6]

Both this bold strategic vision and issues of domestic security underlay the royal governor's speech from the throne to his first assembly. It met in the new capital, Williamsburg, in October 1710 to hear Spotswood deplore the state of the provincial militia. His review of the troops had shown that the militia "on The foot it Now Stands is so Imaginary a Defence, That we Cannot too Cautiously conceal it from our Neighbours and our Slaves, nor too Earnestly Pray That Neither The Lust of Dominion, nor The Desire of freedom May stirr those people to any Attempts." While "Our Neighbours," the French, had ambitions for "universal monarchy" and menaced Virginia from the west, domestic danger came from "our Slaves." Their numbers had recently grown to menacing size. The resistance of the "New Negroes," recently captured and profoundly resentful, was somewhat sporadic but it was ever more alarming. Spotswood's entreaties for a fundamental militia reform to meet the growing threats from Frenchmen without and Africans within obtained no more than an extension of the "Act for Security And Defence of The Country in Times of Danger." This was Virginia's equivalent to the English mutiny act, legislative authorization for martial discipline. Neither the commander in chief nor the assembly made much of its regular renewal. Spotswood's conception of Virginia's strategic situation encompassed far more than its militia, now little more than an ill-equipped constabulary.[7]

His complex corporate, militant imperial vision had been acquired during a lifetime at the forefront of the military revolution. Spotswood had been raised in the context of imperial corporations, crown, commercial, and regimental, all authorized by acts of parliament. These bodies corporate concentrated resources of men and matériel for militant imperial purposes. As an officer in charge of matériel for a British army of 50,000 men and as a preparer of the bills and budgets required to secure legislative appropriations, Spotswood was a comprehensive corporate and political planner. When his scouts found iron ore adjacent to water transportation in the midst of an unexploited and barren territory (then known as "the poisoned fields" and afterward, memorably, as "the Wilderness"), Spotswood instantly proposed a public corporation. Investors from Switzerland, England, and Virginia ought to be incorporated by the Virginia legislature, he said. The assembly, planters to a man, ignored Spotswood's corporate and industrial proposal. So Spotswood patented the Rappahannock lands himself. He recruited German iron miners (who populated another frontier settlement by foreign Protestants). What Spotswood and the Germans developed over the next three decades became the greatest industry, and the major arms manufacturer, of the antebellum South.[8]

The lieutenant governor also outlined to the assembly a naval stores project. Naval stores were expected to be a major American contribution to the

British war machine. Upcountry pine barrens, Spotswood explained, would not support tobacco (the overproduction of which he deplored in any case) or even small farms (which he wished to promote as the nurturers of numerous militia), but the pine barrens would produce naval stores. Pitch, tar, turpentine, and resin were essential to keep the royal navy at sea. Their supply was dangerously dominated by the Scandinavian countries. Pine products were now available from New England and New York, Spotswood admitted. Absent convoys, however, northern naval stores served "only to arm our Enemys at our own cost," whereas royal warships already protected the tobacco fleets from French privateers. Spotswood proposed to import expert producers to Virginia and form a naval stores corporation. Again, the planter-burgesses ignored the governor's corporate plan. Again, Spotswood proceeded on his own, eventually purchasing 45,000 acres of pine barrens and forming a partnership to develop them.[9]

Colonel Spotswood's strategic, corporate, and military headquarters was to be the governor's residence. It was presently only half built. When Spotswood was finished with it, it would be "the Palace." The site of the royal executive residence was sixty-three acres at the eastern end of an avenue laid down by Colonel Nicholson's baroque town plan for Williamsburg. As redesigned by Colonel Spotswood, the town plan echoed the Roman camp, the model that this student of the military renaissance had copied in five campaigns as a quartermaster general in Marlborough's army. The site of Virginia's new capital is a ridge of high ground that slopes down on either side to navigable and defensible creeks, "King's" and "Queen's." Each flows for five miles before reaching the James and the York rivers respectively. So advantaged, the site of Williamsburg had been a place of arms since its inception as "the Middle Plantation," the midpoint of the cross-peninsula palisade of 1628, Virginia's first frontier. In 1677, the barracks and magazine for the regiment of Guards shipped out from London to repress Bacon's revolution were built at the Middle Plantation. There units of the Guards encamped for five years, awing tributary Indians and Berkelean barons alike. There, in the midst of his garrison's camp and well away from Sir William Berkeley's former headquarters at Green Spring, Colonel Jeffreys had convened the council, general court, and assembly. For the next twenty years, the Middle Plantation was the public magazine. As recently as 1702 it had been the distribution point for the royal arms sent out to Virginia's militia on the renewal of the war with France. The Middle Plantation seemed to Colonel Nicholson, then lieutenant governor, the obvious site for the colonial College of William and Mary, founded in 1690, and for a new statehouse when the one at Jamestown, rebuilt after its destruction in Bacon's revolution, burned again in 1698. In 1705, now governor in chief, Nicholson located the colonial capitol a mile from the college down "Duke of Gloucester Street" (which he named after princess Anne's heir, Marlborough's pupil). This avenue was to be the axis of the new capital of Virginia, named "Williamsburg" after the second William the Conqueror. As his plan for Annapolis still demonstrates, Colonel Nicholson favored baroque city plans of circles and avenues. Such plans suited a seventeenth-century royalist whose Virginia partisans called themselves "cavaliers."[10]

It was equally fitting that Colonel Spotswood, a professional soldier of the military renaissance, should overlay Nicholson's cavalier conception with the outline of a Roman camp, the classic material manifestation of military order. The defining structures of every *castra* were the *principia*, or headquarters, the shrine to the state gods, the magazine, and the parade ground. Shelters for soldiers, sutlers, auxiliaries, and artisans were of fixed sizes, proportioned to the ranks of their inhabitants. All dwellings were ordered along uniform setbacks from measured streets. These streets ran at right angles from two axes, the *decium* and the *cardo*. Their intersection was the *forum*, a parade ground, place of arms, and market. The Roman military camp had been reintroduced into the town planning of the British empire at Londonderry, the Irish headquarters of Spotswood's regiment, for almost five years between the peace of Ryswick in 1679 and the renewed war with France in 1702.[11]

The Roman term *capitol* (from the temple of Jupiter Capitolinus, where the senate first assembled) was first used in America to describe the statehouse that now marked Williamsburg's southern *terminus*. The college (from the Latin *collegium*—a priests' school) marked the northern boundary. At the east end of the central axis—the *cardo*—was the shell of the proposed executive residence, the *principia*, presently forlorn foundations in an overgrown field. Like Marlborough's Blenheim Palace, Spotswood's "Palace" (the origin of the label cannot have been far to seek, especially as Spotswood is alleged to have displayed a portrait of himself with Blenheim Palace in the background) became both its builder's recreation and his hostage to fortune. Just as Blenheim was the obsession of the captain general, so directing the completion of "the Governor's Palace," the design and construction of its outbuildings and dependencies, the planning, planting, and cultivating its extensive terraced formal gardens (Spotswood followed the plans of Henry Wise, Marlborough's landscape architect), was Spotswood's recreation, an entertainment fit for an officer and a gentleman. This Spotswood had learned from Marlborough himself, who regularly regaled his staff with the latest improvements he planned for Blenheim. Both Blenheim Palace and Virginia's "Palace," abuilding at the same time, were the work of soldier-architects, Vanbrugh and Spotswood respectively. Both became causes célèbres. Their costs were a deep and continual drain, first on the public purse and then, when political opposition ended public support, on the personal fortunes of their respective soldier-sponsors. When, in March 1711, Spotswood complained about the struggle he had to make "the Income of my Government . . . bear some reasonable proportion to that Representation which was made to me in Europe, before I had quitted my Employments in the Army there," it was the price of "the Palace" that was eating up his profits.[12]

Far more than Blenheim Palace, which was then and which remains to-day a private residence, Virginia's "palace" was and is a public stage on which Spotswood upheld, "by his constant way of Living, the Honour and Dignity of his Majesty's Government." At the palace, he cultivated the loyalty of a people who never saw their prince. Never before had Virginians witnessed "their Sovereign's Birth day celebrated with so much magnificence as in my time and at my Expence." On such public holidays, visitors passed into the palace precincts through great gates of Bath iron hung on columns capped by the imperial crown, flanked by pilasters bearing the royal arms, upheld by stone-carved heraldic beasts. Beyond the elegant wall and balustrade lay the cobbled forecourt flanked by raised flowerbeds, brick office buildings, and the guard-house. Up the Portland stone steps of the palace and through its great doors lay the entry hall armory, modeled on King William's guardroom at Hampton Court Palace. On walnut-paneled walls, 160 stands of the most modern fire-arms, wheels of pistols, and latticeworks of bladed weapons and polearms were "nicely posited by the ingenious contrivance of the most accomplished Colonel Spotswood." Over marble pavements, the visitor passed from the armory—a martial reminder that "the sword . . . will give the law to law"—to elegant par-lors, a state dining room, the billiard room and, if his privilege ran so far, up the great staircase to the governor's own sitting room. An especially valued visitor might be asked to stay overnight in the state bedroom, "the finest chamber in the house."[13]

Out of doors, behind the palace, visitors walked down garden terraces to "falling gardens." They looked across box-lined ponds to vanishing lines (very like the modern west garden sequence at Blenheim). Beyond the garden perim-eter stretched long vistas (cut out of angry neighbors' woodlots). Pond-raised fish fed supper guests. Virginia's first icehouse chilled the syllabub Spotswood served to his visitors during the sultry Williamsburg summer. The palace com-plex made material the cultural elements of Augustan authority. Its offspring along Virginia's rivers show how much the anglicanization of the provincial elite stemmed from the example of the palace that "received its beauty and con-veniencey from the many alterations and decorations of the present Governor, Colonel Spotswood."[14]

The palace, the college, the church, the magazine, the Indian school, even the jail—the set of public buildings that Spotswood designed for the new pro-vincial capital and sited on a Roman plan—manifested imperial authority. As the first and most concentrated expression of "Georgian" building, Spotswood's structures of authority became the models for America's public architecture. This was particularly the case with colleges, beginning with the College of William and Mary. Spotswood announced to his first assembly that the queen would contribute some of her quitrents to rebuilding the college. The ruins of the disastrous college fire (caused not by the students but by members of the

Green Spring faction who, dominating the college board, treated the rooms as their own) had been cleared away when Spotswood arrived. Elected rector of the college, he took charge of the redesign and reconstruction. Between 1710 and 1716, the college was "rebuilt and nicely contrived, altered and adorned by the ingenious direction of Governor Spotswood and is not altogether unlike Chelsea Hospital," the retired soldiers' home in London. Spotswood was constrained by the foundations of 1697 but, adept mathematician as he was, contrived to produce a geometrically satisfying building on a human scale. Classrooms and masters' rooms, dormitories and hall, all were entered through a rather too angular pavilion and opened into disciplined gardens. Occupied by 1716, the College of William and Mary was a fitting setting for the education of "a better polished set of Patriots" than Virginia had yet produced.[15]

Patriots (Roman citizens) were also shaped by the state religion. Every *castra* and *capitol* had its *templum*, the focus of that divine worship which traditionally inculcated obedience to authority, authenticated social rank, and refreshed the crusading spirit. So Spotswood produced an eminently harmonious place of worship, Bruton Parish Church. The old church at the Middle Plantation had been falling down ever since it was "finished" in 1683. It was now wholly inadequate to house the growing congregation consequent upon the construction of the college and the capitol. The vestry asked Spotswood's first assembly for help. Its members, already aware of the new executive's proclivities, asked the governor for a design. With unaccustomed modesty, Spotswood protested that he had not hitherto been involved in ecclesiastical design but, by March 1711, he had produced plans, offered to pay for a third of the building himself, and joined the council president, Edmund Jennings, to beat down the price of bricks. At the end of 1715, the new church was in use, its congregation called to worship by the ship's bell which Spotswood had salvaged from the wreck of HMS *Garland*. As became the representative of the head of the church of England, the queen, the lieutenant governor faithfully graced a state pew, "raised from the floor, covered with a canopy, around the interior of which his name was written in gilt letters."[16]

Across the chancel of the new church, the governor's pew faced the pulpit whose occasional occupant was the fly in Spotswood's ecclesiastical ointment, the rector of Bruton Parish, Commissary James Blair. Spotswood had taken the contract for rebuilding the college from Blair's corrupt control. Spotswood then pointed out that Blair had used the Brafferton legacy for the education of Indian children to buy native students from their families in order to qualify for the endowment. Then Blair had sold the children as slaves. No Indian education, much less Christian conversion, had ever occurred. Besides exposing Commissary Blair's bad behavior, Spotswood publicly doubted the anglican validity of Blair's Scots episcopal ordination. He declined to collate Blair to Bruton Parish. Blair had applied for induction "solely to the Vestry, without his ever making the least application to me for my collation, notwithstanding it was my own parish Church." Busy with his retail store and other "worldly concerns," Blair left sermons and sacraments mostly to his curate, or so Spotswood alleged.[17]

In fact, Blair was a well-published author of sermons, but he certainly neglected his duty, as commissary of the bishop of London, to support the provincial clergy. Spotswood's first act as governor was to collate the clergymen who came out with him into vacant Virginia parishes. Blair encouraged the vestries to resent this intrusion on their self-government. The country party, of which the whiggish Blair was a leader, made Spotswood's efforts on behalf of the anglican clergy a central grievance against the royal executive. On the other hand, Virginia's clergymen, assembled in convocation, were the governor's unswerving and vocal supporters. The president of convocation wrote of the lieutenant governor that "it is difficult to be determined in which respect he chiefly excelled, either in being a compleat gentleman, a polite scholar, a good governor, or a true churchman."[18]

A proponent of the royal prerogative as much in ecclesiastical matters as in civil and military affairs, Spotswood further offended Blair and reduced the autonomy of the colonial church by acting as ecclesiastical "ordinary," issuing marriage licenses and probating wills. Spotswood was an hereditary champion of the church-state. In addition to Archbishop Spotswood, the lieutenant governor was descended from a president of session and secretary of state for Scotland martyred by the parliament as a royalist and an episcopalian. That Spotswood's father was physician to that archroyalist Scot, the earl of Middleton, governor general of Tangier, meant that Spotswood was raised among royal soldiers who esteemed themselves Christian crusaders. To his military upbringing, Spotswood added years of education in cathedral precincts at the Westminster School. For nearly twenty years he served in the royal blue uniform of the 10th Regiment, its officers famously militant churchmen. As a senior staff officer of the duke of Marlborough, Spotswood shared in the ministrations of the duke's chaplain, Francis Hare, bishop of St. Asaph. Colonel Spotswood took Communion with the captain general on the day of battle. Before coming out to Virginia, Spotswood consulted with the American diocesan of the church of England, that veteran cavalryman Henry Compton, bishop of London. Because of his leading role in the coup against the Catholic king James, Bishop Compton embodied the identity of the church, the army, and the constitution. Colonel Spotswood too identified religious uniformity with political order. He was convinced that "when once Schism has crept into the Church, it will soon create Faction in the Civil Government."[19]

Such was the case of North Carolina, Spotswood wrote, "where there's scarce any form of Government" because a bastard form of "Quaker" belief had armed itself in defiance of all authority. In June 1711, civil war broke out in North Carolina. It threatened to spread into Virginia when the rebels tried to recruit servants and slaves from Virginia's Southside counties (ever since Bacon's uprising the refuge of the dominion's dissidents). Spotswood also supported the proprietary governor, Edward Hyde, because he was a representative of the totemic tory family (to whose chief, Lawrence Hyde, earl of Rochester, Spotswood explained the situation). Hyde had been appointed by Spotswood's regimental patrons, the Granvilles, proprietors of both the Carolinas (George Granville was presently secretary at war), but Colonel Edward Tynte, Spotswood's old messmate in the Granville (10th) regiment, the proprietary governor of South Carolina, had died before he could confirm Hyde's command.[20]

Spotswood feared "that Mr. Hyde might expect the same fate Collo. Park had in Antigua." He declared that Bacon's revolt, "the fatal Rebellion in the Country, which formerly cost the Crown a great expence of Treasure to quell, sprang from less dangerous appearances." Spotswood offered mediation. The rebel leader, Thomas Cary, replied that "he was resolved to treat no otherway than with arms." Spotswood then issued a "Proclamation for seizing & apprehending Coll Tho Cary & other Seditious and ffactious persons." He ordered the Southside militia to march into North Carolina to apprehend the rebels. When Cary's retreat beyond the Dan put him out of reach of the militia, Spotswood turned to the royal navy. As usual, the tobacco convoy commodore denied Spotswood's vice admiralty authority but, also as usual, the captains of the ships on the Virginia station obeyed the governor's orders. They crowded their marine detachments into the ships' boats and dispatched them to Albemarle Sound. The royal marines rescued Governor Hyde and flushed out Colonel Cary. He and his heavily armed "Quaker" supporters fled to Virginia's Southside. There the rebel leaders were arrested by Spotswood's militia officers and jailed until they could be sent home aboard the convoy for trial in London. Spotswood explained that "if measures are not taken to discourage such Mutinous Spirits . . . it may prove a dangerous example to the rest of Her Majesty's plantations." He received the strongest commendation from his superiors. They hoped his forceful intervention to repress dissent "will be an Example to other Governors to do their Duty."[21]

Emboldened by the civil strife in North Carolina, the warriors of the southern Tuscarora towns had defied their elders. At first light on September 22, 1711, the young men attacked the softest target, the poor Protestant Palatine refugees in the baron de Graffenreid's settlements along the Neuse River. The hostiles destroyed New Bern and captured the baron himself. Then they struck the Pamlico settlements. Spotswood ordered the Southside militia to occupy the tributary Indian towns along the Roanoke to keep their warriors out of the uprising. The tributaries protested that they were peaceable. They added that the Tuscaroras themselves were divided. The Tuscarora towns north of the Pamlico, whose people traded with and married into the Virginia tribes, had rejected any part "in this bloody Execution." The northern Tuscaroras were anxious to assure Virginia's governor of their peaceful intentions. So Spotswood sent out invitations for a treaty. He suspended all trade with the Indians ("finding they were better provided with Ammunition than we ourselves") and took command of the southern Virginia militia in person. At the militia muster, "there were about 700 horse besides volunteers and about 910 foot, and there were about 30 volunteers, among whom were three parsons." Well supported spiritually, Spotswood used the next five days for organization and drill. "He divided the companies and made them about fifty men each, and made captains over them, though, when he came to Surrey, he found it difficult to get captains because everybody refused the governor and made him so angry that he swore at several, which was a thing he seldom did." Despite Southside dissidence, by the time the Tuscarora and tributary delegates arrived at Colonel Spotswood's camp, he had "brought the Militia under some discipline." The native diplomats "were not a little surprized to find there a great body of men in such good Order." Not since the Guards regiment under Colonel Jeffreys had imposed the Treaty of Middle Plantation on the surviving Powhatan peoples in 1677 had Virginia seen so large and so disciplined a force in the field to support its diplomacy. As in 1677, now in 1711, a soldierly royal executive marched native diplomats along the lines of troops on parade. Impressed, both the tributaries and the Tuscaroras promised peace with Virginia and enmity to the insurgents. They offered to secure the release of de Graffenreid and declared that they would dispatch to Williamsburg diplomats empowered by their peoples to make a permanent peace treaty.[22]

While he waited for the Tuscarora and tributary delegates to arrive, Spotswood had reflected on "the incapacity of this Country for an Offensive or Defensive War. Our Militia are in a manner wholly destitute of Ammunition, and are as ill provided with arms that are useful." Spotswood feared that he could not defend his command against "any considerable attack of an Enemy." If the royal executive were not to risk a repetition of Bacon's uprising, he would have to respond to an Indian incursion with a well-armed force, equipped to take the field in pursuit of a "people more like Wild Beasts than men." Spotswood would need hundreds of stands of uniform arms, field artillery, munitions, and tents (even farmer-fighters could not survive a wilderness campaign without shelter). The board of ordnance (now headed by Orkney's eldest brother, the duke of Hamilton) sent out from the Tower of London in HMS *Nottingham* the finest weapons Colonel Spotswood had ever seen: "it was a particular pleasure to me to see so fine a sett of Arms, for they are far beyond any usually delivered out of the Tower while I served in the Army." To house these splendid weapons, Colonel Spotswood not only made the entry hall of the palace into an elegant and effective armory, he also designed a magazine, the *praetorium* of Williamsburg, and sited it in the *forum*, Williamsburg's Market Square.[23]

The magazine is almost the smallest but perhaps the most satisfying of Spotswood's public buildings. It is an aspiring structure. Its octagonal walls and roof are equal in height, "and the total height from the ground to the apex of the roof is equal to the square constructed on the diameter; thus the whole design is regulated by the Golden section," the mathematical measure of all Spotswood's architecture. Colonel Spotswood improved upon the equation with the beautifully proportioned Palladian windows that light the magazine. Spotswood was so anxious to put the royal arms under cover that he paid for the first cost of the magazine himself. He appointed (and for some years paid out of his own pocket) an armorer and a storekeeper for the royal arsenal. Inspired by the success of his magazine and the history of the Middle Plantation as a place of arms, Colonel Spotswood proposed that Williamsburg become the site of an arms depot for all the colonies on the continent. He made it so for Virginia and both of the Carolinas during the American campaigns of Queen Anne's War.[24]

On August 16, 1711, on news of the Quebec expedition, Virginia's commander in chief proclaimed his queen's American war aims. "Her pious Zeale to propagate the protestant Religion & Extirpate popish Superstition & Idolotry," her "Just Horror of the Rapparies & Murders dayly Committed on her people by the ffrench & Indian Savages," her intention of "Restoring the Crown of Great Brittain to its Antient Rights in North America" had inspired her majesty to send "very considerable part of her fleets & Armys to reduce Canada." Colonel Spotswood ordered that his proclamation of her majesty's war aims, so much, he said, those of her subjects in Virginia, was to be read during divine service in every church in the queen's dominion on September 7, 1711. In the meantime, Spotswood reverted to one of his old duties as quartermaster general. He procured, packed, and shipped north (in Virginia's guardships), 700 barrels of pork for the Canadian expedition. When the queen's quitrents did not suffice to pay for the pork, Spotswood personally advanced most of the deficiency. The shortage of funds owed much to the wartime depression in Virginia's economy but even more to the astonishingly mean and shortsighted policy of the treasury in requiring periodic remissions of Virginia's surplus to help meet England's war debt. There was, Colonel Spotswood wrote auditor Blathwayt, "never greater Occasion since Bacon's Rebellion for leaving some money to answer the Emergencys of the Government." Not only was there a civil war and an Indian uprising on Virginia's southern frontier, but there was also an imminent danger of a French invasion.[25]

Absent the guardships sent to Canada, Spotswood armed a sloop to look out for the French squadron rumored to be en route to attack Virginia. He enlisted lookouts by land as well. He had beacons built to call out the militia (an accidental firing terrified planters as far upriver as Westover, where William Byrd buried his silver). Colonel Spotswood dug to more public purpose. Being the sort of officer who would "eat up a ravelin for his breakfast and afterwards pick his teeth with a palisade," Spotswood indulged his appetite for military engineering. He had batteries built and emplaced seventy guns at Point Comfort, Tindal's Point, Yorktown, and Jamestown. He visited each site half a dozen times. The colonel also staked out a defensive line across the Peninsula below Williamsburg. To bolster the militia's defense of these entrenchments, Spotswood mounted ten pieces of field artillery.[26]

As soon as the sailing season had passed, and with it the menace of a French invasion, Spotswood summoned the assembly to Williamsburg and asked the legislators to pay for his myriad military actions. In his speech from the throne, the commander in chief boasted that few of his predecessors had met so many military emergencies: "The Suppressing a Civill War within a Neighbouring Colony, the preparing to withstand the Attempts of a powerful fleet, at Sea, and ye providing against the mercilless Incurrsions of the Heathen at land, have all been Occurrences of this last half year." The need to defend the sea frontier was a lesson learned from "the Dutch Expedition in 1673." The Carolina intervention had been necessitated by "remembrance of that Dismall Scene here in 1676." Mobilization against the Tuscarora was essential "to guard our own throats." As their commander in chief, Colonel Spotswood, declared, he had "done my part in taking timely measures to Shield you." For their part, in addition to levying the necessary taxes for fortifications, the assembly should support a treaty with the Tuscaroras, pay for Indian hostages to study at William and Mary, appropriate salaries for the frontier rangers (the more necessary because the "late unfortunate disapointment at Canida" would multiply Iroquoian incursions), and accept Spotswood's prescriptions for militia reorganization. Otherwise Virginia, like Carolina, would suffer from "Sword, pestilence and famine."[27]

The burgesses responded in the racist accents of 1676. They not only demanded that the commander in chief "declare Warr against those Tuscarora Indians their Adherents and Abettors," they also called for "extirpating all the Indians, without distinction of Friends or Enemies." Virginians would pay for genocide. Spotswood seized the moment. He offered to raise an expeditionary army of volunteers, drilled by adjutants he trained. The soldiers should be paid by the province, albeit a little less than "the Queen's Regular Troops." Enthusiastic, the burgesses announced that they would raise £20,000. The Green Spring faction were appalled at the prospect of a royal military executive in command of a professionally drilled, regularly paid, middle-class, volunteer provincial army. Once again they raised the reviled names of Oliver Cromwell and James II and their Virginia equivalents, Herbert Jeffreys and Francis Nicholson, all authoritarian advocates of "a standing militia." To sabotage the burgesses' bill, the dissident councilors raised a question of privilege: they offered amendments to what was a money bill. William Byrd explained, "no governor ought to be trusted with £20,000." Spotswood's reply to Byrd's insult was Captain Brazen's: "You can't imagine . . . that I want twenty thousand pounds. I have spent twenty times as much in the service. . . . My head runs much upon architecture. Shall I build a privateer or a playhouse?" Spotswood commissioned both before he was done. He reduced Byrd to his provincial origins into the bargain.[28]

Besides his campaign against the three officeholders Byrd, Ludwell, and Blair, Spotswood moved to challenge what he thought was the faction's ultimate power, its authority over the life and death of Virginians as judges of the general court. The Green Spring faction were a majority of the council, and councilors constituted the supreme court of the province. Spotswood insisted that the crown, that is, he himself, had the power, both inherently and under his 1710 court act, to appoint anyone to sit on courts of oyer and terminer. To those councilors who showed up for the next session of the general court, Spotswood added a slate of judges headed by the speaker of the burgesses, Peter Beverley, Spotswood's business partner and political ally. The Beverley connection was one of the two county families who competed for control of Middlesex and of the Rappahannock valley. The second Middlesex connection was that of the Corbins, kinsmen of the Ludwells and so associates of the Green Spring faction. Spotswood now dismissed their leader, Gawin Corbin, from the naval office for the Rappahannock River for forging the queen's signature. Spotswood's elevation of the Beverleys and his disgrace of the Corbins, his manipulation of militia commissions, his revision of the county court benches, and his reorganization of the sheriffs' roster all were elements of an electoral campaign to replace the "nigardly" burgess clients of the factious councilors with men attuned to expansion and to empire.[29]

Spotswood was convinced that his campaigns in Carolina, which had resulted in the Tuscarora treaty of December 1711 (the majority of the Tuscarora towns agreed to act against the leaders of the hostiles and to send noble children to the college as hostages), and the repression of the Cary rebellion, as well as his defenses against French invasion, would persuade the voters that the commander in chief's martial and diplomatic skills deserved their support. "I have served long enough in her Majesty's victorious Armys to know how to deal with so inconsiderable an Enemy" as the Indians, Spotswood wrote, "if the Assembly will but enable me to w'ch it is probable a little chastizement near home may very much quicken them."[30]

The election of 1712 replaced nineteen of the fifty-one burgesses, all to the advantage of Spotswood's "court party." The executive asked for and the new majority authorized cash and clothing to help North Carolina fight the Tuscaroras. The assemblymen renewed the 1705 defense act. They promised to pay militia called out for extended service. They appropriated salaries for an expanded corps of frontier rangers. The results were disappointing. Spotswood's first attempt to assist North Carolina with 300 men and military aid floundered on that colony's anarchy. His second offer was (characteristically) attended with too high a price: Carolina's cession of south-side border lands to Virginia. Spotswood's effort to take control of the Indian trade, and so of munitions, was

frustrated by the established James River traders, William Byrd and his associates chief among them. Worst of all, the Five Nations, freed from menaces
north and west by a renewed neutrality with the French and with their aboriginal allies, resumed age-old quarrels on Virginia's frontiers. Iroquois incursions
against Indian enemies inevitably meant outrages against neighboring white
settlers. The frontier crisis, Spotswood declared, demanded more than episodic
responses.[31]

So Spotswood imported to America the European concept of "the barrier."
This combination of physical and population obstacles to aggression had been
developed to protect the Netherlands from France. Spotswood had first defended the Dutch Barrier in the army of King William. During his subsequent
years on Marlborough's staff, Spotswood had not only helped extend the Barrier along the Low Countries' frontier with France, he had learned from the
captain general that a barrier could be active as well as passive. That is, it could
be a basis for counterattacks against the French as well as a wall of defense
against the aggression of Louis XIV. It was this sort of barrier that Spotswood
now proposed as the frontier of Virginia. Absent regular garrisons, a barrier required a militant population to defend it. The Tuscarora war had once
again made refugees of de Graffenreid's Palatine settlers. Spotswood wanted
to place them along the upper reaches of the Rappahannock, together with
the German-speaking miners he now settled at the fortified hamlet Spotswood
called "Germanna," the Virginia vanguard of that episodic German frontier
that would extend from General Hunter's Palatines on the Mohawk and Hudson south to the German pioneers of General Oglethorpe's Savannah. Colonel
Spotswood wrote that his German miners and farmers would "prove a strong
Barrier against the incursion of the Indians."[32]

By "Indians" Spotswood meant the Iroquois, incited by the French. Virginia had its own Indian allies. The most militant were Siouian speakers, now
consolidated as the "Saponi" by Spotswood. He moved them all to a new settlement where the Tuscarora path crossed the Meherrin tributary of the Roanoke.
On high ground, Spotswood fortified an administrative center and trading post
for the peoples of Virginia's southwest. This he christened, with his usual identification of religion and royalty, "Christ-anna." From their palisaded village
beneath the bastions of Christanna, ten native nations sent noble hostages to be
educated at William and Mary. At Fort Christanna, native hunting and scouting
parties were joined by companies of Spotswood's rangers to warn of the Iroquois
raiders who made Virginia's tributaries a primary target. Barriers, European or
American, were maintained as much by diplomacy as by force. The tributary
relationship was reinforced by Spotswood's reconfirmation of the "articles of
peace made at Middle Plantation the 29th day of May 1677" by Colonel Jeffreys
and the Guards. Each of the tributary tribes was to acknowledge "its dependence
on the Crown of Great Britain" by presenting three arrows "to the commander
in chief of Virginia . . . on St. George's day at the Palace in Williamsburg."[33]

THE HANOVERIANS

Monarchs, Ministers, and Military Men

George I

Born in 1660, the year of the monarchy's restoration, to the daughter of Elizabeth Stuart, "the Winter Queen" of Bohemia, "the queen of hearts" to Protestants everywhere, and to her husband, a future duke of Hanover, Georg Ludwig was raised to the hunt and to war. Having seen combat in his teens, Georg, like many of his future subjects, fought to raise the siege of Vienna by the Turks in 1683. He commanded troops in the new war with Louis XIV in 1688. Ten years later, Georg succeeded as elector of Hanover and inherited his mother's claim to the throne of England, a claim confirmed by parliament in the act of settlement in 1701 and by the grand alliance against France. Despite his being bypassed militarily by Marlborough, the elector was the bitter enemy of Utrecht, of its English authors, Oxford and Bolingbroke, and, of course, of the jacobite threat they seemed to represent to his succession. On August 6, 1714, just five days after the death of Queen Anne, the parliament of Great Britain proclaimed Georg Ludwig king. On September 18, Marlborough welcomed the new monarch at Greenwich, was recommissioned to all his British commands, and set about to purge the army.

That the royal army constituted the imperial executive was of little interest to a king absorbed by Hanoverian affairs, so the Marlborough connections retained their provincial commands. In domestic politics, Marlborough and all the duke's men were "the king's friends" in the sovereign's bitter quarrel with his heir. His courtiers, headed by the duke of Argyll, saw to it that the prince had a more favorable view of Scots soldiers and a greater concern for the army and the empire than his royal father. George I died in June 1727, at the end of a seven-month residence in Hanover. He apparently preferred death to England.

The official portrait of King George I in his regal robes and garter insignia, by the usual team of Kneller and Smith, dated 1715, did all the artists could to flatter the fifty-five-year-old monarch, but a sourer sovereign it would be hard to imagine.

The same artists, working one year later, achieved a much more attractive portrait of the Prince of Wales. The prince had been favorably introduced to the British public when in 1708 at Oudenarde, he was distinguished in the decisive cavalry charge. His heroics were in marked contrast to the flight from the battle of the Bourbon and Stuart scions. The prince's service under Marlborough followed by his internal exile (it was actually proposed, as it had been in the case of the Mashams, that the prince be sent to command Jamaica, a virtual death sentence) reinforced the prince's determination to personally control and command the royal army, the prop of his prerogative. In imperial terms, the new king's command appeared in his attention to colonial commands, especially at his accession in 1727, and to the appointment of the Cartagena expedition's officers in 1739. George II himself was the last king of Britain to command an army in the field. He was victorious (with the assistance of the earl of Stair) at Dettingen on June 16, 1743. The exchange of the naval and colonial conquest of Louisbourg for a Netherlands barrier fortress, Bergen ap Zoom, in the peace treaty of 1748 demonstrated the priority of Europe in the concerns of the soldier-king. It was the king's ministers and military men, themselves mostly Marlborough's heirs, who responded to the challenge of France when the world war resumed in the backwoods of Virginia in 1754.

George, prince of Wales

Note the hostile contemporary amendments to the titles under the portrait (engraved by Bockman after Gibson's painting) of "the Big Man," Sir Robert Walpole. His honorifics were labeled "*Dis*Honble." He himself was called "*Briber, Coward, Ruiner of England*" in an administration dated "*A.D. 1723 to 1741.*" After the fact though they were, the libels suggest that Sir Robert was not the man to approve of a forward course in America or elsewhere. Born in 1676 to a landed and parliamentary Norfolk family, Walpole was educated at King's College, Cambridge. His tutor was Francis Hare, afterward Marlborough's chaplain, publicist, and biographer. Informed of the talent of the young parliamentarian, Marlborough named Walpole to the admiralty council in 1705. In 1708, he famously defended the council from charges that it had failed to provide American convoys. Marlborough named Walpole his secretary at war. Following Walpole's leading role in the impeachment of Sacheverell in 1710, Marlborough had Walpole made treasurer of the navy. The tory triumph in October, however, meant that the young highflier was dismissed from all his offices, impeached on account of army contracts, expelled from the house, and imprisoned in the Tower (as duly noted in the amendments to his portrait's inscription).

An exact revenge was doubly sweet. At the accession of King George, Walpole became paymaster of the forces, a notoriously profitable post. He led the impeachment of the tory leaders Bolingbroke, Oxford, and Ormonde. In October 1715, Walpole became first lord of the treasury, with immediate profits in excess of £60,000. Splitting from Stanhope and Sunderland over the continental and imperial concerns inherited from Marlborough, Walpole left the ministry and joined the Prince of Wales at Leicester House. The nominal reconciliation of the king and the prince brought Walpole back to minor office, but it was not until the South Sea crisis killed off Walpole's competition—Stanhope, Sunderland, and both Craggs—that Walpole returned to the treasury in 1720. Colossus-like (as the cartoons had it) the "Robinocracy" bestrode the next twenty-one years. With the exception of two brief wars with Spain, Robin's reign was a period of peace. He had, he said, seen war and despised it. Besides, the South Sea bubble in Britain and the Mississippi Company's collapse in France left the major Atlantic powers too poor to mount a major war. Not until March 1738 did the combined crises of Gibraltar, Georgia, and the Guarda Costa put paid to Walpole's peace. Since he had disclaimed all responsibility for the war and its conduct, it was manifestly unfair that the dreadful debacle at Cartagena, the shameful failure at Guantánamo, and the botched attempt on Panama should at last have brought down the exhausted prime minister. His contemporary critic wrote on this portrait that Walpole was "*Turned out too late. Died of Gout and the Stone,*" an agonizing conclusion to the only extensive interval of peace in the hundred years war between France and England for Atlantic mastery.

"It is your war," said Walpole to his colleague and successor, Thomas Pelham-Holles, duke of Newcastle, "I wish you well of it." In 1712, at the age of nineteen, Pelham-Holles had become the wealthiest landlord (and greatest private parliamentary patron) in Britain. His marriage to lady Henrietta Godolphin and his adhesion to the Stanhope-Sunderland ministry began an uninterrupted ascent to power. Named secretary of state for the southern department in 1724, Newcastle did what he could to sustain Marlborough's system of European alliances against France, assaults on the Spanish empire, a closer union with Scotland, and as much attention to the American executive as his ministerial colleagues—and, after 1727, the new king—permitted.

Devious, indecisive, even "a political coward," Newcastle was a bad war leader, as the Caribbean campaign demonstrated, but he was a force in favor of vigorous measures and executives in America, if only because America was ever more clearly of weight in the Atlantic balance of power. "The great war for the empire" was effectively led by others of Marlborough's heirs. It was ended only by the accession of the first civilian king in a century. Newcastle sought a reconciliation with the Americans—whose aggrandizement he had championed for forty years—in the postwar quarrel over the imperial spoils. So he lost his last office in the summer of 1766.

He died within the year.

The duke of Newcastle is pictured here (by Kneller and Smith) as a young man in his first office, lord chamberlain, lavishly robed, wearing the chain and George of the garter, holding his staff of office. In the background, a classical arcade represents the enormous domestic building program that would eventually bankrupt the uncaring aristocrat.

Sir Charles Wager inherited and cultivated an interest in naval empire. His maternal grandfather was William Goodson, the vice admiral enriched in Cromwell's Western Design. Charles's father made a dexterous choice, taking his warship to join the escort of Charles II on his return from exile. Captain Wager saw distinguished service at Tangier, but he died young and Charles was apprenticed to a family friend, a Quaker merchant and seafarer in Rhode Island. Not until he was twenty-three, an advanced age for an apprentice officer, did Wager join the navy of King William. Com-

Sir Robert Walpole

missioned during the officer purge of 1689, distinguished at Barfleur, Wager was quickly promoted captain. He commanded convoys to New England and Virginia until the Peace of Ryswick.

At the outbreak of war in 1702, Commodore Wager's squadron blockaded the coasts of Normandy and Brittany. Sailing to the Mediterranean, he negotiated an Algerine treaty. He shared in the conquests of Gibraltar and Barcelona. Wager took command of the West Indian squadron in 1707. In May following, he engaged the Spanish treasure fleet of Cartagena. Unsupported by his two captains, Wager attacked the three Spanish flagships, sank one, and captured the second. Now rich and famous, lauded by Marlborough and Godolphin, Wager was knighted on his return home in 1709 and elected to parliament on the government interest in 1710. Shelved by the tories, Wager became first comptroller of the navy at the Protestant accession. For the next

Thomas Holles, duke of Newcastle

twenty-four years he was a member of the admiralty board. Admiral Wager did not hoist his flag until 1726, when he took command of a squadron sent to the Baltic to intimidate the Russians. After relieving Gibraltar from the Spanish siege in 1727, and being appointed first lord of the admiralty in 1733, Wager's popularity was such that he was elected to parliament from Westminster in 1734. In 1739, on the outbreak of the third war with Spain, Wager secured the Caribbean command for Edward Vernon and the Pacific squadron for George Anson, but Wager lost office with his friend and patron Sir Robert Walpole and died the next year.

Wager's portrait, subsequently engraved by Faber after Gibson's 1732 oil painting, shows Wager's flag as admiral of the blue flying from the mainmast of his flagship. Most unusually, the admiral is depicted wearing a cavalry officer's breastplate under a civilian velvet coat. The coarseness of his countenance, so a contemporary wrote, belied the gentle Quaker manners Wager acquired in his Rhode Island childhood. His particular interest in America, its relation to the Spanish Caribbean, and of both to English power is reflected in his voluminous papers, abrim with American projects for enhanced naval bases and squadrons, commerce and conquest.

The son of a secretary of state to William III, Edward Vernon began his career in the flagship of Sir George Rooke and served at the Cadiz fiasco in 1702. A lieutenant in Sir Cloudesly Shovell's flagship at Malaga and Barcelona, Vernon had his own command at Tulon. He commanded a ship in Byng's squadron off Dunkirk in 1708 and joined in the pursuit of Forbin's fleet. Seconded to Wager's squadron in Jamaica, Vernon saw two long West Indian tours of duty, divided by the tory administration. After the 1719–21 war with

Sir Charles Wager

Spain, Vernon came home to be elected to parliament. Vernon advocated renewed war with Spain and proposed the capture of Porto Bello, the Panamanian treasure port. Rebuffed by Walpole, Vernon went into opposition. Despite this, Wager secured the Caribbean command for Vernon on the eve of the next war with Spain. Eschewing an attack on the Havana as an army objective, Vernon's squadron took an unprepared Porto Bello in November 1739, less than a month after the declaration of war in Europe. After vainly but destructively cannonading Cartagena, Vernon called for an army, but unsupported by Vernon, the troops died in the assault on Fort St. Lazaro and from epidemic disease on the transports Vernon held at anchor. Vernon then refused to attack Santiago, Cuba. Instead, he dumped the army at Guantánamo Bay. Vernon sabotaged an attack on Panama. Recalled late in 1742, Vernon commanded a Channel squadron briefly in 1745 but, cashiered by the king, never served again.

Vice Admiral Vernon's portrait (engraved by Faber after Bardwell's painting in 1740, © National Portrait Gallery, London) shows the hero of Porto Bello with (engraved) telescope and (lion-hilted) hanger, the insignia of rank before naval officers, inspired by Vernon himself, adopted uniform. In the background is an astonishing scene of wooden ships (and intrepid sailors) assaulting stone fortresses (something Vernon refused to repeat at Cartagena).

The real victor at Porto Bello was an officer of utterly unknown antecedents and the plainest of names, Charles Brown. He joined the navy sometime in the reign of William III and was commissioned lieutenant in 1700, aged about twenty-one. Eight more years of service saw Brown a master and commander. A year later, he became captain of a converted fireship. Brown was captured en route to his next command, at Boston. He tried to mitigate his misfortune in the usual way, by reporting on the French ports through which he passed en route to his exchange. Before peace put him on the beach, Brown commanded convoys to New England and to the West Indies. Reinstated after the Protestant succession, Brown served during the 1720s in the West Indies, ordered to protect merchant shipping from the Spanish coast guards.

War with Spain was in the offing when, in December 1737, Brown was promoted commodore on the Jamaica station. Two years later, Admiral Vernon took command. He ordered Brown to lead the assault on Porto Bello. In failing winds on November 21, 1739, Brown put the *Hampton Court* alongside "the Iron Castle." Her crew took to the boats, scaled the nearly vertical cliffs, and stormed the formidable castle. Brown then personally compelled the surrender of the port's remaining forts and their garrisons. The Spanish governor offered his sword to Brown, but he referred him to his superior officer, Admiral Vernon, who took the surrender—and the credit. In failing health, Brown sailed home in October 1740. He was rewarded with a shore post, commanding the Chatham dockyard until his death in 1753.

One moment of glory marked a career that covered six decades. It is memorialized in this Faber engraving of 1740. Its background completes the picture of Porto Bello which Faber had begun in his Vernon image. In the foreground, Commodore Brown fills out his velvet coat. He grasps his simple cutlass in his big right hand. His plain telescope lies on (an oddly placed) wall beside him. His distinguishing pennant as commodore flies from the foretopmast of the *Hampton Court*. Brown's commonplace countenance is enlivened by his

Edward Vernon
© National Portrait Gallery, London

penetrating eyes, focused by sixty years of service at sea. Here is the portrait of a plain sailor in an aristocratic age.

George Wade, like so many distinguished imperial officers, came from an Anglo-Irish military family. In December 1690, aged seventeen, he was commissioned in the earl of Bath's (10th) regiment. During King William's war, Wade rose rapidly through the regiment's commissioned ranks. He succeeded Roger Elliot as captain of grenadiers in 1695 and served with Elliot's half brother, Alexander Spotswood. At the outbreak of the War of the Spanish, and English, Succession in 1702, Wade's grenadiers obeyed lord Cutts's astonishing orders to storm the citadel at Liège. He succeeded Eliot as major of the 10th, but the campaign of 1703 had been so disappointing that Wade volunteered to serve in Portugal. Marlborough brevetted Wade lieutenant colonel, and Galway made him adjutant general. At Valencia, Wade won a regiment. He escaped from Almanza with much of the brigade he commanded. Promoted brigadier general, Wade was Stanhope's second in command in the conquest of Minorca, led the storm of Fort St. Philip, and was sent home with dispatches.

As a client of Marlborough, Galway, and Stanhope, there could be no command for Wade during the tory ministry but, on the outbreak of the '15, Wade took two regiments of dragoons to overawe Bath and seize the weapons cached there. Wade so established himself in Bath that the formerly tory city returned the general to parliament for the next twenty-six years. From 1724 to 1740, Wade commanded the forces in Scotland. His old comrade in the 10th, Colonel Alexander Spotswood, home from the government of Virginia, was briefly Scots quartermaster general. Wade put the men of his garrison regiments (including the veterans of the American Regiment) to work building 240 miles of military roads. Promoted major general at the

Charles Brown, by Faber

accession of King George II, Wade held four garrison governments, from Fort William to Berwick, reforging the Cromwellian fortress chain. In 1743, Wade succeeded the earl of Stair as field marshal and commander of the British forces in Flanders. He lost four of Marlborough's conquests in a month. Baffled by the '45, General Wade retired, aged seventy-two. He died two years later.

His portrait, engraved by Faber after Van Diest, shows Wade as a cavalry general. In the background runs his road through the highlands to Fort William. A dispatch rider races across one of the thirty bridges Wade's men built. "Had you seen these roads before they were made, / You would lift up your hands and bless General Wade." In this portrait, the general looks every bit the sensualist he was (he acknowledged three illegitimate children). Wade was, as his biographer put it, "a very worthy man where women were not concerned."

Wade's services in Flanders under William III and Marlborough, in Portugal and Spain under Galway and Stanhope, and in his own commands in Scotland and the Netherlands, shared with veterans from every Atlantic theater, spanned more than half a century, from 1690 to 1745. They exemplify the command continuum of the age of Marlborough and obliterate the idea of "salutary neglect."

William Blakeney was another scion of an Anglo-Irish military family. On the frontiers of Ireland, at Castle Blakeney in 1690, aged eighteen, William organized his father's tenants to defend the family plantation from the Irish "natives," excited to revolt by the presence of King James II and the French army. In 1695 Blakeney enlisted in the army of "the deliverer," King William, as an adjutant of the Royal Irish, but he did not achieve commissioned rank until 1701. As a lieutenant and adjutant of the Royal Irish, Blakeney fought at Blenheim. Marlborough

George Wade

promoted him a captain in the hard-hit regiment a week after the battle, brevetted Blakeney major in 1707, and secured him a lieutenancy in the First Guards a year later. Blakeney was promoted captain and lieutenant colonel in 1712. Marlborough retained Blakeney in the Guards in 1715, but he did not receive a regiment in the Irish garrison until 1737. This made the veteran officer, but a junior colonel, and his exiguous corps eligible for the West Indian expedition. As adjutant general, Blakeney won the attention of authority by his speedy organization of the 4,000-man American Regiment and by his perceptive dispatches, written from New York, on related issues of American politics. Promoted brigadier general, Blakeney opposed, in writing with the other veteran officers, the fatal assault on Fort St. Lazaro.

One of the few officers to emerge with credit from the West Indian expedition, Blakeney was promoted major general and commissioned governor of Stirling Castle. He famously defended his post in the '45. Promoted lieutenant general and commissioned lieutenant governor of Minorca, Blakeney commanded the island conquest for a decade. Then, in April 1756, Minorca was attacked by a French expeditionary force. After Admiral Byng failed to relieve him, Blakeney, now aged eighty-five, held out in the citadel, Fort St. Philip, against overwhelming odds for ten weeks. He surrendered at last on honorable terms and evacuated his garrison to Gibraltar. A national hero, Blakeney was dubbed a knight of the bath and created baron Blakeney. He died in 1761 and was buried in Westminster Abbey. William Blakeney was an exemplary soldier of the king on the frontiers of the British empire. He was also an outstanding example of King George II's preference for his former comrades in Marlborough's army, no matter how well along in years.

Blakeney's portrait, engraved by Ryley, © National Portrait Gallery, London, depicts the general as colonel of the Iniskillin foot and lieutenant governor of Minorca standing within the ramparts of Fort St. Philip. Blakeney wears a modern major general's uniform, without armor but with a braided tricorne hat and periwig, and he brandishes the baton of his most famous imperial command.

William Blakeney, by Ryley after Chalmers, © National Portrait Gallery, London

In the spring of 1713, the Christanna scouts found bands of Tuscarora refugees starving in the woods, fugitives from their people's greatest disaster. In March, South Carolina's James Moore had led Catawba and Cherokee warriors to storm the fortified Tuscarora town of Nooherooka. Hundreds of the Hancock band of the Tuscaroras were massacred. Many more were enslaved (to this day their descendants remain distinct elements in South Carolina's multiracial upcountry plantation communities). Those who escaped trekked north along the warriors' path to form the nucleus of the sixth nation of the Iroquois. They drew their league brethren into an unending war against the Catawba "flatheads" of Carolina. That war brought Iroquois fighters down the warriors' path that crossed Virginia above the fall line, a prescription for frontier friction. Although they had taken no part in the war, the Blount bands of the Tuscarora had also fled from their homelands, north across the Roanoke River. Found by Spotswood's scouts, they accepted his invitation to resettle. Although "Blunt King of the Tuskaroodaus . . . told Colonel Spotswood that the country belonged to them before we English came hither; so that he thought they had a better title then we, and ought not be confined to such narrow limits for hunting," nonetheless, in the months and years before they too began to filter north to the shelter of the Longhouse, Blunt's kinsmen helped fill the great barrier gap between the Roanoke and the Rappahannock.[34]

In the autumn of the year, Spotswood traveled the entire length of the new barrier. In six weeks of wilderness travel, covering some 800 miles, Spotswood lost servants, horses, baggage and, in innumerable forest encounters, nearly lost his life. Rather than trusting to a barrier of refugees, red and white, Spotswood would have preferred to act directly against the hostile Tuscaroras and the Iroquois raiders. Indeed, the lieutenant governor and council declared war against these marauders, but Colonel Spotswood found that "the people being unwilling to march from their homes, and not one Officer to be found in the whole Colony that have been in any Employment of Action in an Army," he would have to rely upon the multiethnic barrier to protect the province.[35]

This militant settlement strategy increasingly involved "plantation," in the original sense of the word. From Roman Gaul to English Ireland, as a contemporary "Cato" recalled, plantations were intended "to keep conquered countries in subjection and to prevent the necessity of constant standing armies: a Policy which the Romans practiced, till their conquests grew too numerous, the conquered countries too distant, and their empire too unwieldy to be managed by their native force only." So, too, in Virginia. As Spotswood repeatedly remarked, the Old Dominion was still being seized from its aboriginal owners. As formerly in Ireland, so presently in Virginia, plantations were menaced by as yet unconquered "natives," backed by France. To resist the French and Indians, Spotswood revived the ancient imperial strategy of farmer-fighters manning a frontier of homesteaders, living in government-sponsored settlements, financed by government-favored investors. So Spotswood issued ever-larger grants between the fall line and his outpost at Germanna to his friends and neighbors along the Rappahannock.[36]

The "governor's friends," "the court party," "tories," or "long heads" (that is, full-locked churchmen, not short-haired dissenters, "roundheads"—so long had the tonsorial distinctions of the English civil wars lingered in Virginia)— rallied on Guy Fawkes Day, November 5, 1713. On that day of Protestant patriotic celebration, Spotswood convened the second session of his reformed assembly. In his speech from the throne, he announced the suspension of hostilities in the war with France. "Peace," he declared, "ever comes Attended with innumerable benefits." These he proposed to consolidate with an act for "the better improving the staple of tobacco." It would organize the Virginia tobacco trade to take advantage of the peacetime revival of commerce and to reward the governor's friends in the assembly. The act provided for the inspection and packing of all tobacco offered for sale at official warehouses by forty-seven well-paid tobacco agents, each appointed by the lieutenant governor. The agents would give the planters notes for the value of the inspected crop. These tobacco notes would provide Virginia with its first currency. All public officials, the anglican clergy prominent among them, would receive their salaries and fees in valuable script rather than in trash tobacco. Quality control would both raise the price of tobacco in London and lower the cost of shipping by eliminating trash, by providing uniform barrels, and by ending pilfering.[37]

The political profits were certainly immediate and potentially profound. As Spotswood wrote to his superiors, by the tobacco act he had "clear'd the way for a Govr towards carrying any reasonable point in the house of burgesses, for he will have in his disposal about forty agencies, which one with another are likely to yield nigh 250 pounds P. Ann. each; these my intentions are to dispose of among ye most considerable men of the Colony, and principally to gratify with a Place all the members of the Assembly who were for the bill." Twenty-three burgesses who voted for the bill, and four of their relatives (either councilors who assented to the burgess bill or their dependents) all got tobacco agencies. Like General Hunter, Colonel Spotswood had bought a provincial legislature. The remainder of the session went swimmingly. An act continuing the frontier rangers' pay also authorized the commander in chief to redistribute the force to supervise the new barrier. To defend the barrier, the assembly also reallocated the unused funds appropriated for military assistance of North Carolina. Spotswood's miners and tenants at Germanna were exempted from taxes. So were Spotswood's lands there. But all these acts and their compliant authors were endangered. The name "Germanna" itself signaled another seismic disturbance in "the British Empire."[38]

On October 14, 1714, Spotswood received secretary of state lord Bolingbroke's announcement of the death of Queen Anne and the proclamation of the elector of Hanover as King George. On November 17, Spotswood convened the second session of the assembly that had been bought by tobacco agencies. Sadly for Spotswood, this would be the assembly's last session. All the legislatures of the empire had to be dissolved within six months after the death of the sovereign under whose authority they had been convened. So Virginia would share in the imperial succession crisis. In his speech from the throne, the lieutenant governor lamented the death of the "most Religious Queen," but he declared that Virginians had "unanimously" acknowledged their new king's "undoubted and rightful Title." Spotswood strained to associate King George's foreign identity with an aptness "for Ruling Remote Colonys." He suggested that Virginia, as the crown's most ancient dominion in America, should be the first to congratulate the new king on his accession to the imperial throne. He pledged "that it shall be my care, as it is my duty not only my Self to preserve an inviolable fidelity to his Majesty, but to preserve the Governm't under my charge in a due obedience." Privately, Colonel Spotswood doubtless reminded everyone that he had fought alongside the king's heir, the new prince of Wales, against the French at Oudenarde to extend the Netherlands Barrier.[39]

"The Strength of your Barrier" as Virginia's defense against the French and their Indian allies was the main subject of Spotswood's speech. Now that there was a German prince upon the throne, more of his compatriots should be settled at Spotswood's mining and military settlement "on ye Frontiers of Rappa." To make the tributaries who guarded the southern frontier more reliable allies and to enhance the allegiance of their next generation, the assembly should allocate money to civilize and covert the tributaries' children. The capstone of Spotswood's "Barrier" project was his proposal that the assembly incorporate a Virginia Indian Company. During its twenty-year monopoly of the trade south of the James River, the company would eliminate "the Clandestine Trade carried on by some ill men." These old traders had both brutalized the Indians and supplied them with munitions, Spotswood declared, so they were the major instigators of the recent Indian wars. The Virginia Indian Company (VIC) would cut these renegades out of the fur trade, stop the sale of weapons to hostile Indians and, by fair treatment, win native allegiance. In the service of provincial security the company would also pay for the magazine, the armorer and the storekeeper and, by regulated sales to allied Indians, circulate the gunpowder stockpile, keeping Virginia's powder dry. The VIC would maintain the trading post, the mission school, and the embassy at Fort Christanna. The company would pay the garrison and construct new buildings at the fort. Thence the company would dispatch large, well-directed trading parties south and west. Offering cheap goods bought in bulk, the company's traders would do the diplomatic as well as the economic work of the province. Spotswood was elected governor of the company.[40]

Spotswood's exemplar, Marlborough, had been governor of the Hudson's Bay Company. Its objectives were identical to those of the Virginia Indian Company: to achieve mastery of vast stretches of the American wilderness by economic and diplomatic exchanges with its aboriginal inhabitants at the expense, monetary and military, of the France of Louis XIV. Like the Hudson's Bay Company, the VIC combined economic with strategic objectives. Spotswood had found in the Tuscarora uprising that control of the arms trade was the strongest sanction in Indian diplomacy. Monopolizing trade south of the James, the new company would not only give the commander in chief control of weapons sales but also would ensure fair dealing with the tributary tribes. Company profits would pay the salary of the teacher, the gentle Charles Griffin, and meet the costs of his Indian school and its anglicanization of the native nobility, hitherto supported personally by Spotswood. The Christanna mission school was Spotswood's rebuke to the college's failure in Indian education, that is, to the Green Spring faction. A leader of that faction, William Byrd II, was the leading James River trader by inheritance from his father. When, on December 24, 1714, the subscription lists for the Virginia Indian Company were opened, Byrd and the other old traders boycotted the event. So Spotswood himself invested in company stock, and he recruited his Rappahannock coadjutors in politics and western development, led by Speaker Beverley, to help capitalize the corporation. The VIC was to be more than a fur-trading company or even an anchor of the barrier. It was the base from which Spotswood and the Beverleys could challenge the Green Spring faction for the development of the upper James and Roanoke river valleys.[41]

As soon as the assembly adjourned, on Christmas Eve of 1714, Byrd sailed for London to see if the new regime would change commanders in Virginia, veto the tobacco and Indian trade acts, and so revive the Green Spring oligarchy in the Old Dominion. Byrd's primary supporter was his factor for both tobacco and fur, the elder Micaiah Perry. Perry was a determined whig, as was his son, also Micaiah, who took over the firm on his father's death in 1721, and who became a Walpolean alderman, member of parliament, and lord mayor of London. Perry and company resented everything about Spotswood: Marlborough's legate, a churchman, a royalist, a Scot, a monopolist, an imperialist, a tory. Spotswood had also sinned against merchant priorities by building fortifications with corvée labor, labor that the factors thought should have been devoted to tobacco. Responding to the economic provisions of the union, Spotswood had infiltrated his Scots compatriots into the tobacco trade. He now proposed to control that trade by a provincial act that would both raise the price paid the producers of tobacco and facilitate its taxation by both the crown and the colony. To cap his economic iniquities, Spotswood proposed to monopolize the fur trade by a government corporation.[42]

Church and college, religion and economics were inextricably intertwined. In the nexus of politics and religion, Spotswood had supported the provincial clergy against the famously whig commissary, James Blair. Spotswood had challenged Blair's control, that is, that of the Green Spring faction, over the college. Prior to Spotswood's takeover, Perry had been the college's London financial agent. Spotswood had cashiered the Perry-connected naval officer for the Rappahannock. He would do the same in the James River district. Colonel Spotswood had crafted an aggressive southern strategy based on Indian treaties, Fort Christanna, and the Virginia Indian Company, all to the detriment of the old James River Perry & Co., connection. To the north, Spotswood proposed an industrial frontier centered on Germanna (provincial production was anathema to a mercantilist such as Perry). From Germanna, the lieutenant governor was advancing settlement up the Rappahannock, rivaling the James River fiefdom of the Green Spring faction and their London merchant factors.

Ever since 1676, the country party, its London correspondents, and whig politicians had relied upon the provincial council to check militant governors general and all were furious with Spotswood's challenge to their control of the council. At the moment, Spotswood was resisting the restoration of Edmund Berkeley (the successful suitor of Francis Nicholson's "Delyma," Belinda Burwell), who had lost his seat because of many years of unexcused residence in London. Perry & Co. wanted Berkeley restored to his old seniority. That would permit him to replace Edmund Jennings as president of the council. Jennings, a relative of Marlborough's duchess (so, allegedly, was Spotswood), was much disliked by the faction as a prerogative man, a churchman, and an enemy of Blair and Byrd. Jennings was now in London supporting Spotswood against the planter-merchant faction. "Old Perry really talks impertinently of the breach of my Instructions" in the Berkeley case, Spotswood complained. "If my Superiors think fit to put him at the head of that Board, it shall be entirely indifferent to me in what a Rank he votes," Spotswood wrote, "but I think it is doing little honor to the Government to have its Council appointed in the Virginia Coffee House as an Merchant in London . . . has no other rule to judge a man's merit than by the Number of his Tobacco hogsheads." Worse, the London merchants were pressing the appointment of no fewer than three more members of the Green Spring faction to council seats. Spotswood repeatedly warned his superiors "that the People of Virginia are not well pleas'd when they see so many of one Family [the Burwell connection] on the Gen'l Court Bench," perverting the court's appellate power to favor their personal interests. Spotswood now lit a backfire by nominating as councilors his personal retainers and his clients among the grandees. Eventually, the lieutenant governor permanently altered the balance of the council in favor of the crown.[43]

Meanwhile, the imperial succession crisis rapidly moved toward rebellion in Britain. The combination of a change of dynasties, the accession of a foreigner chosen by parliament, and the monarch-elect's reluctance to leave Hanover for London, all emboldened the jacobite resistance to his succession. The threat of civil war and foreign invasion challenged imperial officialdom, just as the government was convulsed by the most dramatic transformation of office-holding since the restoration of the monarchy fifty-five years previously. In the confusion, neither Perry & Co. nor Colonel Spotswood could get a hearing at

Whitehall. Absent imperial input, Virginia politics was dominated by domestic difficulties: drought and heat, crop failure and Indian war. Food was so scarce that Spotswood had to embargo grain shipments. Planter poverty compelled him to allow the sale of trash tobacco, despite the new tobacco act. The law itself was so hated that the lieutenant governor had to get an act passed to punish the burning of tobacco warehouses.[44]

Worse threatened. On May 15, 1715, a messenger from South Carolina reached Christanna, where Colonel Spotswood was directing the conversion of the fort to five-square form (the same pattern of fortification that Captain John Smith had imposed upon Jamestown!). The South Carolinian reported that at first light on Good Friday, the warriors from the Ten Towns of the Yamasee, in red and black war paint, had overwhelmed Carolina's southern border posts, forced the evacuation of Port Royal by sea, and swept north. The Yamasee had burned every settlement south of Charleston. They drove the survivors into the fortified city. Then, to the north of Charleston, ten more tribes rose as one. First, they tortured the traders living among them (abusive, evil men, the chief cause of the war, so Spotswood's informants told him). The natives then wiped out every settlement more than ten miles west of Charleston. The proprietary governor, Colonel Charles Craven, declared martial law, called out the surviving militia, and personally commanded a counterattack. It "gained some time to build Forts and fortify houses" in a defensive perimeter across the Charleston peninsula. Within the "marked line of Garrisons," there were only 1,500 white men in arms to withstand some 8,000 Yamasee and allied warriors.[45]

Preconditioned by nearly two decades of fighting French ambitions in Europe, Colonel Spotswood believed that the Yamasee war was the first stage of a new Bourbon plan of imperial aggression. He wrote that the attack on South Carolina was "contriv'd by French and Spanish Councils for the . . . driving his Majty's Subjects out of that Province." He dispatched HMS *Valour* to Charleston, loaded with munitions and the vanguard of the 300 volunteers and 30 tributaries whom Colonel Spotswood recruited to reinforce the Carolinians. He ordered the captain of the *Valour* to keep open Charleston's communications by sea. Spotswood urged his fellow vice admirals, Hunter and Dudley, to order their guardships south, freighted with the surplus munitions from the 1711 expedition. Royal ships and arms would both encourage and reinforce the Carolinians in their war against the Yamasees. The station ships would also protect Charleston from French or Spanish assault from the sea. Virginia's commander in chief wrote home "that nigh on 20 years of Service in the Wars of my Country may be taken as an earnest of my Capacity to act here in this Conjuncture." Having twice in four years had to send arms and men to the beleaguered Carolinians, Spotswood wanted more munitions from the royal ordnance, especially as he expected the French to instigate an Iroquois attack on Virginia's fall line frontier. As for Virginia's seacoast, if, as Spotswood feared, the French seized Port Royal and Charleston, "nothing less than a Squadron of Men of War would be able to guard the Bay of Chesapeak and its Trade."[46]

The troops Spotswood sent to Charleston landed just in time to help beat off an attack on the city's defenses. Nonetheless, they were badly treated by the locals. Ill clothed, ill supplied, ill housed, and unpaid, the Virginians were separated from the officers whom Spotswood had commissioned. Their authority, even over their own men, was denied by the Carolina authorities. Spotswood was "more perplexed than ever I was in my life" by Carolina's contempt for "the Obligations of their public Faith." To retrieve his own honor, Spotswood personally paid soldiers' wages to their "distress'd Widdows and indigent Wives and Children." He sent home an officer to beg the imperial authorities to force the Carolina proprietors "to wipe off that eternal blemish it will be on that Country, if so many men must be ruined for venturing their lives in its defence."[47]

In August 1715, the lieutenant governor issued writs for the election of burgesses. He hoped the new assembly would appropriate money for the Virginia volunteers sent to South Carolina and approve Spotswood's proposals to remodel the Virginia militia. "Duty, Honour, and Interest," said Spotswood in his speech from the throne, should impel the assembly to adopt the strategy he had learned from Marlborough: defend at a distance. "Never had Virginia so fair an Opportunity as now, to acquire Glory and appear to the Heathen the most formidable Dominion in America," Spotswood declared. The "Murders, Massacres, and Tortures" inflicted on "our Fellow Subjects" in South Carolina not only demanded Virginia's aid to "our Distress'd Brethren" but also warned Virginia's legislators of the need "to Arm and Secure your People from a Treacherous and Merciless Enemy."[48]

Spotswood's militant charge to the burgesses failed because of an electoral revolution. Drought, depression, and a trade collapse attributed by the opposition to Spotswood's tobacco act envenomed the election mandated by the death of Queen Anne. Not one of the twenty-three burgesses who had accepted the lieutenant governor's appointment as a tobacco agent was returned. Indeed, only fourteen of the fifty-one legislators were reelected. Not a single burgess now held a lucrative office in Spotswood's gift. "The Court Party" fell from a majority in the 1714 house to just six members in 1715. The former speaker, Peter Beverley, Spotswood's legislative leader, had been defeated in Middlesex County. Beverley's backup was the William and Mary College seat, now controlled by Spotswood as rector. "The Country Party" or "Patriots" disenfranchised the college. Then they decided every disputed election against "the Court Party" or the "Friends of the Governor." Nonetheless, the burgesses promised a dutiful consideration of the governor's speech and asked him to submit a detailed plan for the reform of the militia and budgets for the costs of the South Carolina expedition and a military emergency reserve fund.[49]

Spotswood took the bait. He was desperate to reform an undisciplined, unreliable, unwieldy, unfair militia system. The commander in chief had learned
that "the whole burden of defending the country rests upon the poorer Sort
of People." Virtually all propertied men were exempted from service as officeholders, present or former. Compelled to service, poor men could not even
arm themselves, as the 1684 law required, and were therefore subject to fine by
their officers. To attend militia musters, the farmers had to leave their crops,
risking "the entire loss of what should subsist an Indigent family." Spotswood
had proposed a socially equitable and militarily efficient new model. Virginia's
14,000 militiamen were to be reduced to 3,000 foot and 1,500 dragoons, plus
officers. These select militiamen were to be raised from each county in proportion to the number of its taxpayers. The counties would pay their troops by
levies proportioned to property values rather than by regressive poll taxes. The
men would be registered in muster rolls, uniformly armed at public expense,
and drilled by adjutants trained by Colonel Spotswood in the martial forms of
Marlborough's army.[50]

His opponents replied to Spotswood's militia initiative in language borrowed from the country party's antimilitary agitation at home. Given a disciplined force, the commander in chief and his adjutants would "huff and bully the
people." Spotswood's "Standing Army" was denounced as "a means to govern
Arbitrarily and by Martial Law." For twenty-five days, however, the burgesses
strung out the session, collecting their per diem salary while they prepared bills
(which they knew Spotswood would veto) to repeal the tobacco act and to rescind the Virginia Indian Company incorporation. At last, the burgesses voted
down the "Act for Settling the Militia and for the better Regulation thereof
and for Allowing their Pay." Still hoping for some better militia law, Spotswood
kept the burgesses in session for another ten days. The country party took the
time to write a place bill on the model of the 1705 act of parliament. It denied
the holders of any lucrative office a seat in the burgesses. The enemies of the
royal executive then proposed a triennial act, also modeled on a country party
statute. It would eliminate the governor's prerogative of legislative dissolution
and electoral writs. Finally, the burgesses rejected every payment to the soldiers
whom Spotswood had raised to fight in the Yamasee war, and to their suppliers.
The cost of American defense, Virginia's legislators declared, was the responsibility of the British crown.[51]

Spotswood at last understood that he was the victim of a "Trick and Trifle"
planned by the country party councilors and executed by their burgess clients.
Furious, the lieutenant governor dissolved the assembly and denounced those
who "fain to pass for Patriots." These representatives claimed to "Indulge the
poorer Sort of People" but refused to relieve them of the cost of defending
rich men's property, Spotswood declared. These legislators were "obstinately
bent to do nothing for the Safety and Dignity of his Majesty's Government."
Themselves selfish and rich, obstructionist and disloyal, so Spotswood wrote,

the country party burgesses had presented "the Giddy Resolves of the illiterate Vulgar in their Drunken Conventions" as the petitions of the people against the tobacco inspection and the fur-trade monopoly. These shabby compositions, Spotswood declared, were really the work of "the People's Mistaken Choice of a Set of Representatives, whom Heaven has not generally endowed with the Ordinary Qualifications requisite to Legislators." That is, they could neither "Spell *English* or Write Common Sense."[52]

Spotswood was the angrier at the country party's obfuscation, obstruction, and insult because of his anxiety over the succession crisis, not just in Britain but also in Europe and America. Like most of Marlborough's officers, Colonel Spotswood believed that the Utrecht treaties had sacrificed Marlborough's protections for the Protestant states in Europe, thrown away the captain general's prospects of conquering France, abandoned hopes of capturing the Spanish American ports and trade, and lost the best chance in half a century of stabilizing the frontiers of British America. There, failure meant that the Catholic French and Spanish were now free to incite the heathen Indians against the Protestant provinces from Maine to Carolina. In Britain itself, Spotswood feared a counterrevolution that would put a Catholic client of Louis XIV on the imperial throne. Queen Anne's prolonged illness, the delayed accession of King George, pro-Stuart demonstrations in London, jacobite conspiracy in the West Country, risings along the Border, and the invasion of England from Scotland so preoccupied most of the imperial authorities that they ignored the American provinces. Spotswood's dispatches from December 1713 until February 1716 received no reply, either from Queen Anne's commissioners of trade and plantations or from their successors appointed by King George until June 1, 1716.[53]

Then the new board came down decisively on Spotswood's side. They denounced the Virginia council's claim to monopolize the general court or any court of oyer and terminer. They disallowed an older Virginia act reserving provincial offices to creoles. They confirmed Spotswood's controversial land law (which preserved the crown's revenues and rights and imposed actual improvements as a condition of land patents). The commissioners commended Spotswood's efforts to educate, convert, and conciliate the natives. They noted that their predecessors had long since approved Spotswood's requests for munitions. They praised his forwardness in using those munitions to relieve South Carolina. The lords commissioners did write that Spotswood's speech dissolving the 1715 assembly was "so full of sharp expressions" as to impede the restoration of political peace in Virginia, but they assured the lieutenant governor that no credit would be given to his critics until they appeared before the board in person, which they had yet to do. In any case, the commissioners promised to take no action critical of the lieutenant governor until he was fully informed of any charges and given ample opportunity to reply.[54]

The new commissioners' support for Colonel Spotswood reflected a changed political situation in the imperial capital. As his first act reaching

England, the new king had recommissioned the duke of Marlborough as captain general. Although Marlborough was rapidly aging and politically diminished by 1716, he agreed with Spotswood, his former deputy chief of staff, that sooner or later, Virginia would become the focus of the imperial struggle for North America. The duke's present deputy was Spotswood's former chief, Cadogan. He had suppressed the jacobite rebellion, ascended to the peerage, and was in actual command of the army. Cadogan had superseded the duke of Argyll in Scotland for lackluster resistance to the rebellion. Disgraced, the duke was less able to assist his clients, William Byrd among them. Virginia's governor general, the earl of Orkney, was also in disfavor with the new regime for his trimming during the tory ministry and in the succession crisis. Removed from the privy council, Orkney was not able to oust Spotswood had he wished to do so. He could not even contest Spotswood's nominees to the Virginia council, no matter how large the bribe offered lady Orkney by opposition aspirants. Marlborough's son-in-law, the earl of Sunderland, was at the head of the treasury and so effectively prime minister. Spotswood was more pleased by the appointment of a good Marlborough man, General James Stanhope, as secretary of state for the southern department, and so Spotswood's superior officer. Stanhope had endorsed Spotswood's dispatches on the Yamasee war a year before the lords commissioners had done so, and Stanhope, having promoted Marlborough's imperial agenda in Spain, was the imperialist most concerned with making Spanish America subservient to British wealth and power.[55]

Spotswood immediately began to probe the Spanish Caribbean frontier. As vice admiral, Spotswood declared, his authority extended all the way to the Bahamas. Spotswood reported to Stanhope that he had commissioned an armed sloop, the *Virgin of Virginia*, Major Harry Beverley master, with orders to reconnoiter the pirate port at Nassau, seek out salvage opportunities on the Bahama banks (where another Spanish treasure fleet had come to grief) and, partly as a cover for the Bahama probes, develop a trade in Virginia foodstuffs with Jamaica. A storm off the Carolina capes drove the *Virgin* almost to Bermuda. There she was intercepted by a lurking *guarda costa*. The "Spanish" (the captain was French) officers ignored "ye English Ensigns" flown by the *Virgin*, laughed at the Spanish treaties of peace and commerce with Britain (modeled by Stanhope), and disregarded Lieutenant Governor Spotswood's commission and orders to Captain Beverley. The Spaniards stripped the *Virgin*'s crew—red, white, and black—and sent the sloop into St. Augustine. There the Spanish governor declared that, since maize was grown in Spanish America, the *Virgin*'s cargo of Indian corn must be contraband. He condemned the sloop and cargo and imprisoned the master and crew, all without trial.[56]

Somehow, after seven months in a Veracruz jail, Harry Beverley escaped, got home to Virginia, and reported to Colonel Spotswood. Spotswood's subsequent complaints that the Spanish had no "Regard to Justice or the Law of Nations" and his insistence that action must be taken "for the future Security

of the British Commerce in America against the Violence of the Spaniards"
led to a formal protest by British diplomats at Madrid. That failed, as did all
such complaints about the violence and rapacity of the Spanish *guarda costa*, the
injustice of the Spanish governors, and Spanish brutality to British prisoners.
So the stage was set for three wars with Spain before midcentury. Spotswood
anticipated this outcome. In his report on the capture of the *Virgin* and the
imprisonment of its crew (all of whom, Spotswood imagined, would be turned
over as heretics to the tortures of the Inquisition), he recommended an amphibious assault against St. Augustine and an extension of the British empire's
southern frontier to the St. John's River. That is, Colonel Spotswood called for
the conquest and colonization of what became Georgia.[57]

No sooner had he sent Harry Beverley sailing south to beard Spain than
Spotswood himself moved to extend the British frontier westward. He intended
to enrich himself and his clients, displace the Iroquois and their dependents,
and interrupt French commerce and communications. On August 20, 1716,
Colonel Spotswood rode west out of Williamsburg accompanied by a Huguenot officer, Lieutenant John Fontaine, visiting his family and their coreligion-
ists, now naturalized Virginians and armed frontiersmen, and recommended
to Spotswood by Lieutenant Jonathan Atkins, a veteran who had settled in
Virginia and who was now a stockholder in the VIC. Spotswood and Fontaine
rode west and north to the Rappahannock. They were escorted by two troops
of rangers and their Meherrin scouts, commanded by Captain Christopher
Smith, the officer in charge of the northern frontier district, and by Captain
Robert Hicks, his southern district counterpart. Their two troops were a tenth
of the ranger force that patrolled Virginia's frontier from the Potomac to the
Roanoke. The ranger captains themselves were Spotswood's chief links with
Virginia's frontiersmen, red and white.[58]

At the palisaded village of Germanna, the lieutenant governor and his escort were joined by fifty "gentleman adventurers." All of them were members
of Spotswood's Rappahannock connection. Most were Beverleys, by blood or
marriage. They were led by their patriarch, Robert Beverley Jr., the historian
and bitter enemy of Francis Nicholson. The Beverleys had quite a different
opinion of Alexander Spotswood. William Beverley, who codified Virginia's
laws during Spotswood's command, wrote that his administration "is an honor
to Great Britain and the greatest happiness that ever befell Virginia, raising
it from need and indigence to a flourishing plenty and prosperity, with an increase of virtue and good manners." The 13,000 acres that Robert Beverley Jr.
had surveyed "among ye little Mountains" before Spotswood arrived were the
foundation of the governor's Germanna settlement.[59]

Spotswood had commissioned the historian's brother, Peter, surveyor general of Virginia. He had then been reelected as speaker of the house of burgesses. Subsequently, Spotswood would successfully nominate Beverley to the
council. Among Spotswood's suite was Peter Beverley's first assistant surveyor

for the Rappahannock region, James Taylor (grandfather of Zachary). Augustine Smith, Beverley's second assistant surveyor, also rode with Spotswood's party. Smith's older brother, John, was a councilor. Their father had founded Virginia's first professional organization, the Society of Surveyors, exemplars of the emergent upper-middle class of Virginians who were the instruments of imperial expansion. Robert Brooke and Christopher Smith combined the roles of militia officers and Indian diplomats with land surveying, a potent package, productive of transmontane empire. Both Brooke and Smith were clients of the Beverley family. They were joined in Spotswood's entourage by the Robinson brothers, Christopher and John, nephews of the new bishop of London, both married to Beverleys and both Spotswood's nominees to provincial office. Together the Robinsons and Beverleys founded the greatest Virginia dynasty of the next generation. The only missing Beverley brother was Harry, the venturesome voyager, still incarcerated in a Spanish American prison. Also riding with the "gentlemen adventurers" was William Robertson. For thirty-six years clerk of the council, Robertson processed all land grants in Virginia. He was Spotswood's trustee for much of the 93,000 acres the lieutenant governor would patent in the upper Rappahannock region. Spotswood would remove Nathaniel Burwell as naval officer of the Lower York District to make room for Robertson (and to challenge the Burwell-based faction in their heartland). Colonel Jeremiah Clowder, Spotswood's appointee as sheriff of King and Queen County, and his colleague on the county court bench, William Todd, rounded out the party. Almost every one of Spotswood's "Gentleman Adventurers," and many of their relations, subsequently patented vast acreage in the Rappahannock region they now traversed. The only exception, displaying the fastidiousness for which his family was to become famous, was George Mason.[60]

From Germanna, the members of the expedition followed the Rapidan until they turned west up the Swift Run valley. They rode in easy stages, hunting along the way. When they camped each night, a ranger sentry was posted before Colonel Spotswood's military marquee. On the afternoon of September 5, 1716, the party reached the watershed where the Swift Run Gap cuts through the Blue Ridge. A practicable pass through the mountain frontier had been Spotswood's imperial objective since his first summer in Virginia, six years before. Now, standing in the water gap, Spotswood envisioned a protected piedmont behind him, the theater of imperial expansion in the coming generation. Beyond the mountain barrier, Spotswood anticipated an unlimited extension of the British empire. So "we drank King George's health here and all the Royal Family." The rangers thought that the expedition had gone far enough, now that it had reached "Mt. George," but Spotswood insisted that the party follow the Iroquois blazes down the western slope. The Iroquois trail brought the imperial adventurers to the Elk River. This they followed down into a great valley. In its midst ran "a large River which we called Euphrates." On the plains of this river, "Shenandoah" to the Iroquois, Colonel Spotswood "buried a bottle with a paper enclosed in which he writ that he took possession of this place in the name of and for King George 1st of England."[61]

Following a feast of fresh-caught fish, deer, and turkey, the gentlemen "drank the King's health in Champagne" and Tokay. The rangers fired a volley. The adventurers drank "the Prince's health in Burgandy, and [the rangers] fired a volley; all the rest of the Royal Family in Claret, and a Volley. We drank the Governor's health and fired another volley." Ignoring the adage not to mix grape and grain, the gentlemen then consumed "Virginia Red Wine and White Wine, Irish Usquebaugh, Brandy, Shrub, two sorts of Rum, Champagne, Canary, Cherry punch, Cider, Water &c." The next morning, Colonel Spotswood ordered the rangers to scout a route westward to Lake Erie and locate a vulnerable point in the line of French communications between Canada and Louisiana. The gentlemen, doubtless a bit the worse for wear, turned eastward. Passing over "Mt Spotswood," they rode down the river valleys until they reached the mansion of that stalwart of Spotswood's Rappahannock River connection, councilor and colonel William Basset. His boats conveyed the last of the party downriver to a point within an easy ride of Williamsburg.[62]

In the imagination of after ages, Spotswood's gentlemen adventurers became the "Knights of the Golden Horseshoe" because, in the autumn of 1716, Colonel Spotswood presented each of his companions with a keepsake: a little golden horseshoe with garnet "nails." The inscription on the verso read, "Sic juvat ["jurat"?] transcendere mountes" (which, if we are to judge by the wine list, it was). On the obverse was inscribed, "The Transmontane Order." The rules of the order opened membership to "any gentleman . . . that can prove his having drunk his Majesty's health upon Mount George." The officers of the Transmontane Order were the agents of Colonel Spotswood's project by which the piedmont could be developed, the mountain passes seized, the Shenandoah valley claimed, and the country beyond the Appalachians penetrated, first by government-directed traders, then by speculator-sponsored settlers. Finally, French communications between Canada and Louisiana would be cut by British regulars. The banks of Lake Erie, Spotswood anticipated, would become the new frontier of the British empire.[63]

The Iroquois blazes (and, it seems likely, the Meherrin guides, themselves Iroquoians) had reminded Spotswood who actually owned the lands west of the warriors' path across the piedmont, as well as the transmontane territory. Iroquois incursions were the immediate threat to the Virginia frontier. Spotswood ordered Captain Christopher Smith to travel to New York, there to use the good officers of General Hunter to propose to the diplomats of the Five Nations the preliminary articles of a new barrier treaty, an amendment of the Covenant Chain Treaties of 1677 and 1685. Spotswood proposed that the Iroquois move their warriors' path north of the Potomac and west of the Blue Ridge.

Rerouting Iroquois warriors would not just relieve Virginia's Indian tributaries and upcountry pioneers from Iroquois raids, it would practically concede 3 million acres of the Iroquoian sphere to Virginia, that is, to Spotswood and his land-hungry companions.[64]

To negotiate a new Anglo-Iroquois frontier, in August of 1717, Colonel Spotswood set out on a journey of more than 1,000 miles. Virginia's military administrator had obtained the provincial council's approval to declare war unless the Five Nations agreed with Colonel Spotswood's proposal to move the warriors' path north and west. En route to New York, Spotswood met with John Hart, the veteran soldier who was now the royal governor of Maryland. They reviewed that province's long, generally pacific, relationship with the Iroquoian peoples. Hart and Spotswood then went on to Philadelphia to consult the governor, Sir William Keith. An articulate imperialist, Keith published praise of Colonel Spotswood's combination of energy, treaties, and hostage taking in pacifying Virginia's southwestern native neighbors. An illness in Hart's family and Hunter's refusal to leave his cooperative assembly session thwarted Spotswood's "Expectation of a Congress at Philadelphia," so he and Keith conferred with Hunter at New York. Hunter's Scots protégé, Cadwallader Colden, reported that the French had threatened that "their" Indians would attack Iroquoian hunters in the west unless the Iroquois agreed to attack southern targets. The French also tried to thwart any Iroquois negotiation with the British authorities, saying that the British now sought to unite their provinces to destroy the Five Nations because they had supported their Tuscarora kinsmen. French "presents" of arms and ammunition were conditioned on their use in the southern backcountry. In the fall of 1717, Spotswood returned to Williamsburg without having met the Iroquois but more than ever convinced that behind the turmoil on the Virginia frontier lay the imperial aggression of France.[65]

"Having had the honor to serve nine years under my Lord Cadogan as L't Q'r M'r Gen'll of her late Maty's Army in Flanders, I have learned by experience how much the knowledge of a Country contributes . . . to the Execution of Military Projects" so, having reconnoitered the Virginia frontier beyond the Blue Ridge, Spotswood offered to build a road from the Swift Run Gap to Lake Erie and there found a new military settlement. It would immediately take a large share of Indian trade and alliance from the French. It would legalize the British "Right of Possession" over the whole country between the Appalachian Mountains and the Great Lakes. When, inevitably, the war with France for America was resumed, Spotswood's proposed outpost on Lake Erie would "cutt off or disturb the communication between Canada and Louisiana" (the colonel enclosed the detailed itinerary of the posts and distances from Montreal to New Orleans that he had extracted from French prisoners). This westward advance would be financed by the crown's quitrents, vastly increased by the Spotswood expansion of Virginia landholdings. The settlers on those lands would provide the militia required to support the regular garrisons of the chokepoint forts in the Swift Run Gap and at Lake Erie. Colonel Spotswood's western strategy, he wrote, was but his latest contribution to England's empire, he "having been from my Infancy employed in the Service of my Country."[66]

Spotswood had concentrated his imperial energies on the Rappahannock frontier because the Virginia Indian Company act, his scheme for Indian missions and education, trade and alliance, west from the James River, had been disallowed by the privy council on the grounds that it was an illegal monopoly and a restraint on British trade. These arguments had been put forward by the London tobacco traders, those merely mercenary men who "don't care a farthing whether there be either Religion or Government in this Country." They "have Interest enough, Spotswood wrote, by mere Clamour, to disconcert all measures I take for promoting the Christianizing of these Heathen, and thereby securing the future peace of these, his Maty's Dominions." Duly chagrined, the lords commissioners recommended, and the crown ordered, that Spotswood summon an assembly for "the Regulating the Indian trade, the making provision for the Defence of the Frontiers, And reimbursing the Charge of the Indian Company" in maintaining and garrisoning Fort Christanna, building and supporting the mission school there, and refreshing the provincial gunpowder supply. After his experience with the assembly in 1715, Spotswood had no expectations that its successor would repay the Indian Company or, indeed, support any measure of defense whatever. But he had to obey orders.[67]

So, in the spring of 1718, Virginians fought a vigorous election campaign. Spotswood's pamphlets attacked the mean-spirited, plebeian, and partisan burgesses of the 1715 assembly. In their places, the lieutenant governor advised "the People to chuse men of Estates & Families of Moderation [that favorite political term of Marlborough men] & dutiful to their Superiors." In reply, the Green Spring faction posted placards attacking "Torys," "the Court Party," and "Tools of Arbitrary Power." They charged that, if victorious, Spotswood's courtiers would impoverish the people by legislating poll taxes to support Fort Christanna. The ensuing election pushed all moderates, independents, and popular tribunes out of the assembly. The new burgesses were split between Spotswood's "Court Party" and "the faction" burgesses who echoed "the Sentiments of their Directors in the Council." The Green Spring councilors had their burgesses demand that Spotswood restore the councilors' exclusive jurisdiction over life and death, rescind the land law's settlement requirement and quitrent reservation, and abandon to the council the commissioning of surveyors, county clerks, and militia officers. "The Party who have always their Eyes very quick to watch all Advantages for Lessening the power of the Crown" even tacked to a popular fee bill a clause to obstruct the operation of the royal post office in Virginia. The country party argued that "the Parlm't could not Levy any Tax (for so they call ye Rates of Postage) here without the Consent of the General Assembly." Thus early on was charted the rock on which the ship of empire would split.[68]

Spotswood refused to reduce his patronage powers or the crown's judicial authority. He threatened to veto the fee bill if the post office was limited. In reply, "the faction," still a majority of the burgesses, voted to pay William Byrd to act as their London agent against the lieutenant governor. They rejected the recommended recompense to the Virginia Indian Company for its defense, diplomatic, and missionary expenses. They refused to support the maintenance of Indian hostages or the protection of tributary tribes. They blocked regulation of the Indian trade. In short, "all the Measures w'ch have been projected for the Defence of the Country are now overturned . . . the Christianizing the Indians . . . defeated; The King's authority encroached on, his Interest Thwarted and opposed." So, the lieutenant governor declared, the Green Spring councilors and their burgess clients had demonstrated that they were "false to the Interest of the Crown, and very much disaffected to that of Great Britain." Indeed, their "management of the Mob" in opposition to the commands of the crown showed that the country party "would not stick to overturn the Government." Spotswood prorogued the assembly.[69]

The legislature reassembled on November 11, 1718, without a single public grievance being offered. Virginians, Spotswood reported, were "easy under a flourishing Trade, moderate Taxes, an exuberant Treasury, and a profound Peace." Once an antipirate act was passed (which Spotswood used to decapitate Blackbeard), only two items remained on the docket: a review of the condition of the capitol's furniture and a country party bill to revive the disallowed 1705 act that restricted office in Virginia to residents. This Spotswood had publicly promised to veto, "the avowed Design of the Bill being to exclude from Offices all persons recommended from England." "Should the King think fit to . . . send hither Land forces," Colonel Spotswood observed, "No commission could be granted by the Comdr in Chief here, to any Person not qualified by three years Residence, altho such Person ought by the Rules of the Army, Succeed in such Imployment." Residency requirements also reflected on Spotswood's previous appointments of British clergy and professors, armorers and expeditionary officers. So his veto would preserve both the crown's present and prospective patronage in Virginia.[70]

With next to nothing on the docket, some burgesses went off to the races. Others went home for the holidays. Members of the court party found leave from the country party speaker surprisingly easy to come by. Then, without warning on November 20, the plurality of a thin house passed through three readings an address, preprepared on vellum, without discussion or amendment. The address asked the king to remove his lieutenant governor for unspecified "Attempts . . . toward the subversion of the Constitution of our Government, the depriving us of our ancient Rights & privileges, and many hardships which he daily exercises on your Majesty's good subjects of this Colony." William Byrd was appointed agent to present this address. He was to support it with articles of impeachment proving that the lieutenant governor had enforced unfair land laws, lavished money on the palace, interfered with church patronage, neglected the militia (!), vetoed bills passed by the burgesses (whom he had verbally abused), appointed unqualified judges, and intimidated lawyers. Having voted articles of impeachment before reviewing any evidence, the country party was embarrassed the next day. With members back from the races, eight of the fourteen articles were erased as groundless, beginning with the request for Spotswood's removal. Then the rest were dramatically reduced. All that remained was a protest that the governor enforced the land law to collect the king's quitrent (this was the "Attempt to subvert the Constitution") and that he had spent too much on "the Palace."[71]

On December 1, 1718, Spotswood dissolved the assembly and launched a devastating counterattack. From it the Green Spring faction, and the Virginia council's command of provincial politics, never recovered. Spotswood published his dissolution speech as *Some Remarkable* PROCEEDINGS. He declared that "secure under the Protection of my Prince's Justice . . . & tho' I'm a Commander in Chief without A Single Centinel to defend me in this Dominion . . . I dare now tell ye guilty to their faces, that I will still discountenance all such as I discover to be Undutifull to their Prince, or Ungrateful to their Mother Country, and will continue to oppose that restless faction whose Machinations have in all Governors times disturbed the Public Tranquility of the Colony, only to gratify their own private Resentments." This broadside Spotswood not only sent home, he also distributed it to be read aloud in every courthouse, church, and chapel in Virginia. In reply, he received addresses from "the justices, clergy, and inhabitants" of twenty-one of Virginia's twenty-five counties. All condemned the burgesses' proceedings. Typical was the address from Westmoreland declaring that the only "ancient right" on which Spotswood had infringed was "poverty."[72]

The lords commissioners of trade and plantations formally rejected every contention of the burgesses' "illegal address" as complaints not against the lieutenant governor "but against the power invested in him by His Majesty's Instructions." The commissioners assured Spotswood of "all the countenance and support we can give you which we think you have deserved." The law officers of the crown, the postmaster general, and the earl of Orkney (furious that the burgesses had attributed all the evils of Virginia to his absenteeism and anxious to be restored to the privy council) all backed Spotswood. The royal officials agreed with Spotswood that it was time to "put a Stop to the growing Power of a Party to whom not any one particular Govr but Government it self is equally disagreeable."[73]

The lords commissioners recommended that William Byrd be removed from the council (and that every one of Spotswood's nominees be appointed, beginning with Peter Beverley). Byrd was disgraced before the board and discountenanced in the privy council. He sought to save his council seat by promising to give up his agency in London, return to Virginia, and seek a reconciliation with the lieutenant governor, but only the intervention of the duke of Argyll, whom Byrd had long cultivated in hopes of getting the Virginia command, preserved Byrd from utter disgrace. The king had gone back to Hanover, leaving his heir in command. So the prince's party, Argyll prominent among them, had influence enough both to preserve Byrd's seat and to caution Spotswood to accept his submission. On April 26, 1720, the Virginia council met so that, with the worst possible grace, Spotswood could readmit Byrd. When the council met again three days later, Byrd recorded in his diary that "there passed abundance of hard words between the Governor and Council about Colonel Ludwell and Mr. Commissary for about two hours, till all of a sudden the clouds cleared away and we began to be perfectly good friends and we agreed upon terms of lasting reconciliation, to the great surprise of ourselves and everybody else."74

The governor in council immediately approved patents for massive land grants. The upper James valley and the Roanoke corridor were conceded to the country party, a necessary consequence of the collapse of the Virginia Indian Company. Spotswood and his court party associates claimed the upper Rappahannock and its southern tributaries, the Rapidan in particular. They also took out an option on the Shenandoah valley. The lieutenant governor and the councilors of both parties agreed that when a new assembly convened, it would petition the crown to finance and garrison forts at the two mountain passes to defend the king's enlarged dominion against the French and Indians. The king would also be asked to exempt patentees in the two frontier regions from royal fees and rents. The burgesses would pass acts erecting two vast frontier counties to govern the new developments, Brunswick (named for the prince's or country party) south of the James, and Spotsylvania (named for the king's champion, the head of the court party) westward up the Rappahannock and overmountain as far as the "Euphrates." The burgesses would appropriate money for county seats—courthouse, church, jail, and armory—and to purchase weapons for the new counties' militia regiments, the new imperial frontier's first line of defense.75

Patents of 10,000 acres for the Spotswood associates, previously blocked in council, were passed. In exchange, the Meherrin tract, centered on Fort Christanna and controlled by the VIC, was opened to purchase, saving only the Saponi reservation. Next, alternative grants, totaling 27,000 acres, were made along the Roanoke and the Rappahannock. Over the next two years, however, Spotswood and his associates took the lead in development. He alone patented between 86,550 and 93,500 acres of the territory surveyed by the members of "The Transmontane Order." Spotswood insisted that all these patents were designed to extend the empire. "The British Provinces all along the Coast of the American Continent, want People to Seat the vast Deserts on their Backs & to Strengthen their Land-Frontiers; as well as against the French & Span-iards Encroachments as against the Indians Incursions." Yet the ordinary settler would not move into frontier lands "'till the Terror of the Indians is over." Even then, farmers could not pay for patents or for infrastructure. So Spotswood set an example for the speculative developers of the American frontier. He "cleared Grounds, fenced Fields, builded Houses, made Roads and Bridges, set up Mills, drove out Stocks of Cattle, transported Household Goods, removed Families of Women & Children, with all ye Necessaries of Life to support people in the Wild Woods; &, in short, . . . passed through ye immense Troubles, Fatigues, Dangers & Expences, wch are inseparable from new Settlements in America." What Spotswood did on a large scale both his associates and his rivals did on smaller ones. As Spotswood's successor and emulator Major William Gooch put it, these frontier developers "gave encouragement to the meaner sort of People to seat themselves as it were under the Shade & Protection of the Greater." So it was, beginning in the valley of the Rappahannock, that "the meaner sort of the people (in whom consists the strength of all Countrys)" moved west, leav-ing the tidewater to the wealthy planters and their ever-more-numerous slaves. Such was the result of Spotswood's grand scheme to harness the land hunger of Virginians, rich and poor, to do the work of empire.[76]

Spotswood's imperial scheme required provincial legislation. He used all the patronage at his disposal to influence the burgess elections in the autumn of 1720. Clearly, the political truce in the council did not extend to the counties. "The Militia was put into their [Spotswood's "old Creatures'"] hands] tho most rank Tories and Enemies to the Government and Militia Commissions flew about to every fellow that could make two or three votes," so said one faction figure. Spotswood also enlisted county sheriffs and clerks in the cause. Then, in the midst of the election campaign, he convened a grand jury. Spotswood charged them to enforce a law of 1677, enacted in the aftermath of Virginia's civil war and last invoked by Colonel Nicholson, which prohibited sedition and slander. It should now be applied to those who "Misrepresent and Censure every Step of your Chief Ruler" and who "possess the populace with apprehen-sions of Forts, Fortifications, Standing Armies, and other dangerous Designs of a Long headed Governor." Such were "the true Seeds of Rebellion," Spotswood declared. It was akin to "Atheism and Blasphemy, Treason and Treachery" to raise "false and Scandalous Reports to defame Your Chief Ruler and asperse the Administration."[77]

Yet, when the assembly met on November 2, 1720, Spotswood accepted the choice of John Holloway, the faction's lawyer, as speaker of the burgesses. Spotswood endorsed Holloway's claim of parliamentary privilege for the house of burgesses, the more readily because Spotswood's attorney general, John Clayton, was named chairman of the key committee, propositions and grievances. To this evenly balanced assembly, Spotswood announced his own "disposition to peace and Union." He recommended "Moderation and Concord" to Virginia's political nation. They all now knew, Spotswood said, that he intended to make his own future among them. The resurgence of the prince's party at home (signaled by Argyll's protection of Byrd) had put the lieutenant governor on notice that his own tenure of office, already two and a half times the average for royal executives in America, was in danger. In the meantime, as the king's representative, Colonel Spotswood's duty continued "to be Specially mindful of *Great Britain's* Interest" but, as Spotswood told the assembly, he had found a way to unite his imperial program with their provincial self-interest: "Extending your out Settlements to the high Ridge of Mountains . . . the best Barrier nature could form, to Secure this Colony from the Incursions [of the Indians] and more dangerous Incroachments of the *French*."[78]

To define the barrier required the cooperation of the Five Nations. Spotswood asked the burgesses to endorse his demand that the Iroquois move their warriors' path north of the Potomac and west of the Blue Ridge. In their reply, the burgesses offered fulsome praise of the lieutenant governor's "great penetration and . . . Indefatigable application to the Indian Affairs." They endorsed his redefinition of the frontier. They made Spotswood's recommendations for the development of Virginia's west into an address to the crown to build forts at the mountain passes and garrison them with regular troops. The burgesses passed bills to erect two counties to connect the two mountain passes—the Swift Run Gap to the north, the Rock Fish Gap to the south—to the existing frontier, to build a county seat in each, to arm every "Christian tytheable" in the new counties with a modern musket, socket bayonet, cartridge box, powder and ball, all at provincial expense. So the militarized, bureaucratized, royal institutions of the county—clerk and sheriff, militia lieutenancy and county court—were extended, in law at least, all the way west to the Shenandoah and the Roanoke. The assembly exempted every patentee and settler in the new counties from colony taxes for a decade and petitioned the king to remit his quitrents on land in Brunswick and Spotsylvania for the same period. The westward expansion of Virginia had been defined for a generation to come.

Still following Spotswood's lead, the assembly advised King George "how to Extend your Empire" and "Secure our Present Settlements from the Incursion of the Savage Indians and from the more dangerous Incroachments of the Neighbouring *french*" by taking control of the mountain passes with government-sponsored settlement, royal forts, and regular garrisons. The assembly also endorsed Spotswood's aggressive plan to cut French communications "betwixt the Rivers St. Laurence and Mississippi," reminding the king that "our Lieut. Governour Colonel Spotswood . . . has spar'd no fatigue or Expence to visit our Mountains in person and to inform himself of the Exceeding Importance of them both for Your Majesty's Service and for the defence and Security of this Dominion."[79]

The assembly's address marked Virginia's conversion to the empire militant, Spotswood wrote, "when a people who have the greatest Jealousy of and Aversion to a Military Power, so earnestly press for such a Guard to their Frontiers." Spotswood added that if he were the viceroy of New France, he would protect his communications and menace the Virginia frontier by seizing the mountain passes before British forts were built there. "If twenty years' Service in the Wars and if the part I had in the most considerable projects of the last war in Flanders as Lieut QrMaster Genll under the Duke of Marlborough can gain credit with your Lordships as to what I say of the Importance of these Forts to the Security of this Dominion," they would recommend to the king both forts and garrisons. The lords commissioners completely agreed with Colonel Spotswood. They declared that, in general, it was "impossible to improve or even to preserve His Maty's Empire in America without sending a military Force thither." In particular, they stated "that two Companies can not be imployed upon a more important service" than that proposed by the veteran in command of Virginia: garrisoning forts in the passes through the mountain barrier. Indeed, the lords commissioners declared, Spotswood's proposal for imperial expansion should be an example to other British colonies.[80]

Colonel Spotswood's strategy now informed the most comprehensive plan for empire in America since Sir Walter Raleigh inaugurated imperial enterprise with the *Discourse of Western Planting* in 1584. On September 8, 1721, the lords commissioners sent to the king-in-council their recommendations "In Relation to the Government of the Plantations." The 1721 report began with the demand of every English imperialist since Danby's day: the resumption of all colonial charters and every proprietary grant, and the imposition of uniform royal government on every North American province, to secure their "entire, absolute, and immediate Dependency" upon the imperial crown. Dependent on the crown, every provincial government from Nova Scotia to South Carolina should also be made "mutually subservient to each others Support" by adopting the Marlborough ministry's plans of 1702 and 1709. That is, all the North American provinces should be subjected to "the Government of one Lord Lieutenant or Captain General." A lieutenant governor would command each colony, "as it is presently practiced in the Leeward Islands, where each Island had a particular Govr. But one Genl. Over the whole."[81]

The governor general of North America would preside over a legislature composed of two members from each province, paid "independently of ye Pleasure of the Inhabitants." This grand council would legislate levies of men and money from every province, to be applied by the governor general to the common defense. His rule would be enforced, and the North American empire would be protected by large garrisons of regular troops. Four regiments apiece would secure Nova Scotia and South Carolina, the border provinces with New France and New Spain. A full regiment would strengthen New York's frontier with the Five Nations. Two independent companies would garrison Virginia's frontier forts. The plan's premises were those of Marlborough's legates: the eternal enmity of France and Spain to the British empire and the Protestant religion; the incapacity and insubordination of the American provinces; the need to overcome both foreign aggression and provincial indiscipline in order to expand and secure "the King's Empire in America."

British imperial administration was also to be centralized. The plan proposed that a president of the lords commissioners of trade and plantations engross all authority over American affairs. The president would become the sole channel of recommendations to the king-in-council and the sole transmitter of royal orders to the lord lieutenant and governor general of North America. He would be secretary of state for America. Under the command of a single secretary and a governor general, "the King's Empire in America" would burst through the Appalachian barrier and encompass the vast continental expanses bounded by the Great Lakes. The lords commissioners agreed with Spotswood that, while the Appalachian "Mountains may serve at present for a very good Frontier, we should not propose them for the boundary of your Majesty's Empire in America. On the contrary, it were to be wished, that the British Settlements ought to be extended beyond them & some small forts erected on the great Lakes, in proper places, by permission of the Indian proprietors."[82]

Colonel Spotswood consulted the preeminent "Indian proprietors" when touring Five Nations diplomats visited Williamsburg in October 1721. They reported his treaty proposals to Onondaga. It may be assumed the grand council replied in the affirmative for, the preliminary articles having been endorsed by the council and the burgesses of Virginia, Spotswood traveled up to Albany in the summer of 1722. He intended to incorporate the Iroquois, Virginia, and the middle colonies in an American "Ballance of Power" with France and her Indian allies. Tactically, Spotswood hoped to curtail the Iroquois raids that, ever since 1676, had endangered Virginia's domestic tranquility. "A Governor of Virginia," Spotswood wrote, "has to steer between Scylla and Charybidis, either an Indian or a Civil War, for the famous Insurrection in this Colony called Bacon's Rebellion, was occasion'd purely by the Governor and Councill refusing to let the People go out against the Indians." Honored by the "points of war" beaten by the drums of every New York garrison, Colonel Spotswood and the Virginia delegation reached Albany, the traditional place of council with the Five Nations, on August 20, 1722. Nine days later, the paramount chief, Decanisora, "Great Sachem of Onondague," arrived. He was accompanied by the three senior clan councilors of each of the Five Nations and, for the first time in a Covenant Chain conference, three Tuscarora sachems also appeared. The presence and participation of the Tuscaroras, led by the famous Turtle clan sachem Sagayengewarachton, aka "Blawback," marked the reconstitution of the Longhouse League as "the Six Nations."[83]

Despite the lords commissioners' admonitions to Spotswood to treat the Iroquois with "gentleness & fair usage," the colonel threatened Iroquois trespassers beyond the frontier, which he had proposed and that the Five Nations had accepted in preliminary articles, with transportation, enslavement, or hanging, the penalties of a Virginia law he had just obtained. Spotswood also broke diplomatic protocol by addressing the warriors directly. He demanded that these "foolish and ungovernable young men . . . harken better than they have always done to the sage Councils of their Elders and observe more punctually a Treaty wch their Sachims have thought to make for them." He even proposed that the warriors ratify the treaty themselves (which they did not do). Turning to the sachems, Spotswood offered, as from King George, a nobleman's coronet to Ondagsighte, the Oneida speaker. Then Spotswood took from his own lapel a golden horseshoe, the emblem of Virginia's westward march. It was to serve as a pass whenever the Iroquois crossed the new Virginia frontier to negotiate, for the sachems were not to "expect that the Government of Virginia" would ever again travel 600 miles to renew the covenant.[84]

Neither would a full representation of the senior sachems of the Iroquois ever again assemble in a condolence council to polish the covenant chain of multilateral alliance. Now that their frontiers had been pushed westward into the Iroquoian sphere of influence, the three imperial provinces, New York, Pennsylvania, and Virginia, would conduct separate negotiations either with delegations from Onondaga or with the "half kings" (that is, viceroys) who represented the grand council as residents in the dependencies of the Great League of Peace and Power. Decentralization demonstrated that the league had entered its century-long decline. Its conquests were now being transferred from the Iroquois sphere to those of the British provinces. A multimillion-acre Iroquois cession to Virginia was affected by the removal of the warriors' path westward from the fall line to the Shenandoah. This dismantling of Iroquoia was Spotswood's deliberate policy. Complaining that the Iroquois "are grown insolent by perceiving such a value set [on their friendship] during the Course of this War," Spotswood intended to use the interval of peace with France to begin to break up the aboriginal empire. By the treaty of 1722, the Six Nations not only ceded the territory east of the Blue Ridge but, in the Virginia view (finally accepted by the Iroquois at Lancaster in 1744), the Iroquois also yielded the great valley of the Shenandoah, reserving only a right-of-way, the new warriors' path. Indeed, the cession of 1722 was potentially unbounded. While it purported to hold the Iroquois north of the Potomac and west of the Shenandoah, it put no limits on the westward movement of the Virginians. The sachems called Spotswood "Assarigoa," the condolence council name given to lord Howard of Effingham, governor general of Virginia, in 1685. That name, "Long Knife," became the cognomen of all the aggressive and racist Virginians in the coming century. Spotswood had set "the long knives" on that militant and coercive course of conduct which was to last for two generations, until another Virginian ordered the once-mighty Iroquois reduced to mere reservations.[85]

At the Albany conference of 1722, Alexander Spotswood reached the apex of his imperial influence. When he returned to Virginia, he found that he had been replaced by Major Hugh Drysdale. Drysdale was the personal nominee of the new prime minister, Robert Walpole, a civilian crass, corrupt, and commercial. Where Virginia was concerned, Walpole was guided by his brother Horace, auditor general of the plantations. As such, Horace Walpole had inherited an alliance with the Ludwells, his deputy auditors of the Virginia revenue and principals of the Green Spring faction. Auditor Walpole opposed every one of Spotswood's proposals. He was particularly hostile to the fiscal concessions asked of the crown by Spotswood's plan of imperial expansion. Indeed, both brothers Walpole were profoundly anti-imperialist, obsessed with jacobite dangers at home, determined on peace with France abroad, and rivals of Marlborough's heirs, Stanhope and Sunderland, whose ministry's commissioners of trade and plantations had approved Spotswood's militant program of imperial expansion.[86]

In contrast to his predecessor, the new lieutenant governor's military career was remarkably undistinguished. Major Drysdale had slowly risen through the Irish establishment to become a major en second of a marine regiment in 1709. He saw little or no active service. So Drysdale avoided the continental campaigns, the regimental traditions, and the orders and example of Marlborough. It was extended combat service under the captain general's command, that gave both Drysdale's predecessor, Colonel Alexander Spotswood, and Drysdale's successor, Major William Gooch, their concentration on the imperial menace of France (and the vulnerability of Spain), their command presence, and their continental vision. Drysdale had been promoted a reserve major just in time to be disbanded in 1713. He could scarcely claim to be a soldier, still the prerequisite of imperial command. Rather, his major merit was that Drysdale had been the schoolfellow of Bishop Edmund Gibson, "Walpole's pope." Gibson was the new prime minister's dispenser of English ecclesiastical patronage and, as bishop of London (succeeding Spotswood's associate John Robinson), Gibson was the American diocesan. Bishop Gibson was as determined to undo executive control of the Virginia convocation, a diminution of his diocesan authority, as the auditor, Walpole, was to obstruct territorial expansion of Virginia, lest it antagonize the French and endanger the peace. So Major Drysdale became Commissary Blair's creature and Colonel Spotswood's enemy. Advised by the Ludwells, Drysdale systematically attacked Spotswood's property titles. He authorized political, even physical, challenges to Spotswood's authority in his county, Spotsylvania, and his home, the county seat, Germanna. Drysdale discountenanced Spotswood's treaty with the Five Nations. Indeed, he neglected everything to do with the militia, frontier security, the barrier, and the West.[87]

Such profound changes reflected more than a colonial commissary's perennial pique, petty provincial politics, or even the mutation of ministries. Spotswood was replaced and imperial policies were shelved because of a political and economic convulsion, Britain's first stock market crash. The South Sea bubble burst in the autumn of 1720. The bubble had been inflated by exaggerated hopes of vast profits from Spanish American trade following the Utrecht treaties. These hopes were enlarged by the prospects of territorial gains on the renewal of war with Spain in 1718. That conflict had led the lords commissioners to request Colonel Spotswood's strategic advice. Referencing the chief army administrator, Colonel Spotswood replied that "those who knew me in the Army, while I had the hon'r to serve as Lt-Qr-Mr-Genl under my Lord Cadogan, will, I doubt not, allow I have acquired there some reputation in Conducting Military Projects." Although he was "buried in Obscurity in America," Spotswood had "neither been indolent or inactive to informe my Self of such means here as may be of use to my King and Country . . . for enlarging his maty's Dominions in these Parts or Chastizing his Enemys." Having previously proposed the occupation of Spanish Gaule, that is, Georgia, Spotswood now recommended the conquest of Spanish Florida. Apalachicola should be captured and colonized to control the Gulf Coast. Then a fortress should be built on the southernmost keys to command the Straits of Florida and the port of Havana. Finally, St. Augustine should be taken to choke the Bahama Channel.[88]

The speculative climate that bred such "projects" as Spotswood's propelled the price of South Sea stock to stratospheric heights. The Stanhope-Sunderland ministry was inevitably implicated in the subsequent crash. Stanhope died from a stroke suffered in the lords while defending his brother's stockbroking. Marlborough's (and the ministry's) chief political operative, secretary of state Craggs, committed suicide in the midst of the crisis. James Brydges, the army financier, now duke of Chandos, lost £1 million and all his influence. Sunderland, within days of his acquittal of corruption in the South Sea scandal, was replaced by Robert Walpole as first lord of the treasury. Sunderland retained the king's confidence but died during the subsequent general election. Meanwhile, the aegis of the old order, the duke of Marlborough himself, long ailing, perished at last on June 16, 1722. Six days later, the captain general's former deputy chief of staff Alexander Spotswood patented another 40,000 acres, part of the 71,768 he took up in Spotsylvania County in June and July 1722, just before he sailed for Albany and the condolence council with the Iroquois. Spotswood was vulnerable, and he knew it. Stanhope's death and Sunderland's displacement had brought the last Marlborough ministry to an end. On February 5, 1721/22, just two weeks after Robert Walpole became prime minister, Spotswood was "worked out of my Government."[89]

In the new political climate, there was nothing for Spotswood to do but to retire to private life. He populated his Virginia estates with tenants, servants, and slaves. He developed iron mines and forges. He essayed large-scale naval stores production. Pirates and politics excused Spotswood's not returning home to report to his sovereign on a twelve-year tenure in command of

Virginia. The buccaneers would never forgo their revenge on Spotswood for destroying Blackbeard's gang, he said, but Drysdale denied him safe passage in a man-of-war. So Colonel Spotswood bided his time, built his "enchanted castle" at Germanna, the county seat of Spotsylvania, where he "pursues his iron mines strenuously," while waiting for his military patrons to resume power and for the British public to lose patience with the pacific ministry of Robert Walpole. Within the decade, the strategic vision of Alexander Spotswood would again command the respectful attention of imperial-minded ministers, faced with a second war with Spain. Yet another decade, and a third war with Spain in America, would promote Colonel Spotswood major general, second in command of 6,000 troops, 4,000 of them his own regiment, raised in America. General Spotswood's imperial legion was designed to accomplish at last Oliver Cromwell's "Western Design" and the Marlborough plan of 1702, the conquest of the Spanish Caribbean by American troops, and the achievement of Anglo-American hemispheric hegemony.⁹⁰

Epilogue:
The "Golden Adventure"

A

T FIRST LIGHT on June 16, 1722, John, duke of Marlborough, captain general, master of the ordnance, and colonel of the First Guards, died at Windsor Lodge. On July 14, his remains were brought up to Marlborough House to lie in state. Marlborough's last parade began at 12:30 on August 9. From Marlborough House, west along the mall, north through the royal parks, east down Piccadilly, south to Charing Cross, King Street, and the Abbey, the procession was led by detachments of the Horse Guards and Grenadiers. Their kettledrums were decked with black baize. Their trumpets were wound with cypress and bore banners of the Marlborough arms. The Household Cavalry were followed by a train of artillery and by the first battalion of the First Guards, marching without a commanding officer. The Guards' senior grenadier company, commanded by its captain, Colonel Pitt, escorted the mourner in chief, lord Cadogan, and ten other general officers, each distinguished by his loyalty to Marlborough in good times and in bad. Prominent among them were Honywood, Stanwix, Macartney, Erle, and Wade. They were followed by seventy-three military pensioners from Chelsea Hospital, one for each year of Marlborough's life. The Royal Standard was borne before eight caparisoned riderless horses. Next came the duke's standard, the Woodstock quitrent banner (the arms of France), the duke's banner as a prince of the Empire, and Marlborough's own armorial bearings. Each flag was carried by a senior officer flanked by military supporters. The flags were followed by forty mourners in black cloaks.[1]

The focus of the procession was the duke of Marlborough's funeral chariot. A full suit of gilt armor lay atop the coffin, the baton of command held in the right gauntlet, the collar of the order of the garter fastened about the neckpiece. The coffin was surrounded by military trophies. The entire hearse was canopied in black velvet. The eight carriage horses wore the duke's badges. The funeral car was flanked by ten captains, each of whom carried a banner roll with the arms of Marlborough's progenitors. Then came the noblemen of the duke's family, led by the duke of Montagu and the earls of Sunderland and Godolphin, supported by eighteen peers, mourners, and pallbearers.

The entire parade route was lined by the Foot Guards. As the catafalque and its escort passed, the officers of each company lowered their sponsons, the ensigns struck the colors, the privates reversed their muskets. Muzzles pointed toward the pavement, heads bowed toward the stocks, in a drill invented for this occasion and repeated at state funerals ever since, each company of the Guards fell into the ever-growing ranks, marching still with arms reversed, the muffled drums draped with black, the colors furled and wreathed in cypress, the officers with black scarves, all "in such close Mourning as the Military Profession admits." While minute guns boomed from the Tower, the procession was joined by the coaches of the king, his heir, the nobility and gentry, all in order of precedence.

As the captain general's coffin, banners, and mourners entered the west door of the Abbey, the minute guns ceased firing, the muffled drums stopped beating. The Guards passed on to form up on Horse Guards' Parade, the shouted commands startling in the silence. The pallbearers, the choir, and the coffin processed from the west door to Henry VII's chapel. There Bishop Atterbury, dean of Westminster, read the burial service. As the duke's remains were lowered into the tomb of King Henry VII, the garter king-at-arms proclaimed that "thus it has pleased Almighty God to take out of this transitory Life, unto his Mercy, the Most High, Mighty, and Noble Prince, John Churchill, Duke and Earl of Marlborough, Marquis of Blandford, Lord Churchill of Sandford . . . Baron of Aylmer, Prince of the most Holy Roman Empire, Captain General of His Majesty's Forces, Master General of the Ordnance, one of the Lords of his Majesty's Most Honourable Privy Council and Knight of the Noble Order of the Garter." Three signal rockets ascended from the Abbey roof. The ordnance at the Tower fired once, twice, and a third time. At the Horse Guards' Parade, the massed drums rolled. The twenty guns of the artillery train fired three salvoes. The drums rolled again. Two thousand guardsmen fired three volleys. The drums beat for the last time. Then silence fell over the grave of England's greatest general "who, by Military Knowledge, and irresistible Valour, In a long Series of uninterrupted Triumphs, Broke the Power of France."[2]

Marlborough's funeral coincided with the collapse of the South Sea Company. His political enemies had capitalized on the duke's victories by making the price of peace the destruction of the Spanish monopoly of Latin American trade. Given the corporate shell of the South Sea Company and the elusive prospects of Spanish American trade, tory financiers bid to refinance much of England's war debt. They were backed by investors of every description and party. So the bursting of the South Sea "bubble," England's first stock market crash, destroyed the ministry of Marlborough's son-in-law, the earl of Sunder-

land, and of Marlborough's favorite general, lord Stanhope. Stanhope suffered
a stroke on the floor of the house of lords while vehemently rejecting responsibility for the crash. He was replaced as the senior secretary of state by lord
Townshend. Sunderland had to resign the treasury to Townshend's brother-in-
law, Robert Walpole. Because he was at the treasury, Walpole received political
credit for palliating the panic, but he came to power because of the sudden,
nigh simultaneous deaths of Marlborough, the aegis of imperial war, and of
both of his political heirs.[3]

With the death of the captain general and his party, war with the Bourbon
powers for Atlantic empire was suspended. "I have seen how destructive the
effects even of a successful war have been," Walpole declared, and "I am proud
to own it, that I have always been, and always shall be, an advocate for peace."
For a generation, Walpole's pacifism prevailed in Anglo-French relations. The
great imperial enemy was even more enervated than England was by war debt,
by a stock market crash (the Mississippi Company, like the South Sea Company, was premised on the prospect of American trade and empire and it, too,
collapsed when it tried to recapitalize the war debt), by the death of its war
leader, Louis XIV, and by the ascension to power of proponents of European
peace, the regent, Philip, duc d'Orléans, and the chief minister, André Hercule,
cardinal Fleury. Walpole's larger peace policy was thwarted, however, because
French imperialism had a proxy in Spain. The War of the Spanish Succession
had put a French prince upon the Spanish throne. Thrice, in 1718–20, 1727–29,
and 1739–42, Spain and Britain fought over imperial issues in the Mediterranean and around the Atlantic world, and everywhere, behind the hostility of
Spain, British officers saw the specter of France.[4]

British territorial expansion in the American south and aggressive trade in
the Caribbean basin meant continual conflict with Spain, by land on the frontiers of Florida, by sea with the Spanish (often French-captained) *guarda costas*.
One hundred and eighty British and American merchant vessels were captured
in the Caribbean, their cargoes confiscated and their crews imprisoned, and
this in "peacetime." Such mistreatment was typified by the experience of Robert Jenkins, captain of the *Rebecca*, in April 1731. His severed ear was to name
the third Anglo-Spanish war. Spanish executives incited incursions into South
Carolina and Georgia, the new British province carved out of Spanish Guale.
The "family compact" of the Bourbon monarchs in 1733, coincident with the
foundation of Georgia, led quickly to the resumption of formal imperial conflict in the Atlantic world. Intermittent war with Spain was combined with continual friction with France. On the American continent, the French governors
general supplied and directed the assaults of native warriors on the frontiers of
British settlement in Nova Scotia and New England. Given recurrent war with
Spain and constant friction with France in America, the so-called Salutary Neglect of imperial governance, based upon a purported generation of peace, was
little more than postwar fiscal debility. It was poverty that enabled Sir Robert

Walpole and his brother Horace (auditor general of the American plantations) to put sand in the gears of empire.[5]

Walpolean sabotage became much more difficult with the accession in 1727 of a militant prince, George II, the most militant of the Hanoverian "warrior-kings." As prince, he had fought under Marlborough's command at Oudenarde. As king, he was the last British monarch to command troops in battle. Attentive to his army, King George controlled military commissions, whether to regiments or governments. George II invariably chose commanders in chief of American provinces who had either served under Marlborough and succeeded in American commands under his aegis or who had supported the king when he was Prince of Wales. George II's first significant American commission was to General Robert Hunter, formerly Marlborough's major of brigade for the dragoons and governor general of New York and the Jerseys, 1709–22. In 1727, the king promoted Brigadier Hunter major general and governor general of Jamaica. He was ordered to obtain its legislature's renewed fiscal support for imperial governance and defense in return for a refreshed royal concession to provincial self-government (reiterating the exchange formalized by the imperial constitution of 1681). Hunter's political success and his military experience were the more welcome when war with Spain broke out. Raids on Jamaica's north shore apparently anticipated a Spanish effort to recapture Cromwell's conquest.[6]

To carry the war to the enemy, General Hunter again proposed the use of North American manpower. In the autumn of 1726, Hunter reminded lord Townshend that "I was allways of Opinion that the Body of People in No. America, under new Regulations, might be made of considerable use, in case of War." "The Northern Colonies," Hunter declared, were the foundation of any imperial draft, but their legislators had been discouraged "by deep debts and dilatory repayments" for their expenses in raising troops for "two fruitless Expeditions" against Canada, in 1709 and 1711. Therefore, the first of the "new Regulations" must be the crown's promise to meet all the costs of "arming, accoutring, subsisting, or transporting" provincial levies. Second, the king must commission as commander in chief "a Person of honour and Experience," a veteran and an aristocrat, not another Jack Hill. The new general should sail to America in his own squadron, independent of admirals. In a grand progress from north to south, the American commander in chief should assemble each provincial legislature in turn and secure its obedience to royal orders to levy the colony's quota of troops. These recruits were to be disciplined by a corps of half-pay officers accompanying the commander in chief. All expenses should be met by "certain and solid" credits from the treasury, distributed by the commander in chief. The result, a continental army, should assemble at Charleston, South Carolina, its first objective the headquarters of Spanish Florida at St. Augustine. The conquest of the remainder of Spanish Florida would "extend your Territory as far as the Gulf of Mexico." The victorious Anglo-American army would then recapture Providence Island from Spain, taking control of the Isthmian routes to the Pacific Ocean.

The southern campaign, Hunter wrote, would have inured the continental army "to Military Labour and Exercise." Military discipline, together with the promise of a fair share of Spanish plunder, would motivate the American force to join the recruits raised and the garrisons consolidated in the West Indies by the viceroy of Jamaica. Of course, General Hunter wrote, a naval squadron was essential to escort the troop transports to and from Jamaica and to blockade the port of Havana but, he reiterated, the general in command must be superior to the admiral of the squadron, "former Expeditions having miscarried for want of harmony between [them to] their mutual loss." With this prescient prescription, General Hunter concluded his proposal for the conquest of Spain's most strategic Caribbean colonies by an American army under his command.[7]

General Hunter's former command of New York passed to John Montgomerie or, as his kinsman the earl of Loudoun put it, "Our Cousin Mr. Montgomerie" is "to be made a King in the West Indies." Wounded and taken prisoner at Almanza, Montgomerie was now a captain and lieutenant colonel of the Scots Guards, a reward for his having attended the then prince of Wales during his internal exile at Leicester House. Montgomerie was a Scots m.p. as well. To make room for Montgomerie in New York, William Burnet was transferred to Massachusetts. Massachusetts was open because Colonel Samuel Shute (wounded at Blenheim and brevetted major of horse by Marlborough after Oudenarde), having secured a supplementary charter affirming executive authority in Massachusetts, declined to return to the Bay Colony. In Virginia, Major Hugh Drysdale (a marine officer who had seen no service but who was a client of Horace Walpole and of the bishop of London) was now succeeded by Major William Gooch (who had served throughout Marlborough's campaigns and was the son of Robert Walpole's chief borough monger in Norfolk and the brother of the bishop of Norwich). Given Gooch's protection for his estates in Virginia, Colonel Alexander Spotswood came home to receive a royal commendation and a commission as chief of staff in Scotland. Having taken up a Scots seat in the parliament of Great Britain, Lieutenant Colonel John Hope was succeeded in Bermuda by Colonel John Pitt. He had ridden in Marlborough's funeral as the captain general's former master of horse. Colonel Pitt was a son of "Diamond" Pitt, governor of Bombay, by a daughter of General Stanhope. Colonel Pitt's elder brother, Thomas, a colonel of dragoons, raised to the earldom of Londonderry in 1726, now succeeded Colonel John Hart (of the Coldstream Guards) in command of the Leeward Islands and its garrison regiment. The command system of the British empire—military, monarchial, and ministerial—was manifest in the king's commissions of 1727 to American commanders in chief.[8]

Their focus was war with Spain. Their strategy was Cromwell's plan of 1654 (repeated, inter alia, by Marlborough's plan of 1702, Handasyde's plan of

1708, and Hunter's plan of 1726) for the conquest of Spanish American port cities. Their capture would give Great Britain control of the trade and treasure, which sustained Spanish (and French) military might in Europe. "If once Porto Bello and Cartagena are taken," Admiral Edward Vernon predicted, "then all will be lost to them." If the key ports—Porto Bello, the Atlantic terminus of the Panama route to the Pacific; Cartagena, the cynosure of Columbia; and, most important, Havana, "the key to the West Indies"—were opened to British trade, the Spanish American empire would fragment into a mélange of independent, free-trading states, subject financially to British merchant capitalists and naval entrepreneurs and subject politically to the army's garrison government. British strategists observed that only their Atlantic empire—Britain, Ireland, and America—had the sea power required to seize, hold, and service the ports of New Spain; the commercial capacity necessary to supply, and so to dominate, Spanish America; and the military experience in colonial conquest and provincial administration essential to seize and govern the Caribbean choke points. Such were the assumptions that underlay not only General Hunter's proposal in 1726 but also Colonel Spotswood's in 1727.[9]

As members of the duke of Marlborough's staff at the time of General Handasyde's proposal for Caribbean conquest, both Hunter and Alexander Spotswood may have been acquainted with the West Indian option. Spotswood's close connection with the most belligerent British minister of the 1720s, lord Townshend, dated back to their shared service, with Marlborough, during the negotiations of 1709 about the Spanish imperial succession, especially in the West Indies. During his first term as secretary of state, 1714–16, Townshend had been the recipient of Governor Spotswood's dispatches from Virginia on both the menace of France in the American West and the outrages by Spanish *guarda costas* in the Caribbean. In 1727, so Spotswood recalled, the Townshend-Walpole ministry "pitch'd upon him . . . to be the Governor of Jamaica, that by his Skill and Experience in the Art Military, they might be better able to execute their design of taking the Havanna. But the Courage of those worthy Patriots soon cool'd and . . . when the Scheme was drop'd, His Government of Jamaica was drop't at the same time, and then General Hunter was judge'd fit enough to rule that Island in time of Peace."[10]

Having taken a gratuitous slap at his social and military superior, Spotswood listed his own credentials for planning and commanding an American share in Caribbean conquest. These were "Experience in military affairs by 18 years Service in the Army, and chiefly in the Warrs abroad, as well as my knowledge of America, by almost 15 succeeding Years Residence there." So much Hunter could also claim, but Spotswood emphasized his unique "Eight Year Apprenticeship to the forming & Executing Military Dispositions, while I acted as Lt. Quarter Master General under the Duke of Marlborough." Spotswood recalled that from Cromwell to Marlborough, English imperialists had sought and failed to find enough men from America to support the conquest of the

Caribbean. In 1727, however, the war with France had been over for more than a dozen years. During this interval of peace in the long struggle for Atlantic dominion, the American population had increased by a third. Spotswood declared that "the British Dominions in America were now Populous & Powerful enough to afford a considerable Diversion upon any Rupture with Spain." If the British government would pay the fiscal "Charge of a War," the American provinces could provide "a body of at least Eight or Ten Thousand Volunteers." Spotswood explained that disappointed American ambition would motivate provincial volunteers: "the generality of People now in those parts have been led thither by a Spirit of Making their Fortunes, & many Thousands of them not having accomplish'd their ends . . . the very name of an attempt upon the Spanish Settlements in America will carry the [name] of a Golden Adventure which will undoubtedly allure a multitude of brisk Men to venture their Persons." In the homely imaginations of these potential recruits, even the domestic goods of Spaniards were made of precious metal.

> All the tin pots were silver fine,
> And silver wire was used for twine. . . .
> The spits and skewers of ev'ry scullion,
> And wooden cans were solid bullion.[11]

Beyond rankers' lust for loot lay officers' plans of conquest. The Americans' experience of plantation, the instrument of their dispossession of the natives, Spotswood explained, made the provincials "not only the most proper persons for settling & carrying on American Plantations" in the territories to be conquered from Spain, "but also having gained them by their Swords, they will value them the more, & consequently defend them against all future attempts of the Old Proprietors to recover them." The most endangered of the "Old Proprietors" were the Cubans. Cuba's healthy climate, rich soil, large size, strategic location, and splendid harbors inspired Spotswood's calculus of conquest and commerce. The patterns of the trade winds and the currents of the Gulf Stream, he wrote to Townshend, meant that possession of Cuba would curtail both the shipments of American specie that bankrolled the armies of Spain (and France) and the cedar that planked Spain's splendid warships. In their place, "English Shipping may at length come to engross ye Portage of the Wealth of Mexico & Peru." A conquered Cuba would also shield the small and vulnerable islands of the British West Indies from attacks launched from French Hispaniola. Finally, possession of Cuba would threaten St. Augustine in Florida, "a very Dunkirk to our Trade of North America." Because the Chesapeake "Bay-men & all English who have of late years fallen into the hands of ye Spaniards bear a mortal hatred to that Nation for the ill usage they have receiv'd from them," Spotswood told Townshend, "great Numbers in America would heartily engage out of a Spirit of Vengance."

"The proposed American Volunteers" (note Spotswood's novel use of "American"), however greedy, vengeful, and numerous, could not take Spanish possessions by themselves. In addition to an overwhelming British naval force—escorts, transports, and battleships—Spotswood insisted on at least four battalions "of his Majties regular Troops, to sustain & Support such a loose force, & to serve upon Occasions where Order & Discipline is chiefly required & even upon sundry occurrences to oblige those Volunteers to Submit to Rule & Command." Less coercively, in eighteen years in the army Colonel Spotswood had witnessed the role that "the king's coat" and small-unit cohesion played in encouraging uniformity in appearance and behavior. The American volunteers, he wrote, should each be issued "a Red Frock (of some cheap light stuff) & distinguished by their facings & divided into several battalions" so as to make "a much more formidable & Soldierlike Appearance & . . . Keep them to better Order & Discipline."[12]

The crowning lesson Spotswood took from his eight years' service with Marlborough was an appreciation of the character, the competence, and the authority required in a commander in chief. The key component in Spotswood's strategic plan to develop a continental army (as it was in Hunter's) was an "Officer of figure & Service, whose Character for Prudence, Courage, Moderation, & Justice, may render him acceptable to the American Voluntiers." Possessed of Marlborough's virtues, the American commander in chief must take with him the captain general's military currency, blank officers' commissions signed by the king, in numbers sufficient "for engaging ye American Adventurers" to serve themselves and to recruit other Americans. Like the duke in Europe, the general in America must have cash and credit to pay for provisions and transport. Recruiting in a federal system, the general should have royal orders to the chief executives of the American provinces to support the expedition. In particular, the governors general must be ordered to embargo all shipping from American ports lest the Spanish get wind of the expedition. Under pretense of relieving the station ships in North America, the admiralty should double their numbers. The reinforced squadron would escort the troop transports from American ports to a West Indian rendezvous. There, Spotswood wrote, the American convoys would join the royal naval squadron which had escorted transports for four battalions of regular troops, their provisions, and ordnance out to the Caribbean. These British expeditionary troops should be drawn from the royal army's reserves, the garrison of Ireland. Ostensibly, the flotilla and force were to reinforce the garrisons of Port Mahon and Gibraltar, Britain's recent Mediterranean conquests, now subject to repeated Spanish attacks. Actually, they would implement Spotswood's combination of Cromwell's aggression, Marlborough's victories, Americans' militancy, and England's eternal enmity with Spain—in a plan of Caribbean conquest.

Spotswood's plan was shelved in 1727, as he said, on intimations of peace. Hostilities continued, however, and Townshend raised Spotswood's proposal repeatedly until, in 1729, Walpole went behind the secretary of state's back to negotiate peace with Spain. The Treaty of Seville completed Townshend's break with Walpole. In May of 1730, Townshend retired to Norfolk to cultivate his famous turnips and Spotswood sailed back to Virginia and his "enchanted Castle" at Germanna. Colonel Spotswood did receive a consolation prize for his lost expeditionary command: the postmaster general's place for North America. Despite the Virginia burgesses' ominous complaint that postage stamps were an unconstitutional tax by the British parliament on the unrepresented colonists, Spotswood extended the royal postal service from Virginia to Massachusetts. The lynchpin of the new system was the post office in Philadelphia. To run that office Spotswood appointed a young printer named Benjamin Franklin.[13]

Colonel Spotswood's name kept coming up in imperial projects. He had scarcely landed in Virginia when, in April 1730, a syndicate headed by Sir William Keith (who, as deputy governor of Pennsylvania, had supported Spotswood's negotiations with the Iroquois) proposed a new colony to be called "Georgia." It was to extend from the Appalachian frontiers west all the way to the Mississippi, north to Lake Erie, and south to Louisiana. It was to be peopled with German and Swiss immigrants. They would elect a territorial government, but Georgia's commander in chief would be a royal executive, "a Man of Experience in Military as well as Civil affairs, possest of a Character in all Respects Equal to the Trust and likewise upon the Spot to Execute it with Effect." The obvious candidate was Colonel Spotswood, "whose Integrity, and great Abilities are so well known to your Lordships."[14]

The proposal floundered on the western ambitions of the great proprietorial families—Penn, Calvert, and Fairfax—and on the present peace with France. Instead, in 1732, on the eve of the Franco-Spanish "Family Compact," a new "Georgia" was proposed. Its imperial purposes were to push the Anglo-American frontier south into Spanish Florida and to resist French expansion eastward from the Mississippi. The colony was to be commanded by James Edward Oglethorpe. His first military commission, as a child officer on the books of the Foot Guards in 1704, fulfilled Marlborough's promise made to Oglethorpe's older brother, Lewis, as he lay mortally wounded after the storm of the Schellenberg. James Oglethorpe's next commission, in the Horse Guards in 1714, was the captain general's tribute to Oglethorpe's mother, Eleanor Waring, Marlborough's confidante ever since their salad days at Charles II's court and one of Marlborough's links to the exiled royal family. Remarkedly recommended both by Marlborough and by Argyll, James Oglethorpe had received a formal military education in France. In Hungary, he fought with distinction against the Turks as an aide to Prince Eugene. After a decade as a military and social reformer in parliament, the death of his domineering mother freed Oglethorpe to command the Georgia garrison and the South Carolina militia as they advanced into Spanish Guale. By 1736, Oglethorpe's men had established outposts as far south as the St. John's River, the northern border of Florida.[15]

Sir Robert Walpole was prepared to surrender Georgia to Spain to secure peace but, in the 1739 Convention of the Pardo, he thought that he had settled the immediate causes of contention without abandoning the American empire's southern frontier. Spain would recompense British merchants for ships and cargoes lost to the *guarda costas*. The South Sea Company's trading privileges (especially the asiento in slaves) would be extended, provided that the company allocated £95,000 (a part of the company's debts due to the Spanish crown for duties and royalties) to meet British merchants' claims. The Georgians were to withdraw northward, at least to the Altamaha River. Both powers would suspend fortification along the Florida frontier. South Sea Company obduracy (encouraged by parliamentary war fever, most loudly expressed by that "terrible cornet of horse," William Pitt) scuttled the convention. The Walpole ministry was denounced in both the British and the American press as having for twenty years adhered to the maxim "that any, even the most dishonourable Peace, was preferable to a War." In conciliating Spain, Walpole had "negotiated ourselves out of all Reputation." Caribbean conquest was called for.

> Each bold Enthusiast future fame decries;
> And CHURCHILL's Conquests Swim before their Eyes.[16]

In July 1739, in anticipation of war, Admiral Edward Vernon received orders "to commit all sorts of Hostilities against the Spaniards." War was declared on October 19. In November, Vernon fulfilled his boast that he could take Porto Bello with just six ships. The American response to the capture of Porto Bello was novel and belligerent, national and imperial. The news "inflamed every loyal and honest Heart here with a warmpth unfelt before in this infant Country," declared the *Boston Post Boy*. A Bostonian ode, "On the taking Porto-Bello by Admiral Vernon," rejoiced that

> Their Port of War, vain-pompous, empty Name
> At once surrendered when great Vernon came.

Oglethorpe was authorized to draft a regiment from the garrisons of Gibraltar, the north of England, Scotland, and Georgia. Oglethorpe's regiment would spearhead an attack on St. Augustine. Under pressure from the duke of Argyll and other Scots military peers, Colonel Spotswood's plans for a West Indian expedition, to be manned in large part from British America, were dusted off.[17]

Colonel Spotswood himself was promoted major general, commissioned commander of all the forces to be raised in America and, as quartermaster general (chief of staff) of the expeditionary army, was second in command to General Charles, lord Cathcart, eighth baron Cathcart in the peerage of Scotland. Cathcart had been commissioned ensign in Macartney's foot in 1704 and fought with it in Spain at Almanza. Commissioned in the Scots Greys in 1706,

Cathcart was engaged under Marlborough's command at Ramillies and Oude-narde. Cathcart succeeded Robert Hunter, another Ayrshire man (as was their brigadier, Stair), as major of brigade to the dragoons. Returned to service at the Marlborough restoration, Cathcart was distinguished in command of a squad-ron of the Greys against the Scots rebels at Sheriffmuir in 1715. Identified as a Marlborough man, and because Marlborough had been heard to "commend him extremely as a soldier," Cathcart rose steadily. Cathcart was a gentleman of the bedchamber to the prince of Wales, and, when the prince ascended to the throne in 1727, he promised Cathcart that he would succeed his father as a representative peer of Scotland, made him groom of the bedchamber, and gave him the first available regiment of foot. Five years later, the now lord Cathcart was said to be the king's favorite officer. The king commissioned him a colonel of cavalry because "I look upon you to be a man of honour." The king promoted Cathcart brigadier general in 1735 and commissioned him governor of Duncannon Castle in Ireland. Nonetheless, Cathcart had to renounce his association with Stair, vote for the convention of the Pardo, and pledge fealty to Sir Robert Walpole as the price of command of the West Indian expedition. He was promoted major general in July 1739 and named by King George to com-mand the expedition, "the greatest which had ever left England for the West Indies." Recalling their shared service on the captain general's staff, Cathcart esteemed Spotswood, his second in command, as "a very able officer on whose abilities I had great dependence."[18]

Early in June 1740, General Spotswood received royal orders "to take upon him the Command, Conduct, Discipline, Disposition & Embarkation of Our American Troops." He had just obtained leave to come to England for his health. Instead, Spotswood hurried down from Spotsylvania to Williamsburg to consult with the provincial commander in chief, Colonel William Gooch. The lieutenant governor had been ordered, as was every other royal executive from Massachusetts to North Carolina, to give every support to the expedition both personally and through his legislature. Spotswood found that Gooch had already published the royal declaration of war with Spain, forwarded the royal orders for recruiting the American Regiment to the other provincial execu-tives, and convened the Virginia assembly. Remarkably responsive to the royal command, the legislators appropriated £5,000 to feed and transport Virginia's volunteers. The lieutenant governor then ordered every county militia officer to muster his men and read to them the king's offer to arm and uniform, pay and provision every volunteer for the American Regiment on the same basis as the king's regular troops. Recruiting officers reiterated the royal promise that the recruits would be shipped back to Virginia at the conclusion of the expedi-tion unless they chose to stay on as planters or soldiers in their conquests from the Spanish. Gooch added that every recruit would receive two pistoles in cash from Virginia funds as an enlistment bonus. Recruits were also assured that

they would serve only under the officers who recruited them, Virginia gentlemen of their own counties.[19]

Spotswood amplified these incentives for American recruits. "As this was
the first time levies were ever raised on this Continent," he said, Virginia should
set a generous example. Not two but three pistoles would be paid on enlistment. Half a crown "entrance money" was to be added when—it was always a
moment for second thoughts—the recruits boarded the transports. Moreover,
subsistence money would be paid monthly, in cash, at a higher rate than British
regulars received, a recognition of the cost of living in the colonies. Spotswood
observed that his 1716 experience of recruiting men for the relief of South Carolina had shown the necessity of extra allowances and ironclad assurances if
Virginians were to be drawn from their farms. Spotswood also anticipated that
the crown soon would want Americans to enlist in a war with France for the
American West, so good treatment on this inaugural occasion was essential.[20]

More than 400 Virginians immediately enlisted. They were housed at provincial expense (Gooch reminded Spotswood that the compulsory billeting of
troops had been unknown in Virginia since 1682, when the Guards' occupation
of Virginia ended, five years after Bacon's revolution). Nonetheless, desertions
grew as the planting season came on. Volunteers had to be reinforced with conscripts. In May 1740, a law authorized the county courts to draft all "able bod-
ied persons fit to serve his majesty who follow no lawfull calling," that is, time-
expired servants, convicts, and other criminals and vagabonds, mostly Irish
Catholics. William Byrd observed that "tho we do not abound in People, yet it
can be no great loss to part with such as are Idle & Vicious." Still, ex-convicts
and former servants did not dominate the ranks. Rather, most recruits were
younger sons and small planters enlisted by "American Adventurers," men of
good family, well known in their communities. Colonel Gooch was ordered
to agree with General Spotswood which gentlemen would receive warrants to
"raise for rank" Virginia's four companies, each of 120 men, 60 recruited by the
captain, 40 by the lieutenant, and 20 by the ensign.[21]

Spotswood and Gooch selected Lawrence Washington as Virginia's senior
captain. His commission was signed by Governor Gooch on July 10, 1740,
presumably the day that Captain Washington's company mustered complete.
The new captain had been born in 1718. His father was Augustine Washington who, as a schoolboy in England, had rejoiced in the arrival in London
of the Virginian colonel Daniel Parke bearing Marlborough's laconic message
of triumph. Raised in a house called Blenheim with slaves named not Caesar
and Alexander but Marlborough and Eugene, Lawrence Washington was educated in England at Appleby, his father's old school, in the family's ancestral
Westmoreland. Lawrence stayed on after graduation, it is said as an instructor,
more likely to serve an apprenticeship with the family factors, Deane & Co., in
Whitehaven. His subsequent correspondence suggests that Lawrence also built
up that "good acquaintance" in the North Country of Cumberland and West-

moreland so advantageous in later years. When, on the eve of war, Lawrence returned to Virginia, he was already the master of ample lands and numbers of slaves, and a recipient of the patronage of the Northern Neck proprietors, the Fairfax family. Their land claims extended far beyond the Appalachians. Their recommendations for military commissions were heeded both in Williamsburg and London.[22]

Like Captain Lawrence Washington, Captain Richard Bushrod (another name familiar to Washington genealogists) "lived in Virginia upon his own Fortune. Raised his Company there at his own expence, served in the whole Expedition." Bushrod's lieutenant, Hugh Rose (presumably the brother of Spotswood's chaplain and executor), "Lived in Virginia upon his Fortune, and Rais'd 20 men for His Majesty's Service, had an Ensign's commission given him by Col. Gooch, and afterwards was made a Lieutenant." The same British board of general officers which made these assessments reported that Captain James Mercer had "studied law in Virginia, been persuaded to leave his profession and engage in the service at the instigation of Colonel Gooch and raised upward of 130 men in that colony, marched them from 120 to 150 miles at his own expense" to the regimental rendezvous at Williamsburg. Mercer, whose family home was "Marlborough" in Stafford County, was a "clever man of good family who carried arms in the Scotch Dutch [the Scots Brigade in the service of the United Netherlands] . . . and lately in the Scots Fusiliers." James Mercer became an adjutant in the American Regiment, a post otherwise reserved for British regulars. Captain William Fitzhugh reported to Lawrence Washington that "Bollocks Merser . . . with his Hams of Bacon" was the first veteran of the American Regiment to achieve field rank. As major of the Royal Irish, Mercer was killed in the expedition against Ft. Duquesne.[23]

These Virginians were typical of the officers of the American Regiment in having independent means—"living on their own fortunes," as the British generals put it—and enjoying powerful family connections, as did the regiment's captains from other colonies. William Cosby was a son of New York's governor general. Captain Cosby had been sheriff of the city and county of New York among other "employments of considerable profit which he quitted to go upon the expedition to the West Indies." Captain Cosby "raised his company at his own expense." So did Captain John Winslow of Massachusetts, Captain William Hopkins of Rhode Island, Captain Robert Farmar of New Jersey, Captain Thomas Laurie of Pennsylvania, and Captain John Lloyd of Maryland. Their families all had been distinguished from the foundation of their respective provinces, remained prominent through the revolution, and took commands in the United States Army. Even when they raised their companies for the American Regiment in 1740, these officers were already accomplished gentlemen. They included colonial legislators, a provincial secretary of state, and senior officers of militia. Even the subalterns "were recommended by the Governors and by the Gentlemen of the first Rank in the Provinces where the Companies were raised, and were either younger Sons of the principal Families, bred to no Particular Profession, or such of them as had been brought up to the Law, to Merchandize or had served at Sea." All of the American officers were far superior to their characterization by the British naval officer who declared that the American officers were "blacksmiths, tailors, barbers, shoemakers, and all the banditry them colonies affords, insomuch that the other part of the army held them at scorn."[24]

The British regulars had to allow the despised Americans to raise for rank in a royal American regiment because it was thought that provincials would neither be recruited by British officers nor would they enlist in regular regiments. As "strangers to discipline," however, the American officers were not to be promoted beyond captain's rank. The provincials were not even to monopolize subaltern commissions in the "American" regiment. The king reserved to himself "the Nomination of the Field and Staff Officers and also of one Lieutenant [per company] in our American troops." Some of these lieutenants, chosen by lord Cathcart, were "young gentlemen of family, chiefly North Britons, who had learned the rudiments of the military art in Holland and other foreign services, and consequently were the better qualified to discipline a newly raised regiment." These Scots drillmasters were themselves instructed by the expedition's adjutant general, the veteran Colonel William Blakeney. Of a landed Anglo-Irish family, Blakeney had risen through the commissioned ranks of that most professional of regiments, the Royal Irish Regiment. Adjutant in 1699, ensign and lieutenant in 1701, Blakeney won his captaincy at Blenheim. Marlborough brevetted Blakeney major of the Royal Irish after Oudenarde and gave him a lieutenancy (with rank as captain) in the First Guards. Postwar promotion to captain and lieutenant colonel of the Guards attested to Blakeney's political correctness. In the military buildup for the war with Spain, Blakeney, now in his sixties, was appointed adjutant general of the West Indian expedition when another Guards officer, Captain and Lieutenant Colonel Francis Otway, refused the command. As Otway explained to his brother-in-law, the Virginian William Byrd, he was deterred from West Indian duty by fear of yellow jack. Byrd replied that although "a Soldier ought to have a contempt for Death, . . . He may honourably enough not care to dye of disease." So it was Colonel Blakeney who brought out to New York 3,000 stand of arms, 550 sample uniforms, £8,000 cash and unlimited credit, a corps of British adjutants and quartermasters, and thirty newly commissioned lieutenants, one for each company of the American Regiment. While many of these lieutenants were "gentlemen" who had "carried arms," others, like the drillmasters of the provincial troops in the 1711 expedition, had been senior sergeants. One such was Abraham Gee of the Royal Irish, who had been distinguished under Gooch's command at Malplaquet.[25]

Of the eight "Field Officers of Maj. Genl. Spotswood's Regt.," several had seen prior service in America or were presently officers of the independent companies in garrison in New York or Jamaica. Others, like Lieutenant

Colonel Henry Cope, held commands in General Richard Phillips's regiment, beleaguered in Nova Scotia and Newfoundland. Cope had served under Marlborough in Flanders. He was promoted major of Thomas Whetham's regiment in the Marlborough reorganization of 1715. Commissioned lieutenant colonel of the first battalion of Spotswood's regiment, Cope was an officer "very well known in North America, Att present Lt. Governour of Placentia, a cleare cool headed determinate Gentleman." Cope was nominated by another of Marlborough's former subordinates, General Sir John "Legionier" (as imperial chief of staff, Ligonier would recommend the senior commanders for the final war with France for North America). Spotswood's own major, George Martin, had come out to Jamaica in 1718 with Lieutenant Governor Dubourgay's regiment: "he has been all over the West Indies & is Universally Esteem'd for a sensible man and a good Officer." Lieutenant Colonel Merrick had been lieutenant and captain of an independent company in the Jamaica garrison. Edward Clark, son of the lieutenant governor of New York and captain of an independent company there, volunteered to serve in the American Regiment. Such appointments as these manifested the identity of army and empire, the principles of seniority and service, the lasting influence of the duke of Marlborough, and the importance of American experience, even in the era of "Salutary Neglect."[26]

It bears repeating, however, that ninety-nine company-grade commissions and as many as thirty-six additional warrants (in lieu of commissions) were given by the colonial commanders in chief to gentlemen of their own provinces. As Newcastle wrote to Spotswood, this substantial military patronage—at least 135 royal commissions—was put in the hands of the governors general "as an Encouragement to Them to exert Themselves in making their Levys and as a Means to induce the Council, and principle People of each Province, to assist them in it." The political power of military patronage in the North American provinces was immediately apparent. Gentlemen of means and position competed for commands. To keep up the military value of this political currency, Newcastle went out of his way to order the commanders of the expedition to respect the American executives' choices, not only for the blank royal commissions but also for the governors' dozens of warrants to would-be officers. Every governor in the middle and northern provinces reported that—as Spotswood had anticipated—he could have raised at least double the number of men if he had been given more commissions. Six companies had to be disbanded in Massachusetts for lack of commissions (and because Governor Jonathan Belcher, a civilian, a Walpolean, and no friend to the expedition, would not issue warrants). In New York and Pennsylvania, however, ten extra companies were raised. Their officers' warrants, issued by the provincial chief executives, were converted to royal commissions when the four battalions of the American Regiment at last mustered in Jamaica, more than 4,100 strong.[27]

Charged with raising the first American regiment, Major General Spotswood had "entered upon this business with the greatest alacrity." By the end of May 1740, the Virginia companies of the first battalion of Spotswood's American Regiment were being drilled in Williamsburg, on the parade ground Spotswood had laid out, next to the magazine he had designed, perhaps by the adjutants whom he had trained during his long term as commander in chief of the colony. Spotswood's orders required the general to travel north to regiment the other new companies, "& so soon as he had given the necessary Directions here in Virginia, he embarqued on board a wretched vessel, in order to proceed to Maryland. . . . The urgency of the King's orders & his zeale to put them in execution . . . made him go on Board with out necessary conveniences for his voyage. This gave him a most violent cold & afterwards a Fever, which put a Period to his life, in a short time. Thus, Sir, he dyed as much a martyr to His Majesty's Service as if he had fallen in Battle."[28]

General Spotswood's death on June 7, 1740, was fatal to the West Indies expedition. As secretary of state the duke of Newcastle wrote to lord Cathcart, "Mr. Spotswood's Loss . . . is not to be repaired." As the author of the original plan for the Caribbean expedition, Major General Spotswood might have kept the focus on Cuba, his primary objective, avoiding disastrous diversions to Dominica, Cartagena, and Panama. It was also unfortunate that Spotswood's command of the American Regiment passed to William Gooch. He was a brave man and a veteran officer, but Gooch lacked Spotswood's experience on Marlborough's staff and Gooch did not have Spotswood's rank: major general, chief of staff, second in command of the expedition. As a mere colonel and quartermaster, Gooch was not even included in the council of war. He could do nothing to counteract English officers' contempt for the American troops. Nor could he secure promotion for the American officers. Finally, because Spotswood had been Admiral Vernon's schoolfellow at Westminster, he might have tamped down the interservice jealousies that crippled the expedition. Certainly Vernon's tone was much more respectful to Major General Spotswood than it was to his successor, Brigadier General Thomas Wentworth.[29]

Spotswood's death left the raising of the American Regiment in the capable hands of Colonel Blakeney. Following a meeting at New York with Colonel Gooch and the chief executives of the northern colonies, Blakeney dispatched to the provinces thirty British lieutenants—and with them, forty sergeants promoted from the ranks of the New York independent companies—to drill the new companies as they were raised. Blakeney would have preferred a single training camp, but the regimental tents were aboard the ships sailing from British ports to the West Indies, and Blakeney knew that Americans were unused to quartering soldiers. He was the more careful of American sensibilities because, as Blakeney wrote to Newcastle, "from the highest to the lowest, the Inhabitants of these Provinces seem to set a great Value on themselves, and think a Regard is due to them, especially in the Assistance they are able to give the Mother Country on such Occasions, and, as they are a growing Power, should they be disappointed in what is promised them, and what they expect, future

Occasions of the like Nature may suffer for it." "The Affair of Canada," Blakeney wrote, made it essential that American sensibilities be mollified (the 1711 plans for recruiting American troops for an attack on the Canadian maritime provinces and Quebec itself were under review). Colonel Blakeney's first task was to drill and discipline the officers and men of the American Regiment's companies. To this end, he simplified Marlborough's drill for the new American Regiment. The resulting drill book was repeatedly printed in New York and Philadelphia. It instructed not only the American Regiment but also future provincial regiments and militia units in Marlborough's drill method. In England, manuscript copies of Blakeney's abbreviation of *The Duke of Marlborough's New Exercise of Firelocks and Bayonets* (1708) were widely circulated. It is said to have moved George II to commission Blakeney as colonel of his own regiment, the 27th, with its strong American associations.[30]

Blakeney made strenuous efforts to see that the American recruits received their full bounties and subsistence money but he complained that he was thwarted by a lack of a common American currency and by the low volume of intercolonial trade and exchange. Solving such problems, Blakeney wrote to Newcastle, was the more difficult because the provincial legislatures were rife with "factions" and "Parties" whose main concern was thwarting each other rather than serving the public good. Unlike members of the British parliament, Blakeney reported, the American legislators were paid. Their constituents hated taxes. Lest they lose their political jobs, these salaried legislators refused the demands of the royal executives to raise taxes for military expenditures. Even the most modest military services suffered. Blakeney sent Newcastle copies of the proceedings of the New York assembly. It had refused to feed the two New York companies which helped man the New England mast ship (en route to supply vital spars to the British warships in the West Indian expedition) and her escort, HMS *Squirrel* (even though her captain, Peter Warren, had married into the New York elite). Despite the pettiness of provincial assemblies, and the marked particularism of the colonies themselves, Blakeney reported that the prospect of British army pay and provisions, rank and prestige, had attracted more than 4,000 Americans to enlist in the royal service and seek Caribbean conquests. The promise of a militant and imperial future had taken root in American minds and form in the American Regiment.[31]

Undermanned though they were, the *Squirrel* and the other American station ships of the royal navy, as Colonel Spotswood had proposed, escorted the American Regiment's transports to the West Indies, first to the rendezvous off Dominica and then, the British troops having not yet arrived, to Jamaica. Four Virginia companies, three from Maryland, and eight from Pennsylvania had sailed from the Chesapeake in transports chartered by their provinces. Their escorts included the tiny HMS *Wolfe*, whose captain, William Dandridge of Virginia, with many other royal naval officers, now returned to the service after

spending the peacetime years in America (and marrying provincial gentle-
women). Sailing on October 15, the Chesapeake convoy did not wait for Colonel Blakeney. He arrived, with the troops from New York and New England
in fourteen transports, just four days later. Furious with Gooch at being stood
up, Blakeney waited for two weeks (in vain, because they sailed without convoy)
for the companies from New Jersey and North Carolina. Not until the end of
November were all the transports of the American regiment at last anchored in
Port Royal, Jamaica. Nonetheless they prided themselves on arriving ahead of
the British troops at the scene of action.[32]

"The Auspicious Anniversary day of the Battle of Blenheim, the Embarkation was begun." So, on August 13, 1740, from on shipboard in St. Helen's,
wrote lord Cathcart. Himself a veteran of Marlborough's triumph, Cathcart
hoped "that the Consequences of this day's beginning may prove fatal to Spain,
as this day six and thirtie years was to France . . . that great day which decided
the liberty of Europe." But the eighty transports only sailed to Spithead. There
they lay at anchor for more than two months while reports of Spanish and
French reinforcements being sent to the West Indies impelled repeated en-
largements of the escort. Finally, twenty-five ships of the line and eight smaller
warships were assembled, half of England's available fleet. All this time, 7,000
British troops remained packed into transports, subsisting on half rations of salt
provisions, and contracting typhus from newly impressed sailors. The fleet did
not sail until October 26. By January 20, when the ships anchored off Dominica,
541 soldiers were seriously ill, 115 were dead. Casualties among the sailors were
even greater. On January 21, the commander in chief, lord Cathcart, died.[33]

The veteran Scots nobleman was succeeded by "an *English* Gentleman,"
Brigadier General Thomas Wentworth. Because of his skill as a drillmaster
of the six new marine regiments, Wentworth had been promoted second in
command on news of Major General Spotswood's death. Now he succeeded
Cathcart, but Wentworth "had neither experience or judgement." He had
not seen active service under Marlborough—or anyone else, for that matter.
Wentworth's first commission dated only from 1715. In the ensuing twenty-
four years, he had never been in combat or held an independent command.
"My want of experience" appeared in Wentworth's extremes: usual timidity,
occasional rashness, and a desperate determination to do everything by the
book, no matter how long it took or how inappropriate the deliberate dictates
of drill might be to tropical warfare, where the greatest enemies were delay and
disease. The inexperienced general was wholly incapable of standing up to the
veteran admiral, Edward Vernon. Vernon had served in the West Indies from
1708 to 1712. Shelved during the tory ascendancy, Vernon returned to command at the accession of George I, but he was removed once more at that of
George II. After a lapse of a dozen years, Vernon was reappointed as a sop to
the "patriot" parliamentarians, enthusiasts for a Caribbean campaign. Vernon
was a conniving bully, a violent "patriot," a determined enemy of Spain and,

of course, a champion of West Indian war. He believed that the army was only a cumbersome auxiliary to the navy in the Caribbean. Vernon wanted to limit operations to those in which the navy could play the primary role and reap the whole harvest of reputation. Unlike Cathcart (and Spotswood), who had made a long study of potential Spanish targets in the Caribbean, General Wentworth was wholly dependent upon Admiral Vernon. In the council of war that selected Cartagena as a target, "the General declared, that, as he was a Stranger in those Seas, he had no knowledge of the then present State of the City; that he should join with the Admiral in his Opinion; not doubting of his being well informed." A naval officer summed up the two commanders' disastrous defects: "the admiral was a man of weak understanding, boundless arrogance, and over-boiling passions; the general, though he had some parts, was wholly defective in point of experience, confidence, and resolution."[34]

Wentworth's weakness imperiled the army's objective and reduced the American Regiment's role. The leading army officers, Cathcart, Spotswood, and Blakeney, like General Hunter before them, had targeted Cuba. As Blakeney wrote to Newcastle from New York, the conquest of Havana, the military "Key to the West Indies," would also be valuable commercially both to Great Britain and "to these her Northern Colonies." The capture of Havana would have political advantages as well: it "would make his present Majesty's Reign, and the Administration under it, famous to the latest Posterity." The army officers had analyzed the fortifications of Havana and found them strong by sea but weak by land. So they had identified adjacent but poorly defended harbors where troops could be safely landed to assault the city. These officers saw a particular value in the American troops for a Cuban campaign, first as guerilla fighters in the Cuban hinterland, then as experienced planters who could cultivate the conquered island.[35]

Cathcart had taken extraordinary pains to provide for the Americans. He badgered Newcastle to order them pay, tents, and medicine. Cathcart repeatedly promised to honor the warrants of the provincial commanders in chief to officers without commissions, and he pledged to keep the expansive promises made to the American recruits. He called for arms for the eleven overestablishment American companies, and for all the American noncommissioned officers (Blakeney had weapons for only 3,000 privates, leaving more than 1,000 Americans unarmed). Cathcart requisitioned the apparatus of military identity—colors and drums—for every American company and battalion. He proposed to equip 200 of the Americans as dragoons, the army's only cavalry. Cathcart insisted that "the Troops who shall come from North America" should share plunder equally with "the Regular Troops." An additional motive for Cathcart's extraordinary concern for the American recruits may have been the prospect of a commission as commander in chief of British North America.[36]

In 1740, lord Cathcart's name appeared on a set of reflections about "this expedition upon wch I think depend the fate of the King and his Kingdomes

... the preservation of my Country & of the Protestant Succession." King and country, constitution and communion, so the whig ministers believed, were still in danger from internal dissent and foreign invasion, despite Marlborough's victories. The tory betrayal of Marlborough and its consequence, the failed peace of Utrecht, had left English liberty and Protestant freedom at risk by placing all of Spanish America, and leaving most of French America, in the hands of the Bourbon monarchs. The negotiations at Utrecht had also made it clear that America was the crucial theater in the ongoing contest for Atlantic dominion. "The great advantage the King has in an American Warr over all the Nations in Europe," this strategist wrote, "is the very great Number of very good men that is in our Collonies in America which may be used with very great advantage against either France or Spain. It was views of this kind wch made me propose to be appointed Governor General of Our Continent of America."

This would-be viceroy's first concern was how to militarize American manpower. He proposed that every British regiment sent to America should add an American battalion. To recruit their fellow colonists, the company-grade officers of these second battalions must be "proper Inhabitants of the several Colonies," but the field and staff officers should be British regulars, supplied from the double-officered parent battalion. It should also have an extra company of grenadiers. They would "make an excellent head for new Troops." The primary target of these British-American regiments should be Havana, "for that single point *decide de la Guerre*." Next, St. Augustine should be captured. It, together with "a station kept att the Bahama Islands," would mean that "the Bay of Mexico would be effectually shut up." Finally, "if France should take part with Spain in this Warr by the means of our Colonies of New England and New York, we may . . . take Quebeck & Canso." The conquest of Canada by British-American battalions would win a monopoly of the trade in furs and fish, widen the market for British woolens, and give Britain control of the trade in North American timber and provisions on which "the French Suger Islands" depended.[37]

Such spacious views, premised upon an integrated British-American force, died with Cathcart and Spotswood. General Wentworth had no strategic vision. Worse, he exhibited the parochial English officer's characteristic contempt for American troops. After their first battalion's inaugural parade, Wentworth wrote that "they are very little acquainted with discipline." Their officers were no better, being "quite strangers to discipline." Because they were "accustomed to fatigue," Wentworth decided that the Americans should serve as laborers— "pioneers," in English military parlance—working together with slaves conscripted from Jamaican plantations. "From the first review of the American Troops, they were despised," an English officer wrote. English contempt even extended to the colonel of the American Regiment, veteran officer and provincial commander in chief though he was. Wentworth refused to render Gooch "the Honors suitable to the station I have in America," Gooch wrote. He found it "very mortifying after Governing so many years, to be thus managed by Power." Wentworth also denied Gooch any authority as quartermaster general. Wentworth had resented being passed over in favor of Spotswood. He was determined that Spotswood's successor, another officer of American troops, "not approach too near an Equality with himself, and rise Superior to others" of Wentworth's English staff.[38]

Indeed, Wentworth refused to promote any of the American captains to field officer vacancies, even in their own battalions. Twenty-nine American captains, Lawrence Washington included, signed the protest, forwarded to Newcastle by Gooch, that Wentworth's refusal to promote American officers by seniority in their own regiment violated military tradition, the royal promise of equal treatment for Americans, and the secretary of state's assurances to Colonel Gooch. Gooch added that his captains' "Behaviour would have Procurred for them Preferment in any Service." Wentworth's response was to propose Gooch's replacement, breaking up the American Regiment, and the commissioning of English field officers for each of four new American regiments. In the meantime, Wentworth replaced every field officer casualty in the American Regiment—and filled most company-grade vacancies as well—with Englishmen. Rather than promote Americans, Wentworth rewarded English noncommissioned officers and even English volunteers who—like himself—had seen no service with company commands in the American Regiment. So it was that the good intentions of lord Cathcart toward the American Regiment, certified in the king's name by the duke of Newcastle, were lost to the personal limitations, class prejudice, national chauvinism, and military rigidity of General Thomas Wentworth.[39]

The general could maltreat his American subordinates, but he was quite unable to persuade Admiral Vernon to attack Havana, even though that was not only the army's preferred objective but also the apparent inclination of the royal orders (Newcastle, although he was the author of the royal orders and a proponent of an attack on Havana, was habitually, fatally, vague and indecisive). Vernon declared that because the fleet could not attack the harbor fortifications frontally, no assault on Havana was possible. His own preference had long been for Cartagena. There the army would have the chore of capturing the outlying fortifications but the navy would gain the credit of forcing the city to surrender. The admiral refused to consider landing anywhere in Spanish America, however, until he had explored Captain Dandridge's report that a French battle fleet had arrived to prevent "Great Britain forming new settlements and making conquests in the West Indies" and to escort the Spanish treasure ships to Europe. Admiral Vernon ordered the entire expeditionary fleet—twenty-nine ships of the line manned by 15,000 sailors and eighty transports carrying 11,000 troops—to sail from Port Royal to attack the eighteen French ships of the line that Dandridge had reported to be at anchor in Port St. Louis, Santo

Domingo. It took three days to echelon the expedition out of Port Royal and a week to sail to Port St. Louis. There the fleet lay at anchor for another week. Finally, the French governor general sent out an aide to politely explain that the French fleet had sailed home weeks before. Admiral Vernon refused to receive him. At last, General Wentworth undertook his own reconnaissance of the port. He discovered "that all the ships were merchantmen mostly un-rigged except for one frigate of forty guns; and that the supposed [admiral's] flag was no other than the white gable of a house." Only then could Vernon be persuaded to abandon his French focus and up anchor. After this "wild goose Chace," however, the British ships needed wood and water. They anchored off Hispaniola to replenish. "Detachments from the American regiment and from the Negroes were daily sent on Shore to cut Fascines and Pickets" for the siege of Cartagena. Only after having "trifled away three weeks" more, with the troops still packed into the stifling transports, still eating salt provisions, and still drinking unpotable water, both at half rations, did the fleet at last anchor off Cartagena on March 4, 1741. Already the men were dying "like rotten Sheep on a Marsh in a wet Winter." The rainy season, mosquitoes, and yellow fever were just a month away.[40]

The army officers knew, so the naval officers should have known, that both the beaches and the Boca Grande channel adjacent to the city were too shoal- and boulder-strewn for a landing. Vernon had bombarded Cartagena a year earlier. He had wantonly destroyed "two or three Churches besides a great Number of Houses, and killed several Hundred of the Inhabitants" before he concluded that a landing force was necessary to take the city. He claimed that "I know now as much of the avenues to their harbours as they do themselves." Nevertheless, and despite realizing that already "our Forces are daily decreas-ing by Sickness so that slow Matters are certain Ruin," Vernon spent five days reconnoitering off Cartagena. Finally he decided to do as French buccaneers had done forty years before. He would attack the city through its harbor. Of course, in the intervening decades, the Spanish had heavily fortified the deep water entrance. The Boca Chica channel was now protected by "the famous Fort St. Louis" on Bomba Tierra Island. The fort had walls forty-two feet thick, carrying eighty-four artillery pieces served by expert gunners. It was sup-ported by forts San Felipe, Cambria, and Santiago—which covered the landing beaches on Bomba Tierra—by batteries on both sides of the Boca Chica chan-nel into the outer harbor—"the Lake of Cartagena"—and by Fort St. Joseph on a shoal where the channel opened into the lake. Anchored across the channel from Fort St. Joseph to Fort St. Louis lay a boom backed by battleships. All the fortifications were manned with Spanish regular troops. They, like the Spanish ships of force, had been brought across the Atlantic in anticipation of the all-too-well-advertised British attack.[41]

On the evening of March 9, following a naval bombardment to silence the beach defenses, Wentworth led 4,000 troops ashore, or rather, he landed with

MARLBOROUGH'S AMERICA

The duke of Marlborough and Colonel John Armstrong, by Seeman,
courtesy of the duke of Marlborough

John Churchill, duke of Marlborough, was a beautiful young man and a handsome mature one. He was a courageous captain and a cold commander. His sangfroid was remarked upon even by his enemies. He was a master of men, on and off the battlefield. He never forgot a name. He was invariably courteous, never more so than to a fallen foe. Affable, he smiled and he touched. He was deeply informed and astonishingly foresighted. His geopolitical grasp was unsurpassed in his age, extending as it did from the Vistula to the Mississippi; from Hudson's Bay to the coast of Columbia; down the Atlantic to Ghana and the Gold Coast and around the Cape to Bombay and Bengal; and up the Mediterranean to the Adriatic. Marlborough was the greatest European general of the century between Gustavus Adolphus and Napoleon Bonaparte. Only Wellington can be compared to Marlborough among British commanders, having completed the war with France for dominion in the Atlantic world that Marlborough had begun. He ascended from utter obscurity and poverty to fame and riches. The page boy became a prince of the Holy Roman Empire.

Yet Marlborough was, and he remained throughout his illustrious career, deeply insecure. His was the insecurity of a child raised in a literally broken home by men who had lost everything but principle in civil war and revolution. His father was a defeated royal officer. His teacher was a deprived cleric of the church of England. So royalism and anglicanism were Churchill's touchstones. Nonetheless, he advanced himself at the court of the restored king, Charles II, whose chief concern was to avoid a second exile, by being all things to all men. Churchill's particular patron, the king's brother, James, duke of York, afterward James II, was a devout Catholic. Churchill's ascent in the court of an unprincipled king and his overprincipled heir was fueled by sex. In the intervals of his reckless military service, at sea and abroad, in Tangier, France, and Germany, the charming Churchill serviced the king's castoff mistress ("I forgive you, young man," said King Charles, "for you do it for your food"). His vivacious sister, Arabella, prostituted herself to the king's brother ("I never knew what he saw in me, for all I had were brains and he had none").

In a contrast with a wastrel king and a profligate court, Churchill invested all of his profits in annuities and commissions. As his wealth grew, his avarice deepened. It was international news when the duke of Marlborough bought a new coat. On campaign, when his valet cut off the captain general's soaked gaiters, Marlborough admonished him to save the buttons. Trying to decipher one of the duke's semiliterate scrawls, his great colleague Prince Eugene remarked that Marlborough had probably left out the tittles of i and j "to save ink." He spent on himself but a fraction of his enormous military perquisites and shrewd financial investments. These included the Hudson's Bay Company, of which he was governor in succession to James; the East India Company, whose consolidation he facilitated; and the crown corporations for slave trading and fishing, which he helped organize. Marlborough left the love of his life, Sarah Jennings, duchess of Marlborough, the wealthiest woman in Britain, able to complete Blenheim Palace, the greatest private house in Europe and a massive memorial to military merit and to the duke's greatest victory. Marlborough's was the military makeweight that deposed one British sovereign, his patron, James II, and enthroned three monarchs of a greater Britain, William III, Queen Anne, and George I. The maker of the monarchs he served, Marlborough was not just a great general, he was also a distinguished statesman. His foresight and penetration, his clarity and courtesy, his simultaneous mastery of the least details and the largest dimensions made Marlborough, within the limits imposed by his religion and his royalism, a preeminent politician. As "a good Englishman," Marlborough could never be a Cromwell or a king, nor did he want to be. But his dexterity in council, his cogent public address, his knowledge of every politician's pressure points, his financial acumen (Marlborough was almost as much of a contributor to the fiscal as he was to the military revolution of his age), and his enormous prestige would have made Marlborough the first prime minister had his military commands not kept him abroad more than half of each year during "the duke's decade," 1702–12. As it was, his (and Sarah's) best friend, the lord treasurer Godolphin, was, at the height of Marlborough's career, the empire's chief political and fiscal manager. He, and the duchess, were the duke's interlocutors with Anne, crucial roles in an age in which sovereigns ruled as well as reigned. Marlborough, for all his genius, was but "the greatest Subject in Europe."

Marlborough's politics were shaped by his famous "moderation." This tolerant, cosmopolitan, rational ethos made Marlborough anathema to political partisans. Even his own son-in-law, Charles Spencer, earl of Sunderland, the leading whig, despised Marlborough's moderation. In the interests of an aristocratic republicanism, Sunderland undercut his father-in-law at every opportunity. The tories, preeminently the party of church and crown, in awe of France and devoted to divine right monarchy, wanted to cut off Marlborough's head.

Moderation was part and parcel of Marlborough's classical *virtù*. Together with his courage, wisdom, and justice, it made him the Augustus of a new "Augustan" age, the model for the captain general's successful legates in America. Just as his men loved their "Corporal John" for his unequaled care for their material needs, for his courage, manifest at the crisis of every battle, and for the unprecedented series of victories which made the redcoats he drilled and disciplined the world's premier infantry, so his grace's officers respected and, insofar as their talents and commands permitted, emulated the general and the statesman who cultivated their abilities and promoted their careers in army and empire.

> So, when an angel, by divine command,
> With rising tempests shakes a guilty land.
> Such as of late o'er pale Britannia passed,
> Calm and serene he drives the furious blast,
> And, pleased th' Almighty's orders to perform,
> Rides in the whirlwind, and directs the storm.

In this double portrait, Colonel John Armstrong, the engineer officer who succeeded Alexander Spotswood as the captain general's deputy quartermaster general, presents the duke of Marlborough with a plan of Bouchain. The image of the duke, so his duchess said, is "as like him as I ever saw." The portrait, by Enoch Seeman, hangs today in the third state room at Blenheim and is reproduced by the kind permission of his grace the duke of Marlborough. Armstrong, yet another son of an Anglo-Irish military family, was distinguished at Bouchain by his plan to crack that supposedly impregnable fortress. He succeeded Cadogan as quartermaster general in 1712. While superintendent of the destruction of Dunkirk, Armstrong cooperated with Cadogan in planning the coup by which Marlborough intended to effect the Protestant succession. Chief engineer for both George I and George II, Armstrong became colonel of the Royal Irish and died in 1742.

Daniel Parke was passion personified. He was born in Virginia in 1669. His father was the successful planter, colonial councilor, and secretary of state of the same name. His mother was Rebecca Evelyn of the famous family of silviculturists, diarists, and gunpowder manufacturers. As a child, young Daniel was taken to England and raised at Long Ditton among the Evelyn children, his lifelong friends and patrons. Parke's father died when the boy was ten. The Parke estates in Virginia were taken over by his guardian, Philip Ludwell, the chief of the Green Spring faction, Virginia's country party which, following the occupation of Virginia by the Guards in 1676, resisted royal government for half a century. At sixteen, Daniel was sent back to Virginia. To keep Parke's estates in his guardian's family, the boy was married to Jane Ludwell.

When he came of age, Parke rejected his guardian, neglected his wife, and opposed everything that Ludwell stood for: abuse of dependents; assembly autonomy; Bristol (that is, outport) merchants; low church clerics. Parke apprenticed himself to Sir Edmund Andros, the governor general of Virginia. A crusty old tory, Andros had been raised a royalist in the civil wars. As a soldier of the crown, he had fought in the Channel Islands, England, the Low Countries, Barbados, and the Leeward Islands. In America his scope as a royal governor extended from the St. Croix to the Dan. Parke could not have found a more capable imperial tutor. If only to thwart Philip Ludwell and the Green Spring faction, Andros instructed his customs officers to foster Daniel Parke's substantial shipbuilding; assisted his acquisition of land seized from the Rappahannocks after Bacon's revolution (land coveted by the faction); and transferred Parke's tobacco trade from the Bristol smugglers to the aldermanic merchants of London.

Sir Edmund nominated this twenty-three-year-old rake (Parke had brought home from London "Cousin Browne," the first of his publicly announced mistresses) to the royal council of Virginia. Now "Colonel" Parke, the young man became the old executive's enforcer. He

Daniel Parke, by Kneller, reproduced by the kind permission of the
Virginia Historical Society (1985.35)

horsewhipped Francis Nicholson, then the lieutenant governor of Maryland but leader of the opposition to Andros. Parke "sharpened his longest sword" to challenge Nicholson to a duel (Nicholson ducked). Parke (allegedly) dragged from the governor's pew in Bruton Parish Church the (much-tried) wife of Commissary James Blair, clerical counselor of the faction.

When Sir Edmund Andros retired to the government of Guernsey (and a townhouse in London), leaving the Virginia command to Nicholson, Parke perforce went "home." With aspirations to command his native colony, Parke sought the prerequisite military service. He joined King William's army in Flanders as aide-de-camp to the earl of Aaran. When the war resumed in 1702, this ambitious, well-connected, well-constructed, well-to-do young officer was taken into the duke of Marlborough's "military family." Parke's coup was one of the few bright spots in the Antwerp disappointment, caused, Parke wrote with characteristic chauvinism, by Dutch "rats." During the long march to the Danube, there was no fighting. Horribly bored, hot tempered, and an outspoken tory, Colonel Parke disgraced himself by quarreling in the Guards' mess. He redeemed himself at the head of the suicidal assault on the Schellenberg. At Blenheim, Parke's extraordinary service led the captain general to entrust his aide with the news of the victory that altered the balance of power in the Atlantic world. "On the battlefield of Blenheim," Marlborough promised Parke the government of Virginia. In London, an ecstatic queen asked the handsome young officer what reward he desired. Assured of Virginia, Parke winningly replied, "your portrait, your majesty." Parke received as a decoration a miniature portrait of the queen set in a bejeweled frame. Queen Anne also saw that Parke received an unprecedented, unequaled, unrepeated cash reward (the penny-pinching duke thought Parke's pension excessive).

Emboldened by fame, enriched by royal favor, Parke campaigned for a parliamentary seat. Rebuffed by an elections committee, he sailed in his own ship, the great *Indian Queen*, to Antigua, capital of the Leeward Islands. Parke had chosen this government rather than share the profits of Virginia with a titular governor general, the earl of Orkney. As a high tory, irascible (an elbow shattered by a would-be assassin's bullet left Parke in constant pain), a rake, a collector of customs, a policeman, and a champion of the smallholders who constituted his militia, himself the very model of a modern soldier, Parke antagonized the majority of the island's assemblymen: republicans; smugglers; Bristol clients; and amateur strategists. Terrified by the French, excited to revolt by radical clerics, cuckolded husbands, and outraged fathers, the Antigua assemblymen led the island militia—pistols in one hand, pillowcases for plunder in the other—in an assault on the governor general's residence. They overwhelmed his guards and shot his companions. Even as he killed its leader, the mob felled Colonel Parke, ripped Queen Anne's portrait from his neck, broke the back of the helpless executive, and left him to die in the dust of the market square, aged thirty-two.

> This is the Effect of all thy Service done,
> Of Zeal approv'd, and signal Valour shewn
> At Schellenbergh, and on the Danube's Banks?

Kneller's head and his studio's (awkwardly attached) torso depict Daniel Parke as the hero of both the Schellenberg and Blenheim. Parke wears Queen Anne's miniature. He is bracketed by a cavalryman's armor, displayed together with the gold chains and medallions presented to Parke by the cities through which he passed racing home from the Danube. An officer's sash and sword dignify his splendidly brocaded waistcoat, his fine lace cuffs and cravat. The obligatory scarlet coat is of the richest velvet. In the background, a French battery fires point blank at the forlorn hope of the First Guards, led against the ramparts of the Schellenberg by the duke of Marlborough's aide Colonel Daniel Parke.

Robert Hunter was born in Edinburgh in 1666, the son of an impoverished attorney, but Hunter's schoolfellows—with whom he shared an elite education, both classical and modern, in languages and mathematics—included the heir to the marquis of Tweeddale, John, lord Hay, Hunter's closest friend. Hunter summered on his uncle's extensive estate, Hunterston, in Ayrshire. The neighbors included the Dalrymple family, earls of Stair. Hunter's contemporary, afterward one of Marlborough's most trusted generals, the second earl of Stair, became Hunter's "dear good lord," an unfailing patron.

Like so many of his well-bred and well-educated Scots compatriots, Robert Hunter realized that "the only good road in Scotland is the road out." So Hunter entered on the world stage in London. At first light on November 26, 1688, he was "one of the gentlemen who served as a guard under the Bishop of London to the Princess Anne" when, led by Sarah, lady Churchill, the princess fled from the court of her father, James II, to take up titular leadership of "the Glorious Revolution." Hunter returned to Scotland and obscurity. In the spring of 1689, he was commissioned as a junior officer in a regiment raised by the earl of Mar, the first and oldest of Hunter's military and aristocratic Scots patrons. Hunter was at the very bottom of his chosen profession, an ensign of newly raised infantry, fighting in out-of-the-way actions under notorious commanders. Hunter participated in the relief of Londonderry led by Piercy Kirke, soi-disant governor general of New England. Sent by that old Cromwellian John Hill to subdue Highlanders, Hunter was implicated in the massacre of "the thieving tribe of Glencoe." The survivors were sent to slavery in America.

Suddenly, in 1694, after five years of obscure and unrewarding service in Scotland, Hunter jumped to the captaincy of a troop in the Royal Scots Dragoons (afterward, from the mounts Marlborough assigned them, famous as "the Scots Greys") and found himself fighting in Flanders. Within the year, Hunter was an administrative officer, major of brigade to the dragoons. In 1697, escaping demobilization after the Peace of Ryswick, Hunter was promoted major of Charles Ross's Irish dragoon regiment. Dragoons were rough and ready. They wrenched requisitions of food and forage from occupied populations, acted as military police in armies crowded with conscripts and criminals, and subdued riotous, even rebellious, civilians. Hunter excelled at extortion as a policeman and as a combat officer. During his first campaign under Marlborough, the duke made Major Hunter one of his aides and had him brevetted lieutenant colonel in the New Year's list of 1703. On August 13, 1704, Hunter's exiguous command checked an attempted breakout of 12,000 French infantry from Blenheim village. Then, serving under the Scots earl of Orkney, Hunter helped compel the French surrender. He was promoted colonel in the New Year's list of 1705.

At thirty-nine, Colonel Hunter was an officer of distinction. His portrait, painted by Kneller and reproduced from the collection of the New-York Historical Society, shows Hunter in half-armor and leopard skin, the insignia of a cavalry officer. The background depicts Hunter's coup, the defeat of his French opposite number in single combat. Hunter's Latin poems were published (anonymously, of course) in the *Tatler*. He was an intimate of the literati, both whig (Steele) and tory (Swift). Returning to the front in 1706, Hunter carried the battle-winning order at Ramillies but, oversuccessful at Antwerp, he lost the prospect of further advancement in Flanders.

Then lord Hay died at Coutray. Hunter obtained Marlborough's leave to carry Hay's last words to his young widow. She married the messenger. Elizabeth, lady Hay, was twenty, the heiress in her own right of 8,000 well-developed English acres, three London houses, and ample estates in Jamaica. They appeared to offer Hunter an opportunity for promotion. Marlborough could offer Hunter a provincial command, for the union had qualified Scots officers for posts in what was now the British empire. The government of a major royal colony would bring Hunter general's rank and a lucrative garrison to command, but Marlborough had already promised Jamaica to a more senior Scots officer. Modifying his ambition, Hunter obtained the government of Virginia (by arrangement with the absentee governor general, the earl of Orkney). Captured en route to Virginia, Hunter spent two years as a French prisoner, mostly on parole in London. Exchanged at last in the autumn of 1707, Hunter exercised court connections, obtained Marlborough's imprimatur, and was commissioned by the queen as her governor general of New York.

Hunter was sent to New York, so both Marlborough and Godolphin intended, to organize American forces, concentrate American resources, and command the impending expedition to Quebec. The tory counterrevolution of 1710, however, meant that the five regiments extorted from Marlborough for the Quebec operation were consigned to the unready hands of "five-bottle" Jack Hill. Command of the Hudson-Champlain assault on Montreal was given to the tory veteran of American government General Francis Nicholson. Hunter was left to chair the intercolonial congress and mobilize New York, New Jersey, and Connecticut. He built an American brigade, had it disciplined by drill instructors detached from Marlborough's army, amassed provisions, and provided transport. Hunter said that the duty

Robert Hunter, by Kneller, Collection of The New-York
Historical Society

was more demanding than anything he had done in Europe. He was duly promoted brigadier general, but he had now to impose a fiscal revolution on New York to pay for the military one.

Between 1714 and 1717, Hunter directed an inspired exercise in currency finance. A paper currency based on long-term government debt was to be redeemed by long-term levies, taxes which shifted liabilities from agriculture to commerce, from country to city, and from old (tory) merchants to new (whig) ones. The new currency at last repaid the soldiers and supporters of the revolution in New York, relieved Hunter's debts (incurred in resettling Palatine refugees), recompensed military suppliers, and paid the governor general's back salary and costs. Coupled with patronage purges and political prosecutions, the new financial system wiped out the forces of reaction and cemented the revolution in New York. Hunter's career had come full circle since November 26, 1688.

After a decade of command in New York, Hunter spent several years in a Whitehall sinecure, all the while proposing the invasion of Spain's American and Caribbean colonies by North American troops. In 1727, with another Spanish war impending, the new king, George II, promoted Brigadier Hunter major general and commissioned him to command Jamaica. In the viceregal post that he had sought for twenty years, Hunter perpetuated the imperial settlement of 1681, which balanced royal military command and taxation in support of government with local legal and legislative authority. Then Hunter found himself embroiled in another highland resistance to empire. Exhausted by his battle with the Maroons, General Hunter died on the last day of March, 1734, aged sixty-eight.

Renowned in war and no less distinguished in peace,
he passed his days of active service with wisdom and courage,
those of leisure with dignity and refinement . . .
who was careful of the people's health and destroyed his own.

Alexander Spotswood was an army brat. He was born in 1676 in the garrison of Tangier. His father, Robert Spotswood, was the third son of Sir Robert Spotiswoode, Charles I's secretary of state in Scotland, martyred in 1646 by Presbyterian parliamentarians. Robert was an exile, physician to the governor general of Tangier, that veteran Scots royalist Charles, earl of Middleton. Alexander's mother, Catherine Mercer, was said to be a relative of Sarah Jennings, afterward duchess of Marlborough. On Robert Spotswood's death, his widow married Surgeon Elliot of the 2d, Queen's, Royal Regiment. In 1683, Tangier was abandoned. Its hardened garrison regiments took up quarters in London to support the accession of James II. Alexander Spotswood, aged seven, began his education at the famous Westminster School.

Spotswood graduated in 1693. He was immediately commissioned in that famously tory corps the blue-coated regiment of the Granville family, earls of Bath, afterward the 10th foot, in which Alexander's elder half brother, Roger Elliot, was major. Fighting in Flanders, Spotswood was promoted lieutenant within the year. At the Peace of Ryswick, the 10th was garrisoned in Londonderry. The regiment was recalled to Flanders at the outbreak of the war of the English and Spanish successions. The earl of Marlborough immediately brevetted Spotswood captain over the heads of senior officers. In 1703, Captain Spotswood was named deputy chief of staff, a post, as he wrote, usually reserved for much more senior officers. Only after four years of distinguished service, including a long recovery following severe injuries incurred at Blenheim, was Spotswood finally brevetted lieutenant colonel. With General Cadogan, Colonel Spotswood led the allied army's amazing advance to and across the Scheldt. He was severely wounded in the first charge at Oudenarde, in the company of the Hanoverian prince who would become George II. After Ramillies, Spotswood was captured leading the raid into Picardy by which the captain general wished to demonstrate, to allies and enemies alike, how easy it would be to march on Paris. Marlborough's esteem for an officer was measured by the speed of his exchange and the rank of the corresponding officer. In Spotswood's case, the speed was instant and the rank was high. Spotswood even seems to have transmitted Marlborough's peace terms to the French high command. Louis XIV rejected the peace. A final terrible battle was fought at Malplaquet. With the war apparently coming to a close, Spotswood demanded his reward. He reached Virginia on June 1, 1710.

Colonel Spotswood was the most constructive, and the most contentious, of the military executives who, in a generation, transformed Virginia from a tidewater tobacco colony into a transmontane province of empire. Spotswood made that transformation manifest in

Alexander Spotswood, by Bridges,
courtesy of The Colonial Williamsburg Foundation

the public buildings he designed and built at Williamsburg: the palace and the college; the church and the armory; the jail, the archive, and the Indian school. Spotswood was the architect of empire. His "Georgian" structures of authority still are the models of American public and collegiate buildings. His "palace" still shapes elite residences.

As a soldier, Spotswood repressed rebellions, executed pirates, and succored Virginia's neighbors. He reconnoitered the Piedmont, crossed the Blue Ridge, claimed the Shenandoah for King George, and negotiated the northward and westward movement of the Iroquois warriors' path. So Spotswood inaugurated Virginia's imperial expansion. From the Piedmont and Blue Ridge "Barrier" that Colonel Spotswood settled, mapped, and patrolled, he projected an assault against the French empire in the interior from the Ohio to Lake Erie. Against the other Bourbon empire in the Americas, Spotswood planned a campaign by an American army. The Americans would take Spanish Florida, the Keys, and so control the Gulf of Mexico. Then, transported by the British navy, the American army would conquer Cuba.

Meanwhile, a master of modern material cultures, as befit his extended staff experience under Marlborough's command, Spotswood spawned the Virginia Indian Company, analogous to Marlborough's Hudson's Bay Company. Spotswood built ironworks, produced naval stores, and legislated a tobacco regulatory agency. Besides imposing quality control over Virginia's cash crop, a tobacco act was designed to supply Virginia with its first currency, tobacco notes. Spotswood's plan to monetarize the Virginia economy was sabotaged by the succession crisis, economic depression, London merchants, and a dreadful drought. It was not revived for twenty years. Enactment of his plan to modernize Virginia's militia waited for a decade. A royal American regiment, commanded by General Spotswood, was not raised until the outbreak of the next war with Spain, in 1739. Spotswood's plans for Virginia's imperial expansion to the Ohio at the expense of France (and the Iroquois) were finally put into armed action when the officers of Spotswood's American Regiment came home and revived the trading, settlement, and expansionist plans of Spotswood's Virginia Indian Company. Indeed, it can be contended that General Spotswood had both outlined and officered the "great war for the empire."

Not until a generation had passed were Alexander Spotswood's designs for empire effected, but, even before his command of Virginia concluded in 1722, it was already apparent that

> This country is altered wonderfully,
> And far more advanced and improved . . .
> Since the beginning of Colonel Spotswood's lieutenancy,
> than in the whole century before his government.

The portrait of Alexander Spotswood is dated 1736 on the strength of William Byrd II's recommendation to Colonel Spotswood of Charles Bridges as "the Sergeant-Painter of Virginia." The painting is reproduced by permission of The Colonial Williamsburg Foundation. Its subject's military career is suggested by the fortress and camp in the background. Spotswood's architectural achievements are implied by the rolled plan he holds in lieu of the traditional baton of command. Aged sixty, retired for more than a decade, Spotswood was nonetheless about to receive a double promotion to major general and obey orders to raise and to command the four-battalion, 4,000-man American Regiment designed to enact his plan of Caribbean conquest.

Had he lived, Lawrence Washington would have had better credentials to command a continental army and win American independence than his much younger half brother, George. To begin with, the elder Washington had the English formal education and wide acquaintance which gave him the cultural depth and social poise, the affability without familiarity so much in contrast with the coldness and reserve with which his younger sibling masked his educational and social insecurity. Militarily, Lawrence had years of service in a multibattalion, regularly drilled and disciplined royal regiment, a unit sanctioned by disease and hardened by combat. The American Regiment was the model that two military tyros, Robert Dinwiddie and George Washington, tried to reconstitute in the next imperial war. However, it then appeared that the five dozen officers of the American Regiment who with

Lawrence survived the West Indian campaign, took half pay (the substantive mark of their royally conferred rank), and sailed home to make careers in America, had formed a military and imperial brotherhood. Their pride of rank and service drove George Washington to resign his provincial commission rather than subordinate himself.

Contrast with this petulance Lawrence Washington's always-cordial relations with Admiral Vernon and, at last, an affirmative one with General Wentworth. Washington's claim to consideration, beyond the cost of raising his company, equipping himself, and risking death by disease in the West Indies, was his record in combat with the Spanish: the storm of the Baradera battery; possibly the governorship of Fort St. Joseph and clearing the Boca Chica boom; and the repulse of the Spanish flankers at Texar de Gracias. Despite the failure of General Wentworth to promote him or any other provincial officers, Captain Washington declined to come home with Colonel Gooch after the Cartagena disaster. Instead, Washington was distinguished in the invasion of Cuba, winning the praise of Admiral Vernon for the capture of Sta. Catalina. He remained with the expedition until the bitter end. After the American regiment was broken up in Jamaica in the autumn of 1742, Washington brought the 144 Chesapeake survivors home. He retained one of these veterans in his household as a fencing master for young George and another as his own military deputy.

Here, in a portrait attributed to Gustavus Hess Elius, reproduced by courtesy of the Mount Vernon Ladies' Association, Captain Washington is portrayed in scarlet and, green, the regimental color of the Americans, with an officer's gold decoration on the rim of his tricornered hat. His former regimental colonel, Lieutenant Governor Gooch, promoted Washington major as the senior adjutant of the Virginia provincial forces, this despite Gooch's recognition that "making men acquainted with arms" might lead to revolution. He was willing to take the risk in order to keep the appointment of Virginia's military officers in his own hands and in those of the provincial gentry.

Major Washington was now a leader of Virginia's ruling class, having inherited the bulk of the family estates and become the proprietor of the Georgian house he named Mount Vernon. So credentialed, Major Washington made a most advantageous marriage. Ann "Nancy" Fairfax's dowry was an alliance with the greatest and most aristocratic landlords in Virginia. The Fairfax connection carried with it seats in the country court and house of burgesses and an easy access to grants in the Fairfax family's proprietary province, the Northern Neck, all the land between the Potomac and the Rappahannock rivers. The Fairfax interest also opened to Major Washington leadership in an exceedingly ambitious project for trade, diplomacy, and settlement, in a word, empire.

First the clerk and then the president of the Ohio Company, Lawrence Washington promoted to prospective patrons, investors, and settlers the vision of a new western world, purchased from the native proprietors and taken from the French intruders, to be conveyed to yeoman farm families. This was an alternative society to the Virginia that Lawrence Washington deplored as slave-ridden, convict-afflicted, religiously reactionary and, therefore, economically retarded. "Patriotism," Lawrence Washington defined to his English backers, was an imperial policy that, by acquisition of the transmontane region west to the Ohio River and north to Lake Erie, would attract traders and farmers to move west from the Potomac and south from the Susquehanna. In the West, Washington would foster "that delightful liberty," religious freedom. Protestant dissenters would cultivate family farms, pay low taxes, and man a local militia which would protect them from the French and Indians.

In October 1747, Major Washington was a leader among the gentlemen of the Northern Neck who petitioned Governor Gooch and his council for the first grant of land along the Ohio River. In return, Washington and his associates pledged a substantial investment in trade and the construction of a fort, both trading post and settlement protection. A year later, what was now the Ohio Company met for the first time, at Mount Vernon. The directors prepared a petition to the crown for transmontane conquest and colonization. In the spring of 1749, the king's privy council acceded to the Ohio Company request, supported as it was in London by "the military interest," leading merchants, and a new breed of imperial civil servants. Virginia's lieutenant governor was ordered to issue the necessary land patents. Major Washington then asked General Sir William Gooch for arms from Colonel Spotswood's magazine, enactment of a county palatine, a monopoly of the fur trade, and the governor's support for a request for regular troops to garrison the Ohio Company's fort.

Lawrence Washington, by Gustavus Hess Elius,
courtesy of the Mount Vernon Ladies' Association

Even as Major Washington's vision of the West took form, his health failed. His colleagues both in Virginia and in England were increasingly concerned about the consuming
cough Washington had contracted in the Caribbean campaign. After visits to the western
springs and voyages to Barbados and Bermuda failed to effect a cure, Lawrence Washington
succumbed at Mount Vernon on July 26, 1752, aged thirty-four. His house, lands, family
connection, corporation, provincial military rank, and vast imperial ambition were all bequeathed to his ultimate heir, George Washington.

> It has been my opinion, and I hope ever will be,
> that restraints on conscience are cruel,
> in regard to those on whom they are imposed,
> and injurious to the country imposing them.

the grenadiers, apprehended an ambush, reboarded the boats, and lay 200 yards offshore for hours, uncertain what to do. At dusk, no opposition having appeared, the grenadiers relanded. Wentworth went back to sleep on shipboard. The next day, the general, two regular regiments, half of the newly raised marines, and 300 men of the American Regiment, led by Colonel Gooch, came ashore on Bomba Tierra. Although Wentworth was now on an island, with seven miles of water between himself and the Cartagena garrison, he so feared a Spanish counterattack that he stationed most of his force as guards. Gooch recalled that the American troops spent the better part of a week doing guard duty "upon a burning Sand, up to their Anckles." Without tents, sunstruck by day, shivering at night, the men weakened. Finally, Wentworth permitted the troops to build a camp behind a hill that seemed to offer shelter from Fort St. Louis's artillery. Before the fort could be taken, at least one breach had to be made in its walls. The inexperienced British engineers took twelve days to raise a simple battery on the hill. Unfortunately, they sited it in a direct line between the Spanish fort and the English camp. Whatever of the Spanish counter-battery fire overshot the British battery struck the besiegers' camp. Once the Spanish realized their good fortune, they lofted shot over the hill. It ricocheted through the British tents. Not one was left whole. The troops suffered 200 casualties. "Beds & Chairs [were] Shot from under Officers as they ate or slept. Colonel Gooch who commanded the American Regiment received a Contusion in both his Ankles from a spent Ball." Gooch could say, with king William at the Boyne, "it was well that it came no closer," but the colonel of the American Regiment was now badly bruised, he had torn tendons, and his feelings were as hurt as his legs. The choice of campsite should have been his, as quartermaster general. That Wentworth had bypassed Gooch, resulting in both his wounds and his men's suffering, compounded the disrespect shown to Gooch's American Regiment, treated as mere pioneers. Gooch was, as he wrote Newcastle, in "a State of Humiliation."[42]

Americans not under Wentworth's command were given chances to win distinction. The Chesapeake battalion of the American Regiment did duty as marines on the ships of the admiral's own division. As captain of the senior company, Lawrence Washington had "remained on board Admiral Vernon's ship ever since we left Hispaniola, vastly to my satisfaction," for the admiral treated the American officers "like Gentlemen." On March 17, Vernon ordered Washington's men, and the British company commanded by James Murray, with 300 English sailors, to assault the Albanicos (or Baradera) battery. It was bombarding the British camp and battery from a site across the Boca Chica channel from Fort St. Louis. Wentworth had asked Vernon to deal with it. On the night of the 19th the British sailors beached their boats a mile from the battery. They found themselves right in front of a concealed artillery position. Five guns cut swathes in their ranks. The landing party fell back and regrouped. The soldiers replaced the sailors in the lead. Washington's and

Murray's infantry rushed the Spanish position. They took it. Encouraged, they stormed the main battery, spiked its artillery, and blew up the emplacement with its own gunpowder. Veteran officers unanimously "allowed that it was an exceeding good piece of work." The army journalist wrote, "I cannot, without doing Injustice to Capt. Washington, the Honourable Mr. Murry, and the rest of the Land Officers," emulate the navy reporter "in passing over their gallant Behaviour in Silence." Washington himself was most diplomatic. "If the Sailors can claim much honour," Lawrence Washington wrote his father, "I partake of it as Captain of the Soldiers who acted as marines."[43]

By March 25, the twenty twenty-four-pound guns of the British breaching battery had dismounted every artillery piece on the ramparts of Fort St. Louis, but they had only knocked down one corner of a bastion. The rubble was in large chunks, steeply piled, and the breach was backed by a palisade. General Wentworth "judged the breach practicable only because it was the first one he had ever seen." Besides, he was being bullied by Vernon to assault "such a paltry fort that has no outworks" without further delay. At dusk, the breach was attacked. The storming party was commanded by Lieutenant Colonel Macleod, one of the seven Marlborough veterans who died during the Cartagena campaign as field officers either of the marine regiments or of the American battalions. The Spanish garrison fled to their ships. The siege and the assault, American readers were told, had cost "about 300 Men in all. No American Officers Kill'd but the gallant Cap. Provoost of New York." The navy could now occupy the Spanish forts abandoned when Fort St. Louis fell. The chief of these was Fort St. Joseph on an islet at the outlet of Boca Chica. Vernon "put in a Capt of Americans Governour or Commander there." Given Washington's distinction at the Baradera battery, his rank as the senior American officer aboard the flagship, and Vernon's habit of naming his favorite officers as governors of captured fortresses, this "Capt. Of Americans Governour or Commander" is apt to have been Lawrence Washington.[44]

Whoever he was, the governor had the boom cut away from its anchors at Fort St. Joseph. The Boca Chica was clear at last. The fleet kedged, one ship at a time, through the narrows into the vast lake of Cartagena. The city seemed exposed. The American press printed Vernon's premature and vainglorious dispatch (both army and navy officers advised Vernon that it would be time enough to announce victory when Cartagena fell). The *Pennsylvania Gazette* declared that the capture of Fort St. Louis and the opening of the Boca Chica had "so exposed that Town as to make the conquest of it, in all human Probability, but the work of a few Days." The *Gazette* added the formulaic phrases of a new American patriotism: "So Glorious an Event to which we may boast in some Measure to have contributed, inflamed every loyal and honest Heart here with a Warmth, unfelt before, in this Infant Country."[45]

In three days, Vernon's fleet was ready to escort the troop transports up the bay to besiege the city itself. It was another week, however, before the army could be extricated from Bomba Tierra. "Such Americans, as had serv'd on shore, as likewise the Negroes" were the last to embark. Not until dusk on April 5 did 4,000 troops land at Texar de Gracias, two battalions of the American Regiment among them. They were just six miles from the gates of Cartagena. As the vanguard advanced from the beachhead, two ambushes were broken, one by the regulars, using the "street firing" drill beloved of General Wentworth, the other by the American flankers, commanded, it is said, by Lawrence Washington. The Spanish troops fled for the city gates. Rather than follow them into Cartagena, which was now less than a mile away, or seize the key but weakly held and poorly fortified heights of St. Lazaro, only half a mile ahead, Wentworth called a halt. "A number of Americans and Negroes being landed with working tools," he put them to clearing jungle and digging fortifications for a defensible camp. Once again Wentworth ordered the bulk of his army to stand guard day and night ("which harrassed the Men to Death") to resist a Spanish sortie that never came. "Some marauding Americans" took the initiative. They seized the commanding heights on which stood the convent of Madre la Popa while Wentworth's council of war were still debating how to attack them. (Elements of the American Regiment seem to have done all the scouting. "One of our Northern Indians" having finally obtained "Liberty to fight the Spaniards in his own way" was said in the American press to have single-handedly killed twenty-seven "Scouts or Spies of the Enemy" in the brush.)[46]

Wentworth failed to build a battery on La Popa to destroy Fort St. Lazaro, the only obstacle between the invaders and Cartagena. A New York officer wrote home that artillery on La Popa would have commanded not only the fort but the city as well. Instead, in the three days that Wentworth spent fortifying his camp, the Spanish dug entrenchments and built batteries on three sides of the St. Lazaro height (the fourth was covered by the guns of the city, half a mile away). Spanish deserters told Wentworth that the fort was open to assault. He was unmercifully, insultingly pressed by Admiral Vernon to attack. So Wentworth ordered St. Lazaro stormed at night without artillery preparation. Blakeney, now a brigadier general, General Wolfe (detached from his command at Annapolis Royal, Nova Scotia), and Colonel Grant—who was to lead the attack—all objected in writing to "so rash a design." The general overrode their protest, having "a mind to exceed even the great Duke of Marlborough, by attacking stone walls & such a number of cannon with Sword in Hand."[47]

At 3:00 a.m. on April 9, a Spanish deserter led Colonel Grant's grenadiers up a steep slope directly against the strongest point of the Spanish fortifications. Both the colonel and the guide were mortally wounded. Absent directions, the grenadiers halted and threw their grenades. They were too thick-walled to explode. The reserve supply was carried by "a Party of American Soldiers," but during the uphill advance, the Americans "fell back into the Rear." Now they were slow to reach the front lines. Absent grenades, the grenadiers formed up and commenced "street firing" by platoons. The Spanish canister cut swathes in the British ranks, "mowing them down like grass." "For two hours, after everybody but himself was convinced the thing was impractible," Wentworth repeated his orders to continue street firing. By then it was daybreak. The concealed Spanish sharpshooters could see the British officers "down to their shoe Buckles." Artillery from Cartagena began to enfilade the attackers. A Massachusetts officer saw a column of Spanish troops emerging from the city gates to cut off the attackers' retreat. Some 540 Americans were now on the hillside. About 300 of them were pioneers, laden with wool packs and scaling ladders. "Having no arms to defend themselves," many of them had dropped their burdens and fled, "notwithstanding the utmost Endeavours of their Officers to prevent it."[48]

This confirmed General Wentworth's low opinion of Americans and served as an excuse for his failure. He wrote that "what much added to our misfortune was the wretched Behaviour of the Americans, who had the Charge of the Scaling Ladders, working Tools &c, which they threw down in the first Approach of Danger." Of course, Wentworth, leading from behind, did not actually witness the action. A more observant British officer wrote, "seeing the troops falling by whole platoons," the unarmed Americans "refused to advance with their burdens but . . . many of them took up the firelocks which they found on the field, and mixing among the troops, behaved very bravely." Three armed American companies, so a Massachusetts witness reported, "advanced to the Walls of the Fort and raised their Ladders. But alas! They were 8 or 9 Foot too short." Two of the three American captains in that attack were casualties: Thomas Addison of Maryland was wounded; William Clark of New York was killed. The army journalist concluded, "I cannot but add, in Justice to the American Soldiers who were commanded with Arms on that Occasion, they were in no wise wanting to their Duty." The attackers had suffered more than 600 casualties out of 1,400 men engaged. They had stood "like lyons." They were told that "the duke of Marlborough's army never behaved better." Nonetheless, they finally broke and ran. "In the Agonies of Death," Colonel Grant said that "the General ought to hang the Guides, and the King ought to hang the General."[49]

The unengaged men were demoralized by the loss of the army's elite troops. They sickened and died. Water failed and food was short. Vernon, having concluded from the pounding his ships took from the Spanish batteries in the Boca Chica "that no Ships should ever be brought to Batter against Stone Walls," eschewed a cannonade of the city, even though that had been decisive in Pontis's taking Cartagena in 1697 (and in Vernon's own assault on Porto Bello just two years earlier). Vernon also refused to reinforce the army with sailors. In just four days, April 7–10, yellow fever reduced the 6,645 soldiers in Wentworth's camp to 3,569. Of these, 1,200 were "Americans and not fit for service." Yet it was the Americans who dug the entrenchment from the high ground to the seaside that General Wentworth thought necessary to protect his withdrawal. It was a thin battalion of the American Regiment that formed most of the rearguard—"a very disagreeable piece of Duty"—when, on April 16, Wentworth, fearing the Spanish sortie that never came, had the surviving men taken off the beach by night. Naval officers reported that Wentworth left most of his army's equipment behind and thousands of dead soldiers unburied. Army reporters averred that Wentworth got off all of the artillery and that he even made a great show of "taking off five tents and some tools of the Americans" lest the Spanish make trophies of them.[50]

After the evacuation, the wounded and diseased troops were held on crowded transports for three weeks in the lake of Cartagena. A naval surgeon wrote that "the space between decks was so confined that the miserable patients had not room to sit upright in their beds. Their wounds and stumps being neglected, contracted filth and putrefaction, and millions of maggots were hatched in the corruption of their sores. . . . rather than be at the trouble of intering the dead, the commanders ordered them [the sailors] to throw their bodies overboard . . . so that numbers of human carcasses floated in the harbour until they were devoured by sharks and carrion crows." The so-called hospital ships were "destitute of surgeons, nurses, cooks, and proper provision." All were available in Vernon's warships, but "the discord between the chiefs was inflamed to such a degree of diabolical rancour, that the one chose rather to see his men perish than ask help of the other, who distained to offer his assistance unasked, though it might have saved the lives of his fellow subjects."[51]

The reason for the deadly delay in the outer harbor of Cartagena was Admiral Vernon's refusal to convoy the troop transports back to Port Royal until he had produced the semblance of victory. He had the sailors and marines destroy the Boca Chica fortifications just as he had, to much acclaim, demilitarized Porto Bello. On the ruins of Fort St. Joseph, Vernon erected a monument with the motto "Memento las Guardas Costas." On May 12, 1741, the last units of the fleet set sail for a three-week voyage back to Port Royal, Jamaica. There, out of a joint force of 8,676 soldiers who had sailed for Cartagena, only 1,500 mustered fit for duty. Lawrence Washington reported for the Americans that "the enemy killed of ours about six hundred and some wounded and the Climate killed us in greater numbers vast changes we have in each Regiment some are so Weak as to be reduced to a third of their men a great quantity of Officers amongst the rest are dead." Four of the American Regiment's British field officers, two quartermasters, and twelve American captains, twenty-nine lieutenants, and seven ensigns were dead. In the next two weeks, 138 more men of the American Regiment died and 950 fell sick.[52]

"Colonel Gouche, finding that his health declines," so Wentworth wrote to Newcastle on June 30, "has desir'd leave to return to Virginia, which I have consented to: he was upon his first arrival much dissatisfied, at his not being appointed a member of the first council, and, perhaps, at being commanded."

Wentworth claimed to have conciliated Gooch, however, and declared that "he goes away in a very good temper." Colonel Gooch hoped that the king would keep the regiment on foot for service in America, his reward for having "done more towards promoting the Service than any other man engaged in" the expedition. There were precedents. The Nova Scotia and Newfoundland companies had formed Richard Phillips's regiment, the 40th. The South Carolina and Georgia companies had recently been incorporated in General Oglethorpe's regiment. Governor General Hunter had requested and his successor saw the Jamaica companies regimented, with the provincial commander in chief as colonel. Spotswood had recommended regimenting the New York and South Carolina independent companies. "For the Honour of the Corps," Gooch even pledged to clothe the American Regiment "without taking the advantage of it."[53]

Still in Jamaica, Captain Washington also expected "our Regiment paed on the very best footing & that we shall be continued in North America but," he added, "not at the Expence of the Colonies." General Wentworth, however, recommended that either Gooch's four shrunken battalions be consolidated into "a tolerable compleat corps" or that each of the American battalions be "distinguished by the name of ye most considerable provinces and commanded by separate Colonells." So honored, provinces would be expected to support their regiment with men and money, but the regiments, although they bore the names of American provinces, would not be stationed on the continent. Instead, the Americans would be permanently posted in the British West Indies, their men sacrificed to save British lives. Wentworth saw additional advantages to killing American men. "Perhaps the draining so many people from the growing Colonys might be no disadvantage to our mother country," not just because growing provincial populations would propel American manufacturing to the detriment of British trade, but also because the removal of continental troops to the pestilent Caribbean would reduce the threat of armed Americans to British rule. This fear was more clearly articulated by the duke of Bedford, Newcastle's successor as secretary of state. When France, as expected, did enter the war, Bedford advocated the conquest of Canada, but he resisted creation of an all-American force for the attack "on account of the independence it might create in those provinces, when they shall see within themselves so great an army, possessed of so great a country by right of conquest."[54]

All the proposals to keep one or more of the American regiments on foot were quashed. Instead, Gooch complained, "a Succession of Recruiting Officers from Georgia, Jamaica, and South Carolina . . . carried away all the idle Fellows out of a country settled only by Planters." When, in 1746, Brigadier General William Gooch was promoted major general, created a baronet, asked to raise a regiment in Virginia, and offered the command of all the American forces in the latest reiteration of the 1709 plan for "the entire expulsion of the French Out of the Northern Continent of America," he could scrape up only a single company. The Cartagena veterans would not reenlist, Gooch wrote, "they not having digested the hard usage of being Broke in Jamaica and sent Home without a farthing in their Pockets." Sir William Gooch allowed his recruiting officers to promise the few Virginia volunteers that they "are to be commanded by, and continue the whole time, with me," but he had already declined the command, incapacitated by "the wounds and Bruises I gott in the service of my King and Country." He was, Gooch wrote, "fitter for a hospital than a camp. I am next October sixty-six years of age and have served the Crown forty-five of them." Gooch had fought in every one of Marlborough's campaigns. He had taken command of Virginia in 1727, during George II's remilitarization of imperial government. Governing for twenty-two years, an unequaled tenure, Gooch had sustained his old comrade General Spotswood's program of western expansion, succeeded him in command of the American Regiment, and championed Spotswood's plan to turn American expansionism toward the Caribbean. There, Gooch and all of the officers and men of the American Regiment had suffered from the anti-American prejudice of the English officers. So the survivors of the Virginia companies of the American Regiment came home more than ever determined to conquer an empire that they could command themselves.[55]

The officers of the American Regiment, Washington most prominent among them, had seen the prospect of empire in Cuba. Just as Cromwell's officers, after their ignominious defeat on Hispaniola had turned to Jamaica, so the British leaders of the expedition rebuffed at Cartagena had looked about for an easier objective. Captain Washington wrote home from Jamaica that "some talk of the Havanna, others Panama and some Vera Cruz but perhaps others more probably St. Jago de Cuba." The Americans "in their imagination have swallowed up Cuba." They had been fixed on the Havana ever since Spotswood had laid down the plan of the West Indian expedition back in 1727. Its conquest "would strike an universal terror over this part of the world & make them prostrate before us," but Admiral Vernon refused to attempt anything against the batteries of the Havana, nor even those of Santiago de Cuba on the great island's south shore. The most he would agree to was to escort what was left of the troops to Guantánamo Bay, two days' march, he said, from Santiago. Vernon's parliamentary patrons had advised him that "*Take and Hold* is the cry; this plainly points to Cuba." So Vernon now declared that "the chief object of the expedition was the Isle of Cuba."[56]

American enthusiasm for Cuban colonization was again insisted on by both English commanders, equally anxious to make a Caribbean conquest and to depopulate the mainland colonies. As Admiral Vernon put it, "if the Americans could be settled there, it would be much better than their returning home, to a Country overpeopled already, which runs them on setting up Manufactures, to the Prejudice of their Mother Country." Then too, the American Regiment had to be recruited. It now accounted for more than a third of the men fit for service and all of those prepared to colonize Cuba. Wentworth thought the American Regiment could attract recruits if "the Adventurers have any immediate prospect of a settlement." Vernon promised that the fleet would secure the prospective colony's communications with Port Royal. The fleet anchored in Guantánamo Bay on July 18. After taking a week to overcome General Wentworth's fatuous fears of Spanish resistance, a landing was effected on July 23. The American scouts reported that they had broken a Spanish ambush and discovered that Santiago could be reached along the river which they named Augusta (for the princess of Wales). Eighteen miles upriver from Guantánamo, the army set up a classic Roman *castra*, "Georgestadt." Reinforced, the American scouts advanced. They reported that the single-file track to Santiago was ninety miles long, not sixty. Captain Lloyd of Maryland found that the Spanish had already felled trees across the path, broken bridges, and were prepared to ambush any advance in force. Santiago was out of reach, but its very distance from Guantánamo might make a colony there more secure.[57]

From Guantánamo, Captain Lawrence Washington wrote to his father that "Our Regiment has not rec'd that treatment we expected, but I am resolved to persevere in the undertaking. War is horrid in fact, but much more so in imagination." He and his men had "learn'd to live on ordinary diet, & disregard the noise, or shot of Cannon." Refuting General Wentworth's objections that his "Americans" were "mostly composed of Irishmen and some of them convicts," all of them apt to desert, Captain Washington led the Virginia companies to "open a communication" between Georgestadt and the beachhead in Guantánamo Bay by capturing Sta. Catalina. "By the report of Cat. Washington, their Captain, they all went on the Service with great Cheerfulness, and all returned according to your Orders," so Vernon wrote to Wentworth, "without a man deserting and they were concerned to be recall'd and expressed themselves desirous of going again." Washington's conquest, Sta. Catalina, was described by the admiral as a veritable city, with a cathedral and 150 great houses, but the general wrote that Sta. Catalina was "only a sorry Chappell, and a few huts," a minor capture suitable for Americans, Irishmen, and convicts.[58]

Reading this, Vernon told Wentworth that "any thing of a general national Reflection should be studiously avoided." Instead, Vernon observed that Washington's capture of Sta. Catalina had enhanced the possibility of an American settlement, "and the Americans begin to look on it [Cuba] as the land of Promise." General Wentworth, hostile to both the admiral and the Americans, obstructed the proclamation promising free land to American settlers. He wrote that the American soldiers lacked the requisite tools and livestock for settlement. Besides, Wentworth's English officers objected to fighting the Spanish for the benefit of Americans. The general did obey royal orders to detach American officers to the mainland to recruit reinforcements for Cuban colonization, but he sent them only to the northern provinces. Captain Washington had hoped to head a recruiting party to Virginia, but General Wentworth wanted no more of Virginia's riffraff, still believing that "great bodies of them being Irish or British convicts," they would always be "absolute strangers to discipline" and prone to desert.[59]

Yet even Wentworth thought that if the army could manage "to subdue the eastern part of the Island of Cuba," and if it were "peopled from North America," it "would, I conceive, be no despicable acquisition" for the empire. American officers agreed. Enthusiastic letters were carried from Cuba to the colonies by the recruiters from the American Regiment. On August 8, 1740, George Ogilvie of New York wrote from "Cumberland" Bay that 400 Americans were preparing to settle in "a Place as healthy as a Man can wish: we have no want of good beef, Cabaritas, wild hogs, Indian Corn in abundance. Our Men (which before were sickly) in a little [time] we have been here, gather Strength and Vigour daily; and I wish all our old Friends would rigg out and make the best of their way here. . . . now or never for a Plantation on the Isle of Cuba." In the first week of October, Captains "Hipkins" and "Winslaw" (as the *South Carolina Gazette* reported) told the New York legislature that the army was "actually possessed of a rich and fruitful Part of the Island of CUBA. . . . I heartily congratulate my Country Men on this happy Event." New York's chief executive (whose son was now a major in the American Regiment) pointed to public advantages when he urged his legislature to pay a bounty to recruits. An American Cuba would consume the grain and timber, livestock and fish that would otherwise be sold to the French sugar colonies. So the conquest of Cuba would meet the mercantilistic objectives of the molasses act without harming North American trade. Several hundred more Americans enlisted, but they did not find the army in Cuba. In August, the rainy season had set in. A hurricane raised the river and soaked the men. The 1,400 troops at Georgestadt sickened daily. Because General Wentworth again insisted on posting large guards against a Spanish counterattack (that never came), he could not find enough men to advance through the jungle to Santiago. Vernon called up the glorious memory of Marlborough's march to the Danube and his attack through the woods at Malplaquet, but to no avail. By November, that "General for Parade," Thomas Wentworth, declared that he could not even defend Georgestadt. It was evacuated by December 7. Having lost another 1,500 men, the expedition retreated once again to Port Royal.[60]

Another, much more modest conquest was now proposed to exploit the colonizing propensities of the Americans. Jamaica's commander in chief, Edward Trelawney, shared all his predecessors' ambition to widen Jamaica's empire in the western Caribbean. Lieutenant Robert Hodgson, in command of a party of Americans, had refreshed Jamaica's alliance with the Misquito Indians and recruited some settlers for the Honduran coast. Taking Hodgson's advice, Trelawney suggested fortifying a base and building a colony on Roatan Island. The ensuing councils of war exposed the contrasting imperialisms of the navy and army. The admirals saw the prospective seaport at Roatan as an entrepôt for expanded trade, especially in logwood ("which the Dutch now run away with"), with Spanish Guatemala and the Yucatán. These naval spokesmen applauded lucrative commerce carried on with free ports in Spanish America, by English, Irish, and American merchants, all under the protection of the British navy. The naval officers wished to liberate and exploit Spanish America, not to conquer and govern it. They deplored garrison government by army officers as expensive and oppressive. The generals stressed conquest and colonization by the Americans under the command of British army officers. They proposed a military alliance with the Misquitos and other native enemies of Spain, and an overland advance through Honduras and the Yucatán. Here, in an American context, was the perennial quarrel between a "blue water" strategy—naval, commercial, and liberal—and a "continental" strategy—military, territorial, and, in America, conservative.[61]

Strategic differences only deepened service rivalries. General Wentworth complained that "the utmost pains [were] taken, to sow dissention between the land and sea people" by Admiral Vernon and his senior officers. Certainly, these naval officers were determined to reverse the army's political imperial preeminence. "We have so long been considered in a secondary light, as persons of little consequence out of our own element," Vernon wrote to his officers, but "I am not without hope to see the day when Court as well as Country, Ministers as well as Patriots, shall be obliged to acknowledge that you are the only natural Strength of Great Britain." This interservice contest reached the point that, in a quarrel over the danger to the army's provisions from the navy's impressment of American merchant sailors, only the strong arms of servants kept Admiral Sir Chaloner Ogle and Governor General Edward Trelawney from swordplay. Cooperation between the army and the navy now evaporated entirely. The generals and the admirals "began to hold separate councils, drew up acrimonious remonstrances, and sent irritating messages to each other . . . both were in appearance glad of the miscarriage of the expedition in hopes of seeing the other stigmatized with infamy and disgrace." The stakes were high, for it was expected that, as it happened, the failure of the expedition would finally fell the Walpole administration.[62]

The preservation of Georgia, the new British colony on the American frontier with Spain, was bound up with that of Walpole's ministry. So, as the West Indian expedition sailed from England, Newcastle responded to a request from the government of South Carolina for help to protect Georgia, South Carolina's barrier, from the expected Spanish attack. Cathcart was ordered "to detach a part of the American Regiment" to defend Georgia. On its return from Cuba, the army was so reduced in numbers that Governor General Trelawney and Major General Wentworth wanted to send every effective man and the bulk of the battle fleet to join General Oglethorpe. They agreed with him that the best defense of Georgia was the conquest of Spanish Florida. Admirals

Vernon and Ogle objected that the shoal coast from the Carolinas to Florida was no place for battleships. Besides, given the additional troops en route to Jamaica from England and America, the admirals thought that Caribbean conquests, preferably from the French, were still attainable. Instead of the entire army, the admirals only "proposed to send the Americans, according to his Majesty's intention on our first arrival in the country." General Wentworth again objected to any independent service by the Americans. He declared that they were so ill equipped that "their very appearance would greatly prejudice the recruiting." They would not fight, he said, and "I much doubt if many of them would return should they once set foot in N. America." The grudging compromise meant that the navy sent only two twenty-gun ships and a sloop to escort shallow draft transports carrying 577 regulars to Charleston. Arriving in September, they found that General Oglethorpe, in command of the 47th Regiment, the Highland Company, and the Georgia Rangers, had already beaten back the Spanish invaders at the battle of Bloody Marsh. The expeditionary detachment never advanced beyond Charleston.[63]

In mid-January 1742, a reinforcement of two senior regiments, Blakeney's and Guise's (their colonels were already on Wentworth's staff), and drafts from every regiment in England, over 3,000 men, reached Port Royal. They quickly lost nine-tenths of their men to disease. Major elements of Vernon's fleet were ordered to return to England to meet the coming war with France. The admiral demanded that the survivors of the expeditionary army man the warships for the Atlantic crossing. Before the West Indian expedition broke up entirely, Trelawney and Wentworth apparently persuaded Vernon to support an attack on Porto Bello and Panama. They proposed to link up with Commodore Anson's Pacific raiders and perhaps resettle the former Scots colony at Darien. About 3,000 troops sailed from Port Royal in the first week of March 1742. This, the last episode of the "Golden Adventure," was sabotaged by Admiral Vernon. "Because the honour of it, must naturally have fallen to the share of the land forces," the admiral recalled his ships en route to Porto Bello, leaving the transports defenseless. Once again defeated by interservice hostility, all the forces returned to Port Royal in May. "Thus ended the greatest and most Expensive Expedition that ever entered the American Seas, and which Europe gazed on with Attention and Expectation."[64]

The last muster of the American Regiment was taken in Jamaica on October 17, 1742. It included: 314 men discharged in September as aged or infirm ("there not having been the least care taken in choosing the recruits," General Wentworth grumbled); troops now bound for North America; those still serving on board the men-of-war (as the officer closest to Vernon, Washington was sent to extract those of the American troops still on shipboard who wished to go home—he did not entirely succeed); and the 203 Americans in the Roatan garrison. All told, only 1,124 men could be found alive out of the 4,183 Americans who had mustered in January 1741. Nearly three-quarters of the American

Regiment had perished, not counting unnumbered reinforcements. Those of the survivors who insisted upon the terms of their enlistment were discharged in Jamaica, unpaid, on October 24. Late in the autumn, at the close of the hurricane season, they were shipped to North American ports aboard the station ships now detached from Vernon's fleet.[65]

Sixty-four of the American Regiment's provincial officers made it home. They had lost half of their commissioned comrades. All of the surviving officers were granted full pay to the end of 1742 and half pay for life. With this fiscal safety net, and with royal commissions and military titles added to their previous social standing, the former officers of the American Regiment made distinguished careers. For example, Captain Lawrence Washington, the outstanding American officer in the West Indian campaign, landed in Virginia from HMS *Shoreham* with 144 men at the end of 1742. After dispatching the men to their homes, Captain Washington wrote to General Wentworth on January 17, 1743, to report that he had carried out his orders. Washington asked if he should come over to England to protect his rank. Wentworth replied that he was very pleased to learn of Captain Washington's safe return to Virginia and the repatriation of "the solders committed to your charge." The general promised that he had and would do all that could be done for "the reduc'd officers" of the American Regiment. All of them, as they now declared in a petition to the king, were "natural born Subjects, did Cheerfully enter into the Army, Did at great expence raise their Men, Did at great Charges, provide for the late Expedition to go into a Dangerous Climate upon present Action." General Wentworth assured Captain Washington that the British parliament would, as it did, authorize back pay for the officers of the American Regiment to the end of 1742 and, as Washington's agent indicated, half pay for life. Wentworth implied that it would be a waste of time and money for Washington to come over unless he sought active service. Washington, his regiment disbanded, himself in poor health, contemplating marriage, and his ailing father's principal heir, did not intend to rejoin.[66]

As soon as Washington received Wentworth's polite dismissal, he addressed a memorial to Virginia's commander in chief, Brigadier General Gooch, and his executive council "setting forth that he had bore his Majesty's Commission . . . in the American Regiment which is broke by which the Memorialist has been a great Sufferer." By way of compensation, Washington applied for the vacant "post of Adjutant General of this Colony." Naturally, Gooch sympathized with his senior captain, declared Washington "well Qualified," commissioned him adjutant and major over all of Virginia's militia regiments, and gave him a salary, munificent for the Virginia of that day, of £150 per annum. Washington had instantly achieved the field-grade commission in Virginia's forces denied to him in the British army.[67]

The adjutancy to which General Gooch commissioned Major Washington had been requested by the Virginia council in 1728, after Gooch replaced Drysdale. This was a startling reversal of form for a body that had labeled Nicholson's and Spotswood's proposals to discipline the militia by adjutants as the roots of a new Cromwellian military dictatorship, but Drysdale's neglect of the militia had alarmed Virginia's elite. The threat of Spanish raids after 1727, the menace of slave revolts consequent upon the acceleration of human imports from Africa, and the horrifying violence of English convict servants and disbanded soldiers had forced the Virginia gentry to rescind their objections to arming and drilling the commons. The councilors now agreed with the governor that they must arm white freemen from the provincial magazine, and accept the very system of discipline which they had decried in Spotswood's time. Gooch frankly faced the possibility that a well-armed and professionally disciplined militia might be as much a menace to imperial hegemony as it was a necessity for provincial security. "It may be thought dangerous to make Men too knowing in Military Matters," Gooch conceded, but he relied upon "the Loyalty & Fidelity of the Inhabitants to his present most excellent Majesty and that they are engaged by Interest as well as Affection to Great Brittain" to prevent a revolution. General Gooch also relied upon his own military rank, authority, and experience to direct the Virginia provincial forces in the interest of the empire. Moreover, the adjutancy was the key appointment in the lieutenant governor's campaign to keep the military patronage of the province in his own hands, as "Commander in Chief of the Place," and to exclude the absentee titular governor general from nominating British officers to command Virginians.[68]

Now General Gooch's second in command, Major Washington confirmed his place in Virginia's militarized elite when the death of his father, Augustine, in April 1743 left him most of the estate, including the new manor house which Lawrence named Mount Vernon in honor of the admiral, his former commander in chief. An elite marriage was the requisite of rank. From the Appleby School, Lawrence's old teacher, both Latinate and vulgar, wrote, "You tell me, Dear Major Washington, on the 19th of July, that you had taken your residence upon *Mount Vernon*, and give me to understand that in a few hours after writing you might probably be upon your *Mons Veneris*." Indeed, Lawrence had married Ann ("Nancy") Fairfax, the daughter of Colonel William Fairfax, the land agent for the Fairfax family's Northern Neck proprietary and first cousin of the proprietor himself, Thomas, sixth lord Fairfax. Lieutenant Governor Gooch took the first opportunity to commission Major Washington as a justice of the peace for Fairfax County. A year later, following his father-in-law's elevation to the council, Washington succeeded him as a burgess for Fairfax County.[69]

As the greatest proprietors of Virginia's western lands, the Fairfax family were developing the upper Shenandoah valley from a command post in the new town of Alexandria, near the falls of the Potomac. Lawrence obtained Fairfax patronage for his half brother, George, fourteen years his junior, as a surveyor both of town lots in Alexandria and land grants in the Shenandoah. Lawrence also intended to use the Fairfax connection to advance George militarily. Major Washington enlisted Colonel Fairfax to obtain a midshipman's place in the Virginia station ship for George. Lawrence's successful service with Admiral Vernon, Fairfax's own former commission in the navy, the service's social openness, and its congenial relations with American colonists all made the navy an obvious first step for a second son toward an imperial command. George said that he would "be steady and thankfully follow your [Lawrence's] Advice as his best Friend."[70]

George's mother, Mary Ball, was, as she would be throughout her long lifetime, bitterly opposed to any appointment that would remove her son from her side. Fearing to be overcome by the weight of her stepson's advice and the pressure of his friends, she wrote to her brother in London for support. As she was unclear as to what sort of sea service was intended for George, Uncle Joseph covered all the maritime options in his reply. "A common sailor," he wrote, "has by no means the common liberty of the subject; for they [the navy] will press him from a ship where he has 50 shillings a month and make him take three and twenty; and cut him and staple him and use him like a Negro, or rather, like a dog." Even if George escaped the press gang and the dangers of the sea, and rose to be the captain of a Virginia tobacco ship, a middling planter would be as well off and would leave land and slaves to his children besides, "and as for any considerable preferment in the Navy, it is not to be expected, there are always too many grasping for it here, who have interest and he has none."[71]

While his naval appointment remained in contention, George Washington learned how to use his father's surveying instruments. Surveying was Virginia's most lucrative profession, and George now became an insider in the greatest Virginian land grab yet. In April 1745, Walpole having fallen, the "patriot" lord Fairfax at last won royal approval for his extensive interpretation of the western boundaries of his Northern Neck proprietary province. More than 5 million acres, as much land as was patented in all the rest of Virginia, was now his lordship's to dispose of, once it had been surveyed. To chart the westernmost extent of the Northern Neck, from the head of the Rappahannock, across the Shenandoah valley to the very source of the Potomac, commissioners were named for the crown by the governor and council of Virginia and for the proprietor by his agent, Colonel William Fairfax. Then, early in September 1746, the colonel organized an extraordinary echo of Alexander Spotswood's famous reconnaissance of the great valley of the Shenandoah, the 1716 venture of the Knights of the Golden Horseshoe.[72]

The Fairfax expedition assembled in Fredericksburg. Thence Colonel Fairfax wrote to his son-in-law, Major Lawrence Washington, that "George has been with us" to take counsel on how to approach his mother about his midshipman's appointment. This discussion was advanced a week later by the Washington family counselor, Robert Jackson. Besides discussing with Lawrence tactics designed to overcome "the Widow's . . . trifling objections, such as fond and unthinking mothers naturally suggest" to George's naval appointment, Jackson also listed the leading figures of the expedition, the boundary commissioners. Colonel Fairfax, himself commissioner for lord Fairfax, was supported by Colonel William Beverley, reprising the role he had played with Spotswood in 1716. The crown commissioners were Colonel Peter Hedgaman; Lunsford Lomax, afterward a principal of the Ohio Company and negotiator of the 1752 confirmation of Spotswood's 1722 treaty with the Iroquois; and Joshua Fry, professor of mathematics at the college (he would approve George Washington's commission as surveyor, an apprenticeship Washington was just beginning; Washington would succeed Fry as colonel of the First Virginia Regiment). Fry's surveyor was Peter Jefferson, his colleague in Virginia cartography.[73]

The commissioners, so Jackson wrote to Washington, were grandly supported by "surveyors, aid du Camps, valet de Chambres, and a numerous train of Cavalry and Infantry," all led by Robert Brooke, son of the surveyor of that name who had been prominent among Spotswood's corps thirty years before. As in Spotswood's time, Virginia rangers supplied a military escort. They led the commissioners' party west through a trackless, dark, stony, and precipitous wilderness where, "for want of water we could find no other than a standing puddle wherein the Bears used to Wallow." The ranger officers, afterward famous in the western wars fought to secure the claims of these Northern Neck grandees, also planned the expedition's tented camps. There, the gentlemen explorers drank the rundlets of rum thoughtfully provided by Major Washington. As Spotswood's knights had done, the Fairfax party celebrated the royal birthday, here with homely toasts of cider as well as the customary volleys of musketry.[74]

Safely returned from erecting "the Fairfax Stone" at the source of the Potomac, having surveyed the fertile valley of the Shenandoah for the proprietor and for themselves, the commissioners reassembled at Colonel Peter Jefferson's house on January 23, 1747. Working for the next month, they composed the first formal map of Virginia's western empire. Colonel Jefferson's precocious son, Thomas, probably made a nuisance of himself among the instruments and drafts. An expedition bracketed by George Washington, aged thirteen, just picking up the surveyor's tools and the martial ambition that would make him the leader of "the rising American empire," and by Thomas Jefferson, then just five, the founder of "an empire for liberty," was redolent of the imperial future. More immediately, the Fairfax expedition and the Jefferson and Brooke map were the foundations of the next westward venture of the Northern Neck grandees, the Ohio Company, progenitor of the great war with France for America.[75]

In 1747, the Fairfax interest—Thomas Lee, president of the council, others of the great planters of the Northern Neck, and their London merchant-bankers—pressed the crown for an enormous land grant in the Ohio country beyond the bounds of the Northern Neck. This vast region had been opened to Virginians by their expansive reinterpretation, at Lancaster in 1744, of Spotswood's 1722 Albany treaty with the Six Nations. The first surviving record of "the Ohio Company" is dated at "Mount Vernon Octr. The 20th 1748." A year earlier, in October 1747, the clerk of the company, Major Lawrence Washington, had engaged his Northern Neck neighbors, friends, and patrons to sign a petition to the lieutenant governor and council of Virginia seeking the first land grant on the tributaries of the Ohio River. Concerned that the grant "might possibly give umbridge to the French," Sir William Gooch felt that he must write Whitehall for orders "as to granting Lands on the Western side of the Great Mountains." So, as the Mount Vernon memo records, the Ohio Company subscribers had retained John Hanbury, the Quaker London merchant-banker, to apply to the imperial authorities directly.[76]

The subscribers' meeting at Mount Vernon obviously anticipated a favorable outcome. They had arranged a substantial purchase of Indian trade goods, reserved wampum for a treaty with the native proprietors of the soil, and contacted an agent in Rotterdam to procure "Foreign Protestants to settle the Land." To these refugees, Lawrence Washington wrote, the Ohio Company offered not only fertile land but political and religious freedom. "The Advantage of the Act of Toleration," provincial naturalization, political representation, "And the English Laws of Liberty and property" were together "the best in the World for securing the peoples' lives and fortunes against Arbitrary power or any unjust Encroachments whatsoever." Taxes in Virginia were low and did not reach the necessities of life. Finally, Major Washington assured the war-ravaged, religiously persecuted Palatines that "Our Militia renders Soldiers useless and we have no Ecclesiastical Courts."[77]

Hanbury's solicitation (with the august help of John Russell, duke of Bedford) was successful. On April 4, 1749, Sir Thomas Gooch, baronet, was "directed and required" to grant the named petitioners of the Ohio Company 200,000 acres on the Allegheny tributaries of the Ohio. He was to patent a further 300,000 acres when the company fulfilled its engagement to build and garrison a fort at the forks of the Ohio and settle 100 families under its protection. On July 12, 1749, the governor-in-council complied with the king's command. The political, military, and imperial ramifications of the grant instantly appeared. The Ohio Company asked the governor to: commission the company factor as justice of the peace in a new transmontane county, Augusta; exclude the traders of other provinces from the county until they had obtained Virginia licenses; and issue Major Washington "a Dozen or two of Muskets" from General Spotswood's magazine to arm the company's explorers and surveyors. Finally, the company asked the crown to transfer an independent company of regular troops from its Irish garrison to the new fort on the Ohio frontier. At that very moment, the French king's counterclaim to the region was being laid down in lead plates by Captain Pierre-Joseph Céleron de Blainville.[78]

All the while, Major Washington's health was deteriorating. In May 1749, he again received leave from the house of burgesses to treat his enervating cough (the symptom of the tuberculosis Lawrence had contracted during the West Indian campaign). He intended to sail home with Sir William Gooch (who had received the king's leave to recover his health in England) but when the commander in chief was delayed, Major Washington departed for London in July. George did not want his brother to go. He believed that Lawrence's health would be better served in Virginia. There he could deal with such diffi-culties—important to young George—as General Spotswood's son John's plan to divert his family's ferry service to a new landing on Mary Washington's best field. Major Lawrence Washington had bigger fish to fry. Although his health was not improved by London's smog, Washington vigorously promoted the Ohio Company to prospective English investors and politicians. To the likes of the duke of Bedford, the new, militant secretary of state, Major Washing-ton stressed the company's "Interest exclusive of Trade," that is, the strategic implications of western expansion into "the whole Country aback of Pennsyl-vania Virginia and Carolina." "The farther we extend our Frontier the safer we render the Interior Dominions and the French having possession of the Ohio might easily invade Virginia etc.," Washington declared. Such had been Spotswood's strategic arguments two decades earlier. Now Spotswood's im-perialism was a Virginia commonplace. As Spotswood had learned, so Major Washington now observed: the friendship of the Indians was essential to "any Settlement the Crown would think proper to make." "The Indians being no Geographers esteems the honestest who will sell the cheapest," Washington wrote. So the Ohio Company "proposed keeping a large Qy of Goods at the joining of the Ohio and Monongala in a Fortified Store." However, the inves-tors expected the royal government to sponsor a treaty council and pay the Iroquoian viceroys for the lands claimed by the Ohio Company. The respon-siveness of the imperial government was stimulated by granting the duke of Bedford shares in the Ohio Company gratis.[79]

In the fall of 1749, Major Lawrence Washington sailed home to Virginia to begin the company's push westward. So distant a post as the fort proposed on the Ohio required way stations. In November, George Washington, acting "for the Gentlemen of the Ohio Company," surveyed a warehouse site on the upper reaches of the Potomac at Wills Creek, a location afterward famous as Fort Cumberland. Thence the company's Indian traders and diplomats, Chris-topher Gist and Robert Trent, began the exportations and negotiations which brought them up against French advances into the region. Major Lawrence Washington was increasingly responsible for the company's initiatives (he suc-ceeded to the presidency of the Ohio Company on the death of Thomas Lee in November 1750), but Washington's own health continued to decline. He sought relief in Virginia's warm springs. Even there, he advanced the prospects of the Ohio Company. To John Hanbury, Washington wrote that "the Pennsylvania Dutch" whom he had met at Warm Springs had offered to purchase 50,000 acres and bring in 200 families if they were not obliged to tithe for "an English clergyman, when few understand and none made use of him." Lawrence Washington declared that "restraints on conscience are cruel in regard to those on whom they are imposed and injurious to the country imposing them." The British ministry had "shown the true spirit of patriotism, by encouraging the extending of our dominions in America." Now they should extend religious freedom as well. Virginia, still confined by a coercive combination of puritanism and erastianism, Lawrence believed, would never make such a concession. Absent religious toleration, the Old Dominion had grown only "by slow degrees, except negroes and convicts, whilst our neighbouring colonies, whose natural advantages are greatly inferior to ours, have become populous."[80]

Unfortunately, neither warm springs nor liberal sentiments improved Major Washington's health. So he deputized another Cartagena veteran, George Muse, to act as Virginia's adjutant and, in September 1751, sailed with George to Barbados. The younger man was fascinated by an island whose whole white population, as he recorded in his journal, was mobilized to hold down the island's slaves and to defend Barbados against foreign invasion. The entire circuit of the island, George remarked, was fortified either by man or nature. He returned from fortress Barbados in the spring (George's only excursion outside the American provinces), leaving Lawrence to try Bermuda. That island's climate offered Major Washington no relief. He accepted his death sentence, came home and, on July 26, 1752, was buried in the family vault at Mount Vernon. Lawrence left George his heir in Virginia estate, Fairfax patronage, and the prospect of a military career. On November 6, Virginia's governor and council, considering "the great advantage of an Adjutant to this country in instructing the officers and soldiers in the use and exercise of their arms, and in bringing the militia to a more regular discipline and fitting it for service, besides polishing and improving the meaner sort of people, and finding by experience the insufficiency of one, fully to discharge a business of so much importance," divided Virginia into four military districts: one for each neck, and a transmontane frontier district. Three adjutancies went to Cartagena veterans. The fourth, the troublesome southside, was assigned to George Washington. Like the three veterans of the American Regiment, Washington was commissioned a major in the Virginia provincial forces. His elevated rank was supported by a handsome salary. It allowed Major Washington to give up surveying (except to serve his family, the Fairfaxes and, subsequently, to lay out the land grants awarded to veterans of the Great War for the Empire, himself among them). Emulating brother Lawrence, George Washington would concentrate on a military career. A Virginia aristocrat, George Washington had entered provincial military service as a field officer. Novice though he was, Washington never accepted a lesser rank, even in the regulars. It was a measure of Washington's aristocratic arrogance, as well as ignorance, that he should have assumed such an unearned seniority. Major Washington's capacity was immediately tested.[81]

During the spring and summer of 1753, 1,500 French troops fortified posts along a route from Lake Erie to the Allegheny. The French were poised to advance to the forks of the Ohio in the spring of 1754 and drive the Ohio Company traders from their fort. At this crisis George Washington succeeded William Fitzhugh, a veteran officer of the American Regiment, as the adjutant of the Northern Neck. Major Washington assisted Colonel Fairfax in shipping arms to Britain's Indian allies. He elaborated plans to reinforce the Ohio Company's outpost. In October 1753, Major Washington rode to Williamsburg to volunteer to carry west over the mountains Lieutenant Governor Robert Dinwiddie's warning to the French to leave the territory of king George (and the property of the Ohio Company). On October 30, 1753, Dinwiddie commissioned "in the Name of the King my Master . . . George Washington Esqr. One of the Adjutants General of the Forces of this Dominion; to complain" to the French commandant in the Ohio country that "you have lately marcht from Canada with an armed Force, and invaded the King of Britain's Territories." Major Washington was to present Dinwiddie's eviction order.[82]

The French refused to evacuate the Ohio, but the subsequent publication of *The Journal of Major George Washington* made its author Virginia's best-known soldier. His failed attempt to drive the French from Fort Duquesne, however, left Washington subject to the wiles of Tanacharison, the Iroquoian half king. The ensuing assassination of a French envoy was the spark that ignited a world war. Despite what was seen as a blunder in Britain and a crime in France, Major Washington, a hero at home, was promoted lieutenant colonel of the First Virginia Regiment. In July 1754, Colonel Fairfax wrote to Lieutenant Colonel Washington that he was about to be reinforced with troops from New York, Maryland, and North Carolina to help him "prevent the French settling on the Lands of the Ohio." "It will give Me the greatest Pleasure to know from you," his patron wrote Washington, that he, "Colo. Innes, Capts. Clarke, Mackey & Olgvie begin and [are] likely to hold a good Union of Friendship, Councils and joint Operations to fulfil his Majesty's Commands . . . I have no doubt of your friendly Agreement with them on their own Merit, but it may be enlarged from your late Brother's Sake, formerly known to Col. Innes, & Capt. Clark on the Carthagena Expedition."[83]

James Innes, now colonel of the North Carolina contingent, who was formerly "a Capt. In the American regim't on the Expedition to Cathagena, and is an experienced Officer," was commissioned by Dinwiddie as commander in chief. "I rejoice that I am likely to be happy under the Command off an experienced Officer and Man of Sense—it is what I have most ardently wish'd for," Washington wrote. He was the more pleased because the same promotion made him colonel of the Virginia regiment. The new colonel's rank, however, made him the more outraged by the military pretensions of other Cartagena veterans than Innes. Because they held the king's commissions, Mackay, Clarke, Moody, Rutherford, and Ogilvie, officers of the New York independent companies now attached to the expedition, refused "to incorporate or do duty" with Washington's command.[84]

This insult was the more galling to Colonel Washington because he prided himself on his military model, Marlborough. Washington's drill book was Major General Humphrey Bland's *Treatise on Military Discipline*, the official distillation of Marlborough's drill and tactics. Having mastered Marlborough's discipline himself, Colonel Washington mandated it to his officers. Absent regular training, Washington wrote, "let us read. . . . There is Blands and other Treatises which will give the wished for information." From this starting point, Washington would, over a lifetime of service, adapt Marlborough's model to American imperial purposes and his own. In Bland's *Treatise*, Washington read Marlborough's commission as captain general of England, the model and mandate of extraordinary military authority, the power of life and death, the command manual of an imperial army, the palimpsest of Washington's ultimate ambition.[85]

Colonel Washington now strove to reconstitute the Virginia battalion of the Royal American Regiment. Washington and his superior officer, Lieutenant Governor Robert Dinwiddie, insisted that the Virginia Regiment was not a militia unit. Rather, it was a regiment raised by royal authority, paid out of provincial revenues, and officered by gentlemen, many of whom were either Cartagena veterans themselves or, like Colonel Washington, were the younger brothers of the Virginia officers of the American Regiment. Informed by the Cartagena experience, the Virginian officers expected regular pay and allowances for themselves, uniforms (and the martial discipline that was the concomitant of uniform) for their men, and respect for their own rank. Absent royal pay and uniforms, discipline and rank, Washington wrote, many of his officers would resign. He asked Governor Dinwiddie either to accept his own resignation or to allow "me to serve Volunteer, which I assure you will be the next reward to British pay, for as my Services so far as I have Knowledge, will equal those of the best Officers, I make it a point of Honour [not] to serve for less," but in the same breath that he demanded British pay, Washington declared that "I had no view of acquisition but that of Honour, by serving faithfully my King and Country."[86]

Sensitive to the requirements of honor and ambitious to command, Colonel Washington was deeply offended by the attitude of the officers of the independent companies. Dinwiddie had warned Washington that they, "having their Com'o's signed by His M'y, imagine they claim a distinguished rank, and being long train'd in Arms, expect suitable regards." Washington replied that though he and his officers "are greatly inferiour in respect to profitable advantages, yet we have the same Spirit to serve our Gracious King as they have." Insistence on "unreasonable distinction . . . Will be a canker that will grate some Officers of this Regiment beyond all measure to serve upon different terms, when their Lives, their Fortunes, and their Characters are equally, and I dare say as effectively exposd as those who are happy enough to have the King's Commission's." In Virginia, however, as hitherto in Cartagena and Cuba, the regulars "refused Acting in concert" with the provincials "or receiving any direct's or Orders from" their officers. Once again, the regular officers exempted their men from "pioneering" duties and imposed them on the provincial troops. The redcoats, Washington complained, "march at their ease whilst our faithful Soldiers are laboriously employ'd." Even as the redcoated rank and file sneered at provincial "pioneers," the king's officers denied Virginia gentlemen "the rank of Officers, which," as Colonel Washington wrote to Governor Dinwiddie, "to me, Sir, is much dearer than the pay." Finally, in October 1754, Dinwiddie reported to the secretary of state that "Col. Washington on y't account has resign'd his Commission."[87]

In November 1754, William Fitzhugh, a half-pay captain of the American Regiment, former adjutant of the Northern Neck, now a colonel in Maryland's provincial army, conveyed to Washington the proposal of yet another half-pay officer, Maryland's governor, Horatio Sharpe, just named to command on the Virginia frontier. Washington was asked to accept a royal commission as a captain "in the same Manner as was practiced on the Cartagena Expedition." Once again, American officers were to be limited to company-grade appointments. Colonel Washington declared "the disparity between the present offer of a Company, and my former Rank, too great to expect any real satisfaction or enjoyment in a Corps where I once did, or thought I had a right to, command." Still, he wrote, "my inclinations are strongly bent to arms."[88]

Washington's continued search for independent military command, combined with his commitment to continental aggrandizement, resulted in what he would identify to his Continental army officers as "our rising American Empire." That empire realized the ambitions for military distinction and hemispheric hegemony that had been excited in the minds of provincial elites by their service in the first American Regiment. A disaster in itself, the "Golden Adventure" was nonetheless the bridge between Marlborough's America and Washington's America, that is, between the first British and the first American empires.[89]

Notes

Citations to the Blenheim Manuscripts

In 1966, I arrived at Blenheim Palace in hopes that (for the Historical Manuscripts Commission *Report* gave no hint), if my hypothesis about the identity of the army officer corps and the imperial executive were correct, evidence would exist in the papers of the captain general, the first duke of Marlborough. The (10th) duke's secretary and agent were very accommodating. The chief guide and his staff were most welcoming. The duke himself gave a nod. To them all, I remain indebted. I then tried to restore order to the correspondence. Some of it had been annotated by Winston Churchill himself for his *Marlborough*. He had "returned" these selected items in the general direction of the trays which reflected Dr. Stuart Reid's organization. Maurice Ashley had copied extracts to take to Chartwell (*Churchill as Historian* [London, 1968]). Henry L. Snyder was in the last stages of photocopying the Marlborough-Godolphin correspondence for what became his indispensable edition (3 vols., Oxford, 1975).

I settled into Winston Churchill's former dressing room, adjacent to the Long Library. There Cardonnel's letterbooks in their Blenheim bindings, embossed with the double-headed eagle, the duke's crest as a prince of the Empire, stood on the locked shelves. They could be taken down and, as a treat, read in the library's overstuffed insulating chairs, while the priest from Woodstock played Bach on the great organ and the cypress trees around the water gardens outside the great west windows bowed to the wind and rain. On the far side of the palace, much more utilitarian space (in the estate agent's office) gave access to the vast, unlit, chest-encumbered vault where Marlborough's papers were housed.

The palace setting was educational and inspiring. The state rooms offered, among other treasures, the Blenheim Victories. The tapestries are reproduced here, as they were in the first edition of Churchill's *Marlborough*, but now in color. Finally, I discovered Marlborough's extensive, systematic personnel files. Now, I could apprehend the extent, the specificity, and the significance of the duke's role in appointing, promoting, instructing, and acting upon the multitudinous reports he received from the officers of the royal army, many of them members of his staff whom he nominated to command the American provinces of what, in his lifetime, and substantially because of his efforts, became the "British" empire.

Over several seasons in this year and the next, I made extensive notes from the duke's papers, from those of his son-in-law, the earl of Sunderland, secretary of state, and from various of their colleagues and subordinates. Years passed. The prospectus for a multivolume work on army and empire, a "preliminary bombardment" of articles, and the first two volumes of *The Governors-General* were published. Meanwhile, the Blenheim Papers had passed to the state. For a decade, they were sequestered for reorganization in the British Library. Having now drafted a third volume, this one dealing directly with John Churchill, "Marlborough," as he became, I sought to verify my Blenheim researches. I was informed that no correspondence list between the Blenheim shelf marks and the new Add. MS numbers had been kept. Unable to verify particular items, I reread the collection. It was with mixed feelings that I found my notes of three decades earlier were entirely accurate, but, with the inestimable aid of the new *Catalogue of Additions to the Manuscripts: The Blenheim Papers* (London, 1985), I found items not previously noted.

To clarify these stages of discovery, this volume cites the Blenheim shelf marks alone for items not found in the new British Library arrangement. Reference is made to Dean Snyder's volumes and his scholarly notes from *The Marlborough-Godolphin Correspondence* wherever appropriate. Additional Manuscripts numbers are cited for items not found elsewhere. In addition, Archdeacon William Coxe (the first arranger of the Blenheim Papers), *Memoirs of John Duke of Marlborough, with His Original Correspondence: Collected from the Family Records at Blenheim . . .*, 2d ed. (London, 1819) is occasionally cited, usually because of the context Coxe generously provides.

I was grateful to his late grace the duke of Marlborough for his permission to quote and cite the manuscripts of his famous predecessor. I now appreciate the imprimatur of his grace the present duke of Marlborough, particularly with regard to the Blenheim tapestries. I am further indebted to his grace for his hospitality and for gently correcting a tale about Blenheim told to me long ago in the depths of the Adirondacks.

List of Abbreviations

Add. MS	Additional Manuscripts, British Library, London
AHR	*American Historical Review*
AIQ	*American Indian Quarterly*
ANB	*American National Biography*
APCC	*Acts of the Privy Council of England, Colonial Series*, 6 vols., ed. W. L. Grant and J. Munro (London, 1908–12)
BIHR	*Bulletin of the Institute for Historical Research*, London
BJRL	*Bulletin of the John Rylands Library*
CHR	*Canadian Historical Review*
CMNY	City Museum of the City of New York
CO	Colonial Office Group, Public Record Office, Kew, England
CSPC	*Calendar of State Papers, Colonial Series, America and the West Indies*, 20 vols., for 1689–1721, ed. J. W. Fortescue and Cecil Headlam (London, 1901–33)
CSPD	*Calendar of State Papers, Domestic Series*, 13 vols., for 1689–1704, ed. William John Hardy and Robert Pentland Mahaffy (London, 1895–1924)
DHNY	*Documentary History of the State of New York*, 4 vols., ed. E. B. O'Callaghan (Albany, 1849–51)
DNB	*Dictionary of National Biography*, eds. Leslie Stephens and Sidney Lee (London, 1895–1903)
EHD	*English Historical Documents*, vol. 8, *1660–1714*, ed. Andrew Browning (New York, 1953)
EHR	*English Historical Review*
EJC	*Executive Journals of the Council of Virginia*, 5 vols., ed. H. R. McIlwaine and W. L. Hall (Richmond, VA, 1925–45)
GHQ	*Georgia Historical Quarterly*
GM	*Gentleman's Magazine*
HAHR	*Hispanic American Historical Review*
HJ	Historical Journal
HL	Huntington Library, San Marino, CA
HLQ	*Huntington Library Quarterly*
HMC	Historical Manuscripts Commission, *Reports*
JAH	*Journal of American History*
JCTP	*Journals of the Commissioners of Trade and Plantations*, 14 vols. (London, 1920–38)
JHB	*Journals of the House of Burgesses, 1619–1776*, 13 vols., ed. J. P. Kennedy and H. R. McIlwaine (Richmond, VA, 1905–15)
JMH	*Journal of Modern History*
JRUSI	*Journal of the Royal United Services Institute*
JSAHR	*Journal of the Society for Army Historical Research*
LC	Library of Congress, Washington, DC
MHM	*Maryland Historical Magazine*

MVHR	*Mississippi Valley Historical Review*
NCHR	*North Carolina Historical Review*
NEQ	*New England Quarterly*
NLS	National Library of Scotland, Edinburgh
NSHSC	Nova Scotia Historical Society *Collections*
NYCD	*Documents Relative to the Colonial History of the State of New York*, 14 vols., ed. E. B. O'Callaghan and B. Fernow (Albany, 1853–89)
NYHSC	New-York Historical Society *Collections*
NYHSQ	*New-York Historical Society Quarterly*
NYPL	New York Public Library
NYPLB	*New York Public Library Bulletin*
ODNB	*Oxford Dictionary of National Biography* (Oxford, 2004–7)
PCDM	*Private Correspondence of Sarah, Duchess of Marlborough*, 2 vols. (London, 1838)
PGWCS	*Papers of George Washington, Colonial Series*, 2 vols., ed. W. W. Abbot et al. (Charlottesville, VA, 1983)
PMHB	*Pennsylvania Magazine of History and Biography*
PP	*Past & Present*
PSQ	*Political Science Quarterly*
QJNYSHA	*Quarterly Journal of the New York State Historical Association*
SHR	*Scottish Historical Review*
SP	State Papers Group
SRO	Scottish Public Records Office, Edinburgh
T	Treasury Group, Public Record Office, Kew, England
VCRP	Virginia 35th Anniversary Celebration Corporation Colonial Records Project
VMHB	*Virginia Magazine of History and Biography*
WMQ	*William and Mary Quarterly*
WO	War Office Group, Public Record Office, Kew, England
WPHM	*Western Pennsylvania Historical Magazine*

Envoy. "The Sunshine Day"

1. G. M. Trevelyan, *England under Queen Anne*, vol. 1, *Blenheim* (London, 1930), 161–64, 186. Ibid., 177–84 offset Macaulay's notorious character of Marlborough. Marlborough to Heinsius, Mar. 8/19, 1701/2, B. van 't Hoff, ed., *The Correspondence, 1701–1711, of John Churchill, First Duke of Marlborough, and Anthonie Heinsius, Grand Pensionary of Holland* (The Hague, 1951), 10. Marlborough's commission as captain general, dated Mar. 12, 1701/2, is printed in Maj. Gen. Humphrey Bland, *A Treatise of Military Discipline* (London, 1746), 201–3. HMC, *Portland MS*, 4:37. For the queen's speech to parliament on Wednesday, Mar. 11, to which she was accompanied only by the earl and countess of Marlborough, see Edward Gregg, *Queen Anne* (London, 1984), 152–53. For the Denmark-Churchill connection, see Stephen Saunders Webb, *Lord Churchill's Coup* (New York, 1995), 70–73, 143–44, 174–75, 230–31, 248–51, 254–55, 262–65. On the ordnance, see David Chandler, *The Art of War in the Age of Marlborough* (London, 1976), 151, 154–56, 162. Engineering, transport, weapons and munitions manufactures all fell within the purview of the ordnance office and its master general. In 1686, the form of the ordnance had been set for a century to come by James II. Lord Churchill was then James's military favorite and may be presumed to have had a major role in shaping the department of state he now headed. In 1716, Marlborough would preside over the largest eighteenth-century reform of the ordnance. The board named gunners and storekeepers who often served as electoral agents in the garrison towns. Marlborough's "man of business," James Craggs, detailed the electoral ramifications of ordnance appointments to Marlborough, who made his decisions accordingly: Craggs to Marlborough, Mar. 20, 1703, Add. MS 61164, 163ff. On the posts, see the board to the master general, July 4, 1702, Add. MS 61165, 6–7.

2. The West India artillery was ordered Nov. 26, Add. MS 61165, 15–16. Lowther's protest, Feb. 2, 1702(/3?), ibid., 20–21. Stephen Saunders Webb, *The Governors-General* (Chapel Hill, NC, 1979), #14. Newfoundland soon received £2,000 for barracks and fortifications, Add. MS 61165, 33. In time, Marlborough restaffed the board with professional officers such as Michael Richards, formerly the Newfoundland commander and engineer. In the meantime, he "allowed" the principal officers "noe more power then what I could keep from them" when he was abroad, and "when I am in England, the Board can do nothing without my approbation," Marlborough to the countess, May 31, July 1, 1703, Blenheim MS E.2, Snyder, *Correspondence*, 195, 215; same to Godolphin, May 13, 1703, Blenheim MS A.I.14, Henry Snyder, ed., *The Marlborough-Godolphin Correspondence* (Oxford, 1975), 182.

3. The board summarized the year's expenditures, esp. on the plantations, Dec. 19, 1702, Add. MS 61165, 17–19.

4. Marlborough's speech to the states general, Mar. 28, 1702, is in Thomas Lediard, *Life of John, Duke of Marlborough* (London, 1730), 1:142, adapted from *The Lives of the Two Illustrious Generals* (London, 1713), 34–37. W. A. Speck, *The Birth of Britain* (Oxford, 1994), 36.

5. Marlborough did change the composition of the British forces en route to the Netherlands, substituting additional regiments from Ireland for some of the Scots because the queen's hold on the northern kingdom was tenuous. Blathwayt to Yard, Nov. 15, 1701, Add. MS 37992, 264. S. H. F. Johnston, "The Scots Army in the Reign of Queen Anne," *Royal Historical Society Transactions*, 3d ser., 5 (1953): 5, 6, 16. Marlborough voiced an anti-Catholic tone throughout the alliance negotiations: Frances Gardiner Davenport, ed., *European Treaties, Bearing on the History of the United States* . . . (Washington, DC, 1934), 3:78. Nottingham's cabinet minutes of instructions to Benbow, Selwyn, Rooke, and Codrington are in Add. MS 29591, 4b–5, 13, 18.

6. Trevelyan, *Blenheim*, 143–44, 147, 152, 165–67, 172; Lediard, *Marlborough*, 1:149; Nottingham to Marlborough, Apr. 2, 1703, Blenheim MS F.2.4, Add. MS 61118, 167b. On the "new class," see Webb, *Lord Churchill's Coup*, 54, 166, 269; and Geoffrey Holmes, *Augustan England* (London, 1982), 262, 269.

7. Typical of the tory sentiment about Marlborough's changed views was Ailesbury's remark that a continental "war we must have to please the two brothers by alliance [Marlborough and Godolphin] and for their private interest," Thomas Buckley, ed., *Memoirs of Thomas Bruce, Earl of Ailesbury* (Roxburgh Club, 1890), 526–27. Contrast his approval of the policy of Rochester and Nottingham. See also Ian K. Steele, *Politics of Colonial Policy* (Oxford, 1968), 86–89.

8. [Nathaniel Hooke], *An Account of the Conduct of the Dowager Duchess of Marlborough, from Her First Coming to Court, to the Year 1710* (London, 1742), reprinted in William King, ed., *Memoirs of Sarah, Duchess of Marlborough* (London, 1930), 86–91; William Coxe, ed., *Memoirs of John, Duke of Marlborough* (London, 1818–19), 1:154–65n.; Gregg, *Anne*, 164–65, 169–70, 172–76. The queen's appointment of Sarah to the most intimate and profitable posts in the new royal household—groom of the stole; mistress of the robes; keeper of the privy purse—made manifest Sarah's favor. Her daughters became ladies of the queen's bedchamber. Coxe, *Marlborough*, 1:142; Gregg, *Anne*, 153; Frances Harris, *A Passion for Government: The Life of Sarah Duchess Of Marlborough* (Oxford, 1991), 87–88.

9. Coxe, *Marlborough*, 1:153–54, 156–58, 273–81; the countess to Godolphin, May 19, 1702, Snyder, *Correspondence*, 62.

10. The conclusive assessment of Sarah's position is by Harris, *Government*, 89–93. See also Speck, *Britain*, 37. On Defoe and Harley, see HMC, *Portland MS*, vol. 4. Henry L. Snyder, "Godolphin and Harley," *HLQ* 30 (1967): 241–71; Popple to Blathwayt, Aug. 4, 11, 1699, Add. MS 9747, 19, 21–22; Penn to Harley, Pennsylvania, Aug. 27, 1701, May 29, 1702, Feb. 9, 1703/4, Mar. 3, 1704, n.d., HMC, *Portland MS*, 4:19–21, 30–32, 39, 79–81. Webb, "'The Peaceable Kingdom': Quaker Pennsylvania in the Stuart Empire," in Richard S. Dunn and Mary Maples Dunn, eds., *The World of William Penn* (Philadelphia, 1986), 173–94.

11. Blathwayt to Marlborough, Oct. 12, 1703, enc. Col. Robert Quary [to Blathwayt], Philadelphia, June 30, 1703, Add. MS 61133, 81–84. Blathwayt to the lord treasurer, Dec. 31, [1703], T 64/89, 136, and see also 118, 120, 145, 164, 204–9.

12. Marlborough to Godolphin, July 26/Aug. 6, 1703, Blenheim MS A.I.14, Snyder, *Correspondence*, 226; Webb, "Blathwayt," *WMQ*, 3d ser., 26 (1969): 411–13.

13. Marlborough to Heinsius, Apr. 17/28, 1702, 't Hoff, *Correspondence*, 12; same to Godolphin, Mar. 31, June 19/30, 1702; resolution of the states general, June 19/30,

1702, Blenheim MS F.I.17, Snyder, *Correspondence*, 52n, 55, 76; Gregg, *Anne*, 160–61; HMC, *Portland MS*, 4:37–38.

14. *Lives of the Two Illustrious Generals*, 38; Lediard, *Marlborough*, 1:158; John Scot, "The Remembrancer," in James Ferguson, ed., *Papers Illustrating the History of the Scots Brigade in the Service of the United Netherlands, 1572–1782* (Edinburgh, 1901), 3:324; [Orkney to the duke of Hamilton], June 6, 1702, GD 406/1/7173, SRO.

15. Capt. Robert Parker, *Memoirs of the Most Remarkable Military Transactions from the Year 1683 to 1718 . . . in Ireland and Flanders* (Dublin, 1746) is quoted from the edition by David Chandler, *The Marlborough Wars: Robert Parker and Comte de Merode-Westerloo* (London, 1968), 16–18; HMC, Portland MS, 4:40–42; Add. MS 28918, 13–18; C. T. Atkinson, *The South Wales Borderers 24th Foot, 1689–1937* (Cambridge, 1937), 38ff.; Col. Mac Kinnon, *Origin and Services of the Coldstream Guards* (London, 1833), 278; Brig. Gen. Richard Kane, *Campaigns of King William and the Duke of Marlborough* (London, 1735), 38–39; Lediard, *Marlborough*, 1:164–65; Coxe, *Marlborough*, 1:165; Buckley, *Memoirs of Ailesbury*, 539; [Orkney to Hamilton], June 27, 1702, GD 406/1/7295, SRO.

16. *Lives of the Two Illustrious Generals*, 39; Parker, *Memoirs*, 17; Webb, *Lord Churchill's Coup*, 245. Marlborough's comments on Athlone's indecisiveness were scathing. For his part, Athlone claimed coequal status with Marlborough throughout the campaign. Marlborough to Heinsius, Oct. 14, 1702, 't Hoff, *Correspondence*, 35. For the campaign, see the "Eastern Sphere" map accompanying Col. J. Sutherland Brown, "Marlborough's Strategy Preceding Blenheim," *Canadian Defense Quarterly* 2 (1925): 173–80. Most of the actions along the Meuse are diagramed in Winston S. Churchill, *Marlborough* (London, 1947), 1:575–77, 583, 589, 594, 600, 604. On the command, see, Marlborough to Godolphin, Hague, June 2, 10, 16, 1702, Blenheim MS A.I.14, Snyder, *Correspondence*, 70, 71, 74, 75–76; Cardonnel to Cresset, Hague, July 1, 1702: "the States have given directions to all their generals and other officers to obey My Lord Marlborough as their general," Sir George Murray, ed., *The Letters and Dispatches of John Churchill, First Duke of Marlborough, from 1702 to 1712* (London, 1845; repr., New York, 1968), 1:4. Marlborough conveniently blamed the Dutch commonwealthsmen for the refusal of the states general to accept the prince of Denmark as their general. Marlborough to Godolphin, Aug. 16, 20, Snyder, *Correspondence*, 103, 104.

17. Cardonnel to Ingoldsby, Hague, June 10, 1702, Blenheim MS 26:22; M. Gen. Sir F. Maurice, *The 16th Foot* (London, 1931), 16–17; Webb, *Governors-General*, 501, #207, 208; Charles Dalton, ed., *English Army Lists and Commission Registers, 1661–1714* (London, 1960), 4:255–56; Drysdale to Blathwayt, Cork, Aug. 23, 1703, Add. MS 38710, 61.

18. Petition of [lord] George Granville, lieutenant general of the ordnance on behalf of Sir Bevil Granville, to the lord treasurer, T 64/89, 112–13. This is presumably the petition that Marlborough passed on to Godolphin at lord Granville's request, without endorsing it, in July 1703, Blenheim MS, A.I.14, Snyder, *Correspondence*, 217–18n. Selwyn's retention of the Thames governments while serving in command of Jamaica lends support to Granville's contention. Granville's loss was the larger because Godolphin, by taking control of the 4 1/2 percent collected on the "dead commodities" of the West Indies, put Granville's salary on the English exchequer, so he paid English taxes: T 64/89, 114–15; Albert Lee, *The History of the Tenth Foot* (Aldershot, England, 1911) 1:101–2; Add. MS 38710, 134.

19. Narcissus Luttrell, *Brief Historical Relation of State Affairs* (London, 1857), 5:358. Cardonnel to Billingsly, Margate, May 28, and commissions to prepare, Hague, June 9; same to Col. Godolphin, May 25; to Ingoldsby, June 10; and to Blathwayt, July 10, Nov. 17, all 1702, Blenheim MS 26 (Cardonnel's Letter Book), 9, 12, 20, 22, 102, 211. Dalton, *Army Lists*, 3:99, 101, 177; 2:117, 200; list of 3d Troop Horse Guards 1691, Add. MS 61319, 2. Besides Maine, the senior officers were the Marlborough coup's coadjutor, lord John Berkeley, George Churchill, and a Compton (of the bishop of London's family). Note that Marlborough personally arranged army salaries for Billingsly at Berwick and for Nott in Holt's West Indian regiment during the transition in commands, Blenheim MS 27:70, 71. Memorial of Nott to Marlborough [1703], F.2. 19, Add. MS 61692, 156. Webb, *Governors-General*, #204; Webb, *Lord Churchill's Coup*, esp. 222–25.

20. See also Add. MS 38710, 134. Of course, Col. Sidney Godolphin of Scilly wanted a resident lieutenant governor, as Pendennis had received, ostensibly because the islands were exposed to French raids and the garrison companies were frequently rotated. He nominated an islander, William Grills, a captain in the 10th, who in turn negotiated with Marlborough for an exchange (a captaincy in the 10th was worth £350), Add. MS 61288, 169, 171, 173. Selwyn's death was reported on June 15, 1702, HMC, *Downshire MS*, 812. Marlborough lamented Selwyn's death, writing to Godolphin from The Hague, June 19, 1702, Blenheim MS A.I.14, Snyder, *Correspondence*, 75. Nottingham to Marlborough, June 30, 1702, Add. MS 61118, 132. On Selwyn, see Webb, *Governors-General*, #58; Webb, *Lord Churchill's Coup*, s.v. "Selwyn."

21. Marlborough to Godolphin, June 25, 1702, Snyder, *Correspondence*, 76n5; Add. MS 61293, 170. Lt. col. and lt. gov. Richard Brewer's death complicated not only the governmental succession but the regimental command as well. Cardonnel wrote Blathwayt (Oct. 9, 1702, Blenheim MS 26:190) to hold the colonel's commission in abeyance until "the General" came home to finalize the details of the American expedition. For the captain general's authority, see Bland, *Discipline*, 201–3.

22. Marlborough to Heinsius, July 23, Aug. 8, 31, 1702, 't Hoff, *Correspondence*, 23–36; same to Nottingham, July 13, 1702, Murray, *Dispatches*, 1:8; Nottingham to Marlborough, July 7, 1702, Blenheim MS A.1.11, Add. MS 6118, 134; Michell to Marlborough, Aug. 25, 1702, Add. MS 61164, 2; Vernon to Stepney, Feb. 13, 1702, Add. MS 9720, 161–63; Halifax to [Harley], Sept. 19, 1710, HMC, *Portland MS*, 4:596; cabinet minute, July 9, 1702, Add. MS 29591, fol. 35. Draft instructions to Peterborough, Add. MS 29591, 25–27, in Blathwayt's hand. Marlborough to Heinsius, July 18, Aug. 14, Sept. 14; Heinsius to Marlborough, July 21, 't Hoff, *Correspondence*, 18–19, 20, 23, 31. Nottingham to Marlborough, Oct. 6, 1702, Add. MS 61118, 153–54.

23. Marlborough to Godolphin, July 7, Aug. 3, 30, 1702, Blenheim MS A.I.14, Snyder, *Correspondence*, 95, 97. Richard Ingoldsby to Marlborough, Mar. 20, 1705, Nov. 12, 1706 n.s., Dec. 31, Mar. 2, 1707, NS, Add. MS 61163, 14, 24–29, 44–45, 51.

24. Marlborough to Heinsius, Aug. 14, 1702, 't Hoff, *Correspondence*, but Marlborough wrote to Adm. Michell on the same day to suggest that the English detachment mandated a Dutch equivalent, Murray, *Dispatches*, 1:18–19. Vincent T. Harlow, *Christopher Codrington, 1668–1710* (Oxford, 1928), 152. Marlborough remarked to Godolphin on Inchiquin, Aug. 10, 1702, Blenheim MS A.I.14, Snyder, *Correspondence*, 101.

25. Peterborough to lady Marlborough [1703?], Add. MS 61458, 203b. Decades later, an embarrassed Sarah remarked to a would-be historian, "you will wonder to find that I had writt to this man," so obvious a flatterer and such a bitter enemy of her husband (whenever Marlborough was out of power), "but I never did it above twice," ibid., 225. On Mordaunt, see his father's letters to Marlborough, May 23, Aug. 1, Oct. 7, 1704, Add. MS 61154, 35–36, 39, 43. Marlborough to the countess, [July 8/19, 1703], Snyder, *Correspondence*, 219.

26. Marlborough to Godolphin, Aug. 24, 1702; same to the countess, July [9/20, 1704], Snyder, *Correspondence*, 106–7n, 340. Nottingham remarked to Marlborough (Oct. 2, 1702, Blenheim MS A.1.11, Add. MS 61118, 148) that if Portmore did go to America, "such a man may greatly contribute to our Successe." Marlborough had "found it hard to prevail with any considerable officer to go to ye Indies, tho with the Government of Jamaica." If Portmore did take command in America, it was noted by Marlborough's officers that he would have to select another governor general for Cadiz. [Orkney to Hamilton], June 6, 1702, GD 406/1/7293, SRO.

27. On the allied concentration and French efforts to hinder it, see the bulletins of July 6, 10, 1702, Murray, *Dispatches*, 1:6. Orkney [to Hamilton], July 9, 1702, GD 406/1/7244, SRO. The "English" contingent included five regiments of horse, three of dragoons, and seventeen of infantry; a battalion of the 1st Guards; two battalions of the Royal Scots (the 1st of foot); and the 2d, 8th–10th, 13th, 15th–18th, 21st–24th, and 26th regiments. On July 7, commissions were issued to raise nine new regiments for Marlborough's army, the 28th (Gibson's reraised regiment), 29th, 33d–36th, and three others that did not survive long enough to be numbered. For variant tallies, see Sir F. W. Hamilton, *The Origin and History of the Grenadier Guards* (London, 1877), 1:424–25, 431; Lee, *Tenth Foot*, 93–94, 96; Robert J. Jones, *A History of the 15th (East Yorkshire) Regiment . . . 1685 to 1914* (Beverly, 1958), 58; Lt. Col. G. Le Gretton, *The Campaigns and History of the Royal Irish Regiment from 1684 to 1902* (Edinburgh, 1911), 26; Sir Garnet, viscount Wolsey, *The Life of John Churchill, Duke of Marlborough, to the Accession of Queen Anne* (London, 1894), 2:415n; Dalton, *Army Lists*, 4:25n. Marlborough to the states general, July 24, 1702, Murray, *Dispatches*, 1:12; same to Heinsius, July 13, 23, 1702, 't Hoff, *Correspondence*, 17, 20–21. Prior to the outbreak of hostilities, Athlone had garrisoned Maestricht with 12,000 men to protect its vast magazines, Coxe, *Marlborough*, 1:165. Marlborough to Godolphin, July 2/13, 9/20, 1702, Blenheim MS B.2.9; Murray, *Dispatches*, 1:11, 13; Coxe, *Marlborough*, 1:168–69, 171; Snyder, *Correspondence*, 80, 84–85.

28. Snyder, in *Correspondence*, 89n, puts the passage at July 15/26. Bulletins of July 27, Aug. 3, and Marlborough to the states general, Aug. 4, 1702, Murray, *Dispatches*, 1:14–19; Parker, *Memoirs*, 19, 209. Marlborough to Godolphin, July 20/31, July 27/Aug. 7, 1702, Blenheim MS A.I.14, Snyder, *Correspondence*, 90–92, 94.

29. See also Kane, *Campaigns*, 49ff.; Coxe, *Marlborough*, 1:177; Churchill, *Marlborough*, 1:588–90; [Orkney to Hamilton], July 27, 1702, GD 406/1/7152, SRO.

30. Marlborough to Godolphin, Aug. 6[/17], 1702, Snyder, *Correspondence*, 88; Murray, *Dispatches*, 1:20–21, 22; Parker, *Memoirs*, 20, 21; Kane, *Campaigns*, 50; [Orkney to Hamilton], July 27, 1702, GD 406/1/7152, SRO.

31. Bulletin, Camp at Helchteren, Aug. 24, 1702, Murray, *Dispatches*, 1:23–26; Marlborough to Godolphin, Helchteren, Aug. 16[/27], 1702, Blenheim MS A. I. 14, Snyder, *Correspondence*, 103.

32. Sgt. John Milner, *A Compendious Journal of all the Marches, Famous Battles, Sieges…*, (London, 1733), 23–25; Coxe, *Marlborough*, 1:179–82; Orkney to Hamilton, Aug. 2, 31, 1702, OS, GD 406/1/7242, 5015, SRO.

33. Murray, *Dispatches*, 1:19, and bulletin, Camp at Asch, Aug. 31, ibid., 27; Marlborough to Godolphin, Aug. 1/21, 20/31, Blenheim MS A.I.14, Snyder, *Correspondence*, 99–101, 104; same to Heinsius, Sept. 23, 1702, 't Hoff, *Correspondence*, 31–32; same to Nottingham, Aug. 27, 1702, Murray, *Dispatches*, 21; Orkney to Hamilton, Aug. 31, 1702, GD 406/1/5015, SRO.

34. Kane, *Campaigns*, 50, 51; and see Parker, *Memoirs*, 22–23; Marlborough to Nottingham, Sept. 21, 1702, Murray, *Dispatches*, 1:37, see also 36; bulletin, Sept. 25, and Marlborough to Noyelles, Oct. 3, 1702, Murray, *Dispatches*, 39, 42; same to Godolphin, Sept. 10[/21], 14[/25], 1702, Blenheim MS A.1.14, Snyder, *Correspondence*, 113, 115. Marlborough reported that all save a handful of the 800-man garrison were massacred or drowned. Contrast Lediard's laudatory pages about the entrenched peers (*Marlborough*, 1:179–80; likewise Coxe, *Marlborough*, 1:184–85) to the plebeian officer's contemptuous remarks, Milner, *Journal*, 32–33. English casualties were 297.

35. Murray, *Dispatches*, 1:43–45; HMC, *Portland MS*, 4:440; Orkney to Hamilton, Aug. 31, 1702, GD 406/1/5015, SRO.

36. Cardonnel to the dragoon colonels, and to Maj. Hunter, Camp at Sutendal, Sept. 19, 1702, Blenheim MS 26:105, 106, 177, 179, and to Col. Wynn, Sept. 28, 1702, ibid., 13:58. The countryside was called on for "between 30,000 and 40,000 rations a day," delivered to the riverbank for shipment to the allied camps, Murray, *Dispatches*, 1:36; Kane, *Campaigns*, 13. Marlborough to Godolphin, Aug. 31[/Sept. 11], 1702, Blenheim MS A.I.14, Snyder, *Correspondence*, 110.

37. Marlborough to Heinsius, Sutendal, Sept. 23, 1702, 't Hoff, *Correspondence*, 31–32; same to the states general, Oct. 8, 12, 1702, Murray, *Dispatches*, 1:43, 45–46; Lediard, *Marlborough*, 1:185; Churchill, *Marlborough*, 1:599; Marlborough to Godolphin, Sept. 17[/28], 1702, Blenheim MS A.I.14, Snyder, *Correspondence*, 117; Coxe, *Marlborough*, 1:186–87; Marlborough to Nottingham, quoted in Lt. Col. John Davis, *The History of the Second, Queen's Royal Regiment of Foot* (London, 1887–1902), 2:284.

38. Bulletins, Sept. 14, Oct. 16, 1702; Marlborough to the states, Oct. 11, 14, Murray, *Dispatches*, 1:35, 46–47; same to Godolphin, Sutendal, Sept. 3[/14], Before Liège, Oct. 5[/16], Blenheim MS A.I.14, Snyder, *Correspondence*, 111, 121. The trap at Liège is discussed by C. T. Atkinson, *Marlborough and the Rise of the British Army* (London, 1921), 170–71. The absence of the usual bulletin casts some doubt on this description, but Marlborough did write to Boufflers, Oct. 31, 1702, Murray, *Dispatches*, 1:51.

39. Marlborough to Nottingham, Before Liège, Oct. 23, 1702, Murray, *Dispatches*, 1:48, and see 47, 49–51; Buckley, *Memoirs of Ailesbury*, 540–41.

40. Marlborough to Nottingham, Before Liège, Oct. 23, 1702; HMC, *Portland MS*, 4:49; Richard Cannon, *Historical Record of the Tenth or North Lincolnshire Regiment of Foot* (London, 1847), 24; Milner, *Journal*, 42–44, gives English losses as 534. Lt. Col. Elliot's exploit won him Marlborough's help in persuading the regimental agent of the 10th to account with the serving officers, Add. MS 38708, 74–75b.

41. Marlborough to Godolphin, Oct. [21/23], 1702, Blenheim MS A.I.14, Snyder, *Correspondence*, 126; Orkney to Hamilton, [Oct.] 19, 1702, OS, GD 406/1/134, SRO.

42. Orkney to Hamilton, Oct. 19/30, GD 406/1/134, 137n; Orkney to Heinsius, Oct. 14, 1702, 't Hoff, *Correspondence*, 35.

43. *Lives of the Two Illustrious Generals*, 41–42; bulletins, Hague, Nov. 7, 10, 1702, Murray, *Dispatches*, 1:54–55; Milner, *Journal*, 460. Buckley, *Memoirs of Ailesbury*, 543, has Marlborough (presumably shabbily dressed, as usual) passing for a servant of "Goldenwalten" [for M. Gueldermalsen, a political commissar of the states].

44. Marlborough to Godolphin, Hague, Oct. 28[/Nov. 8], 1702, Blenheim MS, A.I.14, Snyder, *Correspondence*, 140; Coxe, *Marlborough*, 1:194.

45. *The Lives of the Two Illustrious Generals*, 43–44, which adds that the Dutch backed their declarations with £10,000 per annum to Marlborough as commander in chief and gave him a patent for the command as well. This is disputed by Corelli Barnett, *The First Churchill* (New York, 1974), ch. 2, n. 2, p. 276. Coxe, *Marlborough*, 1:193, 196; bulletin, Hague, Nov. 10, 1702, Murray, *Dispatches*, 1:54. Appropriately, Marlborough made his quick-thinking servant Stephen Gell commissary for the exchange of prisoners. A ransom was duly paid to the governor of Guelder for the captured cook, Murray, *Dispatches*, 1:57. "I have," Marlborough wrote to Godolphin, Oct. 29[/Nov. 10], 1702, "every reason to be satisfied with the endeavours of every body for the retaking of me," Snyder, *Correspondence*, 141; Parker, *Memoirs*, 25; Martin Joseph, Bishop [Gilbert] Routh, ed., *Burnet's History of His Own Time . . .* (Oxford, 1833; repr., Hildesheim, 1969), 5:31–33; Churchill, *Marlborough*, 1:605–9.

46. Marlborough to the countess, Nov. 4[/15], 6[/17], 1702, Blenheim MS E.2, Snyder, *Correspondence*, 142–44; Coxe, *Marlborough*, 1:201–6; C. Brown, ed., *The Letters and Diplomatic Instructions of Queen Anne* (London, 1935), 97; Henry L. Snyder, "Godolphin and Harley," *HLQ* 30 (1967): 412–17; Gregg, *Anne*, 165–66.

47. Coxe, *Marlborough*, 1:206; Marlborough to Heinsius, Dec. 4/15, 1702, 't Hoff, *Correspondence*, 40–41; HMC, *Portland MS*, 4:53–54; Keith G. Feiling, *A History of the Tory Party, 1640–1714* (London, 1924), 370; Lediard, *Marlborough*, 1:207–9. For the feud at Carlisle, see Webb, *Governors-General*, 80–81, 91–93, 132n. For its continuation during Marlborough's tenure as master general, see Craggs to Marlborough, June 8, 1705, Add. MS 61164, 165–66. Marlborough to Godolphin, same to the duchess, May 31[/June 11], 1703, Blenheim MS, A.I.14, E.2, Snyder, *Correspondence*, 194, 196, but Musgrave had been named teller of the exchequer with Marlborough's approval, 79n, 125. The two tory chieftains' statements are Rochester's 1702 introduction to his father's history, Edward Hyde, earl of Clarendon, *History of the Rebellion and Civil Wars in England*, ed. W. Dunn Macray (Oxford, 1888), 1:xxiv–xxv. Trevelyan, *Blenheim*, 204–5; *Lives of the Two Illustrious Generals*, 45–46; Buckley, *Memoirs of Ailesbury*, 527.

Chapter 1. Grand Designs

1. Snyder, *Correspondence*, 174–75; HMC, *Portland MS*, 4:59; Gregg, *Anne*, 169–70; Cardonnel to Heinsius, 't Hoff, *Correspondence*, 57; Buckley, *Memoirs of Ailesbury*, 558.

2. Marlborough to the duchess, Mar. 6/12, 16/27, 1703, Snyder, *Correspondence*, 152–53, 156–57: Lediard, *Marlborough*, 1:217; Coxe, *Marlborough*, 1:238–39; Webb, "Nicholson," *WMQ*, 3d ser., 23 (1966): 537–39. The Mauritshuis, restored to Marlborough's period and rich with art of the time, is now a public museum at The Hague. Both the governor general and his provincial opponents were up to date on these, the latest rumors of imperial politics: Nicholson to the commissioners, Virginia, July 28, 1703, *CSPC, 1702–3*, #961: "It hath been industriously reported here that H.M. had been pleased to appoint the Earl of Portmore to be my successor, and now lately that the Earl of Grenard should, and that I was turn'd out of the Government for male-administration etc." Even en route to Holland, Marlborough advanced imperial careers, signing promotions for Charles Sybourg and John lord Lovelace, Add. MS 61321, 66; Webb, *Governors-General*, #109, 147, 157.

3. Murray, *Dispatches*, 1:66–67; Marlborough to Godolphin, Apr. 9[/20], 1703, Blenheim MS A.I.14, Snyder, *Correspondence*, 165; Coxe, *Marlborough*, 1:241.

4. On governments as "a just reward and Encouragement to such as are deserving in Her Majesty's Service, of which I know there are many now attending your Grace," see Blathwayt to Marlborough, Apr. 2, 1703, Add. MS 61133, 39. The case in point was Maj. Gen. Wyndham, who proposed to put his commissions as general and colonel at Marlborough's disposal in return for the government of Jersey, Wyndham being too ill to take the field.

5. Dalton, *Army Lists*, 5:64; Webb, *Governors-General*, #37, 206. Granville to Marlborough, St. James, July 2, 1703, and the petition from lord George Granville on behalf of Sir Bevil, lest "yr. Grace's kind intentions in sending him to Barbados will prove mightily to his prejudice," Add. MS 61306, 110.

6. North and Grey to Marlborough, Apr. 13, Dec. 6, 1704, Add. MS 61306, 94, 139. Marlborough's lists of North and Grey's regiment, Add. MS 61319, 1278, 129, and of Granville's, Add. MS 61319, 119, 121, 125, 129. North and Grey to Cardonnel, Mar. 3, Apr. 6 [Apr. 16], 1703, Add. MS 61142, 77, 83, 89. Note that of all these promotions in the 10th, a lieutenant colonel, major, three captains, and nine others, including a quartermaster's and a sergeant's steps to commissioned rank, only one was sold, and that because the company was in debt. Elliot's step to colonel thus promoted fourteen officers of the 10th in his wake. A captaincy in the 10th was worth about £350, Add. MS 61288, 173. North and Grey himself paid the commission fees. Cardonnel to lord North and Grey, Maestricht, Apr. 16, 1703, Blenheim MS 27:111; Blathwayt to the principal officers of the ordnance, Apr. 10, 1703, WO 4/2, 43, to arm Elliot's regiment of twelve companies, each of two sergeants, three corporals, two drummers, and fifty-nine privates. Elliot requested more time to recruit, his officer's commissions having been delayed and his recruiting retarded by the buildup for Flanders, Elliot and William Evans to the prince of Denmark (generalissimo), June 17,

1703, Add. MS 61287, 25. Further recruiting problems followed, as Marlborough was informed, when two companies of Elliot's regiment were picked over for drafts, "being extraordinary good sized," Add. MS 61307, 16. Commissions to be prepared and presented to Her Majesty for General Officers & Brigadiers, dated 1 Jan. 1703/4, St. James's, Apr. 5, 1704, Add. MS 61321, 75. Webb, *Governors-General*, #37.

7. See Cadogan's correspondence with Marlborough, 1703–16, collected from Blenheim MS A.1., B.1., and B.2, in Add. MS 61160. Marlborough to the duchess, Apr. 20/May 1, 1703, Snyder, *Correspondence*, 172; Alexander to John Spotswood, Mar. 15, 1703/4, Lester J. Cappon, ed., "Correspondence of Alexander Spotswood with John Spotswood of Edinburgh," *VMHB* 60 (1952): 221.

8. For examples, see Murray, *Dispatches*. For English antecedents, see Sir Charles Firth and Godfrey Davies, *The Regimental History of Cromwell's Army* (Oxford, 1940); J. W. Fortescue, *A History of the British Army* (London, 1910), 1:310–14; John Childs, *The Army of Charles II* (London, 1976), 5. H. C. B. Rogers, *The British Army of the Eighteenth Century* (London, 1977), 102–4, sketches Marlborough's staff. The fullest accounts of Marlborough's organization are in R. E. Scouller, *The Armies of Queen Anne* (Oxford, 1966), 62–66, and Scouller, "Marlborough's Administration in the Field," *Army Quarterly* 95 (1967–68): 198–99. The best depictions of the duke's staff are in the Blenheim tapestries, woven by de Vos after L. de Hondt. *The Battle of Blenheim* depicts the operational staff, with Cadogan immediately behind the duke, a sergeant orderly at his bridle, and a bareheaded aide, apparently Daniel Parke, to Marlborough's right, attentive to the sweep of his baton, Alan Wace, *The Marlborough Tapestries at Blenheim Palace and Their Relation to Other Military Tapestries of the War of the Spanish Succession* (London, 1968), #42. Son of a soldier, educated in the French army, Holcroft Blood had been Marlborough's chief engineer at Cork and Kinsale. Ordered to the West Indies with Foulkes in 1692, Blood had himself accused of robbing the Royal Mail to avoid the voyage: Dalton, *Army Lists*, 5:8n1.

9. Kane, *Campaigns*, 4, 14, 16, 19–20, 61; Milner, *Journal*, 9; List of Commissions to be for M. G. Earle's Regmt., Jan. 14, 1702/3, Blenheim MS, 27:12.

10. Noyes [to Sharp], Aug. 30, 1703, Maj. S. H. F. Johnson, ed. "Letters of Samuel Noyes, Chaplain of the Royal Scots, 1703–1704," *JSAHR* 37 (1959): 129. Marlborough certainly kept these dreadful facts before his eyes. See the "Pillage" panels of the Blenheim tapestries, Wace, *Marlborough Tapestries*, #23, 24, and see also #32, 33, 57, 68, II, III, some of which are from the three panels of Orkney's set of hangings at Cliveden (a fourth panel is at Brown University). On July 6, 1703, the captain general proclaimed that the penalty for plundering was the summary execution of the plunderers and fiscal restitution by their regiment, Add. MS 61336, 67.

11. See "Recontre" from the First Blenheim Palace set, Wace, *Marlborough Tapestries*, #26, and "Fouragement," #36, 37, from General Lumley's set. Marlborough to the duchess, Apr. 20/May 1, 1703, Blenheim Ms E.2, Snyder, *Correspondence*, 171; Kane, *Campaigns*, 16, 16; Milner, *Journal*, 57, 62. The crossing of the Scheldt was described by an officer of the Jamaica gubernatorial family, R. Molesworth, to his brother, Add. MS 61312, 187b. Milner, *Journal*, 9, 62, 170–71. "Oudenarde," Wace, *Marlborough Tapestries*, #45.

12. Alexander to John Spotswood, Mar. 15. 1703/4, Cappon, "Correspondence," 221. Webb, *Governors-General*, #208. Howe to Cardonnel, Mar. 19, [1703], Blenheim MS F.2.9, Add. MS 61290, 169.

13. Cutts to Marlborough, Jan. 8, 1704, NS, Add. MS 61162, 27; Clifford Walton, *The British Standing Army, 1660–1700* (London, 1894), 408; Rogers, *British Army*, 103; Kane, *Campaigns*, 3–4; Lediard, *Marlborough*, 2:519.

14. Kane, *Campaigns*, 4, 21, 26. On Hunter's American service, see, Mary Lou Lustig, *Robert Hunter, 1666–1734: New York's Augustan Statesman* (Syracuse, NY, 1983). See also Webb, *Governors-General*, #68, 158, 205; Webb, *Lord Churchill's Coup*, 148, 232, 238.

15. Kane, *Campaigns*, 4, 16, 17, 18–19, 27, 63; Dalton, *Army Lists*, 6:291.

16. For another example, see Edward Nott, Webb, *Governors-General*, #204. It was that "he acted as Major of Brigade above eighteen years agoe" which, together with his West India service, provided the official rationale for Marlborough's brevetting this veteran of the 1688 coup and longtime member of the Denmark connection as colonel just prior to his being commissioned to govern Virginia: Memorial of Maj. Edw. Nott, lt. gov. of Berwick, to Marlborough [1703], Add. MS 61692, 56.

17. Bulletins, Apr. 1, 4, 8, May 11, 16, 1703, Murray, *Dispatches*, 88, 90, 94, 96, 99–100; Frank Taylor, *The Wars of Marlborough, 1702–9* (Oxford, 1921), 1:123; Marlborough to Godolphin, [Apr. 13/24, 1703], Snyder, *Correspondence*, 168, n; same to Ormonde, May 12, 1703, Murray, *Dispatches*, 1:96. Th. Hussey to Cardonnel, camp nr. Maestricht, May 1703, on "the want we are in of the Duke's presence here; our Geneerals are so very unsteady here in their resolutions," Add. MS 61412, 101. It is often said that it was the defense of Tongres that won Elliot his regiment, but Marlborough had promoted him months earlier. C. T. Atkinson, "Names, Numbers, and Errors," *JSAHR* 12 (1934): 31; Scot, "Remembrancer," 3:333–36; Milner, *Journal*, 57; Coxe, *Marlborough*, 1:242–43.

18. Davis, *Second, Queen's*, 2:297; Marlborough to the duchess, Camp before Maestricht, May 13[/24], 1703, Blenheim MS E.8, Snyder, *Correspondence*, 182. The duke's depression was widely deplored, Blathwayt to Cardonnel, June 4, 1703, Add. MS 61411, 142.

19. Gregg, *Anne*, 171; Brown, *Letters of Anne*, 125.

20. Davenport, *Treaties*, #92; Coxe, *Marlborough*, 1:233–34, 292; Taylor, *Marlborough*, 1:145; A. David Francis, *The First Peninsular War, 1702–1713* (London, 1975), 75; Murray, *Dispatches*, 1:158–59; Marlborough to Godolphin, July 1, 8, 1703, Blenheim MS A.I.14, Snyder, *Correspondence*, 214, 217.

21. Blathwayt to Cardonnel, May 28, 1703, Add. MS 61411, 138; Portmore to Marlborough, July 23, 1703, Blenheim MS F.2.8, Add. MS 61157, 10–11, protesting that he wished to serve under Marlborough's command and asking him to promote Phillips, Dalton, *Army Lists*, 5:52; Webb, *Governors-General*, #166–70; Portmore to Cardonnel, Apr. 6, 1703, Add. MS 61412, 85; same to Portmore, Aug. 13, 1703, Blenheim MS 13:246. Stanhope to Marlborough, Aug. 2, 6, 1703, Add. MS 61157, 41, 43. On the Stanhope connection, see Webb, *Governors-General*, #130, and see "Stanhope, James" in "Index of Persons."

22. Murray, *Dispatches*, 1:170; Marlborough to Godolphin, July 28/Aug. 9, Aug. 12/23, Sept. 23[/Oct. 4], 1703, Snyder, *Correspondence*, 228, 233, 246, 182n. Nottingham to Marlborough, Apr. 30, July 23, 30, Aug. 6, 20, Oct. 8, 1703, Add. MS 61118, 169, 185–86, 191–92, 195–96, 199, 219; same to [Heinsius] and Marlborough, Apr. 30, *CSPD, 1702–3*, #2,3. See Marlborough's increasingly acerbic replies, culminating in his flat refusal to send his cavalry to Portugal without a direct, written order from the queen in her own hand, *CSPD, 1702–3*, 201–2, 205. For the whig adoption of the slogan "No Peace Without Spain" in Dec. 1707, see Geoffrey Holmes, *British Politics in the Age of Anne* (London, 1967), 77–78. For a (rather charitable) account of the Graydon expedition, see Ruth Ann Bourne, *Queen Anne's Navy in the West Indies* (New Haven, CT, 1939), 154–61.

23. Marlborough to Nottingham, June 19, July 15, Aug. 8, 23, 27, 1703, Murray, *Dispatches*, 1:117, 143, 155–56, 164, 168. Nottingham to Marlborough, July 30, Aug. 30, 1703, Add. MS 61118, 191, 199. Enough troop transports were eventually chartered to release the Virginia fleet. Chandler, *Marlborough Wars*, 119, says only three regiments of foot and Raby's dragoons (the Royals) were sent, but the 2d Queen's (Portmore's), 11th (Stanhope's), 13th (Stewart's), and 17th (Bridges's) appear with the Royal Dragoons on most lists: WO 4/2, s.v. June 8, 1703. Also named as part of the additional 2,000 was "Baltimore's." This regiment's colonel is identified as Charles Calvert (Snyder, *Correspondence*, 255n), but it is clear that the officer in question was James Barry, earl of Barrymore, colonel of the 13th: Dalton, *Army Lists*, 5:17, 68, 69; Marlborough to Hedges, Oct. 30, 1703, Murray, *Dispatches*, 1:203; Sir Henry Everett, *History of the Somerset Light Infantry . . . 1685–1914* (London, 1934), ch. 4; Coxe, *Marlborough*, 1:234–35.

24. Halifax to [Rivers], Jan. 27, 1706[/7], HMC, *Bath MS*, 1:155; Portmore to Marlborough, Lisbon, Mar. 1, 1703/4, May 15, 1704, Add. MS 61157, 14, 17–19. Trevelyan, *Blenheim*, 311; Gregg, *Anne*, 172; Sir John Perceval's report of the lords' debate on Spain, in which Marlborough replied to Nottingham and Rochester with unwonted warmth, Nottingham having argued that "in Flanders wee might war to eternity & never come to anything decisive," HMC, *Egmont MS*, 2:220–21; Davis, *Second, Queen's*, 2:297–99; C. T. Atkinson, "The Penninsular 'Second Front' in the Spanish Succession War," *JSAHR* 22 (1943–44): 223–24, 227, but see *JSAHR* 54 (1976): 231–35; 55 (1977): 40–53. British land forces in Iberia cost £36 million and naval forces £25 million: C. T. Atkinson, "The Cost of Queen Anne's War," *JSAHR* 33 (1955): 174–83.

25. Lediard, *Marlborough*, 1:230–31; Snyder, *Correspondence*, 185n; Johnson, "Letters of Noyes," 37–39, 40; 67; Murray, *Dispatches*, 1:104, 106, 107–8; Taylor, *Marlborough*, 1:129–32; Coxe, *Marlborough*, 1:257–58, 267, 283–84. For Hamilton's expectations that Marlborough would be "more absolute" in 1703, and his disappointment, see GD 406/1/5014, 5139, SRO.

26. Jo. Seymour to Marlborough, June 4, 16, 1703, Add. MS 61295, 12, 14. Marlborough to Godolphin, June 14, 1703, Blenheim MS A.I.14, Snyder, *Correspondence*, 205n.; Webb, *Governors-General*, #119; Cardonnel to Blathwayt, Aug. 6, 1703, Blenheim MS 27.

27. Marlborough to the duchess, Apr. 20/May 1, May 17, same to Godolphin, July 22/ Aug. 3, 1703, Blenheim MS, E.2, A.I.14, Snyder, *Correspondence*, 171, 187, 224–25; Cardonnel to Lauder, July 26, 1703, Murray, *Dispatches*, 1:151–52; John Charnock, *Biographia Navalis*, 4 vols. (London, 1794), 3:16; P. W. J. Riley, *The Union of England and Scotland* (Manchester, England, 1978), 47–48. Orkney to Hamilton, Mar. 24, 1701/2, GD 406/1/5016, SRO; Hamilton to the countess of Marlborough, Mar. 29, 1702, 151; HMC, *Hamilton Supl. MS*, 151; Selkirk to duchess Anne, Apr. 16, 1702, GD 406/1/8439, SRO. Hamilton to Godolphin and to lady Marlborough, June 10, 12, and countess to Hamilton, June 16, 1702, HMC, *Hamilton MS*, 152–55, and see 156. John Carter Brown Library, *Scotland and the Americas, 1600 to 1800* (Providence, RI, 1995). George Pratt Insh, *The Company of Scotland* (London, 1932), 65–67; G. M. Waller, *Samuel Vetch* (Chapel Hill, NC, 1960), chs. 1–2. Riley, *Union*, 34–35, 43; Insh, *Company*, 164–65, 183, 202–4, 212–16, 237–41; John Robertson, "Union, State and Empire," in Lawrence Stone, ed., *An Imperial State at War* (London, 1994), 238. Routh, *Burnet's History*, 5:300, is the classic exposition of the link between Darien and union, but see W. Ferguson, "The Making of the Treaty of Union of 1707," *SHR* 43 (1954): esp. 91; and GD 406/1/5246, 7292, SRO.

28. Orkney to Hamilton, Mar. 3, 1701/2, GD 406/1/5018, SRO, and see 7501, 7419; Selkirk to Katherine (Hamilton), countess of Tullibardine, ibid., 7418; Hamilton to the queen, Mar. 15, and to Marlborough, Mar. 16, 1702, HMC, *Hamilton Supl. MS*, 149–51.

29. And see Marlborough to the duchess, Oct. 19, 1703, Blenheim MS E.2, Snyder, *Correspondence*, 256, 257; Webb, *Governors-General*, #113.

30. *First Discourse on the Affairs of Scotland* (1698), quoted in Johnston, "Scots Army," 1, 3; Riley, *Union*, 52, 56–58, 72. Nicholson to lords commissioners, Mar. 3, 1704/5, CO 5/1314, #43; Stephen Saunders Webb, "Officers and Governors: The Role of the British Army in Imperial Politics and the Administration of the American Colonies, 1689–1722" (PhD diss., University of Wisconsin–Madison, 1965) 274.

31. Marlborough to Godolphin, Aug. 26/Sept. 6, 1703, Blenheim MS A.I.14, Snyder, *Correspondence*, 238 and see 239; Cardonnel to Southwell, Nov. 30, 1703, Blenheim MS 27:374; Churchill, *Marlborough*, 1:683; Orkney to Hamilton, Dec. 29, 1703, GD 406/1/7292, SRO, and see 5246; same to duchess Anne [July 18, 1704], GD 406/1/5032, and see 8101.

32. Churchill, *Marlborough*, 66off.; Coxe, *Marlborough*, 1:244–50; Marlborough to Godolphin, May 8/19, 1703, Coxe, *Marlborough*, 1:245; Snyder, *Correspondence*, 179–8n. Davenport, *Treaties*, 3:78. Orkney to Selkirk, Aug. 15, 1603, MS 1033, NLS.

33. Marlborough to Godolphin, May 20/31, June 21/July 2, 1703, Coxe, *Marlborough*, 1:246–47, 255 (and see 119, 249, 255–57); Snyder, *Correspondence*, 188–89, 210; Marlborough to Heinsius, June 17, 1703, 't Hoff, *Correspondence*, 75; Lediard, *Marlborough*, 1:231–49; Cadogan to Raby, July 27, 1703, Add. MS 22196, 1–2; Parke to Davenant, July 20, 1703, Add. MS 4741, 1. Murray, *Dispatches*, 1:129–31, 135–36; comte de Mérode-Westerloo, *Memoirs*, ed. D. G. Chandler (London, 1968), ch. 1.

34. Johnson, "Letters of Noyes," 37–40. Marlborough to Godolphin, June 14/15, June 24/July 5, 1703, Snyder, *Correspondence*, 205n, 211; same to Heinsius, July 4, 21,

1703, 't Hoff, *Correspondence*, 79, 83; Coxe, *Marlborough*, 1:259, 257; Lediard, *Marlborough*, 1:251; Churchill, *Marlborough*, 1:664, 669.

35. Parke to Davenant, July 20 (OS, July 30, NS) 1703, Add. MS 4741, l.

36. Johnson, "Letters of Noyes," 68–71; Murray, *Dispatches*, 1:159–60, 162–65, 169; Cadogan to Raby, July 27, Aug. 27, 1703, Add. MS 22196, 2, 4; Marlborough to Godolphin, June 14/25, July 22/Aug. 2, 1702, Blenheim MS A.1.14; same, Aug. 6, 1703, Snyder, *Correspondence*, 205n, 224; Coxe, *Marlborough*, 1:250, 264; Churchill, *Marlborough*, 1:664; Lediard, *Marlborough*, 1:256. Orkney to Selkirk, Liège, Aug. 15, 1703, MS 1033, NLS.

37. Murray, *Dispatches*, 1:150, 165–67, 173, 182, 184, 185, 187; Lediard, *Marlborough*, 1:258–65, 269; Coxe, *Marlborough*, 1:283, 285; Marlborough to Heinsius, Aug. 26, 1703, 't Hoff, *Correspondence*, 88–89; Marlborough to Godolphin, Aug. 16; same to the duchess, [Aug. 29/] Sept. 6, 1703, Snyder, *Correspondence*, 235, 240; Marlborough to Nottingham, Sept. 6, 1703, Add. MS 61118, 209b; Orkney to Selkirk, Aug. 11, 1703, MS 1033, NLS.

38. Marlborough to Heinsius, June 8, Aug. 26, 't Hoff, *Correspondence*, 73–74, 89, and see 53; same to Godolphin, May 24/June 3, June 7/18, July 26/Aug. 6, Sept. 9 [/20], 1703, Snyder, *Correspondence*, 190, 199, 226, 242, and see 165; same to Stepney, May 5, Aug. 11, 1704, Murray, *Dispatches*, 1:94, 157. Blathwayt to Cardonnel, May 11, 1703, Add. MS 61411, 120: "People are mightily troubled at ye joining of ye French & Bavarians." See also 126.

39. Marlborough to Heinsius, Sept. 3, 1703, 't Hoff, *Correspondence*, 90. Contrast the characteristic "improvement" in Churchill, *Marlborough*, 1:681. Same, July 21, 1703, 't Hoff, *Correspondence*, 83; Marlborough to Godolphin, [Aug. 26/Sept. 6], Snyder, *Correspondence*, 239; Coxe, *Marlborough*, 1:284, 285.

40. Lediard, *Marlborough*, 1:269–70, 272; Marlborough to Godolphin, July 19, 1703, Snyder, *Correspondence*, 223.

41. Lediard, *Marlborough*, 1:279–80; Marlborough to Godolphin, July 29/Aug. 9, Oct. 11[/22]; same to the duchess, Oct. 11[/22], 1703, Snyder, *Correspondence*, 228, 252, 253. Parke to Davenant, London, Nov. 11, 1703, Add. MS 4741, 5: Parke "went out upon A Party with My Ld at Duseldorp to Meet the K: of Spain & came over with him."

42. Coxe, *Marlborough*, 1:291–92; Marlborough to Godolphin, Oct. 19[/30], 1703, Snyder, *Correspondence*, 255; same to Hedges, Oct. 30, 1703, Murray, *Dispatches*, 1:204.

43. Bulletin, Oct. 22, 1703, Murray, *Dispatches*, 1:202; Marlborough to Godolphin, June 7, 1703, Snyder, *Correspondence*, 199, and see 258n. Handasyde to Marlborough, Jamaica, Aug. 27, 1703, Add. MS 61306, 124. A. D. Francis, "Marlborough's March to the Danube, 1704," *JSAHR* 50 (1972): 86; Lediard, *Marlborough*, 1:280.

44. Marlborough to the duchess, Sept. 30 [Dec. 10?], 1703, Blenheim MS E.2, Snyder, *Correspondence*, 251, 259; Snyder, "Defeat of the Occasional Conformity Bill and the Tack . . . ," *BIHR* 41 (1968): 172–92; King, *Memoirs of Sarah*, 101–2.

45. On the ordnance costs, see Lowther etc. to Marlborough, Nov. 4, 1703, and same to lord treasurer, Sept. 30, 1703, Add. MS 61165, 33–34, 38–39. Cutts, whom Marlborough had left in command of the English in winter quarters, to the duke,

Dec. 11, 1703, NS, Add. MS 61162, 22, downplayed the storm with a politico-military recollection: "It is no more than what happen'd to us when we embark'd for England at the time of the Revolution." Cutts was enthusiastic about the army augmentation: "I shall forthwith acquaint all the Officers what care Your Grace has taken of them in Parliament." Jones, *15th*, 58. See, of course, George Farquhar, *The Recruiting Officer*, ed. Michael Shugrue (1706; repr. London, 1965). Godfrey Davies, "Recruiting in the Reign of Queen Anne," *JSAHR* 28 (1950): 146–59; Coxe, *Marlborough*, 1:308; Trevelyan, *Blenheim*, 331–33, 428; Cardonnel to Blathwayt, Feb. 12, 18, Blenheim MS 28:31, 32; Marlborough to Buys, Dec. 7, 1703, Murray, *Dispatches*, 1:216; Snyder, *Correspondence*, 257n1, places Marlborough's decision to serve in Nov. 1703. The duke's determinations to resign never did last long.

46. Commissions to be prepared and presented to Her Majesty for the General Officers and Brigadiers, St. James, Apr. 5, 1704, Blenheim MS, 10, "New Levies, 1704"; Dalton, *Army Lists*, 5:15; Charles Dalton, ed., *George the First's Army*, vol. 1, *1714–1727* (London, 1910), 35; Marlborough to the duchess, May 8, 1704, Blenheim MS E.2, Snyder, *Correspondence*, 297–98. The Scots dragoons were still styled "Tiviot's," but it was Marlborough who ordered them mounted on the grays that gave the regiment its famous sobriquet, Jan. 11, 1703/4, Add. MS 61396, 14. Cardonnel to Southwell, Feb. 12, 1703/4, Blenheim MS 28:48.

47. Marlborough to Ormonde, same to Erle, Jan. 6, 1704, Murray, *Dispatches*, 1:223–25. The officer-candidate précis are in Blenheim MS 10, Add. MS 61378. List of Officers to be Provided for in the Regts to be Rais'd for the Service of Ireland, Mar. 28, 1704, Blenheim MS F.2.4, Add. MS 61321, 87; Cardonnel to Southwell, Jan. 6, 13, 1703/4, Add. MS 61396, 4, 15; Fr. Parsons to Cardonnel, Mar. 9, 1702/3, Add. MS 61412, 79. On the army in the revolution, see Webb, *Lord Churchill's Coup*, book 2.

48. Add. MS 61378, 9, 36; Meml of Capt Th Fowk to Marlborough, Add. MS 61287, 163; Webb, *Governors-General*, #88; Luttrell, *Brief Relation*, 2:551, 563, 591; Cardonnel to Hedges, Peregren Gally off the Maes, Apr. 9/20, 1704, Blenheim MS 10, 10 (II). On the army demobilization and anglicanization of 1697, see Webb, *Lord Churchill's Coup*, 256–60.

49. Blenheim MS 10:22; Webb, *Governors-General*, #131; Add. MS 61321, 87.

50. Webb, *Governors-General*, #168; Blenheim MS 10:28; Dalton, *Army Lists*, 6:88, 333, 334; Dalton, *George the First's Army*, 209–10.

51. Blenheim MS 10:38, 28:72, 73.

52. List for Sir Charles Hotham's Regiment, Blenheim MS 10 (II):30; Dalton, *Army Lists*, 4:175, 275; 5:192–93; CO 5/1319, #3; CO 5/1365, 220–36; Add. MS 35907.

53. Galway to Erle, Gibraltar, Feb. 27, 1707/8, NS, Add. MS 61158, 71. J. G. A. Pocock, "The Limits and Divisions of British History . . . ," *AHR* 87 (1982): 311–36, esp. 329; Jack P. Greene, ed., "Martin Bladen's Blueprint for Colonial Union," *WMQ*, 3d ser., 17 (1960): 516–30.

54. Blenheim MS 10 (II):37; Dalton, *Army Lists*, 5:192–93; 6:190; Webb, *Governors-General*, #24.

55. Blenheim MS 10 (II):51; A.I.31; Meml of Wm Taylor to Marlborough, Add. MS 61296, 87; Webb, *Governors-General*, #126; Dalton, *Army Lists*, 6:285, 337. This identification is uncertain, but given the name, it would have been a matter of course to promote Taylor, an officer of Erle's foot who had served with credit at Guadeloupe, to a command in Erle's dragoons.

56. Blenheim MS A.26.156; Colonel Whetham's Case, Mar. 2, 1704/5, Add. MS 61297, 105; Harlow, *Codrington*, 170–72; Charles Dalton, "Soldiering in the West Indies," *JRUSI* 42 (1898): 69; HMC, *Ormonde MS*, n.s., 8:52; Webb, *Governors-General*, #78; Parke to Davenant, Nov. 11, 1703, Add. MS 4741, 5. Codrington had appealed to his patron Peterborough for a share in naming his successor and to protect Whetham's right to choose his own officers, Jan. 17, 19, 1704, CO 7/1, #4; HMC, *House of Lords MS*, n.s., 6:7. Webb, *Governors-General*, #74, 77, 78, 80. See generally Harlow, *Codrington*.

57. Marlborough to the duchess, Aug. 16/27, 1703, Snyder, *Correspondence*, 236; Cardonnel to Blathwayt, May 6, 1704, Blenheim MS 28:104. Note, however, that Mathew was regimental agent for the entire Brigade of Guards, a highly lucrative position both for Mathew himself and for his colonel, lord Cutts (Add. MS 61293, 100). Marlborough would dispose of the agency. The Meml of Capt. Mathew to Marlborough, Add. MS 61291, 148, 149; Webb, *Governors-General*, #78, 83.

58. See Braddock's promotion to lieutenant colonel of the Coldstream, Jan. 5, 1703/4, Add. MS 61396, 2. Edward Braddock was commissioned an ensign in the Coldstream Guards in October 1710, while Marlborough was still captain general. Dalton, *Army Lists*, 3:43; 6:56, 57; Col. MacKinnon, *Origin and Services of the Coldstream Guards, 1648–1815*, 2 vols. (London, 1833), 2:473. Lt. Col. Braddock to Marlborough, May 19, 1707, Dec. 19 [n.d.], Add, MS 61284, 64, 66. Douglas Southall Freeman, *George Washington* (New York, 1948), 2:83.

59. Cardonnel to Warre, Feb. 24, 1702/3; same to Ellis, Dec. 21, 1703, Blenheim MS 27:71, 397; C. T. Atkinson, "Queen Anne's War in the West Indies," *JSAHR* 24 (1946): 194.

60. "List of Furlows to Be Prepared by Order of His Grace the Duke of Marlborough for the Four West India Regiments for the Term of Six Months," Add. MS 38709, 30; Dalton, "Soldiering," 66–67; HMC, *Portland MS*, 4:656; Webb, *Governors-General*, #82, 2.

61. Cardonnel to Blathwayt, Oct. 9, 1702, Blenheim MS 26:190; ibid., 27:156. Blathwayt to Cardonnel, Apr. 30, May 28, 1703, Blenheim MS F.2.5, Add. MS 61411, 126, 132. In subsequent years, Marlborough sent out reserve officers to be on hand in Jamaica to take vacancies as they occurred (28:61, 73). He had also sent out three supernumerary officers with Columbine to take places in "the West India Regts." (13:331); Murray, *Dispatches*, 1:211. One of them. Lt. John Fenwick, personified the military professionalism Marlborough preferred, having served for fifteen years under king James, in all of king William's campaigns in Ireland (where Fenwick built an estate), and in Flanders. Invalided out of Selwyn's regiment for wounds in 1697, Fenwick joined the W. I. expedition with certificates of service from Selwyn, Cutts, Churchill, and Mathew, Add. MS 61287, 101, 103, 105. Fenwick and the other volunteers were not commissioned in the W.I., however (another debit in the expeditionary account so far as the duke was concerned). Marlborough took care of the three supernumeraries subsequently, in keeping with the special consideration he offered every officer who "readily offer'd his Service to go to the West Indies," Cardonnel to Blathwayt, Camp near Hanef, July 23, 1703, Add. MS 38710, 12–13. Marlborough followed up on their promotions when the regiments returned to Ireland, Edward Southwell to Marlborough, Nov. 25, 1703, Add. MS 61163, 135. On Handasyde's promotions in regiment and government, see also Atkinson, "War in the West Indies," 88; order to prepare, Feb. 15, 1703/4, *CSPC, 1704–5,* #96; Luttrell, *Brief Relation,* 5:396, Webb, *Governors-General,* #60.

62. [Josiah Sandby, chaplain of Charles Churchill's regiment], "An Account of His Grace the Duke of Marlborough's Expedition into Germany &c," Nov. 11, 1703– Oct. 12, 1704, Add. MS 9114, 1, 6–7 and Add. MS 61408 (2). See William Churchill to Marlborough, London, Mar. 10, 1710/11, who reported that "Dr. Samby" has completed his account of the Hochstadt campaign and forwarded it for Marlborough to review and Steele to edit for publication, Add. MS 61368, 278. On Sandby's ensuing ecclesiastical promotion, see Add. MS 61651, 111b–112. Lediard, *Marlborough,* 1:283; Marlborough to the duchess, Hague, [Jan.] 18/29, [1704]; same to Godolphin, Jan. 21, 1704, Snyder, *Correspondence,* 261; same to Hedges, Feb. 1, 1704, Murray, *Dispatches,* 1:226–27; Orkney to Hamilton, Feb. 19, 1704, GD 406/1/7153, SRO.

63. Marlborough to Hedges, Feb. 18, 1704; same to Bade[n], Feb. 8; same to Savoy, Feb. 10; same to Hop, Mar. 24, 1704, Murray, *Dispatches,* 1:239, 229, 231–32, 245, and see 233. Marlborough to his duchess, Feb. 1[/12], 1704, Snyder, *Correspondence,* 267–68. Add. MS 9114, 8ff.

64. Add. MS 9114, 12; *Lives of the Two Illustrious Generals,* 57. Coxe, *Marlborough,* 1:307–8. On the Circles, see A. D. Francis, "Marlborough's March," *JSAHR* 50 (1972): 91–93; Parker, *Memoirs,* 92; Atkinson, *Marlborough,* 192; Jones, *15th,* 58.

65. Lediard, *Marlborough,* 1:285–87. Coxe, *Marlborough,* 1:317, has this authorization given on the 4th. On the quarrel, see Snyder, *Correspondence,* 271–74.

66. Marlborough to Godolphin, Harwich, Apr. 3, 1704, Blenheim MS A.I.14, Snyder, *Correspondence,* 275–76; *Lives of the Two Illustrious Generals,* 54; Add. MS 9114, 12b–14.

67. Add. MS 9114, 14; Cardonnel to Southwell, Jan. 13, 1703/4, Blenheim MS 28:15; Marlborough to Ormonde, Feb. 22, Mar. 9, 1704, Murray, *Dispatches,* 1:240–41, 243–44.

68. Marlborough to Blathwayt, Harwich, Apr. 8, 1704; same to Hedges, Apr. 6, May 9, June 13, 1704, Murray, *Dispatches,* 1:248, 258, 306–7; Trevelyan, *Blenheim,* 1:335; Godolphin to the duchess, [Apr. 18, 1704]; Marlborough to Godolphin, Apr. 20, 1704, Snyder, *Correspondence,* 280–81, 289; King, *Memoirs of Sarah,* 102; Luttrell, *Brief Relation,* 5:416, 421, 426; Horowitz, *Revolution Politicks* (Cambridge, 1968), 197–99; Snyder, "Godolphin and Harley," 252–54.

69. Cardonnel to Stepney, Hague, Apr. 22, 1704, Add. MS 7063, 44; Webb, "Blathwayt," 413; Gertrude Ann Jacobsen, *Blathwayt, a Late Seventeenth Century Administrator* (New Haven, CT, 1932), 294–95; Trevelyan, *Blenheim,* 339–40; Luttrell, *Brief Relation,* 5:411; Taylor, *Marlborough,* 1:154; Coxe, *Marlborough,* 1:314. Marlborough to St. John, May 11, 1704, Murray, *Dispatches,* 1:260–61. The admiration was mutual: Marlborough to Godolphin, July 13, 1704, Snyder, *Correspondence,* 335. Note that Blathwayt failed to get the transports away in timely fashion, increasing Marlborough's animus, Add. MS 9114, 19; Blathwayt to Marlborough, Apr. 6, 1704, Blenheim MS F.2.12, Add. MS 61133, 91–92.

Chapter 2. The March to the Danube

1. Marlborough to the duchess, Hague, Apr. 24, Oct. 20, 1704, Blenheim MS, E.2, Snyder, *Correspondence*, 287, 385; same to Hedges, Apr. 22, 1704, Murray, *Dispatches*, 1:249.

2. Marlborough to Godolphin, Apr. 11[/21], 18[/29], 21[/May 2], 1704, Blenheim MS A.I.14, Snyder, *Correspondence*, 275n, 278–79, 282. On May 10, Marlborough also intimated his plan to the English envoy at Vienna, Murray, *Dispatches*, 1:258–59.

3. Churchill, *Marlborough*, 1:780; Marlborough to Godolphin, and to the duchess, Apr. 21[/May 2], 1704, Snyder, *Correspondence*, 282–83.

4. Marlborough to Godolphin, Apr. 21, 24, May 4, to the duchess, May 16[/27], Snyder, *Correspondence*, 282, 286, 295, 304; bulletin, May 2, 28, 1704, Murray, *Dispatches*, 1:252–53n, 285n; Coxe, *Marlborough*, 1:320–21, 328–29; Lediard, *Marlborough*, 1:288–89; Kane, *Campaigns*, 54; Taylor, *Marlborough*, 1:154; Add. MS 9114, 18b.

5. Milner, *Journal*, 82; Kane, *Campaigns*, 53; Jones, *15th*, 58n; Churchill, *Marlborough*, 1:751; Dalton, *Army Lists*, 5: pt. 2, "The Blenheim Roll"; Hamilton, *Guards*, 1:443; Webb, *Governors-General*, 468; Webb, *Lord Churchill's Coup*, 14. More mundanely, the Guards colonel managed the most profitable contract for regimental clothing. Marlborough had already rejected one pattern as "too good," i.e., too expensive, reducing the difference between the clothing allowance he received from the Guards' off-reckonings and the price he paid the clothiers. Profitability appears in the price—1,000 guineas—that Capt. and Lt. Col. Stephen Piper offered Marlborough for the regimental agency in succession to Governor General Mathew, Apr. 10, 1704, Add. MS 61293, 100. Marlborough to Godolphin and to the duchess, Apr. 18, 1704, Snyder, *Correspondence*, 279, 281.

6. Webb, *Governors-General*, 468, lists the Guards connections. Meml. of Lt. Col. Andrew Wheeler to Marlborough, Jan. 3, 1705/6; same, June 6, 1708, May 3, 1710, Add. MS 61297, 90, 94, 96. See also the case of Guards captain James Rivers and the West India expedition of 1703, Add. MS 61306, 106–7, Guy to Marlborough, Aug. 2, 1710, Add. MS 61293, 153.

7. Hamilton, *Guards*, 1:225, 228, 247, 427; HMC, *Portland MS*, 4:582; Webb, *Governors-General*, #17; Dalton, *Army Lists*, 5: pt. 2; David P. Henige, *Colonial Governors from the Fifteenth Century to the Present* (Madison, WI, 1970).

8. When it marched with Marlborough from Bedburg, the battalion of the 1st Guards was scandalously underofficered. It remained so until Cutts, etc., at last joined the army, two days after the Schellenberg. Cutts at least had the excuse that he had earned some leave by commanding the English winter quarters in the Netherlands. In public, Marlborough downplayed the difficulty (Murray, *Dispatches*, 1:384), but privately he vowed that "another year I shall make them all goe out of England before mee," Snyder, *Correspondence*, 313; bulletin, May 14, 1704, Murray, *Dispatches*, 1:263. Kane to Cardonnel and enc., May 24, 1704, Add. MS 61291, 50, 51. Hunter's brevet is in Add. MS 61298, 23. Governors general on the march to the

Danube commissioned to command colonies before 1727 are minuted in Webb, *Governors-General*, appendix. Parke's pass, dated at Harwich, April 24, 1704, is in *CSPD, 1703–4*, 336. Parke to Davenant, July 13, 1704, Add. MS 4741, 5.

9. Penn to Harley, HMC, *Downshire MS*, 1: pt. 2, 831–32.

10. Marlborough to the duchess, May 3 [/14], 18[/29], 1704, Snyder, *Correspondence*, 295, 306; Lediard, *Marlborough*, 1:293; Coxe, *Marlborough*, 1:326–27, 331; Churchill, *Marlborough*, 1:746, 747.

11. Marlborough to Lowndes, Apr. 29, 1704, Murray, *Dispatches*, 1:250–51; bulletin, May 14, 19, ibid., 263, 265, and see 256, 379, 381; Francis, "March," 95, 96; Peter Verney, *The Battle of Blenheim* (London, 1976), 46–47; Cadogan to Raby, Add. MS 22196, partially printed in *JSAHR* 50 (1972): 250–51; Add. MS 9114, 18, 26.

12. Kane, *Campaigns*, 4–5.

13. Coxe, *Marlborough*, 1:325; Trevelyan, *Blenheim*, 358n; Add. MS 7063, 481–89; Add. MS 9114, 22–24; Marlborough to the duchess, May 4, 1704, Blenheim MS E.2, Snyder, *Correspondence*, 296; same to Hedges, May 21, 1704, Murray, *Dispatches*, 1:270. The bulletin of May 21, 1704, makes the French force in pursuit of Marlborough thirty-six battalions and fifty-five squadrons, Murray, *Dispatches*, 1:273; Churchill, *Marlborough*, 1:749; Marlborough to Godolphin, May 12/23, 1704, Blenheim MS A.I.14, Snyder, *Correspondence*, 300; same to the council of state, same, Murray, *Dispatches*, 1:274–75, and see 276–78.

14. Bulletin, May 25, 1704, Murray, *Dispatches*, 1:280–81; Add. MS 9114, 25; Milner, *Journal*, 82, 83; Parker, *Memoirs*, 30; Kane, *Campaigns*, 54; Marlborough to Godolphin, May 18/29, 1704, Blenheim MS A.I.14, Snyder, *Correspondence*, 305; Coxe, *Marlborough*, 1:331.

15. Parker, *Memoirs* (Chandler, ed.), 31.

16. C. Churchill to Marlborough, Kernel, May 31, 1704, Add. MS 61163, 166; Murray, *Dispatches*, 1:273; Add. MS 9114, 23b, 26b; *Select Passages from the Diary and Letters of the Late John Blackadder, Esqr., Formerly Lieutenant Colonel of the XXVIth or Cameronian Regiment, Afterwards Deputy Governor of Sterling Castle* (Edinburgh, 1806), 13. Blackadder, son of the famous hill preacher and Williamite agent, had served at Landen and Steinkirk with the brothers Vetch (also sons of a Cameronian leader and principals in the Scots colony of Darien and of Nova Scotia). Blackadder himself was succeeded by Sir John Hope (Bruce), who became governor of Bermuda (1721–27), and Philip Anstruther, colonel of the Cameronians, lieutenant governor of Minorca (1742–43). S. H. F. Johnston, *The History of the Cameronians*, vol. 1, *1689–1910* (Aldershot, England, 1957); Webb, *Governors-General*, #26, 161, 165. Much of the Cameronian mindset is captured by Sir Walter Scott, *The Heart of Midlothian* (Edinburgh, 1818).

17. Add. MS 9114, 27, 31, 34; Add. MS 61163, f.166.

18. Add. MS 9114, 27–29. This is a copy of Add. MS 61408. This "Blenheim Journal" is commonly attributed to Marlborough's chaplain, Francis Hare, but was probably written by Charles Churchill's chaplain and secretary, Josiah Sandby. On this authorship, see Charles to William Churchill, Mar. 16, 1710/11, Add. MS 61368, 27 (which also suggests editing by Richard Steele), and F. R. Harris, "The Authorship of the Ms. Blenheim Journal," *BIHR* 55 (1982): 20–36. Add. MS 9114 is cited here as somewhat more legible. See also, ch 1, n2.

19. Add. MS 9114, 31b; Coxe, *Marlborough*, 1:326, 332–34; Marlborough to Hedges, June 4, 1704, Murray, *Dispatches*, 1:295; bulletin, June 4, 1704, Murray, *Dispatches*, 1:293–94.

20. Lediard, *Marlborough*, 1:303–5; Milner, *Journal*, 86; Marlborough to Godolphin, June 4, 1704, Blenheim MS A.I.14, Snyder, *Correspondence*, 317–18; Churchill, *Marlborough*, 1:763–69. The political stakes were assessed by Harley to Marlborough (May 23/June 3, 1704, Add. MS 61123, 4) when he wrote of this "the most Generous & Gallant Action in the World on which depends the fate of the German Empire." The jealousy of the English dukes at Marlborough's elevation to princely rank was palpable: at the news they "looked Sullen & sate silent," duke of Buckingham to Marlborough, Aug. 28, 1707, Add. MS 61363, 154.

21. Marlborough to Godolphin, May 16/27, May 22/June 2, Snyder, *Correspondence*, 303, 307–8; Lediard, *Marlborough*, 1:303; Parker, *Memoirs*, 31; Add. MS 9114, 32b.

22. Orkney to Selkirk, May 22, 1704, MS 1033, NLS.

23. Murray, *Dispatches*, 1:293–94; Add. MS 9114, 34–35, 37; Marlborough to Godolphin, May 28/June 8, 1734, Snyder, *Correspondence*, 313; same to the assemblies of the circles of Franconia and Suabia, June 16, 19; same to C. Churchill, June 8, 1704, Murray, *Dispatches*, 1:301, 311–18. Marlborough also arranged that his Dutch troops should be supplied from these bases: same to Heinsius, June 25, 1704, 't Hoff, *Correspondence*, 114.

24. Bulletins, June 9, 12, 1704, Marlborough to Harley, June 13, 1704, Murray, *Dispatches*, 1:302, 305, 307; Lediard, *Marlborough*, 1:306; Marlborough to Godolphin, May 28/June 8, Snyder, *Correspondence*, 317. On Eugene and Zenta, see Nicholas Henderson, *Prince Eugene of Savoy* (London, 1964), esp. 40–45, and Derek McKay, *Prince Eugene of Savoy* (London, 1977), 41–47. Marlborough to Godolphin, June 4 [/15], 1704, Snyder, *Correspondence*, 318, and see same to the duchess, May 31[/June 11], June 4/15, 1704 (316, 318); *Lives of the Two Illustrious Generals*, 59–61; Add. MS 9114, 35–35b; Lediard, *Marlborough*, 1:307; Coxe, *Marlborough*, 1:336–37; Milner, *Journal*, 87, 88; Kane, *Campaigns*, 54.

25. Add. MS 9114, 36–37; Marlborough to the duchess, May 31[/June 11], June 4[/15], and to Godolphin, June 4[/15], Snyder, *Correspondence*, 316–19.

26. Hamilton, *Guards*, 1:446; Milner, *Journal*, 88.

27. John Evelyn forwarded Parke's career in Virginia by using his influence with Blathwayt. This dated back to Evelyn's commissionership of plantations in the 1670s. On Feb. 9, 1706, Evelyn recorded, "I went to waite on my L. Treasurer where was the Victorious Duke of Marlborow, who came to me & tooke me by the hand with extraordinary familiarity & Civility, as formerly he was used to doe without any alteration of his good nature. . . . I had not seen him in 2 yeares & believed he had forgotten me," Edmond S. de Beer, ed., *The Diary of John Evelyn* (London, 1955), 5:584. Always courteous, Marlborough never forgot. Parke, as well as Evelyn, benefited. Parke to Cardonnel, June 15, 1704, Blenheim MS A.I.31. The intimacy of the Evelyn and Godolphin families was also helpful to Parke's career.

On the Parke-Evelyn connection, see de Beer, ed., *Diary of Evelyn*, 5:574–75n; Ruth Anne Bourne, "John Evelyn the Diarist and His Cousin Daniel Parke," *VMHB* 78 (1970): 3–33; Helen Hill Miller, *Colonel Parke of Virginia* (Chapel Hill, NC, 1989), 9–11, 73, 78. This connection would produce yet another personal tie between Marlborough's command and Washington's. George Washington Parke Custis, Colonel Parke's great-grandson and Gen. Washington's stepson, memorialized Daniel Parke's career and linked it through his family to his stepfather in *Recollections and Private Memoirs of Washington* (New York, 1860). Custis's mother was Eleanor Calvert of the Baltimore family. In 1831, his daughter married R. E. Lee at the home Parke Custis built, Arlington.

28. Add. MS 9114, 40; Milner, *Journal*, 88, reports a two-day halt because the artillery had bogged down. Churchill to Marlborough, June 18, 20, 1704, Add. MS 61163, 170, 172; Marlborough to Churchill, June 20, 1704, Murray, *Dispatches*, 1:320, and see 291–300, 303, 313–14, 321, for other expressions, to his brother and to the quartermasters general, of Marlborough's concern for his infantry; Lediard, *Marlborough*, 1:316; Marlborough to the duchess, June 14 [/25], 1704, Snyder, *Correspondence*, 324; Blackadder, *Diary*, 16. Bulletin, June 22, 1704, Murray, *Dispatches*, 1:322; Add. MS 9114, 41, 43, Webb, *Lord Churchill's Coup*, 31–36.

29. Parker, *Memoirs*, 32; Lediard, *Marlborough*, 1:312–14. M. De La Colonie, *The Chronicles of an Old Campaigner, 1692–1717*, trans. Walter C. Horsley (London, 1904), 178–79, reports that exact intelligence was given to prince Louis of Baden by a Bavarian corporal. See also Kane, *Campaigns*, 54; Milner, *Journal*, 89, 94; Coxe, *Marlborough*, 1:348, 351n. Estimates of the garrison's size ranged up to 18,000, but 12,000 seems the most likely number. Marlborough's plan pitted 2.5 times that many men against the defense, a bit less than the three to one of present-day practice. The allies counted 96 battalions, 184–202 squadrons, 48 cannon, and 24 pontoons. Of this force, 86 squadrons and 49 battalions were commanded by Marlborough. See also Coxe, *Marlborough*, 1:346; Johnson, "Letters of Noyes," 130; bulletin, June 26, 29, Murray, *Dispatches*, 1:327, 328–29; Marlborough to the duchess, June 18/29, same to Godolphin, July 4, 1704, Snyder, *Correspondence*, 326, 328.

30. Add. MS 9114, 43–44, is followed here on the question of command. On the composition and sources of this, the official account from Marlborough's headquarters, see Cardonnel to Harley, Sept. 25, 1704, Murray, *Dispatches*, 1:409 and n. 18 above. Francis Hare had been tutor to the Marlboroughs' son at Cambridge. Then he was commissioned chaplain general of the army and came out with Cutts's party. They arrived after the battle of the Schellenberg (see Johnson, "Letters of Noyes," 133–34). If Hare composed or helped Sandby compose Add. MS 9114, reference was had to Cardonnel's records. This account is contradicted by Churchill, *Marlborough*, 1:792. In his official account to Harley, July 3, 1704 (Murray, *Dispatches*, 1:330–31), Marlborough simply states that "I resolved to attack." See also Lediard, *Marlborough*, 1:321; Johnson, "Letters of Noyes," 130; Marlborough to Godolphin, [June 22/] July 3, 1704, Snyder, *Correspondence*, 327.

31. See Add. MS 9114, 44b–45 and, in addition to the sources cited in n. 29, see also Kane, *Campaigns*, 54; Milner, *Journal*, 94–95; and Parker, *Memoirs*, 32, all of which reflect the orderly book of the Royal Irish (18th) Regiment.

32. Add. MS 9114, 45. Kane, *Campaigns*, 54, describes the situation at noon. For the advance, see the map in Marcus Junkelmann, *Das greulichste Spectaculum Die Schlacht von Höchstädt 1704* (Augsburg, 2004), 28, copy courtesy of Ms. Cindy Cooper.

33. Marlborough to Harley, July 3, 1704, Murray, *Dispatches*, 1:331; same to states general, July 3, 1704, in Lediard, *Marlborough*, 1:319, 326–27; Add. MS 9114, 46; Coxe, *Marlborough*, 2:40–41.

34. Add. MS 9114, 47–48; Lediard, *Marlborough*, 1:31 and Marlborough's dispatch to the states (1:325–27); Milner, *Journal*, 95; Churchill, *Marlborough*, 1:795; De La Colonie, *Chronicles*, 177.

35. Hompesch to the states, in Lediard, *Marlborough*, 1:329 and see also 1:323, 330, 331–35; De La Colonie, *Chronicles*, 182–93.

36. Add. MS 9114, 48–49; Parke to Davenant, July 17, 1704, Add. MS 4741, 5; Kane, *Campaigns*, 55; Lediard, *Marlborough*, 1:323; Johnson, "Letters of Noyes," 130; Dalton, *Army Lists*, 5: pt. 2, 29–31.

37. Add. MS 9114, 48b–49; Lediard, *Marlborough*, 1:322; Milner, *Journal*, 95; Johnson, "Letters of Noyes," 132.

38. Churchill, *Marlborough*, 1:802; De La Colonie, *Chronicles*, 185.

39. The scene is described in De La Colonie, *Chronicles*, 176, and is depicted in the "Dunawert" panel from the Blenheim tapestries, Wace, *Marlborough Tapestries*, #40. Maps are in Churchill, *Marlborough*, 1:806; Coxe, *Marlborough, Atlas*, #7; Hilarie Belloc, *The Tactics and Strategy of the Great Duke of Marlborough* (London, 1933), 71; Verney, *Blenheim*, 65; Junkelmann, *Höchstädt*, 29.

40. Parke to Davenant, July 13, 1704, Add. MS 4741, 6; Add. MS 9114, 49–51, printed in Murray, *Dispatches*, 1:337; Lediard, *Marlborough*, 1:324, 331.

41. Add. MS 9114, 50–51, Murray, *Dispatches*, 1:338. And see Parker, *Memoirs*, 32, 33; Churchill, *Marlborough*, 1:805. Johnson, "Letters of Noyes," 131, says only 1,800 men survived from twenty-five battalions and six squadrons of French and Bavarians. Lediard, *Marlborough*, 1:323, records the defenders' loss at 5,000–6,000 from a force of 18,000–32,000; Kane, *Campaigns*, 54–55, says 7,000 of the enemy were killed, 2,000 deserted, and 4,008 were taken prisoner, from a force of 18,000. Parke, writing to Davenant ten days after the battle, put the enemy killed at 8,000, Add. MS 4741, 6. Junkelmann, *Höchstädt*, 29, gives D'Arco only 9,000 men, with another 1,000 in the city.

42. Add. MS 9114, 51–52; Johnson, "Letters of Noyes," 132; Blackadder, *Diary*, 19; Webb, *Governors-General*, #156.

43. Lediard, *Marlborough*, 1:334; Marlborough to Godolphin, Sept. 29, 1704, Blenheim MS A.I.14, Snyder, *Correspondence*, 374n, 396n; Luttrell, *Brief Relation*, 5:410, 485. Oglethorpe did not die until November, but he was never able to take up the post of equerry to the queen that Marlborough had promised to him if he survived. Dalton, *George the First's Army*, 126; Marlborough to lady Oglethorpe, Sept. [6/]17, 1705, Murray, *Dispatches*, 2:268; lady Oglethorpe to Marlborough, Godalming, Sept. 12[/25], 1705, Blenheim MS A.I.27; Webb, "Agricola in America," *Reviews in American History* (1978): 318–25.

44. Add. MS 9114, 53–54; Johnson, "Letters of Noyes," 130; Blackadder, *Diary*, 19; Marlborough to Harley, July 3, 1704, Murray, *Dispatches*, 1:331. Hompesch (in

Lediard, *Marlborough*, 1:330) estimated the Dutch loss at 1,600–1,700. The entire allied loss was about 5,474 (1:323, 335), including sixteen generals, forty-five field officers, eighty-eight captains, 247 subalterns, and 4,928 private soldiers. Milner (*Journal*, 96–97) makes the allied casualties 5,304. See Marlborough to Godolphin, Donawert, July 4, 1704, Blenheim MS A.I.14, Snyder, *Correspondence*, 328.

45. See also Add. MS 9114, 54b–55; Parker, *Memoirs*, 33–34; Lediard, *Marlborough*, 1:334, 338.

46. Lediard, *Marlborough*, 1:335, 342–47; Coxe, *Marlborough*, 1:363; Marlborough to Godolphin, July 4, same to the duchess, May 28[/June 8], June 23[/July 4], July [5/]16, 1704, Snyder, *Correspondence*, 329, 314, 328–29, 338; Add. MS 9114, 55–56. The queen left Marlborough in no doubt as to whose victory she thought it was (London, July 4, 1704, Blenheim MS F.2.15, Add. MS 61101, 70), and Harley wrote (July 18/29, 1704, Add. MS 61123, 38) that "the angry people here find the ground begin to fal from under them." He wished Marlborough "a Series of Successes which is so necessary for all our affaires abroad & will make our winter campagne at home less difficult." Harley especially relied on the impact of Marlborough's victory to forward the union negotiation.

47. Marlborough to Godolphin, [June 23/]July 4, [June 25/]July 6, Blenheim MS A.I.14, Snyder, *Correspondence*, 328, 330–31; Kane, *Campaigns*, 55; Johnson, "Letters of Noyes," 145; Add. MS 9114, 59b–60.

48. Marlborough to Godolphin, [June 28/]July 9, July [2/]13, 1704, Snyder, *Correspondence*, 332–33, 334; Coxe, *Marlborough*, 1:369, 370, 371; Add. MS 9114, 57b.

49. Marlborough to Godolphin, May 28/June 8, July [5/]16, [12/]23, 1704, same to the duchess, July [19/]30, 1704, Snyder, *Correspondence*, 313, 336–37, 341, 343, 344; Coxe, *Marlborough*, 1:375; Churchill, *Marlborough*, 1:821–22; Kane, *Campaigns*, 55, 56; Parker, *Memoirs*, 34; Johnson, "Letters of Noyes,"146; Milner, *Journal*, 104; Add. MS 9114, 61b, 64, 72b–73. Lediard, *Marlborough*, 1:349–50, 352, notes that Marlborough refused to accept the enormous ransoms offered him for his forbearance, another indication that in military matters, avarice did not drive him. This destruction Marlborough kept always before him. See the "Horrors of War," in Wace, *Marlborough Tapestries*, #23, 24, as well as the same subject in the tapestries of Marlborough's subordinate Henry Lumley (#32, 33).

Chapter 3. Blenheim

1. Marlborough to Godolphin, July [20/]31, 1704, Snyder, *Correspondence*, 345; same to Heinsius, July 16, 1704, 't Hoff, *Correspondence*, 118, map 12, Hamilton, *Guards*, 1:443; Johnson, "Letters of Noyes," 134, 145; Parke to Davenant, July 17, 1704, Add. MS 4741, 5–5b; Add. MS 9114, 74; Lediard, *Marlborough*, 1:362–63; De La Colonie, *Chronicles*, 224; "Plan of the Movements of the Confederate Army . . . Previous and Subsequent to the Battle of Blenheim," in Coxe, *Marlborough*, *Atlas*, #6; Junkelmann, *Höchstädt*, 36–37.

2. So said the orderly book of the 18th: Parker, *Memoirs*, 35; Milner, *Journal*, 111–12; Kane, *Campaigns*, 56.

3. Marlborough to Godolphin, July [20/]31, 1704, Snyder, *Correspondence*, 344–45; Parker, *Memoirs*, 35; Kane, *Campaigns*, 56; Lediard, *Marlborough*, 1:357.

4. Marlborough to Godolphin, [July 23/]Aug. 3, same to the duchess, [July 30/]Aug. 10, 1704, Snyder, *Correspondence*, 345, 348; Johnson, "Letters of Noyes," 147; Add. MS 9114, 73–74, 75b–76; *Lives of the Two Illustrious Generals*, 66; Parker, *Memoirs*, 35.

5. Add. MS 9114, 77–78, Murray, *Dispatches*, 1:395; Lediard, *Marlborough*, 1:353–54; Coxe, *Marlborough*, 1:383; Hamilton, *Guards*, 1:452–57 and map; Lee, *Tenth Foot*, 24–25. Cardonnel to Stepney, Aug. 10, 1704, Add. MS 7063, 60, gives the same sequence of events, but begins it on the 11th and has Eugene returning at 2:00.

6. Add. MS 7063, 64; Add. MS 9114, 77–79; Murray, *Dispatches*, 1:395–96; Marlborough to Harley and to Hedges, Aug. 14, 1704, Murray, *Dispatches*, 1:390; same to Godolphin, [July 30/]Aug. 10, Snyder, *Correspondence*, 374; Charles Dalton, ed., "The Battle of Blenheim," *JRUSI* 3, no. 2 (1898): 1075; Coxe, *Marlborough*, 1:383, 384; Johnson, "Letters of Noyes," 147; Orkney to [John, lord Hervey], Aug. 17, 1704, "Letters," *EHR* 19 (1904): 307–8; Lediard, *Marlborough*, 1:359, map; Junkelmann, *Höchstädt*, 41.

7. Junkelmann, *Höchstädt*, 362, 364; *Lives of the Two Illustrious Generals*, 67; Add. MS 9114, 80; Orkney to [Hervey], Aug. 17, 1704, "Letters," 307, 311.

8. Add. MS 9114, 83b; *Lives of the Two Illustrious Generals*, 67; Marlborough to Godolphin, June 9/20, 1704, Snyder, *Correspondence*, 321; Webb, *Lord Churchill's Coup*, 31–36.

9. Murray, *Dispatches*, 1:397; Johnson, "Letters of Noyes," 148; Orkney, "Letters," 308; HMC, *Hare MS* (14th Report, app. pt. 9), 200; Coxe, *Marlborough*, 1:385; Churchill, *Marlborough*, 1:842–43; Atkinson, *Marlborough*, 214.

10. Add. MS 9114, 80b–81, 105; Parker, *Memoirs*, 36; Milner, *Journal*, 112; Kane, *Campaigns*, 56. Marlborough (to Harley, Aug. 14, 1704, Murray, *Dispatches*, 1:391) says the allied tents were left standing.

11. Add. MS 9114, 84–85; Murray, *Dispatches*, 1:398; Dalton, "Blenheim," 1076; Lediard, *Marlborough*, 1:367; Milner, *Journal*, 113.

12. One sympathizes with Chaplain General Hare's complaint that "for want of paper I can give you but a short account of the greatest victory that has been won in the memory of man," HMC, *Hare MS* (14th Report, pt. 9), 200. Parker, *Memoirs*, 37; Kane, *Campaigns*, 57; Lediard, *Marlborough*, 1:365; *Lives of the Two Illustrious Generals*, 72.

13. Add. MS 9114, 102b, makes the French 82 battalions and 146 squadrons, and counts the allies as 66 battalions and 160 squadrons. At a nominal strength of 500 men per battalion and 150 per squadron, the French and the Bavarians numbered almost 63,000 and the allies 57,000. Three months into the campaign, actual numbers will have been substantially fewer, but the French superiority of numbers (and, at this juncture, of reputation) was proportionately the same. Orkney measured an even wider disparity: between the 66 battalions and 170 squadrons of the allies and, "as Marshall Tallard told me himself," the 87 battalions and 150 squadrons of the French and Bavarians, "Letters," 307. Lediard, *Marlborough*, 1:366, gives the French 4,000 more troops than the allies. For the armies' deployment, see Lediard,

Marlborough, 1:362; Hamilton, *Guards*, 1: plan 14; D'Ivoy's map in *JRUSI* 42, no. 2; Coxe, *Marlborough*, 1:381 and *Atlas*, #6, 8, 9; Churchill, *Marlborough*, 1:846, 849, 850. Junkelmann, *Höchstädt*, 41, 53, makes the two sides equal in numbers, at 53,000 each.

14. Marlborough to Harley, Aug. 14, 1704, *Dispatches*, 1:391; Mérode-Westerloo, *Memoirs*, 166.

15. Add. MS 9114, 102b–103; *Dispatches*, 1:399–400; Churchill, *Marlborough*, 1:847; De La Colonie, *Chronicles*, 225–26.

16. Orkney, "Letters," 308; Milner, *Journal*, 114; De La Colonie, *Chronicles*, 225; Mérode-Westerloo, *Memoirs*, 168; Lediard, *Marlborough*, 1:370. Today, the Nebel-bach appears a minor obstacle, confined within artificial banks and straight as a string in the plain, shoal and meandering in the upcountry. But, as Louis Laguerre's Marlborough House murals depict, in 1704, beyond its boggy banks, the stream put infantry in up to midchest and horses up to the withers. These depths were ample to break up the linear formations of the allies and to drown the unfortunate, Junkelmann, *Höchstädt*, 40, 42–53, 54, 60. Smaller streams, such as the Meulwagen, and extensive swamps have been filled in recent times.

17. Lediard, *Marlborough*, 1:371; De La Colonie, *Chronicles*, 225–26. The French generals, writing to Michel de Chamillart, minister of war, on Aug. 30, 1704 (Lediard, *Marlborough*, 1:425–26), confirm this as the disposition of Tallard's first line but assert that the second line had a more conventional configuration, with infantry in the center. Presumably, these troops supplied the fourteen-battalion garrison of Oberklau and the nine or ten battalions that perished on the hill crest.

18. Lediard, *Marlborough*, 1:374, 426–28; De La Colonie, *Chronicles*, 225–26.

19. De La Colonie, *Chronicles*, 227; Add. MS 9114, 87; Murray, *Dispatches*, 1:399–400; Lediard, *Marlborough*, 1:369; Coxe, *Marlborough*, 1:395.

20. Marlborough to Harley, Aug. 14, 1704, Murray, *Dispatches*, 1:391; Johnson, "Letters of Noyes," 148; HMC, *Hare MS* (14th Report, pt. 9), 200, 201; Add. MS 9114, 87b–88b; Murray, *Dispatches*, 1:400. The guns and the duke are appropriately juxtaposed in the view from the eastern slope above the Nebel reproduced in the *Blenheim* tapestry, Wace, *Marlborough Tapestries*, #42. See also Laguerre's murals in Marlborough House, Pall Mall, reproduced in Junkelmann, *Höchstädt*, 44, and photographs of artillery details, 51. See also the group portrait of Marlborough's staff at Culford Hall, Junkelmann, *Höchstädt*, 62n.

21. Mérode-Westerloo, *Memoirs*, 168.

22. De La Colonie, *Chronicles*, 226; Alexander Spotswood to John Spotswood, Apr. 17, 1705, Cappon, "Correspondence," 223. Spotswood rejoiced that he had not fallen into the hands of the butchering surgeons (but his recovery took more than a year). Farquhar, *Recruiting Officer*, act IV, scene ii: Butcher: "True, I am a butcher." Sergeant Kite: "And a surgeon you will be. The employments differ only in the name." Lediard, *Marlborough*, 1:371. For the preparation and delivery of fascines by the cavalry, see the "Attaque" from Marlborough's (first) tapestry set, Wace, *Marlborough Tapestries*, #25. From Orkney's set, see #28 55, 70 and plate 2.

23. Milner, *Journal*, 115; Lediard, *Marlborough*, 1:371; Add. MS 9114, 88b–89; Murray, *Dispatches*, 1:401; Blackadder, *Diary*, 22; Churchill, *Marlborough*, 1:853.

24. HMC, *Hare MS* (14th Report, pt. 9), 200; Add. MS 9114, 90. Parker, *Memoirs*, 39, times the attack at 1:15 p.m., whereas Churchill, *Marlborough*, 1:851, has Rowe's brigade seizing the mills and drawing up before Blenheim at 10:00 a.m.

25. See also Add. MS 9114, 91–92; Murray, *Dispatches*, 1:402; Orkney, "Letters," 308; Kane, *Campaigns*, 58; Milner, *Journal*, 116; Dalton, *Army Lists*, 5, pt. 2, 27.

26. Add. MS 9114, 93–93b; Murray, *Dispatches*, 1:403; Coxe, *Marlborough*, 1:401; Parker, *Memoirs*, 40–41.

27. Mérode-Westerloo, *Memoirs*, 169; De La Colonie, *Chronicles*, 227; Lediard, *Marlborough*, 1:429.

28. Dalton, *Army Lists*, 5:239; pt. 2, 51, 52; Webb, *Governors-General*, #207, 131, 208, p. 501. On these and the other imperial officers of the 16th—Clayton, governor of Gibraltar; Doucett, lieutenant governor of Annapolis Royal, N. S.; Irvine, successively governor of Hull and Barbados; and R. Handasyde, lieutenant governor of Minorca and Spotswood's successor as quartermaster general, Scotland—see "Index of Persons," in Webb, *Governors-General*. Maj. Gen. Sir F. Maurice, *The 16th Foot: A History of the Bedfordshire and Hampshire Regiment* (London, 1931), 2, 5–12, 23, 27–31. See also "Epilogue" below.

29. Parker, *Memoirs*, 39–40; Lediard, *Marlborough*, 1:376; Maurice, *16th*, 25–31; Johnson, "Letters of Noyes," 148; Add. MS 9114, 93b; Kane, *Campaigns*, 58–59.

30. Parker, *Memoirs*, 41n; Mérode-Westerloo, *Memoirs*, 169; Kane, *Campaigns*, 60.

31. Add. MS 9114, 93b–94b; Murray, *Dispatches*, 1:401–3; Johnson, "Letters of Noyes," 148, sees this development beginning as early as 1:20; Orkney, "Letters," 308. In retrospect, all observers agreed that it had been a fatal error to let Marlborough's men advance across the Nebel unresisted save by artillery: HMC, *Hare MS* (14th Report, pt. 9), 201; Mérode-Westerloo, *Memoirs*, 171; Milner, *Journal*, 117; Kane, *Campaigns*, 57, 58, 61. De La Colonie, *Chronicles*, 226–27, suggests that Tallard simply lacked time enough to move his men down to the bank of the Nebel.

32. Mérode-Westerloo, *Memoirs*, 171–72; Orkney, "Letters," 308; Add. MS 9114, 94b–95; Orkney to Hamilton, Aug. 14, 1704, GD 406/1/7245, SRO; Milner, *Journal*, 117.

33. Add. MS 9114, 95; Murray, *Dispatches*, 1:401; Milner, *Journal*, 119–20.

34. HMC, *Hare MS* (14th Report, app. pt. 9), 200; Johnson, "Letters of Noyes," 148; Parker, *Memoirs*, 39. For the desperate combat on the allied right, see the 1708 painting in Junkelmann, *Höchstädt*, 57.

35. Add. MS 9114, 95; Murray, *Dispatches*, 1:404–5; Johnson, "Letters of Noyes," 148.

36. Milner, *Journal*, 118; Lediard, *Marlborough*, 1:429.

37. Milner, *Journal*, 119; the French generals in Lediard, *Marlborough*, 1:430. Forty-one of the eighty-two French and Bavarian battalions were committed to the defense of these two villages. Twelve more were tied up in Lutzingen.

38. See the maps in Churchill, *Marlborough*, 1:859 and Junkelmann, *Höchstädt*, 56, 59; the comments of the French generals in Lediard, *Marlborough*, 1:429–30; Parker, *Memoirs*, 42; Add. MS 9114, 97–97b.

39. The author of the *Lives of the Two Illustrious Generals* heard this exchange (77). Kane, *Campaigns*, 60; Add. MS 9114, 97b–98; Murray, *Dispatches*, 1:405–6; Marsin to Louis XIV, in Lediard, *Marlborough*, 1:410; Milner, *Journal*, 118; Johnson, "Letters of Noyes," 148. Note, however, that Lediard, *Marlborough*, 1:380, concluded that Marlborough had been absorbed by the crisis at Oberklau and that the decisive cavalry charge had been organized by Ingoldsby and executed by Lumley and Hompesch (377). The eyewitness testimonies of the author of the *Lives* and of Add. MS 9114 are preferred here.

40. Milner, *Journal*, 119; Add. MS 9114, 97–98; Johnson, "Letters of Noyes," 149; Parker, *Memoirs*, 42. See the dreadfully detailed illustration in Junkelmann, *Höchstädt*, 50.

41. Add. MS 9114, 98–99; Murray, *Dispatches*, 1:406; Marlborough to Hedges, August 17, Murray, *Dispatches*, 1:413–14; HMC, *Hare MS* (14th Report, app. pt. 9), 200. Map in Junkelmann, *Höchstädt*, 61.

42. A copy of Marlborough's note now rests in a glass case, its informality incongruous in the French baroque splendours of the Blenheim Palace state rooms. It is reproduced in facsimilie by Churchill, *Marlborough*, 1:864, by Coxe, *Marlborough*, 1:412–13, and is partially photographed in Junkelmann, *Höchstädt*, 64.

43. Parke to the lords commissioners of trade and plantations, Aug. 4, 1707, *CSPC, 1706–1708*, #1077, p. 519.

44. Davenant to Stepney, Frankfort, Aug. 6, 1704; Stepney to Stanhope, Hague, Aug. 22, 1704, Add. MS 7066, 15; 7069, 171, 172–73; Davenant to Marlborough, Aug. 15, 1704, Add. MS 61363, 1378; Churchill, *Marlborough*, 1:860–70, 960n: Trevelyan, *Blenheim*, 409–11; Coxe, *Marlborough*, 1:414n; 2:38. See Sir Geoffrey Kneller's portrait of Parke with the queen's miniature, and the battle, now in the royal collection, reproduced in Verney, *Blenheim*, 161. The Closterman portrait is reproduced and discussed in Miller, *Parke*, 143. Add. MS 7066, 15; Add. MS 7069, 171–72; Lediard, *Marlborough*, 1:454; Taylor, *Marlborough*, 1:231, 232; de Beer, *Evelyn Diary*, 5:574; Luttrell, *Brief Relation*, Aug. 10, 12, 19, 24, 1704, 5:454, 457, 458, where it was announced that "Her majestie has been pleased to promise the government of Virginia to collonel Parks, in the room of collonel Nicholson, who will be removed." So Nicholson understood (CO 5/1314, #44), as he did also Parke's subsequent disappointment and Orkney's success.

45. Nicholson's proclamation of Dec. 15, 1704, is in W. P. Palmer et al., eds., *Calendar of Virginia State Papers, 1652–1781* (Richmond, VA, 1875–95), 1:86; H. R. McIlwaine and Wilmer M. Hall, eds., *Executive Journals of the Council of Colonial Virginia* (Richmond, VA, 1925–45), 2:413, 444. "Blenheims" were thereupon built across tidewater Virginia. William B. McGroarty, "Four Virginia Blenheims . . . ," *Tyler's Quarterly* 29 (1947–48): 241–48, discusses some of them. The Virginia burgesses chartered a Marlborough on the Potomac. I am indebted to the late Dr. Ruth Anne Bourne for sharing with me her manuscript biography of Daniel Parke and for her valued correspondence and conversation on Virginia in this period.

46. Johnson, "Letters of Noyes," 148; Add. MS 9114, 95b–96b; Murray, *Dispatches*, 1:404–5; Marlborough to Godolphin, Aug. [3/]14, 1704, Snyder, *Correspondence*, 350.

47. Add. MS 9114, 99; Murray, *Dispatches*, 1:406; McKay, *Eugene*, 86–87; Milner, *Journal*, 123.

48. Add. MS 9114, 99–100; Murray, *Dispatches*, 1:406–7.

49. De La Colonie, *Chronicles*, 227, attributes the withdrawal of the elector and Marsin to the menace of the thirty squadrons under Hompesch that Marlborough had ordered up against their flank.

50. Add. MS 9114, 100; Murray, *Dispatches*, 1:407; Parker, *Memoirs*, 42–43; Kane, *Campaigns*, 61.

51. Besides Add. MS 9114, 99b–100, see Orkney "Letters," 309, and the account quoted in Edward Almack, *The History of the Second Dragoons Royal Scots Greys* (London, 1908), 27.

52. Add. MS 9114, 100–100b. Sutton, formerly a candidate for the Jamaica command, afterward a competitor for the government of New York, settled for the lieutenant governorship of Hull. Dalton, *Army Lists*, 5: pt. 2, 42, 43, Webb, *Governors-General*, 482, 497. Sutton was prostrated for four months by his exertions at Blenheim: Memorial of Sutton, Feb. 11, 1705, and further, undated, statement of his case, Blenheim MS, A.I.30, A.I.34. The French generals said that Clérambault committed suicide, Lediard, *Marlborough*, 1:383, 431–32.

53. Add. MS 9114, 100b; Murray, *Dispatches*, 1:407; Almack, *Second Dragoons*, 26–27; Johnston, "Scots Army," 4.

54. Add. MS 9114, 101; Murray, *Dispatches*, 1:406–7; Orkney, "Letters," 309; Coxe, *Marlborough*, 1:415. Churchill, *Marlborough*, 1:868, says Orkney had eight battalions. Orkney to Hamilton, Aug. 14, 1704, GD 406/1/7245, SRO.

55. Orkney to Hamilton, Aug. 14, 1704, GD 406/1/7245, SRO; Orkney, "Letters," 309; Johnson, "Letters of Noyes," 148. One of Marlborough's aides, Lt. Col. Henry Durrell, a captain of the 1st Guards who was promoted adjutant general of the forces immediately after the battle, did arrive with exactly this promise from Marlborough, but not until 9:00 p.m. The confident anticipation of the duke's intent by his staff is usual and instructive about his influence on them.

56. Add. MS 9114, 101b–102, Murray, *Dispatches*, 1:408; Mérode-Westerloo, *Memoirs*, 169, reports the event but, as he takes every chance to do, says that the French had fired the village themselves. So they "were burnt alive amidst the ashes of this smaller Troy of their own making." On the Denonville epsiode, see also Lediard, *Marlborough*, 1:383, 416, 432; Almack, *Second Dragoons*, 27; Trevelyan, *Blenheim*, 1:393–94. Orkney's remarks were reported in Buckley, *Memoirs of Ailesbury*, 571, and see Orkney, "Letters," 310.

57. Orkney, "Letters," 310; Johnson, "Letters of Noyes," 149. HMC, *Hare MS* (14th Report, app. pt. 9), 200, says that these prisoners constituted "the whole body of foot that came with Tallard." In fact, Tallard had forty battalions but, counting the ten slaughtered by the allies during their attack on the center of Tallard's line, and the three cut down in the left attack, Marlborough's men had indeed accounted for Tallard's entire infantry. Milner, *Journal*, 121; De La Colonie, *Chronicles*, 221. That the officer-prisoners were Orkney's is seen in his subsequent disposition of the paroles: Harley to Marlborough, July 20/31, 1705, Add. MS 61123, 176. Galway asked Marlborough to exchange some of the French soldiers for English officers captured in Portalegre, especially Captain J[asper] Clayton, the executive officer who had reorganized Stewart's regiment and who subsequently was commissioned governor of Gibraltar, Hedges to Marlbrough, Jan. 16, 1705[/5], Blenheim MS 1:18; Galway to Hedges, Nov. 30, 1704, Blenheim MS F.2.16, Add. MS 61121, 62, 74. Denonville to Orkney, Mar. 29, 1706, Add. MS 61162, 95; Ingoldsby to Davenant, Aug. 13, 1704, Add. MS 4740, 266; Tallard, who witnessed the surrender from Marlborough's coach, termed it France's darkest hour, Add. MS 7069, 173.

58. Johnson, "Letters of Noyes," 149.

59. Orkney, "Letters," 310–11. Orkney's favor with the Marlborough circle was enhanced when his letters were widely read (but *not* published) in London, E. Burnet to Sarah, duchess of Marlborough, Nov. 3, 1704, Add. MS 61458, 21b. Lady Orkney took the occasion to make up her quarrel with Sarah: E. Orkney to S. Marlborough, Aug. 4, 1704, and reply, Add. MS 61674, 112, 113. Sarah was not convinced of the sincerity of the Orkneys' support for her husband. Johnson, "Letters of Noyes," 150; Parker, *Memoirs*, 44.

60. Add. MS 61298, 65, 67, 81, 83. On Wade's work as commander in chief, Scotland, see Bruce Lenman, *The Jacobite Risings in Britain, 1689–1746* (London, 1980), 221–23. The survivors of the American Regiment's Virginia battalion served with Wade.

61. Marlborough to Godolphin, Aug. [3/]14, 1704, Blenheim MS A.I.14, Snyder, *Correspondence*, 349; Add. MS 9114, 104; *Lives of the Two Illustrious Generals*, 73; Add. MS 61321, 12; Orkney to Hamilton, Aug. 14, 1704, GD 406/1/7245, SRO.

62. Add. MS 9114, 105b; *Lives of the Two Illustrious Generals*, 75.

63. Marlborough to Godolphin, and to the duchess, Aug. [3/]14, 1704, Blenheim MS A.I.14, E.2, Snyder, *Correspondence*, 350–51; same to Godolphin, [Aug. 22/]Sept. 2, 1704, Snyder, *Correspondence*, 361; Add. MS 61363, 147. R. Ingoldsby to Davenant, Aug. 13, 1704, NS: "Yesterday we attaqued the french in theyr camp with that success that has not been heard off in our Eage," Add. MS 4740, 266. On Aug. 16, Cardonnel reported that the number of prisoners, presently 10,000–12,000, increased hourly. "I wish we had some of them in our Plantations for I don't know how else we can dispose of them," Add. MS 7063, 68.

64. Farquhar, *Recruiting Officer*, act II, scene i, reflects such country gentlemen as J. Coke, who rejoiced to Marlborough, June 20, 1704, that after years of paying 4 or 5 shillings in the pound "to no good end," now every campaign brought victory. Marlborough to Godolphin, and to the duchess, Aug. [17/]28, 1704, Snyder, *Correspondence*, 359, 360; Gregg, *Anne*, 184, 188; Queen Anne to Marlborough, Windsor, Aug. 21, 1704, on "the good news Colonel Parke brought me yesterday," Blenheim MS B.11.22, Add. MS 61101, 172, Beatrice Curtis Browne, ed., *The Letters and Diplomatic Instructions of Queen Anne* (London, 1935, 1968), 149–50. The political assessments, domestic and imperial, of Charles Davenant are quoted from his letter to Marlborough, Aug. 15, 1704, Add. MS 61363, 138, and see R. Gwyne to Davenant, Sept. 11, 1704, Add. MS 4741, 18, and Davenport to Stepney, Aug. 6, 1704: "Ye Duke of Marlborough has beyond all dispute saved the Empire," Add. MS 7066, 15. See the far grander conclusions of an English statesman, Sir Winston Churchill, *Marlborough*, 1:844.

65. Add. MS 9114, 103b, 106, 107b, 113, records the results of the author's canvas of the French generals and other officers under the orders of General Churchill:

13,000–15,000 soldier prisoners, 1,000–1,200 officers, and [18] generals captured; an equal number of casualties inflicted; for a total of 28,000–34,000. Captured French dispatches put the number of casualties at 40,000, when the losses of Marsin and the elector are included, Add. MS 7063, 68b, 70. Thousands more deserted to the allies. Milner, *Journal*, 124–26, makes the French and Bavarian force at Blenheim 60,000 and accounts for 38,606 casualties from it. Churchill, *Marlborough*, 1:882, calculated the French investment in Germany as 150,000 men in 1703 and 1704 and estimated that only 16,000 survived to flee across the Rhine ahead of the pursuit led by Marlborough and Eugene.

66. On Malaga, see Capt. Alfred Thayer Mahan, *The Influence of Sea Power upon History, 1660–1783* (New York, 1890, 1957), 186–89; J. H. Owen, *The War at Sea under Queen Anne, 1701–1708* (Cambridge, 1938), 96–98. Rooke was criticized (to Marlborough) for not redistributing the fleet's munitions before the battle, leaving so many battleships toothless, Add. MS 61363, 165–66. The minutes of the council of war, Aug. 14, 1704, after which Rooke withdrew to Gibraltar, are in Sunderland's Malaga papers, Add. MS 61590, 82. On Hamilton's trial and request, see HMC, *House of Lords MS*, n.s., 6: 147, 188; HMC, *Portland MS*, 10:38; Charnock, *Biographia Navalis*, 3:16. Orkney to Marlborough, Oct. 19, 1704, from Wisbaden, whence, as ordered, Orkney reported to Marlborough on the measures he was taking to restore his health after Blenheim, Blenheim MS, F.2.18, Add. MS 61162, 89. On lord Archibald's previous promotion to captain in Orkney's Royal Scots in the Schellenberg promotion list, see same, June 30, 1704, Add. MS 61162, 85. See also the duke of Hamilton to Anne, duchess of Hamilton, Aug. 18, 1704, and reply, Aug. 21, GD 406/1/7985, 7100, SRO. Astutely, the duchess advised against publishing Orkney's letters. She knew better than to dilute Marlborough's glory, so serviceable to the government, GD 406/1/7985, 7102, SRO (see n. 59 above).

67. Marlborough to Godolphin, Aug. 21, 1704, Snyder, *Correspondence*, 353; Milner, *Journal*, 127–28, makes the allied losses 12,484. Sir Charles Hara to Marlborough, Aug. 18, 1704, Add. MS 61307, 127; Orkney to Hamilton, Aug. 14, 1704, GD 406/1/7245, SRO; Dalton, *Army Lists*, 5: pt. 2, 33–38.

Chapter 4. Greater Britain

1. Lediard, *Marlborough*, 1:473; Gregg, *Anne*, 64–65, 195. As Col. Berkeley of princess Anne's Dragoons, lord Fitzharding had been a principal—with prince George and lord Churchill—in the desertion from king James at Salisbury. When the news reached Whitehall, Barbara Berkeley became the sole companion of princess Anne and lady Churchill in their escape from the cockpit: Webb, *Lord Churchill's Coup*, 148.

2. Lediard, *Marlborough*, 1:469, 473–78; Churchill, *Marlborough*, 1:915–17; Coxe, *Marlborough*, 2: 73–74; HMC, *Bath MS*, 1:65. David Green, *Blenheim Palace* (London, 1951).

3. On the commons address to the queen for a Blenheim bounty and the disposition of the money by Marlborough, see Harley to Marlborough, Nov. 1/14, 1704, Blenheim MS F.2.16, Add. MS 61123, 96. The MS bounty list is in Add. MS 61327, 73–83. It is printed, with annotations, by Dalton, *Army Lists*, 5: pt. 2, 1–73. Marlborough assigned his £600 as captain and colonel of the 1st Guards to the regiment's widows' and orphans' fund. Orkney, Hunter, Pitt, and Spotswood were the future American governors general who drew bounty as members of Marlborough's staff, as well as for regimental service and for wounds. See also Coxe, *Marlborough*, 2:66. Alexander to John Spotswood, London, Apr. 17, 1705, Cappon, "Correspondence," 211, and see 223; List of the Bounty Mony, Add. MS 61327, 76, 81; Dalton, *Army Lists*, 5:98; pt. 2, 1, 45; Luttrell, *Brief Relation*, 5:274, 378, 553.

4. Marlborough to Hedges, Camp at Berncastel, Nov. 3, 1704; same to Shrimpton, Mar. 20, 1704; Murray, *Dispatches*, 1:526, 609; Webb, *Governors-General*, 476–78. Shrimpton to Marlborough, Gibraltar, Feb. 3, 1705[/6], OS, Add. MS 61308, 16. The identity with Tangier was made manifest by the use of the Tangier establishment as a model for the garrison of the new conquest: Hedges to Marlborough, Oct. 27, 1704, Blenheim MS F.2.16, Add. MS 61121, 25. See Shrimpton to Marlborough, Oct. 3, 1704, June 8, 1705, Add. MS 61121, 26, 31, on the economic potential of Gibraltar and Dutch jealousy of English control of the conquest. Marlborough had also to respond to Erle's report (June 9, 1705, Add. MS 61158, 19b) that the ordnance had no funds for Gibraltar, Peterborough's American expedition having put it in debt. The Gibraltar estimates, forward contracts, and the board's plea to Marlborough to put the needs of the ordnance before parliament are in Add. MS 61165, 55, 65–66. Having been at the capture of Gibraltar, lord Archibald Hamilton also followed Leake to its relief. Lord Archibald to the duke of Hamilton, Apr. 5, 1705, GD 406/1/7228, SRO. On Tangier, garrison culture, and Churchill, see Webb, *Governors-General*, #172–86, "Index of Places"; and Webb, *Lord Churchill's Coup*, 20–25.

5. Blenheim MS, A.I.30, Add. MS 61291, 124, 126; Dalton, *Army Lists*, 5:188, 269. Even the orphans of officers lost in the 1702 American expedition were nominated to Marlborough for commissions in the new levies: Blenheim MS A.1.31. There was also some raising for rank, when a gentleman was politically acceptable and had "a good Interest . . . for raising of men," as Stanhope and Stanwix put it, Add. MS 61283, 180. On the Wheeler-Foulkes expedition, see Webb, "Blathwayt," 381–94.

6. Blenheim MS, A.I.30. Dalton, *Army Lists*, 5:68, 69, 111, 166, shows Jones's steps: captain, July 2, 1702; brevet (by Marlborough) major, Aug. 1, 1702; bt. (by Marlborough); lieutenant colonel, Aug. 11, 1705.

7. Garth to prince George and two states of Maj. Garth's case, in Blenheim MS F.2.23, F.2.20, A.1.30, Add. MS 61288, 17, 19, 21.

8. Maj. Gen. Holt's Meml., Add. MS 61289, 158. See other cases of "West Indian" service recognized by Marlborough in Blenheim MS A.I.31. Alternatively, to have refused American service was "a great fault," only to be redeemed by the most dangerous and successful service in another theater or by special and scarce skills, such as engineering: Galway to Hedges, Nov. 30, 1704, Blenheim MS F.2.16, Add. MS 61121, 626.

9. Burgess to Cardonnel, Feb. 9, 1705, Blenheim MS, A.I.30, Add. MS 61284, 130–31; Dalton, *Army Lists*, 6:228n13; Dalton, *George the First's Army*, 2:129, 429; Luttrell, *Brief Relation*, 2:41, 43, 44, 61, 63, 68–69, 312; 4:44, 61, 63, 68, 312; 5:550; William, earl Cowper, *The Private Diary*, ed. E. C. Hawtrag (Roxburgh Club, 1933), Feb. 17, 1715; Webb, *Governors-General*, #127.

10. By 1707, Burgess, back in England, applied to Marlborough through intermediaries "because my unhappy Circumstances oblige me at present to be Incognito." He added Argyll and Rivers to his recommenders and found that Sunderland "was pleas'd to take my memorial into his own hands and. . . . sollicit my business himself" with Marlborough: Burgess to [Undersecretary] Thomas Hopkins, Nov. 30, Dec. 10, 21, 1707, Add. MS 61589, 81, 83. His nomination to the Massachusetts command recalls the equally inappropriate designation of Piercy Kirke. Contempt for the puritan colony ran deep in the imperial psyche.

11. On Shute, see Webb, *Governors-General*, #128; Cardonnel to Sweet, nr. Maestricht, May 24, 1703, Blenheim MS, 27:154, and see 12; Dalton, *Army Lists*, 5:168; pt. 2, 16, 17. N.B. Shute's meml. to Sunderland, after Feb. 16, 1709, Add. MS 61589, 120; Wood to same, Oct. 19, 1707, Add. MS 61590, 143–44. Dalton, *Army Lists*, 5: pt. 2, 16, 17; Webb, *Governors-General*, 493; Richard R. Johnson, *Adjustment to Empire; The New England Colonies, 1675–1715* (New Brunswick, NJ, 1981), 353–56.

12. Endorsed "Q Anne to Ld Gd;" dated "Hampton Court, Tuesday/ between four & five aclock," Folger Library, v.b. 267 (interleaved Routh *Burnet's History*), dated as May 1, 1705, by Gregg, *Anne*, 235, 237; Dalton, *Army Lists*, 5:7; 6:365; Marlborough's lists of Hill's regiment, July 4, 1705, May 28, 1709, Add. MS 61319, 137, 143.

13. Handasyde to Marlborough, Jamaica, Feb. 27, 1704/5, Blenheim MS, A.I.26, Add. MS 61308, 21; Add. MS 61283, 122.

14. See also Handasyde to Marlborough, Nov. 20, 1705, Blenheim MS A.I.26; same to commissioners of trade and plantations, June 19, Dec. 17, 1704, Feb. 27, 1705, CO 138/11, 308, 366, 389–90, and see the correspondence of the regimental agent with the paymaster general on the finances of the 22d in Jamaica, and on the provision of barracks in Jamaica on the English and Irish model, CO 138/11, 335, 337, 439, 455–59. *CSPC*, 1704–5, #557, 603, 902, 1459, contain extracts from some of this material. The question of Jamaica barracks and many other issues of fortification, garrisoning, and ordnance for the American provinces are detailed in Dartmouth's report to the lords, as from the commissioners, Nov. 30, 1704, Leo Francis Stock, ed., *Proceedings and Debates of the British Parliament respecting North America* (Washington, DC, 1937): 3:63–85. See, on the Jamaica issues, Stock, *Proceedings* 3:79–80. Handasyde to the commissioners, Jan. 29, 1706, CO 138/12, 73, and see 123–26; *CSPC*, 1704–1705, #399; 740, I, III. See generally Caroline Robbins, *The Eighteenth Century Commonwealthman* (Cambridge, 1959). J. G. A. Pocock, "Machiavelli, Harrington, and English Political Ideologies in the Eighteenth Century," *WMQ*, 3d ser., 22 (1965): 549–83; Bernard Bailyn, *The Ideological Origins of the American Revolution* (Cambridge, MA, 1967).

15. Handasyde to the commissioners, Dec. 17, 1704, CO 138/11, 366; same, Mar. 31, 1708, CO 138/12, 279–89. Handasyde had to accept the tack to the finance bill, "for the life of my Regiment depends on it." Then he asked the plantations commissioners to recommend the queen's veto, CO 138/11, 438; *CSPC*, 1704–1705, #1459. Details of the country program are in CO 138/11, 384–386, 405; *CSPC*, 1704–1705, #929.

16. Handasyde to the commissioners, Dec. 31, 1704, CO 138/11, 379–80; *CSPC, 1704–1705*, #754. Same, June 19, July 28, Dec. 12, 1704, Nov. 20, 1705, Apr. 1, Aug. 2, 1706, CO 138/11, 307, 328–30, 364–65, 438, 466, CO 138/12, 28; *CSPC, 1704–1705*, #400, 1459. Handasyde to the commissioners, Mar. 31, 1708, CO 138/12, 283–84. See Nicholson's identical complaints about the Virginia "Creoles," Webb, "Nicholson," 536–37; CO 5/1312, #19, CO 5/1313, #16(1).

17. Handasyde to commissioners, Dec. 31, 1704. CO 138/11, 380; same, Sept. 17, 1704, Dec. 27, 1706, Mar. 8, 1706/7, CO 138/11, 347, CO 138/12, 63, 79–80; Handasyde to Marlborough, Nov. 20, 1705, Blenheim MS A.I.26.

18. CO 138/11, 367–68; CO 138/12, 73, 79–80, 86, 109–16; Handasyde to commissioners, Apr. 1, Oct. 25, 1706, CO 138/11, 468, 490; same to Hedges, Nov. 20, 1705, CO 138/11, 367–68, 401–3, 431–32; *CSPC, 1704–1705*, #739 (which reads this arrangement as disadvantageous to Handasyde), 1168, 1262, 1334. Handasyde's proposal implicitly had the backing of both the other two regiments (Livesay's in Jamaica and Whetham's in the Leeward Islands), which wanted to be relieved. The Jamaica lobby testified to the privy council "that they thot one Regiment consisting of Eight hundred men, including Officers, would be a Sufficient number to defend that Island." Enclosed in Whetham to Marlborough, Jan. 24, 1704, Add. MS 61297, 103.

19. Handasyde to commissioners, Feb. 16, 1705/6, CO 138/11, 451, noted that his brevet as colonel from king William dated to June 28, 1701, the time of his departure for America. His commission for the regiment was signed by the queen on June 20, 1702, so that "I am now an old Colonel." Same, Aug. 6, 1706, CO 138/12, 25–26. List of the General Officers, Add. MS 61321, 12.

20. Handasyde to commissioners, July 28, 1704; July 18, Aug. 12, 1705; May 12, July 18, Aug. 12, 1706, CO 138/11, 321, 427–29, 433–34, 478; CO 138/12, 12; *CSPC, 1704–1705*, #484, 1262, 1303; Webb, *Governors-General*, #60, p. 481.

21. Handasyde to commissioners, Dec. 17, 1704, June 11, 1705; CO 138/11, 359–61, 403.

22. Commissioners to Handasyde, May 30, Sept. 26, 1706, CO 138/11, 475, CO 138/12, 32; Handasyde to commissioners, June 11, Aug. 12, Nov. 20, 1705, Sept. 16, 1706, CO 138/11, 401–2, 434, 437, CO 138/12, 33. On Roger Handasyde, see Dalton, *George the First's Army*, 1:162. Capt. Thomas Belasyse to Marlborough, n.d., Add. MS 61283, 122. St. John reported to Marlborough, June 14/25, 1706, the arrival of Livesay's and Whetham's officer cadres from the West Indies: Blenheim MS A.I.46.

23. Belhaven to Marlborough [Dec. 1704?], Add. MS 61136, 17–18; Geo. Ramsay to Marlborough, Edinburgh, Jan. 16, 1705, ibid., 19–20, and see Add. MS 61291, 118; Maitland to Marlborough, Feb. 10, 1704/5, Add. MS 61136, 22; Maitland to Marlborough, Memorial, Blenheim MS A.I.34; Marlborough to Godolphin, Hague, Dec. 19, 1704, Snyder, *Correspondence*, 408–9n. On Blenheim and Scotland, see Harley to Marlborough, Aug. 15/26, 1704, Blenheim MS F.2.16, Add. MS 61123, 55, 62.

24. Orkney to duchess Anne, Aug. 26; Selkirk to same, Oct. 14, 17, 28, 1704, GD 406/1/8047, 7238, 7240, 7239, 7142, SRO; Orkney to Selkirk, Jan. 11, 1705/6, MS 1033, 13b, NLS; same, Camp before Menin, Aug. 9, 1706, GD 406/1/9113, SRO. Orkney to Selkirk, Feb. 2, 1706, MS 1033, 16b, NLS; Wace, *Tapestries*, 49, 52n, 82, 123, 124.

25. Murray, *Dispatches*, 1:595; Marlborough to Godolphin, Oct. 6, 1705, Snyder, *Correspondence*, 500, 504. Borthwick and Cranstoun to Marlborough, Blenheim MS A.I.34; Leven to Marlborough, Edinburgh, Sept. 11, Dec. 20, 1705, Jan. 24, 1705/6, Add. MS 61136, 27–28, 31–32, 41–42; Murray to same, n.d., Add. MS 61291, 165. HMC, *Mar and Kellie MS*, 246–49. Leven was named a commissioner for the union, HMC, *Mar and Kellie MS*, 251, and see 252; Riley, *Union*, 255; Johnston, "Scots Army," 19. Selkirk to duchess Anne, Oct. 14, 1704, GD 406/1/7238; Orkney to Selkirk, Nov. 19, 1705, MS 1033, 7–10b, SRO.

26. Marlborough to Godolphin, Oct. 6, 23, Blenheim MS A.I.37, Snyder, *Correspondence*, 500, 504. Marlborough wanted to advance his own staff officers to the command of the new Scots regiments but here, as elsewhere, he had difficulty controlling "the Scots affairs, so subject to alteration," Marlborough to Tiviot, Mar. 25, 1705, Murray, *Dispatches*, 1:613. Lediard, *Marlborough*, 5:534, 555–56. See lady Marlborough's scathing attack on Arygll's opportunism, Add. MS 61101, 161–62. Orkney is quoted to Selkirk, Nov. 19, 1705, MS 1033, 9b, SRO. See also Luttrell, *Brief Relation*, 6:626; Blenheim MS, A.I.34; A. I.28.

27. See also Harley to Marlborough, Apr. 27/May 11, 1705, Add. MS 61123, 142b; Leven to Marlborough, Sept. 11, Dec. 20; Lothian to same, Dec. 8, 27, 1705, Blenheim MS A.1.

28. Orkney to Selkirk, Nov. 19, 1705, MS 1033, 10, SRO; William Ferguson, *Scotland: 1689 to the Present* (New York, 1968), 36–44; Riley, *Union*, 57–58, 98–101, 122, 126. Hamilton to duchess Anne, Dec. 29, 1704; Elizabeth, duchess of Argyll, to Hamilton, Apr. 10, 1705, GD 406/1/8071, 7150, SRO. The alien act was repealed in Dec. 1705 on news that Argyll had obtained a Scots act authorizing the queen to appoint commissioners to negotiate the union. Routh, *Burnet's History*, 5:246–47.

29. Marlborough to Leven, St. James's, Feb. 10; same to Carlisle, Feb. 15, 1705, Murray, *Dispatches*, 1:595–97; G. M. Trevelyan, *England under Queen Anne*, vol. 2, *Ramillies and the Union with Scotland* (London, 1932), 248. Murray, *Dispatches*, 1:595, 597; Anne R to Marlborough, June 12, 1705, Add. MS 61101, 78b. Gen. Thomas Erle, whom Marlborough had brought back from Ireland to be his lieutenant in the ordnance, supervised both the political and logistical functions of the office. Ordnance officers influenced election results. Erle passed their political reports on to Marlborough. Erle also obeyed Marlborough's orders to fill the armories of Berwick, Carlisle, and Hull against the expected troubles in Scotland: Erle to Marlborough, May 1, 18, 1705, Add. MS 61158, 14, 17. On the engineering survey, see the board of ordnance to Marlborough, May 22, 1705, Add. MS 61165, 112.

30. Maine's first entry in Marlborough's personnel records was in 1691 as lieutenant (and colonel) of Marlborough's (3d) Troop of the Horse Guards, Add. MS 61319, 12. Subsequently, Maine appeared in each of Marlborough's promotions lists. Marlborough to Godolphin, June 10/21, 1705, Blenheim MS A.I.37. Snyder, *Correspondence*, 445, has this in Blenheim MS A.I.14. Same to the duchess, June 10/21, 1705, Blenheim MS E.3, Snyder, *Correspondence*, 446; same to Godolphin, June 10/21, July 6, Sept. 10, 1705, Blenheim MS A.I.37, Snyder, *Correspondence*, 445, 454, 455. Luttrell, *Brief Relation*, 5:546; Snyder, *Correspondence*, 703n1, 427n. Maine to Marlborough:

June 30, 1704; Feb. 12, Aug. 2, 5, 1705; Aug. 2, 1707; May 2, 1708, Add. MS 61162, 84, 186, 192, 194, 198, 202; Dalton, *Army Lists*, 5:155, #18; 159; pt. 2, 1, #16.

31. Carlisle to Marlborough, Jan. 13, 1704/5, Add. MS 61308, 11. Stanwix's reward for Blenheim is recorded in Blenheim MS F.2.14, Add. MS 61298, 83. His commission as lieutenant governor of Carlisle is on the list of general officers' commissions ordered Apr. 10, 1705 (as are the governor and lieutenant governor of Chester), Add. MS 61321, 116; Dalton, *Army Lists*, 5:123, 6:182; Dalton, *George the First's Army*, 1:230; Luttrell, *Brief Relation*, 5:556. On Stanwix, see also Webb, *Governors-General*, #38.

32. Riley, *Union*, 146–47, 149–51; Harley to Marlborough, Apr. 27/May 11, 1705, Add. MS 61123, 142b. John Robertson, "Union, State, and Empire: The Britain of 1707 in Its European Setting," in Lawrence Stone, ed., *An Imperial State at War* (London, 1994), 238–39, 242–43; HMC, *Mar and Kellie MS*, 235, 238–39, 243–44, 258–59, 263–64. Lenman, *Jacobite Risings*, 82, calls Hamilton's act "the greatest double-cross of Scottish politics," a distinction indeed! Ferguson, *Scotland*, 46–47. Orkney to Selkirk, Jan. 11, Feb. 2, 1705/6, MS 1033, 14, 16, NLS; Hamilton to Selkirk, Jan. 26, Mar. 22, 1705/6, GD 406/1/7142, 7147, SRO. Riley, *Union*, 182–89; Davenport, *Treaties*, 3: #94; G. P. Insh, *Company of Scotland* (London, 1932), 65.

33. C. T. Atkinson, "Richards," *JSAHR* 46 (1968): 76–87; Richards to Marlborough, n.d., Add. MS 61294, 48; Marlborough to Godolphin, May 18/29, 1705, Snyder, *Correspondence*, 434; *CSPC*, *1704–1705*, #2, 3, 499.

34. Römer was a member of the council of New York. He did what the pervasive corruption of the Cornbury regime would permit to refortify New York and Albany (*CSPC*, *1704–1705*, #643), as he reported to Marlborough (1462). Captured with his son "in his return from New Yorke and New England" in Nov. 1706, Römer pled his ten years' American service to Marlborough to obtain the duke's good offices for an exchange (Römer's former patron, the prince of Hesse, had been killed at Barcelona). It took Römer's promise to return to America to get Marlborough to act: Add. MS 61281, 111, 113, 118, 127, 151. See also Romer to Sunderland, Add. MS 61577, 35–36; Add. MS 61595, 14, 30. Redknap, after serving under William III's command, had fought three campaigns with the Venetians and four with the king of Poland, as he testified to Marlborough when seeking employment in queen Anne's service, Add. MS 61294, 34–35b. *CSPC*, *1704–5*, #260, 417, 600, 966, 968i, 983, 1422. Dudley to Marlborough, New England, Dec. 28, 1703, Add. MS 61306, 145.

35. Dudley to Marlborough, New England, Dec. 28, 1703, Add. MS 61306, 144; same, Sept. 29, 1706, Add. MS 61310, 82–83; same, Nov. 10, 1707, Add. MS 61311, 97; *CSPC*, *1704–1705*, #260, 455, 600, 680.

36. Col. J. Dudley to Marlborough, Boston, New England, Feb. 7, 1705/6, Add. MS 61309, 28; Webb, *Lord Churchill's Coup*, ch. 3. Dudley to Marlborough, Sept. 29, 1706, Add. MS 61310, 82–83. John Shy, *Toward Lexington* (Princeton, NJ, 1965), 14.

37. Blathwayt to Marlborough, July 13, 17, 1705, Blenheim MS A.I.26, Add. MS 61133, 95–98; Dudley to commissioners, July 13, 1704, Mar. 10, 1705, *CSPC*, *1704–1705*, #455, 947; Dudley to Marlborough, Feb. 7, 1705/6, Add. MS 61309, 28; Add. MS 61319, 64b.

38. Dudley to Marlborough, Jan. 30, 1705[/6], Add. MS 61310. The fullest and most perceptive account of Dudley's accomplishment is Johnson, *Adjustment to Empire*. On this period, see esp. 378–81, 384–90, 406. Dudley to Marlborough, Sept. 29, 1706, Add. MS 61310, 82–83.

39. Dudley to Marlborough, Nov. 10, 1707, Add. MS 61311, 97.

40. CO 138/10, 437; *CSPC, 1704–1705*, #1167. CO 138/10, 437. Board of ordnance to Marlborough, Aug. 8, 1704, on Lilly's Jamaica post, Add. MS 61165, 48; Lilly to Marlborough, Barbados, Nov. 12, 1707, Add. MS 61291, 18–19. HMC, *Portland MS*, 4:170–71, 211. Note Erle's return from Ireland, at Marlborough's order, to replace Granville at the ordnance office, and Godolphin's attack on the Granville electoral interest in Cornwall, Luttrell, *Brief Relation*, 5:536; Snyder, *Correspondence*, 423; Webb, *Governors-General*, #12, 30, 116, 148, 201; HMC, *Bath MS*, 1:77.

41. Webb, "Nicholson," 541; Col. Jo. Seymour to Marlborough, Maryland, May 29, 1704, Mar. 2, 1704/5, Blenheim MS A.I.27, Add. MS 61295, 16, 18–21. Circular to governors and proprietors in America, Aug. 25, 1704. Marlborough's old subordinate Cornbury treated the victory proclamation as a matter of routine. Granville in Barbados followed the tory party line and equated Rooke's drawn action at Malaga with Blenheim, *CSPC, 1704–1705*, #538, 897, 937. On Seymour's troubles, see *CSPC, 1704–1705*, #1210, 1316.

42. Luttrell, *Brief Relation*, 5:535. "London the 10 Nov 1704 / From my Ld Orkney / to My Lord Duke," Blenheim MS, F.2.18, Add. MS 61162, 92–93.

43. Parke's credit with Marlborough's staff was still good, as seen in his "fellow Taviller" Cardonnel's compliance with Parke's nomination of "a handsome young Gentleman" for an ensign's commission, he having carried arms for two years as a volunteer in Elliot's regiment, Jan. 15, 1704[/5], Add. MS 61295, 67, 69. Parke to Sunderland, Dec. 10, 1707, Blenheim MS C.2.48, Add. MS 61643, 34. *CSPC, 1704–1705*, #1078, p. 508. The issuance of Parke's commission and instructions for the Leeward Islands was an epic of bureaucratic delay: order to prepare, Mar. 27, *CSPC, 1704–1705*, #980; draft commission, Mar. 29, #997; order of the privy council, Mar. 29, #998; draft instructions, 10 May, #1113; instructions signed June 18, #1186; commission sealed Aug. 10, #1298. On Aug. 30, 1705, Parke reported that his departure would be delayed until the next year by want of conveyance, #1319. Parke to Marlborough, July 26, 1705, Add. MS 61364, 60. Sir William Mathew's exchange of the Guards for the Leeward Islands government (Webb, *Governors-General*, #78) had set off an intense competition for his lieutenant colonelcy and for each of the subordinate steps it opened, Cutts to Marlborough, Nov. 27, 1703, Add. MS 61162, 20; Capt. Wm. Mathew's meml. to Marlborough, Add. MS 61291, 148, 149; Webb, *Governors-General*, #83.

44. *CSPC, 1704–1705*, #1141, 1350, p. 626; West to [Cardonnel], Apr. 10, 1705, Blenheim MS A.I.; Dalton, *Army Lists*, 5:106.

45. Apr. 17, 1705, *CSPC, 1704–1705*, #1039. Contrast Nott's dispatch with Parke's delays. Nott's commission and instructions were ordered on Apr. 2. The commission was drafted by Apr. 13 and the instructions by Apr. 18. Both were signed on Apr. 25. On Apr. 13, HMS *Kingston*, one of the Virginia convoy, had been ordered to await Nott's arrival, which occurred on May 4, 1705. See ibid., #1004, 1011, 1034,

1035, 1123. Nott to Marlborough, Deale, May 4, 1705, Blenheim MS A.I.27, Add. MS 61364, 30.

46. Blathwayt was still auditor general of the plantation revenues and a commissioner of trade and plantations. Miller, *Parke*, 163; Luttrell, *Brief Relation*, 5:611, 620; Parke to Sunderland, Mar. 7. 1707/8, Add. MS 61643, 32–33.

47. Coxe, *Marlborough*, 2:67–71, 73–76.

48. Marlborough to Harley, Hague, Dec. 16, 1704, Blenheim MS A.I.25, Add. MS 61123, 116, attributing the electoral victory to Speaker Harley's "prudent management and zeal for the publick," and endorsed by the grateful recipient, "In a paper by it Self / in my Ld Duke's own/hand." See also Halifax to lady Marlborough, May 12, 1705, Add. MS 61458, 162b. Note their hostility to Crawford, governor of Sheerness, who nonetheless remained in Marlborough's good books for years to come: Add. MS 61589, 163. Marlborough to Godolphin, April 14, 1705, Blenheim MS A.I.14, Snyder, *Correspondence*, 419; HMC, *Portland MS*, 4:180, 189, 250; Luttrell, *Brief Relation*, 5:535, 543, 550; Marlborough to the duchess, Apr. 21, 23, 28, 1705, Blenheim MS E.3, Snyder, *Correspondence*, 417, 426, 428, and see 440. Somerset reported (Apr. 27, 1705) that, as requested by Godolphin, he had sent "an out ffreeman of Woodstock to votte for Brigadier Cadogan." The price for this vote was Marlborough's brevet as major for Capt. Fielding and a troop in Cadogan's regiment for Somerset's heir, Add. MS 61134, 53–54, 63.

49. Halifax to lady Marlborough, n.d., May 12, 15, 22, 1705, Add. MS 61458, 158, 160–66; order of the privy council, Oct. 21, 1706, Add. MS 61598, 26; *APC*, 2, #1618.

50. The electoral balance was reported to Marlborough by his newly chosen paymaster of the army, James Brydges, June 19, 1705, Blenheim MS A.I.26. The closing quotation is from Marlborough to Godolphin, July 6, 1705, Blenheim MS A.I.37, Snyder, *Correspondence*, 453. See the crucial formulation of the nonpartisan policy of royal and ministerial rule by Harley to Marlborough, July 6/17, forwarded by Marlborough to Godolphin and the queen, Blenheim MS A.I.37; Harley to Marlborough, July 6/17 Blenheim MS A.I.14, Snyder, *Correspondence*, 458. Harley to Marlborough, June 15/26, 1705: "The Queen hath wisely & happily delivered her Self from a Party, & I believe she will not easily put herself again into the Power of any Party whatsoever," Add. MS 61123, 166.

51. On the Sunderland crisis, see Halifax to lady Marlborough, May 15, 22, Add. MS 61458, 163–65; HMC, *Hare MS*, 204; Luttrell, *Brief Relation*, 5:533, 536, 560; Coxe, *Marlborough*, 2:70–71, 86; Brown, *Letters of Anne*, 165–66; Snyder, *Correspondence*, 546, 451.

52. Henry L. Snyder, "British Diplomatic Service under the Godolphin Ministry," in Ragnhild S. Hatton and Matthew S. Anderson, eds., *Essays in Honor of David Bayne Horn* (London, 1970), 50–53; Hedges to Marlborough, June 12, 1705, Add. MS 61121, 137, asking for instructions to Sunderland; Harley to Marlborough, Aug. 3/14, 1705, on Marlborough's control of Sunderland's Vienna negotiations, Add. MS 61124, 1. The queen's undated note on "lady Marlborough's unkindness," and on Sunderland, Aug. 30 [1706?], Add. MS 61118, 1, 6. Marlborough to Godolphin, Aug. 6, 1705, Snyder, *Correspondence*, 467; Gregg, *Anne*, 219–31, and see 196, 200–201, on Walpole's entry into government.

Chapter 5. Ramillies and Union

1. The royal instructions to Marlborough, of April 14/25, 1706, are printed in Churchill, *Marlborough*, 2:79–80n. It is striking that as England's wartime prime minister, Churchill advocated the strategy of his famous ancestor. Trevelyan, *Ramillies*, esp. 134, 135; Murray, *Dispatches*, 2:496–97; HMC, *Coke MS*, 72; HMC, *Clement MS* (Molesworth), 223–34; HMC, *Hare MS*, 66; Luttrell, *Brief Relation*, 6:49; Blackadder, *Diary*, 28. "British" encompasses the English, Scots, and Irish units, that is, Queen Anne's troops, under Marlborough's command.

2. Marlborough to Harley, May 4, 7, 17, 1706, Murray, *Dispatches*, 2:485, 487–89n, 493–94n, 513; Parker, *Memoirs*, 58; HMC, *Portland MS*, 4:440–41 (where Cranstoun suggests that Marlborough would have taken only the cavalry with him); Churchill, *Marlborough*, 2:79–84; Coxe, *Marlborough*, 2:319, 321, 323–29, 316–17, 318. Marlborough to Godolphin, Apr. 17/27, 19/30, 28/May 9, 1706, Coxe, *Marlborough*, 2:328–32.

3. Lediard, *Marlborough*, 2:5, 6–9, 11; Marlborough to Harley, May 9, 1706, Murray, *Dispatches*, 2:498, see also 503–4, 509, 512; Coxe, *Marlborough*, 2:325, 332–34; Churchill, *Marlborough*, 2:83; *Lives of the Two Illustrious Generals* (London, 1713), 99; HMC, *Portland MS*, 4:440; Godolphin to Marlborough, Apr. 28, 1706, Coxe, *Marlborough*, 2:333. More particularly, Hanover was concerned that the new acts of regency and naturalization be passed and implemented. On the consultations about union, see also Orkney to Selkirk, Apr. 3, 1707, MS 1033, 21b, NLS.

4. Marlborough to Godolphin, May 4/15, 9/20, Coxe, *Marlborough*, 2:335, 338; *Lives of the Generals*, 99; Lediard, *Marlborough*, 2:10–12.

5. Coxe, *Marlborough*, 2:337; Marlborough to Hop, May 21, 1706, Murray, *Dispatches*, 2:518. See Marlborough's bitter reproach to the Prussians, Murray, *Dispatches*, 2:521–22.

6. Marlborough to Godolphin, May 16/27, 1706, Snyder, *Correspondence*, 552; Milner, *Journal*, 170–71; Scot, "Remembrancer," 376; Coxe, *Marlborough*, 2:340–41; Lediard, *Marlborough*, 2:14, 35–36; Taylor, *Marlborough*, 1:374.

7. Kane, *Campaigns*, 66, and Parker, *Memoirs*, 58, make the allies 117 squadrons and 80 battalions, and the French 132 squadrons and 90 battalions, or roughly 56,000 allies to 62,000 French, Bavarians, and "Spanish." Milner, *Journal*, 170, makes the allies 74 battalions, 123 squadrons, 100 guns, 20 howitzers, or 55,450 men, and the French 76 battalions, 132 squadrons, and 66 guns, or 62,750 men. On p. 177, however, Milner gives the French 82 battalions and 145 squadrons, or 70,000 men. Marlborough to Godolphin, May 24, 1706, Coxe, *Marlborough*, 2:355, estimated the allied strength as 123 squadrons and 73 battalions, the French as 128 squadrons and 74 battalions, or nearly equal numbers. Marlborough to Eugene, May 25, 1706, Murray, *Dispatches*, 2:525; Belloc, *Marlborough*, 120–23, 128; Chandler, *Marlborough*, 175.

8. Lediard, *Marlborough*, 2:14–15; Marlborough to the prince of Denmark, May 24, 1706, Murray, *Dispatches*, 2:522; Churchill, *Marlborough*, 2:97; Coxe, *Marlborough*, 2:340–42n, and *Atlas*, "Plan of the Battle of Ramellies, May 23rd 1706."

9. Camp at Braunchien, May 24, 1706, 7'oclock, Orkney, "Letters," 315; Kane, *Campaigns*, 66–67; Parker, *Memoirs*, 59; De La Colonie, *Chronicles*, 305; Marlborough to Godolphin, May [13/]24, 1706, Snyder, *Correspondence*, 545; Coxe, *Marlborough*, 2:355.

10. Marlborough to Godolphin, May [13/]24, 16/27, 1706, Blenheim MS A.I.37; Coxe, *Marlborough*, 2:355, Snyder, *Correspondence*, 545, 552; Parker, *Memoirs*, 59.

11. Orkney, "Letters," 315. As Marlborough remarked to Godolphin, Orkney, "though he is a brave man, by his own good will he would never venture," May 20/31, 1706, Snyder, *Correspondence*, 554.

12. Atkinson, *Marlborough*, 283n2; Scot, "Remembrancer," 377; Charles Dalton, "The Great Duke of Argyll's Military Career, 1694–1742," *JRUSI* 42 (1898): 632.

13. De La Colonie, *Chronicles*, 312; Lediard, *Marlborough*, 2:15.

14. Lediard, *Marlborough*, 2:16, makes this 1:30. Scot, "Remembrancer," 376. Kane, *Campaigns*, 67. Parker, *Memoirs*, 60, says that Villeroy transferred "an entire line both of horse and foot" from his center to meet the British threat to his left flank. Lettre du Roi a Villeroy, 6 Mai 1706, printed in Taylor, *Marlborough*, 1:377. De La Colonie, *Chronicles*, 308, 313.

15. Marlborough to Godolphin, May [13/]24, 1706, Snyder, *Correspondence*, 545; Lediard, *Marlborough*, 2:16; Orkney, "Letters," 315.

16. Dalton, *Army Lists*, 6:8. The colonel of the 16th, Charles Godfrey Jr., Marlborough's nephew, was not at the front, having replaced the tory Henry Graham as a groom of prince George's bedchamber, July 5, 1706, Gregg, *Anne*, 220–21. Cranstoun to Cunningham, June 10, 1706, HMC, *Portland MS*, 4:310; Le Gretton, *Royal Irish*, 44, 67–70. The brigade was composed of the Royal Scots, a battalion of the 1st Guards, and, as Maurice, *16th*, 38–39, has it, the 16th, 21st, and 26th of the Line. See also Atkinson, *South Wales Borderers* (24th), 59–60; Blackadder, *Diary*, 46.

17. Cranstoun's account in HMC, *Portland MS*, 4:310; Atkinson, *Marlborough*, 289, 290. See also Taylor, *Marlborough*, 371; Churchill, *Marlborough*, 2:111; Marlborough "to Yourself" [Harley] Aug. 30, 1706, HMC, *Bath MS*, 1:96; Orkney, "Letters," 315.

18. Marlborough to Godolphin, May [13/]24, Snyder, *Correspondence*, 545; Parker, *Memoirs*, 60; Coxe, *Marlborough*, 2:347–48.

19. De La Colonie, *Chronicles*, 305, 312–13; Kane, *Campaigns*, 67–68. Churchill, *Marlborough*, 2:98, has eighty-two French squadrons in "the gap of only 1200 paces." Fifty squadrons had been sent to the French left to meet the British. Villeroy also detached twelve squadrons to retake Taviers, leaving only seventy to meet the allied attack. This (Churchill, *Marlborough*, 2:105) was initially delivered by sixty-nine squadrons, but Marlborough brought up eighteen more squadrons for the second charge and added twenty-one fresh squadrons for the final assault. Taylor, *Marlborough*, 2:383, poses forty-eight Dutch and twenty-one Danish squadrons against seventy-eight French. See also Churchill, *Marlborough*, 2:107; Atkinson, "Ramillies," 87n–88.

20. Atkinson, *Marlborough*, 290–91; Cranstoun, June 10, 1706, HMC, *Portland MS*, 4:309–10; Churchill, *Marlborough*, 2:108, has this at 3:30. [Duclos], *Historie de Jean duc de Marlborough*, 3 vols. (Paris, 1808), 2:160–61.

21. *Lives of the Generals*, 100; Marlborough gave Molesworth a regiment and made full provision for Bringfield's family. Marlborough to Godolphin, May [13/]24, Snyder, *Correspondence*, 545; Godolphin to Marlborough, May 17/28, Coxe, *Marlborough*,

2:357; Luttrell, *Brief Relation*, 6:48–49; HMC, *Hare MS*, 211; Lediard, *Marlborough*, 2:17. Parker, *Memoirs*, 61, makes this two incidents, as does Churchill, *Marlborough*, 2:108–10. Orkney's account is in "Letters," 315. Contemporaries viewed the French dragoons' pursuit of Marlborough as attempted murder: Add. MS 61364, esp. 152b.

22. C. Colden to A. Colden, Sept. 25, 1759, William Smith Jr., *The History of the Province of New York*, ed. Michael Kammen, vol. 1, app. B, p. 300.

23. Kane, *Campaigns*, 66, 68; Lediard, *Marlborough*, 2:16; De La Colonie, *Chronicles*, 312–13. C. T. Atkinson and J. W. Wijn, "The Ramillies Battlefield," *JSAHR* 32 (1954): 14–18.

24. Ferguson, *Scots Brigade*, 2:9–10; Scot, "Remembrancer," 378; HMC, *Portland MS*, 4:309; Lediard, *Marlborough*, 2:15, 27; Orkney, "Letters," 315–16; Le Gretton, *Royal Irish*, 44; Milner, *Journal*, 178; Coxe, *Marlborough*, 2:347–48.

25. Quotation in Peter Drake, *Amiable Renegade: The Memoirs of Capt. Peter Drake, 1671–1753* (Dublin, 1755; Oxford, 1960), 79.

26. Lediard, *Marlborough*, 2:19–21, 38–39; HMC, *Portland MS*, 4:311; HMC, *Hare MS* (14th Report, app. pt. 9), 211; Coxe, *Marlborough*, 2:350; C. T. Atkinson, "Cathcart MS," *JSAHR* 29 (1951):20–25, 64–103. The *Wynendael* tapestry at Blenheim shows a sergeant holding a driver to his work with a halberd, Wace, *Marlborough Tapestries*, #46. The abusive relationship was a standard tapestry topic, *Marlborough Tapestries*, #66. Almack, *Second Dragoons*, 31; Atkinson, *South Wales Borderers*, 61.

27. Lediard, *Marlborough*, 2:21, 27, 32; Coxe, *Marlborough*, 2:351–53. The Scots Greys claimed payments for the clothing, accoutrements, and arms for forty troopers lost at Ramillies, and the Royal Irish claimed for thirty lost troopers: WO 4/15, printed in *JSAHR* 15 (1937): 160. Orkney, "Letters," 316; Scot, "Remembrancer," 380. *Lives of the Generals*, 100, has 8,000 of the French army killed on the field, 5,000 captured. Lediard, *Marlborough*, 2:21, 33, makes this 8,000 killed, 6,600 prisoners, plus deserters and wounded to make the French loss 20,000, versus an allied loss of 1,066 killed, 2,567 wounded. Milner, *Journal*, 176–77, details French losses of 21,816, plus 54 cannon, and 2,000 artillery and bread wagons, and counts allied losses of 4,192. Parker, *Memoirs*, 62, makes the French loss 7,000 killed and 30,000 total, against a bit over 5,000 allied casualties.

28. Bruxelles, May 16[/27], 1706, Snyder, *Correspondence*, 553; Lediard, *Marlborough*, 2:29; Parker, *Memoirs*, 62; Milner, *Journal*, 174–75.

29. Cardonnel to Stepney, Louvain, May 25, 1706, Add. MS 7063, 199. Marlborough to Godolphin, May 16/27, 1706, Blenheim MS A.1.37, Snyder, *Correspondence*, 552. Craggs to Marlborough, May 21, 1706, Add. MS 61164, 173, rejoiced at the results of Marlborough's escape from Dutch obstruction: "Their's nothing in this world above your genious nor beyond your reach, when your orders are obeyed."

30. Marlborough to the queen, May 24, 1706, Murray, *Dispatches*, 2:522; Lediard, *Marlborough*, 2:15, 35–36, 42–43, 58, 79. H. T. Dickinson, "Richards," *JSAHR* 46 (1968): 80. Richards's sister was married to Marlborough's London agent, James Craggs Jr. His delight in the victory, when so many of Marlborough's political enemies had said that this campaign, like that of 1705, would come to nothing, was enhanced because the news came by "my Bro.," Craggs to Marlborough, May 17, 1706, Add. MS 61164, 171–72. The ministry's high opinion of Richards and its concentration on retrieving Spanish America from France both appear in Godolphin to [Rivers], Aug. 21, 1706, HMC, *Bath MS*, 1:92–93. For Marlborough's participation, see Churchill, *Marlborough*, 2:81 and the St. John–Erle Correspondence, *JSAHR* 48 (1970) and 49 (1971). Marlborough to Godolphin, May 4/15, 1706, Snyder, *Correspondence*, 536, 545–46.

31. Luttrell, *Brief Relation*, 6:47; the queen to Marlborough, Kensington, May 17, 1606 [1706], Blenheim MS B.II.32, Add. MS 61101, 91, slightly endorsed by lady Marlborough "for some victory," printed in Gregg, *Anne*, 215–16; St. John to Marlborough, May 17/28, 1706, Coxe, *Marlborough*, 2:357–58.

32. Godolphin to Marlborough, May 16, 17, 1706, Blenheim MS A.I.36, Snyder, *Correspondence*, 550–51; Luttrell, *Brief Relation*, 4:48; Marlborough to Sunderland, June 3, 1706, Murray, *Dispatches*, 2:552. Marlborough to Godolphin, May 31/June 11, 1706, Snyder, *Correspondence*, 571, agreed that his conquest of Belgium would make it "very reasonable to insist, that King Charles shall have the intier monarque of Spain."

33. Marlborough to Harley, May 17/28, 1706, Lediard, *Marlborough*, 2:57–58, Murray, *Dispatches*, 2:530n, 537–39; same to Godolphin, Bruxelles, May 16/27, 1706, Snyder, *Correspondence*, 551–52; Lediard, *Marlborough*, 2:43; SP 87/2, fols. 445–56; deputies to the states general, n.d., Lediard, *Marlborough*, 2:50–55.

34. The prince and duke of Marlborough, Ferdinand van Collen, and Sieur Goslinga to the states of Brabant, May 26, 1706, Lediard, *Marlborough*, 2:44–45; Coxe, *Marlborough*, 2:363–64; Churchill, *Marlborough*, 2:121; Chandler, *Marlborough*, 179; "John, Duke and Earl of *Marlborough*, Prince of the *Holy Roman Empire*, Marquis of *Blandford*, Baron *Churchill* of *Aymouth*, One of Her *Brittanick* Majesty's Most Honorable Privy Council, Knight of the Most *Noble Order of the Garter*, Master General of the Ordnance, Colonel of the First Regiment of Her Majesty's Guards, Captain General of Her Land Forces, and Commander in Chief of the Army of the *Allies.* . . . Given in Our Camp at *Beaulieu*, the 26th of *May*, 1706," Lediard, *Marlborough*, 2:55–56. Marlborough to the magistrates of Ghent, May 31, 1706, Murray, *Dispatches*, 2:545; the sovereign council of Brabant to the prince and duke of Marlborough and to the deputies, Brussels, May 27, 1706, and the members of the three estates of Brabant to the same, Lediard, *Marlborough*, 2:46–49.

35. Proclamation by General Churchill, governor of Brussels, June 14, 1706, Lediard, *Marlborough*, 2:84–85; Marlborough to Churchill, June 17, 23, 1706, Murray, *Dispatches*, 2:600–601, 622–23. "I should not much wonder, to hear you had appointed a Governour for Paris, as well as for Brussels & Madrid," K. Chetwood to Marlborough, May 29, 1706, Add. MS 61364, 152b.

36. Marlborough to Churchill, Aug. 6, 1706, and same to Harley, May 28, Aug. 6, 1706, Murray, *Dispatches*, 2:538, 3:56, 69.

37. Marlborough to the queen, Harley, and Hedges, Camp at Grimsby, May 28, 1706, Lediard, *Marlborough*, 2:59; Murray, *Dispatches*, 2:538–39; Lediard, *Marlborough*, 2:79; Webb, *Governors-General*, #63, 86, 128; HMC, *Portland MS*, 4:306. Craggs to Marlborough, May 21, 1706, on Pitt's arrival, with news that subdued political factions, Add. MS 61164, 173. Pitt held colonel's rank and received an aide-de-camp's pay and allowances (£182/10/2) by Marlborough's warrant, Add. MS 61327, 52, 59.

38. Luttrell, *Brief Relation*, 6:48–49; [Anne R. to Marlborough], Kensington, May 21, [1706], Blenheim MS B.II.32, Add. MS 61101, 93; Godolphin to Marlborough, May 26, Marlborough to Godolphin, May 27, 1706, Snyder, *Correspondence*, 562n–63, and see 586–87; Lediard, *Marlborough*, 2:79.

39. Lediard, *Marlborough*, 2:63; deputies to states general, ibid., 2:51; bulletin, Camp at Merelbeck, June 3, 1706, Murray, *Dispatches*, 2:556.

40. Lediard, *Marlborough*, 2:66, 70, 73; Luttrell, *Brief Relation*, 6:51; Colden, in Smith, *History*, 300–301. On Hunter's relationship with Cadogan, see Lustig, *Hunter*, 35–37.

41. Taylor, *Marlborough*, 1:400–401, 405, 407, 419–21; Atkinson, *Marlborough*, 298. Orkney to Marlborough, "Munday eleven a Clock," Camp at Asche, June 7, 1706, Add. MS 61162, 97.

42. Cadogan to Marlborough, [June 2, 4, 6, 1706], Add. MS 61160, 7–9, 13, 17. For a parallel case, see Tacitus, *Annals*, XIII:4. Marlborough to the Marquis de Terracina, June 1, 5, 1706; same to magistrates, June 1, 1706, Murray, *Dispatches*, 2:545–46, 563–64; same to states general, June 1, 3, 1706, Murray, *Dispatches*, 2:548, 558; same to Cadogan, [June 3], 1706, Murray, *Dispatches*, 2:255, 264–66; same to Harley, June 7, 1706, Murray, *Dispatches*, 2:571; same to states of Brabant, June 17, 1706, Murray, *Dispatches*, 2:598. Orkney to Anne, duchess of Hamilton, June 13, 1706, NS, GD 406/1/5302, SRO.

43. Marlborough to Godolphin, May 16–17, 1706, Blenheim MS A.I.36, Snyder, *Correspondence*, 550–51. For the case of Maj. Cranstoun, see his letter of June 10, 1706, HMC, *Portland MS*, 4:309–11, and Marlborough's reactions to Harley, [June 27/] July 8, July 1/12, Aug. 5 [NS], 27, 30, 1706, HMC, *Bath MS*, 1:82, 86, 94, 96. C. Colden to A. Colden, Sept. 25, 1759, Smith, *History*, 1: app. B, pp. 301–2; and see *Collections, N-Y.H.S. 1868*, 195.

44. Lord Bolingbroke, *Contributions to the Craftsman*, ed. Simon Varey (Oxford, 1982), 125; Lediard, *Marlborough*, 2:82–83; Murray, *Dispatches*, 2:546; Marlborough to Godolphin, July 19, 1706, Coxe, *Marlborough*, 2:400, Snyder, *Correspondence*, 615–16.

45. Taylor, *Marlborough*, 1:419ff.; Lediard, *Marlborough*, 2:75–79, 82–85; Coxe, *Marlborough*, 2:385–401, 3:54–55; Marlborough to Godolphin, July 15/26, Oct. 21, 29, and reply, Oct. 13/24, 1706, Coxe, *Marlborough*, 3:58, 75, 76, 79; Marlborough to Godolphin, Oct. 14, 1706, Snyder, *Correspondence*, 2:701. Marlborough to the deputies at Brussels, June 26, 1706; same to estates of city and duchy of Brabant, *Dispatches*, 2:633, 635. Lediard, *Marlborough*, 2:78, suggests that the Dutch deputies and generals had impeded Marlborough's proposed advance, whether against Mons or, by bypassing the French fortresses, against Paris itself, so that the captain general went back to The Hague to refresh his authority. Cadogan and Durrell accompanied Marlborough who, in matters civil and diplomatic, also relied primarily on his military staff. Marlborough to Harley, June 3, 1706, Murray, *Dispatches*, 2:554; Godolphin to Marlborough, May 26, 1706, Snyder, *Correspondence*, 562. The brevity of

Marlborough's visit meant that he had to send Crowe (reporting to Marlborough en route from Spain to England and Barbados) to the states general with Charles III's requests for aid. These would not be honored, as the Dutch left the war in Spain and its imperial potential in the Mediterranean and the Caribbean entirely to England. Crowe to Marlborough, Hague, Aug. 12/23, 1706, Add. MS 61310, 38.

46. Marlborough to Godolphin, June 17, 1706, Coxe, *Marlborough*, 2:380; same to Harley, June 3, 17, 1706; same to Fairborne, June 15, 18, 1706; same to Hedges, July 6, 1706, Murray, *Dispatches*, 2:554, 585, 600, 601, 670. Ross (Hunter's regimental colonel) reported the divisions between the Spanish and French troops in the Ostend garrison, Add. MS 31309, 92–93, 102, 110–12. Fairborne to Marlborough, *Eagle* off Ostend, June 2, 1706, Add. MS 61164, 143, Add. MS 31309, 135, stated that the admiralty had put his squadron under the captain general's command[!] for the capture of Ostend, detailed his ships' bombardment capacity, and reported Captain Delavall's arrival with news from Spain. The remarkably collegial correspondence between the admiral and the general bespoke Fairborne's long reliance on Marlborough's leadership, Add. MS 61164, 150, 159, 161–62; Webb, *Lord Churchill's Coup*, 236, 242, Webb, *Governors-General*, #94. Lediard, *Marlborough*, 2:86–91; Coxe, *Marlborough*, 2:133; Atkinson, *Marlborough*, 300–301; Taylor, *Marlborough*, 1:407; Kane, *Campaigns*, 70; Milner, *Journal*, 184.

47. Marlborough to the duchess, Merelbeck near Gant, May 20[/31], 1706, Snyder, *Correspondence*, 556; same to Salm, Sinzendorff, July 7, 17, 1706, Murray, *Dispatches*, 2:670–72 and see 701; Coxe, *Marlborough*, 2:387–404; Churchill, *Marlborough*, 2:144–54; Marlborough to Godolphin, July 6, 1706, Blenheim MS A.I.37, Snyder, *Correspondence*, 600. Stanhope pressed the commission on Charles III, Stanhope to Marlborough, July 3, 1706, Blenheim MS A.I.47, Add. MS 61157, 61. Marlborough acknowledged Stanhope's agency, Dec. 23, 1706, and promised his brother the next company in the Guards, Murray, *Dispatches*, 3:256–57.

48. Marlborough to Godolphin, June [10/]21, July 1, 6, 1706; Godolphin to Marlborough, June 24, July 4, 1706, Snyder, *Correspondence*, 580, 598–99, 595, 600, 612: "It is amazing that after so much done for their advantage, and even for their safety the States can have been capable of such a behavior. Those of the French faction must have . . . fill[ed] them with jealousy, of your having, and consequently of England's having too much power." Anne R. to Marlborough, July 9, [1706], Blenheim MS B.II.32, Add. MS 61101, 96; Atkinson, *Marlborough*, 299; Churchill, *Marlborough*, 2:141–42, 146; Coxe, *Marlborough*, 2:377, 393; 3:62, 147–48; Marlborough to the prince of Salm, June 30, 1706; same to the deputies, June 30, 1706; same to the emperor, July 12, 1706, and to the king of Spain, July 16, 1706, Murray, *Dispatches*, 2:653, 657, 688–89, 701; same to St. John, June 24, 1706, Blenheim MS 30.13.

49. Simon van Slingelandt to Marlborough, July 3, 1706, quoted in Roderick Giekie and Isabel A. Montgomery, *The Dutch Barrier, 1705–1719* (1930; repr., New York, 1968), 20–21, app. A; Marlborough to Slingelandt Oct. 10, 1706, Murray, *Dispatches*, 3:165–66. Marlborough to Godolphin, Aug. 15, 1706, Snyder, *Correspondence*, 643–44; same to Hedges, July 25, 1706, Cardonnel to Godolphin, July 29, 1796, Murray, *Dispatches*, 3:26, 30–31, 84. Douglas Coombs, *The Conduct of the Dutch . . .* (The Hague, 1958), 138.

50. Marlborough to Hedges, Sept. 3, Nov. 9, 1706, Murray, *Dispatches*, 3:115, 211, and see 168, 194, 223; same to the duchess, Oct. 18, 1706, Snyder, *Correspondence*, 705. HMC, *Bath MS*, 1:105; Atkinson, *Marlborough*, 304–7; Coxe, *Marlborough*, 3:55–56; Marlborough to Portland, July 21, 1706, Murray, *Dispatches*, 3:10–11; Marlborough to Godolphin, Aug. 30, Sept. 20, 1706, Coxe, *Marlborough*, 3:56, 61; Marlborough to Stepney, Dec. 6, 1706, Murray, *Dispatches*, 3:245. Note the administration of Col. William Evans, afterward deputy governor of Pennsylvania, at Tirlemont: Add. MS 61308, 136, 148.

51. Godolphin to Buys, Sept. 3, 1706, Snyder, *Correspondence*, 663–66: "As to England, the Queen's title and the Protestant Succession in the House of Hanover being fully provided for, England must certainly insist upon a treaty of commerce and in that treaty expect to bee relieved from severall encroachments and usurpations on the dominions of England in Newfoundland and Hudson's Bay, and elswere in the Indies . . . the Queen not pretending to any conquest or increase of dominion for herself," so Godolphin told Marlborough (Nov. 8, 1706, Blenheim MS A.I.36, Snyder, *Correspondence*, 730). The American articles "left room for the Queen to lay claim to reparations for incroachments & damages to ye English plantations in America." These were not now specified lest they alarm the Dutch as well as the French. Marlborough declared that "the frute of the Spanish Warr, for the good of England," must include a trade treaty with Spain, including the asiento in slaves, Marlborough to Godolphin, Sept. [9/20], 1706, Snyder, *Correspondence*, 673. HBC directors to Marlborough, Add. MS 61303, 134. The company also supplied Marlborough with a full "Declaration of the Right & Title of the Crown of Great Britain . . . and of the Right and Property of the Hudson's Bay Company derived from the Imperial Crown of Great Britain," Blenheim MS, B.I.30, Add. MS 61358, 50–51; Webb, *Lord Churchill's Coup*, esp. 114–23; J. A. Brandao and William A. Starna, "The Treaties of 1701: A Triumph of Iroquois Diplomacy," *Ethnohistory* 43 (1996): 221–29.

52. Marlborough to Godolphin, July 22, 1706, Blenheim MS A.I.37; Godolphin to Marlborough, Aug. 13/24, 1706, Blenheim MS A.I.36, Snyder, *Correspondence*, 650n; Marlborough to Hedges, Aug. 6, 1706; to Harley, Aug. 30, 1706, Murray, *Dispatches*, 3:51, 110.

53. Memorial of Daniel Parke to Marlborough, [1706]; St. John to same, Blenheim MS A.I.36; Blenheim Establishments, 1705, Add. MS 61317, 22.

54. Coxe, *Marlborough*, 3:3; Marlborough to Godolphin, Sept. 27, 30, 1706, ibid., 3:13–14; Routh, *Burnet's History*, 5:270; Coombs, *Conduct of the Dutch*, 139.

55. Lediard, *Marlborough*, 2:102–3; Churchill, *Marlborough*, 2:179; Chandler, *Art of War*, 39; Parker, *Memoirs*, 109; Kane, *Campaigns*, 89; Marlborough to the duchess, and to Godolphin, Aug. 16, 19, 1706, Snyder, *Correspondence*, 645, 647, 648; Coxe, *Marlborough*, 3:6; Cadogan to Raby, Aug. 17, [1706], Add. MS 22196, 33. Oct. [13/]24, 1706, Blenheim MS A.I.36, Snyder, *Correspondence*, 711; Coxe, *Marlborough*, 3:6–7. See Essex's campaign, fostered by lady Marlborough, to replace Abingdon in the Tower: Essex to Marlborough, May 24, 1705, Add. MS 61308, 175. If Charles Churchill did not take the government of Guernsey, Essex said he would settle for that command, Essex to Marlborough, Lisbon, Dec. 9, [1706], Add. MS 61310, 143. Godolphin to Marlborough, Oct. 21, 1706, OS, Snyder, *Correspondence*, 718–19.

Withers went to Sheerness, Sutton to Hull (as lieutenant governor to Newcastle), and Meredith took over Tinmouth. Lord Hatton having died, Charles Churchill transferred to Guernsey. Lord Essex at last succeeded Abingdon as constable of the Tower and Cadogan became lieutenant. Churchill's appointment was made despite the application of Sir Bevil Granville. Granville had gotten Marlborough to secure his leave from the queen to come home from Barbados, opening the way for the appointment of Col. Mitford Crowe, Godolphin to Marlborough, Sept. 10, Oct. 13, 1706, Blenheim MS A.I.36, Snyder, *Correspondence*, 675, 711; St. John to Marlborough, Sept. 13/22, 1706, Blenheim MS A.I.46. The Granvilles threatened to make trouble about Crowe's appointment unless Marlborough either restored Sir Bevil "to an Old Regiment," he having exchanged the command of the 10th for that of Barbados, or give him the Guernsey appointment, "a very bare equivalent for a Regiment." Either commission would prevent the Barbadian opposition from claiming that their complaints had dislodged Sir Bevil. He mooted the point by dying on the voyage home. He had with him profit "enough to make him easy, though not in any degree such a fortune as governors usually amass." Godolphin to Harley, Sept. 30, 1705, Hedges to Rivers, Nov. 1, 1706, HMC, *Bath MS*, 1:77, 121; Granville to Harley, Nov. 29, 1706, HMC, *Portland MS*, 4:361. The queen was "very uneasy" at granting the Guernsey government to Churchill for life (as Hatton had held it) and Godolphin disapproved of the precedent, but Marlborough had no confidence in his brother's ability to retain the post. In the far more important cases of the Tower commands, the queen and the treasurer expressed their pleasure at the captain general's consolidation of his control of the imperial metropolis. Godolphin to Marlborough, Oct. 13, 16, 22, 27, 1706, Blenheim MS A.I.36, Snyder, *Correspondence*, 707, 711, 719, 722.

56. C. T. Atkinson, "Marlborough's Sieges," *JSAHR* 24 (1946): 83; Parker, *Memoirs* (Chandler, ed.), 64. Coxe, *Marlborough*, 3:2, 5; Taylor, *Marlborough*, 1:408.

57. Orkney to Marlborough, July 15, Aug. 19, 1706, Add. MS 61162, 99, 101; same to Selkirk, Aug. 9, 1706, GD 406/1/9113, SRO. Milner, *Journal*, 188–90; Scot, "Remembrancer," 388–89; Kane, *Campaigns*, 70; Churchill, *Marlborough*, 2:177; Atkinson, *Marlborough*, 301; Taylor, *Marlborough*, 409; Coxe, *Marlborough*, 3:4–5; Chandler, *Art of War*, 160.

58. Dalton, "Argyll's Military Career," 631; Orkney to Marlborough, Menin, Sept. 1, 1706, Blenheim MS A.I.45 [letters to Marlborough, 1706]; Marlborough to Harley, Aug. 30, 1706, Murray, *Dispatches*, 3:110.

59. Same to the duchess, Aug. [1/]12, 1706, Snyder, *Correspondence*, 640. Ben. Bennett to Marlborough, Bermuda, Dec. 30, 1706, Add. MS 61283, 141; Webb, *Governors-General*, #23, 25.

60. Marlborough to Godolphin, [Aug. 29/Sept. 9, 1706], Snyder, *Correspondence*, 659; Godolphin to Harley, [Sept.] 19, [1706], HMC, *Bath MS*, 1:104; Mar to Argyll, May 24, 1706; Dalrymple to Mar, June 14, 1706; Argyll to Mar, July 18, 1706; Mar to Godolphin and to the queen, Oct. 8, 1706, HMC, *Mar and Kellie MS*, 1:263–64, 267, 270, 276, 286–88; Riley, *Union*, 256. Marlborough arranged that Argyll was succeeded as colonel of a Scots-Dutch regiment by lord Tullibardine, Atholl's heir and Orkney's brother-in-law, Snyder, *Correspondence*, 662.

61. Marlborough to Godolphin, July 29/Aug. 9, Sept. 9, 1706, Blenheim MS A.I.37, Snyder, *Correspondence*, 636, 659. Argyll "was so very fickle" that Marlborough feared he "would change his mind on the road," ibid., 655. William Ferguson, "Union Treaty," *SHR* 43 (1905): 106–7.

62. Sir David Nairne to Mar, Sept. 17, 1706, HMC, *Mar and Kellie MS*, 279, and reply 280–81. See ibid., 321, 360, on Argyle's use of the Scots Troop's commissions to reward the military service of unionists. Marlborough replied the next day to Argyll's typically petulant demand for the command of the Coldstream Guards: "My Lord Cutts' death puts it in your Graces power to lett me have some reward as well as Other People," Blenheim MS A.I.45; Add. MS 61136, 47. On Sept. 9, he approached the "Squadrone Volante," Murray, *Dispatches*, 3:17, 125–26; 622n, 703n, 709, 715, 717; Webb, *Governors-General*, #133, 137. To Argyll's American connection, add William Forbes, former lieutenant governor of Barbados (Webb, *Governors-General*, #10), who sought Marlborough's approval of his promotion to serve under Argyll as 2d lieutenant colonel, 4th Troop Life Guards, "the promotion being in course with the Coar," Add. MS 61287, 141. Orkney to Marlborough, "Oct. 1706," Blenheim MS A.I.45, Add. MS 61162, 107. Contrast the tone, and note the success, of Ingoldsby's (that would-be American general) request to transfer from the government of Ghent to Cutts's former command in Ireland, Add. MS 61163, 60–61, 72. Marlborough had to prevent the aggressive Argyll and his astute brother, Archibald Campbell (created earl of Islay as part of the union patronage), from engrossing Scots military promotions lest, as speaker Sir John Smith wrote to Marlborough, the English ministry "suffer a Power to be rays'd soe high in Scotland that can already be soe little depended upon here," Mar. 28, 1710, Add. 61288, 137–38.

63. Maj. J. Cranstoun [to Robert Cunningham], Oct. 11, 20, 1705, HMC, *Portland MS*, 4:250, 264–68; Johnston, "Scots Army," 6; Dalton, *Army Lists*, 5: pt. 2, 66–68.

64. [Nov.] 15, [1706], HMC, *Bath MS*, 1:125, and see 126; Luttrell, *Brief Relation*, 6:129, 130; Marlborough to Godolphin, Sept. 30, 1706, Blenheim MS A.I.37, Snyder, *Correspondence*, 690. The work done since the pioneering effort of John Clive and Bernard Bailyn, "England's Cultural Provinces: Scotland and America," *WMQ*, 3d ser., 11 (1954): 200–213, is ably analyzed in Eric Richards, "Scotland and the Uses of the Atlantic Empire," in Bernard Bailyn and Philip D. Morgan, eds., *Strangers within the Realm: Cultural Margins of the First British Empire* (Chapel Hill, NC 1991), [67–]114.

65. Orkney to Marlborough, Oct. 15, 1706, Blenheim MS A.I.45, Add. MS 61162, 105. Orkney also assured the captain general that lord William Hay had served all the last war with distinction in the Royal Scots. Marlborough to Argyll, Nov. 29, 1706, Murray, *Dispatches*, 3:239. Marlborough balanced his Scots patronage by promoting lord Dalrymple to the colonelcy of the Scots Greys (the purchase price went to the former colonel's widow, lady Hay, and was effectively her dowry for Hunter). Dalrymple was promoted on the nomination of the Scots ministers because of his father's political services and because Dalrymple himself was on active service with Marlborough and high in the duke's favor. See the correspondence of the earl of Tweeddale, Elizabeth, lady Hay, Queensbury, and Mar, to Marlborough, Sept. and Oct. 1706, Add. MS 61136, 51–52, 55–56, 59, 61, and see GD 406/1/7252,

SRO; W. Ferguson, "The Making of the Treaty of Union of 1707," *SHR* 43 (1904): 99–102. Dalrymple was promoted brigadier in six months, "Promotions and Brevets," Add. MS 61321, 6. Besides the Hamilton, Stair, and Hay interests, Robert Hunter also could rely on the queen's physician and confidant, the Scots physician John Arbuthnot. Arbuthnot's role in Hunter's Virginia appointment is unclear, but he was instrumental in Hunter's transfer to New York: C. Colden to A. Colden, Sept. 25, 1759, Smith, *History*, 302. Gregg, *Anne*, 234; Riley, *Union*, 266, 271–72. For Marlborough's approaches to the squadrone leaders, see Murray, *Dispatches*, 3:125; Snyder, *Correspondence*, 647, 703, 715.

66. P. Hume Brown, *History of Scotland* (Cambridge, 1911), 3:75–153; Clerk, "Memoirs," in W. O. Trevelyan, ed. *Select Docs.*, 220; Dalrymple to Mar, Sept. 9; Mar to Nairne, Edinburgh, Sept. 24, Oct. 4–Dec. 28; Campbell to Mar, Sept. 28; Nairne to Mar, Whitehall, Oct. 26–Dec. 19, 1706, HMC, *Mar and Kellie MS*, 276, 281, 282–363. David Crawford to Hamilton, Dec. 1, 1706, GD 406/1/5383, SRO; John Prebble, *The Darien Disaster* (London, 1968), 1–9. See the portrait of the Edinburgh mob in Scott, *Heart of Midlothian*.

67. See also Stair to Harley, Edinburgh, Nov. 26, 1706; report by "Mr. Shute"; Defoe to Harley, Dec. 27, Jan. 4, HMC, *Portland MS*, 4:311, 359, 374, 378. Defoe's reports were circulated to Marlborough and Godolphin. Marlborough to Harley, Oct. 18, 1706, ibid., 4:177. Details from Anne, duchess of Hamilton, to the duke, Nov. 3, 1706, GD 406/1/9732, SRO.

68. Marlborough to Godolphin, Oct. [13/]24, 1706, Blenheim MS A.I.14, Snyder, *Correspondence*, 712, and see 727; Stair to Harley, Nov. 26, 1706, HMC, *Portland MS*, 4:359–60, 353; HMC, *Mar and Kellie MS*, 1:335–36, 353; Johnston, "Scots Army," 17–18.

69. Marlborough to Leven and to Queensbury, Oct. 7, 1706, Murray, *Dispatches*, 3:246–47; Queensbury to Marlborough, Nov. 27, 1706, Blenheim MS, A.I.46. From the chief justice of New York, William Atwood (who recalled "the transporting assurance of your Grace's favour, wth wch I left England for a promising post in America"), Marlborough received a brief on the constitutionality of "a Solid Union" of Scotland with "ye Imperial Crown of this Realm." Atwood reported that he had made the like arguments in Ireland and New York, whose leaders "were against the Revolution, & the Laws of England." A typical whig, Atwood advocated extending the laws of England across the empire, both to protect every subject and to assure the supremacy of the English crown over all the dominions, Add. MS 61365, 49.

70. Leven to Marlborough, Nov. 5; Queensbury to same, Nov. 27, 1706, Blenheim MS A.I.46, Add. MS 61136, 67, 69–70; reply to Leven, Dec. 7, 1706; same to Queensbury, Murray, *Dispatches*, 3:246, 247. See also HMC, *Mar and Kellie MS*, 329, 339, on the suspension of the arming clause (Hamilton pled illness to avoid the vote) and for the opposition claim that the Edinburgh mob was "the genius of the nation." See HMC, *Mar and Kellie MS*, 353, for Marlborough's opinion. Note that most of the Belfast forces were cavalry.

71. Leven to Marlborough, Dec. 31; Queensbury to same, Holyrood House, Dec. 17, 1706, Blenheim MS A.I.46, Add. MS 61136, 75 ("I hope the posting of these troops will confirm all honest men and put others out of hopes to disturb the peace"), 77–78, 79–80; Defoe to Harley, Nov. 30, 1706, HMC, *Portland MS*, 4:362, 364–66. HMC, *Mar and Kellie MS*, 1:296, 297, 323–26, 342–43, 346–47, 350, 352, 358, 363; GD 406/1/5353, 9738, SRO, Orkney to duchess Anne, Dec. 10, 1706, GD 406/1/5353, 6581, SRO.

72. Routh, *Burnet's History*, 5:285, 288, 289–90; William McDowall, *History of the Burgh of Dumfries*, 4th. ed. (Dumfries, 1986), 508–13. I am grateful to the Council of Galloway and Dumfries for this history. Riley, *Union*, 285–92; Speck, *Britain*, esp. 108–13.

73. Routh, *Burnet's History*, 5:291. Loudoun to Marlborough, Eden., Sept. 28, [1706], Add. MS 61286, 14–15b: "Your Grace's glorious victories amongst other good effects will contribute not a little to the promoting of the union." HMC, *Mar and Kellie MS*, 1:340, 351, 359, 382; HMC, *Portland MS*, 4:359, 360.

74. Blenheim MS 19:19, 20, 35, 36, etc.; Murray, *Dispatches*, 3:281–82; 312, 321, 322; Queensbury to Marlborough; Leven to same, Jan. 7, 1706/7, Add. MS 61136, 79–82. The Scots-Dutch soldiers at home also helped swing the Scots parliament toward union, as Argyll reported to Marlborough, Jan. 7, 1706/7, recommending Brig. Gen. George Hamilton's promotion to major general. This Hamilton acknowledged as a favor from Marlborough, Jan. 18, 1707, Add. MS 61289, 21, 23.

75. Dalton, *Army Lists*, 5: pt. 2, 13–14, 6:39; Orkney to Marlborough, Thursday night [Mar. 20, 1706/7], Blenheim MS, A.2.32. Marlborough wanted to control the sale of Hunter's troop so as to open a cornet's commission for queen Anne's page.

76. P. J. W. Riley, *The English Ministers in Scotland, 1701–1727* (London, 1964), 13–15, 90–91; Ferguson, *Scotland*, 53, Davenport, *Treaties*, 3:#94; Leven to Marlborough, [Jan. 7, 1707], Add. MS 61136, 81; Trevelyan, *Ramillies*, 175, 220–22, 236, 243, 248, 264–65. GD 406/1/5492, 5496, 8041, 8052, 8067, 8415, 7255, 8083, SRO; Dalton, *George the First's Army*, 35–38; Marlborough to Godolphin, Sept. 9, 1706, 658, Blenheim MS, A.I. 37, Snyder, *Correspondence*, 659; Webb, *Governors-General*, #203, 205, 206, 67, 68, 62.

77. Nairne to Mar, London, Mar. 6, 1706/7, HMC, *Mar and Kellie MS*, 383; Gregg, *Anne*, 239. As Seafield wrote to Marlborough, Edinburgh, Jan. 25, 1707, only Marlborough's victories, which eliminated hope of support from France against the union, made unconditional ratification of the union treaty possible, Blenheim MS, A.2.31, Add. MS 61136, 89.

Chapter 6. Oudenarde

1. Marlborough to Godolphin, Sept. 29, 1707, Coxe, *Marlborough*, 3:380–81; Snyder, *Correspondence*, 915–16; Speck, *Britain*, 132–34; Lediard, *Marlborough*, 2:231–32; Coxe, *Marlborough*, 4:20–21; Trevelyan, *Ramillies*, 327, 328, 332–33; Marlborough to Sunderland, Oct. 7, 1707, Coxe, *Marlborough*, 3:386; same to queen Anne, n.d., Coxe, *Marlborough*, 4:24, and see 23–28; Gregg, *Anne*, 256–57, 259; Vernon to Shrewsbury, Feb. 10, 14, 1707/8, G. P. R. James, ed., *Letters Illustrative of the Reign of William III* (London, 1841), 343–45, 347–48; PCDM, 2:11; HMC, *Portland MS*, 4:469–70.

2. Thomas Lediard, *The Naval History of England . . . 1066–1734* (London, 1735), 2:287; HMC, *Portland MS*, 4:465–66; Chandler, *Marlborough*, 206; 't Hoff,

Correspondence, 370–77; Marlborough to D'Auverquerque, Lumley, and Cadogan, Feb. 17, 1708; same to D'Auverquerque, Mar. 9, and to Cadogan, Mar. 11; same to Boyle, Apr. 13, 1708, Murray, *Dispatches*, 3:679–80, 689–90, 698, "Paris Advices," Mar. 7, from Cadogan, Mar. 10, 1708, Add. MS 61694; Sunderland to Cadogan, Mar. 5, 1707/8, Add. MS 61162, 128b, 130; Godolphin to Marlborough, Oct. 3, Nov. 19, 1709, Blenheim MS, A.II.38, Snyder, *Correspondence*, 1123, 1153–54. Owen, *War at Sea*, 251–70; HMC, *15th Report*, app. 4:466; Orkney to Selkirk, July 11, 1707, GD 406/1, #5466, SRO; Johnston, "Scots Army,"esp. 14–15. Godolphin to Marlborough, Mar. 1, Oct. 3, 1708, Blenheim MS A.I.38, Snyder, *Correspondence*, 1123; Cadogan to Marlborough, Mar. 20, 1708, NS, Add. MS 61160. King would be colonel of artillery and quartermaster general for the 1711 Canada expedition., Dalton, *Army Lists*, 4: pt. 2, 10n18.

3. Chandler, *Marlborough*, 206, numbers the French force as 6,000 troops, five men of war, fifteen privateers, fifteen transports. Milner, *Journal*, 205; Speck, *Britain*, 139; Coxe, *Marlborough*, 4:34; Marlborough to Leven, Mar. 12, 1708, Murray, *Dispatches*, 3:690–91; Walpole to Marlborough, Apr. 20, 1708, Add. MS 61133, 106. Johnston, "Scots Army," 17.

4. Lediard, *Naval History*, 2:828–29; Coxe, *Marlborough*, 4:37; Marlborough to Robinson, Mar. 2, 1708, Murray, *Dispatches*, 3:686; Orkney to Selkirk, Mar. 10, 1707/8, MS 1033, fol. 40, SRO; lord Archibald Hamilton [to Selkirk], Mar. 18, 1706, MS 1032, fol. 64, SRO; Owen, *War at Sea*, 242–45, makes Byng's squadron twenty-five ships, fifteen of the line.

5. Leven to Marlborough, Mar. 13–15 [1707/8], Add. MS 61136, 99, 101, 103–4; Cadogan to Marlborough, Mar. 20, 28, 1708, Add. MS 61160, 66; Sunderland to Cadogan, Mar. 11, 18, 1707/8, Add. MS 61651, 95; Trevelyan, *Ramillies*, 343; Owen, *War at Sea*, 253, 264–66; Kane, *Campaigns*, 72; Orkney to Selkirk, Mar. 16, 18, 1707/8, MS 1033, fols. 39v, 41r, SRO; J. H. Plumb, *Sir Robert Walpole*, 2 vols. (Cambridge, MA, 1956, 1961), 1:135–36; Maurice Ashley, *Marlborough*, 102. On Marlborough's personal experience of the dangers of the coastal route, see Webb, *Lord Churchill's Coup*, 63–65. For his preservation of the jacobite prisoners, see Marlborough to Berwick, Aug. 24, 1708, Churchill, *Marlborough*, 2:497–98.

6. Lediard, *Marlborough*, 2:237–40; Churchill, *Marlborough*, 2:332; Marlborough to Leven, Mar. 23; same to Stanhope, June 26, 1708, Murray, *Dispatches*, 3:695, 4:84; Cadogan to Cardonnel, Feb. 21, 1707/8, Add. MS 61413, 116; Basil Williams, *Stanhope* (Oxford, 1932), 68–69; Sunderland to Stanhope, Apr. 13, 1708, Add. MS 61651, 98b; Stanhope, memorandum, Add. MS 61651, 198–99.

7. Marlborough to Godolphin, Apr. 22/May 3, May 6/17, 1708, Coxe, *Marlborough*, 4:63, 104; Snyder, *Correspondence*, 960, 965, and see Coxe, *Marlborough*, 4:309–11.

8. Coxe, *Marlborough*, 4:99 has this May 9. Ibid., 4:105, numbers the allies as 112 battalions, 180 squadrons. [Lt. Col. Cranstoun to] Robert Cunningham, Apr. 27, 1708, OS, HMC, *Portland MS*, 4:487.

9. Lediard, *Marlborough*, 2:233; H. L. Snyder, "The Formation of Foreign and Domestic Policy in the Reign of Queen Anne," *HJ* 11 (1968): 144–60. See the plan to put two regiments in Newfoundland and "the proposal of the merchants concerned in the American trade," Marlborough to Boyle, Aug. 2, 1708, Murray, *Dispatches*,

4:143; Coxe, *Marlborough*, 4:161. Marlborough to Godolphin, May 21, 1708, Snyder, *Correspondence*, 977–78; *PCDM*, 1:384, 2:11.

10. Lediard, *Marlborough*, 2:236.

11. Marlborough to Stanhope, June 27, 1708, Blenheim MS 31:405; HMC, *Mar and Kellie MS*, 1:443; Mar to queen Anne, June 14, 1708, HMC, *Mar and Kellie MS*, 1:445–47, 449–50; Sunderland to Roxburghe, HMC, *Mar and Kellie MS*, 1:448; Mar to Stair, June 20, 1708, HMC, *Mar and Kellie MS*, 1:450–51; same to Nairne, HMC, *Mar and Kellie MS*, 1:453; duke of Hamilton to Sunderland, May 8, 19, 1708, PCDM 2:243–49.

12. Duke of Hamilton to Sunderland, May 22, June 7, 1708, Add. MS 61628, 87, 93, and see Montrose to Sunderland, June 1708, ibid., 136–37, 139, 143–45, 148. Riley, *English Ministers*, 104–5, 108; Orkney to Selkirk, Mar. 16, 1707/8, MS 1033, 39–40, SRO; A. Hamilton to same, Mar. 18, 1708, MS 1032, fol. 64, SRO; Marlborough to the duchess, May 17, 1706, Snyder, *Correspondence*, 976; Godolphin to Marlborough, Apr. 26, and reply, May 8, 1709, Snyder, *Correspondence*, 967, 971; Marlborough to Mar, May 31, 1708, Blenheim MS, 21:262, Murray, *Dispatches*, 4:44; HMC, *Mar and Kellie MS*, 1:442; Mar to the queen, June 14, 1708, *Mar and Kellie MS*, 1:446; Marlborough to Seafield, June 4, 1708, Murray, *Dispatches*, 4:49; duke of Hamilton to Sunderland, June 19, 1708, Add. MS 61628, 102–5. See Mar's reports to Marlborough, May 31, June 18, 1708, Add. MS 61136, 113–14.

13. Marlborough to the duchess, May 31, July 23, 1708, Blenheim MS, E.IV, Snyder, *Correspondence*, 976, 1035; Godolphin to Marlborough, June 18, 1708, Blenheim MS, A.II. 38, Snyder, *Correspondence*, 1016; Orkney to Selkirk, Oct. 11, 1707, MS 1033, fols. 34r–35v, SRO; *PCDM*, 1:327; Hunter's case: *CSPC*, *1706–1708*, #1047, p. 97. On Godolphin and the Virginia quitrents, see Webb, "Blathwayt," 414–15.

14. Montrose to Sunderland, [June 1, 1708], Add. MS 61628, 135; Orkney to Sunderland, June 22, 1708, ibid., 176–77. Marlborough to the duchess, [July 12/23, 1708], Snyder, *Correspondence*, 1035.

15. *PCDM*, 1:173–74, 2:103; Masham to Harley, HMC, *Portland MS*, 4:495–96, 499 (which contradicts Gregg, *Anne*, 260–61), and see Marlborough to the queen, May 9, 1708, Blenheim MS, E.2.

16. Godolphin to Marlborough, Apr. 19, 1708, Blenheim MS, A.I.38, Snyder, *Correspondence*, 957; same, June 13, 1708, ibid., 1009. Marlborough to the duchess, Aug. 2, 23, 1708, ibid., 1049n, 1073. Doubt is also cast on the duchess's assertions by Brian W. Hill, *Robert Harley* (New Haven, CT, 1988), 118. Godolphin to Marlborough, May 28, 1708, Blenheim MS, A.II.38, Snyder, *Correspondence*, 995n, 996; Dalton, "Soldiering," 71–73; Marlborough to Walpole, June 18, 1708, Blenheim MS, 21, 365, Murray, *Dispatches*, 4:67. Walpole to Marlborough, June 1, 29, 1708, Add. MS 61133, 111–12, 119. Marlborough's promotion list is in Add. MS 61321, 50. Walpole to Sunderland, June 2, 1708, Add. MS 61589, 97.

17. Cardonnel to Walpole, July 9, 1708, Blenheim MS, 31:399–400; E. Lewis to Harley, June 26, 1708, HMC, *Portland MS*, 4:494; Plumb, *Walpole*, 1:138–40; Godolphin to Marlborough, July 6, 1708, Snyder, *Correspondence*, 1027–28; Walpole to Marlborough, June 22, 1708, Coxe, *Walpole*, 2:9–11; Marlborough to Godolphin, July 9, 1708, Snyder, *Correspondence*, 1022n; Marlborough to the duchess, July 23,

Aug. 6, 1708, Blenheim MS, B.I.2, Snyder, *Correspondence*, 1035, 1052; *PCDM*, 1:146; Coxe, *Marlborough*, 4:190–91, 196–97, 201–2; Marlborough to George Churchill, n.d., Snyder, *Correspondence*, 1083–84; same to Walpole, July 1, 1708, Add. MS 61133, 125.

18. Kane, *Campaigns*, 72–73; De la Colonie, *Chronicles*, 327–28; Coxe, *Marlborough*, 4:100, 127; Lediard, *Marlborough*, 2:247–53; Blackadder, *Diary*, 75; J. R. Jones, *Marlborough* (Cambridge, 1993), 152–54; Chandler, *Marlborough*, 212; Marlborough to Brydges, July 2; same to Boyle, July 9, 1708, Murray, *Dispatches*, 4:92, 100; Atkinson, *Marlborough*, 391.

19. Coxe, *Marlborough*, 4:126, 130–31; Lediard, *Marlborough*, 2:254; HMC, *Hare MS*, 217–18; Chandler, *Marlborough*, 213.

20. Lediard, *Marlborough*, 2:254, 256–57; Coxe, *Marlborough*, 4:131–32; Milner, *Journal*, 214; Chandler, *Marlborough*, map facing 211; Atkinson, *Marlborough*, 335; Marlborough to the duchess, July 9, 1708, Snyder, *Correspondence*, 1023; Murray, *Dispatches*, 4:91; Marlborough to Boyle, July 9, 1708, Murray, *Dispatches*, 4:100–102; Belloc, *Marlborough*, 158–59, map facing 161.

21. Belloc, *Marlborough*, 161, 163; *Historie de Jean Churchill, Duc de Marlborough* (Paris, 1808), 2:332, map appended.

22. Milner, *Journal*, 213–14; Coxe, *Marlborough*, 4:137–38; Lediard, *Marlborough*, 2:259, 282, 286; Belloc, *Marlborough*, 161, 174; Churchill, *Marlborough*, 2:357.

23. To maps cited above, add Coxe, *Marlborough*, *Atlas*, "Plan of the Battle of Oudenarde."

24. Coxe, *Marlborough*, 4:139–40; Milner, *Journal*, 216; Chandler, *Marlborough*, 215; Scot, "Remembrancer," 410; Lediard, *Marlborough*, 2:288–89.

25. Lediard, *Marlborough*, 2:263, 279; Churchill, *Marlborough*, 2:363; Scot, "Remembrancer," 412; [Richard Cannon], *Historical Record of the Eighth or King's Regiment* (London, 1844), 38–39; MacKinnon, *Coldstream Guards*, 317.

26. Lediard, *Marlborough*, 2:264, 279–80; Milner, *Journal*, 216; Atkinson, *Marlborough*, 340.

27. Lediard, *Marlborough*, 2:265; Coxe, *Marlborough*, 4:144–45; Maurice, *16th*, 42–43; Dalton, *Army Lists*, 6:88, 333–34. Webb, *Governors-General*, #207, 208, 159, 168.

28. Chandler, *Marlborough*, 220.

29. Auverquerque's dispatch puts this at 5:00, Lediard, *Marlborough*, 2:282; Coxe, *Marlborough*, 4:147–48; Milner, *Journal*, 217.

30. Coxe, *Marlborough*, 4:147–50; Churchill, *Marlborough*, 2:375; Murray, *Dispatches*, 3:321n; *An Historical Account of the British Regiments . . . Particularly of the Scotch Brigade* (London, 1794), 2:11–12; HMC, *Mar and Kellie MS*, 458–60.

31. Lediard, *Marlborough*, 2:267–68; Milner, *Journal*, 217; Kane, *Campaigns*, 74–75; Rex Whitworth, *Field Marshal Lord Ligonier* (Oxford, 1958), 26; Cannon, *Tenth*, 25; *Historie de Jean Churchill*, 2:339.

32. Coxe, *Marlborough*, 4:152; Lediard, *Marlborough*, 2:269, 272, 284, 286–87, 289, 292.

33. Marlborough to Manchester, July 15; same to Boyle, July 12, 16, 1708, Murray, *Dispatches*, 4:104, 109, 112; same to Godolphin, July 12, 1708, Jan. 23, 1708/9, Blenheim MS, A.II.39, Snyder, *Correspondence*, 1024, 1200; same to the duchess, Jan. 23,

1708/9, Blenheim MS, E.IV, Snyder, *Correspondence*, 1181. Marlborough to Godol-phin, July 26, 1708, Coxe, *Marlborough*, 4:169. Snyder, *Correspondence*, 1038, made French losses 20,000; Milner, *Journal*, 218–19, tallied 19,400 French losses, and 3,041 allied casualties, half of them Dutch. Matthew Bishop, *The Life and Adventures of Matthew Bishop* (London, 1749), 160.

34. Lediard, *Marlborough*, 2:292–93; Marlborough to Boyle, July 16, 1708, Blen-heim MS, B.I.1, Add. MS 61128; Murray, *Dispatches*, 4:109; Milner, *Journal*, 221–23; Bishop, *Life*, 162–63.

35. Lediard, *Marlborough*, 2:297, 299; Murray, *Dispatches*, 4:120, 126; Marlborough to Halifax, July 26, 1708, Add. MS 61134, 198; Murray, *Dispatches*, 4:113, 129, 131–32, 134; Marlborough to Orkney, July 23, 1708, Murray, *Dispatches*, 4:135–37; Milner, *Journal*, 223; Marlborough to Boyle, July 15/26, 1708, Add. MS 61128; same to Go-dolphin, July 26, 1708, Coxe, *Marlborough*, 4:164–65, 167–68, 173, 232, 242–43; Dal-ton, *George the First's Army*, 1:37; *Historie de Jean Churchill*, 2:353, 355–56.

36. Lediard, *Marlborough*, 2:303–4; Murray, *Dispatches*, 4:137; Coxe, *Marlborough*, 4:215–16; Milner, *Journal*, 227–28; Chandler, *Art of War*, 246–48.

37. Marlborough to Orkney, July 29, 1708, Blenheim MS, 44:31; Murray, *Dispatches*, 4:124, 126; Coxe, *Marlborough*, 4:177, 217; Lediard, *Marlborough*, 2:78; Marlborough to Stanhope, June 26, July 15, 1708, Add. MS 61157, 113, Murray, *Dispatches*, 4:84, 108; same to same, Oct. 24, 1708, Blenheim MS, B.I.14, Add. MS 61157, 116; Churchill, *Marlborough*, 2:469–70; Williams, *Stanhope*, 71–73, 74n, 80–82; Boyle to Marlbor-ough, Oct. 19, 1708, Add. MS 61128, 164; Carpenter to same, Add. MS 61158, 199.

38. See also R. G. Thurburn, "The Capture of Minorca, 1709," *JSAHR* 55 (1977): 65–72; Whitworth, *Ligonier*, 31–37; Webb, *Governors-General*, #130–37.

39. Marlborough to Stanhope, Jan. 26, [1708/9], Blenheim MS, B.I.14, Add. MS 61157, 124b, and replies, 130–34, 154; Sunderland to Stanhope [ca. Oct. 19], Dec. 10, 1708, Add. MS 16151, 132, 141b.

40. Erle-Marlborough correspondence, Add. MS 61158, 75ff.; draft instructions to Erle, July 20, 1708, Add. MS 61157, 153. Milner, *Journal*, 223–24; Marlborough to Boyle, Aug. 3, Sept. 10, 1708, Add. MS 61128, 96, 150, and see 105, 109; Coxe, *Marlborough*, 4:175, 221, 223, 225, 233; Andros to Sunderland, July 15, 1708, Add. MS 61546, 106. Webb, *Governors-General*, #30, 116, 148, 201, Stephen Saunders Webb, *1676: The End of American Independence* (New York, 1984), books 2, 4; Webb, *Lord Churchill's Coup*, esp. 181–98, 200–205.

41. Geoffrey Powell, *The Green Howards* (London, 1968), 24, 27; Coxe, *Marlbor-ough*, 4:240–48; Dalton, *Army Lists*, 3:204, 4:276, 5:254, 280–82. Erle also enlisted Marlborough's patronage for Col. Pearne, who found himself commanding Mont-serrat in Douglas's regime, Webb, *Governors-General*, #96, 82. Marlborough to Erle, July 12/23, 1708, Add. MS 61158, 77; Luttrell, *Brief Relations*, 6:337; Penn to Harley, July 14, 1706 ("my son, captain of a foot company, he shall dig potatoes first"), HMC, *Portland MS*, 4:316, and see 80, 287, 551.

42. Sunderland to Popple, June 11, 1708, Add. MS 61653, 163. On the Palatine exo-dus, see ch. 12 below. Webb, *Governors-General*, #157.

43. Pringle to Hunter, n.d.; same to Craggs, Dec. 23, 1709, Add. MS 61653, 193b, 197ff. Add. MS 61594, 39, 69; Sunderland to Cadogan, Jan. 2, Feb. 11, 1708/9, Add.

MS 61651, 80, 151. Hunter to Sunderland, Paris, Dec. 28, Feb. 28, 1709, Add. MS 61595, 58, 72; same to Dr. [Peter] Silvestre, Mar. 28, 1709, Add. MS 61595, 81; Lustig, *Hunter*, 48; Boyle to Marlborough, Apr. 27, May 10, 1708, Add. MS 61128, 27, 37, 56; Commissioners for Sick and Wounded to Sunderland, June 17, 1709, Add. MS 61593, 75–79; Ponchartrain to Sunderland, May 22, July 3, 1709, Add. MS 61593, 49, 53; Hunter to Sunderland, May 5, 1709, Add. MS 61595, 87.

44. The account, misdated to the previous year, is given by Rev. Robert Rose, July 15, 1743, Spottiswoode Papers, MS 2933, 139, NLS; Murray, *Dispatches*, 4:169, 180, 192.

45. Churchill, *Marlborough*, 2:497–504; Marlborough to Townshend, Aug. 13, 1708, Murray, *Dispatches*, 4:164; Ashley, *Marlborough*, 102–5.

46. Godolphin to Marlborough, Aug. 2, 1708, Blenheim MS, A.II.38, Snyder, *Correspondence*, 1057. H. Kamen, *War of the Succession in Spain, 1700–1715* (London, 1969), 185; Ruth Anne Bourne, *Queen Anne's Navy in the West Indies* (New Haven, CT, 1939), 170–72; Charnock, *Biographia Navalis*, 2:432; Josiah Burchett, *A Complete History of the Most Remarkable Transactions at Sea* (London, 1720), 707; Handasyde to Sunderland, Mar. 31, June 14, 17, 1708, Add. MS 61643, 134, 147, 149.

47. Handaysde to Sunderland, June 17, Aug. 6, 1708, Add. MS 61643, 150, 162–63; Macartney to Marlborough, Dec. 14, 1708, Blenheim MS, 1:28; Godolphin to Marlborough, July 30, Aug. 20, Sept. 1, 3, 6, 1708, Blenheim MS, A.II.38, Snyder, *Correspondence*, 1056n, 1079, 1093–95. Peterborough's offer of service to Marlborough, Sept. 26, 1707, Add. MS 61413, 109; HMC, *Portland MS*, 4:503; Handasyde to Sunderland, Sept. 24, Oct. 27, Dec. 4, 1708, Feb. 1, 1708/9, Blenheim MS, C.II.42, Add. MS 61643, 166, 167, 173–74, 178–79.

48. Milner, *Journal*, 226, 229, 234; Maurice, *16th*, 44; Marlborough to Cadogan, Aug. 2, 1708, Add. MS 61160, 81; Atkinson, *Marlborough*, 351, 353; HMC, *Hare MS*, 219–20; Lediard, *Marlborough*, 2:306, 358–59; HMC, *Mar and Kellie MS*, 464; Marlborough to Godolphin, Nov. 29, 1708, Snyder, *Correspondence*, 1152.

49. HMC, *Mar and Kellie MS*, 464; Atkinson, "Marlborough's Sieges," 198; Marlborough to Stanhope, Dec. 10, [1708], Blenheim MS, B.I.14, Add. MS 61157, 122; Milner, *Journal*, 224–25, 233; Kane, *Campaigns*, 76; Lediard, *Marlborough*, 2:328–29.

50. Lediard, *Marlborough*, 2:338–40, 341, 348; Milner, *Journal*, 235–45. Allied casualties were about 900. French losses were 6,000–7,000: Coxe, *Marlborough*, 249; HMC, *Mar and Kellie MS*, 465; Bishop, *Life*, 189, makes the French 24,000, Webb's allied command 7,000. Webb's account is in Lediard, *Marlborough*, 2:341–47. Atkinson, "Marlborough's Sieges," 200. On the tactical importance of the quartermasters (likely commanded on this occasion by Spotswood or Armstrong), see C. T. Atkinson, "Wynendael," *JSAHR* 34 (1956): 28. See also maps in Atkinson, "Wynendael," 27, 31; and Coxe, *Marlborough*, *Atlas*, and "Wynendael," in Wace, *Marlborough Tapestries*, #46.

51. Marlborough to Webb, Sept. 29, 1708, Add. MS 61312, 106, Murray, *Dispatches*, 4:242–43. Webb was also very popular with the troops, Bishop, *Life*, 179–82; HMC, *Portland MS*, 503; [E. Lewis to Robert] Harley, Oct. 5, 7, 15, 1708, HMC, *Portland MS*, 506–9; Sunderland to Marlborough, Oct. 5, 1708, Marlborough to Godolphin, Oct. 8, 9, Nov. 28, Coxe, *Marlborough*, 4:259, 260, 279; Snyder, *Correspondence*, 1152;

Godolphin to Marlborough, Oct. 17, 1708, Blenheim MS, A.II.38, Snyder, *Correspondence*, 1130; Marlborough to Sunderland, Sept. 17/29, [Sept. 20/]Oct. 1, Blenheim MS, B.I.13, 14, Add. MS 61126, 152–53; 61127, 1; Webb to Marlborough, Nov. 1, 1708, Add. MS 61312, 132. As a reward, Webb was commissioned governor of the Isle of Wight. Note Marlborough's constant attention to garrison government appointments on both sides of the Atlantic, even as the siege wore him down. For example, Col. Spicer, the wagon master general, was given Landguard Fort, but "the little Government" of Calshot Castle, "where there is no Salary upon the Establishment whereby it might be a provision for any old officer of the Army," was allowed to pass to a relative of the speaker, Cardonnel to Walpole, Nov. 2, Dec. 17, 1708, Blenheim MS, 32:54–55, 122–23; [Sir John] Smith to Marlborough, Nov. 22, 1708, Add. MS 61297, 180. Marlborough to Godolphin, Oct. 1, reply, Oct. 8, Coxe, *Marlborough*, 4:255–56; Snyder, *Correspondence*, 1106; Dalton, *Army Lists*, 6:17; Lt. Col. E. A. H. Webb, *History of the 12th (the Suffolk) Regiment, 1683–1913* (London, 1914), 41; Godolphin to Marlborough, Dec. 14, 1708, Blenheim MS, A.2.38, Snyder, *Correspondence*, 1175; Atkinson, *Marlborough*, 359; Kane, *Campaigns*, 77; Marlborough to Walpole, [Sept. 20/Oct. 1, 1708], Add. MS 61133, 136.

52. Murray, *Dispatches*, 4:253; Stair to Mar, Oct. 15, 1708, HMC, *Mar. MS*, 466; Marlborough to Sunderland, Oct. 19, 1708, Blenheim MS, B.I.14, Add. MS 61127, 23; Lediard, *Marlborough*, 2:350, 353–55; Coxe, *Marlborough*, 4:257–58. Webb, *Governors-General*, #82, 2, 170.

53. Milner, *Journal*, 237–38; Lediard, *Marlborough*, 2:332–33, 351, 356–57; Coxe, *Marlborough*, 4:262; HMC, *Portland MS*, 508. Erle to Marlborough, Sept. 26, Oct. 15, 17, 19, 25, 29, Nov. 3, 1708, Add. MS 61158, 105, 120, 122, 125, 126; same to Sunderland, July 21, Sept. 6, 10, Oct. 25, 28, 1708, Mar. 2, 1708/9, Add. MS 61577, 137, 141, 144, 155, 161, 185; Sunderland to Marlborough, July 23, Add. MS 61126, 118; same, Sept. 24, 1708, Add. MS 61127, 4b; Marlborough to Sunderland, [Aug. 2/13, 1708]. Add. MS 61128, 121; Marlborough to Erle, Nov. 8, 1708, Add. MS 61158, 143; lngoldsby to Cardonnel, 1 br 16, 1708, Add. MS 61413, 136; Stair to Marlborough, Nov. 16, 1708, Add. MS 61115, 30; Godolphin to Marlborough, Dec. 17, 1708, Blenheim MS, A.II. 61133, 130; Webb, *12th*, 39–40, 42. The fall of the garrison is detailed in Toby Caulfield's letter of Oct. 17/28, Add. MS 61158, 133–34. Gledhill, a client of the earl of Carlisle, was afterward patronized by Orkney and Sutton. Gledhill to Marlborough, Sept. 4, 1707, Add. MS 61288, 55, and see 57, 72; Webb, *Governors-General*, #145. The importance of the loss of Leffinghe is reflected in the extent of the documentation.

54. The news of Port Mahon's surrender arrived together with that of Leffinghe, and nearly coincided with the capitulation for the city of Lille: Sunderland to Erle, Oct. 19, 1708, Add. MS 61651, 467. Marlborough to Sunderland, Oct. 24, Nov. 1, 1708, Blenheim MS, B.I.14, Add. MS 61127, 29–31; Lediard, *Marlborough*, 2:357, 367ff.; Atkinson, *Marlborough*, 361; Coxe, *Marlborough*, 4:263, 273ff.; Marlborough to Godolphin, Nov. 6, 16, 1708, Coxe, *Marlborough*, 4:267, 269; same to Boyle, Nov. 27, 1708, Murray, *Dispatches*, 4:324; Milner, *Journal*, 224, 244; R. Molesworth to his brother, Dec. 3, 1708, Add. MS 61312, 186ff. For an assessment of Marlborough's relation to prince George, see Webb, *Lord Churchill's Coup*, esp. 131–32.

55. Atkinson, *Marlborough*, 362–63; Lediard, *Marlborough*, 2:373–76; Marlborough to the duchess, Nov. 23, 1708, Snyder, *Correspondence*, 1150; Marlborough to Boyle, Nov. 27, 29, 1708, Add. MS 61128, 186–87, Murray, *Dispatches*, 4:326. Marlborough to Stanhope, Dec. 10, [1708], Blenheim MS, B.I.14, Add. MS 61157, 121–23. Lediard, *Marlborough*, 2:371–73, 380, 381; Marlborough to Godolphin, Nov. 29, 1708, Coxe, *Marlborough*, 4:280–88; Atkinson, *Marlborough*, 363; Milner, *Journal*, 245–48; Kane, *Campaigns*, 77–78.

56. Coxe, *Marlborough*, 4:289–90; Milner, *Journal*, 248–49.

57. Lediard, *Marlborough*, 2:403, 409–12; Marlborough to Godolphin, Dec. 10, 27, 1708, Coxe, *Marlborough*, 4:290–91, 195, and see 292–300; Milner, *Journal*, 251–56; Webb, *Lord Churchill's Coup*, 36; Marlborough to Godolphin, Nov. 28, 1708 Snyder, *Correspondence*, 1151.

Chapter 7. Malplaquet

1. Marlborough to the duchess [Dec. 27, 1708/Jan. 7, 1709]; same to Godolphin, Jan. 16, 1708/9, Snyder, *Correspondence*, 1189, 1193–94. Walpole to Marlborough, Feb. 11, 1708/9, Add. MS 61193, 170, on the "easiest" parliament he could recall, thanks to Harley's rebuff at Bewdly and the defeat of Harcourt, the leaders of the "adverse party."

2. Lediard, *Marlborough*, 2:427–29; Coxe, *Marlborough*, 4:375–76, 381.

3. Godolphin to Marlborough, Feb. 11, 1708/9, Snyder, *Correspondence*, 1226; *CSPC*, *1708–1709*, #890.

4. Macartney to Marlborough, London, Dec. 14, 1708, Add. MS 61312, 220 and see 61313, 143; Godolphin to Marlborough, Feb. 7, 1708/9, Blenheim MS B.I.22b, Snyder, *Correspondence*, 1226.

5. Godolphin to Marlborough, Jan. 30, 1708/9, April 1, 1709, Blenheim MS B.I.22b, Snyder, *Correspondence*, 1212, 1237. Marlborough to Godolphin, Feb. 22, 1709, Blenheim MS, A.II.39, Snyder, *Correspondence*, 1225–27. Marlborough to Godolphin, Feb. 21, 1709, Godolphin to Marlborough, Snyder, *Correspondence*, 1224–25. Th. Pulteney to Marlborough, May 2, 1710, Add. MS 61293, 171b; Godolphin to Marlborough, Apr. 1, 1709, Snyder, *Correspondence*, 1237.

6. Marlborough to Walpole, Feb. 4, 1709, Murray, *Dispatches*, 4:424; Marlborough to Chamillard, Apr. 26, 1709, ibid., 4:492. Godolphin to Marlborough, Jan. 30, Feb. 11, 1708/9, Blenheim MS B.I.22b, Snyder, *Correspondence*, 1212, 1226; Macartney to Sunderland [Mar. 1708/9], Add. 61590, 110; Dalton, *Army Lists*, 6:302n7.

7. Vetch Letterbook, [ca. Mar. 11, 1709], 2, CMNY.

8. Marlborough to Heinsius, London, Apr. 29, 1709, Churchill, *Marlborough*, 2:53–56, Snyder, *Correspondence*, 1226; Waller, *Vetch*, 23; Nicholson/Vetch Journal, June 28, 1709, *CSPC*, *1708–1709*, #604; Th. Lloyd to Marlborough, n.d., Add. MS 61208, 225–26. On the capture of St. John's, Newfoundland, Dec. 21, 1708, see *CSPC*, *1708–1709*, #859, 890, 911, 922. Webb, *Governors-General*, 495–96; #139–41, 143.

9. Lediard, *Marlborough*, 2:431–32; Snyder, *Correspondence*, 1220n; Godolphin to Marlborough, Apr. 4, 1709; Marlborough to Godolphin, Apr. 16, 1709; Marlborough to the duchess, Aug. 27/ Sept. 2, 1709, Snyder, *Correspondence*, 1240–41, 1356;

Coxe, *Marlborough*, 4:386–89, 409. Ashley, *Marlborough*, 109, positively asserts that Marlborough sabotaged the Barrier negotiation to preserve his prospective viceroyalty.

10. Coxe, *Marlborough*, 4:391; Churchill, *Marlborough*, 2:534, 539; Davenport, *Treaties*, 2:136.

11. Coxe, *Marlborough*, 4:395, 397–98; Articles 7, 16, Davenport, *Treaties*, 137n26, 138; Marlborough to the duchess, Jan. 26, 1709; the duchess to Marlborough, Jan. 30, Mar. 29, 1708/9, Add. MS 61157, 124–33. Note the replication of the 1702 plan in 1739–41, 1778, and 1798.

12. Rivers to Marlborough, Sept. 9, 1709, Add. MS 61313, 142; Add. MS 61321, 130, 138; Add. MS 61590, 160; Whetham to Marlborough, Jan. 10, 1704/5, Add. MS 61297, 100, 105, Dalton, *Army Lists*, 6:20; Webb, *Governors-General*, #77; Godolphin to Marlborough, June 26, 1709, Blenheim Papers, B.I.22b, Snyder, *Correspondence*, 1294; Marlborough to the duchess, May 21, 1709, Snyder, *Correspondence*, 1252n4. In May, the leadership of the American expedition was informed that Macartney's exchange had failed and that Whetham had taken over the command, with revised orders: Waller, *Vetch*, 150; *CSPC*, *1708–1709*, #492, 497, 498. Sunderland to Marlborough, Apr. 12, 1709, Add. MS 61127, 46. Like British colonels in colonial commands all around the Atlantic, Elliot was lobbying Marlborough to promote him brigadier general on the Gibraltar establishment, Add. MS 61321, 138.

13. Marlborough to Godolphin, May 19, 1709, Blenheim MS A.II.39, Snyder, *Correspondence*, 1250; same to duchess, May 25, 1709, Snyder, *Correspondence*, 1255, for Sunderland's information. Godolphin to Marlborough, May 24, 1709, Snyder, *Correspondence*, 1262; Davenport, *Treaties*, 3:139, #27; William Churchill to Marlborough, May 20, 1709, Blenheim MS B.I.27, Add. MS 61366, 189. William Potter to Marlborough, Hudson's Bay House, Feb. 17, 1709/10, Add. MS 61303, 134; Stephen Evance to Sunderland, Apr. 18, 1709, Add. MS 61647, 131. Note the division between commerce and capital in the contest for Marlborough's support.

14. William Penn to "My Noble friend," Marlborough, Bristol, May 22, 1709, OS, Add. MS 9105, Coxe Papers, XXVIII, quoted in Davenport, *Treaties*, 3:139–40n29; Richard S. Dunn and Mary Maples Dunn, eds., *Papers of William Penn* (Philadelphia, 1981), 4:644–45 et seq.; J. D. Alsop, "William Penn's West India Peace Aims of 1709," *Journal of Caribbean History* 19 (1984): 68–75. Blenheim MS B.I.28; Penn to Marlborough, May 3, 1710, enclosed an antique proposal for free seas in the West Indies, Add. MS 61366, 179–82. Penn anticipated that his American proposals would bring in £1 million per annum to "our poor country": Add. MS 61366, 139, 173, 191–92. Richard Long, who had explored Darien for William III prior to the ill-fated Scots colony, now lobbied Marlborough to include that territory in the peace cessions to England, Jan. 24, Apr. 22, 1709, Blenheim MS B.I.28. Marlborough was also asked to judge Portugal's claims in the Amazon estuary, Add. MS 61127, 50–52; Add. MS 61651, 166. For his prior rejection of France's continental claims, see Webb, *Lord Churchill's Coup*, 114–18.

15. Articles 3, 5, 37, Davenport, *Treaties*, 3:137n25, 138n26; Marlborough to the duchess, May 19, 1709, Snyder, *Correspondence*, 1350–51; Lediard, *Marlborough*, 2:437–38; *Lives of the Generals*, 129; Buckley, *Memoirs of Ailesbury*, 615; Cranstoun to

Cunningham, July 25, 1708 [*sic* for 1709], HMC, *Portland MS*, 4:497; Godolphin to Marlborough, July 6, 1709, Snyder, *Correspondence*, 1304.

16. Cranstoun to Cunningham, July 25, 1708, HMC, *Portland MS*, 4:497; Godolphin to Marlborough, May 31, 1709, Blenheim MS B.I.22b, Snyder, *Correspondence*, 1270.

17. Marlborough to the duchess, June 17, 1709, Blenheim MS E.4. Of course, she thought that the French decision to reject the preliminaries had been encouraged by the tories out of their partiality for the pretender, places, and power. Same to Godolphin, June 7, 1709, Blenheim MS A.I.39, Snyder, *Correspondence*, 1266; Lediard, *Marlborough*, 2:45[1], 454, 433; Jones, *Marlborough*, 173.

18. Hamilton, *Guards*, 2:39; HMC, *Portland MS*, 4:498; Churchill, *Marlborough*, 2:570–71.

19. Marlborough to Godolphin, July 7/18, Sept. 1, 1709, Blenheim MS B.I.22b, Snyder, *Correspondence*, 1305, 1361n; Stanhope to Marlborough, June 15; reply, July 31; Marlborough to Boyle, Aug. 5, 1709, Murray, *Dispatches*, 4:561–62, 568–69.

20. Lediard, *Marlborough*, 2:455–56 [455 is misprinted as 551]; Robert Graves, *Goodbye to All That* (1929; repr., London, 1966), 125; Marlborough to Boyle, June 27, 1709, Murray, *Dispatches*, 4:520; Milner, *Journal*, 260–61.

21. Kane, *Campaigns*, 78; Lediard, *Marlborough*, 2:459–61, 481, 482; G. M. Trevelyan, *England under Queen Anne*, vol. 3, *Peace and the Protestant Succession* (London, 1934), 7; Marlborough to the queen, July 29; same to Boyle, Aug. 12, 15, 1709, Murray, *Dispatches*, 4:556, 572, 574; *Daily Courant*, Aug. 20, 1709, quoted in Lawrence Weaver, *The Story of the Royal Scots* (London, n.d.), 76.

22. For cabinet expectations, see Sunderland to Galloway, May 24, 1709, Add. MS 61651, 168. Vetch to Boyle, New York, June 28, 1709, *CSPC, 1708–1709*, #602.

23. Godolphin to Marlborough, Windsor, Aug. 17, 18, 1709, Blenheim MS B.I.22b, Snyder, *Correspondence*, 1346, 1348. Vetch to Boyle, New York, June 28, 1709, *CSPC, 1708–1709*, #602; Add. MS 61695, 5–10b.

24. Hunter was still a prisoner, his ship having been taken en route to his government of Virginia. On the vexed question of his exchange, see Commissioners for Sick and Wounded to Sunderland, June 17; Ponchartrain to same, May 22, July 3, 27, 1709, Add. MS 61593, 76–78; 61594, 39, 49, 53, 68. Marlborough to Godolphin, Aug. 22, Sept. 9, 1709, Blenheim MS A.II.39, Snyder, *Correspondence*, 1339, 1355. For Halifax on war in the West Indies, see HMC, *Bath MS*, 1:155.

25. Marlborough to Godolphin, Oct. 3, 1709, Blenheim MS A.II.39; Snyder, *Correspondence*, 1381. On Lowther's troublemaking in the ordnance, see Erle to Marlborough, May 6, 1709, Apr. 25, 1710, Add. MS 61158, 164, 170; 61–66, 76–77, 102, 104–9. As Lowther noted, the immediate issue was his use of ordnance patronage to support his parliamentary interest as MP for Westmoreland. Lowther did become governor general of Barbados in 1710 and served until 1721. Marlborough to Lowther, Sept. 19, 1709, Blenheim MS, 23:360; Webb, *Governors-General*, #14. Marlborough to Godolphin, Oct. 3, 1709, Blenheim MS A.II.39, Snyder, *Correspondence*, 1381–82.

26. James Craggs to Marlborough, May 20, 1709, Add. MS 61164, 195–98; Churchill, *Marlborough*, 2:639. Marlborough did get his authority formally extended to Scotland as master general of the ordnance (his officers had been engaged there since the invasion attempt), Add. MS 61166, 35, 39, 47, 69b–71b. Marlborough acted as commander in chief there as well: attorney general Sir Simon Harcourt to Marlborough, July 29, 1709, Add. MS 61365, 153. Atkinson, *Marlborough*, 412–14; Churchill, *Marlborough*, 2:640; Coxe, *Marlborough*, 5:118; and Chandler, *Marlborough*, 270–72, all treat the application for the captain generalcy for life under varying dates. These are disentangled by Henry L. Snyder, "The Duke of Marlborough's Request of His Captain Generalcy for Life: A Re-examination," *JSAHR* 45 (1967): 67, 71, 73. Cowper to Marlborough, June 23, 1709, in Churchill, *Marlborough*, 2:640, and see 642.

27. Marlborough to the queen, Tournai, Sept. 3, 1709, Murray, *Dispatches*, 4:588; Jones, *Marlborough*, 174, 176. S.v. "the ffrench Dominions," Vetch Letterbook, 53, CMNY.

28. Marlborough to the queen, Sept. 11, 1709, Murray, *Dispatches*, 4:59; Milner, *Journal*, 268–69, but see Churchill, *Marlborough*, 2:591. Atkinson, *Marlborough*, 390–91. Coxe, *Marlborough*, 5:20, has Orkney marching on Aug. 31 and Hesse-Cassell early on Sept. 3, followed by Cadogan at 9:00 p.m. and the main body at midnight. For this march and the eight days that followed, see Marlborough to Godolphin, Sept. 19, 1709, Snyder, *Correspondence*, 1369.

29. Lediard, *Marlborough*, 2:490–91; map in Churchill, *Marlborough*, 2:593; Marlborough to Godolphin, Sept. 16, 1709, Snyder, *Correspondence*, 1367.

30. Lediard, *Marlborough*, 2:491; De la Colonie, *Chronicles*, 336–67; Orkney to his brother [Selkirk?], Sept. 16, 1709, "Letters," 317, 318; Atkinson, *Marlborough*, 399; Marlborough to the duchess, [Sept. 10], 1709, Snyder, *Correspondence*, 1359.

31. Orkney, "Letters," 318; Chandler, *Marlborough*, 253; Coxe, *Marlborough*, 5:34, confirms that "the golden moment of attack" was lost on the afternoon of Sept. 9 when Eugene's troops could not join. Atkinson, *Marlborough*, 395; Jones, *Marlborough*, 178; Marlborough to the duchess, [Sept. 10], 1709, Snyder, *Correspondence*, 1359; same to Boyle, Sept. 11, 1709, Murray, *Dispatches*, 4:592; Lediard, *Marlborough*, 2:492, 507–8, 542; De la Colonie, *Chronicles*, 337; Churchill, *Marlborough*, 2:598; Coxe, *Marlborough*, 5: 40–41; Atkinson, *Marlborough*, 397; Bishop, *Life*, 208; Milner, *Journal*, 273.

32. Coxe, *Marlborough*, 5:43. MacKinnon, *Coldstream Guards*, 1:321, makes the armies equal, each with a nominal 100,000 men and an actual 93,000.

33. De la Colonie, *Chronicles*, 337; Orkney, "Letters," 318; Chandler, *Marlborough*, map, 256, 258; Marlborough to Boyle, Sept. 11, 1709, Murray, *Dispatches*, 4:592; Lediard, *Marlborough*, 2:507; Coxe, *Marlborough*, 5:48; Blackadder, *Diary*, 107.

34. Milner, *Journal*, 275; Scot, "Remembrancer," 486, 492; Coxe, *Marlborough*, 5:20, 49, 77–78; De la Colonie, *Chronicles*, 338; Kane, *Campaigns*, 80; Chandler, *Marlborough*, map, 256, and see 258; Trevelyan, *Peace*, 15; [Richard Cannon], *Historical Record of the Third Regiment of Foot, or the Buffs* (London, 1839), 158; Marlborough to the duchess, Oct. 3, 1709, Snyder, *Correspondence*, 1383; Marlborough to Godolphin, Sept. 13, 1709, Blenheim MS A.II.39, Snyder, *Correspondence*, 1363; same to Boyle, Sept. 11, 1709, Lediard, *Marlborough*, 2:508; Bishop, *Life*, 209–13.

35. Coxe, *Marlborough*, 5:51; Churchill, *Marlborough*, 2:608; Jones, *Marlborough*, 179–80; Scot, "Remembrancer," 487, 493–95; Orkney, "Letters," 319. In forty years of war, the Dutch had not suffered such a loss of infantry (8,462), Snyder,

Correspondence, 1377n17; Marlborough to Godolphin, Sept. 26, 1709, Snyder, *Correspondence*, 1376–1377; Atkinson, *Marlborough*, 402; Chandler, *Marlborough*, 269.

36. Churchill, *Marlborough*, 2:603, makes Orkney's command nineteen battalions, of which thirteen were "English." Orkney, "Letters," 319, perhaps to palliate his disobedience, did not recall sending the remainder of his first brigade, the 10th and 37th regiments, to attack the woods on his right flank, but see Cannon, *Tenth*, 28. Chandler, *Marlborough*, 259; De la Colonie, *Chronicles*, 338–39; Coxe, *Marlborough*, 5:56; Milner, *Journal*, 275–76.

37. Orkney, "Letters," 320; De la Colonie, *Chronicles*, 339–40, 341.

38. Marlborough to Godolphin, Sept. 13, 1709, Blenheim MS A.II.39, Snyder, *Correspondence*, 1363; Orkney, "Letters," 319; De la Colonie, *Chronicles*, 342; Scot, "Remembrancer," 496. Coxe, *Marlborough*, 5:59, makes the cavalry order of battle: d'Auvergne's Dutch; Wood's British; Blau's Prussians and Hanoverians; Wirtemberg's and Vehlen's Imperialists.

39. Lediard, *Marlborough*, 2:494, 508, 536; Orkney, "Letters," 320; Marlborough to Godolphin, Sept. 13, 26, 1709, Blenheim MS A.II.39, Snyder, *Correspondence*, 1363, 1377; Milner, *Journal*, 276–77; Scot, "Remembrancer," 488–89, 496; Churchill, *Marlborough*, 2:626; Coxe, *Marlborough*, 5:62–63; De la Colonie, *Chronicles*, 342; Bishop, *Life*, 215.

40. Cadogan to Erle, Sept. 12, 1709, Erle Papers 2/7, 61, Churchill College, Cambridge; Lediard, *Marlborough*, 2:80. Kane estimated the casualties at 18,000 a side. Milner, *Journal*, 279, 280, totals allied losses at something between 13,488 and 19,718, and French casualties at 15,000–16,000. Marlborough's own casualty figure for the allies was 18,353, of whom 1,856 were "English," Snyder, *Correspondence*, 1327n. Lediard, *Marlborough*, 2:500–501, made the British losses 1,806 and the allied total 18,353; Hamilton, *Guards*, 1:325, makes allied losses 20,000 and the French casualties 16,608, not counting prisoners. The allies did take 400 officer prisoners and untold numbers of other ranks: Marlborough to Sunderland, Sept. 30, 1709, Murray, *Dispatches*, 4:611, and see same to Godolphin, Sept. 13, 1709, Blenheim MS A.I.39, Snyder, *Correspondence*, 1363. On the World War I parallel, see Weaver, *Royal Scots*, 76, 80. Scot, "Remembrancer," 499, 500.

41. Milner, *Journal*, 280, gives losses for the twenty British infantry battalions and six cavalry regiments; Kane, *Campaigns*, 80; Lediard, *Marlborough*, 2:502.

42. Marlborough to Godolphin, and to the duchess, Sept. 11, Blenheim MS A.II.30, E.4, and Sept. 13, 1709, Snyder, *Correspondence*, 1359–60, 1363–64.

43. Milner, *Journal*, 279ff.; Marlborough to the duchess, Sept. 26, 1709, Churchill, *Marlborough*, 2:635–36; same to same, Oct. 10, same to Godolphin, Sept. 26, Oct. 3, 21, 1709, Snyder, *Correspondence*, 1376, 1381–82, 1389, 1396; Atkinson, *Marlborough*, 407; Churchill, *Marlborough*, 2:640, 643, 647; Snyder, "Request," 74.

44. Bishop, *Life*, 218; Blackadder, *Diary*, 107, 111.

45. Churchill, *Marlborough*, 2:520. Webb, *Lord Churchill's Coup*, 223. Dalton, *Army Lists*, 6:388, records twenty-nine officers drowned in the Isle of Eggs disaster. Dozens more senior sergeants were commissioned to drill the American Regiment in 1739, some of them Malplaquet veterans. See "Epilogue," below.

46. Churchill, *Marlborough*, 2:612; Chandler, *Marlborough*, 263; Orkney, "Letters," 316. Maurice, *16th*, 52, makes this brigade up of the 8th, 10th, 15th, 16th, and 18th foot. For the 16th's service, see Maurice, *16th*, 46–47.

47. Webb, *Governors-General*, #208, erroneously places Gooch in the 15th. He fought in the 16th in every one of Marlborough's battles. For his service at Cartagena, see Douglas Edward Leach, *Arms for Empire* (New York, 1973), 217–18; Douglas Edward Leach, *Roots of Conflict* (Chapel Hill, NC, 1986), 57, 60; "Epilogue," below. On Doucet, see Webb, *Governors-General*, #166. For Gee, see WO 4/10, 135, 150; Dalton, *Army Lists*, 6:291.

48. Le Gretton, *Royal Irish*, 54–56; (Sterne, on mines). Webb, *Governors-General*, #132; Chandler, *Marlborough as Military Commander* (London, 1973), 264; Churchill, *Marlborough*, 2:616–17. J. A. Houlding, *Fit for Service: The Training of the British Army, 1715–1795* (Oxford, 1981), 176–78. Note also American use of Maj. Gen. Humphrey Bland, *A Treatise of Military Discipline*, 6th ed. (London, 1746), i.e., another iteration of Marlborough's drillbook. For both Kane's and Bland's influence in America, see "Epilogue," below.

49. Johnston, *History of the Cameronians*. [Cranstoun] to Robert Cunningham, July 25, 1709, OS, camp before Tournai, HMC, *Portland MS*, 4:497; Blackadder, *Diary*, 101–2, 106. Sir John Hope (Bruce), lieutenant governor of Bermuda, 1721–27, Webb, *Governors-General*, #26; Philip Anstruther, lieutenant governor of Minorca, 1742–43, Henige, *Colonial Governors*, #162.

50. Dalton, *Army Lists*, 6:355–56. Gerald S. Graham, ed., *The Walker Expedition to Quebec, 1711* (Toronto, 1953), 140, records 884 rank and file lost from the wreck of seven transports. Kane's (ex-Macartney's) lost 200. The 24th (Seymour's) lost 302; the 37th (Windresse's) lost 252; and Clayton's (ex-Honywood's) lost 130.

51. Webb, *Governors-General*, #133. After the war, Argyll was commissioned commander in chief in Scotland and governor of Edinburgh Castle. The actual command was held by Gen. Thomas Whetham, formerly lieutenant general and lieutenant governor of the Leeward Islands (ibid., #77) and commander of the expeditionary force diverted from Canada in 1709, and by Col. Charles Dubourgay, afterward lieutenant governor of Jamaica (ibid., #67). Marlborough superseded Argyll at Edinburgh with Orkney in 1714. For Fermor, see ibid., #131. In the next reign, Thomas Pitt (ibid., #86) would become colonel of the Buffs. He exchanged the regiment for the government of the Leeward Islands. [Cannon], *Third*; Dalton, *Army Lists*, 6:325. Louis B. Wright and Marion Tinling, eds., *William Byrd of Virginia: The London Diary (1717–1721) and Other Writings* (New York, 1958), index, s.v. "Argyll, Duke of."

52. Dalton, *Army Lists*, 6:291; WO 4/10, 135, 137; Lediard, *Marlborough*, 2:592. [Cannon], *Eighth*, makes the brigade 8th, 18th, 21st, and 24th foot. Dalton, *Army Lists*, 6:343–44; Atkinson, *South Wales Borderers*, 89 and ch. 3; Graham, *Walker Expedition*, 140.

53. Dalton, *Army Lists*, 6:291, 318–21; Hamilton, *Guards*, 2:41; WO 4/10, 135, 150.

54. Dalton, *Army Lists*, 5:54, 56; 6:291, 318–19; Webb, *Governors-General*, #58; WO4/10, 135, 150.

55. Houlding, *Fit for Service*, 183, notes that Blakeney added Gen. Bland's text to his own. See "Epilogue," below. Leach, *Roots*, 51, 59. John Dickinson to his father, Aug. 2, 1756, on "the immortal honour of General Blakeney," *PMHB* 86 (1962): 452.

56. On the Guards' regimental connection, see Webb, *Governors-General*, 468. Hamilton, *Guards*, 325–26; WO 4/10, 135, 150; Dalton, *Army Lists*, 6:55n, 291, 318, 320, 321; Henige, *Colonial Governors*, #167, 154. Dalton, *George the First's Army*, 230, 231, 144n9; Webb, *Governors-General*, #99, 144.

57. Cannon, *Tenth*, 28, puts the whole brigade with Lottum's attack; Lee, *Tenth Foot*, 161, 164; Webb, *Governors-General*, #206, 208; Alexander to John Spotswood, Mar. 20, 1711, Cappon, "Correspondence," 229. On Spotswood's American regiment, see "Epilogue," below.

58. Dalton, *Army Lists*, 5:45, 46n2; 6:182, 185, 197, 327; Whitworth, *Ligonier*, 29, 46, 57, 93, 187.

59. Whitworth, *Ligonier*, 202–3, 213, 229, 234, 237, 276, 308.

60. Dalton, *Army Lists*, 6:347–48; Churchill, *Marlborough*, 2:772–73; Webb, *Governors-General*, #169; Graham, *Walker Expedition*, 140.

61. Dalton, *Army Lists*, 5:60–61, 6:291, 323, 341–42; Dalton, *George the First's Army*, 1:347–48; WO 4/10, 135, 150.

62. Add. MS 61285, 135–36; 61308, 38–41; 61309, 18, 125; Dalton, *Army Lists*, 6:19, 144, 351–52, 391; WO 4/10, 135.

63. Dalton, *Army Lists*, 6:349–51.

64. Webb, *Governors-General*, #88, 148; Webb, *Lord Churchill's Coup*, 101–2, 154–55, 223; Dalton, *Army Lists*, 6:331; Jones, *15th*, 76, 81; Marlborough to Somerset, Sept. 30, 1709, Murray, *Dispatches*, 4:607, but the regiment was given to Hereford on Oct. 30, 1709, Dalton, *Army Lists*, 6:8, 196; Marlborough to Godolphin, Oct. 18, 1709, Blenheim MS A.II.39, Snyder, *Correspondence*, 1393–94; same to duchess, Oct. 21, 1709, Blenheim MS E.4, Snyder, *Correspondence*, 1397; Godolphin to Marlborough, Sept. 19, 27; Somerset to same, [ca. Aug. 19, 1709], Snyder, *Correspondence*, 1371–72, 1387, 1394–1395. Dalton, *Army Lists*, 5: pt. 2, 29, 30n4, 6:107.

65. Cardonnel to Erle, June 20, 1709, Erle MS 2/8, 3, Churchill College; Dalton, *Army Lists*, 5:291.

66. Dalton, *Army Lists*, 6:29, 353–54; WO 4/10, 135, 150.

67. Almack, *Second Dragoons*, 33; Webb, *Governors-General*, #39; Orkney, "Letters," 319–20; De la Colonie, *Chronicles*, 342. Dalton, *Army Lists*, 5:27, 6:307, 314–16; Almack, *Second Dragoons*, 29, 34, 35, 36; Churchill, *Marlborough*, 2:603; Orkney, "Letters," 319–20.

68. Webb, *Governors-General*, #128, 127, 63, 86; Dalton, *Army Lists*, 5: pt. 2, 16–17; 6:309; Henige, *Colonial Governors*, #98.

69. Webb, *Governors-General*, 503–4, #15. Alex. Cosby was lieutenant governor of Nova Scotia and Thomas was fort major of Annapolis Royal. Dalton, *Army Lists*, 6:310–11, 312.

70. Dalton, *Army Lists*, 5: pt. 2, 22; 6:313; Webb, *Governors-General*, #109 (as "Sibourg"); May 8, 1722, *JCTP*, 358; Henige, *Colonial Governors*, #167.

71. Dalton, *Army Lists*, 6:200.

Chapter 8. The Duke's Decline

1. Coxe, *Marlborough*, 5:114, 120–22; Brydges to Cadogan, Jan. 6, 1709/10, ST 57, 3:139–40, HL; Lediard, *Marlborough*, 3:26.

2. Coxe, *Marlborough*, 5:123; Speck, *Britain*, 164–175; Snyder, *Correspondence*, 1408n. Geoffrey Holmes, *The Trial of Dr. Sacheverell* (London, 1973); Holmes, *British Politics in the Age of Anne* (London, 1967), 48; Trevelyan, *Peace*, 47–71.

3. Coxe, *Marlborough*, 5:125–28, 131; Cowper to Marlborough, Jan. 17, 1710, Snyder, *Correspondence*, 1410; Speck, *Britain*, 168–69; Lediard, *Marlborough*, 3:20–21; Somers to Marlborough, Jan. 16, [1710], Add. MS 61134, 233.

4. Sarah's note denouncing Somers's insincerity, Add. MS 61134, 287. Coxe, *Marlborough*, 5:142; *An Account of the Conduct of the Dowager Duchess of Marlborough, from Her First Coming to Court, to the Year 1740* (London, 1742), 162–68; James Brydges to John Drummond, Aug. 10, 1710, *HLQ* 3 (1940): 235; Speck, *Britain*, 169–70. The failed attack on Masham was fatal for, to preserve her favorite, queen Anne knew she must rid herself of Marlborough and Godolphin: Godolphin to Marlborough, Aug. 14, 1710, and see same, May 12, 1710, Add. MS 61115, 169b, Snyder, *Correspondence*, 1603, 1494; Coxe, *Marlborough*, 5:132, 145, 148–51; Atkinson, *Marlborough*, 415; Snyder, "Captain General," *JSAHR* 45 (1967): 75–82, esp. 79. On the motion by Sir Gilbert Heathcote, see Lediard, *Marlborough*, 3:1–2.

5. Drummond to Harley, Nov. 11, 1710, HMC, *Portland MS*, 4:621; Brydges to Cadogan, Feb. 28, 1709/10, Apr. 7, 1710, ST 57, 3:172, HL; Cappon, "Spotwood Correspondence," VHMB 60:229.

6. Marlborough to Godolphin, June 27, 1710, Blenheim MS B.II.8, Snyder, *Correspondence*, 1533–34, and see 1480, 1533–34; Dalton, *Army Lists*, 3:284n121 (Franks also cited West Indian and staff service to Marlborough); Dalton, *Army Lists*, 6:98, 160, 351; Cardonnel to Corbett, May 24, 1710, Blenheim MS 33:153. Marlborough insisted that he must approve any regimental command, "for whilst I do serve these employments must not be thought to go by other recomender." Marlborough's permission to governor generals designate to sell their companies in senior regiments was esteemed a favor (Murray, *Dispatches*, 4:697–98; Sunderland(?) to Marlborough, Mar. 21, Apr. 7, 1710, Blenheim MS B.II.5), the more so because these officers retained their rank on the army list and in Spotswood's case (and Hunter's) were promoted general. Other officers were not allowed to sell out because they had "refus'd the West India Service *&* made terms with the Queen," Brig. Tho. Pulteny to Marlborough, May 2, 1710, Blenheim MS B.II.4. It was politically astute of Marlborough to nominate Corbett to Maryland, both the colonel and the colony having jacobite tendencies: Godolphin to Marlborough, May 10, 1710, Snyder, *Correspondence*, 1498; Marlborough to Godolphin, May 19, 1710, Blenheim MS B.II.8; Add. MS 61115, 147, Snyder, *Correspondence*, 1486; Lowther to Marlborough, May 19, 1710, Blenheim MS B.II.4, and reply, B.24.94. On the Barbados command, see also Godolphin to Marlborough, Sept. 5, 1709, Snyder, *Correspondence*, 1366, Apr. 4, 1710, Snyder, *Correspondence*, 1455, Add. MS 61115, 95b–96. On Lowther's disruption of the ordnance office, see Add. MS 61166, esp. 76, 102, 106, 109.

7. Brydges to Drummond, Aug. 24, 1710, *HLQ* 3 (1940): 237, and same to Morice, Aug. 21, 1710, 234; same to Drummond, July 5, Aug. 24, 1710; same to Morice, Aug. 21, 1710, ST 57, 4:56–57, 59, 93, 114, HL; Coxe, *Marlborough*, 5:159. Walpole reported the queen's attendance at the debate on the right of resistance to monarchs, Feb. 28, 1710, Add. MS 61133, 192. Speck, *Britain*, 186, however, observes that the most important and responsible addresses supported the Protestant succession.
8. HMC, *Portland MS*, 4:532; Orrery to Harley, Mar. [14], 1709/10, ibid., 4:537–38, on refusing to repair to the campaign so as to join Argyll in supporting Sacheverell; Churchill, *Marlborough*, 2:674, 704, 708, 723; Lediard, *Marlborough*, 3:17.
9. Jones, *Marlborough*, 185; Marlborough to Godolphin, Apr. 24, May 8, 16, 1710, Snyder, *Correspondence*, 1461, and see 1475, 1481, 1484–85, 1513; Godolphin to Marlborough, Aug. 9, 1710, Snyder, *Correspondence*, 1489–90, and see 1473, 1465–66; Add. MS 61115, 160b–161; Speck, *Britain*, 185; Lediard, *Marlborough*, 3:30–32; Chandler, *Marlborough*, 275, 277; Atkinson, *Marlborough*, 420–22.
10. Atkinson, "War in the West Indies," 108–9; Godolphin to Marlborough, Mar. 3, Apr. 4, 17, 20, May 2, 16, 1710, Blenheim MS B.II.8, Snyder, *Correspondence*, 1427, 1455, 1456, 1464, 1467 (Add. MS 61115, 117), 1482, 1497; Marlborough to Godolphin, May 1, 1710, Snyder, *Correspondence*, 1468; HMC, *Portland MS*, 4:542, 549, 604; Coxe, *Marlborough*, 5:196.
11. May 1, 1710, Blenheim MS E.5; Snyder, *Correspondence*, 1469; same to Godolphin, Blenheim MS B.II.8, Add. MS 61115, 120, Snyder, *Correspondence*, 1468, and see 1487, 1514, 1519, 1552. Hamilton was the third choice, behind two senior serving officers, Macartney in 1709 and Meredyth in 1710. Lt. Gen. Thomas Meredyth was governor of Tilbury and colonel of the Royal Scots Fusiliers, Dalton, *Army Lists*, 6:98; 5: pt. 2, 4n15; Marlborough to the duchess, Mar. 16, 1710, Blenheim MS E.5; duke of Hamilton to Marlborough, June 6, 1710, Add. MS 61136, 149–50. Marlborough to the duchess, Apr. 4, 1710, Snyder, *Correspondence*, 1445–46. Lord Archibald Hamilton to Marlborough, May 2, June 6, 1710, Blenheim MS B.II.4, Add. MS 61136, 143–44, 145–46; Marlborough's gracious reply, June 7, 1710, Blenheim MS 24, 111–12; Murray, *Dispatches*, 5:38.
12. Marlborough to Godolphin, Apr. 24, May 12, 19, 22, 1710, Blenheim MS B.II.8; Add. MS 61115, 108, Snyder, *Correspondence*, 146n6, 1494, 1500, 1502, and see 1508. Churchill, *Marlborough*, 2:713–14. For a full account, see Walpole to Marlborough, Apr. 15, 28, 1710, Add. MS 61133, 196–97, and replies, 198, 202. Marlborough to Walpole, June 26, 1710, Blenheim MS 33, 113. On Marlborough's discretionary use of promotions, see his letter to Stair, May 8, 1710, Murray, *Dispatches*, 5:19.
13. Lediard, *Marlborough*, 3:33–59, 62–64; Marlborough to Godolphin, June 9/20, 1710, Blenheim MS B.II.8; Churchill, *Marlborough*, 2:716; Snyder, *Correspondence*, 1522. Sunderland was temporarily replaced by Henry Boyle and, in September, by St. John, who was "very high in this affair" (Brydges to Cadogan, May 9, 1710, ST 3:271, HL). Speck, *Britain*, 179, 182, 184; queen Anne to the lord treasurer, June 13, 14, Add. MS 61118, 37–38, 41; Marlborough to Walpole, May 5, 1710, Blenheim MS B.III.33. Lediard, *Marlborough*, 3:105–8. Marlborough to the duchess(?), June 27, July 28, 1710, Snyder, *Correspondence*, 1534–35, 1571, and *Conduct of the Dowager Duchess*, 180–82 ; Marlborough to Godolphin, Aug. 2, 1710, Snyder, *Correspondence*, 1575.

14. The Junto (by Halifax) to Marlborough, June 14, 1710, Add. MS 61134, 202–3; Churchill, *Marlborough*, 2:697–98; Mérode-Westerloo, *Memoirs*, 216; Marlborough to Godolphin, [Apr. 27/] May 8, June 12, 1710, Blenheim MS B.II.8, Add. MS 61115, 30; Snyder, *Correspondence*, 1474, 1513. Churchill, *Marlborough*, 2:714, 734, 766, 769, 794–95; Frank H. Ellis, ed., *Swift vs. Mainwaring: The Examiner and the Medley* (Oxford, 1985), 49–57; HMC, *Portland MS*, 4:503, 506, 514; Brydges to Stair, July 3, 1710, same to Drummond, July 5, 1710, ST 57.4:43, 55, HL.

15. Coxe, *Marlborough*, 5:255, 289, 299–300, 407; Marlborough to the queen, June 27, 1710, Murray, *Dispatches*, 5:58; HMC, *Portland MS*, 4:548; Marlborough to Godolphin, [May 8/19], June 2, 12; [July 3/14], 1710, Snyder, *Correspondence*, 1474, 1487, 1504, 1513, 1556; Lediard, *Marlborough*, 3:66; Coxe, *Marlborough*, 5:291–92, 294n; Dalton, "Argyll's Military Career," JRUSI, 42 (1898), 635; Churchill, *Marlborough*, 2:699; "Considerations relating to the Operations for the Rest of the Campagne 1710," Snyder, *Correspondence*, 1555–56.

16. Atkinson, *Marlborough*, 419, 423; Godolphin to Marlborough, Apr. 25, 28, May 2, 5, 9, 23, 26, June 15, July 4, 29, 1710, Snyder, *Correspondence*, 1471, 1475, 1481, 1483, 1489, 1503, 1507, 1529, 1567, 1583 . For Marlborough's opposition to the "West Indies" plan, see his letters to Godolphin, May 16, 19, 1710, Snyder, *Correspondence*, 1484, 1485, and see 1499, 1589.

17. Godolphin to Marlborough, May 23, July 7, 1710, Add. MS 61115, 185–86, Snyder, *Correspondence*, 1503, 1561, and see 1563–64n2, 1569, 1593, on the diversions of the Canadian expedition. Marlborough to Godolphin, Aug. 2, 1710, Snyder, *Correspondence*, 1567; Churchill, *Marlborough*, 2:700. See also Marlborough to Godolphin, [July 31/Aug. 1, 1710], Blenheim MS B.II.9; Snyder, *Correspondence*, 1587. For Marlborough's final veto, see same, Aug. 4, 1710, Snyder, *Correspondence*, 1578; same, [July 7, 10, 1710], Snyder, *Correspondence*, 1545–46, 1550. Yet the duke held out some hope to Godolphin (see Snyder, *Correspondence*, 1555–56). Same, July 10, 1710, Snyder, *Correspondence*, 1550, is quoted.

18. Churchill, *Marlborough*, 2:741; Coxe, *Marlborough*, 5:302–3, 344, 6:2–3; HMC, *Portland MS*, 4:567; HMC, *Bath MS*, 1:198. Godolphin to Marlborough, July 14, 1710, Snyder, *Correspondence*, 1568n; Marlborough to Godolphin, Aug. 2, 1710, Snyder, *Correspondence*, 1575. Speck, *Britain*, 181.

19. Jones, *Marlborough*, 190–91; Marlborough to Godolphin, June 5, 12, 19, Aug. 2, 1710, Blenheim MS B.II.8; Snyder, *Correspondence*, 1506, 1513, 1536, 1575; Atkinson, *Marlborough*, 426; Lediard, *Marlborough*, 23–27, esp. 26.

20. Marlborough to Halifax, Sept. 13; same to the queen, Aug. 31, 1710, Murray, *Dispatches*, 5: 139, 186–87; Lediard, *Marlborough*, 3:72, 75–78; Chandler, *Marlborough*, 380; Marlborough to Godolphin, Aug. 25, 28, 30, Oct. 23, 25, 27, Nov. 9, 1710, Snyder, *Correspondence*, 1604, 1606, 1609, 1645, 1646, 1648, 1652; Churchill, *Marlborough*, 2:701; Coxe, *Marlborough*, 5:363.

21. Churchill, *Marlborough*, 2:702, 749–52; Atkinson, *Marlborough*, 424–25; Lediard, *Marlborough*, 3:72–86, esp. 82–83, 87, 102–3; Atkinson, "War in the West Indies," 94; Atkinson, "Marlborough's Sieges," 86; Bishop, *Life*, 230–34; Scot, "Remembrancer," 547–58; Lee, *Tenth Foot*, 30–31; Godolphin to Marlborough, July 27, 1710, Snyder, *Correspondence*, 1580; Brydges to Drummond, Aug. 24, 1710, ST 57,

4:116, HL, but see same to Cardonnel, Sept. 26, 1710, ST 57, 4:157, and see HMC, *Portland MS*, 4:651 on Marlborough and Hanover. Quotation from Sunderland to Marlborough, Aug. 24, 1710, Coxe, *Marlborough*, 5:735.

22. Churchill, *Marlborough*, 2:758–59.

23. Ibid., 2:769, 819; HMC, *Portland MS*, 4:583–84, 595–96, 652, 637, 649–50, 656.

24. Brydges to Drummond, Sept. 21, 1710, ST 57, 4:151, HL; same to George Brydges, Sept. 29, 1710, ibid., 4:161 and to Coll [Martin] Bladen, Sept. 10, 1710, ibid., 4:144; Marlborough to Godolphin, Oct. 23, 1710, Snyder, *Correspondence*, 1645; same to Walpole, Oct. 16, 20, 1710, Blenheim MS 33:216; Murray, *Dispatches*, 5:191–92; Godolphin to Harley, Nov. 10, 1710, HMC, *Portland MS*, 4:627, and see 652, 649–50; Maj. R. E. Scouller, *The Armies of Queen Anne* (Oxford, 1966), 10–22; Kane, *Campaigns*, 81; Reeves, *Newfoundland*, 52; Parker, *Memoirs*, 93–94. The basic accounts are in ST 8.5, 188–89, 273, 323, HL. St. John's correspondence from this collection is printed in *HLQ* 9 (1936): 119–66.

25. Drummond to Harley, Nov. 7, 11, Dec. 9, 1710, and reply, Nov. 7 (OS), HMC, *Portland MS*, 4:618, 621, 624, 634, and see, ibid., 593, 605, 620, 622, 629, 630, 635; Brydges to Drummond, Nov. 17, 1710, ST 57.4:212–13, HL; J. Craggs to Marlborough, Barcelona, June 21, 1710, Add. MS 61147, 229–34. Ragnhild Hatton, "John Drummond in the War of the Spanish Succession: Merchant Turned Diplomatic Agent," in Hatton and M. S. Anderson, eds., *Studies in Diplomatic History* (London, 1970), 69–96.

26. Orrery to Harley, June 21, Aug. 29, 1710, HMC, *Portland MS*, 4:544, 568–69. On the cultivation of "our friends in the army," see St. John to Harley, Aug. 25, 1710, ibid., 4:575–76. On military leaves for electoral purposes, see Godolphin to Marlborough, June 30, 1710, Blenheim MS B.II.8, Snyder, *Correspondence*, 1552; Seafield to Marlborough, Oct. 1, 1710, Add. MS 61136, 159; Marlborough to the duchess, Sept. 8, 1710, Blenheim MS E.5, Snyder, *Correspondence*, 1617, and on the Gledhill case, see HMC, *Portland MS*, 4:628; Lediard, *Marlborough*, 3:40; Marlborough to Godolphin, May 27, 1710, Blenheim MS B.II.3, and reply, Blenheim MS 24:105, Murray, *Dispatches*, 5:36; Add. MS 61208, 13b, 15, 172–73. Gledhill held the Newfoundland command as late as 1719. See also his connection with the Leeward Islands, ch. 10, below. On discipline and the succession, see Marlborough to Godolphin, Oct. 4, 1710, Blenheim MS B.II.8, Snyder, *Correspondence*, 1638; same to Boyle, Oct. 2, 1710, Murray, *Dispatches*, 5:172; Marlborough to St. John, Oct. 16, 1710, Murray, *Dispatches*, 5:184–85; Cardonnel to Lambert, Oct. 4, 1710, Blenheim MS 33:203; Sunderland to Marlborough, Aug. 11, 1710, Add. MS 61127, 110. Nicholson is quoted from "The Case of Colonel Vetch, Late Governor of Annapolis Royal," Add. MS 61647, 35.

27. Lediard, *Marlborough*, 3:88, and see 92–93; Coxe, *Marlborough*, 5:360–61, 390; HMC, *Bath MS*, 1:199; Churchill, *Marlborough*, 2:791–92; H. T. Dickinson, "Argyle," *JRUSI* 42 (1968): 41; [Drummond] to Harley, Nov. 11, HMC, *Portland MS*, 4:622; Lediard, *Marlborough*, 3:94–95, 115.

28. Coxe, *Marlborough*, 5:404–5, 417, 430; Churchill, *Marlborough*, 2:784–85, 791–93; Lediard, *Marlborough*, 3:93, 95–97, 104–7, 113–14, 116, 119; Gilbert Parke, ed., *Letters and Correspondence, Public and Private, of the Rt. Hon. Henry St. John, Lord*

Viscount Bolingbroke (London, 1748), 1:29, 77; Routh, *Burnet's History*, 6:32–33; [Cannon], *Third*, 161; HMC, *Mar and Kellie MS*, 487–88; HMC, *Portland MS*, 4:630, 660; HMC, *Downshire MS*, 890. The first approaches to France were made Dec. 23, 1710, L. G. Wickham Legg, *Matthew Prior* (Cambridge, 1921), 145–46.

29. HMC, *Downshire MS*, 893.

30. Routh, *Burnet's History*, 6:29–30, 33, 34; Coxe, *Marlborough*, 5:425–39, 431–32; Churchill, *Marlborough*, 2:787–91, 794–95; Lediard, *Marlborough*, 3:99–117; Atkinson, *Marlborough*, 431–34; Ellis, *Swift vs. Manwaring*, 51, 53–56.

Chapter 9. Quebec and Bouchain

1. HMC, *Portland MS*, 4:656; Coxe, *Marlborough*, 6:722; Atkinson, "War in the West Indies," 95–96n; Bishop, *Life*, 235, 239, 241; Davis, *Second, Queen's*, 2:39; L. I. Cowper, ed., *The King's Own: The Story of a Royal Regiment, 1680–1814* (Oxford, 1939), 1:139. It appears that Marlborough had agreed to the withdrawal of only three, not five, regiments from his command in Flanders, ST 57/5, 23, HL. On Brihuega, see Col. Michael Richards to [James] Craggs, Trevelyan, *Peace*, app. D.

2. Lediard, *Marlborough*, 3:94–95, 154; St. John to Harley, Jan. 8, 1710/11, HMC, *Portland MS*, 4:652, and see 622; HMC, *Downshire MS*, 891, 893; Kane, *Campaigns*, 81; Dalton, *Army Lists*, 6:20; Luttrell, *Brief Relation*, 6:687; Atkinson, *South Wales Borderers*, 77–78; WO 4/44–45; Cowper, *King's Own*, 131; Hamilton, *Guards*, 272. Note payments to four of the new lieutenants' wives to transport them to New York, the prerequisite of military family formation in the colony, ST 8/5, 316, HL.

3. St. John to Hunter, Whitehall, Feb. 6, 1710/11, Graham, *Walker Expedition*, 276–78.

4. Ibid., 276.

5. Marlborough himself took 6 percent of the British forces' bread contract. Much of it financed his extraordinary espionage. Trevelyan, *Peace*, 200–201. St. John to Walker, ibid., 171–72, and see 20–21, 274; agent victuallers' demand, Boston, June 30, 1711, ibid., 108. Moore [to St. John], Mar. 4, 1711, *CSPC, 1710–1711*. James Brydges to Henry St. John, and same to Moore, Oct. 20, 1711, ST 57/6, 56–57, HL. For previous profiteering by the same trio, see St. John to [Brydges], Sept. 28, 1707, ST 58/2, 120; [James] Craggs to Brydges, Portella, June 22, 1710, ST 58/8, 10–14. Theopolis Blyke to Brydges, Jan. 31, 1710/11, ST 58/8, 24; Moore to Brydges, May 24, 1711, ST 58/8, 156; Moore to St. John, Mar. 3, 1711, *CSPC, 1710–1711*, #697 [same to Brydges], May 19, 1711, SP 44/213; St. John to Brydges, June 22, 1711, ST 58/8, 185, HL; Parke, *Bolingbroke Correspondence*, 1:252–53.

6. "The Earl of Oxford's Account of Public Affairs, June 4, 1711," HMC, *Portland MS*, 5:465. This figure is confirmed in Brydges's account, June 21, 1711, ST 8/5, 188, HL; St. John to Harley, Jan. 8, 1710/11, HMC, *Portland MS*, 4:652; Nicholson to [Dartmouth], Feb. 26, 1711, *CSPC, 1710–1711*, #681, Graham, *Walker Expedition*, 278; Instructions for the commissary, Apr. 16, 1711, Graham, *Walker Expedition*, 287–89. On Nicholson's forced sale of the corrupt clothing, see George Patterson, "Hon. Samuel Vetch, First English Governor of Nova Scotia," *NSHSC* 4 (1884):

51; Lustig, *Hunter*, 114–15; Hunter to Popple, Oct. 10, 1715; same to Stair, Oct. 18, 1713, *NYCD*, 5:450–52. ST 58/5, 187–89, 323, 341, HL; Graham, *Walker Expedition*, 49.

7. James to William Brydges, Mar. 17, 1710/11, ST 57/5, 28, HL; HMC, *Portland MS*, 4:668–70; St. John to Marlborough, Mar. 13; same to Drummond, June 26, 1711, Parke, *Bolingbroke Correspondence*, 1:94–98, 263–65. Even when Harley recovered, he avoided all meetings about the expedition, having done "all . . . that his duty required to prevent putting the same into execution," Graham, *Walker Expedition*, 411. Dartmouth was the secretary of state in whose jurisdiction America fell, but no one paid much attention to him. As the Imperial envoy wrote, "To talk with Dartmouth is like talking to a brick wall." Churchill, *Marlborough*, 2:816–18, 890. On Mar. 14, Nicholson acknowledged Dartmouth's order to refer all expeditionary matters to St. John, *CSPC, 1710–1711*, #724. On the regiments selected, see Davis, *Second, Queen's*, 2:392, and for the ranks of the colonels, s.vv. "Seymour, Kirk," "Disney [Desaulnais], Hill," "Clayton, Kane," "Windress," and "Grant, Alexander" in Dalton, *Army Lists*. On the royal animus toward Marlborough, see also Brydges to Marlborough, Mar. 26, 1711, ST 57/5:51, HL.

8. St. John to Harley. Jan. 8, 1710/11, HMC, *Portland MS*, 4:652; for "Old Nick Nack," see Robert Hunter, *Androboros, a Biographical Farce in Three Acts*, ed. Lawrence H. Leder, *NYPLB* (1964): 165–67. Nicholson to [Dartmouth?], Portsmouth, Feb. 26, 1711, Graham, *Walker Expedition*, 278–79, *CSPC, 1710–1711*, #681.

9. King to St. John, May 2, 1711, Graham, *Walker Expedition*, 293; Chandler, *Art of War*, 169; Dalton, *Army Lists*, 5: pt.2, 10; 6:43, 45, 182, 196, 306, 351. Perry Miller, *The New England Mind: From Colony to Province* (1953; repr., Boston, 1961), 386.

10. On the Guadeloupe fiasco, see CO 5/152/5; and Harlow, *Codrington*, 165–67. A less critical account is Bourne, *Queen Anne's Navy*, 196–200. Whitewash was liberally applied to Walker by Charnock, *Biographia Navalis*, 2:455–66. W. Thomas to [Edward Harley], Mar. 27, 1708, HMC, *Portland MS*, 4:482; Owen, *War at Sea*, 261. Graham, *Walker Expedition*, 18n1, 59. St. John's rejection of Sir Thomas Hardy and the secretary's exclusion of the admiralty from all information about the expedition were used subsequently both to condemn St. John and to exculpate the navy, Lediard, *Naval History*, 2:855. [Jeremiah Dummer], *A Letter to a Noble Lord concerning the Late Expedition to Canada* (London, 1712).

11. St. John to Hill, Aug. 12, 1711, Graham, *Walker Expedition*, 349–50; H. T. Dickinson, *Bolingbroke* (London, 1970), 85; Dalton, *Army Lists*, 5:46, 66, 157; 6:365. ST 58/5, 46, 187–88; ST 58/8, 44, 99, HL.

12. HMC, *Portland MS*, 4:465, 675–76; Moore to Brydges, Mar. 24, 1711, ST 58/8, 156, HL. Blake and Moore spent £1,000 to get Bolingbroke's patent through the seals.

13. "Line of Battle," Apr. 27, 1711, Graham, *Walker Expedition*, 177. The transports included the *Blenheim*, the *Marlborough*, and the *John and Sarah*, indicating the loyalties of the transport board's contractors. Troop numbers are taken from the review on Noodles Island, July 10, 1711, King, "Journal," in Graham, *Walker Expedition*, 322. These numbers are close to those in Lediard, *Naval History*, 2:851. The Boston alarm was pro forma, for the British fleet was expected, M. Halsey Thomas,

ed., *The Diary of Samuel Sewall, 1674–1729* (New York, 1973), June 23, 1711, 2:664.
[Thomas] Hutchinson, *The History of the Province of Massachusetts . . . 1691–1750*
(London, 1768), 2:142; Herbert L. Osgood, *The American Colonies in the Eighteenth
Century* (New York, 1924, 1958), 1:441–42; *NYCD*, 5:257–61.

14. Governor, Council, and Assembly of Massachusetts Bay to the Queen, Oct. 17,
1711, Graham, *Walker Expedition*, 370–71, *CSPC, 1711–1712*, #123; Governor and
Council of New Hampshire to the House of Lords, Oct. 30, 1711, Graham, *Walker
Expedition*, 372, *CSPC, 1711–1712*, #147; Hutchinson, *History*, 2:142, 147; [Dummer],
Letter to a Noble Lord, 20.

15. Dudley to St. John, Nov. 13, 1711, *CSPC, 1711–1712*, #164; Graham, *Walker Expedition*, 379. The assembly authorized a subsequent issue of £10,000, ibid., 317; Hill
to Dartmouth, July 31, 1711, ibid., 338; Walker, "Journal," July 10, 1711, ibid., 116; Hill
to Dartmouth, July 31, 1711, ibid., 338; King to St. John, July 25, 1711, ibid., 316–17,
and see 344–45; Dudley Proclamation, July 2, 1711, ibid., 192–93; King, "Journal,"
June 28, July 5, 1711, ibid., 319, 322. This source is calendared in *CSPC, 1711–1712*,
#46, as is Hill's journal, Graham, *Walker Expedition*, 61, but the full transcripts
provided by Graham, *Walker Expedition*, are cited. Thomas, *Sewall Diary*, June 28,
1711, 2:665; Hill to Dartmouth, July 21, 1711, Graham, *Walker Expedition*, 336; King,
"Journal," July 28, 1711, Graham, *Walker Expedition*, 319; Hill to Dartmouth, July 31,
1711, Graham, *Walker Expedition*, 336; Walker, "Journal," July 19, 1711, Graham,
Walker Expedition, 121.

16. Graham, *Walker Expedition*, 338, and see 344–45; Bishop, *Life*, 243, 253; Dudley
to Regimental Officers, July 16, 1711, Graham, *Walker Expedition*, 204–8; [Dummer],
Letter to a Noble Lord, 19; *Boston Newsletter*, #379, Graham, *Walker Expedition*, 127.

17. Walker, "Journal," June 26, 29, July 1, 1711, Graham, *Walker Expedition*, 103, 107,
110, and see 115, 116. Walker to St. John, May 4, 1711, ibid., 81; Walker, "Journal,"
May 3, Aug. 3, 1711, ibid., 95, 132–33; Vetch, "Journal," Aug. 8, 1711, ibid., 363–64.
Hutchinson, *History*, 2:143, had read his Dr. Johnson: "Patriotism is the last ref-
uge of scoundrels." King, "Journal," July 29, 1711, Graham, *Walker Expedition*, 326;
Dudley to Walker, July 9, 1711, Graham, *Walker Expedition*, 197; Walker, "Jour-
nal," June 24, July 29–30, 1711, Graham, *Walker Expedition*, 85, 131; King, "Journal,"
July 30, 1711, Graham, *Walker Expedition*, 326; Dudley memo, Oct. 31, 1711, Graham,
Walker Expedition, 374, and see 300–301, 308; Walker to Dudley, July 9, 1711, Graham, *Walker Expedition*, 196–97.

18. Walker, King, and Hill threatened New England with the wrath of parliament,
Graham, *Walker Expedition*, 321, 359, 325, 342, 349–50, 357. See also Walker to Dudley, Boston, July 28, 1711, ibid., 226–27.

19. For this process in New England, see Johnson, *Adjustment*. Waller, *Vetch*, 213;
CSPC, 1711–1712, #44–46; Hutchinson, *History*, 2:142. Francis Parkman, *A Half Cen-
tury of Conflict* (Boston, 1898), 2:161, speaks of these actions as "worthy of a mili-
tary dictatorship." Massachusetts council to [the governor general], July 27, 1711,
Graham, *Walker Expedition*, 223; Dudley to St. John, Nov. 13, 1711, Graham, *Walker
Expedition*, 377–79, *CSPC, 1711–1712*, #164.

20. King's observations on embarkation, July 24, 1711, Graham, *Walker Expedition*, 325.

21. King to St. John, Boston, July 25, 1711, ibid., 315; Brydges to Senserf, July 31, 1711, ST 57/5, 153–54 (reply to 58/9, 7), HL; Hill, "Journal," July 2, 1711, Graham, *Walker Expedition*, 342; St. John to Hill, Aug. 7, 1711, Graham, *Walker Expedition*, 349; Walker to St. John, Aug. 14, 1711, Graham, *Walker Expedition*, 357; St. John to Hunter, Feb. 6, 1710/11, Graham, *Walker Expedition*, 278; King, "Journal," July 2, 1711, Graham, *Walker Expedition*, 321.

22. Walker to St. John, June 28, Sept. 6, 12, 1711, Graham, *Walker Expedition*, 106, 357–59; King to St. John, July 25, 1711, ibid., 315; copies of the intercepted letters are in ibid., 238–50; King "Journal," Sept. 6, 1711, ibid., 332. Costebelle to Pontchartrain, Dec. 3, 1710, in Parkman, *Half Century*, 2:153; Pontchartrain to [Vaudreuil], Aug. 7, 1710, Graham, *Walker Expedition*, 358n. Recall the like assumptions of the Dutch about the Nicolls expedition to Massachusetts and New Amsterdam in 1664. Robert C. Ritchie, *The Duke's Province* (Chapel Hill, NC, 1977), 20; Webb, *Governors-General*, #146; Webb, *1676*, 280–82.

23. Costabella to Pontchartrain, Placentia, July 23, 1711, Graham, *Walker Expedition*, 240; same to same, Dec. 3, 1710, Parkman, *Half Century*, 2:153. Parkman speculates that "la Ronde Denys, who had studied the 'Bostonais' with care," suggested to the French minister Massachusetts' presumed potential for republican resistance to the expedition, 151. Walker, "Journal," June, 1711, Graham, *Walker Expedition*, 100.

24. Dudley to St. John, Nov. 13, 1711, *CSPC, 1711–1712*, #164, Graham, *Walker Expedition*, 379, and see 226; Walker, "Journal," July 2, 1711, ibid., 108–10; King, "Journal," July 24, 25, 1711, ibid., 325; Philip Haffenden, *New England in the English Nation* (Oxford, 1973), 264, 267; Parkman, *Half Century*, 2:160; Osgood, *Eighteenth Century*, 1:441; Hutchinson, *History*, 2:143; the Master of the *Samuel and Anne* [to Walker]. Boston, July 28, 1711, Graham, *Walker Expedition*, 225; Miller, *Colony to Province*, 153ff.; [Dummer], *Letter to a Noble Lord*, 20–21; [Dummer], *Defence of the New England Charters* (Boston, 1721), 18, 19–20. As Brydges [to Senserf, July 31, 1711], put it, "When we are masters of that country [Canada] we shall find a way to make our Northern Plantations more usefull then they have been, but I am apt to think this is not the only thing Mr. Hill is to do," ST 57/5, 154, HL.

25. "Memorie sur la Nouvelle Angleterre," 1710, 1711, Archives de la Marine, Parkman, *Half Century*, 2:155; Dummer, *Defence*, 36–37; Miller, *Colony to Province*, 390; Address of the Governor, Council, and Assembly of Massachusetts to the Queen, Oct. 17, 1711; Dudley to St. John, Nov. 13, 1711, Graham, *Walker Expedition*, 370, 371–380. See the threat by Hill, via King, July 2, 1711, "Journal," Graham, *Walker Expedition*, 342; Samuel Penhallow, *The History of the Wars of New-England with the Eastern Indians . . .* (1726; repr., New York, 1969), 73–74. Dummer, *Letter to a Noble Lord*, 13, 20.

26. King, "Journal," July 30, 1711, Graham, *Walker Expedition*, 326, and see 30; Walker, "Journal," June 30, 1711, ibid., 108. The admiral thought that he had to provision 9,385 men, including the sixteen companies of New England troops, which were transported in ten vessels accompanied by a hospital ship, four provision ships, and forty landing craft.

27. The patriotic captain of a captured French ship, the *Neptune*, told Walker that if he attempted the St. Lawrence, "he would loose all his ships" and that the French had lost eight of the nine vessels they sent upriver in 1710. Lediard, *Naval History*, 2:853n. Walker, "Journal," introduction, Graham, *Walker Expedition*, 74–75, 78.

28. Samuel Vetch, "Journall of a Voyage to Quebec from Boston in New England in July 1711," *NSHSC* 4 (1884): 105–7; Waller, *Vetch*, 222. On the pilot, Paradis, see Graham, *Walker Expedition*, 28–29.

29. Waller, *Vetch*, 223; Walker to Burchett, Sept. 11, 12, 1711, Graham, *Walker Expedition*, 33, 87, 108, 364–65. Brydges to Hammond, Aug. 18, 1711, ST 57/5, 182, HL; Lediard, *Naval History*, 2:854.

30. Graham, *Walker Expedition*, 34–35. George Gauder was Hill's captain lieutenant and quartermaster, Dalton, *Army Lists*, 6:79. His access to the admiral suggests that Gauder was the general's representative aboard the flagship. Characteristically, Admiral Walker took no responsibility for the calamitous course change, blaming fog, contrary currents, and French pilots. Rather, he claimed that his last-minute example saved the remainder of the fleet: Lediard, *Naval History*, 2:854. See also Bishop, *Life*, 248–49.

31. King, "Journal," Aug. 23, 1711, Graham, *Walker Expedition*, 330. Walker, "Journal," Aug. 24, suggests that the *Windsor*, with the *Montage* and the *Eagle*, actually anchored between the Isle of Eggs and the north shore of the St. Lawrence, ibid., 35n, and gives 884 men lost and 499 saved. Lediard, *Naval History*, 2:854, and Gerald S. Graham, *Empire of the North Atlantic* (Toronto, 1958), 99, counts 1,383 soldiers aboard the seven transports, of whom 449 were saved and 864 lost. The entire crew of the *Content*, the New England storeship, was saved. See also Graham, *Empire of the North Atlantic*, 333–34; Hill to Dartmouth, Sept. 9, 1711, Graham, *Empire of the North Atlantic*, 352; Hutchinson, *History*, 2:148n.

32. Graham, *Walker Expedition*, 75, 116–17, Hill to Hunter, Aug. 25, 1711, ibid., 350; Walker, "Journal," July 11, Aug. 25, 1711, ibid., 116–17, 141; King, "Journal," July 9–12, ibid., 323. Jonathan Swift, *Journal to Stella*, ed. Harold Williams (Oxford, 1947), 2:383.

33. Vetch, "Journal," *NSHSC*, 109; Lediard, *Naval History*, 2:853–54; [Resolution of the Sea Officers] on board the Windsor, Aug. 25, 1711, Graham, *Walker Expedition*, 353–54.

34. Vetch, "Journal," *NSHSC*, 110–11; King, "Journal," Aug. 25, 1711, Graham, *Walker Expedition*, 331.

35. King, "Journal," Sept. 11, 1711, Graham, *Walker Expedition*, 334–35. [Dummer], *Letter to a Friend in the Country on the late Expedition to Canada* . . . (London, 1713), 18–20. Dummer's authorship of this pamphlet is questioned by Clifford K. Shipton, *Biographical Sketches of Those Who Attended Harvard College . . . 1690–1701* [Clifford K. Shipton, *Sibley's Harvard Graduates* (Cambridge, MA, 1933), 4 (1690–1700), 467. Costabelle to Pontchartrain, July 23, 1711, Graham, *Walker Expedition*, 238–40; (le Herriot?] to same, July 22, 1711, Graham, *Walker Expedition*, 240–50; King, "Journal," Sept. 6, 1711, Graham, *Walker Expedition*, 331–32; Vetch, "Journal," Sept. 8, 1711, Graham, *Walker Expedition*, 366.

36. Walker, "Journal," introduction, Graham, *Walker Expedition*, 75–76; Lediard, *Naval History*, 2:855–56; Council of War, Sept. 8, 1711, Graham, *Walker Expedition*, 354–55. The tories had great hopes of Newfoundland (Harley's "Silver-Mine,"

Dummer, *Letter to a Noble Lord*, 11), where the fishery "breeds them [the French] upwards of 12000 seamen a year," Brydges to Senserf, July 31, 1711, ST 57/5, 154, HL. Same to Mrs. Masham, Aug. 1711, reflects her devotion to her brother the general, and so the security of his standing with the queen, ST 57/5, 156, HL.

37. On the Forbes disaster, see Vetch to Dartmouth, June 18, 1711, *CSPC, 1710–1711*, #887, and Patterson, "Vetch," 29–30. Hill to Vetch, Aug. [Sept.] 3, 1711, Graham, *Walker Expedition*, 360–61; Webb, *Governors-General*, #164; Waller, *Vetch*, 229–30; Captain H. R. Raymond Smythies, *Historical Records of the 40th (2d Somerset) Regiment . . .* (Devonport, England, 1894), chs. 1–2; King, "Journal," Sept. 7, 1711, Graham, *Walker Expedition*, 332–33; Hill to Dartmouth, Sept. 9, 1711, Graham, *Walker Expedition*, 353; Hutchinson, *History*, 2:148–49. For the 1676 expedition, see Webb, *Governors-General*, 329–71; Webb, *1676*, 127–63. Barry Moody, "Making a British Nova Scotia," in John G. Reid et al., eds., *The "Conquest" of Acadia, 1710* (Toronto, 2004), 146–53; Elizabeth Mancke, "Imperial Transitions," in Reid et al., *"Conquest" of Acadia*, 183–91.

38. Privately, even Mrs. Masham had to recognize that "Mr. Hill and his admiral made wrong steps; however we lay it all to a storm &c.," Swift, *Journal*, 2:378. The colonial provisions were aboard the three storeships which, with HMS *Feversham*, were wrecked on Cape Breton Oct. 7: Hunter [to Dartmouth?], Nov. 12, 1711, *CSPC, 1711–1712*, #162. The pilot issue was squelched, defensively but decisively, by Dudley to St. John, Nov. 13, 1711, *CSPC, 1711–1712*, #164i.

39. Matthew Prior to Sir Thomas Hanmer, Westr., Oct. 9, 1711, Sir Henry Banbury, ed., *The Correspondence of Sir Thomas Hanmer, Bart.* (London, 1738), 131; Swift, *Journal*, 2:383, 385, 394, 397; Routh, *Burnet's History*, 6:66; [Dummer], *Letter to a Friend*, 22; Osgood, *Eighteenth Century*, 2:226; Parkman, *Half Century*, 1:154–62; Arthur Wellesley Secord, ed., *Defoe's Review*, facsimile ed. (New York, 1938), Sat., Dec. 20, 1707, #134; [Dummer], *Defence*, 36. Webb, "Blathwayt," 7; Webb, *Governors-General*, 99–100; Webb, *1676*, 52, 179–80, 188–89, 196–97.

40. [Daniel Defoe], "A Review of the Affairs of France," Tuesday, Feb. 6, 1705, Secord, *Defoe's Review*. See also Dummer: "They fancy us to be a little kind of sovereign state and conclude for certain that we shall be so in time to come," [John Langdon] Shipton, "Jeremiah Dummer," *Sibley's Harvard Graduates*, 4:460; Hutchinson, *History*, 2:142, 146; Luttrell, *Brief Relation*, 6:713; Dalton, *Army Lists*, 4:130; Webb, *Governors-General*, #40; Churchill, *Marlborough*, 2:913, 915. While Walker was ashore, presumably making his excuses to Bolingbroke ("much mortified . . . because this expedition was of his contriving, and he counted much upon it, but lord treasurer was just as merry as usual"), the *Edgar* blew up at Spithead, killing some 500 of its crew, a tragic conclusion to a wasted effort, Swift, *Journal*, Oct. 6, 16, 1711, 2:376, 385. Walker's abuses of the Jamaicans are detailed in Bourne, *Queen Anne's Navy*, 254–59.

41. J. Senserf to Brydges, Jan. 30, 1711, ST 58/7 193, HL; Lediard, *Marlborough*, 3:114–15, 132, 197; Churchill, *Marlborough*, 2:803, 804, 829; Coxe, *Marlborough*, 6:2, 9–10; HMC, *Portland MS*, 4:663; Jones, *Marlborough*, 195, 199–201; *Lives of the Generals*, 152. Stanhope's exchange was deliberately delayed, as his aide-de-camp Captain Cosby reported to Marlborough at The Hague, Murray, *Dispatches*, 5:264–65.

Cosby was a confidential courier for Marlborough and was highly recommended for the promotion (Brydges to Cardonnel, Apr. 16, 1711, ST 57/5, 66, HL) that he finally received in America. On the decline of ministerial support for Marlborough and the army in Flanders consequent on the failed peace negotiations, see same to Marlborough, June 9, 1711, and on the indiscipline of the exhausted army, see Cardonnel to Brydges, Apr. 27, 1711, ST 58/8, 99, HL, and see 208. A committee of general officers, all made privy councilors, now took control of the army in England from Marlborough. Orkney was a member: Add. MS 61134, 10–38; Blenheim MS B.II.15, 19, Add. MS 61158, 178, 182; Murray, *Dispatches*, 5:301, 311, 412. These changes in command and the deprivation of Marlborough's power to promote even a subaltern were announced to the army to publicize Marlborough's loss of authority.

42. Murray, *Dispatches*, 5:270; Lediard, *Marlborough*, 3:132–33, 153; Atkinson, *Marlborough*, 435; map in Churchill, *Marlborough*, 2:838–39, and see 828; Kane, *Campaigns*, 84–85.

43. Marlborough to the duchess, Apr. 30, 1711, Snyder, *Correspondence*, #1742, p. 1663; Coxe, *Marlborough*, 5:58, 6:14–20, quotation, 24, 28–29; Atkinson, *Marlborough*, 436–40, 454; Ant. Hammond to Brydges, July 24, 1711, ST 58/9, 12, HL; Murray, *Dispatches*, 5:319–20, 323, 329; Churchill, *Marlborough*, 833–34; Lediard, *Marlborough*, 3:134, 197–98; Davenport, *Treaties*, 3:141; Hill, *Harley*, 144–45, 152–53.

44. Coxe, *Marlborough*, 6:34–36; Churchill, *Marlborough*, 824–25, 878; Trevelyan, *Peace*, 123–24; [Prior], "Journal of My Journey to Paris," HMC, *Portland MS*, 5:35–36, 38–39.

45. The social forces impelling the peace negotiations were powerfully put by Jonathan Swift, "The Conduct of the Allies," Nov. 27, 1711, Herbert Davis, ed., *The Prose Works of Jonathan Swift* (Oxford, 1939), 6:59; HMC, *Bath MS*, 1:217; Churchill, *Marlborough*, 2:876–81; Lediard, *Marlborough*, 3:126, 137, 199–200; HMC, *Portland MS*, 5:35; Atkinson, *Marlborough*, 455; Jones, *Marlborough*, 221–22; Murray, *Dispatches*, 5:399–400; Prior, "Journal," July 12/23–July 21/Aug. 3, HMC, *Portland MS*, 5:34–42; *CSPC, 1711–1712*, pp. vii–viii. On the revelation of Prior's mission, see Brydges to Marlborough, Aug. 23, 1711, ST 57/5, 184, HL. Prior's prior groveling letters to Marlborough, especially regarding his reappointment to the commission for trade and plantations, are in Blenheim MS, A.II.31, Add. MS 61155, 176–89. See Sarah's bitter comment, 190. Prior's career as Locke's successor on the plantations commission, as Marlborough's pensioner, as secretary for Ireland, and as a diplomat was summarized by Prior himself to Sunderland, Apr. 19, 1720, Add. MS 61603, 159–63.

46. *CSPC, 1711–1712*, p. viii, #219, 300, 326, 385 (where Nicholson, with remarkable foresight, proposed that mutual cessions be made to place the Canadian border south of the St. Lawrence, a position essentially adopted in 1842); St. John to Ottey, Aug. 24, 1711, Parke, *Bolingbroke Correspondence*, 1:337–39; HMC, *Portland MS*, 5:36, 38, 58–159, 6:37, 38, 40; Trevelyan, *Peace*, 29–33; 129, 184; Brydges to Marlborough, June 9, Aug. 23, Sept. 28, 1711, ST 57/5, 91, 184–85, 262, HL; same to Sir David Dalrymple, July 15, 1711, ST 57/5, 132. Francis Bickley, *The Life of Matthew Prior* (London, 1914), 162–77.

47. Reinier Lears to Brydges, Oct. 6, 1711, ST 58/9, 191–92, HL; *CSPC, 1711–1712*, p. vi, #365, 374, 386; Churchill, *Marlborough*, 2:882, 885. Trevelyan, *Peace*, 185–87, 226; Matthew Decker to Brydges, Oct. 10, 1711, ST 58/9, 208, HL. J. Drummond's paean to St. John for securing both the South Sea concessions and the fisheries, July 21, 1711, ST 58/9, 270–71; Reeves, *Newfoundland*, 52–55; B. W. Hill, "Oxford, Bolingbroke, and the Peace of Utrecht," *HJ* 16 (1973): 250, but see 262. The resistance of the Plantations Commission to the proposed American cessions was the more remarkable because, as Marlborough was informed, the commission was recast in a high tory vein the moment peace negotiations were undertaken, Brydges to Marlborough, June 9, 1711, ST 57/5, 92, HL. The peace negotiations took the edge off "the ill news from Quebec," Decker to Brydges, Oct. 10, 1711, ST 58/9, 208, HL.

48. Lediard, *Marlborough*, 3:137–41, 145–48; Churchill, *Marlborough*, 2:834, 843; Coxe, *Marlborough*, 6:23–24, 29–31, 52–56; Kane, *Campaigns*, 78–84; Murray, *Dispatches*, 5:363, 388–89, 408–9, 415, 418–19, 421; Marlborough to Godolphin, May 4, July 20, 27, 1711, Snyder, *Correspondence*, #1743, 1760, 1761, pp. 1663–1664, 1671; Atkinson, *Marlborough*, 438–39.

49. Atkinson, *Marlborough*, 444; Kane, *Campaigns*, 84; Murray, *Dispatches*, 5:425; Belloc, *Marlborough*, 220–23, debates whether the Arleux episode was preplanned by Marlborough or whether he took advantage of the "disgraceful" situation after the fact.

50. Murray, *Dispatches*, 5:425, 427, and especially Marlborough to St. John, Aug. 6, 1711, ibid., 428–29; HMC, *Hare MS*, 232–33; Le Gretton, *Royal Irish*, 61–62; Atkinson, *South Wales Borderers*, 78–79; Lediard, *Marlborough*, 3:151, 161, 206; Kane, *Campaigns*, 85–87; Coxe, *Marlborough*, 6:61–63; map, Belloc, *Marlborough*, facing p. 213, and see 228; Churchill, *Marlborough*, 2:848–51; HMC, *Bath MS*, 1:206; Chandler, *Marlborough*, 78, 288–89, map; Milner, *Journal*, 322–23.

51. Map, Churchill, *Marlborough*, 2:856, and see: 854; J. Senserf to Brydges, Aug. 21, 1711, ST 58/9, 92, HL; Coxe, *Marlborough*, 6:64–65, 68; Robson, ed., "Colville Memoirs," *JSAHR* 25 (1947): 58; HMC, *Portland MS*, 5:68; Lediard, *Marlborough*, 3:157–58. The allied rear guard and the cavalry of the right wing, with the stragglers, did not close up until midnight of the 5th, Lediard, *Marlborough*, 3:162. Atkinson, *Marlborough*, 447–49; Parker, *Memoirs*, 103–6, 126; Churchill, *Marlborough*, 2:854; Kane, *Campaigns*, 87; Blackadder, *Diary*, 149–51. Brydges to Marlborough, June 9/20, 1711, ST 57/5, 89–93, HL, had warned the duke that "there are propositions for a general peace," so that all that might be gained by a risky battle was apt to be lost in negotiations.

52. Lediard, *Marlborough*, 3:156; [Daniel Defoe], *A Short Narrative of the Life and Actions of His Grace John, Duke of Marlborough* [London, 1711], 25; St. John to Drummond, Aug. 14, 1711, ST 57/5, 175, HL; Churchill, *Marlborough*, 2:835, 842, 857, 881; Marlborough to the duchess, May 18, 1711, Snyder, *Correspondence*, #1748, pp. 1666–67; Murray, *Dispatches*, 5:348, 443; Atkinson, *Marlborough*, 463–64; Jones, *Marlborough*, 187, 197, 233. The most damaging assessment of Marlborough's debility is in the supposedly friendly *Lives of the Generals*, 174.

53. Map, Churchill, *Marlborough*, 2:859. Marlborough described the course of the siege to Godolphin, Aug. 13, 14, 17, 20, 27, Sept. 3, 14, 1711. Coxe, *Marlborough*, 6:76–82, excerpts most of them. Full texts are in Snyder, *Correspondence*, 1763–70.

54. Lediard, *Marlborough*, 3:184, 192; Jones, *Marlborough*, 198–99, notes that Cambrai remained a mighty obstacle to an advance along the Lys, but the French were concerned enough to destroy all the forage on their frontier. Trevelyan, *Peace*, 190; Cardonnel to Brydges, Apr. 27, 1711, ST 58/8, 99, HL.

55. Marlborough to Harley, July 27/Aug. 6, HMC, *Bath MS*, 1:206; Lediard, *Marlborough*, 3:153–54, 157, 160, 163, 164, 167, 168, 196, 202–10. Sutton's correspondence with Marlborough on his government and reward is in Blenheim MS B.II.20, Add. MS 61315, 147. Despite Sutton's supposed favor with St. John (HMC, *Portland MS*, 5:68), he was forced to sell out the moment Marlborough was dismissed, ST 57/6, 256–57, HL. Taylor, *Marlborough*, 2:502; Blackadder, *Diary*, 237; St. John to Marlborough, July 31 o.s, 1711, Murray, *Dispatches*, 5:429; Parker, *Memoirs*, 103–4, 106–7n, 163; Le Gretton, *Royal Irish*, 62.

56. Marlborough to Godolphin, Aug. 23/Sept. 3, 1711, Snyder, *Correspondence*, #1768, p. 1678; Murray, *Dispatches*, 5:462n, 486.

57. Lediard, *Marlborough*, 3:177, 180, 185, 201, and see 210; Murray, *Dispatches*, 5:471, 480–81, 490–91, 496; Atkinson, *Marlborough*, 451; Cardonnel to Brydges, Sept. 14, 1711, ST 58/9, HL, 116; Coxe, *Marlborough*, 6:85; *Lives of the Generals*, 156; Marlborough to Godolphin, Sept. 14, 1711, Snyder, *Correspondence*, #1770, p. 1679.

58. Cardonnel to Brydges, Sept. 14, 1711, ST 58/9, 116, HL. On the Stair mission, see ibid., 59/5, 146–47; 59/6, 78; Stair's correspondence with Marlborough in Blenheim MS, B.II.20, Add. MS 61155, 84–85; Coxe, *Marlborough*, 6:46–51. There was some thought that Marlborough himself would stay on the frontier, North and Grey to Marlborough, Oct. 19, 1711, Add. MS 61315, 168. Atkinson, *Marlborough*, 452; Murray, *Dispatches*, 5:554–55; Lediard, *Marlborough*, 3:193–94, 214.

59. Brydges to Marlborough, Sept. 28, 1711; same to Dalrymple, Dec. 8, 1711, ST 57/6, 22, 24, HL; Parke, *Bolingbroke Correspondence*, 2:49. Coxe, *Marlborough*, 6:133, 136, 139, 141–44; Churchill, *Marlborough*, 2:898, but see Atkinson, *Marlborough*, 457–60; Jones, *Marlborough*, 219–20; Lediard, *Marlborough*, 3:213, 215; Anne to Oxford, n.d., Nov. 19, HMC, *Bath MS*, 1:213, 217; Chandler, *Marlborough*, 302.

60. Coxe, *Marlborough*, 6:152, 155–56; Churchill, *Marlborough*, 2:879, 905–13; Trevelyan, *Peace*, 196ff.; Brydges to Sweet; same to Senserf, Jan. 1, 1711/12, ST 57/6, 150, 151, HL; Lediard, *Marlborough*, 3:219–20, 238–40; Atkinson, *Marlborough*, 468–69; Parke, *Bolingbroke Correspondence*, 1:197; Coxe, *Marlborough*, 6:123–27, 130, 132. Marlborough to the duchess, Oct. 22, 1711, Snyder, *Correspondence*, #1779, p. 1684; Edward Gregg, "Marlborough in Exile, 1712–1714," *HJ* 15 (1972): 593–613.

Chapter 10. The Dreadful Death of Daniel Parke

1. On Parke's prior career, see the text above and Webb, *Governors-General*, #80; George French, *The History of Col. Parke's Administration* (London, 1717), 1–2; Ruth Anne Bourne, "John Evelyn, the Diarist, and His Cousin Daniel Parke II," UHMB,

78(1970):2–33; and "Antigua, 1710: Revolution in Microcosm," in John J. Murray, ed., *Essays in European History* (Bloomington, IN, 1950), 85–110; *ODNB*; *ANB*. I am indebted to the late Dr. Bourne for access to her unpublished life of Daniel Parke and for many conversations. The best brief treatment of the Antiguan uprising is John Shy, *Toward Lexington* (Princeton, NJ, 1965), 40–44.

2. Gledhill's letter was enclosed in Maj. William Churchill to Marlborough, London, Mar. 13, 1711, Blenheim MS II:18, Add. MS 61293, 5. *CSPC*, *1706–1708*, #491, 559, 653; *CSPC*, *1710–1711*, #589.

3. *CSPC*, *1710–1711*, #228, 391, p. 200, #809; *CSPC*, *1708–1709*, #182, 531, 589iv, 597i, esp. pp. 387, 391, #597i; *CSPC*, *1710–1711*, #1391, pp. 99, 200. Dalton, "Soldiering," 70–71, says that Johnson, a regimental major and a provincial colonel, was lieutenant governor of Nevis. Bourne, "Antigua," 42, 97. For this and other cases, see French, *History*, 3, 95–96, 148, 193, 334–41, 415–16, 418–19, 421–23; George French, *An Answer to a Scurrilous Libel, Intitled a Letter to Mr. G. French . . .* (London, 1719), 115n; Vere Langford Oliver, *The History of the Island of Antigua* (London, 1894), 1:lxxvi, lxxx,

4. *CSPC*, *1708–1709*, pp. xxxvii–xl, #597i, 741, 852, 875; *CSPC*, *1710–1711*, #161, 228–30, 391, p. 206; Petition of John Buxton enclosed in Parke to Sunderland, Mar. 21, 1709[/10], Add. MS 61643, 66–71, and see same to same, Nov. 25, 1709, 63; Blenheim MS C.II.48; Bourne, *Queen Anne's Navy*, 230; French, *History*, 29–30, 116, 175–77, 180–93, 326, 399–401; French, *Answer*, 41n: "Sandy" received his freedom and fled Antigua. For Tankard's defense by armed slaves, see Oliver, *Antigua*, 1:lxxix, and for Sandy's shooting of Parke, lxxxi.

5. Parke to Marlborough, Nov. 25, 1709, Blenheim MS II.4, Add. MS 61367, 90–91. The political and economic unity of the Atlantic world in the reign of Anne appears in the story of Mr. Vanbell and the ingot of gold. Vanbell's brother, a burgomaster of Amsterdam, asked Marlborough to secure Parke's favor for Vanbell's brother in the Leeward Islands. Parke granted him land on St. Kitts. For this, Parke explained to Marlborough, he subsequently received an ingot of gold by way of acknowledgment. Of course, Parke's enemies made this into a case of extortion: *CSPC*, *1710–1711*, #391, p. 210. Will. Nevine to Sunderland; merchant's memorial, Blenheim MS C.II.48, and see 41; Add. MS 61643, 79, 86; same to same, Add. MS 61643, 78, 81; Jones to Sunderland, "my very good lord," Antigua, Apr. 2, 1709, Add. MS 61644, 69, 72–73; same to same, Nevis, May 28, 1709, Add. MS 61644A, 72–73; Sunderland to Jones, Mar. 25, 1710, *CSPC*, *1710–1711*, #169; Parke to Sunderland, Mar. 7, 1707/8, Add. MS 61643, 33; *CSPC*, *1708–1709*, #91, 116; French, *History*, 186–95; French, *Answer*, ix.

6. Bourne, *Queen Anne's Navy*, 225n; An Abstract of 22 Articles, Add. MS 61643, 72; An Abstract of the Address & Petition, Add. MS 61643, 73; affidavits &c, Add. MS 61643, 74–75; variants in *CSPC*, *1708–1709*, #443, 459, 465, 484, 532, 590; *CSPC*, *1710–1711*, #391, p. 214. The articles and Parke's reply are printed in extenso in French, *History*, 90–199. Here see 90–92, 101, 105–6, 131–32, 149, 150–51, 155, 163, 167, 175, and see 331, 368–71. Parke admitted that he had "appointed Justices of the Peace of the meanest and lowest Ranks and most wretched Characters," that is, he had recommissioned some of his opponents.

7. French, *History*, 167, 177–80, 250; *CSPC, 1708–1709*, #150iii, 459i; Memorial on Lre to be sent Coll. Parke; Meml. by "the subscribing merchants," Add. MS 61643, 76, 84; William Nevine to Sunderland, Add. MS 61643, 79; Blenheim MS II.48; *CSPC, 1710–1711*, #106, 125, 809. For a petition to parliament against Parke by seventeen assemblymen and twenty-five merchants of the Leeward Islands, the mayor and thirty-eight merchants of Bristol, see Oliver, *Antigua*, 1:lxxix.

8. Parke to Sunderland, Mar. 21, 1709[/10], Add. MS 61643, 66; same to lords of trade and plantations, Mar. 21, 1710, *CSPC, 1710–1711*, #161; same, May 4, 1709, *CSPC, 1708–1709*, #487. On the veto, see *CSPC, 1708–1709*, #597i, p. 375; *CSPC, 1710–1711*, #391, pp. 190, 192. French, *History*, esp. 103, 105, 303. The assemblymen were parliamentary illiterates: French, *History*, 115, 119, 218, 225–26, 228–30, 243, 304–6.

9. Parke to Sunderland, June 24, Aug. 4, 1707, Add. MS 61643, 9–12, and see A Proposal relating to the Island of St. Christopher's In America, Add. MS 61644A, 143; *CSPC, 1710–1711*, #391, pp. 196, 208; *CSPC, 1708–1709*, #597i; Bourne, *Queen Anne's Navy*, 226–27; French, *History*, 3–4, 7, 86, 99–100, 103, quotation on 129, and see 168, 197, 202, 220, 222, 302. Oliver, *Antigua*, 1:lxxvi.

10. Parke to Sunderland, May 11, 1710, CO 152/42, fol. 34, *CSPC, 1708–1709*, #597i, pp. 391, 395–96; *CSPC, 1710–1711*, #391, pp. 199–200, 202, 206; French, *History*, 169.

11. French, *History*, 133–45; Parke to Sunderland, Sept. 29, 1708, May 4, June 26, 1709 (Rx. Sept. 11), Blenheim MS C.II.48; Add. MS 61643, 41, 52, 58–59; Address of the Lt. Gov. and Council of St. Christopher's, Oct. 31, same of Antigua, Aug. 24, 1708, Add. MS 61643, 45, 47; *CSPC, 1708–1709*, #150, 589, 597i, p. 303; *CSPC, 1710–1711*, #324, 391, p. 196. Oliver, *Antigua*, 1:lxxxi, declared that Parke's "statements were not as a rule veracious, so of little importance," a fair warning to subsequent historians about Oliver, if not Parke.

12. *CSPC, 1710–1711*, #204i; #391, p. 205; #600; Dalton, "Soldiering," 69–70; Parke to Sunderland, Mar. 10, 1709/10, Blenheim MS C.II.48, Add. MS 61643, 64; *CSPC, 1708–1709*, #193, 487, 597i, p. 395; *CSPC, 1710–1711*, #204, 228–30, 324, 330, 483, 510; *CSPC, 1710–1711*, #204, 229, 230, 483; French, *History*, 28, 194, 293, 297–98; Jones to Sunderland, Antigua, Apr. 2, 1709, Add. MS 61644 A, 69. An investigation of Jones's regimental accounts by the army comptroller was begun in Sept. 1710, CO 152/9, fol. 108. Parliamentary pressure produced a second review: St. John to the lords of trade and plantations, Mar. 21, 1711/12, fol. 377. For the regimental pay, see CO 152/9, fol. 152.

13. French, *History*, 255–56, records the testimony of 106 men. The council of St. Kitts estimated that the regiment actually numbered only 125, ibid., 297–98. The 38th continued to be a byword for the rot that weakened all regiments on foreign service: Houlding, *Fit for Service*. 13–17, 73; J. Guy, *Oeconomy and Discipline* (Manchester, England, 1985), 150–52; Stanley Pargellis, ed., *Military Affairs in North America, 1748–1765* (New York, 1936), 9–11.

14. French, *History*, 289, 179, 342–43, 177–79, 194–95; on the Chester riot, ibid., 383–96. On Newall, see ibid., 179, 392, and French, *Answer*, 75, 222. Dalton, *Army Lists*, 5:182–83.

15. James P. Jones, *A History of the South Staffordshire Regiment (1705–1923)* (Wolverhampton, England, 1923), 5–8. The regiment had arrived in the spring of 1707 from Ireland. On the 40th, see Harry Piers, "The Fortieth Regiment, Raised at Annapolis Royal in 1717; and Five Regiments Subsequently Raised in Nova Scotia," *CNSHS* 21 (1927): 115–83; Smythies, *Historical Records*; Dalton, "Soldiering," 66–75; Atkinson, "Queen Anne's War,"196; Oliver, *Antigua*, 1:ciii.

16. Parke to Sunderland, May 11, 1710, *CSPC, 1710–1711,* #230.

17. Dalton, *Army Lists,* 6:148–50n26; T 221, #8. On Ayon, see *CSPC, 1710–1711,* #324, xv; 390, 589, 821, 841, 899. On Julius Caesar Parke, see Bourne, "John Evelyn," 19–20. On Lt. Philip Welsh, see *CSPC, 1710–1711,* #391, p. 203, and see #324, xxiv. French, *History,* 342–45. Parke is quoted from French, *History,* 175–76. Parke denied that Walsh was "a Dependent on me," he having a prior commission in the 38th, French, *History,* 190, 289. Walsh's deposition and affidavit are in French, *History,* 406–14. But see Oliver, *Antigua,* 1:lxxvi.

18. Atkinson, "War in the West Indies," 195: "Jones was a most unsatisfactory and detrimental colonel." Dalton, *Army Lists,* 6:148, 150.

19. *CSPC, 1708–1709,* pp. 379–83; *CSPC, 1710–1711,* #391, pp. 194–96. On the fortification and strategic issues, see Bourne, "Antigua," Murray, *Essays,* 89–93. Quotation from French, *History,* 379; For the charge and Parke's reply, see French, *History,* 120–31, 204–5, with quotations from 139, 130. See French, *History,* 115–16 on Parke's property.

20. French, *History,* 128, 139; *CSPC, 1708–1709,* #597i, esp. p. 382; *CSPC, 1710–1711,* #391, p. 193. Lilly's report is in French, *History,* 345–47. The assembly rejected Parke's proposal to fortify St. John's. He went ahead regardless. Oliver, *Antigua,* 1:lxxvi, lxxviii.

21. *CSPC, 1710–1711,* #106, 125, 228, 230; French, *History,* 37–39, 47–49, 191, 322, 330–32; Feiling, *Tory Party,* 409. Note also the riotous, antiroyal operations of "the Pope's head Boys," French, *Answer,* 147–48.

22. *CSPC, 1710–1711,* p. xlii, #230, 328, 347, 390; James Jones [to Sunderland], Nevis, June 5, 1710, Add. MS 61644A, 92; Parke to the lords of trade and plantations, May 11, Aug. 1, 16, 1710, *CSPC, 1710–1711,* #228, 324, 330, 344; Parke to Sunderland, July 29, 1710, Antigua, *CSPC, 1710–1711,* #324; Jones to Sunderland, July ? 1710, Nov. 27, 1711, *CSPC, 1710–1711,* #328, 516. Parke's complaint against Jones's maladministration of the 38th was heard in London in Oct. 1710, immediately following the fall of the whig ministry, *CSPC, 1710–1711,* #436. French, *History,* 201.

23. French, *History,* 111–12; Parke is quoted from ibid., 197–99. *CSPC, 1711–1712,* #154ii; *CSPC, 1710–1711,* #390, 391, pp. 192, 204–5.

24. Parke, in French, *History,* 198–99; *CSPC, 1710–1711,* #391, p. 213, #484, 674i(f), 677.

25. *CSPC, 1710–1711,* #674ii, 838; French, *History,* 33, 50; French, *Answer,* 69–70.

26. *CSPC, 1710–1711,* #674ii, 838; French, *History,* 52–54. Oliver, *Antigua,* 1:lxxxi. The grenadier detachment consisted of Lt. Worthington, Sgt. Bowes, and seven private men, the usual detail at the St. John's guardhouse, adjacent to the courthouse, where the governor and council met.

27. *CSPC, 1710–1711,* #683, 809; French, *History,* 33–35, 50–51, 54, 57, 65, 120. Oliver, *Antigua,* 1:lxxx, records both the names of the chief rebels and notes the efforts of the loyalist minority to support Parke. The hypocrisy of the Antiguan assembly-men is obvious: they did not deny to his successor and their accomplice, Walter Hamilton, any of the prerogatives claimed by Parke, French, *Answer,* 87–88. *Truth Brought to Light; or, Murder Will Out . . .* (London, 1713), X79855 (Loudoun Collection), HL, 2. On prior associations in arms, see Webb, *1676,* 9, 48–49; Webb, *Lord Churchill's Coup,* 213–14.

28. *CSPC, 1710–1711,* #483, 674 iv(a), (b), 676, 683, 838; *CSPC, 1711–1712,* #160, 811, ii; *Truth Brought to Light,* 3; French, *History,* 56, 61, 119; Bourne, *Queen Anne's Navy,* 234, and, on Parke's quarrel with Norbury, 223–24, 282. Rookeby was "try'd and broke by a Court of General Officers here [in London]; but by the late Ministry admitted on the Half-Pay Establishment by a special warrant . . . obtain'd . . . from the Queen," French, *History,* 61.

29. Parke's will, *VMHB* 50 (1943): 239; *CSPC, 1710–1711,* #674ii, iv(b), #683, p. 404; French, *History,* 58, 129. The council majority consistently supported Parke, Oliver, *Antigua,* 1:lxxix. Depositions denying Parke's relations with Mrs. Chester are in French, *Answer,* 213–16. The plunder of Parke's house, worth £5,000, was spread far and wide. For the disposition of his queen Anne miniature by the assembly, through its military head, to the widow of a casualty, see French, *Answer,* 235.

30. *CSPC, 1710–1711,* #677i, 683, 809; *Truth Brought to Light,* 3; French, *History,* 59–65, 87, 348–49. Paynter's grievance was a case lost in chancery, French, *History,* 317. The rebels had four killed and thirty wounded, French, *History,* 65; French, *Answer,* 48. On Parke's relationship with Mrs. Chester, see also, French, *Answer,* 46–50. Oliver, *Antigua,* 1:lxxxi–lxxxii, insists that "the Governor was humanely treated af-ter he fell." He records, of Parke's defenders, two officers and thirteen to fourteen soldiers killed, twenty officers and twenty-six men wounded.

31. Yeamans had been an officer in Col. Henry Holt's regiment, disbanded in the Leeward Islands at the peace in 1697 (Dalton, *Army Lists,* 4:90), along with the other officers and governors, Lt. Col. Edward Nott of Berwick and Virginia, Maj. Thomas Delvall, of Montserrat, Nathaniel Blakiston of Montserrat and Maryland, Christopher Codrington of Barbados, and James Norton of Nevis: Webb, *Governors-General,* #74, 90, 93, 94, 111, 118. Piggot had also been a captain in Holt's On Holt's (Bolton's 2d) regiment, see also Webb, *Lord Churchill's Coup,* 155. French, *History,* 66–67, 69, 77–78. *CSPC, 1710–1711,* #730, Mar. 16, 1711 (Gledhill's dispatch received by lords of trade and plantations, who query Hamilton's silence), and see *CSPC, 1710–1711,* #677, 731, 783ii, 821i 826, 827, 899; *CSPC, 1711–1712,* xxxix, #154v, 160, 302; *Truth Brought to Light,* 3; Dalton, *Army Lists,* 6:148n32, 149n64; French, *History,* 69, has Lucas as a captain, a commission he received in 1714, before the regime change. He was promoted major in 1738, lieutenant colonel in 1743, and died on service in France in 1747 while still lieutenant governor of Antigua. On Hamilton, see Rowld Tyson [to Pringle?], 17 Jan. 1709/10; "Draft of Lieutenant Genll. Hamilton's Petition," July 15, 1712, Add. MS 61623, 20, 22–24, and, with due allowance, French, *Answer,* 62, 204. Hamilton was of that ilk, born of Scots parents on service in Germany. He was a trooper with Capt. Sam. Hamilton, a pioneer in Darien, and a captain with Thornhill in the reconquest of the Leeward Islands, where Hamilton married a planter's widow. He was lieutenant governor of St. Kitts. Parke exiled Hamilton to Nevis. He boasted "an awkward Pretension to a military Perfection." See Codrington's comments, CO 154/4, #21, 55. Parke made a fatal error in supporting Hamilton's promotion to lieutenant general of the islands. Subsequently, Hamilton made a composition with the duke of Hamilton to succeed Douglas. French, *Answer*, 131, 204. See also Bourne, *Queen Anne's Navy*, 232.

32. *CSPC*, *1710–1711*, #683; French, *History*, 174; *Forty One in Minature: An Elegiack Poem Inscribed to the Honorable Matthew Prior, Esq* (London, 1711), 4, 7, 12, 14; Oliver, *Antigua*, 1:lxxvi.

33. Lords of trade and plantations to lord Dartmouth, Mar. 22, 1711, *CSPC*, *1710–1711*, #750, and see #809 and p. 434. French, *History*, 11.

34. Dalton, *Army Lists*, 1:314, 5:67, 279, 6:384. *CSPC*, *1710–1711*, #764, 766, 767. Douglas's quotation, French, *Answer*, 156. Douglas took care to report to the duke of Queensbury (as did Samuel Vetch), *CSPC*, *1711–1712*, #154i. On Sir John St. Ledger, see *CSPC*, *1711–1712*, #355; *CSPC*, *1712–1714*, #60, 422; Oliver, *Antigua*, 1:lxxxv. For Queensbury's patronage of Douglas, see French, *Answer*, 131. Douglas's rivalry with Hamilton was a miniature of the contest between their noble Scots patrons.

35. *CSPC*, *1710–1711*, #775, p. 442, #776, 795; *CSPC*, *1711–1712*, #297; Douglas to Oxford, Feb. 9, 1712, *CSPC*, *1711–1712*, #302; Oliver, *Antigua*, 1:lxxxiii, and the full pardon, lxxxiv.

36. *CSPC*, *1710–1711*, #899; Webb, *1676*, 80; *CSPC*, *1711–1712*, #36, 81, 305; *CSPC*, *1712–1714*, #6; Bourne, *Queen Anne's Navy*, 235. The text of Douglas's letter to Erasmus Lewis, Dartmouth's undersecretary, quoted here, is printed in French, *Answer*, xvii–xx. See also French, *Answer*, 56, 116, 221–24; Oliver, *Antigua*, 1:lxxxiii.

37. *CSPC*, *1711–1712*, #63, 176, 194, 225, 302; *CSPC*, *1712–1714*, #6. Hamilton's petition, Add. MS 61623, 22b. On Boar, see Dalton, *Army Lists*, 6:148, 151. Norbury's replacement, Capt. Lyle of the *Diamond*, was just as friendly to the planter-rebels, presumably a testament to the navy's mercantile connection, a transatlantic interest as neglected by historians as the army's. On the complicated history of the new court act, see French, *Answer*, 137–45.

38. *CSPC*, *1711–1712*, #297, 318 (enc.), 350, 355, 434; *CSPC*, *1712–1714*, pp. xxix–xxx, #2, 6, 81, 93, 108, 127, 136, 232; Oliver, *Antigua*, 1:lxxxv. Douglas explicitly denied the charge and publicly renounced any such payments, French, *Answer*, 132–34. There remains, however, the usual question of nominees, but see French, *Answer*, 151–62. The charges against Douglas are repeated in Hamilton's petition, Add. MS 61623, 22, which adds that Douglas had acquired "an Estate Sufficient for the Dignity of a Baronett of Gt. Britain, for the obtaining of wch he hath lately made Application." See, in the same hand, "A Particular of Presents Charged to Have Been Rec'd by Coll. Douglas," Add. MS 61623, 22b. On Lowther vs. Capt. Constable, see Bourne, *Queen Anne's Navy*, 235–36, 241, 252–53. After this, Lowther called for a regular regiment to repress the "rebellious spirit" of the Barbadians. It should be noted, however, that Capt. Constable condemned the Leeward Islanders' "barbarous proceeding against the late Gen. Parks" and vindicated "her Majesty's right and power to send generals to these collonies which they very often despute and have often said before me Her Majesty might save herself the Trouble and Expense of a Generall in those parts," Admiralty Group, PRO, 1:1595, 1596, quoted in Bourne, *Queen Anne's Navy*, 251. The four islanders arrested for Parke's murder were released on bail, French, *Answer*, 134. See French, *Answer*, 145–47 and 221, on Watkins and Mckinnon.

39. *Truth Brought to Light*, mentioned in *CSPC, 1712–1714*, #304i. French, *History*, preface, 21.

40. A full account is in French, *History*, 81–86. A number of witnesses from Antigua were persuaded to change their sworn testimony after they arrived in London. Their evidence against Parke's killers became accusations against Douglas: ibid., 169–78, 225–27. In fact, persons already arrested or fugitives from justice were excluded from the royal pardon. For the judicial proceedings, see also, Oliver, *Antigua*, 1:lxxxviii.

41. French, *Answer*, 151–52, 154, 158, 182, 186–94, 224, 230–33, 239. Bourne, *Queen Anne's Navy*, 237, 251; Bourne, "Antigua," 102.

42. Oliver, *Antigua*, 1:lxxxvi–lxxxvii. Recalling Parke and Douglas and installing Hamilton was said to have cost the Antiguan "patriots" £60,000. So, "as they say themselves while their Sugar Canes grow, and there's Air enough stirring to fill the Sails of their Wind-mills, they can do what they please," French, *Answer*, 78. Douglas was convicted at the King's Bench of maladministration of the Leeward Islands, fined £500, and imprisoned. Oliver, *Antigua*, 1:lxxxix, concludes that "Antigua was certainly unfortunate in having such disrespectable Governors forced on the inhabitants. . . . Parke was killed by the people and Douglas imprisoned five years." Both results were unique.

Chapter 11. Defending the Revolution

1. Anthony Henley to Jonathan Swift, Sept. 16; Swift to Ambrose Phillips, Oct. 20, 1708; same to Hunter, Jan. 12, Mar. 22, 1708/9, Harold Williams, ed., *The Correspondence of Jonathan Swift* (Oxford, 1963), 1:101–3, 132–36; Walter Graham, ed., *The Letters of Joseph Addison* (Oxford, 1941), 121, 210n; William Edward Hartpole Lecky, *England in the Eighteenth Century* (New York, 1892), 1:532; Jonathan D. Fiore, "Jonathan Swift and the American Episcopate," *WMQ*, 3d ser., 11 (1954): 425–33.

2. Ponchartrain to Sunderland, May 22, 1709, Add. MS 61594, 49; commissioners for sick and wounded to same, June 17, 1709, Add. MS 61593, 76–79; same to lord treasurer, Apr. 10, July 11, 1707, Add. MS 61653, 29, 49; *CSPC, 1708–1709*, p. 97. See also Hunter to Sunderland, Dec. 22, 1708 ("I shall certainly not be exchang'd for the Bishop of Quebec"), and Sunderland to the commissioners for the exchange of prisoners, Apr. 17, 21, 27, 1708, Apr. 25, June 28, 1709, Sunderland Letter Book 2: 113, 114, 117, 143, 272, Blenheim MS, Add. MS 61652, 58, 60, 137v, 172; order for the release of the French boat crew, Add. MS 61652, 262. Sunderland to lords commissioners, July 11, 1707, CO 5/1315, #67; Guenin de la Touche, Jan. 16, 1707, VCRP, F.61. Lustig, *Hunter*, 57–58; Cadwallader Colden to his son, #3, Sept. 25, 1759, Smith, *History*, app. B, p. 302; NYHSC, 2:16. Orkney's appointment is calendared in Leonidas Dodson, *Alexander Spotswood . . . 1710–1722* (Philadelphia, 1932), app. 1, but he officially took command on Dec. 10, 1709, Sunderland to lords commissioners, CO 5/1316, #40. On Hamilton, see Marlborough to the duke of Hamilton, June 2, 1710, Murray, *Dispatches*, 5:40.

3. Godolphin to Marlborough, [Aug. 18, 19;] reply, Sept. 7, 1709, Snyder, *Correspondence*, 1346, 1348–49, 1355.

4. *CSPC, 1708–1709*, #721; *NYCD*, 5:91; Sunderland Letter Book 2:334, Blenheim MS, Add. MS 61652, 171v; Marlborough to Godolphin, [Aug. 27/Sept. 7], Sept. [2/]13, [Sept. 22/Oct. 3]; Godolphin to Marlborough, Aug. 19, Sept. 5, 1709, Snyder, *Correspondence*, 1355, 1363, 1366, 1381, 1413.

5. Walter Allen Knittle, *Early Eighteenth Century Palatine Emigration* (Philadelphia, 1937), 3–31, 51; Secord, *Defoe's Review*, 6:22, 25–29, 135–36, 147–49, 179–80, 225; H. T. Dickinson, "The Poor Palatines and the Parties," *EHR* 82 (1967): 465–67, 469; Philip Otterness, "The New York Naval Stores Project and the . . . Poor Palatines, 1710–1712," *NYH* 75 (1994): 135–36; John Murray Graham, ed., *Annals and Correspondence of the Viscount and the First and Second Earls of Stair*, 2 vols. (Edinburgh and London, 1875), 24. For the context of the Palatine migration, see Bernard Bailyn, *The Peopling of British North America* (New York, 1986), 33–34; Paul A. W. Wallace, *Conrad Weiser, 1696–1760: Friend of Colonist and Mohawk* (Philadelphia, 1945), 5. On the ravaging of the Palatinate, see Albert Bernhardt Faust, *The German Element in the United States* (Boston, 1909), 1: esp. 57–60. Lowell Colton Bennion, "Flight from the Reich . . . 1683–1815" (PhD diss., Syracuse University, 1971), 182–90, claims that Davenant and Dayrolle, Marlborough's agents and English diplomats, were immigrant recruiters. [Francis Hare], *The Reception of the Palatines Vindicated in a Fifth Letter to a Tory Member* (London, 1711), 14, 37ff.; Routh, *Burnet's History*, 6:37–38; Sunderland to the lords commissioners, May 5, 1709, Add. MS 61652, fol. 140, p. 237.

6. Knittle, *Palatine Emigration*, 53, 55, 56, 57, 58, 65, 66, 78–79; Sunderland to the commissioners of transportation, Apr. 23, 1709, Add. MS 61652, 269; same to board of ordnance, ibid., 305, and see 150–55, 194; Marlborough to Godolphin, June 24, 1709, Snyder, *Correspondence*, 1293; Marlborough to Boyle, Camp before Tournay, July 15, 1709, Murray, *Dispatches*, 4:547. A. G. Roeber, "'The Origin of Whatever Is Not English among Us': The Dutch-Speaking and the German-Speaking Peoples of Colonial British America," in Bernard Bailyn and Philip D. Morgan, eds., *Strangers within the Realm* (Chapel Hill, NC, 1991), 238–40.

7. Holmes, *British Politics*, 69, 106–8; G. V. Bennett, *The Tory Crisis in Church and State, 1688–1730* (Oxford, 1975), 101–2, 110; same, "Conflict in the Church," in Holmes, ed., *Britain After the Glorious Revolution, 1689–1714* (London, 1969), 168; Secord, *Defoe's Review*, 6:136, 215–18, 246; Caroline Robbins, "A Note on General Naturalization under the Later Stuarts," *JMH* 35:168–72, 176; A. H. Carpenter, "Naturalization in England and the American Colonies," *AHR* 9 (1903–04): 292–293; Knittle, *Palatine Emigration*, 27; Trevelyan, *Peace*, 36–38; Dickinson, "Poor Palatines," 472; [Daniel Defoe], *A Brief History of the Palatine Refugees . . .* [1709; repr., Los Angeles, 1964), 1; A. G. Roeber, *Palatines, Liberty and Property* (Baltimore, 1933), 8–9; Routh, *Burnet's History*, 6:37–39; Feiling, *Tory Party*, 408.

8. Knittle, *Palatine Emigration*, 37–38, 72–73, 77, 78, 79, 82, 84–86, 99; JBT, *1708–1714*, 26; *CSPC, 1708–1709*, #705, 881–82, 883, 891; APCC, *1680–1720*, 553; Sunderland to lords cmrs., May 3, 5, 1709, Add. MS 61652, fol. 74, p. 145; pp. 276–77. Defoe, *Palatine Refugees*, 37–41, 44–45; Secord, *Defoe's Review*, 6:153–54, 167–71, 181–82, 185, 186, 243–44, 267, 271–72; Faust, *German Element*, 212–15.

9. Sunderland to cmrs. of transport, July 8, Add. MS 61652, fol. 74, p. 145; order of the privy council, May 10, 1708, *DHNY*, 3:541–43; I. K. Steele, *Politics of Colonial Policy: The Board of Trade, 1696–1720* (Oxford, 1968), 117–21. On Halifax as a principal exponent of Palatine colonization, see Knittle, *Palatine Emigration*, 125–26, 130, and for his and Somers's involvement in Vetch's plans for Canadian conquest, see J. D. Alsop, "The Age of the Projectors: British Imperial Strategy in the North Atlantic in the War of the Spanish Succession," *Acadiensis* 21 (1991): 43. Hunter to Stair, Oct. 18, 1714, Add. MS 61645, 124. For the entry of Feb. 6, 1709/10, see GD 220/6/1763/6, SRO; Add. MS 61645, 117. Hunter to Stair, Nov. 8, 1714, Add. MS 61645, 128, *NYCD*, 5:454: It was "my most worthy Patrons My Lords Sunderland and Somers" by whose advice "Her Maty Intrusted me with that Affaire." See also Knittle, *Palatine Emigration*, 127–28; *NYCD*, 5:87–88, 112; *CSPC, 1708–1709*, #704, 841–42, 881, 882, 891; JBT, *1708–1714*, 88, 98; APCC, *1680–1720*, 801. Pringle to Col. Hunter: present to the lords commissioners the plan Hunter had offered to Godolphin. Sunderland has ordered the commissioners to entertain it, Add. MS 61653, 193b; Sunderland to lords commissioners, Nov. 29, 1709, Add. MS 61652, 380; Stamford, Dartmouth, et al. to HM, Dec. 5, 1709, Add. MS 61645, 96–102. It may be that Somers put to Hunter the naval stores proposals of Somers's client, the late Richard Coote, lord Bellomont, governor general of New York and New England: see John C. Rainbolt, "A 'Great and Usefull Designe': Bellomont's Proposal for New York, 1698–1701," *NYHSQ* 53 (1969): 339. See also Faust, *German Element*, 73–80; Curtis Nettles, "The Menace of Colonial Manufacturing, 1690–1720," *NEQ* 4 (1931): 240–69; and Daniel A. Baugh, "Maritime Strength and Atlantic Commerce," in Stone, *An Imperial State at War*, 198.

10. Secord, *Defoe's Review*, 544, 545, 547–48; Defoe, *Palatine Refugees*, 4, 16–17.

11. Hunter to lords commissioners Nov. 30, Dec. 1, 1709, *NYCD*, 5:112–14; Sunderland to the president of the New York Council, Nov. 10, Add. MS 61653, 189b; Hunter to Sunderland, Dec. 17, 1709, Add. MS 61645, 85; Sunderland to the lords commissioners, Dec. 19, 1709, Sunderland Letter Book 2:389, Blenheim MS, Add. MS 61652, 192, *CSPC, 1708–1709*, #915–18; Hunter to same, Dec. 1, 1709, *NYCD*, 5:113–14 and covenant in 121–22; Sunderland to Marlborough, Dec. 12, 1709, Jan. 7, 1709/10; same to [Godolphin], Jan. 13, 1709/10, Add. MS 61652, 192v, 198v, 401; Hunter to Sunderland, Dec. 17, 1709, Add. MS 61645, 84.

12. Bennet, *Tory Crisis*, 104, 111; Feiling, *Tory Party*, 409, 411; Holmes, *British Politics*, 133, 137–38; Holmes, *Trial of Doctor Sacheverell*, 65–66; Secord, *Defoe's Review*, 6:427–29.

13. Luttrell, *Brief Relation*, 6:529; Secord, *Defoe's Review*, 6:469–76, 7:137–38 and 142–43n37; Bennet, *Tory Crisis*, 117; Holmes, *British Politics*, 225–32 (n.b. that Orkney's trimming in the Sacheverell case began his split with Marlborough, Holmes,

British Politics, app. B); Feiling, *Tory Party*, 410, 417; Churchill, *Marlborough*, 2:717; Atkinson, *Marlborough*, 427; Lediard, *Marlborough*, 319; Coxe, *Marlborough*, 5:202, 208–9, 230. For Hunter's dependence on Sunderland to support the Palatine scheme, see his last letter (for four years) to Sunderland, New York, July 24, 1710, Add. MS 61645, 121. William Thomas Morgan, "The Ministerial Revolution of 1710 in England," *PSQ* 26 (1921): 189–92.

14. Hunter to Sunderland, July 24, 1710, Add. MS 61645, 121–22; Stanley McCrory Pargellis, "The Four Independent Companies of New York," in *Essays Presented to Charles McLean Andrews by His Students* (New Haven, CT, 1931), 108; Webb, "Nicholson,"523–24; Webb, *Lord Churchill's Coup*, 195–204.

15. Robert Quary to John Pulteney, New York, July 5, [1710], *NYCD*, 5:166; Hunter to [Sunderland], New York, July 24, 1710, Add. MS 61645, 121–22; additional instruction to Hunter, Dec. 26, 1709, GD 220/6/1763/6, SRO.

16. Morgan, "Ministerial Revolution," 184, 208–10; Rev. John Sharpe, "Journal," Aug. 3, 1710, *PMHB* 40 (1916): 293. On the "garrison government" of Albany, see the impressionistic sketch of "a martial poetics of space" by Donna Merwick, *Possessing Albany* (Cambridge, 1990), ch. 6: "A Military Presence on the Land, 1690–1710." Cornbury, typically, had utterly neglected both the Five Nations and the frontier, Colden, "Letters," NYHSC, 2:361–62. Minutes of the commissioners for Indian affairs, Aug. 7, 1710; sachems to Hunter and reply, Albany, Aug. 14, 1710, *NYCD*, 5:217, 220, *CSPC*, *1710–1711*, #834, p. 492; Kaquendero, speaking for the Five Nations, Aug. 19, 1710, *NYCD*, 5:223. Stephen H. Cutliffe, "Colonial Indian Policy as a Measure of Rising Imperialism: New York and Pennsylvania, 1710–1755," *WPHM* 64 (1981): 240–41. The council minutes, Aug. 9–21, are in NY Col. MS 51:6, New York State Library; *CSPC*, *1710–1711*, pp. 490–99. On the frontier situation in 1710, see Yves F. Zoltvany, "France and the West, 1701–1713," *CHR* 46 (1965): 301–22, esp. 304, 315; Charles Howard McIlwaine, ed., *An Abridgement of the Indian Affairs . . . by Peter Wraxall* (Cambridge, MA, 1913; New York, 1968), 65–68, 80. Osgood, *Eighteenth Century*, 3:364, 366–68, 476. While militating against the Albany-Montreal trade, Hunter did try to obtain Caughnawagah promises not to attack New England, *NYCD*, 9:849–50.

17. Hunter to the sachems, Aug. 16, 1710, *NYCD*, 9:222; *CSPC*, *1710–1711*, #834i, p. 494.

18. P. Schuyler et al. to Hunter, Aug. 20, 1710, *NYCD*, 5:228–29; Hunter to BT [Oct. 3, Nov. 14, 1710], *NYCD*, 5:170, 177–79, *CSPC*, *1710–1711*, #414, 517. On the New York mutiny act, see Lawrence H. Leder, ed., "'Dam'me Don't Stir s Man': The Trial of New York Mutineers in 1700," *NYHSQ* 42 (1958): 261, 264–65, 268, 279n, 280–83; Pargellis, "Independent Companies," 114–16, 119; Fortescue, *Army*, 1:335; C. M. Clode, *The Military Forces of the Crown* (London, 1869), 1:147, 149.

19. Francis Harrison to John Champante, New York, Oct. 5, 1710, Rawlinson MS A. F.255, British Library; "The Hard Case of Brigadier Hunter, Governor of New York & the Jerseys in North America" [n.d., but probably Dec. 1714], LO (America), #11, HL. Robert C. Ritchie, *Captain Kidd* (Cambridge, MA, 1988), 169. On sheriffs, see Rex Naylor, "The Royal Prerogative in New York, 1691–1775," *QJNYSHA* 5 (1929): 246–48, 218. Webb, *Officers and Governors*, 87–88, 133–36.

20. See this self-portrait of a tory, sent to Gen. Nicholson in plural as "English men and true members of the Church of England as by law established," *CSPC, 1711–1712*, #14, pp. 3, 9, and see #436; *NYCD*, 5:334–35. Charles Worthen Spencer, "Sectional Aspects of New York Provincial Politics," *PSQ* 30 (1915): 405. English, Scots, and Creoles constituted the triangle of provincial politics, whether in New York or Virginia, see Webb, *Officers and Governors*, 313, 316–17.

21. Thomas Ertman, *Birth of the Leviathan* (Cambridge, 1997), 218–23; Hunter to lords commissioners, Nov. 14, 1710, *NYCD*, 5:180, and see 190–92, 197; lords commissioners to Dartmouth, Feb. 16, 1711, *CSPC, 1710–1711*, #654, and see #693; Robertson, "Union," 247–49. The importance of the precedent provided by Hunter's proposal for parliamentary taxation is discussed by Stanley McCrory Pargellis, *Lord Loudoun in North America* (New Haven, CT, 1933), 27.

22. Hunter to lords commissioners, Nov. 14, 1710, *CSPC, 1710–1711*, #487, p. 269; same, Sept. 12, 1711, *NYCD*, 5:302; lords commissioners to Hunter, Feb. 1, 1711/12, *NYCD*, 5302; *CSPC, 1711–1712*, #231; Pargellis, "Independent Companies," 100, 104, 110–12; JBT, *1708–1715*, 251–52; Lt. John Riggs, Rawlinson MS A, 272, fol. 235, British Library; CO 5/1092, #2. JBT, *1718–1727*, 359. Between 1708 and 1711 alone, the crown spent £89,800 just to support naval station ships in New York: Curtis Nettles, "British Payments in the American Colonies, 1685–1715," *EHR* 48 (1933): 241n, and see 241–44 on troop payments. For cadet education, see *CSPC, 1716–1717*, #561; Pargellis, "Independent Companies," 100, 104, 110–12; JBT, *1718–1722*, 359; William Alfred Foote, "The American Independent Companies of the British Army" (PhD diss., UCLA, 1966), 269–71, 538–41.

23. Arthur H. Buffington, "The Policy of Albany and English Westward Expansion," *MVHR* 8 (1922): 327; Webb, *1676*, 23, 80, 307, 371; John Francis Riggs to [?], Nov. 16, 1716, *CSPC, 1716–1717*, #405; Pargellis, "Independent Companies," 117, 119; lords commissioners to Hunter, June 29, 1711, *NYCD*, 5:252; Hunter to [Dartmouth], Oct. 13, 1710, *CSPC, 1710–1711*, #423; Alex. Strahan [agent for the four companies], to lords commissioners, [Oct. 16], 1712, *CSPC, 1712–1714*, #100; Beverley McAnear, *The Income of the Colonial Governors of British North America* (New York, 1947), 16–27. The vaunted contrast (cf. Baugh, "Maritime Strength," 196) between an allegedly more militant New France and the British provinces suffers when all of New France's 628 regulars are compared to a nominal 400 for New York alone, or 450 redcoats for Nova Scotia. The militia imbalance was 4,484 to some 60,000, Vaudreuil to Orleans, Feb. 1716, *NYCD*, 9:868.

24. Dickinson, "Poor Palatines," 483–85; Knittle, *Palatine Emigration*, 181–84; Lawrence H. Leder, "Military Victualling in New York," in Joseph R. Frese, SJ, and Jacob Judd, eds., *Business Enterprise in Early New York* (Tarrytown, NY, 1979), esp. 25ff., and 44–45.

25. Hunter to lords commissioners, Sept. 12, 1711, *CSPC, 1711–1712*, #95; James H. Kettner, *The Development of American Citizenship, 1608–1870* (Chapel Hill, NC, 1978), 72; Routh, *Burnet's History*, 6:35–40; Holmes, *British Politics*, 69; *CSPC, 1711–1712*, #41, and see p. 194. Hunter to lords commissioners, Sept. 12, 1711, *CSPC, 1711–1712*, #95, pp. 95–99. Cornbury to the lord treasurer (Harley), Nov. 26, 1711, *CSPC, 1711–1712*, #193i; rebuttal by Micaiah Perry et al., Dec. 11, 1711, *CSPC, 1711–1712*,

#210. Hunter's management was endorsed by the lords commissioners and payment was requested from the lord treasurer, Feb. 1, 1712, *CSPC, 1711–1712,* #290. For tory hostility to the Palatines as foreigners, Lutherans, and poor, see Dickinson, "Poor Palatines," esp. 472–73. Otterness, "New York Naval Stores Project," 141–42, 146, 149.

26. *DHNY,* 3:553, 556–67, 656–57, 661, 708; Smith, *History,* 1:138. The lands had been intended for a Scots settlement, according to Knittle, *Palatine Emigration,* 133, and see 169–70; Clarendon to Dartmouth, Mar. 8, 1710, *NYCD,* 5:196–97, and see 253; *CSPC, 1710–1711,* 172, 389; Clarendon to Harley, *Board of Trade Journals,* 2:315, 318, 327, 330–31; CO 5/1122, pp. 459–64; replies by Perry et al., CO 5/1122, pp. 465–75. Petition of John Evans to HM, [Sept. 4], 1711, *CSPC, 1711–1712,* #89; Hunter to lords commissioners, May 7, 1711; Sec. George Clarke to same, May 30, 1711, *NYCD,* 5:211, 238–41; *CSPC, 1710–1711,* #832. JBT, *1718–1722,* 196–97 gives Hunter's view on the whole Palatine project, and see Roeber, *Palatines,* 10–13. Nehemiah, 5.17.

27. Knittle, *Palatine Emigration,* 162, 163, 142, 172–75; Clarke to lords commissioners, May 30, 1711, *NYCD,* 5:239, 240; JBT, *1718–1722,* 195; Colden, in Smith, *History,* app. B., pp. 303–4; Otterness, "New York Naval Stores Project," 151–52, 155, 203–6; *DHNY,* 3:669–74, 683, 707–9; JBT, *1718–1722,* 207; Hunter to St. John, Sept. 12, 1711, *NYCD,* 5:253. For Henry Holland, see Dalton, *Army Lists,* 4:137, 227; JBT, *1718–1727,* 359. Thomas Elliot Norton, *The Fur Trade in Colonial New York, 1686–1776* (Madison, WI, 1974), 67, 76, 137–39. Osgood, *Eighteenth Century,* 2:494–95. Sharpe, "Journal," Aug. 28, 1710, 294; Wallace, *Weiser,* 4, 14–15, 29; Faust, *German Element,* 85–86; Philip Otterness, *Becoming German: The 1709 Palantine Migration to New York* (Ithaca, NY, 2004), 107–12.

28. St. John to Hunter, Feb. 6, 1711, Graham, *Walker Expedition,* 276–78. Hunter to lords commissioners, Sept. 12, 1711, *NYCD,* 5:262–65; Hunter to St. John, Sept. 12, 1711, *CSPC, 1711–1712,* #96; Hunter to Stair, Oct. 18, 1714, *NYCD,* 5:451; Add. MS 61645, 122–23; Colden, in Smith, *History,* app. B, p. 305.

29. Proceedings of the Congress held at New London, June 21, 1711, enc. in Hunter to St. John, Sept. 12, 1711, *NYCD,* 5:257, 260, 261 and, as "Minutes of a Council of War," *CSPC, 1710–1711,* #893; *CSPC, 1711–1712,* p. xiv, #96; Dartmouth to Hunter, July 8, 1712, *CSPC, 1712–1714,* #4. McIlwaine, ed., *Wraxall, Abridgement,* 90–91. Hunter drew bills for £19,584 in New York for the expedition, Nettles, "Payments," 245n2. Only two or three were ever honored and those largely in South Sea stock at par. The mass promotion of NCOs for mobilization was frequent, and so their transmission of the discipline and ethos of Marlborough's army was widespread, Houlding, *Fit for Service,* 103, 166.

30. Beverley McAnear, "Politics in Provincial New York" (PhD diss., Stanford University, 1935), 277; Hunter to lords commissioners, Sept. 11, 1711, *NYCD,* 5:263 and as Sept. 12, *CSPC, 1711–1712,* #95. On Hunter's deference to the assembly as a misstep leading to legislative control of both ordinary and extraordinary revenues, see Naylor, "Prerogative,"240.

31. Act Passed by the General Assembly of New York, July 1711, Evans, 1522, offered a £3 bounty and 18d. per day to volunteers, as well as augmenting the pay of the lieutenants "arrived here from Europe," but each company's captain and one

of its two lieutenants were to be inhabitants. *The Colonial Laws of New York . . .* (Albany, 1894), 1: chs. 224, 227, 228; Charles Z. Lincoln, ed., *State of New York Messages from the Governors* (Albany, 1909), 1:150–53. Hunter reported to Marlborough, May 7, 1711, *CSPC, 1710–1711,* #886i. The lords commissioners were upset at not being copied, as they wrote to Hunter, June 29, 1712, *CSPC, 1710–1711,* #912. See also *CSPC, 1711–1712,* pp. xiv–xv, #308–11; JBT, *1708–1715,* 284. Two thousand small arms, with powder and ball, were left in Hunter's arsenals from the expeditionary stores (Dudley got 1,000). The Palatine soldiers remained the ready reserve for frontier defense: Leder, ed., *Livingston Indian Records,* Feb. 10, 1711/12, *Pennsylvania History* 23 (1956): 220.

32. Webb, *Governors-General,* #156. Council Minutes, Aug. 17, 1711, *NYCD,* 5:265–77; Adolph P. Benson, ed., *Peter Kalm's Travels in North America,* 2 vols. (New York, 1937), 1:361, 366; Colden, "Letters," *NYHSC* (1968), 2:201. Sharpe, present as chaplain to the forces, counted 682 warriors: 155 Mohawks, 182 Senecas, 127 Cayugas, 93 Onondagas, and 99 Oneidas, as well as 26 "Shevenoes," i.e., Shawnees; Colden, "Continuation," *NYHSC* (1937): 338, 402, 404–9; McIlwaine, ed., *Wraxall, Abridgement,* 83–84, 90, and 91, where 132 Hudson valley fighters and 26 Shawnees figure in a total of 682. Zoltvany, "France and the West," 316, records the French raising the western nations against the Iroquois, compelling them to leave large forces at home. For the 1711 battalions, see *NYCD,* 5:254.

33. Hunter to Stair, Feb. 26, 1711/12, June 23, 1712, GD, 135/141/1, 6, 37–38, SRO; Dalton, *Army Lists,* 3:36; same, *George the First's Army,* 1:242; Hunter to Bolingbroke, Oct. 31, 1712, *CSPC, 1712–1714,* #124, acknowledged the commission.

34. Hunter to St. John, Sept. 12, 1711, *NYCD,* 5:256, *CSPC, 1711–1712,* #96, p. 102.

35. James Harrington, *The Commonwealth of Oceana* (London, 1656). The language appears in J. G. A. Pocock's edition (Cambridge, 1992), 16. *CSPC, 1711–1712,* pp. xvii–xviii. Alexander Chalmers, ed., *The Tatler* (London, 1822), #69, pp. 158–59.

36. Steele, *Politics,* 124; GD, 220/6/1763/3, SRO; lords commissioners to St. John, Apr. 23, and to Hunter, June 12, 1712, *NYCD,* 5:329–30, 333; *CSPC, 1711–1712,* #389. Hunter to St. John, Jan. 1, 1711[/12], *NYCD,* 5:296–97, *CSPC, 1711–1712,* #250; Hunter to lords commissioners, Jan. 1, 1711/12, *NYCD,* 5:298, 300, *CSPC, 1711–1712,* #251; "The Hard Case of Brigadier Hunter," LO (America) #11, 6–7, HL. The assembly even declared itself the sole judge of military matters. It took alarm at the priorities and quotas set by the Congress at New London. It denounced gubernatorial commitments at any future congresses, Lincoln, *Messages,* 1:158. Naylor, "Prerogative," 235, 237.

37. Alison Gilbert Olson, "Governor Robert Hunter and the Anglican Church in New York," in Anne Whitman et al., eds., *Statesmen, Soldiers, and Merchants . . .* (Oxford, 1973), 44, 51–52, and see 47 on the tory anglicans of New Jersey versus the Scots proprietors, Hunter supporters. Shipton, *Sibley's Harvard Graduates,* 4:173–79; McAnear, "Politics," 294–96; Hunter to Popple, Nov. 9, 1715, *CSPC, 1714–1715,* #663; *DHNY,* 3:265–68; *NYHSC* (1880): 327–28; Hunter to John Chamberlayne [secretary to the SPG], Feb. 25, 1711/12, *NYCD,* 5:312–15; Hunter to the bishop of London, Mar. 1, 1711/12, *NYCD,* 5:310–12. *William Vesey, A.M. and Rector of the City of New York: A Sermon Preached . . . at the Funeral of the Right Honourable John Lord*

Lovelace . . . Her Majesties Captain General and Governour in Chief . . . , (New York, 1709), NYHSC, 1880 (New York, 1881), 324. For a (characteristic) insistence that Vesey was born to "a jacobite family connected with the Church of England," see Morgan Dix, *A History of the Parish of Trinity Church . . .* (New York, 1898), 1:98–102, 103n. A concise summary of the Hunter-Vesey contest is in Eugene R. Sheridan, *Lewis Morris, 1671–1746* (Syracuse, 1981), 103–4.

38. E. B. Greene, "The Anglican Outlook on the American Colonies," *AHR* 20 (1914–15): 75. Vesey's associates were the warden of Trinity, Thomas Clarke, and the chief justice, Roger Mompesson: Hunter to lords commissioners, Apr. 30, 1716, *NYCD,* 5:477; George Clarke to [William] Popple, Nov. 15, 1715, *NYCD,* 5:464–65; Shipton, *Sibley's Harvard Graduates,* 4:174; Hunter to Stair, Oct. 18, 1714, *NYCD,* 5:453, and see 310–16, 400, 420, 477; Hunter to Chamberlayne, Feb. 25, 1711/12, *NYCD,* 5:315–16. Sheridan, *Morris,* 103–4, 109. Rev. Mr. Jacob Henderson's State of the Church in New York and New Jersey, *NYCD,* 5:334–38, *CSPC, 1711–1712,* #436, and see #449. Sharpe's career in New York is sketched in his "Journal," 257, 258, 261, 277. For the move to the Fort Anne chapel, see "Journal," 412, 414. One sees here, as in James Blair's quarrel with Alexander Spotswood, the origins of what J. G. A. Pocock terms "a certain Scottish flavour to the episcopal communion in North America," Pocock, "The New British History in Atlantic Perspective," *AHR* 104 (1999): 497. E.g., see Ned C. Landsman, *Scotland and Its First First American Colony, 1663–1765* (Princeton, NJ, 1985), 178–79. Note that in the racist act of 1705, the Virginia assembly had also amalgamated Indians and Africans, Edward D. Ragan, "'Where the Water Ebbs and Flows': A History of the Rappahannock People to 1706" (PhD diss., Syracuse University, 2006).

39. For Sharpe's lobbying, see F. E. Ball, ed., *The Correspondence of Jonathan Swift,* 6 vols. (London, 1910–14), 2:41, 42. Hunter, Proclamation, Jan. 12, 1711[/12], Evans #1523; Address of the Provincial Clergy to HE Robert Hunter, Capt. Gen. and Govr. in Chief, &c, May 14, 1712, *DHNY,* 3:129–30; Olson, "Hunter and the Church," 58. Sheridan, *Morris,* 104–16, sees Hunter as less than fully successful. *JBT, 1708–1715,* 424–25. Hunter put the case fully to the SPG secretary, Feb. 11, 1711, *DHNY,* 3:250–56.

40. Hunter to lords commissioners, June 23, 1712, *NYCD,* 5:341–42. The event, and the execution of fifteen slaves, was recorded by Sharpe, "Journal," April 6–21, 1712, 421.

41. Hunter to Dartmouth, June 23, 1712, *CSPC, 1711–1712,* #456. Sharpe, "Journal," June 11, 1712, 422; Hunter [to Popple], Sept. 10, 1713, CO 5/1050, #81. N.B. the central role of prisoners of war, enslaved for complexion, in 1741: [Daniel Horsmanden], *The New York Conspiracy,* ed. Thomas J. Davis ([1744]; repr., New York, 1971), 260–62.

42. Hunter to Popple, Sept. 10, 1713, *CSPC, 1712–1714,* #491; *NYCD,* 5:356, 357, 398, 402, 403; Hunter to lords commissioners, Mar. 14, 1712/13, NYCD 5:355–58, *CSPC, 1712–1714,* #293; Hunter Proclamation, Jan. 11, 1711[/12], Evans #1573; Olson, "Hunter and the Church," 55, 61, 62; Lustig, *Hunter,* 103–6. *Colonial Laws of New York,* 1: chs. 123, 155. The reports reprinted in Dix, *Trinity Parish,* 1:186, are horrifying as regards the torturous execution of innocent slaves but unrevealing as to

Vesey's position. Hugh Hastings, ed., *Ecclesiastical Records: State of New York* (Albany, 1905), 6:1609, 1949–50.

43. Hunter to the lords commissioners, June 23, 1712, *NYCD*, 5:343; McIlwaine, ed., *Wraxall, Abridgement*, 24; Colden, "Continuation," 91–103, 107.

44. *CSPC, 1716–1717*, #405, 507, 551; McAnear, *Income of the Colonial Governors*, ch. 2; Lustig, *Hunter*, 111; John and Frances Riggs to [Charles Delafaye], Nov. 26, 1716, *CSPC, 1716–1717*, #405; and same, May 11, 1717, *CSPC, 1716–1717*, #561; Pargellis, "Independent Companies," 110–11. This account varies somewhat from Leder, "Victualling," 20, but see 36–37. Nettles, "Payments," 245–46. Hunter also received substantial fees for sealing land patents, passes, and civil proceedings of every sort: CO 5/1050, #7ii, 8li. He controlled £3,357 in rent from his wife's English estates.

45. Hunter to lords commissioners, June 23, 1712, *NYCD*, 5:340, *CSPC, 1711–1712*, #454. The commissioners' latest endorsement of Hunter's constitutional position, June 12, 1712, *CSPC, 1711–1712*, #444, was en route to New York. Colden, "Letters," 202. Appropriations for 1711 are in the session laws, Oct.–Nov. 1711, Evans, #39534. For the regular payments for forts and garrisons, see the statutes for April 1712, *Colonial Laws of New York*, chs. 242–44, 246–47.

46. Dartmouth to the royal governors and commanders in chief, Aug. 21, 1712, *CSPC, 1712–1714*, #50, announced the cessation of arms, but its effect was delayed for six months "beyond the line." Hunter to lords commissioners, Oct. 31, 1712, ibid., #122; same, Oct. 13, Dec. 16, 1712, *NYCD*, 5:347–48, 350–51; lords commissioners to Dartmouth, Apr. 1, 1713, *NYCD*, 5:359–60. Hunter to Addison, Nov. 8, 1714, Graham, *Addison Letters*, 493 and, on "the good old earl of Mar," Hunter to Stair, Oct. 18, 1714, *NYCD*, 5:453.

47. "To All Whom These Presents May Concern," New York, 1713, Evans, #1641. For the celebration of Jan. 29, the martyrdom of Charles I, see Sharpe, "Journal," 267, 284, 412.

48. Hunter to the grand jury, May 5, 1713, *NYCD*, 5:363; Evans, #1639, 1641; Lincoln, *Messages*, 1:167–70; Hunter to lords commissioners, Mar. 14, 1713, *CSPC, 1712–1714*, #293; *Board of Trade Journals, 1708–1715*, 461; Sheridan, *Morris*, 108–9.

49. Lords commissioners to Dartmouth, same to HM, Aug. 27, 1712, *CSPC, 1712–1714*, #64, 65; Hunter to lords commissioners, July 8, 1713, *NYCD*, 5:367; lords commissioners to Dartmouth, Apr. 1, 1713, *CSPC, 1712–1714*, #313, again recommended to parliament a bill for New York revenue and supported Hunter's allegations. See also *CSPC, 1712–1714*, #330. The order of the privy council of Apr. 15, revised the New Jersey Council according to Hunter's specifications. Lords commissioners to Hunter, Apr. 23, July 20, 1713, *CSPC, 1712–1714*, #324. Hunter to Addison, Nov. 8, 1714, Graham, *Addison Letters*, 493. Nettles, "Payments," 245n1; JBT, *1708–1715*, 429; Sheridan, *Morris*, 110. Hunter to lords commissioners, July 18, 1713, *CSPC, 1712–1714*, #404.

50. Lords commissioners to Hunter, July 20, 1713, Popple to same, Jan. 1713/14, *NYCD*, 5:367, 377; 15th assembly, 1st session, May 27–July 1, 1713, *Colonial Laws of New York*, 1:779–80. Hunter's speech of Oct. 15, 1713, Lincoln, *Messages*, 1:171. Sheridan, *Morris*, 91–103.

51. Hunter to Popple, May [7], 1714, *CSPC, 1712–1714*, #665, *NYCD*, 5:377; Dalton, *Army Lists*, 6:19, 250, 251; Hunter to lords commissioners, Mar. 28, 1715, *CSPC, 1714–1715*, #311; "The Hard Case of Brigadier Hunter," LO (America) #11, 5, HL; McAnear, "Politics," 293; Gregg, *Anne*, 385–86. Slane's New York package included the usual promotion to brigadier general.

52. Hunter to the assembly, Mar. 24, 1714, Lincoln, *Messages*, 1:172–73; "Brigadier Hunter's Case," GD 220/6/1763/5, SRO; *CSPC, 1714–1715*, #34ii; Sheridan, *Morris*, 111–16. J. H. Plumb, *The Origins of Political Stability: England, 1675–1725* (Boston, 1967), xviii, describes the three factors that established oligarchy in England: "single party government; the legislature firmly under executive control; and a sense of common identity in those who wielded . . . power." For the application of Plumb's model to the British provinces, see *WMQ*, 3d ser., 25 (1968): 631–37.

53. Hunter to lords commissioners, Aug. 27, 1714, *CSPC, 1714–1715*, #34, 35; Hunter to the assembly, July 7, 1714, Lincoln, *Messages*, 1:173; Hunter to Popple, May 7, 1714, *CSPC, 1712–1714*, #665; 15th assembly, 3d session, Mar. 24–July 16, 1714, chs. 273–79, *Colonial Laws of New York*, 1:801–4, 812–14; GD 220/6/1763/2, SRO; Hunter to lords commissioners, Aug. 27, 1714, *NYCD*, 5:379; Lustig, *Hunter*, 118–19. On the balance of taxation and representation in New York's three regions—the Island, the City, and the Valley—see Charles Worthen Spencer, "Sectional Aspects of New York Provincial Politics," *PSQ* 30 (1915): 397–99, 407. Morris, like Hunter, was a Harringtonian in his belief that power should be proportional to landholding, and that merchant oligarchs should be politically discounted. Like Hunter, Morris was an adult convert to the church of England and an active member of the SPG, *ANB*, 15:900–903, and see *DNB*, 39: 287–88.

54. Colden, "Letters," app. B, p. 306, and see 154; 15th assembly, 3d session, ch. 280, Sept. 4, 1714, *Colonial Laws of New York*, 1:815; Sheridan, *Morris*, 111ff., but see Leder, *Livingston*, 234.

55. *Colonial Laws of New York*, 1:815, 826; Clarendon to lords commissioners, Feb. 8, 1714/15, *NYCD*, 5:399; Hunter to same, May 21, 1715, *CSPC, 1714–1715*, #435, and see p. xxvii. JBT, 2:598–99; Sheridan, *Morris*, 113. The inflation caused by bills of credit, beginning with the issue of 1709 in support of the Canada expedition of that year, rose from a basis of £150 New York to £100 sterling to £160: £100 in 1719, John J. McCusker, *Money and Exchange in Europe and America* (Chapel Hill, NC, 1978), 162–63; Leslie V. Brock, "The Currency of the American Colonies, 1700–1764" (PhD diss., University of Michigan, 1941), 66–69, table 4.

56. Hunter to Stair, Oct. 18, 1714, *NYCD*, 5:453; "The Case of Col. Vetch," Blenheim MS D.II.5, Add. MS 61647, 35; *CSPC, 1714–1715*, #122ii.

57. See *CSPC, 1712–1714*, pp. ix–xii, on the enormous range Bolingbroke proposed for Nicholson's enquiries, and ibid., #97, 104, 105, 242, 259, 267, 283, 284, 301, 310, 312, 443i. Nicholson received £4 per diem and salaries for a secretary and three clerks.

58. "The Case of Col. Vetch," Add. MS 61647, 35; *CSPC, 1714–1715*, #122, and see 180, 427, 602; *CSPC, 1712–1714*, #155, 425, 432; Nicholson to Dartmouth, Boston, Dec. 14, 1713, *CSPC, 1712–1714*, #523 (note that Dartmouth was succeeded by Bolingbroke as secretary of state on Aug. 18, 1714, #455); Nicholson to Bolingbroke,

July 23, 1714, *CSPC, 1712–1714,* #731; Hunter to Stair, Oct. 18, 1715, *NYCD,* 5:451–52; same, Nov. 8, *NYCD,* 5:455; Hunter to lords commissioners, Nov. 12, 1715, *NYCD,* 5:462–63. On the clothing, see *CSPC, 1714–1715,* #173, 423, 568vii; *JBT, 1708–1715,* 404, 406, 407. As soon as the regime changed, Hunter sought to be relieved from the cost of the clothing forced on him by Nicholson, *JBT, 1714–1718,* 34. The board, having previously seen Nicholson's clothing, wrote to Stanhope that it was "no ways fit" for HM troops, *NYCD,* 5:470; Hunter to Popple, Oct. 10, 1715, *NYCD* 5:450. Nicholson had more than 4,000 uniforms to dispose of.

59. *CSPC, 1712–1714,* #268, 643, 644, 665; Colden, in Smith, *History,* app. B, p. 305. *JBT, 1708–1715,* 377. Anne R. to Hunter, Apr. 14, 1714, Hastings, *N.Y. Eccles. Recs.,* 3:2041–42. The bishop of London was also asked to review the religious acceptability of colonial councillors, Hastings, *N.Y. Eccles. Recs.,* 3:378. The vestry of Trinity praised Nicholson's appointment, denigrated Hunter's chancery court, and called for the consecration of a bishop for New York, Dix, *Trinity Parish,* 1:189.

60. Lustig, *Hunter,* 116–17; Dix, *Trinity Parish,* 1:180ff.

61. Hunter, *Androboros,* 153–90. For a full discussion of the literary tropes and topical allusions in the play, consult Lustig, *Hunter,* 134–40. See Sheridan, *Morris,* 107, for the rationalist reaction to clerical excess, and on *Androboros,* see 117–18. Sheridan dates the play toward the end of 1715 because of a prefatory mention of Vesey as commissary.

62. Address of the grand jury to Hunter, *CSPC, 1714–1715,* #629vii; Colden, "Letters," 202. On theater and "the imperial project," see Kathleen Wilson, "Empire of Virtue: The Imperial Project and Hanoverian Culture, c. 1720–1785," in Stone, *An Imperial State at War,* 136–43.

63. *CSPC, 1711–1712,* p. xx; *1712–1714,* pp. ix–x; Gregg, "Exile," esp. 596, 599; Churchill, *Marlborough,* 2:893–99, 997; Coxe, *Marlborough,* 6:217, 225, 263; Williams, *Stanhope,* 143.

64. Churchill, *Marlborough,* 2:988, 998; Gregg, "Exile," 601, 609; Coxe, *Marlborough,* 6:264. Hill, "Peace," 258.

65. Gregg, "Exile," 603, 610, 612–16; Coxe, *Marlborough,* 6:270–73, 280, 281, 286–99, 305–7; Churchill, *Marlborough,* 2:999–1003; Gregg, *Anne,* 382–85, 387, 389–90, 391, 392.

66. For whatever reason, Marlborough had refused to sign the association, Coxe, *Marlborough,* 6:274; Churchill, *Marlborough,* 2:1001, 1010–12, 1019, 1020. Williams, *Stanhope,* 143–44; J. M. Kemble, ed., *State Papers* (London, 1857), quoted in Williams, *Stanhope,* 142–43; Marlborough to Robethon, Nov. 30, 1713, Coxe, *Marlborough,* 6:265. Gregg, "Exile," 617.

67. Hunter to lords commissioners, Aug. 13, 1715, Apr. 30, 1716, *NYCD,* 5:420, 477; Hunter to Stair, Oct. 18, 1714, ibid., 5:453. Dix, *Trinity Parish,* 1:190–91, champions Vesey. Hunter to Stair, March 28, 1715, GD 135/141/4 SRO; Hunter to lords commissioners, and to Popple, Oct. 18, 1714, *CSPC, 1714–1715,* #67, 68; Hunter to Popple, Mar. 28, 1715, *NYCD,* 5:400, *CSPC, 1714–1715,* #312; same, Nov. 8, 1714, *CSPC, 1714–1715,* #82.

68. Hunter to [Hugh Campbell, 3d] earl of Loudoun, Dec. 20, 1714, LO (America) #12, HL; Hunter to lords commissioners, Aug. 13, 1715, *NYCD,* 5:421; New York

Quarter Sessions, Nov. 2, 1714, enc. in same, Nov. 8, 1714, *CSPC, 1714–1715*, #83. See also the grand jury statement, *CSPC, 1714–1715*, #83; JBT, *1714–1718*, 44–45.

69. The commission for trade and plantations was converted from tory to whig on Dec. 20, 1714. Hunter's ally William Popple was restored as secretary, JBT, *1708–1715*, 575. See also ibid., 590, 595–97, 601, 602, 606. Secretary (of state for the southern department) James Stanhope to lords commissioners, Jan. 25, 1714/15, draft commission, Feb. 8, 1715, signed Mar. 1; instructions, May 6, 1715, *NYCD*, 5:391–97. Cornbury objected that the award for Leisler's son was recompense for "supporting the rebellion at New York . . . for which Cptain Leisler was condenm'd and executed," JTB, *1708–1715*, 599.

70. Hunter to lords commissioners, March 28, 1715, *NYCD*, 5:399; Samuel Mulford, "A Memorial of Several Aggrievances and Oppressions," *DHNY*, 3:365, 369–70. The assembly's reply, *CSPC, 1717–1718*, #603iii. Sheridan, *Morris*, 115. On Mulford's persecution by Hunter, see McAnear, "Politics," 295–305; and on Mulford's ultimate success, Patricia U. Bonomi, *A Factious People . . .* (New York, 1971), 83n.

71. Hunter to lords commissioners, Aug. 7, 1718, *CSPC, 1717–1718*, #650; same, Mar. 28, 1715, *CSPC, 1714–1715*, #311. See the elegant appreciation of Morris in Smith, *History*, 1:140. Brock, "Currency," 67; Sheridan, *Morris*, 113–14, 118; 16th assembly, 1st session, May 3, 1715 (ch. 290), May 19, 1715, *Colonial Laws of New York*, 1:845–51, and (ch. 293) July 5, 1715, 1:858–63; an act for appointing an agent (ch. 309) July 21, 1715, *Colonial Laws of New York*, 1:881–82. Hunter to lords commissioners, Mar. 14, 1713, *NYCD*, 5:358.

72. Hunter to lords commissioners, May 21, July 25, Aug. 13, 1715, *CSPC, 1714–1715*, #435, 530, 569; Champante to same, Dec. 1, 1715, ibid., #699, Osgood, *Eighteenth Century*, 2:112–13.

73. Lords commissioners to Hunter, Aug. 18, 1715, *CSPC, 1714–1715*, #574; Popple to Atty. Gen., Mar. 7, 1716, *CSPC, 1716–1717*, #81; Hunter to Schuyler, n.d. (but refers to Mar. 17 [1715]), HM 9790, HL.

74. Lords commissioners to Hunter, Mar. 15, 1716, *CSPC, 1716–1717*, #96; JBT, *1714–1718*, 122–23; Williams, *Stanhope*, 179, 384, 399; Lenman, *Jacobite Risings*, 119, 121, 125, 156; W. A. Speck, *Stability and Strife* (Cambridge, MA, 1977), 179–83; Lediard, *Marlborough*, 3:391–400, 405; Cardonnel to Marlborough, June 3, 1715, Add. MS 61315, 222–24.

75. Holmes, *Augustan England*, 271, 273–74; Lediard, *Marlborough*, 3:402–6. Dalton, *George the First's Army*, 1:xxii; Lenman, *Jacobite Risings*, 105; Coxe, *Marlborough*, 6:324. Atkinson, *Royal Dragoons*, 143–44. Oxford was occupied by elements of four regiments.

76. Williams, *Stanhope*, 178, 183. On Stair's dragoons, see Graham, *Stair Annals*, 1:286–89. Coxe, *Marlborough*, 6:325–26; Cadogan to Townshend, enc. in same to Marlborough, Oct. 26, 1715, Blenheim MS 2:26. Atkinson, *Royal Dragoons*, 144–45; Fortescue, *Army*, 2:5–6; Webb, *Lord Churchill's Coup*, 227–28; Riley, *English Ministers*, 252n.

77. Williams, *Stanhope*, 180, 181, 187; Lenman, *Jacobite Risings*, 125; Coxe, *Marlborough*, 6:324, 327, 329–30; Add. MS 61312, 24ff.; Cowper, *King's Own*, 138–42; C. R. B. Barrett, *XIII Hussars* (Edinburgh, 1911), 1:19–22.

78. Mentions and lists of prisoners in *CSPC, 1716–1717*, #128–29, 144, 145, 309–14, and see #215; HMC, *Stuart MS*, 4:87. Riley, *English Ministers*, 194n. Note that the total number of executions, twenty-six (Lenman, *Jacobite Risings*, 158), was the same as Berkeley had inflicted on the Baconians in 1677, Webb, *1676*, 96–101, 124–27, 134–36. Lustig, *Hunter*, 145–47; Lustig, *Privilege and Prerogative: New York's Provincial Elite, 1710–1766* (Madison, NJ, 1995), 36; Stanhope to Hunter, June 22, 1716, *CSPC, 1716–1717*, #227; JBT, *1714–1718*, 90–91; Stanley Nider Katz, *Newcastle's New York . . .* (Cambridge, MA, 1968), esp. 74–77. See Cosby's hostile comments on "the two or three Scotchmen," Katz, *Newcastle's New York*, 79–80; Osgood, *Eighteenth Century*, 2:453ff. On Alexander, see *ODNB*, 1:679, which is identical to *ANB*, 1:721.

79. Hunter to lords commissioners, Oct. 2, 1716, *NYCD*, 5:478–79, *CSPC, 1716–1717*, #348; Webb, *Lord Churchill's Coup*, 270. Bishop of London to David Jamison, Oct. 24, 1710, *CSPC, 1716–1717*, #348ii. Hunter's appointment of Jamison as chief justice of New Jersey was resented by tory "Englishmen and true members of the Church of England by law established," *CSPC, 1711–1712*, #14, pp. 3, 6, 9, 11, and see *CSPC, 1716–1717*, #133ii; *CSPC, 1719–1720*, #538. John Clive and Bernard Bailyn, "Scotland and America: England's Cultural Provinces," *WMQ*, 3d ser., 2 (1954): 200–214. Eric Richardson, "Scotland and the Uses of the Atlantic Empire," in Bailyn and Morgan, *Strangers*, 67–114. For the linkage of Hunter's imperial policies with those developed on the renewal of formal war with France in 1742, see Colden to Clinton, Aug. 8, 1751, *NYCD*, 6:738–47; Cutliffe, "Indian Policy," 263; and Paul Tonks in *ODNB*, 12:495. The allegations of Colden's Jacobism were probably unfounded. Lustig, "Hunter," *ANB*, 5:198, points out that Colden was home to be married when the rebellion erupted. In Oct. 1715, he appears to have raised troops at Kelso to resist a jacobite advance, Alfred R. Hoermann, *Cadwallader Colden* (Westport, CT, 2002), 5–6. See also Alice Mapesden Keys, *Cadwallader Colden* (New York, 1906); and the charming sketch by Brooke Hindle, "A Colonial Governor's Family: The Coldens of Coldengham," *NYHSQ* 45 (1961): 233–50. Hunter's own sizeable household were Scots. Cf. Archibald Kennedy who, like Hunter, was Ayrshire born. Kennedy was commissioned militia lieutenant 1711, regular lieutenant 1712, and adjutant of the four companies and garrison agent in 1721 (JBT, *1718–1722*, 338–42); receiver general, 1722; councilor, 1727. He married into the Schuylers and became a leading negotiator with the Five Nations and a frontier imperialist, *ANB*, 12:564–65; Dalton, *Army Lists*, 6:189. Of course, the Scots character of Hunter's New Jersey regime was even more marked: Landsman, *Scotland's First American Colony*, esp. 125–26, 168–69. On James Alexander's son, William, see Landsman, *Scotland's First American Colony*, 129, 210, 212. On the Scots community in New York, see Joyce D. Goodfriend, *Before the Melting Pot Society and Culture in Colonial New York City, 1664–1730* (Princeton, NJ, 1994), 142–44. On the continuing disproportionate number of Scots in American commands, see Shy, *Toward Lexington*, 352–54.

80. HMC, *Mar and Kellie MS*, 510–15; Riley, *English Ministers*, 254–55, 262–63, 267–68; Speck, *Stability and Strife*, 179–83; Lenman, *Jacobite Risings*, 127, 153; Williams, *Stanhope*, 34, 184, 191; W. L. Burn, "The Scottish Policy of John, Sixth Earl of Mar," *HLQ* 2 (1939): 439–48; Dalton, *George the First's Army*, 1:7–9; Henrietta Taylor, "John, Duke of Argyll and Grenwich," *SHR* 26 (1887): 65–69, 70. Coxe,

Marlborough, 6:322–24, 328, 331. The 11th had been destroyed at Almanza under Hill. He took the reraised regiment to drown at the Isle of Eggs. After Sheriffmuir, the regiment was again cut up at Glenshiel in 1719.

81. Coxe, *Marlborough*, 6:333–37; Argyll to Loudoun, Jan. 2, 1716/17, LO #11180, HL. A full account of the '15 in Scotland is in the correspondence of the 3d earl of Loudoun in HL. Taylor, "Argyll," 65, 69–73. Cadogan to Marlborough, Dec. 9, 1715, Jan. 26, 1715/16, Feb. 21, [23], 1716, Add. MS 61161, 132–34, 184, 191. Note that the invasion of Scotland by 12,000 Swedes under Charles XII was prevented only by the destruction of the Swedish fleet by the Danish and British navies, Churchill, *Marlborough*, 2:1027–28.

82. Churchill, *Marlborough*, 2:1029; Cadogan to Marlborough, Inverness, Apr. 24, 1716, Add. MS 61161, 239b; Charles Cathcart (8th baron Cathcart) to (Hugh Campbell, 3d earl of) Loudoun, Oct. 25, 1716, LO #7961, HL. For the struggle between Cadogan (willing to administer the army as Marlborough's deputy) and Stanhope (who sought Marlborough's offices for himself), see Cathcart to Loudoun, Nov. 8, Dec. 12, 1716, LO #7958, 7959, HL. On Addison, see *CSPC, 1716–1717*, p. vi.

83. Speck, *Stability and Strife*, 183.

84. Hunter to lords commissioners, Apr. 30, 1716, *CSPC, 1716–1717*, #133, 133ii, iii, iv, CO 5/1051, #33, i–iv; and see *NYCD*, 5:476–77; *JBT, 1714–1718*, 290.

85. *JBT, 1714–1718*; Hunter to Popple, Nov. 9, 14, 1715, *CSPC, 1714–1715*, #663, 674. Dix, *Trinity Parish*, 1:191–95, records Vesey's triumphal return and boasts the strength of the church of England party. See also Osgood, *Eighteenth Century*, 3:89–97.

86. Hunter to lords commissioners, June 6, 1716, *CSPC, 1716–1717*, #192iv, and see #195, 195i, "His Excellency's Speech . . . the 5 June 1716," Evans #1846; and Lincoln, *Messages*, 1:177, 178. Richard Aquila, *The Iroquois Restoration . . . 1701–1754* (Lincoln, NE, 1993), 209–15; McIlwaine, ed., *Wraxall, Abridgement*, 118–19, 125, 126, "so that we are surrounded by them," the French.

87. 17th assembly, 1st session, beg. June 5, 1716; 2d session, beg. Aug. 21, 1716, *Colonial Laws of New York*, ch. 315, 1:887–88, and ch. 317, 318, 320, 322, 323, 888–901; Lincoln, *Messages*, 1:180; Hunter to lords commissioners, Oct. 2, 1716, *NYCD*, 5:477–81; *CSPC, 1716–1717*, #348.

88. Hunter to lords commissioners, Oct. 1716, *NYCD*, 5:477–80; same, Feb. 13, 1717, *CSPC, 1716–1717*, #469; Lustig, *Hunter*, 171; Methuen to Hunter: HRH leave for eight months, Oct. 10, 1716, *CSPC, 1716–1717*, #353. John and Frances Riggs to Mr. and Mrs. Charles Delafaye, Nov. 26, 1716, CO 5/1092, #1, partial copy in *CSPC, 1716–1717*, #415, uses "cabinet" to mean the collective executive. This may be the first such American usage.

89. John and Frances Riggs to Charles Delafaye, May 11, 1717, *CSPC, 1716–1717*, #561; *Colonial Laws of New York*, 1:904–18; Hunter to Popple, [May] 13, 1717, *NYCD*, 5:482; *CSPC, 1716–1717*, #565. The social consequences of Hunter's whig, aristocratic policies are anticipated by Rainbolt, "'Great and Usefull Designe,'" 351. Besides the manor of Livingston, Westchester received an (additional) assembly seat, Spencer, "Sectional Aspects," 415. Richard Riggs's commission is in E. B. O'Callaghan, ed.,

Calendar of New York Colonial Commissions (New York, 1929), June 29, 1715, and for John Riggs's captaincy, see under Dec. 19, 1718.

90. *Colonial Laws of New York*, 1:919, 939, 941, 943; Hunter to Popple, Dec. 3, 1717; same to lords commissioners, Jan. 20, 1718; same to Phillips, May 3, 1718; Richard West to lords commissioners, Aug. 20, 1718, *CSPC, 1717–1718*, #236, 317, 519, 603; lords commissioners to lords justices, June 4, 1719, *CSPC, 1719–1720*, #218. *Colonial Laws of New York*, chs. 340–42, 344, 346, 347. By capturing the city delegation, Hunter was able to act for the party of the revolution: lords commissioners to lords justices, June 4, 1719, *NYCD*, 5:524–25. Colden ("Letters," app. B, 307) errs in saying that this act was never confirmed by the crown. See the order of the privy council, [May 19, 1720], *NYCD*, 5:538. Minutes, Feb. 19, 1717/18, Oct. 3, 1718, JBT, *1714–1718*, 340, 434, and see JBT, *1718–1727*, 63–64; Norton, *Fur Trade*, 135.

91. Ch. 347, passed Dec. 23, 1717, *Colonial Laws of New York*, 1:938–91. Hunter to lords commissioners, n.d., Nov. 3, 1718, *NYCD*, 5:508, 519.

92. Colden, "Letters," app. B, 307.

93. Smith, *History*, 1:357n19; Colden, "Letters," 307; Riggs to Delafaye, May 1, 1717, *CSPC, 1716–1717*, #561.

94. Hunter to the assembly, Sept. 24, 1718, Lincoln, *Messages*, 1:185. See, for the first example of the sequential revenue acts, "An Act for a Supply to be Granted to His Majestie for Supporting the Government in the Province of New York," June 24, 1719, *Colonial Laws of New York*, ch. 366, pp. 1013–21.

95. Hunter to Popple, Dec. 3, 1717, *CSPC, 1717–1718*, #236; *NYCD*, 5:494, stated that this, and the 1715 act, "enables the many to venture their stocks in trade to the prejudice of the few who had so long monopolized it." On the "new class," see Milovan Djilas, *The New Class* (New York, 1957) and Webb, *Lord Churchill's Coup*, 269–70. For the pervasive parallels between Hunter and Hamilton, see Ron Chernow, *Alexander Hamilton* (New York, 2004).

96. Hunter to Phillips, Oct. 15, 1718, *CSPC, 1717–1718*, #724i; Riggs to Delafaye, Apr. 18, 1719, *CSPC, 1719–1720*, #153; Hunter to Popple, May 18, June 6, 1719, *CSPC, 1719–1720*, #192, 226; same to lords commissioners, May 27, 1719, *CSPC, 1719–1720*, #203, and see Hunter to Popple, Nov. 22, 1717, *CSPC, 1717–1718*, #223, *NYCD*, 5:493. Lords commissioners to Stanhope, Mar. 15, 1716, *NYCD*, 5:469–70; Williams, *Stanhope*, 203–4. Smith, *History*, 1:156. Hunter's rhetoric was somewhat improved boilerplate. For Spotswood's like language, see Webb, *Officers and Governors*, 307n88.

97. Lincoln, *Messages*, 1:189.

Chapter 12. Alexander Spotswood

1. Spotswood to burgesses, Nov. 24, 1718, CO 5/1318, fol. 305, published as *Some Remarkable PROCEEDINGS*. William Byrd to Charles, earl of Orrery, "William Byrd's Letterbook, 1719–1732," *VMHB* 32 (1924): 25.

2. On Spotswood's birth to the "chirgeon general" of the Tangier garrison and an Englishwoman (variously Catherine or Katherine Murray or Mercer), "a Cousine to the Duchess of Marlborough," see "Pedigrees: Spotiswoode of That Ilk," MS 2933, NLS, 69, and [Rev.] Robert Rose's account, Spotswood, July 25, 1743, ibid., 139. R. A. Brock, ed., *The Official Letters of Alexander Spotswood* (Richmond, VA, 1882), 1:1; Spotswood to commissioners, Aug. 18, 1710, Brock, *Spotswood Letters*, 1:10–11; Leonidas Dodson, *Alexander Spotswood, Governor of Colonial Virginia, 1710–1722* (1932; repr., New York, 1969), 1–5; Webb, *Governors-General*, ch. 7, #206; Webb, *1676*, book 1; Webb, *Lord Churchill's Coup*, 257–60. L. G. Schwoerer, *No Standing Armies!* (Baltimore, 1974); John Trenchard, *An Argument, Shewing That a Standing Army Is Inconsistent with a Free Government* . . . (London, 1697). On the interregnum in Virginia, see Webb, *Officers and Governors*, 313–25.

3. Louis B. Wright and Marion Tinling, eds., *The Secret Diary of William Byrd of Westover, 1709–1712* (Richmond, VA, 1941), Mar. 31, June 22–23, 1710; Spotswood to commissioners, Aug. 18, 1710, Brock, *Spotswood Letters*, 1:7.

4. H. R. McIlwaine, ed., *Executive Journals of the Council of Colonial Virginia*, vol. 3 (May 1, 1705–October 23, 1721), (Richmond, VA, 1928), 252; Spotswood to commissioners, Aug. 18, 1710, Brock, *Spotswood Letters*, 1:11–13; same, July 25, 1711, *Spotswood Letters*, 1:88; Webb, *Governors-General*, 333–34; Dodson, *Spotswood*, 157; Byrd, *Diary*, Sept. 21, 1710; Bertram Wyatt-Brown, *Southern Honor* (Oxford, 1983), 191–92, 354–55. Grace L. Chickering, "Founders of an Oligarchy: The Virginia Council, 1692–1722," in Bruce C. Daniels, ed., *Power and Status Officeholding in Colonial America* (Middletown, CT, 1986), 266. Spotswood's instructions ordered him to organize, arm, and drill the planters and "Christian inhabitants," but these, like all but one of his military instructions, were boilerplate by 1710, mere recitations of the post-Baconian royal reforms of 1679: Leonard Woods Labaree, ed., *Royal Instructions to British Colonial Governors, 1670–1776* (1935; repr., New York, 1987), #552–54, 564, 565, 572, 573, 578, 611. It was clear, however, that "the Crown is obliged to protect them [the provinces] and must necessarily be invested with all the powers requisite for that purpose," Greene, "Martin Bladen's Blueprint," 235. On the invention of rank, see Michael Roberts, "The Military Revolution, 1560–1660," in *Essays in Swedish History* (London, 1956), 212.

5. James L. Bugg Jr., "The French Frontier Settlement of Manakin Town," *VMHB* 61 (1963): 359–94; Robert Beverley, *History and Present State of Virginia*, ed. Louis B. Wright (Chapel Hill, NC, 1947), book 4, p. 457; Richard L. Morton, *Colonial Virginia* (Chapel Hill, NC, 1960), 1:367–69; *EJC*, 3:60, 261–63; Byrd, *Diary*, Sept. 23, 1710. On the Occaneechee episode, see Wilcomb E. Washburne, *The Governor and the Rebel* (Chapel Hill, NC, 1957), 43–46. On the Byrds' fur trade, see Marion Tinling, ed., *The Correspondence of the Three William Byrds of Westover, Virginia, 1684–1776* (Charlottesville, VA, 1977), 1:16; Thomas Perkins Abernethy, *Three Virginia Frontiers* (Baton Rouge, LA, 1940), 32–36, 49–50; Morton, *Colonial Virginia*, 2:425–28. On the Roanoke water gap and its exploitation after 1671, see Fairfax Harrison, *Landmarks of Old Prince William* (Berryville, VA, 1964), 224.

6. On the dispersion and retreat of the Rappahannocks, see Ragan, "'Where the Water Ebbs and Flows.'" Spotswood to commissioners, Dec. 15, 1710, Brock, *Spotswood Letters*, 1:40–41. On Washington's "rising empire," see R. W. Van Alstyne, *The Rising American Empire* (New York, 1960), 1.

7. H. R. McIlwaine, ed., *Journals of the House of Burgesses of Virginia, 1702/3–1705, 1706–1706, 1710–1712* (Richmond, VA, 1912), 240–41, 283, 285; Spotswood to commissioners, Mar. 16, 1710[/11], Brock, *Spotswood Letters,* 1:49–50. Edmund S. Morgan, *American Slavery, American Freedom: The Ordeal of Colonial Virginia* (New York, 1975), 301, 420–23. David A. Williams, *Political Alignments in Colonial Virginia Politics, 1698–1750* (New York, 1989), 125–26, 129–30, 144–45; Anthony S. Parent Jr., *Foul Means: The Formation of a Slave Society in Virginia, 1660–1740* (Chapel Hill, NC, 2003), 50–52; Grace Lawson Chickering, "The Governors' Councils of Virginia, 1692–1722" (PhD diss., University of Delaware, 1978), 195–97.

8. On the corporate empire, see Webb, "'Brave Men . . . ,'" *Perspectives* 8 (1974): 63–65. On Spotswood's iron mining and manufacture, see Dodson, *Spotswood,* 229–31; *JHB, 1702–1712,* 279; Spotswood to commissioners, Dec. 15, 1710, Brock, *Spotswood Letters,* 1:41; Bruce C. Lenman, "Alexander Spotswood and the Business of Empire," *Colonial Williamsburg* 13 (1990): 51–55; Lester J. Cappon, ed., *Iron Works at Tuball . . .* (Charlottesville, VA, 1945), 6–9. On this, "the first commercially successful blast furnace in the Americas," see Ralph C. Meima, "The Giant Who Would Not Stay Buried," *Tools and Technology* 8 (1988): 9–12, 17–21; and, on "the biggest single iron producer in the British Empire," see Bruce C. Lenman, "Spotswood," *ANB.* By 1739, when he left his mines for his last military command, Spotswood was exporting 1,143 tons of iron annually, Peter V. Bergstrom, *Markets and Merchants: Economic Diversification in Colonial Virginia, 1700–1775* (New York, 1985), table 5.2. Note that in iron manufacture, as in other aspects of empire, Spotswood directly inspired the Washingtons. Spotswood's plants operated until they were destroyed in the Civil War. See Ralph Emmett Fall, ed., *The Diary of Robert Rose* (Richmond, VA, 1977), 141–42; Hugh Jones, *The Present State of Virginia,* ed. Richard L. Morton (1724; repr., Chapel Hill, NC, 1965), 73, 171. Spotswood's corporations add an American industrial element to the investment picture painted by P. J. Cain and A. G. Hopkins, "Gentlemanly Capitalism and British Expansion Overseas," *Economic History Review,* 2d ser., 39 (1986): 501–25.

9. For the naval stores project, see Dodson, *Spotswood,* 232–36; Spotswood to commissioners, Mar. 20, 1710/11, CO 5/1315, fols. 240–41; *CSPC, 1710–1711,* #744. See also Sir William Keith, Bt., "A Short Discourse on . . . the Colonies in America," [London, 1728], in *A Collection of Papers . . .* (London, 1740), 172.

10. Graham Hood, *The Governor's Palace in Williamsburg: A Cultural Study* (Williamsburg, VA, 1991); *JHB, 1710,* 240, 275, 285. Houlding, *Fit for Service,* 168n17. Philip Alexander Bruce, *Institutional History of Virginia* (New York, 1910), 2:98–99; Webb, *Governors-General,* 138, 371–72, 374, 381, 391–92, 407, 429, 431, 434–35. See "An Acct. of Arms & Ammunition Belonging to Her Majesty in Virginia," CO 5/1316, fol. 104, for the 1702 distribution. See Ella Lonn, *The Colonial Agents of the Southern Colonies* (Chapel Hill, NC, 1945), 187, for a 1692 shipment lost in the statehouse fire. See Lonn, *Colonial Agents,* 192, 197, for other arms shipments. John W. Reps, *Tidewater Towns* (Williamsburg, VA, 1972), 154, fig. 100; James D. Kornwolf, *Architecture and Town Planning in Colonial North America* (Baltimore, 2002).

11. Albert Harkness, *The Military System of the Romans* (New York, 1887), iv, xlix, lii.

12. Spotswood to commissioners, Aug. 18, 1710, Mar. 6, 1710[/11], Brock, *Spotswood Letters*, 1:10–11, 54. Note that Spotswood had received a detailed account of the revenues and perquisites of Virginia while he considered Marlborough's offer of the command, ibid., 2:192. Marcus Whiffen, *The Public Buildings of Williamsburg* (Williamsburg, VA, 1958), 9–10, 12, 68, 88–93, 94–95. Thomas Tileston Waterman, *The Mansions of Virginia, 1706–1776* (Chapel Hill, NC, 1945), 38–61. On costs, see *JHB, 1702–1712*, xxi, 40, 285. The price of the palace remained a stick to beat Spotswood with: Spotswood to burgesses, Nov. 24, 1718, Aug. 11, 1719, CO 5/1318, 304, 408–13, sec. G. On the Spotswood portrait with an alleged Blenheim background, see Brock, *Spotswood Letters*, 1:viii. On Marlborough's obsession, see David Green, *Blenheim Palace* (London, 1951).

13. Spotswood to commissioners, Jan. 16, 1716, Brock, *Spotswood Letters*, 2:220; Jones, *Present State*, 70; Webb, *Governors-General*, 57.

14. Waterman, *Mansions*, 43, 46. Appropriately, the dining room details in the restored palace are copied from William Blathwayt's Dyrham Park. See Webb, "Blathwayt," 9; Whiffen, *Public Buildings*, 55, 61, 93–94. A similarly balanced and environed house, Chevening, was erected in Kent by Spotswood's superior officer Stanhope, in 1717. See *Country Life*, Apr. 17, 24, May 1, 1920, 512–22, 548, 546, 586–93. At Germanna, Spotswood adopted a plan similar to the palace: Douglas W. Sanford, "The Enchanted Castle in Context," *Quarterly Bulletin of the Archeological Society of Virginia* 44 (1989): 105–6, fig., 3; Historic Gordonville, Inc., *The Enchanted Castle at Germanna* (Somerset, VA, 1987); Bryan Clark Green et al., *Lost Virginia* (Charlottesville, VA, 2001), 12. On Spotswood's "imperial gardening," see Lenman, "'Garrison Government,' Governor Alexander Spotswood and Empire," in Grant G. Simpson, ed., *The Scottish Soldier Abroad* (Edinburgh, 1992), 71, and *ANB*, 20:495. On the royal executive's cultural currency, see Richard D. Brown, *Knowledge Is Power* (New York, 1989), 58. On the building mania of Marlborough's officers (and their aversion to standing timber) see Farquhar, *Recruiting Officer*, II.ii.27–31. John Custis lamented his lost trees to Philip Ludwell II, Apr. 18, 1717, *VMHB* 46 (1939): 244–[45]: "I think he called it a vista." E. G. Swem, *Brothers of the Spade* (Barre, MA, 1957), 15.

15. Pierre Marambaud, *William Byrd of Westover, 1674–1744* (Charlottesville, VA, 1971), 222; Byrd, *Diary*, Apr. 20, June. 16, Aug. 4, Sept. 13, Oct. 31, 1709; Apr. 25, Nov. 7, 1711. Jones, *Present State*, 67. Jones's comparison with Chelsea College would have been more apt if applied to the contemporary design of another military architect, Col. Christian Lilly. His design for Codrington College was being built under the bequest of Gov.-Gen. Christopher Codrington on his former estate in Barbados. See Frank J. Klingberg, ed., *Codrington Chronicle* (Los Angeles, 1949), 27–39. For the College of William and Mary, see Whiffen, *Public Buildings*, 96–112. The method of the design and the timing of the construction of the Brafferton or Indian School (erected 1723) make it quite possible that Spotswood was also its architect. His deep concern for Indian education makes it likely. On the college board, see Chickering, "Oligarchy," 266.

16. Whiffen, *Public Buildings*, 75–85; *JHB, 1710*, 247; *JHB, 1712*, 37. Spotswood to admiralty, Mar. 6, 1710[/11], Brock, *Spotswood Letters*, 1:67. Dell Upton, *Holy Things* *and Profane: Anglican Parish Churches in Colonial Virginia* (New Haven, CT, 1986, 1997), 81–82, dismisses Spotswood's architectural contribution.

17. Spotswood to the bishop of London; to commissioners; and to Dartmouth, Nov. 11, 1711, Brock, *Spotswood Letters*, 1:122, 125, 126; same to commissioners, Dec. 28, 1711, ibid., 1:129. Spotswood to the vestry of St. Ann's, Essex, Sept. 3, 1718, William Stevens Perry, ed., *Historical Collections relating to the American Colonial Church* (Hartford, CT, 1870), 1:205–6, and see 210, 212, 232–34, 246, 247. Blair backed the vestries' independence from English authority. He threatened that the Virginia vestries would fire every clergyman who accepted the lieutenant governor's jurisdiction. Spotswood's position on collation, like so many of his contentions, had previously been Nicholson's, Perry, *Historical Collections*, 1:227. Spotswood to convocation, Apr. 8, 1719, Perry, *Historical Collections*, 1:202. Blair's reply, Perry, *Historical Collections*, 1:228–29, and see 230. Nothing of this is in Parke Rouse Jr., *James Blair of Virginia* (Chapel Hill, NC, 1971). For a full treatment of clerical appointments and the struggle with Blair, see Morton, *Colonial Virginia*, 2:465–71. For criticism of Blair and the "Collegians," see also [William Beverley], *An Abridgement of the Publick Laws of Virginia in Force and in Use, June 10, 1720 . . .* (London, 1722), dedicated "To His Excellency Alexander Spotswood, His Majesty's Leutenant Governor And Commander In Chief Of Virginia, Vice Admiral Of The Same, And All The Adjacent Seas." Morton's account of Spotswood's success in supporting the clergy contrasts with T. J. Wertembaker, "The Attempt to Reform the Church of Colonial Virginia," *Sewanee Review* 25 (1917): 257–82, which depicts the malformation of a stunted provincial branch of the church and is especially informative about clerical "cursing, swearing, Drunkenness or fighting," 263. On Blair's worldly concerns, see Perry, *Historical Collections*, 1:31. On Blair's Scots ordination, see George Mclaren Brydon, *Virginia's Mother Church and the Political Conditions under Which It Grew* (Richmond, VA, 1947), 1:340–53.

18. See also memo of June 28, 1710, Brock, *Spotswood Letters*, 1:2; Spotswood to bishop of London, Aug. 16, 1710, ibid., 1:4–5; same to Blathwayt, ibid., 1:5–6; Jones, *Present State*, 46, 96, 122–25, and see 89n5, 181, 186. Spotswood to bishop of London, Oct. 24, 1710, Mar. 6, 1710[/11], Brock, *Spotswood Letters*, 1:26, 66–67.

19. "Pedigrees: Spottiswoode of That Ilk," MS 2933, NLS, 68b. Perry, *Historical Collections*, 1:237, 239, 245; Spotswood to commissioners, Dec. 15, 1710, Brock, *Spotswood Letters*, 1:38, 39. On Compton in the revolution, see Webb, *Lord Churchill's Coup*, index and "character," book 2 insert.

20. Spotswood to Compton, Aug. 16; same to commissioners and to admiralty, Oct. 24, 1710, Mar. 6, 1710[/11], Brock, *Spotswood Letters*, 1:4–5, 22, 25, 35, 62–63; same to [Lawrence Hyde], earl of Rochester, July 30, 1711, ibid., 1: 107–9; same to Dartmouth, July 15, 1711, ibid., 1:81; same to Col. Edward Hyde, n.d., ibid., 1:47–48; Spotswood's proclamations, Dec. 18, 1710, Jan. 8, 1711, June 10, 1712, CO 5/1337, fols. 56–57, 59; *EJC*, 3: June 13, July 5, 1711; Journal of the Lieutenant Governor's Expeditions, CO 5/1318, fol. 356; Dodson, *Spotswood*, 17–18; David A. Rawson, "The Anglo-American Settlement of Virginia's Rappahannock Frontier," *Locus* 6 (1994): 101–5; Webb, *Governors-General*, #71, 72. Webb, *Governors-General*, 370–71, records Col. Jeffreys's operations in Albemarle and the Southside against Baconian rebels and Indian raiders.

21. Spotswood to Dartmouth, July 15, 28, 1711; same to lords proprietors of Carolina, July 28, 31, 1711; same to commissioners, July 25, 1711, Brock, *Spotswood Letters*, 1:81–86, 91, 92; same to proprietors of Carolina, July 28, 1711, ibid., 101; and to Dartmouth, July 31, 1711, ibid., 107; same to Cary and Hyde, June 20, 1711, CO 5/1337, fols. 35–37; same to Cary, June 21, 1711, CO 5/1337, fol. 36; Spotswood's proclamations, July 24, 29, 1711, CO 5/1316, #29, and fol. 55. See also CO 5/1316, #98. Same to Dartmouth, Sept. 26, 1711, CO 5/1363, fol. 166; commissioners to Spotswood (draft), Feb. 1, 1711/12, CO 5/1335, fol. 168; reprimand to Spotswood from commissioners, Aug. 27, 1712, CO 5/1363, fol. 207. Commanders of station ships were particularly ordered to "consult" with provincial executives, H. W. Richmond, *The Navy in the War of 1739–48* (Cambridge, 1920), 3: app. B. See also Dodson, *Spotswood*, 21; Osgood, *Eighteenth Century*, 2:244–49.

22. Spotswood to commissioners, Oct. 15, Nov. 17; same to Dartmouth, Oct. 15, Nov. 11, Brock, *Spotswood Letters*, 1:115–18, 121–26; CO 5/1318, fol. 356; Byrd, *Diary*, Sept. 4, 20, 29, Oct. 7, 16–21, 1711; Marambaud, *Byrd*, 227. Thomas Parramore, "The Tuscarora Ascendency," *NCHR* 59 (1982): 323–24; Webb, *Governors-General*, 399, 400, #45; Shy, *Toward Lexington*, 10–11.

23. Brock, *Spotswood Letters*, 1:117, 119; Spotswood to commissioners, and to Dartmouth, Feb. 8, 1711[/12], ibid., 1:142, 145; same to Dartmouth, May 8, 1712, ibid., 1:147; commissioners to same, Dec. 6, 1711, CO 5/1337, fols. 27–28; same to same, Apr. 16, 1712, CO 5/1341, 43–44 (repeating Spotswood's alarmist language). Spotswood to ordnance office, Mar. 15, 1713, Brock, *Spotswood Letters*, 2:65–66. Same, May 8, 1716, Brock, *Spotswood Letters*, 2:140, counted 300 muskets, 300 soldiers' tents, 154 barrels of gunpowder, 7 tons and 7 pounds of musket ball; 2 field pieces with carriages and furniture. The 1702 shipment had consisted of 1,013 muskets, 326 carbines, 296 pairs of pistols, 1,017 swords, 798 cartridge boxes, 41 barrels of gunpowder, and 4,300 pounds of musket shot. Of this, Spotswood found in the old Middle Plantation magazine only 173 muskets, 103 carbines, 63 pairs of pistols, 194 swords, 228 cartridge boxes, 10 1/2 barrels of powder, and 1,000 pounds of shot. The weapons were mostly unserviceable and the powder had largely decayed. The bulk of the munitions had long since been distributed to the militia: "An Acct. of Arms & Ammunition Belonging to Her Majesty in Virginia," CO 5/1316, fol. 104. Commissioners to Dartmouth, May 15, 1712, CO 5/1335, fols. 85–86; same, Jan. 29, 1712/13, CO 5/1363, fols. 220–21; Spotswood to Dartmouth, Feb. 6, 1711[/12], CO 5/1316, fol. 314; Dartmouth to commissioners, Apr. 22, 1712, CO 5/1316, fol. 317. The magazine act is in William Waller Hening, ed., *The Statutes at Large: Being a Collection of All the Laws of Virginia . . .* (New York, 1820, 1823, 1969), 4:55–56. This act and the inventories of arms conformed to the royal instructions issued in 1679 (Labaree, *Royal Instructions*, #564, 572), when the Guards were still maintaining barracks and a magazine at the Middle Plantation (Webb, *Governors-General*, 371–74, etc.) and to the instruction (for more frequent reports on munitions) in Spotswood's instructions of 1710, Labaree, *Royal Instructions*, #565. The only royal instructions on military matters not first issued in 1679 were the Lockean, antiprerogative prohibition against martial law in peacetime, issued in 1699, and the reconsideration, issued on the advent of war in 1702, that called for an assembly mutiny act (Labaree, *Royal Instructions*, #562, 563), which Spotswood secured. On the "atrocious" condition of munitions, see Houlding, *Fit for Service*, 137–49.

24. Whiffen, *Public Buildings*, 85–87; Spotswood to commissioners, Jan. 27, 1714[/15], Brock, *Spotswood Letters*, 2:97. Spotswood kept weapons for two full infantry companies in the palace armory. Spotswood to commissioners, June 4, July 15, 1715, Brock, *Spotswood Letters*, 2:115, 120, and see 157, 160.

25. Spotswood's proclamation, Aug. 16, 1711, CO 5/1337, fols. 55–56. Commissioners to Spotswood, Apr. 23, 1713, CO 5/1363, fol. 242v. For the burgesses' protest against the "diversion" of the quitrents, and deputy auditor Ludwell's address of Dec. 1714, see *JHB, 1712–1726*, 109–10, summarized by Spotswood in Brock, *Spotswood Letters*, 2:185; Spotswood to Blathwayt, May 8, 1712, Brock, *Spotswood Letters*, 1:157–59; same to commissioners, June 4, 1715, Brock, *Spotswood Letters*, 2:116, and see 118, 120, 157, 160. See also Webb, "Blathwayt," 414–15; *EJC*, 3:307–8. Again, Nicholson (£900 for the defense of New York in 1703) provided Spotswood's precedent, Morton, *Colonial Virginia*, 1:373. The provisions trade, first organized by Spotswood to supply the Canadian expedition, meant that pork exports, only 97 barrels in 1701, grew to 4,662 barrels by 1727: Bergstrom, *Markets and Merchants*, 132.

26. Byrd, *Diary*, Aug. 28, 1711; CO 5/1320, fol. 57; Farquhar, *Recruiting Officer*, act III, scene i, p. 48; Herbert L. Osgood, *The American Colonies in the Seventeenth Century* (New York, 1904), 3:256–58; Webb, *Governors-General*, 333–34; Webb, *1676*, 18, 21. On the subsequent defense of Spotswood's line, see Alexander S. Webb, *The Peninsula* (New York, [1890]), 71–81.

27. *JHB, 1702–1712*, [301–]3, 309, 314; Spotswood to commissioners, Dec. 8, 28, 1711, Brock, *Spotswood Letters*, 1:129–33, 138–44; same to Dartmouth, Dec. 28, Feb. 8, 1711, Brock, *Spotswood Letters*, 1:134–38, 144–46, CO 5/1337, fols. 27–28.

28. *JHB, 1710–1712*, xliii, 319, 321, 323–25; Spotswood to commissioners, Dec. 28, 1711, Brock, *Spotswood Letters*, 1:130, 131; same to Dartmouth, Brock, *Spotswood Letters*, 1:134–36, and Feb. 8, 1711/12, 145, CO 5/1316, fol. 314; Michael Leroy Oberg, ed., *Samuel Wiseman's Book of Record* (Lanham, MD, 2005), 147–48. Spotswood to commissioners, Sept. 5, 1711, Brock, *Spotswood Letters*, 1:110–12. Byrd, *Diary*, Jan. 9, 15, 20, 21, 24, 29, 1712. Oligarchic fear of the cooperation of the governor and the burgesses in a popular military project was articulated by Keith, "Present State" (1721), in *Collection*, 181. The £20,000 jibe and its social consequences are remarked on by Brown, *Knowledge*, 53–54. Farquhar, *Recruiting Officer*, V. iv. 17–21. Osgood, *Eighteenth Century*, 3:229.

29. On the oyer and terminer issue, see Worthington Chauncey Ford, ed., *The Controversy . . . on Commission of Oyer and Terminer* (Brooklyn, 1891); Williams, *Political Alignments*, 172–75. On the royal introduction of these courts to punish the rebels of 1676, see Webb, *1676*, 149–56. On Rappahannock rivalries, see the evocative study by Darrett B. Rutman and Anita H. Rutman, *A Place in Time: Middlesex County, Virginia, 1650–1750*, 2 vols. (New York, 1984). Spotswood to commissioners, Dec. 28, 1711, Feb. 2, 1711[/12]; same to Dartmouth, Dec. 28, 1711, Feb. 8, 1711[/12], Brock, *Spotswood Letters*, 1:132, 137, 139, 140, 141, 144, 145. *EJC*, 3:304–5. On the changing composition of the burgesses, see Morgan, *American Slavery, American Freedom*, 358–62, 366–67.

30. Spotswood to commissioners, and to Dartmouth, Dec. 28, 1711, Brock, *Spotswood Letters*, 1:133, 137–38. He did assume that the victorious British army would have troops to spare for America once the war was won in Europe.

31. Cynthia Miller Leonard, ed., *The General Assembly of Virginia, July 30, 1619–Jan. 11, 1978* . . . (Richmond, VA), 65–67; Webb, *Officers and Governors*, 344; Dodson, *Spotswood*, 24–31, 71–72, 82, 161; William L. Saunders, ed., *The Colonial Records of North Carolina* (Raleigh, NC, 1886), 1:834–35, 861–63, 866–69; Verner W. Crane, *The Southern Frontier, 1670–1732* (1929; repr., Ann Arbor, MI, 1956), 159–60; *JHB, 1712–1726*, xviii, 36; Hening, *Statutes*, 4:30; Spotswood to Dartmouth, Dec. 28, 1711, May 8, July 26, 1712; same to commissioners, Feb. 8, 1711[/12], May 8, July 26, 1712, June 2, 1713, Brock, *Spotswood Letters*, 1:137, 141–42, 146–47, 169–71, 173, 2:25.

32. Giekie and Montgomery, *Dutch Barrier*, 968. Treaty with the Saponi Indians, CO 5/1313, fols. 515–16; Spotswood to Dartmouth, Feb. 8, 1711[/12], CO 5/1337, fol. 28; same, July 26, 1712, Brock, *Spotswood Letters*, 1:169, 171, 173; Spotswood to commissioners, July 26, 1712, Brock, *Spotswood Letters*, 1:169; same to bishop of London, Jan. 27, 1714, Brock, *Spotswood Letters*, 2:88; Dodson, *Spotswood*, 73–76; Byrd, "History of the Dividing Line," in Wright and Tinling, *London Diary*, 591–92. *EJC*, 3:296, 310, 363, 364; Saunders, *Colonial Records of North Carolina*, 1:828–29, 861, 874, 882, 974; Morton, *Colonial Virginia*, 2:432. On frontier posts and non-English pioneers as constituents of American expansion, see Frederick Jackson Turner, *The Frontier in American History* (New York, 1920, 1958), 16–17, 22–23, 86, and, on the German frontier, 102–3.

33. The Saponi and Tutelo subsequently joined the Cayuga, according to Marian E. White, William E. Engelbrecht, and Elizabeth Tooker, "Cayuga," in *Handbook of North American Indians*, ed. William C. Sturtevant, vol. 15, *Northeast*, ed. Bruce G. Trigger (Washington, DC, 1978), 501. However, it was Senecas who took responsibility for preserving Tutelo songs and dances until their dancing floors were flooded by the U.S. Corps of Engineers. Brydon, *Virginia's Mother Church*, 2:341–42. On the origin of the rangers and their joint patrols with the tributaries, see Webb, *Governors-General*, 370. For a summary of Spotswood's westward push, see Thomas Perkins Abernethy, "The First Transmontane Advance," in James S. Wilson, ed., *Humanistic Studies in Honor of John Calvin Metcalf* (New York, 1941), 120–23. On the tributary treaties and Spotswood's realignments, see W. Stitt Robinson, *The Southern Colonial Frontier, 1607–1763* (Albuquerque, n.d.), 129–31. Spotswood's efforts here were singled out for praise in the 1721 Report, *NYCD*, 5:623. Edward P. Alexander, "An Indian Vocabulary from Fort Christanna, 1716," *VMHB* 303–13; Mary C. Beaudry, "Fort Christanna: Frontier Trading Post of the Virginia Indian Company," in Albert E. Ward, ed., *Forgotten Places and Things* . . . (Albuquerque, 1983), 133–40; Edward P. Buford, *Fort Christanna* (Laurenceville, VA, 1924).

34. Dodson, *Spotswood*, 31–32, 75–77; Spotswood to commissioners, Feb. 11, 1712[/13], Brock, *Spotswood Letters*, 2:12; CO 5/1318, fol. 56v.; same, July 20, [1714], CO 5/1316, fol. 524v. and, under July 21, 1714, Brock, *Spotswood Letters*, 2:70–72. Matthew Lawson Rhoades, "Assarigoa's Line: Anglo-Iroquois Origins of the Virginia Frontier, 1675–1774" (PhD diss., Syracuse University, 2000), 75–80; Douglas W. Boyce, "'As the Wind Scatters the Smoke': The Tuscaroras in the Eighteenth Century," in James H. Merrell and Daniel K. Richter, eds., *Beyond the Covenant Chain: The Iroquois and Their Neighbors, 1600–1800* (Syracuse, NY, 1987), 154–56, 160–63; Jones, *Present State*, 61 and #47; Morton, *Colonial Virginia*, 2:431; Crane, *Southern Frontier*, 161.

35. CO 5/1318, #209 D, and see fols. 356–56v; Spotswood to Dartmouth, Sept. 14, 1713; same to commissioners, Sept. 14, Nov. 16, 1713, Brock, *Spotswood Letters*, 2:34, 37, 41–42; *JHB, 1712–1714*, 70.

36. "No. 106. Saturday, December 8, 1722. Of Plantations and Colonies," in Ronald Hamoway, ed., *Cato's Letters . . . by John Trenchard and Thomas Gordon* (Indianapolis, 1995), 2:748.

37. Spotswood's speech, Nov. 6, 1713, *JHB, 1712–1726*, 47–48; proclamation of truce with France, Oct. 15, 1712, CO 5/1344, fol. 66, and of peace, fol. 243. On tobacco notes as currency, see Leslie V. Brock, *The Currency of the American Colonies, 1700–1764: A Study in Colonial Finance and Imperial Relations* (New York, 1975), 10–15; Brydon, *Virginia's Mother Church*, 2:332–38. Spotswood to commissioners, Dec. 29, 1713, Brock, *Spotswood Letters*, 2:47–50. Morton, *Colonial Virginia*, 2:423–24. Note the anticipation of the "two penny" controversy.

38. "The Present State of Virginia for the Year 1714," CO 5/1317, #46; *VMHB* 2 (1894): [1–]15. Of course, membership in the burgesses was a function of social position. Spotswood was buying up much of Virginia's political nation outside the Green Spring faction. Only one of the forty-seven agents was recommended just by his burgess seat. Of course, every one of the twenty-five "yea" voters received an agency. Thirty-one agents also held places on the country courts (twenty were of the quorum; five were first in the commission). Eight agents were coroners, five were county clerks, and one was a councilor. All, save the last, were Spotswood appointees. *JHB, 1712–1726*, 73; Dodson, *Spotswood*, 52; Spotswood to commissioners, Dec. 19, 1713, Brock, *Spotswood Letters*, 2:48. Slightly different numbers of appointees are given in Williams, *Political Alignments*, 149–50.

39. Spotswood to commissioners, Oct. 25, 1714, Jan. 27, 1714[/15]; same to Bolingbroke, Oct. 25, 1714, Brock, *Spotswood Letters*, 2:75, 76, 94; Linda Colley, *In Defiance of Oligarchy: The Tory Party, 1714–1760* (Cambridge, 1982), 180–83, 338–39, #16, 17; Spotswood to commissioners, Oct. 25, 1714, Brock, *Spotswood Letters*, 2:76, CO 5/1317, fols. 110–11.

40. Spotswood to Bishop Robinson, Jan. 27, 1714[/15], Brock, *Spotswood Letters*, 2:90. Writing to Blakiston, Dec. 1, 1714, Spotswood stressed the king's personal knowledge of mining and observed that "these mines are to be wrought by persons of the same Nation and Religion," Brock, *Spotswood Letters*, 2:78. CO 5/1317, fol. 108, 110v; *JHB, 1712–1726*, 80–81. Osgood, *Eighteenth Century*, 3:234, sees the VIC as a burgess initiative. Spotswood to commissioners, Jan. 27, 1714[/15], Brock, *Spotswood Letters*, 2:94–95. Morton, *Colonial Virginia*, 2:436, insists that the VIC was not a monopoly, since anyone could invest and any investor could trade. The act is printed in W. Neil Franklin, ed., "Act for the Better Regulation of the Indian Trade, Virginia 1714," *VMHB* 72 (1969): 141–51, from CO 5/1386, fols. 61v–64r. Robinson, *Southern Colonial Frontier*, 131–32. Dodson, *Spotswood*, 83–87. Spotswood suspected that Byrd incited Iroquois raids on the Virginia frontier in order to stimulate the munitions

trade, Richard Acquila, "Warriors' Path," *AIQ* 40 (1983): 215. See also Brydon, *Virginia's Mother Church*, 2:342–43.

41. Webb, *Lord Churchill's Coup*, 3–4, 118–25; Proclamation regarding the Indian Trade, June 10, 1712, CO 5/1337, fols. 59v–60; lists of subscribers, Williams, *Political Alignments*, 160–61; *EJC*, 3:301–11, Apr. 26, 1712. Spotswood to Popple, Apr. 16, 1717, Brock, *Spotswood Letters*, 2:230–38; same to commissioners, Jan. 22, 1714[/15], Brock, *Spotswood Letters*, 2:93. On Griffin, see Morton, *Colonial Virginia*, 2:436–37. The previous fur trade monopoly, which excluded William Byrd I, had been a country party criticism of Gov. Berkeley in 1676, Webb, *1676*, 30; Henrico County Grievances, Oberg, *Samuel Wiseman's Book*, 241. A Namierist would reduce this contest to a family quarrel between the seven Burwells, who connected the members of the Green Spring faction, and the seven Beverleys, who constituted the court party linkage. For the Burwell-Ludwell connection, see Chickering, "Oligarchy," 1, 2; Brock, *Spotswood Letters*, 2:54–55, 60–61, 77–80, 157, 285, 314–16.

42. Jacob M. Price, *Perry of London* (Cambridge, MA, 1992), 54–59, 64–65, [72–] 77. Alfred James Henderson, *London and the National Government, 1721–1742* (Durham, NC, 1945), 127–31, 135, 165–66, 204–7, on Micajah Perry II. For his subsequent influence on the Walpole ministry, see Williams, *Political Alignments*, 276–77. On Spotswood's sponsorship of Scots in the tobacco trade, see Warren M. Billings, John E. Selby, and Thad W. Tate, *Colonial Virginia* (White Plains, NY, 1986), 201. Spotswood to Blakiston, Dec. 1, 1714, Brock, *Spotswood Letters*, 2:79.

43. Webb, "Nicholson," 535, #38. *EJC*, Nov. 4, 1714; Spotswood to commissioners, same to Blakiston, Dec. 1, 1714, Brock, *Spotswood Letters*, 2:76–79; Ford, *Controversy*, 27. On Spotswood's first round of council nominations, see Spotswood to Dartmouth, Mar. 9, 1713, CO 5/1341, 45–46, Brock, *Spotswood Letters*, 2:54–55; same to commissioners, Mar. 9, 1713, Dec. 1, 1714, Brock, *Spotswood Letters*, 2:58–61, 77–78; same to Blakiston, Dec. 1, 1714, Brock, *Spotswood Letters*, 2:78–80. Williams, *Political Alignments*, observes that seven of nine council appointees in Spotswood's tenure were his first choices, 148–49, 275.

44. Spotswood to commissioners, January 27, 1714[/15]; same to Stanhope, May 27, July 15, 1715, Brock, *Spotswood Letters*, 2:96, 111, 120–21.

45. See also Verner W. Crane, *The Southern Frontier, 1660–1732* (Ann Arbor, MI, 1929, 1956), 162–86; Morton, *Colonial Virginia*, 2:437–38.

46. Spotswood to commissioners, June 4, July 15; same to Josiah Burchett, secretary of the admiralty, July 16, 1715, Brock, *Spotswood Letters*, 2:116, 120–21, 126–27; commissioners to [Stanhope], Sept. 6, 1715, CO 5/1342, 3–4; CO 5/1335, fols. 125–26.

47. Spotswood to commissioners, Oct. 24, 1715, May 24, 1716; same to Stanhope, July 15, 1715, Brock, *Spotswood Letters*, 2:120, 125, 131–32, 136, 165–66.

48. Spotswood's speech, *JHB, 1712–1726*, 122–23. Crane, *Southern Frontier*, 176.

49. The doleful economic situation is analyzed by Billings, Selby, and Tate, *Colonial Virginia*, 173–75, and see 181–83. Williams, *Political Alignments*, 163–64, has one burgess/inspector reelected, one inspector newly elected, and fifteen members reelected. See his analysis of the committee chairs, 165–66. On the extraordinary value of naval (customs) offices and revenue collectorships, see Chickering, "Oligarchy," 267. Compare "The Present State of Virginia for the Year 1714," CO 5/1317,

#46, with the lists of burgesses in JHB. The burgesses of 1714 held an average of 1.4 appointive offices, those of 1715 but 0.7. Spotswood states the size of the court party in *JHB, 1712–1726*, 169. Yet many justices refused to certify petitions against the tobacco act. Some courts refused to levy burgesses' salaries. Instead they praised the executive. See *JHB, 1712–1726*, 122, 124, 132–33, 136, 140, and see 127, 128, 168; CO 5/1412, Oct.–Nov. 1715, Spotswood to commissioners, Aug. 9, 1715, Brock, *Spotswood Letters*, 2:128–29; same, Mar. 20, 1717/18, CO 5/1318, #167; Osgood, *Eighteenth Century*, 3:236. In Middlesex, the Robinson brothers were replaced by nonentities in 1715, attesting to the popular nature of the electoral revolt (Rutman and Rutman, *A Place in Time*, 227–28), but the new men were not reelected, attesting to the revolt's short duration.

50. "Propositions for a New Regulation of the Militia," CO 5/1318, fols. 101–2, CO 5/1315, #136; Spotswood's answer, #11, to "A.N.," Brock, *Spotswood Letters*, 2:212. See also Spotswood's remarks of Mar. 15, 1719, CO 5/1318, #208, and see the Essex County case in *JHB, 1712–1726*, 338, 346–47, where Spotswood threatened to cashier abusive officers. The well-to-do were heavily armed as cavalry captains and they armed their own troopers. If Col. Carter is typical, these cavalry commanders were obsessive about the maintenance and security of their weapons. They maintained several sets of arms at various "quarters," Robert Carter, Orders to John Johnson, June 22, 1721, Wright, ed., *Carter Letters*, 105.

51. Spotswood to commissioners, May 23, 1716, Brock, *Spotswood Letters*, 2:152, 154, and see 209, 212; *JHB, 1712–1726*, 147, 152, 162,168–69; Shy, *Toward Lexington*, 13–14. As in so many cases, the Nicholson administration was a rehearsal for Spotswood's, the two governors' proposed militia reforms and the "country" objections to them being much the same: Webb, "Nicholson," 539–41. For these antimilitary arguments in England, see Schwoerer, *No Standing Armies!* and comments in Webb, *Lord Churchill's Coup*, 256–60. Once again "under a Necesity of putting an unequal Militia law in Execution," Colonel Spotswood "so contrived, that by cantoning the Counties into small Districts and forming the Troops and Companies in those Cantons," he "made that easy to the People, which all along had been burthensome and unequal." Spotswood reduced the march to muster from thirty or forty miles to ten miles or less. Quotation from [Beverley] *An Abridgement*, dedication to Spotswood, and from Keith, "Present State" (1728), in his *Collection*, 180.

52. *JHB, 1712–1726*, 168–69, 170; Spotswood to Stanhope, same to commissioners Oct. 24, 1715, May 23, 1716, Brock, *Spotswood Letters*, 2:130, 133–35, 154, 157. For Turner's characteristic comment that Spotswood was struggling with frontier democracy, see *Frontier*, 247–48.

53. Spotswood to commissioners, May 25, 1719, CO 5/1318, #209, sec. H; commissioners to Spotswood (draft), June 1, 1716, CO 5/1335, fols. 130–36. Lediard, *Marlborough*, 3:391–406; Basil Williams, *The Whig Supremacy, 1714–1760* (Oxford, 1965), 157–64; Speck, *Stability and Strife*, 179–83.

54. CO 5/1317, #12, 84; Spotswood to Stanhope, Oct. 24, 1715, Brock, *Spotswood Letters*, 2:131, 133. Commissioners to the king, Mar. 3, 1717/18, CO 5/1365, fols. 27, 39; Spotswood to commissioners, Aug. 6, 1718, CO 5/1365, fols. 41–60, and see commissioners to Spotswood, June 1, 1716, Aug. 30, 1717, CO 5/1335, fols. 136, 143, 145.

55. On the transformation of the commission, Dec. 20, 1714, see *JCTP*, Feb. 17–Mar. 8/9, 1714/15, p. 575; and Steele, *Politics*, 149–51. The first substantive Virginia matter (the limitation of officeholding) was considered on July 15, 1715, JLCTP, Mar. 1714/15–Oct. 1718, p. 50. Spotswood's dispatches to Stanhope about the Yamasee War were read on July 8, JLCTP, Mar. 1714/15–Oct. 1718, p. 51. Spotswood was written to on Aug. 17, 1715, JLCTP, Mar. 1714/15–Oct. 1718, p. 72. Spotswood to Stanhope, Mar. 20, 1715[/16], Brock, *Spotswood Letters*, 2:109–10.

56. Spotswood to admiralty, same to commissioners, July 3, 1716; same to Stanhope, Oct. 14, 1715, Spotswood to commissioners, May 1, 1717, Brock, *Spotswood Letters*, 2:168–71, 182–83, 245; lieutenant governor and council to commissioners, [May 31, 1717], CO 5/1342, fol. 118, and see fol. 120 for Spotswood's vice admiralty jurisdiction. Beverley's memo is in William P. Palmer, ed., *Calendar of Virginia State Papers . . .* (Richmond, VA, 1875), 1:188. Spotswood's legal minutes are in Palmer, *Calendar of Virginia State Papers*, 1:186. On the *guarda costa* depredations, see Richard Pares, *War and Trade in the West Indies, 1739–1763* (Oxford, 1936), 14–28.

57. Spotswood to commissioners, May 1, Aug. 29, 1717, Brock, *Spotswood Letters*, 2:245, 259; commissioners to Secretary [Addison], Aug. 6, 1717, CO 5/1342, fol. 112, enclosing Spotswood to commissioners, May 31, 1717, CO 5/1342, fols. 113–21. N.B. the use of this very language by the duke of Newcastle to Spotswood and Gooch ordering them to raise American troops for the war on Spain in 1739, Add. MS 32693, 18. For the representation by HM envoy to Spain, see [commissioners to Spotswood], Jan. 29, 1717/18, CO 5/1365, fol. 21. See also Morton, *Colonial Virginia*, 2:463–64.

58. *EJC*, 3:428, June 17, 1716; CO 5/1318, fol. 54; ranger accounts, Oct. 22–Dec. 6, 1716, CO 5/1318, fols. 99–100; CO 5/1365, fol. 54. The rangers of this period traced their origin to Col. Jeffreys's 200-man establishment of 1679. Their successors were recruited from the redcoats disbanded in 1681. They were converted from riverine garrisons to mounted patrols in 1682 and expanded to four troops of thirty rangers each by Sir Edmund Andros in 1694. Nicholson proposed ranger-based frontier settlements in 1701. These Turner (*Frontier*, 87) saw as the antecedents of the Kentucky "stations." See Turner, *Frontier*, 85, 86; and Bruce, *Institutional History*, 2:104–22; Webb, *Governors-General*, 370. Edward Porter Alexander, ed., *The Journal of John Fontaine* (Williamsburg, VA, 1972), 9, 37–43, 84–85, 88, #116, 179; Perry, *Historical Collections*, 1:193–95, 247–48; Ann Maury, ed., *Memoirs of a Huguenot Family* (New York, 1853); Robinson, *Southern Colonial Frontier*, 27. Dalton, *Army Lists*, 6:230. Fontaine was still drawing half pay in 1740. Atkins is not to be confused with the officer of the Coldstream Guards killed in Spain in 1706, Dalton, *Army Lists*, 3:43, #5. Warren R. Hofstra, "'The Extention of His Majesties Dominions': The Virginia Backcountry and the Recasting of Imperial Frontiers," *JAH* 84 (1998): 1287, 1289–91.

59. Rawson, "Anglo-American Settlement," 94–98. On the "Germa-anna" settlement on the "Rapid-anna" River, see also Raymond E. Meyers, "The Story of Germanna," *Filson Club History Quarterly* 48 (1974): 27–42. On the two German migrations to Spotswood's development, called "St. George's Parish," migrations afterward celebrated as the fountain of the western movement, see also John W.

Wayland, *Germanna Outpost of Adventure, 1714–1956*, (Staunton, VA, 1956), 9–13, 17. Wayland records a third German migration as well as noting the importance of the Germanna ford site, a tactical objective down to "the battle of the Wilderness" in May 1864. Louis B. Wright, *The First Gentlemen of Virginia* (San Marino, CA, 1940), 306; Jones, *Present State*, #214, p. 239; [Beverley], *Abridgement*, dedication. Dodson, *Spotswood*, 280–81; CO 5/1320, p. 225; Morton, *Colonial Virginia*, 2:444–46.

60. Jones, *Present State*, #190, 194, 204, 213, pp. 243, 244, 264. Peter Beverley and John Robinson were Spotswood's choices to succeed Ludwell as receiver general, Spotswood to Blathwayt, July 3, 1716, Brock, *Spotswood Letters*, 2:174. Christopher Robinson was Spotswood's choice to replace Gawin Corbin, whom Spotswood fired as naval officer for the Rappahannock, Williams, *Political Alignments*, 268. On Spotswood's substitution of Robertson for Burwell, see Williams, *Political Alignments*, 272, and, for the lament by Robert Carter for his son-in-law, to Micajah and Richard Perry, July 3, 1720, see Wright, *Carter Letters*, 6. On the Beverley-Robinson connection, their quarrel with Corbin, and their search for a patron, all of which antedated Spotswood's arrival, see Rutman and Rutman, *A Place in Time*, 217–26. For John Robinson's formation of the Greenbriar Company, and William Beverley's 100,000-acre development in the Shenandoah Valley, see Hofstra, "'Extention,'" 1298, 1311. On the Society of Surveyors and the advent of an upper middle class, see Sarah S. Hughes, *Surveyors and Statesmen: Land Measuring in Colonial Virginia* (Richmond, VA 1979), 179–80. On the middle class and imperial authority, see Webb, *Governors-General*, index, s.vv. "Jeffreys" and "Hutchinson," and Webb, "Nicholson," 539–40. Note the place of surveyors in every western expedition. On the frequent sequence of surveyor, soldier, statesman, see Philander D. Chase, "A Stake in the West: George Washington as Backcountry Surveyor and Landholder," in Warren R. Hofstra, ed., *George Washington and the Virginia Backcountry* (Madison, WI, 1998), 160–61. Hofstra, *The Planting of New Virginia* (Baltimore, 2004), 21–22, 56–64, 109–12, 115.

61. CO 5/1318, fol. 356v; Delma R. Carpenter, "The Route Followed by Governor Spotswood in 1716 . . . ," *VMHB* 73 (1965): 405–42; Porter, *Fontaine*, 105–6; W. W. Scott, "The Knights of the Horseshoe: Their Route," *WMQ*, 2d. ser., 3:145–53. David C. Roller and Robert W. Twymen, eds., *The Encyclopedia of Southern History* (Baton Rouge, 1979), 692. See also Wayland, *Germanna*, 36, who notes the near neighborhood of the headwaters of the James. So this expedition was not too far afield from Spotswood's original proposal for a westward advance up one bank of that river, Spotswood to commissioners, Dec. 15, 1710, Brock, *Spotswood Letters*, 1:40.

62. Porter, *Fontaine*, 107.

63. Ian Marshall, "Landscape Aesthetics and Literary History . . . ," *Mississippi Quarterly* 44 (1990–91): 69; Jones, *Present State*, 58–59. Jones's testimony gives a quietus to Bruce Lenman's argument in "'Garrison Government,'" 74. And see Spotswood's presentation of a golden horseshoe badge to the speaker of the Six Nations, *NYCD*, 5:675. On the whole episode, see Morton, *Colonial Virginia*, 2:447–49. See also Lyman C. Draper, "Life of Daniel Boone," Draper MS, ser. B, vols. 1–5, p. 115, State Historical Society of Wisconsin, Madison. For the development of the Shenandoah by William Beverley, John Robinson, and others of the "knights," see n. 60 above and Thomas Perkins Wertembaker, "The First Transmontane Advance," in James S. Wilson, ed., *Humanistic Studies in Honor of John Calvin Metcalf* (New York, 1941), 133, 137. Note that the projected boundary of Virginia and New York, the Niagara frontier, was proposed conjointly by Spotswood and Hunter.

64. Spotswood to commissioners, Aug. 29, 1717, CO 5/1318, fol. 139, and see fol. 357, #16; same to Peter Schuyler, Jan. 25, 1719/20, *Pa. Council Minutes*, 3:84; *NYCD*, 5:490–92.

65. On Hart, see Webb, *Governors-General*, #120; Spotswood to commissioners, Feb. 27, 1717/18, Brock, *Spotswood Letters*, 2:261–62, CO 5/1318, fol. 171; Lustig, *Hunter*, 151–52; Journal of the Lt. Govrs. Travells & Expeditions, CO 5/1318, fol. 357; Dodson, *Spotswood*, 101; Keith, "Report to the Lords Commissioners" (1718), in *Collection*, 191; Cadwallader Colden, "Continuation" (of the *History of the Five Indian Nations Depending upon the Province of New York*) Colden Papers, 9, NYHSC (1937): 380, 413–14, 425–34; Acquila, "Down the Warrior's Path," 212–215; Richard Acquila, *The Iroquois Restoration* (Detroit, 1983), ch. 7; McIlwaine, ed., *Wraxall's New York Indian Records*, Albany, Jan. 21, 1716/17, 48, 117–18.

66. Spotswood to commissioners, Aug. 14 [Sept. 27], 1718, Brock, *Spotswood Letters*, 2:295–304.

67. OPC, July 31, 1717, enc. in commissioners to Spotswood, Aug. 30, 1717, CO 5/1335, 143–46; Spotswood to commissioners, June 24, Sept. 27, 1717; same to Popple, Apr. 16, 1717, Brock, *Spotswood Letters*, 2:276, 301–2, 238. The eloquent and well-researched protest by (unnamed) Virginia and Maryland merchants against the principle of monopoly, allegedly manifested by the VIC, was ideologically as well as economically important to the repeal of the VIC act, CO 5/1317, fol. 90. See Keith, "Report to Commissioners," 198–99, on the view, a country shibboleth since 1628, that "monopoly" was the hallmark of absolutism. That the merchant motivation was more political than economic is shown by their lack of investment (other than Perry's supplies to Byrd) in the fur trade, Spotswood to commissioners, Sept. 27, 1718, Brock, *Spotswood Letters*, 2:301–3. See the Virginia Merchant's Memorial, CO 5/1318, #105, and see 70, 79, 89, 111, 115; CO 5/1317, #75, but see #40. For the Perrys' assistance to Ludwell, see Spotswood to Blakiston, Apr. 16, 1717, and see same to commissioners, Sept. 27, 1718, Brock, *Spotswood Letters*, 2:243, 301–2. For the accomplishments of the VIC in frontier security and Indian education, see Robinson, *Southern Colonial Frontier*, 133–34, and for the damage done to frontier security by the VIC's disbandment, see Brock, *Spotswood Letters*, 2:302–3.

68. Spotswood's "Advice to Freeholders" [Apr. 1718], CO 5/1318, #170, printed by Jack P. Greene, ed., "The Opposition to Lieutenant Governor Alexander Spotswood, 1718," *VMHB* 70 (1962): 39–41. "Narrative of Proposals Made for Reconciling the Differences between Colonel Spotswood and the Council of Virginia," CO 5/1318, #193. Spotswood to commissioners, June 24, 1718, Brock, *Spotswood Letters*, 2:276–77, 279–81; *JHB, 1712–1726*, 173. Faction lists are in Byrd, *Diary*, Feb. 5–13, Apr. 21, 24, 29, Dec. 13–16; confirmed by Spotswood to commissioners, Dec. 22, 1718. CO 5/1318, fols. 291–98; Osgood, *Eighteenth Century*, 3:247; Williams, *Political Alignments*, 182–83; Rutman and Rutman, *A Place in Time*, 228.

69. Instructions to William Byrd by the burgesses, May 30, 1718, CO 5/1318, fol. 214, *JHB, 1712–1726*, xxxvi–xxxvii, 216; "Narrative of Proposals," CO 5/1318, #193; Spotswood to commissioners, June 24, 1718, Brock, *Spotswood Letters*, 2:282–83. The social split between the parties was politically suggestive. The Green Spring faction refused to join the governor's celebration of the king's birthday on May 28, declining to come to the palace reception or attend the theatrical performance Spotswood sponsored at the new playhouse. Instead, the faction hosted a drunken mob at "the Burgesses House," Spotswood to commissioners, June 24, 1718, Brock, *Spotswood Letters*, 2:284; Whiffen, *Public Buildings*, 112–17.

70. Spotswood to commissioners, Dec. 22, 1718, CO 5/1318, fols. 291–301; same to Craggs, Oct. 22, 1718; same to commissioners, Mar. 25, 1719, Brock, *Spotswood Letters*, 2:306–10; council minutes, Dec. 24, 1718, CO 5/1318, #61(i), fol. 299.

71. *JHB, 1712–1726*, 228–29; Spotswood to burgesses, CO 5/1318, #61(v), fol. 305v; same to commissioners, Dec. 22, 1719, CO 5/1318, fol. 292. Morton, *Colonial Virginia*, 2:415–16; Greene, "Opposition to Spotswood," 35–39; Greene, *The Quest for Power: The Lower Houses of Assembly in the Southern Royal Colonies, 1689–1776* (Chapel Hill, NC, 1963), esp., 28–29, 187, 279–80; Billings, Selby, and Tate, *Colonial Virginia*, 188. Williams, *Political Alignments*, 190, suggests that the burgesses realized that they were being used by the councilors of the faction, headed by Ludwell, and revolted against this dictation. In this protest, as in every episode of his entire administration, Spotswood was supported by Virginia's official agent, Col. Nathaniel Blakiston, officer of a regiment (the 15th, Bolton's 2d) with unequaled imperial experience. Blakiston had been brevetted colonel as (deputy) governor of Montserrat. He commanded Maryland before becoming agent for both the Chesapeake colonies. Blakiston was a Marlborough man to whom Spotswood was introduced before his commission was announced. Dodson, *Spotswood*, 113; Webb, *Governors-General*, #93, 118; Webb, *Lord Churchill's Coup*, 154–55; Lonn, *Colonial Agents*, 60, 89–90, 158, 159, 182, 208, 381–82, 387.

72. *Some Remarkable PROCEEDINGS*, printed broadside, State Historical Society of Wisconsin, Madison; Spotswood to burgesses, Nov. 28, 1718, CO 5/1318, #61(v), fols. 303–5; Spotswood to commissioners, Mar. 26, May 26, 1719, Brock, *Spotswood Letters*, 2:311, 314, 320. "The present contention is with a Party, & not with the Country," same to Popple, Feb. 5, 1718/19, CO 5/1318, #203; Addresses against the proceedings of the burgesses: CO 5/1318, #205, 225. In Apr., Spotswood also persuaded the clerical convocation to denounce Commissary Blair and to endorse Spotswood's right to collate, Brydon, *Virginia's Mother Church*, 1:349–51; Spotswood's letter of Aug. 14, 1718, Brock, *Spotswood Letters*, 2:292–93.

73. "Remarks on the Articles . . . Rejected by the House of Burgesses," CO 5/1318, fols. 334–39; Spotswood to commissioners, Aug. 11, 1719, ibid., #73, fol. 413; commissioners to Spotswood, June 26, 1719, CO 5/1365, fols. 100–104, *CSPC, 1719–1720*, #271, p. 142; Spotswood to commissioners, Aug. 1, 1718, CO 5/1365, fol. 60; commissioners to Craggs, Apr. 10, 1719, rejecting the address of the house of burgesses, CO 5/1365, fols. 95–97; Spotswood to commissioners, Mar. 5, 1719/20, CO 5/1318, #213; Orkney to same, May 3, 1720, CO 5/1318, #214; same, May 31, 1719, CO 5/1365, fol. 94, and commissioners to the king, same. Mr. Solr. Genl's Report [Mar. 1718/19],

CO 5/1365, #198; postmaster general's secretary to commissioners, May 8, 1719, CO 5/1365, #205. On the completeness of Spotswood's victory, see Morton, *Colonial Virginia*, 2:460; Williams, *Political Alignments*, 191, 193–94; Dodson, *Spotswood*, 198–200; Parent, *Foul Means*, 202–3.

74. Commissioners to the king, Apr. 9, 1719, recommending the replacement of William Byrd, AWOL from the council of Virginia, by Peter Beverley, CO 5/1365, fol. 94; order of the privy council, June 25, 1719, CO 5/1318, #212. Orkney vehemently opposed Byrd's agency (Byrd, *Diary*, Nov. 17, 1718) and supported Spotswood's council nominations. For the commissioners' anger at Byrd's presumption in opposing Spotswood's recommendations, see Byrd, *Diary*, Dec. 11, 1718. Spotswood to commissioners, Dec. 22, 1718, CO 5/1318, #199; order of the privy council, May 9, 1719, CO 5/1318, #204; Spotswood to commissioners, Mar. 5, 1719/20, and privy council orders, June 28, 1720, CO 5/1319, #1,2. Plumb, *Walpole*, 1:288–92, 294–357; Speck, *Stability and Strife*, 196; Dodson, *Spotswood*, 279. Letter to Mr. King, Oct. 5, 1721, CO 5/1319, fols. 41–42. For Byrd's delaying actions, see his *Diary*, Dec. 4, 1718, and Byrd to commissioners, Dec. 4, 1718, CO 5/1318, #189. For his solicitation of ministers, see Byrd, *Diary*, Apr. 20, 1719, and of Argyll, Byrd, *Diary*, Oct. 24, 1719. See also Byrd to duke Dulchetti [Argyll], Nov. 4, 1719, Maude H. Woodfin, ed., Marion Tinling, transcriber, *Another Secret Diary of William Byrd*, (Richmond, VA, 1942), 368–71. Spotswood to commissioners, Aug. 11, 1719, CO 5/1318, #226. Byrd, *Diary*, Apr. 29, 1720. Interestingly, just three days earlier, the "Whig schism" had ended with "great hugging and kissing" between Stanhope and Walpole, Sunderland and Townshend, Philip Woodfine, "Walpole, Horatio," *ODNB*, 57:73.

75. *EJC*, 3:515–27, 532, 538–41. The exception was a grant to Gawin Corbin, a faction leader but a Rappahannock grandee, in what was now Spotsylvania County, ibid., 539. For the seating of Beverley and Digges, see ibid., 518, 528, 533, 540. The land grants were the more easily passed because three of Spotswood's nominees— John Robinson, Peter Beverley, and Cole Digges—had been added to the council, and because Byrd and Ludwell boycotted the council when grants to Spotswood and his associates were passed. Rhoades, "Assarigoa's Line,"103; Rawson, "Rappahannock Frontier," *Locus* 6 (1994): 112–15; *JHB*, 1720, 290; Hofstra, "'Extention,'" 1285–86, 1291–92. The literary monument to Byrd's development of the James River/Roanoke frontier is his "History of the Dividing Line," 533–600. The land grant process, controlled by Spotswood, who acted as secretary of the province himself following Cocke's death, was in two stages: preemption warrants presently; then, from May to July 1722, patents. See John Grymes's statement, May 25, 1724, CO 5/1320, fol. 32; Manning Curlee Voorhis, "The Land Grant Policy of Colonial Virginia" (PhD diss., University of Virginia, n.d.), 140–41.

76. See *EJC*, 3 for these grants. See also Abernethy, "Transmontane Advance," 127, 128; Voorhis, "Land Grant Policy," 142. It is true, as an anonymous critic wrote in Oct. 1721 (CO 5/1319, fols. 41–42), that the immediate advantages were all Spotswood's. In his namesake county he controlled the surveyors. His companies developed both mines and settlements. The county seat was in Spotswood's new palace at Germanna. It was the base for developing a grant of 20,000 acres running up to the Swift Run Gap. Spotswood admitted that he knew nothing about

"Brunswick" or its purported pass. Its development was delayed for a decade, until Byrd moved in, CO 5/1319, "Q." For the land grants, see CO 5/1319, #93, 73, 74, fols. 177, 182; CO 5/1344, p. 1; CO 5/1365, fol. 166, and, most fully, "The Case of Col. Spotswood with Respect to His Lands, [Feb. 1726/27], CO 5/1320, fols. 97–102. See also Gooch to commissioners, Nov. 6, 1728, CO 5/1321, fol. 106. Morton, *Colonial Virginia*, 2:482–83; Harrison, *Landmarks*, 224–25. Deputy auditor Corbin declared that Spotswood held 93,391 acres in Spotsylvania. Spotswood admitted to 86,850, CO 5/1319, fol. 184. He had held just 25,181 before the great carve-up began in 1720. The names of these grants—Germanna, Wilderness, and Spotsylvania—will authenticate to students of the second "war of the rebellion" Spotswood's contention that much of his holdings were scrub pine, good for nothing but naval stores. See Ulysses S. Grant, *Personal Memoirs*, ed. James M. McPherson (1885; repr., New York, 1999), 425–26, 440–55.

77. Anon. to Mr. King, Dec. 5, 1721, CO 5/1319, #16, fols. 41–42. Webb, *Governors-General*, 366, records Col. Jeffreys's use of this statute against the first generation of the Green Spring faction. "The Governor's Charge to the Grand Jury and Their Address," Oct. 19, 1720, CO 5/1319, Q 16. In another of the parallels in his administration with Spotswood's, see Nicholson's prosecution of Byrd and Beverley under this statute, Webb, "Nicholson," 537. Spotswood's militia purge ran into trouble in Col. Carter's lieutenancy. There were not enough literate candidates to replace the captains Spotswood left out of the commission (Carter to Spotswood, Aug. 12, 1720, Wright, *Carter Letters*, 43, and see 62). Carter wrote the Perrys that "there have been mighty struggles through the country who should be our Parliament men," Sept. 19, 1720, Wright, *Carter Letters*, 47. See also Williams, *Political Alignments*, 200–201.

78. Robert Carter made it clear that the opposition was deeply chagrined at Spotswood's vindication at home and that only mutual self-interest led to the unanimous support of the assembly for his western program, "as far as will be consistent with the country's ability." Carter to William Dawkins, July 15, and to the Perrys, Nov. 8, 1720, Wright, *Carter Letters*, 30, 58. *JHB, 1712–1726*, 249–52. Holloway had sought the speakership since he entered the burgesses in 1710. Spotswood's clerical champion, Hugh Jones, was named chaplain. Morton, *Colonial Virginia*, 2:475. The transfer of burgess salaries and allowances from county to provincial levies greatly increased legislators' independence of their constituents even as it made it imperative that the burgesses cooperate with the executive to pass a budget, CO 5/1319, Q 16; Rhoades, "Assarigoa's Line," 100–101. Recall the same result in New York, another example, perhaps, of Hunter's advice to his colleague. The preliminaries of the peace can be traced in *EJC*, 3:532, 533–34, 549–50, 552–55. *JHB, 1712–1726*, 262, 274, 260–61, 270–71, 277, 283–84, 297–99, 300–301, 313.

79. The laudatory address was written by Clayton. The assembly offered to pay for all of Spotswood's expenditures on the palace and its gardens, and voted him funds for his work on the public buildings. The acts, including the constitution of Brunswick and Spotsylvania, are in Hening, *Statutes*, 4:77–79, 81–83.

80. Spotswood to commissioners, Jan. 16, 1720/21, CO 5/1319, #3; commissioners to Carteret, July 17, 1721, CO 5/1365, fol. 118.

81. CO 5/1365, fols. 117–18, 229–36. Richard Hakluyt, *Discourse of Western Planting*, ed. David B. Quinn and Alison M. Quinn, (London, 1993), esp. 115–20. A list of plans for military, consolidated American government is given in Webb, "Nicholson," 542–43, #52, and see Culpepper's proposal, Webb, *Governors-General*, 399. Commissioners to the king, "In Relation to the Government of the Plantations," Sept. 8, 1721, Add. MS 35907; *NYCD*, 5:591–630. Mutual defense was a persistent theme of Spotswood's dispatches. See, for example, Brock, *Spotswood Letters*, 1:108, 143, 146–47, 151, 2:124–25. See also Pargellis, *Loudoun*, 9n, 12n.

82. *NYCD*, 5:607, 624–25: "We would particularly recommend the building of a fort on the Lake Erie, as hath been proposed by Colonel Spotswood, your Majesty's Lieut. Governor of Virginia, whereby the french comunications from Quebec to the River Mississippi may be interrupted, a new trade opened with some of the Indian nations, and more of the natives engaged in your Majesty's interest." Spotswood's Florida design, Keith's Pennsylvania plan, and a plan for multiple forts and garrisons on the western and southern borders of South Carolina were also included in the report.

83. *EJC*, 3: Oct. 19–21, 1721, pp. 552–54; *JHB, 1712–1726*, 346–47, 350, 353–54. Commissioners to Spotswood, July 14, 1720, CO 5/1365, fol. 111; account of £1,602/16/4 disbursements, July 29–Oct. 26, 1722, CO 5/1322, fol. 78, and see 139; *JHB, 1712–1726*, 319–54; Hening, *Statutes*, 4:103–6. "Articles of Peace Made & Concluded at Albany wth. the Five Nations . . . by Alexander Spotswood Esqr His Majestys Lt Governor of the Colony & Dominion of Virginia in the Year 1722," CO 5/1319, 151–57. The Tuscarora settlement, is noted in CO 5/1319, 154v. This was, as it has remained, a tentative incorporation. Elsewhere in the treaty, the Tuscarora are merely listed as one of the many refugee tribes resettled along the Susquehanna as a buffer for the homeland of the Longhouse. Totem signatures appear, CO 5/1319, 155v. Printed in *NYCD*, 5:673–77. Spotswood's report, Oct. 31, 1722, *EJC*, 4:22–23; Morton, *Colonial Virginia*, 2:479–80; Acquila, "Warriors Path," 216.

84. Commissioners to Spotswood, July 14, 1720, CO 5/1365, fol. 111; Articles, CO 5/1319, 154, 156, 157; *NYCD*, 5:673–77; Hening, *Statutes*, 4:103–6. The pin pass was symbolic. Actual passports for Iroquois parties of more than ten were to be issued by the commander in chief of New York.

85. Articles 2, 4, CO 5/1319, fols. 153–54; Proposal 6, ibid., fol. 156. Spotswood to Dartmouth, May 15, 1713, Brock, *Spotswood Letters*, 2:19; Newcastle to commissioners, July 26, 1726, CO 5/1319, fol. 29v. Anthony F. C. Wallace, *Jefferson and the Indians* (Cambridge, MA, 1999), ch. 1. Wallace, *The Death and Rebirth of the Seneca* (New York, 1979): Barbara Graymont, *The Iroquois in the American Revolution* (Syracuse, NY, 1972); Alan Taylor, *The Divided Ground* (New York, 2006).

86. Commission to Drysdale, Apr. 20, 1722, CO 5/1365, fol. 129; announced Dec. 30, 1722, ibid., 124; Orkney to Newcastle, May 5, 1726, CO 5/1344, #7, recalled Drysdale's nomination by Sir Robert Walpole. Commissioners to Drysdale, June 19, 1723, CO 5/1365, fol. 124v, p. 246; Dodson, *Spotswood*, 246–47; Henderson, *London*, 92, 109–11; Plumb, *Walpole*, 1:262–63, 270; "Mr. Auditor Walpole's Objections," CO 5/1319, #35; *JCTP, 1718–1722*, 279–80, and see 246–47, 298; Order of the privy council, Aug. 27, 1723; Drysdale to commissioners, Nov. 17, 1723, CO 5/1319, #52, 91.

Walpole pressured Orkney into supporting the faction, Orkney to commissioners, Dec. 30, 1725, CO 5/1319, #92. Voorhis, "Land Grant Policy," 136–38.

87. Drysdale to the bishop of London, Fulham Palace Papers, Virginia, box 1, #67, VCRP, Speck, *Stability and Strife*, 210; "Mr. Auditor [Walpole] to Commissioners," Apr. 5, 1722, CO 5/1365, p. 242, and his objections, 244; commissioners to Drysdale, June 19, 1723, CO 5/1365, fol. 24v, p. 126; Drysdale's attack on "Exorbitant Grants of Land in Virginia," June 6, 1724, was referred to the law officers, CO 5/1365, fol. 140; queries about Spotswood's grants, CO 5/1319, fols. 186–87. *EJC*, 4:63–65, includes a revision of the commission of the peace for Spotsylvania. Spotswood to commissioners, "Virginia (Spotsylvania County) June 16th 1724," CO 5/1319, fols. 190–92; same, Mar. 4, 1727/28, CO 323/8, pp. 250–51, and see CO 5/1322, fol. 77. Abernethy, "Transmontane Advance," 128. On Gibson and Walpole, see *ODNB*, 57:78–79, 83. Blair was in London when Drysdale was commissioned. Much is made of this by Rouse, *Blair*, 206–8. See also Morton, *Colonial Virginia*, 1:348; Billings, Selby, and Tate, *Colonial Virginia*, 139–40, 196–97; Williams, *Political Alignments*, 24, 188–89, 199.

88. Spotswood to commissioners, Feb. 1, 1719[/20], May 20, 1720, Brock, *Spotswood Letters*, 2:328–37; commissioners to Spotswood, June 26, 1719, July 14, 1720, CO 5/1365, fols. 104–5, 110; Dodson, *Spotswood*, 242–44. Spotswood's proposed Key fortress became Fort Jefferson.

89. Virginians observed the simultaneous collapse of John Law's Mississippi Company in France, Carter to the Perrys, July 13, 1720, Wright, *Carter Letters*, 5. Carter, for example, repeatedly predicted "ruin to the nation" from the South Seas speculation, July 22, 23, 1720, Feb. 13, 1720/21, ibid., 35, 39, 72, 93. It was the Anglo-French fiscal convulsion of 1720 that compelled the imperial retrenchment by both kingdoms subsequently called "Salutary Neglect." Plumb, *Walpole*, 1:363–89; Speck, *Stability and Strife*, 196–202; Williams, *Whig Supremacy*, 176–79; P. M. G. Dickson, *The Financial Revolution in England . . . 1688–1756* (London, 1967), 90–205; Dodson, *Spotswood*, 272–73, 282; John Grymes to [Peter] Lehup, May 25, 1724, CO 5/1320, fol. 32; Draper, "Life of Boone," Draper MS, ser. B, vols. 1–5, pp. 118–19, State Historical Society of Wisconsin, Madison. On land grants, see above and CO 5/1319, fols. 184–85; Spotswood to Orkney, Mar. 22, 1727, CO 5/1320, fol. 123. Randall Shrock, "Maintaining the Prerogative," (PhD diss., University of North Carolina, 1980), 66–67, observes that Spotswood's correspondence with imperial authorities diminished in volume and executive emphasis immediately after the reconciliation of 1720. [Rev.] Robert Rose, writing from "Spotswood," July 25, 1743, Spottiswoode Papers, MS 2933, NLS, recorded what he doubtless heard from Spotswood: "In 1722 he was superseded for the same Reason he was not advanced in the Army; He scorned to purchase any Great Man's favour, nor ever sold his own." Extortion was a commonplace to auditor Walpole. He made thousands out of a post with an annual salary of just £250. He was in London at the time of Spotswood's supersessions: Woodfine, "Walpole," 47.

90. On the "enchanted castle," see Byrd, "A Progress to the Mines in the Year 1732," *London Diary*, 628–31; Douglas W. Sanford, "The Enchanted Castle in Context," *Quarterly Bulletin, Archaeological Society of Virginia* 44 (1989): 97–115. The quotation

is from Carter to the Perrys, Mar. 25, 1721, Wright, *Carter Letters*, 90. See same to Edward Tudor, May 27, 1721, on the pirate menace, Wright, *Carter Letters*, 97. See also Marcus Rediker, *Between the Devil and the Deep Blue Sea* (Cambridge, 1989), 134, 254, 269, 277. Ronald L. Lewis, *Coal, Iron, and Slaves* (Westport, CT, 1979), 20–21, 25.

Epilogue. The "Golden Adventure"

1. Lediard, *Marlborough*, 3:411–25; *London Gazette*, Aug. 7–11, 1722; "An Exact Representation of the Solemn and Magnificent Funeral Procession of His Grace John Late Duke of Marlborough . . . Thursday the 9th of August 1722 . . . ," BM, reproduced in Dalton, *George the First's Army*, 2:110–14; Fortescue, *Army*, 2:10–13; Plumb, *Walpole*, 2:53–56.
2. Bolingbroke's epitaph, Lediard, *Marlborough*, 3:439.
3. Dickson, *Financial Revolution*, 149, 153, 160, 164, 174, 198–99; Plumb, *Walpole*, 1:293–309, 344–47, 377–80, 2:7–9, 232; James A. Henretta, *"Salutary Neglect": Colonial Administration under the Duke of Newcastle* (Princeton, NJ, 1972), 15; Osgood, *Eighteenth Century*, 3:491; *GM* 11 (1741): 422–23. Philip Woodfine, *Britannia's Glories: The Walpole Ministry and the 1739 War with Spain* (London, 1988), 192.
4. Dickson, *Financial Revolution*, 141, 153, 157, 173, 188, 200; Claude Sturgill, "From Utrecht to the Little War with Spain," and Philip Woodfine, "The Anglo-Spanish War of 1739," in Jeremy Black, ed., *The Origins of War in Early Modern Europe* (Edinburgh, n.d.), 176–84, 185–209. See the typically trenchant summary by J. R. Jones, *Britain and the World, 1649–1815* (Sussex and New Jersey, 1980), 187, 191, 199. For a contemporary connection between the Marlborough campaigns and the 1739 war with Spain, see *A Proposal for Humbling Spain Written in 1711 . . . to Which Are Added, Some Considerations on . . . the Present War* (London, [1739]), 56–62. Fortescue, *Army*, 2:16, 18; Pares, *War and Trade*, 62; H. W. Richmond, *The Navy in the War of 1739–1748* (Cambridge, 1920), 1:24, 118–19; Daniel A. Baugh, *British Naval Administration in the Age of Walpole* (Princeton, NJ, 1965), 15–19. Recall that in 1719, Spanish troops landed with jacobites in Scotland, leading to the retaliatory raid on Vigo. Following the British blockade of Cadiz in 1726, Gibraltar was besieged by the Spanish. Houlding, *Fit for Service*, 178. Fortescue, *Army*, 2:9–10.
5. Hunter's complaints (to Stanhope) about French-captained, Spanish-commissioned, *guarda costas* were discussed in parliament as early as Mar. 1715/16, Stock, *Proceedings* 4:70n, and see iii–ix, 35n, 195–97, 369, 422–24, 426n, 427, 453, 458, 537, 543, 719, etc. See also Spotswood to the lord commissioners, May 3 1721, Brock, *Spotswood Letters*, 2:346–50. Lord Archibald Hamilton lost the government of Jamaica in the purge of 1716, ostensibly because of his retaliation against the *guarda costa*, Pares, *War and Trade*, 14–15, but Hamilton's policy was continued by his successors. Fortescue, *Army*, 2:37, 39, 40, 43, 48; Osgood, *Eighteenth Century*, 3:496; Baugh, *Naval Administration*, 495–96; Sir Herbert Richmond, *The Navy as an Instrument of Policy, 1558–1727*, ed. E. A. Hughes (Cambridge, 1953), 389–97. Speck, *Stability and Strife*, 234; Woodfine, "War of 1739," 191, 193–95; Jones, *Britain and the World*, 199. The documents on the Jenkins incident, edited by J. K. Laughton, are

in *EHR* 4 (1889): 741–49, and see Robert Beatson, *Naval and Military Memoirs of Great Britain from 1727 to 1783* (1804; repr., Boston, 1972), 1:43–56.

6. On the royal monopoly of military patronage, see the decisive remarks of Horatio Walpole to Richard Trevor, Feb. 22 [Mar. 4], 1739/40, Apr. 29 [May 2], 1740, HMC, *14th Report, Part IX*, (London, 1895), 40, 44–45, 46–47. On the militancy of the Hanoverians, see James Hayes, "The Royal House of Hanover and the British Army, 1714–60," *BJRL* 40 (1957–58): 328–57: "They preserved the army . . . from parliamentary influence and interference and from the hazards of peace." See also Sir Lewis Namier, *The Structure of Politics at the Accession of George III* (London, 1965), 28, 253–54; Richard Pares, *King George III And the Politicians* (Oxford, 1953), 17–18; Shy, *Toward Lexington*, 68–69, 234–36; Tony Hatner, *An Eighteenth Century Secretary at War: The Papers of William, Viscount Barrington* (Oxford, 1988), 13, 275, 277, 355–56, but see #239. The king made his command clearest in the case of garrison governments, Hatner, *Eighteenth Century Secretary*, #217. See also the interesting case of Chatham's son, John, viscount Pitt, commissioned to attend Gen. Murray in the government of Quebec (Hatner, *Eighteenth Century Secretary*, #218–21), the first step toward being, successively, first lord of the admiralty, master general of the ordnance, and governor of Plymouth, Jersey, and Gibraltar. On George II in particular, Guy, *Oeconomy and Discipline*, 19–22, 32; Houlding, *Fit for Service*, 102–3, 115–16, 154–55, 179–81; Richard Harding, "Lord Cathcart, the Earl of Stair and the Scottish Opposition to Sir Robert Walpole," *Parliamentary History* 11 (1992): 195, 204, 206, 210, 212, 215; and even Henretta, "*Salutary Neglect*," 172. The accession of George II coincided with the national recovery from the South Sea bubble and renewed fiscal capacity for imperial projects, Dickson, *Financial Revolution*, 204. Lustig, *Hunter*, 124–26, 163, 174–75, 263–92, 306–7; Webb, *Governors-General*, #63, 68, 86, 159, 207, 208, pp. 299–312, 324–26; Dalton, *George the First's Army*, 2:335, 351; Agnes M. Whitson, *The Constitutional Development of Jamaica, 1660–1729* (Manchester, England, 1929), 10–11, 17, 40, 41, 57–59; *CSPC, 1723*, #226, 597; *1726–1727*, #217, 435, 437; APCC, #45, 68; Henretta, "*Salutary Neglect*," 49–52, 70–71, 108–9, 130, 172–73n. The king's informed control of military commissions also controlled the next wave of gubernatorial appointments in 1737, on the eve of the next war with Spain, Henretta, "*Salutary Neglect*," 176–77; Philip Haffenden, "Colonial Appointments and Patronage under the Duke of Newcastle, 1724–1739," *EHR* 78 (1963): 424, 433; Whitworth, *Ligonier*, 187–91.

7. Ro. Hunter to Charles, lord Townshend, Charlton, Nov. 12, 1726, Vernon-Wager Papers, LC, 44805–96 (not "Charleston," pace William Chauncey Ford, ed., *List of the Vernon-Wager Manuscripts in the Library of Congress* [Washington, DC, 1904], 14). Webb, *Governors-General*, 153, 165–67.

8. On Montgomerie, see [Hugh Campbell, 3d earl of] Loudoun to [Alexander Montgomerie, 9th] earl of Eglington, n.d.; same to James Ferguson, Aug. 5, 1729, LO #9978, 9964, HL. See the charming description of the prince of Wales's court in Col. Montgomerie to Loudoun, Hampton Court, Sept. 10, 1716, LO #9222, HL. On Col. Shute's protest that the Massachusetts representatives "had endeavoured to wrest the Sword out of your Royal Hands," see APCC, 3:#75. Shute's memorial to the king, *CSPC, 1722–1723*, #683i, pp. 324–30, printed in *EHD*, 9:260–64.

Supplementary Charter, Ellis Ames and Abner Cheyney Goodell, eds. *The Acts and Resolves, Public and Private, of the Province of Massachusetts Bay* (Boston, 1889), 1:21–23. On the lieutenant colonelcy of the 4th Horse, a post worth £3,000–4,000, which Shute exchanged for the Massachusetts command, see Whitworth, *Ligonier*, 36. On the place of governorships in the imperial command structure, see Whitworth, *Ligonier*, 187–88, 191. On Massachusetts' governance, see also Richard L. Bushman, *King and People in Provincial Massachusetts* (Chapel Hill, NC, 1985), 111–14, 117n87; 122–23; William Pencak, *War, Politics and Revolution in Provincial Massachusetts* (Boston, 1981), 65, 66, 71, 76, 79; [Thomas] Hutchinson, *The History of the Province of Massachusetts . . . 1691–1750* (London, 1768), 2:196–246. Osgood, *Eighteenth Century*, 3:144, 156–57, 160, 164–71, 177–78; Webb, *Governors-General*, #66, 171, 128, 167, 158, 206; Henretta, *"Salutary Neglect,"* 61–63, 69–70. Protection for Spotswood, APCC, 3:#129, 181; Spotswood to lords commissioners, June 16, 1724, CO 5/1319, fols. 190–92; same, Mar. 4, 1728/29, CO 323/7, 247; Dodson, *Spotswood*, 280–89, 294–96.

9. Vernon to Wager, June 6, 1741, Vernon-Wager Papers, LC, 46588–605. Charles E. Nowell, "The Defense of Cartagena," *HAHR* 42 (1962): 482; Ceasaro Fernandez Duro, quoted in Cyril Hughes Hartmann, *The Angry Admiral: The Later Career of Edward Vernon* (London, 1953), 53, 93, Richmond, *Navy*, 33–34. Recall the parallel projects by Samuel Vetch and Francis Nicholson.

10. Godolphin to Marlborough, Aug. 17, 18, 1709, and replies, Aug. 22, Sept. 9, Blenheim MS, B.I.22b; A.II, 39; Snyder, *Correspondence*, #1346, 1348, 1339, 1355. Marlborough saw this, as he saw every West India expedition, as little more than "an excuse to plunder." So it still was. Baugh, *Naval Administration*, 22. Dodson, *Spotswood*, 302; Byrd, *London Diary*, 368–69.

11. Spotswood [to Townshend, 1727], Add. MS 32, 694, 3–7. *The Statistical History of the United States from Colonial Times to the Present*, sec. Z, 1–19. [Thomas Kirby of Canso], "Carthegen's Downfall," in David Shields, *Oracles of Empire* (Chicago, n.d.), 191; Shy, *Toward Lexington*, 15–16, on motivation: rank and pay for officers; land and loot for other ranks.

12. Spotswood to Townshend, Add. MS 32, 694, 3–7. Albert Harkness Jr., "Americanism and Jenkins' Ear," *MVHR* 37 (1950): 88–90, elaborates the distinctions between "American" and "European" that arose, a dozen years after Spotswood's dispatch, during the expedition of 1739–42. On the uniforms of the American Regiment, see W. Y. Baldry and A. S. White, "Gooch's American Regiment of Foot, 1739–1742," *JSAHR* 16 (1937): 237. H. Charles McBaron Jr., William A. Foote, and John R. Elting, "The American Regiment, 1740–1746," *Military Collector and Historian* 21 (1969): 85, pl. #325. On "uniformity," see Michael Roberts, *The Military Revolution, 1560–1660* (Belfast, 1956), 11–12.

13. Plumb, *Walpole*, 2:121–22, 171, 185–87; Dodson, *Spotswood*, 182–83, 300–301; Pargellis, *Loudoun*, 10–11. Spotswood to Newcastle, Sept. 5, 1739, CO 5/1337, 1, 216.

14. Thomas Gould et al. to lords commissioners, Apr. 6, 1730, CO 5/1322, fols. 102–4; Sir William Keith to same, Apr. 7, 1730, ibid., 105–6; same to king, n.d.; same to commissioners, Aug. 30, 1731, *VMHB* 29 (1921): 183–229; Charles E. Kemper, ed., *VMHB* 35 (1926): 175ff., 185–87; Morton, *Colonial Virginia* 2:543–44; and see Keith

&c. to the king, CO 5/1322, pp. 167–68; same to lords commissioners, Aug. 30, 1731, CO 5/1322, pp. 177–78. Note the "Georgia" project's extraordinary anticipation of the Northwest Ordinance of 1787, itself the stud link in the chain that connected Britain's imperial policy with America's.

15. Ann V. Strickler Milbourne, ed., "Colony West of the Blue Ridge . . . Additional Documents," *VMHB* 35 (1926): 259–65; Amos Aschbach Ettinger, *Oglethorpe: A Brief Biography*, ed. Phinzy Spaulding (1906; repr., Macon, GA, 1989); Ettinger, *James Edward Oglethorpe* (Oxford, 1936), 50–58, 67–68, 127–28; Dalton, *Army Lists*, 6:51, 53, 391; Dalton, *George the First's Army*, 1:126–27; Rodney M. Baine and Mary E. Williams, "James Oglethorpe in Europe: Recent Findings of His Military Life," in Spaulding and Jackson, eds., *Oglethorpe in Retrospective*, 113–16, and Baine and Williams, "Oglethorpe's Early Military Campaigns," *Yale University Library Gazette* 60 (1986): 63–76; Webb, *Lord Churchill's Coup*, 39, 90; Leach, *Arms for Empire*, 187–89; HMC, *Egmont MS* (London, 1920–23), 1:12, 26–27, 39; Plumb, *Walpole*, 2:144–45, 184, 209–11, 214; Osgood, *Eighteenth Century*, 3:36–37, 39–40, 41, 43–45; Henretta, *"Salutary Neglect,"* 177, 193; Colley, *In Defiance of Oligarchy*, 211; Trevor Richard Reese, *Colonial Georgia: A Study in British Imperial Policy* (Athens, GA, 1963), 55–58; Webb, "Agricola in America," *Reviews in American History* (1978): 318–25; Shy, *Toward Lexington*, 31–33. These sources describe the American continental campaign of 1739–42, the attacks on St. Augustine, and the defense of Georgia. Like the West Indian campaign, Oglethorpe's imperial venture is instructive as to the limited duration of "Salutary Neglect," the fall of Walpolean mercantilism under anti-Spanish and Anglo-American imperial pressure, and the continual continental aspirations of the colonists and their sponsors.

16. George R. to Vernon, July 16, 1739, Add. MS 32, 692, 128–32; *Verses Addressed to Admiral Vernon* (London, 1744); Tobias Smollett, "An Account of the Expedition against Carthagena," in James P. Browne, ed., *The Works of Tobias Smollett* (London, 1872), 8:428; Richmond, *Navy*, 1:135; Pares, *War and Trade*, 14–19, 22–28, 43–58, 65–68, 85; Harold W. V. Temperley, "The Causes of the War of Jenkins' Ear, 1739," Royal Historical Society *Transactions*, 3d ser., 3 (1909): 197–236, esp. 226–27; Woodfine, "War of 1739," 202 ff. Even if Walpole had been ready to abandon Georgia, his ministerial colleagues were not: Reed Browning, *The Duke of Newcastle* (New Haven, CT, 1975), 88. See Browning, *Newcastle*, 92–95, on the machinations of the South Sea Company and Pitt's speeches. The Convention of the Pardo, Jan. 3/14, 1739, is in Charles Oscar Paullin, ed., *European Treaties Bearing on the History of the United States* (Washington, DC, 1937), 4:#129. The failure of Seville to halt "Spanish depredations" on American trade was the causus belli, Beatson, *Memoirs* 1:35–42. On the remobilization of 1727–29, see Holmes, *Augustan England*, 1:35–42. William Pulteney to Vernon, Aug. 17, 1740, *GM* 18 (1748): 302–3; Pitt's speech in Stock, *Proceedings*, 5:viii, 773–75, 780n; John Tate Lanning, *The Diplomatic History of Georgia . . .* (Chapel Hill, NC, 1936), ch. 7; Fortescue, *Army*, 2:56; Leach, *Arms for Empire*, 207, 210; R. Harding, "Vernon," in LeFevre and Harding, eds., *Precursors of Nelson*, 167–68. For several plans to employ North American troops in the West Indies, see anon. to Wager, Jan. 14, 1739, Ford, *List*, 59. Speech of Apr. 15, 1740, *Pennsylvania*

Gazette, Oct. 23, 1740. Verse, *Boston Evening Post*, reprinted in *Pennsylvania Gazette*, Oct. 3, 1740. See also the British verse addressed to Vernon "to raise thy fame / Beyond victorious Churchill's deathless name," Shields, *Oracles*, 188.

17. Pares, *War and Trade*, 16–50, 47–49, 54–55, 106, 121, 165; Newcastle to Vernon, Mar. 26, 1740[/41], M. B. McL. Ranft, ed., *The Vernon Papers* (Greenwich, CT, 1958), 77–79, and see 8–9, 11; Kathleen Wilson, "Empire, Trade and Popular Politics in Mid-Hanoverian England: The Case of Admiral Vernon," *PP* 121 (1988): 74, 77; *GM* 10 (1740): 144–45; letters to Vernon from Newcastle and Wager, *GM* 18 (1748): 68–70, and Pulteney to same, 302–9; Richard Harding, *Amphibious Warfare in the Eighteenth Century* (Rochester, 1991), 37, 39–40, 42, 46; *Boston Post Boy*, quoted in John Tate Lanning, "American Participation in the War of Jenkins' Ear," *GHQ* 11 (1927): [191]. The exact language reappeared to celebrate the capture of Ft. St. Louis in *Pennsylvania Gazette*, May 14, 1741, #48. Shield, *Oracles*, 186–87. Cromwell's instructions to Gen. Robert Venables and Adm. William Penn, [Dec. 9, 1654], Ford, *List*, 7; *A True Copy of Cromwell's Manifesto* (London, 1741); *Proposal for Humbling Spain*, 52–53; Webb, *Governors-General*, ch. 4; Jones, *Britain and the World*, 198; instructions for Vernon, July 16, 1739, Vernon-Wager Papers 45797–99, LC; July 10, letters of marque and reprisal (which produced a swarm of American privateers), and the declaration of war with Spain, APCC, 3:#468.

18. Sir William Pulteney to Vernon, Aug. 17, 1740, Ranft, *Vernon Papers*, 121. Opening the debate on the Cartagena disaster on Dec. 4, 1741, lord Chesterfield complained about "new raised soldiers, a sickly major general [Cathcart], and one who was a brigadier too young to have experience," i.e., Wentworth. Argyll, once again on the outs, demeaned the commanders: "Lord Cathcart had never served but as a major in Flanders and a lieutenant colonel in the Rebellion. And they skipt over 45 general officers to come at him. Spotswood served under my eye, was a captain and under quartermaster general. But never commanded more than a platoon," Stock, *Proceedings*, 5:111. Argyll's vindictiveness did illuminate the command problem consequent on a generation of peace with France. Marlborough's surviving generals (the angry Argyll was the exception) were either too old to serve, politically unacceptable, or both. Marlborough's junior officers, distinguished as their service had been, now, after a lapse of twenty-five years, saw their first active service as general officers. On the active service of Marlborough's former officers through the 1740s, see Holmes, *Augustan England*, 265, and a dozen other examples, with service into the 1770s, in Hatner, *An Eighteenth Century Secretary*, "Biographical Notes." On Cathcart as an example of Marlborough's Scots disciples in war and union (including the Dalrymple earls of Stair and their clients, such as Robert Hunter, and the Montgomerie earls of Eglington and their client John Montgomerie), see W. L. Burn, Memorandum, Oct. 10, 1933, Loudoun Catalogue, and Col. Montgomerie to the earl of Eglington, Hampton Court, Sept. 10, 1716, LO 9222, HL. Harding, "Cathcart," *Pennsylvania History*, 11:194–98, 204, 206, 209, 214–17; Guy, *Oeconomy and Discipline*, 20. Spotswood's commissions, Dec. 26, 1739, Add. MS 32693, 184. And see Add. MS 28132, 100; *GM* 9 (1741): 148; Richmond, *Navy*, 1:35; Pares, *War and Trade*, 85; Plumb, *Walpole*, 2:75–76, 276–77, 281; Henretta, *"Salutary Neglect,"* 121–23, 176; Dalton, *Army Lists*, 5:36, 224, 6:33–34, 180, 197, 300, 314–15; Cathcart to

Andrew Stone, Oct. 12, 1740, CO 5/41, 194–95; Blakeney to Newcastle, July 3, 1740, CO 5/41, 223–36; Cathcart to Newcastle, July 25, 1740; same, "6 at night," CO 5/41, 68, 70. Newcastle warned Cathcart against undue "preference to one particular Part of His Majesty's subjects," Henretta, *Salutary Neglect,"* 133. Newcastle's dislike of Scots was notorious, Browning, *Newcastle*, 85.

19. Instructions to Spotswood, Apr. 2, 1740, CO 318/3, fols. 245–51; instructions to provincial commanders in chief, ibid., fols. 252–56, esp. #18, fol. 255; instructions to Gooch, and Newcastle to same, Jan. 5, 1739/40, Add. MS 32693, 16–17, 180; reply, Apr. [10], 1740, CO 5/1337, fol. 224; Gooch to Newcastle, May 2, June 14, Aug. 30, CO 5/1337, fols. 229, 230–31, 232, 234; Dodson, *Spotswood*, 302–3; *EJC*, June 14, 1740; *VMHB* 15 (1907): 4.

20. Spotswood [to George Clarke], Annapolis, Apr. 26; same to Newcastle, Maryland, June 26; Blakeney to Newcastle, July 8, [Sept. 25], 1740, CO 5/41, 217–20, 221–22, 251. Fairfax Harrison, *Landmarks of Old Prince William*, 162–64; Hall, "Maryland's Part," *MHM* (1907): 150; Osgood, *Eighteenth Century*, 3:498.

21. For the Guards' occupation of Virginia, see Webb, *Governors-General*, index, s.v. "Army, Guards-based Battalions," and Webb, *1676*, 147–48, 163, 189, 216–20. On the composition of the "American" regiment's rank and file, see *A Journal of the Expedition to Carthagena, with Notes. In Answer to a Late Pamphlet; Entitled, An Account of the Expedition to Carthagena*, 2d ed. (London, 1744), 55. This publication, hereafter cited as *A Journal of the Expedition*, was the army's defense of Gen. Thomas Wentworth from the charges levied by the naval spokesmen, Capt. Charles Knowles. Knowles's work was technically anonymous. It was enclosed "in Capt. Knowles's of Sept. 10, 1741," CO 5/41, 280–96. It is cited here as Knowles, "Expedition." It was subsequently published as *An Account of the Expedition to Carthagena, with Explanatory Notes and Observations* (London, 1743). Knowles's double alphabet of notes was answered, letter by letter, by the army journalist. Both authors apparently thought this system of footnote commentary both novel and conclusive. Gooch to Newcastle, Aug. 30, 1740, CO 5/1337, fols. 240–41; Blakeney to Newcastle, [Sept. 25], 1740, CO 5/41, 251; Labaree, *Royal Instructions*, #1017; instructions to the lieutenant governor of Virginia, Jan. 5, 1739/40, Add. MS 32693, 17; W. Byrd to Col. Fr. Otway, Feb., 1740, "Letters of the Byrd Family," *VMHB* 37 (1929): 29; Freeman, *Washington*, 1:65n, 120; Morton, *Colonial Virginia*, 2:532; E. Alfred Jones, "The American Regiment in the Carthagena Expedition," *VMHB* 30 (1922): 1–2; the king to the governors, Apr. 2, 1740, SP 42/85, 295–96; CO 5/41, 24–25, 36–41, 154–55, 217–20; Gooch to Newcastle, May 2, Aug. 30, 1740, CO 5/1337, fols. 229, 230–31, 240–41; Fairfax Harrison, "When the Convicts Came," *VMHB* 30 (1922): 256; Shy, *Toward Lexington*, 16–17n. On the illegality of Irish recruits, see Guy, *Oeconomy and Discipline*, 124. The army was still anglican, by law and in practice. N.B. that the nominal recruiting number of 120 men was just that. Service establishment for the American Regiment was 100 men per company.

22. "A List of the Names of Gentlemen, to Whom His Majesty's Commission to Command the Forces Raised in Virginia Were Given, with the Dates of Their Severally Receiving Them. In Lieut. Govr. Gooch's Letter of Sept. 13th 1740," CO 5/1337, fol. 244; Newcastle to lieutenant governor of Virginia and Maj. Gen.

Spotswood, Apr. 5, 1740, Add. MS 32693, 190; Freeman, *Washington*, 1:32, 41, 56, 73. It is not clear if the £100 Lawrence Washington promised Gooch's son was payment for Washington's commission (Freeman, *Washington*, 1:66–67), but the timing is suggestive. "Arms were his avocation": Freeman's character sketch of Lawrence Washington, is in Freeman, *Washington*, 1:76. Lawrence's portrait, with commentary, is between Freeman, *Washington*, 1:95–96. Lawrence Washington to Augustine Washington, Jamaica, May 30, 1741, George Washington Papers (Microfilm), MSS. & Archives Section, NYPL. See the Fairfax-Washington correspondence printed in Moncure Daniel Conway, *Barons of the Potomac and the Rappahannock* (New York, 1892), esp. Jos. Deane to Capt. Washington, Wt. Haven, Nov. 6, 1744; William Fairfax to Maj. Washington, Whitehaven, July 6, Oct. 12, Conway, *Barons*, 109–11, 282–86.

23. General Officers of the Army to the Lords Justices, May 16, 1743, WO 71/7; "List of the Officers of Colonel Gooche's Late Regiment of Americans . . . ," CO 5/41, 38; Jones, "American Regiment," 8, 10, 30; and see *VMHB* 15 (1908): 6; 16 (1909): 234ff. On the Mercer-Washington connection, see Freeman, *Washington*, 1:66n, and, for the service of three of James Mercer's nephews with Col. George Washington in the Virginia Regiment, see Donald Jackson and Dorthy Twohig, eds., *The Diaries of George Washington* (Charlottesville, VA, 1976–79), 1:247. John Fenton Mercer, James's nephew, also "of Marlborough," was an officer in Washington's regiment, served Fort Necessity and, as a captain, was killed at the head of his company in Aug. 1756. *PGWCS*, 1:210n5. T. Stafford to Lawrence Washington, Nov. 13, 1749, *VMHB* 30 (1932): 19–20; Conway, *Barons*, 111–12, also confirms Mercer's continued service. Mercer was especially recommended by Vernon to Newcastle, Francis Berkeley Jr., "The War of Jenkins's Ear," in Darrett B. Rutman, ed., *The Old Dominion* (Charlottesville, VA, 1964), 60n. On Bushrod, see "Return [of the American Regiment]," May 30, 1741, CO 5/42, fol. 50; "To the Walls of Cartagena . . . ," *Virginia Cavalcade* 5 (1955): 5; and, on the family in relation to Washington, Freeman, *Washington*, 1:526, 5:491, 6:14, 19, etc. On Rose and Mercer, see minutes of "The Board of General Officers . . . Horse Guards, Jan. 2, 1743," T 1/315, fols. 3–5. This board included generals Wentworth, Guise, Blakeney, and Cope of the expeditionary force, James Edward Oglethorpe, commander in chief of Georgia and South Carolina, and lord Archibald Hamilton, former governor general of Jamaica and brother of the late earl of Orkney, governor general of Virginia. Another board met on May 1, 1744, to review the records of the officers of the American Regiment who had subsequently reached England, T 1/315, fols. 6–9. See also Murtie Jane Clark, ed., *Colonial Soldiers of the South, 1732–1741* (Baltimore, 1983), 249, 253. Fitzhugh's promotion depended on his paying the £100 owed the company by its former captain.

24. Knowles, "Expedition," CO 5/41, 294v. For a critique of Knowles's work, see Harding, *Amphibious Warfare*, 73–75, 77. See also *A Journal of the Expedition*, 54, 55; List of the Officers, May 16, 1743, WO 71/7; T 1/315, 4; *Pennsylvania Colonial Records*, 4:396–97; Robert R. Rea, *Major Robert Farmar of Mobile* (Tuscaloosa, AL, 1990), 4, 8–12, 5. Like Mercer, Farmar achieved a regular majority. In command of the 34th Regiment, Farmar occupied and colonized the "uniquely terrible" west Flor-

ida. Fulfilling the ambitions of the American Regiment's officers, Farmar became a planter patriarch at Mobile. Shy, *Toward Lexington*, 151, 154–57, 280, 282–84n. That the mistreatment of the Americans alienated them from Great Britain is the leitmotif of Douglas Edward Leach, "The Cartagena Expedition, 1740–1742, and Anglo-American Relations," in Maarten Ultree, ed., *Adapting to Conditions: War and Society in the Eighteenth Century* (Tuscaloosa, AL, 1986), 43–55.

25. *A Journal of the Expedition*, 54–55; Dalton, *Army Lists*, 5:54, 56; Labaree, *Royal Instructions*, #1017, 1018. The 1711 precedents (themselves developments of the Whetham expedition of 1709 and Shannon's in 1710) were recorded in Add. MS 32,694, 101–4, Pargellis, *Loudoun*, 12–13. Spotswood's instructions #6, 8, CO 318/3, 242v, 248v; "A Schedule of the Particulars Carried by Colonel Blakeney," CO 318/3, 253; Gooch's instruction #6, CO 318/3, 254; "Names of Gent. Carrying Arms," "Field Officers of Majr. Genl. Spotswood's Regt.," Cathcart to Newcastle, Sept. 14, 1740, CO 5/41, fols. 36–37, 40–41, 154–55. Blakeney would famously command the defense of Ft. St. Philip, Minorca, when he was eighty-three! Whitworth, *Ligonier*, 233n. Byrd to Otway, Feb. 1740, "Byrd Family Letters," *VMHB* 37 (1929):28–29, added that Otway should use his influence with Virginia's new governor general, brigadier general the earl of Albemarle, to become lieutenant governor of Virginia.

26. "Field Officers of Major Genl. Spotswood's Regiment," CO 4/41, 40–41; "List of the Officers," WO 71/1, printed in Clark, *Colonial Solders*, 249–58; and see *VMHB* 30 (1922): 7; SP 42/85, fol. 296; Cathcart to Newcastle, Sept. 14, 1740, CO 5/41, 154–55; the king to the governors, Apr. 2, 1740, SP 42/85, fol. 296. On Phillips's troops in Nova Scotia and Newfoundland, see APCC, 3:#478; Reid et al., *Conquest of Acadia*, 153, 182–91. On Whetham, a figure in the coup of 1688, an officer and governor in the West Indies, and putative governor of Canada in 1709, see Webb, *Lord Churchill's Coup*, 102, 155; Webb, *Governors-General*, #77, and index. Promoted general in 1739, Whetham died in 1741. Harding, *Amphibious Warfare*, 72. Hall, "Maryland's Part," *Md. Hist.* 4 (1907): 151; Harkness, "Americanism," 65; WO 4/10, 135, 150; Dalton, *Army Lists*, 6:291.

27. Newcastle to Spotswood, Apr. 5, 1740, CO 5/5, fol. 159; same to governors, Jan. 5, 1739/40, SP 42/85, fol. 294; Blakeney to Newcastle, New York, July 31, 1740, CO 5/41, 223–26. Same, Sept. 11, 1740, CO 5/41, 231–32, counted forty-one companies raised, i.e., 1,100 over the 3,000 quota. This muster did not include four companies from North Carolina. Then there were another 1,000 or more recruits. So, some 5,500 American troops were enlisted for the West Indian expedition. Harding, *Amphibious Warfare*, makes the American total 4,183. See also the summary of Newcastle's correspondence with the North American governors, Add. MS 32695, 53–54, 473–74. Henretta, *"Salutary Neglect,"* 200–201, 210–15. Belcher's (Walpolean) sabotage of recruiting and Shirley's (Pelhamite) success led to the former's replacement by the latter. Report of the General Officers, Jan. 2, 1743, T 1/315; s.v. Ensign Ammi Wise; Osgood, *Eighteenth Century*, 3:497n1; John A. Schultz, *William Shirley* (Chapel Hill, NC, 1961), 36–37. Newcastle to the Governors, Circular Letter, Dec. 4, 1740, John C. Van Horne, ed., "The Correspondence of James Blair as Acting Governor of Virginia, 1740–1741," *VMHB* 84 (1976): 42. Harkness, "Americanism," 69–70. See the authoritative article by William A. Foote, "The Pennsylvania Men of the American Regiment," *PMHB* 87 (1963): 31–38; Rea, *Farmar*, 12. On the seductiveness of the British army to Americans, see Shy, *Toward Lexington*, 15, 392–94; Pargellis, *Loudoun*, 14–15, 106, 271.

28. William Byrd to Sir Charles Wager, June 1, 1740, *VMHB* 37 (1929): 105–6. For Wager's American upbringing, see Daniel A. Baugh, "Wager," in LeFevre and Harding, *Precursors*, 105–07, 113. Wager's files are crowded with American projects (Ford, *List*), some probably passed on to the leaders of the West Indian expedition: Newcastle to Vernon, Oct. 15, 1741, Ranft, *Vernon Papers*, 245. See also Henretta, *"Salutary Neglect,"* 50, on Wager's "extensive following in the colonies, many of them fellow officers" of the royal navy who intermarried into the provincial elites, Henretta, *"Salutary Neglect,"* 158, 190–92, 222. As the naval equivalent of Ligonier, Wager was the key figure in the increase in the number of naval governors general.

29. Newcastle to Cathcart, July 24, 1740, Add. MS 32694, 256–57; same to "Lieut. Govr. Gooch at Jamaica," and same "at Virginia," July 24, 1740, ibid., 283–86; minute of Gooch's commission, Dec. 26, 1740, Add. MS 32623, 184; Newcastle to Gooch, Jan. 5, 1739/1740, Add. MS 32693, 15; Blakeney to Newcastle, June 25, 1740, CO 5/41, 215; Gooch to Newcastle, Aug. 9, 1740, CO 5/1337, fols. 238–39. Vernon [to Spotswood], Sept. 28, 1740, Ford, *List*, 82; Vernon to Wager, Oct. 7, 1740, Ranft, *Vernon Papers*, 135; Dodson, *Spotswood*, 30; Beatson, *Memoirs*, 1:69. On the importance of Westminister School ties, see Browning, *Newcastle*, 102–3.

30. Gooch to Newcastle, Aug. 9, 1740, CO 5/1337, fols. 238–39; Blakeney to Newcastle, July 8, 31, Aug. 2, Sept. 11, 1740, CO 5/41, 219–20, 223–25, 227–28, 232. Houlding, *Fit for Service*, 176, 188–89; Pargellis, *Loudoun*, 14–17, 42. Warren to Burchett, New York, Aug. 28, 1740, Julian Gwyn, ed., *The Royal Navy and North America: The Warren Papers, 1736–1752* (London, 1973), 23.

31. Blakeney to Newcastle, Sept. 11, 1740, CO 5/41, 231–32. Warren was a most successful scout and raider and, subsequently, the cooperative commodore who, with the New England provincial forces, captured Louisbourg in 1745. Having married into the New York gentry, Warren shared plunder and prize money with the New York company on board the *Squirrel*: Michael Tyrell to William Johnson, Port Royal, Jamaica, May 28, 1741, James Sullivan, ed., *The Papers of Sir William Johnson* (Albany, 1921), 1:10. On Warren, see *ODNB*; and Julian Gwyn, *The Enterprising Admiral* (Montreal, 1974).

32. Instructions to lieutenant governor of Virginia, Apr. 5, 1740, Add. MS 32693, 154; Blakeney to Newcastle, [Sept. 25], Oct. 13, Dec. 14, 1740, CO 5/41, 250–52, 253–55; Gooch to same, Dec. 8, 1740, Jan. 7, 1740/41, CO 5/41, 260–63; Vernon to Newcastle, Oct. 14, 20, 28, Dec. 12, 1740, SP 42/85, fols. 360–62, 376–77, 382–87; order of Mar. 28, 1740, SP 42/185, fol. 295. Report from Williamsburg, Oct. 24, 1740, and from New York, Jan. 29, 1741, *Pennsylvania Gazette*, Nov. 13, 1740, Jan. 25, 1741. Richmond, *Navy*, 1:57–58; Fortescue, *Army*, 2:43, 62; Harding *Amphibious Warfare*, 72. It would be surprising if the naval officers on half pay in America between the wars did not profit from the victualing contracts for the station ships, Baugh, *Naval Administration*, 399. William Dandridge was a Virginia councilor by Spotswood's nomination and he was Martha Dandridge's uncle. "The Petition of the Officers of the Late American Regiment," May 16, 1743, CO 71/7. "The troops from North America were a very seasonable reinforcement to the garrison of Jamaica against an expected Bourbon attack," Beatson, *Memoirs*, 1:84–85.

33. Cathcart to Newcastle; same to Harrington, Aug. 13, 1740; same to Newcastle, Sept. 14, 1740, CO 5/41, 77–78, 108, 154; Wager to Vernon, May 29, 1740, Ranft, *Vernon Papers*, 103; Fortescue, *Army*, 2:58–62; Baugh, "Wager," 124; Baugh, *Naval Administration*, 116–18. On manning problems, Baugh, *Naval Administration*, 164–69; on typhus, 179–80, 185, 186, table 2; on sailing delays, 199–201; on Ogle's squadron, 192–93, 197–198, 403; and see Beatson, *Memoirs*, 1:68, 86. The fleet included nearly every battleship then in England. "Wager, Sir Charles," *ODNB*; *South Carolina Gazette*, Jan. 22, Mar. 26, 1741; Hugh Whiteford's report, N. Dominica, Dec. 24, 1740, CO 5/41, 210–11; "Return," Dec. 23, 1740, CO 5/42, 20. *A Journal of the Expedition*, 52–53. Smollett, "Account," 428–29. The land forces included the four battalions of the (61st) American Regiment and, from England, the 15th and 24th Foot, and 1st–6th Marines, Houlding, *Fit for Service*, 414.

34. Wentworth's commission, Stock, *Proceedings*, 5:161n; Cathcart to Harrington, Aug. 13, 1740, CO 5/41, 108–10; Wentworth to Newcastle, Oct. 3, Dec. 20, 1740, Jan. 20, 1740/41, Dec. 6, 1741, CO 5/42, fols. 15, 16, 26–29, 95–96; *GM* 11 (1741): 11; HMC, *Egmont MS*, 3:270–71; Smollett, "Account," 448; Harding, *Amphibious Warfare*, 73, 89–90, 91; Harding, "Vernon," 157, 160, 162; Pares, *War and Trade*, 86–87; Richmond, *Navy*, 1:44–45, 103, 110, and, for his laudation of Vernon, 39–40. On Wentworth's inexperience, Richmond, *Navy*, 103. Ranft, *Vernon Papers*, 4–5, #61; Vernon to Wager, Apr. 21, May 26–31, 1740, Ranft, *Vernon Papers*, 89–90, 101, 133, felt a large force could not be provisioned and cited the (supposed) hunger experienced by Adm. Walker in the expedition of 1711. On the circumstances of Vernon's commission, see also Baugh, *Naval Administration*, 131n, 503. Vernon-Wager Papers, 46555, LC, indites Wentworth's "unpardonable Indolence in not . . . reading & digesting Lord Cathcart's Papers." So Wentworth was without weight in the council of war. On Cathcart's preparations, see Beatson, *Memoirs*, 1:69. For the six marine regiments, all commanded by Marlborough's veterans, see Guy, *Oeconomy and Discipline*, 128.

35. Blakeney to Newcastle, New York, July 8, 31, 1740, CO 5/41, 217–18, 223. Webb, *Governors-General*, ch. 4.

36. Memorandum for His Grace, the Duke of Newcastle, from Lord Cathcart, n.d.; Cathcart to Newcastle, July 15, Sept. 30, 1740, CO 5/41, 52–55, 56–57, 122–23; Cathcart to [Andrew] Stone (an undersecretary of state), Oct. 12, 1740, ibid., 194. Cathcart may even have intended to promote deserving American officers to field-grade commissions, same, Oct. 3, 12, 1740, ibid., 174–75, 194–95. Pares, *War and Trade*, 88, 91–92; Baugh, "Wager"; and Harding, "Vernon," 108, 122–23.

37. The memo has been attributed to Cathcart: ("Ld. Cathcart to Newcastle . . . Has Suggested Himself . . . as Governor General of the Whole Continent"), VCRP, SR 7141, 2; Joseph Aloysius Devine, "The British North American Colonies in the War of 1739–1748" (PhD diss., University of Virginia, 1968), 23. However, the only identification in the document is the endorsement: "Ld S to Cathcart, 1740," Add. MS 32692, 544–45.

38. Wentworth to Gooch, Jamaica, July 24, 1741, Add. MS 32,694, 283–86; bishop of Norwich (Thomas Gooch) to Newcastle, Aug. 11, 1740, ibid., 254; Gooch to Newcastle, June 1, 23, 1741, CO 5/41, 264–65; Cathcart to Newcastle, Camp at Carrisbrooke, July 25, 1740, CO 5/41, 68; Wentworth to Newcastle, Jan. 20, 1740/41; June 20, 1741, CO 5/42, fols. 26–27, 28–29. Wentworth was "a Gentleman by Descent and possessing Lands by Inheritance (Circumstances which in a Country like this render you the more proper for military Rand & Command)," 2d lord Barrington to Maj. Gen. Gansell, WO Apr. 18, 1770, Hatner, *Eighteenth-Century Secretary*, 238.

39. Gooch to Newcastle, Sept. 16, 1741, CO 5/1337, fol. 258, enclosing American Captains to Wentworth, CO 5/41, 260. Wentworth even refused to promote the British lieutenant colonels of the American Battalions to colonel rank in the new marine regiments, Wentworth to Newcastle, June 30, 1741, CO 5/42, fol. 54. *A Journal of the Expedition*, [3–5]. Newcastle to Vernon, Apr. 18, 1740, SP 42/85, p. 190; same to Wentworth, Aug. 14, 1740, Add. MS 32694, 472; Wentworth to Newcastle, Jan. 20, 1740/41, CO 5/42, fol. 277. On English "gentleman volunteers," see Guy, *Oeconomy and Discipline*, 91; Houlding, *Fit for Service*, 103; Pargellis, *Loudoun*, 310–11. See also Shy, *Toward Lexington*, 370–71, 380–81.

40. Etched in acid, Richard Pares's sketch of Newcastle as "a political coward" is in *War and Trade*, 44–46. Vernon to Newcastle, Feb. 25, Apr. 1, 1740, *Original Papers Relative to the Expedition to Carthagena*, 2d ed. (London, 1744), 31–33, 70–71; orders to Vernon, July 4, 1719, Ford, *List*, 9. Sir Charles Wager's memo of the force required for attacks on Cartagena, Panama, and St. Jago, n.d., Ford, *List*, 69; Vernon to Wager, Feb. 24, 1740, Ford, *List*, 71; council of war, Feb. 8, 1740, Ford, *List*, 70. Council of war, Feb. 16, 1740; Vernon to Wager, Feb. 24, 1740, Vernon-Wager Papers, 46014, 46021–25, LC. On the Havana target, see Vernon-Wager Papers, 46014, 46021–25, 85, and on the Ft. St. Louis mistake, Beatson, *Memoirs*, 1:87–88. On Dandridge's mistake, see also Vernon-Wager Papers, 46563, LC; Vernon to Dandridge, Jan. 14, 1740/41, and councils of war, Feb. 8, 23, 1740/41, Ranft, *Vernon Papers*, 163–64, 171. Vernon to Newcastle and Wager, Feb. 24, 1740/41, Ranft, *Vernon Papers*, 177–80. Richmond, *Navy*, 1:54–57, 106–10. Pares, *War and Trade*, 163–78; Richard Pares, "American versus Continental Warfare, 1739–1763," *EHR* 51 (1936): 430; Fortescue, *Army*, 2:63; William Laird Clowes, *The Royal Navy* (London, 1898), 3:64–65, 67–68; Nowell, "Defense of Cartagena," 488–89; Baugh, *Naval Administration*, 23. John R. McNeill, "The Ecological Basis of Warfare in the Caribbean, 1700–1804," in Ultree, *Adapting to Conditions*, 26–42, esp. 35. Browning, *Newcastle*, 99–101. Vernon was correct that d'Antin's intention had been to attack the expeditionary fleet and Jamaica as well, but disease destroyed his force: Jones, *Britain and the World*, 200–201.

41. Vernon to Wager, Feb. 25, 1739, Vernon-Wager Papers, 45719, LC; Vernon to Sir Chalioner Ogle, Mar. 6, 1740, *Original Papers*, 37; Smollett, "Account," 442; "A Plan of Carthagena," *GM* 10 (1740): 201, noted that the city and its approaches had been refortified since they were stormed by the baron de Pontis' buccaneers in 1697. De Pontis' action was reprised in *An Account of the Taking of Carthagena* (London, 1740). See also Vernon to Cathcart, Oct. 14, 1740, *Original Papers*, 6; Clowes, *Royal Navy*, 3:58, 61, 68–70; Beatson, *Memoirs*: 1:61, 63, 66, 89, details the Spanish buildup in 1740. "Carte topographique de Le Baye et Faubourg de Cartagene avec les forts et batteries nouvelle etablies pour servit a sa defense," reproduced in Richmond, *Navy*, 1: facing p. 22. See also the "Plan of the Harbour, Town, and Several Forts of *Cartagena*," Richmond, *Navy*, 1: facing p. 112. Nowell, "Defense," 490–91, denies that there had been Spanish reinforcements and (492) excuses Vernon's delay. Harding, "Vernon," 157, 168; "Vernon," *ODNB*; Vernon-Wager, Feb. 25, 1739, Ford, *List*, 58; instructions to Vernon, July 16, 1739, Ford, *List*, 62; dispatches, Apr. 3, May 12, printed in *Pennsylvania Gazette*, May 15, June 12, 1740; Vernon to Newcastle, Apr. 5, 1740, published June 29, *London Gazette*, and in *Pennsylvania Gazette*, Sept. 18, 1740. See officers' letters in *Pennsylvania Gazette*, Sept. 18, Nov. 13, Dec. 11, 1740, July 9, 1741; *South Carolina Gazette*, May 28, June 7, Aug. 1, 16, 1740, Mar. 19, 1741; Patrick Burns, Report on Cartagena fortifications, Jan. 17, 1739, enc. by Wager to Vernon, Jan. 18, 1739, Ford, *List*, 57, 58; Warren to Vernon, Feb. 24, 1740, Ford, *List*, 71. Pares, *War and Trade*, 111. Maps: Fortescue, *Army*, 64, and facing p. 78; *GM* 10 (1740): facing p. 145; Harding, *Amphibious Warfare*, 93–96; and app., Richmond, *Navy*, 1:52–54.

42. "Lord Elibank's Journal," CO 5/41, fol. 302v. That Elibank, the Scots major of Bland's regiment, was the only regular officer not promoted at Cartagena presumably gave an edge to his criticism of the English general Wentworth. Even for a Scot, the major had a remarkable degree of sympathy for the Americans he commanded. On the delay in encamping and the exposure of the troops see Vernon and Ogle to Wentworth, Mar. 11, 1740, ibid., 46049–50; on excessive guard duty, same, Mar. 25, ibid., 46060. See also the narrative, enclosed by Vernon to Newcastle and Wager, Apr. 1, 1741, ibid., 46442; anon. account, ibid., 46557–59. The correspondence is printed in Ranft, *Vernon Papers*, #132, 150, 154. See also Vernon [to Trelawney], Mar. 20, 1740/41, Ranft, *Vernon Papers*, 194–96, and Vernon's orders to his captains, n.d., Ranft, *Vernon Papers*, #135–37. Wentworth to Newcastle, Mar. 31, 1741, CO 5/42, fols. 36–37; Gooch to Newcastle, Sept. 16, 1741, CO 5/1337, fol. 258; Vernon and Ogle to Wentworth, Mar. 11, 1740, *Original Papers*, 43; same, Mar. 23, 24, 25, Ford, *List*, 73.

43. *A Journal of the Expedition*, 13–15n1. Vernon to [Trelawney], Mar. 20, 1740/41, Ranft, *Vernon Papers*, #142, pp. 195–96, where Washington appears as "Lawrence." Washington was not named in Vernon's account to Newcastle, Apr. 1741, Ranft, *Vernon Papers*, p. 209. Other elements of the American regiment may have joined the attack. Ens. Marshall of Pennsylvania "received a severe Wound at the Barraderra Battery" and was promoted lieutenant: "A List of Officers May 16, 1743," WO 71/7. Vernon to Wager, Apr. 1, 1741, Vernon-Wager Papers, 46445–46, LC, mentions only the naval officers (as does Richmond, *Navy*, 1:114–15). Vernon to Wentworth, Apr. 1, 1741, *Original Papers*, 49. See also Vernon and Ogle to Wentworth, Mar. 24, 1740, Vernon-Wager Papers, 46058, 46060, LC, and the anon. account, Vernon-Wager Papers, 46557–59; Smollett, "Account," 438–39; Vernon to Newcastle, July 29, Nov. 3, 1741, *Papers relating to the Expedition to Cuba* (London, 1744), 37, 41, 152. Lawrence Washington to Augustine Washington, Jamaica, May 30, 1741, NYPL; Harding, *Amphibious Warfare*, 104–5; Beatson, *Memoirs*, 1:91–95. The Scots nobleman was James Murray, afterward one of Wolfe's brigadiers at Quebec.

Murray took command of the city, fought a second battle on the plains of Abraham, led the advance to Montreal, and became military governor of the Quebec district.
44. *A Journal of the Expedition*, 19. Vernon, Ogle, and Lestock to Wentworth, Mar. 25, 1741, Ranft, *Vernon Papers*, #150, p. 202. See also the anon. account in Vernon-Wager Papers, 46559, LC. The report of Provost's death (*Pennsylvania Gazette*, May 14, 1741) may have been incorrect. He was not listed as killed on the "Return" of Mar. 31, 1740, CO 5/42 fols. 32–33, but he was listed on the regimental roster as "still abroad in North America" on May 16, 1743, WO 71/7. On MacLeod, see Smollett, "Account," 440; *GM* 11 (1741): 499. For the survivors of Malplaquet killed at Cartagena, see Dalton, *Army Lists*, 6: Malplaquet Roll, and WO 4/10. These veterans included: Maj. Benjamin Gregg of Gooch's and Blakeney's old regiment, the 16th (the Royal Irish) Regiment; John, lord Colville, a lieutenant colonel of the American Regiment; and Christopher Ganey, killed commanding a company of grenadiers in the assault on Ft. St. Lazaro. See also Harding, *Amphibious War*, 105; Vernon to Wager, Apr. 2, 1740, Ford, *List*, 89, Richmond, *Navy*, 1:116–18. Beatson, *Memoirs*, 1:96, has a naval officer, "Captain Coates," left to command this fort.
45. Vernon's April Fool's Day dispatch (Ranft, *Vernon Papers*, #154, pp. 206–14) was a classic example of selling the skin of a bear not yet killed. Adm. Ogle and Gen. Wentworth, concerned about the strength of the Spanish, the sickness of the British, and the onset of the rainy season, advised that a victory dispatch should wait the conquest of the city, ibid., 24. For the patriotic formulation, see Newport declaration of May 13, 1741, reprinted *Pennsylvania Gazette*, June 4, 1741, and the *Boston Post Boy*, Lanning, "Participation," [191].
46. "Lord Elibanks' Journal," CO 5/41, fol. 310v. *A Journal of the Expedition*, 25, 30, u, rebuts the contention that a push would have overwhelmed Ft. St. Lazaro and, perhaps, have reached the city gates. On the guards and American laborers, see *A Journal of the Expedition*, z, pp. 33–34. Richmond, *Navy*, 1:119–20. For Lawrence Washington's supposed service at La Quinta, see Hartman, *The Angry Admiral*, 215. On the Americans in the landing force and the unnecessary guards, see also the anon. account in Vernon-Wager Papers, 46561, LC. "Lord Elibanks' Journal," CO 5/41, fol. 311v; Vernon and Wentworth to Newcastle, Apr. 26, 1740; *GM* 6 (1747): 305, and see 310, 384; Vernon to Newcastle, Mar. 31, 1741, CO 5/42, fol. 37v. Richmond, *Navy*, 1:57, 120–22; Fortescue, *Army*, 2:66–67; council of war, Mar. 30, 1741, Ford, *List*, 89; Lanning, "Participation," 194, 195; Harding *Amphibious Warfare*, 94; *Pennsylvania Gazette*, July 23, 1741.
47. *A Journal of the Expedition*, 30–36; army council of war to Vernon, Apr. 7, 1741, Vernon-Wager Papers, 46474–45, LC; Vernon and Ogle to Wentworth, Apr. 6, 17, Vernon-Wager Papers, 46456–57, *Original Papers*, 91, 152–53; anon. account, Vernon-Wager Papers, 46561, LC; Smollett, "Account," 450; Clowes, *Royal Navy*, 3:73–74, Richmond, *Navy*, 1:119–20. Michael Tyrell to William Johnson, May 28, 1741, Sullivan, *Johnson Papers*, 1:11–12; James Deane to Lawrence Washington, July 24, 1741, Conway, *Barons*, 101. Harding, "Vernon," 169. Wentworth and Guise to Vernon, Apr. 2, reply, Apr. 3, 1741; Ford, *List*, 89; Vernon and Ogle to Wentworth, Apr. 4, 1741, Ford, *List*, 90; Wentworth to Vernon, Apr. 6/7, Ford, *List*; Lawrence Washington to Augustine Washington, Jamaica, May 30, 1741, NYPL. A

Spanish Officer's Acct., Add. MS 22680, ed. James Alexander Robertson, *HAHR* 2 (1919): 65–66. Wolfe's son, James, afterward Marshal Ligonier's choice to lead the (seventh) assault on Quebec, had been too ill to accompany his father's regiment to the West Indies.

48. The army officer's *A Journal of the Expedition*, 38, 55, insists that the grenades were not defective, but rather that the naval commentator (Knowles) was ignorant. A List of the Officers . . . of the American Regiment, WO 71/7; Smollett, "Account," 451–52; minutes of the council of war, Mar. 30, 1741, Vernon-Wager Papers, 46440, LC. On the second American landing, see Wentworth and Guise to Vernon, Apr. 2, 1741, calling for "a Detachment of Fifteen hundred men, under proper Officers from the American Regiment Commanded by Colonel Gooch," Vernon-Wager Papers, 45456. The admiral refused to put so many men ashore (Vernon-Wager Papers, 46459), but two elite American companies, one of which appears to have been Lawrence Washington's, were among the first troops landed. Subsequently, 600 American "pioneers" landed to build a camp and to act as porters for the assault on Ft. Lazaro, Wentworth to Vernon, Apr. 6, 1741, Vernon-Wager Papers, 46466. On the assault, see also the anon. account in Vernon-Wager Papers, 46561–62 and "Lord Elibanks' Journal," CO 5/41, 313v, 315v. Richmond, *Navy*, 1:121–23. The "horrid mistakes" of devotion to platoon firings was deplored at this time by Marlborough's veterans, Houlding, *Fit for Service*, 192–95. Lawrence Washington reported to his family's factors and friends at Whitehaven "from ye Harbour of Catagena ye 31st of March lost" (1741). Joseph Deane replied on July 24, congratulating Washington on his escape from "misfortunes and mortality," reporting that Gooch had accused the Virginian of cowardice, that Vernon had failed, and that (San Lazar) had been stormed without a breach in its fortification, Conway, *Barons*, 100–101.

49. Wentworth to Newcastle, Apr. 26, 1741, CO 5/42, fol. 34; Nowell, "Defense," 499; Fortescue, *Army*, 2:69–71; Harding, *Amphibious Warfare*, 114–15; Hall, "Maryland's Part," *MHM* (1907): 157; Rea, *Farmar*, 14–15; *South Carolina Gazette*, June 25, 1741; *Pennsylvania Gazette*, July 9, 1741, reprinting letters received at Boston, June 29. On total casualties, see New York lieutenant Michael Tyrell to William Johnson, May 28. 1741, Sullivan, *Johnson Papers*, 1:10, who counted 648; Warren, as reported in *Pennsylvania Gazette*, June 25, 1741, numbered 642 killed in the assault. For Addison's wound, see T 1/315, 4. Ens. Thomas Marshall of New Jersey was "shot through the body," T 1/315, 9.

50. "Lord Elibanks' Journal," CO 5/41, fol. 315v; *A Journal of the Expedition*, 43–47, e.g., recorded 4,340 rank and file reduced to 3,569, "including 1140 American Soldiers, of whom 600 were employed upon no other Service but on Working Parties." On ships and stone walls, see *A Journal of the Expedition*, 50, and the anon. account, Vernon-Wager Papers, 46557, LC. Vernon seems to have forgotten the success his squadron had had against the forts of Porto Bello. Creswell, *Admirals and Generals*, 45 #1, estimates that 6,600 men were reduced to 3,200 between Apr. 7 and 10, and declares that "hundreds more were sickening daily, few of them to recover," 50–51. The American Regiment here lost nine more officers to disease, Return for April 1741, CO 5/42, #38. Army council of war, Apr. 10, 1741, Vernon-Wager Papers,

46484, LC; naval council of war, Apr. 12, 1741, Vernon-Wager Papers, 46488; Vernon to Wager, Apr. 20, 1741, Vernon-Wager Papers, 46532; same to Wentworth, Apr. 15, 16, 17; naval council of war, Apr. 12; army council of war and joint council, Apr. 14, *Original Papers*, 101–2; Ford, *List*, 91–93. Vernon to Wentworth, March 18, 1740/41, Ranft, *Vernon Papers*, #40. The lack of food and water is laid to Vernon's account by Beatson, *Memoirs*, 1:97. Harding, *Amphibious Warfare*, 123–24, table 1; *South Carolina Gazette*, Sept. 19, 1741; J. R. McNeill, "Yellow Jack and Geopolitics," in Alf Hornberg et al., eds., *Rethinking Environmental History* (Lantham, MD., 2006), 199–209; Smollett, "Account," 456.

51. Vernon to Wager, Apr. 21, May 9, 30, Ford, *List*, 74, 75, 94; same, June 6, enc. May 30, 1741, Vernon-Wager Papers, 46575–85, LC; Vernon to Newcastle, May 30, Dec. 6, 12, 1741, *Original Papers*, 131; Fortescue, *Army*, 2:72–73; Harding, *Amphibious Warfare*, 123–24; Beatson, *Memoirs*, 1:98–99. See also Cathcart to Newcastle, Oct. 18, 1740, CO 5/41, 198. The dire and deadly situation of the sick in British naval "hospitals" and sick bays was hardly better, Baugh, *Naval Administration*, 180–85. Tobias Smollett, *The Adventures of Roderick Random* (New York, 1907), 2:116, 119.

52. Naval council of war, Apr. 12, 1741, Vernon-Wager Papers, 46490, LC; Vernon to Wager, Apr. 26, 1741, ibid., 46534, 46536; Wager to Vernon, May 23, 1741, ibid., 46565. Lawrence Washington to Augustine Washington, Jamaica, May 30, 1741, NYPL. Wentworth to Newcastle, [Feb. 11, 1741/42], CO 5/42, fols. 164–65, enc. #3; A List of the Officers of the Honble. Colon. Gooch's Regiment of Foot who have been killed since they left America, May 30, 1741, CO 5/42, fol. 50, and see June 19, 57. Harding, *Amphibious Warfare*, 123–24, table 1. One of Richmond's (rare) criticisms of Vernon is his failure to retain these forts, *Navy*, 1:124–25.

53. Wentworth to Newcastle, June 30, 1741, CO 5/42, fol. 54v; Gooch to Newcastle, Sept. 23, 1741, CO 5/1337, fol. 159v. The estimate for an American Regiment was put before parliament in 1742 (Stock, *Proceedings*, 5:118), but left on the table. The eight Jamaica independent companies, the garrison of Roatan (two American companies, one of Wolfe's), and a force of Americans in Belize were regimented under Gov.-Gen. Trelawney as the 49th foot. Letter of Aug. 24 in *South Carolina Gazette*, Sept. 19, 1741.

54. Lawrence to Augustine Washington, Jamaica, May 30, 1741, NYPL. Wentworth's proposal was to Newcastle, Nov. 2, 1741, CO 5/42, fols. 83–85. See same, Dec. 20, 1741, CO 5/42, fols. 105–7. Arthur F. Buffington, "The Canada Expedition of 1746: Its Relation to British Politics," *AHR* 45 (1940): 555; Baugh, *Naval Administration*, 26, 71–72, 74; *ODNB*, "Russell, John, Fourth Duke of Bedford"; Harrison, "Convicts," 256–57.

55. Gooch to Newcastle, June 13, Aug. 26, 1746, CO 5/1338, # 2, 4; Gooch transcripts, Virginia Historical Society, 838, 865. Henretta, *"Salutary Neglect,"* 252; Harding, *Amphibious Warfare*, 163. Among other demands on provincial manpower, three independent companies were raised to garrison South Carolina and "to avoid the Charge of Transportation . . . levied in . . . North America," APCC, 3:780. Virginia was the nearest recruiting ground to the southern frontier. Virginia sent only one company, but once again, more than 5,500 Americans enlisted for the 1746 expedition, Pargellis, *Loudoun*, 14. Gooch to Newcastle, Apr. 9, June 13, 1746,

Feb. 12, 1746/7, CO 5/1338, #2, 6; Virginia Historical Society *Transactions*, #839–40, 869; recruiting proclamation by Gooch, June 10 1746, Virginia Historical Society *Transactions*, # 841. Dalton, *Army Lists*, 5: 5, pt. 2, 51; 6:333; Dalton, *George the First's Army*, 1:156; Percy Scott Flippin, "William Gooch," *WMQ*, 2d ser., 5 (1925): 225–28, 6:1–38; Webb, *Governors-General*, #208 (where the 16th foot is erroneously labeled 15th). Henretta, "*Salutary Neglect*," 252, 279–82; Morton, *Colonial Virginia*, 2:534–35, 596, 597.

56. Lawrence to Augustine Washington, Jamaica, May 30, 1742, NYPL; [William Dummer], "Some Considerations about Forming a Descent in the Spanish West Indies," [1730], Ford, *List*, 30; J. Hamilton, "Proposal for Taking Cuba by a Force to Be Raised in America," [May 14, 1739], Ford, *List*, 60. *South Carolina Gazette*, July 16, 1741; Harding, *Amphibious Warfare*, 106, and see 125–28; Pares, *War and Trade*, 92, and see 66, 68, 75, 77–81. Webb, *Governors-General*, 151–52. Trelawney to Wager, Aug. 29, 1740, Vernon-Wager Papers, 46252, 46253, LC; Ford, *List*, 80; council of war, May 26, 1741, Ford, *List*, 94. Pulteney to Vernon, Aug. 17, 1740, *GM*, 18 (1748): 303–30, Ranft, *Vernon Papers*, #81, Richmond, *Navy*, 1:56, 126–27. Horatio Walpole (to Robert Trevor, Oct. 3, 1740, Aug. 10, 1741, HMC, *Trevor MS*, 57, 59, 75) argued that while England might take it, it could not hold a West Indian conquest against the united forces of France and Spain. Therefore, there was no achieving the "patriot" proposal "of our *carving some good slice out of America that may secure a door and inlet for our commodities and manufactures in the New World.*"

57. Vernon-Wager, Apr. 26, 1741, Vernon-Wager Papers, 46534, LC. Vernon (to Newcastle, Nov. 3, 1741, *Expedition to Cuba*, 152) understood "the principal Motive of all the American Officers engaging in the Service, the hopes of being settled in the West Indies, and in Cuba preferably to all other Places." Wentworth to Newcastle, Nov. 2, CO 5/42, 96ff., on recruiting, and see "State of the War in America," *GM* 11 (1741): 587–88. Return Aug. 26, 1741, CO 5/42, 75–77. Pares, *War and Trade*, 82, 83, 92–93.

58. Lawrence to Augustine Washington, May 30, 1741, NYPL; Wentworth to Newcastle, Aug. 28, 1741, CO 5/42, fol. 72, same, Dec. 20, 1741, SP 42/90, fols 429–32. Lanning, "Participation," 200–201; Harkness, "Americanism," 78–80; Pares, *War and Trade*, 93; Harding, *Amphibious Warfare*, 53. Wentworth was not altogether mistaken: half a dozen of the Irish soldiers in the American Regiment did desert to the Spanish: Return of Gooch's Regiment, Oct. 3, 1741, CO 5/42, fol. 82.

59. Vernon to Wentworth, Aug. 19, 1741, *Expedition to Cuba*, 70–72; Wentworth to Newcastle, June 2, Aug. 13, 28, Oct. 8, Nov. 2, 1741, CO 5/42, fols. 42, 69, 74, 80v, 97–98. Council of war, June 28, 1742, CO 5/42, fol. 241. Laurence to Augustine Washington, May 30, 1741, NYPL; Pares, *War and Trade*, 93. Capt. William Hopkins, formerly a Rhode Island assemblyman and lieutenant colonel of militia, "being a Diligent Officer was employ'd by his [Wentworth's] order in recruiting at New York, Rhode Island &c and did good Service," List of Officers, WO 71/7. General Officers Report, May 1, 1744, T1/315, s.v. "Hopkins," "Farmar," Rea, *Farmar*, 16. The royal orders conveyed by Newcastle to Vernon (and Wentworth), Oct. 15, 1741, (Ranft, *Vernon Papers*, 243–46), called for recruiting the Americans. So "it is extremely to be wished that these American troops may be well satisfied with their treatment . . . that the terms and conditions upon which they were raised may be constantly and punctually complied with . . . and that all possible encouragement may be given them for making settlements in any part of the enemy's country . . . and that they may be treated in the same manner with the other forces, that they may be encouraged to enlist and incorporate with them." These orders reiterated previous commands. Entirely ignored by Wentworth, they were partially observed by Vernon.

60. Wentworth to Newcastle, June 7, Aug. 13, 28, Oct. 8, 1741, CO 5/42, fols. 42, 69, 74, 80v; *Pennsylvania Gazette*, Oct. 1; *South Carolina Gazette*, Oct. 10, 1741. Pares, *War and Trade*, 80–82, 88, 90–91; Richmond, *Navy*, 1:127–28, 130. On the Oglivies, the New York military family descended from one of the thirty sergeants promoted lieutenants for the 1711 expedition, see Dalton, *Army Lists*, 6:291–92. Despite their public enthusiasm, some of the recruiters did not return to Cuba or the expedition, Rea, *Farmar*, 16. On the evacuation, and Wentworth's label, see Edward to James Vernon, Ranft, *Vernon Papers*, #179.

61. Council of war, May 16, 1741, Vernon-Wager Papers, 46569–70, LC; Vernon to Wager, June 6, 1741, ibid., 46588–605; same to Newcastle, Nov. 26, 1741, CO 5/42, 90ff., quoted by Harding, *Amphibious Warfare*, 153, and see 132–33, 145. Council of war, June 28, 1742, Ranft, *Vernon Papers*, 253–54. Council of war, Jan. 22, 23, 28, 1741/42, CO 5/42, fols. 124, 237–38. Wentworth to Newcastle, and to Courald, Mar. 1, 1741/42, CO 5/42, fols. 201–3; "An Account," July 22, 1742, CO 5/42, fols 245. Carteret put it pithily: "Royal Navies are kept by the merchants, and must protect the merchants." This remark was true literally as well as figuratively. Pares, *War and Trade*, 48, 119. On maritime empire, see also Bob Harris, "'American Idols': Empire, War and the Middling Ranks in Mid-Eighteenth-Century Britain," *PP* 150 (1996): 127–30, 138–39. Nicholas Rogers, "Caribbean Borderland: Empire, Ethnicity, and the Exotic on the Mosquito Coast," *Eighteenth-Century Life* 26 (2002): 123–25, 128. For the American garrison, see W. Y. Baldrig and A. S. White, "Gooch's American Regiment of Foot, 1739–1742," *JSAHR* 16 (1937): 237. On Roatan, see also Pares, *War and Trade*, 94–95, 261–62; Richmond, *Navy*, 1:16, 130, 133; Harding, *Amphibious Warfare*, 137, 145, 146. For a recent reiteration of the debate between naval "soft power" and army conquest, see Robert D. Kaplan, "Obama Takes Asia By Sea," *New York Times*, November 12, 2010, A 123.

62. Trelawney did all that he could to mediate the conflict between Vernon and Wentworth, the current example of the army-navy hostility that, as Hunter noted, had doomed all the recent West Indian expeditions. Trelawney went so far as to propose a united armed service: "Such a scheme . . . would do more lasting good at least to the nation than the Duke of Marlborough's victories," Hartman, *Angry Admiral*, 122, and see 85, 121. An Account of the Altercation between Sir Chaloner Ogle & Mr. Trelawney, July 22, 1742, CO 5/42, fol. 245; Vernon-Wager Papers, 46714, LC; Smollett, "Account," 448. The case went to court and Ogle was convicted of assault. For the impressment of American merchant sailors, especially by Knowles, see Baugh, *Naval Administration*, 20, 221. Trelawney feared that "any thing that looks like an Impress" would scare off the Northward folks," whose manpower was vital to privateering and whose provisions could not be replaced, Baugh,

Naval Administration, 216–17. For the ministerial collapse following the Cartagena debacle, see Stock, *Proceedings*, 5:111–112n; Wilson, "Empire, Trade and Popular Politics," 106; *ODNB*, "Holles, Thomas Pelham"; and see Robert Harris, *A Patriot Press* (Oxford, 1993), 101–2. For the transatlantic military/political issue, see Edward to James Vernon, Nov. 17, 1741, Ranft, *Vernon Papers*, #178, pp. 247–48: "Our great men are endeavouring . . . to make the disputes between you and the land forces in the West Indies, a Party quarrel between land & sea officers here." On the (lessening) social distinctions between the services, see Holmes *Augustan England*, 286–81.

63. Instructions to Vernon, Oct. 2, 1740, SP 42/85, fol. 361; Lanning, "Participation," 204; Cathcart to Stone, Oct. 3, 1740, CO 5/41, 174; Harding, *Amphibious Warfare*, 147–48, 202. Wentworth to Newcastle, Sept. 5, 1742, CO 5/42, fols. 280–81; Vernon and Ogle correspondence with Trelawney and Wentworth, Aug. 5–Sept. 3, ibid., CO 5/42, fols. 254–58, 272–79; William Bull to the expeditionary commanders, Charleston, South Carolina, July 7, 1742, CO 5/42, fols. 259–61; council of war (naval officers only), Aug. 4, 1742, CO 5/42, fol. 267; same, Aug. 7, 1742, Ranft, *Vernon Papers*, 198. Phinzy Spaulding, *Oglethorpe in America* (Chicago, 1977), 127–50; John Jay TePaske, *The Governorship of Spanish Florida, 1700–1763* (Durham, NC, 1964), 139–54; Larry E. Ivers, *British Drums . . .* (Chapel Hill, NC, 1974), 151–62.

64. The model for this venture was the seizure of Porto Bello and Panama by Henry Morgan's 500 buccaneers in 1670 (Webb, *Governors-General*, 245–49; Hartman, *Angry Admiral*, 113–14), just as de Pontis's exploit was the buccaneering example at Cartagena. The speed and audacity of the age of licensed piracy contrasted with the delays of modern regularity and bureaucracy. These delays were fatal now that yellow fever had arrived from Africa with the slaves, an African revenge. Pares, *War and Trade*, 93–96; Harding, *Amphibious War*, 137, 139–44; Trelawney to Wager, Sept. 12, 1740, Oct. 5, 1742, Ford, *List*, 81, 97; Richmond, *Navy*, 1:33, 131–33; Newcastle to Vernon, Oct. 15, 1741, Ranft, *Vernon Papers*, 244. The isthmian plan, like all its predecessors, was reported fully in the American press. See the Boston report, dated Apr. 27, reprinted in *Pennsylvania Gazette*, May 7, and *South Carolina Gazette*, July 16, 1741. On the drafting of soldiers to man the fleet, see Creswell, *Generals and Admirals*, 39n, and, on the failed Panama adventure, 23–24, 53; Baugh, *Naval Administration*, 218–19; Beatson, *Memoirs*, 1:138–40, who blamed the army's apprehensions for the fiasco. Wentworth to Couraud, Feb. 5, 1741/42, CO 5/42, fol. 112; same to Newcastle, Feb. 11, 1741/42, Mar. 31, Sept. 5, 1742, CO 5/42, fols. 166–67, 207–10, 280. On Anson's voyage and the ministry's criminal coercion of 259 Chelsea pensioners to be a "marine regiment," see Leo Heaps, ed., *Log of the Centurion* (London, 1973), 29–30, and Philip Sumarez's log, passim. Beatson, *Memoirs*, 1:42–43, 56–58; Richmond, *Navy*, 1:97–100, and an impassioned defense of Vernon, 133ff.; Pares, *War and Trade*, 104–8. For the famous circumnavigation, see George Anson, *A Voyage round the World* (London, 1748). It was only fitting that given the Anglo-American disaster in the Caribbean, the peace treaty with Spain did not mention the *guarda costa* and that the asiento was not renewed: Browning, *Newcastle*, 135.

65. Return of the American Regiment, Aug. 3, 31, Oct. 17, 1742, CO 5/42, fols. 36, 79, 225, [286]. The Petition of the Officers of the late American Regiment, rec'd

16 May 1743, WO 71/7; Stock, *Proceedings*, 5:126, 134–35; T. Stafford to Lawrence Washington, Nov. 13, 1749, Conway, *Barons*, 111; *New York Weekly Journal*, Jan. 17, 1743; Foote, "Pennsylvania," 37. Vernon insisted "that without the Aid of some of the American troops, we could not get our Ships to Sea," Vernon to Wager, June 6, 1741, Vernon-Wager Papers 46586, LC. Wentworth had to appeal to the royal promise and use Washington's good offices with Vernon to get those who wished to go home released: Wentworth to Newcastle, May 24, 1742, CO 4/42, 218–19; Vernon to Wentworth, Oct. 9; same to Newcastle, Nov. 3, 1741, *Expedition to Cuba*, 113, 152; Hartman, *Angry Admiral*, 119–20; Lanning, "Participation,"204; Rea, *Farmar*, 17; Harding, *Amphibious Warfare*, 149, 193; *GM* 16 (1746): 404; HMC, *Egmont MS*, 3:160. Guy, *Oeconomy and Discipline*, 129–30. Others of the American Regiment, the equivalent of a single understrength battalion, still serving as marines under their own officers, had sailed to England. There, on Oct. 25, 1742, the last companies of the American Regiment were disbanded. Thirty-nine officers and perhaps 200 men were incorporated into Gen. Pulteney's regiment; "our regiment," they called it when they wrote home to their comrades in America. They served in Flanders against the French and in Scotland against the jacobites. There, "pioneers" once again, they helped build the first roads through the tribal Highlands, the last frontier in Great Britain.

66. Thos. Wentworth to Captain Washington, Apr. 17, 1743, Conway, *Barons*, 104; Alex. Wilson to Lawrence Washington, Nov. 6, 1742, photo reproduction of the document bound in Conway, II, LWS Collection, Morristown National Historical Park, Morristown, NJ, printed in Conway, *Barons*, 102–3, accounted for Washington's pay from the date of his commission until Dec. 24, 1740. Clearings from that date until the disbandment of Gooch's regiment, Wilson wrote, would be delayed at least until the summer of 1743. Wilson presumed that Washington would not come over, the American Regiment being reduced. American officers in England, application, Jan. 26, 1743, WO 71/7. Freeman, *Washington*, 1:71n. Board of general officers to the lords justices, May 16, 1742, WO 71/7; "Officers of the Regiment . . . Remaining in America," and "Observations," WO 71/7. "Charge for a [four-battalion] Regiment of Foot Raised in America for Service in the West Indies, for the Year 1742," Stock, *Proceedings*, 1:118. At £91/1/5 per annum, (Guy, *Oeconomy and Discipline*, table 4.7) half pay was a substantial income. For its foundation of army officers' social and professional status, see Holmes, *Augustan England*, 263. Not having purchased their commissions, the officers of the American Regiment could not sell out, Houlding, *Fit for Service*, 102–4. Hatner, *Eighteenth Century Secretary*, 275–82. The fullest treatment of purchase in an Anglo-American context is in Pargellis, *Loudoun*, 306–14. Fifteen officers of the former American Regiment were still drawing half pay even after the peace of Paris in 1763, Devine, "British Colonies," 99–100. On the paradox of the prestige of an army commission in a (supposedly) antimilitary polity, see Shy, *Toward Lexington*, 346–49.

67. Washington Memorial, Apr. 30, 1743, *EJC*, 5:117. Fairfax Harrison, "George Washington's First Commission," *VMHB* 31 (1923): 272. In his sketch of Lawrence Washington, Jared Sparks, *The Writings of George Washington* (New York, 1847), 2:422, asserts that Washington declined British half pay "on the ground that he could not conscientiously take the oath required, while he held the adjutancy in Virginia." On the responsibilities—recruiting, regulating, reports, drill, and discipline—of the adjutant general, see Guy, *Oeconomy and Discipline*, 29–30; Houlding, *Fit for Service*, 155–56.

68. Webb, "Nicholson," 539–41; Dodson, *Spotswood*, 204–5. On the menace of Spanish privateers, see Gooch to Newcastle, Sept. 15, 1741, CO 5/1337, fol. 254. On convict outrages, see Harrison, *Landmarks*, 157–73. On slave unrest, see Parent, *Foul Means*, esp. 59–72. For slave numbers (in the 1730s, Virginians "imported more slaves than ever before or again"), see Philip D. Morgan, *Slave Counterpoint* (Chapel Hill, NC, 1998), 81 and table 10. Gooch to lords commissioners, Mar. 20, 1729, CO 5/1321, 110ff.; same to Albemarle, Sept. 3, 1739, CO 5/1337, fols. 208–11; Henretta, *"Salutary Neglect,"* 249–50; Morton, *Colonial Virginia*, 2:507; "Keppel, William Anne," *ODNB*. See Fortescue, *Army*, 2:37, 39–40, on the "national militia" of the American provinces which, Fortescue believed, operated "with an efficiency unknown to the militia of England."

69. Ri. Yates to Major Washington, Appleby, Nov. 13, 1743, Conway, *Barons*, 106–8; Freeman, *Washington*, 1:77; *EJC*, 5:132.

70. On the Northern Neck investors, see Alfred P. James, *The Ohio Company* (Pittsburgh, 1959), ch. 1; Lois Mulkearn, ed., *George Mercer Papers relating to the Ohio Company of Virginia* (Pittsburgh, 1954), 1–7: "Resume of the Proceedings of the Ohio Company, October 24, 1747–May 24, 1751." Kenneth P. Bailey, *The Ohio Company of Virginia* (Glendale, CA, 1939), 126–37; Patrice Louis-Rene Higonnet, "The Origins of the Seven Years War," *JMH* (1968), 61; Rhoades, "Assarigoa's Line," 156–63, 170–73; Fred Anderson, *Crucible of War: The Seven Years' War and the Fate of Empire in British North America, 1754–1766* (New York, 2000), 23, 27–28; Eric Hinderaker, *Elusive Empires: Constructing Colonialism in the Ohio Valley* (Cambridge, 1997), 136–37; Francis Jennings, *The Ambiguous Iroquois Empire* (New York, 1984), 356–63. William Fairfax to Lawrence Washington, Federicksburg, Sept. 9; Robert Jackson to same, Sept. 18, 1746, Conway, *Barons*, 238–40; Freeman, *Washington*, 1:194–95; Baugh, *Naval Administration*, ch. 3, esp. pp. 94–96.

71. Freeman, *Washington*, 1:198–200, 202n46. *PGWCS*, 1:54n.Uncle Joseph did not exaggerate midshipmen's dreadful circumstances: Edward Thompson, *Seamen's Letters* (London, 1756), 1:140, quoted in Clowes, *Royal Navy*, 3:21–22; Baugh, *Naval Administration*, 118–20, 139, 145. Even so well-connected a naval officer as George Clinton despaired of flag rank and begged the government of New York for compensation for twenty-five years drudgery as a captain, Baugh, *Naval Administration*, 138n158. That naval officers were an increasingly large proportion of the governors general shows that they were taking Vernon's admonition to heart.

72. Freeman, *Washington*, 1:186–89, 447–513, 520–25. Fairfax Harrison, "The Northern Neck Maps of 1737–1747," *WMQ*, 2d ser., 4 (1924), 8.

73. Col. William Fairfax to Maj. Lawrence Washington, Fredericksburg, Sept. 9, 1746; Robert Jackson to same, "18 7bre 1746," Conway, *Barons*, 236–40.

74. J. W. Wayland, ed., *The Fairfax Line: Thomas Lewis's Journal of 1746* (New Market, VA, 1925), esp. 22–23, 25, 29–32, 41–42n, 46–47.

75. Dumas Malone, *Jefferson the Virginian* (Boston, 1948), 23–24; Harrison, "Northern Neck Maps," 10–11, 13.

76. Hughes, *Surveyors and Statesmen*, 179–80. The Treaty of Lancaster, whose origins lay in the Onondaga/Oneida action in Augusta County, Dec. 18, 1742 (James Titus, *The Old Dominion at War* [Columbia, SC, 1991], 7–10), marked the end of the Onondaga's century-old southern strategy, Webb, *1676*, 252. Note that Virginia's representatives at Lancaster, councilors Thomas Lee and Robert Beverley, headed families prominent in Spotswood's land company and its successor, the Ohio Company, and that the Lancaster Treaty was ratified at Onondaga. Mulkearn, *Mercer Papers*, 3–4, 6–7; Ohio Company to Hanbury, June 21, 1749, Mulkearn, *Mercer Papers*, 140–42, 145–46, 171; James, *Ohio Company*, 14–15; Bailey, *Ohio Company*, [35]–60, amplifies the company's membership. He attributes Gooch's lack of support for the Ohio Company to his alliance with Speaker John Robinson and his Greenbrier Company, and with the councilors Thomas and William Nelson, principals of the Loyal Land Company, 65–68; and see Charles Royster, *The Fabulous History of the Dismal Swamp Company* (New York, 1999), 34–36. Gooch to lords commissioners, June 16, 1748, CO 5/1327; Higonnet, "Origins," 60, 74, is criticized by T. R. Clayton, "The Duke of Newcastle, the Earl of Halifax, and the American Origins of the Seven Years' War," *HJ* 24 (1981): 571–603. Hanbury's petition to the king, and the resulting OPC, are printed in Bailey, *Ohio Company*, 298–303. Hanbury stressed that the grant was conditioned on "Erecting a Fort and Maintaining a Garrison." Henretta, *"Salutary Neglect,"* 281–85, 293, 300, 306–9.

77. Washington to [Hanbury], n.d., Sparks, *Writings of Washington*, 2:481. Dinwiddie to Washington, Mar. 20, 1730/31, Conway, *Barons*, 278–79.

78. James, *Ohio Company*, 16, 22, 25, 27; Mulkearn, *Mercer Papers*, 169, 250–51; *EJC*, 5:296–97; Morton, *Colonial Virginia*, 536ff.; Freeman, *Washington*, 1:236; W. W. Abbott et al., eds., *The Papers of George Washington, Colonial Series* (Charlottesville, VA, 1983), 1:59; Jackson and Twohig, *Diaries of George Washington*, 1:120–22; Osgood, *Eighteenth Century*, 4:286–87, 291–92, 295; Clayton, "Newcastle," 48. Ohio speculation, dating back to Spotswood's penetration of the Blue Ridge, is laid out by Lawrence Henry Gipson, *Zones of International Friction . . . , 1748–1754: The British Empire Before the American Revolution* (New York, 1939), 4:226–34, 241–68. Titus, *Old Dominion at War*, 11–14, 16, concludes that "it was the activities of the Ohio Company that brought to a head the conflicting claims of France and Britain."

79. Freeman, *Washington*, 1:229–31, 233; George to Lawrence Washington, May 5, 1749; same to Anne Fairfax Washington, n.d., *PGWCS*, 1:6, 38; Conway, *Barons*, 272–77; Ron Chernow, *Washington* (New York, 2010), 16–17; Bailey, *Ohio Company*, 27–31; James, *Ohio Company*, 31; Lawrence Henry Gipson, *The British Empire Before the American Revolution* (New York, 1939), 4:247. "Russell, John, Fourth Duke of Bedford," *ODNB*. Henretta, *"Salutary Neglect,"* 282. Bedford had just replaced Newcastle as secretary of state for the southern department (which included the American provinces), 1748–51. Bedford, a militant imperialist, was "head of the military interest," succeeding the royal duke of Cumberland.

80. George Washington's survey is recorded in *PGWCS*, 1:8, 45; and see Bailey, *Ohio Company*, 70, 73–81. Freeman, *Washington*, 1:236, 244–45; Lawrence Washington to Thomas Hanbury, n.d., Sparks, *Writings of Washington*, 2:481. Washington wrote in the same vein to Robert Dinwiddie, the professional imperial administrator who was one of the Ohio Company's British members and who succeeded Gooch as lieutenant governor of Virginia. Dinwiddie replied that an exception from tithes was unlikely, Sparks, *Writings of Washington*, 2:482; Conway, *Barons*, 278. Lawrence Washington was an early American exponent of the idea that "Britain was to spread liberty in the world, using her constitution as a model," the antecedent of the Jeffersonian "empire of liberty," Jeremy Black, *America or Europe? British Foreign Policy, 1739–63*, 182; Wilson, "Empire of Virtue," 128–84; Robert W. Tucker and David C. Henderson, *"Empire of Liberty": The Statecraft of Thomas Jefferson* (New York, 1990), esp. ch. 16.

81. Freeman, *Washington*, 1:247ff., 264, 268; on the southside adjutancy, see *PG-WCS*, 1:53; Jackson and Twohig, *Diaries of George Washington*, 1:25–26, 34, 118, 120–26; *EJC*, 5:413; *VMHB* 31 (1923): 272; Chernow, *Washington*, 8–9, 15, 18–19, 22–23, 26, and for his transfer to the Northern Neck adjutancy, 27.

82. George Washington to Robert Dinwiddie, June 10, 1752, *PGWCS*, 1:50, 53; Freeman, *Washington*, 1:266–67, 272ff.; *EJC*, 5:444–45; Holderness to Dinwiddie, Aug. 28, 1753, CO 5/1344, n.p., printed in Bailey, *Ohio Company*, 189, [201]–203n, from CO 5/211, 21–30; Dinwiddie to the French commander on the Ohio, Oct. 30, 1753, Jackson and Twohig, *Diaries of George Washington*, 1:126–29. Higonnet, "Origins," 64–68; Clayton, "Newcastle," 584; Gipson, *British Empire*, 4:288–96; Anderson, *Crucible*, 31–32, 37–38, 40–41.

83. *The Journal of Major George Washington . . .* (1754; fasc. ed., Williamsburg, VA, 1959); Freeman, *Washington*, 1:259–50. J. Fredrick Fauz, "'Engaged in Enterprises Pregnant with Terror': George Washington's Formative Years among the Indians," in Hofstra, *George Washington and the Virginia Backcountry*, 115–55; Lois Mulkearn, "Half King, Seneca Diplomat of the Ohio Valley," *WPHM* 37 (1954): [65]–81; Washington's speech to the Indians at Wills Creek, Apr. 23, 1754, John C. Fitzpatrick, ed., *Writings of Washington* (Washington, DC, 1931), 1:38–39. Gipson, *British Empire*, 4:296–99; Anderson, *Crucible*, 5–7, 42–65; Jones, *Ohio Company*, 29–71, 84–85. Bailey, *Ohio Company*, 179, notes that Jacob Van Braun, George Washington's interpreter, had served under Lawrence Washington in the Cartagena expedition and been kept on in the Washington household as George Washington's fencing master. And see Bailey, *Ohio Company*, 180–82. Fairfax to Washington, Alexandria, July 5, 1754, *PGWCS*, 1:174; Jackson and Twohig, *Diaries of George Washington*, 1:3.

84. Washington to Dinwiddie, May 29, 1754, *PGWCS*, 1:129, 136; R. A. Brock, ed., *The Official Records of Robert Dinwiddie*, Virginia Historical Society *Collections*, n.s., 3 (Richmond, 1883), 1:48, 179–81. Dinwiddie did ask for two majors' commissions, one for Innes and the other for Innes's second in command, George Washington: Dinwiddie to Sir Thomas Robinson, Nov. 16, 1754, ibid., 409. Dinwiddie to Washington, June 4, and reply, June 10, 1754, *PGWCS*, 1:126, 129. Fairfax had reported to Sir Charles Wager on West Indian affairs, Nov. 26, 1729, Ford, *List*, 27. A British officer himself, Fairfax had married an officer's daughter, connections that deepened the British military context of George Washington's youth.

85. On Washington's use of Bland's *Treatise*, see Col. Oliver L. Spaulding Jr., "The Military Studies of George Washington," *AHR* 29 (1924): 675–76. Washington first used the edition of 1727, but by 1775, he specificed the edition of 1762, ibid., 678. Washington to his officers, Jan. 8, 1756, *PGWCS*, 2:257; Virginia Steele Wood, "George Washington's Military Manuals," http://www.loc.gov./rr/genealogy/bib_guid/WashingtonMilitaryManuals.pdf, [1], 3, 8. Freeman, *Washington*, 2:150, and bibliographic note on Bland's work as "the basic text of the American Army," 2:290–93. Marlborough's commission as captain general appears on pp. 201–3 of the 1746 edition of Bland's *Treatise*. Russell F. Weigley, *History of the United States Army* (Bloomington, IN, 1984), 11, and see 13–15, 28–30. On Bland, see Dalton, *Army Lists*, 6:176n; Whitworth, *Ligonier*, 57n. Hatner, *Eighteenth-Century Secretary*, 377. Houlding, *Fit for Service*, 179–87, 191–92, comments on Bland's *Treatise* as evidence of the prevalence of Marlborough's systems throughout the period, and as the chief text of young officers in Britain and often in simplified colonial versions in America. Second in influence was the work of "Marlborough's Drillmaster" Brig. Gen. Richard Kane's *Campaigns*. It was owned by Washington in the 1757 edition. Then there was Lt. Gen. Richard Molesworth's *Short Course*, written prefatory to his projected life of Marlborough. Another of Marlborough's veterans, Brig. Gen. and Adj. Gen. Adam Williamson, refected his commanding formative service under Turenne (Webb, *Lord Churchill's Coup*, 31–36) in his widely read *Maxims of Turenne* (1740, 1744). For Washington's study of Turenne, see Spaulding, "Military Studies of Washington," 680. Washington's subsequent military reading is noted in Houlding, *Fit for Service*, 201–2n96, 281, and see 213–16 for the American response to the 1764 *Regulations*. See also n. 34 above. Houlding, *Fit for Service*, 169, also comments on colonial editions and on governorships awarded to Bland and to subsequent officer-authors. Bland was governor of Fort William and of Edinburgh Castle (while commander in chief in Scotland, having been governor general of Gibraltar). For his service with Marlborough, see above.

86. Dinwiddie to Innes, Mar. 23; same to Washington, Mar. 15, May 4; same to Henry Fox, secretary at war, July 24; same to Capt. John Rutherford, Oct. 5; same to Sir Thomas Robinson, Nov. 16; Washington to Dinwiddie, June 4, 1754, Brock, *Dinwiddie Records*, 1:106–7, and see 125–26, 197–98, 246, 349, 403–4. Capt. Gen. the duke of Cumberland resolved the issue of seniority raised by Washington's conflict with the captains of the independent companies by amending the articles of war to erase the rank of provincial field officers. Washington's refusal to serve on such degrading terms was echoed by every provincial field officer in America, Pargellis, *Loudoun*, 86–87, 90. Dinwiddie to Fox, July 24; same to Rutherford, Oct. 5, 1754; list of officers; Washington to Dinwiddie, "From Our Camp at the Great Meadows," May 24, 1754, Brock, *Dinwiddie Records*, 1:246, 354, 112–15, 176–82, *PGWCS*, 1:109. On "honor" in these circumstances, see Shy, *Toward Lexington*, 344.

87. Dinwiddie to Washington, June 4, 25; Washington to Dinwiddie, June 10; same to Rutherford, Oct. 5; Dinwiddie to Robinson, Nov. 16, 1754, Brock, *Dinwiddie Records*, 193–94, 198–99, 218, 350, 403; *PGWCS*, 1:126–27, 129–40, 148–49, 157, 224n1; and on the refusal of the independent companies "to Lend a Hand" or "do Duty as Pioneers," see Adam Stephen's autobiography, *PGWCS*, 1:157. On this occasion, as later, George's mother was delighted that her son could now devote himself to her welfare, Conway, *Barons*, 81. See the identical language of British officers, resentful of Hanoverian preferences, Hayes, "Hanover and the British Army." On the view of provincial troops as peasant laborers, see Shy, *Toward Lexington*, 100.

88. W. C. Ford, ed., *The Writings of George Washington*, 14 vols. (Washington, DC, 1889–93), 1:137; Freeman, *Washington*, 1:104, 440. Fitzhugh, a Virginia captain in the American Regiment with Lawrence Washington, was also George Washington's predecessor in the Northern Neck adjutancy. Washington to Dinwiddie, June 10, 1752, *PGWCS*, 1:50–51; Washington to Col. William Fitzhugh, Belvoir, Nov. 15, 1754, *PGWCS*, 1:225–27. Fitzhugh received his British half pay even while he was a colonel of Maryland militia in the war with France. Fitzhugh had been assisted by Lawrence Washington in securing half pay "to establish my Rank in the Army, which is all I want." He resigned his royal commission to become a member of the Maryland revolutionary council and a councilor of the new state government of Maryland. Aged and blind though Fitzhugh was, the British troops burned his home, Rouseby Hall, but Fitzhugh survived the war. Conway, *Barons*, 204–10, includes Fitzhugh's correspondence with Lawrence Washington. He is alleged to have participated in the military funeral of Gen. George Washington, ordered by Pres. John Adams. In fact, Fitzhugh had died the previous year, on Feb. 11, 1798, the last surviving officer of the American Regiment, *VMHB* 8 (1900): 91–92. On Sharpe's commission to command as "lieutenant colonel of foot in the West Indies," see Dinwiddie to Clark, Oct. 20; same to Granville, Oct. 25, 1754; same to Sir Thomas Robinson, Nov. 16, 1754, Brock, *Dinwiddie Records*, 1:350, 372–73, 463n–64. Clayton, "Newcastle," 589n85; Pargellis, *Loudoun*, 24n; Gipson, *British Empire*, 6:50–53.

89. The phrase is from the famous Newburgh Address, "Speech to the Officers of the Army," Mar. 15, 1783, George Washington, *Writings*, ed. John Rhodehamel (New York, 1997), 500.

Acknowledgments

Marlborough's America, the fourth volume of *The Governors-General*, is the first to reach back to the founding doctoral dissertation, "Officers and Governors," supervised by the late Merrill Jensen, and completed in 1964 at the University of Wisconsin, Madison. The dissertation's thesis, about the identity of the imperial executive and the royal army, was confirmed by research in the Marlborough Papers at Blenheim Palace in 1967 and 1968. This work was undertaken as a fellow of the Institute of Early American History and Culture, Williamsburg, and with the support of Lester J. Cappon, the institute's director. Further research in British repositories made it apparent that the imperial impulse and its armed executors, which reached their apotheosis in the age of Marlborough, had their origins in the consolidation of the English state and its inaugural overseas ventures in the reign of Elizabeth I. The enlarged project was outlined in "Army and Empire Garrison Government in England and America, 1569 to 1763," published in the *William and Mary Quarterly*, 3d ser., 29 (1977): 1–31, edited by W. W. Abbott and Michael McGiffert.

There followed *The Governors-General: The English Army and the Definition of the Empire, 1569–1681*, edited by Norman S. Fiering, first published in 1979. The manuscript had benefited greatly from a searching reading by Bernard Bailyn. The required reconstruction took place in two fellowship terms, 1971–72 and 1974–75, in the Charles Warren Center for Studies in American History at Harvard. These terms were supported by a fellowship from the National Endowment for the Humanities.

The research and writing of the second volume of *The Governors-General, 1676: The End of American Independence*, first published in 1984, was supported by a fellowship from the John Simon Guggenheim Memorial Foundation. Renewed research in the Harvard College Library was enriched by the hospitality of the Warren Center and of the masters and fellows of Leverett House and Adams House. *1676* exposed the consequences of armed English imperialism and of its officer-executives for the colonial and aboriginal peoples of eastern North America during "the time of troubles" epitomized by Bacon's revolution in the Chesapeake and the Algonquin uprising in New England called King Philip's War.

Both *1676* and the third volume of *The Governors-General, Lord Churchill's Coup: The Anglo-American Empire and the Glorious Revolution Reconsidered*, first published in 1995, were much enhanced by the editing of Jane N. Garrett and the work of her colleagues at Alfred A. Knopf. *Lord Churchill's Coup* traced the ascent, in the English and French armies and at the court of St. James, of John Churchill, the ensign of the Guards who rose to become the general officer most responsible for the military coup of 1688. This volume was enriched by a review of the Blenheim Papers, at last available (and meticulously cataloged) in the British Library. The manuscript was further improved by the reading of a late draft by Professor J. R. Jones of the University of West Anglia and Professor W. A. Speck of Leeds University. I have also to acknowledge the award of a Mellon Fellowship by the Henry E. Huntington Library and the innumerable courtesies of the library staff and Robert C. Ritchie, Keck Director of Research.

Marlborough's America, the fourth volume of *The Governors-General*, embodies the insight of the dissertation: that the English empire, in the British Isles, in America and, as it now appears, in the low countries of northern Europe, was an expression of English nationality, expanded around the Atlantic world by professional army officers, linked by the chain of command. At its head was the sovereign but, from 1702 to 1712 (and from 1714 to 1716), the royal army was effectively headed by the captain general, the duke (as he now became) of Marlborough. His legates in American commands personified the attributes of their commander, the Augustus of a new Augustan age. This galaxy of imperial executives, all Marlborough's veterans (many of them his staff officers), found their American commands underdeveloped colonies but left them maturing provinces, the frontiers of the British empire. The military executives nurtured provincial officers. These elites' shares of the continuing wars with the Bourbon powers for American hegemony were clearly anticipated by their service in the Cartagena expedition and the American Regiment. Subsequently, these veteran officers underwrote an empire of their own. It was founded on the drill and discipline, the imperial accomplishments and the professional example, of John Churchill, first duke of Marlborough.

For more than four decades, the gestation of *Marlborough's America* has been supported by the Maxwell School of Citizenship and Public Affairs at Syracuse University and by its Department of History. I am especially indebted to Dean John L. Palmer, who appointed me to the Maxwell professorship and who supported the chair with research funds. I also appreciate continued support from the associate deans of Maxwell, Robert D. McClure and Michael J. Wasylenko. The department of history, led by Carol Faulkner, chair, and her predecessors, has continuously sustained the work. My friend and colleague, David H. Bennett, has patiently followed the ups and downs of this project for more than half a century. This work could not have been completed without the extraordinary editorial skills of Mrs. Frances U. Bockus. I also appreciate the tireless research work of my former student and present assistant,

Dr. Gregory K. Scott. The inter-library loan staff of the Ernest Stevenson Bird Library of Syracuse University were indispensable.

Marlborough's America owes its publication by the Yale University Press to its editorial director, Christopher Rogers. His instant and informed appreciation of the manuscript and his astute attention to its revision underlie this work. Christina Tucker, assistant editor for history, has been an able and sympathetic guide through the publication labyrinth. The work benefitted immeasurably from copy editing by Robin DuBlanc. Margaret Otzel, senior editor at Yale University Press, liberally applied her taste and talent in getting this work into print. Mary Valencina cast and recast elegant designs. Bill Nelson drew the maps. The manuscript was read for the press by Professors Richard R. Johnson of the University of Washington and Steven C. A. Pincus of Yale. Their initial assessments and subsequent correspondence were important to reconsiderations and revisions.

I have also to thank the individuals and institutions who supplied many of the images which enrich these pages. First, of course, I am indebted to his grace, the duke of Marlborough, and his staff Blenheim Palace: the archivist, John Forster; the house manager, Kate Ballenger; and the education officer, Karen Wiseman. Nicole Contaxis of the New-York Historical Society; Tom Morgan and Emma Butterfield at the National Portrait Gallery, London; Jennifer Van Horn and Dawn Bonner at Mount Vernon; the staff of the Virginia Historical Society; Barbara R. Luck and Marianne Martin at the Colonial Williamsburg Foundation, supplied essential portraits of protagonists. I have also to thank David Paul Broda of the Syracuse University Photographic and Imaging Center for expert assistance.

The author of *Marlborough's America* owes most of all to Dr. Margaret E. Webb. To her, this work is dedicated, with love.

Index

Pairs of numerals in *italics* refer to the illustration inserts:

insert 1 follows page 24
insert 2 follows page 152
insert 3 follows page 248
insert 4 follows page 344
insert 5 follows page 392

The first numeral in each pair identifies the insert; the second identifies the (unnumbered) page in that insert. Thus, "*3/2*" refers to insert 3, page 2.